In an age of migration, this *International Handbook of Migration Studies* is a magnificent achieve-ment. The editors have brought together four dozen original essays by leading scholars that illuminate this vast and fascinating field, as rapidly changing as the world on the move it seeks to grasp. Global in scope, innovative in design, with wide-angle multidisciplinary lenses, this timely volume is an essential reference for scholars, students, and informed publics alike.

Rubén G. Rumbaut, co-author of *Immigrant America: A Portrait, and Legacies: The Story of the Immigrant Second Generation*

A gem of a book, packed with thoughtful and well-written essays, that brings together an interdisciplinary group of scholars to survey a broad range of topics, theoretical approaches, and methods in the field of international migration. Full of fascinating information and valuable insights, Gold and Nawyn have produced an indispensable resource for students and scholars alike.

Nancy Foner, Distinguished Professor of Sociology, Hunter College and the Graduate Center of the City University of New York

International migration is a highly complex issue, but this handbook offers the reader a clear and comprehensive introduction into thinking about this and doing scientific research. The hand-book draws together important and diverse writings, mainly but not exclusively by American authors, and provides an essential resource for students of international migration.

Jan Rath, University of Amsterdam

Patterns of migration change over time. So do patterns of studying them. This impressive and wide-ranging survey of the most up-to-date approaches in the field of migration studies has entries on everything from sexuality to elite migration, to the view from sending states to international adoptions and climate-induced migration. The *Handbook* also examines concepts and methods, from assimilation to transnationalism to comparative approaches. It has something for everyone: smart syntheses of your own specialty and smart useful overviews of those you know less about. This book is a must for every migration scholar's shelf.

Nancy L. Green, École des Hautes Études en Sciences Sociales

Routledge International Handbook of Migration Studies

The current era is marked by an unparalleled level of human migration, the result of both recent and long-term political, economic, cultural, social, demographic, and technological developments. Despite increased efforts to limit its size and consequences, migration has wide-ranging impacts upon social, environmental, economic, political, and cultural life in countries of origin and settlement. Such transformations impact not only those who are migrating, but those who are left behind, as well as those who live in the areas where migrants settle.

The Routledge International Handbook of Migration Studies offers a conceptual approach to the study of international migration, exploring clearly the many modes of exit, reception, and incorporation which involve varied populations in disparate political, economic, social, and cultural contexts. How do these movements also facilitate the transmission of ideologies and identities, political and cultural practices, and economic resources? Uniquely among texts in the subject area, the *Handbook* also provides a section devoted to exploring methods for studying international migration.

Featuring 47 essays written by leading international and multidisciplinary scholars, *The Routledge International Handbook of Migration Studies* offers a contemporary, integrated, and comprehensive resource for students and scholars of sociology, politics, human geography, law, anthropology, history, urban planning, journalism, and health care.

Steven J. Gold is professor and associate chair in the Department of Sociology at Michigan State University. His interests include international migration, ethnic economies, qualitative methods, and visual sociology. The past chair of the International Migration Section of the American Sociological Association, and the International Visual Sociology Association, Gold is the author, co-author or co-editor of six books, including *The Store in the Hood: A Century of Ethnic Business and Conflict* (Roman and Littlefield, 2010). Together with Rubén G. Rumbaut, he is the editor of *The New Americans* book series from LFB Publishers.

Stephanie J. Nawyn is an assistant professor in Sociology at Michigan State University. Her research and teaching areas of expertise are in gender and immigration, with a focus on forced migration, families, and social incorporation. Dr Nawyn conducts research on community development among immigrants and the importance of social networks and social capital to immigrant and refugee incorporation, as well as the socioeconomic advancement of African-born immigrants in the United States.

Routledge International Handbook of Migration Studies

Edited by
Steven J. Gold and Stephanie J. Nawyn

LONDON AND NEW YORK

First published 2013
by Routledge
2 Park Square, Milton Park, Abingdon, Oxfordshire OX14 4RN

Simultaneously published in the USA and Canada
by Routledge
711 Third Avenue, New York, NY 10017
First issued in paperback 2014
Routledge is an imprint of the Taylor & Francis Group, an informa company

British Library Cataloguing in Publication Data
A catalogue record for this book is available from the British Library

Library of Congress Cataloging in Publication Data
Routledge international handbook of migration studies / edited by Steven J. Gold and Stephanie J. Nawyn.
    p. cm.
  Includes bibliographical references and index.
    1. Emigration and immigration. 2. Emigration and immigration–History. 3. Immigrants–Social conditions. 4. Immigrants–Economic conditions. 5. Emigration and immigration–Research. I. Gold, Steven J. (Steven James) II. Nawyn, Stephanie J. III. Title: International handbook of migration studies.
  JV6035.R68 2012
  304.8–dc23
                          2011051865

ISBN13: 978-0-415-77972-2 (hbk)
ISBN13: 978-1-138-78773-5 (pbk)

Typeset in Bembo and Stone Sans by
Taylor & Francis Books

Contents

Contents

Contents

Tables

Figures

Contributors

Ramona Fruja Amthor is an Assistant Professor of Education at Bucknell University, teaching courses on social foundations, multicultural education, and immigration. In her research, she examines the intersections among educational contexts, immigration, and identity, focusing on immigrants' transitions and their experiences with education and citizenship in their multiple forms.

Fredrik N. G. Andersson has a Ph.D. in Economics from Lund University where he is currently employed as a researcher. His main research field is long term economic growth: its causes, consequences, and possibilities.

Anny Bakalian, Ph.D. is the Associate Director of the Middle East and Middle Eastern American Center, at the Graduate Center, CUNY. She is the author of *Backlash 9/11: Middle Eastern and Muslim Americans Respond* with Mehdi Bozorgmehr, and *Armenian Americans: From Being to Feeling Armenian*.

Irene Bloemraad examines immigration and politics. Her books include *Becoming a Citizen*, *Rallying for Immigrant Rights* (edited with Kim Voss) and *Civic Hopes, Political Realities* (edited with Karthick Ramakrishnan). She is Associate Professor of Sociology at the University of California, Berkeley and a Scholar with the Canadian Institute for Advanced Research.

Marc H. Bornstein is Senior Investigator and Head of Child and Family Research at the Eunice Kennedy Shriver National Institute of Child Health and Human Development. Bornstein has published in experimental, methodological, comparative, developmental, and cultural science as well as neuroscience, pediatrics, and aesthetics. Visit *www.cfr.nichd.nih.gov* and *www.tandfonline.com/HPAR*.

Mehdi Bozorgmehr is Professor of Sociology and Co-Director of the Middle East and Middle Eastern American Center at the Graduate Center, City University of New York. He is the co-author of *Backlash 9/11: Middle Eastern and Muslim Americans Respond* (University of California Press, 2009) with Anny Bakalian, which received an honorable mention for best book from the International Migration Section of the American Sociological Association.

Alin M. Ceobanu is an Assistant Professor of Sociology and European Studies at the University of Florida. His research explores cross-nationally the links between anti-immigrant sentiment and national attachments, extension of rights to immigrants and citizenship regimes, and perceptions of immigrants' impact on crime and crime rates.

Becky Conway is a doctoral student in Sociology at Vanderbilt University, where she earned her masters' degree. Her area of specialization is the sociology of culture, with an additional interest in research methods.

Flavia Cristaldi is an associate professor at the "Sapienza" University of Rome, where she teaches Geography of Migrations. Her research interests are urban geography, residential segregation, migration, commuting, and gender studies.

Joe T. Darden is Professor of Geography at Michigan State University and former Dean of Urban Affairs Programs from 1984–1997. He is a former Fulbright Scholar, Department of Geography, University of Toronto, 1997 to 1998. Dr Darden's research interests are residential segregation, immigrant incorporation and socioeconomic neighborhood inequality in multi-racial societies.

Héctor L. Delgado is Associate Professor of Sociology at University of La Verne. He is the author of *New Immigrants, Old Unions: Organizing Undocumented Workers in Los Angeles* (Temple University Press 1993) and several articles on unionization, immigrants, and race and ethnicity.

Cristián Doña-Reveco is a doctoral candidate in Sociology and History at Michigan State University. His research focuses in the intersection of history and biography in the migration process from the Southern Cone of America to the United States. He also does research on using cinema in teaching Sociology and History.

Astrid Eich-Krohm is an assistant professor of sociology at Southern Connecticut State University. Her research and teaching interests are international migration with a special interest in highly skilled migration, gender, medical sociology, and qualitative research methods.

Xavier Escandell is an Associate professor of Sociology at the University of Northern Iowa. His research explores attitudes towards immigration policies in Europe, and overall immigrant settlement processes and their socio-political incorporation into the host societies. His most recent work examines how Bolivian migrants in Spain are transformational forces for the receiving and sending communities.

Yen Le Espiritu is Professor of Ethnic Studies at the University of California, San Diego. She has published widely on Asian American panethnicity, gender, and migration, and US colonialism and wars in Asia.

Thomas Faist is Professor for the Sociology of Transnationalization, Development and Migration in the Department of Sociology at Bielefeld University. He is also deputy chair of the Collaborative Research Center "From Heterogeneities to Inequalities". He held visiting appointments at Malmö University and the University of Toronto.

Kathryn Farr is Professor Emerita in the Department of Sociology at Portland State University. Her research interest is in the organization of transnational forms of gender-based violence. She is the author of *Sex Trafficking: The Global Market in Women and Children*.

Patricia Fernández-Kelly is Senior Lecturer in Sociology and Research Associate in the Office of Population Research at Princeton University. Her research focuses on immigration, race, ethnicity, and gender. She is the author of *For We are Sold, I and My People* (State University of New York Press, 1983) and *Out of the Shadows* (Penn State University Press, 2006).

Donna Gabaccia is Professor of History at the University of Minnesota, where she teaches world history. She is the author, most recently, of *Foreign Relations: Global Perpectives on American Immigration*.

Solomon Addis Getahun is an associate professor of history at Central Michigan University. His research is on African and African Diaspora history, with a focus on contemporary Ethiopian refugees and immigrants in the US. Urbanization, political violence and identity politics in Ethiopia are his other interests.

Linda Gjokaj is a PhD candidate of Sociology at Michigan State University. Her research interests are immigration, gender, and families. Linda is working on her dissertation titled, "Community, Ethnicity and Assimilation: The Case of Albanians in Metropolitan Detroit," which explores how disparate groups of Albanians create a cohesive ethnic community.

Chien-Juh Gu is Associate Professor of Sociology at Western Michigan University. She received her Ph.D. from Michigan State University. Gu is author of *Mental Health among Taiwanese Americans: Gender, Immigration, and Transnational Struggles* (LFB, 2006) and has published several articles on immigration, gender, culture, and social psychology.

Jacqueline Maria Hagan is a professor of sociology at the University of North Carolina at Chapel Hill. Her research interests include international migration with a focus on labor markets, policy, religion, and human rights. She is author of *Deciding to be Legal* (Temple 1994) and *Migration Miracle* (Harvard 2008).

Pierrette Hondagneu-Sotelo is Professor in the Department of Sociology at the University of Southern California. Her published research has focused on gender and immigration, informal sector work, Latina/o sociology, and religion and the immigrant rights movement. She is currently writing a book about immigrants and gardens.

Emily Noelle Ignacio is an Associate Professor of Sociology in Ethnic, Gender, and Labor studies at the University of Washington Tacoma. Her most recent book is *Building Diaspora: Filipino Community Formation in the United States* (2005, Rutgers University Press). She is currently completing a book entitled *Racial Projects in the United States, 1790 to the Present*.

Hiromi Ishizawa is an Assistant Professor of Sociology at George Washington University. Her research focuses on sociology of language, immigration, social demography, and urban sociology. Her current research project examines the effect of political context on the levels of English proficiency among foreign-born Hispanics.

Thomas Janoski is Professor of Sociology at the University of Kentucky. He is the author of *Citizenship and Civil Society* (1998, Cambridge University Press) and *The Ironies of Citizenship: Naturalization and Integration in Industrialize Societies* (2010, Cambridge University Press). He teaches courses in international migration at the undergraduate and graduate levels.

Guillermina Jasso is Silver Professor of Sociology at New York University. She specializes in sociobehavioral theory, distributive justice, mathematical modeling, and international migration.

She is the author of *The New Chosen People: Immigrants in the United States* (with Mark Rosenzweig) and numerous articles.

Peter Karpestam has a Ph.D. in Economics from Lund University where he currently works as a researcher and lecturer. His Ph.D. thesis explores the economic consequences of migration. He teaches macroeconomics and international economics. His current research is about economic growth, financial crises and greenhouse gas emissions.

László J. Kulcsár is an Associate Professor of Sociology at Kansas State University. His field of expertise is social demography and regional development, with an emphasis on migration, urbanization, and spatial inequalities. He does research on rural population dynamics and the social and demographic transformation of post-socialist Eastern Europe.

Guofang Li is an associate professor in the Department of Teacher Education at Michigan State University. Li specializes in ESL/EFL education, family and community literacy, and Asian education and has conducted research in these areas in international settings. Li is the recipient of the 2010 Early Career Award of AERA.

Matthew Light is assistant professor at the Centre for Criminology and Sociolegal Studies, University of Toronto. His doctoral dissertation (Department of Political Science, Yale University, 2006) compared the migration policies of regional governments in contemporary Russia. His most recent research focuses on policing and law enforcement in the Republic of Georgia.

Andrea Louie is an Associate Professor in the Department of Anthropology at Michigan State University. She has conducted research exploring how ideas constructed around "Chineseness" have been reworked as transnational processes. Her book *Chineseness Across Borders: Re-negotiating Chinese Identities in China and the US* (Duke University Press, 2004) won the Association for Asian American Studies Social Sciences book award.

Jan Lucassen is senior researcher at the International Institute of Social History in Amsterdam and Professor of History at the Free University in Amsterdam. He specializes in global labor relations and migration history. He is the editor (with Leo Lucassen) of *Migration, Migration History, History: Old Paradigms and New Perspectives* (1997) and (with Leo Lucassen and Patrick Manning) *Migration History in World History: Multidisciplinary Approaches* (2010).

Leo Lucassen is professor of Social History and chair of the History Department at Leiden University. He published extensively on (global) migration history and urban history. He is the editor (with Jan Lucassen) of *Migration, Migration History, History: Old Paradigms and New Perspectives* (1997) and (with Jan Lucassen and Patrick Manning) of *Migration History in World History: Multidisciplinary Approaches* (2010).

Eithne Luibhéid is an Associate Professor of Women's Studies at the University of Arizona; author of *Entry Denied: Controlling Sexuality at the Border* (U. Minnesota Press, 2002); co-editor of *Queer Migration: Sexuality, US Citizenship, and Border Crossings* (U. Minnesota Press, 2005); and editor of a *GLQ* special issue, "Queer/Migration" (2008).

Adam McKeown is a Professor of History at Columbia University, where he offers courses on the histories of world migration, globalization, and drugs. He wrote *Melancholy Order: Asian*

Migration and the Globalization of Borders (2008), and "Chinese Emigration in Global Context, 1850–1940," *Journal of Global History* 5 (2010): 95–124. He is now working on the history of globalization since 1760.

Cecilia Menjívar is Cowden Distinguished Professor of Sociology in the School of Social and Family Dynamics at Arizona State University. Her immigration research has focused on the effects of the law on various spheres of life primarily among Central Americans in the United States.

Pyong Gap Min is Distinguished Professor of Sociology at Queens College and the Graduate Center of CUNY, and Director of the Research Center for Korean Community at Queens College. The areas of his research interest are immigration, ethnic identity, ethnic business, religion, and family/gender, with a special focus on Asian/Korean Americans. He is the author of several books and numerous articles.

Charlie V. Morgan is an Assistant Professor in the Sociology and Anthropology Department at Ohio University. His research interests include immigration, race and ethnicity, and inter-marriage. He is currently conducting research on foreigners in Japan.

Brendan Mullan is an Associate Professor of Sociology at Michigan State University. His current research focuses on the socio-economic, socio-demographic, and socio-cultural dynamics of globalization, the causes, content, and consequences of international migration, and the interplay between globalization and migration.

Julie Park is Assistant Professor in Sociology and Asian American Studies at the University of Maryland, College Park. Her research examines the socioeconomic, spatial, and health/epidemiological adaptation process of immigrants and their children in the US.

Rigoberto Rodriguez is an urban geographer specializing in the use of Action Research to promote social policies that improve conditions for immigrants and people of color in Southern California, and an Assistant Professor in the Chicana/o and Latina/o Studies Department at California State University, Long Beach.

Janet W. Salaff (deceased 2010) was professor emerita of Sociology at the University of Toronto and the author, co-author or editor of eight books including *Working Daughters of Hong Kong: Filial Piety or Power in the Family*, and *Hong Kong Movers and Stayers: Narratives of Family Migration*.

Sara Salman is a Ph.D. student in Sociology at the Graduate Center, CUNY.

Mariano Sana holds a Ph.D. in Demography from the University of Pennsylvania. He is an associate professor of Sociology at Vanderbilt University. Most of his research is in the field of international migration, with an emphasis on data collection methodology, immigrant economic behavior and impacts of immigration on labor markets.

Nandita Sharma, Associate Professor of Sociology at the University of Hawai'i at Mānoa, researches the relationship between nationalism, migration policies and processes of capitalist globalization. She co-edited (with Bridget Anderson and Cynthia Wright) a special issue on "No Borders as Practical Politics" for the journal *Refuge* (26:2, 2010).

Gabriel (Gabi) Sheffer is Professor of Political Science at The Hebrew University of Jerusalem. His current research foci are: ethnic politics, with special emphasis on ethno-national diasporas, including the Jewish diaspora. He has published numerous books, edited volumes, journal articles and chapters in edited volumes. Among his books are: *Modern Diasporas in International Politics, Middle Eastern Minorities and Diasporas,* and *Diaspora Politics: At Home Abroad.*

Thomas Soehl is a doctoral candidate in Sociology at the University of California, Los Angeles. He specializes in international migration, comparative race and ethnicity, and quantitative research methodology. His current research centers on the incorporation of migrants and their homeland connections. He received support from a US Department of Education grant awarded to UCLA and the ZEIT-Stiftung Ebelin und Gerd Bucerius.

Miri Song is Professor of Sociology at the University of Kent in England. Her research interests include migration and the second generation, ethnic and racial identities, racisms, and multiraciality. She is completing a book, *Mixed Race Identities* (with Peter Aspinall), which is coming out with Palgrave/Macmillan in 2012.

Gillian Stevens is Professor of Sociology and Executive Director of the Population Research Laboratory at the University of Alberta, Canada. Her research usually focuses on issues of immigration and language in American and Canadian society.

Roger Waldinger is Distinguished Professor of Sociology at UCLA. His work focuses on a broad range of topics within international migration, including immigrant entrepreneurship, labor markets, assimilation, the second generation, high-skilled immigration, immigration policy, and public opinion. He is the author of six books, most recently, *How the Other Half Works: Immigration and the Social Organization of Labor* (University of California Press, 2003).

Charles Watters is Professor of Childhood Studies at Rutgers University. His research interests focus on the impact of migration and globalization on children, encompassing asylum seeking and refugee children, health and well-being, identity, and education. He is the author of the 2008 book *Refugee Children: Towards the Next Horizon.*

Karen A. Woodrow-Lafield is Research Professor and Faculty Associate in the Maryland Population Research Center at the University of Maryland College Park specializing in the demography and sociology of immigration and citizenship. She has long studied population change from legal and unauthorized migration and recently evaluated immigration assumptions and methods for actuarial projections in social security programs. Her research also addresses influences of social and human capital for becoming naturalized citizens.

Min Zhou is Professor of Sociology & Asian American Studies and the Walter and Shirley Wang Endowed Chair in US-China Relations & Communications at the University of California, Los Angeles.

Maxine Baca Zinn is Professor Emeritas of Sociology at Michigan State University. Her books include *Diversity in Families and Globalization: The Transformation of Social Worlds* (with D. Stanley Eitzen). In 2000, she received the American Sociological Association's prestigious Jessie Bernard Award in recognition of achievements in the study of women and gender.

Introduction

Steven J. Gold and Stephanie J. Nawyn

The current era is marked, despite increased efforts to harden nation-state borders, by an unparalleled level of human migration, which is the consequence of both recent and long-term political, economic, cultural, social, demographic, and technological developments. These include the end of the Cold War; the efforts of corporations, states, social movements, and religious organizations to increase both their access to and control over populations, resources, and finances; the global expansion of production, commerce, consumption, and communications and entertainment media; the need for both inexpensive and highly skilled labor; and the growing availability of low-cost and high-speed modes of transportation. Migration is also initiated by intergroup conflicts, environmental disasters, economic transformations and ethnic cleansing. These occurrences have brought previously isolated peoples and cultures much closer together than ever before.

The resulting patterns of contemporary migration are unprecedented in both the sheer numbers of people involved as well as their diversity. In 2011, the International Organization for Migration estimated that there were a total of 214 million migrants internationally, some 3.1 percent of the world's population or 1 in every 33 persons (IOM 2011). Such migrants, who remitted approximately $325 billion to their homelands in 2010, represent almost every motive and social category imaginable (Mohapatra *et al.* 2011). They seek work and economic opportunities, reunification with family members, a more congenial environment or, most poignantly in the case of war-weary refugees, a safe place to live. Adding to the challenges of border crossing, migrants find themselves targeted as marks, consumers, and recruits by merchants, employers, religious proselytizers, criminals, human traffickers, social control apparatuses, and the leaders of a wide variety of social and political movements. While some carry on unscathed, others are scarred en route. Still others, including migrants, non-migrants, and former migrants, engage in occupations ranging from resettlement staff and smugglers to travel agents. In so doing, they find ways to benefit from their ties to the global migration stream (Cohen 1969; Safran 1999).

International migration encompasses widely varied forms of population movement, from both sanctioned and covert labor migrations, to contract labor and "guest-worker" programs, to network-driven chain migrations that link communities across international borders. Flows of highly skilled professionals traverse industrialized and developing countries, low-skilled workers

1

risk their lives to access better labor opportunities, and displaced asylum seekers struggle to gain legal recognition in both developing and developed countries. The study of international migration explores these many modes of exit, reception, and incorporation which involve varied populations in disparate political, economic, social, and cultural contexts.

More than just a demographic shift in population, these movements also facilitate the transmission of ideologies and identities, political and cultural practices, and economic resources. These transformations impact not only those who are migrating, but also those who are left behind, as well as non-migrants who live and work where migrants settle.

Reactions to migration and the types of change with which it is associated take many forms. The political outcomes of migration range from declarations of global human rights, to the extension of dual citizenship to expatriates, to "extraordinary rendition," selective incarceration and profiling, to internal exile, mass killings, and expulsions of entire populations. Whatever the shape these political reactions to migration have taken, however, migration patterns often resist policies intended to mold them according to plan (Massey 1993; Castles and Miller 2009).

Migration and its aftereffects have wide-ranging impacts upon nearly every aspect of social, economic, political, and cultural life in countries of origin and settlement—altering dietary habits, tastes in clothing and music, economic patterns and religious, racial, ethnic, familial, gender, and political practices, and identities. Many contemporary social problems—including racial, ethnic, national, and religious conflicts, economic inequalities, and the unraveling of political structures and practices—are themselves the product of previous migrations.

While sometimes generating problems, migration also provides benefits and solutions. Some migrant groups record remarkable achievements. They compensate for population decline and contribute inestimable resources to host societies while also remitting prized assets, ranging from economic support to political leadership to their countries of origin (Levitt 2001; Morawska 2001; Portes 2001; Saxenian 2006).

The causes and consequences of international migration have long been among the focal concerns of social scientists, historians, legal scholars, political activists, and social reformers. Hence, there is major precedent and a wide body of available theory, methods, and archival literature through which these topics can be investigated. At the same time, many new forms of contemporary migration defy established categories, models, and methods. Consequently, migration research demands a mastery of both conventional and cutting-edge approaches.

According to available evidence, current patterns of migration—and the many critical issues associated with it for both sending and receiving environments—will become even more prominent in the future, and more consequential both for social policy and scholarship. Given the social, economic, political, and ideological importance of international migration in the contemporary world, this handbook has been devised in such a way as to provide students, scholars, policy makers, and general readers with the basics of what they need to develop a sound, wide ranging, and forward looking understanding of the phenomenon.

Central themes

Of the many factors that have recently transformed the study of international migration, we identify four as bases for the organization of this handbook. First is the vast and diverse number of persons currently living outside of their countries of birth. Second are the innumerable types of international migrants, the unprecedented ways that immigration is affecting human lives, and the myriad settings in which migrants can be found.

Third is the growth and transformation in the ways that academics, policy makers, journalists, artists, and other observers study international migration. The earliest students of international migration relied almost entirely on the theories and methods of economics, demography, and sociology. At present—reflecting both the diversity of migrants and the expansion of intellectual life and technology—international migration is explored via a whole catalogue of approaches, including, but not limited to the gaze of the social and natural sciences, humanities, journalism, and the creative arts. The consequence has been the generation of a vast body of analytical materials based in multiple perspectives and the collection of plentiful and varied caches of data.

Finally, we acknowledge the change that has occurred among the students of international migration. In the past, the academy was among societies' most exclusive institutions, barring participation by women, racial, and ethnic minorities, immigrants, and those of humble birth. Several processes have altered this pattern. Academics in general, and migration scholars in particular, are now diverse in their nationality, class, gender, religion, race, life experience, and sexual identity. A considerable number are themselves immigrants (Rumbaut 2000). These investigators ask questions, maintain loyalties, and hold perspectives that were largely absent among an earlier generation of migration scholars. The handbook makes a conscious effort to both acknowledge and draw upon the innovation and diversity brought to migration studies by these recent transformations.

A conceptual focus

This handbook examines international migration from a conceptual, multidisciplinary, and international perspective. Based upon in-depth essays written by both leading scholars and up-and-coming specialists, the book is organized around key concepts in the study of international migration. This strategy allows us to transcend the disciplinary, geographical, and methodological limitations that often hinder scholarly investigation. Accordingly, the book cites and brings together an eclectic range of disciplinary foci, methodological techniques, and regional pre-rogatives. It allows readers to understand basic theories and principles that can be applied to multiple cases, rather than selecting only those that conform to the assumptions and conventions associated with particular outlooks.

Existing readers on the topic of international migration tend to be organized around parti-cular cities or countries, or specific social categories (race, ethnicity, generation, social class, gender, religion, or occupation). Further, such compendia tend to rely on a narrow range of disciplinary perspectives and methodological approaches. While providing useful and well-integrated information, such studies restrict the full diversity of perspectives and approaches to migration research used by the broader community of migration scholars. Moreover, by relying on models and concerns inherited from other disciplines or topics of study, such analyses treat the key issues in the study of international migration as secondary to those favored by other projects and bodies of literature. Such an approach obscures our understanding of international migration as an important social phenomenon in its own right.

In contrast, *The Routledge International Handbook of Migration Studies* is organized around the field of international migration *per se*. Towards this end, it stresses an interdisciplinary, eclectic, complementary, and integrative approach rather than relying upon the concerns and definitions derived from other fields. Chapters are written by a wide range of experts on the topics they know best. Authors explain central issues according to their own vision, using incisive reviews of pertinent literature. Moreover, in many chapters they draw upon data acquired from their own research, conducted in a globe-spanning array of locations and disciplines. Chapters reflect upon key debates and competing and contradictory approaches to the field.

In introducing readers to the diversity of perspectives, methods, topics, and disciplines that are currently applied to the study of migration, this book offers a realistic and nuanced grasp of perspectives on both international migration as well as a indication of the intellectually dynamic climate maintained by scholars who examine it.

The Routledge International Handbook of Migration Studies is sizeable—featuring 47 chapters—and is intentionally diverse in scope. Nevertheless, it cannot attend to every worthy topic or perspective in this expanding field. Accordingly, while covering central themes, we made special efforts to represent contemporary, leading-edge works that are shaping the field's growth. These include migration control, host hostility, transnationalism, and diasporas, migrant families, cultural conflict, multiculturalism, citizenship, climate change-induced migration, and the experience of migrants during the global "war on terror."

Each chapter includes between 20 and 40 references that direct readers to canonical texts. This provides access to key findings while also opening up the space we require to emphasize current topics, approaches, and findings.

The book's organization

The book is organized according to what we regard as a natural history of the process of international migration and adjustment to the host society. While we don't directly cover internal migration, we wish to point out that many of the forms of social, economic, and cultural adjustment experienced by international migrants are very similar to those of internal migrants. Accordingly, many of these chapters are relevant to the study of internal migration.

We begin with a summary of several Theories and Histories of International Migration, outlining their focus, assumptions, and methodologies.

By identifying foundational theories on international migration, the text enables readers to understand assumptions about migration that underlie the thinking of scholars and policy makers associated with specific disciplines and topics of study. The book's introduction also allows readers to link interpretations of migration with various academic disciplines' central methodological, ideological, and epistemological traditions. Finally, brief regional histories of migration in four world regions—our sole use of locality as an organizing principle in the book—provide a background for current concerns and contexts.

The next section concerns Forced Migrants. As of 2005, about 17 million persons worldwide were in flight from their countries of residence due to political and ethnic conflicts, wars, revolutions, and natural disasters. Some of these persons receive refugee status and, with it, financial assistance, health care, and legal residency status in another country. Others, who may be in equally dire straits, are denied refugee status and must endure in a stateless condition (Salomon 1991; Watters 2008).

The next section addresses Migrants in the Economy. A considerable fraction of international migration is motivated by various economic goals, including obtaining increased earnings, acquiring funds that will be sent back home to support relatives, communities, or social movements; and improving one's own or family members' education. Even those who migrate for other purposes—to obtain health care, for family unification, for a change of scene, to escape violence or oppression, or to pursue religious activities or an artistic or cultural calling—must find ways of supporting themselves.

The economic activities and fates of international migrants are extraordinarily diverse. The most privileged of these include the skilled and professional workers who are recruited to develop advanced technology, some of whom are involved in creating global centers of production and wealth including California's Silicon Valley. Another economic category, risk-taking immigrant entrepreneurs, establish their own businesses, often drawing on group-based resources and overseas sources of business expertise, capital, labor, and goods (Light and Gold

2000; Rath 2001). Their willingness to locate enterprises in impoverished areas sometimes yields conflicts with local residents (Zenner 1991; Min 1996; Chua 2003).

Labor migrants often fill jobs and tolerate wages that the native-born are reluctant to accept. Undocumented workers perform a variety of tasks without the benefit of regulation, rights or stability. Return migrants transfer resources, skills, capital, cultural practices, and networks back to their countries of origin or to a third location. In this way, migrants' diverse economic involvements tell us much about their own goals and prospects, how they fit into the host society, and their likelihood of return or further migration (Piore 1979).

Following from our account of the disparate economic fates encountered by immigrants, the next section addresses Intersecting Inequalities in the Lives of Migrants. Bearing distinct racial, cultural, linguistic, religious, familial, and dietary practices from members of the host society, migrants find themselves to be targets of ridicule or harassment. For them, housing, recreation, and basic social services (education, housing, health care) are difficult to acquire in the crowded and expensive settings where they often settle. Competition over scarce resources may spark turf wars with established residents or other migrants. Migrant youth, persons of stigmatized status, and those associated with political, sexual, and other marginalized subcultures are especially vulnerable to mistreatment. On the other hand, newcomers who are able to achieve rapid mobility and a modicum of comfort may inspire jealously and resentment from some while receiving kudos from others (Gold 2010). Finally, disadvantaged groups such as immigrant minorities and indigenous groups may engage in conflicts with regard to the ideological dimensions of victimization and self-assertion. And migrants do not just enter existing hierarchies of inequality; their presence and actions within the receiving society reshape those hierarchies, which effect social inequality among non-migrants.

Given their encounters with inequalities, immigrants build lives, communities, and identities in the host society, even if they must do so under condition that the Marxist aphorism describes as "not of their own choosing." The section on Creating and Recreating Community and Group Identity explores this process.

As migrants establish communities in the host society, they often seek to compensate for what they lack. Those who are impoverished devise means of financial survival (Cohen 1969; Tienda and Raijman 2001). Those deficient in status build systems of prestige (Min 1996). Cognizant of their past, migrants frequently work to preserve aspects of the life back home that they miss. They often maintain active ties and links to the country of origin and keep in touch with co-nationals, co-religionists, and relatives in other settings (Smith 2005). They also endeavor to improve prospects for their children (Zhou and Bankston 1998). Finally, because time-tested means of socialization are often altered in the course of migration, migrant organizations are committed to forms of identity formation, especially for youth (Andezian 1986; Wolf 1997; Portes and Rumbaut 2006; Kasinitz et al. 2008). These topics are examined in chapters on community patterns, panethnicity, and immigrant religion.

Drawing on their shared communities and identities, as well as other resources, migrants Socially Reproduce themselves. This occurs in several realms including family formation and maintenance, marriage and intermarriage, and the nurturance of immigrant children (Pedraza 1991; Gabaccia 1994; Zlotnick 2003). A chapter on international adoption addresses an important but understudied form of social reproduction that involves both families and immigrant children.

Migrant communities do much to help their members find jobs, deal with inequalities, build communities, and negotiate their position in the new society. However, the resources and limitations encountered by migrants—both individually and collectively—are to a considerable degree shaped by the Actions of Nation States.

In many instances, the host society has the most direct access to and control over resident migrants. However, other countries exert influence as well. For example, countries of origin often act on behalf of expatriates, and encourage or prevent their return (Faist 2000; Fitzgerald 2009). Further, countries seeking to import workers or exclude undesirables wield considerable influence over migrant populations (Borjas 1990).

States regulate a variety of activities associated with immigrants' presence, including primary and secondary education, language training, recruitment, emigration control, naturalization, political incorporation, regulation of health, and access to various public benefits. This section examines how governments and nation states act with regard to immigrants.

Until relatively recently, most scholars and policy makers assumed that migrants maintained extensive relations with only a single nation state—that of their country of origin (for short-term sojourners) and the host society (for longer term settlers) (Gordon 1964). However, a growing body of research and theorizing has come to recognize that various communities maintain international social, economic, political, familial, religious, and identificational links. Consequently, Maintaining Links Across Borders has become a vital area of migration research (Portes 1991; Basch *et al.* 1994; Massey *et al.* 1994; Guarnizo and Smith 1998; Faist 2000; Glick Schiller 2005).

To better understand such relationships, scholars have advanced an approach called "transnationalism." Stressing the globalization of political, economic, social, and cultural life, the speed and low cost of modern communication and transportation, the rights revolution that has opened opportunities for incorporation and self-determination among the women and men of formerly excluded ethnic and nationality groups, and the acceptance of expatriates in the polity of many nations, the concept of transnationalism emphasizes the various networks and links (demographic, political, economic, cultural, familial) that exist between two or more locations. From this perspective, migration is not a single, discrete event involving movement from one geographically and socially bounded locality to another. Instead, transnational communities embody and exchange concerns, relationships, resources, needs, and often people immersed in multiple settings.

An alternative model for understanding the interconnection of dispersed people is diaspora. Originally associated with groups encountering forced exile from their homeland—as in the case of Jews, Africans, Armenians, and Indians—in recent years, scholars have applied this concept in a broader if less specific manner to codify a range of interconnections between people, cultures, and nations to represent feelings of longing and displacement but also the potential for reconnection, advancement, and liberation common to migrants and exiles many in settings (Cohen 1997; Safran 1999). Some individuals and groups are able to maintain citizenship in several countries, but even those who do not regularly cross borders often sustain involvements with several groups and locations (Nonini and Ong 1997; Clifford 1998; Gold 2002). The book's section on crossing national boundaries includes chapters on diasporas, transnationalism, and return migration.

Finally, the book concludes with a section that summarizes and offers practical descriptions of Methods for Studying International Migration. Exploring international migration requires researchers to deal with crossing cultural and linguistic boundaries, and to resolve ethical dilemmas associated with collecting information from groups lacking knowledge about and power within the host society. Some of the most effective approaches integrate and triangulate multiple types of data. Despite these specific needs, literature describing methods developed specifically for the study of international migration is scarce (Massey *et al.* 1997, Gold 2007; Iosifides 2011).

This handbook works to fulfill this need with a section dedicated to several research methods with special application to the study of international migrants. Included are chapters on the use of census analysis, surveys, and ethnosurveys, participant observation, interviews, measuring time, visual sociology, on-line sources, comparative methods, and action research.

References and further reading

Andezian, S. (1986) "Women's roles in organizing symbolic life." In R. J. Simon and C. B. Brettell (eds), *International Migration: The Female Experience*. Totowa, NJ: Rowman, pp. 254–65.

Basch, L., Glick Schiller, N., and Blanc-Szanton, C. (1994) *Nations Unbound: Transnational Projects, Postcolonial Predicaments, and Deterritorialized Nation States*. Basel, Switzerland: Gordon and Breach Publishers.

Borjas, G. (1990) *Friends or Strangers: The Impact of Immigrants on the US Economy*. New York: Basic Books.

Castles, S. and Miller, M. (2009) *Age of Migration*, 4th edition. New York: Guilford

Clifford, J. (1994) "Diasporas" *Cultural Anthropology* 9(3): 302–38.

Cohen, A. (1969) *Custom and Politics in Urban Africa*. Berkeley, CA: University of California Press.

Cohen, R. (1997) *Global Diasporas*. Seattle, WA: University of Washington.

Chua, A. (2003) *World on Fire: How Exporting Free Market Democracy Breed Ethnic Hatred and Global Instability*. New York: Doubleday.

Faist, T. (2000) *The Volume and Dynamics of International Migration and Transnational Social Spaces*. Oxford, UK: Oxford University Press.

Fitzgerald, D. (2009) *A Nation of Emigrants: How Mexico Manages its Migration*. Berkeley, CA: University of California Press

Gabaccia, D. (1994) *From the Other Side: Women, Gender, and Immigrant Life in the US, 1820–1990*. Bloomington, IN: Indiana University Press.

Glick Schiller, N. (2005) "Long distance nationalism." In M. Ember, C. R. Ember and I. Skoggard (eds), *Encyclopedia of Diasporas: Immigrant and Refugee Cultures Around the World*. New York: Springer Science and Business Media, pp. 570–80.

Gold, S. J. (2002) *The Israeli Diaspora*. Seattle, WA: University of Washington Press/Routledge.

——(2005) "Migrant networks: A summary and critique of relational approaches to international migration." In M. Romero and E. Margolis (eds), *The Blackwell Companion to Social Inequalities*. Malden, MA: Blackwell, pp. 257–85.

Gold, S. J. (2007) "Using photography in studies of immigrant communities: Reflecting across projects and populations." In Gregory C. Stanczak (ed.), *Visual Research Methods: Image, Society and Representation*. Los Angeles, CA: Sage, pp. 141–66.

Gold, S. J. (2010) *The Store in the Hood: A Century of Business and Conflict*. Lanham, MD: Rowman and Littlefield.

Gordon, M. (1964) *Assimilation in American Life*. New York: Oxford.

Guarnizo, L. E., and Smith, M. P. (1998) "The locations of transnationalism." In M. P. Smith and L. E. Guarnizo (ed.), *Transnationalism from Below*. New Brunswick, NJ: Transaction, pp. 3–34.

International Organization for Migration (IOM) (2011) *About Migration: Facts and Figures*. www.iom.int/jahia/Jahia/about-migration/facts-and-figures/lang/en (accessed November 21 2011).

Iosifides, T. (2011) *Qualitative Methods in Migration Studies: A Critical Realist Perspective*. Burlington, VT, Ashgate.

Kasinitz, P., Mollenkopf, J., Waters, M., and Holdaway, J. (2008) *Inheriting the City: The Second Generation Comes of Age*. New York: Russell Sage Foundation.

Levitt, P. (2001) *The Transnational Villagers*. Berkeley, CA: University of California Press.

Light, I. and Gold, G. (2000) *Ethnic Economies*. San Diego, CA: Academic Press.

Massey, D. S., Arango, J., Hugo, G., Kouaouci, A, Pellegrino, A., and Taylor, J. E. (1993) "Theories of international migration: A review and appraisal" *Population and Development Review,* 19(3): 431–66.

Massey, D. S., Goldring, L. and Durand, J. (1994) "Continuities in transnational migration: An analysis of nineteen Mexican communities" *American Journal of Sociology* 99(6): 1492–533.

Massey, D. S., Alarcon, R., Durand, J., and Gonzalez, H. (1987) *Return to Aztlan*. Berkeley, CA: University of California Press.

Min, P.-G. (1996) *Caught in the Middle: Korean Communities in New York and Los Angeles*. Berkeley, CA: University of California Press.

Mohapatra, S., Ratha, D., and Silwal, A. (2011) "Outlook for remittance flows 2011–13. Remittance flows recover to pre-crisis levels." *Migration and Development Brief Migration and Remittances Unit* Vol 16, World

Bank. http://siteresources.worldbank.org/EXTDECPROSPECTS/Resources/476882–1157133580628/MigrationandDevelopmentBrief16.pdf.

Morawska, E. (2001) "The new-old transmigrants, their transnational lives, and ethnicization: A comparison of the 19th/20th- and 20th/21st-century situations." In N. G. Gerstle and J. Mollenkop (eds), *Immigrants, Civic Culture and Modes of Political Incorporation*. New York: Russell Sage, pp. 47–96.

Nonini, D. and Ong, A. (1997) "Introduction: Chinese transnationalism as an alternative modernity." In A. Ong and D. Nonini (eds), *Ungrounded Empires: The Cultural Politics of Modern Chinese Transnationalism*. New York: Routledge, pp. 3–33.

Pedraza, S. (1991) "Women and migration: The social consequences of gender" *Annual Review of Sociology* 17, 303–25.

Piore, M. J. (1979) *Birds of Passage*. New York: Cambridge University Press.

Portes, A. (2001) "Introduction: The debates and significance of immigrant transnationalism" *Global Networks* 1(3): 181–93.

Portes, A and Rumbaut, R. G. (2006) *Immigrant America: A Portrait*, 3rd edition. Berkeley, CA: University of California Press.

Rath, J. (ed.) (2002) *Unraveling the Rag Trade: Immigrant Entrepreneurship in Seven World Cities*. Oxford: Berg.

Rumbaut, R. G. (2000) "Immigration research in the United States: Social origins and future orientations." In N. Foner, R. G. Rumbaut, and S. J. Gold (eds) *Immigration Research for a New Century: Multidisciplinary Perspectives*. New York: Russell Sage Foundation, pp. 23–43.

Safran, W. (1999) "Comparing diasporas: A review essay" *Diaspora* 8(3): 255–91.

Smith, R. C. (2005) *Mexican New York: Transnational Worlds of New Immigrants*. Berkeley, CA: University of California Press.

Salomon, K. (1991) *Refugees in the Cold War: Towards a New International Regime in the Early Postwar Era*. Lund, Sweden: Lund University Press.

Tienda, M. and Raijman, R. (2000) "Immigrants' income packaging and invisible labor force activity" *Social Science Quarterly* 81(1): 291–311.

United Nations, Department of Economic and Social Affairs, Population Division (2009) *Trends in International Migrant Stock: The 2008 Revision*. United Nations database, POP/DB/MIG/Stock/Rev.2008. http://esa.un.org/migration/p2k0data.asp

Watters, C. (*2008*) *Refugee Children: Towards the Next Horizon*. London: Routledge.

Wolf, D. L. (1997) "Family secrets: Transnational struggles among children of Filipino immigrants" *Sociological Perspectives* 40(3): 455–480.

Yoon, I. J. (1997) *On My Own: Korean Businesses and Race Relations in America*. Chicago, IL: University of Chicago Press.

Zenner, W. P. (1991) *Minorities in the Middle: A Cross-Cultural Analysis*. Albany, NY: SUNY Press.

Zhou, M. and Bankston, C. III. (1998) *Growing up American: How Vietnamese Children Adapt to Life in the United States*. New York: Russell Sage Foundation.

Zlotnick, H. (2003) *The Global Dimensions of Female Migration*. Washington, DC: Migration Policy Institute.

Part I
Theories and histories of international migration

Summary theory chapters

This section offers an overview of several of the major theoretical and disciplinary perspectives applied to international migration (economic, environmental, psychological). It also offers summaries of migration history in four major world regions—Africa, Europe, Asia, and the Americas. These broad perspectives introduce readers to many of the disciplinary and conceptual distinctions and assumptions around which studies of international migration have been constructed. It also provides regional and historical backgrounds that trace the origins and trends that underlie contemporary migration.

Economic approaches

In their chapter on economic theories of international migration, Peter Karpestam and Fredrik N. G. Andersson assert that economics literature on the topic has three distinct characteristics. First, it focuses almost entirely on labor-migration, while largely ignoring other types of migrants, such as refugees. Second, it reflects a well-known, but seldom discussed, division between internal migration (migration within countries) and international migration. Third, it emphasizes the determinants of migration rather than their consequences.

The chapter explores six common economic theories of international migration, evaluates empirical support for them and examines their policy implications. Despite the many types of labor migration theories advanced by economists, the authors suggest that they can be classified into either of the two following categories: (1) theories that concern the initiating causes of migration and (2) theories regarding the self-perpetuation of migration. Neoclassical theory, the new economics of labor migration theory, and dual/segmented labor market theory represent the first category. Network theory, cumulative causation theory, and institutional theory denote the second.

Karpestam and Andersson assert that migration theories should be seen as complementary rather than contradictory and point out that the analysis of macroeconomic data yields empirical support for several theories depending on the time when data is collected, a supposition that is commonly ignored in the empirical literature.

Psychological approaches

Much scholarship regards international migration as group or collective phenomenon. However, Marc Bornstein, in his chapter on Psychological approaches to international migration points out that individuals live outside countries of origin, not just groups. Accordingly, this chapter's goal is to develop a psychology of individual acculturation in a manner that complements the group-based focus most commonly applied to the study of international migration.

For the vast majority of international migrants, leaving their native country and settling in a new one requires them to contend with very different ways of life associated with the country of origin, on one hand, and the host society on the other. When considered in this way, migration and acculturation constitute thoroughly transforming forces on individual people. Bornstein contends that a comprehensive understanding of acculturation must embrace dual processes of group cultural and individual psychological adjustment that result from contact between two or more groups and their individual members. He goes on to differentiate individual-level from group-level acculturation, stressing that individual-level acculturation is not a uniform process as is often implied by group-level analysis and demonstrates that the psychological study of acculturation raises methodological, disciplinary, and policy considerations that are neglected in group-level approaches. Next, the chapter distinguishes and discusses *variability* of different sorts that constitutes the heart of individual psychological acculturation. Finally, the chapter points to promising future directions for the development of theory and empirical inquiry in the study of psychological acculturation.

Climate/environment

In this chapter on environmental theory, László J. Kulcśar describes the history of relations between ecology, environment, and migration. He details how topical concerns associated with particular periods shaped theorizing and areas of investigation. In the most general terms, climate change should be understood as part of the dynamic environmental context in which human actions take place. Recently, there has been an emphasis on developing interdisciplinary perspectives to understand the links between human and natural systems. Demography has a crucial role in this endeavor, drawing from the long history of research on the links between population dynamics and the environment by examining case studies of environmental disasters such as the 1906 San Francisco Earthquake, the Dust Bowl of the 1930s in the USA—an extensive drought that caused thousands of people to abandon the great plains—and Hurricane Katrina which flooded New Orleans in 2005.

Using social demography, Kulcśar provides a conceptual framework to understand the links between migration and climate change. He discusses the mechanisms through which climate change, such as changing temperature and humidity, sea-level rise, and extreme weather hazards, impacts migration behavior. The chapter examines motives for flight, resources available to migrants, and the temporary or permanent status of environmentally driven migrations. Finally, the chapter discusses some of the unique features of environmentally-motivated migrations. While socially or economically determined travel abroad can offer migrants a degree of freedom with regard to the timing of their departure, major environmental disasters like floods, earthquakes, tsunamis, or volcanic eruptions often preclude the exit of those most directly impacted. If residents wait until models that can accurately predict the timing and impact of such events to depart, their flight may be too late. Accordingly, preventative action must be taken before comprehensive analysis is complete.

Historical approaches by world region

A considerable body of the literature on international migration has been created by historians. The products of this research are essential for understanding the origins of contemporary migration, the nature of the migration process and in order to compare the experience of today's migrants to those moving during earlier periods.

The historical perspective is indispensable because other scholarly disciplines that examine international migration—most notably the social sciences—address only the present. This is a consequence of disciplinary and institutional pressures to address immediate social problems, inform and influence social policy, in response to the dictates of funding agencies (which regard historical research to be lacking in practical application), and because cutting-edge research techniques do not lend themselves to the analysis historical data (Mills 1959; Wallerstein 1997).

Despite the clear value of historical studies of international migration, historians have themselves become increasingly critical of many aspects of their discipline, noting that established scholarship is insufficiently complex, has failed to attend to the full variation of migrant process and populations, and is "limited and skewed" (Hoerder and Harzig 2009: 1). Focusing excessively on migrants to the USA, the field has neglected women and non-white people, has ignored return migration, makes ill-informed and arbitrary distinctions between various conceptual categories and world regions, and devotes insufficient effort to recording the myriad social processes in countries of origin (Hoerder and Harzig 2009).

In an effort to address the origins and current trends of migration, four chapters provide a historical summary of migration patterns in four world regions—Europe, by Leo and Jan Lucassen, Asia by Adam McKeown, Africa by Solomon Getahun, and the Americas by Donna Gabaccia. These chapters offer a framing and contextualization of international migration while also addressing the diversity and complexity that is too often elided in existing literature.

References and further reading

Hoerder, D. and Harzig, C. with Gabaccia, D. (2009) *What is Migration History?* Cambridge, UK: Polity Press.

Mills, C. W. (1959) *The Sociological Imagination*. New York: Oxford University Press.

Wallerstein, I. (1997) "Eurocentrism and its avatars: The dilemmas of social science" *The New Left Review* I/226, November-December: 93–107.

Economic perspectives on migration

Peter Karpestam and Fredrik N. G. Andersson

Introduction

The economic literature on migration has grown rapidly over the last decades. Although the literature covers a wide range of different topics which are all related to migration, it has three distinct characteristics. First, it focuses almost entirely on labor migration, and other types of migrants (e.g. refugees) are typically ignored. Second, it contains a well-known, but often unexpressed, division between internal migration (migration within countries) and international migration (King and Skeldon 2010). Third, it emphasizes on the determinants of migration rather than their consequences (Greenwood 1985). However, because the causes of migration and its consequences are closely related, the same theories can be used to explain both international and internal migration.

There are numerous theories that explain migration. Because motives to migrate are complex, these different theories should be viewed as complementary rather than contradictory. In this chapter we explore six common theories, discuss their policy implications, and their empirical support. We end the chapter by reflecting on a commonly ignored issue in empirical surveys, i.e., we discuss the importance of accounting for different time horizons when evaluating causes and effects of migration empirically. This discussion highlights the importance of viewing migration theories as complementary rather than contradictory.

Despite the existence of numerous labor migration theories, these can effectively be classified into either of the two following categories: (1) theories of the initiating causes of migration and (2) theories of the self-perpetuating causes of migration (Massey *et al.* 1993). At least three theories can be placed in the first category; neoclassical theory, the new economics of labor migration theory and dual/segmented labor market theory. And, at least three theories can be placed in the second category; network theory, cumulative causation theory, and institutional theory.

In neoclassical theory, individuals will migrate when the expected income is higher at the destination than at their current residence. The New Economics of Labor Migration (NELM) theory, on the other hand, stresses the importance of the household as the decision maker rather than the individual, and hypothesizes that individuals are not indifferent to risk (i.e. they are risk-averse). Therefore, population movements can take place even if there are no perceived differences in the expected income between regions, which are not possible in neoclassical models. Dual Labor Market Theory studies migration at a higher level of aggregation than the former theories, and emphasizes basic structural characteristics (e.g. the wage formation process) in the economy, which creates a demand for immigrant labor. The Dual Labor Market theory was mainly developed to explain some empirical observations, typically unexplained by other models. For example, the income distribution in many economies is not entirely explained by the fact that different individuals have different talents and levels of education (Cain 1976).

The second category of theories involves explanations of the self-perpetuating mechanisms of migration. Simply put, these theories explain how current migration flows can cause future population movements. Network theory, for instance, belongs to this category as it acknowledges the fact that migrants provide friends and relatives back home with support and information about the destination area. Connections between migrants and relatives back home therefore induce more migration.

Cumulative Causation theory explains several self-perpetuating forces of migration, for instance the effects of migration on the income distribution and agricultural production in origin areas. Institutional theory focuses on the necessary institutions, which assist both legal and illegal (typically international) migration. One example relates to the fact that many countries restrict immigration, which generates a need for services that can assist the "underground migrants." Therefore, former migration leads to more migration because of the formation of different underground activities such as smuggling of migrants and providing the migrants with false documents (visas, passports, etc.).

In the remainder of the chapter we discuss, more extensively, each of the mentioned theories one by one. In the second section we discuss theories of the initiating causes of migration. In the third section, we discuss the self-perpetuating forces of migration. In the fourth section we elaborate on empirical issues and exemplify by drawing from our own work on migrant remittances.

Theories of the initiating forces of migration

Neoclassical theories of migration

For a long period of time, neoclassical theory was the dominating paradigm in economics. In neoclassical theory, it is assumed that individuals are rational, risk-neutral, and that they maximize their utility (which typically implies maximizing their income). Under these assumptions, it has been possible to establish different hypotheses, which explain migration from both a micro- and a macroeconomic perspective.

The early microeconomic neoclassical theories of migration states that individuals migrate when the wage is higher elsewhere than at the current residence (Sjaastad 1962). Todaro (1969) and Harris and Todaro (1970), which are two of the most significant contributions to neoclassical migration theory, extend this proposition by suggesting that instead of actual wage differential, migration is *de facto* driven by the expected wage differences between regions. To illustrate this point, assume an individual considers migrating in order to increase her income. If she evaluates that the benefits exceeds the costs, she migrates. Assume she has a real wage of 10 dollars at her current profession and residence. Further assume that if she chooses to migrate, she has a chance to double her real wage to 20 dollars. However, migrating may also result in unemployment. Let p denote the probability of being employed if she migrates and, consequently, $(1-p)$ the probability of being unemployed. The expected income from migrating equals $p \times 2\varphi + (1-p)\chi\theta$. If this expected income exceeds her present income of 10 dollars she migrates, otherwise not. This simple calculation can be made more complicated by, for example adding the costs of migration. If migrating is associated with traveling expenses, the expected income from migrating equals $p\times 2\varphi+(1-p)\chi\theta-$traveling costs. Her migration choice is consequently based on her perceived probability of being employed at the destination, her expected income if employed, and the costs of traveling to the destination. The greater the probability of employment and the lower the traveling cost, the higher incentives to migrate. The higher the costs to migrate, the fewer who will afford to move. This means that individuals who arguably have the highest incentives to migrate (i.e. the poor) may end up staying at home.

At the macroeconomic level, the neoclassical models shifts focus from the individual toward supply-side growth theories. At the macroeconomic level, migration is an essential part of a developing country's transition toward a developed economy. According to neoclassical growth models, there are three main sources of growth: technology advancement, capital accumulation, and labor accumulation. Lewis (1954) and Ranis and Fei (1961) expand the neoclassical growth model to take into account the initial development stages that transition countries goes through in their transformation toward a developed economy. A large part of the labor force is employed in agriculture at the initial stages of the transition period. The agricultural sector is assumed to be overpopulated with surplus labor, and the amount of land available is not enough to occupy the available labor in farming. Agricultural wages are thus driven down to a subsistence wage. Wages in industry are higher, but limited capital availability restricts the expansion of this sector. Capital accumulation in the industry sector generates an increased labor demand. Because the industry sector offers higher wages than the traditional sector, labor migrates from agriculture to the industry. This way, labor migration constitutes an essential part of the growth process in developing countries and the accumulation of capital is fundamental for sustained economic growth.

Certainly, the Lewis model is relevant for many aspects but is still unable to explain the population movements from rural to urban areas that occur "despite the existence of positive marginal products in agriculture and significant levels of urban unemployment."[1] In the Lewis model, the urban sector is assumed to be able to absorb all labor coming from rural areas, and therefore there should be no urban unemployment, which is clearly unrealistic. By introducing the concept of minimum wages in the urban sector, the Harris–Todaro model is able to explain how urban unemployment arises. Harris and Todaro state that the legally determined minimum wage in many countries is considerably higher than the wage that otherwise arises when the labor markets are unregulated. Firms in the industrial sector therefore cannot afford to absorb all rural–urban migrants.

Attempts to empirically evaluate the neoclassical models involve statistical testing of whether wages and unemployment rates at the origin and destination areas influence migratory flows. Several studies support that both higher incomes and better employment possibilities create incentives to migrate (see e.g. Todaro 1980; Greenwood 1985; Pederzen et al. 2004). But, the early neoclassical models have been criticized for their simplifying and restrictive assumptions. For example, in the Harris–Todaro model it is assumed that all individuals are homogeneous and therefore have an equal chance of finding employment when they migrate. However, because individuals are heterogeneous and individual characteristics such as age, gender, education, etc., affect wages and the chances of employment, these attributes should also affect the decision to migrate as well.

There are several attempts to account for heterogeneity among individuals in the neoclassical models. Borjas (1987), a major contributor in this field, suggests that the income distribution in both origin and destination areas influences migration. An unequal income distribution normally implies high economic returns (wages, etc.) to education and entrepreneurial activities. Therefore, if the income distribution is more unequal at the destination than at the origin, this induces a "positive selection" of migrants. Positive selection refers to the situation where the average migrant is more skilled, more entrepreneurial and has more education than the average native at the origin. Positive migrant selection implies a "brain drain," which retards the economic development in origin areas. In contrast, a more equal income distribution at the destination than at the origin implies that migrants are "negatively selected," meaning that the average migrant is less able than the average native in the origin country. Negative selection contradicts the "brain drain" hypothesis as it rather implies a "brain gain" for origin areas. Under these circumstances, it is more likely that the typical migrant is unemployed and uneducated rather than highly educated and skilled. Which type of migrant selection that dominates clearly influences how well migrants are assimilated in destination areas.

The empirical research regarding migrant selection yields mixed results and support both the existence of positive and negative selection of migrants. For example, Chiswick (1978) finds support of positive selection of immigrants in the USA based on the 1970 population census. Immigrants earn less than Native-born Americans when they arrive, but they are able to catch up and go beyond after 10–15 years in USA.[2] In later years, however, the quality of immigrants reflected in for example t, have decreased which probably is a result of the 1965 Immigration and Nationality Act. The 1965 Immigration and Nationality Act reformed the US immigration policy by abolishing national origin criteria. Further, Mexican immigrants have a higher return on education in Mexico than in the USA (Taylor 1986), which implies that Mexican emigrants are negatively selected.

Besides accounting for the selection process of migrants, there are additional discussions in the literature. One specific example concerns the impact on migration of welfare systems in destination countries. Borjas (1999) argues that generous welfare systems can compensate for a high risk of unemployment and help to attract immigrants. However, the empirical evidence on this topic is mixed (Zadovny 1997; Urrutia 2001; Hatton and Williamson 2002). For example, there is little evidence of any effect on population movements from old to new member states when the European Union (EU) accepted additional members back in the 1980s. Further, the recent widening of the EU in 2004 did not result in large migratory flows from post-communist Eastern Europe to Western Europe. Despite this, the majority of the EU 15 member states restricted migrant workers' access to the labor markets and the immigrants' eligibility to social benefits when ten countries joined the EU in 2004.

Despite these extensions of neoclassical theory, some criticism remains. For example, recall the neoclassical prediction that individuals migrate as long as the expected income is higher at the destination than the certain income at the origin. This proposal originates from the assumption that individuals are indifferent to risk. But, to migrate is associated with both risks (e.g. ending up unemployed) and the possibility to improve the standard of living. Arguably, because of risk aversion, potential migrants can refrain from migrating, even if the expected income is higher at the destination than the origin, which is not a possible scenario in the neoclassical models. Supplementary theories have been developed to account for this and additional aspects which, given the neoclassical theories' assumptions, cannot be incorporated in the neoclassical models.

The new economics of labor migration

The new economics of labor migration (NELM) originates from the observation that rural–urban migration in developing countries started to increase from the 1970s, and as the rate of immigration into cities exceeded the pace of urban job creation, this resulted in accelerating urban unemployment. Up to this point, migration had been perceived as purely positive phenomenon,

15

which reallocates labor from low to high productive activities (i.e. as in the Lewis–Ranis–Fei model). But, alongside with growing unemployment rates in the cities, the increase of rural–urban migration resulted in hygiene problems, increased crime rates, and a growing urban informal sector (Todaro 1980). The large flow of internal migrants in developing countries could not be explained based on neoclassical assumptions alone and additional theories with complementary explanations were needed.

The NELM became a popular theory in the 1980s as it responded to the critique against neoclassical models along at least three dimensions: (1) that migration often takes place despite lower expected income at the destination area than at the origin, (2) that migration is not always permanent, but can also be temporary (see e.g. Stark and Levhari 1982), and (3) that households (and individuals) are risk-neutral. Neoclassical theory focuses on the individual and does not account for migrant ties with family and friends back home. One implication of the neoclassical theory is that migrants do not have any incentives to return as long as they do not perceive that they can increase their income this way. However, NELM stresses the importance of family ties, and assumes that decisions to migrate take place at the household level, as opposed to the individual level in the neoclassical models.

The unique contribution of NELM is the assumption that households, and not individuals, are the main decision-makers to analyze. NELM also relaxes the neoclassical assumption that individuals are risk-neutral. Instead, NELM assumes that households are risk-averse. Given the NELM assumptions, three main hypotheses about the determinants of migration have been formulated: (1) the insurance hypothesis, (2) the investment hypothesis, and (3) the hypothesis of relative deprivation.

The insurance hypothesis posits that households in rural areas send migrants to diversify their sources of income for the purpose of insuring themselves against unforeseen economic shocks such as cattle disease, crop failure, or a tropical storm. Households in poor countries have more uncertain incomes than in richer countries and typically lack social benefits such as unemployment insurance and public health care. If households are unable to acquire an insurance policy, NELM suggests that they will use other strategies, such as sending a migrant to work in the city.

The investment hypothesis posits that households engage in migration in order to overcome malfunctioning credit markets, which are typically apparent in developing countries. If households cannot obtain bank loans, they can send migrants in order to increase their income, income that they then can use for productive investments in the family business.

The relative deprivation hypothesis states that households send migrants to reduce their sense of relative deprivation compared to other nearby households. If households feel that they are poor compared to other households, this motivates them to send migrants elsewhere in order to increase their relative income.

From NELM, we can draw the following conclusions. First, migration does not stop when there are no regional differences in expected income. Other factors such as the local income distribution and the income volatility (i.e. not the level of income) of households are also important determinants of migration. For example, households with highly uncertain incomes are more inclined to send migrants. Moreover, policy-makers are able to influence migration flows by adjusting the share of population which is eligible for different types of social benefits (e.g. unemployment compensation) or giving farmers proprietorship to their land because they can use their land as collateral when applying for a loan.

NELM was first developed to explain rural–urban migration in developing countries but has become a popular theory to explain international migration, in particular migration from developing countries to developed countries. Several empirical studies find support of either one or several hypothesis of NELM (see e.g. Ryan et al. 2010; Willis and Yeoh 2010). An early and one of the most influential studies (Lucas and Stark 1985) found that remittances to rural households in Botswana increased during times of droughts (i.e. evidence of the insurance hypothesis). This supports that migrated relatives provide their families with economic assistance when times are hard. Moreover, numerous studies show that households use remittances for productive purposes such as schooling and entrepreneurial activities which supports the investment hypothesis (see e.g. Cox-Edwards and Ureta 2003; Woodruff and Zentono 2007; Adams *et al.* 2010). The alternative perspective offered by NELM and the existing empirical support make NELM an important complement to the neoclassical theories.

Segmented/dual labor market theory

The segmented labor market theory (SLM theory) was developed to explain social problems that are often associated with labor migration, such as poverty, labor market discrimination, and the observed ineffectiveness of education to render higher earnings among migrants (Cain 1976). The perseverance of these social problems in the USA in the 1960s "despite anti-poverty and training programs," motivated researchers to develop additional theories.

SLM is foremost a labor market theory, which has been extended to consider the consequences of labor migration. Both the neoclassical theory and the NELM theory are mainly microeconomic theories with a focus on individuals and households. SLM, on the other hand, stresses several complex macroeconomic structural features in destination countries, which contribute to create a segmented labor market and a demand for immigrant labor. For example, SLM theory divides the economy into a primary and secondary sector (Souza-Posa 2004). In the primary sector, wages are high, jobs are secure, and there are significant returns to education whereas the secondary sector employs low-wage, unskilled labor, has a low degree of job security and low returns to education. The distinction between a primary and a secondary sector is motivated theoretically by the existence of institutional regulations (e.g. minimum wages) which protects the primary sector from uncertain elements, e.g. business cycle fluctuations (see Piore 1975). Some countries have established minimum wages by law while other countries adhere to negotiations between employers and labor unions. Monetary and fiscal policies are frequently employed by policy-makers to minimize fluctuations in national incomes and unemployment rates.

The two sectors are linked because the regulations in the primary sector influence the secondary sector's recruitment of labor as well. Consider, for example, the determination of wages. In most industrialized countries, the wage setting process is a combination of the negotiations between individual employers and employees on the one hand, and between employer organizations and unions on the other. This means that when employers are in need of unskilled low-wage labor, it is expensive to try to attract this category of workers by raising their wages because other categories of workers will respond by demanding higher wages too (so that their social status and prestige is maintained). Therefore, the employers are forced to find unskilled labor in other ways, for instance by hiring immigrants, which are not equally concerned about their social status. This way of describing the recruitment process of labor is in contrast to neoclassical theories, which assume one complete and competitive labor market.

SLM theory is able to provide an explanation of migration because the poor working conditions and low wages associated with the secondary market does not attract native workers and employers therefore make use of immigrant labor instead (Piore 1979). Historically, women and teenagers have supplied employers with low-skilled labor, but the increase in female labor participation and the decline in birth rates in later years have reduced the available native labor stock willing to occupy these jobs (Massey *et al.* 1993).

In many ways, SLM appears both logical and appealing, because it emphasizes perspectives which are typically neglected in other theories. But, to validate SLM empirically has proven problematic. Empirical validation of SLM requires being able to confirm that wage differentials are not the mere results of differences in individual skills but also arise because of a segmented labor market. However, this requires defining the dual structures of the economy in an objective and non-arbitrary manner. Empirical studies often find that the labor market is segmented along some particular dimensions (e.g. age, gender) but results are often mixed and typically depend on the exact criteria used to define the duality of the labor market (Cain 1976; Leontaridi 1998; Souza-Poza 2004). Nonetheless, the underlying logic in SLM theories constitute and essential part of understanding the labor market, and have gained increased interest since the 1980s and the 1990s when labor market conditions started to deteriorate in many industrialized countries.

Theories about the self-perpetuating mechanisms of migration

As previously mentioned, several empirical surveys show that socioeconomic variables in both destination and origin areas are important determinants of migration. Moreover, empirical surveys also show that current migration flows is positively influenced by the population movements that have occurred in the past. In this sector we therefore focus on the self-perpetuating forces of migration.

Network theory

Social network theory and its effects on migration has mainly been used in sociology, but it can be extended into economics. Social network theory is related to NELM in two important ways; first it assumes risk-averse individuals, and second it assumes that migrating individuals remain in touch with their family and friends back home. If individuals are risk-averse, they are reluctant to migrate even if the expected income is higher at the destination than at their current residence. However, individuals, who have already migrated can provide friends and family with relevant information about jobs and traveling. This information reduces the potential migrant's risk of unemployment if she migrates, and consequently increases the probability that she migrates. Migration can therefore increase future migratory flows.

The explanatory power of network theory can be assessed at both the community/regional level and at the individual level. At the community level, migration should be more common from regions which have a history of high outmigration (Taylor et al. 2003). On the individual level, increasing the number of contacts (i.e. social networks) in destination areas should raise the propensity among individuals to migrate.

As discussed previously, international migrants and internal migrants are likely to have similar reasons to migrate. But, as emphasized by Massey et al. (1993), social networks are arguably more important for international migrants than for internal migrants. Barriers to moving should be higher and more complex when migrating abroad. To move to another country often involves learning a new language and adapting to a new culture, which is typically not necessary when moving within the same country. Consequently, international migrants rely more on connections and networks with friends and relatives than internal migrants.

Network Theory implies that as the migrant stock in destination areas increases, the migration process should become less selective. Initial migrants do not have any connections with people in the destination area, but as more and more people move, the social connections between the origin and the destination area start to grow. This means that social networks become increasingly important in explaining the migration process and that the characteristics of individuals gradually become less significant. Researchers agree that social networks today comprise one of the most important determinants of population movements (Taylor 1986; Gurac and Cases 2002; Ramamurthy 2003).

Cumulative causation theory

The term cumulative causation, initially coined by Myrdal in 1957, is a general term which refers to any reinforcing chain of events. For example, how poverty generates more poverty or how economic growth can spur even more economic growth. In our context, cumulative causation refers to additional factors, besides social networks, which can explain the self-perpetuating forces of migration. As the reader might notice, some of these explanations are developed from the same assumptions as the theories mentioned in section two. For instance, recall NELM, which predicts that as households send migrants and start to collect remittances, migrant households will become richer than non-migrant households. This will increase the sense of relative deprivation among non-migrant households, which induces additional households to engage in migration (see e.g. Selby and Murphy 1984). Another explanation relates to "brain-drain," which can occur when migrants are positively selected. If migrants are more productive and entrepreneurial than the average non-migrant at the origin, this will reduce the economic growth in source regions compared to the destination areas, inducing even more people to leave. This pattern is confirmed in Mexico, where the youngest and most productive household members are typically the ones who migrate from rural areas (Reichert 1982).

A third explanation concerns agricultural activities. For example, migrants may use their income from abroad to buy land back home. But, migrants are more likely than local residents to buy land primarily for the purpose of increasing their social status, and they therefore do not make the necessary investments to preserve the land. Moreover, because migrant households have access to more capital (earned from migrant remittances) than non-migrant households, they will adhere to relatively capital-intensive methods (fertilizers, machinery, etc.) when farming (Massey 1987). Therefore, agricultural investments generated from migrant income will reduce the demand for farm labor, causing unemployment and even more outmigration. Other explanations which overlap with other disciplines besides economics relate to cultural and normative factors. Massey *et al.* (1993) explain how immigrants are assimilated into destination areas and as they are starting to work the jobs they are occupying are increasingly perceived as "immigrant jobs" among natives. Hence, the presence of immigrants generates a demand for additional immigrants because certain professions are no longer desirable among natives.

Cumulative causation theory has proven particularly useful for rural communities, which is explained by the fact that there are higher incentives to migrate from rural areas than urban areas in the first place. This, in turn, implies that the cumulative causation mechanisms of migration described above are stronger for rural than urban areas. For example, migrants from rural areas may use their incomes from abroad to purchase land back home, whereas the remittances and savings of urban migrants are more likely to be used for non-productive consumption.

As migrants acquire land back home, this can affect origin areas and render more migration because the migrants may let the land fallow and/or shift towards more capital-intensive methods. However, in urban areas, when migrant incomes are mainly used for consumption this is not likely to generate further population movements. Also, there are higher incentives for the well educated to migrate from rural than from urban areas, because cities have more diversified labor markets. For example, Fussell and Massey (2004) find no evidence of cumulative causation effects on migration between urban areas in Mexico and the USA.

Institutional theory

In economics, institutions are typically defined as entities or communities which share the same rules, norms, and conventions. Consequently, institutions is a broad concept and includes public authorities as well as private firms and different ethnic groups. There is a strong focus in economics on the role of institutions in the general international development process. Popular applications include the impact of institutional development on economic growth and the impact of the current globalization process on the design of political institutions. Institutional theory can contribute to the economic literature on migration through its emphasis on the creation of institutions in the migration process. For instance, international migration can speed up the establishment of cheap flight connections between emigrant and immigrant countries. Lower transportation costs induce more people to migrate. Moreover, when rich countries restrict immigration, this creates an incentive for people to migrate illegally. This encourages the formation of different "underground institutions," which facilitate undocumented migration. These "underground institutions" can provide immigrants with false documents (e.g. passports, visas) and smuggle them across the border (see Massey *et al.* 1993). The number of asylum seekers has soared in recent years and estimates suggest that illegal immigrants increase the foreign-born population in OECD countries by 10–15 percent (Hatton and Williamson 2002), which underlines the relevance of institutional theory as a complement to established theories.

An alternative economic perspective on the empirical literature: an example of migrant remittances

Empirical evaluations of different migration theories often rely on the use of microeconomic data, normally household surveys. Often, these are cross-sectional surveys which means that they only have information about a sample of households and individuals during one specific time period (e.g. a year). Although there are longitudinal studies in the literature, these studies are typically limited to only a few observations. An alternative is to use macroeconomic data, which is often available for several years. Further, by using macroeconomic data, it is possible to make inferences about the aggregated effects of migration, which are relevant for policy-makers. It should be mentioned that microeconomic data, on the other hand, is more detailed than macroeconomic data, and therefore allows for more complex analysis. The remainder of this chapter will discuss the fact that most empirical studies neglect accounting for different time horizons when evaluating causes and effects of migration empirically. We will exemplify this by drawing from our own work on migrant remittances.

Migrant remittances are a significant source of income for many households in low- and middle-income economies. With a total of US$316 billion in 2009, remittances to developing countries exceed official development assistance and are of the same magnitude as foreign direct investments.[3] The empirical economic literature on remittances has explored the effects and consequences of remittances. Although it is compelling to think that remittances generate positive effects for the sending economies by increasing sending households' disposable income. It is not entirely possible to separate between the causes and effects of remittances. Because remittances are partially sent to compensate for low incomes, this creates a problem of "reversed causality."

Reversed causality arises because the compensatory nature of remittances can induce a negative correlation between remittances and different indicators of economic welfare, even if remittances have a positive effect on welfare. Poor households may receive more remittances than rich because they are poor, at the same time as remittances increase the incomes for anyone who receives them. Also, existing theories have different predictions regarding the relationship between remittances and socioeconomic variables in recipient countries. Therefore, it is difficult to use statistical methods to assess whether the economic conditions in remittance receiving areas explain the amount of remittances they are receiving, or if there is a reversed causality involved. The empirical literature has typically dealt with the reversed causality problem by using the instrumental variable technique.

Although using instrumental variables is a conventional econometric technique, which is commonly accepted among researchers, we wish to complement this with an additional and commonly overlooked perspective. In line with conventional macroeconomic theory (see e.g. Samuelson 1954; Goodfriend and King 1997; Woodford 2003), it is reasonable to assume that the correlation between different macroeconomic variables, for example remittances and economic growth, depend on the time horizons (i.e. the short run, the medium run, and the long run). For instance; if remittances are used for consumption, an increase in remittances can cause a temporary boom in demand, but will have no growth effects in the long run. A long-run growth effect only occurs if remittances are used for productive purposes.

Support for the assertion that the relationship between macroeconomic variables depends on the time horizon can also be found in migration theories. Recall NELM, which argues that migration is the outcome of collective decisions made by households. The insurance hypothesis, which belongs to NELM, postulates that households try to diversify their income sources in order to insure themselves against unanticipated economic shocks, and therefore send migrants (Lucas and Stark 1985, 1988). Researchers have investigated whether the insurance motive is relevant in explaining remittance flows or if there are other reasons why migrants remit. The insurance motive is, however, not the only possible explanation for why migrants remit. An alternative explanation is the altruism hypothesis, which states that migrants remit because of emotional ties to relatives back home (see e.g. Karpestam 2009).

When trying to separate between these two motives empirically, there is one important difference between the implications of the altruism and the insurance hypotheses. According to the altruism hypothesis, the amount of remittances is reduced as income and consumption in the receiving country increases and the need for assistance thereby gradually decreases. The insurance hypothesis has no such implications (Rapoport and Docquier 2005), because households are assumed to send migrants to insure themselves against unexpected events, but not to increase their overall income. Both theories, however, suggest that remittances increase when households are exposed to a temporary economic decline. Consequently, if the insurance hypothesis is true, we can expect a negative correlation between remittances and consumption/ income in source countries in the short run, but not in the long run. In contrast, we can find support for the altruism hypothesis if there is a negative correlation between remittances and income/consumption both in the short run and the long run.

Analyzing the correlation between macroeconomic variables over different time horizons yields fruitful insights and is a growing field of research in in macroeconomics (see e.g. Andersson 2008). To illustrate our point, we use data from 50 low and middle income countries covering the period 1980–2006. The data were collected from the World Development Indicators. For this exercise, we are interested in analyzing the relationship between received remittances and consumption of goods and services in remittance receiving countries.

The estimated model is a one way fixed effects panel data model:

$$c_{it}^h = \alpha + y_{it}^h \beta^h + r_{it}^h \gamma^h + \varepsilon_{it}^h \tag{1.1}$$

where i denotes the country, t is time, h is the horizon, c is per capita consumption, y per capita GDP and r per capita remittances. β^h and γ^h are the parameters that that will be estimated which show the relationship between remittances and consumption and GDP and consumption. For instance, if γ^h is positive, consumption and remittances are positively correlated. To be more specific, if $\gamma^h = 0.5$, a one-dollar increase of remittances is coupled with a 50 cents increase of consumption. Note that it is not possible to identify the causal chain, i.e. we cannot infer when a 50 cent increase causes a one-dollar increase in remittances or if it is the other way around.

Even though we cannot make inferences about causal patterns, we can make inferences on whether the correlation between remittances and consumption at different time horizons supports one specific theory or several theories at the same time. We divide the data into a trend component (the long-run) and two cycles (short and medium run).[4] The lengths of the cycles are 2 years (short run), 2–16 years (medium run) and 16 years and beyond (long run). We further divide the sample into growing economies, declining economies, low-income, and middle-income economies. In rapidly growing economies, GDP per capita at least doubled between 1980 and 2006. In declining economies, GDP per capita fell over the same period. Low income countries have an average of less than 10,000 dollars per capita over the period and middle income economies have more than 10,000 dollars per capita on average. The relationship between remittances and consumption is likely to differ between these categories. For instance, rapidly growing economies are likely to have a more developed financial infrastructure than declining economies, which affect how remittances are used and the channels that migrants choose to send remittances through.

Tables 1.1–1.3 show the results from our statistical calculations when the data was decomposed into short-run (1–2 year horizon), the medium-run (2–16 year horizon) and long-run (>16 years) components. Starting with the short-run (1–2 year horizon), Table 1.1 shows a negative and statistically significant relationship between consumption and remittances (−0.37) for rapidly growing economies. This result is consistent with both the altruism hypothesis and the insurance hypothesis, possibly indicating that a decrease in consumption causes an increase in remittances in order to compensate for this fall.

We do not find any significant relationships between consumption and remittances for any of the other subpanels (i.e., declining economies, middle income economies and low income economies) in the short run. The significant parameter for rapidly growing economies may be explained by these economies having more developed financial institutions, which allow rapid support through remittances during economic shocks, for instance a recession.

Table 1.2 presents the regression results for a 2–16 year long cycle (the medium-run). For all sub-panels except declining economies, there is a positive and significant correlation between remittances and consumption. As previously mentioned, it is not possible to draw certain conclusions about causality, but a possible explanation is that remittances help to increase consumption in all countries except for declining economies. Declining economies may not have the necessary financial institutions to allow for rapid increases of remittances during economic downfalls. Also, declining and low income economies generally receive fewer remittances than middle income economies and rapidly growing economies, implying that effects of remittances is small in these countries.

It is interesting to note that there is a stronger positive relationship between remittances and consumption in low income countries than in middle income countries. Moreover, the parameter is particularly high for rapidly growing economies (1.4, Table 1.2). Possibly, the design of institutions allows for a more optimal allocation of financial means in developed countries and rapidly growing economies compared to less developed economies. Remittances can be saved, consumed or invested and it is generally acknowledged that poor households use a relatively large share of their income (including remittances) for non-productive consumption and less for productive investments. If households in the more developed economies use a higher share of

Table 1.1 Regression results short-run (horizon 1–2 years)

Dependent variable	Consumption		
	Estimate	SD	P-value
All countries			
GDP	0.533***	0.123	0.000
Remittances	0.001	0.227	0.498
R²	0.645		
Rapidly growing economies			
GDP	0.509**	0.274	0.032
Remittances	−0.372***	0.101	0.000
R²	0.598		
Declining economies			
GDP	0.284	0.433	0.256
Remittances	1.812	1.676	0.140
R²	0.501		
Low income economies			
GDP	0.291***	0.069	0.000
Remittances	0.108	0.179	0.273
R²	0.607		
Middle income economies			
GDP	0.536***	0.126	0.000
Remittances	0.016	0.225	0.471
R²	0.646		

their received remittances for productive investments, remittances can increase economic growth and consequently consumption more in the developed countries compared to less developed countries. Possibly, this effect may be best captured at the 2–16 year horizon. Although we cannot make certain statements about causality, this is one possible explanation which suggests that the causal relationship of how remittance affects consumption is best represented when the data is decomposed into a 2–16-year horizon, and that the reversed effect, i.e., how the level of consumption affects the remittances that will be received is best captured when the data is decomposed into either a 1–2-year or a >16-year horizon. This would indicate that the process through which remittances boost GDP growth and consumption lasts between 2 and 16 years, but that the effect has vanished after 16 years and that the impact of remittances have not reached their full effect before 1–2 years.

Table 1.3 shows the estimated regression results for the long-run (>16 year horizon). There is a negative relationship between remittances and consumption for rapidly growing economies and middle income countries (−0.35 and −0.51, respectively). This is supportive of the altruism hypothesis but not the insurance hypothesis. However, for low income economies there is a significant positive relationship (0.317) and for declining economies the correlation is insignificant (−0.085). The combination of these results suggests that as the national income increases beyond a certain level of development, remittances start to decrease. Before countries have reached a specific level of income, migrants will continue to remit. Because these countries are poor, the need for remittances does not cease until a certain level of development is reached.

Table 1.2 Regression results medium-run (horizon 2–16 years)

Dependent variable	Consumption		
	Estimate	SD	P-value
All countries			
GDP	0.600***	0.108	0.000
Remittances	0.893***	0.291	0.001
R^2	*0.785*		
Rapidly growing economies			
GDP	0.692***	0.260	0.000
Remittances	1.424***	0.204	0.000
R^2	*0.908*		
Declining economies			
GDP	0.561***	0.165	0.000
Remittances	0.003	0.316	0.462
R^2	*0.704*		
Low income economies			
GDP	0.319***	0.061	0.000
Remittances	1.127***	0.430	0.005
R^2	*0.753*		
Middle income economies			
GDP	0.602***	0.109	0.000
Remittances	0.872***	0.288	0.001
R^2	*0.783*		

As illustrated by our results, different theories are supported at different time horizons. This suggests that individuals/households have a more complex behavior than predicted by only one theory. From this result, we can draw two conclusions; First, different theories should be seen as complementary rather than contradictory. Second, when analyzing macroeconomic data, it is important to consider different time horizons.

Summary

In this chapter, we have explored common economic migration theories and discussed their different implication regarding the socioeconomic consequences of migration for origin areas as well as emigration areas. We have discussed neoclassical theories, the New Economics of Labor Migration, Segmented Labor Market Theory and different theories about the self-perpetuating forces of migration (i.e., Network Theory, Institutional Theory and Cumulative Causation Theory). The overall conclusion is that migration theories should be seen as complementary rather than contradictory. Empirical research supports the finding that poverty constraints in source countries, wage gaps between rich and poor countries and the migrant stock in destination areas are all fundamental in explaining world migration patterns since the nineteenth century (see e.g. Hatton and Williamson 2002). The nineteenth century is often perceived as the initiating epoch of "mass migration." Between 1820 and 1913, more than 50 million migrants left Europe, crossed the Atlantic Ocean and arrived in "the New World." Ever since, immigration to the western hemisphere has been significant, with labor migration being the dominant form during

Table 1.3 Regression results long run (>16 years)

Dependent variable	Consumption		
	Estimate	SD	P-value
All countries			
GDP	0.445***	0.045	0.000
Remittances	−0.347***	0.133	0.005
R^2	0.801		
Rapidly growing economies			
GDP	0.330***	0.095	0.000
Remittances	−0.510***	0.174	0.002
R^2	0.655		
Declining economies			
GDP	0.580***	0.034	0.000
Remittances	−0.085	0.316	0.394
R^2	0.983		
Low income economies			
GDP	0.317***	0.118	0.004
Remittances	0.687*	0.481	0.077
R^2	0.834		
Middle income economies			
GDP	0.446***	0.046	0.000
Remittances	−0.349***	0.134	0.005
R^2	0.801		

the first half of the twentieth century but with refugee and family reunification being on the rise during the second half. We have also shown that when using macroeconomic data, there is empirical support for several theories at different time horizons, an issue which is typically ignored in the empirical literature. Our precognition is that this is going to be an important topic in the economic literature on migration as well as within other sub-disciplines of economics in the future.

Notes

1 Harris and Todaro (1970), p. 126.
2 This pattern is found extensively in the literature, see e.g. Vijverberg and Zeager (1994).
3 www.worldbank.org, June 1, 2010.
4 For this purpose, we use a maximal overlap discrete wavelet transform (see Percival and Walden 2006).
5 Harris and Todaro (1970) p. 126.
6 This pattern is found extensively in the literature, see e.g. Vijverberg and Zeager (1994).
7 www.worldbank.org, June 1, 2010.
8 For this purpose, we use a maximal overlap discrete wavelet transform (see Percival and Walden 2006).

References and further reading

Adams, Jr., Richard, H., and Cuecuecha, A. (2010) "Remittances, household expenditure and investment in Guatemala" *World Development* 38(11): 1626–41.
Andersson, F. N. G. (2008) "Wavelet analysis of economic time series" *Lund Economic Studies* No. 149.

Borjas, G. J. (1987) "Self-selection and the earnings of immigrants" *The American Economic Review* 77(4): 531–53.

Borjas, G. J. (1999) "Immigration and welfare magnets" *Journal of Labor Economics* 17(4): 607–37.

Cain, G. C. (1976) "The challenge of segmented labor market theories to orthodox theories: A survey" *Journal of Economic Literature* 14(4): 1215–57.

Catrinescu, N., Leon-Ledesma, M., Piracha, M., and Quillin, B. (2009) "Remittances, institutions, and economic growth" *World Development* 37(1): 81–92.

Chiswick B. R. (1978) "The effect of the Americanization on the earnings of foreign-born men" *Journal of Political Economy* 86(51): 897–921.

Cox-Edwards, A and Ureta, M. (2003) "International migration, remittances and schooling evidence from El Salvador" *Journal of Development Studies* 72(2): 429–61.

Fussell, E. and Massey, D. S. (2004) "The limits to cumulative causation: International migration from Mexican urban areas" *Demography* 4(1): 151–71.

Goodfriend, M and King, R. C. (1997) "The new neoclassical synthesis and the role of monetary policy" *NBER Macroeconomic Annual* 12: 231–83.

Greenwood, J. M. (1985) "Human migration: theory, models, and empirical studies" *Journal of Regional Science* 25(4): 521–44.

Gurac, D. and Cases, F. (2002) "Migration networks and the shaping of migration systems." In M. Kritz, L. L. Lim, and H. Zlotnik, *International Migration Systems: A Global Approach.* Oxford: Clarendon Press, pp. 150–76.

Harris, J. and Todaro, M. (1970) "Migration, unemployment and development: A two-sector analysis" *American Economic Review* 40: 126–42.

Hatton, T. and Willamson, J. G. (2002) "What fundamentals drive world migration?" *NBER Working Paper* No. 9159.

Karpestam, P (2009) "Economics of migration." *Lund Economic Studies* No. 153.

King, R and R. Skeldon (2010) "'Mind the gap!' Integrating approaches to internal and international migration" *Journal of Ethnic and Migration Studies* 36(10): 1619–46.

Leontaridi, M. R. (1998) "Segmented labour markets: Theory and evidence" *Journal of Economic Surveys* 12(1): 63–101.

Lewis, W. A. (1954) "Economic development with unlimited supplies of labour" *The Manchester School of Economics and Social Studies* 22(2): 139–91.

Lucas, R. E. B. and Stark, O. (1985) "Motivations to remit: Evidence from Botswana" *Journal of Political Economy* 93(5): 901–18.

Lucas, R. E. B. and Stark, O. (1988), "Migration, remittances, and the family" *Economic Development and Cultural Change* 36(3): 465–81.

Massey, D. S. (1987) "The Ethnosurvey in theory and practice" *International Migration Review* 21(4): 498–522.

Massey D. S., Arango, J., Hugo, G. Kouaiuci, A., and Pellegrino, A. (1993) "Theories of international migration: A review and appraisal" *Population and Development Review* 19(3): 465–81.

Myrdal, G. (1957) *Rich Lands and Poor.* New York: Harper and Row.

Pederzen, J., Pytlikova, M. and Smith, N. (2004) "Selection or network effects? Migration flows into 27 OECD countries 1990–2000" IZA Discussion Papers.

Percival, D. B. and Walden, A. T. (2006) *Wavelet Methods for Time Series Analysis.* New York: Cambridge University Press.

Piore, M. J. (1975) "Notes for a theory of labor market stratification." In R. Edwards, M. Reich, and D. M. Gordon (eds), *Labor Market Segmentation.* Lexington MA: D. C. Heath.

Piore, M. (1979) *Birds of Passage: Migrant Labor Industrial,* Cambridge: Cambridge University Press

Ranis, G. and Fei, J. C. H. (1961) "A theory of economic development" *American Economic Review* 51(4): 533–65.

Ramamurthy, B. (2003) International labour migration: Unsung heroes of globalization. *SidaStudies* No. 8.

Rapoport, H. and Docquier, F. (2005) "The economics of migrants' remittances." In *Handbook of the Economics of Giving, Altruism and Reciprocity.* Vol. 2, pp. 1135–98.

Reichert, J. S. (1982) "Social stratification in a Mexican sending community: The effect of migration to the United States" *Social Problems* 29(4): 422–33.

Ryan, L., Sales, R. Tilki, M., and Bernadetta, S. (2010) "Family strategies and transnational migration: Recent Polish migrants in London" *Journal of Ethnic and Migration Studies* 35(1): 61–77.

Samuelson, P. (1954) *Economics.* New York: McGraw and Hill.

Selby, H. A. and Murphy, A. D. (1984) "The Mexican urban household and the decision to migrate to the United States, Occasional Papers in Social Change." No. 4, Philadelphia, PA: Institute for the Study of Human Issues.

Sjaastad, L. (1962) "The costs and returns of human migration" *Journal of Political Economy* 70S: 80–3.

Souza-Poza, A. (2004) "Is the Swiss labor market segmented? An analysis using alternative approaches" *Labour* 18(1): 131–61.

Stark, O. and Levhari, D. (1982) "On migration and risk in LDCs" *Economic Development and Cultural Change* 31(1): 191–6.

Taylor, J. E. (1986) "Differential migration, networks, information and risk." In O. Stark (ed.), *Research in Human Capital and Development, 4 Migration, Human Capital, and Development.* Greenwhich, CT: JAI Press, pp. 147–71.

Taylor, J.E, De Brauw A., and Rozelle, S. (2003) "Migration and income in source communities: A new economics of migration perspective from China" *Economic Development and Cultural Change* 52(1): 75–101.

Todaro, M. P. (1969) "A model of labor migration and urban unemployment in less developed countries" *The American Economic Review* 59(1): 138–48.

Todaro, M. (1980) "Internal migration in developing countries: A survey." In R. A. Easterlin (ed.), *Population Change in Developing Countries.* Chicago, IL: University of Chicago Press, pp. 361–402.

Urrutia, C. (2001) "On the self-selection of immigrants" Manuscript, Universidad, Carlos III Madrid.

Vijverberg, W. P. M. and Zeager, L. A. (1994) "Comparing earning profiles in urban areas of an LDC: Rural-to-urban migrants vs. native workers" *Journal of Development Economics* 45: 177–99.

Willis, K. D. and Yeoh, B. S. A. (2010) "Gender and transnational household strategies: Singaporean migration to China" *Regional Studies* 34(3): 253–64.

Woodford, M. (2003) *Interest and Prices, Foundations of a Theory of Monetary Policy.* Princeton, NJ: Princeton University Press.

Woodruff, C. and Zenteno, R. (2007) "Migrant networks and micro-enterprises in Mexico" *Journal of Development Economics* 82(2): 509–28.

Zadovny M. (1997) "Welfare and the locational choices of new immigrants" *Economic Review—Federal Reserve Bank of Dallas*; Second Quarter 1997.

2

The day after tomorrow

Migration and climate change

László J. Kulcsár

Introduction

Climate change has attracted considerable academic attention over recent years. The first emphasis was on the description and correct measurement of the phenomenon as well as the development of appropriate models to predict its course. Later the discourse was extended to the global and local inequalities regarding the impact of climate change and the political economy surrounding it.

In the most general terms, climate change should be understood as part of the dynamic environmental context in which human actions take place. Changing environmental conditions have been migration drivers throughout human history. Climate change is the most current example of this, and it is important to investigate its unique dynamics related to migration. Recently, there has been a clear emphasis on developing interdisciplinary perspectives to understand the links between human and natural systems. In this endeavor demography has a crucial role, building on the long history of demographic research on the links between population dynamics and the environment.

In this chapter, using the perspective of social demography, I provide a conceptual framework to facilitate the understanding of the links between migration and climate change. Following an overview of scholarship on population, migration, and the environment, I discuss the mechanisms through which climate change impacts migration behavior, such as changing temperature and humidity, sea-level rise and extreme weather hazards.

Population, migration, and the environment

The population–environment nexus has intrigued demographers since the time of Malthus and his pessimistic predictions about population and food production. The academic discourse on population and environment had three major phases (Pebley 1998). The first was the original Malthusian concern about food production, most clearly represented in its modern form by Ehrlich (1968), running parallel with the debate on the link between population growth and economic development (Boserup 1965; Coale 1976; Simon 1981; Keyfitz 1990; Gaburro and Poston 1991; Tiffen 1993; McNicoll 2003). The alarmist tone of the debate determined the public perception of population issues following World War II, but especially in the 1960s and 1970s.

In the 1970s, with the onset of the Green Revolution, the emphasis has shifted to investigate the impact of human activities on the environment, but it kept the general alarmist tone. Following the report "The Limits to Growth" (Meadows *et al.* 1972) and the global oil crisis of 1973, public and academic attention turned to non-renewable energy sources and pollution at the global scale. The theoretical outcome of this debate was the inclusion of concepts such as sustainability and carrying capacity to academic discourse (Boserup 1976; Gilland 1983; Rees 1996). At the same time, the conceptual understanding of this impact was condensed into the IPAT formula (Ehrlich and Holden 1971; Ehrlich and Ehrlich 1990) IPAT (I = PAT or I = $P \star A \star T$) is an abstract formula illustrating how the human impact on environment (I) is a function of population (P), affluence (A), and technology (T). IPAT was not a mathematical equation, and while various attempts were made to elaborate this formula (Commoner 1972; York *et al.* 2003), the conceptualization and operationalization of affluence and technology seems to be elusive enough to remain a major obstacle for a working mathematical model.

The emphasis on pollution led to the third major phase of the debate in the late 1980s, first about the ozone layer and then gradually shifting to the issues of global warming and climate change in general. Originally, it investigated and emphasized the global impact of climate change. Then as the climate models have become more sophisticated, the discourse shifted to the local impacts of climate change, understanding that different regions will be affected in very different ways.

The demographic aspect of the discourse has shifted away from resources to impact, using climate change as the independent variable. Considerable attention was given to the health risks of climate change, as one particular mechanism through which changing temperature and humidity can affect population trends (Haines and Patz 2004; Patz *et al.* 2005; McMichael *et al.* 2006). This impact could be either direct, for example the deaths from the 2003 heat wave in Europe (Haines *et al.* 2006), or indirect by increasing the risk for other health problems.

Migration as a study area has been present in ecological analysis for quite some time (see Poston and Frisbie 2005 for an overview). It was added to the population and environment debate in the 1970s, when Lester Brown has coined the term "environmental refugees" (Massey *et al.* 2010), referring to people who are displaced due to extreme weather hazards. The estimates about the number of environmental or climate refugees/migrants have been increasing (Myers 1993; 1997) parallel with efforts to better specify the population at risk (Black 2001; Castles 2002). This discourse was the first to explicitly address global environmental factors behind migration dynamics, using the alarmist tone which has always characterized the population—resources—impact debates.

The best-known examples for environmental drivers of migration from modern history are usually those that captivated public imagination because they were catastrophic in proportions. The 1906 San Francisco earthquake destroyed half of the housing stock and displaced more than 300,000 people of whom 75,000 never returned (Haas *et al.* 1977). It was clearly a catastrophic event, but only a temporary one from which the city recovered within a few years. Hurricane Katrina in 2005 seemed equally catastrophic with all the destruction, but from a simple long-term demographic perspective, it can also be seen as temporary. Just like San Francisco, New Orleans did not disappear from the map, although the composition of the population can change significantly, especially if the impact is not evenly distributed among the residents.

There is one significant difference between the two cases though. The San Francisco earthquake was a natural disaster with no connection to climate change. Katrina on the other hand was a hurricane, more easily perceived as part of the changing climate conditions with an increasing risk for similar occurrences. This perception is crucial for influencing migration decisions. From this perspective, it is less relevant whether the event has a clear causal connection to climate change, as Hurricane Katrina was as much a man-made disaster as a climate-induced one.

The Dust Bowl in the United States is often cited as the textbook example for changing environmental conditions that induce mass migration. It is also the textbook example of the perfect storm triggered by misunderstood climate cycles and unsustainable farming practices boosted by short-term economic gain. This was a different type of environmental driver compared to Katrina and the San Francisco earthquake, as it lasted for years and impacted a large geographic area. Thus, instead of a shock event of which several are usually needed to fundamentally alter migration streams, the Dust Bowl was a prolonged period of unfavorable conditions, which from a more historical perspective was rather the return of a dry cycle—except that by this time the farming practices destroyed the original land conditions. The resulting mass migration out of the region was permanent, and most of the migrants had not returned when the dry cycle ended in the 1940s.

When migration is a response to changes in environmental conditions, it is sometimes seen as an adaptation procedure (Bardsley and Hugo 2010). Some argue that migration is the evidence for the failure of adaptation (Heine and Petersen 2008). Others state that migration is in fact the procedure of successful adaptation (McLeman and Smit 2006; Tacoli 2009). In either case, there seem to be a clear causal link between the dependent and independent variables.

However, these conditions are not perceived as purely environmental, rather a deterioration of general living conditions (Adamo 2009; Massey *et al.* 2010). This means that people do not necessarily move because of unfavorable weather. Rather weather, or climate in general, becomes one component in migration decision making. The strength of this component depends on many factors of the impact mechanisms, therefore operates differently in various situations. For those displaced by destructive flooding, there is no choice regarding the move and may not be many alternatives regarding the destination either. At the other end of the spectrum are people who worry about air conditioning and water bills in the arid southwest or maybe the increasing home insurance costs around the Gulf of Mexico. For these people, climate change is just one of many indirect factors influencing their migration decision.

Climate change and migration drivers

The fundamental question in the climate change—migration nexus is the causal mechanism between the two, or in other words the dynamics of how climate change works as an independent variable. The most basic understanding of migration uses push and pull factors to describe why people move (Lee 1966). Climate change almost exclusively influences push factors, in contrast to environmental amenities that largely operate through pull factors.

As mentioned before, climate change is usually not the sole factor behind migration decisions. Apart from climate change induced displacement following shock events, it is simply one driver of migration behavior. Thus, if one wants to study the impact of climate change, the task is to find those components of migration decision making that are sensitive to climate conditions, keeping in mind that these components carry different weights in different situations and contexts.

Migration decision making involves two separate decisions, one about the move itself, and one about the destination. While these decisions are often made at the same time, it is important to separate them to see how climate change affects them. If a migration decision is made based on push factors, destination considerations usually come second. Climate changes makes people move who otherwise would not want to, therefore it is likely that they have not thought about destinations in advance. Destination decisions are contingent on social networks in general and the impact mechanisms in this particular case. Extreme weather hazards push people to the nearest safe destination. Gradually rising sea level or increasingly common droughts may leave more time for considering various destinations.

What further complicates the understanding of the climate change–migration nexus is the dynamics of voluntary vs. involuntary migration. Since climate change mostly operates through the push factors, it puts those who move for climate change related reasons to the involuntary migration category as they are pushed rather than pulled into the migration stream. As mentioned before, one of the most common images of climate change and migration is that of climate refugees, in other words, environmental displacement. This non-voluntary migration can be either temporary or permanent based on the conditions. Annual droughts or flooding can lead to both permanent and temporary displacement based on many factors, while gradual sea-level rise eventually displaces everybody in the impact area.

Over time, a series of temporary displacement can lead to permanent migration when the individuals or households decide that it is no longer possible to sustain their everyday lives under the new climate conditions. This blurs the distinction between voluntary and involuntary migration. Climate hazards for example make people leave who have not planned doing so, indicating involuntary migration. But beyond the general context, the timing and the destination may leave more agency at the individual or household.

The importance of the difference between voluntary and involuntary migration is in the social composition of the migrant population. Voluntary migration is usually a result of planning when resources are allocated to offset the costs of migration, establish new life at the destination, and invest in future social capital. Involuntary migration can be the exact result of disasters eliminating people's assets and stripping them off even the most basic resources, making them move without planning and intention.

This means that while voluntary migrants in most cases tend to be comparatively resource-rich and therefore seen as assets,[1] involuntary migrants are usually poor and often create burdens for the destination community or country. Theoretically, one could imagine a climate change induced migration stream in which resourceful residents are the first to move away, mostly by choice and leaving those with fewer resources behind. This is similar to a situation where new industrial developments, such as a nuclear plant or a highway, would make the more affluent population move away based on their residential preferences, leaving those that cannot afford to look for better places behind (Szasz and Meuser 2000). Similarly, as the example of Hurricane Katrina has shown, there are significant differences in the impact across socioeconomic groups (Finch et al. 2010; Fussell et al. 2010).

Apart from the presence or absence of resources, another important consideration for the voluntary–involuntary migration theme is the difficulties of integration at the destination. Voluntary migrants have an easier time integrating, because they wanted to move there in the first place, therefore they are more prepared and informed. For most involuntary migrants, the first destination is temporary, and many may move to several places before resettling somewhere, with little motivation and great difficulties to integrate.

The difference between seasonal and permanent migration is also important, because seasonal migration is often left out of migration statistics, despite that its dynamics can provide crucial information about potential permanent changes in the future. In the literature, the terms seasonal and temporary are mostly used interchangeably, although temporary migration is often reserved to discuss guest workers in industrial and postindustrial societies. Seasonal migration refers to moves that are determined by (agricultural) seasons and connected to land use practices, especially pasture management and grazing. When pastures or water availability changes due to climate change, and triggers a different seasonal migration pattern while keeping the main residence the same, it seldom registers in the migration statistics. Yet, such changes can mean fundamental shifts in livelihoods, putting pressure on the environment and leading to conflict, such as in the case of Darfur.

Migration decisions are as complex and diverse as the characteristics of decision making actors and places involved in the move. Population demographics and place characteristics make every move unique, thus the impact of climate change on migration decisions will be unique as well. With that caveat, from a theoretical perspective it may be possible to identify two major groups of reasons why people move voluntarily: economic opportunities and residential preferences. These usually operate in combination with each other, but from the climate change perspective there are some important differences.

Many of the moves are related to economic reasons, when the actors expect their economic situation (jobs, livelihoods, and costs of living) to improve either right after the move or over time. In this scenario, climate change drivers weaken or eliminate economic opportunities at the origin. Examples can include desertification in Sudan, frequent floods in Bangladesh, Venice and its tourism industry slowly submerging, or the Dust Bowl putting farms out of business in Oklahoma. In some cases, people can find alternative opportunities and stay, but in other cases they may decide or be forced to leave. This mostly applies to climate change drivers that shape decisions gradually, leaving enough room for the migration to be considered voluntary.

Residential preferences are usually related to the pull factors. Environmental and cultural amenities are important components of migration decisions. If we consider climate change as the driver of migration, residential preferences will work as push factors, making places less attractive. Increasing temperature and humidity, the growing likelihood of extreme weather hazards, and the generally increasing unpredictability and variability of weather are particularly important in such cases.

These examples clearly indicate that while there are some general patterns in how climate change influences migration, the actual dynamics are contingent on the location, the characteristics of the migrant actors, and the impact mechanisms. In the next section I discuss three of the impact mechanisms: extreme weather hazards, sea-level rise, and changing temperature and humidity.

Impact mechanisms

Extreme weather hazards

Extreme weather hazards include hurricanes, tornados, floods, droughts, wildfires, and heat and cold waves. While they can have devastating direct impact on mortality, their connection to migration, apart from immediate displacement, is less clear. In most cases, these extreme weather events share two important characteristics: they are temporary in a sense that they last for a finite period although their destructive impact may be permanent; and they are extreme because they do not occur on a regular basis.

The temporary aspect of extreme weather refers to the occurrence, which may last for hours, days or weeks, but not for a prolonged period. Once the event vanishes, conditions usually resume to what is normally experienced at the given location. In that sense, although extreme weather can displace many people, it usually does not change established migration streams. The impact has to be proportionate to the size of the place to affect the majority of the population and fundamentally change migration dynamics. The Dust Bowl or Hurricane Katrina can be considered as examples of this. Smaller events could have the same impact on small communities. An example for this is the 2007 tornado in Greensburg, Kansas.[2] But even with the destruction of a large tornado or flood, places seldom disappear if they are sustainable otherwise. Hence, from this perspective the study of migration dynamics should focus on population composition, as even if the size of the population will rebound, the composition may not be the same.

The nature of extreme weather refers to these events not occurring frequently. The importance of this is in the migration threshold of push factors. While the temporary aspect of extreme weather induces displacement if the destruction is substantive, the frequency of extreme weather works in a different way, influencing voluntary migration considerations. Extreme weather is just one factor behind a migration decision, but its increasing frequency, which seems to be one of the characteristics of climate change (Solomon *et al.* 2007), definitely works toward a greater likelihood of outmigration. If extreme weather becomes the regular weather, many people may decide to look for greener pastures. Over time, this affects the sustainability of the place.

Similarly to the frequency of extreme weather, the increasing degrees of uncertainty of weather patterns make people re-evaluate their residential preferences. Regional climate models have become more important and more accurate in recent years. In certain regions, climate change means clear cooling or warming, but in many areas it is the increasing uncertainty and variability of weather patterns, including extreme weather, which seems to be the outcome (Van Aalst 2006). Uncertainty is an unattractive factor in residential preferences, and in combination with other drivers, may also contribute to increasing outmigration from an area.

It is important to note that residential preferences not only account for the physical attractiveness and amenities of an area, but also for the costs of living which could go up fast if insurance costs increase due to extreme weather. And the ability to bear the costs and take the risks *vis-à-vis* the general popularity of a place varies across groups with different social and economic status.

Sea-level rise

Sea-level rise is probably the most captivating image of climate change. This is partly because the climate change discourse grew out of global warming discourse, and the melting of the ice caps and the subsequent sea-level rise were the easiest to imagine as direct impacts of warming temperatures.

Coastlines have been densely populated areas throughout human history. Approximately 10 percent of the world's population lives in low elevation coastal zones, areas that are less then 10 meters above sea level (McGranahan *et al.* 2007). A large share of this population is in crowded urban areas that emerged by utilizing long-distance trade routes over history. Moreover, coastline populations continue to increase. To use the United States as an example, according to the US Bureau of Census estimates, the population in coastline counties has increased from 47 million to 87 million between 1960 and 2008, exceeding the population growth rate of the United States (Wilson and Fischetti 2010). The increase was particularly high (150 percent) in Gulf of Mexico coastline counties. This growth also means that the population affected by hurricanes is larger as well. When Hurricane Donna hit in 1960, 11 million people were affected. The same hurricane today would affect more than 24 million people (Wilson and Fischetti 2010).

Similarly to international trends, the coastline population of the United States is increasingly urbanized. In 2008, 254 of the 3,142 counties were considered coastline counties. Of these, 153 are metropolitan counties and an additional 46 are micropolitan.[3] Only 55 counties are non-metropolitan, or rural, and these counties have only one percent of the total coastal population (Wilson and Fischetti 2010).

According to recent estimates, sea-level rise can affect 20 million people in the United States alone by 2030 (Curtis and Schneider 2011). In the United States, and in other countries, the immediate attention is usually given to the direct displacement effect. Of course, sea-level rise will not occur overnight, and people will have some time to adjust to the changes. Accordingly, the intensity of outmigration from coastal areas will not be the same during the time over which the given coastal habitat disappears. The dynamics of migration will depend on the resources of residents, push factor thresholds, and various individual characteristics, including the extent of information they have about the change.

One thing is sure though: sea-level rise will make people move, and a 100 percent impact will result in a 100 percent outmigration. More complex questions are where these people will move and how that would change existing migration streams and networks. General wisdom tells that additional migration follows existing and established channels (Hugo 2010). However, a new surge of migration may become large enough to alter the original conditions that established the migration stream, and can led to the development of new streams, creating strong ripple effects (Curtis and Schneider 2011).

Consider the following theoretical example. There is a two-way migration stream between inland county A and coastal county B, based on long established networks. If coastal county B is threatened by sea-level rise, the migration stream first becomes unidirectional (from B to A), and that changes conditions in county A. People who migrated from A to B cannot do that anymore, so they either stay in A, or move away to another inland county C, likely creating changes in the migration streams of that county. Conditions in county A will definitely change, which may make some people in coastal county B change their plans and move to someplace else, creating additional ripple effects and so on.

As it can be seen, the destination aspect of migration is a complex phenomenon, and the ripple effects caused by sea-level rise will affect locations well beyond the coastal places. This picture then is further complicated by the composition of migrants. Affluent populations can move almost solely based on their preferences, but those with fewer resources will look for the most affordable, typically short distance move, likely to neighboring locations. These locations would experience a large influx of less affluent populations, as well as the social and economic challenges that are the results of that move.

Changing temperature and humidity

Similarly to extreme weather hazards, changing temperature and humidity also have a demographic impact beyond migration. These conditions can cause increasing health risks both directly and indirectly. Higher average temperatures and increasing humidity can contribute to health problems, especially among the elderly. At the same time, changing temperature and humidity can also shift disease habitats and seasons. Locations that were not affected by malaria for example may become suitable new habitats for mosquitoes. And even if there is no geographic expansion of disease habitats, longer or more humid disease seasons can increase infection rates solely based on the temporal aspect.

In terms of the migration impact, the changing temperature and humidity work through the threshold mechanism. These changes (including the changing health risks above) occur over a longer period, therefore the migration impact will be similar to the other impact mechanisms in terms of the gradual impact on population mobility. On the other hand, increasing temperature would contribute to more frequent droughts and desertification, making some places eventually unsuitable for human habitat. The human response will be based on the prevailing social organization of the location. In developed countries and urban locations where livelihoods are based on industries and services, residential preferences will motivate migration behavior in response to changing temperature and humidity. In places where the economy is more closely connected to agriculture, migration decisions will be based on land use conditions. This is where the changing seasonal migration streams can provide crucial insights to future trends.

Another similarity to extreme weather hazards is the increasing uncertainty of how climate change will unfold in various localities. Thus, the way in which people will perceive this variability and uncertainty of temperature and humidity will be similar to how they think about the impact of extreme weather hazards on their migration decision making. Again, in some places it will be a residential preference issue, while in other places the basic livelihoods will be threatened by unpredictable weather patterns.

Conclusions

Climate change influences migration in two major ways. One is the direct impact of environmental displacement, which usually occurs after extreme weather events but will eventually be a crucial factor in sea-level rise and desertification. The other is the indirect impact where the components of changing climate contribute to migration decisions together with other factors. Thus, when studying the impact, the drivers of migration decisions have to be isolated and individually examined to determine whether they are sensitive to climate change. Climate change may not be the only factor behind migration, but could operate as the tipping point among many factors.

Climate change seldom makes places more attractive. It mostly influences migration through the push factors, and therefore the move could be seen as involuntary at least to some extent. In a paradoxical way, the future migration streams influenced by climate change may be the exact opposite of those developed in past decades where coastal areas or places with insufficient water supply became attractive locations for millions of people. To some extent, this is similar to how the arid Great Plains in the United States became settled during a wet climate cycle resulting in unsustainable farming practices and the eventual exodus during the Dust Bowl era. This brings up the considerations about national and local development policies and land management practices that often make locations more vulnerable.

Until recently, the academic discourse on climate change focused on global impacts. Studies investigating extreme weather hazards, for example Hurricane Katrina, have a local focus, but systematic attempts to analyze gradual changes are missing from the literature. The reason for this is the lack of reliable regional climate models.[4] As climate scientists refine their models for smaller geographic units, demographic research should keep up and provide regional analysis and estimates. It is also important to remember that the impact mechanisms of climate change are not isolated. Sea-level rise can only affect coastal locations, but extreme weather and changing temperature/humidity can have more complex and interlinked impacts. This complexity also means greater unpredictability, which in turn can be an important factor in migration decision making.

The public discourse has often been focusing on environmental displacement following extreme weather because these cases are easy to understand and receive high media attention. However, the gradual impact of climate change on migration will probably affect more people. The question is how gradual this impact will be. Locations continuously have to adapt to changing environmental conditions that may or may not alter migration streams. One may argue that as long as climate changes, an example for dynamic environmental conditions, would not trigger mass migration over a short period, it should not be any different. However, exactly because climate change works through push factors and results in involuntary migration, the populations in migration streams are more likely to be resource poor, vulnerable groups, posing considerable national and local policy challenges.

Vulnerability to climate change varies tremendously across populations living in impact areas, adding further complexity to the study of the climate change–migration nexus. On the one hand, there is uncertainty about the regional or local impact of climate change, while on the other hand there is the complexity of human reactions to this change. Research and policy should address both parts of this dynamic. And while migration is the dependent variable in this equation, it does not mean that social scientists can wait until reliable small-scale climate models are developed. As Curtis and Schneider (2011) clearly stated, understanding the composition and vulnerability of populations as well as their migration networks and potential migration behavior prior to the environmental impact is crucial. Among the lessons we learned from Hurricane Katrina, the most important is that we cannot wait until the levees break.

Notes

1 In reality, this is of course a much more complex picture. A sudden influx of migrants, no matter how resourceful, would pose challenges to any community. In-migration of low-income populations to poor (and therefore more affordable) places is another example for social challenges.
2 The Greensburg tornado was an EF-5 twister, killing 12 people in the town of 1,500. Practically the whole town was destroyed, including all municipal buildings and structures. While the town was largely rebuilt, and even reinvented (as a "green" town), its current population is around 1,000, and its composition has changed too.
3 Micropolitan is a label introduced in 2003, and used for county based statistical areas that have a core place with a population of 10,000–50,000 (irrespective of the size of the area population).
4 One exception from this is the models about sea level rise excellently utilized by Curtis and Schneider (2011).

References and further reading

Adamo, S. B. (2009) *Environmentally Induced Population Displacements*. IHDP Update 1, 2009. Bonn, Germany: International Human Dimensions Programme on Global Environmental Change.
Bardsley, D. and Hugo, G. (2010) "Migration and climate change: examining thresholds of change to guide effective adaptation decision-making" *Population and Environment* 32(2–3): 238–62.
Black, R. (2001) "Environmental refugees: Myth or reality" *United Nations High Commissioner for Refugees Working Papers* 34: 1–19.
Boserup, E. (1965) *The Conditions of Agricultural Growth: The Economics of Agrarian Change under Population Pressure*. Chicago, IL: Adline.
——(1976) "Environment, population, and technology in primitive societies" *Population and Development Review* 2(1): 21–36.
Castles, S. (2002) *Environmental Change and Forced Migration: Making Sense of the Debate*. Geneva: United Nations High Commissioner for Refugees.
Coale, A. (ed.) (1976) *Economic Factors in Population Growth*. London: Macmillan.
Commoner, B. Y. (1972) "The environmental cost of economic growth" *Chemistry in Britain* 8(2): 52–65.
Curtis, K. and Schneider, A. (2011) "Understanding the demographic implications of climate change: Estimates of localized population predictions under future scenarios of sea-level rise" *Population and Environment* www.springerlink.com/content/x12463470750910g.
Ehrlich, P. (1968) *The Population Bomb*. New York: Ballantine Books.
Ehrlich, P. R. and Holdren J. P. (1971) "Impact of population growth" *Science* 171(3977): 1212–17.
Ehrlich, P. R. and Ehrlich A. H. (1990) *The Population Explosion*. New York: Simon and Schuster.
Finch, C., Emrich, C. T., and Cutter, S. L. (2010) "Disaster disparities and differential recovery in New Orleans" *Population and Environment* 31(4): 179–202.

Fussell, E., Sastry, N., and Vanlandingham, M. (2010) "Race, socioeconomic status, and return migration to New Orleans after Hurricane Katrina" *Population and Environment* 31(1–3): 20–42.

Gaburro, G. and Poston, D. L. Jr. (eds) (1991) *Essays on Population Economics: In Memory of Alfred Sauvy*. Padova: CEDAM.

Gilland, B. (1983) "Considerations on world population and food supply" *Population and Development Review* 9(2): 203–11.

Haas, J. E., Kates, R. W., and Bowden, M. J. (eds) (1977) *Reconstruction Following Disaster*. Cambridge, MA: MIT Press.

Haines, A. and Patz, J. (2004) "Health effects of climate change" *JAMA* 291(1): 99–103.

Haines, A., Kovats, R. S., Campbell-Lendrum, D., and Corvalan, C. (2006) "Climate change and human health: Impacts, vulnerability, and mitigation" *Lancet* 367(9528): 2101–9.

Heine, B. and Petersen, L. (2008) "Adaptation and cooperation" *Forced Migration Review: Climate Change and Displacement*, 31(31): 48–50.

Hugo, G. J. (2010) "Climate change induced mobility and the existing migration regime in Asia and the Pacific." In J. McAdam (ed.), *Climate Change and Displacement: Multidisciplinary Perspectives*. Oxford: Hart Publishing.

Hurt, D. R. (1981) *An Agricultural and Social History of the Dust Bowl*. Chicago, IL: Nelson Hall.

Keyfitz, N. (1990) "Toward a theory of population-development interaction." In K. Davis and M. S. Bernstam (eds), *Resources, Environment and Population. Population and Development Review*. A Supplement to Vol. 16. New York: Oxford University Press.

Lee, E. (1966) "A theory of migration" *Demography* 3(1): 47–57.

Massey, D., Axinn, W. G., and Ghimire, D. J. (2010) "Environmental change and out-migration: Evidence from Nepal" *Population and Environment* 32(2–3): 109–36.

McGranahan, G., Balk, D., and Anderson, B. (2007) "The rising tide: Assessing the risks of climate change and human settlements in low elevation coastal zones" *Environment and Urbanization* 19(1): 17–37.

McLeman, R. and B. Smit (2006) "Migration as an adaptation to climate change" *Climatic Change* 76(1–2): 31–53.

McMichael, A. J., Woodruff, R. E., and Hales, S. (2006) "Climate change and human health: Present and future risks" *Lancet* 367(9513): 859–69.

McNicoll, G. (2003) *Population and Development: An Introductory View*. Population Council, Working Paper No. 174. New York.

Meadows, D., Randers, J., and Behrens, W. (1972) *The Limits to Growth: A Report for the Club of Rome on the Predicament of Mankind*. New York: Universe Books, pp. 56–60.

Myers, N. (1993) "Environmental refugees in a globally warmed world" *BioScience* 43(11): 752–73.

——(1997) "Environmental refugees" *Population and Environment* 19(2): 167–82.

Patz, J. A., Campbell-Lendrum, D., Holloway, T., and Foley, J. A. (2005) "Impact of regional climate change on human health" *Nature* 438: 310–17.

Pebley, A. (1998) "Demography and the environment" *Demography* 35(4): 377–89.

Poston, D. and Frisbie Parker, W. (2005) "Ecological demography." In D. Poston and M. Micklin (eds) *Handbook of Population*. New York: Springer.

Rees, W. E. (1996) "Revisiting carrying capacity: Area-based indicators of sustainability" *Population and Environment* 17(3): 195–215.

Simon, J. (1981) *The Ultimate Resource*. Princeton, NJ: Princeton University Press.

Solomon, S., Qin, D., Manning, M., Marquis, M., Averyt, K., Tignor, M. M. B., LeRoy Miller, H., Chen, Z. (eds) (2007) *Climate Change 2007: The Physical Science Basis. Contribution of Working Group I to the Fourth Assessment Report of the Intergovernmental Panel on Climate Change*. New York: Cambridge University Press.

Szasz, A. and Meuser, Michale. (2000) "Unintended; inexorable: The production of environmental inequalities in Santa Clara County, CA" *American Behavioral Scientist* 43(4): 602–32.

Tacoli, C. (2009) "Crisis or adaptation? Migration and climate change in a context of high mobility" *Environment and Urbanization* 21(2): 513–25.

Tiffen, M. (1993) "Productivity and environmental conservation under rapid population growth: A case study of Machakos District" *Journal of International Development* 5(2): 207–21.

Van Aalst, M. (2006) "The impacts of climate change on the risk of natural disasters" *Disasters* 30(1): 5–18.

Wilson, S. and Fischetti, T. (2010) "Coastline population trends in the United States: 1960 to 2008" *Current Population Reports* 25–1139.

York, R., Rosa, E. A., and Dietz, T. (2003) "Footprints on the earth: The environmental consequences of modernity" *American Sociological Review* 68(2): 279–300.

3

Psychological acculturation

Perspectives, principles, processes, and prospects

Marc Bornstein

Introduction

Acculturation traditionally includes "those phenomena which result when *groups* of individuals having different cultures come into continuous first-hand contact, with subsequent changes in the original culture patterns of either or both *groups*" (Redfield *et al.* 1936: 149–50, emphasis added). Since this formative definition was first advanced, the sociological and anthropological origins of acculturation theory and research have engendered continuing and appropriate focus on group-level acculturation. However, it is well to recall that *individuals* do the actual migration and adjustment. More than 200 million people today are said to live outside their country of origin. That number tallies to 1 in ~30 individuals living on earth.

For the vast majority of international migrants, leaving their native country to settle in a new country engenders daunting alternatives between allegiance to and association with one way of life that includes family, social, and economic connections against usually contrasting economic, philosophical, religious, and political conditions or investments. When considered in this way, migration and acculturation constitute thoroughly transforming forces on individual people. On this argument, we contend that a more encompassing approach to acculturation must embrace dual processes of group cultural and individual psychological adjustment that result from contact between two or more groups and their individual members.

This brief chapter outlines some prominent principles, processes, and prospects of this perspective on individual-level *psychological acculturation*. We first review relevant general theory about migration and acculturation. We then differentiate individual-level from group-level acculturation. Individual-level acculturation is not a uniform process as implied by a group-level approach. Next, we distinguish and discuss *variability* of different sorts that constitutes the heart of individual psychological acculturation. For brevity's sake, we provide selected, rather than exhaustive, illustrations. Psychological acculturation raises methodological, disciplinary, and policy considerations, and we overview those also. Finally, we point to some profitable future directions of theory development and empirical inquiry in the area of psychological acculturation. Migration signifies physical relocation between geographic locales; acculturation signifies psychological adjustment. Acculturation is certainly a group phenomenon, and some aspects of acculturation submit to group-level analysis; acculturation is also an individual phenomenon, and other aspects are better understood at an individual level. This chapter focuses on the latter.

Acculturation: a group *and* individual phenomenon

Acculturation

When an individual from one culture emigrates to a new one, that individual conveys his or her original culture. Acculturation is the study of how people with one culture negotiate adjustment as they settle and adapt in a new culture. Twentieth-century theory and research on acculturating groups and individuals was initially characterized by unidimensional and unidirectional models of change where immigrants were seen to relinquish their culture of origin as they acquired a new culture of destination. In short, acculturation equated to assimilation (Gordon 1964). Accumulating evidence eventually suggested that most acculturating individuals adopt cognitions and practices of the new culture while simultaneously retaining those of their old (e.g., celebrating holidays of the culture of destination as well as holidays of the culture of origin). That is, individual immigrants have (varying degrees of) competence in two cultures.

Group and *individual*

Acculturation takes place on both group and individual planes. Group-level processes and effects provide a deeper understanding of global acculturation experiences and help to identify social forces (e.g., attitudes toward immigrants, immigration policies) and aggregate acculturation trajectories. However, just as different immigrant groups retain and adopt culture-specific cognitions and practices differently, so too do different individual immigrants in a group. Indian migrants to the United Kingdom may be considered to have acculturated because a large proportion of Indians have, for example, learned to speak English. However, individuals within the migrant Indian community vary widely in the ways they have adapted and differ considerably in their level of acculturation, as for example in their English-language proficiency.

From the example just given, it is plain that the two planes of acculturation do not necessarily change in lockstep, and there are good reasons for adopting a multi-level perspective of individuals nested within groups—and therefore of acculturation transpiring at the two levels. Furthermore, each level certainly informs and influences the other. Compare the acculturation histories of newer Mexican immigrants in New York City with more established Dominicans. Mexicans are scattered across neighborhoods with low co-ethnic concentration, compared to Dominicans many of whom have lived in a predominant urban enclave for over 50 years (Yoshikawa 2011). Mexicans arrived in a period without a pathway to citizenship; in contrast, many Dominicans experienced amnesty in the late 1980s following the Immigration Reform and Control Act. Recent migrants from the Dominican Republic are much more likely to have family members in the United States with residency or citizenship and accompanying language and systems navigation skills than recent migrants from Mexico. Mexican parents and their young children have lower availability of supports for child care and finances as well as fewer multi-generational family networks. For children, this means that grandparents and other older family members with English-language skills are far more likely to be present in Dominican households than in Mexican households. In this way, individual acculturation patterns are influenced by group histories of migration. Individual immigrants from the former Soviet

Union (FSU) to Israel in the 1990s experienced reduced migration-related trauma because their exodus comprised whole families.

In brief, acculturation involves complex processes that occur in individuals and in groups. On the group plane, acculturation involves changes in social structures and institutions and in cultural practices. On the individual plane, acculturation involves changes in a person's cognitions and practices broadly construed. At the group level, acculturation encompasses social change in demographic, health, and economic systems in society and affects civic, educational, social service, and legal systems. At the individual level, migrants often think, feel, and behave differently from the native-born in a culture of destination and they also differ from one another on indices of health, well-being, education, and so forth.

Psychological acculturation

International migration is not a single, discrete event involving movement from one geographically and socially bounded locality to another. Rather, international migration entails dynamic exchanges, multiple domains, diverse resources, and imperative needs that are simultaneously unique and indigenous to multiple settings. Migration and acculturation are inherently individual experiences that precipitate thoroughgoing changes of social identity and self. Immigrants must negotiate new cultures and learn to navigate new systems. Just to communicate effectively in their culture of settlement requires of immigrants new competencies in speaking, listening, reading, and writing. Such transformations entail gaining new knowledge as well as adjusting ingrained life scripts. Immigrants face multiple challenges in acculturating to a new society—including deciding which cognitions or practices to retain from their culture of origin and which to adopt from their culture of destination.

Not every individual enters into, participates in, or accommodates in acculturation in the same way; one individual in a group may follow a course toward fuller assimilation, whereas another in the same group may strive for a bicultural equilibrium. Individual differences are the hallmark of psychological acculturation, and there is great variability in the ways individuals go about acculturating as well as in the levels and types of acculturation they achieve. Here, we discuss several kinds of variability that principally define psychological acculturation. Migration transcends identity in the sense of who am I, and raises considerations of where do I fit and what are my present and future roles within my new society. Individual level analyses focus on images of self within place or context.

Along the way, considerations of variability elicit methodological, disciplinary, and policy questions. For example, most studies measure acculturation at a single point in time and generally employ a cross-sectional research design. This methodological orientation leads to an artificially cropped "snapshot" of acculturation and invariably to portrayals of acculturation status as static. In reality, however, acculturation in individuals is dynamic and nonlinear, as acculturating individuals retain some cognitions or practices of their culture of origin and undergo periods of stabilization as well as change. Immigrants' modes of acculturation may vary over time as a function of ongoing experiences in their new culture, or new developments in the original culture. Examinations of acculturation true to its process nature call for microgenetic and longitudinal designs, preferably with multiple waves.

Within-group variability

Migrants vary in many general individual-difference characteristics that likely affect acculturation (e.g., age, gender, personality) as well as specific acculturation-related characteristics (e.g., motives for migration, commitment to the adopted homeland, length of settlement). Psychological acculturation is concerned with both, and how immigrants acculturate is a product of combinations of individual-difference and acculturation-related factors. Within-group variability is as likely in relevant resources as in acculturation strategies or options.

Here we explore some main sources of variability that likely shape psychological acculturation. Learning new cultural norms and values, adjusting behaviors according to those norms and values in social interactions, and building competencies based on multiple, perhaps even conflicting, standards, are common individual tasks of immigrants. Individual adjustment generally is an ongoing dynamic process in which personal characteristics and learning experiences interact to contribute to mental and socioemotional functioning. Moreover, people are not passive registrants of their experiences (*read* new culture), but rather play active roles in self-socialization (Bornstein *et al.* 2011). The constructive and agentic parts immigrants play in their acculturation (*read* resocialization) are reflected in their in maintaining or jettisoning past culture, adapting or rejecting the surrounding culture, and constructing a new culture. What are some of the principal individual characteristics that channel the course of immigrant acculturation?

Age and developmental status

From a lifespan perspective, immigrants appear to acculturate differently depending on their age or developmental status. That is, acculturation is developmentally sensitive. When Richman *et al.* (1987) explored acculturation among migrants to Peru, they learned that age at the time of migration was associated with level of acculturation achieved. Not only do migrants enter the acculturation stream at different points in their own development, but the course of subsequent currents of both acculturation and development can also be expected to eddy differently downstream for those who start the process at different life stages. Individuals who enter into acculturation in childhood may embrace culture-of-destination cognitions and practices as a way of fitting in and lose or reject those of their culture of origin (Benet-Martínez and Haritatos 2005; Schwartz *et al.* 2010). Thus, young people immigrating to ethnic enclaves are more likely to be bicultural whereas adults are less likely to acquire the new culture (Schwartz *et al.* 2006). Few studies directly examine how processes of acculturation differ depending on the developmental status of the child, adolescent, or adult (Bernhard 2010). Indeed, the intersection of development and migration is an oddly neglected issue in light of the fact that children constitute a large proportion of migrants and often fill unique roles in mediating between cultures of origin and destination. Being more acculturated, children frequently language "broker" for adults, for instance.

Life's developmental stages are intrinsically associated with certain developmental tasks. As children enter adolescence, for example, their improved capacity for self-reflection, coupled with the task of forming a socially acceptable identity, herald increased sensitivity to the opinions of significant others and constant re-assessment of social relationships. Formation of a socially approved identity might therefore present special challenges for migrant adolescents who are exposed to alternate visions of a healthy identity in the family and the wider society. Even younger and older adolescents respond differently to conflicting demands from cultures of origin and destination: Younger adolescents tend to navigate between cultural ecologies more fluidly than do older adolescents, perhaps because they are developmentally more flexible and open to new experiences (Berry *et al.* 2006).

Processes of acculturation also vary for people at different stages of life; parents and children do not necessarily acculturate in similar manners. Immigrant parents often have less contact with the wider society and may experience more difficulty in learning the new language than do their children. Immigrant children are usually more frequently and intensively exposed to their new culture through peers and school, contributing to their greater acceptance of that new culture. Thus, children of immigrants typically acculturate faster and begin to function trans-culturally more rapidly than their parents. In brief, lifespan developmental processes inform acculturation in individuals.

Gender

Gender is often treated as a nuisance variable or covariate in acculturation research. However, research points to distinct pathways of acculturation by gender (Güngor and Bornstein 2009). First-generation women often carry the heritage culture perhaps because of their typically more limited connection to the wider mainstream society beyond the home (Ward *et al.* 2001). However, girls are more likely to be bicultural, perhaps because of their greater sensitivity and adaptability to new social networks (Berry *et al.* 2006). A study on the transmission of gender role values in Turkish German immigrant families showed that Turkish daughters are more egalitarian than their mothers and their male peers whereas sons are not more egalitarian than their fathers. Among Vietnamese Australians and Chinese Canadian university students, boys score more similarly to their parents in terms of traditionalism than girls. In brief, acculturative change is in differential evidence among girls and boys, and women and men.

Personality

Choosing to emigrate may reflect certain personality characteristics (assertiveness, ego control), and acculturating, or developing a bicultural identity through internal processes of change, may be facilitated in certain (open, extraverted) personalities more than others. As individuals, immigrants naturally possess different constellations of personality characteristics that help or hinder their acculturation. Differences in attitude, risk taking, and level of anxiety tolerance doubtlessly contribute to variability in individual acculturation.

Cognition

Before following any feasible course of acculturation, individuals with one culture need to be exposed to and incorporate information from a new culture (Padilla and Prez 2003). Many possible processes have been proposed. Social-learning theory emphasizes the roles of observation and modeling in the acquisition of new and culturally appropriate skills, for example. In all cases, individual differences in cognitive functioning must come into play. Educated immigrants adapt more proficiently, just as educated immigrant parents are better positioned to advance their children, to help with homework, and to negotiate on behalf of their children with teachers and school administrators, whereas parents (even in the same immigrant group) with limited education may lack both experience and knowledge to provide similar support. Individual differences in language proficiency further condition acculturation. Speaking the language of the culture of destination is requisite to success for children enrolled in mainstream schools and in the labor market and other settings for adults. New language use is the most important explanatory predictor of individual differences in ethnic friendship homophily (Titzmann and Silbereisen 2009). As proficiency in the new language improves, homophily bias decreases, a finding that stands independent of length of stay in the host country and opportunity structures. In brief, accounting for individual personality and cognition fleshes out a conceptual framework that improves understanding of individual acculturation.

Generation

Acculturation has in the past been equated to generation of immigration. Individuals in different generations face different issues *vis-à-vis* their cultures of origin and destination and thus likely follow different trajectories of acculturation. People born outside the culture of destination often self-identify with their culture of origin, in contrast to those born and reared their whole lives in the culture of destination. For example, second-generation (just like younger) Latin immigrants to the United States adjust better to the majority culture than first-generation (like older) immigrants (Sabogal *et al.* 1987). Parents and children who share the same language and birth country may still differ in their acculturation (McQueen *et al.* 2003). Even siblings within the same family—who are titularly the same generation—do not necessarily acculturate in the same ways or to the same degree.

Generational discrepancies in acculturation are therefore common in immigrant families because the primary socialization of parents transpired in their culture of origin, whereas, depending on their age of arrival, children may experience primary socialization in the culture of destination. This discrepancy between immigrant parents and their children is referred to as the acculturation gap (Farver *et al.* 2002; Birman 2006). Parents and children can undergo differential rates of acculturation and these differential processes can account for significant sources of intergenerational differences, sometimes leading to increased conflict and stress and to problematic adaptation. In consequence, acculturation study needs to differentiate and to examine the variability associated with 1, 1.5, 2, and successive generations. In brief, generations likely vary in acculturation in ways that have consequences for individual immigrant adjustment.

Domain

Acculturation is multifaceted, impacting individuals in affective, cognitive, and behavioral spheres of functioning. Individuals do not necessarily acculturate in all domains of life on the same timetable or in the same direction. Rather, different psychological domains can and do show different patterns and rates of acculturation. Parenting practices appear to acculturate more readily than parenting cognitions. For example, Bornstein and Cote (2001, 2004) found that US Japanese immigrant mothers' cognitions resembled cognitions of mothers in Japan, or were intermediate between those of Japanese and European American mothers, whereas their behavioral interactions with children resembled those of European American mothers more closely than practices of Japanese. Insofar as they acculturate differently, acculturation attitudes do not necessarily predict acculturation behaviors. Ethnic behaviors may decrease from the first to the second generation, although attitudes do not change. Individual immigrants may embrace certain aspects of the culture of destination (e.g., language, dress, and music) and actively reject others (e.g., religious practices, customs, and emotions).

Perhaps the most widely acknowledged illustration of domain variability in psychological acculturation comes from the observation that immigrants tend to acculturate differently in public and private spheres of life (e.g., Arends-Tóth and van de Vijver 2004). Generally, the public domain involves participation in the social lives of both cultures of origin and destination, contacts with nationals, use of mass media, and schooling, whereas the private domain involves personal and value-related matters like preferences in socializing children, language spoken at home, and sanctioned ethnicity of persons to marry. Cultural adaptation is often preferred in the public domain and cultural maintenance in the private domain. For example, Phalet and Swyngedouw (2003) found that Turkish and Moroccan immigrants in The

Netherlands attributed more importance to cultural maintenance in the home and family (private domain), whereas adaptation was more important in school and at work (public domain).

When acculturation investigators focus on general processes or orientations, the more differentiated domain-specific nature of individual acculturation is masked. Domain variability suggests that acculturation is flexible and sensitive to situation-specific norms or demands. Thus, immigrants may seek economic assimilation, linguistic integration, and relationship separation. In brief, acculturation does not affect all aspects of the psyche in an identical way, and domain specificity predicts that different aspects can and will vary in their course of adjustment.

Motives and means

Migrants vary in their motives to emigrate and acculturate. For some, international migration is voluntary, for others, it is involuntary. Some individuals emigrate with a goal to retain the ways of their culture of origin, and some with a goal to embrace those of their culture of destination; others with a plan to bridge the two cultures as best they can, and still others with no plan at all (Berry 2007). Each individual motive conditions acculturation. Refugees, sojourners, and permanent immigrants vary with respect to their reasons for migrating (which can affect their psychological profiles) and plans for remaining in the culture of destination (which can affect their motivation to acculturate), and so follow different trajectories of acculturation. Foreign-born individuals also arrive in new cultural settings via multiple different mechanisms, each of which may portend unique consequences for their acculturation. One frequent migrant pathway is through family reunification; other policies that may account for different patterns of international migration include employment-based programs, diversity-based immigration, border policies, and humanitarian programs. In brief, individual motivations and means to acculturate inform psychological explanations of acculturation.

Time

Each individual's length of stay in their new country relates to their acculturation experience. Silbereisen and Titzmann (2007), who studied ethnic German immigrants from the FSU, found friendships were nearly 100 percent intra-ethnic in the period shortly after arrival in the country of destination.

Context

Individual differences in acculturation derive not only from variability in what people bring to the process of acculturation but also variability in the structural affordances of the situations in which individual migrants find themselves and those which they left. Consider variability associated with each context. People tend to emigrate from developing nations, and sending societies (and so their emigrants) represent a wide range of national origins and cultures that uniquely shape the nature of acculturation. The relation between parental harshness and child aggression is positive for Canadians of European ancestry but negative for Canadians of South Asian ancestry. Acculturation studies tend to lump sub-groups together when in actuality they demand differentiation: Hong Kong Chinese differ from Mainland Chinese arriving on Canadian shores, and Chinese migrants to the United States differ depending on whether they emigrated from rural or urban areas. Harwood et al. (2002) discussed in detail variability found among Latin American families in socialization goals that reflect their individual country of origin. Communities of Turkish immigrant worker families in European societies are generally more cohesive (e.g., showing higher levels of ethnic density, associational life, language retention, and co-ethnic marriages) than otherwise similar Moroccan immigrant communities (Phalet and Heath 2011). Accordingly, Turkish immigrant parents are more effective in transmitting cultural values and religious beliefs and practices to their children than Moroccan parents (Phalet and Schönpflug 2001). Obviously, in each case individuals in the group vary along the dimension in question.

For their part, modern, Western, industrialized receiving societies differ in their cultures, policies, and so forth and are themselves inhomogeneous, many having experienced socio-political changes associated with past immigration. An individual's path in acculturating is affected by whether the receiving context encourages or discourages interaction with and acquisition of the mainstream culture. Some receiving contexts suppress migrant diversity; others segregate or marginalize immigrants; whereas still others promote pluralism and support diversity (Berry and Kalin 1995). Societies with a positive multicultural ideology provide more positive settlement contexts for individual migrants through social supports from institutions (e.g., culturally sensitive health care and multicultural curricula in schools), and they are less likely to enforce cultural change (through assimilation) or exclusion (through segregation and marginalization). Individuals within these varying contexts are positioned to take differential advantage of them. Compare three groups of countries in Europe: countries with long histories of considerable and diverse immigration (England and The Netherlands), countries with guest-worker histories (Germany and Austria), and countries with short immigrant histories (Norway and Finland). Different immigrant groups have gravitated to these countries, where they are treated differently. In historical immigration countries, such as Australia, Canada, and the United States, heritage and mainstream cultural orientations are more compatible and less conflicting, hence biculturalism is more prevalent, than in more recent (especially South and Central) European receiving countries where integration policies are less developed or absent.

Local context too exerts an impact on individual acculturation. In longstanding migration gateways, like Amsterdam and New York City, neighborhoods incorporate successions of multiple immigrant groups, promoting contact and comingling. Here, individual immigrants may find multi-cultural networks that provide a range of choice as to whether and how much to participate in the mainstream society. In some ethnic communities immigrants can purchase items from, converse entirely in the language of, and lead a life that differs little from their place of origin. By contrast, immigrants who settle in less multi-cultural areas are likely to follow different patterns of acculturation. For example, lower co-ethnic concentrations experienced by newer immigrants, in comparison to well-established ones in larger ethnic enclaves, afford services and support networks that differentially cater to the ethnic community. They in turn shape individual ethnic vitality.

A related factor that may affect individual acculturation is the cultural distance between the two contexts. For example, for Peruvians migrating to Chile the same continent and shared language presumably constitutes a closer distance to acculturate than Chinese migrating to Chile across continents and languages. The further evaluation of ethnic groups according to social distance is called the "ethnic hierarchy." In The Netherlands, Surinamer and Antillean immigrants are evaluated more positively than Turks and Moroccans. Distance can be measured by country-level indicators, such as gross domestic product or Hofstede measures, or by examining perceived cultural distance (how similar or different cultures of origin and destination are perceived to be).

In brief, individuals from diverse contexts of origin migrate to diverse contexts of destination, and so migrants acculturate in unique combinations of the two, and where individual immigrants come from, where they arrive, and the intercultural distances between the two all matter to their psychological acculturation.

Processes in psychological acculturation

Individuals acculturate. How? What processes are involved? At base, acculturation entails some internal negotiation between the cognitions and practices of (at least) two cultures. Eventual adaptations therefore must have core psychological features (Ward *et al.* 2001). Different processes have been proposed that accord with different theoretical perspectives of acculturation. Early unidimensional models of acculturation presumed additive/subtractive processes. Newer bicultural models pose questions about how individual immigrants integrate cultures. Individuals might combine—alternate, balance, or merge—contrasting cultural orientations generally or do so for specific situations or domains. Different process models of individual acculturation harbor idiosyncratic assumptions and implications. For example, alternation rests on the assumption that it is possible to maintain positive relations with two (or multiple) cultural systems without having to choose (permanently) between them. Immigrant adolescents from the FSU to Israel have been reported to balance their established Russian cultural identity with their new Israeli identity rather than reject one at the expense of the other. It is also feasible that immigrants create new cultures with unique features that are atypical of either culture of origin or destination. Indian immigrant mother-infant dyads in the United States engage in vocal interaction patterns that differ from both Indians in India and European Americans in the United States (Gratier 2003).

Risks and rewards in psychological acculturation

A focus on the individual in acculturation has almost from the start raised mental health concerns, and that long-standing clinical orientation has rather consistently stressed deficits, disorders, and disabilities. Not unexpectedly, healthcare practitioners are occupied with immigrants who seek help for their psychosocial struggles. However, acculturation is as much a well-spring of opportunities as a source of problems and entails individual rewards as well as risks. In dwelling on challenges, it has been easy to overlook immigrant successes.

Risks

The tendency to "pathologize" acculturation is partly attributable to roots of its study in psychiatry. Theories and research on acculturation were initially strongly influenced by medical fields concerned with pathological symptomatology believed to accompany "culture shock." It was widely accepted that immigrants inevitably encounter problems that are presumptive of poor psychological adaptation. Living in two cultures was deemed problematic because managing the complexity of dual reference points generates identity ambiguity, confusion, and anomie. Migration can cause or is at least associated with stress and increased risk of mental health problems, such as anxiety, alienation, psychosomatic symptomatology, depression, and identity diffusion (Berry and Kim 1988). Turkish children in The Netherlands reportedly manifest higher levels of internalizing and externalizing problem behaviors, than their native peers.

Because immigrant families straddle two cultures, intergenerational discrepancies can also arise, as we have seen, between parents, who wish to inculcate traditions of their culture of origin in their children, and children, who wish to conform to and be accepted by peers in the culture of destination (Kaplan and Marks 1990; Szapocznik and Kurtines 1993; McQueen *et al.* 2003). Asian Indian immigrant parents attempt to engage their American-born adolescents in Indian cultural practices, observe religious rituals and beliefs, feel a sense of pride and moral commitment to their ethnic group, and they may take them to visit India. But their adolescent children often prefer to speak primarily English, participate in American culture activities, have mostly American friends, want an unarranged marriage, and refer to themselves as American or Asian American (Farver *et al.* 2002). Thus, within immigrant families, individuals often differ with respect to their acculturation, and this gap in acculturation statuses can generate inter-generational tension and conflict (Birman 2006), socioemotional difficulties in adolescents, and parenting challenges characterized by poor communication, uncertainty, and diminished satis-faction. Chinese immigrant parents who adhere to the importance of education and the hier-archical parental role at home and emphasize superficial, performative levels of traditional Chinese parenting in their new American cultural context tend to have distressed Chinese American adolescents, whereas those who adapt the broader, general principles and tenets of Chinese parenting (e.g., importance of respect, education, and self-cultivation) tend to have non-distressed Chinese American adolescents (Qin 2006, 2008).

Manifold other psychological challenges attend individuals who rear children transnationally. At the individual level, attachment difficulties have been noted because children withdraw from parents from whom they have been separated, and some transnational parents bear hardships because they are unable to live up to their own (cultural) expectations of providing appropriate care. Focusing on children left behind by their parents (especially mothers) highlights emotional consequences, problems with managing decision-making and power sharing between parents and grandparents or other caregivers, and problems that arise if parents start a new family in their new country.

Rewards

Stressing troubles associated with immigrant status obscures successes that individual immigrants may achieve in self-esteem, cognitive functioning, and life satisfaction. Filipino and Chinese immigrant youth may suffer elevated familial problems, but they are often accompanied by high academic achievement. Asian Americans, including Hmong, Burmese, and Cambodians, do not have high incomes, but Koreans, Japanese, and Taiwanese do. People who live in two cultures need not inevitably suffer; indeed, some authors have asserted unique advantages that accrue to living in two worlds. Individuals who effectively blend cultures reportedly exhibit higher cog-nitive functioning and greater mental health status (Rogler *et al.* 1991). Cross-cultural experiences open one to self-discovery, personal growth, and escape from social roles and culturally restrictive perceptions. Numerous immigrants build good lives in their new cultures, as history amply attests. Contemporary research has unveiled a plethora of immigrant strengths, including large majorities of intact two-parent families, a strong work ethic, and notable commitments to the culture of destination. These dual views of risks and rewards have consolidated in an emerging perspective that acculturation is a multidimensional and bidirectional process in which individuals can forge cognitions and practices from cultures of origin and destination in a positive framework.

Policy implications of psychological acculturation

These theoretical, empirical, and clinical considerations have implications for policy *re* citizenship, social welfare, health, and education that touch individual immigrants (Yoshikawa 2011). Immigration policies vary across countries (www.mipex.eu), just as public acceptance of immigrant diversity varies.

Norms of the heritage context may be construed as problematic when practiced in the mainstream context. Head covering in French schools is a notable example. Many policy factors affect individual immigrants' acculturation, and also their well-being. Immigrants who live in an undocumented legal status hesitate to seek medical attention unless in emergency or acute situations; as a result, they fail to benefit from preventative healthcare (Bernhard *et al.* 2007).

The assumptions of researchers, practitioners, and policymakers about the lives of immigrants matter for the interventions and programs they provide, the conclusions they draw, and the regulations they develop and implement. When their assumptions are misplaced, the effects on immigrants may be adverse. Insofar as systematic relations exist between how individuals acculturate and how they adapt, the possibility exists for the development of some "best practices" in how to promote positive psychological acculturation. Policies and programs, as macro-level influences on the individual, often operate through the family level from effects that originate in higher ecological spheres, such as communities, neighborhoods, and social networks (Yoshikawa and Hsueh 2001).

Future directions in psychological acculturation

We have so far hinted implicitly or discussed explicitly several future directions of an individual psychology of acculturation. Acculturation is today treated holistically, but an individual-level analysis calls for disaggregation. Research has neglected how bicultural competencies originate at the level of the individual, processes by which bicultural skills develop and are expressed in the individual, and the psychological sequelae of biculturalism for individuals. In the future, we need to look more carefully as well at the speed, completeness, and felt comfort with acculturation within and across domains of psychological functioning. In this connection, longitudinal research will likely yield unique insights into so-far under-researched temporal processes and trajectories of individual acculturation.

As acculturation research becomes sensitive to the dizzying array of global emigration and immigration actualities, and spreads its net to examine a greater multiplicity of migration contents and contexts, similarities and differences in processes of individual acculturation and associated adjustment or maladjustment of individuals will rise to challenge accepted notions that derive from group acculturation research. Findings in one cultural arena or area of the world do not necessarily generalize to others. As our knowledge of the individual in the midst of international migration experiences advances we will need to alter our acculturation conceptions and theories. To paint a more complete picture of individual acculturation, future research will do well too to focus on positive migration and acculturation and identify keys for individual successes.

Conclusions

The numbers of individuals living outside their country of birth is large and will continue to grow. Recent surveys indicate that perhaps 700 million individuals would migrate to a new country permanently if they had the chance. The demographic, political, economic, religious, and familial networks that exist through individuals who are situated between two (or more) cultures has mushroomed based on the globalization of contemporary life, the speed, ease, and economy of communication and transportation, and the worldwide rights revolution. Acculturation has consequently become one of the most salient individual-difference constructs in psychology, and the burgeoning psychological literature has begun to refine our understanding of immigrants and their individual acculturation. This individual perspective is requisite to understand psychological processes of continuity and change attendant to migration and acculturation.

Given contemporary circumstances, immigrants are likely to gain competence in two cultures, move from one to another flexibly, and maintain transcultural ties blurring historical boundaries of social and psychological space. Still, immigrants need to master key skills to function optimally in different worlds—this fundamental individual aspect of acculturation endures. Major theories of acculturation in the past have tended to neglect the raft of individual differences we have discussed that facilitate, inflect, or retard acculturation. How international migrants acculturate psychologically is a product of many factors. Ours is not the first or only exposition of psychological acculturation (Social Science Research Council 1954; Graves 1967; Teske and Nelson 1974), and in this chapter we have intended neither a comprehensive nor exhaustive account of psychological acculturation. Rather, our goal has been to alert the reader and acculturation theorist and researcher alike to some not unimportant guideposts that constitute a psychology of individual acculturation, one that complements historical focus on the group.

Acknowledgment

We thank E. Stano and R. Tamaroff. Supported by the Intramural Research Program of the NIH, NICHD.

References and further reading

Arends-Tóth, J. and van de Vijver, F. J. R. (2004) "Domains and dimensions in acculturation: Implicit theories of Turkish-Dutch" *International Journal of Intercultural Relations* 28(1): 19–35.

Benet-Martínez, V. and Haritatos, J. (2005) "Bicultural identity integration (BII): Components and psychosocial antecedents" *Journal of Personality* 73(4): 1015–50.

Bernhard, J. K. (2010) "From theory to practice: Engaging immigrant parents in their children's education" *Alberta Journal of Educational Research,* 56(3): 319–34.

Bernhard, J. K., Goldring, L., Young, J., Berinstein, C., and Wilson, B. (2007) "Living with precarious legal status in Canada: Implications for the wellbeing of children and families" *Refuge* 24(2): 101–13.

Bernhard, J. K., Landolt, P., and Goldring, L. (2009) "The institutional production and social reproduction of transnational families: The case of Latin American immigrants in Toronto" *International Migration* 47(2): 3–31.

Berry, J. W. (2007) "Acculturation strategies and adaptation." In J. E. Lansford, K. Deater-Deckard, and M. H. Bornstein (eds), *Immigrant Families in Contemporary Society*. New York: Guildford Press, pp. 69–82.

Berry, J. W., and Kalin, R. (1995) "Multicultural and ethnic attitudes in Canada" *Canadian Journal of Behavioural Science* 27(3): 310–20.

Berry, J. W. and Kim, U. (1988) "Acculturation and mental health." In P. Dasen, J. W. Berry, and N. Sartorius (eds), *Health and Cross-cultural Psychology*. Newbury Park, CA: Sage, pp. 207–36.

Berry, J. W., Phinney, J. S., Sam, D. L., and Vedder, P. (2006) "Immigrant youth: Acculturation, identity and adaptation" *Applied Psychology: An International Review* 55(3): 303–32.

Birman, D. (2006) "Measurement of the acculturation gap in immigrant families and implications for parent-child relationships." In M. H. Bornstein, and L. R. Cote (eds), *Acculturation and Parent-Child Relationships: Measurement and Development*. Mahwah, NJ: Erlbaum, pp. 113–34.

Bornstein, M. H., and Cote, L. R. (2001) "Mother-infant interaction and acculturation: I. Behavioural comparisons in Japanese American and South American families" *International Journal of Behavioral Development* 25(6): 549–63.

——(2004) "Mothers' parenting cognitions in cultures of origin, acculturating cultures, and cultures of destination" *Child Development* 75(1): 221–35.

Bornstein, M. H., Mortimer, J. T., Lutfey, K., and Bradley, R. (2011) "Theories and processes of life-span socialization." In K. Fingerman, C. Berg, T. Antonucci, and J. Smith (eds), *Handbook of Life-span Development*. New York: Springer, pp. 27–55.

Farver, J. M., Narang, S., and Bhadha, B. (2002) "East meets west: Ethnic identity, acculturation, and conflict in Asian Indian families" *Journal of Family Psychology* 16(3): 338–50.

Gordon, M. (1964) *Assimilation in American Life: The Role of Race, Religion and National Origins*. New York: Oxford University Press.

Gratier, M. (2003) "Expressive timing and interactional synchrony between mothers and infants: Cultural similarities, cultural differences, and the immigration experience" *Cognitive Development* 18(4): 533–54.

Graves, T. (1967) "Psychological acculturation in a tri-ethnic community" *South-Western Journal of Anthropology* 23(4): 337–50.

Güngör, D. and Bornstein, M. H. (2009) "Gender, development, values, adaptation, and discrimination in acculturating adolescents: The case of Turk heritage youth born and living in Belgium" *Sex Roles: A Journal of Research* 60(7–8): 537–48.

Harwood, R., Leyendecker, B., Carlson, V., Asencio, M., and Miller, A. (2002) "Parenting among Latino families in the US." In M. H. Bornstein (ed.), *Handbook of Parenting Vol. 4 Applied Parenting*, 2nd edn. Mahwah, NJ: Erlbaum, pp. 21–46.

Kaplan, M. S. and Marks, G. (1990) "Adverse effects of acculturation: Psychological distress among Mexican American young adults" *Social Science and Medicine: An International Journal* 31(12): 1313–19.

Lerner, Y., Kertes, J., and Zilber, N. (2005) "Immigrants from the former Soviet Union, 5 years post-immigration to Israel: Adaptation and risk factors for psychological distress" *Psychological Medicine* 35(12): 1805–14.

Lin, C. C. and Fu, V. R. (1990) "A comparison of child-rearing practices among Chinese, immigrant Chinese, and Caucasian-American parents" *Child Development* 61(2): 429–33.

Marín, G. (1993) "Influence of acculturation on familialism and self-identification among Hispanics." In M. E. Bernal and G. P. Knight (eds), *Ethnic Identity: Formation and Transmission among Hispanics and other Minorities* Albany, NY: State University of New York Press, pp. 181–96.

Masgoret, A. M. and Ward, C. (2006) "Culture learning approach to acculturation." In D. L. Sam, and J. W. Berry (eds), *The Cambridge Handbook of Acculturation Psychology*. Cambridge, MA: Cambridge University Press, pp. 58–77.

McQueen, A., Getz, J. G., and Bray, J. H. (2003) "Acculturation, substance use, and deviant behavior: Examining separation and family conflict as mediators" *Child Development* 74(6): 1737–50.

Mendoza, F. S., Javier, J. R., and Burgos, A. E. (2007) "Health of children in immigrant families." In J. E. Lansford, K. Deater-Deckard, and M. H. Bornstein (eds), *Immigrant Families in Contemporary Society*. New York: Guildford Press, pp. 30–50.

Ngai, M. (2004) *Impossible Subjects: Illegal Aliens and the Making of America*. Princeton, NJ: Princeton University Press.

Padilla, A. M. and Perez, W. (2003) "Acculturation, social identity, and social cognition: A new perspective" *Hispanic Journal of Behavioral Sciences* 25(1): 35–55.

Phalet, K. and Heath, R. M. (2011) In R. Alba and M. A. Waters (eds) *New Dimensions of Diversity: The Children of Immigrants in the US and Europe*. New York: Russell Sage.

Phalet, K., Lotringen, C., and Entzinger, H. (2000) *Islam in de multiculturele samenleving* [Islam in the multicultural society]. Utrecht, The Netherlands: Ercomer.

Phalet, K. and Schönpflug, U. (2001). "Intergenerational transmission of collectivism and achievement values in two acculturation contexts. Special issue: Perspectives on cultural transmission" *Journal of Cross-Cultural Psychology* 32(2): 186–201.

Phalet, K. and Swyngedouw, M. (2003) "A cross-cultural analysis of immigrant and host values and acculturation orientations." In H. Vinken and P. Esther (eds), *Comparing Cultures*. Leiden, Holland: Brill, pp. 185–212.

Phinney, J. S. (2006) "Acculturation is not an independent variable: Approaches to studying acculturation as a complex process." In M. H. Bornstein and L. R. Cote (eds), *Acculturation and Parent-Child Relationships: Measurement and Development*. Mahwah, NJ: Erlbaum, pp. 79–95.

Qin, D. B. (2006) "Our child doesn't talk to us anymore: Alienation in immigrant Chinese families" *Anthropology and Education Quarterly* 37(2): 162–79.

——(2008) "Doing well vs. feeling well: Understanding family dynamics and the psychological adjustment of Chinese immigrant adolescents" *Journal of Youth and Adolescence* 37(1): 22–35.

Redfield, R., Linton, R., and Herskovits, M. J. (1936) "Memorandum for the study of acculturation" *American Anthropologist* 38(1): 149–52.

Richman, J., Gaviria, M., Flaherty, J., Birz, S., and Wintrob, R. (1987) "The process of acculturation: Theoretical perspectives and an empirical investigation in Peru" *Social Science and Medicine* 25(7): 839–47.

Rogler, L. H., Cortes, D. E., and Malgady, R. G. (1991) "Acculturation and mental health status among Hispanics: Convergence and new directions for research" *American Psychologist* 46(6): 585–97.

Sabogal, F., Marin, G., Otero-Sabogal, R., Marin, B. V., and Perez-Stable, J. (1987) "Hispanic familialism and acculturation: What changes and what doesn't?" *Hispanic Journal of Behavioral Sciences* 9(4): 397–412.

Schwartz, S. J., Unger, J. B., Zamboanga, B. L., and Szapocznik, J. (2010) "Rethinking the concept of acculturation: Implications for theory and research" *American Psychologist* 65(4): 237–51.

Schwartz, S. J., Pantin, H., Sullivan, S., Prado, G., and Szapocznik, J. (2006) "Nativity and years in the receiving culture as markers of acculturation in ethnic enclaves" *Journal of Cross-Cultural Psychology* 37(3): 345–53.

Silbereisen, R. K. and Titzmann, P. (2007) "Peers among immigrants—Some comments on 'Have we missed something.'" In R. C. M. E. Engels, M. Kerr, and H. Stattin (eds), *Friends, Lovers and Groups. Key Relationships in Adolescence*. Chichester: Wiley, pp. 155–66.

Social Science Research Council (1954) "Acculturation: An exploratory formulation" *American Anthropologist* 56(6): 973–1000.

Szapocznik, J. and Kurtines, W. M. (1993) "Family psychology and cultural diversity" *Hispanic Journal of Behavioral Sciences* 48(4): 400–407.

Szapocznik, J., Scopetta, M. A., Kurtines, W. M., and Arnalde, M. A. (1978) "Theory and measurement of acculturation" *Interamerican Journal of Psychology* 12(2): 113–30.

Teske, R. H. C., and Nelson, B. H. (1974) "Acculturation and assimilation: A clarification." *American Ethnologist* 17(2): 218–35.

Titzmann, P. and Silbereisen, R. K. (2009) "Friendship homophily among ethnic German immigrants: A longitudinal comparison between recent and more experienced immigrant adolescents" *Journal of Family Psychology* 23(3): 301–10.

Ward, C., Bochner, S., and Funham, A. (2001) *The Psychology of Culture Shock*, 2nd edn. London: Routledge.

Yoshikawa, H. (2011) *Immigrants Raising Citizens: Undocumented Parents and their Young Children*. New York: Russell Sage.

Yoshikawa, H., and Hsueh, J. (2001) "Child development and public policy: Toward a dynamic systems perspective" *Child Development* 72(6): 1887–903.

4

European migration history

Jan Lucassen and Leo Lucassen

Introduction

Traditional overviews of migration in Europe in the modern era are based on the so-called mobility transition. This still influential interpretation claims that until "modernization"— meaning roughly the Industrial Revolution and the accompanying massive population growth and urbanization—European societies were largely static and levels of migration therefore low. Only through the modernization process did people become uprooted and in large numbers leave the countryside to flock to the city, not only within Europe, but also overseas. This explains the disproportionate attention in many studies on migration of the 50–60 million Europeans who went to the Americas and Oceania. Only after World War II, so the conventional view goes, did migration to Europe become significant. [High levels of immigration occurred through the decolonization of Western European countries like the UK (from South Asia and the Caribbean), France (Africa, South East Asia, and the Caribbean), Belgium (Congo), Portugal (Mozambique and Angola) and the Netherlands (Indonesia and Surinam).] Another large immigration consisted of guest workers and their families from Northern Africa and Turkey and finally the number of asylum seekers from Africa, Asia, and the Middle East increased significantly from the 1980s onwards.

This standard history, however, is highly selective as it largely ignores intra-European migrations and important internal flows within countries. Furthermore it is not very consistent as it strongly favors emigration to the Americas over people who left Europe to Siberia, Central Asia and the Middle East, and furthermore it ignores circular and return migrations. Finally it is completely silent about unfree migrations from, to, and inside Europe. In this chapter we use a different perspective that builds on the vast new historiography of the last decades which started with the pioneering work in the 1980s of historians like Klaus J. Bade, Gérard Noiriel, Dirk Hoerder, Nancy L. Green, Leslie Moch, and others. Moreover, we follow the recent theoretical approach of Patrick Manning, who developed a cross-community approach to migration. In contrast to people who move within their "home community," whose members share the same language and culture, the migration of people who join or invade another community is fundamentally different and often leads to social and cultural change. As people from different communities in isolation have developed different ideas, technologies, and artifacts, cross-community migration easily leads to innovation and change. Whereas Manning defines community in linguistic terms we also include social and cultural parameters. For the long nineteenth century, ending with World War I this means that we not only focus on people who leave (*emigration*) or enter (*immigration*) Europe, but also include *internal migrants* who move to cities, because they entered a different socio-cultural world. Because nation states become much more homogeneous in the course of the nineteenth century and cultural differences between the countryside and the city within nation states became less significant, we decided for this chapter to exclude internal migrants in the "age of extremes" that started with World War I. From that time onwards we concentrate on rural–urban moves of an international and later on intercontinental nature, for example Italians from the Sicilian countryside and Moroccans from the Rif mountains to Paris, Brussels, and Amsterdam.

Furthermore we discuss *seasonal migrants* who moved between more traditional and highly commercialized regions, sometimes across national boundaries, but not necessarily so. Third, we will pay serious attention to the migration of *soldiers* (and *sailors*) who moved over national boundaries, a category that is often overlooked. These moves may often have been temporarily, but the cross-community experience did influence both the migrants as well as the societies they entered, in the case of soldiers either as combatants or as occupiers/peace keepers. One can think of intra-European wars, but also the migration of millions of soldiers within the many empires, including Russia and the Ottoman empire, who left for Asia and Africa. But also of Americans, Australians, Canadians, and colonial soldiers from all continents who fought during World War I and World War II, and part of whom functioned as occupying forces, like Americans in postwar Germany and Russians in Eastern Europe. Finally our cross-community approach also includes *colonization migrations*, which we define as people who settled in different ecological settings in rural areas, often in different countries. In the modern era this form of cross-community migration was rather small and largely limited to Eastern and southeastern Europe.

The mobility transition

In 1971 the geographer Wilbur Zelinsky published a seminal article in which he launched the idea of a mobility transition that would have unchained Europeans and hugely stimulated migration. At the same time he fully acknowledged that we should not value international over internal moves. He rightly argued that black families moving a city block into a white district experience often a more dramatic social shift than families moving over thousands of miles by their employer and ending up in a duplicate of their former neighborhood. Furthermore he considered early modern mobile scholars, merchants, soldiers, sailors, and so on as "full-fledged" migrants, only assuming that these were exceptions to the sedentary rule. And given the state of the art in historical migration studies at the time, he could not be blamed for underestimating migration in early modern Europe.

Forty years later, however, there is ample proof of worldwide structural mobility and migration long before the so-called modernization set in and we have become aware of the structural function of migration for the human species from the very beginning when people left Africa some 60,000 years ago. This does not rule out, however, an increase during the nineteenth century as a result of the transportation (steamships and railways) and communication (telegraph, telephone, newspapers) revolutions, which made travel cheaper and faster, enabling massive intercontinental and other long distance moves. And this is indeed what we see when we estimate cross-community migrations in Europe between 1500 and 1900: already high levels before 1800 and an increase especially after 1850 (Table 4.1).

J. Lucassen and L. Lucassen

Table 4.1 Total migration rates in Europe 1501–1900

	Total average population (millions)	Total migrations (millions)	Migration rate (%)
1501–50	76	9.0	13.0
1551–1600	89	13.2	14.8
1601–50	95	19.1	20.1
1651–1700	101	18.9	18.7
1701–50	116	20.5	17.7
1751–1800	151	26.3	17.4
1801–50	214	48.5	22.7
1851–1900	326	100.4	30.8

Source: Lucassen and Lucassen 2011: p. 304.

Different from what Zelinsky assumed this increase did not start from scratch, so that the term "transition" is misleading. Instead what we see is in the first place shifts in scale, not in the nature of migration. How migration rates developed in the twentieth century still has to be calculated, but there are good arguments to expect total mobility rates to fall, because of healthier cities (thus lower mortality and higher natural increase), fast transportation (enabling commuting), more fixed jobs (decreasing circulatory moves between the countryside and cities), and less seasonal and colonization migrations (mechanization of agriculture, less "empty land"). It remains to be seen whether this decrease is balanced by colonial migrations, "guest workers," and especially by the huge migrations of soldiers as well as the forced migrations of refugees and the massive deportations of demonized minorities (especially Jews, but also huge numbers of politically and ethnically untrustworthy Russian citizens under Stalin) and forced laborers during and after the many wars that scourged the continent. The impact of tourism, since the 1960s, is another form of mobility which still has to be assessed.

In the remainder of this chapter we will use the four basic sub-categories of cross-community migration to give a thematic/diachronic overview of the major migrations in, to and from Europe. This diverges from the standard story and introduces different comparisons and relationships, that stress the structural and systemic dimension of migration for human societies. At the same time it explicitly acknowledges the contingent political and cultural factors that shaped and colored migrations within the context of nation states, empires, welfare states, warfare and repression, economic and political inequalities, and changing family systems and gender roles.

Seasonal migrants

Seasonal labor was widespread throughout Europe since the Middle Ages, especially in the western and southern parts. Annually large numbers of peasants left their small farms to work for higher wages in areas where labor was in great demand, especially during harvest times. Thanks to a systematic attempt to quantify this form of migration during the Napoleonic period the numbers around 1811 are well known. For the nineteenth century we have some good additional data. Absolute numbers of Europeans who were involved in this type of migration increased from an estimated half million in the seventeenth century to almost 25 million in the second half of the nineteenth century. Around 1800 the largest systems (attraction poles with their hinterland) were to be found in France, Italy, and Spain. Smaller systems could be found in the Western part of the Netherlands (attracting Germans) and around London (attracting Irish).

In the course of the nineteenth century not only did numbers swell in Europe, but we see important shifts: shrinkage in Southern and Western Europe and a huge increase in Germany (mainly Polish speaking Russians) and Russia. Especially the Russian empire is of interest, because it is often assumed that because of the second serfdom peasants were tied to the soil. We now know however, that mobility restrictions notwithstanding, Russian peasants were very mobile and that this increased tremendously in the second half of the nineteenth century up until World War I, from half a million around 1800 to 7 million a century later. The reason for this growth is not so much the abolishment of serfdom in 1861, but the opening up of farmland in the southern parts of the quickly expanding Russian empire.

Seasonal migration systems also changed through the transport revolution. As soon as cheap and fast shipping lines developed between Southern Europe and the Americas, large numbers of Italians, Spaniards, and Portuguese (mainly men) joined the transatlantic great migrations to work part of the year in Argentinean agriculture and in North American mines. At least initially this work was combined with a small farm in their countries of origin where spouses and children remained. Although in the longer run this often resulted in permanent settlement overseas, it explains partially the very high rates of return migration of Southern European migrants until World War I.

After the Great War total numbers fell quickly as seasonality diminished and machines took over, but the phenomenon did not vanish entirely. In a way new forms of seasonal labor developed that fit in our cross-community approach. This is most obvious in Spain and Italy (and to a lesser degree Greece), where in the last decades of the twentieth century Moroccans as well as Rumanians and Albanians have found work in both agriculture and construction. Other systems have sprung up in North Western Europe, where since the end of the 1990s large numbers of Poles have filled vacancies in the same economic sectors. Strictly speaking these migrants differ from the prototypical seasonal migrant, because they do not combine this work with a small plot of land back home, nor is all the work of a seasonal nature. Finally, the role of the state has changed. Not so much for the Poles who since 2005 as EU citizens can move freely, but for North Africans the situation is quite different. Many of them entered the "weak southern belly" of Europe as illegals, and those who were not so lucky to become regularized have a very vulnerable position.

Colonization

In contrast to the Chinese empire since the High Middle Ages colonization migration has been of minor importance in Europe. An exception were the Ottoman and Russian empires. We are especially well informed about the latter, where imperial policies since Catharina the Great opened up vast territories in the South and the East. A conservative estimate is that between 1750 and 1900 some 10 million peasants settled in the Forest heartland and the Steppe regions of European Russia. To some extent the massive population movements in South Eastern Europe, in the wake of the crumbling Ottoman empire might also be subsumed under the heading of colonization. In most cases this involved forced population exchanges between Greece (1922/1923) and the Balkans on the one hand and the new Turkish state on the other. Many of these migrants ended up in cities, but a considerable number involved rural to rural moves, which reshaped the rural landscape in this part of Europe.

Other colonization migrations concerned Europeans moving outward, especially to the American and Siberian frontiers. Also here, this involved in each case at least ten million migrants, who as emigrants settled in sparsely populated lands where the native population was either killed or marginalized.

Moves to the city

During the early modern period considerable numbers of Europeans flocked to cities. Their numbers were especially high because of the high urban mortality, which necessitated a constant stream of migrants, as well as the spectacular urbanization in the area that covered Northern Italy, Southern Germany, and the North West (Belgium, Netherlands, and England). This urbanization process intensified and spread in the nineteenth and twentieth centuries, to a large extent due to the settlement of country folk, is often studied and discussed separate from the "great migration" to the Americas. This mental membrane often hides more than it reveals. There are good reasons to consider the Atlantic, including Europe and the Americas, as one migratory space from the mid-nineteenth century onwards. Especially the transportation and communication revolutions expanded the geographical scale of European migrations and brought the Americas, as well as other imperial spaces (especially within the British and French global empires), in direct reach of potential migrants. Moreover, as economic historians have shown, the "first round of globalization" quickly led to a gradual convergence of wages and created a common space in which the bright lights of the city could be Vienna, Paris, Amsterdam, but also Chicago, Buenos Aires, or Toronto.

Seen in this light it makes perfect sense to analyze the bulk of the great transatlantic migrations together with the cityward moves within and between European countries. Good examples offer the well know emigrations of ten of millions of Italians, Poles, and Irish to the Americas, especially the United States. Between 1870 and 1940, however, almost as many Italians migrated to countries like France, Switzerland, the Austrian–Hungarian Empire, and Germany. Poles also settled in large numbers in Germany and France, and a minority of Irish (but still hundreds of thousands) chose the UK and not the United States as a destination. Their motives often did not differ fundamentally. In all cases the search for work and a better living dominated.

Labor migrants before World War I

The same was true for many internal migrants up to World War I. Especially the low skilled of them were seen as different by their co-patriots and stigmatized as country bumpkins who lacked basic cultural refinement and whose dialects were incomprehensible. Well known are the Bretons and peasants from the Massif Central who in the nineteenth century were considered as dangerous and alien nomads wrecking the social fabric of the city. Only gradually did these peasants turn into Frenchmen, Germans, etc. And for some countries, like Italy, this process of internal cultural and national homogenization lasted until the 1950s and 1960s, when millions of Southern "*bruti, sporchi, e cattivi*" (ugly, dirty, and bad) Italians moved to northern cities like Turin and Milan. It is no coincidence that the new social sciences were captivated by the assumed dramatic uprooting effects of rural to urban migrations, as the work and preoccupation of Tönnies, Weber, Durkheim, and the founders of the Chicago School, like Robert Park, testifies, and which buttressed the latter on developed modernization paradigm that guided Zelinsky's idea of a modernization transition. We now know that alienation, anomy, and uprooting were largely smoothed by the cushioning effects of migrant networks and urban institutions, and furthermore that many peasants combined rural with urban work, because of the volatile nature of both labor markets. Only after World War I did urban and industrial jobs become more stable and did most rural migrants settle permanently in cities.

Apart from low skilled peasants, European cities bustled with skilled workers, artisans and career migrants, and civil servants, who navigated various urban networks and added to the very high mobility. Especially in the Austrian–Hungarian Empire networks of journeymen, working in small-scale urban workshops, have been studied, showing very high levels of circular mobility and multiple moves in the life course of millions of Europeans. This concerned both men and women. Well known are young women who found employment in small and large cities as domestics, factory workers, or shop assistants, throughout Europe. In the twentieth century this type of migration decreased, partly because formal education became more important, and new technologies replaced manual labor. Moreover, as we explained earlier on the increasing national integration and cultural homogenization, most internal migrants no longer qualify for the cross-community criteria.

For the larger part of the twentieth century our attention therefore shifts to foreign migrants who move to cities. Most Europeans who went for shorter or longer periods to other European countries ended up in cities. Either as workers in mines and industries, as domestics, artists, skilled workers, or merchants. Some settled for good, others—like the Poles in the Ruhr area and Italians in French industrial areas—moved on when industry declined, whereas many moved on a temporary basis. A good example of the latter are the almost 200,000 German (and Austrian) young women who crossed the Dutch border to work as domestics in Dutch house-holds. Due to the dismal German economy and towering inflation in the 1920s they were very cheap and came in the reach even of the lower Dutch middle classes. Most of them returned in the course of the 1930s when the German labor recovered, although some 15 percent in the end married a Dutch man and settled definitely.

Forced migrations and mass killings

Internal European labor migrations gained massive proportions during the two World Wars, in which both captives and forced laborers were needed to keep the labor market buoyant. During both wars Germany developed the most extensive system, but also in France some 200,000 colonial workers were imported from South East Asia and Africa, to fill the gaps that the drafted men had left. The most pernicious systems, however, developed under the rule of Hitler and Stalin. Nazi Germany developed a systematic policy to force men from occupied countries to work in German factories, mines, and agriculture, which amounted to almost 10 million Europeans (75 percent being civilians) who spent years against their will in Germany. They were vital for the German economy as they made up 50 percent of the total labor force in agriculture and munitions factories and one third in the metal, chemical, mining, and construction industries. Most of them came from Eastern Europe (Poles and Russians), but France and Italy also contributed heavily. It concerned both men and women, in the case of Russians and Poles half of them were (young) women. Apart from them the Nazis sent some 2.5 million political prisoners, homosexuals, and other "unwanted elements" to concentration camps (85 percent from abroad). All of them were used as workers for shorter or longer periods and at least a third of them died. Finally at least 3.5 million German and foreign Jews were sent to death camps, many of whom were put to work before they were killed.

The large-scale forced displacement (and killing) of people is also well documented for Soviet Russia, where Stalin instigated a systematic policy of forced migrations of various kinds of ethnic groups (from descendants of German migrants in the Volga region to Korean migrants in the south-east) to Central Asia and Siberia. Furthermore "class enemies," like the Kulaks, were massively deported to Gulags, where they were put to work under atrocious circumstances. In total some 12 million people were forcefully moved to often remote areas of Soviet Russia. These deportations started already on a small scale under Lenin in the 1920s with Cossacks from the Terek region as well as Kulaks and assumed massive proportions from 1930 onwards, especially of Kulaks, but also through the cleansing of the western (Poles, Finns) and eastern frontiers (Koreans). During the war followed a plethora of groups from the Caucasus, "Germans," Jews and members of "punished religions," like "old believers"(orthodox Christians).

Guest workers and beyond

After World War II the demand for migrant labor soon made itself felt. In Germany this was partly met by the large-scale immigration of so-called "Aussiedler" and "Volksdeutsche" from Eastern Europe, but these "returnees" were soon insufficient to meet the demand. Like in Belgium, France, and the Netherlands in the course of the 1950s agreements were concluded with Southern European countries (Greece, Spain, Italy, Yugoslavia) and soon also with Turkey, Tunisia, and Morocco, whereas in France this group mainly consisted of workers from Algeria, which until 1961 was an integral part of the nation. In most cases these migrants came from the countryside and settled predominantly in cities. This was also the case in the UK, where the bulk of the migration to cities like London, Birmingham, Liverpool, Leicester, and Manchester were colonial migrants from India, Pakistan, Bangladesh (after 1971), and the Caribbean. So in a way we can consider these postwar cross-community migrants as rural to urban moves, whose motives to migrate and settlement process shows more similarities with earlier internal cityward newcomers than one might think at first sight.

These on average low-skilled migrants are only one part of the migration puzzle. It is one that dominates the public and political discussion, but which easily makes us forget the almost equally large migrations of higher skilled, both between European countries as those coming from other parts of the world. In the Netherlands, for example, in 2010, 154,000 people officially settled in the country. Almost 30,000 of them were born there and may be called "return migrants." Of the rest two-thirds were classified as "western" migrants (born in Europe, North America, Japan, and Indonesia) and only a third as "non-Western." Studies on these western migrants are conspicuously lacking and many people do not consider them as migrants in the first place, showing how much in the public discourse "migration" was equated with lower class non-western migrants causing "problems."

Again the large majority of all immigrants from abroad in European countries settled in cities and both the lower and higher skilled contribute to the very diverse nature of these cities. A diversity which often stimulates creative and cultural industries and has a much greater added economic value than is normally assumed. As Saskia Sassen has shown, both the unskilled and problematized and the (high) skilled are part of the same system. Whereas the elites among the migrants earn high incomes, they increase the need for all kind of personal services, running from restaurants to ironing services, domestics, and doormen. Cities like Paris, London, Frankfurt, Rome, and Amsterdam are well-known examples.

Soldiers

In the period 1500–1800 soldiers constituted the most important category of cross-community migrants, which is not so strange given the constant warfare between European states and the widespread practice of foreign mercenaries. Nevertheless it is often overlooked that many people, until recently only men, experience cross-community migration as soldiers and sailors. The first group encounters new cultures while fighting or by being part of an occupying force abroad. This could mean Europeans inside their continent as well as in other parts of the world including the colonies, or non-Europeans fighting on European soil. At the beginning of the nineteenth century this mainly concerned millions of French, Dutch, English, Germans, and Austrian–Hungarians enlisted in or fighting against the French revolutionary army. Russians also fought, but remained largely within their own empire. Apart from the Crimean (1856) and French–German (1870) wars, the long nineteenth century was a rather peaceful interlude between the early modern period and the "age of extremes." The only exception were the colonies which drew hundreds of thousands of European soldiers through imperial circuits.

During the Great War some 65 million soldiers were enlisted, of whom 10 million died, 21 million were wounded, and some 8 million were taken captive. The cross-cultural contacts and exchanges were largely limited to bullets and grenades, due to the narrow battlefield in the West (Belgium and Northern France) and the East (Ukraine). Moreover, most soldiers were sentenced to a gruesome stay in the trenches and apart from a few surreal football matches against the enemy between the front lines during Christmas breaks, they had little contact with either the local population or the enemy. This was quite different during World War II. In 1939 and 1940 the Blitz reduced the period of actual fighting to a few weeks and—at least on the Western front—the war consisted mainly of Germans occupying and administering large stretches of Europe. It brought millions of German soldiers to foreign lands where they stayed for years at a time, as well as West European volunteers for the Waffen SS on the Eastern front. Led by general Rommel hundreds of thousands of German soldiers also ventured into Northern Africa until their retreat in 1943. This year also marked the inflow of increasing numbers of English, Canadian, Australian, and American forces, first in Southern Italy and from D-day onwards also in Western Europe, until Germany's defeat in May 1945. In the East Russian soldiers reached Berlin and beyond.

The interaction between foreign soldiers and the local European population did not end with the armistice. The whole of Germany was occupied and divided into four zones (English, American, French, and Russian) and with the outbreak of the Cold War millions of soldiers from these countries set up camps and bases most of which were finally closed after the Fall of the Berlin Wall in 1989. Americans like Elvis Presley and many others spent years of their adulthood in a foreign country and continent, adding to the global spread of American popular and consumer culture and the dominance of the English language. Furthermore, especially at the end of World War II, they befriended local women, many of whom followed fiancées to overseas destinations, adding to the postwar emigration wave from the Netherlands and Belgium in particular. Furthermore, Western European forces, like the Dutch army, used the Northern German plain to exercise and prepare for the final tank war with the Russians, establishing large-scale bases and establishing—albeit limited—contact with the local population.

In the second half of the twentieth century European soldiers fought decolonization wars outside Europe, which involved hundreds of thousands of young men: Dutch in Indonesia between 1945 and 1949, French in Indochina in the beginning of the 1950s and subsequently in Algeria during the savage war of independence (1954–61), Portuguese in Angola and Mozambique until 1975, Belgian soldiers in Central Africa, and Europeans enlisted in the French Foreign Legion, active in Africa, to mention the most important forces. In France the frustration of losing their North African colony also had long-term effects on the settlement process of Algerian workers and their families in metropolitan France, which already started in the interwar years. Think of French soldiers (like Jean Marie Le Pen) but also some 200,000 French colonials ("pieds noir") who had to leave Algeria and many of whom soon occupied important positions in the French state. Especially in institutions that dealt with the Algerian immigrants they greatly added to the negative attitude towards them, which was further stimulated by a series of terrorist bomb attacks by the Algerian Liberation Movement during the war of independence.

59

Finally, in more recent years European soldiers were found in large (British troops in Iraq) or small (various countries serving in UN missions) numbers in Africa and Asia, as well as in Yugoslavia since the breakup of this federation in 1989.

Less numerous, but not insignificant were European sailors. Their numbers quickly dwindled in the course of the nineteenth century with the shift from sailing to steamships. In the twentieth century, we saw a gradual shift in recruitment from Western and Northern European sailors to Greece and the Middle East. They predominantly manned the international fleets who more recently were relieved by Asians (Chinese, Filipinos) and Africans (Cape Verdians). Apart from working at ships, a number of them also became the pioneers of important chain migrations and permanent settlement in European port cities, both before and after World War II.

Settlement processes

How migrants settle in new societies depends on the prevailing "membership regime" that sets the rules. In Europe since the Middle Ages different regimes can be distinguished: multi-ethnic empires (Ottoman, Austrian Habsburg, Russian), mono-religious territorial states, as well as republics (like the Dutch) that accommodate ethnic and religious differences. In the course of the nineteenth century these three regimes converged into the dominating nation state model, inspired by the principles of the French Revolution, expecting migrants to integrate or assimilate. Furthermore, in the course of the nineteenth century these states started regulating international migration. Especially after World War I, the monitoring and regulation of migration increased, stimulated by the emergence of nationalism and state-induced welfare states. Nevertheless, millions of migrants settled in European states, partly enabled through the increasing (embedded) social and legal rights of migrants in liberal democracies which restricted the power of nation states to regulate migration. Finally we saw a gradual liberalization of the intra-European migration as the European Union expanded from the 1960s onwards, shifting the migration controls to the outer border of the EU.

The combination of the nation state model and a heightened attention to the immigration and settlement of foreign migrants in the twentieth century has made immigration and integration into a salient political topic. In particular, attention to non-European and culturally distinct newcomers, however, obscures the continuity in settlement processes in the last two centuries. Thus, it is almost considered common knowledge that the settlement process of postwar migrants from African, Asian, and Caribbean origin, often subsumed under the Eurocentric label of "non-western migrants," have greater trouble adjusting to their new environment than their intra, let alone internal, European precursors. Or, the more optimistic version, that their settlement process at least evolves along different lines than before.

The problem with these assumptions is, first of all, that it is too early to tell. At least if we accept the historical analogy that the settlement process takes place over several generations. That of many recent groups, including many colonial migrants, is far from completed and the third generation is only in its infancy. Second, these predictions are based on unproven and untested assumptions about the past. For example we know that all kind of internal migrants, like the Bretons and Auvergnats in Paris, at least the first two generations, were confronted with similar problems (both in terms of finding their place and the way they were viewed) as more recent newcomers from other continents. Also earlier migrants were often low skilled and through their different dialects and customs perceived as culturally distinctive. This is even more true for European migrants who crossed national borders like the Italians, Poles, and Irish. Especially in the latter case there were violent clashes between the first generation and native workers. Furthermore the receiving states often perceived them as a threat to the national identity.

This was especially the case with Polish-speaking migrants who settled in the German Ruhr area. Technically speaking they were German citizens, living in the Eastern part of the German empire that had been united in 1871. The powerful chancellor Bismarck, however, was afraid that their virulent Polish nationalism would stimulate the claims for an independent Polish state. Poland had been divided among Russia, Prussia, and Austria–Hungary at the end of the eighteenth century and its resurrection would have serious territorial and geopolitical consequences. Many "Poles," however, did indeed resist assimilation and established a vibrant Polish associational life and tried their best to shield their children from becoming Germans. In reaction the German police kept a strict watch on all Polish cultural and political activities and tried to break their nationalism.

In the long run this repressive policy was successful. At least, the second and third generations did become much more German than their parents and grandparents would have liked and within half a century these Poles were much more integrated than many would have held possible. Whether this was the direct effect of repression is doubtful. Integration processes have a logic of their own and are to a large extent autonomous, at least when migrants and their descendants share the key institutions (schools, public space, media, the army, shops, etc.) with the native population. Part of these Poles, after World War I for economic reasons, moved on to France, where they were joined by new fellow countrymen who were recruited by French organized employers. Also in France, a vibrant Polish life soon developed during the first decades of their stay, but also here within two generations they became more French than many could have predicted.

This conclusion also extends to the hundreds of thousands of Italians who left for France from the 1870s onwards to work in mines and industry in the east, north-east, and the Paris basin. Initially they were treated with great distrust and hostility, only in their case not so much by the French state, but by French workers who accused them of strike breaking and accepting low wages. Moreover, Italians were seen as footloose, as "nomads," because they were single young men who seemed to have no intention of taking root. This was considered extra problematic because their very mobile life style made it difficult to integrate them in French unions. Italians and French workers shared the same workplaces, but initially the Italians kept to themselves and indeed did occasionally weaken the bargaining position of their French coworkers. In the 1890s this led to a series of violent clashes, which cost dozens of Italians their lives. After the turn of the century relations became better and many Italians started their own families, mostly marrying Italian women, joining French unions, and quickly integrating through the workplace.

The third telling example of "old" mass migrations within Europe are the Irish who settled in the UK from the 1830s onwards. Although most of them chose the United States as their destination, especially during the potato famines of the 1840s, some 300,000 preferred a shorter trip across the Irish Sea and ended up in Scotland, the Midlands (Manchester, Liverpool), and London. Like the Poles they posed a threat to the nation (due to separatist leanings) and like the Italians they were accused of strike breaking and lowering the standards of the working class. On top of this, however, came a religious threat. The great majority of the Irish were Catholics who had settled in a Protestant country and Catholics, ruled by the pope in Rome, were seen as fundamentally different and a menace to the core values of British society. Catholics were accused of being anti-democratic, anti-national, and anti-liberal. Catholicism was presented as an authoritarian, repressive religion that left their members no room for deciding for themselves. Finally many Protestants believed that Catholics were planning to rule the world, by—among other things—reproducing much quicker than Protestants.

These ideas, which show remarkable similarities with the anti-Islam rhetoric of the last decades in Europe, were mobilized by zealous political entrepreneurs whose activities (e.g. lecture tours in cities with a large Irish minority) led to pogrom-like situations in the 1860s in various English cities, such as Stockton and Birmingham. As in the other two cases, with time the animosity between the immigrants and the native population diminished, although anti-Irish sentiments lasted well into the twentieth century, partly fueled by terrorist activities of the IRA and its precursors.

Postwar immigration: the liberal phase until 1973

These three large-scale immigrations roughly occurred between the middle of the nineteenth century and World War I, and in France the immigration continued during the 1920s due to a deliberate policy of the state and employers. The second wave started after the war and—apart from large numbers of displaced persons—consisted initially of young male Southern Europeans and later on North Africans and Turks who were recruited for low-skilled mining and industrial work in Western Europe, except for the UK. As they were meant to stay only temporarily, it took until the 1970s before a full-scale integration process really started by way of family reunification.

Fortress Europe 1973 to now

The long economic downturn, triggered by the Oil Crisis of 1973, urged many a migrant not to return, despite massive unemployment, but rather to bring over wives and children. This unexpected and unforeseen mass immigration of Turks, Algerians, and Moroccans, to mention the three largest groups, can be explained by acknowledging the changed nature of the state, which became visible in three ways. First of all the effects of the welfare state, which enabled guest workers to build up social rights; second, the principle of equality which strengthened the residence rights of aliens as they stayed on longer; and finally the unintended consequences of the restrictive aliens policy that most countries adopted after 1973. It was only then that guest workers from outside the European Union realized that returning to their countries of origin meant giving up their social and legal rights. As a result many of them decided to stay and exercise their rights to reunite with their families, which started the ill-timed mass immigration at the beginning of a long period of recession.

For colonial migrants the timing of their migration followed political dynamics, as they were the product of independence movements within the colony. During the decolonization process European states were often slow to limit the entrance of people from the former colonies, either because of their inclusive imperial ideology (the UK, France, and to a lesser extent Belgium and Portugal), or because of large mixed Eurasian populations who were considered to belong to the mother country (Eurasians in the Netherlands). Hence some groups arrived at an economically favorable moment, at the beginning of the long postwar economic boom (Dutch Eurasians from Indonesia, some Algerians, and the West Indians in the UK), whereas the immigration of others coincided with the recession of the mid-1970s (Surinamese in the Netherlands in 1975, some Algerians in France, and some Pakistani and Bangladeshi in the UK). Their settlement process was further influenced by pre-migration socialization, in terms of language, religion, and education. "Black" migrants who already spoke the language and had converted to Christianity, like the Creoles from Suriname, identified much more quickly with the culture at destination (and were seen as belonging to that society) than for example "white" Turkish Muslim guest workers, differences that among other things transpire at the level of mixed marriages.

At the same time Europe increasingly closed its borders, turning into a "Fortress Europe," and started to question the loyalty of its newly won migrants. Events like the Rushdie Affair and 9/11 in particular made Muslim immigrants highly suspect. To what extent the settlement process of these newcomers from Asia, Africa, and the Americas in the long run will differ fundamentally from earlier (European) migrants remains to be seen. Apart from acknowledging the increasing possibilities to build transnational spaces, the effect of the recent transport (cheap flights) and communication (cell phones, internet) revolutions, it is clear that also the role of the state has changed, and therewith to some extent the migration dynamics.

References and further reading

Bade, K. J. (2003) *Migration in European History*. Oxford: Blackwell Publishing.

Bade, K. J., Emmer, P. C., Lucassen, L., and Oltmer, J. (eds) (2011) *The Encyclopedia of Migration and Minorities in Europe. From the 17th Century to the Present*. New York: Cambridge University Press.

Freitag, U., Fuhrmann, M., Lafi, N., and Riedler, F. (eds) (2011) *The City in the Ottoman Empire. Migration and the Making of Urban Modernity*. London: Routledge.

Gabaccia, D. R. (2000) *Italy's Many Diasporas*. London: UCL Press.

Green, N. L. (1997) The comparative method and poststructural structuralism: New perspectives for migration studies. In J. Lucassen and L. Lucassen (eds), *Migration, Migration History, History: Old Perspectives and New Paradigms*. Bern: Peter Lang, pp. 57–72.

Herbert, U. (1997) *Hitler's Foreign Workers. Enforced Foreign Labor in Germany under the Third Reich*. Cambridge: Cambridge University Press.

Hoerder, D. (2002) *Cultures in Contact. World Migrations in the Second Millennium*. Durham, NC: Duke University Press.

Lucassen, J. and Lucassen, L. (2009) "The mobility transition revisited, 1500–1900: What the case of Europe can offer to global history" *The Journal of Global History* 4(4): 347–77.

——(2010) *The Mobility Transition in Europe Revisited, 1500–1900: Sources and Methods*. IISH Research Papers. M. v. d. Linden. Amsterdam,:International Institute of Social History, nr. 44.

——(2011) "From mobility transition to comparative global migration history" *The Journal of Global History* 6(2): 299–307.

Lucassen, L. (2005) *The Immigrant Threat: The Integration of Old and New Migrants in Western Europe since 1850*. Urbana, IL: The University of Illinois Press.

Manning, P. (2005) *Migration in World History*. New York: Routledge.

Moch, L. P. (2003) *Moving Europeans. Migration in Western Europe since 1650*. Bloomington, IN: Indiana University Press.

Noiriel, G. (1988) *Le creuset français: Histoire de l'immigration, XIXe-XXe siècles*. Paris: Éd. du Seuil.

Polian, P. (2004) *Against their Will: The History and Geography of Forced Migrations in the USSR*. Budapest: CEU Press.

Sassen, S. (1991) *The Global City: New York, London, Tokyo*. Princeton, NJ: Princeton University Press.

Zelinsky, W. (1971) "The hypothesis of the mobility transition" *The Geographical Review* 61(2): 219–49.

5

Migration history in the Americas

Donna R. Gabaccia

Most studies of migration focus either on North or South (or Latin) America or on the few countries of the Americas (Canada, Argentina, and the United States) that have made immigration central to their national histories. This chapter offers a very long-term perspective on migrations in the Americas. It draws on world historians (who use archaeological, genetic analysis, and historical linguistics in order to describe prehistoric movements), on historians of the early modern Atlantic and modern era of migrations from Europe and Asia, and on social scientific studies of contemporary migrations. Those studying the most recent of these migrations are far more likely than historians to emphasize their unprecedented size and significance. Historians agree that the origins of recent migrants in the Americas are more diverse than in the past but otherwise view recent migrations as merely the latest phase in much older processes of social, economic, and cultural transformation accompanying human mobility.

The peopling of the Americas

At least 38 autonomous nation states with the addition of a few remaining European territories in the Caribbean make up the modern Americas. Concepts such as emigration and immigration, which have been developed to analyze movements of people in such national settings, are not as useful for the study of earlier times. Thus, many world historians prefer to write about the mobility of people rather than about emigrants and immigrants.

Studies by natural scientists and archaeologists suggest that humans originated in Africa around 200,000 years ago; the process whereby humans walked or traveled by boats, "peopling the earth," proceeded slowly over more than 60,000 years. Peopling the earth involved millions of incremental moves made by small kin-based groups as their populations expanded, segmented socially, and split or separated spatially. Small groups moved peacefully or fled from conflict into adjoining regions, adapting to new ecological conditions and differentiating themselves culturally and linguistically as they traveled.

It is now widely accepted that humans first arrived in the Americas over a land bridge from Siberia into Alaska, some time between 12,000 and 30,000 years ago. The exact routes by which early humans traveled to Tierra del Fuego and eastward from the first Pacific routes are disputed, with both seaside movements and movements through the valleys of the long mountain chains of North and South America considered as possible. Archeologists describe most of the early human groups occupying the Americas as living highly mobile lives. Hunting, fishing, foraging, and gathering meant that small groups moved seasonally over large territories in North and South America. Shifting cultivation of domesticated crops was integrated into the cycle of seasonal moves, first in northern South America and in Middle America, and eventually elsewhere in southwestern, central, and eastern North America, too. After 3000 BCE, more intensive cultivation of corn and of potatoes created the basis for population growth, larger, more sedentary settlements and early states in coastal and central Mexico and in the Andes mountains. Long-distance trade accompanied the development of the Olmec, Toltec, Incan, Mayan, and Aztec civilizations, but trade also created long-distance contacts among groups of hunters and gatherers and seasonal cultivators everywhere. Although poorly understood and intensively debated, the lives of Americans remained mobile even after the rise of agriculture: foraging, hunting, raiding, conquest, and population growth could produce social segmentation, colonization of unoccupied or defeated territories, and relocations in response to climatic change or social conflict.

By 1490, the population of the Americas has been estimated at between 25 and 100 million persons. The outcome of millennia of shorter and longer distance migrations, cultural differentiation was pronounced in the Americas: several hundred languages, along with thousands of local variations, were spoken. Outside of a few large empires, identities were very local, with many people calling themselves simply, in their native tongues, "men" or "humans."

Conquest, coercion, and colonization: early modern histories of Atlantic empire building, 1492–1776

Massive death accompanied the introduction of new germs by the Europeans arriving from Europe after Christopher Columbus's first voyage in 1492. The total population of the Americas declined by 80–95 percent in the century between 1500 and 1600 as Spain's empire quickly expanded from the Caribbean to include much of South America, Central America, and the southern parts North America. By the 1530s the Portuguese claims in South America too had expanded to support more permanent colonization in Brazil. England, France, and the Netherlands established permanent colonies in the Caribbean and in North America somewhat later, in the 1600s.

Because of these devastating demographic consequences, some historians refer to this era of European empire building as peopling the Americas while others refer to it instead as the transformation of the Americas into a neo-Europe. Most scholars prefer to describe the migrations from Europe that accompanied empire building as conquest or colonization. Whatever they are called, the voluntary migrations of relatively small numbers of Portuguese, Spanish, Dutch, French, and British merchants, soldiers, gold- or adventurer seekers, and missionaries set in motion a far more massive migration of coerced, forced, and enslaved laborers, mainly from Africa. Frequently European conquest transformed surviving indigenous peoples into refugees or exiles, fleeing the territories claimed and occupied by Europeans.

The migrants from Europe to the Americas were surprisingly few in number. Estimates of Spaniards arriving in the Americas before 1700 fall well under 1 million, and the numbers of Portuguese traveling to Brazil before 1700 probably did not exceed 100,000. The exercise of European power did not rest on numbers but on superior weaponry and transportation technologies. Both advantages allowed Europeans to organize the coercive and brutal recruitment of laborers, producing the gold, silver, sugar, and timber that had motivated European exploration and conquest.

The slave trade was an unprecedented forced migration of 12 million people who were treated as exchangeable commodities and "shipped" under particularly horrific conditions across the Atlantic. The slaves transported constituted about 3 percent of total world populations in 1500 and 0.5 percent in 1700. Until 1800, Africans crossing the Atlantic outnumbered Europeans by a factor of four. More than 200,000 Africans arrived in the Americas to work on plantations in the sixteenth century; 2 million in the seventeenth century; and well over 7 million in the eighteenth century. High rates of death and low rates of childbearing among enslaved laborers continuously drove demand for new "importations." Only as abolitionist campaigns tackled the immorality of the slave trade did the numbers of slaves captured and transported decline; nevertheless, 2 million more slaves arrived after 1800. Over the entire colonial era, 40 percent of all slaves worked in Brazil; most of the rest labored in French, Spanish, and Dutch sugar-raising colonies in the Caribbean. About 300,000 were brought to British North America to cultivate tobacco, indigo, rice, and, later, cotton.

In the 1700s, Britain's, France's, and Portugal's colonization efforts expanded and the balance of African and European migrants changed. About 600,000 Portuguese migrated to Brazil, where many worked in new mining regions; migrants to British North America numbered over 100,000. Alone among Europe's empire builders, Britain's rulers encouraged colonization by their most marginal subjects, including Catholic, Jewish, Quaker, Pietist, and Puritan minorities, prisoners, and even foreigners from Germany. Many impoverished men and women traveled under indenture; by embracing seven years of servitude, "servants" worked to pay off the debts they incurred for the transatlantic passage. As Europeans settled the eastern provinces of North America and expanded inland in search of farmlands, natives resisted or fled inland, precipitating new alliances and conflicts among indigenous peoples.

The early modern migrations of conquest, missionizing, slave trade, and settlement redrew the cultural map of the already diverse Americas. In tropical areas, unbalanced migrant sex ratios and huge variations in personal power exercised by Europeans, natives, and slaves encouraged sex between white males and African or native females. In the Spanish and Portuguese empires, governing elites attempted to categorize the linguistic and physiognomic variations that resulted, using the new language of racial taxonomy—creoles, Africans, Indians, and mixed-race peoples of many kinds. In Mexico and in the Andean mountains of South America, native populations again began to grow and intermarried with persons of European descent. In British and French North America, by contrast, populations of both indigenous peoples and slaves of African origin remained small; both law and English culture discouraged biological mingling among peoples of differing origins. Far from imperial capitals, new ways of life emerged, creating many local but American identities. By the time imperial wars among the French, Spanish, and British Empires began in the 1700s, the foundations for political rebellion and the reorientation of the imperial-era migrations had been established.

To populate is to govern: nations states confront settlers and labor migrants from Europe and Asia, 1776–1940

Hemispheric analysis of the modern Americas reveals the close relationship of nation building and "immigration." In the years after 1776, nationalist revolutions began to unravel the European empires built during the early modern era. Beginning in British North America, continuing with the Haitian independence from France in 1804, and rendering most of Spanish America independent by 1824, these revolutions produced a patchwork of politically unstable new states. Civil wars, revolutions, and border battles were common in both South and North America; each conflict generated refugees and exiles who fled to, and then sometimes also plotted, from adjoining countries.

The rise of nation states transformed imperial patterns of labor recruitment as newly independent nations gradually substituted for the importation of enslaved laborers with competitive searches for settlers, potential citizens, and wage workers. To entice migrants, the new nations of the Americas promised relatively easy naturalization procedures that allowed foreigners to become citizens and that declared to be citizens all infants born to free people on their national territories. Many of the new countries of the Americas were shaped by the vast international migrations of the nineteenth and early twentieth centuries. Still, national mythologies diverged sharply as historians and political elites interpreted the mixing of peoples that had made each individual nation. While many nationalists embraced the principles of liberalism, few nations proved willing to accept and welcome all persons arriving on their shores.

Between 1820 and 1940 as many as 60 million persons migrated to the Americas. More than 32 million went to the United States, while Argentina attracted over 6 million, Canada over 5 million, Brazil over 4 million, Cuba almost a million, and Chile and Uruguay over 700,000 each. The vast majority of migrants originated in Europe; however, roughly 3 million came from India, China, Japan, or Africa. This means that rates of international, long-distance migration equaled or slightly surpassed those of our own times, with 60 million migrants constituting over 5 percent of the world's population in 1820 and about 3 percent of that population in 1940. (Today, UN statistics suggest that in 2005, around 3 percent of the world's population lives outside its country of birth.)

The early modern empires left a migratory legacy, too. The slave trade continued but diminished as first Haiti and the British Empire and then other new American nations abolished it and slavery itself, until the final abolition of slavery in Brazil in 1888. Imperial Atlantic shipping and trade routes also persisted, but ships plying these routes increasingly profited by carrying passengers. Since Spain, Portugal, the Dutch, France, and Britain had all also acquired early modern colonies in Asia; Asians too began to travel across the Pacific to the Americas. Until the 1890s, the largest groups of migrants to the United States and Canada still traveled from the lands of their former imperial ruler in the British Isles (England, Scotland, Ireland), with smaller numbers coming from Germany and the Scandinavian countries. Migrations to Brazil and to Argentina more often originated in Portugal, Spain, and Italy. By the last years of the nineteenth century these two systems were converging somewhat, with increasing numbers traveling to the Americas from all the southern and eastern peripheries of Europe and from first China, and then Japan, Korea, and India. Migrants from Italy moved in large numbers along both North and South Atlantic shipping routes, while Japanese went to both North and South America.

Abolition of slavery transformed older schemes for labor recruitment. In the Caribbean, abolition forced landowners to seek new sources of labor, often under indenture or other forms of contract. Looking beyond Africa, imperial networks directed recruitment toward Chinese and South Asian "coolies." Newly emancipated slaves often sought to leave plantation districts where they worked, moving inland to take up subsistence farming or seeking construction work elsewhere. Thousands of indentured workers from India and China replaced slave labor in cultivating and harvesting sugar in Cuba and in Trinidad. The building of the Panama railroad, and later Canal, first under French and later under US management, also raised demand for newly emancipated African-origin laborers. For Panama Canal labor bosses, too, China, the nearby islands, and the peripheries of Europe seemed plausible sites for recruitment. In Brazil, Italians immigrants were recruited to replace African slaves. More generally across the Americas, however, immigrants from Europe and Asia avoided settlement and work in areas where slavery persisted or where large populations of newly emancipated workers of African-descent crowded local labor markets.

Throughout the nineteenth century, the identification of agricultural "frontiers" in Argentina, Canada, and the United States created enormous incentives to rural European migrants suffering through the consequences of agriculture's commercialization and the onset of industrialization in their homelands. While settlers perceived these frontiers as empty, nation states were typically in the midst of forcing indigenous peoples to ever-more marginal regions in order to encourage settlement by Europeans. Called "emigrants" in English-speaking countries and "inmigrantes" in most parts of Latin America, settlers hoped to recreate their threatened traditions of family subsistence farming and artisanal production. Many migrants hoped to become landowners or to recreate close-knit communities of friends and family members from the old country. But the growing demands of export-driven and large-scale commercial agriculture, especially on the pampas of Argentina and on the North American Great Plains, did not often allow such dreams to be realized. By the late nineteenth century, men traveled to the agricultural frontiers of Argentina, the United States, and Canada to work as seasonal harvesters for wages on large farms or estates. Other migrants combined agricultural harvest work with seasonal labor in industry or construction, often on the vast railroad systems being built to unite new nations and to connect their inland agricultural regions to cities and ports where beef or wheat were processed and exported.

Across the Pacific, Chinese and Japanese wage-seekers also sought employment in large-scale commercial agriculture, especially on the west coast of North America, as well as in construction, logging, fishing, and mining. For many Asian migrants, the only escape from exploitative conditions as wage-earners was in petty trade and commerce, including the operation of small grocery stores, restaurants, and laundries.

By the end of the nineteenth century employment in a few economic sectors—construction, food processing, mining, industry, and domestic service—was reshaping migrations of would-be settlers across the Americas. As wage-earning replaced settlement, the proportion of female among international migrants dropped (only 10 percent of migrants from China and from the Balkans, for example, were female) and the representation of job-seekers from Asia and the southern peripheries of Europe increased. Circulation and return became common as migrant men called "sojourners" or *golondrini* ventured out and back home again. As the volume of transatlantic migrants again rose after the depression of the 1890s, urban centers and workplaces in southern Brazil and in Argentina, in Toronto and Montreal, and in New York, Chicago, and San Francisco became largely immigrant sites, with their populations in constant flux. However some sojourners transformed themselves into permanent settlers once they had gained familiarity with local labor markets, often when they married or called for family members and children from their home countries.

In Canada, Argentina, and the United States, natives objected that newcomers threatened to alter the nature of the new nations, undermining the fragile foundations of cultural solidarity by introducing new customs and ideas. Especially in countries with republican systems of governance, fiercely xenophobic movements of citizen voters soon emerged and demanded that national legislatures offer greater protection against such foreign threats. Citizens saw threats not only in competition on the labor market but also in the attraction of migrants believed to have foreign political ideologies (notably anarchism, socialism, and syndicalism) or in the tendency of immigrants to continue their own religious and cultural customs and to create institutions and businesses where they could continue to speak their own languages.

Along with Catholics in Protestant North America, migrants from China initially faced the greatest levels of hostility. Beginning already in the early 1850s, soon after the first Chinese arrived in the United States in search of gold, Anglo Californians began to insist that the Chinese were racially incapable of acquiring the habits of western, civilized life. With the legislators of the United States leading the way, restrictive laws began to limit the liberty of workers to enter from China or, once in the United States, for example, to seek work, rent homes, marry, or purchase property. The United States forbade entrance to Chinese laborers in 1882; it secured an agreement from Japan's government to end the migration of Japanese laborers (the so-called Gentlemen's Agreement) in 1908. After 1921, by act of Congress, the United States excluded all immigrants from Asia. Many other nations, including Canada and Australia, followed suit in the 1920s and 1930s, as World War I, the Bolshevik Revolution in Russia, and global depressions intensified nationalist passions and fears of labor market competition.

In the United States, restrictions soon spread to other groups, especially as the origins of settlers and workers shifted away from Protestant northern Europe toward the south and eastern margins of Europe, where large number of Catholics, Jews, and Orthodox Christians lived in relative poverty. Between 1885 and 1903, the United States, prohibited entry to contract laborers, anarchists, and "those likely to become a public charge" (that is, to require assistance because of unemployment or poverty). In 1906 it raised its requirements for naturalization to include English-language facility. Restrictions against workers and radicals also spread throughout the Americas—Argentina excluded anarchists, for example—and by 1936 even Mexico prohibited entry to laborers. The walls against immigration were high enough that refugees fleeing from Civil War in Spain and fascism in Germany or Italy in the 1920s and 1930s faced enormous difficulties in finding asylum; for refugees, only Mexico held open its welcome.

Although the transatlantic migrations attracted the greatest attention (for their enormous size) and the transpacific migrations fueled widespread and successful movements to racialize and then to exclude Asians, movements of people within the Americas were also significant, even if less often the focus of scrutiny. The largest movements within the Americas linked neighboring countries, although most nations did not bother even to count those departing or to register migrants entering from a neighboring country. In the nineteenth century, movements of farmers, workers, and family members across the largely unmarked border between the United States and Canada were so substantial that differences between citizens of the two countries struck many as meaningless. Persons born in the United States were 4 percent of Canada's population in 1910, while the numbers of Canadians living in the United States equaled a quarter of Canada's total resident population.

No easy co-mingling occurred along the border between Mexico and the United States, although there too movement itself was relatively free, and the number of Mexicans traveling north to find work increased after 1880. Americans from the United States became the largest of the foreign populations of Mexico. Indigenous peoples too frequently relocated across borders when they found advantage in doing so. Thus, when Mexico at the turn of the century sought to remove the Yacqui from northern Mexico to hemp plantations in the south, many Yacqui crossed over into Arizona.

Such intra-American movements were even more likely to be temporary and circular than were the longer distance Atlantic or Pacific migrations. North and South American border areas experienced largely unregulated daily commuting in both directions. As the economies of first northeastern, then Great Lakes and prairie Canada and the United States were integrated by rail lines in the nineteenth century, Canada's population moved toward the largely unpatrolled international border. After the Mexican revolution, by contrast, the new government of Mexico sought to limit emigration of its citizens to those possessing a valid contract for temporary labor in the United States. By the 1940s, the US and Mexican governments began to cooperate in recruiting temporary workers in exactly this fashion. Four and a half million Mexican men eventually traveled to the United States as braceros until the program was discontinued in 1963.

Restrictions placed on first Pacific and then Atlantic migrations succeeded in diminishing the east–west and west–east circuits of nineteenth-century labor recruitment only by generating new circuits that pulled rural residents toward prospering cities such as Buenos Aires or Sao Paulo and, especially in North America, from the poor rural South toward the industrial powerhouses of Chicago and New York. The fact that the United States refrained from restricting the numbers of immigrants admitted from other American nations also proved a powerful influence. The building of the Panama Canal reoriented circum-Caribbean labor-seeking toward New York, which by the 1920s had a large Jamaican population. The cities of the northern United States increasingly drew labor from the southern states: the so-called "Great migration" of African Americans, which had begun after the Civil War, with movements toward the cities of the upper south, now replaced foreign-born workers in northern cities with new arrivals from South Carolina and Alabama. Under unsettled conditions in revolutionary Mexico, too, small migrations of men seeking work in Texas and in California soon grew into large streams. Although the Great Depression also forced large numbers of Mexican workers out of the United States again, the Mexican-origin population of the United States declined only temporarily and the bracero program set off a new round of chain migrations that continues to the present. Within large countries such as the United States, significant internal population shifts responded to changes in international migrations. For example, the "Great Migration" of African Americans from the southern to the northern, industrial areas of the United States began after war and restriction reduced the numbers of immigrant laborers arriving from Europe after 1914.

As had been true during the early modern era of European empire-building, the vast migrations of the nineteenth and early twentieth centuries generated enormous levels of both cultural conflict and cultural creativity. For many new nations, the place of migrants in the nation required careful consideration. Throughout the Americas historians and social scientists, alongside philosophers and political leaders, began to offer new post-colonial stories of how their nations had been and were being built or constructed as independent and separate from Europe. These stories of nation building differed considerably from country to country. The United States took pride in being a nation of immigrants or a melting pot that both tolerated religious and cultural diversity (for example in the form of hyphenated African-, Native-, Asian-Hispanic, or various kinds of Euro-Americans) while also expecting assimilation into its English-speaking and British-rooted political and civic traditions. To the north, Canada acknowledged its bilingualism and origins in two warring empires—the French and the British—while making room in a multicultural mosaic for postwar newcomers and its First Nations—the indigenous peoples with deeper American roots. Argentina spoke of its long history as a "crucible of races," while insisting that the product of its marital melting pot were Argentineans without hyphens. Brazil too emphasized its long history of racial amalgamation, contrasted its "racial democracy" based on intermarriage to the segregation of races and ethnic groups in the United States. Mexico, along with most of the newer nations of the Caribbean, also differentiated themselves from North Americans by emphasizing the limited salience of color in their systems of governance and in their national cultures. Mexicans referred to their own cosmic race—understood to be the cultural product of *mestizaje*, or mixing—while in Cuba, theorists instead discussed how Africans, indigenous peoples, Chinese, and Europeans had all been transformed through the interactions of everyday life—a phenomenon they called transculturation. It was with such national myths that the countries of the Americas would confront the new migrations of the late twentieth century.

Refugees, exiles, and job-seekers in the contemporary Americas

Recent discussions of globalization portray contemporary world migrations as unprecedented and transformative. Certainly the short-term moves of tourists, businessmen, and corporate managers and international students are unprecedented in today's world. By contrast, mobile wage-earners and refugees more often encounter firm barriers to movements.

Migrations in the Americas were nevertheless transformed in the middle years of the twentieth century through a combination of a global depression in the 1930s, restrictive legislation worldwide, and the subsequent international hot and cold wars of the 1940s, 1950s, and 1960s. Trans-oceanic migrations collapsed; what replaced them were hemispheric moves from the so-called "global south" toward a "global north" composed of North America, Australia, and Europe. In the Americas, inter-American, local, regional, and hemispheric movements of refugees, exiles, and laborers have not completely replaced trans-oceanic migrations. Asia continues to generate sizeable migrations to Canada and to the United States, and Latin Americans now migrate to Europe. However, throughout the Americas, migrants from immediately neighboring countries are still often the largest groups—a pattern that discussions of globalization often miss.

Although the harshest and most racist of restrictive measures aimed especially at migrants from Asia were gradually abandoned during the 1960s and 1970s, immigration remained restricted numerically throughout most of the Americas. Restrictions on the migration of laborers remain stringent, making unauthorized entry or work, and illegality, especially common among construction and farm and factory workers and domestic servants throughout the hemisphere. Simultaneously, however, the proportion of highly educated migrants seeking professional and technical positions outside their home countries has increased, and many immigration policies in the Americas now seek to admit more of these workers.

Just as the persistent and tightening restrictions on migrations in the twentieth century worked to transform temporary labor migrants within the Americas into "illegal aliens," so too restriction created a new category of migrants called refugees and asylum seekers. In response to the horrors of the Holocaust, the United Nations sought to "manage" refugees, overseeing the creation and management of camps for them, especially in Asia and Africa. In the Americas, however, those fleeing political discrimination in central and south America and the Caribbean before 1990 typically encountered US laws and immigration practices that denied entry to asylum-seekers from non-Communist countries. The distinction between labor migrants and asylum-seekers is especially hotly disputed and often difficult to draw.

However ineffective rising rates of illegality make immigration restriction seem, the numbers of immigrants living in the Americas suggest that they work. Compared to the past, the numbers of foreigners seeking jobs or homes in the Americas is not particularly impressive. The United States continues to attract the largest number of immigrants; about a third of all international migrants live in the United States. Nevertheless, in 2005 the 35 million foreign-born in the United States constituted only 12.4 percent of the resident population, which is slightly below the historical peak of 14.8 percent. With only 5.6 million immigrants, Canada is more heavily impacted, with foreigners constituting over 18 percent of its population. Once important migrant magnets Argentina and Brazil draw migrants—many of them of indigenous and rural origin—mainly from their nearest neighbors. Argentina's 1.5 million foreigners are only 4.2 percent of its population—a far cry from the turn of the last century, when a third of the country's population was foreign born. Brazil's 600,000 immigrants constitute a minuscule 0.3 percent of the nation's residents. Today, Mexico has as almost as many immigrants as Brazil, although in Mexico, too, the foreigners are a small proportion (0.6 percent) of its population. Many of these foreigners, Mexico believes, are in transit northward, hoping to gain entry into the United States. Chile, too—where 184,000 foreigners constitute 1.2 percent of its population— has diminished in importance as a magnet for international migrants in our own times.

Most social scientists who study migrations in the Americas focus exclusively on immigration and thus on the United States and Canada. The immigrant populations of the two countries are strikingly different. In 2008, Mexicans constituted 30 percent of all immigrants living in United States, dwarfing the next largest groups from the Philippines, India, and China (which each contribute about 4 percent of the foreign-born US population), from Vietnam, El Salvador, Cuba, and Korea (at about 3 percent each) and from Canada and the Dominican Republic (2 percent each). Among these large groups are many refugees: Cubans arrived in large numbers after the Cuban revolution and Vietnamese fled in the aftermath of the US withdrawal from its anti-communist war there. Filipino and Korean immigrants come from countries with long-standing ties to the United States, established through investment, empire building, and the continued presence of US military bases. Many of the other largest immigrant groups are labor migrants seeking work at both the bottom and the top of the US job market. Mexicans and Dominicans are more likely to work in blue collar jobs, while migrants from China are more occupationally mixed and migrants from India are most likely to work in professional and technical occupations. As economic development in the United States shifted from the border with Canada to the border with Mexico border, both US and Mexican citizens moved toward that border, creating the so-called US "sunbelt." The result has been increases in the already-heavy flow of people in both directions, provoking intensifying fears of unauthorized crossings by migrants, drug dealers, and terrorists. The sunbelt includes large areas, such as the southeastern states, which in the past had almost no history of immigration but which now see proportions of foreigners rising.

Canada, a country of many smaller immigrant groups, also carefully controls entry. The largest of its immigrant groups still hails from the United Kingdom. But even this group constitutes only 11 percent of the foreign born in Canada. The next largest groups—from mainland China, India, Italy, and the United States—each contributes less than 5 percent to the foreign-born population. While cities such as Vancouver and Toronto have become multi-cultural icons of the impact new immigration has had, large parts of rural and western Canada have experienced little settlement by newcomers. Internationally, Canada is known for a relatively generous refugee policy but none of its largest immigrant groups arrived as refugees. Less constrained than the United States by geo-political Cold War pressures, Canada, unlike the United States before 1980, granted asylum to small numbers fleeing military dictatorships in Central America in the 1960s and 1970s. Confronting the country's need for labor, Canada has also created a temporary work program that is understood to be flawed, yet still superior to the policies of other countries. Canada's immigration point system—which privileges as desirable those immigrants who are highly educated persons with professional training—is also sometimes seen as a model for other countries hoping to attract "the best and brightest." Such groups make up at least a third, and possibly more, of Canada's immigrant population.

The "southern cone" of South America is now understood to be an emerging region of "South–South" migrations. Most of the immigrants in Argentina, for example, come from Uruguay, Paraguay, Bolivia, and Chile. Italy and Spain continue among the largest groups in the country, however, largely because of migrations that occurred already a half-century ago. Along with Argentina, Chile and Venezuela number among the "magnets" for other South Americans, while Bolivia, Paraguay, Peru, and Columbia generate more of the emigrants.

Once magnets attracting large numbers of immigrants, some of the countries of South America have instead become generators of emigrants. The harsh authoritarian regimes of Argentina and Central America in the 1970s and the collapse of the Allende Socialist government in Chile in 1973 resulted in the departure of substantial numbers of political activists seeking refuge in Europe and North America. In 2000, almost 800,000 Brazilians—mainly labor migrants—lived in the United States. Under the nationality laws of countries such as Japan and Italy, furthermore, the children and grandchildren of immigrants in Brazil and in Argentina can reclaim their citizenship with relative ease. Faced with the economic crises of the 1980s and 1990s, over 200,000 Brazilians of Japanese descent sought work in Japan. By 2009, Japan's government began offering such workers cash settlements to return to Brazil. The other countries of the European Union expressed displeasure with Italy's nationality policies once, for example, Spain discovered that many Argentines entering Italy quickly relocated there.

Departures from Latin America for Japan or Italy—much like the migrations to the United States from Canada of highly educated workers—do not fit neatly within the post-colonial frameworks that seek to explain south–north migrations. By contrast, departures for the United Kingdom or the Netherlands from Jamaica or Curacao in the years after World War II definitely retraced the routes of imperial rule—and were sometimes labeled as "the empire striking back." Historians of North America also sometimes view the vast migrations from Mexico to the United States initiated under the bracero program (1943–63) as resembling post-colonial migrations and guest worker migrations into Europe.

The emigrant nation par excellence of the contemporary Americas is, of course Mexico. The vast majority of Mexico's migrants follow a century-old path into the US southwest and often to worksites that became familiar under the bracero program. Soon after the bracero program ended in 1963, the United States for the first time imposed numerical limits on the numbers of visas granted to citizens of Mexico and other American nations. With migration and employments patterns already well-established, the numbers of persons working in the United States without authorization rose during every subsequent period of economic expansion. Workers from Mexico form a large part of this population of the so-called illegal or undocumented alien workforce. Estimates of unauthorized entry into the United States from Mexico spiked after the implementation of NAFTA (North American Free Trade Agreement) but declined sharply during the financial crises of 2009–10.

Estimates of Mexican nationals living in the United States constitute about 15–20 percent of Mexico's resident population. Mexico's government both cooperates with the United States in seeking to find a solution to unauthorized border-crossing and seeks ways to encourage migrants in the United States to maintain ties to their birthplace through remittances (which totaled over $26 billion in 2006), through voting rights, and through participation in hometown associations.

In sharp contrast to the European Union, efforts at economic integration in the Americas have not allowed for freer movement of people across borders. The series of trade agreements established in the late twentieth century between Canada and the United States, Canada, the United States, and Mexico, nations in the Caribbean, and nations in the southern cone of South America encouraged and strengthened regional commercial ties. But economic integration has done little to stem the mobility of people; if anything, rates of border-crossing (often illicit) have increased with economic integration. The long-term consequences of this disjuncture between neo-liberal economic plans and national restrictions on migration policies are still not obvious. While critics claim that the paradox works to create form of global apartheid within the United States the most immediate consequence of this paradox seems to be a widespread belief that systems designed to govern migration are broken, undermining citizen support for their own national governments.

References and further reading

Altman, I. and Horn, J. (eds) (1991) *"To Make America": European Emigration in the Early Modern Period*. Berkeley, CA: University of California Press.

Baily, S. and Míguez, E. (eds) (2003) *Mass Migration to Modern Latin America*. Wilmington, DE: Scholarly Resources Books.

Kalia, K. (ed.) (2010) "Country Resources." *Migration Information Source*. [Online]. Available: http://www. migrationinformation.org/Resources/ [September 15, 2010.]

Hoerder, D. (2002) *Cultures in Contact: World Migrations in the Second Millennium*. Durham, NC: Duke University Press.

Hoerder, D. and Harzig, C. (2009) *What is Migration History?* Cambridge: Polity Press.

Hoerder, D. and Faires, N. (eds) (2001) *Migrants and Migration in Modern North America: Cross-Border Lives, Labor Markets and Politics in Canada, The Caribbean, Mexico and the United States*. Durham, NC: Duke University Press.

Knowles, V. (1992) *Strangers at our Gates: Canadian Immigration and Immigration Policy, 1540–1990*. Toronto: Dundurn Press.

Lesser, J. (1999) *Negotiating National Identity: Immigrants, Minorities and the Struggle for Ethnicity in Brazil*. Durham, NC: Duke University Press.

Massey, D., Durand, J., and Malone, N. (2002) *Beyond Smoke and Mirrors: Mexican Immigration in an Era of Economic Integration*. New York: Russell Sage Foundation.

Moya, J. (1998) *Cousins and Strangers: Spanish Immigrants in Buenos Aires, 1850–1930*. Berkeley, CA: University of California Press.

Nugent, W. (1992) *Crossings: The Great Transatlantic Migrations, 1870–1914*. Bloomington, IN: Indiana University Press.

Portes, A. and Rumbaut, R. (2006) *Immigrant America: A Portrait*. Berkeley, CA: University of California Press.

Rodriguez, M. (2005) *Repositioning North American Migration History: New Directions in Modern Continental Migration, Citizenship, and Community*. Rochester, NY: University of Rochester Press.

Spickard, P. (2007) *Almost All Aliens: Immigration, Race, and Colonialism in American History and Identity*. New York: Routledge.

Waters, M. and Ueda, R. (eds) (2007) *The New Americans: A Guide to Immigration since 1965*. Cambridge, MA: Harvard University Press.

6

Asian migration in the *longue durée*

Adam McKeown

Looking at Asian migration over the *longue durée* helps us to remember that Asia is an arbitrary space. There is no form of "Asian" migration that is different from mobility in other parts of the world. Asia has encompassed a huge variety of mobilities and regional migration systems. And many of the most important migratory movements in human history have crossed the borders of what we now know as Asia. At best, Asia has emerged as an imaginative construct out of the minds of Europeans over the past 700 years, and the minds of Asians over the past 200 years.

But that exercise of imagination has had its effects. By the 1880s they resulted in a series of migration laws and racist policies that excluded Asians from most non-Asian destinations and confined their migration to separate Asian systems. This segregation came hand in hand with an erasure of the historical memory of Asian mobility over the last two centuries. Although Asians continued to migrate at rates comparable to Europeans, they were depicted as immobile land-bound peasants without the resources or structures necessary to migrate. When Asian migration was recognized, it was usually in small numbers as "coolies," "sojourners," victims of famine and corruption, or other forms of tradition-bound mobility that made Asians distinct from the modern and free mass migrations thought to characterize the Atlantic world.

The segregation of Asian mobility from the rest of the world was brief. It has broken down rapidly since the 1940s, as Asians have moved in increasingly large numbers both within and outside of Asia. Historical memory, on the other hand, has not changed so rapidly. Much current migration policy, historical accounts and social scientific research is based on assumptions that mass migration in Asia is a recent phenomenon. Contemporary mobility is then presented as a new challenge for regions long thought be characterized by relative immobility, "coolies," and isolation from the trends of modern history and globalization.

This account will place Asian migration within long-term trends of human migration around the globe. It will note the ways in which mobility has linked "Asia" to other parts of the world, the similarities in the organization of human mobility around the world, and the extent to which all of the human communities we now know are the products of mobility and hybridity. It will then look at the rise of distinct systems of Asian mobility in the late nineteenth century, and conclude with a discussion of the effects of that segregation on our understandings of contemporary migration.

75

A. McKeown

Early human movement

Our picture of early human movements out of Africa that probably started around 60,000 BCE is still murky. It is likely that one of the most important early movements followed the southern coast of Asia, arriving in Australia by about 50,000 BCE. But our picture is constantly changing in the wake of new genetic, linguistic, and archaeological research. Dates for the initial migration of Asians into the Americas range from 25,000 to 12,000 BCE. Speculations about the geographic origins of the first migrants into Europe include Africa, Central Asia, the Middle East, and North India. Despite these uncertainties, this research does point to the fact that we have to look at early human mobility in terms of multiple waves and diverse directions that often folded back on previously settled and traversed regions.

Geneticists and historical linguists have used statistical techniques to postulate the existence of a handful of major groups in Asia. Geneticists have identified three major human groupings (Cavalli-Sforza and Cavalli-Sforza 1996; Tishkoff *et al.* 2009).

1 A group ranging from southern China through Southeast Asia into the Pacific Islands, of which New Guineans and Australians are distinct subgroups.
2 A group that includes native Americans, northeastern Asians (including Japanese, Koreans, and northern Chinese), and Arctic peoples, with the Americans being the most distinct.
3 A group that spreads from South Asia through the Middle East and North Africa and across Europe, with South Asians being the most distinct.

Historical linguists, some following the methods of Joseph Greenberg, have also identified several major linguistic groupings as of 1500 CE (Dolgopolski 1998; Greenberg 2000–2002; Manning 2005).

1 *Eurasiatic/Nostratic*, which spreads across the northern latitudes from western Greenland to Western Europe. They spread south into Iran and north India about 3–4000 years ago, and more recently (post 1500) into the Americas and Australia.
2 *Dene-Caucasian*, which is mostly comprised Sino-Tibetan speakers but may include a handful of Caucasian and central Siberian languages as small islands within the Eurasiatic sea of northern Asia.
3 *Austric*, which covers most of mainland and insular Southeast Asia as well as the Pacific Islands, with the exception of interior New Guinea and parts of Melanesia.
4 *Dravidian*, which probably once predominated in India but now restricted to southern India.
5 *Afroasiatic*, which predominates in North Africa and spread to the Arabian peninsula as the Semitic languages.

Regardless of whether any these groupings survive later research, they already point to a principle to guide further investigation: that the movement of people (genes) may or may not correspond with the movement of culture (as represented by language or archaeological findings). For example, the core areas of the northern and southeastern Asian gene groups have significant overlap with the Eurasiatic and Austric language groupings, respectively. But Chinese speakers cross these genetic groups, including equally large chunks of each. And the third genetic grouping from northern India to Europe includes portions of at least three major language groupings: Eurasiatic, Afroasiatic, and Dravidian. This kind of research also points towards the existence of frequent and layered movements over time as a key aspect of human history. Few peoples in the world can trace both their genetic and linguistic heritages back to the original settlers of their region.

The movements of Indo-European and Austronesian speakers are two of the most recent and well studied of these early (i.e. before large agricultural states and written records) migrations. The Austronesian migrations were a movement of both genes and language into Southeast Asia and the Pacific, often by sea. By about 1000 CE they had arrived in New Zealand, Hawaii, and Easter Island, some of the last unsettled frontiers in the world. The Indo-European migrations left a stronger legacy of language and culture than of genes. They spread overland across much of Central Asia and Europe by 1000 BCE. Both migrations were associated with new forms of technology, and the spread of cultural and linguistic forms that have shaped the world to the present.

Austronesian speakers probably emerged in what is now southern China, and spread to Taiwan by 3000 BCE. Their expansion was associated with outrigger canoes, rice, terraced agriculture, pottery, stilt houses and tattoos. After moving to the Philippines, Borneo, and Java by 2000 BCE, Astronesians divided into two main groups. Malay speakers spread through maritime Southeast Asia, where they still dominate many of the coastal areas to this day. They migrated as far as East Africa and Madagascar during the first millennium CE. The languages of Madagascar still show a strong Malay influence and the gene pool is nearly half Malay in origin. The second branch had its origins in the Lapita culture that began around 1500 BCE in what is now called the Solomon Islands east of New Guinea. It was clearly a mix between Austronesian immigrants and pre-existing residents (the linguistic and genetic perseverance of which can be found in highland New Guinea). Over the next 2,500 years, Austronesian speakers used their sea-going skills to spread to nearly all the islands of the Pacific, while losing some of their early technologies such as pottery and rice. Inter-island voyaging and communication probably continued until after 1600 CE (Bellwood 1997; Kirch 2002).

Indo-European speakers emerged around 4–3000 BCE in the area to the north of the Black Sea that was a frontier between expanding agriculturalists and hunter-gatherers. This region was associated with horse domestication, and horse-riding and pastoralism became a dominant mode of life by the third millennium BCE, with some groups living exclusively as pastoral nomads by the first millennium. The rise of Indo-European language was also associated with a cultural complex characterized by patriliny, militaristic culture, large entourages (*comitatus*), hero myths, hospitality, wealthy graves, and a polytheistic pantheon mediated by shamans (Anthony 2007; Beckwith 2009).

While large groups of Indo-European speakers may have moved across the Central Asian steppes, migration beyond the steppes was mostly made up of smaller groups of elites as mercenaries, conquerors, or through alliances with local elites. In this way, languages and cultural practices spread more than the actual genes. Indo-European speakers first began to spread into Europe around 3000 BCE. The appearance of wealthy graves suggests their elite status, but there is little evidence of violence or conquest. The development of saddles and chariot warfare in Central Asia after 2000 BCE was associated with the expansion of Iranian and Indic speakers through Central and into South Asia. The culture of chariots and wealthy burial was also apparent in the rise of the Shang Dynasty in China around 1200 BCE, although there was limited linguistic and genetic impact from Indo-European speakers. Altaic speakers such as Turks, Mongols, and Manchus also began to adopt Indo-European cultural forms. Genetic exchange between the two groups was extensive, and cultural and linguistic interactions were probably quite complex. The resultant Central Asian cultural complex was a dominant feature of Asia until the eighteenth century, and shaped many of the empires and political structures of western, southern, and eastern Asia to this day (Beckwith 2009).

States, agriculture, and armies

After the third millennium BCE, Central Eurasian horse cultures dominated movement in the interior of Asia, as did Austronesian seafaring culture in much of maritime Asia. The space between them, from the coast to a few hundred kilometers inland, was increasingly dominated by agricultural states that were associated with forms of mobility that were different from the nomadism and communal relocation that was common in the hills, steppes, and littoral areas. In many ways, these states and the rise of agriculture reduced mobility by fixing the homes and villages of previously mobile hunter-gatherers and swidden agriculturalists. But the concentration of wealth and power in cities and the military also created new kinds of mobility (Manning 2005). Except for some merchants, this mobility rarely crossed the long-distances of migrants in maritime and Central Asia. But the emergence of the silk roads as a space of human mobility, interaction between states and between the peoples of inner and peripheral Asia, and as a route for the spread of universalizing regions did help to create a common Eurasian space that was unmatched in size and scope by any other part of the world. Patterns of trade, labor, peasant, elite, and coerced migration were forged within this space that still shape much migration to this day.

The concentration of wealth and military power facilitated many forms of migration. Conquest often caused pre-existing populations to flee. Those that did not flee could be coercively relocated near capitals or to distant border areas for security or to contribute to economic development. The armies themselves were major sources of mobility in their constant recruitment of slaves, prisoners, and subjects for army service and public works. This was an important link with Central Asian peoples, who remained one of the major sources of both slaves and soldiers for the agricultural empires. Soldiers and their families were often settled in frontier areas both as garrisons and agricultural colonists. These pacified frontiers also attracted the immigration of independent farmers and merchants, who were sometimes encouraged through state subsidies and tax breaks.

Even without direct military coercion, corvée labor (unpaid labor required by states or local lords), tribute transport, public works, active slave trades, and elite circulation were important aspects of many of these states. The concentration of wealth required a constant flow of labor and craftsmen into cities, palace construction, canal and wall maintenance, and other works. The administration of power also encouraged the circulation of elites into new administrative positions and as beneficiaries of land grants in return for services. The specifics varied from place to place. In many states, the peasantry were obliged to perform labor corvée. In western Asia, slaves were a common form of labor and military migration. In India by the second millennium CE, castes and distinct groups who engaged in perpetual itinerant labor mobility emerged (Ludden 1985; Kerr 2006). Large states also supported the formation of regional markets that encouraged less coercive mobility. Sometimes entire villages or itinerant castes and groups would specialize in the training of certain crafts and professions such as stonework, acting, or construction, and travel the circuits from markets to manors to practice their crafts. The transportation routes themselves became a further cause of migration, requiring the labor of numerous porters, animal drivers, guides, guards, and sailors (Skinner 1976).

Eurasian exchange

The concentration of wealth and military power also facilitated long-distance trade by securing trade routes and markets, and creating a clientele for expensive products. Common motifs found on merchant seals show the existence of trading networks stretching from northern India to the eastern Mediterranean by the second millennium BCE—the same space that would be conquered by Alexander the Great in 323 BCE. By the beginning of the common era, these trade routes reached across Asia to China, India, and the Mediterranean, both overland and via the oceans. This expansion of trade routes was made possible through interaction between the peoples of Central Asia and the peripheral states (Beckwith 2009).

The integration of these trading routes supported the rise of two interrelated phenomena: trade diasporas and the spread of universal religions. Although the states provided some security against bandits and fraud, long-distance trade was still plagued by problems of trust, information, and balance of payments. Agents linked across great distances by ties of kinship, adoption, religion, and ethnicity had more incentive to maintain trust and think of their endeavors as a long-term, even multigenerational project. Their personal futures were bound up with the success of their groups. And the success of their groups helped to identify them as people to whom rulers and other merchants would turn when looking for information, loans, and goods. This success was best maintained through control of knowledge and opportunities, a control that could be buttressed by the maintenance of unique culture and bloodlines (Curtin 1984).

Distinct forms of religious worship often helped bind these trading diasporas together, as has been the case for Jews and Parsis. But these trading diasporas also interacted well with the universalizing religions such as Buddhism, Christianity, Manicheanism, Islam, and some forms of Brahmanism that have spread throughout Eurasian trading networks over the past two millennia. These religions not only broke ties with local and family gods, but also developed institutional structures delinked from particular states (as opposed to, say, Confucianism or Zoroastrianism, which retained strong institutional ties to the Chinese and Iranian states) and could move easily with merchants. Most of them also developed ideologies of thrift, self-control, and family virtues that fit well with the behavior of successful merchants (Foltz 1999).

These religions, especially in their more missionary incarnations, developed at major cross-roads of world trade. Most of the monotheistic religions developed out of the contact between people in the region between Iran and the Levant. Similarly, Mahayana Buddhism—a more populist and missionary form of Buddhism—developed around 100 BCE in the Kushan Empire. The Kushan was located at the heart of the silk roads in what is now Afghanistan, and was home to a mix of Greek, Indian, Persian, and Central Asian cultures. Buddhist monasteries and temples soon spread along the trading routes in conjunction with wealthy traders. They offered places for merchants and transportation workers to rest, exchange information, and mediate disputes with people who shared common values. In return, the monasteries and temples flourished with the help of generous donations from the merchants. Initially associated with merchant enclaves in the first centuries of its spread, Buddhism eventually spread to local societies in East and Southeast Asia (Liu 1996). Tibet, located off the main trade routes, was one of the last states to adopt Mahayana Buddhism.

Monotheistic sects from Western Asia followed these same routes, including Nestorian Christian, Manichean, and Jewish traders and proselytizers. Islam appeared in the trading centers of Mecca and Medina. It followed the trade routes in its initial expansion, embracing a generous portion of Persian and Hellenic culture along the way. Throughout much of Asia east of Iran, however, it continued to remain just one religious alternative out of many until after the thirteenth century when sufis (who emerged from Central Asia), scholars, and merchants began to deepen and extend its reach. Wandering sufis did much of the hard work of attracting peasant converts. Migrant scholars accepted jobs and advisory positions at states throughout Asia. And merchants were often the cutting edge of expansion. Much as with Buddhist monasteries, Islamic *ummah* (communities), and occasionally mosques provided spaces for merchants to net-work and display trustworthy behavior. Islamic law and resident scholars established common guidelines to judge disputes and inheritance issues. The elites of some Southeast Asian states converted precisely because of the access to trade offered by adherence to Islamic law and communities. By the mid-sixteenth century, Islamic states and traders were established across a huge swath of Eurasia from the Philippines to West Africa. Pilgrimage to Mecca also became more common in this period, establishing a concrete mode of interaction between these disparate regions (Chaudhuri 1985; Eaton 1996).

Much is often made of the over 3,000 years of military conflict between agricultural states and nomadic peoples as an important theme in world history. But the mobility and interactions between these peoples were just as important. The skills and knowledge of pastoral peoples in Central Asia and Arabia in navigating the steppes and deserts were a crucial part of these trade routes. Central Asia was not only a space of nomadic peoples, but also of settled agriculturalists, merchant, and rulers who also had a strong interest in the wealth that could be gained through trade. Sogdian traders residing in the cities of Central Asia were often the main translators of major religious texts. And the repeated conquest and rule of landed empires by nomadic peoples helped Central Eurasian political practices spread across the whole of Asia (Beckwith 2009).

The Mongol conquest was the culmination of this interaction. By the 1260s, Mongol rule spanned the trade routes of Asia, integrating confederacies of pastoral peoples with bureaucratic states in China, Russia, and Iran. Even the conquest itself was made possible by the integration of Central Asian cavalry and siege warfare experts from settled states. With the establishment of the Mongol Empire (divided into four sections) trade and the movement of experts flourished even more (Abu-Lughod 1991). This was the context in which famous travelers such as Ibn Battuta and Marco Polo crossed the continent. The routes followed by travelers and merchants were the same routes followed by the Black Death as spread from southeastern China to India and the Mediterranean in the middle of the fourteenth century. The mass deaths catalyzed the fall of the Mongols and the emergence of a new world of mobility that shifted decisively to the oceans and peripheral states.

Early modern mobility

In the half-millennium after the spread of the Black Death in the 1340s and 1350s, two major changes happened with respect to migration. The first was that maritime routes overtook the overland routes as the main channels of long-distance trade and mobility. The second was the massive expansion of agricultural empires in China, Russia, India, Iran, and the Middle East. These states gradually overwhelmed the Central Asians and pastoral peoples. They also supported the expansion of peasant frontier settlement, urban migration, and domestic labor and craft migration, often with reduced state coercion and control. This mobility of individuals and their families for the sake of new land or work became the dominant framework for human mobility in the early modern world.

The rise of maritime mobility came hand in hand with proliferation of port cities from East Africa, around the South Asian peninsula, across Southeast Asia and up to Nagasaki, replacing the inland oases as the main centers of global trade. Most of these entrepots—with the exception of European, Japanese, and Chinese ports—actively encourage the business of as many different traders as possible. New trade diasporas also spread throughout Asia, including Armenians, Bugis, Chinese, Dutch, Gujaratis, Hadhramis, Iranians, Jews, Portuguese, and Sindhis (Dobbin 1996; McCabe et al. 2005). The ports worked to accommodate these merchants, and many of these travelers took up positions in local governments, leading to the growth of a common culture of hospitality and trading norms across the Asian Oceans from Amsterdam to the East Indies.

The large empires benefited from this trade but remained focused on the development of agricultural revenue. In an age of growing population and competition between empires, this often meant the encouragement of massive frontier settlement, as well as increased urbanization and growing labor markets. The details looked different in each empire. In China, after evicting the Mongols, the early Ming resettlement of the depopulated Yangtze valley and the area around Beijing was one of the last great examples of mass state-sponsored migration. By the time of the Qing (1644–1911), however, the massive settlement of some 30 million people in western China, Taiwan, and the hill areas of central China was largely through independent migration or mild state encouragements such as tax breaks for new settlers. Chinese cities became some of the largest cities in the world, and a large periodic market system and networks of migrant merchant associations spread through much of the empire (Skinner 1976; Cao *et al.* 1997; McKeown forthcoming). In Russia and some Southeast Asian states like Siam, on the other hand, state control continued to predominate and even intensified. The czarist government allowed escaped serfs to settle freely on empty frontiers. But most mobility came in the form of serfs granted to elite estates, and the regulated transfer of population to eastern regions (Hellie 2002).

All of these states increasingly clamped down on uncontrolled nomadic and semi-nomadic mobility at their borders. Russia and Qing China were the most aggressive and successful, militarily subduing most of their Central Asian enemies by the late eighteenth century (Perdue 2005). The so-called "gunpowder" Islamic empires of western Asia also put intense pressure on these unregulated spaces with their forms of repeated and unstable communal mobility (Streusand 2010). China and the states of mainland Southeast Asia increased pressure for the assimilation of the mobile people of highland Southeast Asia. Many of these peoples responded by packing up their villages and relocating to where labor recruiters, armies, and tax collectors could not find them. But by the late nineteenth century even this option was becoming untenable (Scott 2010).

By 1800, migration across Asia looked much more like the kinds of migration we now know. They were migrations of families to settler frontiers, of workers and craftsmen to cities, mines, local markets, and transportation work, of peasants into armies, and of traders, workers, and soldiers to increasingly distant locations across the face of the planet.

The creation of Asia, 1840–1940

Migration boomed around the world in the century after the 1830s. European industrialization generated a mutually reinforcing expansion of labor needs, markets, resource demands, and mass communication technologies. All of these both produced and benefited from a rapid expansion of urban and long-distance migration. The impact of these transformations was global. Asians made up more than half of this long-distance migration. They moved to work in ports, mines, and plantations, to grow and mill rice for laborers to eat, and as traders, shopkeepers, and moneylenders who expanded the reach of industrial markets into the farthest corners of the globe. The great bulk of this migration—both in the Atlantic world and in Asia—was of independent individuals, organized through family, fellow villagers, and informal recruiters. Asians were fully a part of this transformation of global mobility in the nineteenth century (Bose 2009; Amrith 2011).

Most of this long-distance migration moved from the most highly populated parts of the world to the less populated frontiers. Three main systems can be identified, two of which were in Asia (McKeown 2004).

1 *The transatlantic system*: 60 million people moved to the Americas, nearly 3 million of whom were from China, Japan, India, and the Middle East. These flows peaked during 1903–13 at an average of 1.5 million per year.
2 *The Southeast Asian system*: 30 million Indians (mostly from southeastern India) and 20 million southern Chinese moved mostly into Southeast Asia, but also to islands around the Pacific

and Indian Oceans. This migration grew concurrently with the transatlantic migrations, but at slightly lower rates. It did not peak until the 1920s, averaging over 1 million per year.

3   *The North Asian system*: about 13 million Russians migrated to Central Asia and Siberia, 30 million northern Chinese to Manchuria, and a few million Japanese and Koreans moved throughout the region. This migration only started to reach massive numbers in the 1890s, and peaked in the late 1920s and 1930s at about 1.3 million per year.

These migrations contributed to a redistribution of the world's population towards the frontier regions. From 1850 to 1950 the proportion of the world's population in the three main sending regions decreased from 76 percent to 60 percent, while the proportion in the main receiving regions increased from 10 percent to 24 percent.

These migrations around the globe were similar and connected. When we compare emigration regions of similar population and size, we find that peak annual emigration rates were quite similar. Counties in south and north China and northeastern India ranged from 13–15 emigrants per thousand in the late 1920s, rates that are similar to peak years in Norway, Great Britain, Portugal, and Italy. And although Asian migrants are often remembered as indentured "coolies" in the service of European planters, only a small fraction of them signed indenture contracts with Europeans. Less than 3 percent of Chinese emigrants (about 750,000) were ever indentured. The great majority of Chinese migrants worked for family or Chinese employers and profit-sharing ventures. And while over 95 percent of Indians traveled to destinations within the British Empire and over half of them worked on European plantations, most were still recruited by Indian gang bosses and family. Less than 10 percent (about 3 million) signed indenture contracts directly with Europeans. And with the exception of coerced Korean labor in Japan during World War II, the vast majority of Asian migration to North Asia was free and independent (unlike Russian migration, much of which was highly regulated and coerced). Their mobility was supported through a variety of debt and sentimental obligations to friends, family, and employers. In other words, their mobility was not much different from that of European migrants (Treadgold 1957; Gottschang and Lary 2000; McKeown 2010).

The most striking example of the growing connectedness of migration around the globe is the convergence of return rates (return migrants as a proportion of outbound migrants) over the nineteenth century. Economists have shown that return migration corresponds well with business cycles. When employment abroad is good the return rates are low, and vice versa. Asian migrants are often depicted as "sojourners" who only intended to migrate temporarily, as distinct from European settlers in the Americas. In the Middle of the nineteenth century there was some truth to this distinction, when an average of 60–70 percent of Chinese and Indian migrants returned each year, compared with rates that varied from 20 to 60 percent for European migrants to the United States. By the 1880s, however, both the timing of return cycles and the average numbers of returns for all three groups started to converge, averaging about 60 percent for all groups by the early twentieth century. The cycles and proportions of return migration from Manchuria joined this convergence in the 1920s. Whatever differences existed between Asian and Atlantic migration in the middle of the nineteenth century, the aspects of migration shaped by economic forces were increasingly similar by the end of the century (McKeown 2010).

At the same time, migration destinations were becoming segregated. In the 1850s and 1860s, migrant destinations were truly global and integrated. Nearly 40 percent of Chinese and 20 percent of Indians traveled to destinations beyond Asia. By the 1880s, Asians were increasingly restricted to Asian destinations. By the early twentieth century, less than 5 percent of all Chinese and less than 1 percent of Indians traveled beyond Asia. This happened even as overall Asian emigration increased eightfold. Japanese emigration bucked this trend a bit. The Japanese fought hard and bitterly against discriminatory immigration laws, and the majority of Japanese emigrants traveled to Hawaii, North America, Brazil, and Peru. But this ultimately amounted to less than 750,000 emigrants, not a big dent in the overall trends from Asia.

Asian migration was compelled into these regional systems by the erection of exclusionary laws and other migration controls that kept them hemmed within the continent. In just the brief period from 1881 to 1883 the United States, New Zealand and several Australian colonies enacted anti-Chinese immigration laws; the Ottoman Empire set up a quarantine station at the entrance to the Red Sea and imposed a head tax on pilgrims (encouraging the rise of a passport regime that made it more difficult for Asians to pass through the Suez Canal); the Russian and Qing empires both passed laws promoting settlement and fortification of the Russia–Chinese–Korea border area so as to block the expansion of each other; and the Indian Emigration Act consolidated past legislation on Indian migration and defined "emigrant" as migrants who travel beyond India to destinations other than Ceylon or the Straits Settlements. Latin American countries soon followed with their own Asian exclusion laws. Asia became encased within borders, and the idea of "Asian" migration became a reality (Zolberg 1999; McKeown 2008).

The segregation of Asia and the creation of three systems had a concrete impact on the context of Asian migration. Atlantic migration was associated with a virtuous circle of development, in which investment followed labor migration, creating profits that were then invested both in America and back in Europe. Over the course of a century, migrant-sending regions shifted from northwestern to southeastern Europe, as wages in the original sending regions began to converge with those in the Americas. In Asia, on the other hand, migration was less associated with economic dynamism. The same villages and counties that sent migrants in the 1850s were still sending migrants in the 1930s. There is little evidence of any wage convergence between sending and receiving regions. The flows of migration and money were cross-cutting rather than a virtuous circle, as much investment came from Europe and profits were returned there. There was also much less urban migration within Asia. In both India and China, the dynamic global economy of the second half of the nineteenth century was largely experienced as war, famine, and flood. Only in the early twentieth century did migration within China and India start to resemble nineteenth-century European patterns of intensive urbanization and domestic labor mobility.

Into the present

Asia has been an integral part second wave of global mass migration since the 1950s. Urbanization has overtaken that in Europe and North America. Asians have also had an important role in the rise of global long-distance migration since the 1960s. Now the majority of Asian emigrants are likely to leave rather than remain in Asia, with net emigration amounting to 1.3 million a year. But large numbers also travel within Asia. As is the trend around the world, they no longer travel to frontier areas but to more developed economies like Japan, Malaysia, Taiwan, and Thailand. Indeed Asia has some of the states with the highest proportions of immigrants in the world: over 40 percent of the population in Singapore, and more than 70 percent in smaller Gulf states such as Qatar and the UAR (IOM 2010).

One legacy remains from the earlier era of segregation: the erasure of historical memory. Most accounts of the first wave of mass migration in Asia still reproduce the same characterizations that had justified the exclusions and racist policies of the 1880s: that Asians were sojourners, coolies, tied to the land, unable and unwilling to migrate without European intervention, not "true" immigrants. There is little sense of immigrant heritage in most Asian countries. And policies are often rooted in the idea that contemporary migration is a break from longstanding patterns of immobility, an unprecedented challenge caused by current globalization.

To some extent this historical forgetting is understandable because of the relatively meager demographic legacy of Asian migrants and their descendants. In the 1950s, only 11 million Chinese could be found outside China and 4.5 million Indians outside of India (Davis 1951; Poston and Yu 1990). This was less than the European-descended population of Argentina alone. From this perspective, Asian migration had a much smaller impact on the world than did European.

But we must understand this difference as a product of different historical contexts. Nearly all emigrants to Southeast Asia moved into tropical areas with well-established native or colonial states. In contrast, Europeans tended to move into sparsely populated temperate areas where they became the majority and held political power. Tropical plantations and mines were much less amenable to long-term settlement and families than small farms on temperate frontiers or the new cities of the Americas. Asian return rates were also higher than European before the 1880s, giving the descendants of those early European settlers more generations to proliferate. Also, far fewer Asian women migrated than Europeans throughout the entire first wave. Asian women generally ranged from 5 percent to 20 percent of emigrants until the 1920s, while European women were more likely to range from 25 percent to 50 percent women. There was also a much larger and better established native population in Southeast Asia. When Asian immigrants intermarried with locals, their descendants were just as likely to be considered Burmese, Vietnamese, or Thai as to be considered Chinese or Indian.

The Manchurian migrations resemble European migrations much more closely. This was an example of migration to a temperate frontier with substantial urbanization, where the natives were almost entirely displaced and where, despite interludes of Russian and Japanese intervention, Chinese ultimately maintained political control (not least because they overwhelmed the place with migrants). Fifty million Chinese resided in Manchuria by 1953, nearly five times as many Chinese as could be found abroad. This happened despite the fact that average rates of return and female migration were similar for the southern Chinese emigrants. On the other hand, both the United States and Manchuria started with populations of about 6 million in 1800 and received similar numbers of migrants over the next 140 years, yet this produced a population of 134 million people of European descent in the United States by 1955. Lower return rates, higher rates of female migration, and greater economic growth in the United States all conspired to produce this disparity.

The lack of memory about migration has contributed to immigration policies in Asia that are some of the most restrictive and discriminatory in the world. They are grounded in state-based developmentalism and temporary labor emigration schemes at the expense of immigrant rights (Oishi 2005; Seol and Skrentny 2009). A broader appreciation of the fundamental role of migration in Asian history could help to moderate the fear and discomfort that surrounds contemporary mobility.

References and further reading

Abu-Lughod, J. L. (1991) *Before European Hegemony: The World System A.D. 1250–1350*. Oxford: Oxford University Press.
Amrith, S. S. (2011) *Migration and Diaspora in Modern Asia*. Cambridge: Cambridge University Press.
Anthony, D. (2007) *The Horse, the Wheel and Language: How Bronze-Age Riders from the Eurasian Steppes Shaped the Modern World*. Princeton, NJ: Princeton University Press.
Beckwith, C. (2009) *Empires of the Silk Road: A History of Central Eurasia from the Bronze Age to the Present*. Princeton, NJ: Princeton University Press.

Bellwood, P. (1997) *Prehistory of the Indo-Malaysian Archipelago*, 2nd edition. Honolulu, HI: University of Hawai'i Press.

Bose, S. (2009) *A Hundred Horizons: The Indian Ocean in the Age of Global Empires*. Cambridge, MA: Harvard University Press.

Cao, S. J., Ge, J. X., and Wu, S. D. (1997) *Zhongguo Yimin Shi* (China's Immigration History), 6 vols. Fujian: Fujian Renmin Chubanshe.

Cavalli-Sforza, L. L. and Cavalli-Sforza, F. (1996) *The Great Human Diaspora: The History of Diversity and Evolution*. New York: Perseus Books.

Chaudhuri, K. N. (1985) *Trade and Civilization in the Indian Ocean: An Economic History from the Rise of Islam to 1750*. Cambridge: Cambridge University Press.

Curtin, P. D. (1984) *Cross-cultural Trade in World History*. Cambridge: Cambridge University Press.

Davis, K. (1951) *The Population of India and Pakistan*. New York: Russell and Russell.

Dobbin, C. (1996) *Asian Entrepreneurial Minorities: Conjoint Communities in the Making of the World-economy 1570–1940*. Richmond, VA: Curzon.

Dolgopolski, A. (1998) *The Nostratic Macrofamily and Linguistic Paleontology*. Cambridge: Institute for Archaeological Research.

Eaton, R. M. (1996) *The Rise of Islam and the Bengal Frontier, 1204–1760*. Berkeley, CA: University of California Press.

Foltz, R. (1999) *Religions of the Silk Road: Overland Trade and Cultural Exchange from Antiquity to the Fifteenth Century*. New York: St Martin's Press.

Gottschang, T. and Lary, D. (2000) *Swallows and Settlers: The Great Migration from North China to Manchuria*. Ann Arbor, MI: The University of Michigan, Center for Chinese Studies.

Greenberg, J. (2000–2002) *Indo-European and its Closest Relatives*, 2 vols. Stanford, CA: Stanford University Press.

Hellie, R. (2002) "Migration in early modern Russia, 1480s-1780s." In D. Eltis (ed.) *Coerced and Free Migration: Global Perspectives*. Stanford, CA: Stanford University Press, pp. 292–323.

IOM (2010) *World Migration Report. The Future of Migration: Building Capacities for Change*. Geneva: International Organization for Migration.

Kerr, I. J. (2006) "On the move: circulating laborers in pre-colonial, colonial and post-colonial India" *International Review of Social History* 51(suppl): 85–109.

Kirch, K. V. (2002) *On the Road of Winds: An Archaeological History of the Pacific Islands before European Contact*. Berkeley, CA: University of California Press.

Liu, X. R. (1996) *Silk and Religion: An Exploration of Material Life and the Thought of People, AD 600–1200*. Oxford: Oxford University Press.

Ludden, D. (1985) *Peasant History in South India*. Princeton, NJ: Princeton University Press.

Manning, P. (2005) *Migration in World History*. London: Routledge.

——(2006) "*Homo sapiens* populate the earth: A provincial synthesis privileging linguistic data" *Journal of World History* 17(2): 115–58.

McCabe, I. B., Harlaftis, G. and Minoglou I. P. (eds) (2005) *Diaspora Entrepreneurial Networks: Four Centuries of History*. London: Berg.

McKeown, A. (2004) "Global migration, 1846–1940" *Journal of World History* 15(2): 155–89.

——(2008) *Melancholy Order: Asian Migration and the Globalization of Borders*. New York: Columbia University Press.

——(2010) "Chinese emigration in global context, 1850–1940" *Journal of Global History* 5: 95–124.

——(forthcoming) "A different transition: Mobility in Qing China, 1600–1900." In J. and L. Lucassen (eds), *Globalising Migration History: The Eurasian Experience (16th to 21st Centuries)*. Leiden: Brill.

Oishi, N. (2005) *Women in Motion: Globalization, State Policies and Labor Migration in Asia*. Stanford, CA: Stanford University Press.

Perdue, P. C. (2005) *China Marches West: Qing Conquest of Central Eurasia*. Cambridge, MA: Belknap Press of Harvard University Press.

Poston, D. L. and Yu M. Y. (1990) "The distribution of the overseas Chinese in the contemporary world" *International Migration Review* 24(3): 480–508.

Scott, J. C. (2010) *The Art of not Being Governed: An Anarchist History of Upland Southeast Asia*. New Haven, CT: Yale University Press.

Seol, D. H. and Skrentny, J. D. (2009) "Why is there so little migrant settlement in East Asia?" *International Migration Review* 43(3): 578–620.

Skinner, G. W. (1976) "Mobility strategies in late imperial China: A regional systems analysis." In C. A. Smith (ed.), *Regional Analysis*, vol. 1, *Economic Systems*. New York: Academic Press, pp. 327–64.

Streusand, D. E. (2010) *Islamic Gunpowder Empires: Ottomans, Safavids and Mughals*. Boulder, CO: Westview.

Tishkoff, S. A., Reed, F. A., Friedlaender, F. R., Ehret, C., Ranciaro, A., Froment, A., Hirbo, J. B., Awomoyi, A. A., Bodo, J.-M., Doumbo, O., Ibrahim, M., Juma, A. T., Kotza, M. J., Lema, G., Moore, J. H., Mortensen, H., Nyambo, T. B., Omar, S. A., Powell, K., Pretorius, G. S., Smith, M. W., Thera, M. A., Wambebe, C., Weber, J. L., and Williams, S. M. (2009) "The genetic structure and history of Africans and African Americans" *Science* 324(5930): 1035–44.

Treadgold, D. (1957) *The Great Siberian Migration: Government and Peasant Resettlement from Emancipation to the First World War*. Princeton, NJ: Princeton University Press.

Zolberg, A. (1999) "The Great wall against China: Responses to the first immigration crisis, 1885–1925." In J. and L. Lucassen (eds), *Migration, Migration History, History: Old Paradigms and New Perspectives*. Bern: Peter Lang, pp. 291–305.

7

Charting refugee and migration routes in Africa

Solomon Getahun

Introduction

The continent of Africa has more than 54 countries with diverse geography, culture, economy, and history. Owing to this, it is difficult if not impossible to chart the routes of African migration and places of destinations. Even if we try, since society is in constant motion and change, today's route and destination might not be true for tomorrow. It is with this understanding that the route and destination of migration in contemporary Africa should be considered. It is also worth noting that the causes of African migration, within and outside of the continent, are far more intricate than the linear interpretation associated with economic inequalities. Prior to colonialism, the rise and fall of empires, long-distance trade (the slave trade can serve us as an excellent instance in illuminating the role of external impulses in reorienting trade routes, to say the least), trans-human lifestyle, and external impulses such as Muslim–Arab and European traders influenced patterns of migration within Africa and to other parts of the world.

Under colonial rule, faster modes of communication were launched, and yet artificially created African states with arbitrarily delineated boundaries also came into existence. As a consequence, while colonialist-regulated male-dominated labor migration for the sole purpose of profit was introduced, customary movement of people was restricted and reoriented. The caravan trade routes that crisscrossed the continent were redirected from the interior to the coast and hitherto unknown urban centers evolved and the coast became the destination of migrants at the expense of indigenous African towns in the interior. Africans also left their continent for Europe and the Americas as dock workers, sailors, students, and soldiers. In the latter instance, hundreds of thousands of African soldiers partook in World War I and World War II.

African migration patterns within the continent since the 1960s

During the post-colonial period, determinants of African migration were as diverse and as complex as the previous periods. Following independence, political turmoil swept across the continent. Despite independence, many Africans viewed the state as an alien institution imposed upon them by colonial powers. They considered the state as a relic of the colonial past without historical or political legitimacy. Ethnic, clan, and religious allegiances superseded loyalty to the newly manufactured "nation-state." Corruption, nepotism, and mismanagement further aggravated the situation in the newly independent countries. It was during such circumstances that the military, which considered itself as a viable alternative institution that is free from corruption and parochialism, began involvement in politics. Initially, its involvement was by invitation (Lefever 1970; Assensoh 2002). The new rulers of Africa who lack traditional sources of authority or the necessary ballot increasingly began relying on the armed forces to squash protest against their rule. The military, who noticed that the state is feeble without its assistance, took matters into its own hands. Soon after independence, the continent was enveloped by a series of military *coups d'état*. Hope for a better political future and economic progress was replaced with disillusionment and despair. To add insult to injury, the continent became a battleground for the Cold War rivals, the USA and the Soviet Union, who exploited the instability to their geo-political advantage. Coupled with this, World-Bank induced structural adjustment policies, and the energy crisis, famine, and civil wars affected millions of Africans. They became displaced persons, refugees, and asylum seekers within and outside of the continent (Getahun 2007a,b).

Events of the post-Cold War period also influenced causes, patterns, and destinations of African migrations. This period has contradictory features that sharpened existing problems while presenting Africans with new opportunities and challenges. The period is dominated by globalization and the rise of ethno-nationalism, which are apparently contradictory yet inter-related phenomenon. On the one hand globalization—which is witnessed through increased migration, technological developments that narrowed the physical and psychological distance between individuals, nations, and continents and enhanced interaction among them at various levels—brought nations, people, and different cultures increasingly closer. The global citizen has multiple citizenships with multiple passports. The world is also becoming a level playing field. Technological invention, innovation, and production are no longer the domains of the very few centers or states. The world market is no longer under the prerogatives of the G-7/8. It has fallen into the hands of the G-20 and more. In short, the world has become multi-polar. Divided states such as East and West Germany, North and South Yemen, etc., are reunited to become one state.

On the other hand, however, the resurgence of ethnicity and nationalism in the global age challenged ideas of the homogeneous state. It questioned and redefined existing relationships and notions of the nation-state and the citizen thus necessitating the emergence of new identities and boundaries (Nieguth 1999). Such developments, therefore, triggered the formation of new states and diasporas; and still some are in the making. For instance, the former Soviet Union splintered into many states. Yugoslavia, too, was partitioned, and still continues to be so. Though not acute and violent like that of Eastern Europe, Western Europe has gone or is going through similar metamorphosis. The British Empire, which collapsed on the immediate aftermath of World War II, has continued to splinter. Northern Ireland is divided between Catholics and Protestants, while the Scots are discussing secession from the British parliament. Northern Italians are complaining about the less developed south. In Canada, the Quebec issue is not yet resolved (Harris 1996; Hobsbawm 1997; Keating 1997; McCormick and Alexander 1997). Doubt in the nation-state, which I call "the reverse process," also impacted Asia: Indonesia is besieged by the crisis in Timor, while Taiwan is pushing for the final enactment of its divorce from China. Tibet and Mongolia have become a stumbling block for the rising global power, China.

Africa, too, had its share secessionist movements. Congo and Nigeria, though they look relatively calm, are beset with secession. The crisis in Ivory Coast almost split the country into two, North and South. In January 2011, the people of Southern Sudan voted to secede from the North. Somalia has imploded while one of the longest secessionist wars in the African continent, the Eritrean struggle against Ethiopia, finally ended with the independence of the former in 1991.

The aforementioned events, globalization, and its discontents (contradictions)—to use Saskia Sassen's phrase (1998)—have impacted Africa in two major ways. First, either due to the cumulative effects of earlier events or newer developments that can be specifically attributed to globalization or both, the number of refugees from Africa continued to be significant even after many of the conflicts in the continent had wound down in the new century.

As it could be seen from Figure 7.1, in the 1960s, due to the relatively peaceful processes of decolonization, Africa's share of refugees was smaller than in the years to come. At that time, Africa accounted for less than one in six of all refugees in the world. The events of the 1970s such as civil wars, military putsches, rising oil prices, and IMF-driven economic adjustment policies resulted in socio-economic and political dislocation that created, among other things, an enormous refugee population. During this period, two in every five refugees were African. The scenario in the 1980s was no better than the previous years. In the 1980s, more than a third of the refugees in the world were Africans. As of 2011, of the top 10 refugee-producing countries more than half are African. These countries are Sudan, Somalia, Eritrea, the Democratic Republic of Congo, Burundi, and Angola. These African refugees include victims of drought, famine, flood, arbitrary demarcation of boundaries, decolonization, post-independence conflicts, apartheid, inter-guerrilla warfare, flight from recruitment into the military, or guerrilla forces, etc. (Weis 1978; Adepoju 1982; Cimade 1986; Bakwesegha 1994; Matlou 1999).

Some of the aforementioned victims moved across international borders seeking asylum to a third country, mainly the USA, Canada, Australia, and to some degree Western Europe. Usually 90 percent of asylum seekers are rejected and hence forced to stay in refugee camps within Africa for years. Such practice, which is commonly referred to as "refugee warehousing" is partly attributed to the benevolence of Africans in accepting and accommodating fellow

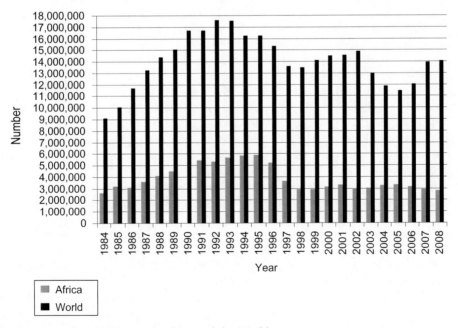

Figure 7.1 Number of refugees in Africa and the World
Source: US Committee for Refugees, *World Refugee Survey* (2009)[1]

Africans who are in distress. It is also partly the consequence of the reluctance shown by Europeans, North Americans, and Australians in admitting refugees from Africa. While the USA tightened its door against immigrants after the events of 9/11, Western Europe too has closed its doors to immigrants and refugees from Africa especially after the establishment of the "Eurozone." Though the establishment of the "zone" made it easier for Europeans to travel within Europe, it made it more difficult for the *others*—non-European immigrants—to cross into Europe. Western Europe was able to benefit from the collapse of the Soviet Union and Eastern Bloc countries politically and economically. In the latter instance, Western Europe was able to get highly skilled yet cheap labor from the former Eastern Bloc countries including the Soviet Union. Cold War politics, which often involved portraying the other party undemocratic, cruel, etc., usually compels states to keep the semblance of "political correctness." The attempt to be politically correct, in either Eastern or Western Bloc countries, includes accepting refugees and immigrants. This pretense ceased to exist with the end of the Cold War. Thus, West European countries can now reject, with no qualms, refugees and immigrants from African countries and others. Also, because of the availability of cheap labor from former Eastern Bloc countries, African labor has become redundant. Growing xenophobia and racism also encouraged West European countries to shut their doors tight against African immigrants, asylum seekers, and refugees.

Second, as a consequence of the aforementioned developments, African refugees and immigrants are compelled to devise ways in circumventing "refugee warehousing" and tighter immigration regulations—Africans changed their routes, agents, and destinations of migration. African migration to the Middle East and beyond, using the caravan routes, has been a common practice since ancient times, now took a newer twist and with it a newer challenge. Stricter immigration laws prompted West African immigrants and refugees to employ traffickers and smugglers to reach their destination. The latter revived the ancient caravan routes that connected sub-Saharan African countries with North Africa to smuggle and traffic individuals across the desert into North Africa and thence Europe. Owing to their geographic proximity and historic ties to southern Europe, North African countries such as Libya, Morocco, Tunisia, and Algeria, in addition to being destinations of African migrants and refugees, are also used as gateways into Europe by smugglers and traffickers. Though the majority of Africans, especially from West Africa, traveled on foot to inland destinations like Agadez (one of the ancient trading centers), there are few Africans that enter via air into the Maghreb countries. From places like Agadez, Africans were taken to the Sebha oasis in Libya, then to Tripoli and other coastal cities in Libya. From there, they were smuggled/trafficked into either Malta or other Italian Islands. From Tamanrasset (southern Algeria), the illegal migrants were taken into Algiers or other northern coastal cities or enter Morocco and thence, crossing the Straits of Gibraltar into Spain (Adepoju 2004; Haas 2006).

So much is the smuggling of Africans through North African countries, across the Mediterranean Sea into Europe, that the European Union is demanding that Spain tighten its southern border and tasked it with guarding southern Europe from being a thoroughfare for "illegal" immigrants. Spain, on its part, urged Morocco to do something about these illegal immigrants—passing the task of guarding the gates of Europe to the Africans. On the other hand, African leaders like Muammer al-Gaddafi openly demanded Europe pay billions of dollars if it wanted to be saved from turning Black (Traynor 2010; Pisa 2010). All attempts seem to have failed to stave off the tide of African migrants sneaking into Europe.

This is partly due to the insatiable Western European demand for prostitutes from all over the world. As a consequence, trafficked women from Eastern Europe, Southeast Asia, sub-Saharan Africa, and Latin America supply the prostitution market in Western Europe. In Africa most of the trafficked persons are victims of civil war and forced displacement. Though there is no specific figure for trafficked and smuggled persons from Africa, it is one of the bourgeoning "migration industries." Trafficking and smuggling is also the outcome of increasingly restrictive immigration laws, low fertility rates and an insatiable demand for labor in the western world. Lack of social mobility in many of the Third World countries and the prevalence of conspicuous consumption as the result of remittances builds pressure for migration (Castles 2004; Getahun 2011).

African countries, Ghana, Senegal, and Nigeria, are the main sources of prostitutes in Europe. Of these, the Nigerians account for the largest share of sub-Saharan African prostitutes in Western Europe for the following reasons. Trafficking and smuggling should not be viewed outside of the broader context of migration. Though barely studied, there are some 200,000 Nigerian legal residents in Europe. In addition, though poverty and unemployment are not unique to Nigeria and although Nigeria is relatively peaceful and prosperous compared with some of the West African countries, corruption, violence, and organized crime are higher in Nigeria than in other parts of Africa. However, not all parts of Nigeria are affected by human trafficking. Studies indicate that women's trafficking is concentrated in the south-central part of the country, which further explains why human trafficking is rampant in this particular region. The Edo province, whose capital is Benin, is noted for its local tradition of slavery. The gender inequality in the province and the desire to have luxury goods and the higher social status associated with them is also another driving force for human trafficking. In the Edo province in particular and in many parts of Africa in general working abroad is viewed as the only way out of poverty (Carling 2005).

As Europe (Spain) tried to further tighten its border, the traffickers and smugglers also perfected their tactics and began employing newer routes. They used Senegal (West Africa) as an exit point to go to Spain and thence to other parts of Europe via the Canary Islands. Thus, these days it is not uncommon to hear about stranded Africans being rescued by the coast guard of this or that European country on the Mediterranean Sea. European measures to tightly shut its doors, however, have also resulted in the following. Besides making the smugglers and traffickers more sophisticated, it made the life of the smuggled /trafficked Africans more dangerous. It has become common to read media reports regarding the "discovery" of deceased African bodies floating on international waterways. This is in addition to the continued discovery of Africans caught while trying to illegally enter a neighboring African country's territory in an attempt to reach Europe (Abbink 2006; Tremlett 2007; Totaro 2008; Reuters 2010; Getahun 2011).

Lately, Egypt has evolved as another North African conduit through which African immigrants and refugees, primarily from countries in the Horn of Africa and to a limited degree from other parts of the continent, pass through. The route through Egypt, however, is not primarily directed to Europe but to Israel. Africans are smuggled into Gadarif, Kasela, etc., (Sudan) and thence to Egypt. From there, refugees and immigrants are tracked into Israel through Sinai. This new phenomenon, in addition to the earlier mentioned reasons, can be partly attributed to the presence of large number of Ethiopian Jews in Israel. A sizeable number of Ethiopian Jews left Ethiopia for Israel through Sudan and advised some of their Ethiopian acquaintances and relatives to do the same. Unlike many Middle Eastern countries, Israel is a country of immigrants with strong democratic credentials—about 20 per cent of the Israeli population is non-Jewish. The presence of non-Jewish immigrants in Israel and the existence of a sizeable black population attract refugees from other parts of Africa. The increasing presence of non-Jewish immigrants in Israel has become a political issue and a security concern in Israel, and the smuggling of African immigrants across the Sinai into Israel and the ordeals that these African immigrants and refugees suffer under the Egyptian police and the smugglers have attracted some media attention (AFP 2000; Gardner 2000; Getahun 2007a,b; AFP 2010; Seth 2010).

In addition to Israel, the oil-rich countries of the Middle East, encouraged by their newly acquired petro-dollars, attracted African migrant laborers of all sorts. Some of these laborers, however, are trafficked and smuggled women and children for *harams* and domestic work. While most of the trafficked and smuggled persons from West Africa were destined for prostitution in Western Europe, it is East Africans, especially people from the Horn of Africa who provide prostitutes to the Middle East. Smugglers and traffickers from East Africa employed dhows and other modes of transportation to smuggle people across the Red Sea and the Indian Ocean into Yemen and thence beyond. Hargessa and Basoso, which are ports on the Somali coast, and Mombasa (Kenya), serve as exit points to Aden, one of the major port cities on the Yemeni coast, and beyond (Nation Correspondent 2005, 2008; Murdock 2010). The existence of repressive regimes and failed states in the Horn of Africa further created a bonanza for smugglers and traffickers in the region. Print media and the internet report hundreds of Ethiopians, Eritreans, and Somalis who are risking their lives to cross the Red Sea, through war-torn Somalia, into Yemen illegally.

People of the Horn also attempt their refugee-immigrant odyssey by crossing the border town Moyale in southern Ethiopia and entering Kenya, and thence to southern Africa and beyond. In this context, Southern Africa, especially South Africa, Botswana, and Angola emerge as another destination and as a point of exit for African immigrants and refugees. The end of apartheid in South Africa and the booming economics of Botswana and Namibia attracted migrants (both unskilled and highly professional) from throughout Africa. One has to note that southern Africa, especially South Africa, had been a magnet for labor migrants from around the neighboring countries and beyond for a while. Not all African immigrants in southern Africa are legally admitted, however. Owing to geographic proximity and common political heritage—apartheid—thousands of Zimbabweans crossed into South Africa and Botswana, while others from the continent either legally migrated or were smuggled into South Africa for a price. For instance, smugglers charge between $1,000 and $1,500 to smuggle an Ethiopian through Ethiopian Moyale into Kenya. Then, disguised as a Masai, the Ethiopians pass into Uganda or Tanzania, from where they move into troubled Zimbabwe. From there, depending on the security situation at the Zimbabwe–South Africa border, Ethiopians are smuggled into South Africa. If and when the security on the Zimbabwe–South Africa border becomes very tight, the smugglers will take the Malawi route into Mozambique (Tate) and thence to South Africa. Malawi had been "warehousing" refugees and asylum seekers from Somali, Ethiopia, Democratic Republic of Congo, Burundi, Rwanda, Eritrea, etc., at its Dzaleka refugee camp in Dowa (Northern district of Malawi). Some estimates have it that the number of people who enter South Africa from the Horn of African countries alone is more than 17,000 annually (Getahun 2007a,b; Nyasa Times 2009a,b; Nyakairu 2010).

Some African immigrants will remain in South Africa while others, who can afford to pay the hefty sum (it is said that it will cost a total of US$10,000 for an Ethiopian to be smuggled from Ethiopia into the USA), will continue their journey to the USA, or from South Africa, they will depart for Australia. The journey to the USA is through Brazil, Colombia, and Mexico (Getahun 2011). These days, Africans in Brazil account for more than 65 percent of the refugees in the country, while Argentina reported receiving refugees and asylum seekers from Africa in the thousands. These Africans are accidental refugees and asylum seekers who were stranded in these countries while attempting to reach the USA. The Africans are primarily from the Horn of Africa countries such as Djibouti, Eritrea, Somalia, and Sudan—known havens for terrorists, including al-Qaida—according to an internal [US] government assessment obtained by The

Associated Press (Getahun 2006; Romero 2008; Sullivan: July 13, 2008; Henao 2009). However, there are also Africans from all parts of Africa. Like Europe and the Middle East, the service sector in South Africa and Botswana, in addition to other professionals, attracts sex workers and hence trafficked women and children from Africa and beyond.

Conclusion

The abovementioned developments inform us that despite the rhetoric of globalization, which was supposed to facilitate travel, the developed West is tightly closing its doors to African immigrants. This has resulted in charting new routes of migration and new global yet illegal agencies, human smugglers, and traffickers.

The presence of African immigrants, refugees, and asylum seekers in southern and western Africa does not mean that these places are final destinations for Africans. They also serve as a stepping ground for destinations beyond Africa. For instance, while northern and southern African countries serve as destination points for Africans, they are used as a springboard for destinations in Europe and the USA.

The existence of immigrant African professionals in Africa reveals another development—the brain drain that beset the continent since the 1960s is now changing into brain circulation. Owing to the presence of stable and relatively democratic and wealthy African nations, more and more Africans are choosing to stay in the continent than leave for Europe and the Americas. Therefore, the earlier pattern of migration, which had been established as a result of colonialism, was superseded by the selected migration destinations such as the USA, Canada, and Australia. The emergence of global cities also created a different type of immigrants, the "privileged citizens." These are professionals from other countries who, however, are not seeking permanent settlement. Transnational corporations brought them. Their presence, meanwhile, attracts the less skilled and other service-giving people: chauffeurs, dancers, prostitutes, waitresses, etc., which partly explains the presence of illiterate and lower class African immigrants in different parts of the world. Migration, which often was a privilege reserved for the affluent class and the educated African, is no longer.

Despite the presence of brighter spots in the continent, civil war, recurring drought, poor economic performance, and lack of democratic governance in many parts of Africa will continue to produce millions of refugees and displaced people who would risk their lives to leave their homes seeking a better future or safety either in neighboring countries or outside of the continent. And despite European, American, and Middle Eastern countries' reluctance to accept African immigrants and refugees, and despite the American and European attempts to curtail African migration by placing harsh anti-immigrant laws, Africans will find ways to reach these places. Migration once started, legal or illegal, will evolve itself into network migration such as family reunification. On the other hand, the introduction and imposition of strict immigration laws will encourage Africans to increasingly rely on smugglers and traffickers while persuading smugglers and traffickers to improve and perfect their smuggling and trafficking techniques.

Note

1 Compiled by the author from the US Committee for Refugees, *World Refugee Survey* (Washington, DC) 1980–2008. The figure on Africans does not include internally displaced persons (IDPs). If that is included, the number of refugees in Africa could be much higher. For instance, in 1981, Africa had 3,589,000 refugees and 2,735,000 IDPs. In that same year, the total figure for the IDPs in the world was 3,562,200.

References and further reading

Abbink, J. (2006) "Slow awakening? The Ethiopian diaspora in the Netherlands, 1977–2007" *Diaspora: A Journal of Transnational Studies* 15(2/3); 361–80.

Adepoju, A. (1982) "The dimension of the refugee problem in Africa" *African Affairs* 81(322): 21–35.

——(2004) "Changing configurations of migration in Africa" *Migration Information Source*, September 1.

Agence France Presse (AFP) (2010) "Six Eritreans shot dead on Egypt-Israel border" *AFP*, August 14.

——(2000) "Israeli population rises to 6.4 million, almost 19 percent Arab" *AFP*, December 31.

Assensoh, A. B. (2002) *African Military History and Politics: Ideological Coups and Incursions, 1900-Present.* New York: Palgrave Macmillan Press.

Bakwesegha, C. (1994) "Forced migration in Africa and the OAU Convention." In H. Adelman and J. Sorenson (eds), *African Refugees: Development Aid and Reinterpretation.* Boulder, CO: Westview Press.

Castles, S. (2004) "Confronting the realities of forced migration" *Migration Information Source*, May 1.

Carling, J. (2005) "Trafficking in women from Nigeria to Europe" *Migration Information Source*, July 1.

Cimade, I. M. (1986) *Africa's Refugee Crisis: What's To Be Done?* Michael John (trans.). London: Zed Books Ltd.

Gardner, G. S. (2000) "Filipino workers to be assured minimum wage" *Jerusalem Post*, April 4.

Getahun, S. A. (2007b) "Determinants of Ethiopian refugee flow in the Horn of Africa." In T. Falola and N. Afolabi (eds), *The Human Cost of African Migration.* New York: Routledge, pp. 359–80.

——(2011) "Ethiopian immigrants." In Ronald H. Bayor (ed.), *Multicultural America: An Encyclopedia of the Newest Americans*, 2. New York: Greenwood Press, pp. 657–700.

——(2006) "Brain drain and its impact on Ethiopia's higher learning institutions: Medical establishments and the military academies between 1970s and 2000" *Perspectives on Global Development and Technology* 5(3): 257–75.

——(2007a) *The History of Ethiopian Immigrants and Refugees in America, 1900–2000: Patterns of Migration, Survival and Adjustment.* New York: LFB Scholarly Publishers.

Haas, H. (2006) "Trans-Saharan Migration to North Africa and the EU: Historical Roots and Current Trends" *Migration Information Source*, November 1.

Henao, L. A. (2009) "African immigrants drift toward Latin America" *Reuters*, November 17.

Harris, J. (1997) "The dynamics of the African diaspora." In A. Jalloh and S. E. Maizlish (eds), *The African Diaspora*. Arlington, TX: Texas A&M University Press.

Hobsbawm, E. (1997) "Anti-nationalist account of nationalism since 1989." In M. Guibernaum and J. Rex (eds), *The Ethnicity Reader: Nationalism, Multiculturalism and Migration.* Malden: Polity Press, pp. 69–72.

Keating, M. (1997) "Canada and Quebec: Two nationalisms in the global age." In M. Guibernaum and J. Rex (eds), *The Ethnicity Reader: Nationalism, Multiculturalism and Migration.* Malden: Polity Press, pp. 171–80.

Lefever, E. W. (1970) *Spear and Scepter: Army, Police, and Politics in Tropical Africa.* Washington, DC: Brookings Institution.

Matlou, P. (1999) "Upsetting the chart: Forced migration and gender issues, the African experience." In D. Indra (ed.), *Engendering Forced Migration: Theory and Practice.* New York: Berghahn Books, pp. 128–134.

McCormick, J. and Alexander, W. (1997) "Scotland: Towards devolution." In M. Guibernaum and J. Rex (eds), *The Ethnicity Reader: Nationalism, Multiculturalism and Migration.* Malden: Polity Press, pp. 156–63.

Murdock, H. (2010) "Smuggled goods dominate ancient Ethiopian trade route," *Voice of America (VOA)*, June 21.

Nation Correspondent (2005) "Team questions held Ethiopians" *The Daily Nation* (Nairobi), July 13.

——(2008) "Ethiopians hiding in a container seized" *The Daily Nation*, October 14.

Nyakairu, F. (2010) "Thousands flee south every year from Somalia, Ethiopia" *Reuters*, February 8.

Nyasa Times (2009a) "Ethiopian refugees give Malawi police tough task" *Nyasa Times* (Malawi), May 3.

——(2009b) "Malawi police arrest 169 Ethiopians" *Nyasa Times*, July 1.

Nieguth, T. (1999) "Beyond dichotomy: Concepts of the nation and the distribution of membership" *Nations and Nationalism*, 5(2) (April): 155–73.

Pisa, N. (2010) "'Pay me 4bl. pounds a year and I'll stop Europe from turning black' Col. Gaddafi demands EU Cash to stop immigration through Libya" *Mail* online, August 31.

Reuters (2010) "Libya denies mistreatment of Eritrean migrants" *Reuters*, July 8.

Romero, J. (2008) "Drunk driver suspected of killing foreign cab driver" *MyFOXColorado.com*, September 8.

Sassen, S. (1998) *Globalization and its Discontents.* New York: The New Press.

Seth, F. (2010) "The long road of death, a massacre in Sinai" *The Jerusalem Post*, August 18.

Sullivan, E. (2008) "Smuggling rings possible US terror threat" *Associated Press,* July 13.

Tremlett, G. (2007) "Spain intercepts 180 African immigrants in single vessel" *Guardian Unlimited*, July 30.

Traynor, I. (2010) "Gaddafi wants $7b to stem migration" *The Sydney Morning Herald*, September 3.

Totaro, P. (2008) "All at sea in a leaky boat" *The Sydney Morning Herald*, September 19.

US Committee for Refugees, (1980–2008) *World Refugee Survey*, Washington DC.

Weis, P. (1978) "Convention refugees and de facto refugees." In G. Melander and P. Nobel (eds), *African Refugee and the Law*. Uppsala: The Scandinavian Institute of African Studies, pp. 15–22.

Part II
Refugees and forced migrants

The scholarly literature on forced migration is often divorced from the broader field of migration studies. This is because refugee studies came into being as a line of inquiry independent of the study of other migrants, with a focus on policy-relevant empirical findings and few theoretical concerns (Black 2001). This development coincides with (and one may argue is in response to) policy makers' need for understanding refugee migrations in order to cultivate responses to increases in refugee populations around the world. In the 1980s, refugee scholars moved to consolidate the field in order to increase its coherency (see Zetter 1988 for an example). Since then, refugee studies has increasingly become an autonomous field of inquiry, establishing a rich multi-disciplinary and methodological conversation that is global in geographic scope but limited in its cross-pollination with other realms of migration scholarship.

Studies of trafficking are even more isolated from the larger field of migration studies, with their development influenced by anti-slavery and anti-sex work scholarship and activism (see Limoncelli 2010 for an historical account of anti-trafficking social movements). Current research on trafficking continues to exhibit multidisciplinary influences from studies of violence against women and international labor rights. But trafficking also represents a specific form of migration that is either forced, coerced, or in other ways exploitative. Responses to trafficking frequently address migration dynamics. Examples are efforts to mitigate "push" factors such as providing girls in developing countries with economic opportunities so that they are less vulnerable to trafficking, and the United States' creation of the T-visa, which extends legal temporary resi-dency to trafficking victims who are willing to testify against their traffickers.

In this volume, we endeavor to bring forced migration studies back into conversation with the broader field of international migration. Scholars have aptly criticized the dichotomy between forced and economic migrants, arguing that many migrants have limited options when they choose to migrate, few migrants have no options at all (even a choice between life and death is a choice), and many migrants feel compelled to move for a combination of reasons that include political, environmental, and/or economic incentives (Richmond 1993; Coutin 2007). Thus, we argue that better integration of forced migration scholars with the broader field of migration studies will be beneficial to researchers studying all types of migrants.

In this section we start with Charles Watters' chapter on forced migration. In it, Watters connects empirical data on refugees and asylum seekers with broader theoretical frameworks.

He notes the multiple events that may initiate displacement, and the similarities between refugees and other migrants in how they are received by natives in points of settlement. Watters also upends the notion that forced migrants lack agency, and calls for more attention to the interaction of macro-structural forces with the micro-processes of migration decisions made by individuals, families, and communities.

In her chapter on refugee resettlement, Stephanie Nawyn provides a view of the state and supra-state institutions that demarcate refugees from other migrants. Resettlement validates the displacement experiences of refugees and grants them an opportunity to remake their lives in another country, but not without costs. Decreasing material support and enhanced host hostility make resettlement an increasingly difficult process for refugees. Further, there are vast differences in the level of resettlement assistance offered by different countries, ranging from complete non-assistance to programs that are heavily funded but highly proscriptive. But again, refugees are not without agency, and they develop their own strategies and interpretations for what it means to resettle and integrate into a host society.

Finally, Kathleen Farr reviews the literature on human trafficking, demonstrating the range of coercion and agency available to trafficked individuals. She details the debates among feminist scholars who split over the construction of trafficked women as either passive victims or constrained agents, and summarizes contradictory views regarding the legitimacy of sex work as a strategy for women's economic survival. She details the different kinds of labor derived from trafficked persons, including trafficked children, and assesses the global dynamics that sustain trafficking. Finally, she reviews policy responses to trafficking, noting the expansion of legal definitions that categorize voluntary prostitution as trafficking while law enforcement focuses less attention on other forms of forced labor.

References and further reading

Black, R. (2001) "Fifty years of refugee studies: From theory to policy" *International Migration Review* 35(1): 57–78.

Coutin, S. B. (2007) *Nations of Emigrants: Shifting Boundaries of Citizenship in El Salvador and the United States*. Ithaca, NY: Cornell University Press.

Limoncelli, S. A. (2010) *The Politics of Trafficking: The First International Movement to Combat the Sexual Exploitation of Women*. Stanford, CA: Stanford University Press.

Richmond, A. (1993) "Reactive migration: Sociological perspectives on refugee movement" *Journal of Refugee Studies* 6(1): 7–24.

Zetter, R. (1988) "Refugees and refugee studies: A label and an agenda" *Journal of Refugee Studies* 1(1): 1–6.

8

Forced migrants

From the politics of displacement to a moral economy of reception

Charles Watters

Introduction

The late twentieth and early twenty-first centuries have witnessed a remarkable growth in the extent and in the diversity of international migration. More people are on the move from a wider diversity of countries. The pattern of migration has changed from large-scale migration from one country to a particular destination—for example, the large-scale movement of populations in the mid-twentieth century from former colonies of European powers such as India and Algeria to the UK and France—to more diverse forms of migration not explicable in terms of colonial histories. Part of this phenomenon is, of course, the result of a more globalized economy or what Castells (2000) terms the "network society," linking the production of goods and services to an ever-expanding interdependent global economy.

While migration in general has increased and diversified, forced migration in particular has undergone a comparable range of transformations. The diversification of forced migration is due in no small part to the changing nature of war in which large-scale conflicts involving battle between soldiers of opposing armies has given way to a plethora of "low-intensity conflicts." These mirror shifting power dynamics in the post Cold War age. Conflicts between a number of "great powers" and their allies jostling for strategic and material advantage has in many instances given way to a more fractured form of conflict between the USA and its European and Australasian allies, and disparate but networked groups that resort strategically to civilian targets such as subways, trains, buses, and aircraft as evident, for example from the 9/11 attacks on the World Trade Center, the 2004 Madrid train bombings, and the 2007 subway bombings in London.

Arguably the diversity of forced migrants in recent times reflects this changing pattern of conflict. According to 2010 figures provided by the United Nations High Commission for Refugees, 43.3 million people were forcibly displaced at the end of 2009, the highest figure since the mid-1990s. This figure includes a significant number of internally displaced persons with the number of people uprooted in their own countries growing by 4 percent to 27.1 million (UNHCR 2010). It is also exacerbated by a very low proportion of those crossing international borders feeling able to return to their own countries owing to ongoing violence and upheaval. The origin of refugees reflects the changing face of global conflict with over half coming from Afghanistan and Iraq alone. The broad impacts of displacement are also illustrated in the multiple destinations of refugees showing, for example, that the 2.9 million Afghani refugees are present in no less than 71 countries. Evidence that all parts of civilian society experience the impact of armed conflicts is provided by breakdown of the refugee population by age and gender: 47 percent of refugees and asylum seekers were women and girls and 41 percent children under the age of 18 (UNHCR 2010).

Current trends point to the fact that forced migration is a growing phenomenon in the modern age. It is increasing in terms of the sheer numbers of persons involved, in the types of forced migration that is taking place, and in the diversity of migrants' nationalities, ethnicities, and religions as well as their gender and age. Despite its numerical growth and increasing global impact, theoretical reflection on the phenomenon of forced migration is often embedded in orientations more broadly applicable to migration in general. I will examine the usefulness of these theories before considering further the particularities of forced migration and the theoretical approaches that may be most illuminating.

Theoretical orientations

A useful outline of theories of migration is provided in Castles and Miller's (2003) influential book, *The Age of Migration*. The authors provide a range of theoretical perspectives from neo-classical push–pull theory, to historical structural theories and migration systems theory. Push–pull theory presents particular challenges in terms of consideration of the phenomenon of forced migration. Migration here is viewed in terms of rational choice involving assessing the circumstances within one's home environment, or "push factors," and weighing up the potential benefits of moving to another locality, so-called "pull factors." It generates a vision of individuals and groups making calculated decisions in circumstances in which a period of reflection is possible. For those who are forced migrants, the decision to move may be sudden and based on immediate threats to individuals and group well-being. An aerial onslaught in the proximity of a village, may, for example, lead the population of the village to flee for their lives, little caring about potential destinations provided they are seen to offer an opportunity for immediate safety. However, in other circumstances an element of deliberation may be present. Thousands of young people in Somalia, for example, have felt their situation in the homeland to be filled with danger and an absence of opportunities. These push factors have led to decisions to flee the homeland in pursuit of better lives. They have not only decided to leave Somalia but have developed aspirations to reach countries that they envisage providing them with good opportunities, for example education and decent livelihoods. In these circumstances one can detect a mixture of push and pull factors and the movement of forced migrants cannot be adequately explained without reference to both dimensions. To take another example, the past two decades has witnessed the converging of tens of thousands of migrants at French and Belgian ports such as Calais and Zeebrugge, enduring extremely harsh living conditions while desperately seeking passage to the UK. A high proportion of these migrants have come from dangerous war-affected countries such as Iraq and Afghanistan and as such one can envisage compelling push factors that may have led them to flee. However, these ports offer a further specter, of migrants in the ostensibly safe countries of France and Belgium daily risking their lives to reach the UK. The pursuit of a measure of safety is here mixed with powerful aspirations towards better lives; thus invoking both push and pull factors.

A further theoretical orientation is provided by what Castles and Miller define as historical-structural theories. These theories center analysis on global economic disparities and their impact on patterns of migration. Uneven geographical development encompassing legacies of colonialism and exploitation give rise to huge economic differences between and within countries and regions. These economic and geo-political factors go some way toward explaining large-scale migratory patterns in the modern age, for example the movement of millions of people from former colonies such as India, the West Indies, Congo, and Algeria to seek prosperity in the former colonial powers of Britain, Belgium, and France (Hobsbawn 1994). Moreover, this perspective highlights a perennial and rapacious movement of global capital in seeking to create optimum global conditions for maximizing profit, gives rise to circumstances in which areas of the world are devastated and traditional forms of livelihood destroyed (Harvey 2006). This movement gives rise to what Bauman (2004) refers to as migrants with "wasted lives" and Castells (2000) refers to as a "fourth world." In these present-day dystopias poverty and displacement are simultaneously deterritorialized and ubiquitous.

Internal migration has seen a massive movement of people from the countryside to ever-burgeoning cities eking out livelihoods at the margins, as low-paid workers, street children, waste pickers, and so on. Within this context Bauman pointedly refers to those displaced by poverty and instability as "human waste" invoking an image of powerless people swept along by the flotsam and jetsam of global capital. As I noted elsewhere, Castells (2000) offers a comparable analysis in writing of the impact of global capitalism on children. In contrast to the push–pull dichotomy proposed by some migration theorists, he depicts children as caught between "supply and demand" factors. On the one hand, there is supply of children brought about by a breakdown of family structures, poverty, and misery resulting in children being sold for survival, being sent to the streets to help out, or running away from the hell of their homes to the hell of their non-existence (Castells 2000: 163). The demand is created by the processes of globalization, business networking, criminalization of a segment of the economy, and advanced communication technologies. A further crucially interrelated factor in children's exploitation and exclusion is the "disintegration of states and societies, and the massive uprooting of populations by war, famine, epidemics, and banditry" (Castells 2000: 164).

Historical-structural theories can tell us much about migration in general and forced migration in particular. Forms of labor migration, for example the movement of Turks to work in the German automobile industry in the 1960s, can be theorized in relation to the strategic political and economic interests of Turkey and Germany. While uneven geographical development produced by global capitalism has certainly been, and continues to be, a highly significant factor in migratory flows, it may tell us little about the specific decisions taken by individual migrants. Why for example, do some Afghanis seek asylum in France while others risk their lives to try to get to the UK? Why do Congolese asylum seekers present their applications in London rather than in Belgium, their former colonial power? The numerous questions that arise in the study of forced migration call for an analysis that examines both what may be referred to as the macro-level of international politics and economics and a micro-level concerned with the examination of forced migrants individual and collective aspirations and the opportunities that may be available to them in the process of flight.

The importance of a multi-level approach underpins Castles and Miller's advocacy for what they term "migration systems theory." According to them:

> The basic principle is that any migratory movement can be seen as a result of interacting macro and micro structures. Macro-structures refer to large-scale institutional factors, while micro-structures embrace the networks, practices, and beliefs of the migrants themselves.
>
> (Castles and Miller 2003: 27).

In addition to macro- and micro-levels they suggest study of a meso-level that could include the role of intermediate actors such as border guards, immigration officials, and smugglers. This form of multi-level approach is certainly promising in relation to the study of forced migrants. To take one of numerous potential examples, the allied invasion of Iraq is appropriately studied at both a geo-political and economic level and at the level of the opportunities and decisions made by individual Iraqis to flee their country and seek better lives elsewhere. The hazardous journeys undertaken by forced migrants involve contact with a range of "meso"-level actors whose actions may have a critical influence on the migrants opportunity for safety and well-being. As I have observed elsewhere, the ongoing practices of border guards and shipping police may have decisive impacts on migrant children at the ports of Zeebrugge in Belgium and Dover in the UK (Watters, 2008). To take another example, the Mediterranean country of Malta has witnessed tens of thousands of arrivals from migrants trying to reach Europe from North Africa. These migrants, mostly from the Horn of Africa who have traveled to Libya in attempting to reach Europe generally have no idea of Malta and simply have the aspiration to reach a European shore. Their arrival in Malta is crucially conditioned by the seaworthiness of the boats they travel in as they generally arrive in Malta having been rescued by the Maltese navy after getting into distress in Maltese waters. Thus while global geo-political and national events may have led to their decision to flee and individual and collective agency may have been crucial factors in aspiring to reach particular countries, the role of intermediate actors may have been crucial in determining their entry into Malta (Pace *et al*. 2009).

As such, I have, in borrowing a phrase from V. S. Naipaul characterized these migrants as experiencing the "enigma of arrival." Their place of arrival may well be a hitherto unknown and largely unanticipated territory in which they experience the disturbing and enigmatic process of being viewed as people whose intention is to reap the benefits of the welfare systems available to the taxpaying locals. Within the context of the European Union countries, they also experience the impact of the Dublin Convention under the provision of which, after making a claim for asylum, they are required to remain on the territory of the first country they enter until their claim is concluded. There are widely differing success rates for such claims across the EU and failure to be granted refugee status may result in the asylum seeker being deported. In 2009 for example the UK accepted 26.9 percent of claims in the first instance, Germany 36.5 percent, and Denmark 47.9 percent while Ireland accepted 4 percent of claims and Greece 1.2 percent (European Commission 2010). These examples suggest the importance of viewing forced migration through both the lens of global economic disparities and political violence and that of human aspiration.

Migration systems theory offers a capacious and compelling alternative to the limitations of push–pull and historical structural theories. It offers a potential synthesis of the dichotomies implicit in the juxtaposition of push–pull and historical structural theory; the rational choice and role of agency implicit in the former and the role of an overdetermining structure in the latter. Also of value here is the insights provided by Zolberg (1989) in his seminal paper "The Next Waves," in which he points to the importance of the shifting laws and policies of nation states that provide changing possibilities for would be migrants. In elaborating on Zolberg's contribution, I have likened this to a series of doors, some growing in size while others shrink, in offering opportunities to different categories of potential migrants. A country may for example have laws and policies that provide generous opportunities for persons assessed to be refugees to enter its territory while being very strict in treatment of asylum seekers. One thinks for example of Australia, which accepts large numbers of refugees, whose status is determined before entering the country, while having a reputation for strict policies of deterrence toward would-be asylum seekers (Silove *et al*. 2000).

Reviewing the strengths and limitations of these theoretical formulations in the light of the lived realities of forced migrants provides an opportunity to articulate the outlines of an integrated theoretical and methodological orientation. First, on a macro-level it is important to identify the political and economic forces that have given rise to people fleeing their homes. If one considers any population of forced migrants, from Afghanis on the Pakistan border, to Somalis in Northern Europe and the USA or Zimbabweans in the UK, a broad engagement with what Castles and Miller have called the historical-structural perspective is essential for understanding. However, within this it is important to engage with contemporary political and economic dynamics regarding the ways in which laws and policies generate what I have described as "avenues of access" for forced migrants (Watters 2001b). Moreover, these may be enacted, or superseded within what Agamben, following Benjamin refers to as "states of exception—a point of imbalance between public law and political fact" (Saint-Bonnet, 2001: 28, quoted in Agamben 2005: 1) that exists at an "ambiguous, uncertain borderline fringe between the legal and the political." Commenting on the contemporary situation in Europe, Agamben argues that government "instead of declaring the state of exception prefers to have exceptional laws issued" (Agamben 2005: 21). For asylum seekers and refugees, a set of political considerations, not least those construed as linked to terrorism and security, and media-induced scares regarding the country being "flooded by migrants, routinely provoke the implementation of increasingly draconian laws and policies."

These avenues are both geographical and categorical; geographical in the sense of the ways in which asylum seekers' journeys may be diverted owing to shifting policies within and between countries. One can consider for example, how passage to Europe from North Africa has been filtered through the Spanish territories in Spain and the Canary Islands. In 2011, the conflict in Libya generated thousands of arrivals in the Italian island of Lampedusa and the then Italian Prime Minister Berlusconi announced plans for their immediate expulsion. Macro-level developments not only influence the scale of migration but also the national and ethnic compositions of migrants. The extent to which one side in a conflict gains the upper hand (and in certain circumstances the role of western powers in achieving this), influences the population that feels compelled to flee their homes.

The avenues are also categorical in that the recognition of forced migrants in countries of reception shifts historically, giving rise to changing politics of compassion and laws and policies. As Fassin (2005) noted, earlier decades witnessed widespread admiration and support for refugees. They were celebrated and admired as heroes who had successfully escaped persecution from repressive communist regimes. The extent to which refugees are welcomed differs from country to country as does the reception of asylum seekers. An aspect of the latter is the widely diverging acceptance rates for those making asylum claims from country to country. These vagaries of law and policies are not met mutely or impassively by forced migrants and, where circumstances allow a degree of calculation, decisions regarding countries of destination may be influenced by perceptions of the fairness or otherwise of countries treatment of would be refugees. This appears to be a factor for example in migrants on the coast of France resisting opportunities to claim asylum until they manage to travel to the UK.

Forced migration and the limits of compassion

The specter of thousands of people being forced to flee their homes and countries in seeking safety ordinarily provokes feelings of compassion. However, the sentiment of compassion has been eroded in recent times by a depiction of asylum seekers as not legitimate refugees but cynical economic migrants, ruthlessly exploiting the governments and populations of host counties. As Fassin (2005) has observed, compassion has, in recent decades given way to a widespread culture of mistrust. A feature of this has been the displacement of the heroic figure of the refugee as a courageous person fleeing repressive (typically communist) governments for sanctuary in the West, to an image of the asylum seeker as the embodiment of an enemy within. With large numbers of asylum seekers in the past decade arriving in Western countries from Afghanistan, Iraq, and Somalia, they have been depicted in Western media as a Muslim "other," part of a population linked to enemy combatants or as pirates who pose a threat to Western interests and embodying a primitive zealotry and barbarism antithetical to human rights.

As I have argued elsewhere, a historically situated dialectical relationship between belongingness and otherness may be appropriately seen within the context of a moral economy. A moral economy in this sense does not only govern the relationships between members of a group or community bounded by moral codes and mutual obligations, but is always crucially linked to ideas of the "deserving" or "undeserving" (Watters 2001a, 2007). I have linked the idea to medieval notions in England of the deserving and the undeserving poor with the deserving poor legitimized through the wearing of "pauper" badges assigning them as appropriate subjects for charitable support. Arguably, a similar movement has taken place in modern times. As discrimination toward settled members of minority ethnic and racial groups has increasingly become illegal and publically unacceptable, asylum seekers and undocumented migrants constitute a new "other" occupying a marginal space outside the limits of compassion. Within this context the forced migrant represents what Agamben (1998) has termed "bare life." His or her rights are not those of a citizen but reside in the sphere of human rights. The rights thus accorded are viewed by Arendt (1968) as residual, only available as a result of most fundamental of human attributes-being human.

A contemporary shift towards a discourse of human rights in relation to forced migrants is manifest in reductions in the numbers of asylum seekers receiving refugee status in industrialized countries but simultaneously having enhanced opportunity to be allowed to remain in countries of asylum under humanitarian provisions. Fassin (2001), for example, writing on the situation *sans papiers* in France, observed the declining numbers receiving political asylum while noting that concomitantly similar numbers were receiving leave to remain on the grounds of ill health and in particular mental ill health. Asylum seekers thus occupy specific "problem spaces" in which it is not their political bodies, the traditional route of legitimation, but their "sick bodies" that offer avenues of access toward legitimacy in receiving countries. As I have argued elsewhere, within these circumstances, those working as advocates for would-be refugees adopt processes of "strategic categorization" in which they respond to these predefined opportunities for legitimacy by highlighting the problems forced migrants face that are most likely to achieve successful outcomes (Watters 2001b). In practical terms this may involve highlighting the presence of mental health problems, for example post-traumatic stress disorder (PTSD) in forced migrants. In doing so I am not suggesting that those offering support to forced migrants are operating by deception and trying to present conditions that are not present. Rather they are alive to the situation facing the forced migrants and are strategically categorizing their problems to enhance their opportunities for support and legitimacy. This is, I believe, a dimension often missed by authors preoccupied by the ubiquity of concerns with PTSD and other mental health problems among refugee populations (Summerfield 1999). In some ways writing on this topic echoes limitations inherent in the historical-structural approaches discussed above in that there is a preoccupation with top-down macro-level factors in which forced migrants are merely passive recipients of global political and economic forces.

What this orientation fails to engage with is the role of refugees themselves in interpreting and responding to the very problem spaces that they are placed within or, in terms employed by de Certeau (1984), their use of tactics within the strategic spaces available to them. Not only refugees but the various intermediaries or what Castles refers to as "meso"-level actors who represent forced migrants in various institutional contexts, be they health centers, social work offices, or immigration courts, and so on, respond to and may resist political and economic structures. Like the Cambodian refugees in Ong's study of the interfaces between refugees and institutions in one American city, they do not simply absorb the designations and problems ascribed to them but respond to them often in astute ways to enhance their own life chances (Ong 2003). Accounts of the meanings migrants make of the circumstances they find themselves in are, of course, nothing new and are pervasive in the humanities and social sciences. In the case of forced migrants such accounts are less common owing to a view of this population as passive victims of circumstances.

A further reason relates to the phenomenon of what I have referred to above as "strategic categorization" (Watters 2001b). The political discourse surrounding forced migrants in industrialized countries creates a sharp division between "genuine refugees" deserving of the support and protection of host countries and what are variously referred to as "economic migrants," "scroungers," or "queue jumpers," terms used to refer to migrants who are seen as arriving spontaneously and who may seek asylum. The first category and the one representative of the deserving poor who should be entitled to the host societies' support, consists of those who are seen to have fled persecution. As such, they are viewed *de facto* as not exercising agency in choosing a country of destination. To suggest that they may have exercised a degree of rational choice has the potential to undermine their asylum claims. This thinking underlies the Dublin Convention within the EU, which is explicitly in place to deter economic migrants "shopping around" to find a country in Europe with the best living conditions. If asylum seekers are genuinely fleeing persecution, so the thinking behind the measure goes, they will be happy to have their claims considered by the first safe country they arrive in. Within this context, to talk of those seeking asylum as having aspirations toward life in particular countries and not only preoccupied with questions of their own safety is to potentially undermine the arguments that are the basis of their asylum claims. In my view, this polarization between a view of "genuine" refugees as lacking agency and "bogus" refugees who are making choices with respect to potential destinations is deeply flawed.

Is it not the case that, save for circumstances of immediate danger, such as just before or during an attack on a village, within processes of flight there is always an intermingling of fears and aspirations? Moreover, just as agencies such as the UNHCR seeks "durable solutions" to refugee problems, is it not the case that forced migrants seek both freedom from persecution and the chance of experiencing living conditions in which there are opportunities for education, jobs, and housing? What I refer to as this "aspirational" dimension of forced migration is present in the well-documented movement of migrants across Europe and in the large-scale secondary migration of migrants who had received refugee status in Sweden, Denmark, and the Netherlands to the UK (Derluyn and Broekhaert 2005; Watters, 2008).

Conclusion

The above discussion has highlighted some of the complexities of contemporary forced migration and tentatively indicated ways forward in terms of theoretical and methodological approaches. As recent UNHCR data indicate forced migration is a growing phenomenon but not one growing in any straightforward manner. The shifting nature of global conflicts has resulted in highly diverse populations seeking asylum by crossing international borders. These can range from large-scale displacements to neighboring countries such as the millions who have crossed the border between Afghanistan and Pakistan, to protracted processes of flight resulting in forced migrants crossing numerous countries to seek durable solutions for themselves and their families.

These movements are governed by a politics of displacement that has wide-ranging theoretical and methodological implications. Attempts to reduce our understanding of the phenomenon of forced migration to considerations of rational choice as implicit in push–pull formulations are unsatisfactory as are formulations associated with historical-structuralist orientations. I have argued for an approach that recognizes the complexity of forced migration through engagement with different levels; from the macro-level of global political and economic factors to a micro at which decisions are made by individuals, families, and communities and an intermediate level that examines the role of various actors that mediate the relationships between forced migrants themselves and the national and international institutions that have decisive impact on migrants' futures. Moreover, I argue that this approach must be cognizant of the role of nation states and international bodies in presenting or constricting "avenues of access" through which forced migrants seek protection. These are manifested within the context of a politics of compassion in which receiving states view forced migrants as "deserving" or "undeserving" in ways that may be decisive for their future prospects.

References and further reading

Agamben, G. translated by Attell, K. (2005) *State of Exception*. Chicago, IL: University of Chicago Press.
——(1998) *Homo Sacer: Sovereign Power and Bare Life*. Stanford, CA: Stanford University Press.
Arendt, H. (1968) *The Origins of Totalitarianism*. New York: Harcourt.
Bauman, Z. (2004) *Wasted Lives: Modernity and its Outcasts*. Cambridge: Polity Press.
Castells, M. (2000) *End of Millennium: The Information Age: Economy, Society and Culture*. Second Edition. Oxford: Blackwell.
Castles S. and Miller M. (2003) *The Age of Migration*, 3rd edition. London: Macmillan.
Castles, S. (2003) "Towards a sociology of forced migration and social transformation" *Sociology* 37(1): 13–34.
De Certeau, M. (1984) *The Practice of Everyday Life*. Berkeley, CA: University of California Press.
Derluyn, I. and Broekhaert, E. (2005) "On the way to a better future: Belgium as a transit country for trafficking and smuggling of unaccompanied minors" *International Migration* 43(4): 31–56.
European Commission (2010) *Asylum Decisions in the EU27*. Brussels: Eurostat. http://ec.europa.eu.
Fassin, D. (2005) "Compassion and repression: The moral economy of immigration policies in France" *Cultural Anthropology* 20(3): 362–87.
——(2001) "The biopolitics of otherness: Undocumented foreigners and racial discrimination in French public debate" *Anthropology Today* 17(1): 3–7.
Harvey, D. (2006) "Notes towards a theory of uneven geographical development." In D. Harvey (ed.), *Spaces of Global Capitalism*. London: Verso, pp. 69–116.
Hobsbawm, E. (1994) *The Age of Extremes: The Short Twentieth Century 1914–1991*. London: Abacus.
Ong, A. (2003) *Buddha is Hiding: Refugees, Citizenship, the New America*. Berkeley, CA: University of California Press.
Pace, C. Carabott, J., Dibben, A., and Micallef, E. (2009) *Unaccompanied Minors in Malta*. Valetta: European Migration Network.
Silove, D., Steel, Z., and Watters, C. (2000) "Policies of deterrence and the mental health of asylum seekers" *Journal of the American Medical Association* 284(5): 604–11.
Saint-Bonnet, François (2001) *L'état d'exception*. Paris: Presses Universitaires de France
Summerfield, D. (1999) "A critique of seven assumptions behind psychological trauma programmes in war affected areas" *Social Science and Medicine* 48(10): 1449–62.
UNHCR (2010) *2009 Global Trends: Refugees, Asylum Seekers, Returnees, Internally Displaced and Stateless Persons*. Geneva: United Nations High Commission for Refugees.
Watters, C. (2001a) "Emerging paradigms in the mental health care of refugees" *Social Science and Medicine* 52(11): 1709–18.
——(2001b) "Avenues of access and the moral economy of legitimacy" *Anthropology Today* 17(2): 22–23.
——(2007) "Refugees at Europe's borders: The moral economy of care" *Transcultural Psychiatry* 44(3): 394–417.
——(2008) *Refugee Children: Towards the Next Horizon*. London: Routledge.
Zolberg, A. (1989) "The next waves: Migration theory for a changing world" *International Migration Review* 23(3): 403–30.

9

Refugee resettlement policies and pathways to integration

Stephanie J. Nawyn

While many migrants have limited choices regarding if and when they migrate, refugees have been recognized by a state or international body as having left their country and as being unable to return because of persecution or a well-founded fear of persecution based on their race, religion, nationality, political belief, or membership in a particular social group. Once recognized as a refugee, one option for achieving permanent protection from persecution is resettlement. In this chapter I will explain what resettlement is, give a brief history of resettlement and related policies for managing refugees, and describe the different approaches countries have to resettlement. I will then provide a summary of the existing research on how refugees have experienced resettlement, and what needs refugees have that resettlement policies have (or have not) attempted to meet. Finally I will lay out new directions in which the study of refugee resettlement could move.

What is resettlement?

As defined by the UNHCR (United Nations High Commissioner for Refugees), resettlement is the transfer of refugees from the country in which they have first sought asylum (often referred to as the country of asylum or host country) to another country for permanent settlement (generally referred to as the resettlement country). Asylum seekers differ from refugees in that they arrive in a country of (potentially) permanent settlement and then request asylum, which is different from refugees who request permanent settlement before arriving in the resettlement country. However, both groups may flee their home country for similar reasons, and asylum seekers who are granted asylum are generally given the same rights (including rights to resettlement assistance) as refugees. Countries that provide resettlement assistance only do so for individuals that they recognize as refugees, so forced migrants who enter a resettlement country will not receive resettlement assistance without recognition as refugees from that state. Examples of state non-recognition are the Central American migrants who fled to the United States in the 1980s, and North Koreans fleeing to China since the mid-1990s. In the case of Central Americans, some were allowed to reside legally in the United States but few were ever eligible for resettlement assistance. In the case of North Koreans, they either remain in China without authorization or have been deported.

International human rights law does not guarantee resettlement as a right, but refugees have the right to seek and receive protection, and for many refugees resettlement is the best (and only) solution for permanent protection. Resettlement countries, through negotiations with the UNHCR, commit to accepting particular numbers of refugees each year, and according to their own national criteria choose the particular refugees they will accept. These national criteria vary, but often are related to the particular country's national interests and which refugees they feel they can best incorporate.

So while protection is the key concern for the UNHCR, states are primarily concerned with how best to fulfill their international obligations and to incorporate refugees into their societies. In most resettlement countries, this involves social welfare assistance programs designed to facilitate the integration of refugees into their new societies, with the level of the assistance reflecting the generousness of the resettlement country's social welfare apparatus. For example, in the Netherlands where there is a strong social welfare system, state assistance for refugees to integrate is quite extensive. Comparatively, in Italy which has a weak social safety net, state-provided refugee assistance is nearly non-existent (Korac 2003). The cultural acceptability of social welfare assistance also shapes the kinds of assistance provided in resettlement. In Western European countries where state welfare support for individuals is considered a right of citizenship, refugees receive assistance for a relatively long period of time but are often barred from finding employment so that they do not compete with natives. Conversely, in the United States where welfare usage is stigmatizing, refugees receive cash assistance for a short period of time and resettlement services are directed primarily at moving refugees into employment (Nawyn 2011).

Resettlement is among three durable solutions that the UNHCR uses to protect refugees, the other two being voluntary repatriation and settlement in the country of first asylum. Resettlement is the least often used durable solution, available only to a small number of the total refugee population. For example, in 2010 about 1 percent of the total worldwide refugee population was resettled (UNHCR 2011a). The vast majority of refugees reside in developing countries, often those bordering the countries from which the refugees fled. Some are integrated and are given citizenship or other similar rights in the host country, but most are either dispersed and working without authorization or living in refugee camps in what many have described as refugee warehousing (Hathaway and Neve 1997). Developed countries have long been reluctant to admit refugees for resettlement, fearing economic costs as well as the public's negative opinion of refugees and conflation of refugees with economic migrants (Stein 1986). While this reluctance has intensified with the growing number of refugees from developing countries, tensions around resettlement of refugees has a long history.

History of resettling refugees

While the category of refugee predates the twentieth century, it was not until World War I that the number of refugees became large enough to prompt state concern about how to handle such migrants. Prior to that time, population displacement either involved small numbers of people or occurred in regions with few restrictions against movement across state borders. It was only during World War I in Europe that we saw mass migrations of displaced people coupled with a hardening of state borders that necessitated states to develop policies for permanently settling refugees. Poles, Germans, Ukrainians, and Russian Bolsheviks were among the first groups displaced at the outbreak of war in 1914, with the numbers of displaced people increasing exponentially as the war progressed and genocidal attacks on minority populations increased, like those against Armenians and Jews (Marrus 2002).

Over concern about the social disruption caused by not only refugees but the millions of war prisoners around Europe following World War I, the newly formed League of Nations created the "High Commissioner on Behalf of the League in Connection with the Problem of Russian Refugees in Europe" in 1921 (Marrus 2002). The individual chosen as the first High Commissioner was Fridtjof Nansen, a Norwegian explorer and scientist who had developed a world-wide reputation for humanitarian assistance for refugees. The League tasked the High Commissioner with solving the "refugee problem" by negotiating with states to resettle some refugees but repatriating most of the Russian refugees and prisoners of war back to Russia. But amid states' resistance to opening their borders to refugees, insufficient funds to repatriate individuals back to their home countries, and continued military conflicts around Europe that displaced even more people, Nansen achieved only modest success in reducing the numbers of refugees in Europe within the 10-year period the League envisioned for the High Commission's existence (Marrus 2002).

World War II similarly created new and more intense pressures on states to address the masses of refugees displaced by conflict and the national border re-mapping that occurred after the war. The member states of the newly formed United Nations (UN) instituted several measures intended to manage future refugee problems. Included in these measures was the 1951 Convention on the Status of Refugees. The 1951 Convention was designed to define international obligations to refugees, and to institute the rule of *non-refoulement*, or the requirement that states not send a person back to their country of origin if that deportation could lead to the person being harmed (Marrus 2002). The UN formed the UNHCR, which they originally tasked to protect refugees but which now has an expanded mission of determining refugee status and providing humanitarian assistance to not only refugees but internally displaced persons, stateless people, and others groups that UNHCR refers to as "persons of concern." UNHCR currently plays a pivotal role in managing resettlement at the international level. While not the only agency that determines refugee status, they are critical in the management of the large refugee camps in East and West Africa and the Great Lakes region of Africa, and in Thailand, Bangladesh, and Malaysia, and wields considerable influence in negotiations with developed countries asked to resettle some of these refugees. Their most recent success in these negotiations was to convince Japan to become a resettlement country; in September 2010 Japan resettled refugees for the first time (UNHCR 2011a).

The United States has historically, and continues to be, a major receiving country for refugees. The first large groups of refugees admitted into the United States were refugees from World War II. In 1948, 409,696 refugees from Germany, Poland, the Baltic states, and Russia were admitted (Hein 1993). As the Cold War developed, the United States continued to take in refugees from various communist countries, particularly Russia, Hungary, and later Cuba (Hein 1993; Marrus 2002). The fall of Saigon to communist forces led to the evacuation of well-educated, elite members of the old Vietnamese regime, but soon to follow were tens of thousands of poor Vietnamese, Cambodians, and Laotians. With the passage of the 1980 Refugee Act, US resettlement policy was ostensibly disconnected purely from political interests (i.e. resettling refugees ad hoc from regimes hostile to the United States) and was replaced with a process for determining an annual commitment to resettle a certain number of refugees and for determining which refugees the United States would resettle. However, political and military interests continue to influence which refugees the United States takes in. The fall of the US-backed Shah in Iran led to the migration of thousands of Jewish, Baha'i, Christian, Zoroastrian, and moderate Muslim Iranians to the United States. The break up of the Soviet Union led to large increases of refugees from that region, as did the dismantling of the Former Yugoslavia and the genocide in Bosnia-Herzegovina that followed (and in which the US military intervened). Since the late 1990s the number of refugees from Africa (largely from East Africa/ African Horn and the Great Lakes region) to the United States has increased, but Asians (largely Burmese and Bhutanese) and Cubans were the largest refugee groups resettled in the United States (Office of Refugee Resettlement 2011).

Goals of different resettlement regimes

Resettlement countries work with the UNHCR and other international bodies to intentionally bring refugees into the country, whereas host countries often reluctantly accept refugees in a time of crisis when thousands of displaced people show up at their borders. So while Pakistan *hosts* the largest number of refugees (largely from neighboring Afghanistan), the United States *resettles* the largest number of refugees. Other significant resettlement countries are the United Kingdom, Canada, Australia, Sweden, and Norway (UNHCR 2011a). While the number of refugees that are resettled is small compared with the global refugee population, a large proportion of research on refugees focuses on resettlement and the particular infrastructure of different resettlement regimes.

Most resettlement states design resettlement policies around achieving a particular version of integration; rather than excluding or isolating refugees, policies are intended to incorporate them into national life and minimize their impacts on receiving communities. This most often includes permanent settlement with rights comparable to citizens. This approach differs from that directed at other types of migrants for which states often enact policies designed to discourage permanent settlement. However, individuals who enter a country as refugees can and have been deported, such as the deportation of Cambodians from the United States who originally entered the country as refugees (Hing 2005). Countries in Europe now frequently detain asylum seekers or bar them from entering the country altogether (Bloch and Schuster 2005) in order to exclude them from resettlement eligibility and thus limit the state's responsibility to provide them permanent settlement.

Research across different resettlement regimes reveals distinct outcomes from the various approaches. In Australia, an emphasis on mental health needs has encouraged refugees to take a "passive" approach to resettlement, in which refugees tend to think of themselves as helpless victims (Colic-Peisker and Tilbury 2003). The United Kingdom has a decentralized resettlement program which some scholars argue allows for more active involvement of refugees themselves to determine what constitutes successful resettlement (Majka 1991). However, the UK has taken an aggressive stance toward dispersing refugees since 2000 in the hopes of discouraging the formation of insular migrant communities (Bloch and Schuster 2005), and as the state has increasingly relegated basic service provision to private agencies, serious gaps in assistance have resulted (Wren 2007). The Canadian resettlement regime is also largely decentralized and incorporates ethnic organizations in its service delivery structure to refugees (Lawrence and Hardy 1999), which has generally been successful in integrating refugees without requiring them to abandon their cultural identities. The weaker social welfare systems in Southern Europe mean refugees are largely left to fend for themselves (Korac 2002). In some instances, detention centers are built to warehouse asylum seekers in an effort to keep them from entering other parts of Europe (Hathaway and Neve 1997).

In the United States, the resettlement program is funded mostly by the federal government but services are administered almost entirely by voluntary agencies (referred to as VOLAGS), with a primary goal of resettlement being to help refugees achieve economic self-sufficiency as quickly as possible (Nawyn 2011). The US government forms partnerships with VOLAGS to provide services intended to facilitate refugees' incorporation. VOLAGS do provide social welfare services beyond those mandated by resettlement policies, but most are still funded by the government, often using federal social welfare dollars allocated to state agencies to use at their discretion. VOLAGS partner with other non-governmental organizations (NGOs) that do not have a contractual relationship with the government as a strategy for maintaining services while receiving shrinking government funding. Faith communities, particularly Christian church congregations, have played a large role in resettlement by providing sponsorship and volunteer labor towards resettlement (Nawyn 2006). However, there is evidence that church volunteers sometimes exploit their relationship with refugees, predicating their assistance on the refugees' participation in their congregation; this most often happens when church volunteers receive little or no supervision by the resettlement agency (Kenny and Lockwood-Kenny 2011).

From 1975 until 1982, refugees in the United States received up to three years of assistance. Over time, the length of assistance and amount in real dollars has steadily decreased (Gold 1992: 62). Resettlement programs vary widely by state, ranging from 90 days to generally no more than eight months. Resettlement is also intertwined with other social service provision programs which vary by state and are supplemented by services from a range of NGOs, producing a complicated set of overlapping structures through which refugees move to access resources, and presenting a complex picture for scholars trying to assess the short- and long-term effects on different refugee populations (Rumbaut 1989). While the resettlement program is highly proscriptive, the non-governmental and immigrant community infrastructures in the United States provide flexibility in how refugees can integrate. In smaller, emerging locations of resettlement, the non-governmental infrastructure is usually limited, and the immigrant community infrastructure is sometimes weak or non-existent. In larger traditional gateways with long-settled immigrant communities, refugees can benefit from existing immigrant assistance infrastructure but they also face greater competition with other immigrants in the job and housing markets.

Most countries that take an active role in resettlement attempt to residentially disperse refugees and discourage residential concentration into ethnic enclaves. States enact these policies with the hope of encouraging interaction with the host society and quickening the acquisition of the host language. However, some scholars suggest that dispersal distances refugees from important co-ethnic support, leaving refugees feeling socially isolated (Allen 2007). However, dispersed refugees are more likely to develop social ties extending outside their ethnic community, which can provide them advantages in earnings (Majka and Mullan 2002; Allen 2009). Refugees usually can make their own choices about where to live after they arrive in a resettlement country; significant patterns of secondary migration in the United States have resulted in previously dispersed refugee populations concentrating in particular states, e.g., Cubans in South Florida, Vietnamese in California and Texas, and Somalis in Minnesota.

Refugees' experiences with resettlement

In his assessment of resettlement studies, Stein (1981) divides this subfield into two categories: the studies that focus on the system (the services and processes to which refugees are exposed) and the subjective experiences and expectations of the refugees. Stein argued that what refugees expect from resettlement shapes how they behave within the resettlement process, and that their expectations are often "romantic and unrealistic" (p. 325). Assuming that he is correct that what refugees expect from resettlement is unrealistic, that they will not receive the assistance they expect or hope for, why would that be the case? Research on the discursive positioning of refugees provides at least one compelling explanation: while refugees may see themselves as people with rights, resettlement countries and receiving communities view them as people with needs (Gold 1992; Verdirame and Harrell-Bond 2005). This discursive position reflects the institutional shift of resettlement from identifying people as refugees (i.e. people with a right to protection) to their entrance into a resettlement country (i.e. people who need assistance from that country). By and large the conception of refugees as people with rights disappears once refugees arrive in the resettlement country, which privileges the goals of the resettlement country (usually minimizing the burden of refugees on the state or local community) over the goals refugees have for themselves. Thus, in the United States where the resettlement program requires refugees to acquire employment very quickly after arrival, any rights refugees have are predicated on their success in finding a job and being economically self-sufficient (Nawyn 2011).

Refugee scholars have widely criticized resettlement policies and programs for serving largely as mechanisms of social control over refugee recipients of assistance. Ong's (2003) work makes a pointed critique of state resettlement policies and the NGOs enacting those policies, arguing that these entities have actively contributed to disruptions to traditional Cambodian refugee families through their mandate from the state as social welfare agents. In order for refugees to receive assistance from these agencies, Cambodian refugees were required to adhere to cultural- and class-specific expectations of the welfare state. For example, welfare policies in California required assistance to be distributed only to nuclear family members of an eligible household, discouraging co-residence of extended family, and some public aid workers would push birth control use on young Cambodian women and expect them to invest in increasing their earning potential rather than focus on motherhood. These expectations, Ong argued, disrupted the traditional Cambodian refugee families and led to the dissolution of Cambodian cultural community. In my research on resettlement in several different states in the United States, I show how the push to employ refugees quickly leads to the reproduction of gendered and ethnic employment enclaves that provide refugees little social mobility (Nawyn 2010).

But refugees are not mere victims that passively accept assistance from Western nations or Western NGOs. Refugees are agents that manipulate their surroundings to maximize their resources (Kibria 1994; Holtzman 2000). They have their own expectations for what successful resettlement means; they may adopt goals that run contrary to the goals of their particular resettlement program. Ong (2003) showed that Cambodian refugees in the United States strategically use institutions like religious communities to garner resources for upward mobility, participating in congregations not because of heartfelt religious beliefs but rather to improve their business relationships. Gold's (1992) study of Vietnamese and Soviet Jewish refugees described the conflicts between refugees and their resettlement service providers, with refugees often relying more upon their own ethnic networks than the agencies tasked with assisting them. My own work (Nawyn 2010) illustrates the ways in which refugees often, through organizations like mutual assistance associations, develop their own integration practices that go beyond the state's agenda for resettlement.

The needs of refugees in resettlement

Refugees, like all international migrants, face a host of challenges to successfully integrating into the receiving society, with varying definitions of what "successful integration" means to them. These challenges bring with them particular needs that theoretically could be met through resettlement policies. While no country that offers resettlement assistance does so for a length of time sufficient to fully meet the integration needs of refugees, there are particular needs that different resettlement programs attempt to address, and around which research assessing these programs tends to cluster.

Employment

Refugees need to find a job that will support their households in societies that almost always have a much higher cost of living than the refugees were accustomed to in their home countries, their host country, and of course refugee camps. Refugees that have spent a long time in protracted refugee situations (living for a decade or more in refugee camps or without authorization in a host country) often find it particularly difficult to acquire employment because they often lack necessary language skills, education, or work experience (since few camps include educational institutions or have economies that have developed beyond small-scale entrepreneurial activities). Conversely, refugees with considerable levels of pre-migration education and urban experience, like the Soviet Jews or first-wave Cubans who were resettled in the United States (Gold 1989, 1992), have a much easier time adjusting to job markets in developed countries.

In countries that provide resettlement assistance for a short period of time, refugees have an acute need to acquire employment sufficient to financially support themselves and their household. This is especially important in the United States, which has a thin social welfare net and a culture that prizes economic productivity (Potocky-Tripodi 2003; Nawyn 2011). Conversely, refugees in European countries are banned from employment for a significant length of time so as not to compete with citizens, which may slow down their integration (Valtonen 2004; Wren 2007).

Learning the dominant language

Refugees find it critical to acquire language skills in their receiving society, as the ability to speak and read the dominant language affects a range of daily experiences and greatly facilitates their material survival. In addition to the opportunity to find better employment, refugees without dominant language skills frequently feel social isolation (Allen 2007), particularly when they do not know many people who speak the dominant language and they live in communities with insufficient interpretation services (Nawyn *et al.* 2012). Additionally, parents who remain non-dominant monolingual frequently experience conflicts with their children who learn the dominant language much faster (Gold 1989).

Mental health

Refugees frequently suffer from mental health problems, with serious mental health problems like post-traumatic stress disorder endemic among particular groups of refugees such as the recent group of Iraqi refugees (Jamil *et al.* 2002). Scholars and mental health professionals most often attribute these problems to the violence, upheaval, and personal or familial loss experience as part of refugee flight. However, research also indicates that challenges following resettlement such as economic hardship also contribute to refugees' mental health problems (Simich *et al.* 2006). Additionally, refugees are often reluctant to seek mental health services because of cultural taboos surrounding mental health or because they cannot find culturally appropriate mental health services. Years of untreated mental illness like post-traumatic stress disorder manifest into a range of health and socio-economic problems that sometimes spill over into the second generation (Marshall *et al.* 2005).

Gender-specific needs of refugees

Research on women refugees and gender within resettlement and in forced migration studies more broadly is quite extensive; in this chapter I can only touch upon some of the major themes in this body of work. For a beginning introduction to this body of literature, readers should consult the edited volume by Doreen Indra (1999).

Gender relations within refugee families often differ from gender norms in the resettlement country, and the gender dynamics that have sustained families are often challenged by resettlement. Prior to resettlement, men may have taken primary responsibility for supporting the family's material needs and women's contribution to the household may have been confined to the home. New economic demands after resettlement usually require all able-bodied adult household members to work, and refugee men may feel frustrated and diminished by their dependence on the economic contributions of wives (Martin 2004). Men from a variety of cultures define masculinity largely through having a "good" job and being able to support a family, and refugee men after resettlement frequently find achieving this definition of masculinity a major challenge (McSpadden 1999). State challenges to patriarchal family relations such as resettlement caseworkers instructing refugee parents that they cannot physically punish their children (Nawyn 2010) not only challenge men's authority in the family but also women who rely on patriarchy to control their children's behavior (Kibria 1993).

Men and women often organize their lives differently, and as is true of women in industrialized countries, refugee women generally take on more reproductive or domestic responsibilities than do men. Refugee women who care for small children may have little time to take language instruction classes. They may have also come from societies in which extended kin helped care for their children or in which the state provided childcare for working mothers, and losing those support systems may put additional stress on refugee women, particularly if they work for pay outside the home (Martin 2004).

Men's and women's experiences of pre-migration violence also differ; both men and women refugees frequently experience violence, but for women this often takes the shape of sexual violence. Refugee women frequently feel inhibited from talking about their experiences with rape or sexual assault because of taboos around sexual purity, family honor, or simply the fear and shame that women of any culture might feel after such victimization. Resettlement programs do not always include sufficient mental health services or culturally appropriate outreach to women who have experienced sexual violence, so the needs of women who have been victimized too often go unmet.

Areas for future investigation

There are many areas in which resettlement studies could expand, and many gaps that need to be filled. Here I highlight just a few that I think are particularly important for scholars to consider given the current state of resettlement policies and politics.

Family unity

The process of forced migration frequently upends families and damages family ties and support systems. Refugees may lose family members who are killed in violent conflicts, or lose track of where family members are during flight. Once approved for resettlement, remaining family ties may be severed again by policies that do not allow extended family members to be resettled together. The UNHCR defines family members eligible for resettlement generally as spouses and dependent children, although aged parents and married children living with a primary householder who has refugee status may also be granted resettlement with the rest of the household (UNHCR 2011b). However, this definition excludes extended family who may provide critical material and non-material support to the refugees being resettled, and it allows for only one spouse (so that polygamous families are excluded).

Some scholars have conducted research on the importance of family unity and maintaining family ties post-resettlement (Simich *et al.* 2006), but more work is needed particularly on transnational family relations post-resettlement. For example, the Somali Bantu resettlement produced a diaspora of usually tight-knit Bantu kin networks, presenting new challenges to the Bantu in maintaining family relations and rituals across great distances. The Tanzanian government's decision to grant citizenship to Burundian refugees has meant that those Burundians in Tanzania are not likely to be resettled with other family members in resettlement countries, solidifying the transnational status of families that had hoped to eventually reunite. The strategies that these Somali Bantu and Burundian families enact to maintain family relations, and the health of those families in the future, will provide scholars evidence of both the positive and detrimental effects that resettlement can have on refugee families.

Long-term social integration

Integration is a process that unfolds over a long period of time, with no clear endpoint at which "successful" integration can be measured. Yet, those people who design and implement resettlement policy would benefit from understanding how different resettlement strategies shape integration opportunities and barriers of different refugee groups. As I noted earlier in this chapter, the variability between different resettlement regimes, and even the variable ways in which the same regime administers resettlement in different localities, makes the task of assessing the long-term effects of one strategy versus another on different refugees herculean, to say the least. However, it is an important task to attempt given resettlement countries' concerns about the adaptability of various refugee groups post-resettlement.

Some possible strategies are to compare some of the basic approaches used in resettlement (such as intensive versus laissez-faire government intervention or dispersal versus ethnic residential enclave), conduct cross-group and cross-national comparisons, and to measure the integration of refugees over a long duration (including the integration of their native-born children). Korac (2002) has done this with her cross-national comparison between interventionist Netherlands and laissez-faire Italy. Colic-Peisker and Tilbury (2003) compare different approaches that refugees have to the same resettlement program and identify different trajectories that come from those approaches. Haines (2002) and Marshall *et al.* (2005) studied the long-term integration of Vietnamese and Cambodian refugees in the United States, respectively. Much more work like this needs to be done in order to understand the trajectories that different refugees take as they attempt to build a new life in their resettlement country, and what effects those early resettlement experiences might have on long-term integration.

Expanding protection outside of resettlement

Because of the high economic cost of resettlement and the reluctance of resettlement countries to receive more refugees, some refugee policy makers are increasingly considering the costs and benefits of resettling refugees compared to other durable solutions. One route policy makers are considering is to put more resources into integrating refugees in the host country or country of first asylum. Rather than spending money on bringing refugees to their country for resettlement, developed countries could put those resources into helping host countries absorb their refugee populations. This strategy would provide the benefit of settling refugees into a country that is closer to their home country (not just geographically but economically and culturally), would avoid the dispersal of extended family that often results from resettlement, and might be more politically expedient for resettlement countries that face native opposition to receiving more refugees. However, the ability of host countries to provide adequate protection to refugees would need to be established, and researchers would need to investigate whether such a program would actually result in lower costs in the long term (particularly since the remittances sent by resettled family members has served to economically sustain refugees in host countries).

Another strategy that UNHCR has begun to pursue is to use labor migration paths to find refugees permanent employment. For refugees who are in camps and have labor skills desired by other countries, UNHCR would work to bring those refugees to other countries as economic laborers. UNHCR is considering this strategy in part because of the paths of irregular labor migration that many refugees take when they self-settle (working outside the framework of the UN and the international resettlement regime to seek permanent protection on their own). However, a great deal more research needs to be conducted before determining whether such a strategy will provide the protection to which refugees, by law, are entitled.

Further reading

Allen, R. (2007) "Sometimes it's Hard Here to Call Someone to Ask for Help": Social Capital in a Refugee Community in Portland, Maine. PhD thesis, Massachusetts Institute of Technology.
——(2009) "Benefit or burden? Social capital, gender, and the economic adaptation of refugees" International Migration Review 43(2): 332–65.
Bloch, A. and Schuster, L. (2005) "At the extremes of exclusion: Deportation, detention and exclusion" Ethnic and Racial Studies, 28(3): 491–512.
Colic-Peisker, V. and Tilbury, F. (2003) "'Active' and 'passive' resettlement: The influence of support services and refugees' own resources on resettlement style" International Migration 41(5): 61–91.
Gold, S. J. (1989) "Differential adjustment among new immigrant family members" Journal of Contemporary Ethnography 17(4): 408–34.
——(1992) Refugee Communities: A Comparative Study. Newbury Park, CA: Sage.
Haines, D. W. (2002) "Binding the generations: Household formation patterns among Vietnamese refugees" International Migration Review 36(4): 1194–1217.
Hathaway, J. C. and Neve, R. A. (1997) "Making international refugee law relevant again: A proposal for collectivized and solution-oriented protection" Harvard Human Rights Journal 10, 155–69, 173–87.
Hein, J. (1993) States and International Migrants: The Incorporation of Indochinese Refugees in the United States and France. Boulder, CO: Westview Press.
Hing, B. O. (2005) Detention to deportation – Rethinking the removal of Cambodian refugees. UC Davis Law Review 38: 891–971.
Holtzman, J. D. (2000) Nuer Journeys, Nuer Lives: Sudanese Refugees in Minnesota. Boston, MA: Allyn and Bacon.
Indra, D. (ed.) (1999) Engendering Forced Migration: Theory and Practice. New York: Berghahn Books.
Jamil, H., Hakim-Larson, J., Farrag, M., and Jamil, L. H. (2002) "A retrospective study of Arab American mental health clients: Trauma and the Iraqi refugees" American Journal of Orthopsychiatry 72(3): 355–61.
Kenny, P. and Lockwood-Kenny, K. (2011) "A mixed blessing: Karen resettlement to the United States" Journal of Refugee Studies 24(2): 217–38.
Kibria, N. (1993) Family Tightrope: The Changing Lives of Vietnamese Americans. Princeton, NJ: Princeton University Press.
——(1994) "Household structure and family ideologies: The dynamics of immigrant economic adaptation among Vietnamese refugees" Social Problems 41(1): 81–96.
Korac, M. (2002) "The role of the state in refugee integration and settlement: Italy and the Netherlands compared" Forced Migration Review 14(June): 30–32.
——(2003) "Integration and how we facilitate it: A comparative study of the settlement experiences of refugees in Italy and the Netherlands" Sociology 37(1): 51–68.
Lawrence, T. B. and Hardy, C. (1999) "Building bridges for refugees: Toward a typology of bridging organizations" Journal of Applied Behavioral Science 35(1): 48–70.
Majka, L. (1991) "Assessing refugee assistance organizations in the United States and the United Kingdom" Journal of Refugee Studies 4(3): 267–83.
Majka, L. and Mullan, B. (2002) "Ethnic communities and ethnic organizations reconsidered: South-east Asians and Eastern Europeans in Chicago" International Migration 40(2): 71–92.

Marrus, M. R. (2002) *The Unwanted: European Refugees from the First World War through the Cold War.* Philadelphia, PA: Temple University Press.

Marshall, G. N., Schell, T. L., Elliott, M. N., Berthold, S. M., and Chun, C.-A. (2005) "Mental health of Cambodian refugees two decades after resettlement in the United States" *JAMA: Journal of the American Medical Association* 294(5): 571–79.

Martin, S. F. (2004) *Refugee Women.* Lanham, MD: Lexington Books.

McSpadden, L. A. (1999) Negotiating masculinity in the reconstruction of social place: Eritrean and Ethiopian refugees in the United States and Sweden. In D. Indra (ed.) *Engendering Forced Migration: Theory and Practice.* New York: Bergahn Books, pp. 242–60.

Nawyn, S. J. (2006) "Faith, ethnicity, and culture in refugee resettlement" *American Behavioral Scientist* 49(1): 1509–27.

——(2010) "Institutional structures of opportunity in refugee resettlement: Gender, race/ethnicity, and refugee NGOs" *Sociology and Social Welfare* 37(11): 149–67.

——(2011) "'I have so many successful stories': Framing social citizenship for refugees" *Citizenship Studies* 15(6–7): 679–93.

Nawyn, S. J., Gjokaj, L., Agbényiga, D. L., and Grace, B. (2012) "Linguistic isolation, social capital, and immigrant belonging" *Journal of Contemporary Ethnography* 41(3): 255–81.

Office of Refugee Resettlement (2011) *Report to Congress, FY 2008* Washington, DC: US Department of Health and Human Services.

Ong, A. (2003) *Buddha is Hiding: Refugees, Citizenship, the New America,* Berkeley, CA: University of California Press.

Potocky-Tripodi, M. (2003) "Refugee economic adaptation: Theory, evidence, and implications for policy and practice" *Journal of Social Service Research* 30(1): 63–91.

Rumbaut, R. G. (1989) "The structure of refuge: Southeast Asian refugees in the United States 1975–85" *International Review of Comparative Public Policy* 1: 97–129.

Simich, L., Hamilton, H., and Baya, B. K. (2006) "Mental distress, economic hardship, and expectations of life in Canada among Sudanese newcomers" *Transcultural Psychiatry* 43(3): 418–44.

Stein, B. N. (1981) "The refugee experience: Defining the parameters of a field of study" *International Migration Review* 15(1/2): 320–30.

Stein, B. (1986) "Durable solutions for developing country refugees" *International Migration Review* 20(2): 264–82.

UNHCR (2011a) *60 Years and Still Counting: UNHCR Global Trends 2010.* Geneva, Switzerland.

UNHCR (2011b) *UNHCR Resettlement Handbook.* Geneva: United Nations High Commissioner for Refugees.

Valtonen, K. (2004) "From the margin to the mainstream: Conceptualizing refugee settlement processes" *Journal of Refugee Studies* 17(1): 70–96.

Verdirame, G. and Harrell-Bond, B. E. (2005) *Rights in Exile: Janus-faced Humanitarianism,* New York: Berghahn Books.

Wren, K. (2007) "Supporting asylum seekers and refugees in Glasgow: The role of multi-agency networks" *Journal of Refugee Studies* 20(3): 392–413.

10

Human trafficking

Kathryn Farr

Every year millions of people are trafficked within and across national borders for commercial sex and forced labor. Their exploitation is organized and managed by an ever-growing trafficking industry that brings in high profits at relatively low risk. Like other business operations, the human trafficking industry depends on an accessible supply, an efficient marketing system, and high demand. Conditions were near-perfect for meeting these requirements with the fall of the Soviet Union in the early 1990s. Widespread joblessness and service cutbacks left many women in the region without the income or aid to support themselves and their children. State failure was accompanied by a breakdown in law and order that allowed established Soviet crime groups—many of whom already trafficked weapons, alcohol, cigarettes, and other products—to gain an even stronger foothold. Such groups, along with newer entrepreneurs, saw in the increasingly desperate female population a sizeable source for high-demand sex markets in nearby countries. In short time, a lucrative trafficking industry evolved in the region, and women from the former Soviet republics were dispersed in formidable numbers into sex markets to the west in Europe and the Middle East, and to the east in Japan and elsewhere.

Since the fall of the Soviet Union in the early 1990s, the trade in humans has expanded, as have the conditions under which the human trafficking industry flourishes. This chapter provides an overview of the worldwide human trafficking phenomenon and the factors that support and promote it.

Definitional issues and debates

By the late 1990s, there was a growing literature on the trafficking of women and girls into prostitution, spurred in part by radical feminists such as Kathleen Barry (1995) and Donna Hughes (2000), who characterized sex trafficking, as well as prostitution itself, as violence against women. Because, from this perspective, prostitution is something done to women by pimps and customers, it cannot be constructed as a behavior of "choice." Accordingly, the campaign against sex trafficking should promote not only the rescue of prostituted women, but the abolition of prostitution itself.

Countering this discourse, other feminist scholars (see, for example, Doezema 2002; Agustin 2007; Davidson 2010) wrote about sex trafficking from a labor or civil rights perspective, arguing that many putative sex trafficking victims are actually women who have made a choice—however constrained—to enter into sex work. The "enslaved victim" construction, these scholars have suggested, not only deprives these women of agency and interferes with their livelihood, but also ignores abuses against sex workers carried out by state authorities. Sex workers' self-defined labor and civil rights, then, should be the focal point of activism.

A related claim of abolition critics is that portrayals of prostitutes from source countries in the global South as "wounded victims" in need of feminist rescue are racist and aimed at "advancing certain feminist interests, which cannot be assumed to be those of third world sex workers themselves" (Doezema 2002, p. 20).

Indeed, in recent years, the enslaved or wounded victim view has informed the campaigns of an often religious-tinged rescue industry. An example of this thrust is the anti-trafficking work of the International Justice Mission (IJM). Operating in the United States and other countries, IJM is well-known for its organized brothel raids and the delivery of rescued girls to shelters, many of which are run by Christian organizations. Located in Cebu City in the Philippines, one such shelter, Happy Horizons, provides "daily, Bible-based counseling to restore self-esteem and confidence that comes with the realization that one is a precious, beloved child of God … " (quoted in Thrupkaew 2009). Critics of a hyper-rescue strategy as part of a moral crusade also note that many young women have fled from the shelters and that post-rescue services are frequently lacking.

Another issue divides feminists in these often contentious debates: some argue that prostitution—constructed as (sex) work—is no different from and should not be set apart from other forms of trafficked labor. Others, however, note that when women and men are trafficked into domestic, agricultural, or industrial work, it is their labor (as service) that is sold, but when women and girls are trafficked for commercial sex, their body (as commodity) is the object of sale. Purchasers may select from the lot on the basis of the commodity's sexualized self as it reflects local or foreign-exotic standards of sexual attractiveness (or idiosyncratic "tastes"). That is, the sexual commodification of women can be construed as a special case of the people trade, one which is consistent with transnational cultural objectifications of women as sexual body and men's entitlement to her/it.

More generally, some scholars are critical of the hyper-attention to sex trafficking and its "innocent" victims, arguing that this focus overshadows the much larger problem of forced labor trafficking, feminizes the victim population, and ignores human trafficking's relationship to migration. Adults and children of both sexes are routinely trafficked internally and internationally, often ending up in conditions of enslavement not only in domestic, agricultural or industrial work, but also in criminal activities such as drug dealing and begging. Victims of labor trafficking are typically people attempting to migrate in search of better life opportunities or to escape a dangerous life. The construction of human trafficking as enslavement rather than (would-be) migration, notes Davidson (2010), leads to the identification of a relatively small population of enslaved and thus deserving victims, unlike the masses seeking to migrate, who are characterized as "free" and thus undeserving of protection. Penttinen (2008) eschews this either–or take, noting that conventional dichotomies constructing the trafficked person as *either* a passive victim *or* a conspiring migrant ignore the subtleties that negate the existence of a single, stable trafficking subject.

Regardless of the characterization of the trafficking subject, however, the movement of people is usually central to definitions of human trafficking in the academic and human rights literature. As sex trade researcher Donna Hughes (2000) puts it, sex trafficking includes "any practice that involves moving people within and across local or national boundaries for the purpose of sexual exploitation" (p. 626).

Yet, current criminal codifications of human trafficking have distanced human trafficking from migration and even rendered the choice/consent issue moot. As set forth in the 2000 United Nations Protocol to Prevent, Suppress and Punish Trafficking in Persons, especially Women and Children (often used as a guideline for criminal legislation in individual states), human trafficking is:

> the recruitment, transportation, transfer, harbouring or receipt of persons, by means of the threat or use of force or other forms of coercion, of abduction, of fraud, of deception, of the abuse of power or of a position of vulnerability or of the giving or receiving of payments or benefits to achieve the consent of a person having control over another person, for the purpose of exploitation.
>
> Exploitation shall include, at a minimum, the exploitation of the prostitution of others or other forms of sexual exploitation, forced labour or services, slavery or practices similar to slavery, servitude or the removal of organs.
>
> (Article 3a)

Importantly, this internationally-accepted definition does not insist upon population movement as a criterion for the offense—recruitment or harboring suffices. The US Department of State (2009) has made this explicit, stating in the US Victims of Trafficking and Violence Protection Act (TVPA), that a "victim need not be physically transported from one location to another in order for the crime to fall within these [trafficking] definitions." This definition would also seem to exclude another facet of migration, i.e., human smuggling, in which would-be-migrants pay a price for a transportation service (although smugglers sometimes exploit their customers after delivering them to their destination, and as such would most likely qualify as traffickers). Article 3b of the Protocol states further that the "consent of a victim of trafficking in persons to the intended exploitation" is "irrelevant where any of the means set forth" in Article 3a have been employed.

Both the UN and US codes seem to identify the transactional component of the exploitation as the criminal act, and such a designation actually expands the potential victim and offender classes. If, for example, any woman recruited into prostitution by any other person is considered a trafficking victim, then the great majority of women working in the sex industry are trafficked women, and all who recruit or harbor them are traffickers. Again, however, consistency is elusive. In a shift that favors viewing human trafficking as a labor condition, the UN Office on Drugs and Crime (2009) has recently suggested that the term "trafficking" can be misleading in that "it places emphasis on the transaction aspects of a crime that is more accurately described as enslavement" (p. 6).

While most agree that trafficking in humans constitutes exploitation—be it transactional or labor enslavement, most who statistically describe its extent measure the movement of people across borders by traffickers. From their review of these latter efforts, Gallagher and Holmes (2008) conclude that there are "compelling claims" that trafficking across borders is increasing and that the trafficking industry is becoming ever-more global, professional, and well organized.

Extent, forms, and flows of human trafficking

Determining the number of trafficking victims is, like counting any illegal behavior, notoriously problematic. Frequently cited estimates place the number of persons annually trafficked across national borders at somewhere between 700,000 and 2 million (with a few estimates as high as four million); from 2 to 4 million more are trafficked domestically (see, for example, UNIFEM 2007; US Department of State 2007; UNESCO 2009). According to the International Labor Organization (ILO) (2009), at least 12.3 million persons are in forced or enslaved labor worldwide, some 2.4 million of these as a result of trafficking. Many sources state that the great majority (some 70–80 percent) of trafficking victims are women and girls.

Sex trafficking is often reported to be the most common form of human trafficking. At one international conference, a UN representative referred to UN data indicating that about 75 percent of trafficking involved women and children for sexual exploitation (Dujisin 2009) And, a global report based on criminal justice and victim assistance data from 155 countries found that 79 percent of trafficking cases involved sexual exploitation (UN Office on Drugs and Crime 2009). In the United States, an examination of certified victims of trafficking also found that the great majority of cases involved sex rather than forced labor (US Department of Justice 2008). Others question the accuracy of these percentages, pointing out that vast numbers of forced labor cases are concealed and that the lesser attention to labor trafficking contributes to a serious undercounting of it. Moreover, they argue, statistics on women said to be sex trafficking victims include large numbers of women who willingly migrated to do sex work. Indeed, the ILO now claims that the majority of human trafficking worldwide actually involves forced labor (US Department of State 2009).

Forms of human trafficking

Sex trafficking

Women and girls may be sold or abducted into the sex trade, but the most common form of recruitment is a deceitful job offer. Often relying on local contacts to gain credibility with potential recruits and their families, traffickers promise a job in a foreign country or in another part of their own country doing restaurant, hostess, domestic or office work. Some women do know that the promised job is in the sex industry, but few are aware of the terms of their trafficking or the conditions of their living and work environment.

Sex trafficking is profitable in large part because of the debt bondage system under which it operates. Upon arrival at her destination, the woman is told that she owes a considerable debt for the planning and execution of her trip and the "job" arrangements. Southeast Asian women trafficked for sex to the United States, Canada, and Japan tend to have sizeable debts, ranging on average from $25,000 to $30,000. Intra-regional trafficking usually involves lower debts (one study (Caldwell *et al.* 1997) found debts of $6,000 to $18,000 for Russian women trafficked to Germany in the late 1990s). There are other costs for her—earnings are taken by traffickers for her room and board, and there are often medical fees as well as fines for a variety of minor behavioral violations (see Farr 2005). Passports and other identification documents are commonly held by the traffickers and must be bought back if and when the woman is able to pay off her debt and free to leave. Prior to the termination of her debt, however, she can be sold to a new owner and acquire a new debt. That is, she is a re-usable commodity that can be sold and re-sold for new profits.

For internationally trafficked women, taken to a country where they don't speak the language, are not familiar with the culture, know no one, and are working in an illegal industry, the options are few. Traffickers use a variety of additional control mechanisms, including keeping the women under guard and on the business premises, assaulting and raping them, or threatening violence against their family back home. Living conditions are often abysmal and workloads (serving as many as 25–30 men a day) excessive. Health issues, including HIV/AIDS and other sexually transmitted infections, are a serious problem, particularly in countries and regions with high rates of infectious diseases. For very young girls, physical vulnerability to STDs is especially high, and it is the younger girls who typically have less power to negotiate the terms of the sexual transactions (such as the use of condoms). Around the world, the age of sex trafficking victims has been declining, as male customers seek sex with younger and younger girls. In some places, sex with a young or virginal girl is believed to enhance male potency or even cure an STD.

Forced or enslaved labor

Like sex trafficking victims, women and men trafficked into forced labor are exploited in many ways, including wage withholding or under-payment, no time off, severe health and safety risks, sub-standard living conditions, and assaults. Would-be migrants and undocumented immigrants are particularly vulnerable to being trafficked into forced or enslaved labor, and their precarious status is used to keep them from reporting or escaping the exploitation.

Forced labor occurs throughout the world, but much of it transported across borders ends up in affluent countries in the global north, where demand is high. From a study of forced labor in the United States covering the period from January 1998 to December 2003, for instance, Bales *et al.* (2004) reported that there were at any given time at least 10,000 forced laborers in the United States. Most were trafficked in from one of 35 countries—China accounted for the largest number of victims, followed in order by Mexico and Vietnam.

A sizeable number of women are trafficked from developing to more affluent countries for domestic labor. Major destinations are countries in Europe, North America, the Middle East, and wealthier Asian sites, such as Japan, South Korea, Malaysia, Hong Kong, and Singapore. In many countries, including the United States, domestic workers are not fully included under national labor laws and thus lack even minimal protections. One review of migrant domestic workers in the Middle East (Saudi Arabia, Kuwait, UAE, Bahrain, Lebanon, and Jordan) and Singapore and Malaysia (Varia 2010) found that reforms were slow to come. Migrant domestic workers were still not allowed to leave their workplace without their employer's permission. Recruiters in the workers' home country gave deceitful job information and often charged excessive fees; in the destination countries, trafficking brokers charged elevated fees, made changes in contracts that had already been signed by the job seeker in her own country, and forced workers to stay in exploitative work situations.

Another problem involves the recruitment and transport of domestic workers by foreign diplomats, who are often protected from legal redress due to diplomatic immunity. In the United States, foreign diplomats and international organization employees can bring domestic workers into the country on special (A-3 and G-5) visas; from 2005–9, about 3,000 such visas were issued annually (Department of Homeland Security 2009). One such visa was awarded to Mani Kumari Sabbithi, an Indian national trafficked to Virginia by a Kuwaiti diplomat and his wife. Her employers forced Sabbithi to work 16–19 hours per day every day, took her passport, confined her to the house, severely beat her, and withheld medical care from her. Sabbithi filed suit against her employers for trafficking and forced labor in January 2007 (Frederickson and Leveille 2007). In March of 2009, the suit was dismissed by a US District Court (Civil Action No. 07–115), which ruled that the defendants "were entitled to diplomatic immunity and could not be sued in the United States" and that the Trafficking Victims Protection Act "does not override diplomatic immunity." Referring to the opinion of the US Department of State (see also, Sabbithi, 605 F. Supp. 2d at 125–30), the Court also ruled that "hiring domestic employees" does not "constitute commercial activity."

Child trafficking

Child trafficking is included among the "worst forms of child labor" in the 2000 ILO Convention (No. 182). In a 2010 report, the ILO summarized its most recent findings, showing that of some 215 million children in (largely unpaid) child labor overall, over half are in the most egregious forms of child labor, and approximately 5.7 million are in forced or bonded labor. While their numbers are high in all regions of the world, children trafficked into enslaved or bonded child labor are found in the largest numbers in South Asia and sub-Saharan Africa. They are trafficked not only for domestic, sexual, agricultural, and industrial labor, but also for organized, illicit street work. One recent study, for instance, uncovered over 6,000 young boys in Senegal trafficked into forced begging by religious leaders known as *talibe* who had promised to be their educators. Other boys were trafficked into forced labor in gold mines within Senegal and across the border into Mali and Guinea (US Department of State 2009). Also, tens of thousands of children (some estimates have been as high as 200,000–300,000) around the world are used as soldiers or sex and domestic slaves for combatants in armed conflicts. Some have been recruited through persuasion, but many have been abducted and transported to combatant field bases.

International flows

Throughout the 1990s and into the 2000s, developing countries in the global South and countries in transition, such as the former Soviet republics and countries in the former Yugoslavia, served mainly as sources or suppliers of humans for trafficking. Major destinations were affluent countries in several regions—the US and Canada in North America; numerous Western European countries; Japan, Singapore, and Hong Kong in East Asia; and Gulf countries, such as Qatar, the UAE, Kuwait, and Israel. Some countries were active transit sites or hubs, either because of their positioning between source and destination countries (e.g., Albania, the Czech Republic, Turkey, Pakistan), or because of well-established sex industries there (e.g., Thailand, the Philippines), or both (India). While these trajectories still stand, international flows have become more diversified, with a number of developing countries serving as hubs and destinations for trafficking victims.

Traffickers have taken advantage of the potential supply of women in sub-Saharan Africa, where both domestic and cross-border migration have historically been a normative part of the search for work. Nigeria is an active source of women and girls trafficked into Western Europe for sexual exploitation; additionally, women have for some time been routinely trafficked from countries in East Africa for domestic labor in the Gulf states. South Africa, with a flourishing tourism industry, has become a major destination for women and girls trafficked from elsewhere in Africa, as well as from East Asia and Eastern Europe. Kenya's growing tourism (and thus sex) industry has also attracted traffickers. Multiple ongoing armed conflicts in Africa further feed the human trafficking problem by creating an even more desperate supply of potential recruits; war-related lawlessness provides traffickers virtual impunity (Farr 2010).

As in Africa, migration for work has a lengthy history in many parts of Latin America, thus opening the door to human trafficking. Mexico has well-established networks of traffickers who bring women into the United States for sexual and domestic service, and both men and women for agricultural labor. Colombia has long been a major source of women and girls trafficked internationally—including to Western Europe, the Middle East, and East Asia—for sex and domestic service; Colombia also has a sizeable child soldier problem. Guatemala is a notable source of women and children trafficked to Mexico and to the United States, and more recently, with its own burgeoning sex industry, Guatemala has also become a destination for trafficked women.

Because trafficking in humans is so profitable, the search for new markets, new routes and new forms of exploitation should not be surprising. Moreover, the organization of the trafficking industry is particularly amenable to expansion and change.

The human trafficking industry

In its last global report (Belser 2005), the ILO estimated that of the US$44.3 billion in annual profits from forced labor worldwide, some US$32 billion came from the labor of trafficking victims, and more than US$15 billion of this latter sum came from the labor of persons trafficked into affluent countries in the global north. The money made from this exploitative industry provides a vast array of traffickers with comfortable incomes.

The human trafficking industry operates as a network system with tentacles that reach into all regions and most countries in the world. The networks consist of groups and individuals in a variety of roles. In Phil Williams' (2008) typology, network groups include transnational criminal organizations (with "broad portfolios of activity"), traditional criminal organizations, ethnically based trafficking organizations (such as the Albanian and Kosovo Albanian networks), criminal-controlled businesses, and opportunistic amateurs. Also critical to the success of the industry are "corrupt guardians" (Farr 2005), such as border patrol agents, police officers, immigration officers, and embassy officials, who either aid or purposefully ignore trafficking activity. Trafficker roles include recruiters, brokers, employment, and travel agents, document thieves and forgers, transporters, club owners or other employers, premise guards, money launderers, and contractors (overseers, who organize and administer a particular trafficking operation). Not every trafficking episode utilizes all of these actors, but they all play an integral part in the smooth functioning of the industry overall.

The organization of human trafficking networks is more lateral than hierarchical, and positions are dynamic rather than fixed. In fact, flexibility and adaptation are key organizational components. Groups and persons may quickly change their way of doing business and even their business partners in order to maximize opportunities or thwart law enforcement efforts. Redundancy is typically built into the networks so that if one back-up plan fails, another is available, and so that those in positions central to a particular operation are protected by multiple outside layers. Technological know-how and accessibility contribute to the ability to adjust and adapt to changing conditions and markets.

Economic and political factors contributing to human trafficking

Globalization, neo-liberal market policies, and inequality

Privatization and deregulation polices that have produced a globalized "free" market economy have also led to economic instability in many developing and transition countries and growing income inequality between and within countries. In an effort to offset economic downturns and build toward a better future, a number of poorer countries have accepted sizeable loans from international financial institutions. Heavily indebted countries are encouraged or required by their lenders (e.g., the World Bank, the International Monetary Fund) to implement austerity programs and, where amenable, to build up tourism industries. Austerity efforts have often consisted of cutbacks in social services, such as welfare, health, and child care, on which women rely, along with reductions in service jobs heavily filled by women. On the other side, the growing affluence of upper classes in industrialized as well as some developing countries has yielded not only more discretionary income among them but also a rising demand for cheap labor—for households and businesses alike.

Global economic inequalities have also been a factor in the outsourcing of labor in the global south. In 2009, international migrants from developing countries sent home some US$315 billion in remittances (www.worldbank.org/prospects/migrationandremittances). Over the last few years, remittances to developing countries have accounted for some 75 percent of the total value of remittances from international migrants. Remittances account for substantial portions of GDP in several major trafficking source countries: 50 percent of GDP in Tajikistan, 31 percent in Moldova, and 28 percent in the Kyrgyz Republic (Ratha et al. 2009). Moreover, several countries in the Persian Gulf that are major destinations for trafficked labor have particularly high percentages of migrants workers: 85 percent of Qatar's population are migrants, as are 70 percent of the populations of Kuwait and the United Arab Emirates.

The trafficking industry has also benefited from technological advances that allow for easy transnational communication, immediate monetary deposits, and the efficient movement of the (human) commodity. As Williams (2008: p. 126) has pointed out in regard to sex trafficking, globalization has expedited the "transshipment process, making it easier and cheaper to link the supply of women for commercial sex with centres of demand."

Migration policies

Although national borders have opened for the transnational flow of goods and money, many countries have "increasingly and forcefully asserted their sovereign right to control the movement of people across their borders" (Dinan 2008, p. 67). While some view efforts to limit immigration as anti-trafficking measures, others note that coupled with the pressures to migrate, restrictive immigration policies actually foster growth in a "migration mediation industry," pushing would-be-migrants directly into the hands of traffickers. Playing upon undocumented workers' fears regarding the sending of money home through legal channels, traffickers profit further from providing this mailing service for fees at inflated rates, in some instances as high as 20 percent (Ratha 2004, referred to in Dinan 2008, p. 70).

Patriarchal exploitations of women and girls

While men and boys are also victims, women and girls have certain vulnerabilities that increase their risk of falling prey to traffickers. To begin, economic downturns in developing and transition countries often hit women faster and harder than men. In the first years following the 1991 collapse of the Soviet Union, for example, women accounted for 80 percent of those in the former Soviet republics who lost their jobs (Caldwell et al. 1997). Wage gaps increased as well. In Russia alone, women's wages went from 70 percent of men's in 1989 to 40 percent of men's in 1995 (Hunt 1998). Such economic losses account in great part for the 1990s surge of women trafficked from the Soviet region.

Militarized prostitution is another factor in the modern-day expansion of sex trafficking. World War II, the Korean War, and the Vietnam War lay the ground for the build-up of sex industries in, as well the sex trafficking of women to, war-affected areas in Asia. In one of the more infamous modern military atrocities, an estimated 200,000 Asian women were abducted and forced into prostitution to service Japanese troops during World War II. These "comfort women" were widely trafficked, "shipped ... like military supplies throughout the vast area of Asia and the Pacific that Japanese troops controlled from the Siberian border to the equator," and listed on military supply lists under headings such as "ammunition" and "amenities" (Case Watch 2003, pp. 2–3). The Vietnam War also brought a sex industry explosion in that country; by the late 1960s the demand from US and other troops began to outstrip the local supply, and women were trafficked into Vietnam from neighboring countries such as Laos and Thailand to supply the sex industry.

Today, war-affected women and children in armed conflicts across regions engage in "survival sex" (i.e., exchanging their bodies for food and other necessities, or for services such as passage across the border into another country). Women in war-related displacement camps form a "captive pool" for traffickers, particularly in extended refugee settlements, such as those along the border between Myanmar and Thailand. Displaced women are also especially vulnerable in places in which trafficking networks have become established—such as Albania, where organized-crime groups take Kosovar women from refugee camps and sell them into prostitution in Italy and other parts of Western Europe.

Demand has also been enhanced through globalization-related increases in migratory male labor and the expansion of sex tourism. That is, in addition to local demand, the traveling of men—whether for soldiering, civilian labor, or recreation—is accompanied by the trafficking of women for sexual exploitation.

Responses: advances, challenges, and strategies

In the 2000s, attention to human trafficking increased notably. The UN Office on Drugs and Crime reported that of the 155 countries that provided data for its 2009 Global Report, 63 percent had enacted laws criminalizing trafficking for sexual exploitation and forced labor of victims of all ages and both genders. An additional 16 percent of the countries had passed laws addressing some forms of human trafficking, albeit limited in certain cases to child or female victims. That is, almost 80 percent of the countries had anti-trafficking laws at the end of 2008, compared to only one-third of the surveyed countries in 2003. Moreover, the 2009 Report found that over half of the data-providing countries had a police unit devoted solely to human trafficking. Yet, throughout the world, law enforcement and judicial activity lags in regard to trafficking arrests, prosecutions, and convictions.

Additionally, the law enforcement focus is largely on sex trafficking, and in many countries (notably so in the United States) on the domestic recruitment of minor girls into prostitution. This focus slants the demographic profile of victims of human trafficking and reinforces the perception that most victims are women and girls trafficked for sexual exploitation. Although the UN Report issues a caveat regarding the serious under-reporting of trafficking for forced labor, the picture that emerges and plays throughout the media is of the pimped-out teen or pre-teen girl. Greater media attention to forced and enslaved labor could contribute to public awareness regarding the scope of the human trafficking problem.

More effort could be applied toward dismantling the human trafficking industry itself. One strategy involves increasing risks for traffickers, e.g., hardening the certainty and severity of criminal penalties for trafficking activities. Another option is the employment of civil strategies for making the industry less lucrative, e.g., using RICO-like laws to confiscate illegally gained trafficking profits. Strengthening monitoring and regulatory activities to combat the illegal sale and purchase of sexual or other trafficked labor through the Internet is an additional industry-weakening strategy. The pursuit of criminal and civil actions against customers and employers of trafficked labor may also help reduce demand—a critical component for a profitable industry.

Services for potential and actual victims of trafficking comprise another countering strategy. Awareness and education campaigns for vulnerable women and girls, would-be-migrants, and other susceptible groups could help reduce the trafficking supply. The provision of shelter, financial, and legal services to survivors of trafficking is not only humane, but also blunts the trafficking industry's predatory ability. Input from local communities is advised, as the targeting of such services to meet specific needs in particular places is critical to their effectiveness.

Finally, human trafficking relies on deeply-entrenched structural arrangements and cultural beliefs that oppress and divide human groups. Policies that better protect against poverty and inequality would, of course, be useful, as would stronger protections of the legal and civil rights of citizens and migration seekers alike. Campaigns to address elitist and discriminatory perceptions of particular groups of people as expendable commodities should be an integral part of any anti-trafficking effort.

References and further reading

Agustin, L. M. (2007) *Sex at the Margins: Migration, Labour Markets and the Rescue Industry*. London and New York: Zed Books.

Bales, K., Fletcher, L., and Stover, E. (2004) *Hidden Slaves: Forced Labor in the United States*. Berkeley, CA: Human Rights Center, September

Barry, K. (1995) *The Prostitution of Sexuality*. New York: New York University Press.

Belser, P. (2005) "Forced labour and human trafficking: Estimating the profits" Working paper 42, March. Geneva: International Labour Office.

Caldwell, G., Galster, S., and Steinzor, N. (1997) *Crime & Servitude: An Expose of the Traffic in Women for Prostitution from the Newly Independent States*. Washington, DC: Global Survival Network.

Case Watch (2003) www.atimes.com. Japan's mass rape and sexual enslavement of women and girls from (1932–45: The "comfort women" system, retrieved from Case Watch, www.cmht.con/casewatch/cases/cwcomfort2.htm.

Davidson, J. O'C. (2010) "New slavery, old binaries: Human trafficking and the borders of 'freedom'" *Global Networks: A Journal of Transnational Affairs* 10(2): 244–61.

Department of Homeland Security (2009) *Yearbook of Immigration Statistics 2009*. Washington DC, www.dhs.gov/xlibrary/assets/statistics/publications/ni_fr_2009.pdf.

Dinan, K. A. (2007) "Globalization and national sovereignty: From migration to trafficking." In S. Cameron and E. Newman (eds) *Trafficking in Humans: Social, Cultural and Political Dimensions*. New York: United Nations University Press, pp. 58–79.

Doezema, J. (2002) "Who gets to choose? Coercion, consent and the UN Trafficking Protocol" *Gender and Development* 10(1): 20–27.

Dujisin, Z. (2009) *Europe: More to Trafficking than Prostitution*. IPS Inter Press Service, www.ipsnews.net/asp?idnews=46980.

Farr, K. (2010) "No escape: Sexual violence against women and girls in central and eastern African armed conflicts" *Deportate, Esuli, Profuhe:Rivista Telematica di studi sulla memoria femminile* [*Deportees, Exiles, Refugees: Online journal of studies on women's memory*] 13–14: 85–112.

——(2005) *Sex Trafficking: The Global Market in Women and Children* [Contemporary social issues, series ed., George Ritzer]. New York: Worth. www.newesweek.com

Frederickson, C. and Leveille, V. (2007) "Eradicating slavery: Preventing the abuse, exploitation and trafficking of domestic workers by foreign diplomats and ensuring diplomat accountability. ACLU statement to the House Foreign Affairs Committee, A hearing on International Trafficking in persons: Taking Action to Eliminate Modern Day Slavery," Washington, DC, October 18.

Gallagher, A. and Holmes, P. (2008) "Developing an effective criminal justice response to human trafficking: Lessons from the front line" *International Criminal Justice Review* 18(3): 318–43.

Hughes, D. M. (2000) "The 'Natasha' trade: The transnational shadow market of trafficking in women" *Journal of International Affairs* 53(2): 625–51.

Hunt, S. (1998) "For east bloc women, a dearth of democracy" *International Herald Tribune* July 7.

International Labour Organization (2009) "The cost of coercion. Global Report under the follow-up to the ILO Declaration on Fundamental Principles and Rights at Work" International Labour Conference, Report IB, ILC, 98th session, Geneva.

Penttinen, E. (2008) *Globalization, Prostitution and Sex-trafficking: Corporeal Politics*. London: Routledge.

Ratha, D., Mohapatra, S., and Silwal, A. (2009) "Migration and Remittance Trends 2009" *Migration and Development Brief 11*, World Bank, November 3.

Thrupkaewe, N. (2009) "Beyond rescue" *The Nation* October 26: 21–4.

UNESCO Trafficking Statistics Project. (2009) www.unescobkk.org.

UNICEF. (2003) *Trafficking in Human Beings, Especially Women and Children in Africa.* Florence: UNICEF Innocenti Research Centre.

UNIFEM (United Nations Development Fund for Women) (2007) "Trafficking in women and girls" *Facts and Figures n VAW,* www.unifem.org/gender_issues/violence_against_women/facts_figures.php.

United Nations Office on Drugs and Crime (2009) "Executive summary" *Global Report on Trafficking in Persons,* February.

US Department of Justice (2009) *Attorney General's Annual Report to Congress and Assessment of US Government Activities to Combat Trafficking in Persons Fiscal Year 2008,* www.justice.gov/ag/annualreports/tr2008.

US Department of State (2009 and 2007) *Victims of Trafficking and Violence Protection Act: Trafficking in Persons Report 2009; Victims of Trafficking and Violence Protection Act: Trafficking in Persons Report 2007.* Washington, DC: Office to Monitor and Combat Trafficking in Persons.

Varia, N. (2010) *Slow Reform: Protection of Migrant and Domestic Workers in Asia and the Middle East.* Human Rights Watch, April. www.time.com.

Williams, P. (2008) "Trafficking in women: The role of transnational organized crime." In S. Cameron and E. Newman (eds), *Trafficking in Humans: Social, Cultural and Political Dimensions.* New York: United Nations University Press, pp. 126–57.

Part III
Immigrants in the economy

Economic factors are basic to international migration. Indeed, increasing one's standard of living or at least accessing a survival income is among the major motives for going abroad. While the goal of economic improvement motivates international migration, a sizeable body of research suggests that non-economic factors—including migrants' geographical and social location, demographic characteristics, and embeddedness in communal and family networks—shape it.

Employers and the host society more generally evaluate migrants in terms of their nationality, age, gender, race, language skills, legal status, and educational background as well as imputed cultural characteristics. Such appraisals often place migrants at an economic disadvantage as they compete with the native born. This is why migrants trained as doctors or engineers sometimes drive taxis or clean toilets in the point of settlement. Certain employers, however, prefer migrant workers over natives because they are believed to be harder working, more compliant or more accepting of low wages. Migrant workers endure wages and working conditions intolerable to natives because at least initially, their point of reference is to the country of origin, where circumstances are even worse.

In order to compensate for their disadvantages, migrant workers rely on various forms of cooperation—involving family members, co-nationals, and others—through which employment-related information and resources are shared. Such trust-based organizations allow migrants to control economic niches ranging from donut shops and jewelry stores to child care and construction work in numerous settings. Despite these collective achievements, the record shows that migrant communities are hardly immune from exploitation and abuse.

Aware of their disadvantages, immigrants often gravitate toward jobs that native workers find degrading, dangerous or poorly remunerated. At the same time, highly skilled immigrants command generous salaries, excellent working conditions and expedited residency status through their mastery of the advanced knowledge and education vital to high technology industries. Despite the generous rewards associated with such skills, young people in developed countries often eschew STEM (Science, Technology, Engineering, and Mathematics) fields. As a consequence, with government approval, leading universities offer the brightest international students scholarships, supplemented by the option of staying on to work after graduation. Because of the global demand for professional and technical workers, high tech industries and academic departments in many countries are characterized by an international workforce.

Hector Delgado's chapter on migrant workers and unions examines the history of relations between immigrant workers, unions, and employers. Noting that unions commonly regard immigrants as a threat to their control over jobs, wages, and working conditions, Delgado points out that employers and their political allies have long exploited this conflict in order to control the entire labor force.

At least since the era of Asian exclusion in the mid-1800s, racial and ethnic prejudice has inspired this "divide and rule" strategy in the USA, where only the most radical unions sought to organize racial minorities. European workers were sometimes accepted on the basis of the whiteness they shared with natives. However, during hard times, Hungarians, Italians, Russians, and others were also condemned.

Despite native workers' fears that cooperating with immigrants would be harmful to their interests, migrants, who were often immersed in cultures of solidarity, contributed much to the American labor movement. Recalling this record, Delgado points out that in recent years, the growing number of migrant workers, coupled with the decline of US union membership has stimulated efforts to organize migrants in service industries. (In fact, the professional associations to which many migration scholars belong have a recent record of relocated their annual conventions in order to support labor actions by immigrant-heavy service workers unions).

There were few migrant workers in Europe until the mid-twentieth century. However, unionists there tend to be more embedded in cultures of labor activism that are those in North America. Consequently, they are more open to organizing migrants. As Delgado concludes, in both the USA and Europe, union members increasingly realize that they can do little to regulate the presence of migrants. Further, legal restrictions against newcomers only reduce their wages and make organizing them more difficult. In contrast, when immigrants join local unions, the entire workforce stands to benefit.

Pyong Gap Min describes how ethnically defined middlemen minority groups—Jews in Medieval Europe and in US ghettos in first half of the twentieth century, Chinese in Southeast Asia, Armenians in the Middle East and Koreans in American cities from the 1970s through the 1990s—function as economic intermediaries between elites and masses, colonizers and the local population and between major corporations and minority consumers. Trading minorities often encounter hostility and develop ethnic solidarity among their members as a means of support. Min outlines the social conditions associated with enhanced or attenuated levels of conflict between dominant groups, middleman minorities, and low status consumers in contemporary societies.

Finally, Astrid Eich-Krohm's chapter reviews skilled migration. Beginning with the notion of brain drain, whereby developing societies were seen losing their most highly skilled workers to more affluent nations, she shows how multidisciplinary research has broadened our understanding of this phenomenon. The landscape has been changed by globalization, the increased power of multinational corporations, and various incentives extended by both states and employers to recruit a proficient labor force. Accordingly, a growing number of skilled workers now receive offers from localities beyond their initial point of settlement as well as the possibility of a subsidized return home.

Rather than focusing only on males, as has been customary in migration studies, Eich-Krohm asserts that women now play important roles in shaping the experience of skilled migrants, both as professionals in their own right, as well as important determinants of where and how family life will be conducted. Reflecting the transformations encountered by skilled migrants, she suggests that the *brain drain* terminology be replaced with the more open-ended moniker, *brain circulation*.

11

Unions and immigrants

Héctor L. Delgado

For well over a century, organized labor in the United States came down on the side of restriction in the immigration debate. But in 2000, the Executive Council of the AFL-CIO, the oldest and largest federation of labor unions in the United States, adopted a pro-immigrant resolution in favor of a new amnesty program for undocumented immigrants and the repeal of the employer sanctions provision of the Immigration Reform and Control Act (IRCA) of 1986. The shift was reflected in the AFL-CIO's and Change to Win's *The Labor Movement's Framework for Comprehensive Labor Reform* (2009), which included support for

> [a]n independent commission to assess and manage future flows, based on labor market shortages that are determined on the basis of actual need; a secure and effective worker authorization mechanism; rational operational control of the border; adjustment of status for the current undocumented population; and improvement, not expansion, of temporary worker programs, limited to temporary or seasonal, not permanent, jobs.

One critic of the AFL-CIO's shift is the labor economist Vernon M. Briggs, Jr. By focusing on the organization of immigrant workers, and thereby tying itself to immigrant causes, Briggs (2001) avers, the federation robs native workers of the only protection they have from unfair competition by the undocumented for low-skilled jobs. This issue is not unique to organized labor in the United States. Trade unions in Europe are confronted as well with the challenge of what to do about *and with* large numbers of immigrant workers in the labor market. This chapter focuses on and compares the relationship between labor unions and immigrants in the United States and Europe, beginning with and focusing principally on the US case.

The economic, political, and social climate in which unions are operating today in the United States is very different from the one in which the nascent labor movement operated in the nineteenth and for much of the twentieth centuries. Globalization and the virtually unfettered movement of capital and workers across borders has changed the playing field, and a growing local and international human rights movement, including advocacy groups for immigrants and workers in the United States and Europe, have emboldened immigrant workers and have pressured trade unions and states to adopt more relaxed immigration positions and policies. Unable to influence immigration policy and the enforcement of immigration laws effectively, organized labor in the United States has chosen to organize both documented and undocumented immigrants in order to reduce employers' incentive to hire them. Labor unions in several European countries have arrived at the same conclusion, but given the United States' unique immigration experience, the road has been a much longer one for the US labor movement.

Unions and Immigrants in the United States: survival over solidarity

In the late eighteenth century, the new republic generally welcomed immigrants. In a country that had just divested itself of British rule, there were many who believed that the United States should be a refuge for people fleeing tyranny. Furthermore, expansion and security required immigration. But the period was not completely free of fears and prejudices. All of the colonies denied the franchise and the right to hold office to Roman Catholics and Jews, and concerns about the immigration of paupers was widespread, as were fears among artisans about wage and price competition. Increasingly, industrialization was robbing artisans of their independence and control over the means of production, placing them in more direct competition with immigrant workers. Initially, artisans recognized that the "enemy" was not the immigrant, but rather capitalists and financiers, and they formed organizations to protect their interests. But in the face of the Panic of 1837 and the five-year depression that ensued, a rapidly growing nativist movement, mechanization and the de-skilling of work, and an expanding pool of unskilled labor, principally immigrant, solidarity gave way to survival and ethnic antagonism (Bonacich 1972; Lane 1987).

The second half of the nineteenth century and early twentieth century witnessed the rapid growth of the factory system and the demand for more and more labor that native workers alone could not meet. Immigrants would have to make up the difference, and they did. Industrialization created enormous wealth, but those who performed the backbreaking work in the factories saw relatively little of it. Workers recognized as they never had before that they had to organize and did so at a pace not previously seen. In city after city, labor organizations formed, including the Knights of Labor, whose membership exceeded 700,000 in the 1880s. Some of these organizations, including the Knights, were short lived, and they and others eventually affiliated with the American Federation of Labor (AFL). While the Knights of Labor was much more inclusive in its membership, the AFL, founded in 1886 and modeled after Britain's Trade Union Congress (TUC), focused on the skilled crafts. Most new immigrants were unskilled. Meanwhile, immigration into the United States in the decade of the 1880s nearly doubled from the previous decade, so that by 1890 the foreign-born population surpassed 9 million.

Unions' reluctance, immigrants' willingness

The AFL was slow to take up the fight for strong immigration restrictions, but in its 1897 convention adopted a resolution in support of a literacy test for immigrants, which found its way into the Immigration Act of 1917. In fact, the AFL-CIO supported, and in some cases helped to initiate, virtually every piece of restrictive immigration legislation passed in the first two decades of the twentieth century. In 1902 organized labor supported the reenactment of the Chinese Exclusion Act and in 1907 the "Gentleman's Agreement," designed to curb Japanese immigration. In 1905 in San Francisco, over 60 labor unions formed the Asiatic Exclusion League to restrict immigration from Asia for the "preservation of the Caucasian race upon American soil ... " (Takaki 1989: 201). In 1921, organized labor welcomed the passage of the Immigration and Naturalization Act (INA), enacted to curtail dramatically immigration from Eastern and Southern

Europe, and in 1924 the Johnson–Reed Act, which, in addition to reducing quotas even further, barred the immigration of "aliens" ineligible for citizenship. The national origins quota system established by the 1921 and 1924 acts, and the Immigration Act of 1917, guided immigration policy in the United States until 1952.

While the restrictive immigration reforms of the 1920s placed numerical quotas on European immigrants, they did not establish quotas on immigrants from Mexico. The literacy test and fees and taxes, however, made it more difficult for Mexicans to enter the country legally. Consequently, a growing number entered without the proper immigration credentials. This was a boon for employers who wanted cheap and disposable workers. As one foreman put it, "'When we want you. We'll call you; when we don't—git'" (McWilliams 1939, 125). During economic downturns, Mexican workers were pushed out, as they were during the Great Depression, but when the economy rebounded they were "welcomed" back. Meanwhile, little effort was made by the AFL to organize them. The federation's reluctance to organize these workers, however, did not prevent them from striking, sometimes with the help of communist labor organizations and organizers, but for the most part by forming their own organizations (Weber 1963; Jamieson 1976). Between 1933 and 1939, for example, California farms witnessed over 180 strikes (Maciel 1981). Mexican workers comprised the bulk of the strikers. Efforts by the Congress of Industrial Organizations (CIO) to organize Mexican workers were only marginally better than the AFL's, despite the fact that Mexican workers had demonstrated a high level of militancy and receptivity to unionization. This was true of European immigrants as well. Despite the mainstream labor movement's persistent attempts to exclude them, immigrants played an important role in organized labor's development.

Immigrants' contributions to the labor movement

Organized labor had its roots in previous immigrant communities and some of the most important early labor leaders were themselves immigrants or the children of immigrants. Among them were Samuel Gompers, the first president of the AFL, who was born in London and immigrated to the United States as a teenager, and Eugene Debs, a founder of the International Workers of the World (IWW) and the son of French immigrants. Prior to 1900 large numbers of skilled workers had immigrated to the United States with union experience. One example was English mill operatives from Lancashire who struck on several occasions during the 1870s in Fall River, Massachusetts. Skilled English immigrants brought with them labor organizing skills they had honed during a period of substantial union activity in England during the mid-1800s and tactics such as the creation of cooperatives to reduce living expenses, selective strikes, and levies on the wages of workers who continued to work during strikes. Some of these English craft unions were transplanted in the United States. In 1872, Illinois passed a mine safety statute as a result of a campaign by immigrant coal miners. Several of these miners' leaders, themselves immigrants from Staffordshire, helped form the American Miners' Association, the first national miners' union in the United States. English miners, in fact, played a prominent role in the formation of United Mine Workers of America. But English immigrants were not alone in this regard. In Chicago, for example, German immigrant workers, under the leadership of seasoned union activists from Germany, also formed trade unions (Bodnar 1985: 85–8).

Union membership increased dramatically at the end of the nineteenth century and the beginning of the twentieth, accompanied by a dramatic surge in immigration. In 1900, union membership was just below 1 million, but by 1915 exceeded 2.5 million. Meanwhile, nearly 450,000 immigrants arrived in 1900, but between 1905 and 1915 the number of immigrants entering the country averaged roughly a million a year (Table 11.1)

This called into question the assertion that immigrants had a dampening effect on union-ization; an assertion based in part on numerous instances in which high levels of immigration coincided with low levels of unionization. But as Hourwich (1922: 30) observed in his study of immigration, first published in 1912, "The fact is ... that the origin and growth of organized labor in the United States are contemporaneous with the period of 'new immigration,' and that the immigrants from Southern and Eastern Europe are the backbone of some of the strongest labor unions." Unions, in turn, played an important role in the "Americanization" of immigrants.

Unionization, Americanization, and whiteness

At the turn of the twentieth century, the process of "Americanization" was in full gear. Americanization was "a kind of crusade as employers, nationalist groups, and various state and federal agencies" attempted to remake immigrants in the American mold (Barrett 1992: 997). The process took place in many settings, including the workplace, where workers from different ethnic and racial groups labored side by side. When ethnic groups formed their own unions, as they did their own churches and fraternal and other organizations, the Americanization process was retarded. Racism, nativism, and chauvinism in the labor movement in the late 1800s and early 1900s had a similar effect. In explaining unionism to workers, organizers also had to explain the basic "values and ideas that gave the movement its rationale, its soul" (Barrett 1992: 1009). Foremost among these values were the freedoms of association and speech. And it was in labor unions that many immigrants learned not only that solidarity could be achieved across ethnic lines, but that it was *essential* if they were to improve their conditions of work.

Americanization often meant defining and protecting whiteness. The AFL more readily embraced eastern and southern Europeans than it did non-Europeans, conferring on them what Roediger (2005) calls an "inbetween" status. This unique status provided them with a foot in the door to "whiteness." Most AFL unions "were 'exclusionary by definition' and marshaled economic, and to a lesser extent political, arguments to exclude women, Chinese, Japanese, African Americans, the illiterate, the noncitizen, and the new immigrants from organized workplaces, and, whenever possible, from the shores of the United States" (Roediger 2005: 79). Citing work by Robert Lee (1999), Gwendolyn Mink (1990), and Andrew Neather (1993), Roediger (2005) argues that AFL campaigns to restrict immigration were not driven solely by economic concerns, but by racial ones as well. Opposition by craft unions to Chinese immigrants in the second half of the nineteenth century was especially pronounced and racist, but "much"

Table 11.1 Unionization rates and immigration to the United States

Year	Private sector union membership	Percentage of private sector employees	Immigration to the United States
1900	917,000	6.51	448,572
1901	1,167,000	7.70	487,918
1902	1,500,000	9.26	648,743
1903	1,908,000	11.47	857,046
1904	1,995,000	12.19	812,870
1905	1,923,000	11.07	1,026,499
1906–10	2,109,000	10.47	4,962,310
1911–15	2,508,000	12.23	4,457,831

Source: "US Private Sector Trade Union Membership" (2003) for the union figures and the Immigration and Naturalization Service (INS) for the immigration numbers.

of the same rhetoric "was fastened onto the Hungarian immigrant in the 1880s and then recycled in the AFL's campaign to restrict the 'new immigrant' generally over the next four decades" (Roediger 2005: 80).

Hungarians were referred to as "filthy Huns" in union trade union publications and pasta joined rice as an un-American and uncivilized food. Eugene Debs, also a founder of the American Railway Union, the first industrial union in the United States, said of Italians that they lived "far more like a wild beast than the Chinese" (Roediger 2005: 80). Another argument for restriction was the Russian Revolution and the rise of communism, in which eastern and southern Europeans were especially suspect. Changes in technology and the relations of production, and the availability of a large pool of unskilled workers, predominantly immigrant, eventually forced AFL unions to organize Italians, Slavs, and even the "filthy Huns." This, in turn, called for changes in the way unions organized, including the hiring of organizers from workers' ethnic groups. In Los Angeles today most unions that organize Latina/o immigrant workers have several, some a preponderance, of organizers who are Latinas/os.

Organizing immigrant workers

After WWII, and prior to its merger with the CIO in 1955, the AFL held to its restrictionist position on immigration, while the CIO adopted a more liberal one based largely on humanitarian grounds. The CIO, unlike the AFL, for example, called for the abolition of the national origins quota system. Stating the CIO's position, Walter Reuther said before a Senate committee in 1955, "'Our unions are open to all, and all are accorded equal treatment, equal rights, and equal opportunity,'" (Haus 2002: 71). After the merger, the AFL-CIO adopted a position more in line with the CIO's position prior to the merger, but was slow to organize immigrants initially, despite a steady decline in membership since the late 1950s, when nearly 40 percent of private sector workers were unionized. By 1980, slightly over 20 percent were unionized. This started to change in the 1980s, when the AFL-CIO, led by unions such as the Service Employees International Union (SEIU), started to form coalitions with immigrant advocacy groups, among them the National Immigration Forum, and to accelerate their efforts to organize undocumented immigrant workers. They had little choice.

Immigrant workers, especially in some cities and sectors of the economy, simply comprised a portion of the workforce too large for organized labor to ignore. In 2006, the number of foreign-born wage and salary workers was approaching 20 million, a nearly 66 percent increase from 1996. During the same period, their share of all wage and salary workers rose from 11 percent to 15 percent.

In 2006, 10.3 percent of foreign-born wage and salary workers were covered by a union contract, compared to 13.7 percent of their native-born counterparts (Table 11.2). While native-born workers are more likely to be unionized than immigrant workers, between 1996 and 2006 the number of native-born union workers declined 9 percent while foreign-born union workers increased 30 percent. In 1996 foreign-born workers made up 8.9 percent of workers covered by a union contract, by 2007 it had risen to 12.1 percent (Table 11.2). However, the proportion of union members among both foreign- and native-born workers both declined between 1996 and 2006 (Velma Fan and Batalova 2007). The labor movement in the United States recognizes that its ability to make up lost ground rests in some, if not considerable, measure on its ability to organize immigrant workers. As Ruth Milkman (2000: 1) observes, " ... recruiting immigrants is an increasingly urgent imperative for the besieged labor movement."

The economic downturn that began in earnest in 2007 stalled modest gains in union membership. The percent of workers unionized in 2009 was 12.3 percent, a 0.1 percent drop from

Table 11.2 Foreign-born workers and native-born workers covered by a union contract by nativity among union-represented workers 1996–2007

	Foreign-born wage and salary workers	Native-born wage and salary workers	Foreign-born wage and salary workers	Native-born wage and salary workers
1996	13.6	16.5	8.9	91.1
1997	13.1	16.0	9.4	90.6
1998	12.1	15.8	9.1	90.9
1999	12.6	15.6	9.7	90.3
2000	12.0	15.3	10.3	89.7
2001	12.0	15.2	10.6	89.4
2002	11.4	15.1	10.3	89.7
2003	11.3	14.8	11.5	88.5
2004	10.8	14.4	11.4	88.6
2005	11.1	14.1	12.2	87.8
2006	10.3	13.7	12.1	87.9

Source: Adapted from Tables 1 and 2 in 'Foreign-Born Wage and Salary Workers in the US Labor Force and Unions' by Velma Fan and Batalova (2007).

the previous year, but the number of wage and salary workers belonging to unions was 15.3 million or 771,000 fewer members than the previous year. Another 1.6 million workers, half of whom are government workers, are covered by a union contract. But even the 12.3 percent is misleading, since, despite employing fewer workers than the private sector, 7.9 million of 15.3 million union members in 2009 were employed in the public sector. The rate for private industry was 7.2 percent compared to 37.4 percent in the public (*Bureau of Labor Statistics*). The task for organized labor is a formidable one, especially in the private sector, but if recent attacks on public-sector unions by Republican governors and legislators are any indication, organized labor in the United States will be engaged in a fight for survival on both fronts.

Union campaigns

In some parts of the country, organized labor took up the task of organizing the undocumented before the AFL-CIO announced its new policy. In *New Immigrants, Old Unions: Organizing Undocumented Workers in Los Angeles*, I provide an in-depth deviant case analysis of one of these campaigns in the mid-1980s, in which the International Ladies Garment Workers Union (ILGWU) organized a factory in which virtually its entire workforce was undocumented (Delgado 1993). Milkman's (2000) edited volume, *Organizing Immigrants,* contains in-depth analyses of other campaigns in the Los Angeles area prior to 2000. These campaigns revealed unions' desire and willingness to change in order to organize immigrant workers, immigrants' receptivity to unionization, and the difficulties, not entirely unique to immigrant workers, entailed in organizing them.

Perhaps the best known and heralded of these campaigns was the Justice for Janitors (JFJ) campaign orchestrated by the Service Employee's International Union (SEIU) in 1990. But there were others. Miriam Wells's study of the Hotel Employees and Restaurant Employees International Union (HERE) in San Francisco found that immigrant workers in the city's hotel industry were receptive to unionization and the local in turn reshaped its practices and programs to organize them. HERE was among the first unions to target immigrant workers, in part, because of the rapidly changing demographics of the work force in the industry over the previous 20 years. Between 1970 and 1990, for example, the immigrant share of cooks increased from 43 percent to 77 percent, food preparers from 67 percent to 80 percent, and room cleaners, who comprise 27 percent of all hotel workers, from 15 percent to 85 percent (Wells 2000: 116–17).

In the same volume, Carol Zabin (2000) analyzes a successful organizing campaign in the Los Angeles area by the International Association of Machinists and Aerospace Workers (IAM) of an overwhelmingly immigrant workforce at American Racing Equipment Company which resulted in a contract in 1991. Highlighting the militancy of the immigrant workers and the role played by their strong social and family ties, Zabin underscores the substantial commitment in resources by the IAM. A year later, drywallers, the vast majority of them immigrants, waged a successful campaign in southern California. In November of 1992 the Pacific Rim Drywall Association (PRDA), an organization of drywall firms north of San Diego ratified a union contract with drywall workers. But as Milkman and Wong (2000) observe, San Diego's residential drywall industry remained steadfastly nonunion and the campaign did not lead to the level of organizing that some hoped this campaign, American Racing, and the Justice for Janitors campaigns would spur. While organizing them was possible, it was not easy, and it would not get any easier.

The undocumented and the law

The majority of people in the United States want the federal government to control the country's borders, especially after 9/11. Business and the state generally have resisted calls for more restrictions, although there have been exceptions. Employers seek to reduce their costs and increase profits; and cheap, more malleable, unskilled, and semi-skilled immigrant workers, in a union-free environment, allow them to do this more easily. The federal government's reluctance to enact more restrictive immigration and worker protection legislation, like the Employer Free Choice Act (EFCA), strengthens employers' hands and weakens labor's. Unions have all but given up on closing the border, but are now trying to make undocumented immigrant workers less attractive to employers by advocating for strong worker protections for *all* workers, including the undocumented. This was at the crux of a case in Alabama in the late 1980s.

In *Patel v. Sumani Corp., Inc.*, a judge in Alabama ruled in 1987 that undocumented workers were *not* protected by the Fair Standards Labor Act (FLSA), contending that by protecting them it would encourage them to cross the border illegally. The following year, in *Patel v. Quality Inn South* (1988), the 11th circuit court reversed the decision, noting that by not protecting them, the result would be an increase in both the demand for and supply of these workers. Furthermore, the Supreme Court of the United States in 1984 had ruled in *Sure-Tan, Inc. v. NLRB* that undocumented workers were "employees" under the National Labor Relations Act (NLRA) and therefore entitled to *employee* protections. In 2002, however, in *Hoffman Plastic Compounds, Inc. v. NLRB* (2002), the conservative majority on the Supreme Court ruled that undocumented workers were not entitled to back pay remedies under the NLRA. The ruling did not deny undocumented workers wages for work performed, but rather wages they *would have earned* had they not been fired illegally, a remedy applied many times in the past by the NLRB. The majority based its decision principally on what it claimed was a contradiction between immigration and labor law.

Writing for the majority, Chief Justice Rehnquist observed that when *Sure-Tan* was decided in 1984 it was not illegal to hire undocumented workers, but that changed with IRCA two years later. IRCA required employers to verify applicants' eligibility to work and to fire individuals they discovered were not authorized to work in the United States. Employers who knowingly employed undocumented workers were subject to penalties. On the other hand, the

Chief Justice noted, workers who used fraudulent documents to obtain work also were violating federal law. There was no question that the worker in question used fraudulent documents to obtain work. The majority reasoned that awarding him back pay would subvert the policies underlying the IRCA; policies the NLRB had "no authority to enforce or administer." Consequently, the Court held that the award lay "beyond the bounds of the Board's remedial discretion." Awarding the undocumented worker back pay, the Court held, "would have unduly trenched upon explicit statutory prohibitions critical to federal immigration policy, as expressed in the IRCA." Furthermore, the Court noted that the NLRB could not impose punitive remedies on employers. It could only compensate individuals harmed, but, technically, Rehnquist wrote, the worker in this case could not be harmed because he was in the country illegally. There was no reason to believe, Rehnquist added, that Congress wanted someone who used false documents to receive back pay. But the legislative history of the IRCA and a section in IRCA appropriating funds to enforce the law on behalf undocumented workers "in order to deter the employment of unauthorized aliens and remove the economic incentive for employers to exploit and use such aliens," suggests rather strongly, contrary to Rehnquist's assertion, that it was not Congress' intent to limit undocumented workers' labor law protections.

While union and immigration activists were relieved that the *Hoffman* decision did not change the designation of undocumented workers as "employees" under the NLRA, this designation and the protection that accompanied it would not have any teeth without the back pay remedy. In fact, in his dissent, Justice Breyer argued that by not penalizing the employer more severely, there was little disincentive to hire undocumented workers—and this, in turn, did more to undermine immigration policy than a back pay remedy. Breyer wrote, "As *all* the relevant agencies (including the Department of Justice) have told us, the National Labor Relations Board's limited backpay order will *not* interfere with the implementation of immigration policy. Rather, it reasonably helps to deter unlawful activity that *both* labor laws *and* immigration laws seek to prevent." He then added that without back pay in its arsenal of remedies, "employers could conclude that they can violate the labor laws at least once with impunity." Breyer reminded his colleagues that the Court in *Sure-Tan* recognized the need to protect undocumented workers in order to make them less attractive to employers. A back pay award, Breyer continued, did not serve as a magnet of any significance, "for so speculative a future possibility could not realistically influence an individual's decision to migrate illegally." In *Hoffman*, immigration law trumped labor law, despite the fact that the enforcement of both is not only possible, but, arguably, *necessary* if the desired result is to discourage employers from hiring undocumented workers. While *Hoffman* may weaken unions' ability to organize undocumented workers, it has done little to stem the flow of undocumented immigrants crossing the border, as has an "enforcement-only" policy at the border.

The failure of an enforcement-only border policy

In a critique of comprehensive immigration reform and an "enforcement only" approach to immigration reform, Hinojosa-Ojeda (2010: 3) observes that declines in authorized immigration to the United States from Mexico have occurred only during economic downturns, as they have in the last two years, adding that "declining birth rates in Mexico will likely accomplish what tens of billions of dollars in border enforcement clearly have not: a reduction in the supply of migrants from Mexico who are available for jobs in the United States." Between 1990 and 2008, the number of undocumented workers in the United States has more than tripled, from an estimated 3.5 million to an estimated 11.9 million, *while at the same time* the Border Patrol's budget has increased 714 percent and the cost per apprehension has increased from $272 in 1992 to $3102 in

2008. As many as 98 percent of unauthorized immigrants keep trying until they make it, but not as many try when the jobs on the US side of the border dry up, as has been the case since 2007. During the recession, the number of undocumented immigrants crossing the border has actually decreased (Hinojosa-Ojeda 2010).

Enforcement-only border policies have had the unintended consequences of making the border more dangerous, especially for undocumented immigrants, and the people-smuggling business even more lucrative. According to the American Civil Liberties Union of San Diego and Imperial Counties and Mexico's National Commission of Human Rights, an estimated 5600 immigrants lost their lives crossing the border between 1994 and 2000 (Hinojosa-Ojeda 2010). The border enforcement strategy adopted after the passage of IRCA in 1986 is one that Massey *et al.* (2002) contend has not only *not* achieved the goal of deterring undocumented immigration, it has also yielded unforeseen negative consequences for people on both sides of the border. These policies, they contend, "have had less to do with stopping undocumented migrants than with pushing them into remote sectors of the border where they will be neither seen nor heard, and most important, where they will not be videotaped" (Massey *et al.* 2002: 106). There are other unintended consequences as well.

The more difficult it becomes to cross the border without the required documents, the more dispersed the points of entry, therefore converting a regional problem into a national one, and the more permanent this workforce becomes because of growing fears of apprehension at the border. Instead of risking apprehension and other dangers by crossing the border repeatedly, immigrants increasingly settle on the northern side of the border (Massey *et al.* 2002). This, in turn, means an increase in the number of family members coming to join their spouses, siblings, grandparents, children, and grandchildren, whom they would not see as frequently as they did when the border posed fewer risks. This also increases the number of unemployed undocumented immigrants.

Another consequence of these policies, and one especially important to organized labor, has been a lowering of wages paid to the undocumented, which employers justify by pointing to risks and costs they incur as a consequence of these policies. The tendency toward permanent settlement, however, is a boon for organized labor, if it wants to take advantage of it. Once a worker decides to stay indefinitely, the worker is more receptive to unionization overtures. In Europe, immigrants, including undocumented immigrants, increasingly are settling and becoming permanent fixtures in the workforce, thereby presenting organized labor in these countries with some of the same opportunities as and challenges facing organized labor in the United States.

Immigrants and unions in Europe

With minor exceptions, Western European countries did not become importers of labor until the 1950s, a century after the United States opened its doors to millions of foreign workers. Trade unions in Western Europe feared, as did their counterparts in the United States, that immigrant workers would drive down wages and depreciate working conditions. At the same time, they recognized the demand for foreign labor, especially in some sectors of the economy. The response initially was a system of temporary employment, in part, to prevent industries that relied heavily on immigrant workers from outsourcing their work. Many of these workers returned home, but as the United States saw at the turn of the century, many more remained and became "a structural part of the West European labour markets" (Pennix and Roosblad 2000: 5). They formed their own communities, with their own organizations, just as European and Mexican immigrants at the turn of the twentieth century in the United States had done, and this infrastructure and social ties made it easier for others to follow and stay.

With settlement, and the passage of time, immigrants became part of new networks that not only made it easier for them to find work, but also, as noted earlier, for unions to organize them. Within a relatively short period of time, they no longer compared themselves to others in their homeland, but rather to workers in their *new* home. "The shift from temporary migration to permanent settlement," as Piore (1979: 109) observes in his classic *Birds of Passage*, "implies a fundamental change in perspective, which has repercussions in political and other forms of organizations." I found clear evidence of this in my own study of the unionization of undocumented workers in Los Angeles. This change in perspective was welcomed by labor unions, since the new comparisons changed expectations and contributed to a growing dissatisfaction among these workers which they could, and did, tap.

While labor unions in the nineteenth century in the United States opted rather quickly to turn a cold shoulder to immigrant workers, European trade unions initially were friendlier, in part because of a widely held ideological belief that a labor movement must attend to the needs of *all* workers (regardless of borders). In the end, however, organized labor in Europe chose practicality over solidarity as well. As Pennix and Roosblad (2000: 187) observe, "although trade unions may commit themselves verbally in varying degrees to the international solidarity of all workers, the dominant frame of reference is that of the nation state and the national arena." During the Cold War especially, any talk of international solidarity smacked of communism. The rebuilding effort after the war "demanded" *national*, not international solidarity (including solidarity between workers, employers, and the state). But organized labor in Europe, and in the United States, discovered that they could do little to prevent immigrants from entering their respective countries, principally because of the demand for their labor by politically powerful employers. Once they were here and as their numbers grew, organized labor could not afford to ignore them.

Inclusion over exclusion

In a comparison of France and the United States, Haus (2002) analyzed why unions in these two countries changed their positions on immigration. Immediately following the end of World War II (WWII), the French labor federation *Confédération Générale du Travail* (CGT) supported restrictive immigration policies. By the end of the century, the CTG and AFL (prior to its merger with the CIO) had changed their positions in the face not only of the internationalization of labor markets, but also a new international human rights regime that "called into question the ability and/or right of the state to fully control migration" (Haus 2002: 156). Restriction, in the eyes of organized labor, seemed ineffective or undesirable, or both, under these conditions, so it opted for the carrot over the stick. In her study of immigration and unions in France, Italy, and Spain, Watts (2002) arrives at a similar conclusion, and observes that, unlike unions in the United States, unions in these countries have been able to influence immigration policy in favor of a more relaxed border for legal immigration and legislation protecting immigrant workers. Unions in the United States are now attempting to do the same.

For organized labor in Europe and the United States, then, as immigrant worker numbers swelled and immigrant workers' propensity to settle increased, the question turned increasingly from how to keep them out to whether they should organize and extend to them the same rights and protections enjoyed by native workers. Owen Tudor (2010), Head of the TUC's European Union and International Relations Department, wrote in a recent blog, "Attempts to close the border and crack down on illegal immigrants don't work. What is needed, instead, is to ensure that everyone working in the US is treated fairly, and migrants should be offered a path to citizenship so that they don't disappear into the informal economy. This is pretty much the same prescription as the TUC and others have advocated for the UK." Union leaders on both sides of the Atlantic ultimately chose to organize immigrant workers, including the undocumented, and clearly globalization was a pivotal factor (Haus 2002; Watts 2002).

States' capacity to regulate immigration has become extremely difficult with the onset of globalization, given the demand for immigrant workers in labor-intensive sectors of developed countries' economies and the social networks that facilitate both documented *and undocumented* immigration. Furthermore, if unions push for or otherwise support restrictive and punitive immigration policies, they place themselves at odds with the very workers they are trying to organize. Only by organizing them can they prevent them from undercutting wages and working conditions, and avoid deepening a divide between native and immigrant workers that employers can exploit. "In fact, many labor leaders in Western Europe and the United States have come to believe that restrictive policies do little more than force immigrants into a precarious legal and economic position, which ultimately undermines the wages and working conditions of all workers" (Watts 2002: 2). If they are correct, then the rising tide of anti-immigrant sentiment in Europe, fueled by fears of "creeping Islamification" in a continent where many of the new immigrants are Muslim, is not good news for organized labor.

Rising anti-immigrant tide

In the last two years an anti-immigrant party in Sweden won seats for the first time, Britain's new prime minister is moving on his pledge to restrict immigration and increasingly workers are demanding "British jobs for British workers," France is "repatriating" Romas and attempting to ban burqas, surveys show that Germans would seriously consider supporting a new party promising to be tougher on immigrants and Chancellor Merkel proclaimed that multiculturalism had "utterly failed" in Germany, Italy's anti-immigrant Northern League has made substantial electoral gains recently, and in the Netherlands the anti-immigrant Freedom Party made strong gains in June of 2010 (Reuters 2010). Immigrants are convenient scapegoats during economic downturns, but in Europe, at least, economic growth requires immigrant workers. As the head of the Parisian international migration unit of the Organization for Economic Cooperation said to *Bloomberg News* reporter Gregory Viscusi (2010), "If you look beyond the noise, you don't hear anyone saying there shouldn't be any immigration at all. They can't. Parts of the economy would grind to a halt." Europe's low population growth rate, coupled with a rapidly aging citizenry, *requires* a substantial infusion of immigrants to satisfy labor needs. As Leiden University's Costica Dumbrava (2008) aptly put it, "Rather than accepting immigration or rejecting it, the question is how to manage it, how to design proper policy frameworks to make full advantage of its benefits and to avoid its main risks."

Some of the measures being proposed to manage immigration are familiar to students of immigration in the United States and are likely to be equally successful, which is to say not very. Chancellor Merkel may have sensed at least this much when she said to young members of the Christian Democratic Party, "Now they live with us and we lied to ourselves for a while, saying that they won't stay and that they will have disappeared again one day. That's not the reality." The dilemma is an old one. How do you exploit the labor of foreigners and at the same time withhold from them political and other rights and maintain cultural purity. Benjamin Franklin said of the Germans ("Palantine Boors"), "Why should Pennsylvania, founded by the English, become a Colony of Aliens, who will shortly be so numerous as to Germanize us instead of our Anglifying them, and will never adopt our Language or Customs ... " In the more recent past, white South Africans created homelands, or *bantustans*, where blacks could enjoy rights denied to them by the apartheid regime in white areas where their labor was essential. And it was the hope of some, if not many employers and politicians in the United States that Mexico would serve as a kind of *bantustan* to which Mexican workers would eventually return after laboring north of the Rio Grande (Burawoy 1976). But they didn't always return to their homeland and with time fewer and fewer did—and even fewer when the border became more dangerous and difficult to cross. They are here to stay, as are immigrants (and their children) in Europe; and as long as they are here, organized labor has opted more often than not, and with little choice, to try organize them.

Conclusion

On May Day in 2006, millions of immigrants, many of them undocumented, marched in numerous cities across the United States to protest a bill making its way through Congress criminalizing them and anyone helping them. Many of these immigrants worked in low-wage industries and jobs, where unionization rates, even during good times for organized labor were low. In unions' stead a growing number of worker centers have been formed in the United States to address the needs of these workers and their families. In 1992 there were only five centers in the country, but by 2006 there were 140 worker centers in 80 different cities, towns, and rural areas (Fine 2006). These centers reached out to unions. Unions' response, tepid at first, improved with the creation of a partnership between the AFL-CIO and the National Day Laborer Organizing Network (NDLON), the largest association of worker centers in the country. NDLON's Executive Director observed, "I don't think it's possible to do it without labor's participation. Community organizations had been pushing hard before the AFL-CIO decided to join, but I felt it was an impossible task; when the AFL-CIO got in it became real" (Gallagher 2010: 4). In the final analysis, however, workers' centers cannot get for immigrant workers what labor unions have managed to get for workers for generations. Workers' fortunes are much more likely to improve with a revived labor movement. And short of unlikely immigration reform that seals the border and repatriates immigrants, a revival depends substantially on organized labor's ability to organize immigrant workers.

Unions in most of Europe and the United States recognize that there is little they can do to regulate immigration, but they can organize immigrants. As long as a demand exists for the labor of immigrants, and the demand especially in Europe is indisputably substantial, they will come; and the more difficult it becomes to cross a border, the more likely it is that they will settle. The rising anti-immigrant tide and increase in racial fears and hatred in the United States and Europe, and a temporary decrease in the demand for immigrant labor, may result in a reduction in international migration. Another consequence, and one especially detrimental to unions, is that undocumented workers will be driven further underground and become much more difficult to organize. In this scenario, the principal losers will be workers and labor unions.

References and further reading

AFL-CIO and Change to Win (2009) *The Labor Movement's Framework for Comprehensive Labor Reform.* www.aflcio.org/issues/civilrights/immigration/upload/immigrationreform041409.pdf.
Barrett, J. R. (1992) "Americanization from the bottom up: Immigration and the remaking of the working class in the United States, 1880–1930" *The Journal of American History* 79(3): 996–1020.
Bodnar, J. (1985) *The Transplanted: A History of Immigrants in Urban America.* Bloomington, IN: Indiana University Press.
Bonacich, E. (1972) "A theory of ethnic antagonism: The split labor market," *American Sociological Review* 37(5): 547–59.
Briggs Jr., V. M. (2001) *Immigration and American Unionism.* Ithaca, NY: Cornell University Press.

Burawoy, M. (1976) "The functions and reproduction of migrant labor: Comparative material from Southern Africa and the United States" *The American Journal of Sociology* 81(5): 1050–87.

Delgado, H. L. (1993) *New Immigrants, Old Unions: Organizing Undocumented Workers in Los Angeles*. Philadelphia, PA: Temple University Press.

Dumbrava, C. (2008) "Labour immigration policy in Europe? What kind?" *Network Migration in Europe*. www.migrationedution.org.

Fine, J. (2006) "Finding a place for immigrant workers in today's labor movement." www.afl-cio.org/mediacenter/speakout/janice_fine.cfm (accessed 2010).

Gallagher, T. (2010) (February) "A more perfect union: Organized labor's critical role in comprehensive immigration reform." Sebastopol, CA: Grantmakers Concerned with Immigrants and Refugees. www.gcir.org/publications/gcirpubs/union.

Haus, L. (2002) *Unions, Immigration, and Internationalization: New Challenges and Changing Coalitions in the United States and France*. New York: Palgrave Macmillan.

Hinojosa-Ojeda, R. (2010) "Raising the floor for American workers: The economic benefits of comprehensive immigration reform" Center for American Progress, American Immigration Council (January).

Hoffman Plastic Compounds, Inc. v. NLRB. (2002) 122 S. Ct. 1275.

Hourwich, I. A. (1922) *Immigration and Labor: The Economic Aspects of European Immigration to the United States*. New York: G. P. Putnam's Sons.

Jamieson, S. (1976) *Labor Unionism in American Agriculture*. New York: Arno Press.

Lee, R. G. (1999) *Orientals: Asian Americans in Popular Culture*. Philadelphia, PA: Temple University Press.

Lane, A. T. (1987) *Solidarity or Survival? American Labor and European Immigrants, 1830–1924*. New York: Greenwood Press.

Maciel, D. (1981) *La Clase Obrera en la Historia de Mexico: al norte del rio bravo (pasado inmediato) (1930–1981)*. Mexico: Siglo Veintiuno Editores.

Massey, D. S., Durand, J., and Malone, N. J. (2002) *Beyond Smoke and Mirrors: Mexican Immigration in an Era of Economic Integration*. New York: Russell Sage Foundation.

McWilliams, C. (1939) *Factories in the Field: The Story of Migratory Farm Labor in California*. Boston, MA: Little, Brown and Company.

Milkman, R. (ed.). (2000) *Organizing Immigrants: The Challenge for Unions in Contemporary California*. Ithaca, NY: Cornell University Press.

Milkman, R. and Wong, K. (2000) "Organizing the wicked city: The 1992 Southern California Drywall Strike." In R. Milkman (ed.), *Organizing Immigrants: The Challenge for Unions in Contemporary California*, Ithaca, NY: Cornell University Press, pp. 169–98.

Mink, G. (1990) *Old Labor and New Immigrants in American Political Development: Union, Party and State, 1875–1920*. Ithaca, NY: Cornell University Press.

Neather, A. (1993) "Popular Republicanism, Americanism and the Roots of Anti-Communism, 1890–1925" (Ph.D. dissertation, Duke University).

Patel v. Quality Inn South. (1988) 846 F.2d 700 (eleventh circuit court).

Papel v. Sumani Corp., Inc. (1987) 660 F.Supp. 1528 (N.D. Ala.).

Penninx, R. and Roosblad J. (2000) "Introduction" and "Conclusion." In R. Penninx and J. Roosblad (eds), *Trade Unions, Immigration, and Immigrants in Europe, 1960–1993: A Comparative Study of the Attitudes and Actions of Trade Unions in Seven West European Countries*. New York: Berghahn Books, pp. 1–19, 183–211.

Piore, M. J. (1979) *Birds of Passage: Migrant Labor and Industrial Societies*. Cambridge: Cambridge University Press.

Reuters (2010) "Factbox: Immigration Backlash Spreads in Europe." September 19. http://uk.reuters.com/article/2010/09/19/uk-europe-immigrants-idUKTRE68I2ER20100919.

Roediger, D. R. (2005) *Working Toward Whiteness: How America's Immigrants Became White*. New York: Basic Books.

Sure-Tan, Inc. v. NLRB. (1984) 467 US 883, 81 L. Ed. 2d 732, 104 S. Ct. 2803.

Takaki, R. (1989) *Strangers from a Different Shore: A History of Asian Americans*. Boston, MA: Little, Brown & Company.

Tudor, O. (2010) "Immigration: what makes it work" *Touch Stone* (January 12). www.touchstoneblog.org.uk/2010/01/immigration-what-makes-it-work.

"US Private Sector Trade Union Membership" (2003) The Public Purpose, Labor Market Reporter. www.publicpurpose.com/lm-unn2003.htm

Velma Fan, C. and Batalova, J. (2007) "Foreign-born wage and salary workers in the US labor force and unions" Migration Information Source, Migration Policy Institute (MPI) (August 28).

Viscusi, G. (2010) "Illegal immigrant inconvenient truth shows few dispensable" Bloomberg (October 13). www.bloomberg.com/news/2010-10-13/illegal-immigrants-inconvenient-truth-shows-no-nation-can-do-without-them.html.

Watts, J. R. (2002) *Immigration Policy and the Challenge of Globalization: Unions and Employers in Unlikely Alliance.* Ithaca, NY: Cornell University Press.

Weber, D. A. (1973) "The organizing of Mexicano agricultural workers: Imperial Valley, and Los Angeles 1928–34, An oral history approach" *Aztlan* 3: 307–47.

Wells, M. J. (2000) "Immigration and unionization in the San Francisco hotel industry." In R. Milkman (ed.), *Organizing Immigrants: The Challenge for Unions in Contemporary California.* Ithaca, NY: Cornell University Press, pp. 109–29.

Zabin, C. (2000) "Organizing Latino workers in the Los Angeles manufacturing sector: The case of American racing equipment." In R. Milkman (ed.), *Organizing Immigrants: The Challenge for Unions in Contemporary California.* Ithaca, NY: Cornell University Press, pp. 150–68.

12

Middleman entrepreneurs

Pyong Gap Min

When two or more ethnic/racial groups live together in a society, they have almost always maintained ethnic stratification. The dominant group has controlled subordinate minority groups, both politically and socioeconomically. Social scientists interested in ethnic and race relations have recognized that certain alien groups have played an intermediary role in host societies between the dominant group and subordinate minorities. They use the concept "middleman minorities" or "middleman entrepreneurs" to characterize these minorities' inter-mediate economic role, bridging what they call the "status gap" in particular societies. Since the 1960s, the concept has been popularly used in the social science literature (Rinder 1958–59; Blalock 1967: 79–84; Eitzen 1971; Loewen 1971; Bonacich 1973; Zenner 1991).

The literature has often cited the following groups as typical cases of middleman minorities: Jews in the Medieval Europe, Poland, and other Eastern European countries before World War II, and in the United States in the first half of the twentieth century; Chinese in Southeast Asian countries (Vietnam, the Philippines, Thailand, and Malaysia); Indians in West and South Africa; Parsees and Jains in the caste-ridden Hindu India; Christian Armenians in the Middle East; Scots in the British Isles; and Koreans in the United States during the 1970s through 1990s. The literature also shows that middlemen entrepreneurs exhibit the following three characteristics that mutually influence one another: (1) concentration in trade and other types of occupations involving the intermediary economic role such as money-lending, (2) subjection to host hostility, and (3) ethnic solidarity. This essay examines historical cases of middleman minorities, their central characteristics, and the major causal factors contributing to this minority adaptation based on a literature review.

The status gap and the intermediary economic role

The idea of the middleman minority can be found in the original writings of Weber (1952), Simmel (cited in Cahnman 1974), Becker (1950), and other classical theorists. In particular, Becker coined the term "middleman minority" (Zenner 1991: 7). These classical writers con-sidered Jews and other trading minorities as representative of a pre-modern form of capitalism because their enterprises depended upon ethnic and family ties. Although they found many parallels in cultural characteristics of such middleman minorities as the Jews in Medieval Europe and Chinese in Southeast Asian countries, a shared social position or similar social status is a more important cause of their middleman minority adaptation than their cultural characteristics.

Rinder's (1958) article published in *Social Problems* was the first major sociological work that emphasized the status gap in the host society as the central factor for middleman minority adaptations of various groups in different societies. He argued that trading minorities, such as Jews in the Medieval Europe and the Chinese in Southeast Asia, historically existed in societies characterized by the status gap. Rinder (1958) said "The status gap is economically dysfunctional in terms of maximum economic rationality. It impedes the flow of goods and services by imposing an arbitrary barrier of social distance between segments of the same society" (p. 254). In other words, the ruling group needed to bring an alien group for the purpose of distributing goods and services to the masses, since there was no intermediate group in these societies that would bridge the status and economic gaps.

In the 1960s, sociologists studying ethnic and racial stratification (Shibutani and Kwan 1966: 191–97; Blalock 1967: 79–84) devoted several pages to middleman minorities. They too considered the status gap in the host society as the main determining factor for the middleman minority pattern. Social scientists and historians have further clarified the characteristics of middleman minorities since the 1960s (Eitzen 1971; Loewen 1971; Bonacich 1973; Bonacich and Modell 1980; Turner and Bonacich 1980; Sengstock 1982; Zenner 1982, 1991; Min 1996, 2008). These studies have indicated that middleman merchant minorities existed in two types of societies. First, middleman minorities developed in pre-industrial agrarian societies, such as Medieval Europe and pre-war Poland, where a small number of the ruling class controlled the consuming masses with no middle class to bridge them (Eitzen 1971; Zenner 1991). Second, they existed in colonized societies where the colonial ruling group did not want to give economic power to the native population. The ruling groups brought alien minorities to specialize in commerce to bridge them and the consuming masses. For example, the Chinese focused on internal trade in the Spanish-controlled Philippines (Wickberg 1965; Eitzen 1971) while Indians specialized in businesses in South Africa and West African countries (Tinker 1973; Moodley 1980).

In contrast, the United States population in the second half of the twentieth century was predominantly middle class. Thus a typical middleman minority was not likely to develop in the society. However, Rinder (1958) suggested that the United States might need a middleman minority to bridge the huge white–black racial status gap, and pointed out that in "the urban Negro ghettoes, Jews have been prominent in venturing into this gap to service the commercial needs, even as they did for the medieval peasant" (p. 257). Later, Loewen (1971) tried to explain the concentration of Chinese immigrants in the Mississippi Delta in the black-oriented grocery business based on the white–black status gap. He argued that because of the racial status gap before 1960, few white people were willing to operate grocery stores in black neighborhoods and that this social structure provided Chinese immigrants with an opportunity for the grocery business in the black community.

Sengstock (1982) described Iraqi Christians in Detroit as middleman merchants serving black neighborhoods with grocery items. Min (1996) extensively examined Korean immigrants' active business involvement in black neighborhoods in New York and Los Angeles in the 1980s and early 1990s, using the middleman minority perspective. In his view, structural factors in lower income black neighborhoods, such as high crime rates and the lower spending capacity of the residents, discouraged corporations and white independent business owners from investing there. This provided opportunities for many Korean immigrants to run retail businesses, such as grocery, produce, and clothing stores, in black neighborhoods.

About 15 years later, Min (2008: Chapter 5) tried to explain Korean retail store owners' experiences of black boycotts in New York City, using the serial middleman minority theory.

In his view, unlike in colonized or pre-industrial agrarian societies, the American middleman immigrant group can achieve the intergenerational social mobility, moving into the mainstream economy. Thus a newer disadvantaged immigrant group continues to replace the earlier middle-man group concentrating in retail businesses in black neighborhoods. In the process of ethnic succession, Korean immigrants replaced Jews and Italians as middleman merchants in the 1980s, and in turn, Koreans were replaced by more recent immigrant groups, such as Indians and Pakistanis during the early 1990s. Min's ethnographic research in lower income black neighborhoods in New York City showed that other immigrant groups, such as South Asians, Middle Easterners, and African/Caribbean black immigrants, have moved in black neighborhoods. More significantly, he also found their immigrant business activities in black neighborhoods were hampered by a large number of megastores that were encouraged to move to these neighborhoods as part of the New York City government's larger initiative for urban renewal. He concluded that black neighborhoods in New York City no longer needed middleman merchants because the government-initiated urban renovation had contributed to the development of many mega retail stores there.

In her theory of middleman minorities, Bonacich (1973) posits that it is the middleman minority group's sojourning orientation, rather than the status gap of the host society, that is the main cause of the middleman-type adjustment. With this theory, she does not confine middleman minorities to those that bridge the status gap, but also includes other minority groups with high self-employment rates. Bonacich and Modell (1980) treat Japanese truck farmers, as well as Japanese wholesalers and retailers of farm products in California, as middleman merchants. Light and Bonacich (1988: 17) define middleman minorities as "entrepreneurial ethnic minorities [who] cluster in commercial occupations, especially in Third World societies." But I believe that the term "trading minorities" should be used to refer to immigrant and minority groups that concentrate in commercial occupations in various societies. Following the above-mentioned original theorists, I believe that the term "middleman minorities" should be reserved for immigrant and ethnic minorities that play an intermediary economic role in highly stratified societies.

Host hostility and scapegoating

Middleman minority theorists have suggested that the vulnerable economic position of middleman minorities, along with their visibility, cohesion, and outside status, provoke host hostility and scapegoating (Rinder 1958; Blalock 1967: 79–84; Zenner 1991: 22–5). Sandwiched between the two, middleman minorities are hated by both the ruling group and other minority or lower class groups in the host society. Owing to their lack of power, they often become easy targets, especially by lower class minority groups that suffer from exploitation and discrimination by the dominant group. The ruling group can also use a middleman minority as a scapegoat to protect its political and economic interests. During periods of economic and political distress, reactions to middleman minorities include boycotts, riots, expulsion, and genocide.

Many social scientists and historians have documented the hostility that middleman merchants encountered. For example, Palmer (1957) showed that Asian Indians in West Africa who specialized in middleman commercial activities were victimized by violent riots and even expulsion. Rinder (1958) opened his article by focusing on the status gap as the main determinant of the middleman minority role, citing a *New York Times* article about the 1949 riots in Durban and its suburbs in South Africa that resulted in thousands of Indian casualties and widespread property damage. In his comprehensive socioeconomic study of Indians in Africa, Chattopadhyaya (1970: 402) documented how European and African traders' organizations tried to instigate both whites and blacks to exclude Indians from the economic life in Kenya.

Eitzen (1971) and Wickberg (1965) indicated that Chinese merchants in the Philippines faced hostile reactions by local residents. Especially after many Southeast Asian countries became independent from Western colonial rulers after World War II, did the Chinese residents there encounter hostile reactions of economic nationalism. For example, in 1954 the Filipino government passed the Retail Trade Nationalization Act according to which aliens with the exception of Americans were able to engage in retail trade only until death or retirement of the owners, while other anti-Chinese legislation restricted import and foreign exchange licenses to Filipinos (Heidhues, 1974: 22).

Zenner (1991) focuses more on anti-middleman stereotypes of Jews than on physical violence and riots. He said that the stereotypes of European Jews as moneylenders or money-mongers were similarly applied to the Chinese in Asian countries in the form of references to the Chinese as the "Jews of Siam" (Zenner 1991: 55).

There are many materials that have documented the hostility that middleman merchants in the United States endured. Porter (1981) pointed out that Jews in the United States, as merchants filling the gap between the residents of African American and Latino neighborhoods, and the dominant classes controlling banks, other economic institutions, and powerful political power structures, were vulnerable to hostility. Several studies have documented the boycotts and riots that victimized Jewish merchants in African American neighborhoods (Cohen 1970; Gold 2010: 82–85). In his book focusing on the middleman role of the Chinese grocers in the Mississippi Delta, Loewen (1971: 175–76) also devoted a few pages to discussing Chinese-owned stores singled out for attack by black rioters in the 1960s.

In addition, Korean immigrant retail store owners in black neighborhoods in New York City, Los Angeles, and other major cities received national and international media attention in connection with the severe conflicts with black customers in the 1980s and early 1990s. Using various theoretical perspectives, a dozen books examined black boycotts of Korean stores and the victimization of Korean merchants during the Los Angeles riots (Min 1996, 2008; Kim 2000). Since Korean retail store owners in black neighborhoods heavily depend upon white corporations for supplying merchandise (Light and Bonacich 1988, part 4), Korean merchants in black neighborhoods can be considered middleman merchants. In his two books, Min (1996, 2008) used middleman minority theory to explain conflicts between Korean merchants and black customers. During the 1992 Los Angeles riots, the police did not respond to the urgent requests for help by Korean store owners surrounded by rioters. This seems to support the proposition of middleman minority theory that the ruling group would like to use middleman merchants as a bulwark to protect itself from violent reactions by a subordinate group.

In explaining black boycotts and other forms of rejection of Korean merchants in black neighborhoods, Min (1996, 2008) cited Black Nationalism as the major anti-middleman ideology against outsiders' commercial activities in black neighborhoods. In his view, just like colonized nations, African Americans as a colonized minority in the United States developed a nationalist ideology that blacks should control their economy in their neighborhoods. Although Black Nationalism is too diverse to allow a coherent generalization, one important idea that has been consistently emphasized by Black Nationalists is community control of educational, social, economic, and political institutions. Min considers the stress on the economic autonomy of the black community inseparably linked to black boycotts of Korean stores. He emphasized the role of Black Nationalism in black boycotts of Korean stores by showing that all major long-term boycotts of Korean stores in black neighborhoods were organized by Black Nationalists such as

Sonny Carson and emphasized the removal of non-black merchants from black neighborhoods as the major goal of the boycotts (Min 1996: 109–17).

In his most recent book, Min (2008) reported that black boycotts and other forms of rejection of Korean stores in black neighborhoods had almost disappeared in Los Angeles and other cities since the mid-1990s. Furthermore, there was no evidence of boycotts of other non-Korean immigrant businesses in black neighborhoods. This is an important finding because in the 1980s and early 1990s no researcher or no Korean community leader would have imagined that black boycotts of Korean stores would actually end.

To explain the disappearance of black boycotts of Korean and other immigrant-owned stores, Min (2008: 89–96) emphasized two types of changes in the structure of lower income black neighborhoods, such as Harlem and Flatbush in New York City. First, since there is no prominent middleman group in black neighborhoods as a result of the ethnic and racial diversity of business owners (as already noted above), black residents may have had difficulty in targeting Korean merchants or any other immigrant business group as outsiders. Second, and more significantly, the increasing racial and ethnic diversity among residents in black neighborhoods also has made it difficult for black residents to consider historically black neighborhoods as their own communities. The racial diversity of residents in lower income black neighborhoods has increased with the settlement of Mexican and other immigrants, and even native-born whites. The fundamental causes of increasing racial diversity in black neighborhoods are the ethnic and racial diversity of contemporary immigration and government-initiated urban renovations.

Ethnic solidarity on the part of middleman minorities

Middleman minority theorists posit that there are triadic causal relations among a middleman group's ethnic solidarity, its intermediary economic role, and its subjection to host hostility (Bonacich and Modell 1980; Turner and Bonacich 1980; Zenner 1991). Ethnic solidarity facilitates a middleman minority's commercial activities, which generate host hostility. Host hostility further enhances a middleman minority's ethnic solidarity. As noted above, there is an abundance of the literature documenting the host hostility and stereotypes that middleman minorities encountered, but middleman minority studies have neglected to empirically examine the effect of business-related intergroup conflicts and host hostility more generally on ethnic solidarity.

Jews, Chinese, and other minority groups serving as middleman merchants in different societies generally maintained strong ethnic ties and had low levels of assimilation to host societies (Bonacich and Modell 1980, 2008; Turner and Bonacich 1980; Zenner 1991: Chapter 4; Min 1996). Because of stereotypes such as being "clannish," "a separatist complex," and having "double standards," these middleman groups are believed to have maintained culturally determined ethnic solidarity. However, strong ethnic ties and lack of assimilation on the part of middleman minorities were mainly reactions to prejudice and discrimination by host societies and hostility encountered in connection with their commercial activities.

We can concede that middleman minorities' cultural traditions partly contributed to ethnic attachment and lack of assimilation. For example, Jews, who served as a prototypical middleman minority in different societies, had advantages in preserving their cultural traditions and ethnic networks by virtue of their Jewish religious rituals, while their rituals discouraged interactions with non-Jewish citizens. Nevertheless, we need to remember that Jews in Europe, especially in Eastern Europe, were subjected to formal discrimination in occupations and forced segregation (Zenner 1991: 62–6). They chose middleman occupations as survival mechanisms. Jews in the United States were treated better than those in Europe, but American Jews had also encountered prejudice and discrimination until the first half of the twentieth century, which is one of the factors for their high concentration in the garment industry and retail businesses. The same can be said of the Chinese, which is another prominent example of a middleman minority in many Asian countries. Under the impact of Confucianism, they had strong family and kin ties, which facilitated their commercial activities (Willmot 1960; Zenner 1991: 78–81). But overseas Chinese, like Jews, also were not allowed to hold desirable occupations by the colonial governments in Asian countries, although they were somewhat encouraged to specialize in internal trade.

Members of a middleman minority encounter not only the initial discrimination in choosing their occupations by the ruling group, but also rejection and even physical violence, especially by the subordinate group, due to their commercial activities in alien countries. Especially when their economic survival is threatened, members of a minority group are likely to unite in order to protect their common economic interests. Thus, the latter form of host hostility can further strengthen ethnic solidarity on the part of middleman minorities. It is important for studies of middleman minorities to systematically examine the effect of middleman merchants' conflicts with customers and the ruling group on their ethnic solidarity, but as already pointed out above, there are limited studies.

In order to examine the effect of middleman merchants' business-related inter-group conflicts on their ethnic solidarity, it is important to make a conceptual distinction between ethnic attachment and ethnic solidarity. As I have clarified elsewhere (Min 1996: 5, 2008: 2), ethnic attachment indicates the cultural, social, and psychological attachments of its members to an immigrant/ethnic group. It is based on an individual's personal identity. By contrast, ethnic solidarity indicates use of ethnic collective action to protect common economic, political, and security (against physical violence) interests. It is based on a collective, political identity. All types of immigrant/ethnic entrepreneurship can enhance ethnic attachment to the extent that entrepreneurship is based on ethnic ties, but only the middleman type of businesses that involve a great deal of business-related intergroup conflict can enhance ethnic solidarity (use of ethnic collective action).

A dozen studies have examined the effect of immigrant entrepreneurship on ethnicity (Bonacich and Modell 1980; Reitz 1980; Light and Bonacich 1988, Chapter 12; Fugita and O'Brien 1991; Min 2008). However, most of these studies focus on demonstrating the effect of immigrant entrepreneurship on what I defined above as "ethnic attachment." For example, Bonacich and Modell (1980) showed that Japanese Americans in California in the ethnic economy maintained higher level of Japanese cultural traditions and Japanese social networks. Thus they demonstrated the effect of Japanese businesses on what is defined here as ethnic attachment, although they used *The Economic Basis of Ethnic Solidarity* as the main title of their book.

By contrast, research on the effect of immigrant entrepreneurship on ethnic solidarity had been neglected in literature until most recently. But Min (1996, 2008) extensively investigated the effect of immigrant merchants' business-related conflicts with other groups on ethnic solidarity using the middleman minority perspective. Using the Korean communities in New York City and Los Angeles, he examined in detail how Korean merchants' conflicts with black customers, white suppliers, Latino employees and government agencies unified not only Korean merchants, but also the entire Korean community (Min 1996, 2008). His research reveals that black boycotts of Korean grocery, liquor, and produce retail stores, and the victimization of many Korean merchants during the 1992 Los Angeles race riots are very similar to the victimization of middleman retail store owners in other societies, and that they contributed more to ethnic solidarity in the entire Korean community than other types of Korean merchants' intergroup conflicts. His research in New York City (Min 2008: Chapter 4) reveals that Korean produce retail store owners' conflicts with white suppliers strengthened their class solidarity, but not Korean community solidarity as a whole.

Concluding remarks

As reviewed in this essay, middleman minority theory is useful in explaining many cases of alien minorities that played an economically bridging role between subordinate minority groups or subordinate classes, and the ruling groups in different societies. There is no case in which all members of a particular minority group played an intermediary economic role as middleman minority theory seems to suggest. However, we have found many cases of minority groups where the majority of members have played this role and had similar experiences in terms of strong ethnic ties, experiences of host hostility, and the intergenerational transmission of commercial occupations. Although typical middleman minorities existed in pre-industrial agrarian or colonized societies, Jews, Koreans, and other groups played a similar role in the United States, economically bridging white producers and consumers in lower income black neighborhoods. Thus, middleman minority theory has been useful in understanding both patterns of ethnic and racial stratifications in particular societies and particular minority experiences.

Middleman minority theory is useful for both ethnic studies to understand particular minority groups' adaptations in particular host societies (descriptive) and patterns of ethnic and racial stratification (analytical and theoretical). No contemporary society seems to have a radical class stratification system, similar to Poland before World War II, to the extent that there is no merchant class. Moreover, all colonized societies in Africa and Asia have been liberated from Western colonial powers, and thus many Indian and Chinese merchants settled in these colonized countries have re-migrated to the United States and other Western countries to escape from emerging nationalism there. Thus the colonial pattern of race relations that needs a merchant minority seems to exist in no contemporary multiethnic society.

As noted above, the black neighborhoods in New York City in twenty-first-century America do not have a prominent middleman minority due to the movement of mega stores and the increasing ethnic and racial diversity of their residents. However, inner-city black neighborhoods in rustbelt cities, such as Detroit, Michigan, and Gary, Indiana have not gone through similar urban renovations. Thus large numbers of immigrants continue to play the role of middlemen merchants in black neighborhoods in these American cities even in the twenty-first century (see Gold 2010: 212–19).

References and further reading

Becker, H. (1950) *Through Values to Social Interpretations.* Durham, NC: Duke University Press.
Blalock, H. (1967) *Toward a Theory of Minority Group Relations.* New York: Wiley.
Bonacich, E. (1973) "A theory of middleman minorities" *American Sociological Review* 38(5): 583–94.
Bonacich, E. and Modell, J. (1980) *The Economic Basis of Ethnic Solidarity: Small Business in the Japanese American Community.* Berkeley, CA: University of California Press.
Cahnman, W. (1974) "Pariahs, strangers and the Court Jews—A conceptual classification" *Sociological Analysis* 35(3): 155–66.
Chattopadhyaya, H. (1970) *Indians in Africa: A Socio-Economic Study.* Calcutta, India: Bookland Private Limited.
Cohen, N. (1970) *The Los Angeles Riots: A Sociological Study.* New York: Praeger.
Eitzen, S. (1971) "Two minorities: The Jews of Poland and the Chinese of the Philippines." In D. Gelfand and R. Lee (eds), *Ethnic Conflicts and Power: A Cross-National Perspectives.* New York: John Wiley and Sons.

Fugita, S. and O'Brien, D. (1991) *Japanese American Ethnicity: The Persistence of the Community*. Seattle, WA: University of Washington Press.

Gold, S. J. (2010) *The Store in the Hood: A Century of Ethnic Business and Conflict*. Lanham, MD: Rowman and Littlefield Publishers.

Heidhues, M. S. (1974) *Southeast Asia's Chinese Minorities*. Hawthorn, Victoria: Longman.

Kim, C. J. (2000) *Bitter Fruit: The Politics of Black-Korean Conflict in New York City*. New Haven, CT: Yale University Press.

Light, I. and Bonacich, E. (1988) *Immigrant Entrepreneurs: Koreans in Los Angeles 1965–1982*. Berkeley, CA: University of California Press.

Light, I. and Gold, S. (2002) *Ethnic Economies*. San Diego, CA: Academic Press.

Loewen, J. (1971) *The Mississippi Chinese: Between Black and White*. Cambridge, MA: Harvard University Press.

Min, P. G. (1996) *Caught in the Middle: Korean Communities in New York and Los Angeles*. Berkeley, CA: University of California Press.

——(2008) *Ethnic Solidarity for Economic Survival: Korean Greengrocers in New York City*. New York: Russell Sage Foundation.

Moodley, K. (1980) "Structural inequality and minority anxiety: Responses to middleman groups in South Africa." In R. M. Price and C. G. Rotberg (eds), *The Apartheid Regime: Political Power and Racial Discrimination in South Africa*. Berkeley, CA: University of California, Institute of International Studies, pp. 217–35.

Palmer, M. (1957) *The History of Indians in Natal*. National Regional Survey, vol. 10. Capetown: Oxford University Press.

Porter, J. N. 1981. "The urban middleman: A comparative analysis" *Comparative Social Research* 4: 199–215.

Reitz, J. G. 1980. *The Survival of Ethnic Groups*. Toronto, Canada: McGraw-Hill.

Rinder, I. (1958) "Strangers in the land: Social relations in the 'status gap'" *Social Problems* 6(3): 253–60.

Sengstock, M. (1982) *Chaldean Americans: Changing Conceptions of Ethnic Identity*. Staten Island, NY: Center for Migration Studies.

Shibutani, T. and Kwan, K. (1966) *Ethnic Stratification: A Comparative Approach*. New York: Macmillan.

Stryker, S. (1974) "A theory of middleman minorities: A comment" *American Sociological Review* 38: 281–82.

Tinker, H. (1974) *A New System of Slavery: The Export of Indian Labor Overseas, 1830–1920*. London, UK: Oxford University Press.

Turner, J. (1973) "The sociology of black nationalism." In J. Ladner (ed.), *The Death of White Society*. New York: Random House, pp. 232–52.

Turner, J. and Bonacich, E. (1980) "Toward a composite theory of middleman minorities" *Ethnicity* 7: 144–58.

Weber, M. (1952) *Jews and Modern Capitalism*. Glencoe, IL: Free Press.

Wickberg, E. (1965) *The Chinese in Philippines Life, 1850–1898*. New Haven, CT: Yale University Press.

Willmot, D. (1960) *The Chinese of Semarang*. Ithaca, NY: Cornell University Press.

Zenner, W. (1982) "Arabic-speaking immigrants in North America as middleman minorities" *Ethnic and Racial Studies* 5(4): 457–76.

——(1991) *Minorities in the Middle: A Cross-Cultural Analysis*. Albany, NY: State University of New York Press.

13

Twenty-first-century trends in highly skilled migration

Astrid Eich-Krohm

Introduction

This chapter gives an overview of key research on highly skilled migration. Highly skilled migrants either have special skills based on experience in a specific field or a tertiary higher educational degree such as a Masters or PhD. For the last 50 years a growing global economy has encouraged the migration of the highly skilled around the world. Researchers have focused on the interests of key actors in the migration process: the nation state, multinational corporations, and migrants themselves. Nation-states have been increasingly concerned about a "brain drain," in which the best and the brightest individuals emigrate to other countries either temporarily or permanently. Although this phenomenon used to be a concern primarily for developing countries, it now affects post-industrialized countries as the global competition for highly skilled employees continuous to increase. International corporations readily encourage highly skilled migration to ensure research, innovation, and development for their businesses. These goals work in tandem with national strategies to attract and retain successful businesses and employees. The motivations and career goals of the highly skilled migrants themselves play a significant role as individuals consider their place in the global world. Highly skilled migrants are often portrayed as a fortunate group based on their education and skills. However, discrimination, unemployment, offshoring of skilled jobs, and non-transferable degrees are a growing concern for this group.

The overall conditions of highly skilled migration changed dramatically with the introduction of information technology (IT) and its rapid spread throughout industrialized countries. Emerging markets have led to a high demand for the highly skilled and also renewed interest in their movements. Castells (2000) argues that information technology was necessary to create a shift from a world economy based on industrial production to the development of a global economy rooted in technology and information. The global economy "includes financial markets, international trade, transnational production, and, to some extent, science and technology, and specialty labor" (Castells 2000: 101). Productivity, development, and growth are dependent on workers who have special skills and/or a high level of education. Furthermore, sectors of society will be based and transformed by knowledge and information technology leading to a new occupational structure (Castells 2000).

Notably, much of the research about highly skilled migrants features men. It tends to neglect women's mobility as professional migrants in their own right as well as the significant role women play in a family's migration decisions. The numbers of highly skilled women migrants have risen substantially during the last 10 years but research about this group is still lacking (Docquier *et al.* 2009).

Defining highly skilled migrants

The concept of highly skilled migration is rather complex and difficult to define. Many researchers agree that a tertiary education (e.g. a university degree) should be the norm for defining highly skilled migrants. That is, a migrant with a Bachelor's degree or post-tertiary education with a Master's or a Doctorate degree would typically be considered as highly skilled. But this definition is problematic because educational degrees are not always easily transferable between countries, and a migrant with a graduate degree might work as a cab driver, because the degree obtained in the native country is not accepted in the host country. Additionally, migrants who have a high level of experience and special skills in a given field (i.e., through apprenticeship education that is common within some European countries) may not have a higher educational degree. Furthermore, there are different terms for this population based on the professional domain in which the migrants work. The terms Human Resources in Science and Technology (HRST) and Science, Technology, Engineering, and Mathematics (STEM) are used interchangeably to describe the highly skilled workforce in IT and the natural sciences. Finally, skilled professionals and entrepreneurs in management, business, accounting, and banking also belong to the group of highly skilled migrants.

Because of conceptual variations in the classification of migrants as highly skilled, it is difficult to estimate their migration flows. Statistics are relatively incomparable within and between countries (Koser and Salt 1997; Pellegrino 2001). Neither large data sets (i.e., population data from the US Census or the United Nations) nor visa statistics are created for the purpose of counting highly skilled migrants. They often exclude information on education, occupation, or employment that would be crucial for determining this classification. For this reason, some studies of highly skilled migration focus exclusively on only one or two professions (e.g., doctors and nurses) or they include all occupations and persons that fit into a singular definition based on predetermined criteria such as the educational degree (Pellegrino 2001).

Context of highly skilled migration

Sparked by the flow of students from developing to developed countries after World War II, highly skilled migration captured the interest of researchers. In order to spur development in non-industrialized countries, students were sent to study in developed countries as an investment in human capital. However, developing countries were not able to offer employment and a rewarding salary as an incentive for return. As a result many international students looked for, and found, job opportunities in their host countries. This one-way migration flow known as "brain drain" refers to the exodus of human capital from developing to developed countries, especially to the United States (Parlin 1976).

The 1965 changes in US immigration law had a profound impact on the overall composition of immigrants to the United States, which shifted from European countries to migrants from Asia and Latin America. Asian immigration had been severely restricted for some decades, and earlier Asian immigrants were mostly low-skilled workers. The new Asian immigration to the United States brought an increase in professionals from middle-class backgrounds and urban areas (Ong *et al.* 1994; Smith and Edmonston 1997).

Coinciding with changes in US immigration law was the development and restructuring of the Pacific Rim region, which included China, the Philippines, South Korea, India, and Vietnam. Such changes tied Asian countries to a global market system in which many of the highly skilled Asian migrants were trained either at US universities abroad or at their own universities based on a Western style curriculum (Ong and Liu 1994). Ong and colleagues (1994: 27) argue that, "these Asian immigrants are manifestations of a globalizing economy, in which national boundaries no longer confine business activities." These developments created economic networks between multiple countries in different regions, thereby expanding the world economy.

The economic need was politically supported, allowing for an increase of immigrant professional and technical workers (Parlin 1976). The influx through *skill-based non-immigrant visa* admissions (temporary) grew steadily during the 1980s (Jasso and Rosenzweig 1990). From 1978 to 1988 the number of visas issued in these categories tripled (Jasso and Rosenzweig 1990). In contrast, the influx through occupational preference by *immigrant visas* (permanent) accounted only for less than 4 percent during the same period (Jasso and Rosenzweig 1990). Furthermore, the development of the aerospace and other technical industries was a pull factor for highly skilled migrants.

Multinational corporations (MNCs) contributed significantly to the increase of highly skilled migration. These corporations developed during the 1980s and 1990s based on three conditions: privatization, opening national markets to foreign companies, and greater participation of local companies in the global economy (Sassen 2005). Multinational companies are active in more than one country with manufacturing, development, production, and financial branches dispersed globally (Castells 2000; Sassen 2005). MNCs are in great need of a highly skilled workforce to stay innovative and competitive. These companies hire new highly skilled workers and at the same time, exchange employees between branches in core countries of the global economy (Findlay 1995). Findlay (1995) argues that these movements are increasingly temporary in nature because international companies need mobile managerial staff that know the job and the company. The global market enables MNCs to have access to a large pool of highly skilled employees and professionals through their own company's networks.

Despite the desire to have a global pool of highly skilled employees from abroad, economic difficulties—such as the tech/internet bubble burst in 2000 and the global financial crisis that started in 2008—have increased the unemployment rate in the STEM workforce. There are competing interests between policy makers, corporations, native-born professionals, and highly skilled migrants that contribute to different employment situations for the highly skilled. MNCs are powerful players and important sources of revenues at national levels and therefore able to put pressure on governments to support highly skilled migration. Some global corporations, for instance, laid off highly skilled workers during the recession but at the same time lobbied policy makers to raise the cap of H-1B non-immigrant visas to hire more STEM workers from abroad (Hira 2010). Iredale calls this "industry led where employers are the major force behind the selection and migration of skilled immigrants" (2001: 16). Thus, Hira (2010) concludes that education levels alone are insufficient for determining which migrants fit the classification of the highly skilled. Furthermore, highly skilled workers in advanced countries have become more vulnerable through off-shoring jobs to emerging markets such as India and China where salaries are lower and fast-developing technologies require continued education on the part of the STEM worker that is rarely provided by companies (Hira 2010). Thus, it is difficult to estimate the number of, or demand for, highly skilled workers in a given labor market (Hira 2010).

Additionally, migrants' chances of successful employment in a foreign labor market are directly related to the evaluation and acceptance of foreign degrees. If a degree is not recognized by the host country, a university-educated migrant may end up working in a different occupation for a much lower salary (Portes and Rumbaut 1996). Doctors, nurses, lawyers, and teachers frequently experience such under placement when the occupational system of the host country is not compatible with the system in the sending country. Often host countries require additional training and/or exams (re-accreditation) for professions such as these, which imply considerable money and time before migrants may work in their professions again and some never do.

Despite those constraints highly skilled migrants are presumed to integrate fairly easily into the host country's society based on their financial situation, language, knowledge, and professional abilities (Findlay 1995; Portes and Rumbaut 1996; Hardill 2002). Compared with low-skilled migrants, these economic and cultural resources make the highly skilled less dependent on networks from their native communities. In fact, some researchers consider the highly skilled to be relatively "invisible" in the host country. However, this assumption is misleading. Although human capital is important, host countries are not equally welcoming highly skilled migrants from around the world.

Race and ethnicity shape the integration process of highly skilled migrants and play an important role in how professionals from abroad are perceived in the host country (Yeoh and Khoo 1998; Purkayastha 2005). Ong's (1999) research about Chinese and Hong Kong business professionals and entrepreneurs in California shows that wealth and skills alone cannot "buy" acceptance into American society. Cultural knowledge is crucial. For these professional migrants, training in Western culture starts early in childhood by attending international schools in their native country or spending extended time abroad with the family. Many Chinese and Hong-Kong expatriate families ensure that their children receive degrees from a university in North America, Great Britain, or Australia to gain greater cultural knowledge of the West and increase their chances for success in the future (Ong 1999). Still, highly skilled migrants from non-Western countries may still be less employable than US citizens or immigrants originating from Western countries. In his case study of employment opportunities of highly skilled migrants compared with natives, Parlin (1976) found that highly skilled migrants from non-Western countries were less employable than US citizens or immigrants originating from Western countries and that employer rejections were not based on the skills of the applicant. Instead they were based on discrimination. Similarly, according to Alarcón (1999) engineers from Mexico and India employed in the United States enjoy higher salaries, better research opportunities and middle-class status compared with their own countries but at the same time experience a glass ceiling that prevents them from obtaining higher management positions.

Migration motivations of the highly skilled

Highly skilled professionals are active agents in the migration process. Their motivations are both professional and personal. A temporary work commitment in another country has the potential to deepen one's knowledge in a specific field and expand professional networks that could lead to further employment (Alarcón 1999). Highly skilled migrants who move with their families often view the temporary stay in another country as a chance for their children to be raised in a global world (Ong 1999; Eich-Krohm 2012). Technological advances such as air-travel and the Internet facilitate the maintenance of social networks with family and friends in the native country as well as professional networks. Portes and Rumbaut (1996) suggested that professionals with a middle-class lifestyle were much less inclined to move to another country. This might have been true years ago, but with an increasing number of students studying abroad and international doctoral graduates and post-doctorate positions offered around the world, ideas about global work are shifting. More people are introduced to different cultures and settings that spark their interests in careers offering global employment and the excitement and challenge that comes with it. Having the flexibility to move and engage with different cultures is a key characteristic of highly skilled migration today.

Key immigration research by Cheng and Yang (1998) identified five motivations for the highly skilled to migrate: (1) the desire for better living conditions; (2) improvement in work and research conditions (i.e., including funding, research facilities, equipment, books, and libraries); (3) better educational resources for children; (4) greater political conditions; and, (5) more employment opportunities, especially if the home country does not have enough jobs for the highly trained, or it does not offer social mobility. The economic argument particularly dominates research discussions of the highly skilled. Economic incentives tend to explain highly skilled migration from developing countries, but they do not fully explain skilled migration from developed countries with a similar standard of living.

Personal motivations are increasingly important for the highly skilled in post-industrialized countries. Participants in a study of German highly skilled migrants in the United States emphasized a generational shift in perspective about the meaning of work. In stark contrast to their parents' focus on economic security through life-long loyalty to one employer, professionals valued interesting challenges, flexibility, and greater responsibility. As a result, half of the participants in this study did not migrate to obtain a higher salary or career advancement but for cultural reasons and interesting work challenges (Eich-Krohm 2012). Similarly, Ong (1999) describes Chinese business professionals in the United States who offer valuable insights into Asian countries as new markets for global corporations.

In contrast, highly skilled migrants from Latin America seem to migrate more often for economic advantages. Migration of skilled migrants from Latin America has quadrupled between 1970 and 1990 (Pellegrino 2001). The debt crisis of the 1980s was a key factor for the emigration of the highly skilled and some Latin American countries absorbed highly skilled workers from neighboring countries. Overall, Mexican highly skilled migrants are the largest group from all Latin American countries in the United States. It is unclear though if Latin America is experiencing a brain drain or brain circulation. Some countries produce highly skilled people at a very high rate suggesting over-education of some populations (Pellegrino 2001).

The role of women in skilled migration

Even though the number of women migrants is increasing around the world, research on this group is still lacking. Women have either been neglected completely in studies of migration or were viewed as non-essential. Existing research on women in professional migration can be divided into two categories: women who move because of their own careers and women who move as so-called "tied migrants" because their husbands accepted a job offer abroad. Professional women on assignment in foreign countries who have a husband as the *tied migrant* are still a minority (Adler 1994; Goyette and Yu Xie 1999).

Despite the efforts by some countries to increase the number of women in STEM fields the gains have been small (Hira 2010). A gender segregated job market based on patriarchal ideas of women's and men's roles in public and private life shapes the science pipeline as well as the professional choices of those who may aspire to it. Given that international experiences are essential in many professional environments, gender expectations still prevent women from reaching top positions. As a result, companies not only have a smaller pool of women to choose from nationally and internationally for skilled positions, there is evidence that companies support stereotypical beliefs that women will not be as successful internationally as men are (Adler 1994).

157

Much recent immigration research on women focuses on socioeconomically disadvantaged groups and has ignored "what we know about gender in the migration of the many highly educated professional and entrepreneurial immigrants" (Hondagneu-Sotelo 1999: 571). When women migrate as spouses their skills are not recognized and they might even be prevented from paid work due to immigration regulations or professional accreditation (Kofman and Rahguram 2006). For example, spouses of H-1B visa holders are not eligible for work permits and cannot apply for paid jobs until the family is eligible for the green card, a process that can take up to five years or longer (Eich-Krohm 2012).

Although women migrants often have similar educational levels to their husbands, they tend to face more barriers to career progression. These include career breaks while having children as well as supporting their husband's career development instead of their own (Hardill 2002; Kurotani 2005). Japanese companies who send employees to the United States expect the wives to join their husbands in order to take care of the household. The wives' work is to create a relaxing home environment for the husband and children (Kurotani 2005). Because it is mostly unclear how long temporary migrations will last, wives face breaks in their careers thereby making it difficult for them to return to their own professions. Hardill (2002) concludes that temporary migration can be as detrimental to a woman's career as having children. Analyzing highly skilled migration on the micro-level reveals that men have more and better chances than do women to establish a successful career abroad.

Policy issues

Researchers tend to agree that highly skilled workers are important to any country's development and wealth (Hira 2010). Nation-states create the framework in which corporations encourage highly skilled migration, by developing trade agreements with other countries, investing in and subsidizing specific industries, and creating barriers or incentives for companies to do business. Immigration laws enable corporations to hire the human capital they need in order to stay competitive. Alternatively, they may also prevent access to migrants. The United States supports highly skilled migration in myriad ways. As a result most of the research about this group originates from there. The United States has structural advantages that support the inflow of highly skilled migrants. These include (1) a variety of non-immigrant visa categories that allow at least a temporary stay in the country; (2) policy makers and businesses that work together to fill the demand for skilled labor as indicated by increasing the number of H1-B visas if necessary; and (3) the United States has the greatest number of universities, colleges, and research facilities in the world.

Tables 13.1–13.3 present an overview of the numbers of visas issued in different *non-immigrant visa* categories that specifically target highly skilled migrants. These visa categories allow employees a temporary stay to work and live in the United States. The visas of greatest interest to employers are H-1B "Workers with Specialty Occupations;" which are mostly used in the STEM workforce; L-1 "Intracompany Transferees," which are found in both the STEM workforce and in business/management; and E-1 to E-3 "Treaty Traders and Investors," which is mostly found in business, banking, and the managerial workforce. Employees' families can join the main visa holder and spouses can also apply for a work permit except in the H-1B visa category. The dependents—family members—are included in these numbers.

Asian countries are taking the lead of supplying the United States with migrants in this category. Highly skilled migrants from India take an impressive lead of receiving H-1B visas. Canada and Mexico are increasingly becoming source countries for highly skilled migrants to the United States. They share a border and strong business ties with the United States. In contrast, European countries take a distant third place compared to Asian and North American countries. Germany's H-1B applicants dropped sharply between 2005 and 2010. A reason might be that Germany developed initiatives to attract German scientists working in the United States and spur their return. During the last five years, European and South American countries sent fewer highly skilled migrants to the United States, and one factor may have been the global economic downturn.

Business ties play an important role in the Intracompany Transferee (L-1) visa category. These numbers show how many employees were transferred between production sites of other countries and the United States. Canada and Mexico are taking the lead followed closely by Asian countries, with India having the highest increase in L-1 visas in 10 years. Strengthening business ties with emerging markets in Asia and trade agreements with Canada and Mexico may have supported this development. The European region is third in the ranking but with overall

Table 13.1 Workers with specialty occupations from selected region/countries

Region and country	2000	2005	2010
Asia	166,877	174,728	222,117
Europe	107,366	109,676	72,164
North America	32,497	50,999	112,138
South America	31,728	51,892	32,936
China	14,874	11,801	19,493
India	102,453	102,382	138,431
Japan	11,989	14,858	12,099
Korea	5,647	10,041	11,815
France	14,745	15,403	10,804
Germany	13,533	14,022	8,380
UK	32,124	30,755	17,099
Canada	12,929	24,086	72,959
Mexico	13,507	17,063	30,571

Source: United States, Department of Homeland Security, *Yearbook of Immigration Statistics*: 2000, 2005, 2010.

Table 13.2 Intracompany transferees from selected region/countries

Region and country	2000	2005	2010
Asia	104,003	81,570	154,368
Europe	210,426	139,603	136,788
North America	53,318	37,367	163,670
South America	37,367	35,794	29,335
India	18,056	28,460	68,445
Japan	54,433	30,899	44,902
Korea	5,654	10,041	11,815
France	30,075	17,604	19,893
Germany	32,564	21,776	19,912
UK	76,707	52,745	45,293
Canada	26,694	16,569	109,732
Mexico	21,883	16,279	49,650
Brazil	13,042	10,198	10,679

Source: United States, Department of Homeland Security, *Yearbook of Immigration Statistics*: 2000, 2005, 2010.

decreasing numbers during the last 10 years. This might be due to the expansion of the European Union, which created stronger business networks among those countries, and the creation of the Euro currency. Of all South American countries only Brazil scored above 10,000 visas issued in this category regularly.

The next category (Table 13.3) is the smallest among the *non-immigrant visa* categories: Treaty Traders and Investors (E-1 to E-3). The Asian region is presented the strongest because Japan accounts for two-thirds of the visas in this category. Mexico is another source country for this type of visa and overall North America is the second source region for this type of migrant to the United States. The European countries lag behind these regions. France and Germany saw slight increases in this category and the numbers from the UK have decreased over the last 10 years.

Tables 13.4–13.6 present another important category in the *non-immigrant visa* distribution— international students and exchange visitors. These include researchers, academics, and post-doctoral students. Students and exchange visitors may try to find employment in the United States after they finish their studies or when their research appointments have ended. The source countries in these categories are much more diverse and numerous than in the categories mentioned before. Both groups are also allowed to bring their families and those are included in these numbers.

Table 13.3 Treaty traders and investors from selected region and countries

Region and country	2000	2005	2010
Asia total	83,529	95,534	138,361
Japan	66,277	72,606	93,303
North America	6,673	13,159	134,764
Canada	3,216	4,477	35,176
Mexico	3,034	7,903	98,291
Europe	73,298	74,338	85,635
France	9,107	10,376	12,787
Germany	22,819	25,294	31,597
UK	17,900	17,233	14,738

Source: United States, Department of Homeland Security, *Yearbook of Immigration Statistics*: 2000, 2005, and 2010.

Table 13.4 Student and exchange visitors from Asia

Region and country	2000	2005	2010
Asia	*472,175*	*457,147*	*822,551*
China	89,823	54,574	221,820
India	47,773	61,146	99,786
Japan	113,102	93,588	67,862
Korea*	79,549	117,755	172,523
Saudi Arabia	12,579	3,925	41,646
Taiwan**	N.A.	42,819	45,117
Thailand	15,253	16,714	21,130
Turkey	20,717	22,340	31,799
Israel	10,962	10,935	12,328

Source: United States, Department of Homeland Security, *Yearbook of Immigration Statistics*: 2000, 2005, and 2010.
*Korea includes South and North Korea prior to 2004. Numbers of 2005 and 2010 only apply to South Korea.
**In the 2000 statistics Taiwan was included in China.

Students and exchange visitors from China, Korea, and India have substantially increased whereas Japan's numbers have at the same time decreased. Taiwan is another strong contributor to this category compared with the size of its overall population. Saudi Arabia, Thailand, Turkey, and Israel are small contributors to the other visa categories but are recognizable source countries for student and exchange visitors.

North America is an especially large contributor of students and exchange visitors. Canada and Mexico share almost equally high numbers that no other country matches. Short distance may be one reason, and another is social networks that already exist through earlier migration to the United States. Whereas South America is a small contributor in the other *non-immigrant visa* categories, Brazil, Venezuela, and Columbia are source countries for students and exchange visitors.

Among the European countries, France, Germany, and the UK continuously send students and exchange visitors to the United States, followed by countries such as, Italy, Russia, and Spain who have had an increase in these visa categories during the last 10 years. At the same time, there has been a decrease in students and researchers from Ireland and Sweden. The numbers of students and researchers from the Ukraine has more than doubled during the last five years.

Despite the recent economic downturn, the United States still attracts many highly skilled migrants and seems to be well positioned to compete for the best and the brightest. However, other countries have realized that they need to invest in programs or change immigration laws

Table 13.5 Student and exchange visitors from North and South America

Region and country	2000	2005	2010
North America	93,424	110,963	717,552
South America	86,084	81,904	106,792
Canada	26,323	33,949	335,327
Mexico	26,855	34,442	335,544
Brazil	29,180	27,433	38,961
Venezuela	13,357	9,990	14,141
Columbia	15,312	12,201	18,479

Source: United States, Department of Homeland Security, *Yearbook of Immigration Statistics*: 2000, 2005, and 2010.

Table 13.6 Student and exchange visitors from European countries

Region country	2000	2005	2010
Europe	342,409	319,916	362,674
France	37,268	29,576	41,876
Germany	55,670	44,452	53,003
UK	43,087	39,659	45,060
Ireland	16,717	11,730	12,332
Italy	16,273	15,418	21,822
Russia	19,305	26,842	32,773
Spain	19,526	16,085	22,885
Sweden	14,302	9,368	11,952
Ukraine	4,659	5,955	13,141

Source: United States, Department of Homeland Security, *Yearbook of Immigration Statistics*: 2000, 2005, and 2010.

to encourage their own citizens to return from abroad or to attract highly skilled migrants from other countries.

Brain drain or brain circulation?

Whereas "brain drain" suggests negative consequences for the sending and positive outcomes for the receiving country, studies now use the term "brain circulation" or "brain exchange" to refer to temporary flows of skilled migrants specifically among post-industrialized countries that are considered mutually beneficial (Guellec and Cervantes 2002). There is no conclusive evidence yet about the impact of brain drain on source countries or if brain drain has turned into a more healthy brain circulation/exchange.

Germany's businesses have argued for many years that they experience a shortage of highly skilled workers suggesting a brain drain. A high number of Germans with tertiary and higher degrees are leaving the country at least temporarily (Eich-Krohm 2012). As the fourth largest economy in the world Germany needs to attract highly skilled workers and professionals to secure the nation's future development and competitiveness. The status of highly skilled migrants among post-industrialized countries encourages German-trained professionals to migrate abroad and take their skills with them. The discussion has sparked new government strategies designed to motivate German scholars who are abroad to return home (Eich-Krohm 2012).

Brain drain is a problem for Italy as well. However, the nation-state has not responded with effective policy changes or incentives. Morano (2006) concludes that there is a disinterest on the part of politicians to retain Italian scientists, attract foreign scientists, or even motivate Italian scientists to return to Italy after being abroad.

Australia seems to be a success story of the brain circulation/exchange discussion accomplished through immigration policy reforms. A high number of skilled migrants arrived in Australia between 1986 and 1991 but only 30 percent found a job in the first five years. Between 1997 and 2002 the Australian Government implemented new immigration policies that focused on these problems. The new policies included mandatory English language testing, pre-migration qualifications screening, and better incorporation of international students as a potential pool of skilled employees. Since these policies have been enacted the unemployment rate among the highly skilled fell below 10 percent and, at the same time, the income levels of those employed rose substantially (Hawthorne 2005).

As a former developing country India has suffered from a brain drain. However, India is now considered an emerging market due to the development of large urban and research centers. Realizing that its stock of highly skilled citizens in the United States could help to build and strengthen India's economy the Indian government established dual citizenship for non-resident Indians and a ministry to attend to their needs (Harvey 2008). Such efforts support return migration for India. Even though there is no evidence yet that the Indian brain drain has turned into healthy brain circulation, Indian scientists are more positive about India's prospects and their future professional opportunities there (Harvey 2008).

This review would not be complete without including China's brain drain. China has been an important source country for highly skilled migrants to the United States. Similarly to India, China is also viewed as an emerging market with rapid economic growth. But whereas India's government is based on democratic principles, China is a socialist country under one party rule with a strong ideological basis. Wang (2005) argues that China's political ideology contributes not only to the emigration of Chinese but that it effects the decision to return or to stay abroad as well. Cao (2008) concluded that political connections still play a significant role to attain research positions and prevent highly skilled Chinese from returning. There are also worries that the Chinese government will interfere with science and educational goals and a system of corruption that does not help to persuade first-rate Chinese academics to return (Cao 2008).

Another consideration for countries with a substantial outmigration of skilled workers is remittances. Remittances sent by migrants to their native countries are viewed as a positive outcome of emigration. According to Faini (2007) this is not the case for highly skilled migrants from developing countries who are often from wealthy families and do not need the financial support. They might use their skill set instead to reunite with their family in the host country. Docquier and Rapoport (2007) conclude in their analysis that there is an optimum rate of emigration of the highly skilled for any given country that has a positive effect. They call for sensible immigration policies that do not restrict emigration of the highly skilled instead to use sensible incentives to spur return migration.

Conclusion

The research on highly skilled migrants seems to spark more questions than it answers. What exactly contributes to brain drain and what supports brain circulation? As a first step, a more detailed and comparative analysis about strategies that different nation-states employ to attract or foster return migration of the highly skilled would be helpful. Equally important is the question of supply and demand. What are the skills that are most in need, and how can the real demand be determined and successfully satisfied?

Research also needs to focus on the micro-level. What are the issues for the highly skilled to move abroad and what motivates them to move back to their home country? This review also raised the question of discrimination based on race/ethnicity, gender, and age. Increasing flows of temporary migrants raise questions for theoretical assumptions as well. What impact does it have on one's life to live abroad? In what ways do these concerns impact temporary migration? The advancement of information technologies during the last 10 years and the ease with which information flows between different actors raises the question of identity. How much does this information flow influence the adaptation processes of migrants and their families? How important is it for highly skilled migrants to identify with the values and traditions of the host culture? Migration research about the highly skilled has to be more inclusive of women and different racial/ethnic groups. How can this knowledge contribute to the expansion of existing migration theories such as transnationalism and assimilation?

Finally, this review reveals that there is a disconnection among migration researchers because there is no agreement of who exactly the highly skilled are. As discussed this group is very heterogeneous and diverse in terms of skill levels, degrees, gender, race/ethnicity, and age and, therefore, questions the idea that the migration experience is similar for the whole group regardless of origin. Thus, there is a need for more collaborative projects to compare findings within and among countries and to foster new directions for research.

References and further reading

Adler, N. J. (1994) "Competitive frontiers: Women managing across borders" *Journal of Management Development* 13(2): 24–41.

Alarcón, R. (1999) "Recruitment processes among foreign-born engineers and scientists in Silicon Valley" *American Behavioral Scientist* 42(9): 1381–97.

Borjas, G. J. (1999) *Heaven's Door: Immigration Policy And The American Economy*. Princeton, NJ: Princeton University Press.

Cao, C. (2008) "China's brain drain at the high end: Why government policies have failed to attract first-rate academics to return" *Asian Population Studies* 4(3): 331–45.

Castells, M. (2000) *The Information Age: Economy, Society, and Culture Volume I, The Rise of the Network Society*. Oxford: Blackwell Publishing.

Chappell, L. and Glennie, A. (2010) "Show me the money (and opportunity): Why skilled people leave home—and why they sometimes return" Migration Policy Institute. www.migrationinformation.org/Feature/display.cfm?ID=779.

Cheng, L. and Yang, P. Q. (1998) "Global interaction, global inequality, and migration of the highly trained to the United States" *International Migration Review* 32(3): 626–53.

Docquier, F., Lowell, B. L., and Marfouk, A. (2009) "A gendered assessment of highly skilled emigration" *Population Review* 35(2): 297–321.

Docquier, F. and Rapoport, H. (2007) "Skilled migration: The perspective of developing countries" IZA Discussion Paper No. 2873.

Eich-Krohm, A. (2012) *German Professionals in the United States: A Gendered Analysis of the Migration Decision of Highly Skilled Families*. El Paso, TX: LFB Scholarly Publishing LLC.

Faini, R. (2007) "Remittances and the brain drain: Do more skilled migrants remit more?" *The World Bank Economic Review* 21(2): 177–91.

Findlay, A. M. (1995) "Skilled transients: The invisible phenomenon?" In R. Cohen (ed.), *The Cambridge Survey of World Migration*. Cambridge: Cambridge University Press, pp. 515–22.

Fix, M. and Passel, J. S. (1994) *Immigration and Immigrants Setting the Record Straight*. Washington, DC: The Urban Institute.

Glick-Schiller, N. (1995) "From immigrant to transmigrant: Theorizing transnational migration" *Anthropological Quarterly* 68(1): 48–63.

Guellec, D. and Cervantes, M. (2002) "International mobility of highly skilled workers: From statistical analysis to policy formation." In *Mobility of Highly Skilled Workers: From Statistical Analysis to the Formulation of Policies*. OECD Publications: France, pp. 69–96.

Goyette, K. and Xie, Y. (1990) "The intersection of immigration and gender: Labor force outcomes of immigrant women scientists" *Social Science Quarterly* 80(2): 395–408.

Hardill, I. (2002) *Gender, Migration and the Dual Career Household*. New York: Routledge.

Harvey, W. S. (2008) "Brain circulation? British and Indian scientists in Boston, Massachusetts, USA" *Asian Population Studies* 4(3): 293–309.

Hira, R. (2010) "US Policy and the STEM Workforce System" *American Behavioral Scientist* 53(7): 949–61.

Hondagneu-Sotelo, P. (1999) "Gender and contemporary US immigration" *American Behavioral Scientist* 42(4): 565–76.

Hondagneu-Sotelo, P. (ed.) (2003) *Gender and US Immigration: Contemporary Trends*. Berkeley, CA: University of California Press.

Hawthorne, L. (2005) "Picking winners: The recent transformation of Australia's skilled migration policy" *International Migration Review* 39(3): 663–96.

Iredale, R. (2001) "The migration of professionals: Theories and typologies" *International Migration* 39(5): 8–24.

Jasso, G. and Rosenzweig, M. R. (1990) *The New Chosen People: Immigrants in the United States*. New York: Russell Sage Foundation.

Kofman, E. and Raghuram, P. (2006) "Gender and global labor migrations: Incorporating skilled workers" *Antipode* 38(2): 282–303.

Koser, K. and Salt, J. (1997) "The geography of highly skilled international migration" *International Journal of Population Geography* 3(4): 285–303.

Kurotani, S. (2005) *Home Away from Home: Japanese Corporate Wives in the United States*. Durham, NC: Duke University Press.

Morano Foadi, S. (2006) "Key issues and causes of the Italian Brain Drain" *Innovation* 19(2): 209–23.

Ong, A. (1999) *Flexible Citizenship: The Cultural Logics of Transnationalism*. Durham, NC: Duke University Press.

Ong, P., Bonacich, E., and Cheng, L. (1994) "The political economy of capitalist restructuring and the New Asian immigration." In P. Ong, E. Bonacich, and L. Cheng (eds), *The New Asian Immigration in Los Angeles and Global Restructuring*. Philadelphia, PA: Temple University Press, pp. 3–35.

Ong, P. and Liu, J. M. (1994) "US Immigration Policies and Asian Migration." In P. Ong, E. Bonacich, and L. Cheng (eds), *The New Asian Immigration in Los Angeles and Global Restructuring*. Philadelphia, PA: Temple University Press, pp. 45–73.

Pellegrino, A. (2001) "Trends in Latin American skilled migration: 'Brain Drain' or 'Brain Exchange'?" *International Migration* 39(5): 111–32.

Parlin, B. W. (1976) *Immigrant Professionals in the United States: Discrimination in the Scientific Labor Market*. New York: Praeger Publishers.

Portes, A. and Rumbaut, R. G. (1996) *Immigrant America, A Portrait.* 2nd edition. Berkeley, CA: University of California Press.

Purkayastha, B. (2005) "Skilled migration and cumulative disadvantage: The case of highly qualified Asian immigrant women in the US" *Geoforum* 36(2): 181–96.

Sassen, S. (2005) "The network of global cities: A space of power and empowerment" *Journal of Social Affairs* 22(86): 13–31.

Smith, J. P. and Edmonston, B. (1997) *The New Americans: Economic, Demographic, and Fiscal Effects of Immigration.* Washington, DC: National Academy Press.

United States Department of Homeland Security (2001) *Yearbook of Immigration Statistics 2000.* Washington, DC: US Department of Homeland Security, Office of Immigration Statistics.

——(2006) *Yearbook of Immigration Statistics 2005.* Washington, DC: US Department of Homeland Security, Office of Immigration Statistics.

——(2011) *Yearbook of Immigration Statistics 2010.* Washington, DC: US Department of Homeland Security, Office of Immigration Statistics.

Wang, W. (2005) "Ideological orientation and the PRC academic migration: A theoretical and longitudinal analysis" *Sociological Inquiry* 75(2): 216–48.

Yeoh, B. S. A. and Khoo, L.-M. (1998) "Home, work and community: Skilled international migration and expatriate women in Singapore" *International Migration* 36(2): 159–86.

Part IV
Intersecting inequalities in the lives of migrants

As immigrants encounter host societies, they generally confront a new system of stratification. As newcomers, immigrant and minorities who lack citizenship, language skills, and contacts in the new setting, they are often disadvantaged. However, due to social norms, resources, eligibility for benefits, and other factors, some groups find themselves in a relatively privileged position in the new society. Regardless of the impact of the host society's patterns of social inequalities, migrants must understand its meaning to function effectively. This section summarizes the impact of several forms of social inequality as they are encountered by international migrants in points of settlement.

Miri Song notes that post-World War II international migration commonly involves racial issues as immigrants from Asia, Latin America, Africa, or the Middle East enter nations whose majority is of European origins. Asserting that globalization has transformed the meaning of race from a generally static and geographically fixed category to one that integrates groups, meaning systems, and networks in multiple settings, the author identifies six central trends in the field of race and migration, offers case study material from the USA and UK, and suggests ways of re-thinking race and migration to capture contemporary realities.

Pierrette Hondagneu-Sotelo observes that decades after ambitious efforts to increase the awareness of gender in the academy, the major topics in international migration continue to neglect or ghettoize its importance. Despite this trend, she observes five areas of investigation that continue to contribute knowledge about gender in migration. These include general efforts of scholars to include gender as a main-stream issue in migration studies, research about the importance of gender to care work, the investigation of sexuality in international migration, research on sex trafficking, studies of borderlands and migration, and analyses of gender, migration, and children.

In their chapter, Mehdi Bozorgmehr, Anny Bakalian and Sara Salman integrate theoretical, historical, and contemporary literature collected in several locations to create a basic under-standing of host hostility. Reviewing economic, political, and social-cultural explanations of the phenomenon and focusing on recent instances of Islamophobia in Europe and the USA, they contextualize the three most common outcomes of anti-immigrant movements: exclusion, forced assimilation, and the development of ethnic solidarity among those targeted.

Noting that all migrants need a place to live, Joe Darden and Flavia Cristaldi observe that migrants tend to be concentrated within specific locations in host societies. Drawing upon theoretical materials, historical data and case studies of migrant settlement within major cities in Europe and North America, they introduce basic methods for studying residential segregation. Using these tools, the authors examine the role of socioeconomic status, self-segregation, and discrimination in determining migrants' residential patterns. They find that while patterns of segregation vary between groups and countries, the role of discrimination appears to the most convincing explanation for this process, especially since 1965, when the majority of immigrants to Europe and North America became racially distinct from resident populations.

Eithne Lubheld notes that migration scholarship has traditionally ignored, marginalized or trivialized sexuality or subsumed it under established academic topics like gender, deviance, and morality. Rejecting status quo assumptions that define sexuality as either a natural drive or a private matter, scholars examining the topic assert that sexuality is inevitably expressed and experienced through social, economic, and cultural mediation and comprises a locus of power and struggle. Accordingly, sexuality and migration scholarship concerns the role of state, employers, families, communities, and individuals in strategically mobilizing sexualities to organize, govern, and contest migration processes at multiple levels and in relation to changing social, political, and economic agendas and hierarchies. Because the topic is often suppressed and treated distinctly from other migration-related concepts, it both challenges and connects to existing theory and research. As revealed by her summary of important scholarship on migration and sexuality, the examination of the topic demands innovative approaches and has the potential to provide a wealth of inventive insights.

In her unique contribution about migrants and indigenous nationalism, Nandita Sharma draws on literature about racism and de-colonialism to reframe the role of nationalism in resolving conflicts between migrants and indigenous populations. Rejecting the nationalistic link between ownership of territory and political rights, she emphasizes the notion of shared access—*the commons*—as a means to end exploitation and expropriation. In so doing, she brings the experience of the migrant and the indigenous into a single analytic field that recognizes the spatial dimensions of power and the needs, vulnerability, and humanity of both categories.

14

The changing configuration of migration and race

Miri Song

The terms migration and race are often mutually constitutive. The coupling of these two concepts is based upon historical events in which, especially post-World War II, migration to Western societies has effectively meant the migration of mostly non-white people from post-colonial societies, such as former British "subjects" in Pakistan, or Turkish "guest workers" moving and settling in (then) West Germany, or Algerians moving to France. The term migration has also been used by many analysts as strongly linked with the dynamics of racisms, disadvantaged status, and the representation and positioning of the "other."

While I can only scratch the surface about the multifaceted and highly complex relationship between migration and race in this chapter (especially given all the different types of studies about migration—transnational processes, immigrant adaptation and ethnic businesses, the dynamics of sending and receiving societies, etc.), I will map out the changing relationship between migration and race, as evidenced by changing social and political developments and/or documented and theorized by various analysts. In doing so, I will broadly address the relationship between migration and race in Western, advanced capitalist societies, such as in North America and Western Europe. Since both these terms are extremely broad, and can refer to many different bodies of literature, this overview will be necessarily schematic. And while I do not distinguish between ethnic and racial groups in this short chapter, my discussion of "race" will also tend to subsume references to ethnicity, as many groups comprise both ethnic and racial groups.

Following the work of urban sociologist Robert Park and his race relations cycle, classical theories of assimilation were emblematic of a particular understanding of migration to Western societies, in that "classical" theories (based upon the experiences of white European migrants, such as Italians or Germans, to the USA) of assimilation posited a relatively straightforward trajectory for European migrants: upon arrival, they would encounter some prejudice and various forms of social and economic barriers, but that with the rise of the second generation, who would have benefited from "native" language and schooling, and acculturation more generally, a full-blooded "structural assimilation" into a dominant culture would be virtually assured (though, of course, this is a highly simplified rendering of such an argument)—see Milton Gordon (1964).

But with the large scale immigration of people into the USA from Latin America and Asia in the post-1965 period, a considerable body of literature has argued that race and the racialized experiences of certain non-white immigrant groups could fundamentally shape their

169

incorporation, opportunities, and experiences (albeit in various possible ways) in their "host" society. Thus so-called "segmented assimilation" theory, pioneered by Alejandro Portes and Min Zhou (1993), among others, located "race" firmly in relation to migration. According to this way of thinking, black Haitians who settled in Miami (or Chinese who settled in New York), encountered very different experiences (and treatment) as migrants to the USA, in comparison with the German or Irish migrants who arrived earlier in the twentieth century. The significance of race and racial barriers in shaping the experiences of new immigrants to the USA, however, has been questioned by some analysts who argue that post 1965 immigrants' experiences were not that different from white European immigrants in early twentieth century, who also suffered prejudice and a variety of social and economic barriers.

Scholarship concerning the relationship between migration and race has witnessed debates, too, about whether structural or cultural variables were more significant in explaining the differential outcomes for disparate migrant groups (see Steinberg 1989). Scholars advocating intersectionality have, importantly, and over many decades, contested what they regarded as overly rigid and uni-dimensional understandings of racial and gender disadvantage and oppression, in which class dynamics were regarded as primary in explaining most forms of subordination and oppression, including racial oppression, as exemplified by certain orthodox Marxist approaches (like that of Oliver Cox).

In the last several decades, vast bodies of literature on globalization, transnationalism, and diasporas have fundamentally shaped contemporary debates which concern the relationship between migration and race (and/or ethnicity). As denizens of an increasingly global, interconnected world, competing arguments have been made about the effects of globalization in every sphere of life, including debates about dialectical tendencies toward cultural homogenization *and* cultural differentiation (Hall *et al.* 1992). Some analysts have argued that national identities are declining, and new hybridized identities are emerging (e.g., see Appadurai 1990), while others (e.g., see Smith 1990) argue that globalization can engender emotionally laden forms of nationalisms and a return to mythic certainties.

The dynamics associated with globalization, and modernity more generally, are said to destabilize established identities. Increasingly, people's sense of their ethnic identities and affiliations are said to be relativized and shaped by our greater consciousness of the interconnections of people and societies around the world. Although there is much debate about the concept of diaspora, it can be defined as the imagined condition of a "people" dispersed throughout the world, by force or by choice. Diasporas are transnational sociocultural formations of people who share real and/or symbolic ties to some distant "homeland" (Ang 1994). Contemporary international migration is significantly different from that of previous periods, and this is most evident in studies of transnationalism, which emphasize the economic, cultural, political, and familial networks and links between two or more locations (Gold 2000).

Thus people's sense of belonging and identity are complicated by increasingly complex migratory trajectories and potentially multiple transnational and diasporic ties. And given the complicated trajectories of many ethnic minority groups and individuals, in terms of moving from one place to another, one's ethnic and/or racial identity and affiliations need not be territorially bounded to one's birthplace or any one place. However, it is not possible to generalize about the transnational ties and experiences of disparate migrant groups; nor can we assume a homogeneous experience within each group, without reference to individuals' specific settlement histories, gender, and class locations. In fact, in some of the literature on globalization and diaspora, the postmodern emphasis on fluid identities and positionings is far too celebratory, emphasizing the freedom with which diasporic minorities are able to fashion desired and multiple positionings and identities (see Bhabha 1994).

Why should we re-evaluate the relationship between migration and race, and "difference" more generally? Given the major changes discussed above, especially in relation to what we call globalization, and all its attendant processes, we need to rethink both the structure and agency underlying migrants' diverse and multiple experiences. While overly celebratory and sanguine discourses about movement and reinvention are problematic and simplistic, overly rigid, orthodox understandings of how contemporary migrants are constrained by overwhelming global and state structures are equally problematic.

The study of migration and race, broadly conceptualized, is now carried out at a major historical conjuncture, where, according to theories of late modernity and individualization (Giddens 1991; Beck 1992), traditional, communal ties in countries such as Britain are weakened, and traditional class solidarities have allegedly eroded. At the same time, contemporary multi-ethnic Western societies such as the USA and Britain (and Western European countries) are marked by entrenched forms of "identity politics," in which racialized and visible migrant and minority groups mobilize around their ethnic and racial and religious identities as a means of making claims upon the state and upon the wider society. Many such Western societies, possibly with the exception of Canada, are in almost constant and controversial discussions about the pros and, more typically, cons of immigration. Thus the specter of difference, and the migrant as other, continue to dominate social and political debates.

I now turn to six major currents and developments which are re-shaping the way we think about the historical (and often presumed) coupling of migration and race. This discussion is highly generalized, and while not specific to any one country, pertains primarily to multiethnic Western societies such as Britain and the United States. I will occasionally draw upon particular examples from Britain to illustrate my points.

Growing attention to second-generation inclusion and belonging

Studies of the second generation (and even 1.5 generation!) are now myriad in multiethnic Western societies. Multiple studies on both sides of the Atlantic have investigated the variable educational and labor market outcomes of disparate minority groups, whether it be the differential educational attainments of Dominican or Indian second-generation individuals in the USA or the attainments of Turkish versus Moroccan second-generation people in the Netherlands. Other studies have examined the linguistic retention (or not) of Mexican Americans versus Chinese Americans. Such studies have been complemented by perspectives which stress the importance of intersectionality in making sense of individuals' gendered, classed, and regional selves (Anthias and Yuval-Davis 1992). Furthermore, there is growing attention to the fact that specific minority groups can be quite heterogeneous, prompting the need to consider intra-group diversity. For instance, the group "Asian" in Britain now includes Indian origin Britons who significantly outperform Pakistani or Bangladeshi Britons in education and income. As "super-diversity" emerges in London, and other large, cosmopolitan metropolitan areas, more attention is being paid to specific sub-groups within groups (Vertovec 2007).

But where some of the most interesting work is emerging is in studies which investigate qualitative measures of well-being and inclusion, which are more difficult to capture and measure for social scientists: e.g., do second-generation individuals feel that they belong (and in what ways) in society? Do they participate in mainstream politics or other forms of civic activity? So while questions of socioeconomic attainment are still tremendously important, more studies are addressing inclusion and belonging (Song 2003). For instance, while the British Chinese are regarded as a successful minority group, given their high educational attainment, there is also evidence that some British Chinese people do not feel "British," or that they belong in Britain. Nevertheless, as will be discussed below, there can be mixed evidence, where different indicators of inclusion and participation can suggest rather different outcomes. Many more studies are needed about issues which go beyond education and labor market attainment, as important as they are.

Older studies of migration and race relations, for example in the Chicago School, tended to be characterized by top-down studies of, and about, migrant groups (however sympathetically they may have been portrayed), but these more contemporary studies concerning migration and race, especially qualitative studies of particular groups, have tended to privilege the voices and experiences of individual migrants themselves. So in recent years, there is now a wealth of both quantitative and qualitative approaches to the study of migrant experiences. Furthermore, increased interest in various qualitative measures of well-being and inclusion can engender a critical rethinking of existing theoretical orthodoxies about racial disadvantage and racial hierarchy, especially in the USA, where such an orthodoxy has explicitly distinguished between "voluntary" and "involuntary" migrants. While such a distinction is still important and tenable in certain respects, it is only one (perhaps limited) way of understanding the complex manifestations of advantage and disadvantage, or the complex intertwining of specific disadvantages with specific privileges.

Questioning the presumed salience of "race" and ethnicity

While older studies of "the second generation" tended to focus upon their structural disadvantage, as discussed above, others also tended to articulate the now rather unfashionable view that this generation was effectively "between two cultures," so that second-generation individuals could face difficulties in navigating different languages, cultural practices, and norms in the so-called public and private spheres. Also, as noted in studies of "ethnic options" (Waters 1990), non-white minority individuals' identity options can be highly constrained by rigid, racialized notions about whether someone looks "American" or "British" (among other variables), according to prevailing social norms. These approaches, to name only a few, point to the continuing salience of ethnic and racial difference in the lives of many visibly different individuals.

Nevertheless, more recent studies in both North America and Europe have mapped out the assertive ways in which second-generation individuals and groups are asserting their public presence, including their insistence upon complex meanings and modes of belonging. Many studies show that, in the context of globalization and the transnational and diasporic communities associated with it, second-generation men and women can assert affiliations in relation to multiple societies and groups—all of this aided not only by travel, but also the ubiquitous Internet. Increasingly, the presumed salience of and meanings associated with "race" or ethnic identity for second-generation individuals must be questioned and investigated. Many studies now show complex, multiple, and layered forms of belonging, whether it is partial, "conditional subjectivities of belonging" (Parker 1995), or skillful modes of code switching (Hall 1997).

Also, in what ways may second-generation individuals attach meanings to, and mobilize around, their ethnic/racial/religious backgrounds? For instance, how do second-generation British Muslims mobilize around their Muslim identities and faith? In what ways do their religious beliefs and practice intertwine with their ethnicities? Many studies still demonstrate the ways in which second-generation status is racialized for particular groups, whether this is manifested through the social encounters across a Chinese take-out, between the customer and the Chinese server, or in terms of British-born Indian young people subject to forms of Islamophobia in their encounters with others in schools or public spaces. But growing numbers of studies reveal that, even among second-generation individuals, the centrality and importance of their ethnic ancestries can differ considerably, according to their locality, class background, and the specificity of their ethnic or racial background. For instance, many second-generation individuals engage in daily forms of code-switching, drawing on different cultural repertoires, languages, and sensibilities, depending upon their specific social network and context. For many such individuals, multiple modes of belonging—at the local, national, and transnational levels—are navigated on a regular basis, and are not mutually exclusive of one another.

And in Europe in particular, the high profile attached to the rise of second-generation Muslim identification requires analysts to think about how race, ethnicity, and religion may combine. For instance, some studies in Britain now suggest that while the specific ethnic ancestry of second-generation Muslims (e.g., Bengali) is less important than it was to their parents, a panethnic sense of being Muslim is growing in importance and resonance for many young people—even if it may be only symbolic. So in addition to constant and gradual forms of ethnogenesis, we must also be mindful of the blurring of ethnic, racial, religious, and national identifications and affiliations, and their highly diverse manifestations in disparate localities throughout each country.

Whiteness, white migrants and the white working classes

The changing relationship between migration and race also needs to be examined in the context of social and political changes concerning white migrants and the white working classes. Major political undercurrents which concern the status of the white working (and to a lesser extent, the white middle) classes in Western European countries, such as in Britain and France, are highly prominent in the national agendas of these countries—especially in terms of histrionic fears about both legal and illegal immigration. The rise of various right-wing parties, such as the British National Party in Britain, is symptomatic of the contemporary political climate. In comparison with the post-war period, the class diversification and socioeconomic success of certain migrant groups has not been lost upon politicians and representatives of white working class people who attest to feeling "left behind." And in the USA, the growing numbers and influence of the black middle class has not gone unnoticed in poorer, rural white communities. For instance, in Britain, recent studies show that white working class boys' educational attainment is worse than that of minority boys, and in certain sectors of the media and popular culture, caricatures of white working class people appears to be largely socially acceptable. In any case, a simple equation in which "white" status is said to signal privilege, socially and economically, is clearly untenable—though the privileges of whiteness, in certain settings, can still be considerable (Lipsitz 2006).

The automatic coupling of migrant = non-white-raced person requires rethinking, of course, not only for academics, but also in the popular imagination. New streams of "white" migration from the enlargement of the European Union, for instance, has meant that Polish and Russian workers throughout the cities of London or Paris are now commonplace. Former sending societies are now becoming receiving immigration destinations—e.g., Italy, Spain, Greece—and this results in new understandings and meanings of "difference," migrant, and of racial hierarchies.

The arrival (and in some cases, settlement) of white Eastern European migrants to Western European destinations thus raises interesting and important questions about their incorporation. Will their integration trajectories be similar to that of white European immigrants to the USA in the early to mid-twentieth century? Does their visible whiteness shield them from prejudice, and allow them, at least in the next generation, to integrate relatively unproblematically into the white mainstream of European nations? Or does their arrival signal a more complex (and as yet unknown) conjuncture of migrant status, ethnicity, nationality, and geopolitics which has not yet been sufficiently studied?

Furthermore, the study of new white migrants is especially important in a context where blatant expressions of racist beliefs (e.g., in the alleged inferiority or superiority of some groups over others) is now socially unacceptable in most Western societies. The coupling of migration and race has also been complicated by the subtle refashionings and renaming of racial concerns into "ethnic" and "cultural" concerns. For instance, the discourse of national culture and belonging has gradually replaced the socially unacceptable articulations of the putatively 'different' migrant as an undesirable, raced person (Gilroy 1987)—what Michael Billig (1995) has called "banal nationalism." Instead, seemingly innocuous articulations about preserving and honoring national culture has effectively enabled the continuation of exclusionary and essentialising discourses to circulate in relation to "others," even if they may be "native" speakers and raised in that society. In this respect, white migrants who speak different languages, have identifiably different names, and "foreign" cultural repertoires can be targeted as not only foreign and undesirable, but also, to some, undeniably "different." Their arrival and gradual settlement, over time, engenders new thinking about the constantly changing and redrawing of ethnic and racial boundaries, with some bright boundaries turning into blurred boundaries, or new boundaries forming along the way (Alba 2005).

Islamophobia as the bright line of discrimination/disadvantage

In comparison with the USA, where "race" is still paramount as the key "bright" boundary of difference, especially with black people, Muslims (whether they be Pakistanis in Britain, Moroccans in France or the Netherlands, or Turks in Germany) constitute a key racial/ethnic/religious target in Western Europe. Governments in France, the Netherlands, and states in Germany have or are contemplating the banning of the veil from public institutions and settings.

In Britain, Tariq Modood in particular has stirred up controversial debate by suggesting that working class Muslims are the most racially oppressed group in Europe. Not only did this foment passionate debate about whether one can posit a "hierarchy of oppression" (a term used by one of his critics), but it engendered debate about the differential nature and experience of what we understand to be racisms and racial disadvantage. According to Modood, Muslims tend to be reviled for their putative cultural and religious foreignness, and their visibility (e.g. via the veil) makes them easy targets, especially in our post-9/11 world.

This huge focus on "problematic" Muslims has reshaped people's understandings of the "migrant"—not only is this migrant typically raced as either South Asian (e.g. Pakistani) or Middle Eastern, but this migrant is deemed a religious zealot, and possible suicide bomber as well. This obsession with Muslims in our midst has recast wider understandings of who belongs and who does not—so that, as Modood has pointed, black Britons, most of whose ancestors arrived in the post-war period from former British colonies such as Nigeria or Jamaica, are now seen as not quite *so* "different" as Muslims, especially given the valorization of certain black cultural forms in wider mainstream popular cultures.

In the aftermath of 9/11 and the July 7, 2005 bombings in London, there was particular horror and incredulity expressed about the fact that many of the bombers had been born and raised in Britain. Rather than bearded men burning the *Satanic Verses*, as happened in 1989, widespread concern was expressed about the fact that these men were British and in higher education. So the entire political context in which discussions about migration and racial and ethnic and religious difference occur is one in which the perceived excesses of an overly liberal multiculturalism are seen to be, by many, to be a terrible mistake. As discussed earlier, the disaffection of British born Muslims has illustrated the need to study not only economic disadvantage and blocked opportunities, but also the need to investigate the lack of "social cohesion" or "community cohesion" in many urban centers, where white and South Asian communities are said to live parallel lives. The widespread concern about disaffected "home-grown" Muslims in European societies also signals the need to rethink the assumed and straightforward weakening of ethnic and racial ties and affiliations in the second generation; in fact, there is considerable evidence that politicized assertions of public ethnicity and public assertions of Muslim identity are growing, at least among some sectors of second-generation Muslims. Needless to say, there are many second-generation Muslims who neither practice nor feel particularly strongly about Islam or their religious identities.

But the overriding concern about "foreign" and alienated Muslims, coupled with evidence of economic deprivation, has fundamentally shaped thinking about not only which types of migrants are deemed racial targets, but also the nature of the discrimination and prejudice they encounter. This dominant social and political focus upon minority Muslims has thus led to growing debate about the need to identify disparate and specific forms of racialization and racism(s). Attention to the experiences of Muslim groups in Western multiethnic societies reveals the increasingly blurred boundaries between racial/ethnic/religious/national affiliations, meanings, and markers.

Rethinking of multiculturalism and citizenship

The reconfiguration of migration and race is also being shaped, as discussed above, by not only the now-omnipresent preoccupation with Muslims and Islam in many Western societies, but also the many criticisms of multiculturalism, which is increasingly regarded as misguided and problematic by politicians, policy analysts, and the wider population. Although there is no singular definition of multiculturalism, it refers, broadly speaking, to a set of ideas, policies, and practices which espouse ethnic and cultural diversity and distinctiveness. In recent years, critics of multiculturalism have argued that it has both hindered social cohesion, and encouraged the formation of separate, parallel minority communities who do not share the core values of mainstream society.

In his preface to the 2002 White Paper called "Secure Borders, Safe Haven: Integration and Diversity in Modern Britain," the then Home Secretary David Blunkett wrote: "To enable integration to take place and to value the diversity it brings, we need to be secure within our sense of belonging and identity and therefore to be able to reach out and to embrace those who come to the UK … " (p. 1). The title of this White Paper reflects not only the intense security concerns in the aftermath of 9/11, but also the ongoing controversies about the viability and desirability of ethnic diversity and multicultural policies in Britain and other Western European societies.

For the past two decades, the British state (and various other Western European countries) has had to address both the recognition of growing ethnic diversity, and the need to foster social cohesion (and combat forms of radical extremism, whether actual or imagined). Thus a number of European states have emphasized the civic and cultural integration of immigrants and their second-generation offspring (Joppke 2004), and this has been evident in the reformulation of both policies concerning multiculturalism and citizenship policies (Modood 2007).

Cultural assimilation into the nation has been deemed desirable to ward off racialized segregation and disaffection, whether in reference to preventing urban disturbances in the north of England between Asian and white Britons, or in the Paris suburbs. Too much "difference" is said to be alarmingly manifest in a number of ways, particularly in relation to Muslim groups, whether it is the language spoken, beliefs about a secular society, or gender practices. Perceived failures of some groups to advance or integrate are then taken to be a function not of a dominant boundary, restriction, and exclusion, but of the absence of certain kinds of values on the part of the group itself (Steinberg 1989).

In the context of criticisms against multiculturalism, conceptualizations of citizenship have become increasingly central to government's policies surrounding integration and social cohesion. Under New Labour, more demanding citizenship tests were aimed at not just the formal acquisition of citizenship, but also a fostering of a cultural and national sense of belonging within the nation. Citizenship education was also introduced in Britain in 2002, so that schools' roles in "civil enculturation" became more explicit (Schiffauer et al. 2004).

Thus, a nation is not only a political entity but a symbolic and cultural community shaped by the ways in which people think about and enact ideas about the nation and its national culture (Anderson 1983). Yet modern nations are not only culturally hybrid, but comprised of different genders, classes, ethnicities, and religions. Contemporary attempts to refashion citizenship in Britain acknowledges the culturally hybrid nature of post-colonial Britain, but in pointing to areas of "core culture" and values, a dominant (and in practice, often a racially exclusionary) discourse of the nation unfolds. Increasingly, public policy and academic scholarship reflects this preoccupation with citizenship, and how minority individuals are expected to be "active citizens" who work at their inclusion. As a result, the discourses of race and racial difference are side-lined, or obscured, by an emphasis upon a seemingly race-neutral and concerned citizen who is, and wants to be, a part of the mainstream. Thus the ongoing furor about immigration is ultimately about the type of society we want to live in, as well as the extent to which immigrants can and should participate in the wider society (Kymlicka 1995).

Growth in intermarriage and "mixed race" people

Another key development which is reshaping how we conceive of migration and race is the growth in interethnic relationships and mixed race people. What do interethnic relationships, and the growth of second- and third-generation "mixed race" people suggest for our understandings of migration, race, and "integration"? In the USA rates of intermarriage for groups such as Asian Americans and Latino Americans are significant, where the percentages of Asian or Latino husbands or wives with spouses of another race or ethnicity surpassed 30 percent by the late 1990s, with most of these married to a white partner. Current demographic projections in Britain and even the USA suggest that while ethnic boundaries will not disappear overnight, they will grow ever more complex and blurred (Song 2010). To provide some sense of the burgeoning unions between white and non-white Britons, there are *more* "mixed" black Caribbean/white Britons under the age of 5 than children of this age with two black Caribbean parents.

Seen in the broader context of group relations, intermarriage is considered, by many analysts, to be *the* litmus test of integration. It is said to signal a significant lessening of "social distance" between a minority group and the white majority (since most interethnic unions involve white partners). Why should we be interested in rates of interethnic unions? First, it is noteworthy if some groups intermarry with whites, while others do not—this would suggest that some groups are more socially acceptable in the white mainstream than are others. For instance, some American analysts have suggested that the growing numbers of Asian/white unions, and their Eurasian offspring, suggest the emergence of a kind of honorary white group, with the boundaries between Asian (and light-skinned Latino) Americans and white Americans increasingly softening. Also, because marriage is regarded as a mechanism for the transmission of ethnically specific cultural values and practices to the next generation, intermarriage may fundamentally affect the boundaries and distinctiveness of ethnic minority groups.

Studies of multiracial people note a recurrent societal preoccupation—an expectation that they choose one race as their primary basis of identification. Historically, one race has typically been seen as the primary, dominant race of a multiracial person (Spickard 1989). For instance, the USA has traditionally enforced the "one drop rule," so that part-black people are expected to see themselves as black. While the very existence of multiracial people might seem to herald a profound rethinking of existing racial categories and their legitimacy, as well as the everyday belief that there are such things as "pure" and distinct races, multiracial people themselves are subject to racial discourses (both in the wider society and in their family lives) which constrain and shape the ways in which they are able to assert their desired ethnic and racial identifications (Song 2003).

Nevertheless, more recent studies have demonstrated that mixed people can and do make choices about their ethnic and racial identities. Studies have shown that mixed people do assert preferred identity options, so that while some individuals may adopt a singular racial identification (e.g., as black), others may opt for a blended, mixed identification, in which they refuse to choose one category over another; yet others may claim an identification which transcends racial categorization and thinking altogether (Rockquemore and Brunsma 2002). So while some individuals may seek inclusion in an existing racial category, others may try to contest, refute or shift racial boundaries or classifications.

In fact, the emergence of a multiracial movement in the USA (DaCosta 2007) has shown the ways in which minority groups and individuals, from the ground up, are challenging existing classifications and policies. If the numbers of interethnic relationships continue to grow, as they almost certainly will, it may be that our awareness of and meanings attached to notions of ethnic and racial difference may be blunted. There is now a question mark about the automatic salience of one's mixedness and/or racial/ethnic ancestry, especially for mixed people in large, cosmopolitan settings, where being mixed is increasingly ordinary. But we must avoid an overly sanguine view that mixing and the existence of mixed people somehow signals an unproblematic integration and social acceptance.

Conclusion

Given all the major developments discussed above—(a) the diverse experiences and identification of the second generation, (b) the questioning of the presumed salience of ethnicity and race, (c) the attention to white ethnicity and experiences, especially that of the white working classes, (d) growing forms of Islamophobia and its implications for our understandings of racialized experiences, (e) the ongoing criticisms of multiculturalism and the emphasis upon active citizenship, and finally, (f) the growing numbers of mixed relationships and individuals—we need to rethink the configuration of migration and race. In a context in which so many social dynamics are simultaneously in play, and in which analysts can marshal multiple and sometimes conflicting forms of "evidence," it is less and less likely that social scientists can proclaim neat and definitive trends and outcomes. It is imperative that scholars consider both the structure and agency underlying migrants' diverse and multiple experiences. All this complexity and multiplicity of forces and variables suggests that much scholarship concerning migration and race may become ever more specialized, as scholars investigate particular aspects of social experience, in relation, perhaps, to ever-more specific groups and sub-groups!

Generational status is still key in understanding the relationship between migration and race, but it's a less predictable relationship than in the past—being second or third generation may or may not mean being "raced" depending upon regional location, one's parentage (mixed or not), one's appearance, one's class background, etc. When does the marker of generational status—the key marker of migrant status—become less salient? Up to now, the most significant divide has been that between first and second generation, both in terms of structural incorporation and broader investments in belonging in the "host" society. What is a fascinating question for the future is the status of the third generation and beyond, especially for migrant groups which are traditionally seen as visible, "raced" minorities. For example, is a third generation Briton of Indian descent, who is married to a white English person, a 'migrant' still? And to what extent, and in what ways, will one's non-white status matter? Will a "multi-generation" Briton of Chinese or Pakistani origin, as in the case of multi-generation Asian Americans in the USA (Tuan 1998), still be seen as "foreign," and thus a perennial "migrant" of sorts?

As discussed above, the issue of intermarriage and growing numbers of mixed people is also important for the configuration of migration and race because both of these concepts have relied centrally upon the identification and delineation of clear boundaries between distinct named groups of people. Since the state has historically employed classifications and terms to distinguish between various minority and majority groups, it will have to think critically and carefully about the legitimacy of existing ethnic and racial classification schemes to denote ethnic and racial difference, and mixedness, in the population. Various methodological and theoretical concerns, which will inform policy decisions, are increasingly pressing. For instance, how should states classify the marriages of mixed people? Is it an intermarriage if, for instance, a mixed Chinese/ English person marries a white person, or would this count as a marriage between two members of the majority society? If this same mixed person married someone who was "purely" of Chinese heritage, would this, then, count as intermarriage? These are not merely technical questions, for, on the ground, lay people (and analysts) will be asking themselves the same questions.

It is doubtful that one's migrant status (however distant this may be in actual generational removes) will simply erode in a linear fashion, at least in terms of how that "migrant" may be seen in the wider society. But the meanings associated with such migrant status will be mediated by many different factors which will or will not render one's migrant (i.e., not fully belonging) status meaningful or noticed in a given situation. Visibility, as a marker of raced difference, will still continue to matter in a variety of contexts, but its effects may be less predictable or less consistently salient than in the past. It is now commonplace for analysts to note the socially constructed and contingent nature of both race and ethnicity. Despite numerous scholarly pronouncements about the multiplicity and fluidity of racial identifications, on the ground, "ordinary" people inhabit worlds where essentialist racial attributions are rife. In this sense, understandings of race, migration, and migrant, have remained all too real.

References and further reading

Alba, R. (2005) "Bright versus blurred boundaries" *Ethnic and Racial Studies* 28(1): 20–49.
Anderson, B. (1983) *Imagined Communities*. London: Verso.
Ang, I. (1994) "On not speaking Chinese," *New Formations* 24, November, 1–18.
Anthias, F. and Yuval-Davis, N. (1992) *Racialized Boundaries*. London: Routledge.
Appadurai, A. (1990) "Disjuncture and difference in the global cultural economy." In M. Featherstone (ed.) *Global Culture*. London: Sage, pp. 295–310.
Beck, U. (1992) *Risk Society*. London: Sage.
Bhabha, H. (1994) *The Location of Culture*. London: Routledge.
Billig, M. (1995) *Banal Nationalism*. London: Sage.
DaCosta, K. (2007) *Making Multiracials*. Cambridge, MA: Harvard University Press.
Giddens, A. (1991) *Modernity and Self-Identity*. Cambridge: Polity Press.
Gilroy, P. (1987) *There Ain't No Black in the Union Jack*. London: Routledge.
Gold, S. (2000) "Transnational communities: Examining migration in a globally integrated world." In P. Aulakh and M. Schechter (eds), *Rethinking Globalizations(s)*. New York: St Martins Press, pp. 73–90.

Gordon, M. (1964) *Assimilation in American Life*. New York: Oxford University Press.

Hall, S. (1997) *Representation*. Milton Keynes: Open University Press.

Hall, S., Held, D., and McGrew, A. (1992) *Modernity and Its Futures*. Milton Keynes: Open University Press.

Joppke, C. (2004) "The retreat of multiculturalism in the liberal state" *British Journal of Sociology* 55(2): 237–57.

Kymlicka, W. (1995) *Multicultural Citizenship*. Oxford: Clarendon Press.

Lipsitz, G. (2006) *The Possessive Investment in Whiteness*. Philadelphia, PA: Temple University Press.

Modood, T. (2007) *Multiculturalism*. Cambridge: Polity Press.

Parker, D. (1995) *Through Different Eyes*. Aldershot: Avebury Press.

Portes, A. and Zhou, M. (1993) "The new second generation: Segmented assimilation and its variants" *Annals of the American Academy of Political and Social Science* 530: 74–96.

Rockquemore, K. and Brunsma, D. (2002) *Beyond Black*. Thousand Oaks, CA: Sage.

Schiffauer, W., Baumann, G., Kastoryano, R., and Vertovec, S. (2004) *Civil Enculturation*. New York: Berghahn Books.

Smith, A. (1990) "Towards a global culture?" In M. Featherstone (ed.), *Global Culture*. London: Sage, pp. 171–92.

Song, M. (2003) *Choosing Ethnic Identity*, Cambridge: Polity Press.

——(2010) "Is there 'a' mixed race group in Britain? The diversity of multiracial experiences," *Critical Social Policy*, 30(3): 337–58.

Spickard, P. (1989) *Mixed Blood*. Madison, WI: University of Wisconsin Press.

Steinberg, S. (1989) *The Ethnic Myth*. Boston, MA: Beacon Press.

Tuan, M. (1998) *Forever Foreigners or Honorary Whites?* New Brunswick, NJ: Rutgers University Press.

Vertovec, S. (2007) "Superdiversity and its implications" *Ethnic and Racial Studies* 30(6): 1024–54.

Waters, M. (1990) *Ethnic Options*. Berkeley, CA: University of California Press.

15

New directions in gender and immigration research

Pierrette Hondagneu-Sotelo

Immigration studies has grown vastly in the last 30 years, but glance at the principal journals and publications in the United States, and immediately you get it: gender is still ghettoized in immigration scholarship. Basic concepts like gender, sex, power, privilege, sexual discrimination, and intersectionalities are regularly absent from the vocabulary and the study designs. The cottage industries of segmented assimilation, transnationalism, and citizenship—with a few significant exceptions—remain like hermetically sealed steam trains from another century, chugging along oblivious to developments in gender scholarship of the last 30 years. I went through all of the recent issues of the *International Migration Review*, the premier social science journal in this field, and I found that in 2007, 2008, and 2009, there were a total of seven articles with "women" or "gender" in the title. In 2006, there were none except those included in a special issue on gender. Why is that? Gender remains one of the fundamental social relations that anchors and impacts immigration patterns, including labor migration as well as professional class migrations and refugee movements. Gender is deeply implicated in imperialist, military, and colonial conquests, which are widely recognized as the roots of global international migration flows. Once immigration movements begin, they take form in markedly gendered ways. In addition, immigration processes bring about life-impacting changes, de-stabilizing and remodeling the gendered way daily life is lived.

Sociology experienced an increase in feminist research in the 1980s and 1990s. In the 1970s, feminist research projects had emphasized the ways in which institutions and social privileges are constructed in ways that favor men. Since then, most feminist-oriented scholars have dispensed with unitary concepts of "men" and "women." Multiplicities of femininities and masculinities are recognized today, as interconnected, relational, and intertwined in relations of class, race-ethnicity, nation, and sexualities. The focus on intersectionalities in immigration studies is palpable in gender and immigration studies elsewhere around the globe too, but from what I can see, it is perhaps less institutionalized in Europe, Asia, and Latin America. Outside of the United States, there is also less focus on men and masculinities, and sexualities (with the exception of trafficking, which I discuss below).

Looking at scholarship on gender and migration today, I see two seemingly contradictory trends. On the one hand, an androcentric blindness to feminist issues and gender remains. It is business as usual, the missing feminist revolution. Morakvasic made this observation in 1984, and Silvia Pedraza in 1991. That's now an old song, and I don't want to sing it here. On the other hand, there *is* a vibrant scholarship on gender and migration, but not only is it not reaching or shaping some of the debates at the core, but it is also balkanized. In fact, there are several distinctive arenas of gender and migration scholarship, and there appears to be a lack of communication among these arenas. Researchers working on, for example, the subject of migration and transnational sexualities may not be aware of the research on migration and care work. As I see it, there are at least five different streams of gender and migration research. In this chapter I provide a brief overview of these areas.

Gender and migration: carrying the flag

In the first category of "gender and migration" scholarship, I see researchers—almost all of them women—pursuing what some might call a mainstream social science approach. Here, the goal is to make gender an institutional part of immigration studies. It is not, as is often mistakenly suggested, solely about gauging gender gains for immigrant and refugee women. Rather, a small group of intrepid scholars are carrying the flag to establish legitimacy for gender in immigration studies. In the United States this includes prominent scholars such as sociologist, demographer and co-editor of the *American Sociological Review*, Katharine Donato, as well as historian and former president of the Social Science History Association Donna Gabbacia, and anthropologists Patricia Pessar and Sarah Mahler. This is not only a US issue of concern. In Spain, the anthropologist Carmen Gregorio Gil has published numerous articles on feminist debates in gender and migration, as has geographer Brenda Yeoh, on the topic of migrant women domestic workers in Singapore, and Marina Ariza and Ofelia Woo Morales and others on Mexico. In Europe, Annie Phizacklea and Mirjana Morakvasic published some of the earlier works on this topic, followed by Elinor Kofman, Helma Lutz, and others.

In the United States Donato, Gabbaccia, and others edited a special issue of the *International Migration Review* (*IMR*) in 2006, with the title of "A Glass Half Full? Gender in Migration Studies." This was a 20-year follow up to a 1986 special issue of the journal that had focused on the category of immigrant *women*. By the 1990s, the research had shifted away from a focus on "women" and was emphasizing migration as a gendered process. This research sought to break simplistic gender binaries, and drew attention to gendered labor markets and social networks, the relationship between paid work and household relations, changes in family patriarchy and authority that come about through migration, and gendered and generational transnational life (Grasmuck and Pessar 1991; Kibria 1993; Hondagneu-Sotelo 1994). Later, Stephanie Nawyn (2010) emphasized the ways that refugee resettlement non-governmental organizations (NGOs) shape refugee women's ability to challenge patriarchy in the home, yet simultaneously reaffirm patriarchal capitalism in the workplace, and Cynthia Cranford's (2007) research emphasized how economic restructuring, and workplace and union politics allow Latina immigrant janitors to challenge gendered constraints in multiple spheres. All of these works emphasize that gender is a dynamic and constitutive element of migration and immigrant integration.

In the special issue of *IMR*, Donato *et al.* (2006) addressed some of these key themes and offered a multidisciplinary review of the field of migration and gender, and the results reflect the pattern identified by Stacey and Thorne (1985) more than two decades ago: more openness in anthropology, less change in the more quantitative fields of demography and economics. Scholars such as Donato and Gabbaccia seek to discover what they call the "gender balance" of major migration movements around the world and in different time periods. They seek to measure when migration flows tip from being primarily male to majority female. In the United States, that happened at an aggregate level in the early twentieth century.

In Europe, especially Spain, there is burgeoning new research on transnational motherhood, and South American women's labor migration to Spain and their roles as pioneers in family migration (Escriva 2000). Research in Asia focuses on gender, migration, and the state (Piper and Roces 2003; Oishi 2005), and there is diverse gender research in Mexico, the nation with the longest continuously running transnational labor migration (e.g., Arias 2000; Oehmichen 2000). In the United States, a new book by Gordillo (2010) focuses on Mexican women's gendered transnational ties, and a 2009 book edited by Seyla Benhabib and Judith Resnick (2009) carries the gender flag into the territory of debates about citizenship, immigration law, sovereignty, and legal jurisdiction. The topic of domestic violence in immigrant women's lives has also garnered deserved attention (Menjivar and Salcido 2002). These are some varied and ongoing efforts that seek to reform immigration scholarship so that it acknowledges gender as fundamental to migration processes.

Migration and care work

A second stream has focused exclusively on the relation between women's migration, paid domestic work, and family care. The key concepts here are "carework," "global care chains," "care deficits," "transnational motherhood," and "international social reproductive labor." The development of this literature has been made possible by theories of intersectionality. Beginning in the 1980s, and guided by paradigm changing work of feminist scholars of color in the United States, the unitary concepts of "men" and "women" were replaced with the idea that there are multiplicities of femininities and masculinities, and that these are interconnected, relational, and intertwined with inequalities of class, race-ethnicity, nation, and sexualities.

In this body of research, the focus shifts away from relations between women and men, to inequalities between immigrant women and nation, the way these are constituted by the international unloading of domestic reproductive work from women of the post-industrial, rich countries to women from the less-developed, poor countries of the global south. Often, this mandates long-term family separations between migrant women and their children. This is a big literature, and still growing, but key contributors have included Hondagneu-Sotelo and Avila (1997), Chang (2000), Parrenas (2001), and Hondagneu-Sotelo (2007) on the United States; Constable (1997) and Lan (2006) in Asia; Anderson (2000), Escriva (2000), Parrenas (2001), and Lutz (2008) in Europe and the UK; and Hochschild and Ehrenreich's (2003) edited book, covering global ground. Newer research examines the integration of immigrant men in domestic jobs, such as Polish handymen in London (Kilkey 2010) and Mexican immigrant gardeners in Los Angeles (Ramirez and Hondagneu-Sotelo 2009).

Why did this literature begin emerging around 2000? The late twentieth century was marked by the rapid increase in women migrating for domestic work. During the peak periods of modernization and industrialization, migrants were mainly men—usually men from poorer, often colonial societies—recruited to do "men's work." Chinese, Filipino, Japanese, Irish, Italian, and Mexican men, for instance, all took turns in being recruited and brought to build infrastructure in the industrializing United States. In some instances, family members were allowed to join them, but in many cases, especially those involving immigrant groups perceived as non-white, the family members (women and children) were denied admission. Government legislation enforced these prohibitions on the permanent incorporation of these workers and their families. The Bracero Program and the Guest Worker Program are the exemplars of these modern gendered systems which relied on male labor recruitment and subjugation, and the exclusion of families.

Things have changed today. Factories migrate overseas in search of cheaper labor, and high-tech and highly educated professionals have joined labor migrants. But among them are legions of women who crisscross the globe, from south to north, from east to west in order to perform paid domestic work. Consequently, in some sites, we are seeing the redundance of male migrant labor, and the saturation of labor markets for migrant men. In places as diverse as Italy, the Middle East, Taiwan, and Canada, Filipina migrant women caregivers and cleaners far outnumber Filipino migrant men. The demand is activated in different ways by different nations, raising questions of how state policies facilitate women's migration, and here there is a lot of variation. What is clear is this: women from countries as varied as Peru, Philippines, Moldavia, Eritrea, and Indonesia are leaving their families, communities, and countries to migrate thousands of miles away to work in the new worldwide growth industry of paid domestic work and elder care. What remains puzzling is marginalization of this literature in immigration scholarship. That could be explained because the topic draws together three elements usually thought to be unimportant: women, the domestic sphere, and carework.

Sexualities

A third branch of gender and immigration research has been more related with the humanities, queer studies, and cultural studies. Here, the focus is on sexualities, including gay and queer identities, as well as hetero-normativity and compulsory heterosexuality, employed both as a form of legal immigration exclusion as well as inclusion. The posthumously published book by Lionel Cantu, *The Sexuality of Migration* (2009), edited by his former mentor Nancy Naples and colleague Salvador Ortiz, shows how sexual relationships among Mexican gay men are related to international tourism, transnational networks and sometimes, legal asylum. The debates over gay marriage also resonate in immigration policies that deny entrance to queer and LBGT immigrants. Eithne Luibheid (2002) takes up these themes in *Entry Denied: Controlling Sexuality at the Border,* where she shows how implicit and explicit definitions of heteronormativity have been integral to laws that govern immigration control. In most nations, heterosexual citizens can sponsor their foreign partners for legal residence. But only 19 countries around the world permit lesbian and gay citizens to sponsor their foreign partners. The United States is not among those 19 nations. The 1965 Immigration Act made heterosexual marriage the most important avenue for legal entry to the United States. We usually think of the 1965 Immigration Act as liberalizing immigration legislation, as it ended the Asian racial exclusions and institutionalized legal family immigration— but it is also exclusionary because it reifies a narrow heterosexual definition of family. Another book that addresses the longstanding invisibility of gay and queer immigrants is Martin Manalansan's (2003) *Global Divas: Filipino Gay Men in the Diaspora,* an ethnography conducted in New York City.

Too often "sexualities" gets translated as a focus on queer sexualities, and a book that makes an important intervention in studying up is Gloria Gonzalez-Lopez's (2005) *Erotic Journeys: Mexican Immigrant Women and their Sex Lives*. This book looks at normative heterosexual practices and values of Mexican immigrant working class women and men in order to reveal how processes of invisible power organize Mexican immigrant women's lives. Rather than taking the familiar approach of focusing on social problems such as teen pregnancy, or the transnational transmission of HIV, Gonzalez-Lopez examines Mexican immigrant women's sexual practices and how they feel about them. It's the sociological imagination at it's best, making visible the socially constructed and problematic nature of something previously taken as normative and acceptable.

Sex trafficking

The fourth stream of gender and migration research is centered on debates about sex trafficking, and migrant women working in sex work. In Europe, this is a huge area of scholarship and activism, one where the moral crusade often masks structures of labor exploitation. One of the strongest critics of the "rescue industry" is the scholar/activist Laura Agustin (2007). Originally from Latin America, but based in the UK, she examines sex tourism, sex work migration, and crackdowns by police and immigration authorities. Sex work draws migrant women from Eastern Europe, the Caribbean and Latin America, Asia, and Africa. Highly influenced by Anzaldua's borderlands thinking, Agustin seeks to break down the duality of seeing migrants as unwanted intruders or powerless victims. She views migrant women's sex work through the lens of labor markets and informal economies, and she favors a perspective that is devoid of moralizing, one that favors agency over victimization.

The US-based scholar Rhacel Parrenas is best known for her work on transnational Filipina domestic workers and their family forms, but her most recent research focus is on Filipina migrant entertainers and hostesses in Japan. Some of this writing has already appeared as a chapter in her 2008 book, *The Force of Domesticity*.

Like Agustin, she views migrant women sex workers through the lens of labor markets and structural constraints, rather than as immoral women or hapless victims of exploitation. Unlike Agustin, Parrenas provides a close-up ethnography of the Japanese sex industries' reliance on Filipino women and transgender hostesses and entertainers. Until very recently, there was an entire visa system set up to facilitate temporary labor contracts for Filipina/o hostesses in Japan, but this ended with US pressure from the "war on trafficking," which assumes that all commercial sex transactions are tantamount to exploitation, regardless of consent. The United States funds over 100 projects around the world to stop sex trafficking. Parrenas and Agustin are in agreement: many of these US campaign are tools to control women, and to disperse American colonialist culture and morality.

Borderlands and migration

The fifth arena is a broad one that owes its legacy to Gloria Anzaldua's classic *Borderlands/La Frontera: The New Mestiza*, published in 1987. The scholarship which it generated brings together a Chicana studies focus on the hybridity of identities, and the hybrid space of borderlands. Influenced by socialist feminist thought, and internal colonialism, the focus here is on both mestiza identity, *and* on spaces that defy easy opposition between dominant and dominated, here and there. *Women and Migration in The US-Mexico Borderlands*, edited by Denise Segura and Pat Zavella (2007), best exemplifies this stream. Here the contributors argue that there are feminist borderlands and theoretical emphases: structural, discursive, interactional, and agentic. New destinations research that focused on the gendered reception for Mexican immigrants in the South and Midwest also highlights diverse borders and crossings (Deeb-Sossa and Binkham Mendez 2008; Schmalzbauer 2009).

The notion of a "gendered borderlands" reverberates in research far beyond the US–Mexico border zone. As already noted, Laura Agustin, the scholar/activist who focuses on sex trafficking, is also inspired by Anzaldua, and very deliberately employs border thinking, challenging the supposed oppression and victimization of migrant women sex workers, and rethinking women's migration rights in a broader framework. Bandana Purkayastha's (2003) research on South Asian immigrant women also brings together intersectionalities and transnational social life. And Yen Le Espiritu (2003), underscoring the role of US imperialism, military intervention, and multinational corporations in fomenting refugee movements and labor and professional class migration, also calls attention to the United States as the primary border crosser. It is a scholarly twist on the old Chicano T-shirt slogan: "We didn't cross the border. It crossed us." And it resonates with the political slogan used by Caribbean and South Asian immigrant activists in the UK, signaling the colonialist legacies of contemporary migration and demographic transitions: "We're here because you were there."

Gender, migration, and children

An emergent area of scholarship focuses on gender, migration, and children. Less cohesively developed than the other arenas reviewed here, the research on children and the gendered ramifications of transnational migration is nevertheless a critical emergent field. Gendered social constructions of childhood mediate transnational migration processes and childhoods (Orellana *et al.* 2003; Thorne *et al.* 2003). Researchers have examined gendered dynamics surrounding "the children left behind" as their mothers migrate as transnational domestic workers (Parrenas 2005); the negotiated narratives of sexuality and purity among second-generation young women (Espiritu 2001), the gendered and racialized work experiences of second generation youth (Lopez 2003), and the gendered concerns and strategies that immigrant parents employ in organizing their children's transnational trips home (Smith 2005). Another body of scholarship looks at the gendered labor performed by the children of poor and working class Mexican immigrants (Estrada and Hondagneu-Sotelo 2011). Research has also examined children's gendered expectations for family migration projects (Pavez Soto 2010) and more generally the gendered options of pursuing education versus migration (Paris Pombo 2010).

Concluding thoughts

Gender and migration research momentum is advancing in many directions. This includes new and continuing research on the global care chains, on labor market processes and activism around sex work and anti-sex trafficking campaigns, on women and borderlands hybridity, continuing projects on the gendered and generational processes of transnational migration, gendered social constructions of childhood, and sophisticated tabulations in demography. I think these are all valuable. But two trends are notable: researchers in these different spheres are mostly not in conversation with one another. Second, there is a continued and near total deafness from scholars working on other core areas of immigration studies, on segmented assimilation, immigrant religion, transnationalism, and citizenship. The former is due to the increasingly specialized and balkanized nature of social science research today, and the latter remains a concern that should be remedied.

We can also detect a subtle shift away from a "migration and development" paradigm toward one that focuses on "immigrant integration." I think future scholarship in gender and migration must also grapple with the fact that we are living in a national and global crisis of immigration restrictionism. Transnationalism is a way of life for many, but unlike some of the celebratory commentators, I do not believe transnationalism or post-nationalism provides a viable framework for immigrant rights. We do not appear to be approaching the erosion of nation-state borders, so with that reality, it is important to focus on immigrant integration. And in this regard, I think we need new young feminist scholars dedicated to unraveling the gendered processes and institutions that promote immigrant restrictionism, exclusions and violence, and prohibit immigrant integration.

Along these lines, I want to conclude by noting how gender is used in the current vilification of immigrants. Since the beginning of immigration legislation in the United States, gender and race have been used as central categories of exclusion. The Page Act of 1875, the first precursor to US federal immigration law, excluded Chinese women who were held to be immorally suspect prostitutes. The big mid-twentieth-century contract labor programs in the United States and Western Europe, the Bracero Program and the Guestworker Program prohibited women and selected prime working age men as the ideal labor migrants, as they would not bring social reproduction costs nor, it was thought, contribute to demographic transformations. During the 1980s and early 1990s, the "immigrant danger" was largely seen as feminine one. The bodies of immigrant women—namely poor immigrant women, women of color, and especially Mexican women—were seen as a threat to the United States. Perceived as pregnant breeders, they were also construed as racial threats to demographic homogeneity, social welfare drains on public schools and hospitals, and as the culprits responsible for the social reproduction of immigrant children and entire communities.

In the last decade, we've seen a switch in the gendered construction of immigrant danger. The new danger is a masculine one, one personified by terrorist men and "criminal aliens." These are racialized men. Muslim terrorists, Mexican narco-traffickers, and gang bangers are the new racialized and gendered immigrant danger. The majority of criminologists agree that there are no obvious connections between criminality and the foreign born, but in spite of this, we have seen a rapid increase in the number of immigrant men detained and deported. Between 1980 and 2005, the proportion of incarcerated immigrant men in the United States increased fourfold. Why? It is largely due to draconian immigrant restrictionist legislation, IIRIRA (Illegal Immigration Reform, and Immigrant Responsibility Act) of 1996, aggressive practices of imprisoning those awaiting asylum decisions, and ways in which many drug crimes—even possessing a small amount of pot or cocaine—are now considered deportable crimes for legal immigrants. The increasing rate of incarceration of immigrant men also corresponds with the rise of private, for-profit prisons run by corporations. The popular mass media has covered these issues in such a way that lead to the conflation of undocumented immigrants, "criminal aliens," and terrorists, all of them configured as dangerous men.

It's a moment in history where racialized and gendered xenophobia have greased the chutes of deportation, and blocked the ladders of immigrant integration. This is an issue of great urgency for women, men, and children of all nations. As this review essay suggests, gender and migration scholarship has flourished, but it has remained somewhat balkanized. The next generation of gender and migration scholars has a strong scholarly foundation on which to build, and given the current social and political climate, the challenges of understanding the gendered dimensions and repercussions of immigrant restrictionism should emerge as the among the pressing new arenas of focus.

References and further reading

Agustin, L. (2007) *Sex at the Margins: Migration, Labour Markets and the Rescue Industry*. London: Zed Books.
Anderson, B. (2000) *Doing the Dirty Work: The Global Politics of Domestic Labour*. London: Zed books.
Anzaldúa, G. (1987) *Borderlands. La Frontera: The new Mestiza*. San Francisco, CA: Aunt Lute Books.
Arias, P. (2000) "Las migrantes de ayer y de hoy." In D. Bassols and C. Oehmichen (eds), *Migración y relaciones de género en México*. México: GIMTRAPUNAM/IIA, pp. 185–202.
Benhabib, S. and Resnick, J. (eds) (2009) *Migrations and Mobilities: Citizenship, Borders and Gender*. New York: New York University Press.
Cantu, L. (2009) *The Sexuality of Migration: Border Crossings and Mexican Immigrant Men*. N. A. Naples and S. Vidal-Ortiz (eds), New York: New York University Press.
Chang, G. (2000) *Disposable Domestics: Immigrant Women Workers in the Global Economy*. Cambridge, MA: South End Press.
Constable, N. (1997) *Maid to Order in Hong Kong: Stories of Filipina Workers*. Ithaca, NY: Cornell University Press.
Cranford, C. J. (2007) "It's time to leave machismo behind!: Challenging gender inequality in an immigrant union" *Gender & Society* 21(3): 409–36.
Deeb-Sossa, N. and Mendez J. B. (2008) "Enforcing borders in the Nuevo South: Gender and migration in Williamsburg, Virginia and the Research Triangle, North Carolina" *Gender & Society* 22(5): 613–38.

Donato, K. M., Gabaccia, D., Holdaway, J., Manalansan IV, M., and Pessar, P. R. (2006) "A glass half full? Gender in migration studies" *International Migration Review* 40(1): 3–26.

Escriva, A. (2000) "Empleadas de por vida? Peruanas en el servicio domestico en Barcelona" *Papers* 60: 327–42.

Espiritu, Y. L. (2001) "'We don't sleep around like white girls do': Family, culture, and gender in Filipina American lives" *Signs* 26(2): 415–40.

——(2003) *Home Bound: Filipino American Lives Across Cultures, Communities, and Countries*. Berkeley, CA: University of California Press.

Estrada, E. and Hondagneu-Sotelo, P. (2011), "Intersectional dignities: Latina immigrant adolescent street vendors in Los Angeles" *Journal of Contemporary Ethnography*, 40(1): 102–131.

Gonzalez-Lopez, G. (2005) *Erotic Journeys: Mexican Immigrant Women and their Sex Lives*. Berkeley, CA: University of California Press.

Gordillo, L. M. (2010) *Mexican Women and the Other Side of Immigration: Engendering Transnational Ties*. Austin, TX: University of Texas Press.

Grasmuck, S. and Pessar, P. R. (1991) *Between Two Islands: Domincan International Migration*. Berkeley, CA: University of California Press.

Hochschild, A. and Ehrenreich, B. (eds) (2003) *Global Woman: Nannies, Maids and Sex Workers in the New Economy*. New York: Metropolitan Books.

Hondagneu-Sotelo, P. (1994) *Gendered Transitions: Mexican Experiences of Immigration*. Berkeley, CA: University of California Press (4th printing).

——(2007) *Domestica: Immigrant Workers Cleaning and Caring in the Shadows of Affluence*, 2nd edition. Berkeley, CA: University of California Press.

Hondagneu-Sotelo, P. and Avila, E. (1997), "'I'm here, but I'm there': The meanings of Latina transnational motherhood" *Gender & Society* 11(5): 548–71.

Kilkey, M. (2010) "Domestic-sector work in the UK: Locating men in the configuration of gendered care and migration regimes" *Social Policy and Society* 9(3): 443–54.

Kibria, N. (1993) *Family Tightrope: The Changing Lives of Vietnamese Americans*. Princeton NJ: Princeton University Press.

Lan, P.-C. (2006) *Global Cinderellas: Migrant Domestics and Newly Rich Employers in Taiwan*. Durham, NC: Duke University Press.

Lopez, N. (2003) *Hopeful Girls, Troubled Boys: Race and Gender Disparity in Urban Education*. New York: Routledge.

Lubheid, E. (2002) *Entry Denied: Controlling Sexuality at the Border*. Minneapolis, MN: University of Minnesota Press.

Lutz, H. (2002) "At your service madam! The globalization of domestic service" *Feminist Review* 70: 89–104.

Manalansan, M. (2003) *Global Divas: Filipino Gay Men in the Diaspora*. Durham, NC: Duke University Press.

Menjivar, C. and Salcido, O. (2002) "Immigrant women and domestic violence: Common experiences in different countries" *Gender and Society* 166: 898–920.

Morakvasic, M. (1984) "Birds of passage are also women … " *International Migration Review* 18(4): 886–907.

Nawyn, S. J. (2010) "Institutional structures of opportunity in refugee resettlement: Gender, race/ethnicity, and refugee NGOs" *Journal of Sociology & Social Welfare* March, 37(1): 149–67.

Oehmichen, C. (2000) "Las mujeres indígenas migrantes en la comunidad extraterritorial." In D. Barrera and C. Oehmichen (eds), *Migración de género en México*. Mexico City: GIMTRAP and UNAM, pp. 319–49.

Oishi, N. (2005) *Women in Motion: Globalization, State Polices, and Labor Migration in Asia*. Stanford CA: Stanford University Press.

Orellana, M. F., Thorne, B., Chee, A., Shun, W., and Lam, E. (2003) "Transnational childhoods: The participation of children in processes of family migration" *Social Problems* 48(4): 572–91.

Parrenas, R. (2001) *Servants of Globalization*. Stanford CA: Stanford University Press.

——(2005) *Children of Global Migration: Transnational Migration and Gendered Woes*. Stanford CA: Stanford University Press.

——(2008) *The Force of Domesticity: Filipina Migrants and Globalization*. New York: New York University Press.

Paris P. and Dolores, M. (2010) "Youth identities and the migratory culture among Triqui and Mixtec boys and girls" *Migraciones Internacionales* 5(4): 139–64.

Pavez Soto, I. (2010) "Peruvian girls and boys as actors of family migration in Barcelona: Generational relations and expectations" *Migraciones Internacionales* 5(4): 69–99.

Pedraza, S. (1991) "Women and migration: The social consequences of gender" *Annual Review of Sociology* 17: 303–25.

Piper, N. and Roces, M. (eds) (2003) *Wife or Worker? Asian Women and Migration*. Oxford: Rowman and Littlefield Publishers.

Purkayastha, B. (2003) "Skilled migration and cumulative disadvantage: The case of highly qualified Asian Indian immigrant women in the US" *Geoforum* 36(2): 181–96.

Ramirez, H. and Hondagneu-Sotelo, P. (2009) "Mexican immigrant gardeners in Los Angeles: Entrepreneurs or exploited workers?" *Social Problems* 56(1): 70–88.

Schmalzbauer, L. (2009) "Gender on a new frontier: Mexican migration in the rural mountain west" *Gender & Society* 23(6): 747–67.

Segura, D. and Zavella, P. (2007) *Women and Migration in the US-Mexico Borderlands*. Durham, NC: Duke University Press.

Smith, R. C. (2005) *Mexican New York: Transnational Lives of New Immigrants*. Berkeley, CA: University of California Press.

Stacey, J. and Thorne, B. (1985) "The missing feminist revolution in sociology" *Social Problems* 32(4): 301–16.

Thorne, B., Orellana, M. F., Shun. W., Lam, E., and Chee, A. (2003) "Raising children, and growing up, across national borders: Comparative perspectives on age, gender, and migration." In P. Hondagneu-Sotelo (ed.), *Gender and US Immigration: Contemporary Trends*. Berkeley, CA: University of California Press, pp. 241–62.

16

Host hostility and nativism

Mehdi Bozorgmehr, Anny Bakalian, and Sara Salman

Introduction

Host hostility and nativism have not received much conceptual and theoretical attention from researchers. Consequently, there are few publications on the topic. The purpose of this chapter is to survey and bring together the disparate descriptive and historical literatures. We focus on hostility and nativism directed against immigrants and refugees (i.e., the foreign born) or people of immigrant stock (first and second generation). We examine the US experience in detail and compare it with other major immigrant-receiving advanced industrial countries in Europe. We first define concepts that are subsumed under the rubric of host hostility such as nativism, racism, xenophobia, and its specific variant Islamophobia. We compare and contrast how newcomers were treated during the two massive immigration waves that occurred both at the turn of twentieth century (1880–1930) and in the twenty-first century (1965 to present) in the USA. We use landmark cases to illustrate how the interests of the host population (majority and native-born minorities) resulted in hostility against immigrants at various periods triggered by economic, political or social motives. Next, we review the key sociological theories of intergroup conflict. We conclude with a discussion of the consequences of host hostilities. While restrictive immigration laws that limit entry to migrants are exclusionary, they do not directly pertain to immigrants already living in host societies and therefore are not included in our analysis.

Conceptual definitions and clarifications

The "host" in host hostility has been traditionally conceptualized from the perspective of a society *vis-à-vis* newcomers (Jaret 2002). This has sometimes but not often encompassed the state and its policies (Joppke 2010). While the host society is viewed as a monolith, in reality it is highly stratified by power relations between majority and minority groups. The majority population wields greater power because it has access to valued, yet scarce, resources. Minority groups are disadvantaged in comparison to the powerful majority population adversely affecting their upward mobility (Olzak and Nagel 1986).

Racism is exercised when the members of a group are treated unequally based on their affiliation instead of their individual characteristics and qualities. It is a practice that subordinates victimized groups and hinders their upward mobility. Traditional racism is the belief that some groups are inherently superior to others in intelligence, temperament, and attitude as well as physically. "New racism" is cultural rather than biological, using the values of the dominant society to marginalize groups that resist assimilation. While prejudice and discrimination are often used simultaneously and interchangeably, prejudice refers to attitude while discrimination signifies action and behavior. Prejudiced attitudes often take the form of scapegoating and stereotypes. Discriminatory behaviors include bias incidents, which are motivated by the offender's prejudice against the group, and hate crimes, which are acts of violence committed against people, organizations, or property. Starting in the 1980s, hate-crime statutes were first enacted in the USA and the UK, acknowledging that a significant number of crimes against persons and property were motivated by hate (Min 2005).

In his classic book, *Strangers in the Land*, John Higham (1955) defined nativism as zealous opposition to minorities because of perceived un-American characteristics. Nativists draw on ethnocentric assumptions about outsiders and seek to protect a nation's values and traditions from foreigners and intruders. In other words, nativism is not simply a synonym for racism; it is a sentiment that is imbued with threatened nationalism. Nativism is exogenous, whereas racism can be both endogenous and exogenous. Xenophobia is a form of racism that is characterized by the hatred or fear of foreigners. Islamophobia, the dread of Islam and all Muslims, is a specific example of xenophobia (Modood 2005) which has intensified in the aftermath of 9/11 and 7/7 in the UK.

Old and new nativism

Despite the fact that the USA is a nation of immigrants, newcomers continue to face hostilities from native-born Americans. Ironically, members of ethnic groups whose immigrant ancestors were discriminated against are capable of engaging in hostility and violence against the newest arrivals. Studying immigration history in the USA demonstrates recurring nativist sentiments and discriminatory behaviors. We use two major waves of immigration in American history—the first during the turn of the twentieth century (1880–1930) and the second post-1965—to compare and contrast old and new nativism (also see Jaret 2002). By the 1880s, the national origins of the majority of immigrants had shifted from Northern and Western Europeans to Southern, Central, and Eastern Europeans. Moreover, this wave was mostly Catholic, Jewish, and Orthodox Christian, making them different from the dominant White Anglo-Saxon Protestant (WASP) population. The newcomers were mostly peasants or artisans, generally with little formal education and knowledge of English.

By the first decade of the twentieth century, there were already signs that the economic boom was slowing, almost to a halt. Immigration was partly blamed for the woes of the nation. There were attempts to curtail new immigration, but legislation had to await the end of World War I. The National Origin's Act of 1924 established immigration quotas for each country using the 1890 census as a yardstick for the desirable composition of the nation. Since there were few immigrants from Southern and Eastern Europe before the 1880s, a new influx from these regions was dramatically curtailed until 1965 when these laws were revoked. In the decades between the first large wave of immigration and the second, the USA suffered the Great Depression and World War II (Zolberg 2006). During this period, with the immigration door almost shut, migration chains between the pioneers and subsequent waves were broken. Allowing enough time for full assimilation was part of the original motivation to stem the tide of immigration.

In contrast to the first wave, the post-1965 immigrants have been coming from Asia, South and Central America, the Caribbean, Africa, and the Middle East. Moreover, unlike their predecessors, newcomers' socioeconomic characteristics are more diverse. While some are highly educated professionals admitted under employment preferences, others are labor migrants with minimal education. Additionally, larger numbers of immigrants have arrived with some English fluency (Portes and Rumbaut 2006). In terms of religiosity, today's immigrants cover a wide range of religious persuasions.

The most recent immigrants to the USA enter a post-industrial society where the dual economy requires highly specialized workers in the primary sector as well as cheap labor in the secondary sector. Consequently, contemporary immigrants include professionals in health care, information technology, as well as entrepreneurs. At the other end of the spectrum, labor migrants have found menial employment as maids, manicurists, busboys, and garage attendants.

Globalization as a phenomenon has further changed the profile of new immigrants. Today, most arrive with prior exposure to technology, travel, and communication skills. Not only are the immigrants entering a society that is more welcoming and multicultural, they are also able to maintain transnational relations with their homelands, thereby resisting assimilation. As importantly, since the civil rights movement of the 1960s and the ethnic revival movement in the 1970s and 1980s, pluralism is now the dominant current ideology, as opposed to assimilation and Americanization during the classic era of immigration (1880–1930) (Alba and Nee 2003). All these differences have implications for the new immigrants and the society as a whole in the face of old and new nativism.

At the turn of the twentieth century, religious difference was a major source of nativism (Jaret 2002). The majority Protestant population and elites believed that Catholics were incapable of independent thought because they confessed to a priest and obeyed the Pope, their spiritual father. In contrast, Protestants believed that they were more rational and free because of their unmediated relationship with God. While anti-Semitism has been prevalent in US history, it escalated when over two million Jews arrived from Eastern European *shtetls*. In contrast to the affluent German Jews who had preceded them, the newcomers were less educated, Yiddish speaking, and congregated in tenements in New York City. The Americanized Jews established self-help organizations to change their coreligionists' peasant manners and help them assimilate. Nonetheless, anti-Semitism from the host society persisted affecting the social mobility of second generation Jews. In the early decades of the twentieth century, social clubs and resorts banned Jews from membership, big law firms and corporations denied them employment, and Ivy League universities imposed a quota on Jewish students (Diner 1999). Anti-Semitism against European Jews has a long history, but everything pales when compared to the Nazi ideology that cost the lives of over six million Jews in the Holocaust. Yet after Germany acknowledged its wrongdoing and paid reparations, German neo-Nazi and far-right skinheads have made a comeback, many decorated with symbols smuggled from America. Since the 1990s, they have been attacking refugee centers, murdering Turkish women, and terrorizing visibly Muslim persons and places (Castles and Miller 2008).

Antiradicalism was another nativist sentiment that emerged in the first half of the twentieth century. Their targets were Bolsheviks, anarchists, and communists. Many native-born Americans believed that foreigners would bring about the destruction and destabilization of the country's institutions and threaten American democracy. In 1919, when bombs were mailed to prominent national leaders across the country, including one that partially destroyed the house of US Attorney A. Mitchell Palmer, the Bolsheviks or "the Red Menace" were believed to be the culprits. Palmer and J. Edgar Hoover, his young assistant, imprisoned and deported many Bolsheviks and radicals (Camp 1995; Gerstle 2004).

Even though the USA has been a more welcoming society to the post-1965 immigrants, hostilities continue to erupt at times of economic and political crises. Economic crises can be felt at both local and national levels, whereas political crises are often felt at the national level. In particular, immigrants who share the ethnic and religious characteristics of the "enemies" of the state become the victims of backlash. The internment of Japanese Americans was one of the most egregious episodes of host hostility in US history, built on exclusionary legislation and rampant anti-Asian racism in the West. After the attack on Pearl Harbor in 1941, President Roosevelt passed Executive Order 9066, mandating approximately 120,000 Japanese Americans to be sent to "war relocation camps" for about four years on the grounds that they can spy for the Japanese government. The order detained all men, women, and children of Japanese descent in the western coastal regions. Two-thirds were the US-born (*nisei*) and citizens (Daniels 1972, 1988).

In the first decade of the twenty-first century, Islamophobia has emerged as a dominant form and has been fueled by at least two factors. First, like Catholicism and Judaism in American history, Islam is confronting hostility as a new religion. Second, since the end of communism, radical Muslims have become the new nemesis of the USA. The backlash against Middle Eastern and Muslim Americans is not new. At least since the 1973 Arab oil embargo, anti-Americanism in the Middle East has ushered backlash. Other notable incidents include the Iran hostage crisis, the 1983 bombing of the US embassy in Beirut and the US marine barracks, the First Gulf War (1990–1), and the 1993 World Trade Center bombing. In particular, the 9/11 terrorist attack, the US involvement in wars in Afghanistan and Iraq, and the continuing Arab–Israeli conflict have made the backlash against Muslims in America particularly virulent (also see Shryock 2010).

In 2010, plans to establish an Islamic Center, the Park 51 project, a few blocks from the World Trade Center site of the September 11 2001 terrorist attacks in New York City sparked controversy and anti-Muslim sentiments. The center has been supported by many politicians at the local and national levels, including New York City Mayor Michael Bloomberg and President Barack Obama, as well as by religious leaders of many faiths. However, conservative politicians, Tea Party activists, and some of the 9/11 families and survivors opposed it, labeling it the "Ground Zero mosque." They argued that a mosque at this hallowed place would prevent the nation from healing. While the Park 51 project planned to include facilities for athletics, performances, and weddings, as well as a space for prayer, the opposition has been focused on "the mosque." These sentiments were fueled by fear of Islam and a belief that it is a violent religion that threatens the security of the USA.

While there is no unified "European response" to the perceived anxiety regarding Muslim immigrants, many countries have witnessed host hostility. Until the 1970s, France welcomed immigrants to fill labor demands. However, when the second generation demonstrated in 1983 for equality and end of racism, "Marche des Beurs," the French questioned their integration in intense debates (1983–5). Having established Le Front National (FN) far-right, nationalist political party in 1972, Jean-Marie Le Pen used immigration as a wedge issue in electoral campaigns. For example, in 1983, FN managed to change the outcome of small municipal elections in spite of its minuscule membership. His daughter, Marine Le Pen, continued this legacy in 2011.

Likewise in the UK, immigration was unrestricted for Europeans for most of the twentieth century, thus filling the gap in the unskilled labor market. Even the 1948 British Nationality Act enabled former empire subjects to live and work in the UK without a visa. In 1968, however, Conservative MP Enoch Powell began agitating for immigrants' stronger connections to the UK. He alleged that visa applicants established families with partners they never met because they were motivated by welfare benefits. While Powell was dismissed from his post as Shadow Defence Secretary for his racism, soon thereafter restricted citizenship codes for immigrants from the colonies were enacted. In the next section, we identify various causes of nativism and group them under political, social/cultural, and economic categories.

Often hostilities emerge during periods of mass migration and economic downturns. There-fore, we compared the two main large-scale immigration waves to the USA at the turn of the twentieth century (1880–1930) and the turn of the twenty-first century (1965 to the present). Immigration to the USA has reoriented from South, Central, and Eastern Europe in the first wave to Asia, South and Central America, the Caribbean, Africa, and the Middle East in the second wave, resulting in far more diversity in contemporary immigration. The new immigrants are also more diverse in socioeconomic origins, with only some immigrants starting at the bottom of the ladder. In addition, the new immigrants are diverse religiously and have intro-duced new religions to America (e.g., Buddhism, Hinduism, Islam, and Sikhism). The outcome of all this diversity is that the immigrants no longer fit a simple stereotype and thus cannot be subjected to the same type of nativism that the pioneers encountered.

The dominant ideology of immigration has also changed from assimilation during the first wave to pluralism during the second. The new ideology does not expect immigrants to com-pletely shed their cultural heritage or otherwise be subjected to societal ostracism. This does not mean that the assimilationists have disappeared from the scene. There is still a strong anti-immigrant current in the USA, though the nativists' targets are more specific. Undocumented migrants are the newest and the easiest targets.

Economic causes of nativism

While theories of intergroup relations are not specifically geared at explaining hostilities against immigrants, they are useful in examining the relationship between foreign and native-born groups. These theories have attributed the cause of conflict to competitive minority–majority relations in the host society. The "structural theory of ethnic competition," as formulated by Olzak and Nagel (1986), for example, deals with some form of economic or political contestation between groups. It demonstrates that ethnic conflict is caused by increased rivalry when inequalities between groups diminish. This would explain the rise of hate crimes in the 1980s as new immigrants attempted integration in predominantly white neighborhoods and institutions, threatening whites' privileged position and access to the scarce societal resources. It also explains anti-immigrant ordinances passed in small-town America as Latino immigrants have spanned across the nation to new destinations since the inception of the twenty-first century. For instance, Hazleton, Pennsylvania passed an anti-immigrant ordinance in 2006 which allowed businesses to investigate the immigration status of their employees, penalizing employers who did not comply with the ordinance. After it was struck down by a federal judge, Hazleton attempted to pass other anti-immigrant ordinances, unsuccessfully.

Edna Bonacich posited that ethnic hostility is derived in many instances from economic conflicts created by capitalist economies. She coined the term "split labor market theory" to explain this conflict, which she argues is an immediate result of high-priced labor (traditionally white males), and cheap labor (typically composed of new immigrants and ethnic minorities) in the USA (Bonacich 1972). In an attempt to minimize labor costs and increase profit, employers hire immigrant and ethnic minorities as cheap labor power. This creates animosity and frustration among the native-born labor force, which has historically led to anti-immigration sentiments and actions. The anti-Asian sentiment in the nineteenth century is a case in point. Initially, Chinese laborers were welcomed into the USA because of their cheap and cooperative labor. However, shortly after they became visible, white workers felt threatened by the competition. They began lobbying to restrict Chinese immigration to the USA and from working in mines and on the railroads.

Even after the passage of Civil Rights laws (1964, 1965) and the fact that two US presidents apologized for the Japanese internment during World War II, Asians continued to be targeted as the US economy suffered a downfall. In the 1980s and early 1990s, US industries began to lose to global competition, and never fully recovered. Politicians and media outlets blamed cheap imports, especially Japanese cars, for the failure of American industries. The imbalance of US–Japanese trade fueled anti-Japanese sentiments among natives resulting in "Japan bashing." The brutal murder of Vincent Chin, a 27-year-old Chinese American in Detroit in 1982, was a vivid example of scapegoating. The assailants, two autoworkers (one recently laid off), called him a "Jap," and blamed him for the loss of their jobs. They received no time in jail.

Theorists have argued that "middleman minorities"—small business owners who straddle producers and consumers in modern economies—face host hostility because of their visible concentration in business. Their economic success can provoke hostility by the majority population and envy by disadvantaged minority groups (Bonacich and Modell 1980; Turner and Bonacich 1980; Gold 2010). The Los Angeles Riots of 1992 constitute a glaring American example of hostility against middleman minorities. Having established small businesses in predominantly African-American neighborhoods in South Central Los Angeles, Korean storeowners were resented by African Americans for hiring co-ethnics and Latino labor migrants, taking capital away from the black community, as well as ill treatment and lack of trust of black customers. About 2,300 Korean stores were destroyed at a cost approximately $785 million. Leading Korean American scholar Pyong Gap Min has maintained that the anti-Korean hostility was due to their precarious middleman minority role (Min 1996).

In the post-1965 era, undocumented migration to the USA has emerged in the public imagination as the new economic threat. Douglas Massey notes that Mexican "illegal" migration began in 1965 and steadily increased from the mid-1960s in response to the collapse of both the Mexican economy and the end of the Bracero Program (Massey *et al.* 2002). The program was based on a binational treaty between the USA and Mexico that imported Mexican labor contractors to work in the agricultural sector in the USA because of the shortage of American farm workers during World War II (also see Ngai 2005).

In the 1990s, undocumented immigrants were accused of tapping into and depleting public resources despite the fact that many researchers have debunked the "loafer" myth. Available evidence shows that the undocumented shy away from using welfare programs out of fear of being caught and deported. Nonetheless, undocumented immigrants are scapegoated with a variety of policies and laws (Chavez 2008). Examples include the anti-immigration measures of the 1996 Welfare Reform Act, which restricted the access of even legal and permanent residents to services and public assistance. Another noteworthy example is Proposition 187 in California, euphemistically called the "Save our State" proposition. Proposed by Pete Wilson, the former governor of California in 1994, this anti-immigration measure sought to restrict illegal immigrants from accessing public services such as education and health care, except in emergency cases. It also charged social service agencies with gatekeeper responsibilities, thus criminalizing illegal immigrants. Proposition 187 was bogged down in the courts and was not passed as law on the grounds that immigration law is a federal not state matter (Sabagh and Bozorgmehr 2002).

Undocumented migrants are accused of not only exploiting public resources, but also taking jobs from hardworking Americans. In April 2010, Arizona passed the anti-immigration legislation SB 1070, which authorizes local law enforcement agents to check the immigration status of individuals suspected of being illegal immigrants. While the law is being challenged by the US Justice Department on the grounds that immigration law is federal not local, almost half of Americans oppose the Justice Department's actions. In August 2010, nativist proponents of SB 1070 sought to change the Fourteenth Amendment of the Constitution, which grants citizenship to children born in the USA. They feared that illegal immigrants would enter America's borders to give birth and thus gain naturalization through their children who have birthright citizenship.

Christian Joppke (2010), a specialist on immigration and citizenship in Europe, suggests that the tightening of immigration legislation coincided with economic downturns. Indeed, across Europe since the 1980s, states are deregulating their economies and dismantling their welfare system. Health care, postal services, public utilities (electricity, gas), public transportation, and telecommunication (telephones and the Internet) have been privatized. Even before these changes, many Europeans were feeling "compassion fatigue." For decades, many European states had open door policies and generous benefits toward refugees and asylees which attracted persons fleeing war and political crises. As a result, native Europeans became more anti-immigrant, blaming newcomers for numerous problems.

Political causes of nativism

Suspicion of new immigrants intensified during World War I (1914–18) because many originated from countries that had become the enemies of the USA. In particular, German immigrants, who were called "enemy aliens," were required to register and to be monitored by the state. Fifteen states passed laws making English the official language. Past admiration for German scientific and artistic accomplishments soon turned into hostility and race-based vilification of "Huns" or barbarians. German ethnic organizations were attacked, and nativist anger was aimed at all things German. The hysteria led to the banning of Beethoven's music in Boston, and the burning of German books in Lima, Ohio. Many German American institutions and organizations conformed to the demands of super-patriots. For example, Lutheran churches switched their service to English and many German Americans Anglicized their names. The upshot was their expedited assimilation (Kennedy 1980).

Political refugees and exiles who leave their country of origin because of their opposition to the regime often become scapegoats in the host society. Generally, political refugees tend to be caught in the middle of conflicts between sending and receiving societies. The Iranian case perhaps best exemplifies tenuous relations between sending and receiving nations in contemporary times.

After the Iranian Revolution of 1978–9, relations between the USA and Iran became strained, as Washington was a longtime supporter of Mohammad Reza Shah Pahlavi. When the exiled Shah entered the USA in October 1979 for medical care, many Iranians feared a repetition of the US-assisted coup that had put the Shah back on the throne in 1953. This concern instigated the "Iran Hostage Crisis," where a crowd of about 500 militants stormed the US embassy in Tehran on November 4 1979 and captured about 90 employees who were inside. Of these, 52 Americans were held hostage for 444 days until January 20, 1981. In retaliation, the federal government and several states enacted measures that specifically targeted Iranian students in the USA. In November 1979, the Attorney General, upon the direction of President Carter, required all Iranian nationals who were in the USA on student visas to report to the Immigration and Naturalization Service (INS) for registration by mid-December. Each non-immigrant alien was required to provide proof of residence, full-time school enrollment, and a passport with a valid visa. The regulation implied that non-compliance would be considered a violation of the conditions of the alien's stay in the United States, thus grounds for deportation under the Immigration and Nationality Act. The hostage crisis prompted a presidential order known as the "Iranian Control Program," which screened almost 57,000 Iranian students, the single largest group of foreign students in the USA at the time. However, the program has had long-term consequences of restricting Iranian immigration to the USA. The closure of the

American embassy in Iran to date forces Iranians to first travel to a transit country to obtain a US visa (Bozorgmehr 2000).

Bakalian and Bozorgmehr (2009) develop a theoretical model of backlash for the causes and consequences of host hostility during periods of war and/or political/ideological crises. In these hostile periods, the state tends to target a minority population that happens to share the same immigrant/ethnic or religious background as the "enemy." Such repressive measures rarely happen in a vacuum. The targeted group generally suffers from widespread scapegoating and stereotypes. Thus, there is a feedback loop between the hate crimes and bias incidents perpetrated by common people and the repressive policies of the state; both are mediated and reinforced through deeply seeded prejudice and discrimination. Backlash is defined as the combination of stereotypes, scapegoating, hate crimes and government initiatives. Backlash may give rise to mobilization or claims making in the short or long term. In the 9/11 case, the mobilization of the Middle Eastern and Muslim populations was relatively quick due to the existence of opportunity structures, namely the passage of civil rights laws, the Japanese redress movement, the emergence of oversight organizations such as the American Civil Liberties Union (ACLU), and the culture of pluralism in the USA (Schain 2008).

Political scientist Martin Schain argues that immigration dynamics on both sides of the Atlantic are politicized differently; they vary in how issues are framed and in their salience (Schain 2008). Since 9/11, Muslim immigrants' traditional behavior and religiosity have been perceived as a threat to national identity in France, Germany, and Great Britain (Joppke 2009), whereas the USA has problematized the undocumented (mostly from Latin America) and the porous Mexico border. Women donning the *hijab,* or more radically the *niqab*, in school and the workplace, have been subject to harassment, especially in France. In the 1990s, a number of girls were suspended from school for refusing to remove their *hijab*. The debates came to be known as *l'affaire du voile*. Teachers and others argued that displaying one's religious identity harms the unity and laïcité (secularism) of the French Republic. In 2011, the French center-right government banned the wearing of *niqab* or *burqa*. Those breaking the law would be fined 150 Euros or made to enroll in mandatory lessons in French citizenship. Immigration has also been an electoral hot-button issue in contemporary Europe. The emergence of small far-right political parties in the Netherlands, Austria, Denmark, and Luxembourg has forced moderates or centrists to accommodate to extremists to win elections. With the FN in France and the Conservative Party in Britain, the immigration of Muslims has been politicized, resulting in re-examination and critique of immigration and citizenship policies. In contrast, immigrants from Europe are seen as necessary for the labor market.

Social and cultural causes of nativism

Nativists believe that non-English languages are not part of the American culture and that language differences pose a threat to the American nation. This fear has been demonstrated throughout the twentieth century with calls for monolingualism and "English only" legislation, which gained national prominence in the 1980s and 1990s. These campaigns, led by politicians such as Japanese American senator S. I. Hayakawa, called for a constitutional amendment to make English the official language of the USA. Nativists fear that multilingualism is going to destabilize and balkanize the USA, like Canada for instance (Zolberg and Woon 1999). However, these fears are unwarranted. The consensus of researchers is that immigrant languages are lost altogether within three generations. Indeed, there is a decided preference for English speaking among the second generation and English monolingualism by the third (Portes and Rumbaut 2006).

In the Netherlands, the pillarization system was used as the basis for the social institutions of the Dutch society according to religious groupings of Protestants and Catholics. The influx of Muslim immigrants in the 1960s and 1970s—mostly from Turkey and North Africa (Morocco, Algeria, and Tunisia)—coincided with the decline of the pillarization system. As a result, they were not able to develop a distinctive Muslim pillar, and have subsequently faced obstacles to their institutional claims for accommodation. Dutch society experienced several dramatic incidents of intergroup conflict such as the murder of film maker Theo van Gogh by a Dutch Moroccan in 2004, heralding much dread and debate about Islam in Holland. Muslims in the Netherlands have a long history, with the earliest wave of Muslim immigrants arriving from the Dutch East Indies in the nineteenth century. Labor shortages in the 1960s forced the government to import guest workers from Turkey and Morocco (Rath 2011). Even when the program ended in 1973, immigrants continued to arrive under family reunification provisions. Since the 1990s, the majority of newcomers have been refugees or asylum seeker from Muslim countries. Tolerance is a cherished value for the Dutch, who are proud of the harmonious coexistence that the Protestants and Roman Catholics in the Netherlands have and continue to enjoy. However, once the Muslims were no longer confined to their ethnic enclaves, especially the second generation, Dutch tolerance began to wane. The Dutch reacted with fear and hostility. The Muslims, who were seen as guests, were settling permanently and in large numbers, posing a threat to the Dutch way of life. Not surprisingly, when the Minister of Justice suggested in 2006 that the Netherlands should accept Shariah law, a massive outrage resulted.

Consequences of nativism: exclusion, forced assimilation, and ethnic solidarity

Throughout the history of American immigration, the first tendency of nativists has been to keep undesirable groups out by stopping all forms of immigration, expel illegal immigrants and constrain legal immigrants by depriving them of full citizenship rights bestowed upon native-born citizens. This ideology exhibits anxieties about the impact of the new waves of immigrants on American society. The 1924 quota law, Proposition 187 in California and SB 1070 in Arizona are examples.

The second nativist trend is "forced assimilation" (Portes and Rumbaut 2006). The classic example is the response of the USA to the massive wave of immigration at the turn of the twentieth century. As the economic well-being of the USA declined in the first two decades of the twentieth century, there were concerns that immigrants would not be able to adapt to the American way of life. To assuage their anxieties, the One Hundred Percent Americanization Movement was created. The Hundred Percenters became very popular, and was endorsed by President Theodore Roosevelt who warned against the dangers of "hyphenated Americans." Federal and state agencies embarked on a massive educational program including classes in the English language, citizenship, American history, and politics. The campaign to Americanize the uncouth masses involved lessons on personal and household hygiene, diet, fashion, and etiquette. The Anglo-Saxon middle class mainstream culture formed the standard for everyone and everything.

Advocates of Americanization recognize US immigrant history and the success of the immigrant experience in abandoning one's culture. Nativists believe that since the old immigrants, including their ancestors, assimilated rapidly, the cultural traditions and the languages of the newcomers are also expected to disappear by the second generation. They favor "English only" policies and often have unreasonable expectations of immigrants to speak unaccented English. While this movement appears to be inclusive, it has been counter-productive.

Furthermore, what forced assimilationists neglect is that in an increasingly globalized world, knowledge of languages other than English is beneficial for citizens and nation states alike. For instance, America has a vital need for fluent Arabic speakers to fill intelligence services positions in the aftermath of 9/11. Bilingualism and even multilingualism should be seen as an asset for the USA in the world. Although pluralism has replaced assimilation as the dominant ideology of majority–minority relations in the USA, the proponents of forced assimilation persevere.

In 2005, the European Union adopted a common agenda for integration. Jan Rath, a leading scholar of European immigration at the University of Amsterdam, notes that the Dutch expect immigrants to change and that the government has the power to enforce integration (Rath 2011). Germany, the Netherlands, and the UK have even developed citizenship tests, which suggest that there is a single national and cultural standard for citizenship and belonging. This is strongly implied in the material covered in the test preparation kits. For example, test takers should know that nude swimming is legal in the Netherlands. To sensitize them to become tolerant Dutch, immigrants are shown images of topless women and men kissing. In Germany, a draft test queried the opinion of applicants on forced marriage, homosexuality, and women's rights, all of which were questions that extend beyond knowledge of civic duties. Migrants are increasingly tested on their value systems in the path to becoming citizens.

Nonetheless, in spite of the fear of Muslim extremists and anti-Islamic rhetoric, the immigrant populations are integrating. In France, the rate of intermarriage among the second generation is relatively high. Moreover, states have been silently accommodating many of the claims of their Muslim citizens through human rights litigation. For instance, a German *hijabi* woman sued a well-known department store company for firing her as a cosmetic salesperson. The success of her case has opened the door to other claimants to defend their individual rights to practice their religion in a liberal democratic state. While most European societies assume that integration is one-sided, astute entrepreneurs realize that there is a lucrative market to serve. Albert Heijn, the largest supermarket company in Holland, has its Turkish, Moroccan, and Pakistani employees wearing headscarves in the company's colors, symbolizing that their business is Muslim-friendly. In France, there are newly established *halal* retail stores that feature non-pork pate and sausages for upwardly mobile native Muslims.

Intransigent nativism often has the opposite effect for the host society. It gives rise to ethnic solidarity, defined as collective action on the part of minority groups to advance their goals and objectives. For instance, the Japanese American Citizens League (JACL) mobilized Japanese Americans after the war for the recognition of and reparation for the internment camps, and formed the Commission on Wartime Relocation and Internment of Civilians. Their campaign culminated in the Civil Liberties Act of 1988, which provided monetary compensation of $20,000 to each victim if alive, or an heir if deceased and a formal apology.

The well-known Simmel–Coser theorem states host hostility creates internal group solidarity (Coser 1956). While true in terms of group cohesion and ethnic retention, ethnic solidarity has only recently taken effect in response to new nativism. This is mainly due to structural conduciveness of post-Civil Rights America to ethnic and racial minority claims making. The post-9/11 backlash illustrates a new trend in mobilization among targeted populations. Civil Rights Laws (1964, 1965) have changed the playing field for all minority groups by creating a more conducive environment for claims making. While it took the Japanese a long time to mobilize against their internment, Middle Eastern and Muslim Americans immediately mobilized against the 9/11 backlash and claimed their rightful place in American society. Middle Eastern and Muslim Americans distanced themselves from the terrorists and condemned the 9/11 terrorist attacks. They demonstrated their allegiance to the USA by engaging in outreach, educating the American public about both the Middle East and the Muslim faith, and engaging their community members in political advocacy (Bakalian and Bozorgmehr 2009).

Other examples of ethnic solidarity include the collective mobilization by Mexican and Hispanic communities in California against Proposition 187 in 1994. The Mexican American Legal Defense and Educational Fund (MALDEF), organized naturalization and voting registration campaigns, producing a shift in the electoral power of Mexican Americans in California by electing young Democratic Mexican politicians costing conservative Republican politicians their seats. In 2005, Republicans sponsored the bill H.R. 4437, Border Protection, Antiterrorism and Illegal Immigration Control Act, in an attempt to criminalize undocumented workers, their employers and anyone who provides them with assistance. The bill also sought to build a fence along the entire US–Mexican border. In response, Mexican and Mexican American groups and civil right organizations, labor unions, and the Catholic Church organized large civic protests and marches in Los Angeles, Chicago, Phoenix, and Washington, DC, as well as other metropolitan areas in the USA. The bill never became law (Hondagneu-Sotelo 2008).

Conclusion

This chapter has dealt with host hostility in major immigrant-receiving advanced industrial countries. While the main focus is on the USA, we have used Europe to show similarities and differences. Nativism has been used as a concept to depict host hostility. In spite of keen interest in nativism and its persistence, there are few publications on the subject, and much of it is historical and descriptive in nature. Our goal was to review the existing literature on host hostility and nativism, and organize it conceptually and theoretically. We started by mapping the landscape of hosts, guests, and hostility. Although often treated as a homogeneous entity, the host comprises several components, namely the state, the majority population and the native-born ethnic/racial minorities, each of which can engage in anti-immigrant animosity. The guests are immigrants, refugees, and their descendants (ethnic minority groups). Hostility and nativism run the full gamut from scapegoating, stereotypes, prejudice, discrimination, and racism, to hate crimes, bias incidents, and government initiatives.

There are at least three major sources of nativism: economic, political, and social/cultural. Although these reasons are often combined in reality, we examine each separately for analytical purposes. Economic reasons entail labor market competition, middleman minority status, global economic competition, undocumented migration and in general some form of intergroup competition for scarce resources. Some of these economic roots of conflict are more theoretically developed than others, so we summarize them here. The wage and salaried immigrants allegedly compete for menial jobs with the native-born minorities in inner cities. The self-employed who hold a middleman minority position, face conflict with native-born minorities and are accused of hiring co-ethnics and labor migrants rather than unemployed native-born minorities. Political reasons often involve hostilities between the sending and receiving countries, especially during times of war and international crises.

American and European societies have manifested their persistent nativism in a variety of ways. Two dominant forms are forced assimilation and integration of immigrants (English-language only movements) or exclusion of the newcomers (anti-immigrant legislation). One of the new and unintended consequences of hostility has been ethnic solidarity among the targeted groups, defined as collective action or claims making to achieve specific aims. While in the old days, nativism resulted in involuntary and forced assimilation, it now may result in ethnic solidarity. Nativists unintentionally help immigrant groups and especially their descendants to lay claims to their rights and find a place in host societies. Hopefully, in the long run, this will reduce if not eradicate host hostility and nativism in the USA and Europe.

References and further reading

Alba, R. and Nee, V. (2003) *Remaking the American Mainstream*. Cambridge, MA: Harvard University Press.

Bail, C. A. (2008) "The configuration of symbolic boundaries against immigrants in Europe" *American Sociological Review* 73(1): pp. 37–59.

Bakalian, A. and Bozorgmehr, M. (2009) *Backlash 9/11: Middle Eastern and Muslim Americans Respond*. Berkeley, CA: University of California Press.

Blalock, H. (1967) *Toward a Theory of Minority Group Relations*. New York: John Wiley and Sons.

Bonacich, E. (1972) "A theory of ethnic antagonism: the split labor market" *American Sociological Review* 37(5): 547–59.

Bonacich, E. and Modell, J. (1980) *The Economic Basis of Ethnic Solidarity: Small Business in the Japanese American Community*. Berkeley, CA: University of California Press.

Bozorgmehr, M. (2000) "Does host hostility create ethnic solidarity? The experience of Iranians in the United States" *Bulletin of the Royal Institute for Inter-Faith Studies (BRIIFS)* 2(1): 159–78.

Brimelow, P. (1995) *Alien Nation: Common Sense about America's Immigration Disaster*. New York: Random House.

Camp, H. C. (1995) *Iron in Her Soul: Elizabeth Gurley Flynn and the American Left*. Pullman, WA: Washington State University Press.

Castles, S. and Miller, M. (2008) *Age of Migration*, 4th edition. New York: Guilford.

Cesari, J. (2004) *When Islam and Democracy Meet: Muslims in Europe and the United States*. New York: Palgrave.

Chavez, L. R. (2008) *The Latino Threat: Constructing Immigrants, Citizens, and the Nation*. Stanford, CA: Stanford University Press.

Cornell, S. E. and Hartmann, D. (1998) *Ethnicity and Race: Making Identities in a Changing World*. Thousand Oaks, CA: Pine Forge Press.

Coser, L. A. (1956) *The Functions of Social Conflict: An Examination of the Concept of Social Conflict and its Use in Empirical Sociological Research*. New York: The Free Press.

Daniels, R. (1972) *Concentration Camps USA: Japanese Americans and World War II*. New York: Holt, Rinehart and Winston.

——(1988) *Asian Americans: Chinese and Japanese in the United States since 1850*. Seattle, WA University of Washington Press.

Diner, H. R. (1999) *Jews in America*. New York: Oxford University Press.

Foner, N. and Alba, R. (2008) "Immigrant religion in the US and Western Europe: Bridge or barrier to inclusion?" *International Migration Review* 42(2): 360–92.

Gold, S. J. (2010) *The Store in the Hood: A Century of Ethnic Business and Conflict*. Lanham, MD: Roman and Littlefield.

Gerstle, G. (2004) "The immigrants as threat to American security: A historical perspective." In J. Tirman (ed.), *The Maze of Fear: Security and Migration after 9/11*. New York: New Press, pp. 87–108.

Higham, J. (1955) *Strangers in the Land: Patterns of American Nativism, 1860–1925*. New Brunswick, NJ: Rutgers University Press.

Hondagneu-Sotelo, P. (2008) *God's Heart Has No Borders: Religious Activism for Immigrant Rights*. Berkeley, CA: University of California Press.

Jaret, C. (1995) *Contemporary Racial and Ethnic Relations*. New York: Harper Collins.

——(2002) "Troubled by newcomers: Anti-immigrant attitudes and actions during two eras of mass migration." In P. G. Min (ed.), *Mass Migration to the United States*. Walnut Creek, CA: Altamira Press.

Joppke, C. (2009) *Veil: Mirror of Identity*. Boston, MA: Polity Press, pp. 21–63.

——(2010) *Citizenship and Immigration*. Boston, MA: Polity Press.

Kennedy, D. M. (1980) *Over Here: The First World War and American Society*. New York: Oxford University Press.

Koopmans, R., Statham P., Giugni M., and Passy, F. (2005) *Contested Citizenship: Immigration and Cultural Diversity in Europe*. Minneapolis, MN: University of Minnesota Press.

Massey, D. S., Durand J., and Malone, N. J. (2002) *Beyond Smoke and Mirrors: Mexican Immigration in an Era of Economic Integration*. New York: Russell Sage.

Min, P. G. (1996) *Caught in the Middle: Korean Communities in New York and Los Angeles.* Berkeley, CA: University of California Press.

Min, P. G. (ed.) (2005) *Encyclopedia of Racism in the United States [Three Volumes].* Westport, CT: Greenwood Press.

Modood, T. (2005) *Multicultural Politics: Racism, Ethnicity, and Muslims in Europe.* Minneapolis, MN: University of Minnesota Press.

Ngai, M. (2005) *Impossible Subjects, Illegal Aliens and the Making of Modern America.* Princeton, NJ: Princeton University Press.

Olzak, S. and Nagel, J. (eds) (1986) *Competitive Ethnic Relations.* Orlando, FL: Academic Press.

Portes, A. and Rumbaut, R. G. (2006) *Immigrant America: A Portrait,* 3rd edition. Berkeley, CA: University of California Press.

Rath, J. (2011) "Debating multiculturalism: Europe's reaction in context" *Harvard International Review* http://hir.harvard.edu/debating multiculturalism (accessed January 6 2011).

Sabagh, G. and Bozorgmehr, M. (2002) "From 'give me your poor' to 'save our state': New York and Los Angeles as immigrant cities and regions." In D. Halle (ed.), *New York and Los Angeles: Politics, Society and Culture.* Chicago, IL: University of Chicago Press, pp. 99–123.

Sanchez, G. (1999) "Face the nation: Race, immigration, and the rise of nativism in late twentieth century America." In C. Hirschman, P. Kasinitz, and J. DeWind (eds), *The Handbook of International Migration: The American Experience.* New York: Russell Sage, pp. 371–82.

Schain, M. A. (2008) *The Politics of Immigration in France, Britain and the United States: A Comparative Study.* New York: Palgrave.

Shryok, A. (2010) *Islamophobia/Islamophilia: Beyond the Politics of Enemy and Friend.* Bloomington, IN: Indiana University Press.

Turner, J. and Bonacich, E. (1980) "Toward a composite theory of middleman minorities" *Ethnicity* 71(1): 144–58.

Vertovec, S. and Wessendorf, S. (eds) (2009) *The Backlash Against Multiculturalism: European Discourses, Practices and Policies.* London, UK: Routledge.

Zolberg, A. R. (2006) *A Nation by Design: Immigration Policy in the Fashioning of America.* New York: Russell Sage.

Zolberg, A. R. and Litt Woon, L. (1999) "Why Islam is like Spanish: Cultural incorporation in Europe and the United States" *Politics and Society* 27(1): 5–38.

17

Immigrants and residential segregation

Joe T. Darden and Flavia Cristaldi

Introduction

The concept of residential segregation

Residential segregation refers to unequal access of two population groups to housing. Housing is a basic necessity to life. All immigrants seek access to it when they arrive in their host country. What most immigrants find is that equal access to housing tends to be a function of the differences between their characteristics and those of the larger society. Because access is unequal, the residential pattern of housing tends to be segregated on the basis of race, ethnicity, class, religion, gender, and age. The overall pattern of immigrant housing in global metropolitan areas in the United States, Canada, and selected metropolitan areas in Europe is one of residential segregation. Thus, the most important question is not whether residential segregation exists, but how much exists? The second important question is what are the causes of immigrant residential segregation in the various countries? For sure, segregated housing can lead to segregation in other areas of life—schooling, employment, recreation, and access to quality neighborhoods. Thus, residential segregation can lead to inequality and subordination and limit the options for social mobility of an immigrant group by consigning the group to inferior schools and neighborhoods of low-paying jobs and housing.

Key issues in historical and contemporary patterns of immigrant residential segregation

Because the historical patterns of immigrants to the United States, Canada, and selected European countries have been different from contemporary patterns, researchers have had to adopt different theories or conceptual frameworks to explain these. For example, whereas historical patterns of residential segregation of immigrants from selected European countries to the United States and Canada could be explained by spatial assimilation theory, contemporary patterns of residential segregation of recent immigrants from non-European countries require a different theory or conceptual framework. We have adopted the conceptual framework of differential incorporation. This conceptual framework will be discussed later in this chapter.

Measuring residential segregation

Regardless of the country of destination of the immigrant groups, in order to determine how much residential segregation exists, measurement is required. We have chosen the most common and most widely used measure of residential segregation—the index of dissimilarity. The index assesses the degree to which two groups (immigrants versus native born or non-immigrants) are unevenly distributed over neighborhoods (e.g., census tracts or wards).

The basis on which unevenness is determined is the percentage of the immigrant and the percentage of the native born or non immigrant population in the metropolitan area as a whole. If the percentage of Filipino immigrants is 30 percent and 70 percent of the total population is native born in the metropolitan area as a whole, then the expected criterion for non-segregation or evenness would be that the percentage of total Filipino immigrants and the percentage of total native born population would be 30 percent and 70 percent in each neighborhood (census tract or ward). As each neighborhood deviates from the percentage compositions of the metropolitan area as a whole, the index of dissimilarity increases. The index ranges from "0" reflecting no segregation (i.e., evenness of the two groups over neighborhoods) to "100" indicating complete segregation or unevenness. The higher the index, the greater is the degree of residential segregation.

Comparative immigrant residential segregation and contextual differences among countries

In conducting comparative immigrant research, it is important to select the *same* immigrant group in both countries and the same spatial unit of measurement (e.g., census tracts or wards) (Darden and Fong 2011). This will enable one to systematically examine any contextual differences in residential segregation. As this chapter will reveal, as a rule, each immigrant group experiences a higher level of residential segregation in New York than in Toronto and the selected European metropolitan areas. This may be due, in part to, size of the immigrant groups in each metropolitan area. The immigrant groups are generally larger in New York. It may also be due to the structure of the governmental unit and local control versus regional governmental control over housing. Whereas New York is more fragmented as a metropolitan area with each municipality under local governmental control, different tax policies, and zoning restrictions, metropolitan Toronto is characterized by regional control of housing policies. A similar pattern of regional versus local control exists in selected metropolitan areas in Europe (London, Paris, Rome, Madrid). Residential segregation is usually higher in fragmented metropolitan areas.

Finally, residential segregation of immigrants may be influenced by differences in subsidized housing policies. In the United States, public housing has a history of being restricted to the central city and to poor neighborhoods of metropolitan areas. It has also been associated with racial segregation, where most residents are non-white (including both immigrants and the native born). On the other hand, in Toronto and selected European metropolitan areas, social or public housing has been more spatially dispersed throughout the metropolitan area, including the suburbs. Public housing in Canada and Europe may also include a higher percentage of native-born working class white people as well as immigrants. These housing policies may have contributed to lower levels of residential segregation in Toronto and the selected metropolitan areas in European countries.

In the first part of this chapter, we discuss some of these critical issues in detail. In the second part, we present a case study of comparative immigrant residential segregation in metropolitan areas in Canada, the United States, England, Italy, France, and Spain.

The issue of the old versus the new immigrant residential segregation

We refer to the "old immigrant" residential segregation as the residential segregation of European immigrants in the United States and Canada. Europe was primarily a region of emigration although some immigration between European countries did occur during the nineteenth and early twentieth centuries. Little research has been done of the residential segregation of European immigrants to other European cities during that time. In contrast, between 1880 and 1920, millions of immigrants, from Eastern and Southern Europe, arrived in United States (Massey and Denton 1993) and Canadian cities (Darden 2004) in search of employment in the growing manufacturing industries. Many were unskilled and lacked a high level of education. The key barriers to their residential integration and incorporation were a lack of education, skills, language, and culture, and, in some instances, religious differences. The socially constructed factor of race was not considered to be a major barrier since they were racially white, i.e., similar in color to the native-born population in the United States and Canada.

Both the United States and Canada had imposed racially restrictive immigration policies on non-European immigrants, e.g., from Asia, Africa, the Caribbean, and Latin America. These policies, which allowed European immigrants to enter the "gates" while denying non-European immigrants entry, were not changed until 1965 in the United States (Daniels 2007) and 1967 in Canada (Darden 2004).

Thus, during the era of industrialization, researchers were essentially engaged in trying to understand the extent of and the factors related to the residential segregation of white immigrant groups from European countries. They employed spatial assimilation theory to explain why some immigrant groups were more residentially segregated from the native born population than others (Massey and Denton 1993). Spatial assimilation theory assumes that immigrants who arrive in the host country are of low socioeconomic status compared to the native-born population. As a result, they settle in the least desirable neighborhoods of the metropolitan area—often in the poorest areas of the central city. As the immigrant group acquires more social and economic resources—i.e., education, a higher status occupation, and higher income—the immigrant group moves to a more desirable residential location, which is often in the suburbs among a higher percentage of the native-born, high status white population (Massey and Denton 1993; South et al. 2005). According to spatial assimilation theory, the only barrier immigrants need to overcome is socioeconomic status or class.

This theory was useful in explaining the residential segregation of white immigrants from Europe to North America. However, when researchers attempted to apply the theory to non-European groups, i.e., non-whites, it failed (Darden and Kamel 2000). The reason the theory was inadequate for explaining the residential segregation of most non-white immigrant groups is because the theory does not take race or color discrimination in housing into account. Such discrimination operates independently of socioeconomic status (Darden and Kamel 2000).

Thus, in order to adequately explain the residential segregation of the "new immigrants," i.e.,post-1965 immigrants from non-European countries, a different conceptual or theoretical framework is needed.

The new immigrant residential segregation

The "new immigrant" residential segregation started after the post-industrial era commenced, and globalization increased the demand for immigrant labor (both skilled and unskilled). European immigrants could no longer fill the void as immigration was declining from Europe. Thus, both the United States and Canada changed their racially restrictive immigration policies to meet the labor demands. As a result, more immigrants from Latin America, Asia, Africa, and elsewhere started to move to the United States and Canada to meet the labor demands. Others moved to countries that are now part of the European Union. The general immigration pattern is the movement from less developed to more developed countries.

It is correct to say that the new immigration and consequent immigrant residential segregation is related to globalization. The process of globalization resulted in an increased demand for labor which resulted in an increase in immigration from less developed countries influenced by the need for such labor (which includes many highly skilled and highly educated immigrants). In order for the United States, Canada, and selected countries in the European Union (England, France, Italy, Spain) to fulfill their labor demands, they had to change their restrictive immigration policies to allow more immigrants from non-European countries to enter. Unlike traditional immigrants of European origins, many of these immigrants are not white and many are not poor.

Immigrants arrive with different levels of education, skills, experience, language, culture, and religion. Such social capital and economic resources influence the speed and success to which they become incorporated into the mainstream of global metropolitan areas (Price and Benton-Short 2007).

Unlike past immigrant settlement patterns, more recent patterns of immigrant settlement reveal that many immigrants bypass cities and settle directly in the suburbs. Thus, for the following reasons, we argue for a different conceptual or theoretical framework to explain the residential segregation of the new immigrants, and we reject the traditional spatial assimilation theory. We argue instead for employing the conceptual framework of differential incorporation.

Differential Incorporation

Differential incorporation is conceptualized as a two-way process. One process relates to the internal characteristics of the immigrant group. The focus of the internal-characteristics process is on the group's strengths and weaknesses. In other words, the group's social capital and resources as measured by education, skills, and experience (Darden and Teixeira 2009). Each immigrant group possesses a quantity of social capital and economic resources, and arrives in their new country with that social capital and economic resources. The other process involves the external forces imposed on the immigrant group by the white host majority group, despite the internal characteristics of the immigrant group. Racial discrimination is a major form of these external forces (Darden 2004).

Conducting comparative international immigrant residential segregation research

The issues related to conducting international immigrant research are national differences in the classification and definition of immigrant groups by race and ethnicity as well as the combination of groups into a single category. Thus, the challenge is to select the same immigrant groups for analysis and to disaggregate each group to examine their residential segregation pattern. It is also a challenge to select the same geographic sub-unit, which may vary from country to country. This is sometimes referred to as the scale problem.

Additionally, there is the issue of a lack of geographical disaggregation. Fragmentation of metropolitan areas may result in different levels of residential segregation at the municipal level. This is often overlooked because residential segregation is examined by most researchers at the metropolitan level only (Iceland, *et al.* 2002; Darden 2009). We discuss these issues here in the hope of improving residential segregation research in a comparative context.

Several researchers have indicated the difficulty of conducting comparative international research on residential segregation (Musterd 2005; Johnston, *et al.* 2007; Peach 2009). The first problem is that various countries define racial groups, ethnic groups, and national origin groups according to different classification systems. Thus the compositions of the same group in one country may be different in another country, or race, for example, may not be a classification at all (Darden 2004).

Ideally, it is important to ensure that the comparative analysis of residential segregation is based on the selection of the *same* group in terms of composition. For example, the broad category "Asian," which is often used by researchers in the United States, is very heterogeneous, including groups such as Chinese and Japanese, but also Indians, etc. If one country's Asian population is 80 percent Chinese and another country's Asian population is 80 percent Indian, the results of residential segregation measures are likely to be highly different. Thus, comparing Asian residential segregation between countries would be very misleading and would reveal little about differential residential segregation and incorporation except confusion. Therefore, the researcher should choose the same national or ethnic group—i.e., compare Chinese in one country with Chinese in another. In other words, disaggregate the groups.

The second challenge is related to the sub-units countries use to collect both demographic and socioeconomic data by race and ethnicity. Often neighborhood type sub-units vary from country to country. This variation may influence the index of dissimilarity that determines the amount of residential segregation. It is a basic rule that the smaller the spatial sub-unit, the higher the level of residential segregation revealed by the index of dissimilarity. Thus, an index computed on the basis of census tracts (used in the United States and Canada), which are comparable to neighborhoods and constitute on average 4,000 people, would be different (and generally higher) than an index based on wards (used in the UK), which range from 8,000 to 10,000 people and are therefore larger than census tracts (Peach 1996).

Moreover, Italy, France, and Spain do not provide demographic and socioeconomic data by either census tracts or wards for each immigrant (nationality) group. Instead, data are presented using other geographic sub-units or scales. A third challenge to conducting comparative international research on residential segregation is related to the fact that a single index of residential segregation of metropolitan areas does not capture the varying levels of residential segregation at the municipal level. This issue is best demonstrated in metropolitan Detroit, which in 2000 was the most racially segregated metropolitan area in the United States, with an index of dissimilarity for the metropolitan area of 85 (Darden 2009). Metropolitan Detroit, like most metropolitan areas, is highly fragmented politically, demographically, and socioeconomically. Such fragmentation results in different levels of residential segregation *within* the metropolitan area at the municipal level. In other words, it is not sufficient to evaluate the level of segregation of metropolitan areas unless additional information about segregation at the municipal scale is also provided (Darden 2009). To be sure, metropolitan areas are complex socioeconomic and demographic entities not governed by a single political unit. Instead, metropolitan areas are comprised of numerous villages, townships, and cities. Since housing and neighborhood preferences and exclusion often vary from municipality to municipality, it is important to examine immigrant residential segregation at the municipal level. It is at this level that housing and land use policies, zoning regulations, local property taxes, and fiscal policies are established and implemented (Darden 2009). Public service delivery also often occurs at this level, involving police protection and safety, garbage collection, school quality, parks and recreation, and other amenities which influence the housing search process and neighborhood choice.

The level of black/white residential segregation for the Detroit metropolitan area as a whole is quite high, yet it is quite low for many adjacent suburban municipalities where the housing and neighborhood choice decision is actually made by the home seekers.

The issue of immigrant category

The classification or category of immigrant groups can influence their level of residential segregation and incorporation in the host country. There is a hierarchy of immigrants entering a host country which may influence the ease or difficulty of incorporation and therefore influence the level of residential segregation. At the top of the hierarchy are the highly skilled, professionals or investors. In Canada, for example live-in care givers, provincial nominees, and entrepreneurs are also included. Economic immigrants are the most preferred by policy makers and other stakeholders and such preferences are related to immigration policies. Second are the family immigrants who enter as part of the family reunification process. Third are the refugees who enter due to some political reasons or other hardship which demands a humanitarian response. Finally there are the undocumented who are not invited but enter usually in search of jobs or economic survival. They are the least preferred by the host country in general. Because the race and class characteristics of immigrants in each of the categories above may vary, it is important to control for all characteristics except place of destination in any comparative study of immigrant residential segregation. In other words, independent immigrants in one country should be compared with independent immigrants in another while controlling for all characteristics. It is not appropriate to compare immigrants that are predominantly refugees in one country with immigrants that are predominantly independent in another and expect similar levels of residential segregation.

The inclusion of gender in immigrant residential segregation research

In the study of immigrants from Europe during the period of industrialization (the "old immigrant" residential segregation era), researchers often excluded gender—i.e., women—from immigrant residential segregation research. An analysis of residential segregation which includes gender may reveal a different pattern of residential segregation. Under the "new immigrant" residential segregation of the post-industrialization era, gender should not be ignored, as women constitute a large share of the immigration pool due to globalization and the labor demands that have resulted from the economic transformations process. Women are estimated to comprise about half the world's immigrant population (Morokvasic 2003). Since women may work disproportionately in different occupations from the occupations of men (e.g., live-in domestic workers) women may be obligated to live in the residence of the host family. Many Filipino women immigrants are employed under such conditions. Their occupation as live-in domestic workers influences their residential patterns and degree of segregation from native-born white people (Cristaldi 2004b). Thus, when data on gender are available, it should be included in immigrant residential segregation research. Whereas current policies on immigration by many advanced countries are beginning to recognize the feminization of the immigration process, they have not addressed the different experiences due to the gender of immigrants (Cristaldi 2002; Ho 2006).

The causes of residential segregation

The major causes of residential segregation are socioeconomic status, voluntary segregation or preferences for residential segregation, and discrimination in housing and steering by neighborhood composition (Darden 2003; Cristaldi, 2012). Most research suggests that socioeconomic status difference between non-white and white people (whether immigrant or native-born) is not the major cause of residential segregation (Peach 1996; Darden and Kamel 2000; Musterd 2005;

Iceland and Wilkes 2006). Peach (1999) demonstrated that social class explained only 10 percent of the residential segregation between Bangladeshi immigrants and white people in London. Musterd (2005) documented similar results about the influence of socioeconomic status on residential segregation for other groups in European cities. Given that social class is a poor predictor, other factors must be considered. We discuss two of the factors below.

Voluntary residential segregation or preferences for residential segregation must be examined in two ways. First, there is the preference for residential segregation by the white host majority from the immigrant or non-white minority. Research suggest that white preferences for all-white or predominantly white neighborhoods does influence the level of immigrant residential segregation. This is because many if not most white people prefer to reside only with other white people and are reluctant to move into neighborhoods with more than a few non-white people (Darden 2003).

The second reason preferences must be examined is to understand the inclinations of ethnic/immigrant groups (which often differ from those of the host or majority group). The research suggest that although ethnic minorities may express a preference for co-ethnic neighborhoods that ranges from up to 50 percent, their preference must be considered within the context of perceived or actual racial hostility and/or racial discrimination (Darden 2003). Finally, among the three causes, discrimination in housing, i.e., the exclusion of ethnic minority immigrants from white majority host neighborhoods, is a *major* cause of residential segregation (Turner, *et al.* 2002; Darden 2003; Cristaldi, 2012). In sum, the causes of residential segregation are connected to the three factors—socioeconomic status, voluntary preferences, and discrimination in housing and steering. Among the three factors, discrimination seems to be the most important contributor. However, the intensity of housing discrimination against each immigrant group varies. Given similar socioeconomic characteristics, it is usually greater against those with darker skins and less against those with lighter skins (Darden 2004).

In the remainder of this chapter, we present a case study of the new immigrant residential segregation in a comparative context.

International comparisons of immigrant residential segregation

We limit our study to only three immigrant groups that are all Asian, but from different countries. We have taken into account the size of each of these immigrant groups in six global metros since the small size of the group may present technical problems related to the spatial distribution of the group over sub-units in the global metros (Peach 1996).

We note, however, that caution is still advised in interpreting some of the indexes where the sub-units differ substantially in size between countries, e.g., census tracts, wards, and urbanistic zones. We reiterate that the larger the size of the spatial sub-unit, the greater the probability of a lower level of residential segregation revealed by the index of dissimilarity.

Data

The data for the analysis were obtained primarily from the governmental agencies that collect statistical (i.e., census) demographics and socioeconomic data by geographic sub-unit on the immigrant population and total population for the following global metros: London, Madrid, New York, Paris, Rome, and Toronto.

The immigrant groups examined included Chinese, Indians, and Filipinos. These groups were selected in order to ensure that the same non-European immigrant groups (i.e., non-white) were compared in each global metro.

Method of analysis

To determine the extent to which each non-European immigrant group was residentially segregated from the host group in the global metro, we used the index of dissimilarity (D). The index measures residential segregation that is defined as the overall unevenness in the spatial distribution of two groups. The index of dissimilarity is be stated mathematically in Equation 17.1:

$$D = 100(\tfrac{1}{2}\sum_{i=1}^{k}|x_i - y_i|)$$ (17.1)

where x_i = the percentage of a global metro's total European (white) population living in a given geographic sub-unit (e.g. census tract/neighborhood, ward for Toronto, New York, and London). For Madrid, Paris, and Rome, we substituted the total European (white) group for total citizens living in urbanistic zones. y_i = the percentage of a global metro's total non-European (non-white) immigrant group population living in the same geographic sub-unit in Toronto, New York and London. For Madrid, Paris, and Rome, we substituted non-European (non-white) immigrant group for non-citizens living in the same sub-units. k = the number of sub-units. D = the index of dissimilarity, which is equal to one-half the sum of the absolute differences (positive and negative) between the percentage distributions of the European (white) population and non-European (non-white) immigrant population in the global metro of Toronto, New York, and London and total citizens versus non-citizens in the global metro of Madrid, Paris, and Rome. The index value may range from 0, indicating no residential segregation, to 100, indicating complete residential segregation. The higher the index, the greater the degree of residential segregation. Conceptually, the index of dissimilarity measures the minimum percentage of a group's population that would have to change residences for each geographic sub-unit to have the same percentage of that group as the global metro area as a whole.

Census socioeconomic data was used where available to assess the extent to which the non-European immigrant groups were reaching parity with the host population. This data was combined with previous studies to measure comparative progress in this area.

The foreign-born (immigrant) population of the global metros

Table 17.1 shows the number and percentage of foreign-born population of each global metro selected. Toronto has the highest percentage (44 percent) of foreign born, and the second highest total number. New York is second with 36 percent, and first in the number of foreign born. Madrid, with 5 percent, is the global metro with the lowest percentage of immigrants.

The next section examines the profile of each global metro.

Metro Toronto

As indicated in Table 17.1, metro Toronto had the highest percentage of immigrants among the six global metros. The three non-European groups of Chinese, Indians, and Filipinos started to arrive in Toronto in large numbers only after Canada changed its racially restrictive immigration policy to the present class-based system in 1967 (Darden, 2004, 2005, 2006). Compared to Indians and Filipinos, the Chinese are the most residentially segregated from the white population in Toronto, with an index of dissimilarity of 57.6 in 2001 (Table 17.2) (Darden 2004).

Metro New York

Table 17.1 indicates that the New York metro area has the second highest percentage (36 percent) of the foreign born population and the largest number (2.8 million). As with Toronto, Chinese, Filipinos, and Indians arrived in large numbers in the New York metro area after the United States changed its racially restrictive immigration policy in 1965.

Many arrived with a high level of education and skills which has enabled them to bypass the poor neighborhoods of the central city, where traditional immigrants from European countries located when they first arrived in the New York metropolitan area(Allen and Turner 2009). Among the three non-European immigrant groups, the Chinese is the largest and has been in the New York metropolis longer than Indians or Filipinos. Yet the Chinese are the most

Table 17.1 Metropolitan areas in selected countries of study and the percent foreign born

Rank	Metropolitan area	Number foreign born	Total population	Percent foreign born (year)
1	Toronto	2,032,960	4,647,960	44.0 (2001)
2	New York	2,871,032	8,008,278	36.0 (2000)
3	London	1,940,390	7,172,091	27.1 (2001)
4	Paris	1,081,611	6,161,887	17.5 (1999)
5	Rome	169,064	2,655,970	6.4 (2000)
6	Madrid	272,692	5,423,384	5.0 (2001)

Sources: Strategic Research and Statistics (2005). *Recent Immigrants in Metropolitan Areas: Toronto – A Comparative Profile Based on the 2001 Census.* Retrieved July 1, 2010 (www.cic.gc.ca/english/resources/research/census2001/toronto/intro.asp).
National Institute of Statistics Census for France, Italy, Spain, United Kingdom.
US Bureau of the Census. 2003. Summary File 4. Washington, DC Data User Services.

Table 17.2 Residential Segregation of Filipinos, Indians, and Chinese in six global metro areas as measured by the index of dissimilarity*

Global metro area	Geographic unit	Filipinos	South Asians (Indians)	Chinese	Year
Toronto	Census tracts (averaging 4,000 population)	48.1	53.4	57.6	2001
New York	Census tracts (averaging 4,000 population)	56.0	59.0	62.5	2000
London	Wards (averaging 11,000 population)	–	44.0	26.6	2001
Paris	Triris (averaging 45,000 population)	–	29.7	53.4	1999
Rome	Urbanistic zones (averaging 18,000 population)	36.1	38.3	39.9	2004
Madrid	Districs (averaging 10,000 population)	51.4	30.3	34.0	2001
Mean		**47.9**	**42.5**	**45.6**	

Source: Computed by the authors from data obtained from Statistics Canada; the United States Bureau of the Census; the National Institute of Statistics for Italy, Spain, and France; Peach (2009), and (Rees and Butt, 2004).
* The index ranges from 0, indicating no segregation, to 100, or complete segregation. The higher the index, the greater the degree of residential segregation.

residentially segregated from whites. Table 17.2 shows that the Chinese had an index of dissimilarity of 62.5 compared to 59 for Indians and 56 for Filipinos.

The London Metro area

Unlike Canada and the United States, the census for England and Wales uses wards instead of census tracts for spatial sub-units to measure residential segregation. As indicated earlier, wards are larger in geographic scale on average than census tracts. This will influence the level of residential segregation, resulting in lower overall averages when compared to the level of residential segregation for the same groups using census tracts.

Metro London has continued to be the global metro of choice for non-European immigrant groups. Within metro London, the level of residential segregation of the Chinese from the white population was much lower than the level between Indians and whites. The index of dissimilarity for Chinese and whites was 26.6 compared to 44 for Indians (Table 17.2). A separate census category for Filipinos was not found in the British census. For Indians, socioeconomic status did not seem to be the major reason for their level of residential segregation.

Paris Metro area

Immigrants from China and India are increasing. In 1999 (the most recent census), there were 22,764 Chinese and 3,891 Indians in Paris (Simon 1999). No specific data were provided on Filipinos.

Unlike New York and Toronto (where census tracts are used) and London (where wards are used), the geographic units in Paris are called *triris*. They cover 123 municipalities, Paris plus the first ring, i.e., *Petite Couronne* for a total area of 762 km. Based on these large spatial sub-units, the index of dissimilarity for Chinese in Paris was 53.4. It was 29.7 for Indians.

Metro Rome

Rome has been the preferred destination for Filipino, Chinese, and Indian immigrants who settled in Italy. According to the Municipality of Rome, there were 22,195 immigrants born in the Philippines who resided in metropolitan Rome in 2000 (Cristaldi 2002). They constituted 13.4 percent of the foreign-born population (the largest of any immigrant group) and 0.8 percent of the total population of metropolitan Rome (Cristaldi 2004a). The Chinese numbered 5,637, or 3.3 percent of the foreign born population and 0.2 percent of the total population. There were 4,326 Indians, representing 2.5 percent of the foreign born population and 0.16 percent of the total population of metropolitan Rome (Cristaldi 2004a).

Instead of census tracts or wards, the dissimilarity index for Rome is based on urbanistic zones, which is the spatial sub-area defined by the municipality of Rome for planning purposes. There are 155 urbanistic zones for the extensive municipality of Rome (Cristaldi 2004b).

The Italian government does not provide socioeconomic data on immigrant groups at the neighborhood or even the urbanistic zone level. Thus, it is difficult to assess the influence of socioeconomic status on the three immigrant groups' spatial distribution all over the extensive municipality (Cristaldi 2004b).

Owing in part to their occupation, which has been disproportionately live-in domestic work, Filipinos are the least residentially segregated among the three groups. The index of dissimilarity for Filipinos was 36.1. It was 38.3 for Indians and 39.9 for Chinese. The Chinese are more residentially concentrated in the East section of the municipality of Rome (Cristaldi and Lucchini 2007; Cristaldi 2009).

Madrid

In Madrid, there were 11,573 Chinese and 6,124 immigrants from the Philippines in 2000 (Instituto Nacional de Estadistica 2004). Unlike Rome, the most highly segregated immigrant group in Madrid was the Filipinos (Echazarra 2010). The index of dissimilarity between Filipinos and the total Spanish population of Madrid was 51.4. The index was 34.0 for Chinese and 30.3 for Indians.

Similar to Italy, Spain has not provided socioeconomic data at the neighborhood level on immigrant groups. Therefore, we cannot examine the relationship of each immigrant group's socioeconomic status and their level of residential segregation.

Conclusions

This chapter has examined the critical issues related to the "new immigrant" residential segregation. The discussion of issues was followed by a comparative international immigrant case study, examining levels of residential segregation of three immigrant groups—Chinese, Indians, and Filipinos—in six global metropolitan areas, located in the United States, Canada, and the European Union. These are Toronto, New York, London, Rome, Paris, and Madrid. These are all gateway global metros for international migrants.

Our objective was to examine the pattern of residential segregation of the three immigrant groups to see whether place mattered. For example, was any one group consistently less residentially segregated than the other immigrant groups in all of the global metros?

Our analysis using the index of dissimilarity to measure residential segregation revealed that in general, the mean level of residential segregation was low, i.e., below 50 for all three groups. The mean was slightly higher for Filipinos at 47.9, followed by the Chinese at 45.6. The least segregated immigrant group was Indians, with an index of 42.5. However, no one immigrant group was consistently the most or least segregated among the six metro areas examined. Caution is advised, however in interpreting the index of dissimilarity between metro with different spatial sub-units (i.e., census tracts and wards). Because the index of dissimilarity is based on census tracts which are smaller spatial sub-units than those used in other global metros reveals a higher level of residential segregation in general. Except for Toronto, where census tracts were used, each of the three immigrant groups experienced a lower level of residential segregation than in New York.

Filipinos were the least segregated in Rome (36.1). Indians, like the Filipinos, experienced the highest level of segregation in the New York metro area (59). They experienced the lowest level of residential segregation in Paris (29.7).

The Chinese experienced their highest level of residential segregation in New York (62.5) and their lowest level in London (26.6). The evidence suggests that the pattern of residential segregation for each non-European immigrant group varies between global metro areas. However, in general, it is below 50.

Finally, socioeconomic data (where available) indicates that socioeconomic status as measured by occupation and educational attainment does not adequately explain the level of residential segregation of the immigrant groups. Discrimination may be more of an explanation. Further study in a comparative context is needed.

More studies of discrimination in housing and steering are needed in Canada and countries of the European Union in particular. Presently, only the United States maintains strong discrimination in housing studies based on the paired test audit method (Darden 2004). Thus, international comparative studies of immigrant residential segregation due to housing discrimination are not an option due to a lack of comparable data.

References and further reading

Allen, J. P. and Turner, E. (2009) "Ethnic residential concentrations with above-average incomes" *Urban Geography* 30(3): 209–38.

Cristaldi, F. (2002) "Multiethnic Rome: Toward residential segregation?" *GeoJournal* 58(2–3): 81–90.

——(2004a) "The settlement pattern of immigrants: From the metropolitan area to the inner city of Rome." In D. Wastl-Walter, L. A. Staeheli, and L. Dowler (eds), *Rights to the City*. IGU-Home of Geography Publication series Vol 3. Rome: Societa Geografica Italiana, pp. 155–68.

——(2004b) "Roma città plurale: Del diritto alla casa alla segregazione spaziale degli immigrati" *Geotema* 23: 16–25.

——(2009) "The immigration space in Rome: Residential and productive features." In R. Morri and C. Pesaresi (eds). *Migration and Citizenship: The Role of the Metropolis in the European Union Process of Enlargement*. Ricerche e Studia 20, pp. 117–29.

Cristaldi, F. (2012) *Immigrazione e territorio. Lo spazio con/diviso*. Bologna: Pàtron Editore.

Cristaldi, F. and Darden, J. (2011) "The impact of immigration policies on transnational Filipino immigrant women: Comparison of their social and spatial incorporation in Rome and Toronto" *Journal of Urban History* 37(5): 694–709.

Cristaldi, F. and Lucchini, G. (2007) "Cinesi a Roma: una comunita di ristoratori e commerciantia" *Studi Emigrazione* 165: 197–218.

Daniels, R. (2007) "The Immigration Act of 1965: Intended and unintended consequences." In *Historians on America*. Washington, DC: US Department of State, pp. 76–83.

Darden, J. T. (2003) "Residential segregation: The causes and social and economic consequences." In C. Stokes and T. Melendez (eds), *Racial Liberalism and the Politics of Urban America*. East Lansing, MI: Michigan State University Press, pp. 321–44.

——(2004) *The Significance of White Supremacy in the Canadian Metropolis of Toronto*. Lewiston, NY: The Edwin Mellon Press.

——(2006) "The impact of Canadian immigration policy on the structure of the black Caribbean family in Toronto." In E. Fong (ed.), *Inside the Mosaic*. Toronto: University of Toronto Press, pp. 146–68.

Darden, J. T. (2009) Geographic racial equality in America's most segregated metropolitan area: Detroit. In J. Frazier, J. T. Darden, and N. Henry (eds), *The African Diaspora in the United States and Canada at the Dawn of the 21st Century*. Binghamton: Global Academic Publishing, pp. 135–45.

Darden, J. T. and Kamel, S. (2000) "Black residential segregation in the city and suburbs of Detroit: Does socioeconomic status matter?" *Journal of Urban Affairs* 22: 1–13.

Darden, J. T. and Tabachneck, A. (1980) "Algorithm 8: Graphic and mathematical descriptions of inequality, dissimilarity, segregation or concentration" *Environment and Planning A* 12: 227–34.

Darden, J. T. and Teixeira, C. (2009) "The African diaspora in Canada." In J. Frazier, J. T. Darden, and N. Henry (eds), *The African Diaspora in the United States and Canada at the Dawn of the 21st Century*. Binghamton, NY: Global Academic Publishing, pp. 13–34.

Darden, J. and Kamel, S. (2005) "Filipinos in Toronto: Residential segregation and neighborhood socioeconomic inequality" *Amerasia Journal* 30(3): 25–38.

Darden, J. and Fong, E. (2011) "The spatial segregation and socioeconomic inequality of immigrant groups." In C. Teixeira, W. Li, and A. Kobayashi (eds), *Immigrant Geographies of North American Cities*. Don Mills, ON: Oxford University Press, Chapter 4.

Echazarra A. (2010) "Segregación residencial de los extranjeros en el área metropolitana de Madrid. Un análisis quantitativo" *Revista Internacional de Sociología* 68: 165–97.

Ho, C. (2006) "Migration as Feminisation? Chinese women's experiences of work and family in Australia" *Journal of Ethnic and Migration Studies* 32(3): 497–514.

Iceland, J., Weinberg, D., and Steinmetz, E. (2002) *Racial and Ethnic Segregation in the United States: 1980–2000*. Washington, DC: US Bureau of the Census.

Iceland, J. and Wilkes, R. (2006) "Does socioeconomic status matter? Race, class and residential segregation" *Social Problems* 53(2): 248–73.

Instituto Nacional de Estadistica (2004) *Madrid Foreign Born, 2002*: INE.

Johnston, R., Paulsen, M., and Forrest, J. (2007) "The geography of ethnic residential segregation: A comparative study of five countries" *Annals of the Association of American Geographers* 97(4): 713–38.

Massey, D. and Denton, N. (1993) *American Apartheid: Segregation and the Making of the Underclass*. Cambridge, MA: Harvard University Press.

Morokvasic, M. (2003) "Transnational mobility and gender: A view from a post-wall Europe." In M. Morokvasic, U. Erel, and K. Shinozaki (eds), *Crossing Borders and Shifting Boundaries, Vol. 1: Gender on the Move*. Opladen: Leske and Budrich, pp. 101–33.

Musterd, S. (2005) "Social and ethnic segregation in Europe: Levels, causes and effects" *Journal of Urban Affairs* 27(3): 331–48.

Peach, C. (1996) "Does Britain have ghettos?" *Transactions of the Institute of British Geographers* 21: 216–35.

——(1999) "London and New York: Contrasts in British and American models of segregation" *International Journal of Population Geography* 5: 319–51.

——(2009) "Slippery segregation: Discovering or manufacturing ghettos?" *Journal of Ethnic and Migration Studies* 35(9): 1381–95.

Rees, P. and Butt, F. (2004) "Ethnic change and diversity in England" *Area* 36(2): 174–86.

Price, M. and Benton-Short, L. (2007) "Immigrants and world cities: From the hyper-diverse to the bypassed" *GeoJournal* 68(2–3): 103–17.

Simon, P. (1999) "Nationality and origins in French statistics: Ambiguous categories" *Population* 11: 193–220.

South, S., Crowder, K., and Chavez, E. (2005) "Migration and spatial assimilation among US Latinos: Classical versus segmented trajectories" *Demography* 42(3): 497–521.

Turner, M., Ross, S., Galster, G., and Yinger, J. (2002) *Discrimination in Metropolitan Housing Markets: National Results from Phase 1 HDS 2000*. Washington, DC: The Urban Institute.

18

Sexualities and international migration

Eithne Luibhéid

Introduction

The ways that sexuality shapes and is reshaped by international migration has long been implicitly acknowledged, including by scholarship on "marriage migration" and on the linkages among late nineteenth-century industrialization, immigration, and the sex industry. Nonetheless, the major social science disciplines have generally addressed sexuality and international migration as separate areas. In recent decades, however, scholars have increasingly situated sexuality and international migration in critical conversation. In the process, they have drawn on and transformed key theories, methodologies, and research practices within and across the disciplines.

Historically, migration scholarship—including immigration, emigration, diaspora, and transnationalism research—has ignored, marginalized, or trivialized sexuality, or else subsumed it under rubrics like gender, deviance, or morality (Manalansan 2006). In recent decades, however, scholars have begun to insist that sexuality must be analyzed as a distinct axis that structures all migration processes. Although groundbreaking scholarship often focused on gay migrant experiences, scholars' purpose was never to simply "add" lesbians, gay men, or other figures to existing migration histories, theories, and methods. Instead, they have shown that sexuality structures all migration experiences, and migration theories, methodologies and epistemologies must be reformulated accordingly. Illustrating this insight, several recent works explore how normative heterosexuality and marriage, and the affective bonds that characterize them, become reformulated across transnational circuits that span international borders. Other scholarship explores how diasporas and borderlands may be conceived without reinscribing sexually normative logics that often inform theories of race, ethnicity, culture, and space.

Sexuality: neither "natural" nor private but an axis of power

Such scholarship has been enabled by the recognition that sexuality is neither a "natural" drive nor a private matter; instead, sexuality is invariably expressed and experienced through social, economic, and cultural mediation, and comprises a locus of power that is continually struggled over. Thus, states, corporations, and powerful groups intervene in and deploy sexuality for varied aims, including through immigration policies, practices, and ideologies. Individuals also deploy sexuality to construct flexible migration, legalization, and citizenship opportunities. Sexuality and migration scholarship therefore centers the role of states, employers, families, communities, and individuals in strategically mobilizing sexualities to organize, govern, and contest migration processes at multiple levels and in relation to changing social, political, and economic agendas and hierarchies.

Scholars caution that sexuality categories and concepts are burdened by histories and legacies "that must be interrogated, do not map neatly across time and space, and become transformed through circulation within unevenly situated local, regional, national, and transnational circuits" (Luibhéid 2008: 170). Thus, although this essay uses terms such as lesbian, gay, bisexual, transgender, queer, heterosexual, and sex worker to discuss migration histories, experiences, and struggles, the categories should nonetheless be understood as contingent, provisional, incommensurate with categories in other locations and histories, and always requiring critical interrogation.

Through exploring the interrelationship between sexuality and migration, scholars have broken with the robust research on gender and migration, and insisted that sexuality must be analyzed as separate from (though deeply intertwined with) gender. As Eve Sedgwick (1990: 31) explains, it is important to distinguish sexuality from gender because gender concepts frequently uphold heteronormative models of sexuality. These are models that valorize sexuality that is channeled into childbearing within patriarchal marriage, especially among members of the dominant racial/ethnic and class group. At the same time, heteronormative thinking obscures the gendered, racial/ethnic, class, and geopolitical relations of power that produce such a system, and instead characterizes the system as "natural," timeless, and world saturating. Heteronormativity is evident in migration scholarship that conflates sexuality with gender, which in turn is often equated with women, which means that only women have sexuality/gender and gender or sexuality are normed as heterosexual. Critical attention to heterosexism therefore shifts the analytic lens away from sexual identities conflated with gender categories and understood as essential, stable, relatively unchanging, to instead theorize the production of sexual subjectivities that variously relate to gender categories, and to explore the creation of the distinction between normative and non-normative sexualities. Immigration processes and nation-state immigration control apparatuses are centrally implicated in these dynamics, since nation-states are often popularly imagined and materially governed through logics of "family" that are (hetero)sexist, racist, colonialist, and bourgeois.

Challenging models of sexual assimilation, acculturation, or normative development

Recent scholarship about sexuality and migration importantly builds from queer of color, feminist of color, ethnic studies, postcolonial, and public health scholarship showing that sexuality upholds relations of power that are not only gendered and sexualized, but also materially constituted through racial, class, religious, and geopolitical hierarchies. This insight has enabled scholars to challenge Eurocentric paradigms of assimilation, acculturation, or normative development that have often guided research about migrant sexualities. For example, migration is frequently conceived within spatial and temporal binaries as a movement from "tradition" to "modernity." Thus, gay men, lesbians, and heterosexual women who migrate from the global south to the global north are typically viewed as moving from "repression" to "liberation." Sexuality in migrants' countries of origin is conceived as "backward," unidimensional, unchanging, and inherently different from sexuality in countries of destination. Migration is therefore expected to transform migrants into sexually "modern" or "liberated" people through exposure to "western" ways.

216

Lionel Cantú (2009: 76–80) describes that this framework "others" migrants; constructs them as backward; erases their internal difference; and ignores the ways that globalization has reconfigured sexualities within migrants' own countries. Moreover, given the complex, historically long-standing, and frequently unequal ties between nation-states as a result of colonialism, capitalism, warfare, and asymmetrical cultural exchange, migrants often arrive not to begin a process of assimilation, but rather to continue their engagement with economic, social, cultural, and political systems that have already profoundly affected their lives (Manalansan 2003). Some sexually marginalized migrants, rather than finding "liberation" in "destination" countries, instead enhance their status among family members and friends in their countries of origin as a result of migration; other migrants experience new sexual constraints, limitations, and dangers such as lack of access to reproductive health care and sexual harassment or abuse including in workplaces. As they confront issues like racism, (hetero)sexism, economic marginalization, language barriers, and sometimes undocumented status, migrants commonly experience restructured asymmetries rather than "liberation."

"Exposure to mainstream ways" is therefore deeply inadequate for understanding how and why migrants reconstruct their sexual understandings, practices, and ideologies. Instead, the negotiation of intersecting structural barriers and possibilities, combined with migrants' own agency, offers a more useful conceptual framework. For instance, according to Manalansan, queer Filipino migrants, who remain caught between the racism of mainstream gay and lesbian communities and the homophobia of migrant communities, create "multiple hybrid cultures and … spaces for community activities and new cultural 'traditions' that depart from both their own migrant communities and from mainstream 'straight' and 'gay and lesbian' cultures" (2006: 236). Ongoing ties between migrants and family or community members who live scattered along transnational circuits that span international borders further ensure that sexuality transformations circulate multi-directionally. Overall, scholars have significantly challenged simplified notions of "migration as liberation," and in the process, complicated and recast time/space binaries (e.g., Alexander 2005: 189–95). Eurocentric and "step-ladder" models of how sexual cultures become transformed and diffused through transnationalizing and globalizing processes have been similarly rethought (Oswin 2006).

Discourses of migrant sexualities: subjective, ideological, and material effects

Migrants may nonetheless narrate their own experiences in terms of sexual "liberation" or "modernity/modernization." Such discourses perform important subjective, ideological, and material work. For example, Jennifer Hirsh discovered that heterosexual Mexican migrants in the United States may claim "modern bodies, modern loves, and modern sex" in order to challenge racist and colonialist stereotypes; reposition themselves spatially and temporally relative to family, friends, and co-workers left behind and those in the United States; and as a strategy of mobility, self-protection, and ongoing negotiation of (bi or trans)national identities (Hirsh 2003: 280, 255). Alternatively, Yen Espiritu showed that some migrants challenge racism and (neo)colonialism by constructing mainstream cultures and dominant racial/ethnic/class groups as sexually immoral (Espiritu 2003). In these circumstances, migrant women (and daughters) are compelled to uphold strict sexual standards as a means to signal the worthiness of the entire migrant community and the retention of its (often invented or reconstructed) cultural heritage, in contrast to the "immorality" of the mainstream. Failure to uphold community sexual standards becomes viewed as cultural or racial betrayal, enacted in gendered terms. Yet, challenging racism and xenophobia through policing sexuality in these gendered ways reinforces patriarchy, heterosexism, and moral discourses that marginalize many *within* migrant communities. Overall, migrants' varied approaches to understanding how migration alters sexuality are deeply intertwined with mainstream narratives that demonize migrants through claims about their supposedly aberrant sexualities, "excessive fertility," potential threat to the nation's cultural and biological heritage through sexuality, and transmission of sexual disease and disorder.

Discourses about migrants' sexualities also allow states to (re)position themselves within the global order. This is particularly evident when migrants seek asylum based either on persecution because of their sexualities, or based on persecution that took sexual form (which are two different, though sometimes inter-related, issues). In theory, asylum is available to migrants who can prove persecution, or well-founded fear of persecution, on account of their race, religion, nationality, political opinion, or membership in a particular social group. Feminist advocates, attorneys, and scholars have waged a fierce struggle to ensure that persecution that takes sexualized form (e.g., rape, sexual torture) is recognized *as* persecution (rather than being dismissed as the unfortunate, essentially private actions of single individuals). The widespread use of rape as a weapon of war in Bosnia, Rwanda, Haiti, and elsewhere contributed to acknowledgment that sexual violence may serve as a tool for persecution.

Recognition that sexual identity may provide a basis for asylum was slower in coming, particularly for lesbians and gay men. Many nation-states insist on treating lesbians and gay men as "deviants" rather than as members of a "particular social group" who may be eligible for asylum if they have been persecuted on that basis. For example, until 1990, lesbians and gay men were barred from legal admission to the United States precisely because their sexualities were viewed as deviant and undesirable. A considerable shift in perspective was required to view them as belonging to a "social group" that might be persecuted and merit protection. Similar contradictions were evident in the rules around migrants seeking asylum because they were persecuted on account of their HIV or transgender status—immigration law often sanctioned their exclusion, but asylum law sometimes permitted their admission. However, admission primarily occurred when migrants were able to present themselves as totally victimized; in conformity with dominant cultural stereotypes (including stereotypes of gay, lesbian, or trans identities, and of migrants' countries of origin); and as unlikely to lead to a "flood" of other applicants should they succeed. Asylum seekers from "friendly" countries were unlikely to secure recognition, no matter how strong their claims were. Kristen Walker characterizes asylum as a "violent gift" (cited in Miller 2005: 144), since it requires applicants to paint their countries of origin in thoroughly negative terms, while ignoring the ways that geopolitically powerful nation-states are implicated in these conditions. Moreover, asylum seekers' narratives are frequently recuperated to advance racist, colonialist claims about countries of origin, and to allow destination countries to assert their superiority, while ignoring that lesbians, gay men, women, people of color, poor people, and/or migrants frequently suffer violence and discrimination in destination countries, too. In these ways, asylum cases involving sexuality provide opportunities for nation-states to engage in what Miller describes as transnational looking and judging that has important ideological and material effects, and to (re)position themselves within the global order while usually doing little to address actual migrants' needs (Miller 2005: 143). Non-governmental organizations (NGOs) have become important actors in these dynamics, too, since asylum has become a primary mechanism through which discourses of sexuality circulate at different scales and remake complex hierarchies. These changing and contradictory discourses concern not just gay men and lesbians, but also such issues as female genital cutting, forced abortion and sterilization, HIV, and rape. At the same time, the vast majority of the world's displaced and asylum-seeking peoples remain located in the global south, which has far fewer resources for their assistance.

Discourses and practices associated with HIV transmission have similarly provided grounds for "transnational looking and judging" that have significant ideological and material effects where migrants are concerned. As Meredith Raimundo (2003) describes, the production of knowledge about HIV/AIDS has frequently reinforced neocolonial geographies, relationships, and imaginaries; marked out certain migrants as legitimate targets for the discriminatory application of immigration rules and workplace practices, while at the same time failing to ensure conditions for health and care and perpetuated normative images of "innocent" heterosexual victims (often white, middle class, and sometimes children) in opposition to those who "deserved" to become ill.

In sum, narratives about migrant sexualities, whether produced by migrants, mainstreams, nation-states, NGOs or anyone else, cannot be treated as transparent reflections of empirical "facts," but instead, as conditioned by (and further conditioning) available ideological and material relations.

Why migration? Intertwining sexual and economic factors

Another important area of scholarship concerns whether sexuality not only structures (and becomes restructured by), but also directly impels, migration. Manuel Guzmán (1997) coined the term "sexile" to describe those who feel forced to migrate because of sexual alterity. Scholarship often conceived sexile as being entirely separate from (and less important than) economic considerations. Thus, sexual "minorities" who felt forced to migrate were effectively inscribed as bourgeois subjects who were defined entirely by sexuality. However, recent scholarship challenges the separation of sexuality from political economy, and instead demonstrates that sexual and economic factors intertwine to impel and shape migration processes and experiences. For instance, Lionel Cantú interviewed Mexican migrant men who had sex with men (not all of whom identified as gay, bisexual, or a similar category). He found that all informants, "in one form or another gave financial reasons for migration to the United States" (Cantú 2009: 132). Yet, their financial reasons were interconnected with sexuality, including because sexual minorities often face marginalization and discrimination in the labor market. Gender, class, and cultural factors further shaped migration possibilities, desires, and decisions among Cantú's informants. For example, some economically privileged men who were able to maintain gay or bisexual lifestyles with minimal cost were less likely to migrate; at the other end of the spectrum, some gay or bisexual men who wanted to migrate lacked the necessary resources. Thus, the connections between sexuality, economics, and migration are multiple and complex. Debates about these connections significantly transform our understanding of migrant sex work and marriage migration, too.

Emerging areas of research

Sexual norms and migrant legal statuses

Important emerging areas of research promise to deepen our understanding of the interconnections between sexuality and migration. For example, scholars are exploring how nation-states come to designate migrants as authorized or unauthorized. Although unauthorized status is conventionally portrayed as reflecting migrants' undesirable characters, scholars have shown that this designation derives from and extends relations of power that are grounded in histories of colonialism, global capitalism, patriarchy, and racism. Contemporary neoliberal economic globalization processes have rearticulated these histories by mobilizing growing numbers of people for migration, even while nation-states have developed increasingly restrictive regimes for migrant selection, and expanded and diversified the grounds on which migrants become designated as unauthorized after admission. Some scholars have begun to explore how sexual norms, specifically, fit into these dynamics as states redraw the line between authorized and unauthorized migrant status—and how migrants may take up, strategically inhabit, and seek to transform sexual norms in order to reconstruct their legal statuses and migration opportunities.

Research on marriage migration and migrant sex work has often been at the forefront of these discussions. Many nation-states admit migrants based on male–female marriages, while at the same time refusing to admit similarly situated same-gender couples, and thus gay men and lesbians must find grounds other than their relationships for legal admission. The contrasting treatment of male–female versus same-gender relationships perfectly illustrates how sexual norms may shape access (or not) to legal admission. Similarly, sex work is criminalized in many nation-states, with the result that anyone who has ever sold sex is likely to be denied legal admission. Moreover, anyone who is caught selling sex after admission is liable to become criminalized and deported—which reminds us that legal statuses need to be maintained through "proper" behavior, and that migrants may transition from authorized to unauthorized status (or vice versa) after admission including through normative sexual regimes.

Nationalist sexual norms certainly shape designations of authorized and unauthorized status, but labeling certain kinds of migration as unauthorized does not prevent it from occurring. Thus, when nation-states designate sex work, for example, as an activity that renders one ineligible for legal admission, or results in criminalization and deportation after admission, this designation serves less to deter migrants than to heighten the dangers of their journeys and reinforce their exploitability, while reducing their avenues for recourse in cases of abuse. Indeed, scholars suggest that the designation of sex work as an activity that renders migrants illegal or deportable does little to address the conditions that brought them into the sex industry in the first place, on terms ranging from consent to coercion; and often fuels anti-trafficking campaigns and exclusionary legislation that strengthen the hand of the state and serve the interests of capital (Kempadoo 2005).

A growing scholarly literature also theorizes how sexual violence, frequently perpetrated with impunity, attempts to further inscribe powerlessness on unauthorized migrants' bodies. This includes through systemic practices of rape, sexual abuse, and sexual coercion at national borders, in migrant workplaces, and within migrant detention facilities. An important strand of the scholarship explores how neoliberal globalization processes, in conjunction with Mexican and United States complicity, have given rise to the systemic disappearance, sexual torture, and murder of hundreds of young, mostly dark-skinned, poor young women, many of whom had migrated internally and were employed in global export processing zones in Cuidad Juárez, Mexico, across the border from El Paso, Texas (e.g. Fregoso 2007).

Incorporating migrants through norms of sexuality, intimacy, and affect

Another important area of emerging scholarship explores how migrants are not just excluded but also differentially included and governed by states, employers, and others on the basis of sexuality. Differential incorporation and governance occurs along a spectrum. At one end are modes of incorporation that render migrants maximally vulnerable and exploitable, with minimal recourse to rights or protections, as occurs for many migrants engaged in sex work. At the other end of the spectrum are modes of incorporation that seek to ensure that migrants become good, entrepreneurial, responsible subjects of neoliberalism. The privileging of heterosexual marriage as a basis for admission—whereby migrants are not only admitted on the basis of marital heterosexual ties, but also contractually mandated to turn to these relationships rather than the state for material support, and to remain in the relationships for a duration sufficient to establish "genuine love" in the eyes of state officials—demonstrates how heteronormativity produces modes of incorporation that serve neoliberalism.

The exploration of differential migrant incorporation through sexual regimes builds on and contributes to the "affective turn" in migration studies. For instance, the editors of *Love and Globalization* argue for a "political economy of love" framework that links "macro-level political-economic transformations" with subjective experiences of love, sexuality, and intimacy (Padilla *et al.* 2007: xii). Historically, norms of love, sexuality, and intimacy have been central to capitalist transformations, dynamics of individualization, and practices of consumption. They also remain "fundamentally linked to social and economic inequalities" at different scales (Padilla *et al.* 2007: xii). The differential incorporation of migrants certainly works through their affective, sexual, and intimate ties. States' investment in promoting particular kinds of ties is shown not only by the privileging of heterosexual marriage as a basis for legal admission, but also by the fact that some nation-states now admit same-sex couples—yet usually on the condition that they demonstrate that their intimate and sexual bonds remain private (rather than political) and tied to domesticity and consumption in ways that that mirror the heterosexual norm. Thus, alternative formations of affect, sexuality, intimacy, and obligation, which are evident in queer and non-normative communities, remain ignored, invalidated, or actively disallowed under state regimes for migrant admission and continued residence. Moreover, the denial of legal admission to low-income heterosexual spouses, as well as to families that do not match dominant cultural norms/expectations, further shows how affect, intimacy, and sexuality are deployed to produce class-specific, racial, and patriarchal modes of migrant incorporation and subject formation.

Recent changes in immigration law, which have significantly expanded the grounds on which migrants may be criminalized and deported after entry, while reducing migrants' ability to present their state-recognized heterosexual family ties as mitigating factors, indicate the importance of the prison-industrial complex and the expanding carceral archipelago in mediating migrants' incorporation and governance. At the same time, the expanding criminalization, detention, and deportation of migrants illustrates that borders and immigration controls are not confined to territorial land borders, but instead are increasingly everywhere, linked at different scales, and tied to both carceral and citizenship regimes—including through affect, sexuality, and intimacy.

Yet, migrants' lives are never reducible to regimes or purviews of states or employers. Furthermore, migrants are aware of state regimes of desired affect, intimacy, and sexuality and they strategize accordingly. For example, Denise Brennan has shown how some poor women from the Dominican Republic sell sex and romance to tourists, hoping that a tourist will sponsor their migration as a fiancée or wife. Marriage rather than sex work therefore emerges as the women's last ditch effort at economic survival in a context where powerful nation-states grant legal admission to poor women for purposes of marriage, but not for seeking work (Brennan 2004: 213). At the other end of the economic spectrum, Aihwa Ong (1999) argues that well-to-do families strategically deploy familial regimes in ways that intersect with economic opportunities and nation-state migration regimes, in order to forge new possibilities for their members in a context of globalization. Under varied conditions, gay, trans, and queer migrants also renegotiate affective ties and financial obligations toward families of birth across borders, while also forming "complex fictive family networks of friends and lovers" (Manalansan 2006: 236). Research explores how the internet, as a critical element in the transnational flow of information, images, imaginaries, and commodities, may mediate the linkages between love, intimacy, sexuality, and international migration.

Transmigration

Another important emerging area of scholarship concerns what we may describe as "transgender" migration. "Transgender" (or trans) has varied meanings and histories, but here I use it as a provisional umbrella term to designate people who, in various ways, don't conform to gender norms. Within migration scholarship, transmigrants are often placed into one binary gender category or another, based on their biological gender, who they have sex with, and/or their gender performance—but these often arbitrary classifications overlook the theoretical and political benefits of remaining open to gender systems that are not binary or stable. Openness to complex gender systems admittedly presents challenges. For example, contemporary European and North American models of "sexual object choice" (whereby the gender of one's sexual partner supposedly defines one's own gender and sexual identity) do not map neatly onto gender/sexual systems in other locations (e.g., in many Latin American nations, men's gender status is not affected by same-gender sexual encounters if a man takes the sexually active role). Illustrating these complexities, Vogel describes that Venezuelan trans sex workers in Europe viewed themselves as having been born male homosexuals (*maricos*), and conceived homosexuality as the basis for their desire to accomplish a sexy, hyper-feminine appearance—including through breast augmentation but not surgical removal of their genitals. Yet, they did not want to be women, and "were not very much interested in how an average woman would be" (Vogel 2009: 373). Vogel expresses reservations about conceiving these migrants as transgender, instead preferring the term "*transformista*" or "*travesti*." Her thoughtful explication of the histories, complexities, and limits of the terminologies through which these migrants' lives may be apprehended illustrates why analysis of transgender migration promises to enrich scholarship on sexuality and migration—including by pushing us to better understand the intricate, varied ways that sexuality and gender co-construct one another. Thus, my use of the category "transgender" or "trans" to describe Vogel's informants is not intended to denigrate her or their perspectives, but rather as a stand-in term to mark the existence of migration situations like (and unlike) those studied by Vogel.

Nascent research suggests the importance of theorizing transmigration across transnational fields, and in relation to multiple trajectories, imaginaries, hierarchies, and changing possibilities. Research also suggests the intertwining of economic, gender, and sexual factors in shaping transmigration. For example, migration offers opportunities to both earn money and try out new gender practices; indeed, migrant earnings provide the means to purchase forms of sexualized gender enhancement such as breasts, and these enhancements in turn may improve migrants' earning possibilities. Clare Sears (2008) concludes that transgendering practices and discourses shape, and become reshaped by, migration; have multiple genealogies; involve experiences of pleasure and dispossession; and have multiple, disparate, and contradictory effects that require careful specification (including reinforcing and undoing gender norms as they intersect with racial, class, and geopolitical hierarchies).

Thus, I began this review by describing the importance of separating sexuality from gender as a heteronormative category. However, the return of gender—by way of transmigrants whose lives and practices open up gender—allows us to ask new, nuanced questions about the ways gender and sexuality inscribe, articulate, co-produce, and transvalue one another. This sharpens sexuality and migration (and gender and migration) analyses, including by alerting us to questions of normalization and unequal power, and the interplay of race, class, culture, and geopolitics.

Juggling contradictory mandates

The developing scholarship on sexuality and international migration reflects and further contributes to significant social and academic transformations. In the United States, social transformations include the expansion and diversification of global migration; restructured racial, ethnic, and religious landscapes; the impact of decolonial, civil rights, feminist, gay, and transgender

rights movements; the AIDS pandemic; the emergence of sexuality as an arena of sharp contestation in political life; the so-called War on Terror that has significantly reshaped the policing
of immigration; the globalization of sexual politics and institutions including those addressing
human rights; and the restructured prison–industrial complex with its dense linkages to immigration control. Academically, sexuality research became institutionalized in universities in the
late 1980s, initially under the rubric of Lesbian and Gay Studies, and subsequently as Queer
Studies in some instances. Major social science disciplines continued to significantly contribute to
sexuality research. Feminist and queer of color scholarship made clear how hierarchies of race,
class, gender, and geopolitics are enforced through sexual regulation. In the 1990s, sexuality
scholarship underwent "transgender" and "transnational" turns. The stunning expansion of
migration scholarship, including under the rubrics of transnationalism, globalization, and diaspora
studies; the institutionalization of Ethnic Studies programs; and the emergence of clinics and law
programs that particularly address gender and sexuality, has also significantly enabled the research.

The research on sexuality and migration continues to juggle complex and contradictory
mandates (Luibhéid 2008). This includes recovering and honoring histories that have been
rendered invisible and unintelligible within both sexuality and migration scholarship, in a
manner that challenges dominant structures of power and knowledge that erased those histories
in the first place yet without producing new erasures and closures. Scholars have also paid close
attention to the social categories through which systems and individuals understand and
experience their lives, while refusing to reify the categories. Instead, they have analyzed how
social categories circulate (or do not), who takes up the categories, in what ways, and for what
kinds of work, and what histories get enabled or erased in the process. While remaining focused
on grounded experiences, social struggles, and a vision of social transformation, scholars have
also insisted that research on sexuality and migration involves questions that extend beyond
identity-based politics, theories, and modes of representation. Scholars have also sought to
juggle concerns about multiple, rather than singular, axes of power and inequality. Finally and
perhaps most importantly, scholars have struggled to ensure that their research contributes to
social change, rather than being recuperated to serve the violence of capital and the state. These
are significant challenges, yet research about the interconnections among sexuality and migration is flourishing within disciplines, across disciplines, and as a horizon of possibility for exciting
new modes of intellectual and political engagement.

References and further reading

Alexander, M. J. (2005) *Pedagogies of Crossing. Meditations on Feminism, Sexual Politics, Memory, and the
    Sacred*. Durham, NC: Duke University Press.
Brennan, D. (2004) *What's Love Got to do With it? Transnational Desires and Sex Tourism in the Dominican
    Republic*. Durham, NC: Duke University Press.
Cantú, L. (2009) *The Sexuality of Migration*. N. Naples and S. Vidal-Ortiz (eds), New York: New York
    University Press.
Espiritu, Y. L. (2003) *Homebound: Filipino American Lives Across Cultures, Communities, and Countries*.
    Berkeley, CA: University of California Press.
Fregoso, R. (2007) "Toward a planetary civil society." In D. Segura and P. Zavella (eds), *Women and
    Migration in the US-Mexico Borderlands. A Reader*. Durham, NC: Duke University Press, pp. 35–66.
Guzmán, M. (1997) "'Pa' la escuelita con mucho cuida'o y por la orillita: A journey through the contested
    terrains of the nation and sexual orientation." In F. Negrón-Muntaner and R. Grosfoguel (eds), *Puerto
    Rican Jam; Rethinking Colonialism and Nationalism*. Minneapolis, MN: University of Minnesota Press, pp.
    208–29.
Hirsh, J. (2003) *A Courtship After Marriage. Sexuality and Love in Mexican Transnational Families*. Berkeley,
    CA: University of California Press.

Kempadoo, K. (ed.) (2005) *Trafficking and Prostitution Reconsidered: New Perspectives on Migration, Sex Work, and Human Rights.* Boulder, CO: Paradigm Press.

Luibhéid, E. (2002) *Entry Denied: Controlling Sexuality at the Border.* Minneapolis, MN: University of Minnesota Press.

——(2008) "Queer/migration. An unruly body of scholarship" *GLQ* special issue on "Queer/Migration" 14(2–3): 169–90.

Manalansan, M. F., IV. (2003) *Global Divas: Filipino Gay Men in the Diaspora.* Durham, NC: Duke University Press.

——(2006) "Queer intersections: Sexuality and gender in migration studies" *International Migration Review* 40(1): 224–49.

Miller, A. (2005) "Gay enough? Some tensions in seeking the grant of asylum and protecting global sexual diversity." In B. Epps, K. Valens, and B. Johnson González (eds), *Passing Lines: Sexuality and Immigration.* Cambridge, MA: Harvard University Press, pp. 137–87.

Ong, A. (1999) *Flexible Citizenship: The Cultural Logic of Transnationality.* Durham, NC: Duke University Press.

Oswin, N. (2006) "Decentering queer globalization: Diffusion and the 'global gay'" *Environment and Planning D: Society and Space* 24(5): 777–90.

Padilla, M., Hirsch, J., Muñoz-Laboy, M., Sember, R., and Parker, R. (eds) (2007) *Love and Globalization: Transformations of Intimacy in the Contemporary World.* Nashville, TN: Vanderbilt University Press.

Raimundo, M. (2003) "'Corralling the virus': Migratory sexualities and the 'spread of AIDS' in the US media" *Environment and Planning D: Society and Space* 21(4): 389–407.

Sears, C. (2008) "All that glitters: Trans-ing California's gold rush migrations" *GLQ* 14(2–3): 383–402.

Sedgwick, E. (1990) *Epistemology of the Closet.* Berkeley, CA: University of California Press.

Vogel, K. (2009) "The mother, the daughter, and the cow: Venezuelan transformistas' migration to Europe" *Mobilities* 4(3): 367–87.

19

Migrants and indigenous nationalism

Nandita Sharma

Introduction

Over the last decade, at least two discourses concerning the relationship between people variously constituted as either "migrants" or as "indigenous" have intensified (and in some places emerged anew). One presents this relationship as one of potential and fruitful solidarity. Not only have many of those constituted as either "indigenous" or as "migrants" experienced both the linked processes of expropriation and exploitation under processes of colonial (and postcolonial) rule, hostility towards "migrants" and the "indigenous" are understood to be interlocking sets of ideological practices for the maintenance of contemporary injustices. In this vein, solidarity between these two groupings is not only desirable, it is necessary to end practices of domination.

The other increasingly dominant discourse sees the relationship between "migrants" and the "indigenous" as one *of* colonialism. That is, "migrants" and their movements into places identified as "indigenous" are seen as *a part of* the process of colonialism. In this discourse migrants are colonizers. From this perspective, decolonization becomes the assertion of "indigenous" sovereignty over place.

These amount to be quite different understandings of colonialism and present starkly different strategies for achieving decolonization. The belief that "migrants" and the "indigenous" *share* experiences of colonialism is one that situates migration as one of the *outcomes* of people's experience of colonization. Such a view also sees processes of colonialism as not fully contained within any particular place but as traversing and effecting a broad and deep network of connected sites. Colonialism is recognized as a process occurring *across* space and as drawing people into a shared field of power. The anti-colonial project, from this perspective, is a global one, one that focuses on ending the practices that led to people dispossession, displacement, and subsequent exploitation.

Seeing migration as an act *of* colonialism, on the other hand, relies on the assumption of a strong, essential relationship between particular groups of people and particular lands. This is what I call a *territorialized understanding of colonization and imperialism*. Land, a key means of production and bases of life, becomes territorialized when ideas of membership or "belonging" are understood as inherently *limited* to a select group of people, usually based on ideas of "blood" and "soil." Land often also becomes racialized or ethnicized through such ideas. Such a perspective understands colonialism to be ultimately about the expropriation of specific territories and the dispossession of people constituted as "indigenous" to it. The anti-colonial project, in this case, comes to be about reclaiming particular lands for particular groups. Colonialism is understood to be a set of isolated and unrelated events. This is the nationalist anti-colonial project. It sees decolonization as bringing about the rule of the "natives."

Evaluating both of these sets of arguments should clarify our understanding of processes of colonialism as well as the politics of decolonization. By bringing the experiences of "migrants" and the "indigenous" together into one analytic field, we can better see that the problem of colonialism is not fundamentally the problem of the imposition of "foreign" rule over "natives." Instead, if we understand colonialism not inherently as a process of "foreign" control but, rather, as a process of expropriation and exploitation *full stop*, our temporal as well as spatial understanding of colonialism changes—as do our strategies for decolonization. This change, I believe, strengthens movements working to end people's oppression and exploitation. Such a change requires an ontological shift regarding who we think we are and how we imagine our connections to one another.

The theories developed under the rubric of postcolonialism, especially those incorporating the insights of the scholarship on transnationalism, are useful in this regard, for they allow us to see the historical as well as contemporary *connectivity* people have with each other. These connections have been forged *across* the places claimed by colonial empires and *within* any given colonial administrative space. In making these connections, other crossings have had to be made: people have had to connect *across and against* different spatial imaginaries of "race" or "nation". These connections have and continue to exist at economic, political, and social levels as well as affective ones. Postcolonial theories are further useful in revealing the development of territorialized notions of space and place that both "migrants" and "indigenous" people encounter, indeed, in the very constitution of people into these supposedly separate, distinct, and, for some, antagonistic, groups.

I begin this chapter with a discussion of the arguments made by those advancing an autochthonous discourse in which all places are presented as being "native" to certain identifiable people and where the "indigenous" are said to have inherent rights of sovereignty over and against those imagined as "non-native." It is within such autochthonous discourses that the argument that all "migrants" are colonizers is asserted. I maintain that these arguments can best be understood as part of the development and expansion of neo-racist praxis and, indeed, that neo-racist ideologies rationalize the absolute conflation between migration and colonialism.

I conclude by offering an alternative to autochthonous discourses, one rooted in a deep opposition to nationalisms. Instead of having a territorialized understanding of colonialism—and decolonization—I argue for viewing the *commons* as the object of colonial possession and the *commoners* as the subjects of colonial rule and as the agents of decolonization. In this, the political and intellectual project for decolonization is the gaining of our commons and our effective assertion of common rights. A focus on the commons and commoners allows us to more fully address the contemporary relationships of capitalism as well as offering us a route away from the quagmire of territorial and imaginative colonial states shaped through ideologies of nationalism and the (neo)racist turn.

Autochthony

Since the late-1980s, representations of "belonging" have increasingly relied on autochthonous discourses and their negative counterpart, discourses of alien-ness or foreign-ness. As Jean and John Comaroff (2000: 128) argue, by " ... elevating to a first-principle the ineffable interests and connections, at once material and moral, that flow from 'native' rootedness, and special rights, in a place of birth," autochthonous discourses place those constituted as "natives" at the top of a hierarchy of the exploited, oppressed, and colonized and insist on the centrality of the claims of "natives" for the realization of either decolonization or justice. Within the negative duality of "natives" and "non-natives" that such discourses put into play, origins (and in some contexts, claims to original human settlement) becomes the key determinant of who belongs in any given place today—and who does not.

The quintessential "alien" or "foreigner" within autochthonous discourses is the figure of the "migrant" and, indeed, within such discourses, migrants are simply *figures*. Since the hegemonic understanding of what it means to be a "migrant" in the modern and postcolonial world assumes movement away from one's "native" land, migrants come to stand as the ultimate "non-native." Increasingly *irrelevant* within autochthonous discourses are the circumstances that lead to people's migration so that all "migrants" can be represented as colonizers by virtue of their "non-native-ness."

Such a move works to shift the focus away from colonialism, where the historical dynamic is one of expropriation and exploitation and the key relationship is one between expropriators and the expropriated, to one where the dichotomy between "native" and "non-native" becomes central to both analysis and politics. Patrick Wolfe (2008) asserts this when he says:

> the fundamental social divide is not the color line. It is not ethnicity, minority status, or even class. The primary line is the one distinguishing Natives from settlers—that is, from everyone else. Only the Native is not a settler. Only the Native is truly local. Only the Native will free the Native. One is either native or not.

This is a territorialized perspective of land and belonging in which being "native" is both *spatially* and *temporally* dependent. While those constituted as "migrants" may also be identified as "natives" to some given space, once they have moved away from places where such identities may be claimed, they become "*not natives*" in the place they move to. Thus, "migrants" may retain their claims to indigeneity but only to the places where they no longer live. Thus, some argue that "migrants" can continue to claim "native" rights to places they have moved from if they are able to show descendancy from those claiming to be the original human inhabitants (see Kauanui 2008: 637). Within discourses reliant on the primacy of autochthony, claims to native-ness require more than birth in a given space; they require a lineage traceable to the claimed first inhabitants. Consequently, dominant understandings of "native-ness" become racialized and ethnicized. This essentialization of belonging is dependent upon nationalist ideas of primordial "homelands." This is evident in Candace Fujikane's (2005: 77) argument about the inherent "foreign-ness" of "Asians" in the United States:

> Indigenous people are differentiated from settlers by their genealogical, familial relationship with specific land bases that are ancestors to them. One is either indigenous to a particular land base or one is not. Asian Americans are undeniably settlers in the United States because we cannot claim any genealogy to the land we occupy, no matter how many lifetimes Asian settlers work on the land, or how many Asian immigrants have been killed through racist persecution and hate crimes, or how brutal the political or colonial regimes that occasioned Asians' exodus from their homelands.

In the mode of representation of indigeneity there exists an elision between "native" as a colonial state category of subjugation and "indigenous" as a subjectivity of resistance. This is because while the more contemporary subjectivity of "indigeneity" emerged in the post-World War II era and largely from the perspective of those within this category, it is based upon the underlying logics of the colonial (and, later, postcolonial) state's distinction between "natives," "colonials" and, when necessary, "migrants." Today, it brings together very diverse people across the world, under a single, shared subjective understanding of being "indigenous" (Niezen 2003). Arguably, it is a form of subjectivity that has come into being because of the devastation wrought in the aftermath of 1492 and, arguably, before. It is, however, also a form of subjectivity that interpellates people into ruling relations through an attempt to gain national "sovereignty." Indeed, autochthonous modes of belonging are significant in articulating the methods of colonial rule with the national state form, including the racialized/ethnicized basis upon which political rights and rights to property, especially property in land and natural resources, are to be apportioned within any claimed national space.

Today, a rhetoric of autochthony is evident throughout the world and across the Left–Right political spectrum, including in diverse sites in Europe, Southern Africa, Central Africa; Asia, Latin America; North America, and in the Pacific. It is expressed and experienced more or less intensely in these various places but in all of its manifestations, the conflict is one between "native" and "non-native." Hence, while ostensibly about stasis, autochthonous discourses are mobilized through constant reference to migration. As such it is crucial for migration scholars to understand it especially since autochthonous discourses have informed anti-immigrant politics throughout Europe, the expulsion of "non-natives" (e.g., in Uganda in the 1970s), military *coups d'etat* in Fiji in the 1980s, genocidal practices in Rwanda, violent attacks on "migrants" in South Africa, and in an increasingly popular rhetoric that asserts that there is no distinction between processes of migration and processes of colonization in the USA, New Zealand, Australia, and Canada (which is the focus of this chapter).

Along with a popular rhetoric associating "native-ness" with ancestral "rootedness" in particular lands, the position that all "migrants" are "settler colonists" has been advanced in a number of recent scholarly works in Canada and the USA. In a special issue of the journal *Amerasia* entitled "Whose Vision? Asian Settler Colonialism in Hawaii" edited by Fujikane and Okamura (2000) (also see Fujikane and Okamura 2008), the essayists claim that "Asians" in Hawai'i (by which they primarily mean the descendants of indentured plantation workers who began arriving from various sites across Asia in the mid-1800s) are "settler colonists." This, it is argued, makes them *active* in the colonization of "native Hawaiians." In particular, the contributors focus on the anti-racism politics of "Asians" in Hawai'i which demand an end of White, American hegemony. This, they assert, not only serves to "mask Native struggles against Asian settler colonialism" but to further the process by which indigenous Hawaiians remain colonized. This is because anti-racist demands are said to invariably fall into the "civil rights" framework that the essays contend serves to legitimize the power of the USA (Fujikane 2000: xvii). Thus, any engagement with the USA by "Asians" is seen as support for it. However, such an engagement does not carry the same consequences of complicity for "indigenous" people, however, since their engagements are represented as an essential part of "nation-to-nation" negotiation.

In a 2005 journal article in *Social Justice*, Bonita Lawrence and Enakshi Dua make some of the same arguments. They contend that in Canada:

> [p]eople of color are settlers. Broad differences exist between those brought as slaves, currently working as migrant laborers, are refugees without legal documentation, or émigrés who have obtained citizenship. Yet people of color live on land that is appropriated and contested, where Aboriginal peoples are denied nationhood and access to their own lands.
> (Lawrence and Dua 2005: 134).

They analyze the politics of anti-racism to make a clear distinction between "natives" and "people of color." They claim that anti-racist praxis has historically excluded "aboriginal" (or indigenous) peoples' perspectives. The result, they claim, is twofold: aboriginal people "cannot see themselves in antiracism contexts and Aboriginal activism against settler domination takes place without people of color as allies." For this reason, they assert anti-racist praxis has actually "contribute[d] to the active *colonization* of Aboriginal peoples" (Lawrence and Dua 2005: 122–3, emphasis added). Indeed, they contend that "antiracism is *premised* on an ongoing colonial project" (2005: 123, emphasis added).

Their examples of the ways in which anti-racist praxis is a colonial practice include postcolonial critiques of national liberation and social constructivist critiques troubling the "naturalness" of "communities" and "nations" (such as Stuart Hall's (1993) critique of "ethnic absolutism". See Valaskakis (2005) for an aboriginal scholar using Hall to theorize indigenous identities). Lawrence and Dua maintain that such analyses further the *colonization* of indigenous people by "contribut[ing] to the ongoing delegitimization of Indigenous nationhood" (2005: 128). *Critiques* of nationalisms, thus, are portrayed as *attacks* against indigenous people and their contemporary efforts for sovereignty. Politically, they argue, "people of color" ought to refrain from such critiques and, instead, recognize that they are "settlers" and, as such, a "*part of* the ongoing project of colonization" (Lawrence and Dua 2005: 122, emphasis added).

Similarly, Cynthia Franklin and Laura Lyons (2004: 17) argue that social historical accounts of the connections amongst people within the space of the "Revolutionary Atlantic," as Peter Linebaugh and Marcus Rediker (2000) put it, are also part of a broad, *anti-indigenous* stance. Arguments reliant on theories of diaspora and hybridity, Franklin and Lyons argue, work to minimize the significance of nationalism to the success of "native" sovereignty movements and in doing so are, in and of themselves, *colonizing* gestures (Franklin and Lyons 2004: 51).

It is important to note that, autochthonous discourses, such as those found in these three texts, argue for the theoretical centrality of "nativeness" as part of the political discourse and practice of "native" nationalisms. This helps to explain not only why all "non-natives" are conceptualized as colonizers, but also why the (varied) critics of nationalisms or those who reject ideas of race or ethnic purity or those whose scholarship uncover acts of solidarity *across* or even *against* such lines are conceptualized as colonizers as well.

In the special issue of *Amerasia*, "native" Hawaiian struggles are exclusively framed as a *nationalist* struggle in the tradition of Third World national liberation movements. Haunani Kay Trask conceives them to be " … but the latest stage in the revolutionary era that advanced the freedom of African, Latin American, and Asian peoples" (Trask as quoted by Leong 2000: vi). Likewise, Lawrence and Dua state that indigenous people in Canada must "regenerate nationhood" to realize decolonization for "[a]t the heart of Indigenous peoples' realities … is nationhood" (2005: 124).

As in other nationalist movements with their always-limited sense of belonging to the "nation," autochthonous arguments for national liberation require a unified, homogeneous nation set against its Others. In the *Amerasia* issue as well as in Franklin and Lyon's essay, the nation's Others are constituted primarily as "Asian settler colonists," including non-Hawaiian Pacific Islanders (see Kosasa cited by Fujikane 2000: xvi–xvii). In Lawrence and Dua's essay, they consist primarily of all "migrants" but especially "people of color" fighting racism.

Not only do these texts promote a nationalist politics, they also advance a *statist* one. Both Trask (2000: 13–14) and Lawrence and Dua (2005: 124) cite Article 1 of the United Nations Charter as a central basis for the difference between indigenous and anti-racist struggles and hence between "natives" and "non-natives." By conferring legitimacy to the UN Charter and its recognition of the right of self-determination for "peoples" alone, non-whites who are also

229

constituted as "non-natives" are not only evacuated from the project of decolonization, their agency is made secondary to that of native-nationals. Racialized minorities, in the nationalist logics of the UN model of "self-determinacy" are relegated to being "mere" subjects of various "nations" and their existing or hoped-for national sovereign states.

Significantly, because they are not "people" as defined by the global system of power, non-white people in Hawai'i, or elsewhere in the USA and Canada, are cast as *not-colonized* and, therefore, as incapable of acting as *agents* of anti-colonial (or other liberatory) projects. As a result, not only are bodies and lands racialized, but the nationalization and racialization/ethnicization of the *politics* of decolonization is secured as well. Only "natives" are the "nation's" subjects and only the nation's subjects are legitimate agents in its self-determination. All those constituted as "migrants" are framed as colonizers or, once the "sovereignty" of any "native nation" is granted, as *its* racial/ethnic minorities. Not only is their racialization left unquestioned, so is the broader field of racism that both "natives," "people of color" and, of course, "whites" operate in.

By legitimizing the national state project, what is also legitimized is the "right" of "nations" to exclusively determine their membership, a right granted to national state officials through the same United Nations Charter cited as a basis of legitimacy for "native" nationalisms. This right of "national sovereignty" allows for both the state's regulation of people's movement in and across nationally defined territories as well as the differential allocation of hierarchically organized statuses within the nationalized polity.

Such a nationalist and statist logic is celebrated. Trask (2000: 13), in her *Amerasia* article, "Settlers of color and 'immigrant' hegemony: 'Locals' in Hawaii," advances an explicitly statist, even neoliberal, vision of a decolonized Hawaiian "nation." She states:

> Once Hawaiians reclaim these lands, public and private relationships between Natives and non-Natives will be altered. For example, settlers will have to pay taxes or user fees to swim at Native-owned beaches, enjoy recreation at Native-owned parks, drive on Native-owned roads, fly out of Native-owned airports, educate their children at public schools on Native-owned lands, and on, and on. Above all, non-Natives will have to live alongside a Native political system that has statutory authority to exclude, tax, or otherwise regulate the presence of non-Natives on Native lands. The potential shift here frightens non-Natives because it signals the political and economic ascendance of Natives. At the least, Native power means no more free access by non-Natives to Native resources.

Such statements do a kind of *political* work. By accepting the logics of the national state system with its powers to exclude (or, better, to "differently include"), this time based on the hard distinction between "native" and "non-native," as well as the nationalist logics of terri-torialization, those working against colonialism *outside* of an autochthonous and/or nationalist framework are silenced by being labeled as colonizers. Indeed, as discussed above, within autochthonous discourses, any challenge to nationalist politics aimed at securing sovereignty is portrayed as support for colonization. In short, critics of nationalism are condemned in order to *depoliticize* a particular, nationalist response to colonization. In this sense, "native" nationalisms and the autochthonous discourses they advance can be seen as a form of *border politics*. As with all border politics, the intent is to construct a negative duality between national subjects said to rule and foreign objects to be ruled over. Both rely on the denunciation of both migrants portrayed as transgressors of "national" space and developments in historical and cultural studies that de-naturalize the existence of "nations."

Neo-racism and the conflation between migration and colonialism

Autochthonous discourses positing "all migrants are colonizers" necessarily renders as a serious problem the entire process of human migration while denying that "natives" have also moved and continue to do so. Within such a perspective, the only way to *not* be a "colonizer" is to not move, something that many people have been unable or unwilling to do in the past and that a growing number of people find impossible or undesirable to do today (see Hansen and Stepputat (2005) for critiques of the idea that there is a "land" to which one "naturally" belongs). The failure to recognize that migration is an oft-used strategy to escape subjugation, destitution, and death and to gain life—by people *across* the identifications of "native" and "non-Native"—is also a failure to recognize the significance of *territorializing* one's access to the stuff of life.

In this regard, it is worthwhile noting the historical relationship between border controls regulating people's mobility and the early period of expropriation in Europe. The original Poor Laws in England were designed to both control the mobility of peasants fleeing their now-expropriated commons as well as to coerce those criminalized as "vagabonds" into working (Papadopoulos *et al.* 2008). Indeed, capturing and containing a potential workforce by compelling them to *not move*, was a key element in making nascent capitalist ventures within England possible. Criminalizing people's mobility and denying needed resources/services to those deemed to be "illegally" migrating, was an important part of how the modern proletariat was formed.

Mobility, then, was defined as a major problem by and for those who needed a sedentary workforce. Thus, as Papadopoulos *et al.* (2008: 55) note, "It is no coincidence that the word mobility refers not only to movement but also to the common people, the working classes, the mob". It was this mob and their attempts to flee expropriation and exploitation that posed one of the greatest threats to the success of capitalism.

Restrictions on mobility also worked to *territorialize* people's relationship to space and to land. One's wage rates, access to employment, to rights, etc. were all bound to one's recognized legal residence in particular spaces. Thus, through attempts at rendering people immobile, "[b]odies become territorialized; people become subjects of a specific territory, of a sovereign power" (Papadopoulos *et al.* 2008: 48). Coerced *immobility* acted to discipline the unruliness of the expropriated in order to make them productive workers whose labor power could be exploited. It is in part for this reason that early passports were designed to control people's *exits*, not their arrivals into, the territories controlled by various ruling groups (Torpey 2002).

Essential to the process of imposing capitalist social relations, however, is, as ever, the process of expropriation and displacement. As capitalism expanded in Europe and in the European trade networks that were increasingly becoming capitalized, securing a needed workforce came to increasingly depend upon moving people to potential sites of production. Migration, therefore, came to be seen as a means by which to both dispel the rebelling mob and to ensure the possibility of successful capitalist ventures. The processes of containment, immobilization, and territorialization on the one hand and displacement and dispersal, came to be inextricable from one another through the territorialization of rights and belonging.

These processes are intensifying today, as we can see with the growing securitization of states' policies on cross-border movement. Indeed, it seems that as capitalist social relations have expanded, the presence of "foreigners" has taken on even greater urgency and generated increasingly heated controversies. However, this is now as much of a strategy for those who see themselves as resisting capitalist colonization as it is for those promoting it.

For nationalists, since it is capitalist colonialization (or imperialism) that gave rise to ideas of "nationhood," *anti-colonialism* is the avenue through which the "native nation" can be born. As with all nationalist strategies, "native" nationalisms depend on the existence of a "foreign"

Other *in* the "nation" to give meaning to the limited character of its membership. The obvious "foreigner" in the historic White settler colonies is that group identified as "European" or "white" and this, primarily, was the case in earlier periods of "native" nationalisms. However, today, "native" nationalisms have seen it necessary to respond to the co-existence of non-white "migrants" as well. The contemporary development of a "native" nationalism, therefore, has re-cast these migrants as not *also-colonized* but as *also-colonizers*. Autochthonous discourses privileging (or "centering") the "native" provide meaning to the claim that all "non-natives" are the quintessential threat to the realization of "national sovereignty." Such a re-presentation, in part, is what continues to breathe life into the "native" nation.

Far from being a contradiction or a mere reaction, such moves toward autochthony are deeply embedded within the processes of capitalist globalization, particularly in its current neo-liberal phase. Problematizing the presence of those who don't "belong," along with calls for people to stay fixed in "their" space, have gained legitimacy precisely as capital, commodities, ideas, and people have become increasingly mobile and as there have been reductions in the material benefits of citizenship resulting from neoliberal policies of liberalization, privatization, and de-regulation (see Balibar 1991b; Mamdani 1998; Mallon 2006: 285).

The ideological terrain of neo-liberalism is very much racialized. It is a racism that can best be characterized as one where "differences" between *cultures* and *traditions* are seen as insurmountable. This differs from previous hegemonies of racist ideologies for it does not rely on a biological concept of "race" or even a racialized vertical hierarchy *per se*. Instead, this form of racism mobilizes a horizontal difference that contends that "different" people should be in "their own" places (which, not coincidentally, often coincide with the boundaries of the existing or aspired-for nation states). This form of racism has been called a "differentialist racism" (Taguieff 1990) or, simply, "neo-racism" (Balibar 1991a). While Robert Miles (1993) points out that these racisms may not be so new, it is certainly true that today's racist practices are "largely based on the argument that it is futile, even dangerous, to allow *cultures* to *mix* or insist that they do so" (Hardt and Negri 2000: 192). This stems from its basic assumption that *ethnic* boundaries are "natural borders" (see Mamdani 1998).

The centering of "culture" or "ethnicity" within neo-racist discourses ensures the continuation of the devotion to genealogy (and, therefore, to anti-miscegenation) held by the "old" racisms. Such a devotion has its material moorings: origin stories within the neo-racist imagination lay the basis for making *historical* claims to contested lands by ethnicizing group rights which are said to be held solely by those "native" to the place (Mamdani 1998; Hall 2005). Such notions work to make "native" identity a "possessive identity," since it is this identity that is often the only avenue within existing systems to make group claims to resources (Lipsitz 1998). In this regard, it is mainly a possessive identity of the poor and dispossessed since the rich have other, more market- and law-based means by which to gain land. Processes of neo-liberalism have exacerbated this process as access to needed resources has become even more diminished by the further entrenchment of market relations.

The ideology of neo-liberalism directs antagonism away from the poor against the rich and, in its stead, divides the poor (and sometimes the rich) into antagonistic groups (Mamdani 2001: 202). With such a "naturalization of xenophobia," as Comaroff and Comaroff put it (2000: 140), it is, therefore, entirely unsurprising that the demonization of contemporary as well as past migrations constitutes a central characteristic of the autochthonous character of neo-racist thought. As Étienne Balibar (1991b: 52) points out, within this neo-racist sensibility, "migrants" come to stand in for the subordinated "race."

That such a flexible Othering is related to the neo-liberalization of state practices is evident in the *ideological* character of the criteria of belonging—and not-belonging. That is, the neo-racist fetishization of autochthony should by no means be confused with either the disavowal of racialized hierarchies or the *actual* spatial separation of "different people." Border-talk, and the state policies and ideas of "community" mobilized through it, while responsible for the increased precariousness of many people's global migrations, is largely aimed at creating categorical juridical distinctions *between* "different" people *within* the same social space (Sharma 2000; 2006).

Thus, whilst the distinction between "native" and "non-native" *appears* to be spatially organized (i.e. demands for fixed ethnicized boundaries that coincide with spatial territory through greater border control), autochthonous discourses are primarily concerned with sorting out distinctions *within* shared spaces. This ensures the neo-racialization of the polity, of politics writ large and of social movements. In an act of high irony, such neo-racializations are often formulated as a kind of *anti*-racist response that "centralizes indigeneity" (as Lawrence and Dua 2005, call for) by demanding "a place" for "each people." It is in this way that the historical articulation of racism and nationalism is mobilized through autochthonous discourses (Balibar 1991b: 50). Neo-racist arguments of this kind, therefore, ought to be seen as linked to both new or old nation-building projects as well as to neo-liberal practices since both are reliant on forms of "differential inclusion" (Deleuze and Guattari 1987).

It is for this reason that within discourses of autochthony, it is paramount that the concerns of "natives" and "non-natives" *not* be seen to be *commensurate*. For instance Franklin and Lyons (2004: 10) argue that attempts to recognize the correspondence between people's dispossession across the world works to threaten the claims of specifically "native" dispossession. In a sense, this is true, for recognizing the deep *connections* between various experiences of colonization does indeed challenge any nationalist narrative of singularity. However, this is a problem for nationalist politics, *not* for the project of decolonization. Decolonization is not dependent upon nationalism. Indeed, nationalist efforts have not been able to achieve anything that resembles the end of colonialism (Scott 2004; Prashad 2007).

Against nationalism

While those constituted as "migrants" or "foreigners" provide nationalists with an Other whose presence can be used as a spur for nationalist activity, their presence has also posed the greatest *challenge* to nationalist narratives. Nora Rathzel (1994: 91) notes that migrants are threatening precisely because they: "make our taken-for-granted identities visible as specific identities and deprive them of their assumed naturalness." In this, the mobility of those racialized/ethnicized as being "different" from the national subject " ... becomes a basic form of disorder and chaos—constantly defined as transgression and trespass" (Cresswell 1996: 87). A comment by a Cambodian woman refugee in Paris captures this well: "we are a disturbance ... Because we show you in a terrible way how fragile the world we live in is" (in Morely 2000: 152).

People who cross national borders thus reveal the *global* character of ruling social relations—and the systems of governance and identification that sustains it. Modern migrations and the displacements wrought by the relations organized through global capitalism and the equally globalized system of nation-states are integrally related experiences. Just as people's migrations from one space to another has been part of their experience of colonialism (think of the forced movement of enslaved people from Africa or the Trail of Tears in the US), people's migrations also arise from their attempts to *escape* from colonialism. Migration is an oft-used survival strategy utilized by people across all divides of "race," "ethnicity," and "nation." Over the last several hundred years, it is a strategy that both those constituted as "natives" and as "non-natives" have, and continue to, engage in.

Refusing to recognize this and to incorporate those constituted as "migrants"/"foreigners" into movements for decolonization is therefore an historical failure. It is a failure of historical understanding of how the growing number of expropriated and exploited people across the globe were brought together within, through, and sometimes against, capitalist colonizing projects (see Wynter 1995). Refusing to acknowledge how migrations and migrants are often borne of colonial experiences is to replace their lived realities with an ideological narrative and consciousness of *nationalism* that privileges *disconnections*, both of the past and today. Conversely, recognizing our interconnections may help us develop a politics capable of realizing a project of decolonization worthy of its name.

Projects of decolonization, therefore, need, I think, to challenge capitalist social relations *as well as those* organized through the nation state, such as sovereignty, and, crucially, have as their goal the gaining of a global *commons*. The commons is an organization of human activity that " ... vests all property in the community and organizes labor for the common benefit of all" (Linebaugh 2007: 6). Thus, the commons is much more than a resource: it is a *practice*, a practice of commoning (Linebaugh 2007: 6). Key to the realization of a commons is the nurturing of relationships of mutuality with fellow commoners. As Peter Linebaugh (2007: 45) puts it, "Commoners think first not of title deeds, but of human deeds." He further notes four key principles historically evident in the practice of commoning and in the rights held by commoners, rights that differ substantially from the modern, territorialized nation state regime of land rights and "human rights."

First, common rights are "embedded in a particular ecology" reliant on local knowledge. In this sense common rights are neither abstract nor essentialist but based in practice. Second, "commoning is embedded in a labor process" and is "entered into by labor." Third, "commoning is collective." Fourth, commoning is "independent of the state" and the law. Within common rights there are no sovereigns. In sum, commoning is the realization of not only political rights but also social and economic rights of the *commoners*, a practice that resolves the capitalist separation of falsely divided spheres. Common rights have historically included the principles of: neighborhood; subsistence; travel; anti-enclosure; and reparations (Linebaugh 2007: 45). These remain not only valuable principles for which to struggle today but viable, everyday practices engaged in by people escaping ruling relations.

Contrary to a nationalist common-sense, ending the ongoing, global practice of expropriation is not possible when we deny or even try to sever our links with one another through a neo-racist politics of autochthony with its notion of "historical continuity of title." Indeed, if we understand *colonialism* to be the theft of the commons, the agents of decolonization to be the *commoners* and decolonization as the gaining of a *global commons*, we are likely to have a much clearer sense of *when* we were colonized, *who* colonized us and *how* to decolonize ourselves and our relationships.

Understanding colonialism as taking place each time the commons is expropriated and the commoners turned into an exploitable labor force would expand our understanding of colonialism and who has been colonized. However, instead of pitting one racialized, ethnicized, and nationalized group of expropriated commoners against another in the struggle for decolonization, it would re-invigorate the contemporary struggle against *all* "possessioners" (some of whom are *part* of the group defined as "Native") the world over.

The implications for migration scholars of such a reconceptualization of colonialism and the associated reconceptualization of space, belonging, and forms of national governance are significant. First, by bringing the "indigenous" and "migrants" into the same analytical field of study, we can see the work done by colonial categorical divides in the legitimization of globalizing capitalist social relations and the related territorialization of social imaginaries. Such reconceptualizations also expand the conceptual tools available to understand many existing social divides and the kinds of social claims that people make to space, belonging, rights, and to the means of production (land, control over labor, etc.). By insisting on the importance of studying nationalist discourses and practices, the insights wrought by the excellent work done on racism can be extended to include the *spatial* dimensions of power. In particular, since nationalist practices are concerned both with issues of the "right" spatial allocation of people and with the social space accorded to various differentiated people *within* national states, analyzing nationalist practices allows us to deconstruct the false divide between the nationalisms of the powerful and those of the oppressed. Instead, we can see that both rely upon neo-racist practices of spatial management. Such forms of management are central to the practice of border controls today.

References and further reading

Anderson, B., Sharma, N., and Wright, C. (2009) "Editorial: Why no borders?" *Refuge* (Special Issue on "No borders as a practical political project"), 26(2): 5–18.

Balibar, É. (1991a) "Is there a neo-racism?" In É. Balibar and I. Wallerstein (eds), *Race, Nation, Class: Ambiguous Identities*. London: Verso, pp. 17–28.

——(1991b) "Racism and nationalism." In É. Balibar and I. Wallerstein (eds), *Race, Nation, Class: Ambiguous Identities*. London: Verso, pp. 37–67.

Comaroff, J. and Comaroff, J. L. (2005) "Naturing the nation: Aliens, apocalypse, and the postcolonial state." In *Sovereign Bodies: Citizens, Migrants, and States in the Postcolonial World*. T. B. Hansen and F. Stepputat (eds), Princeton, NJ: Princeton University Press, pp. 120–47.

Cresswell, T. (1996) *In Place/Out of Place*, Minneapolis, MN: University of Minnesota Press.

Deleuze, G. and Guattari, F. (1987) *A Thousand Plateaus: Capitalism and Schizophrenia*. B. Massumi (translation), Minneapolis, MN: University of Minnesota Press.

Franklin, C. and Lyons, L. (2004) "Remixing hybridity: Globalization, native resistance, and cultural production in Hawai'i" *American Studies* 45(3): 49–80.

Fujikane, C. (2000) "Introduction: Asian settler colonialism in Hawai'i" *Amerasia* 26(2): xv–xxii.

——(2005) "Foregrounding native nationalisms: A critique of antinationalist sentiment in Asian American studies." In Kent A. Ona (ed.), *Asian American Studies After Critical Mass*. Oxford: Blackwell Publishing, 73–97.

Fujikane, C. and Okamura, J. Y. (eds) (2000) "Whose vision? Asian settler colonialism in Hawai'i." Special Issue of *Amerasia*, 26(2).

Fujikane, C. and Okamura, J. Y. (eds) (2008) *Asian Settler Colonialism: From Local Governance to the Habits of Everyday Life in Hawaii*. Honolulu, HI: University of Hawai'i Press.

Hall, A. J. (2005) *The American Empire and the Fourth World: The Bowl With One Spoon*. Montreal/Kingston: McGill-Queen's Press.

Hall, S. (1993) "What is this 'black' in black popular culture?" *Social Justice* 20(1/2): 104–14.

Hansen, T. B. and Stepputat, F. (2005) "Introduction." In T. Blom Hansen and F. Stepputat, (eds), *Sovereign Bodies: Citizens, Migrants, and States in the Postcolonial World*. Princeton, NJ: Princeton University Press, pp. 1–38.

Hardt, Michael and Negri, A. (2000) *Empire*. Cambridge, MA: Harvard University Press.

Kauanui, K. J. (2008) "Colonial in equality: Hawaiian sovereignty and the question of US civil rights" *The South Atlantic Quarterly* 107(4): 635–50.

Lawrence, B. and Dua, E. (2005) "Decolonizing antiracism" *Social Justice* 32(4): 120–43.

Leong, R. (2000) "Whose vision? Asian settler colonialism in Hawai'i" *Amerasia Journal* 26(2): xii–xiv.

Linebaugh, P. (2007) *The Magna Carta Manifesto: Liberties and Commons For All*. Berkeley, CA: University of California Press.

Linebaugh, P. and Rediker, M. (2000) *The Many-Headed Hydra: Sailors, Slaves, Commoners, and the Hidden History of the Revolutionary Atlantic*. Boston, MA: Beacon Press.

Lipsitz, G. (1998) *The Possessive Investment in Whiteness: How White People Profit from Identity Politics*. Boulder, CO: Westview Press.

Mallon, F. E., 2005 "Pathways to postcolonial nationhood: The democratization of difference in contemporary Latin America." In A. Loomba, S. Kaul, M. Bunzl, A. Burton, and J. Esty, (eds) *Postcolonial Studies and Beyond*. Durham, NC: Duke University Press, pp. 272–92.

Mamdani, M. (1998) "Understanding the crisis in Kivu." *Report of the Council for the Development of Social Research in Africa (CODESRIA) Mission to the Democratic Republic of Congo*, September. www.codesria.org/spip.php?rubrique4&lang=en (accessed May 1 2007).

Miles, R., (1993) *Racism after 'Race Relations'*. London: Routledge.

Morley, D. (2000) *Home Territories: Media, Mobility and Identity*. London: Routledge.

Niezen, R. (2003) *The Origins of Indigenism: Human Rights and the Politics of Identity*. Berkeley, CA: University of California Press.

Papadopoulos, D., Stephenson, N., and Tsianos, V. (2008) *Escape Routes: Control and Subversion in the 21st Century*. London: Pluto Press.

Prashad, V. (2007) *The Darker Nations: A People's History of the Third World*. New York: The New Press.

Raibmon, P. (2005) *Authentic Indians: Episodes of Encounter from the Late-Nineteenth-Century Northwest Coast*. Durham, NC: Duke University Press.

Rathzel, N. (1994) "Harmonious Heimat and disturbing Auslander." In K. K. Bhavani and A. Phoenix (eds), *Shifting Identities and Shifting Racisms*. London: Sage, pp. 81–98.

Scott, D. (2004) *Conscripts of Modernity: The Tragedy of Colonial Enlightenment*. Durham, NC: Duke University Press.

Sharma, N. (2000) "Race, class and gender and the making of difference: The social organization of migrant workers in Canada" *Atlantis: A Women's Studies Journal* 24(2): 5–15.

Sharma, N. and Wright, C. (2009) "Decolonizing resistance, challenging colonial states" *Social Justice* 35(3): 120–38.

Taguieff, P.-A. (1990) "The new cultural racism in France" *Telos* 83: 111-14, 116–22; trans. Russell Moore.

Torpey, J. (2002) *The Invention of the Passport: Surveillance, Citizenship, and the State*. Cambridge: Cambridge University Press.

Trask, H. K. (2000) "Settlers of color and 'immigrant' hegemony: 'Locals' in Hawai'i." In "Whose Vision? Asian Settler Colonialism in Hawai'i. Special issue of *Amerasia Journal* 26(2): 1–26.

Valaskakis, G. G. (2005) *Indian Country: Essays on Contemporary Native Culture*. Waterloo: Wilfred Laurier Press.

Wolfe, P. (2008) Back Cover Comment. In C. Fujikane and J. Y. Okamura (eds), *Asian Settler Colonialism: From Local Governance To the Habits of Everyday Life in Hawai'i*, Honolulu, HI: University of Hawai'i Press.

Wynter, S. (1995) "1492: A new world view." In V. L. Hyatt and R. Nettleford (eds), *Race, Discourse and the Origin of the Americas: A New World View*. Washington, DC: Smithsonian Institution Press, pp. 5–57.

Part V
Creating and recreating community and group identity

A combination of culture, host environment, and communal factors lead to the transformation of group identity among immigrant populations. Immigrants create lives, communities, and identities in the host society, often in a context of disadvantage and unfamiliarity with the local environment. Migrants seek to build viable communities and provide members with resources that they require for adapting to and functioning—politically, economically, and culturally—within the host society. Such activities are often oriented toward managing and transmitting knowledge about the group to its own members—especially youth, to the host society, and to the country of origin.

Yen Espiritu describes instances where multiple migrant nationalities consciously create shared identities that facilitate the achievement of political and other goals in the host society. Such panethnic movements and organizations bring groups with seemingly distinct histories and separate identities together in cooperation around shared political and economic agendas, including protecting and advancing their collective interests. Drawing on evidence from the USA and other countries, this chapter examines the ways by which individuals experience, understand, and respond to the panethnic label.

Min Zhou develops a perspective on immigrant/ethnic communities that integrates various groups' particular characteristics, collective cultural values and practices, and broader structural factors to explain variation in immigrant groups' mobility. She draws on existing research to build a conceptual framework and illustrates it by contrasting two kinds of ethnic communities: old Chinatowns and newer suburban enclaves.

In her chapter on immigrant religion, Jacqueline Hagan shows how an awareness of transnationalism has focused scholars' interest in the actions of "migrants in motion across territories," on a global level, thus supplanting previous concerns with religion and migrant adaptation in European and North American nation states. She reveals how religion plays a vital role in shaping migrants' decision-making while providing spiritual support and guidance to satisfy the needs of migrants as well as their loved ones remaining in communities of origin. Established organizations advocate for migrant rights and contest abuses meted out by nation-states during a historical period marked by increasing hostility to those crossing international borders.

Religious organizations—including those formed by migrants themselves—help migrants to express claims of membership in the host society and in so doing foster cultural and religious diversity. Shifting away from a longstanding concern with denominations and congregations to a focus on "lived" or "everyday" religion, these innovations provide fresh insights into the ways through which migrants express their faith, navigate religious and secular organizations, and remain connected to family, community, and homeland.

20
Panethnicity

Yen Le Espiritu

Panethnicity refers to the development of bridging organizations and the generalization of solidarity among ethnic subgroups that are perceived to be homogeneous by outsiders (Lopez and Espiritu 1990: 198). Contemporary research on panethnicity indicates that panethnic identities are self-conscious products of political choice and actions, not of inherited phenotypes, blood-lines, or cultural traditions. Panethnic movements and organizations bring groups with seemingly distinct histories and separate identities together in cooperation around shared political and economic goals—to protect and advance their collective interests. While institutional paneth-nicity has been extensively studied, far less attention has been paid to the ways in which indi-viduals experience, understand, and respond to the panethnic label. The available evidence indicates that panethnic identity is generally a secondary identity that coexists, at times uncomfortably, with ethnonational identities. The chapter focuses primarily on panethnic groups in the United States, but ends with comparative examples of how panethnicity operates in other countries and globally.

Panethnic organizing and racialization

Panethnic organizing in the United States was prompted by the social struggles that swept across the country in the 1960s. In particular, civil rights and the subsequent minority movements had a profound impact on the racial ideology of minority groups, sensitizing them to racial issues. Moreover, as a result of the 1960s movements, antidiscrimination legislation moved away from emphasizing the equality of individual opportunities to focusing on the equitable distribution of group rights. This move led to the implementation of government-mandated affirmative action programs designed to ensure minority representation in employment, in public programs, and in education. Since numbers count in the American political structure, many racialized groups have determined that their efforts to promote social change are more effective when they organize panethnically (Cornell 1988; Espiritu1992; Saito 1998).

Racial lumping drives the formation of panethnic organizations and social practices. Unwilling or unable to listen to myriad voices representing particular subethnic groups, government bureau-cracies (and the larger society) often lump diverse racial and ethnic minority groups into the four umbrella categories—blacks, Asian Americans, Hispanics/Latinos, and Native Americans—

and treat them as single units in the allocation of economic and political resources (Lowry 1982, 42–3). In response to these state-offered incentives, members of the subgroups within each category begin to act collectively as panethnic groups to protect and to advance their interests. In other words, panethnic mobilization is "partly a construction of the state" (Jones-Correa 1998, 111). The pervasive system of racial and ethnic classification in the United States creates incentives for ethnic groups to develop panethnic political and cultural projects:

> The data-gathering methods of the census and its use by government agencies in allocating resources, the mobilization techniques of political parties and lobbies, the organization of charities and nonprofit groups, the marketing techniques of the media—all these categorize and appeal to people as members of large ethno-racial groups, thereby fostering a sense of panethnic identity.
>
> (Itzigsohn 2004: 197)

Since the 1970s, panethnic organizations such as the National Council of La Raza, Asian Pacific American Labor Alliance and the National Urban Indian Development Corporation have played an important role in securing rights and services for their respective communities such as fair wages, safe working conditions, affordable housing and economic opportunities (Okamoto 2006: 1). The case of Native Americans is unique because federal Indian policies pursue a two-pronged strategy. On the one hand, they recognize tribes as geopolitical units and the foci of various government programs and legislation, thus making tribal affiliation essential. On the other hand, the government insists that Indian-ness is the relevant ethnic distinction for political policy purposes, thus making pan-Indian organization necessary (Nagel 1982). In other words, the various levels of American Indian mobilization "are responses to a particular incentive structure largely determined by US Indian policies" (Nagel 1982: 39).

When manifested in racial discrimination and violence, racial lumping necessarily leads to cross-group solidarity (Espiritu 1992). In the case of black Americans, the "one-drop rule," which was developed and violently enforced to protect slavery and to bolster Jim Crow segregation, allocates any person with any known African black ancestry to the stigmatized "black" category. By 1925, the one-drop rule was firmly established, adopted, and affirmed by not only white but also black America. The black pride movement of the 1960s and the harsh and uncompromising black-white model in American society greatly strengthened black unity, rousing black Americans to downplay color and class differences and to affirm blackness (Davis 1989). As Dawson (1994) reports, a linked fate—a shared race and a shared history of racial discrimination—explains why African Americans, regardless of class divisions, have remained largely a politically cohesive group. Like African Americans, many Native Americans are racially mixed. The degree of racial mixture figures in government definitions of who is Indian, and is certainly a recognized dimension of individual variation within Indian nations. But whites rarely make distinctions between different Indian groups, especially in urban areas, and when distinctions are made, they are on the basis of tribe, not race (Cornell 1998: 132–8).

For Asian Americans, anti-Asian violence often takes the form of "mistaken identity" hate crimes. The most notorious case of mistaken identity was the 1982 killing of Vincent Chin, a Chinese American who was beaten to death by two white men who allegedly mistook him for Japanese. Because the public seldom distinguishes among Asian American subgroups, anti-Asian violence concerns the entire group, crosscutting class, cultural, and generational divisions. Therefore, regardless of one's ethnic affiliation, anti-Asian violence requires counter-organization at the pan-Asian level (Espiritu 1992, ch. 6). The belief that all Asian Americans are potential victims propels Asian Americans to join together in self-defense to monitor, report, and protest anti-Asian violence. As an example, in the 1990s, when large numbers of Southeast Asian immigrants in Detroit began experiencing problems with racist violence, educational inequality, and poor housing, a small group of East and South Asian American activists created a successful youth leadership-training program organized around a pan-Asian identity and radical critiques of institutionalized racism. The group's success enabled it to move from panethnic to inter-ethnic affiliation through an alliance with a Puerto Rican youth group also plagued by hate crimes, police brutality, and prosecutorial racism (Espiritu *et al.* 2000: 132).

Racial violence has also forged theretofore-unlikely alliances. Since September 11, 2001, in response to the conflation of Middle Eastern and South Asian-descended peoples, these two groups have begun to form political coalitions to combat hate crimes against their communities. Spickard (2007: 602–3) describes the racial lumping that provided the impetus for the coalition: "It is tragic, but not accidental, that several of the people murdered or attacked in hate crimes just after September 11 were not Muslims, nor Arabs, nor Middle Eastern Americans at all, but rather Sikhs."

Racial variation is greatest among and across Latino subgroups in the United States. As a result, Latinos "face the challenge of imagining themselves as a composite race that encompasses an assortment of diverse national origins, various cultural heritages, and disparate phenotypes" (Torres-Saillant 2003). Many Puerto Rican migrants are "black" by mainland definition and have experienced direct racism approaching that suffered by non-Latino black Americans (Rodriquez 1980). In contrast, most Cubans and South Americans, reflecting their middle-class backgrounds, look European, and can blend into white America. Although Mexican Americans are racially diverse, most Americans consider them "brown" or "mestizo" (Lopez and Espiritu, 1990: 204). The class-color link tends to divide Latino subgroups, breeding intra-Latino racism and inequalities. Mexican American activists have advocated a version of Latino panethnicity that valorizes "brownness;" for "phenotypically distinctive Latinos," affirmation of brownness has become a way to assert an antiracist racial solidarity while at the same time maintaining distance from blacks (Foner and Fredrickson 2004: 7). Some scholars have linked Latino reluctance to embrace a distinct panethnic identity with the insufficient strides for full citizenship that Latinos have made in American society (Torres-Saillant 2003).

Panethnicity is thus largely a product of racial categorization, a process that is intimately bound up with power relations. The American racial classification system ignores subgroup boundaries, lumping together diverse peoples in a single, expanded panethnic framework. Excessive categorization is fundamental to racism because it permits "whites to order a universe of unfamiliar peoples without confronting their diversity and individuality" (Blauner 1972: 113). In other words, racialization is the driving force leading national origin groups to collectively organize as panethnic groups. Even when those in subordinate positions do not initially regard themselves as being alike, "a sense of identity gradually emerges from a recognition of their common fate" (Shibutani and Kwan 1965: 208). This is not to say that panethnicity is solely an imposed identity. Although it is originated largely in the minds of outsiders, the panethnic concept has become a political resource for insiders, a basis on which to mobilize diverse peoples and to force others to be more responsive to their grievances and agendas.

Panethnicity and internal diversities

Although racialization fuels panethnic mobilization, it does not automatically produce panethnic outcomes. That is, "even if the state imposes a racial structure on groups or if ethnic groups experience discrimination and racism, panethnicity does not always occur" (Okamoto 2006: 2). Asian Americans and Latinos, two groups that continue to be transformed by new immigration, face a special challenge: how to bridge the class, ethnic, and generational chasms dividing the immigrants and the US born? Such internal diversities, and a lack of shared histories in the United States, weaken the groups' abilities to speak with a unified political voice.

A key obstacle to panethnic formation is internal class differentiation. Reflecting their diverse origins and experiences of incorporation into the US class structure, Latino subgroups have the most diverse average class positions, which have limited their potential for panethnic organization, especially between the largely white and middle-class Cubans and poor people of black, Indian or mixed race from parts of Central America and the Caribbean (Lopez and Espiritu 1990). In the same way, contemporary Asian immigration to the United States is bifurcated along class lines: many recent Asian immigrants are uneducated, unskilled, and poor, while others are highly educated, skilled, and affluent. In 2000, Japanese, Chinese, and Asian Indians consistently held more wealth at the top end while non-Vietnamese Southeast Asians settled at the bottom end (Ong and Patraporn 2006).

However, Asian Americans, due to occupational segregation and spatial concentration, have been more successful relative to Latinos at forging panethnic alliances (Lopez and Espiritu 1990). Although great disparities exist within the Asian American grouping, overall, the major Asian American groups face relatively similar economic challenges. An analysis of 55 national Asian American organizations that were formed from 1970 to 1998 indicates that the occupational segregation of Asian Americans heightens panethnic consciousness, leading to the formation of pan-Asian institutions (Okamoto 2006). More than one-quarter of these pan-Asian organizations shared the common goals of promoting civil, economic, and political rights for Asians in the United States as well as in their countries of origin (Okamoto 2006, 20). Linda Vo's (2004) study of the Asian Business Association in San Diego provides an example: the city's Asian Americans joined the association because of shared professional interests and shared experiences of economic exclusion and employment discrimination. In another example, Leland Saito (1998) reports that Japanese and Chinese Americans in Monterey Park, California united to protest xenophobic attempts to remove Asian-language business signs. Overall, these studies suggest that as Asian Americans find themselves without economic opportunities and fair treatment, they establish supportive pan-Asian alliances from which to strategize about their collective class interest (Okamoto 2006).

Spatial concentration also facilitates the establishment of panethnic institutions (Okamoto 2006). Since interests, competition, and conflict in the United States tend to be strongly regionalized, it follows that cooperation is more likely when subethnic groups are concentrated in the same area. Asian Americans are far more concentrated geographically than the general US population. Data from the 1997–8 State and Metropolitan Area Data Book, published by the Census Bureau, show that almost 66 percent of all Asian Americans live in just five states: California, New York, Hawai'i, Texas, and Illinois. Remarkably, close to 55 percent of all Asian Americans live in just six metropolitan areas: Los Angeles, New York, San Francisco, Honolulu, Washington DC, and Chicago. These data indicate that although the Asian American population as a whole may seem relatively small on a national level, in many of the most dynamic states and metropolitan areas, Asian American numbers show that they constitute a vital part of that population (Le 2010). Their spatial concentration, rough numerical equity and relatively small numbers in these spaces have made it both possible and necessary for them to establish panethnic organizations to combat economic exclusion and discrimination. There is also suggestive evidence of pan-Asian bloc voting in Asian-dense districts. For example, Vietnamese Americans in Orange County, California consistently voted for Japanese American and Korean American candidates who ran against White candidates at a level comparable to that which they gave to Vietnamese American candidates (Collet 2005).

In contrast, the regional separation among the three major Latino groups—Mexican Americans in California and the Southwest, Puerto Ricans in New York and New Jersey, and Cubans in South Florida—has made it more difficult for them to organize panethnically. However, evidence from one major point of overlap, Chicago, suggests that Mexican and Puerto Rican residents were able to "transcend the boundaries of their individual ethnic groups and assert demands as a Latino population or group" in efforts to improve schools and job opportunities for their respective communities (Padilla 1985: 163). Padilla (1985) concluded that a common sense of economic deprivation and political exclusion and an objectively similar class position were the essential factors for this panethnic co-operation.

The possibility of a common identity depends on local contexts. Panethnic mobilization appears to work best when there is no majority group dominating the coalition. As an example, in a working-class neighborhood in Queens, New York City, where the different Latino groups were roughly equal in size, research indicates that repeated interactions between residents fostered a new overarching identity that enabled the establishment of institutional panethnicity. Living in small, often overcrowded spaces, these Spanish-speaking residents developed an "experiential panethnicity" (Ricourt and Danta 2003) as they interacted with each other in the daily-life settings of residence, neighborhood, and workplace. These day-to-day interactions eventually led to the institutionalization of panethnicity, in which community leaders created religious congregations, senior citizen centers, social service programs, cultural organizations, and political groups that served all Latinos in Queens (Ricourt and Danta, 2003: 10). In contrast, in San Francisco, the dominance of Mexicans—and Mexican culture—undermined the fragile Latino coalition and marred efforts by community leaders to promote cross-group cultural events. Given the growing diversification of the city's Latino population, the dominance of Mexican salsa as a public symbol of Latinismo at Latino cultural festivals has led to "accusations of cultural cooptation on the part of some Mexicans and of cultural exclusion and domination on the part of some Central Americans" (Sommers 1991: 42).

The media constitute one of the most important institutional sites for the forging of panethnic identities. Mainstream media outlets have a powerful interest in creating panethnic market segments to which they appeal and sell (Rodriquez 1999). At the same time, ethnic media—radio stations, TV programs, and newspapers and magazines—provide a vehicle for the expression of a shared cultural identity and the construction of panethnic projects and solidarity. As Itzigsohn (2004: 210) reports, the Latino and Latina media "go way beyond simply creating a market segment and play an important role in promoting community institution building." As an example, since its inception, *Latina* magazine, a bilingual women's magazine that was launched in 1996 for college-educated Latinas, has served as a site through which Latinidad has been constructed and reconfigured. Promoting an imagined panethnic Latino community, the magazine approaches standard topics such as celebrity portraits, love and romance, entertainment-oriented stories with a strong investment in validating the Latinidad of both the celebrities and magazine readers, celebrating the inclusion of Latinas in the US entertainment industry and challenging the stereotypes of Latino men and women (Martínez 2004).

Individual panethnicity

As with institutional panethnicity, individual panethnicity emerges as a reaction to the forces of racial labeling and exclusion in American society. Upon entering the United States, immigrants discover that they are expected to be part of a broader panethnic group whose existence many did not know prior to arrival. As part of a larger process of incorporation into American society, many immigrants and their children gradually adopt the more inclusive panethnic

Y. L. Espiritu

identities. As an example, Itzigsohn and Dore-Cabral (2000) report that as Dominican immigrants integrate themselves into American life, they react to being labeled Hispanic or Latino by adopting this panethnic identity and constructing social, cultural, and political projects based on it. However, since Latinos are a multiracial group, individual experiences with racism diverge according to how each person looks in relation to the norms of whiteness (Itzigsohn 2004: 203). Similarly, in a study on "pan-Asian ethnogenesis," Nazli Kibria (2002) finds that for second-generation Chinese and Korean Americans, the shared experience of being labeled *Asian* by others has driven them to adopt Asian American as a basis of affiliation and identity (Kibria 2002). For immigrants from the Caribbean and Africa who find themselves labeled *black*, this process of racial ethnogenesis may be most complete given the rigid black-white distinction in the United States—a distinction that renders specific ethnonational affiliations invisible (Waters 1999).

As expected, US-born, American-educated individuals appear to be much more receptive to panethnicity than their immigrant parents and foreign-born counterparts. This receptivity stems from their perceived common ground of culture and race and shared experiences of growing up in the United States as a racial other (Moore 1990; Oboler 1992; Flores-Gonzalez 1999; Kibria 2002). It was often in college that panethnicity became more than a label imposed from the outside but an identity to be actively embraced. The presence of panethnic student associations and ethnic studies programs and centers on college campuses is critical to the development of panethnic identity. According to Kibria (2002), the Chinese and Japanese American college students whom she interviewed identified their joining of pan-Asian student organizations and enrolling in Asian American studies courses as watershed events in the development of their Asian American identity. Involvement in pan-Asian activities provided "an umbrella for social-izing, self-exploration, and political activity" and "brought with it participation in pan-Asian friendship and social circles" (Kibria 2002: 113). The development of pan-Asian friendships and incorporation into pan-Asian social networks provided the basis for Asian American college students to understand Asian America not only as a political but also a social and cultural community (Kibria 2002: 115).

Intermarriage between ethnic subgroups is a good measure of panethnicity on the level of individuals. Just as intermarriage between major ethnic categories suggests the breaking down of social boundaries, so intermarriage within these categories can consolidate subgroups into one panethnic identity. There is evidence that intermarriage is occurring at substantial levels among Asian American subgroups and among Latino subgroups. Analyses of 1980 and 1990 census data on marriage patterns in major metropolitan areas confirm that Asian American and Hispanic identities are "truly significant in the socially important process of mate selection" (Rosenfeld 2001: 172). Importantly, in most cases, the tendency to marry panethnically is just as strong for the college-educated as for the non-college-educated, suggesting that panethnicity has "far-reaching consequences for personal preferences and identities" (Rosenfeld 2001: 173). The enduring strength of panethnic marital associations among US-born Asian and Latino couples suggests that panethnicity should remain strong and viable into the next generation, regardless of changes in immigration levels and patterns (Rosenfeld 2001: 173). Cuban Americans seem to deviate from this pattern. A large survey of high school children of Cuban immigrants in the Miami/Ft. Lauderdale area found that the less acculturated students were more likely to adopt the Hispanic label while the more acculturated ones preferred hyphenated American identities (Portes and Macleod 1996). This finding bespeaks the specificities of the Miami's Cuban case: the concentrated political and economic power of the city's acculturated Cubans enable them to disassociate from less privileged Latino groups and to focus instead on their national identity (Cortina 1990).

Panethnicity in transnational context

The scholarship on US-based panethnicity suggests that panethnic identity is associated with immigrants and their children, the product of migration to a new society. However, once formed in the diaspora, panethnic identities may be extended transnationally to migrant-sending societies. Bridging studies of panethnicity and the literature on transnationalism, Roth (2009) shows that many non-migrants in San Juan, Puerto Rico and Santo Domingo, the Dominican Republic, have adopted the Latino panethnicity first established by their compatriots in the United States. Through multi-sited ethnography and qualitative interviews with Puerto Ricans and Dominicans who have never lived abroad, Roth (2009) reports that the extension of panethnicity to migrant-sending societies is facilitated by transnational linkages: through recurring individual contact with migrants and via the deliberate efforts of transnational media to foster panethnic identification in order to expand the appeal and consumption of their cultural products.

To sum up Roth's findings: non-migrants that have the most frequent face-to-face contact with migrants from the United States typically express the strongest panethnic identification. But the history of political relations between the migrant-sending and-receiving societies matters: it provides the infrastructure and shapes the mechanisms for the transmission of pan-ethnicity from one context to another. According to Roth (2009), Puerto Rico's formal affiliation with the United States produces transnational connections that are supported by political and institutional infrastructure, enabling the transmission of panethnicity. This affiliation facilitates personal and business visits between the two sites, supports the movement of transnational Spanish networks into Puerto Rican markets, and subjects non-migrants to the American racial classification system that categorizes people as members of panethnic groups on census forms, federal college loan applications and other government documentation. As a result of the century-old relationship between Puerto Rico and the United States, awareness of American society and Latino panethnicity is an everyday reality for Puerto Ricans on the island. On the other hand, because the Dominican Republic does not have formal affiliation with the United States, Dominican non-migrants are unlikely to reach the same level of panethnic identification found in Puerto Rico. However, as Dominican migration to the United States continues, and as the likelihood of face-to-face interaction between Dominican non-migrants and migrants rises, American society will become an increasingly important point of reference for the production of new panethnic identities at home.

Diaspora Africans have also created broader pan-African kinship alliances. Lake (1995) reports that while most diaspora repatriates identified with their specific African nationalities, they also adopted pan-African identities in order to more effectively struggle against European and European American colonialism and racism. Indeed, invented by black diasporan intellectuals, pan-Africanism, which advocated the liberation of Africa, was the fundamental political philosophy of black modernity in the twentieth century. Paul Gilroy's influential book *Black Atlantic: Modernity and Double Consciousness* insists upon a notion of blackness that is "explicitly transnational and intercultural," and that travels through and alongside Africa, Britain, and the United States (Gilroy 1993: 15). Focusing on a group of black intellectuals that traversed national boundaries both in their lives and in their writing, Gilroy traces how this network for oppositional exchanges from one oppressed black group to another was held together by a politics of racism that helped to establish specific notions of blackness linked to but also outside of "Africa."

Similar to diaspora Africans, First Nation people have crafted panethnic solutions to their shared history of exploitation, broken treaties and decimation (Trottier 1981). Established in 1982, the United Nations Working Group on Indigenous Populations (WGIP) brings together indigenous delegates from the Americas, and from Europe, Australia, New Zealand, Africa, and

Asia to demand and develop international legal standards for the protection of the rights of indigenous peoples (Muehlebach 2001). This "global indigenous caucus" has been remarkably consistent in crafting a discourse that emphasizes their shared "histories of economic, political, ecological, and cultural oppression," that insists on their specific meaningful relationships to the environment and nature, and that demands their fundamental right to self-determination (Muehlebach 2001: 423).

Even as scholars document the presence of transnational panethnic groupings, they simultaneously stress the import of the national context for the development of panethnicity. As an example, while Eleanor Rose Ty and Donald Goellnicht propose the umbrella term Asian North American to bring together Asians residing in the United States and Canada, they also note that the Asian Canadian panethnic coalition has received less institutional support and thus has been slower to expand than their counterpart in the United States. In the early 1970s, like Asians in the United States, Chinese and Japanese Canadians developed an Asian Canadian consciousness as they became politically aware that they shared a common psychological and historical experience. However, some two decades later, Canadian universities still offer no equivalent of Asian American studies, a key institution in the development of Asian American panethnic identities in the United States. Moreover, since Canada is a British Commonwealth country, Canadian scholars tend to classify Asian Canadian literary texts, especially writing by Canadians of South Asian origin, as Commonwealth or postcolonial literature, rather than Asian Canadian literature (Ty and Geollnicht 2004: 6). The underdevelopment of Asian Canadian studies and Asian Canadian literature—two key institutions in the formation of panethnic identities—has thus slowed the expansion of pan-Asian consciousness and organizing in Canada.

Finally, given the internationalization and feminization of the labor force in recent decades, some Asian women in the United States and in Asia have begun to conceive of themselves as similarly situated racial, gendered, and classed subjects. For many Asian immigrant women, instead of gaining access to a better, more modern, and more liberated life in the United States, have been confined to low-paying service jobs and factory assembly-line work, especially in the garment and microelectronics industries. The similarities in the labor conditions for Asian women here and in Asia, brought about by global capitalism, constitute the "shifting groups for a strategic transnational affiliation" (Kang 1997: 415).

Challenges and possibilities

In the United States, panethnicity is both a political response to the American racial stratification and classification system and a form of assertive panethnic identity. In all, researchers report the emergence of a dual identification pattern, in which both panethnic and ethnic identities and affiliations co-exist. Although panethnicity is likely to grow in size and significance, it is not expected to supersede the specific ethnicities, but to become part of a range of available ethnic options—an identity that can be invoked or set aside in different situations for different cultural and political projects (Itzigsohn and Dore-Cabral 2000; Kibria 2002). The boundaries between panethnicity and ethnicity are thus porous rather than rigidly separate. This finding corroborates the current scholarship on ethnic identity, which emphasizes "its multiple, fluctuating, and situational character" (Kibria 2002: 102). This multitiered and seemingly flexible pattern poses this challenge: how to affirm and define the broader panethnic boundary that acknowledges a racialized similarity in the interests of shared goals, while at the same time maintaining and asserting the individuality of specific ethnic identities?

The existing evidence suggests that panethnicity has been an efficacious but contested category, encompassing not only cultural differences but also social, political, and economic inequalities.

Although outsiders may have drawn the panethnic boundary, the task of "bridging" belongs to the ethno-national groups. The panethnic group can be exclusive, ignoring diverse viewpoints and subsuming nondominant groups, or it can be inclusive, incorporating conflicting perspectives and empowering less established communities. Class, ethnic, and generational divisions can be obscured and perpetuated or they can be recognized and addressed. A study of second-generation Asian American leaders at four public universities suggests that as the Asian population in the United States has grown and diversified, the term "Asian American" itself has transformed and pluralized. The pluralization of the term's definition enables Asian Americans of diverse backgrounds to identify with the racial label by appropriating a variety of meanings to it. While the availability of these alternative meanings encourages some individuals to identify with "Asian American," it can also disengage others precisely because it can refer to any number of meanings (Park 2008: 557).

One issue that appears to tie seemingly diverse groups together, not only in the United States but also internationally, is US (and also European) colonialism and imperialism around the world, and the resultant racial hierarchies both abroad and at home. Although different Latino groups have vastly different immigration histories, socioeconomic profiles, and cultural traditions, their lives have all been greatly impacted by US foreign policy—an impetus for Latino migrants and non-migrants uniting around the Latino concept (Calderon 1992: 39). In the same way, the disruptive and often-violent effects of American expansionism and militarism in the Asia Pacific region, created a historical basis for solidarity among seemingly diverse groups such as Japanese, Filipinos, Southeast Asians, Koreans, Pacific Islanders, multiracial Asians and Asian adoptees (Spickard 2007). US colonialism, orientalism, and racism may also form the basis of larger and shifting coalitions. Today working-class immigrants of diverse backgrounds coexist with African American and US-born Latinos in urban communities across the country. This "social geography of race" has produced new social subjects and new coalitions. For example, young Laotian women in northern California joined Chinese and Japanese Americans in panethnic struggles against anti-Asian racism and also against the "neighborhood race effects" of underfunded schools, polluted air and water, and low-wage jobs that they and their families share with their African American, Latino, Arab American, and poor white neighbors (Espiritu et al. 2000; Shah 2002). In the same way, recognizing their common histories of political fragmentation and disfranchisement, Japanese, Chinese, and Mexicans in the San Gabriel Valley of Los Angeles County formed political alliances to work together on the redistricting and reapportionment process in the Valley (Saito 1998: 10). The recognition of shared histories of oppression has also led to the formation of panethnic groupings across national borders.

In all, the examples cited in this chapter call attention to the plural and ambivalent nature of panethnicity: it is a highly contested terrain on which ethnonational groups merge and clash over terms of inclusion but also an effective site from which to forge crucial alliances with other groups both within and across the borders of the United States in their ongoing efforts to effect larger social transformation.

References and further reading

Blauner, R. (1992) *Racial Oppression in America*. New York: Harper & Row.
Calderon, J. (1992) "'Hispanic' and 'Latino': The viability of categories for panethnic unity" *Latin American Perspectives* 19(4): 37–44.
Collet, C. (2005) "Bloc voting, polarization, and the panethnic hypothesis: The case of Little Saigon" *Journal of Politics* 67(3): 907–33.
Cornell, S. (1988) *The Return of the Native: American Indian Political Resurgence*. New York: Oxford University Press.

Cortina, R. (1990) "Cubans in Miami: Ethnic identification and behavior" *Latino Studies Journal* 1(2): 60–73.

Davis, F. J. (1989) *Who Is Black?: One Nation's Definition*. College Park, PA: Penn State University Press.

Dawson, M. C. (1994) *Behind the Mule: Race and Class in African American Politics*. Princeton, NJ: Princeton University Press.

Flores-Glonzalez, N. (1999) "The racialization of Latinos: The meaning of Latino identity for the second generation" *Latino Studies Journal* 10(3): 3–31.

Espiritu, Y. L. (1992) *Asian American Panethnicity: Bridging Institutions and Identities*. Philadelphia, PA: Temple University Press.

Espiritu, Y. L., Fujita Rony, D., Kibria, N., and Lipsitz, G. (2000) "The role of race and its articulations for Asian Pacific Americans" *Journal of Asian American Studies* 3(2): 127–37.

Foner, N. and Fredrickson, G. M. (2004) "Introduction: Immigration, race, and ethnicity in the United States: Social constructions and social relations in historical and contemporary perspective." In N. Foner and G. M. Fredrickson (eds), *Not Just Black and White: Historical and Contemporary Perspectives on Immigration, Race, and Ethnicity in the United States*. New York: Russell Sage, pp. 1–19.

Gilroy, P. (1993) *The Black Atlantic*. Cambridge, MA: Harvard University Press.

Itzigsohn, J. (2004) "The formation of Latino and Latina panethnic identities." In N. Foner and G. M. Fredrickson (eds). *Not Just Black and White: Historical and Contemporary Perspectives on Immigration, Race, and Ethnicity in the United States*. New York: Russell Sage, pp. 197–216.

Itzigsohn, J. and Dore-Cabral, C. (2000) "Competing identities? Race, ethnicity and panethnicity among Dominicans in the United States" *Sociological Forum* 15(2): 225–47.

Jones-Correa, M. (1998) *Between Two Nations: The Political Predicament of Latinos in New York City*. Ithaca, NY: Cornell University Press.

Kang, L. and Yi, H. (1997) "Si(gh)ing Asian/American women as transnational labor" *Positions* 5(2): 403–37.

Kibria, N. (2002) *Becoming Asian American: Second-Generation Chinese and Korean American Identities*. Baltimore, MD: John Hopkins University Press.

Lake, O. (1995) "Toward a pan-African identity: Diaspora African repatriates in Ghana" *Anthropological Quarterly* 68(1): 21–36.

Le, C. N. (2010) "Population statistics & demographics" *Asian-Nation: The Landscape of Asian America*. www.asian-nation.org/population.shtml (July 28, 2010).

Lopez, D. and Espiritu, Y. (1990) "Panethnicity in the United States: A theoretical framework" *Ethnic and Racial Studies* 13(2): 198–224.

Lowry, I. S. (1982) "The science and politics of ethnic enumeration." In W. A. Van Horne (ed.), *Ethnicity and Public Policy*, vol. 1. Madison, WI: University of Wisconsin Press, pp. 42–61.

Martínez, K. Z. (2004) "*Latina* magazine and the invocation of a panethnic family: Latino identity as it is informed by celebrities and *Papis Chulos*" *The Communication Review* 7(2): 155–74.

Masuoka, N. (2006) "Together they become one: Examining the predictors of panethnic group consciousness among Asian Americans and Latinos" *Social Science Quarterly* 87(8): 993–1011.

Moore, J. (1990) "Hispanic/Latino: Imposed label or real identity?" *Latino Studies Journal* 1: 33–47.

Muehlebach, A. (2001) " 'Making place' at the United Nations: Indigenous cultural politics at the UN Working Group on indigenous populations" *Cultural Anthropology* 16(3): 415–48.

Nagel, J. (1982) "The political mobilization of native Americans" *Social Science Journal* 19(3): 37–46.

Portes, A. and MacLeod, D. (1996) "What shall I call myself? Hispanic identity formation in the second generation" *Ethnic and Racial Studies* 19(3): 523–47.

Oboler, S. (1992) "The politics of labeling: Latino/a cultural identities of self and other" *Latin American Perspectives* 19(4): 18–36.

Oboler, S. (1995) *Ethnic Labels, Latino Lives*. Minneapolis, MN: University of Minnesota Press.

Okamoto, D. (2006) "Institutional panethnicity: Boundary formation in Asian-American organizing" *Social Forces* 85(1): 1–25.

Ong, P. and Pataporn, V. (2006) "Asian Americans and wealth." In J. G. Newbhard and R. Williams (eds), *Wealth Accumulation and Communities of Color in the United States*. Ann Arbor, MI: University of Michigan Press, pp. 173–90.

Padilla, F. (1985) *Latino Ethnic Consciousness*. Notre Dame, IN: University of Notre Dame Press.

Park, J. Z. (2008) "Second-generation Asian American pan-ethnic identity: Pluralized meanings of a racial label" *Sociological Perspectives* 51(3): 541–61.

Ricourt, M. and Danta, R. (2003) *Hispanas de Queens: Latino Panethnicity in a New York City Neighborhood*. Ithaca, NY: Cornell University Press.

Rodriguez, A. (1999) *Making Latino News: Race, Language, Class*. Thousand Oaks, CA: Sage.

Rodriguez, C. E. (1980) "Economic survival in New York City." In C. E. Rodriguez, V. Sanchez Korroll, and J. O. Alers (eds), *The Puerto Rican Struggle*. New York: Puerto Rican Migration Research Consortium, pp. 31–46.

Rosenfeld, M. J. (2001) "The salience of pan-national Hispanic and Asian identities in US marriage markets" *Demography* 38(2): 161–75.

Roth, W. (2009) "'Latino before the world': The transnational extension of panethnicity" *Ethnic and Racial Studies* 32(6): 927—47.

Saito, L. (1998) *Race and Politics: Asian Americans, Latinos, and Whites in a Los Angeles Suburb*. Urbana and Chicago, IL: University of Illinois Press.

Shah, B. (2002) "Making the 'American' subject: Culture, gender, ethnicity, and the politics of citizenship in the lives of second-generation Laotian girls." Ph.D. diss, University of California at Davis.

Shibutani, T. and Kwan, K. (1965) *Ethnic Stratification*. New York: Macmillan.

Sommers, L. K. (1991) "Inventing Latinismo: The creation of 'Hispanic' panethnicity in the United States" *The Journal of American Folklore* 104(411): 32–53.

Spickard, P. (2007) "Whither the Asian American coalition?" *Pacific Historical Review* 76(4): 585–604.

Torres-Saillant, S. (2003) "Inventing the race: Latinos and the ethnoracial pentagon" *Latino Studies* 1(1): 123–51.

Trottier, R. (1981) "Charters of panethnic identity: Indigenous American Indians and immigrant Asian Americans." In C. F. Keyes (ed.), *Ethnic Change*. Seattle, WA: University of Washington Press, pp. 271–305.

Ty, E. and Goellnicht, D. (2004) "Introduction." In E. R. Ty and D. Goellnicht (eds), *Asian North American Identities: Beyond the Hyphen*. Bloomington, IN: Indiana University Press, pp. 1–14.

Vo, L. Trinh. (2004. *Mobilizing an Asian American Community*. Philadelphia, PA: Temple University Press.

Waters, M. (1999) *Black Identities: West Indian Immigrant Dreams and American Realities*. Cambridge, MA: Harvard University Press.

21

Understanding ethnicity from a community perspective

Min Zhou

Past and recent research finds that ethnicity results in varied outcomes of social mobility among different immigrant groups. Such divergent outcomes in turn lead to further changes in the character and salience of ethnicity. Much of the intellectual debate on ethnic differences takes place along the following lines: *the cultural perspective*, which emphasizes the role of internal agency and the extent to which ethnic cultures fit the requirements of the mainstream society; and *the structural perspective*, which emphasizes the role of social structure and the extent to which ethnic groups are constrained by the broader stratification system and networks of social relations within it.

Social scientists from both perspectives have attempted to develop statistical models to quantitatively measure the effects of "culture" and "structure" on the upward social mobility of immigrant groups. Under ideal circumstances, these models would include indicators illuminating pre-migration circumstances such as home-country values and norms and pre-migration socio-economic characteristics. But because of data limitations, researchers typically control for "structure" by documenting specific contexts of exit, identifying aspects of post-migration social structures, and operationalizing those components for which they have data. This is not only a conventional practice but also a reasonable approach, since many post-migration socioeconomic differences of adult immigrants are likely either to reflect or be carryovers from, pre-migration differences. However, even the most sophisticated statistical model accounts for only some of the variance, leaving a large residual unexplained. More intractable are questions of how to conceptualize and measure ethnicity. Given data limitations, researchers often try valiantly to create measures that are ingenious, though not fully convincing, and have to place much weight on the effect of a dummy variable for ethnicity. However, the exact meaning or contents of this dummy variable remains ambiguous.

I argue that ethnicity cannot be simply viewed as either a structural or a cultural measure; rather it encompasses specific cultural values and behavioral patterns that are constantly inter-acting with both internal and external structural exigencies. Unpacking the ethnicity black box, therefore, necessitates a new conceptual framework from a community, rather than an individualist, perspective. Informed by the abundance of multidisciplinary research on international migration and ethnic communities, I have attempted to develop a community perspective that takes into account the interaction of individual characteristics, group-level cultural values and practices, and broader structural factors in explaining inter-group variations in immigrant mobility out-comes. In this chapter, I draw on existing research to sketch a conceptual framework from this community perspective and illustrate it with a case study.[1]

The ethnic community revisited

Ethnicity is not lodged in the individual but in a socially identifiable group, and, more generally, in a community. What then is a community? In the broadest sense, a community is defined by a group of interacting people sharing a common physical or social space, similar beliefs, values, norms, and meanings, and a considerable degree of social cohesion. As a sociological construct, a community entails meaning making, interaction, and action among members of a group with shared identity, goals, expectations, and behavioral patterns. An ethnic community by the same token is a group of people identified with one another by a common heritage that is real or imagined. To understand ethnicity in a community context, the concepts of ethnic enclaves, institutional completeness, and social capital are most helpful.

Ethnic enclaves as communities

The idea that ethnic enclaves are significant contexts for immigrant adaptation stems from classical assimilation theories. The classical assimilation perspective suggests that ethnic enclaves are not permanent settling grounds and that they are beneficial only to the extent that they meet immigrants' survival needs, reorganize their economic and social lives, and ease resettlement problems in the new land. Such classical assimilation theories predict that ethnic enclaves will eventually decline and even disappear as coethnic members become socioeconomically and residentially assimilated, or as fewer coethnic members arrive to replenish and support ethnic institutions. Indeed, old Jewish, Polish, Italian, and Irish enclaves in America's major gateway cities have gradually been succeeded by native or immigrant minorities. Here, ethnic enclaves in this sense overlap with communities defined by common heritages or national origins. However, the term "ethnic enclave" is often loosely defined and used interchangeably with the term "immigrant neighborhood" to refer to a place where foreign-born and native-born racial/ethnic minorities predominate. Urban America has witnessed rapid neighborhood transition: some old immigrant neighborhoods are declining into ghettos or "super-ghettos" where poverty trumps ethnicity to become a defining characteristic, while others have remained vibrant and resilient enclaves where a certain ethnicity dominates despite increasing ethnic diversity.

Classical assimilation theories fail to explain why such ethnic succession transpires, much less why patterns of neighborhood change differ by race/ethnicity or national origin. Past research generally cites economic restructuring and white flight as principal causes of inner-city ghettoization (Wilson 1978; Massey and Denton 1995). However, today's immigrant neighborhoods in urban America differ from past and present native-minority neighborhoods. Among the distinctive characteristics are a large share of noncitizen immigrants, both legal and undocumented; the diverse national origins and social class backgrounds; and the significance of immigrant entrepreneurship, which transcends ethnic and national boundaries. Today's immigrant neighborhoods encompass multiple ethnic communities and thus may not be easily dichotomized as either a springboard or a trap for upward social mobility. Rather, they may contain a wider spectrum of both resources and constraints which vary by ethnicity.

Institutional completeness

To distinguish between an immigrant neighborhood and an ethnic enclave analytically, it is important to study local social structures, namely all observable establishments that are located in a spatially bounded neighborhood. The local social structures may range from social service and human service organizations, civic organizations, and religious organizations, to various ethnic organizations (e.g., family, kin, clan, or hometown associations, mutual aid societies, professional associations, homeland high school or college alumni associations). The concept of "institutional completeness" is thus particularly relevant for examining the interaction between local institutions and ethnicity in immigrant neighborhoods. Breton (1964) examined the conditions under which immigrants became interpersonally integrated into the host society. Defining "institutional completeness" in terms of complex neighborhood-based *formal* institutions that sufficiently satisfied members' needs, Breton measured the degree of social organization in an ethnic community on a continuum. By focusing on the organizational structure and the interaction between individuals interacting in this structure, two concepts—that of the ethnic enclave and that of the ethnic community—become overlapped. At one extreme, the ethnic community consisted of an informal network of interpersonal relations, such as kinship, friendship, or companionship groups and cliques, without formal organization. Towards the other extreme, the community consisted of both informal and formal organizations ranging from welfare and mutual aid societies to commercial, religious, educational, political, professional, and recreational organizations and ethnic media (radio or television stations and newspapers). The higher the organizational density within a given ethnic community, the more likely was the formation of ethnic social networks, and the higher the level of institutional completeness. Breton found that the presence of a wide range of formal institutions in an ethnic community (i.e., a high degree of institutional completeness) had a powerful effect on keeping group members' social relations within ethnic boundaries and minimizing out-group contacts. However, ethnic institutions affected social relations not only for those who participated in them but also for those who did not, and the ethnic community did not prevent its members from establishing out-group contacts. Like classical assimilation theorists, Breton concluded that the ethnic community would fade progressively given low levels of international migration because even a high degree of institutional completeness would not block members' eventual integration into the host society.

In the US context, ethnic communities vary in the density and complexity of organizational structures but few show full institutional completeness. In my approach to the ethnic community, I borrow Breton's concept of "institutional completeness" and measure it in terms of the density and diversity of local institutions.[2] I add two additional dimensions: coethnicity and mixed-class status (Zhou 2009b). The coethnic dominance of an institution's ownership, leadership, and membership strengthens within-group interpersonal interaction. Diverse class statuses of participants in local institutions alleviate the negative effects of social isolation. In an ethnic community in which there is a high degree of institutional completeness, those who have residentially out-migrated are likely to maintain communal ties through routine participation in its institutions and thus promote interpersonal relationships across class lines. In my view, an ethnic community's institutional completeness, along with a significant presence of the coethnic middle class, positively influences immigrant adaptation through tangible resources provided by ethnic institutions and intangible resources, such as social capital, formed by institutional involvement.[3]

Social capital

Although the concept of "social capital" has come into wide use in recent years, scholars have debated over how to define and measure it and at what level of analysis to locate it. Coleman defines *social capital* as consisting of closed systems of social networks inherent in the structure of relations between persons and among persons within a group—a "dense set of associations" within a social group promoting cooperative behavior that is advantageous to group members (Coleman 1988). Portes and Julia Sensenbrenner (1993) define it as "expectations for action within a collectivity that affect the economic goals and goal-seeking behavior of its members," even if these expectations are not oriented toward the economic sphere. Sampson (2004) describes it as having variable utility values, arguing that not all social networks are created equal and that many lay dormant, contributing little to effective social action, social support, or social control. Putnam (1993) treats civic organizations as the main source of social capital because these organizations provide a dense network of secondary associations, trust, and norms, thereby creating and sustaining "civicness," or a sense of civic community that facilitates the workings of the society as a whole. Demographic characteristics, such as socioeconomic status (SES) or race and ethnicity, can also be part of the social capital process. For example, family educational background, occupational status, and income are usually considered forms of human or financial capital. However, family SES can also connect individuals to advantageous networks and is thus related to social capital (Bourdieu 1985). As Loury (1977) suggests, social connections associated with different class status and different levels of human capital give rise to differential access to opportunities.

Despite the lack of a uniform definition, scholars seem to agree that social capital is embedded not in the individual but in the structure of social organizations, patterns of social relations, or processes of interaction between individuals and organizations. That is, social capital does not consist of resources that are held by individuals or groups but of processes of goal-directed social relations embedded in particular social structures. In the case of immigrants, social capital often inheres in the social relations among coethnic members; it is also embedded in the formal organizations and institutions within a definable ethnic community that structure and guide these social relations. Because of the variability, contextuality, and conditionality of the process, social relations that produce desirable outcomes for one ethnic group or in one situation may not translate to another ethnic group or situation. Thus, social capital is embedded in and arises from institutions in a particular community, one in which the organizational structure and member identification are based on a shared ancestry and cultural heritage: the ethnic community.

Analyzing the formation of social capital in institutional and ethnic contexts is important in two respects. First, former social relations in families, friendship, or kinship groups, and other social networks are often disrupted through the migration process. Many newcomers today experience difficulty in connecting to the larger host society and institutions because of their lack of English-language proficiency and cultural familiarity. Among coethnics in their own ethnic community, however, even as total strangers, they can reconnect and rebuild networks through involvement in ethnic institutions because of their shared cultural and language skills. Second, ethnic institutions differ from pan-ethnic, multi-ethnic, and mainstream institutions at the local level in that they operate under similar cultural parameters, such as values and norms, codes of conduct, and, most importantly, language. In theory, immigrants can participate in and benefit from any local institutions in their new homeland. But many are excluded from participation in mainstream institutions, such as local government and "old-boy" networks or schools and parent–teacher associations, because of language and cultural barriers. Ethnic institutions, in contrast, not only are more accessible but also more sensitive than other local institutions to group-specific needs and particular ways of coping. Further, they are more effective in resolving cultural problems. Thus ethnicity interacts with local institutions to affect the formation of social capital and other forms of resources.

As the existing research suggests, immigrant neighborhoods are constantly changing. Out-migration of upwardly mobile residents negatively affects social organization, social networking, and social life at the local level. However, contemporary immigration and immigrant selectivity have shaped immigrant neighborhoods in diverse ways that both reinforce old constraints and create new opportunities. To explain inter-group differences in community development, we need to consider a dual-level analytical framework. One is at the level of institutions—how neighborhood-based institutions generate resources—and the other at the level of ethnicity—how patterns of interpersonal relationships are structured by ethnicity to create community resources and access to these resources in a given neighborhood. From this community perspective, we can begin to see the complexity of group processes and the interplay between cultural and structural factors that determine adaptation by ethnic groups sharing the same physical space. I elaborate on this perspective by a case study—a comparative analysis of the creation of ethnic resources in old Chinatown and new Chinese ethnoburbs.

The dynamics of ethnic capital for community building

Old Chinatowns versus new Chinese ethnoburbs[4]

In twenty-first-century, urban America, many immigrant neighborhoods encompass multiple ethnic communities, some of which are more resourceful than others. To explain the inter-ethnic variations in community development at the local level, we frame the concept of "ethnic capital" (Zhou and Lin 2005). Ethnic capital involves the interplay of financial capital, human capital, and social capital within an identifiable ethnic group. Financial capital simply refers to tangible economic resources, such as money and liquidable assets. Human capital is generally measured by education, English proficiency, and job skills. While financial and human capital may be held by individual group members, social capital is more complex, entailing social relations, processes, and access to resources and opportunities. Old Chinatowns and new Chinese ethnoburbs are two ideal types that can illustrate the ethnic capital dynamics.

Ethnic capital in old Chinatowns

The Chinese are the oldest and largest ethnic group of Asian ancestry in the United States. These earlier immigrants were uneducated peasants and came almost entirely from the Pearl River Delta region in South China as contract labor, working at first in the plantation economy in Hawaii and in the mining industry on the West Coast and later on for the transcontinental railroads west of the Rocky Mountains. Most intended to stay for only a short time to "dig" gold to take home, but few realized their golden dreams. Instead, many found themselves easy targets of discrimination and exclusion. In the 1870s, white workers' frustration with economic distress, labor market uncertainty, and capitalist exploitation turned into anti-Chinese sentiment and racist attacks against the Chinese. In 1882, the US Congress passed the Chinese Exclusion Act, which was renewed in 1892 and later extended to exclude all Asian immigrants until World War II.

Legal exclusion, augmented by extralegal persecution and anti-Chinese violence drove the Chinese out of the mines, farms, woolen mills, and factories on the West Coast. As a result, Chinese laborers already in the United States lost hope of ever fulfilling their dreams and returned permanently to China. Many gravitated toward San Francisco's Chinatown for self-protection. Others traveled eastward to look for alternative means of livelihood. Chinatowns in the mid-West and on the East Coast grew to absorb those fleeing the extreme persecution in California. From the passage of the Chinese Exclusion Act of 1882 to its repeal in 1943, Chinese immigrants in the United States were largely segregated in Chinatowns in major urban centers, such as San Francisco, Los Angeles, New York, and Chicago. In this sense, Chinatown is an American creation, a direct outcome of racial exclusion.

When an ethnic group is legally excluded from participating in a mainstream host society, effective community organizing can mobilize ethnic resources to counter the negative effects of adversarial conditions. Old Chinatowns displayed several distinctive features: (1) a small merchant class established a firm foothold at the outset of the enclave's formation; (2) interpersonal relations were based primarily on blood, kin, and place of origin; (3) economic organizations were interconnected to a range of interlocking ethnic institutions that guided and controlled interpersonal and interorganizational relations; and (4) the ethnic enclave as a whole, operated on the basis of ethnic solidarity internally and interethnic exclusivity externally.

In old Chinatowns, despite a severe lack of financial and human capital, social capital was relatively abundant. Social capital, formed through the same origin, a common language, and a shared fate, along with intimate face-to-face interaction and reciprocity within the enclave, provided uniform support for economic and social organization, which in turn facilitated the accumulation of human capital in job training (and also, to a lesser extent, children's education) on the one hand, and the accumulation of financial capital through ethnic entrepreneurship and family savings on the other hand. Table 21.1 reveals the interactive processes of ethnic capital in old Chinatowns.

The process of financial and human capital accumulation based on strong social capital in old Chinatowns heightens the significance of ethnic businesses and institutions. During the exclusion era, old Chinatowns experienced parallel developments in the ethnic enclave economy and social structures. Facing external hostility, the lack of financial and human capital combined with a sojourning orientation would constrain community development. But ethnic businesses in the enclave grew under certain conditions. First, an ethnic merchant class was formed prior to Chinese exclusion. Second, legal exclusion prohibited the Chinese from being hired in the mainstream economy and thus pushed them into pursuing small businesses in their own enclave and seeking occupational niches unwanted by natives, such as the laundry business in the pre-World War II era. Third, ethnic segregation created a tremendous demand for ethnic-specific goods and services on the one hand and the availability of low-wage labor to supply to the enclave economy on the other. Chinese entrepreneurs were able to raise financial capital and mobilize other economic resources to establish businesses not simply through family savings or overseas investment, but also through coethnic members' sentimental and instrumental ties to the social structures of Chinatown. The access to low-cost coethnic labor gave ethnic entrepreneurs a competitive edge. Although ethnic businesses within the enclave were often short-lived and lasted only one generation, they nonetheless opened up a unique structure of opportunities that corresponded to the sojourning goals of early Chinese immigrants (Zhou 1992).

Regarding institution building, ethnic concentration led to the consolidation of Chinatown's social structures. Various neighborhood-based organizations emerged to organize economic activities, meet the basic needs of sojourners, such as helping them obtain housing and employment, and mediate social relations at individual and organizational levels. The most visible and influential of these organizations included family, clan or kinship associations, district associations, and merchants' associations, also called "tongs" (Zhou and Kim 2001). The Chinese Consolidated Benevolent Association (CCBA) was an apex organization, also referred to as Chinatown's unofficial government. The relationships between the elite and masses, between

Table 21.1 Interactive processes of ethnic capital in old Chinatowns

Components	Strength	Relations
Social capital	Strong	Basis
Human capital	Weak	Outcome
Financial capital	Weak	Outcome

individuals and associations, and between associations and the CCBA in old Chinatowns were interdependent. The power structure was vertical and relatively unified for several reasons. First, the early Chinese immigrants came from a few tightly-knit rural communities in South China. Although there were variations in dialects and bases of networks, most of them were Cantonese, came from similar socioeconomic backgrounds, arrived in America in groups as contract laborers, and had similar jobs. They lacked human capital, English language proficiency and information on employment, and thus were dependent on a small group of coethnic labor brokers or merchants, and later on coethnic organizations. Second, most of them were sojourners who did not intend to settle in the United States. Without their families, they were highly dependent on one another for social support and companionship. Third, the hostility of the host society and legal exclusion from the larger society meant that only a few were able to venture beyond their own ethnic enclaves.

Developments of the enclave economy and ethnic social structures resulted in a high level of institutional completeness in old Chinatown. Such structural constraints strengthened immigrant networks, created opportunities for community organization, and gave rise to an interdependent organizational structure. Personal and organizational interdependence, in turn, allowed social capital to emerge by virtue of the immigrants' shared cultural bonds and shared experiences of exclusion—bounded solidarity—and their heightened awareness of common values, norms, and obligations—enforceable trust. Bounded solidarity and enforceable trust, however, did not inhere in the moral conviction of the individual or the culture of origin; rather, they interacted with structural factors in the host society in order to help immigrants organize their social and economic lives in disadvantaged or adverse situations (Portes and Zhou 1992).

Ethnic capital in new Chinese ethnoburbs

Contemporary Chinese immigration drives much of ethnic population growth and reshapes patterns of community development. Between 1960 and 2000, the number of Chinese Americans grew more than 10-fold—from 237,292 in 1960 to 2,879,636 in 2000, and to nearly 3.8 million in 2010. Unlike their earlier counterparts, contemporary Chinese immigrants come from diverse origins. The three main sources of Chinese immigration are mainland China, Taiwan, and Hong Kong, as well as the greater Chinese Diaspora in Southeast Asia and the Americas. Chinese immigrants from different origins or different regions of the same origin do not necessarily share the same culture or lived experiences.

Contemporary Chinese immigrants also come from diverse socioeconomic backgrounds. They now constitute not only "the tired, the poor, and the huddled masses yearning to breathe free," as is inscribed in the Statue of Liberty, but also the affluent, the highly skilled, and the entrepreneurial. The 2000 Census showed that young foreign-born Chinese (aged 25 to 34) with four or more years of college education were more than twice as common as young US-born non-Hispanic whites (65 percent vs. 30 percent). The influx of large numbers of resource-rich immigrants creates new modes of settlement, the most remarkable of which being the detour from inner-city ethnic enclaves to white middleclass suburbia as well as the newly emerged ethnoburbs (Li 1997).[5] Residential patterns of the Chinese are now characterized by concentration as well as dispersion. Geographical concentration, to some extent, follows a historical pattern: Chinese Americans continue to concentrate in the West and in urban areas. One state, California, by itself, accounts for 40 percent of all Chinese Americans (1.1 million). New York accounts for 16 percent, second only to California, and Hawaii accounts for 6 percent. However, other states that historically received fewer Chinese immigrants have witnessed phenomenal growth.

At the local level, traditional Chinatowns continue to exist to receive newcomers and attract economic investments from coethnics, but they no longer serve as primary centers of initial settlement as the majority of new immigrants, especially the affluent and highly skilled, are bypassing inner cities to settle into suburbs immediately after arrival. As of 2000, less than 3 percent of Chinese in Los Angeles, 8 percent of Chinese in San Francisco, and 14 percent of Chinese in New York lived in old Chinatowns. However, demographic changes impacted by international migration do not appear to be associated with the disappearance or significant decline of old Chinatowns, which have actually grown and expanded. In 2009 in New York City's old Chinatown, 7 out of 14 census tracts had a Chinese majority. Likewise, 4 out of 7 census tracts in LA's Chinatown had a Chinese majority.

The majority of the Chinese American population is spreading out into the suburbs outside of traditional immigrant gateway cities as well as in new urban centers of Asian settlement across the country. As of 2000, half of all Chinese Americans lived in suburbs. There are few new urban Chinatowns in the country where more than half of the residents are coethnics. For example, in New York City's Flushing, known as the "second [urban] Chinatown," only two of the 11 census tracts contained 25 percent or more Chinese and none had a Chinese majority. In Los Angeles' Monterey Park, known as "the first suburban Chinatown," 10 of the 13 tracts contained 25 percent or more Chinese but only one tract had a Chinese majority. Suburbs in Los Angeles, San Francisco, San Jose, Chicago, Houston, and Washington, DC, have witnessed extraordinarily high proportions of the Chinese Americans in the general population and the emergence of a new and distinct phenomenon—"ethnoburbs" (Li, 1997; Zhou *et al.* 2008).

The pattern of ethnoburb development is distinct from that of old Chinatown. Rather than an ethnic minority being pushed into an urban area for mere self-protection and survival, it involves an incoming ethnic minority that arrives with higher than average education and economic resources and with the capability of creating its own economy. The new Chinese ethnoburbs share certain common characteristics with old Chinatowns, but are distinct from Chinatowns in many ways (and they also differ from one another). Like old Chinatowns, new middle-class immigrant communities serve the needs of new arrivals unmet in the mainstream society and provide opportunities for self-employment and employment. But unlike China- towns, they are better connected to the host society, the homeland, and the global on eco- nomic, social, and political terms. Moreover, they can no longer be narrowly defined as their "ethnic enclave" or "staging places" just for the poor and the unacculturated. While they are started by affluent and educated immigrants, investors, and professionals, however, ethnoburbs gradually become magnets for coethnic members from lower socioeconomic backgrounds who arrive either to reunite with families or to feed the labor demand of the growing enclave economy.

The processes of ethnic capital formation in new Chinese ethnoburbs differ. Compared with old Chinatowns, contemporary Chinese ethnoburbs have distinct features: (1) they are popu- lated by a significant entrepreneurial class equipped with foreign capital; (2) interpersonal rela- tions within the community are less likely to be based on strong ties defined by blood, kin, and place of origin, and more likely to be based on secondary, weak ties defined by common socioeconomic status or other economic and professional characteristics; (3) economic organi- zations are less interconnected to the local ethnic social structure and more diversified in type and more connected to mainstream and global economies; and (4) even though the enclave as a whole continues to operate on the basis of bounded solidarity and enforceable trust defined by a common ethnicity, it does not necessarily preclude interethnic cooperation and social integration. Table 21.2 reveals the interactive processes of ethnic capital in new Chinese ethnoburbs.

Table 21.2 Interactive processes of ethnic capital in new Chinese ethnoburbs

Components	Strength	Relations
Financial capital	Strong	Basis
Human capital	Strong	Basis
Social capital	Weak	Outcome

As shown, the interactive processes of ethnic capital in new Chinese ethnoburbs are initially not based on social capital because localized ethnic organization is relatively weak. Instead, the enclave is built on strong financial and human capital. Social capital formation through ethnic interaction and organization comes *after* the formation of ethnoburbs.

The comparative analysis of the dynamics of ethnic capital in old Chinatowns and new Chinese ethnoburbs suggests an alternative way to unpack ethnicity from a community perspective. Although all ethnic groups are capable of developing their own communities, development outcomes vary depending largely on the interaction between individual- and group-level socioeconomic characteristics and larger structural forces pertaining to globalization, immigration selectivity, culture, and host society reception.

Conclusion

As I have shown in the above comparative analysis, old Chinatowns have been, and will continue to be, instrumental in facilitating immigrant adaptation, as their strong social capital repertoire supports the formation and accumulation of human capital and financial capital. New Chinese ethnoburbs also function to facilitate immigrant adaptation as they provide newer sites and opportunities for coethnic members to reconnect and rebuild social networks conducive to upward social mobility. Thus, the concept of *ethnic capital* opens up an alternative way of approaching and studying contemporary immigrant enclaves.

The above case study also suggests that social organization in immigrant neighborhoods varies by ethnicity and that the vitality of an ethnic community and its ability to generate resources conducive to social mobility depends largely on the development of the enclave economy and local social structures. In the case of the Chinese immigrant community in Los Angeles, social developments at the local level, whether in Chinatown or Chinese ethnoburbs, produce unique local social environments, in which the availability of and access to neighborhood-based resources are constrained by ethnicity (i.e., benefiting Chinese immigrants to the exclusion of non-Chinese residents members living in the same neighborhood). I believe that this community perspective offers a more nuanced and precise explanation of how social resources are produced and reproduced in the ethnic community and why ethnicity may positively affect outcomes for some groups but have negative consequences for others.

Notes

1 The chapter draws on my published work from the introductory chapter of *Contemporary Chinese America* (Zhou 2009a) and Chapter 2 of *The Accidental Sociologist in Asian American Studies* (Zhou 2011).
2 I use "institution" and "organization" interchangeably to refer to registered (formal) and non-registered (informal) establishments that exist in a given neighborhood.
3 This is the basic argument I am developing in *The Accidental Sociologist in Asian American Studies* (Zhou 2011).
4 This section draws from Zhou and Lin 2005.
5 "Ethnoburbs" are of relatively recent vintage, referring to multiethnic middleclass suburbs.

References and further reading

American Community Survey (2009) U.S. Bureau of the Census.

Bourdieu, P. (1985) "The forms of capital." In J. G. Richardson (ed.), *Handbook of Theory and Research for the Sociology of Education*. New York: Greenwood, pp. 241–58.

Breton, R. (1964) "Institutional completeness of ethnic communities and the personal relations of immigrants" *American Journal of Sociology* 70(2): 193–205.

Coleman, J. S. (1988) "Social capital in the creation of human capital" *American Journal of Sociology* 94: 95–120.

Li, W. (1997) *Spatial Transformation of an Urban Ethnic Community from Chinatown to Chinese Ethnoburb in Los Angeles*. PhD dissertation, University of Southern California.

Loury, G. (1977) "A dynamic theory of racial income differences." In P. A. Wallace and A. Le Mund (eds), *Women, Minorities, and Employment Discrimination*. Lexington, MA: Lexington Books, pp. 153–86.

Massey, D. S. and Denton, N. A. (1995) *American Apartheid: Segregation and the Making of the Underclass*. Cambridge, MA: Harvard University Press.

Portes, A. and Sensenbrenner, J. (1993) "Embeddedness and immigration: Notes on the social determinants of economic action" *American Journal of Sociology* 98(6): 1320–50.

Portes, A. and Zhou, M. (1992) "Gaining the upper hand: Economic mobility among immigrant and domestic minorities" *Ethnic and Racial Studies* 15(4): 491–522.

——(1993) "The new second generation: Segmented assimilation and its variants" *The Annals of the American Academy of Political and Social Science* 530: 74–96.

Putnam, R. D. (1993) *Making Democracy Work: Civic Traditions in Modern Italy*. Princeton, NJ: Princeton University Press.

Sampson, R. J. (2004) "Neighborhood and community: Collective efficacy and community safety" *New Economy* 11: 106–13.

Wilson, W. J. (1978) *The Truly Disadvantaged: The Inner City, the Underclass, and Public Policy*. Chicago, IL: University of Chicago Press.

Zhou, M. (1992) *Chinatown: The Socioeconomic Potential of an Urban Enclave*. Philadelphia, PA: Temple University Press.

——(2009a) *Contemporary Chinese America: Immigration, Ethnicity, and Community Transformation*. Philadelphia, PA: Temple University Press.

——(2009b) "How neighborhoods matter for immigrant children: The formation of educational resources in Chinatown, Koreatown, and Pico Union, Los Angeles" *Journal of Ethnic and Migration Studies* 35(7): 1153–79.

——(2011) *The Accidental Sociologist in Asian American Studies*. Los Angeles, CA: UCLA Asian American Studies Center Press.

Zhou, M. and Kim, R. (2001) "Formation, consolidation, and diversification of the ethnic elite: The case of the Chinese immigrant community in the United States" *Journal of International Migration and Integration* 2: 227–47.

Zhou, M. and Lin, M. (2005) "Community transformation and the formation of ethnic capital: The case of immigrant Chinese communities in the United States" *Journal of Chinese Overseas* 1(2): 260–84.

Zhou, M., Tseng, Y.-f., and Kim, R. (2008) "Rethinking residential assimilation through the case of Chinese ethnoburbs in the San Gabriel Valley, California" *Amerasia Journal* 34(3): 55–83.

22

Religion on the move

The place of religion in different stages of the migration experience

Jacqueline Maria Hagan

Because research on religion and migration has historically developed separately, we have only recently begun to understand their interrelationships. With the mass movements of individuals with diverse religious experiences from the global south since the mid-1960s, social scientists in the United States and Europe have taken a renewed interest in the connections between migration and religion. Most of the scholarship that has emerged in recent decades focuses on the immigrant experience and the role of religion in facilitating incorporation and ethnic identity, reflecting the academy's concern with the ways in which immigrants of diverse backgrounds and cultures are integrating into American and European societies. With the development of trans-nationalism as a new theoretical lens on the migration experience, research has broadened and shifted from a discussion of immigrants in national context to one of migrants in motion across territories. This new perspective has removed religion from a more restricted study of the immigrant experience and placed it within the broader context of the migration process. This chapter will provide an overview of the old and new scholarship that connects religion and migration. It will focus both on the place of migrants' religious beliefs, activities, and institutions in the different stages of the migratory circuit, and, conversely, it will examine the ways in which migrant religion is transformed by migratory behavior and practices.

Religion and the migration undertaking

Decision-making and departure

The migration undertaking is usually examined as a secular process. Theories explaining why people leave and where people go tend to be based on economic and social models. According to these accounts, individuals alone or together with family make a cost–benefit analysis between the places of origin and potential destinations and they migrate if the net benefit anticipated— usually higher wages—is greater at the destination. According to network theory, when migrants are all set to move, they will, if they can, activate their personal networks at areas of destination. Yet the decision to migrate in the contemporary world is even more complex than presented in economic or social network models of decision-making. For many migrants, especially the growing number of irregular migrants and refugees, who face enormous danger in their journeys and uncertainty in their futures in new lands, their religion guides the decision-making process.

A growing number of studies in the Africa–EU and Latin America–US migratory systems have demonstrated the central role of religion in the decision-making and journey stages of the migration undertaking. Religion in community of origin provides both resources for spiritual support and guidance in the decision-making process, and clergy and places of worship in home communities have adapted their practices to meet the needs of prospective migrants. The personal and institutional religious practices that bear on the migration undertaking are strongly shaped by place and culture. In his study of Ghanaian Pentecostalism, Rijk Van Dijk (1997) found that prospective Pentecostal migrants in Ghana and Nigeria turn to healing and deliverance rituals held for them at prayer camps for spiritual counsel and protection during their travel to Europe. These religious practices are not limited to Pentecostal communities in Africa. In their study of Guatemalan Pentecostalism, Jacqueline Hagan and Helen Rose Ebaugh (2003) found that prospective migrants turn to *ayunos* (fasts), retreats, and prayer camps to prepare for the hardships of the journey to the United States. Catholic communities also practice departing rituals. In Catholic communities throughout Central America and Mexico, departing migrants often make pilgrimages to familiar shrines where they deposit petitions requesting safety during their trip and well-being for their families, and make promises to saints and leave *ex votos* in exchange for safe travel and return (Wilson 2010; Durand and Massey 1995; Hagan 2008).

Migration also transforms institutional religious practices in communities of origin. Church clergy and caretakers of shrines in the Americas have created rituals and transformed sacred images to mark the departures of their flock and to encourage them to remain close to their faith and home. Recognizing a tradition of migration in their communities and motivated to keep their flocks linked to home, local dioceses, parishes, and priests accommodate emigration. In this way religious institutions in communities of origin sustain international migration (Hagan 2008; Fitzgerald 2009). In many migrant sending communities, including those in Nigeria, Ghana, Mexico, and Central America, trusted clergy provide counsel for departing migrants without papers. Approval from local clergy, often in the form of final blessings, sanctions migration and offers psychological empowerment to prospective migrants. These blessings constitute a spiritual travel permit that, in the mind of the receiver, may come close to if not exceed the value of an official visa. In this sense, migration counseling sanctions what is otherwise an unauthorized act. In parishes throughout Mexico and in some sending communities in El Salvador and Honduras, clergy celebrate the Day of the Migrant to commemorate in part the hardships that migrants endure and the Day of the Absent Sons to provide solace to family and to encourage a homecoming. Some churches in Mexico promote migration devotion by framing successful migrations as miracles, and profit from its material dimensions by selling to departing migrants physical mementos—medals, devotionals—to comfort them on their journey north. Local religious leaders in communities of origin also promote migration by incorporating the plight of migrants into their weekly services and transforming and then framing local saints as protectors and companions of migrants. For example, in Santa Ana Guadalupe, the local diocese transformed St Toribio, a martyr of the Cristero Wars, into a *coyote* saint, thus providing a powerful spiritual and moral narrative for undocumented migrants (Hagan 2008; Fitzgerald 2009).

The journey

Worldwide there are more than 212 million migrants, including a growing number of whom are impoverished and have no choice but to cross borders to find work to feed their families. Others are forced out because of political strife in their homelands. In an era of accelerated globalization, militarized borders, and involuntary migration, employers, smugglers, and private detention facilities profit from the vulnerability of migrants. Lacking resources, many of today's migrants must trek over thousands of miles of desert and traverse treacherous waterways to reach their destinations. Many risk and even lose their lives. Since 1995 an estimated 15,000 migrants and refugees have died attempting to reach Europe and North America, most of them who have drowned at sea or perished in deserts.

The changing conditions and dangers of contemporary migration journeys have resulted in the phenomenal growth of civil society organizations that deal with transit migration issues and, within civil society, the proliferation of faith-based organizations and churches along major crossing corridors in the Latin America and Africa migratory systems. Journeying migrants and refugees, who lack the resources or personal networks to assist them in their travels, now turn to these churches, shelters, and religious workers for help. Indeed, it is hard to imagine how refugees fleeing political turmoil in Egypt, Libya, and Nigeria, or escaping poverty in Honduras and El Salvador could have overcome the hardships of their journeying without the assistance of churches and faith-based organizations. In this way, religious institutions assume an increasingly important mediating role in migrant and refugee journeys (Coutin 1993; Hagan 2008).

Many of these churches and faith-based shelters have migrant and refugee programs that are supported by transnational religious congregations and faith-based organizations (e.g., Jesuit Relief Services or Church World Service,) and their secular civil society partners (UNHCR and IOM). The involvement of local religious organizations and churches in providing for the humanitarian needs of journeying migrants and protecting their rights has become especially important in some transit countries in Africa, where government policies and actions increasingly restrict the political space for secular civil society organizations, such as UNHCR, to meet the needs of vulnerable populations. Because of their higher level of credibility with both the people and the government, faith-based organizations, and local churches can engage more directly with political actors to resolve migration issues and respond to the needs of transit migrants.

In the Americas, a hierarchy of religious organizations mediates the dangerous journey for those migrating from Latin America to the United States. Once limited to occasional churches offering migrants help, now multiple organizations, churches, and programs along the migratory route provide for the needs of journeying and deported migrants. They include the Scalabrini Missionaries, a transnational religious congregation devoted to protecting and serving journeying migrants, programs sponsored by the US Catholic Bishops Conference, and multiple churches of various denominations that straddle both sides of the US–Mexico border (Hondagneu-Sotelo *et al.* 2004; Menjívar 2006; Hagan 2008).

Faith-based shelters provide numerous services to migrants to facilitate their journeys from the global south. They provide direct material assistance in the way of food, shelter, clothing, and medical attention. They also provide migrants with the spiritual, psychological, and social capital to continue on their journey. The clergy who care for these shelters offer services, blessings, and counsel to migrants to sanction their migration, help them endure the separation from family and community, and fortify them for the hardships of the remaining journey. From trusted faith workers and lay staff who run the shelters, migrants learn about the dangers of crossing international borders and, in some cases, are directed to alternative and safer routes than they would otherwise use. Those who travel alone sometimes network with other migrants at these shelters. Such non-kin migrant networks, forged in the shelters, buffer against the disruption and isolation, and offer solidarity, social support and protection on the road (Christensen 1996; Hagan 2008).

Religious organizations have become more than providers. They are also advocates of the rights of migrants and watchdogs of state policies. At multiple levels of church hierarchy, from the Bishops Conference to interfaith organizations to local churches and shelters in Central America, Mexico, and along the US–Mexico border, faith workers are increasingly involved in issues of international transit migration that transcend national borders. Motivated by a theology of migration, and as advocates for the rights of migrants to cross borders to find work, these religious workers and the transnational organizations in which they operate, have emerged as important vehicles for contesting nation-state activities and monitoring the regulatory practices of state institutions and policies. They challenge the migration state by documenting human rights abuses and crossing risks associated with current border enforcement policies. Along the US–Mexico border, cross-border interfaith coalitions challenge US immigration policy by providing humanitarian assistance to crossing migrants and encouraging social and political protest among followers (Hoover 1998; Groody 2002; Hondagneu-Sotelo *et al.* 2004; Menjivar 2006; Hagan 2008).

Collectively, the activities of these organizations suggest the emergence of a new sanctuary movement. Unlike the 1980s sanctuary movements in the southwest United States and southern Mexico whose primary goal was to provide refuge for Central Americans fleeing political strife, today's sanctuary efforts transcend national borders. In the absence of a retreat in state enforcement policy, these sanctuary efforts are unlikely to recede as they constitute a countervailing refuge from the expansive smuggling industry and vast military operations with which they share the migratory route. These sanctuary initiatives attest not only to the particular salience of religion and the church in the lives of migrants from Latin America, but also to the growing public role of religion in secular and political life in the United States today (Casanova 1994).

Religion and the immigrant experience

By far, most historical and contemporary scholarship on religion and migration focuses on the place of religion in immigrant incorporation, with an emphasis on explaining how religious institutions help immigrants face the challenges of adaptation to a new land. Both historical and contemporary accounts in the United States describe the ways in which religious institutions in receiving areas act as vehicles through which immigrants weather the hardships and traumas of immigration and, at the same time, preserve their cultural heritage and reaffirm their ethnic identities. Indeed, it is precisely because of the psychological traumas and hardships of immigration that immigrants turn to religion—the familiar—for comfort. Religion is so central to the immigration experience that the historian Timothy Smith describes it as a "theologizing experience" (1978: 1175). In classic studies of European immigration to the United States, for example, Oscar Handlin (2002 [1951]) and William Herberg (1955) singled out the psychosocial benefits of religious affiliation and participation for newcomers.

The large influx of diverse immigrants to Europe and the United States since the 1960s has renewed scholarly interest in the intersection between immigration and religion. Case study accounts in Europe emphasize the problems associated with the religious diversity of its newcomers and its implications for European society. This problematic account is explained by the largely Muslim composition of Europe's immigrants and the secular stance of the native population (Foner and Alba 2006).

In direct contrast, American scholars emphasize the positive and functional role of religion in immigrant incorporation, pointing to the centrality of religious organizations as sources of social and economic support in the settlement experience of a variety of newcomer immigrant groups. Churches, synagogues, and temples provide a variety of resources to ease settlement for newcomer members. Virtually all studies of immigrant churches and faith based organizations discuss the many services provided to newcomer immigrants and refugees, from food to housing, language training, and job referrals (Warner and Wittner 1998; Ebaugh and Chafetz 2000; Nawyn 2005; Hirschman 2006). In addition to direct material assistance, religious organizations also provide the children of immigrants with access to networks and information that facilitate social and economic adaptation and upward mobility. Min Zhou and Carl Bankston (1998) found that participation in ethnic religious centers protected Vietnamese immigrant youth in New Orleans from neighborhood gangs and strengthened their integration into the Vietnamese ethnic community and encouraged parental aspirations for educational advancement. David Lopez (2008) found that churches that offer formal education training such as English language and SAT classes encourage study habits, which in turn facilitate upward mobility. Studies have also demonstrated that through participation in such activities as event planning, coalition building, and group religious rituals and commemorations, immigrant churches and congregations can inspire civic and political participation (Jones-Correa and Leal 2001; Ecklund 2005), and political mobilization (Hondagneu-Sotelo 2008).

Religious centers, which are often erected or transformed by immigrants, also provide fellowship among co-nationals. In this way they reinforce ethnic identity, thereby creating more religious and cultural diversity across America's religious geography. American pluralism has also encouraged immigrant communities to reproduce their icons from homeland and erect their own places of worship, which further provides solace and refuge from the hardships of the migration experience (Tweed 1997; Orsi 2002). Within the walls of ethnic churches, in the comfortable company of family and friends, immigrants pray in their native languages and practice familiar cultural rituals, including the reproduction and transformation of revered icons from homeland.

Another consistent finding in the literature is that religion helps immigrants become Americans and offers them and their children a feeling of belonging in the United States. In the social settings of religious institutions, immigrants and their children can express and articulate claims for membership in American society (Kurien 1998; Portes and Rumbaut 2006; Alba et al. 2008). The central role of religion to the identity formation of newcomer immigrants led Oscar Handlin (2002 [1951]), over a half a century ago, to conclude that immigrants become Americans by first becoming ethnic Americans, a process nurtured through ethnic churches.

A number of US scholars have shifted their focus from the role of host religious institutions in adaptation to instead examine how immigrants themselves negotiate with religious institutions and continue to use their agency in the settlement stage of the migration process. One way that migrants negotiate the religious landscape of their new environment is by incorporating themselves into multiple religious traditions and organizations. Immigrants often mix and match religions to benefit themselves, taking advantage of geographical proximity and network ties. As Peggy Levitt (2007) reminds us, syncretism is often the norm among immigrants, not the exception.

Nor are the religious practices of immigrants confined to specifically religious settings. They extend to other social spheres, such as workplaces, civic and political associations, neighborhoods, and households. Referred to as "everyday religion" or "lived religion," this perspective places emphasis on religion as practice. Robert Orsi (1997) explains that this perspective constitutes a reorientation of religious scholarship away from static concepts of Catholicism and Protestantism, and from the academy's long-standing fixation on denominations and congregation. It shifts the attention to "a study of how particular people, in particular places and times, live with, through, and against the religious idioms available to them in culture" (1997: 7). Adopting this perspective, Bender and Smith (2004) show how south Asian Muslim taxi drivers in New York City practice their daily religious rituals while on the job by frequenting restaurants that offer informal prayer services. Similarly, in her study of the undocumented migration journey from Latin America to the United States, Hagan (2008) found that in the absence of places to worship along the migrant trail, some migrants improvised and spontaneously erected shrines from stones and materials found on the journey.

Religion and transnationalism

There is a general consensus among American and European scholars that we need to move from the study of immigrants to one of migrants and from the issue of religious identity within migration to that of the movement of religions and hyphenated identities (Assayag 2000; Levitt 2003; Bava 2011). This requires moving beyond the nation state as a unit of analysis and studying persons in sending and receiving societies as participants in a single social arena (Vasquez and Williams 2005). The recognition that migrants are embedded in two nations through sustained and enduring relations across borders is what scholars term "transnational migration" (Glick Schiller 1999).

Scholars argue that religion is a key social field of transnational migration because it enables migrants to stay closely connected to homeland and to members of shared culture, tradition, and faith throughout the world (Levitt 2007). Studies that take a transnational approach to the place of religion in migration situate their work at different levels of analyses, from global institutions to organizations to communities to individual migrants. Numerous studies have shown how global transnational religious organizations foster migrant inclusion in both home and host countries (Casanova 1994; D'Agostino 1997; Levitt 2007; Fitzgerald 2009). The Catholic Church provides social capital to migrants through the resources available to new members. At the same time the Catholic church has encouraged migrants to stay connected to nonmigrants in homeland, sending clergy to immigrant communities abroad to meet with migrants from their home communities. The Catholic Church in home communities also encourage nonmigrants to stay connected with migrants abroad by accommodating emigration through celebrations such as the Day of the Migrant to commemorate in part the hardships that migrants endure and the Day of the Absent Sons to provide solace to family and to encourage a homecoming. Catholic transnational religious orders, such as the Scalabrini keep migrants close to their faith and homeland as they accompany them on the migrant trail.

Global religious networks also unite religious followers around the world. Many migrants from Latin America participate in transnational rituals and form organizations and brotherhoods far from their homelands to bring their patron saints to them, to re-create the presence of their icons. In this way followers in their new homes can honor their icons through customs such as annual processions and do not have to travel to the shrine to feel the presence of their icons and remain connected to homeland. Second-generation Ticuanense in New York City commemorate their patron saint to identify with their home community in Mexico (Smith 2006). The Peruvian Brotherhood of the Lord of Miracles regularly performs the procession to their patron Christ to help Peruvian migrants maintain religious identity and create a public space for themselves (Paerregaard 2001). The global community of the Guatemalan based Brotherhood of Hermano Pedro commemorate the plight of his undocumented followers as they pray over the migration petitions requesting assistance on their journeys (Hagan 2008).

Transnational relationships and structures also develop at the intermediate level of analysis, among institutions and organizations whose activities extend across borders. Indeed, much of the activism in opposition to the US border policies described in the journey section of this chapter is coordinated at this intermediate level, by religious leaders and civil society organizations on both sides of the US–Mexico border, and is directed at providing life-saving efforts for journeying migrants, educating the public about the human costs of US enforcement campaigns, and ultimately calling for reform in US immigration policy. Collectively, they are becoming a transnational sanctuary and advocacy movement.

Transnational activities are also created from the ground up, from the everyday activities of the migrants themselves (Smith and Guarnizo 1998; Levitt 2001). A number of case studies recognize the importance of religious practices in the creation of immigrant identity in the host country and for the maintenance and ongoing sense of belonging in the home community. For example, to make sense of their identity and confirm their membership in the home community, migrants have long transferred religious rituals and holy images from home to host country (Tweed 1997; Orsi 2002). In her transnational study of the undocumented journey from Latin America to the United States, Hagan (2008) discusses the transnational ritual of *promesas*, pledges made by the departing in exchange for a safe crossing. These rituals ease the departure, sustain and nurture hope on the journey and assure the return of the migrant who must fulfill the pledge of returning to the shrine to give an offering to the saint or icon that made the migration possible.

Conclusion

In the past two decades, scholars have learned a great deal about the relationships between migration and religion. One of the major advances in the field has been a shift from the study of the immigrant experience from the perspective of the host society to the study of religion throughout the migration experience, from a focus on decision-making through the journey and settlement to a focus on the development of transnational ties. Building upon this knowledge, there are several directions for future research. The field could be enriched by moving beyond case studies to more analytical comparisons to fully understand how migration shapes religious traditions (i.e., migrants and nonmigrants, migrants of different faiths and cultures). Scholars also need to continue to move beyond studying religion in national context and in specific religious settings. Studying religion through a transnational lens and adopting a lived religion approach will provide insights into the different social fields in which migrants practice their religion, navigate religious and secular organizations in host countries, and remain connected to family, community, and homeland.

References and further reading

Alba, R., Roboteau, A., and DeWind, J. (2008) "Introduction." In R. Alba and A. Roboteau (eds), *Religion, Immigration and Civic Life in America*. New York: New York University Press, pp. 1–24.

Assayag, J. and Bénéï, V. (2000) "A demeure en diaspora. Asie du Sud, Europe, Etats-Unis" *L'Homme* 156: 15–28.

Bankston, C. L. and Zhou, M. (2000) "De facto congregationalism and socioeconomic mobility in Laotian and Vietnamese immigrant communities: A study of religious institutions and economic change" *Review of Religious Research* 38: 18–37.

Bava, S. (2011) "Migration-religion studies in France: Evolving toward a religious anthropology of movement" *Annual Review of Anthropology* 40: 493–507.

Bender, C. and Smith, E. A. (2004) "Religious Innovations Among New York's Muslim Taxi Drivers." In T. Carnes and F. Yang (eds), *Asian American Religions: Borders and Boundaries*. New York: New York University Press, pp. 76–97.

Cadge, W. and Ecklund, E. (2007) "Immigration and religion" *Annual Review of Sociology* 33: 359–79.

Casanova, J. (1994) *Public Religions in the Modern World*. Chicago, IL: University of Chicago Press.

Christiansen, D. (1996) "Movement, asylum, borders: Christian perspectives" *International Migration Review* 30(1): 7–17.

Coutin, S. B. (1993) *The Culture of Protest: Religious Activism and the US Sanctuary Movement*. Boulder, CO: Westview Press.

D'Agostino, P. R. (1997) "The Scalabrini Fathers, the Italian emigrant church, and ethnic nationalism in America" *Religion and American Culture* 7(1): 121–59.

Durand, J. and Massey, D. S. (1995) *Miracles on the Border: Retablos of Mexican Migrants to the United States*. Tucson, AZ: University of Arizona Press.

Ebaugh, H. R. and Chafetz, J. S. (2000) *Religion and the New Immigrants: Continuities and Adaptations in Immigrant Congregations*. New York: AltaMira Press.

Ecklund, E. H. (2005) "Models of civic responsibility: Korean Americans in congregations with different ethnic compositions" *Journal of the Scientific Study of Religion* 44(1): 15–28.

Fitzgerald, D. (2009) *A Nation of Emigrants: How Mexico Manages Its Migration*. Berkeley, CA: University of California Press.

Foner, N. and Alba, R. (2008) "Immigrant religion in the US and Western Europe: Bridge or barrier to inclusion?" *International Migration Review* 42(2): 360–92.

Glick Schiller, N., Basch, L., and Szanton Blanc, C. (1992) "Transnationalism: A new analytical framework for understanding migration." In N. Glick Schiller, L. Basch, and C. Szarton Blanc (eds), *Towards a Transnational Perspective on Migration: Race, Class, Ethnicity and Nationalism Reconsidered*, New York: Annals of the New York Academy of Sciences, pp. 1–24.

Groody, D. G. (2002) *Border of Death, Valley of Life: An Immigrant Journey of Heart and Spirit*. New York: Rowman & Littlefield.

Hagan, J. M. and Ebaugh, H. R. (2003) "Calling upon the sacred: The use of religion in the migration process" *International Migration Review* 37(4): 1145–62.

Hagan, J. M. (2008) *Migration Miracle Faith, Hope, and Meaning on the Undocumented Journey*. Cambridge, MA: Harvard University Press.

Handlin, O. (2002 [1951]) *The Uprooted: The Epic Story of the Great Migrations That Made the American People*. Philadelphia, PA: University of Pennsylvania Press.

Herberg, W. (1955) *Protestant, Catholic, Jew: An Essay in American Religious Sociology*. Garden City, NY: Doubleday and Company.

Hirschman, C. (2004) "The role of religion in the origins and adaptation of immigrant groups in the United States" *International Migration Review* 38(3): 1206–33.

Hondagneu-Sotelo, P., Gaudinez, G., Lara, H., and Ortiz, B. C. (2004) "There's a spirit that transcends the border: Faith, ritual, and postnational protest at the US–Mexico border" *Sociological Perspectives* 47(2): 133–59.

Hoover, R. (1998) "Social theology and religiously affiliated non-profits in migration policy." PhD dissertation, Texas Tech University, Lubbock.

Jones-Correa, M. A. and Leal, D. L. (2001) "Political participation: Does religion matter?" *Political Research Quarterly*. 54(4): 751–70.

Kurien, P. (1998) "Becoming American by becoming Hindu: Indian Americans take their place at the multicultural table." In R. S. Warner and J. G. Wittner (eds), *Gatherings in the Diaspora: Religious Communities and the New Immigration*. Philadelphia, PA: Temple University Press, pp. 37–70.

Levitt, P. (2001) *The Transnational Villagers*. Los Angeles, CA: University of California Press.

Levitt, P. (2003) "'You know, Abraham was really the first immigrant': Religion and transnational migration" *International Migration Review* 37(3): 847–73.

Levitt, P. (2007) *God Needs No Passport: Immigrants and the Changing American Religious Landscape*. New York: The New Press.

Lopez, D. (2008) "Whither the flock? The Catholic Church and the success of Mexicans in the United States." In R. Alba, A. Roboteau, and J. DeWind Religion (eds), *Immigration and Civic Life in America*. New York: New York University Press, pp. 71–98.

Menjivar, C. (2006) "Introduction: public religion and immigration across national contexts" *American Behavioral Scientist* 49(11): 1447–54.

Nawyn, S. (2005) *Faithfully Providing Refuge: The Role of Religious Organizations in Refugee Assistance and Advocacy*. Working Paper 15. The Center for Comparative Immigration Studies, San Diego CA: University of California.

Orsi, R. A. (2002) *The Madonna of 115th Street: Faith and Community in Italian Harlem, 1880–1950*, 2nd edition. New Haven, CT: Yale University Press.

——(1997) "Everyday miracles: The study of lived religion." In D. Hall (ed.), *Lived Religion in America*. Princeton, NJ: Princeton University Press, pp. 3–21.

Portes, A. and Rumbaut, R. (2006) *Immigrant America*, 3rd edition. Berkeley, CA: University of California Press.

Smith, M. P. and Guarnizo, L. E. (eds) (1998) "Transnationalism from below." Special Issue of *Comparative Urban and Community Research*, 6.

Smith, R. (2006) *Mexican New York: Transnational Lives of New Immigrants*. Berkeley, CA: University of California Press.

Smith, T. L. (1978) "Religion and ethnicity in America" *American Historical Review* 83(5): 1155–85.

Tweed, T. A. (1997) *Our Lady of Exile: Diasporic Religion at a Cuban Shrine in Miami*. New York: Oxford University Press.

Van Dijk, RA. (1997) "From camp to encompassment: Discourses on transsubjectivity in the Ghanaian pentecostal diaspora" *Journal of Religion in Africa* 27(2): 135–59.

Vasquez, M. and Williams P. J. (2005) "The power of religious identities in the Americas" *Latin American Perspectives* 32(1): 5–26.

Warner, R. S. and Wittner, J. G. (eds) (1998) *Gatherings in the Diaspora: Religious Communities and the New Immigration*. Philadelphia, PA: Temple University Press.

Wilson, T. (2010) "The culture of Mexican migration" *Critique of Anthropology* 30(4): 399–420.

Yang, F. and Ebaugh, H. R. (2001) "Transformations in new immigrants religions and their global implications" *American Sociological Review* 66(2): 269–88.

Zhou, M. and Bankston, C. L., III. (1998) *Growing up in America: How Vietnamese Children Adapt to Life in the United States*. New York: Russell Sage Foundation.

Part VI
Migrants and social reproduction

Migration transforms the processes by which social groups reproduce themselves. The greatest changes are encountered by those who go abroad, but those remaining in the country of origin and residents of the host society also experience altered circumstances. Through this process, established relationships and social patterns are often challenged and strained, but in many cases ties endure. The outcome, while traumatic, may yield new opportunities for migrant individuals, families, and communities in points of origin and settlement.

The forms of social reproduction transformed through migration that we explore here include marriage and family relations, language learning and use, intergenerational relations, and the patterns and meanings associated with intergenerational mobility. Because migrants transform patterns of social reproduction as they adapt to the new setting, the issue of assimilation is inextricably associated with migrants' social reproduction.

Guofang Li's chapter on immigrant language acquisition reviews the individual, collective, and contextual factors that both facilitate and limit immigrants' ability to acquire fluency in the host society's language. The author calls for increased attention to developing approaches that will better assist immigrants' acquisition of dominant language skills. She also emphasizes the importance of studying the intergenerational transmission of language acquisition. A case in point is "subtractive assimilation," a process that involves immigrants' children losing the ability to speak their parents' native language which depresses both social mobility and well-being (Feliciano 2001; Portes and Rumbaut 2006).

The next chapter by Linda Gjokaj, Maxine Baca Zinn, and Stephanie Nawyn highlights key areas in which family and migration scholars have contributed to migration studies. The authors stress the transformed relations that occur within migrant families as they encounter different stages of the migration process, starting from the decision to migrate and extending after settlement. They note the importance of transnationalism as a conceptual lens for understanding family migration, and conclude by suggesting several areas for future study.

Exploring another dimension of family relations, Charlie Morgan analyzes marriage and intermarriage among migrant populations. Morgan reviews the key conceptual areas addressed by scholarship on immigration and intermarriage, identifies methodological contributions and limitations in this area, and describes how intermarriage has changed patterns of ethnic and racial identification among both migrant populations and host societies.

In her chapter on international adoption, Andrea Louie summarizes the history of this growing form of international migration—which is generally not regarded as such—and summarizes the outlooks of both its proponents and critics, noting that it is important to specifically examine how adoptees are positioned both legally and socially in relation to other types of migrants. Observing that the countries receiving the highest number of international adoptees in 2004 were affluent nations in North America and Europe, and that the top sending countries to the USA are generally located in Asia, Latin America, and Eastern Europe but *are not* characterized by extreme poverty or the greatest birth rates, she shows that international adoption is mediated by governmental policies and reflects social, cultural, and historical factors, including gender, race, and nationality. Drawing upon her own research on how white and Asian American parents who adopted Chinese children conceive of Chineseness as a racial and cultural form as they help their adopted children craft identities in the USA, she gleans a wealth of knowledge regarding popular understandings of belonging, authenticity, and kinship that are relevant to the broader study of international migration. Finally, the chapter concludes with accounts of social activism mounted by international adoptees themselves.

The section ends with Julie Park's chapter on the educational and economic advancement of the children of immigrants. Park identifies central theories and findings in this area of scholarship, describes the major datasets commonly used to study the fate of children, and summarizes the possible trajectories described in the literature on the assimilation of the "1.5" and second generation of post-1965 immigrants. She closes by suggesting trends that immigrant children and the children of immigrants are likely to encounter in the future, including unprecedented levels of ethnic/racial and socioeconomic diversity, as well as increasing geographical mobility with migrants congregating less in gateways cities and instead, dispersing into communities little associated with migrant settlement.

References and further reading

Feliciano, C. (2001) "The benefits of biculturalism: Exposure to immigrant culture and dropping out of school among Asian and Latino youths" *Social Science Quarterly* 82(4): 865–79.

Portes, A., and Rumbaut, R. G. (2006) *Immigrant America: A Portrait*, 3rd edition. Berkeley, CA: University of California Press.

23

Immigrant language acquisition

An international review

Guofang Li

Recent statistics show that despite recent economic downturn in many countries around the world, international migration is still growing. In the United States, the foreign-born population reached about 38.1 million in 2007 with legal immigration flow standing at 1,107,126 annually (Papademetriou and Terrazas, 2009). In the same period, other modern industrial countries including Canada, the UK, Australia, New Zealand, The Netherlands, Germany, France, and Norway also continued to admit historically high number of immigrants from Asia, Latin America, the Caribbean, North Africa, and the Middle East (Ben-David, 2009). According to UNDP (2010), by mid-2010 there were about 200 million international migrant workers and their families who had chosen voluntarily to reside outside their country of birth for employment and education, in addition to 15 million refugees who had been forced to move across borders for fear of persecution or violence in their country of origin.

Accompanying the persistent upward trends in international migration are the persistent economic mobility and integration problems troubling the receiving countries. One of the major barriers to successful integration of the immigrants into the host country is immigrants' language acquisition, as the ability to speak and write in the target language in the host culture is a basic step to enable them to participate in the life of the host culture, further their education, get a job, obtain health care and other social services, and apply for citizenship (Portes and Rumbaut 2006). Lack of target language proficiency has been noted to contribute to a myriad of problems for both government agencies and workplaces in providing services and creating work for them in the host countries as well as to immigrants themselves in their adaption to new life styles and cultures. Further, with historically high inflows of immigrants, the schools in a number of receiving countries are also experiencing a sudden and steep rise in the numbers of children of these immigrants. To these children, to succeed in school and beyond also depends on their proficiency in the language of instruction. Therefore, to immigrants and their children, language acquisition plays a key role in their integration into the host culture.

While much research has focused on immigrants' language acquisition in different countries or regions, little is known on the issues and trends across international contexts. In this chapter, drawing on research studies conducted in international settings, I review findings on immigrants' language acquisition. Given the magnitude of the field and the limited space here, I have chosen to do a conceptual review by describing how researchers frame and investigate issues concerning immigrant language acquisition to gain new insights of the field. I have identified four diverse but interrelated theoretical perspectives that researchers used to frame their investigations: the individual perspective, the contextual perspective, the human capital perspective, and the ethnicity perspective. The individual perspective examines how individual factors and characteristics such as age at migration, length of residence, education level, and gender affect destination language acquisition and development. The contextual perspective investigates factors such as the familial context and the contexts of countries of origin and destination on immigrant language acquisition. The human capital perspective sees language acquisition as an act of personal and economic investment and examines the economic returns and earnings brought about by immigrants' investments in learning the destination language. Finally, the ethnicity perspective associates immigrant destination language acquisition with their ethnic identity and commitment. This line of research mainly addresses how immigrant settlement patterns in relation to ethnic networks and group size affect destination language acquisition. For each perspective, exemplars of work that reflect that perspective are reviewed.

Patterns and issues of immigrant language acquisition: diverse perspectives

This section reports findings on immigrant language acquisition from the individual characteristics perspective, the contextual perspective, the human capital perspective, and the ethnicity perspective. Although these perspectives are discussed separately, many of the studies reviewed address multiple themes.

Immigrant language acquisition as an individual phenomenon

The individual characteristics perspective examines language acquisition as an individual phenomenon. Research from this perspective mainly examines how individual factors and characteristics such as age at migration, duration of stay, education level, immigration status, and gender affect destination language acquisition and development. Owing to the limited space in this chapter, only the major factors such as age at immigration, length of stay, educational level, and gender are reviewed.

Age at immigration

Age at immigration or arrival is one of the most researched factors in second-language acquisition. The general conclusion is that age at immigration is an important factor that influences immigrants' language acquisition at the destination country; however, whether a critical period in second-language acquisition exists and how the age factor influences immigrant language acquisition is still subject to debate.

Some researchers such as Birdsong (2004, 2005) believe that the Critical Period does not exist and adults exposed to the target language can also attain native-like proficiency. Birdsong (2004) conducted an experiment in France on 20 native speakers of English who were near-native speakers of French, and 20 native speakers of French to understand the age effects on second language attainment. The participants were asked to perform three linguistic tasks (interpretation of decontextualized ambiguous sentences and of *bien* in decontextualized sentences, and the judgment of the acceptability of French sentences chosen). The comparative analysis between the performances of the two groups offers convergent evidence that native competence can be achieved by postpubertal learners. In a subsequent critical review of research on age effects in second-language acquisition, particularly those related to the age effects on immigrants' attainment of native-like proficiency, Birdsong (2005) further argues that the decline in attained second language proficiency is not due to maturational milestones but persists over the age spectrum during which a myriad of exogenous and endogenous variables are in play. Based on this conclusion Birdsong suggests that interpretation of the age factor need not be bound to the "ill-suited constructs such as the critical period hypothesis/second language acquisition and to received notions such as insignificant incidences of nativelikeness" (pp. 124–25). Rather, understanding of the age effects may benefit from "principled, granular investigations of linguistic variables that may interact with the age factor" (p. 124).

In contrast to Birdsong's perspective, many other researchers believe there is a clearly identifiable Critical Period, and younger starters are advantaged relative to older starters in language acquisition. They also believe that the age factor has differential effects on learners' destination language proficiency. For example, in a study on the performance on English phonology (i.e., foreign accent) and knowledge of morphosyntax (i.e., grammatical rules) by 240 native Korean participants who arrived in the United States between the ages of 1 and 23 years, Flege and Liu (1999) found that although age of arrival may have an effect on phonology, an increase in age of arrival did not result in a decrease in the native Korean participants' knowledge of English morphosyntax. That is, the age at immigration has differing effects on the Korean immigrants' destination language acquisition. Based on her analysis on the 1990 US census data, Stevens (1999) also found that proficiency in a second language among the foreign-born adult immigrants in the United States is strongly related to age at immigration, but the relationship in large part may due to the timing of immigration within the life-course that sets immigrants onto certain life-course trajectories because of a variety of influential social and demographic variables such as amount of exposure to the target language and further education opportunities. For instance, immigrants who enter the country earlier in life are more likely to go school in the United States and are more likely to marry a native-born American than those who enter the country at older ages. In a recent study that focuses on the age factor on bilingual development, Esser (2008) conducted an analysis of the age factor using the German Socio-Economic Panel (GSOEP) dataset that includes the members of the "guest worker generations," ethnic German immigrants from different East European countries as well as all immigrants from non-German speaking West European countries. Esser found that the age at immigration impedes both immigrants' first language and second-language development. That is, a too low age at immigration hinders first-language acquisition, whereas a too high age thwarts second-language acquisition. Esser suggests in order to become competent bilinguals, immigrants must have interethnic contacts at an early stage in order to provide simultaneous exposure to different language environments during the period when learning aptitude is highest.

Length of residence

Studies investigating the possible effects of age at immigration on second-language acquisition among immigrants often explicitly take the effect of length of residence in the destination country into account (Stevens, 2006). Immigrants' length of stay or residence in the destination country is directly linked to exposure to opportunities to learn the target language and hence to immigrants' destination language proficiency. While some research indicated no significant effect of the number of years of exposure on language performance for learners beyond the first few years of exposure (usually 5–10 years) (e.g., Johnson and Newport, 1989), other research has found that persons who have been resident in the destination country for a considerable amount of time (i.e., beyond 5 or 10 years of residence) generally have better language proficiency (Stevens 1999;

Tubergen and Kalmijn 2005). Regardless of these different conclusions, researchers have argued that language learning is a social process and that experiences and input matter. For example, Fledge and Liu (2001) compared the performances on three experiments (a word identification test, a grammaticality judgment test, and a listening comprehension test) by Chinese adults living in the United States with long and short length of residence in the United States and with different primary occupation (students vs. nonstudents). They found that significantly higher scores were obtained for the students with relatively long length of residence (LOR) than for the students with relatively short residence in all three experiments, the difference between the nonstudents differing in LOR was nonsignificant in each experiment. They concluded that the adults' performance in a second language will improve measurably over time, but only if they receive a substantial amount of native speaker input.

Another important focus of this research is on the rate of academic language acquisition for immigrant children. Several studies have studied how long it takes to acquire oral and academic language proficiency (Collier and Thomas 1989; Hakuta et al. 2000). For example, Collier and Thomas (1989) analyzed the length of time required for 2014 limited English proficient students to become proficient in academic English based on data in the United States; and Hakuta, et al. (2000) investigated the same issue using data from four districts in Canada and United States. All these studies conclude that, for most students, oral proficiency takes 3–5 years to develop, and academic English proficiency can take 4–7 years or longer to develop. An important factor that affects the rate of acquisition is students' bilingual schooling experiences. As Collier and Thomas (1989) conclude, immigrant children who receive their formal schooling in two languages generally reach national norms in standard tests after 4–7 years; for students who study exclusively in a second language, it may take as long as 7–10 years or they may never reach national norms.

Education level

In terms of the influence of educational level, it is found that persons with a higher education generally have better language proficiency. Researchers have found that there is a mutual influence between education and language proficiency and that several factors interact with the education factor to influence language proficiency. For example, in their analysis of the Canadian census data, Schaafsma and Sweetman (2001) found that educational attainment (and related earnings) varies systematically across age at immigration with those arriving around age 15–18 obtaining fewer years of education and having lower earnings and lower language proficiency than those who arrive either slightly earlier or later. In another study that used a multilingual phone survey data on four ethnic groups (Somalis, Hmong, Russian, and Mexican) conducted in metropolitan Minneapolis/St Paul in the United States, Fennelly and Palasz (2003) found that whether immigrants return to higher education upon immigration has a major impact on their language proficiency. Their sample indicated that immigrants with a college degree are 29 times more likely than non-high school graduates to speak English well and more than 20 times likely to read well. Further, female immigrants were found to benefit more than males from completing college in terms of spoken English proficiency. Similar findings were also observed in data from Australia and other European countries (Schnepf 2006; van Tubergen and Kalmijn 2009). For example, Schnepf (2007) in her analysis of three sources of achievement data, PISA, TIMSS, and PIRLS, across 10 OECD countries found there are significant gaps in educational achievement between immigrants and natives and these educational gaps were attributed to poor destination language skills (and vice versa) as well as factors such as socio-economic status and school segregation.

Gender

Gender is an important factor that affects immigrant language acquisition. Although research has found that female immigrants often benefit more from higher education and/or language classes in their spoken English proficiency, in general, women have fewer opportunities to learn English upon immigration due to a number of factors such as familial responsibilities, cultural and religious beliefs, and economic constraints (Mora and Davila 1998; Beiser and Hou 2000; European Commission 2003). Beiser and Hou (2000) in their study of Southeastern Asian refugee women in Canada found that female refugees are not only less likely to speak English or French at arrival but also have fewer opportunities than men to learn English after immigration. Similarly, using the 1980 and 1990 Public Use Microdata Samples on Hispanic workers in the United States, Mora and Davila (1998) found gender-related differences in Hispanic workers' English skill acquisition, which in turn influences their labor market earnings—Hispanic women are found to be less proficient in English and therefore earn less. Further, they found that English fluency appears to serve as a stronger occupational sorting mechanism for women than men. In many European countries (e.g., Belgium, Italy, and Germany), poor destination language skills are found to be one of the major barriers for female immigrants to integration into host countries and there are major obstacles for women attending language classes offered by the host countries due to low income and/or domestic responsibilities; thus, many of them are rendered socially invisible (European Commission 2003).

Immigrant language acquisition in contexts

A second perspective explores contextual factors such as the familial context and the contexts of countries of origin and destination on immigrant destination language acquisition.

The family context

In addition to studying individual characteristics, a few studies have examined the family as the context for immigrant language acquisition. In their seminal study using a sample of the Longitudinal Survey of Immigrants to Australia (LSIA), Chiswick *et al.* (2005a) for the first time examined the role of family dynamics, particularly relationships among family members on immigrant language acquisition. They found that there is a strong correlation in the English speaking skills of spouses among recent immigrants to Australia, generated from commonalities in many personal characteristics (such as birthplace, schooling, and even age) and in many determinants of English speaking skills (such as educational attainment, age at migration, country of birth, and visa category). In another study by van Tubergen and Kalmijn (2009) on Turkish and Moroccan immigrants' destination language use and proficiency in the Netherlands, it was found that the second language skills of the partner strongly affect language use and language proficiency. For example, immigrants married to a native Dutch, a second-generation immigrant, or a higher educated spouse clearly use Dutch more often, and these effects on language usage are significantly stronger than on language proficiency.

In addition to studying the relations of immigrant husbands and wives on language acquisition, several studies have also focused on relations between parents and children and among siblings. In their subsequent analysis, Chiswick *et al.* (2005b) considered the links among the dominant language skills of mothers, fathers, their children and sibling relationships among the children using a large sample from the 1996 Australian Census of Population and Housing data. In terms of links between parents and children's language skills, they found that the presence of children might lower parental destination language proficiency if children serve as translators for their parents, if children lower their parents', especially their mother's, labor supply, and if parents use the origin language at home to transmit it and the origin culture to their children. On the other hand, because of the greater exposure to the destination language in school and the greater ability of youths to acquire destination language skills, they may serve as their parents' teachers and role models in the destination language. Moreover, the relationship between a parent's and a child's proficiency may be stronger for the mother because of the greater time input of mothers in the rearing of children. In terms of links among siblings, they found that the larger the number of siblings the greater the linguistic interactions in the home with destination language speakers, and the less the interaction with their foreign-speaking parents, especially for the youngest as distinct from the oldest child.

Focusing on parent–adolescent language use and relationships among families with East Asians, Filipino, and Latin American backgrounds, Tseng and Fuligni (2000) found that despite great variation in the patterns of language use across immigrant families of diverse backgrounds, there is a strong association between parent–adolescent language use and cohesion, discussion, and conflict. It is found that adolescents who spoke in different languages with their parents reported less cohesion and discussion with their mothers and fathers than did their peers who spoke the same language with their parents; adolescents who mutually communicated in the native language with their parents reported the highest levels of cohesion and discussion. Also focusing on parent-adolescent relationship, in a recent analysis, Liu *et al.* (2009) examined the link between mothers' self-reports of English and heritage language proficiency in youth's academic and emotional adjustment among 444 Chinese American families. They found that mothers who were English proficient tended to have children with higher academic achievement and fewer depressive symptoms, and mother–adolescent match in heritage language proficiency was related to higher math achievement scores and overall GPA.

Contexts of countries of origin and destination

Both immigrants' home and host country matter for their destination language acquisition. Several studies have examined how the contextual factors of the "origin effect," the "destination effect," and the combination of both. According to van Tubergen and Kalmijn (2005), the destination effect examines the role of political regimes and anti-immigrant sentiments in the host societies; the origin effect examines the characteristics of the sending countries such as economic conditions. The combination of these two effects such as the size of an immigrant group relative to the destination population is called the "setting" or "community" effects.

In their analysis of the cross-national data set that included more than 186,000 immigrants from 182 origin groups, in nine destinations: Australia, Belgium, Denmark, Germany, Great Britain, Italy, the Netherlands, Norway, and the United States, van Tubergen and Kalmijn (2005) found that contextual effects play an important role in the destination language proficiency of immigrants. In terms of the destination effect, they found that in societies with a left-wing legacy and with a high degree of prejudice toward immigrants, immigrants have poorer command of the destination language. The former is because the political climate in these countries is more tolerant toward immigrants, resulting in fewer incentives to learn the host language; the reason for the latter finding is that in societies with anti-immigrant sentiments social interaction decreases between natives and immigrants, which in turn decreases immigrants' exposure to the official language and hampers their process of language learning.

In terms of the origin effect, van Tubergen and Kalmijn (2005) found that immigrants from countries with more globalized economies speak the destination language better because immigrants from more economically globalized societies are more strongly exposed to the foreign language before immigrating. Further, they found that those who moved from politically suppressed societies have a poorer command of the destination language. Finally, in terms of the setting or community effect, van Tubergen and Kalmijn (2005) found that geographic distance between the country of origin and the destination country has a negative effect on immigrants' language proficiency. That is, immigrants whose origin country is close to the destination country have better command of the destination language. Further, they found a negative relationship between immigrants' language proficiency and the distance between their native language and host language and between the size of the immigrant group in the destination country and immigrants' language skills.

Several other studies have also addressed similar setting effect. For example, the effect of linguistic distance between country of origin and destination country was also examined by Beenstock *et al.* (2001) by using the 1972 Census of Israel and the Immigration Absorption (panel) Surveys conducted in the 1970s. Their analysis also suggested that country of origin and language of origin matter for destination language proficiency (i.e., Hebrew), especially in the longer term. Specifically, they found that by country of origin, those from North Africa are the least proficient; by language of origin, Arabic speakers with a small linguistic distance from Hebrew are the most proficient, but immigrants from English-speaking origins with a large linguistic distance are the least proficient in Hebrew.

Immigrant language acquisition as human capital

A third perspective sees language acquisition as a process of acquiring human capital and an act of personal and economic investments. Research from this perspective mainly focuses on economic returns and earnings brought about by immigrants' investments in learning the destination language.

Seeing destination language proficiency as an important economic asset that is associated with increased workforce participation, researchers around that world have conducted research to examine the relationship between destination language proficiency and earnings in the labor market. The findings from the United States, Canada, Israel, Germany, UK, and Australia all suggest that destination language proficiency is an important determinant of immigrants' earnings in the labor market—the higher their skills in the destination language, the more occupational success they have. Shields and Price (2002), for example, in their analysis of the ethnic minority immigrants' wages in the UK found that immigrants' fluency in English increases the mean hourly occupational wage by as much as 20 percent. Further, a common finding is that even among those who have high-paying jobs, those with low language proficiency levels will earn substantially less than their linguistically fluent counterparts and that this gap is larger than that observed in lower paying jobs; and sometimes destination language fluency had almost no effect on wage growth in the low-skill occupations. Overall, studies have shown complementarity between immigrants' linguistic capital or language skills and other forms of human capital (such as earnings of schooling, total labor market experience, duration in the United States, being married, being a citizen and weeks worked in the year) in affecting immigrants' earning in the labor market (Chiswick and Miller 2002; Berman *et al.* 2003).

Research has also examined the relationship between destination language proficiency and earnings in the labor market from different angles. For example, while most research focused on language fluency (speaking), Ferrer *et al.* (2006) explored the effect of immigrants' literacy skills (reading, writing, and cognitive skills) on their earnings and the sources of lower return to education and experience among immigrants in Canada. They found that literacy skills also have a significant impact on earnings and that lower immigrant literacy levels contribute to immigrant–native-born earnings differentials; and immigrants receive a lower return to foreign-acquired university education than native-born returns to a host country-acquired university education.

In an analysis of data from the 1990 US census data, Bleakley and Chin (2004) examined the relationship between destination language proficiency and earnings from the angle of age at immigration effect. They found a significant positive effect of English proficiency on wages among adults who immigrated to the United States as children (i.e., arrive up to age 11) and much (approximately 90 percent) of the effect of English-language skills on wages works through changing educational attainment or years of schooling in the host society.

Another angle of analysis is from the length of residence or stay in the host society. Dustmann (1999) in his analysis of data from the first wave of the German Socio-Economic Panel differentiated temporary or contract immigrants from permanent immigrants and examined whether country-specific linguistic capital is sensitive to the duration in the host country labor market. He found that destination language fluency is negatively and significantly affected by immigrants' return propensity. That is, immigrants who plan to stay longer in the host society labor market tend to invest more intensively in their human capital, particularly in the destination language learning (see also Chiswick and Miller, 1999).

Gender differences are also examined in relations to language proficiency and economic returns. As described in the section of gender, several studies have revealed that women immigrants tend to have fewer opportunities to learn English after immigration, earn less, and face more barriers in promotion in the host society labor market than their male counterparts (see Mora and Davila 1998; Beiser and Hou 2000). However, for women who are proficient in both speaking and reading, their earnings are much higher than those who lack both skills. For example, in their analysis of both adult male and female immigrants from the 1989 Legalized Population Survey (LPS) in the United States, Chiswick and Miller (1999) found that earnings are higher by about 8 percent for men and 17 percent for women who are proficient in both speaking and reading English, compared to those lacking both skills.

Immigrant language acquisition and ethnicity

A fourth perspective associates immigrant destination language acquisition with their ethnic identity and commitment. This line of research mainly addresses how immigrant settlement patterns in relation to ethnic networks and group sizes affect destination language acquisition.

Since immigrants typically choose to locate in cities with similar ethnic concentrations, one key question researchers have tried to address from this perspective is whether ethnic enclaves (networks) impede destination language acquisition. The findings have been inconsistent in literature. While some studies suggest that ethnic enclaves negatively affect immigrants' destination language acquisition (and educational attainment) in many countries such as USA, Canada, Germany, and UK (e.g., Chiswick and Miller 1996; Danser and Yaman 2010; Waldorf et al. 2010), other studies have found that the issue is more complex as it depends on immigrants' choice of location, the size of the ethnic communities, and the assimilation and networking behaviors of the members of the communities.

In terms of the size of ethnic concentration, several studies such as Florax et al. (2005) have found that immigrants living in areas with large immigrant enclaves are less likely to invest in learning the destination language than those living in areas with small immigrant enclaves. The issue of size is also closely linked with immigrants' choice of location. Bauer et al. (2005), for example, using the Mexican Migration Project (MMP) that included individuals from more than 7,000 households in 52 Mexican communities in the United States, explored the relationship between the location choice of migrants and connected the location decision with their language proficiency. They found that location decisions are conditioned in important ways on linguistic ability. Those migrants with limited English proficiency tend to direct themselves disproportionately to destinations that already contain substantial numbers of Mexicans, thus providing an environment where they can get by in Spanish, whereas those with English ability are more likely to go to places with small immigrant populations. Therefore, ethnic enclaves seem to have the strongest effect on those with the lowest language abilities and the least effect on those who have the highest language proficiency. Similar findings are also revealed in studies of immigrants in other countries. In Chiswick and Miller (2003) analysis of adult male immigrants in Canada, for example, it is found that residence in ethnic enclaves in which the origin language is spoken more intensely is associated with both a higher probability of being unable to speak an official language and mother tongue retention in the home even when the immigrant speaks an official language. That is, the higher the concentration of co-ethnic groups in areas where an immigrant lives, the more likely he or she will avoid the use of the official languages and speak the mother tongue at home.

The impact of ethnic enclaves on destination language acquisition is also dependent on factors such as assimilation behaviors involving contacts with the host society and networking behaviors within the own immigrant community (Florax *et al.* 2005). Drawing on the survey in a representative national sample of 804 post-1989 Russian immigrants in Israel, Remennick (2004), for example, argues that the Russian community did not impede but facilitated Russian immigrants' Hebrew learning, especially among younger immigrants. This is because the Russian community in Israel, though autonomous with its own labor market, consumer services, media, and social networks, promotes additive bilingualism that encourages the incorporation of the elements of Hebrew into their everyday communications and cultural/media consumption. The formation of new ethnic identity and entity—Russian Israeli—has resulted in the improvement of Hebrew skills among young and middle-aged immigrants.

Another key question addressed from the ethnicity perspective is how language proficiency is mediated through ethnicity affects immigrants' earnings and economic mobility. Several studies have found negative returns associated with ethnicity. Pendakar and Pendakar (2002) examined the earnings differentials for men and women associated with language knowledge in three Canadian urban markets: the Census Metropolitan Areas (CMAs) of Montreal, Toronto, and Vancouver. They found that knowledge of minority languages is correlated with lower earnings for men and women in Canada's three largest cities; people who speak both a majority language and a minority language earn less than those who speak only a majority language. Further, they found knowledge of Southern European and Asian languages such as Greek, Spanish, Arabic, Hindi, Punjabi, Tagalog, and Vietnamese is associated with larger negative earnings differentials than knowledge of Northern and Eastern European languages such as German, Polish, and Ukrainian. These findings suggest that there exists labor market discrimination that is based on culture in addition to color.

Using data on adult foreign-born men from non-English speaking countries from the 1990 Census of Population of the United States, Chiswick and Miller (2002) revealed the importance for earnings of English language. For example, the foreign born from non-English speaking countries who are fluent in English earn about 14 percent more than those lacking this fluency. Further, they found although there is an adverse effect of linguistic concentration on immigrants' earnings, it seems to affect the immigrants differently: the adverse effect is more pronounced among those immigrants more fluent in English than those who are not. That is, for those who are not fluent in English, ethnic enclaves provide relatively greater earnings opportunities than outside the enclaves.

Conclusions and future research directions

The four perspectives that reviewed in this chapter suggest the complex nature of the issue of immigrant destination language acquisition as it is related to not only immigrants' individual backgrounds but also a set of socio-cultural, socio-economic, socio-geographical, and socio-political factors. Though immigrants' agency and choice can be a powerful influence on where they settle in the host societies and how much they will invest in destination language learning, a myriad of external factors such as the nature and size of the ethnic communities, the contexts of reception and the situations of the labor market in the host society often become constraints and barriers for their language learning. While these findings reveal much about what influences immigrants' language acquisition, they also suggest the need to investigate effective practices and programs that help immigrants overcome these barriers and influences to succeed in learning the destination language in the host society. In addition, more research is needed on how destination immigration policies are shaping or are being shaped by these external, contextual factors.

Another important finding is that immigrants' first language proficiency and their ethnic communities are often found to have a negative influence on their destination language acquisition and their earnings in the host society, a factor that often leads to a language shift to second language from first-generation immigrants to their next generations and "the loss of anything else immigrants might have brought with them" (Portes and Rumbaut, 1996, p. 230). To counteract this type of subtractive assimilation, future research must investigate inter-generational language acquisition and transmission models and patterns in both destination and heritage languages. As well, more efforts must devote to fostering additive bilingualism in host societies. For example, one such effort is research on hybrid immigrant community identity formation and social networking (such as that of Russian Israel described by Remennick 2004) that promotes additive bilingualism.

References and further reading

Bauer, T., Epstein, G. S., and Gang, I. N. (2005) "Enclaves, language, and the location choice of migrants" *Journal of Population Economics* 18(4): 649–62.
Beenstock, M., Chiswick, B. R., and Repetto, G. L. (2001) "The effect of linguistic distance and country of origin on immigrant language skills: Application to Israel" *International Migration* 39(3): 33–60.
Ben-David, E. (2009) "Europe's shifting immigration dynamic" *Middle East Quarterly* Spring: 15–24.
Berman, E., Lang, K., and Siniver, E. (2003) "Language-skill complementarity: Returns to immigrant language acquisition" *Labour* 10(3): 265–398.
Beiser, M. and Hou, F. (2000) "Gender differences in language acquisition and employment consequences among Southeast Asian refugees in Canada" *Canadian Public Policy* 26(3): 311–30.
Birdsong, D. (2004) "Second language acquisition and ultimate attainment." In A. Davies and C. Elder (eds), *The Handbook of Applied Linguistics*. Malden, MA: Blackwell, pp. 82–105.
——(2005) "Interpreting age effects in second language acquisition." In J. Kroll and A. M. B. de Groot (eds), *Handbook of Bilingualism: Psycholinguistic Perspectives*. Oxford: Oxford University Press, pp. 109–27.
Bleakley, H. and Chin, A. (2004) "Language skills and earnings: Evidence from childhood immigrants" *Review of Economics and Statistics* 86(2): 481–96.
Chiswick, B. R., Lee, Y. L., and Miller, P. W. (2005a) "Family matters: The role of the family in immigrants' destination language acquisition" *Journal of Population Economics* 18(4): 631–47.
——(2005b) "Parents and children talk: English language proficiency within immigrant families" *Review of Economics of the Household* 3(3): 243–68.
Chiswick B. R. and Miller, P. W. (1996) "Ethnic networks and language proficiency among immigrants" *Journal of Population Economics* 9(1): 19–35.
——(1999) "Language skills and earnings among legalized aliens" *Journal of Population Economics* 12(1): 63–89.
——(2002) "Immigrant earnings: Language skills, linguistic concentrations, and the business cycle" *Journal of Populations Economics* 15(1): 31–57.

——(2003) "The complementarity of language and other human capital: Immigrant earnings in Canada" *Economics of Education Review* 22(5): 469–80.

Collier, V. P. and Thomas, W. P. (1989) "How quickly can immigrants become proficient in school English?" *Journal of Educational Issues of Language Minority Students* 5(Fall): 26–38.

Danser, A. M. and Yaman, F. (2010) *Ethnic Concentration and Language Fluency of Immigrants: Quasi-experimental Evidence from the Guest-worker Placement in Germany*. Germany: The Research Institute of the German Federal Employment Agency.

Dustmann, C. (1999) "Temporary migration, human capital, and language fluency of migrants" *Scandinavian Journal of Economics* 101(2): 297–314.

European Commission (2003) *Migration and Social Integration of Migrants*. Luxembourg: Office for Official Publications of the European Communities.

Esser, H. (2008) "Language acquisition and age at immigration: The difficult conditions for bilingualism." www.iza.org/conference_files/AMM_2008/esser_h1665.pdf (accessed February 21 2011).

Fennelly, K. and Palasz, N. (2003) "English language proficiency of immigrants and refugees in the twin cities metropolitan area" *International Migration* 41(5): 93–125.

Ferrer, A., Green, D. A., and Riddell, W. C. (2006) "The effect of literacy on immigrant earnings" *The Journal of Human Resources* 41(2): 380–410.

Flege, J. E., and Liu, S. (2001) The effect of experience on adults' acquisition of a second language. *Studies in Second Language Acquisition* 23(4), 527–52.

Florax R. J. G. M., de Graaff, T., and Waldorf, B. S. (2005) "A spatial economic perspective on language acquisition: Segregation, networking, and assimilation of migrants" *Environment and Planning*, 37(10): 1877–97.

Hakuta, K., Butler, Y. G., and Witt, D. (2000) "How Long Does It Take English Learners to Attain Proficiency. Policy Reports, University of California Linguistic Minority Research Institute," UC Berkeley. http://escholarship.org/uc/item/13w7m06g (accessed March 2 2011).

Johnson J. S. and Newport, E. L. (1989) "Critical period effects in second language learning: The influence of maturational state on the acquisition of English as a second language" *Cognitive Psychology* 21(1): 60–99.

Liu, L. L., Benner, A. D., Lau, A. S., and Kim, S. Y. (2009) "Mother-adolescent language proficiency and adolescent academic and emotional adjustment among Chinese American families" *Journal of Youth Adolescence* 38(4): 572–86.

Mora, A. and Davila, M. T. (1998) "Gender, earnings, and the English skill acquisition of Hispanic workers in the United States" *Economic Inquiry* 36(4): 631–44.

Papademetriou, D. G. and Terrazas, A. (2009) "Immigrants in the United States and the current economic crisis." www.migrationinformation.org/usfocus/display.cfm?ID=723 (accessed February 21 2011).

Pendakur, K. and Pendakur, R. (2002) "Language as both human capital and ethnicity" *International Migration Review* 36(1): 147–77.

Portes, A. and Rumbaut, R. G. (2006) *Immigrant America: A Portrait*. Los Angeles, CA: University of California Press.

Remennick, L. (2004) "Language acquisition, ethnicity and social integration among former Soviet immigrants of the 1990s in Israel" *Ethnic and Racial Studies* 27(3): 431–54.

Shields, M. A. and Price, S. W. (2002) "The English language fluency and occupational success of ethnic minority immigrant men living in English and metropolitan areas" *Journal of Population Economics* 15: 137–60.

Schaafsma, J. and Sweetman, A. (2001) "Immigrant earnings: Age at immigration matters" *Canadian Journal of Economics* 34(4): 1066–99.

Schnepf, S. V. (2006) "Immigrants' educational disadvantage: An examination across ten countries and three surveys" *Journal of Population Economics* 20(3): 527–45.

Stevens, G. (1999) "Age at immigration and second language proficiency among foreign-born adults" *Language in Society* 28(4): 555–78.

——(2006) "The age-length-onset problem in research on second language acquisition among immigrants" *Language Learning* 56(4): 671–92.

Tseng, V. and Fuligni, A. J. (2000) "Parent-adolescent language use and relationships among immigrant families with East Asian, Filipino, and Latin American backgrounds" *Journal of Marriage and Family* 62(2): 465–76.

UNDP (2010) "Human development report 2010: The real wealth of nations: pathways to human development." http://hdr.undp.org/en/reports/global/hdr2010 (accessed March 18).

G. Li

Van Tubergen, F. and Kalmijn, M. (2009) "Language proficiency and usage among immigrants in the Netherlands: Incentives or opportunities?" *European Sociological Review* 25(2): 169–82.

——(2005) "Destination-language proficiency in cross-national perspective: A study of immigrant groups in nine Western countries" *American Journal of Sociology* 110(5): 1412–57.

Waldorf, B. S., Beckhusen, J., Florax, R. J. and De Graaff, T. (2010) "The role of human capital in language acquisition among immigrants in US metropolitan areas" *Regional Science Policy and Practice* 2(1): 39–49.

24

Connecting family and migration

Linda Gjokaj, Maxine Baca Zinn, and Stephanie J. Nawyn

Introduction

Migration has produced tremendous changes in the structures and functioning of families, and the dynamic experiences of family life. Families are central to decisions about when, how, and which people migrate, playing an important role in migrants' ability to navigate the receiving society, and are vital to continuing relationships across borders. In making the decision about who migrates, early theorists conceptualized households as homogeneous units wherein the interests of the collective "family" were prioritized. However, feminist migration scholars have critiqued such conceptions of households for ignoring conflicts and power differences between household members (Grasmuck and Pessar 1991; Hondagneu-Sotelo 1994). Additionally, migration creates a compression of time and place that brings into high relief the dynamics of globalization that affect all families, making migrant families an important site for both family scholars and those studying migration. In this chapter, we describe the importance of the family as a set of social relationships that shape (and are shaped by) the experiences and conditions of migration.

The relationship between family and migration has long been recognized in social science, but has only recently become an area of specialization in its own right. The expanding literature makes it clear that geographic mobility implicitly and explicitly involves families (Bailey and Boyle 2004). We identify seven clusters of family migration research, and highlight the prominent issues and debates that scholars are addressing within each area. We contend that like other social practices and relations, families are always in motion, continuously transforming and being transformed by transnational spaces. We define transnationalism as social interconnectedness that crosses national boundaries, with continuous exchanges across borders. We argue that transnationalism has been the most influential analytic lens for recent studies of migration and families, and so we have focused this chapter on transnational families to reflect that influence, although we do attend to other commonly used frameworks within the literature.

This review of issues related to migrant families focuses on research produced over the last few decades, which offers a look at families as part of transnational networks and communities. Current family migration scholars use transnationalism as their primary lens, and this literature on migrant families is largely focused on transnational ties and families within the United States. The issues we address in this chapter are occurring in family lives in different parts of the world today. However, this chapter is not a comprehensive review of what is now a vast body of research. Instead, we present selected scholarly works to illustrate how family and migration are connected. Although our framework is transnational, the chapter's emphasis is on immigrant families in US contexts.

The United States has been, and continues to be, a central destination and place of settlement for immigrants and their families. Immigrants are also more racially, ethnically, culturally, linguistically, and socio-economically diverse than in previous periods of US immigration (Lee and Bean 2010), making the United States an important site for examining how family patterns are transformed through migration. With this focus we do not intend to foster Western bias in understandings of families. While much of the central scholarship in migration and family has developed in the United States, scholars in other nations are also studying family/migration connections. For example, freedom of movement principles in the European Union make family migration a critical topic in European migration research (Bailey and Boyle 2004). The flourishing body of international scholarship is especially important for our understanding of how different political, economic, and demographic contexts shape migrant families.

Family and migration processes

This section highlights how immigration is largely a family-based process. Family members make decisions, albeit unevenly, about who, why, and how people migrate and settle within the context of the broader political and economic conditions in the country of origin and destination (Hondagneu-Sotelo 1994). We explain how the family is an important social unit that shapes migration decisions and trajectories by looking specifically at transnational employment and state policies. Next we consider the intersection in the literature on work and migration, looking at how migration processes tightly link work and family issues through ongoing transformations in the global economy that often demands migration and family changes.

Transnational employment

Major transformations in the global economy and its international division of labor produce transnational migration to pursue employment. One of the most important features of global capital's search for cheap labor is the recruitment of women from less developed countries. This has many consequences for family roles, family dynamics, and even the distinctive shapes that families manifest in different social locations. Women who have not been in the labor force before will enter wage work, often transforming gender relations and giving them greater power within families. In other cases, family boundaries expand as the demand for immigrant women's work increases and women must leave their families and children in order to provide for them. The strong effects of transnational labor on family life have become increasingly evident as more family members seek employment across national boundaries. Around the world, families are becoming more dispersed. Families are transnationally located, spread out over several countries and continents.

The past two decades have seen a proliferation of research and scholarship on how gendered and racialized labor demands affect women and their families. This literature illustrates striking interconnections between families in a global stratification system. Family arrangements of particular categories of people in one society are intricately linked with family arrangements of particular categories of people in other societies. In the United States, for example, the labor of immigrant women meets demands for domestic work, emotion work, and carework in households, businesses, and other institutional settings. Women's labor migration from poor countries to rich ones enables women in privileged families to have private lives and careers, while immigrant women serve those families by working worlds away from their own families (Hondagneu-Sotelo 2001; Parreñas 2001; Ehrenreich and Hochschild 2003; Karraker 2007), producing what some scholars have referred to as a "care drain" in which the children of transnational mothers are left without adequate care (Ehrenreich and Hochschild 2003).

Few macrostructural discussions of transnational labor flows put family at the center of analysis. Here, Kibria's (2011) analysis of the globalization–family nexus is instructive. The family, she explains, is typically seen as a recipient of globalization, a sphere that is "acted on" by globalizing forces with little concern for how globalization itself may be shaped by the family. Globalization shapes the family and the family is a critical *mediating structure* of globalization. Although the work/family field has not treated migration itself as a family strategy for families in the developing world, survival strategies may likely include the international labor migration of one or more members to the more prosperous segments of the world (Kibria 2011: 243–45). As Dreby (2010: 211) observes in her study of Mexican migrant families, "Mexican parents' migration is ultimately an effort to reconcile the demands of work and family in a global economy." Migration is not simply a global economic matter; it is a work/family matter as well for both skilled and unskilled labor migrants. Although ongoing trends toward the feminization of migration account for the current focus on race, class, and gender disadvantages in labor migration, skilled migrants and their family strategies should also be recognized (Raghuram 2004). The formation of families and their opportunities for movement across borders are also shaped and restricted by the power of the state to control who emigrates (and for how long they can stay) by narrowly defining family in law.

State policies

State policies, both in the sending and receiving countries, shape family migration flows through regulating and influencing labor migration. Sending countries have a vested interest in maintaining expatriate loyalties for political and financial reasons, and while sending states welcome the remittances that citizens laboring overseas send, they also seek to minimize the costs to families that come with having family members divided by nation-state boundaries. For example, the Philippines requires potential women labor migrants to complete a training program instructing them on how to be better transnational mothers if they have children, and as stressing the importance of not marrying or becoming pregnant overseas in order to maintain their familial ties with the sending country (Rodriguez 2010).

Receiving countries also have an interest in dissuading migrants from putting down roots, enacting policies that discourage the formation of familial ties within the receiving country. Such policies have been common in the United States and Europe with regards to temporary workers, barring workers from bringing family members with them. States assume that denying access to family members will prohibit the formation of permanent ties with the receiving society, and ensure that temporary workers will return to their home country at the end of their contracted work period. However, research on the effects of temporary or "guest" worker programs on return migration and settlement patterns show uniformly that such policies do not deter permanent settlement, and in fact often facilitate the migration of temporary workers' family members to the receiving country (Castles 1986). Once migrant families establish ties in the receiving country, increases in immigration law enforcement frequently leads to extreme family hardship in mixed-status families, as unauthorized family members are deported, sometimes leaving behind citizen dependent children (Menjivar and Abrego 2009).

There is also the issue of state policies that define what constitutes "family," limiting how familial relationships can be mobilized for migration through authorized means. Receiving countries generally allow relatively narrow definitions of family, systematically excluding kin ties outside of heterosexual, nuclear families from reunification opportunities (Luibhéid 2005). Family members falling outside the definition of "nuclear" (including non-dependent adult children) are also excluded from receiving refugee status with other family members and must instead file their own petition. This latter category is particularly problematic, as it leads to dividing family members with highly interdependent relationships across vast distances in different resettlement countries, the ramifications of which are under-explored in migration research. The literature on transnational employment and state policies reveals how migration is entangled with family matters. In the next section we examine the links in the context of assimilation processes.

Family and immigrant assimilation

The theoretical orientation of US migration scholarship during the 1920s to the early 1960s centered on the classic, or linear, assimilation model. This model predicted that immigrants and their offspring would eventually move up in the socio-economic ladder by integrating into mainstream society and adopting a modern family structure, particularly of white, Protestant, middle-class families (Kibria 1993: 16). However, significant developments occurred in our scholarly understandings of immigrant families since the dominance of classical assimilation model. Migrant families are viewed more as places of "conflict and negotiation" (Foner 2005), with race, nativity, gender, and class as significant structural and interactional features within the ongoing research on assimilation and immigrant families.

Race

Given the preoccupation with assimilation in migration studies, it is not surprising that the subject of intermarriage occupies a prominent place in the field.[1] Restrictions and laws about marriage and family are vital in maintaining racial boundaries. Social scientists view marriage between people of different racial and ethnic groups as the litmus test for assimilation (Lee and Bean 2010). Although the field in general shares this view on race, intermarriage, and assimilation, their interconnections remain controversial and raise many unanswered questions about changes in the color line. For example, do rising patterns of intermarriage among Asians and Latinos alter their place in the US racial hierarchy? If so, do Asians and Hispanics fall on the black side or the white side of the color line? A study by Lee and Bean (2010) addressing immigration and the color line in America uses intermarriage as a main indicator of changing racial boundaries. Their study offers evidence that the color line in an increasingly diverse American society is no longer between whites and non-whites, but rather between blacks and all others, as Latinos and Asians are accepted into the dominant social group.

Matters of racial and ethnic identity occupy growing importance in migration studies, and families are significant in how immigrants and their descendants view themselves racially. Ongoing research reveals that racial and ethnic identities are imposed, chosen, and rejected in families. Vasquez (2011) for example, describes the family as "the cornerstone of racial identity." Her recent study of three generations of Mexican American families finds two patterns of racial identity formation in families. In "thinned attachment" families, commitment to and familiarity with Mexican heritage wanes over time. In contrast, families exhibiting "cultural maintenance" continue Mexican cultural practices through three generations (Vasquez 2011).

Negative stereotypes of immigrant families have long been part of scholarly and popular thought. In early social science, immigrant families and mythical "standard families" were viewed as opposites. Immigrant families were thought to be products of racial and ethnic traditions alone. Not only were they out of step with the demands of modern society; they were implicated in turn-of-the century urban problems. New historical studies offer a different picture of immigrant family life. The social problems model of immigrant families has been replaced with a broad understanding of families as products of their cultures *and* the communities in which they settled, and as vital resources for recruitment, labor placement, and settlement of migrants. Some research (Zhou and Bankston III 1998) has exposed the stereotype in the United States that particular immigrant groups have superior cultural values to Americans, especially native-born minorities. This positive stereotype coexists with popular images of immigrant families as socially deficient, and a source of social disorganization. Receiving nations often use racialized family images to define national boundaries. In the United States, opposition to Latino immigration often calls on stereotypes of Latinos as breeders draining public resources (Hondagneu-Sotelo 1995).

A large body of literature emphasizes that various family patterns of immigrants are not passively handed down from generation to generation. Instead, immigrants selectively choose and actively use varied cultural resources. Within particular social contexts and constraints, they create new family traditions. This perspective draws attention to immigrant families as sites of resistance against racial domination (Baca Zinn 2010: 375). Scholars apply the term "family strategies" to the behaviors family members use in responding to social barriers. In addition to maintaining cultural identity, the literature highlights strategies such as migration itself, and adapting family, kinship, and household configurations as circumstances require. For example, Glenn (1983) underscores the flexibility of Chinese Americans in devising a range of different family types corresponding to prevailing historical conditions, testifying to the resilience and resourcefulness of Chinese American families in overcoming obstacles. Family strategies are complicated because families are not unitary settings. Struggles for cultural resistance may also generate family conflict. As Kibria (1993) discovered for Vietnamese immigrants, using family traditions to build cultural autonomy also produce struggles between women and men. As we illustrate in the next section, migration is a gendered process wherein power relations between men, women, and children play out in households and families.

Gender and immigrant families

A burgeoning literature within migration investigates how gender shapes (and is shaped by) decisions to migrate, who migrates and why, household and family relations, social networks, social policies, and global and local labor systems (Hondagneu-Sotelo 1994, 2001; George 2005). This body of scholarship reveals how gender, a central organizing component of social relations, is reinvented, transformed, and also reaffirmed throughout migration and settlement processes, inevitably (re)configuring family dynamics and (re)fashioning familial experiences in new ways.

Feminist migration scholars have been at the forefront of contesting uniform notions and images of families (Hondagneu-Sotelo 1994; Baca Zinn et al. 2010). This scholarship departs from conventional interpretations of households and "the family" as a moral economic unit wherein members are motivated to migrate solely for economic gain and make rational, collective decisions about migration, settlement, and possibly return migration. This work has not only challenged static, uniform notions of families, but also the idea that women in migration are dependents who merely follow men (Hirsch 2003; George 2005).

Feminist migration scholars unraveled how men, women, and families experience and work out the tensions arising from shifting gender relations and challenges to patriarchy through and after migration, especially when immigrant women enter the labor market (Hirsch 2003;

George 2005; Parreñas 2005). One key finding emerging from this research is that through migration, men's patriarchal power diminishes and women experience increased decision-making authority and economic power in their household and spousal relations, albeit unevenly and sometimes in contradictory ways (Kibria 1990; Hondagneu-Sotelo 1994; Toro-Morn 1995). Darvishpour's (2002) study of Iranian immigrants in Sweden shows that changes to gender relations after migration wherein women experience more power in their households and families has led some immigrant women to initiate divorce, which would have been extremely difficult in Iran.

Other scholars found similar shifts in gender relations and family dynamics by paying attention to both the challenge *and* reaffirmation of gender and patriarchy in relation to other systems of difference such as class, ethnicity, and culture. Kibria's (1990) research with Vietnamese families in the United States shows that while migration increases women's status, power, and authority, patriarchal family structures and gender relations of inequality are reconstituted through the influence and internalization of Confucian-based ideologies. Instead of significantly challenging unequal gender relations within the family through their increased status and men's decreased socio-economic status and privilege, women drew from female-based social networks and groups to cope with male privilege because maintaining patriarchal family relations offered women greater control over their children and more economic security.

Some research has examined how men cope with challenges to their masculinity and shifting power relations, particularly how they develop strategies for reproducing unequal gender relations because of, and after migration. George's (2005) research on female Kerali nurses who migrated before their husbands illustrates how the status men had in Kerala, as heads of household and breadwinners, diminish in the host-society context. However, "nurse-husbands" re-establish traditional gender roles through the male-controlled church environment. Through church, men create new roles for themselves that are considered the traditional responsibilities of women, such as cooking, serving food and caroling (129–30). Toro-Morn's (1995) study also illustrates the "durability of patriarchy" (George 2005: 20). She finds that Puerto Rican middle- and working-class women in Chicago, who migrated with a different set of motivations and hold somewhat distinctive views of their family and work obligations, still had to "confront the duality of being responsible for the reproductive work that takes place at the home and the productive work outside the home" (713).

This research has not only yielded important insights about gender relations, but also about the ongoing complexities and realities of family lives within a global context. Next we continue to look at how family strategies, power dynamics, struggles for cultural resistance and family conflicts are manifested in immigrant families and households by looking at the relationship between immigrant parents and their children.

Parenting and intergenerational relations

Migration scholars have become increasingly interested in investigating the challenges migration brings to parenting practices and intergenerational relationships, especially how migration experiences influence the children of immigrants over time. In many families, intergenerational relationships are a significant arena of tension and conflict, but also are ties that bind, support, and inspire positive trajectories. Global, transnational, and local conditions frame these relationships and interactions wherein space, time, and transnational extended family networks enter into parent/caregiver–child relations in novel ways, affecting not only intimate household relations and survival strategies, but also how families, particularly children, fare in school and the labor force.

Segmented assimilation, adaptation, acculturation, and/or transnationalism are some of the more common frameworks used to understand intergenerational relations and their implications on families, parents, and children (Zhou and Bankston 1998; Portes and Rumbaut 2001). From the segmented assimilation perspective, researchers focus on how the children of immigrants fare in terms of their socio-economic mobility patterns (Portes and Rumbaut 2001). Parental control, family, and ethnic community resources, in addition to race, nativity, and host-country reception, affect how generations confront the socio-economic challenges they face in cross-cultural contexts, with the second generation following divergent, contradictory paths of "assimilating" to various segments of US society (Portes and Rumbaut 2001). Researchers found that parents draw upon ethnic community resources in order to reinforce cultural strategies of their parenting and discipline in ways that shape positive educational and economic trajectories of the immigrant offspring growing up in the United States (Zhou and Bankston 1998).

Several researchers examine the conflicts arising from the tensions between maintaining immigrant parents' culture, the socialization and assimilative processes, and pressures children experience as they grow up in host-society contexts (Zhou and Bankston 1998; Espiritu 2001; Portes and Rumbaut 2001; Karraker 2007). In this popular line of research, for instance, scholars investigate how immigrant parents exert more pressure on their daughters than sons to exemplify conventional ideals of behavior in part because they worry their daughters will adopt the sexual mores of American culture. Espiritu's (2001) research best exemplifies this tension in the context of race, culture, and assimilation. Her research shows that Filipina immigrant mothers resist assimilation to US society by controlling and exercising power over their daughters so they do not grow up like white "American" girls. The differential pace of assimilation between parents, children, and the larger ethnic community stir up other sources of tension and conflict between immigrant parents and their children in which immigrant families and communities confront issues of courtship, marital choices, parental discipline and obligation, and the educational and economic futures of generations in distinctive ways (Zhou and Bankston 1998; Kibria 1993).

More recent research on intergenerational relations reveals the influences of current transnational forces separating children and their parents. The literature shows how migration makes it both possible and difficult to fulfill parental obligations over time and across national borders. The global economy and the international division of labor are not the only factors shaping these emerging transnational relationships. Menjívar and Abrego (2009: 163) refer to migrant parents in transnational situations as making a "generational sacrifice."

Menjívar and Abrego's (2009) research reveals how legal instability, economic uncertainty, separation and reunification, and "mixed-status families" are some of the significant emerging issues in contemporary families, particularly how they work to (re)shape inter- and multi-generational relationships. For example, immigrant parents who leave their children behind send remittances as one way to fulfill their parental obligations across borders. With lengthy separations and economic instability in the receiving society, however, it becomes difficult for parents to continue to send financial and material resources. Children often report resentment towards their transnational parents, particularly mothers, and express feelings of abandonment (Parreñas 2005; Menjívar and Abrego 2009; Dreby 2010), sometimes refusing to call their parents "mom" or "dad," withholding emotion from parents, or refusing to defer to parental authority (Dreby 2010).

Despite children's often negative reaction to transnational parenting (and transnational mothering in particular), Hondagneu-Sotelo and Avila (1997) found that transnational Latina mothers came to define the economic support that they provided through remittances as "good mothering," and developed creative ways of caring for their children across national borders.

Still, migrant fathers and mothers report painful emotions resulting from contact with their non-migrant children, who often express wanting to join their parent (Schmalzbauer 2004). Migrant parents, and especially mothers, express concern about how their children will be cared for during their absence. Migrant fathers often leave their children with their wife or female partner, but migrant mothers more often leave their children in the care of "other-mothers" (Schmalzbauer 2004: 1323) such as their own mother, their mother-in-law, sisters, or even daughters.

Parents more commonly migrate without their children than the reverse. Yet, there are parents who send their children overseas without accompanying them. These "parachute children" come from wealthy families who seek legal avenues for the entire family to migrate (Orellana Faulstich *et al.* 2001). This dynamic reverses the more typical power dynamics in families by giving children a valuable resource that their parents cannot directly access.

Current migration and intergenerational family research focuses on relations between parents and children. Studies on grandparents and grandchildren are needed to better understand how generational relations and migration are linked.

Migration, family changes, and intimate relationships

Because migration is a significant life event and process for both migrant and non-migrant family members, it is not surprising that immigration and settlement experiences activate major family changes that shape paths to family formations and intimate relationships and create stress for individuals. This section highlights how changes to some of the intimate arenas of family life are intensified through migration and settlement in cross-cultural contexts. Tension, agency, resistance, resilience, and choice characterize these experiences and interactions.

Marriage

Research on marriage among immigrants often concerns intermarriage between immigrants and those of other racial and ethnic groups. As discussed earlier, intermarriage is a defining feature of assimilation and a much-studied topic in migration studies. Moderate levels of intermarriage with non-Hispanic whites among many immigrant groups are well documented, as are differential patterns across groups. Research finds generational differences in the intermarriage rates of all immigrant groups. It also finds new patterns of decreased intermarriage among Hispanics, which are explained in terms of immigrant replacement. Questions about marriage rates and their meaning are likely to expand in the coming period. Definitions of marriage are also shifting in the United States and many other societies, making other routes to family formation, such as non-marital cohabitation, acceptable.

Marriage and the desire to form families have long been an important part of global migration, with increasing numbers of marriages in which the spouses are of different nationalities. Marriage migration is strongly gendered. When arranged by broker agencies, unions reflect economic disparities between wives and husbands. The world-wide phenomenon of trans-national marriage is also grounded in global interconnections (including war) and international migration patterns (Karraker 2007: 56–9).

In the past three decades, marriage of resident aliens to US citizens has been a primary path for migration to the United States. This reveals the preference for married couples in US immigration policies, which have family reunification as a primary goal. In recent years, more legal immigrants entered the United States through marriage than any other means. Hidalgo and Bankston (2008: 167–8) point out that migration through marriage poses an interesting reversal in the standard sequence of events. Here, marriage occurs before migration and most of the process of fitting into the new homeland takes place *after* marriage, in other words, the last stage of assimilation is one of the first!

Migration and marriage are momentous life events with unique parallels, often taking place in close relation to one another. In both marriage and migration, individuals make a commitment to a new object, a new environment, a new atmosphere, and a new world (Youakim 2004: 155). The study of marriage among immigrants, like the study of marriage in general, reveals wide-ranging relationships patterned by locality, law, religion, gender expectations, kinship networks, and work opportunities for men and women. Additional processes within the political economy of migration itself shape marriage among immigrants. This context heightens conflict and the need for negotiation in such critical areas as the division of household labor, the spending of money and the adaptation of household and kin relations across national borders.

Migration is widely assumed to contribute to union instability and dissolution. Divided households, gendered migrations, and extensive time away from home loosen the norms and social controls that provide cohesion. These conditions contribute to union dissolution (Frank and Wildsmith 2005). Other research, however, finds that migration has positive as well as negative effects on marital relations. For example, in a study of Ethiopian immigrants in Toronto (Hyman *et al.* 2008), couples reported increased marital conflict and communication problems. But on the positive side, they also reported increased mutual dependence and autonomy, improved intimacy, and more decision-making.

Exactly why migration brings some unions to the breaking point while other unions endure family division and separation requires further study. Attention to marital ideals is important in this regard. Hirsch's (2003) study of Mexican migration finds a striking shift in the basis for marriage—from marriages rooted in obligation and respect to marriages based on companionship and intimacy. In both sending and receiving communities, changes in what spouses *expect* from marital relationships strongly affect the immigrant family experience (Hirsch 2003), as do transformations in and challenges to sexual identities, sexual behaviors, and courtship and mate selection practices in country of origin and reception.

Sexualities and intimacies

Sexuality and intimate relations as arenas of popular and scholarly investigation are often relegated to the "internal" sphere of families and relationships. However, this budding area of migration research illuminates the way sexual power relations intertwine with the public and global features of social life to shape migration decision-making, family structures, intergenerational relations, settlement experiences, and construction of communities, households, and families across national borders (Espiritu 2001; Hirsch 2003; Gonzalez-Lopez 2005; Acosta 2008; Cantú 2009). The view that sexuality is a "dimension of power" (Cantú 2009: 75) diversifies our understandings of families in migration and global contexts.

While the gender and immigrant family literature challenges the uniform notions of families as they relate to masculinity and femininity, the sexualities literature exposes how familial relations are permeated by notions of heteronormativity in ways that intersect with gender relations. For example, Cantú's (2009) pioneering work shows how traditional heteronormative family relations, gay and queer social networks and support systems, and economic uncertainty work together to influence migration decisions, job acquisition, and the settlement experiences of Mexican men who have sex with men. These factors also intersect to form households and families based on sexual orientation, which Cantú refers to as "safe houses" and a "landing pad" in the receiving context, away from the heterosexual constraints of their family household in Mexico (Cantú 2009: 135).

Research shows that through migration, gay immigrant men and lesbian women create new family structures and household arrangements in creative response to strained biological family relations, discrimination based on sexual orientation in the country of origin, and the desire for sexually liberal spaces (Acosta 2008; Cantú 2009). In both scholarly and popular circles, the notion that sexual orientation is one motivation for migration and reason for building new families and communities of support in the receiving context are rarely examined and understood in immigration research.

Scholars have focused on how sexuality is regulated through family and ethnic community power relationships (Espiritu 2001; Gonzalez-Lopez 2005). One line of research highlights parental control of female (hetero)sexuality in the context of "family honor" where mothers typically hold primary responsibility for being the "mediator of sexual morality" within their families (Gonzalez-Lopez 2005: 241). This research shows how sexuality is used as a source of familial control in ways that dictate not only who moves across national borders and settles in new places and spaces, but also the experiences and expressions of sexuality, sexual identities, and intimate relations across borders and generations.

Conclusion

Families are vital to our understanding of migration, settlement, and transnationalism. We have used a broad array of research to show how family, household, and kinship patterns have far-reaching relevance for migration and how migration is studied. The seven arenas of family immigration research we have identified illuminate how family patterns are transformed through immigration. The chapter summarizes the major concepts and issues from within these key arenas of immigrant families that help us better understand migration experiences as well as families more generally.

A central idea is that families are continuously changing and being altered by transnational forces of which migration is a key component. Using research produced over the last few decades, we have described the intricate connections between migratory processes and family life. We have explored such transnational forces shaping and stretching families across national borders. These forces capture how one of the major challenges to migrant family life is the separation of close family members when one or more members migrate while others stay behind. For instance, we have explored how transnational families form based on the necessity (often economic) for one or more family members to migrate, and have identified the ways in which social policies separate families based on narrow definitions of families in law. Work has always been a key factor in producing varied kinship, household, and domestic arrangements, and the family migration literature clearly demonstrates how labor profoundly influences family life. Most notably, labor relegates families to different social locations with varied opportunities to meet family requirements in sending and receiving societies, profoundly shaping spousal and intimate relations, as well as intergenerational relationships. The literature also reveals that families and households are not unitary settings.

Connecting families, as well as households, with migration brings into sharp view the dynamic relationship between the intimate aspects of families and other social institutions, structures, and processes in profound ways. The literature reveals that through migration and settlement, families and households are central sites through which power relations are played out, and racial, ethnic, and gendered social structures and identities are (re)fashioned, demanding more research and raising new questions about gender relations, marriage, courtship, sexuality, and the shifting US color line. Migration, in short, cannot be viewed as disconnected from family processes.

Note

1 Refer to Chapter 25 in this volume for an in-depth discussion of the trends and debates in the study of migration and intermarriage.

References and further reading

Acosta, K. L. (2008) "Lesbianas in the borderlands: Shifting identities and imagined communities" *Gender and Society* 22: 639–59.

Baca Zinn, M. (2010) "The family as a race institution." In P. H. Collins and J. Solomos (eds), *The Sage Handbook of Race and Ethnic Studies*. Thousand Oaks, CA: Sage, pp. 357–82.

Bailey, A. and Boyle, P. (2004) "Untying and retying family migration in the new Europe" *Journal of Ethnic and Migration Studies* 30(2): 229–41.

Cantú Jr, L. (ed.) (2009) *The Sexuality of Migration: Border Crossings and Mexican Immigrant Men*. New York: New York University Press.

Castles, S. (1986) "The guest worker in Western Europe—an obituary" *International Migration Review* 20(4): 761–78.

Darvishpour, M. (2002) "Immigrant women challenge the role of men: How the changing power relationship within Iranian families in Sweden intensifies family conflicts after migration" *Journal of Comparative Family Studies* 33(2):, 271–96.

Dreby, J. (2010) *Divided by Borders: Mexican Migrants and their Children*. Berkeley, CA: University of California Press.

Ehrenreich, B. and Hochschild, A. R. (2003) *Global Woman: Nannies, Maids, and Sex Workers in the New Economy*. New York: Metropolitan Books.

Espiritu, Y. L. (2001) "'We don't sleep around like white girls do': Family, culture, and gender in Filipina American lives" *Journal of Women in Culture and Society* 26(2): 415–42.

Foner, N. (2005) "The immigrant family: Cultural legacies and cultural changes." In C. Suarez-Orozco, M. Suarez-Orozco, and B. Qin-Hilliard (eds), *The New Immigration: An Interdisciplinary Reader*. New York, Routledge, pp. 157–66.

Frank, R. and Wildsmith, E. (2005) "The grass widows of Mexico: Migration and union dissolution in a binational context" *Social Forces* 83(3): 919–48.

George, S. M. (2005) *When Women Come First: Gender and Class in Transnational Migration*. Berkeley, CA, University of California Press.

Glenn, E. N. (1983) "Split household, small producer, and dual wage earners: An analysis of Chinese American strategies" *Journal of Marriage and the Family* 45(1): 35–46.

Gonzalez-Lopez, G. (2005) *Erotic Journeys: Mexican Immigrants and their Sex Lives*. Berkeley, CA: University of California Press.

Grasmuck, S. and Pessar, P. R. (1991) *Between Two Islands: Dominican International Migration*, Berkeley, CA: University of California Press.

Hidalgo, D. A. and Bankston III, C. L. (2008) "Military bride and refugees: Vietnamese American wives and shifting links to the military, 1980–2000" *International Migration Review* 46(2): 167–88.

Hirsch, J. S. (2003) *A Courtship after Marriage: Sexuality and Love in the Mexican Transnational Families*. Berkeley, CA: University of California Press.

Hondagneu-Sotelo, P. (1994) *Gendered Transitions: Mexican Experiences of Immigration*. Berkeley, CA: University of California Press.

——(1995) "Women and children first: New directions in anti immigrant policies" *Socialist Review* 25: 169–90.

——(2001) *Domestica: Immigrant Workers Cleaning and Caring in the Shadows of Affluence*. Berkeley, CA: University of California Press.

Hondagneu-Sotelo, P. and Avila, E. (1997) "'I'm here, but I'm there': The meanings of Latina transnational motherhood" *Gender and Society* 11(5): 548–71.

Hyman, I., Gruge, S., and Mason, R. (2008) "The impact of migration on marital relationships: A study of Ethiopian immigrants in Toronto" *Journal of Comparative Family Studies* 39(2): 149–63.

Karraker, M. W. (ed.) (2007) *Global Families*. Boston, MA: Allyn and Bacon.

Kibria, N. (1990) "Power, patriarchy and gender conflict in the Vietnamese immigrant community" *Gender and Society* 4(1): 9–24.

——(1993) *Family Tightrope: The Changing Lives of Vietnamese Americans*. Princeton, NJ: Princeton University Press.

——(2011) "The globalization-family nexus: Families as mediating structures of globalization." In A. I. Garey and K. V. Hansen (eds), *At the Heart of Work and Family: Engaging the Ideas of Arlie Hochschild*. New Brunswick, NJ: Rutgers University Press, pp. 243–49.

Lee, J. and Bean, F. D. (2010) *The Diversity Paradox: Immigration and the Color Line in Twenty-first Century America*. New York: Russell Sage Foundation.

Luibhéid, E. (2005) "Introduction: Queering migration and citizenship." In E. Luibhéid and J. R. L. Cantu (eds), *Queer Migrations: Sexuality, US Citizenship, and Border Crossings*. Minneapolis, MN: University of Minnesota Press, pp. ix–xlvi.

Menjivar, C. and Abrego, L. (2009) "Parents and children across borders: Legal instability and inter-generational relations in Guatemalan and Salvadoran Families." In N. Foner (ed.), *Across Generations: Immigrant Families in America*. New York: New York University Press, pp. 160–89.

Orellana Faulstich, M., Thorne, B., Chee, A., and Lam, W. S. E. (2001) "Transnational childhoods: The participation of children in processes of family migration" *Social Problems* 48(4): 572–91.

Parreñas, R. S. (2001) *Servants of Globalization*. Stanford, CA: Stanford University Press.

——(2005) *Children of Global Migration: Transnational Families and Gendered Woes*. Stanford, CA: Stanford University Press.

Portes, A. and Rumbaut, R. G. (2001) *Legacies: The Story of the Immigrant Second Generation*, Los Angeles, CA: University of California Press and Russell Sage Foundation.

Pyke, K. (2007) "Immigrant Families in the US." In J. Scott, J. Treas, and M. Richards (eds), *The Blackwell Companion to the Sociology of Families*. Malden, MA: Blackwell Publishing, pp. 253–85.

Raghuram, P. (2004) "The difference that skills make: Gender, family, migration strategies and regulated labour markets" *Journal of Ethnic and Migration Studies* 30(2): 303–21.

Rodriguez, R. M. (2010) *Migrants for Export: How the Philippine State Brokers Labor to the World*. Minneapolis, MN: University of Minnesota Press.

Schmalzbauer, L. (2004) "Searching for wages and mothering from afar: The case of Honduran transnational families" *Journal of Marriage and the Family* 66(5): 1317–31.

Toro-Morn, M. I. (1995) "Gender, class, family and migration: Puerto Rican women in Chicago" *Gender and Society* 9(6): 712–26.

Vasquez, J. M. (2011) *Mexican Americans across Generations: Immigrant Families, Racial Realities*. New York: New York University Press.

Youakim, J. (2004) "Marriage in the context of immigration" *American Journal of Psychoanalysis* 64(2): 155–65.

Zhou, M. and Bankston, III, C. L. (1998) *Growing up American: How Vietnamese Children Adapt to Life in the United States*. New York: Russell Sage Foundation.

25

Immigrant intermarriage

Charlie V. Morgan

Introduction

Immigrants from Latin America and Asia since the 1960s have forced us to reconceptualize how we study race relations in the United States. The same is true for intermarriage. Interracial marriages have increased from 150,000 marriages in 1960 to 3.1 million in 2000, accounting for 6.2 percent of all marriages compared to less than 1 percent in 1960. In 2008, the percentage had further increased to 7.6 percent, representing one in every 13 marriages (Lee and Bean 2010). Moreover, intermarriage has always been the litmus test for the social distance between people from different racial and ethnic groups, assimilation of the various groups into US society, the color line, and panethnicity. While there are still important lessons to be learned from black–white intermarriages in the United States, immigrants from Latin America and Asia are changing the way we measure, conceptualize, theorize, and research intermarriage. Moreover, these intermarriages inform public policy decisions in profound ways. This chapter focuses on the ever-expanding role of "immigrant intermarriage," which, broadly defined, includes any marriage in which an immigrant, or his or her child, marries someone from a different racial *or* ethnic group in the United States.

I first look at the major theoretical contributions that scholars have provided for understanding immigrant intermarriages: assimilation, social distance, color line, and panethnicity. Second, I examine the methodological considerations of studying these intermarriages, specifically the range of datasets as well as the different analytical techniques used. Third, I will highlight the key empirical findings of the most recent studies. Finally, I talk about future developments and directions in studies on immigrant intermarriage.

This chapter highlights four general themes: first, a move from dichotomous and linear concepts to multicategorical and multidimensional concepts, which depict richer and more realistic models of interrelationships; second, the need for datasets that include smaller subgroups and provide more detail about immigration and marital history; third, innovation in multivariate models and mixed methods; and fourth, the importance of understanding not only the changing nature of intergroup relations across time and generations, but also the intersection of these changes with social class, gender, and religion.

Theoretical notes on immigrant intermarriage

Assimilation

In 1964, Milton Gordon wrote *Assimilation in American Life*, his seminal book on the various types of assimilation. Despite its publication over four decades ago, it remains the standard reference on intermarriage and its role in assimilation. Gordon focused on social structure and group life as a way to understand how ethnic groups assimilate in the United States. Gordon traced the concept of assimilation from its earliest days and proposed a comprehensive way to think about the various subtypes of assimilation and how these subtypes interact, both empirically and theoretically. Gordon also divided the assimilation process into seven types: cultural, structural, marital, identificational, attitude receptional, behavior receptional, and civic assimilation. This chapter focuses particularly on his third step, marital assimilation.

Gordon's assimilation model has often been referred to as a straight-line model, even though he never used this terminology nor stated it as such. He conceptualized the assimilation process as an ideal type, which is made clear by the fact that he continually emphasizes that for immigrants, structural assimilation has typically not fully taken place. Therefore, even if we assume that he was advocating a "straight-line" assimilation model, it is clear that he does not believe that this model represents the reality of the United States experience regarding racial, religious, or national origin groups. Regardless of our interpretation, many scholars view Gordon's ideal type as a straight-line assimilation model. Indeed, it appears that immigrants and their children are assimilating into a white mainstream (Qian and Lichter 2007: Fu and Hatfield 2008; Gonsoulin and Fu 2010). For example, a recent study focusing on native-born Asian Americans and their marital patterns found that Asian Americans (for the most part) are highly acculturated and structurally assimilated (Min and Kim 2009).

There are many scholars, however, who are critical of the straight-line approach to assimilation. Among immigration scholars, a segmented approach to assimilation has gained traction in the literature. This discussion has also made its way into the immigrant intermarriage literature. The segmented approach claims that there are three paths to assimilation: one into a white mainstream (measured by how many immigrants and their children intermarry with white people), another into the ethnic community (also seen as an upwardly mobile path achieved through marrying co-ethnics within the ethnic enclave), and finally a downward path measured by the outmarriage to non-white minority groups (Yancey 2003; Fu and Hatfield 2008; Song 2009; Gonsoulin and Fu 2010). A number of intermarriage researchers have therefore used marital assimilation of immigrants as a test of segmented assimilation.

The first hint of segmented marital assimilation was seen in the form of "a retreat from intermarriage" (Qian and Lichter 2007: Lichter *et al.* 2011). As a result of changes in racial classification (2000 Census), the continued influx of immigration, a rise in cohabitation rates, and the effect of education composition on intermarriage, the last decade of the twentieth century (1990–2000) displayed decreases in immigrant intermarriage with white people and increases in marriage between native-born and foreign-born co-ethnics (Qian and Lichter 2007). A follow-up study found that intermarriage among Latinos and white people declined for the first time in the 1990s. Second-generation Latinos are more likely to marry first-generation Latinos than to marry third-generation Latinos or white people, whereas the third generation is more likely to marry other third-generation Latinos or white people. This could indicate a retreat from intermarriage among the second-generation Latinos, or at least a slowing of the pace of assimilation (Lichter *et al.* 2011).

A couple of articles directly test straight-line marital assimilation against segmented marital assimilation (Fu and Hatfield 2008; Gonsoulin and Fu 2010). Fu and Hatfield (2008) found evidence to support at least three different paths of assimilation: (1) into a white mainstream, (2) into panethnic groups by marrying other Asian ethnics, and (3) into an ethnic enclave through marrying co-ethnics (but still a path of assimilation, given that they are structurally assimilating). They did not find evidence to support downward assimilation into an underclass. Gonsoulin and Fu (2010) found more evidence to support a segmented assimilation model than a straight-line assimilation model (2010: 274).

Whether there are segmented marital assimilation paths and to what degree they are segmented are empirical questions that are unsettled and vary depending upon the dataset and analytical techniques used (a topic discussed below). There are even those who call into question the assumed link between intermarriage and assimilation, claiming that this assumed connection is much more tenuous and complex than is currently recognized by scholars, and that it needs to be critically reassessed (Song 2009).

Social distance

Building on Weber's concept of status group closure, intermarriage offers an important look at how open or closed groups are, based on how willing they are to form intimate and long-term relationships with people from outside their group (Kalmijn 1998): "Increasingly permeable and blurred social boundaries—and intermarriage with whites—is clearly a key dimension of the contemporary assimilation process in America" (Qian and Lichter 2007: 89). For example, 55 percent of native-born Asian Americans are outmarrying with non-ethnic partners, which points to a high level of acculturation and a weakening of the boundary and social distance between Asian Americans and white people (Min and Kim 2009).

Social distances between racial groups in the United States are shrinking, but still persist, indicating that a racial hierarchy remains in our society (Yancey 2003; Qian and Lichter 2007; Min and Kim 2009; Lichter *et al.* 2011). There is also a need to distinguish social distances between races, between ethnic groups within the same racial category, and within generations from the same ethnic group. Marital patterns speak to the social distances between not only white people, but between the various Asian ethnic groups. Furthermore, social distances indicate the degree to which pan-Asian or panethnic formation is happening among Asian American groups (Min and Kim 2009). Even when we do see declines in intermarriage between second-generation Latinos and third-plus generation Latinos, there is little evidence to suggest that cultural preferences (in the form of social distances) are driving these marital patterns; rather, it appears that changing marriage markets and other such structural factors explain these gaps (Lichter *et al.* 2011).

Most of the studies indirectly address social distance *vis-à-vis* intermarriage patterns. Yancey (2003) is one of the few scholars that directly links social distance and intermarriage. He uses attitudinal data from a variety of racial groups (European Americans, African Americans, Latino Americans, and Asian Americans) to measure social distances. This data is then extrapolated to show how the author believes that we are moving from a black–white color line to a black–non-black color line.

Color line

America has a long history of representing a black–white color line in a number of social, economic, and political arenas. Given that race is socially constructed, scholars are interested in how this color line will shift, especially given the high numbers of immigrants and the high rates of intermarriage among immigrants and their children. Various scholars have suggested that we are moving toward a black/non-black color line, while others suggest that we are headed toward a more complex color line, such as a tri-racial divide with white people, honorary white people (i.e., Latinos and Asians), and black people. However, most of these arguments, especially when it comes to intermarriage, still need to be tested empirically.

One of the largest proponents of the black/non-black color line is George Yancey (2003). He argues that Latinos and Asians (i.e., non-black minorities) are experiencing structural, marital, and identificational assimilation to the extent that they are accepting majority group status (at the very least, their racial and ethnic identities are thinning to the extent that they can identify with the majority group). On the opposite end of the spectrum, black people have not been able to assimilate, experience a high degree of alienation, and are likely to remain at the bottom of the social hierarchy. Therefore, the measuring stick will not be whether or not these new immigrant groups will be "white" or not, but whether they are "black" or not.

One of the key assumptions of the black/non-black divide is that Latinos and Asians will continue to intermarry at increasing rates, or at least at the same pace. This relates to Gordon's proposed definition of marital assimilation as occurring on a "large-scale" (p. 125). It is therefore hard to argue if the intermarriage glass is half-full or half-empty. The recent finding that we are experiencing a "retreat from intermarriage" certainly calls this assumption into question (Qian and Lichter 2007; Lichter *et al.* 2011). On the other hand, attitudinal-based data suggest that the "experience and social status of Asians and Latinos are closer to those of whites than to those of blacks at this point in time" (Lee and Bean 2010: 99).

On the other side of the debate is Bonilla-Silva (2004), one of the strongest proponents of a tri-racial system of stratification similar to Latin American countries, consisting of "whites," "honorary whites," and "collective black." The white category includes white people, new white immigrants, assimilated white Latinos, some multiracials, assimilated Native Americans, and "a few Asian-origin people." Honorary whites include light-skinned Latinos, Asian American groups, Middle Eastern Americans, and most multiracials. The collective black would include Vietnamese, Hmong, and Laotian Americans, dark-skinned Latinos, black people, new West Indian and African immigrants, and "reservation-bound Native Americans." The critical aspect of this approach is the honorary white category:

> "Honorary" means they will remain secondary, will still face discrimination, and will not receive equal treatment in society. For example ... albeit substantial segments of the Asian American community may become "honorary white", they will also continue to suffer from discrimination and be regarded in many quarters as "perpetual foreigners."
>
> (2004: 944)

The reference to Arab Americans relates to key assumptions by both Yancey and Bonilla-Silva. Yancey states that the "assimilation of nonblack minorities assumes that there will not be a social event that dramatically increases the amount of racial tension between those groups and the majority group" (Yancey 2003: 139). Bonilla-Silva states that the category of honorary whites "is the product of the socio-political needs of whites to maintain white supremacy" (2004: 942). While both of these assumptions are difficult to prove, they lie at the heart of the color line debate. Are the perceptions that Latinos are "illegal aliens" pervasive enough to increase racial tensions? What about the recent backlash against Muslims in the United States? A comparison of intermarriage in Britain and Europe is instructive in that the critical divide appears to be between Muslims and non-Muslims—a religious divide rather than a racial divide (Song 2009). Song states that "scholars may put too much store by what interracial relationships (with whites) afford in terms of privilege and social acceptance into the (still predominantly) white mainstream—

especially in relationships with working-class whites" (2009: 343). Either way, Latino and Asian immigrants and their children will be the key to solving this theoretical puzzle.

Panethnicity

Panethnicity is an important concept that examines the degree to which ethnic groups within a certain racial category associate with each other, or identify with each other. Intermarriage, especially interethnic marriage (e.g., Japanese–Filipino or Cuban–Mexican couples) is a good indicator of whether ethnic groups are forming panethnic groups in our society. Shinagawa and Pang (1996) were among the first to claim that the rise in interethnic marriages among Asians in the United States is a sign of an Asian panethnicity, where a racial consciousness is more important than an ethnic consciousness. More recently, Fu and Hatfield (2008) found evidence to support a path of assimilation into panethnic groups through intermarriage with other Asian ethnics, especially in the case of the Chinese, Japanese, and Koreans.

The formation of panethnic relations through intermarriage, at least as a monolithic group of Asian ethnics, is not without its critics. Min and Kim (2009) found little evidence for panethnic relations, especially in the form of ethnic solidarity. What they do find, however, is that according to interethnic marriage trends, there are likely three panethnic groups: East (Chinese, Korean, and Japanese), South (Asian Indian, Pakistani, and Bangladeshi), and Southeast (Vietnamese, Cambodian, Lao, and Hmong). Filipino Americans, due to their history, language, and religion, have links to all three of these pan-Asian formations.

Whether or not the rising rate of interethnic marriages is a sign of panethnicity is still an empirical question. Asian ethnics may be less likely to cross a racial boundary as opposed to an ethnic boundary, which could signal the importance of race and a shared racial consciousness. On the other hand, this may merely be an indication of the importance of preferences for similar cultures, in which case Asian ethnics view other Asian ethnics as closer in cultural traits than other races, and thus ethnicity could be more salient than race for some groups (Morgan 2009).

Methodological innovations and limitations

Most of the work on intermarriage has been descriptive rather than theoretical. Social scientists use a variety of datasets to examine intermarriage patterns and trends, although the decennial Census is the most widely used. Since 2000, the US Census Bureau administered the American Community Survey (ACS) every year to three million people. This allows for a more timely national survey. The Current Population Survey (CPS) is another national dataset that is becoming more heavily utilized in studying immigrant intermarriage. This is the only major national survey that asks the parental nativity of the respondents since the Census Bureau dropped this question the 1980 decennial census. The parental nativity question is critical to isolating the second generation as opposed to distinguishing only between foreign-born and US-born respondents.

There are also regional surveys, such as the Children of Immigrants Longitudinal Study (CILS) and the Immigration and Intergenerational Mobility in Metropolitan Los Angeles (IIMMLA) survey, that include information about spouses and partners, allowing for analyses of intermarried couples (see Morgan 2009; Gonsoulin and Fu 2010 for analyses of these regional surveys). Other similar surveys also exist that are of limited use, either because they do not have questions for spouses or because the sample sizes are too small to generalize to a larger population.

A major weakness of the above-mentioned datasets is that they rely on prevalence measures (surveying all of the intermarried couples *at* a given time) as opposed to incidence measures (surveying all of the intermarried couples who married *in* a given time). Thus, most of the limitations lie in the nature of these quantitative datasets. Qualitative datasets are helpful, but it is difficult to find and interview interracial couples, and we cannot generalize the findings to the larger population. Given the above-mentioned difficulties, the largest hurdle to understanding immigrant intermarriage lies in our datasets. Another complication is the issue of how we count intermarriages. Do we follow the norm and stick to "interracial" couples, or do we also include "interethnic" couples? And what about cohabiting couples? Should we expand the scope of inter-marriage and study interethnic and interracial partnering instead of just interracial marriages?

Given the types of datasets used, combined with the difficulty of finding and interviewing intermarried couples, most of the intermarriage studies employ quantitative analyses. These analyses vary from simple percentages and cross tabulations to the more complex odds ratios and log-linear modeling (see pp. 404–6 of Kalmijn 1998 for a detailed discussion of measures and models). Percentages and cross-tabulations have the advantage of easy interpretation, but have no reference points and do not control for the size of the group. Presenting odds ratios from logistic regression models are preferred because they provide a reference point and are inde-pendent of group size. Recently, however, log-linear models have become the "statistical method of choice" and the "gold standard" (Batson *et al.* 2006; Qian and Lichter 2007). One problem with log-linear models is that they are difficult to interpret (Rosenfeld 2008). One way to ease the interpretation is to transform the log-linear estimates into odds ratios (see Batson *et al.* 2006 for an example of this technique).

One solution to highlighting advantages and minimizing disadvantages is to triangulate by using a number of the above-mentioned analytical methods. Fu and Hatfield (2008) offer a good example of triangulation using descriptive statistics, multinomial logistic regressions, and log-linear models. Rosenfeld (2008) not only uses a number of different datasets, but also uses percentages, odds ratios, and a saturated log-linear model. Another original method is the use of a multilevel approach that incorporates individual and contextual variables (Kalmijn and Van Tubergen 2010). No amount of sophistication, however, can make up for the difficulty of conceptualizing immigrant intermarriage: "[I]f the boundaries between groups are in flux and are fundamentally messy, how are we to know which marriages count as incidents of intermarriage?" (Song 2009: 338).

Empirical claims about immigrant intermarriage

Aside from major theoretical debates, there are also less common theoretical ways of thinking about the empirical questions surrounding immigrant intermarriage. It is these mid-range theoretical frameworks that help researchers examine data and test some of the larger questions raised above. One of the greatest contributions in this area is the theoretical framework laid out by Kalmijn (1998). He identified three causes of endogamy: preferences, third parties, and marriage markets. These three causes can be further contrasted through their links to either cultural or structural factors (Kalmijn and Van Tubergen 2010; Lee and Bean 2010; Lichter *et al.* 2011). Cultural factors are often associated with individual preferences and third-party influences, whereas structural factors are often associated with marriage markets. There are, however, multiple ways to interpret and operationalize the three factors that Kalmijn outlined. For example, some scholars separate individual and contextual factors, further breaking down contextual factors into cultural and structural determinants (Kalmijn and Van Tubergen 2010). I use these frameworks to highlight the empirical findings on immigrant intermarriage.

Race and ethnicity

The literature on intermarriage can be divided into four traditions: racial, ethnic, socioeconomic (often measured as education), and religious intermarriage (Gordon 1964; Kalmijn 1998; Rosenfeld 2008). Race is common in the literature, while ethnicity (or national origin as a proxy for ethnicity) has gained some attention as of late. Among these traditions, however, race appears to be the greatest barrier to intermarriage (Shinagawa and Pang 1996; Rosenfeld 2008).

Racial endogamy has declined significantly during the twentieth century, but still remains stronger than any of the other types of endogamy: "The relatively high power of racial endogamy, even at the end of the 20th century, means that well more than 90 percent of all marriages in the United States continue to be racially endogamous" (Rosenfeld 2008: 15). Virtually all of the racial groups marry within their own group at a higher rate than we would expect: black people (95 percent), Asians (75 percent), Latinos (65 percent), American Indians (45 percent), and Europeans of the same nationality (25 percent) (Kalmijn 1998). Given the various parameterizations of models, we must interpret these statistics in terms of the model that is estimated and classifications that are used. For example, others have found that only 15 percent of Latinos out-married (i.e., married persons other than Latinos) (Lichter *et al.* 2011).

There are even signs that racial endogamy is growing stronger. Intermarriage among Latinos and white people declined for the first time in the 1990s (Lichter *et al.* 2011). Moreover, the last decade of the twentieth century (1990–2000) ushered in decreases in intermarriage with white people and increases in marriage between native-born and foreign-born co-ethnics (Qian and Lichter 2007). These changes are attributed to racial classification in the Census, an influx of immigrants, increases in cohabitation, advances in educational attainment, and possibly the recent rise in anti-immigrant sentiment.

Structural factors lead people from various racial and ethnic groups to come into contact, whereas cultural factors affect how they will react to and get along with people from different racial and ethnic groups. In combination, these factors ultimately influence people to cross racial and ethnic lines to form intimate relationships. Intermarriage among immigrants only becomes important if ethnic differences (i.e., race, religion, and national origin) have meaning to the people who cross these boundaries (Gordon 1964). From a qualitative analysis of interracial couples, Lee and Bean (2010) found that Asians and Latinos do not perceive many differences between themselves and white people, thus indicating that the boundaries between whites and Asians and Latinas people are fading. Aside from racial differences, however, Morgan (2009) found important ethnic differences among interracial and interethnic couples.

Shinagawa and Pang (1996) were among the first researchers to conceptualize and document the rise in interethnic marriages among the Asian American population. They found that the number of interethnic marriages from 1980 to 1990 approached, and, for some groups, sur-passed, interracial marriages on a national level. Few authors have explored the growing ethnic diversity of Asians (Shinagawa and Pang 1996; Fu and Hatfield 2008; Min and Kim 2009), Latinos (Jacobs and Labov 2002), black people (Batson *et al.* 2006), and even white people (Kalmijn and Van Tubergen 2010), which is especially odd given the massive influx of immigrants since the 1960s.

A couple of examples should suffice to highlight important ethnic differences within racial groups. For example, while Asian Indians tend to marry other Asian Indians, and Filipinos to marry other races, Chinese, Japanese, and Koreans have a strong tendency to intermarry with each other (Fu and Hatfield 2008). Among black immigrants, Puerto Ricans are the most likely to intermarry with white people, followed by African Americans. West Indians are the least likely to intermarry with white people, but are much more likely to marry African Americans

(Batson *et al.* 2006). Findings from an analysis of 94 national-origin groups in the United States show a lot of variation in intermarriages across world regions, highlighting the importance of looking at individual national-origin groups (Kalmijn and Van Tubergen 2010).

Generation

Increased intermarriage across generations is one of the key assumptions made by proponents of a straight-line assimilation model (Lee and Bean 2010). Countless studies have found that inter-marriage increases with each subsequent generation (Shinagawa and Pang 1996; Song 2009; Gonsoulin and Fu 2010). Generational gaps can be structural (i.e., relating to population com-position) and/or cultural (i.e., relating to social distance) in nature: "Almost two-thirds of the group-level variance in the choice between endogamous and native-stock partners can be attributed to the cultural and structural factors that were incorporated" (Kalmijn and Van Tubergen 2010: 475). Lichter *et al.*'s (2011) evidence favors structural explanations; however, even generational gaps due to structural factors can turn into cultural factors over time.

Generation is perhaps one of the least studied and most difficult factors to understand. Few datasets have the proper variables to compute meaningful generational distinctions, and even when we do have the correct variables (such as parental nativity), how do we measure genera-tional differences? There is a key distinction between the 1.5 generation (migrated to the United States as a child) and the second-generation (US born). For example, Gonsoulin and Fu (2010) found that second-generation Latinos displayed very similar marriage patterns to 1.5-generation Latinos, whereas second-generation Asians were almost three times more likely to outmarry than 1.5-generation Asians. The "new second-generation" (1.5 and second gen-erations) are likely the key to understanding issues of assimilation, social distance, the color line, and panethnicity.

There is also a need to separate the native-born from the second generation and the third-plus generations. We are particularly interested in understanding how many native-borns are intermarrying with first-generation immigrants, especially compared to native-borns inter-marrying with white people. The last decade of the twentieth century (1990–2000) ushered in decreases in intermarriage with white people and increases in marriages between native-born and foreign-born co-ethnics (Qian and Lichter 2007). A groundbreaking study by Lichter *et al.* (2011) further clarifies the above finding, showing that intermarriage among Latinos and white people declined for the first time in the 1990s. Second-generation Latinos were more likely to marry first-generation Latinos than third-generation Latinos or white people, whereas the third-generation are more likely to marry other third-generation Latinos and white people. This could indicate a "retreat from intermarriage" among the second-generation Latinos. This can be attributed to growing numbers of Latino immigrants. Min and Kim (2009) confirm this finding, showing that native-born Asian Americans are outmarrying with immigrant co-ethnics at high rates. They attribute this to three factors: increasing immigration flows that have encouraged social interactions, increasing transnational ties, and reduced cultural barriers via globalization (see also Kalmijn and Van Tubergen 2010 for evidence of globalization).

Gender differences

We see vast gender differences when it comes to immigrants and their children intermarrying. A key division is between the immigrant first generation and the second generation. For example, Latino and Asian women are more likely to outmarry with white people than are Latino and Asian men (Jacobs and Labov 2002; Lichter *et al.* 2011). Once we exclude the first generation immigrants, native-born Latino men are more likely to outmarry with white people than are Latino women, but Asian women are still more likely to outmarry white people compared to Asian men. Among black immigrants, black men are more likely to intermarry with white people than are black women (Batson *et al.* 2006).

Accounting for war brides is crucial in understanding gender differentials in intermarriage (Jacobs and Labov 2002). This partially explains why the first and second generations look so different. Jacobs and Labov state, "Excluding marriages involving those with US military experience and foreign spouses substantially reduces the female share of intermarriages previously observed among nearly all groups of Asian women" (2002: 632). For example, it is estimated that among various intermarried immigrant women in the US, a very large fraction are war brides. 75 percent of intermarried Korean women, 64 percent of intermarried South East Asian women, 58 percent of intermarried Vietnamese women, 52 percent of intermarried Filipino women, 45 percent of intermarried Japanese women, 26 percent of intermarried Chinese women, and 22 percent of intermarried Asian-Indian women in the United States are war brides among the first generation. For those in the second generation under age 40, there are more Asian women (especially Chinese, Filipino, Japanese, and Pacific Islanders) married to non-Hispanic white people than Asian men, whereas there are more Latino men (especially Mexicans, Puerto Ricans, and Cubans) married to non-Hispanic white people than Latino women.

Of more importance are the possible reasons why we see these gender differences, especially among Asian women (even when we account for war brides). Kalmijn states, "A speculative interpretation of this exception is that Asian-American women are attractive marriage candidates for white men because of their physical appearance and presumed acceptance of more traditional power relationships in marriage. A more plausible interpretation lies in the role of opportunity: the presence of American soldiers in Japan and Korea" (1998: 412–13). We have already seen that war brides cannot account for all of the differences, giving some credence to "speculative interpretations." Min and Kim (2009) found that the remaining gap can be explained according to three factors: (1) "native-born Asian women are more likely than their male counterparts to consider the benefit of egalitarian gender relations in selecting non-ethnic partners" (2009: 457), (2) white men seek Asian wives due to stereotypes of their submissiveness, and (3) Asian men have a hard time marrying white people due to negative stereotypes of Asian men regarding gender issues. Morgan (2009), relying upon in-depth interviews, also found that some Asian American women are more likely to marry white people and less likely to marry other Asians because of perceptions of patriarchy among co-ethnics resulting from their parents and previous dating experiences with Asian men.

Religion

In one of the first articles to document the importance of religion among immigrants intermarrying, Kennedy (1944) found that ethnic boundaries were weakening: "Cultural lines may fade, but religious barriers are holding fast" (p. 334). She predicted that religion would play a large role in the intermarriage of future immigrants. This prediction has apparently not borne out, but it is unclear if this is because religion is not as important for today's immigrants and their children or because we do not have adequate data to empirically test this idea.

More recently, Kalmijn (1998) found that religious groups tend to have higher rates of endogamy, mainly as a result of third-party control: "That the boundaries between religious groups in Europe and the United States have weakened during the twentieth century is consistent with the notion of declining third-party control and matches long-term processes such as secularization and depillarization" (1998: 411). Christians are more likely to marry other Christians, whereas Hindu and Buddhists are less likely to outmarry. Islamic men are also less likely to outmarry (no significant differences were found for Islamic women). In addition, group size affects religious endogamy: "When there are more persons in religiously similar groups in a state, persons are more likely to marry with other national-origin groups" (Kalmijn and Van Tubergen 2010: 472).

Religious divisions between Catholics and Protestants have been relatively weak since the early 1900s (Rosenfeld 2008). Divisions between Jews and Christians, however, are still high when it comes to religious endogamy, suggesting that social barriers remain strong despite their decline over the years. Furthermore, we have already seen that there is a critical divide in Europe between Muslims and non-Muslims (Song 2009). Rosenfeld (2008) claims that "the marriage market isolation of Buddhists, Muslims, and other non-Christian groups in the United States cannot be reliably determined from the currently available data" (p. 24). This is a crucial point, given that many of the immigrants are coming from Asia with a variety of religious orientations that are non-Christian. While there are not as many Muslims, given the post-9/11 environment in the United States, this group is of particular interest. The issue of religious endogamy is of utmost importance, and yet there are few datasets with both partners' religious affiliations that would enable us to understand this issue.

International focus

A number of countries (especially Asian countries such as Japan, South Korea, and Taiwan) have started bringing in a large number of mail-order brides from other countries as a way to meet the demand for brides. This is a relatively recent phenomenon (it started in Japan in the late 1980s) and is historically understudied. These international intermarriages involve many of the factors mentioned above, but in different structural and cultural contexts. This phenomenon is not confined to Asian countries, but is also becoming more prevalent in the United States (especially in the form of brides from Russia, the Philippines, and a number of Asian countries found through various Internet sites).

Related to this topic are intermarriage studies in other countries. Lucassen and Laarman (2009) summarized a wide range of intermarriage studies among immigrants in five European countries (Netherlands, Germany, France, Belgium, and England). This study offers important comparisons within European nations, but also with immigrant intermarriage in the United States. For example, the authors found that religion was more important than race or color in Europe, compared to the United States. Part of this can be explained by the tradition of slavery in US history, but part can also be explained by the immigrants' experience as guest workers, the distinctness of Islam, and whether or not they were once a colonial subject of the European country to which they migrated. Even though a "systematic comparison of intermarriage patterns throughout Western Europe is lacking" (Lucassen and Laarman 2009: 58), we can learn a lot about immigrant intermarriage from comparative studies. For example, "intermarriage patterns in Great Britain, problematises the sweeping assumption that increased intermarriage rates coincides with upward social mobility, and thereby structural integration" (Lucassen and Laarman 2009: 62).

Another unique international study was conducted by Jacobson and Heaton (2008), who examined census data and compared intermarriage rates across six different locations with different histories of immigration, racial composition, and racial subjugation: the United States, Hawaii as a special case within the United States, Canada, New Zealand, South Africa, and Xinjiang Province in China. They found varying degrees of intermarriage both across the six contexts, as well as within the different groups in these contexts. They explain these differences using structural opportunities (in the form of segregation, geographical isolation, and local marriage markets), which lead to more intermarriage, and juxtapose those opportunities with third-party influences (in the form of group identification, group sanctions, and religion), which lead to less intermarriage. They also examine age as a key factor, showing that in all of the societies they studied, younger people tend to outmarry at higher rates than do older people. Despite obvious limitations with data in comparative studies of immigrant intermarriage, much is to be gained through these international studies.

The future of immigrant intermarriage

In summary, there are a number of important theoretical areas in immigrant intermarriage that need to be explored. Do intermarriage trends among immigrants and their children point to a straight-line assimilation pattern (similar to European immigrants in the early 1900s) or a segmented assimilation pattern? What do we know about the social distance between groups based on their intermarriage? Do intermarriage patterns point to a tri-racial color line, or are we moving toward a black/non-black divide? Finally, are these immigrant groups and their offspring forming panethnic entities through intermarriage?

When it comes to empirical studies on immigrant intermarriage, current studies point to important areas of further exploration. How does the meaning of intermarriage change depending on whether or not we examine racial categories or ethnic categories? What role does religion play in how immigrants and their children decide to intermarry? Generation is also a critical factor to understanding intermarriage. Since most of the immigrants who arrived after 1960 have children who are still in their teenage years, the emerging third generation will become one of the most interesting topics in intermarriage studies in the next decade.

Despite the fact that most of this chapter has focused on immigrant intermarriage in the United States, we have a lot to learn from cross-national, comparative studies from around the world. The United States receives the highest number of immigrants from around the world and thus has an abundance of intermarried couples, but there are a number of other countries that also have high proportions of immigrants. Moreover, given the ease of travel, communication, and business in the form of globalization, there are few countries that do not have immigrants, and where there are immigrants, there are intermarriages.

References and further reading

Batson, C. D., Qian, Z., and Lichter, D. T. (2006) "Interracial and intraracial patterns of mate selection among America's diverse black population" *Journal of Marriage and Family* 68(3): 658–72.

Bonilla-Silva, E. (2004) From bi-racial to tri-racial: Towards a new system of racial stratification in the USA" *Ethnic and Racial Studies* 27(6): 931–50.

Fu, X. and Hatfield, M. (2008) "Intermarriage and segmented assimilation: US-born Asians in 2000" *Journal of Asian American Studies* 11(3): 249–77.

Gonsoulin, M. and Fu, X. (2010) "Intergenerational assimilation by intermarriage: Hispanic and Asian immigrants" *Marriage and Family Review* 46(4): 257–77.

Gordon, M. M. (1964) *Assimilation in American life: The Role of Race, Religion and National Origins.* New York: Oxford University Press.

Jacobs, J. A. and Labov, T. G. (2002) "Gender differentials in intermarriage among sixteen race and ethnic groups" *Sociological Forum* 17(4): 621–46.

Jacobson, C. K. and Heaton, T. B. (2008) Comparative patterns of interracial marriage: Structural opportunities, third-party factors, and temporal change in immigrant societies" *Journal of Comparative Family Studies* 39(2): 129–49.

Kalmijn, M. (1998) "Intermarriage and homogamy: Causes, patterns, trends" *Annual Review of Sociology* 24: 395–421.

Kalmijn, M. and Van Tubergen, F. (2010) "A comparative perspective on intermarriage: Explaining differences among national-origin groups in the United States" *Demography* 47(2): 459–79.

Kennedy, R. J. R. (1944) "Single or triple melting-pot? Intermarriage trends in New Haven, 1870–1940" *The American Journal of Sociology* 49(4): 331–39.

Lee, J. and Bean, F. D. (2010) *The Diversity Paradox: Immigration and the Color Line in Twenty-first Century America*. New York: Russell Sage Foundation Publications.

Lichter, D. T., Carmalt, J. H., and Qian, Z. (2011) "Immigration and intermarriage among Hispanics: Crossing racial and generational boundaries" *Sociological Forum* 26(2): 241–64.

Lucassen, L. and Laarman, C. (2009) "Immigration, Intermarriage and the changing face of Europe in the post war period" *The History of the Family* 14(1): 52–68.

Min, P. G. and Kim, C. (2009) "Patterns of intermarriages and cross-generational in-marriages among native-born Asian Americans" *International Migration Review* 43(3): 447–70.

Morgan, C. V. (2009) *Intermarriage Across Race and Ethnicity Among Immigrants: E Pluribus Unions*. New York: LFB Scholarly Pub Llc.

Qian, Z. and Lichter, D. T. (2007) "Social boundaries and marital assimilation: Interpreting trends in racial and ethnic intermarriage" *American Sociological Review* 72(1): 68–94.

Rosenfeld, M. J. (2008) "Racial, educational and religious endogamy in the United States: A comparative historical perspective" *Social Forces* 87: 1–31.

Shinagawa, L. H. and Pang, G. Y. (1996) "Asian American panethnicity and intermarriage" *Amerasia Journal* 22(2): 127–52.

Song, M. (2009) Is intermarriage a good indicator of integration?" *Journal of Ethnic and Migration Studies* 35(2): 331–48.

Yancey, G. (2003) *Who Is White? Latinos, Asians, And the New Black/nonblack Divide*. Boulder, CO: Lynne Rienner Pub.

26

Prospects for the children of immigrants in the twenty-first century

Julie Park

During the first decade of the twenty-first century, immigrants continued to significantly contribute to the population growth in many developed nations in Europe, North America, and Australia. Although immigrants make up nearly 20–25 percent of the population in countries like Australia, Switzerland, and Canada, the United States has the largest number of foreign-born persons with 3.5 times more immigrants than the country with the second largest immigrant population (UN 2009). The United States is home to nearly 40 million foreign-born people according to the 2010 American Community Survey, which translates to more than one in eight persons. More importantly, almost one in four children in the United States are living with foreign-born parents. In some states with a significant immigrant population like California, nearly half of all children live in immigrant families (Mather 2009). Beyond the demographic importance of immigrants and their children in the United States, much of the previous research on the children of immigrants and their assimilation has been conducted in the US context. Therefore, much of this chapter will focus on the socioeconomic prospects for the children of immigrants and the assimilation literature in the US context.

With so many children living in immigrant families, researchers and policy-makers are interested in the various aspects of their well-being and achievements in the present as well as in the longer term. To appreciate the contexts that directly produce or at least influence these outcomes, it is particularly important to better understand the families in which they grow up, the schools in which they begin their socioeconomic attainment, and the community contexts in which they live. The primary focus of this chapter is on all children of immigrants, but it is important to note that there are differences between immigrant children who are foreign born and have a migration experience of their own and the second generation, namely the native-born children of immigrants.

The children of immigrants today may face much of the same challenges and opportunities as their predecessors in the past century; however, the twenty-first century may also introduce circumstances that diverge from the past. The past century of research has shown that, compositionally, the post-1965 children of immigrants in the United States differed from those growing up during the earlier half of the century. They came from racially and socioeconomically diverse backgrounds with the vast majority arriving from Latin America and Asia as well as increasingly from other parts of the world. Unlike the turn of the twentieth century, immigrant parents are arriving with increasingly varied immigration statuses (temporary worker, undocumented, or refugee/ asylee status) which fundamentally impacts the life chances of their children.

More specifically, the circumstances for the turn of the twentieth-century children of immigrants differ from those of the post-1965 era in several ways. First, they entered in a relatively narrow window of time with most arriving during the 1900s and 1910s. The Johnson and Reed Act of 1924 ushered in the silent era of immigration when very few immigrants arrived for several decades. Therefore, there is a distinct cohort of the second generation that came of age together through the same economic and social circumstances. On the other hand, among those in the post-1965 era, there is a constant replenishment of immigrants and their children. Therefore, it is difficult to make generalizations about the new second generation because different cohorts are facing different contexts and socioeconomic circumstances.

Second, earlier children of immigrants came of age at a time of rapid economic and education expansion in the United States. On the other hand, post-1965 children of immigrants have been arriving or growing up during an era of economic restructuring toward an hour-glass economy. Zhou (1997) argues that there are very few opportunities within this economic structure for upward mobility. Most recently, children of immigrants are growing up during an era of intensified globalization and continued economic restructuring. Many scholars have speculated that the changing economic and social contexts in the last few decades generate more socioeconomic uncertainty for immigrant families and their children.

The sociohistorical context's impact on the socioeconomic prospects of the children of immigrants is not only important in the United States but in any country experiencing mass immigration and settlement. For instance, Crul and Vermeulen (2003) find that different European national contexts of reception can yield different socioeconomic outcomes for the Turkish second generation. The Turks may have higher education levels in France than in Germany, which reflects the broader differences in educational attainment between the two countries. However, the unemployment rate of second-generation Turks is also higher in France than in Germany because the German apprenticeship system yields higher employment among youth. This kind of comparative or cross-national research provides invaluable insights into the importance of the context of reception. As Boyd (2002) points out in her research on the second generation in Canada, it is with cross-national research that we begin to uncover differences in structural contexts and their consequences on the children of immigrants as well as on the applicability of theories of assimilation across time and space.

At the beginning of the twenty-first century, the children of immigrants are once again situated in a unique context that may again alter their prospects for long-term socioeconomic attainment, acculturation, or assimilation. This chapter first lays out the various ways in which immigration scholars have conceptualized the socioeconomic prospects for children of immigrants. Second, I review the various contexts in which these children are being socialized and to what extent they may impact the various aspects of their well-being and prospects for socioeconomic advancement or upward mobility. Third, I examine the ways in which the familial, social, and geographic contexts that the immigrant children of today are diverging from contexts of the past.

Theories of acculturation, assimilation, and socioeconomic upward mobility

As the second generation of the turn of the twentieth-century immigration era in the United States was coming of age, many scholars began to speculate how immigrant generations would eventually fare. Park and Burgess (1921) offered an ecological model of assimilation that assumed each successive generation would be more culturally, socioeconomically, and spatially integrated with the mainstream. Their concept of assimilation is nested in cultural terms as spatial (residential) and temporal dimensions measure the pace of assimilation. Warner and Srole (1945) further expanded this linear upward progression of immigrants, or straight-line assimilation, by going beyond culture to explicitly include racial and ethnic subsystems in mediating the pace of assimilation. They linked the upward social mobility of eight immigrant groups to assimilation with "ethnic-ness" dissipating especially for the second generation. However, ethnicity was still defined in very cultural terms (religion and language) with upward mobility necessarily meaning becoming less ethnic. They also distinguished race from ethnicity by arguing that race groups least like white "old Americans" may be "doomed to a permanent inferior ranking" (Warner and Srole 1945: 284). This distinction becomes quite salient as immigrants went from being ethnically diverse in the beginning of the twentieth century to being racially diverse in the latter part of the century.

Gordon (1964) refined this straight-line assimilation theory by laying out seven stages or types of assimilation. They include cultural or behavioral assimilation (change of cultural pattern to those of host society), structural assimilation (large-scale entrance into cliques, clubs, and institutions of host society, on primary group level), marital assimilation (large-scale intermarriage), identificational assimilation (development of sense of peoplehood based exclusively on host society), attitude receptional assimilation (absence of prejudice), behavior receptional assimilation (absence of discrimination), and civic assimilation (absence of value and power conflict). Distinguishing acculturation from structural assimilation, Gordon conceived that acculturation could occur without being subsequently followed by structural assimilation. This partitioning of how immigrant generations assimilate becomes particularly useful in conceptualizing how the children of immigrants can grow up completely immersed in the host country's culture and yet can remain unassimilated.

According to this straight-line assimilation model, each subsequent generation should experience more upward mobility and assimilation than the previous generation. However, many researchers consistently found evidence to the contrary. In fact, some researchers observed that the second generation is not doing much better than the first generation in what has been termed by Herbert Gans (1992) as the "second-generation decline." This decline occurs as the children of immigrants become Americanized enough to expect upward mobility out of low-paying, low-status jobs that their parents hold. However, with pervasive economic restructuring and limitations to their educational achievement, their expectations clash with the kinds of jobs that are made available or accessible to them. These children of immigrants do not see opportunities in the mainstream economy and yet they are not willing to take the same jobs as their parents leaving them to be marginalized and excluded from upward mobility. The mismatch between rising aspirations and socioeconomic opportunities may lead to a "second-generation revolt" (Perlmann and Waldinger 1997) by which these children of immigrants might end up with a chronically tenuous position in the labor market, engage in criminal activities or drug/alcohol abuse, or other detrimental activities. A poignant example of this is illustrated by the 2005 riots in France by second-generation youth who were particularly vulnerable in a labor market riddled by high unemployment (Silberman 2011). Beyond unmet aspirations and expectations, there are other factors that may also hinder upward mobility or assimilation. Growing up in poor or unsafe neighborhoods, having undocumented status, or being racialized in certain ways can contribute to what has also been termed downward mobility or downward assimilation (Gans 1992; Portes and Zhou 1993; Waters 1999).

With evidence refuting the straight-line assimilation model and with findings such as second-generation decline, Portes and Zhou (1993) introduced the segmented assimilation theory that is widely accepted and used in the immigration literature today. Instead of assuming that upward mobility is experienced by all children of immigrants, Portes and Zhou argue that the new second generation is incorporated in the US system of stratification that tracks them on divergent trajectories. Three possible patterns of adaptation are most likely to occur among contemporary immigrants and their children. One of them replicates the time-honored portrayal of growing acculturation and parallel integration into the white middle class; a second leads straight into the opposite direction to permanent poverty and assimilation into the underclass; still a third associates rapid economic advancement with deliberate preservation of the immigrant community's values and solidarity (Portes and Zhou 1993: 82). Segmented assimilation theory highlights the importance of the context of reception or what they refer to as the modes of incorporation. The outcomes for the children of immigrants are contingent upon the policies of the host government, the strength and resources of the co-ethnic community, and the values and prejudices of the receiving society (Portes and Zhou 1993). In earlier conceptions of assimilation, the context of reception was largely assumed or ignored but Portes and Zhou contend that the locational context as well as race-ethnicity varies across immigrant groups. Therefore, upward mobility and entrance into the white middle class can no longer be assumed for the post-1965 children of immigrants.

Alba and Nee (2003) also acknowledge the importance of the context of reception or what they refer to as mainstream society. However, in their formulation of a new theory of assimilation, the mainstream is also continually altered by immigrants and ultimately, assimilation is a two-way process in which both immigrants and the mainstream change in response to the other. Like other researchers who track the socioeconomic attainment of the children of immigrants (Kasinitz et al. 2008; Park and Myers 2010; Alba and Waters 2011), Alba and Nee (2003) find consistent evidence of upward mobility. Simultaneously, they acknowledge that racial stratification persists in the American context. They just question the extent of its rigidity as suggested by Portes and Zhou (1993).

Lastly, Rubén Rumbaut (1997) points out that the concept of assimilation is simultaneously both descriptive and prescriptive with the implicit assumption that assimilation always produces positive outcomes for immigrants and their children. Rumbaut explains that inherently within the assimilation perspective, there is a "patronizing ethnocentrism built into assumptions about immigrant adjustment that equated 'foreign' with 'inferior' and the ways of the 'host or 'core' society and culture with 'superior'" (1997: 487). He describes several examples in which assimilation produces negative results for immigrants or their children and these are referred to as a paradox of assimilation. One of the most well-known examples of this is the epidemiological paradox where numerous studies have shown that immigrants may arrive healthier than the mainstream population. With increasing duration of US residence, immigrant and especially their children may begin to adopt the eating habits and sedentary lifestyles of the mainstream which then results in the deterioration of their health. Other areas include mental health and ethnic self-identity.

The conceptions, extensions, and revisions of assimilation theory affords researchers the theoretical framework with which to understand the socioeconomic prospects of the children of immigrants as they come of age in the twenty-first century. More recent theoretical contributions have largely departed from earlier conceptions of assimilation that were explicitly normative and prescriptive. Instead, they provide the conceptual tools to understand and explain the patterns of change for immigrant generations with the changing contexts of reception.

Large studies and other datasets on the children of immigrants

The US Census Bureau is the main source for demographic data on children of immigrants in the United States, and is the most frequently used publically accessible data source for tracking their socioeconomic assimilation. The decennial census has historically contained the largest sample of households with immigrant children and this remained true up the 2000 decennial census. With the decision to do away with the long-form for the 2010 decennial census, the American Community Survey (ACS) is now conducted annually with 3 million households in its stead since 2005. Besides the general demographic characteristics of immigrant children (age, sex, race–ethnicity), these data also provide a wealth of other information that are of keen interest to researchers. For instance, the ACS provides data on their household structure, family economic status, when they or their parents entered the United States to stay, language spoken at home and English proficiency, their parents' employment status and occupation, or the racial and economic composition of where they reside just to name a few. Along with the ACS, the Current Population Survey (CPS) is also commonly used since it contains questions about the nativity of mothers and fathers (crucial in distinguishing the second generation from other native-born children) as well as most of the variables contained in the ACS. These data not only provide basic demographic profiles of immigrant children but they also make statistical analyses possible and at various levels of geography.

The landmark study on children of immigrants was led by Alejandro Portes and Rubén Rumbaut. It is called the Children of Immigrants Longitudinal Study (CILS) and in 1992, it interviewed over 5,200 youth in Miami and San Diego from eighth and ninth grade. In 1995, they re-interviewed as many original respondents as they could find as the children of immigrants were nearing high school graduation and this wave of interviews also included a parental survey. The third wave of data was collected in 2001–3. The study included both quantitative questionnaires as well as qualitative in-depth interviews. The study focused on patterns of acculturation, family and school life, language, experiences of discrimination, self-esteem, aspiration, and achievement. Some of the key findings from this study are reported in an edited volume (Rumbaut and Portes 2001).

Between 1998 and 2000, John H. Mollenkopf, Philip Kasinitz, and Mary C. Waters conducted a study of second-generation immigrants in New York City (Kasinitz et al. 2008). The study includes a telephone survey (sample included 3,415 young adults aged 18 to 32), in-depth interviews with 333 of the telephone respondents and several ethnographies (Kasinitz et al. 2004). Though the study does not directly study children, the respondents were asked about the families and neighborhood in which they grew up as well as their experiences transitioning from high school to either college or the labor force. These aspects of the study help bridge our knowledge about how children of immigrants grow up to how they transition into early adulthood and what their early socioeconomic attainments are.

Most recently, the Immigration and Intergenerational Mobility in Metropolitan Los Angeles (IIMMLA) study was conducted from 2004 to 2008 by Rubén G. Rumbaut, Frank D. Bean, Leo Chávez, Jennifer Lee, Susan K. Brown and Louis DeSipio of the University of California, Irvine, and Min Zhou of the University of California, Los Angeles. Similar to the New York study the 4,780 telephone survey respondents were between the ages of 20 and 39 which means that the study does not directly interview children but asks about their history.

In several other immigrant-receiving countries like Canada and parts of Europe, some large government-sponsored datasets allow for comparative research on the socioeconomic outcomes of the children of immigrants. However, there is a need for comparable data-collection projects in other countries on the other aspects of life for the second generation as they enter adulthood (e.g., identity formation, aspirations and perceived barriers to success, the role of the ethnic community, etc.). Beyond the average socioeconomic attainment levels of the children of immigrants, the experiences and narratives of the second generation are also important in understanding the processes of and the meanings attached to assimilation.

Demographic variables or measurements of adaptation

The adaptation process of children of immigrants is not only contingent upon their ascribed characteristics (e.g., race, ethnicity, and gender), the human capital they or their parents bring (e.g., educational attainment or dominant language proficiency), and the context in which they live but it also depends on the amount of time they have been in the destination country. This is especially true for immigrant children since they are arriving during their formative developmental and educational years. Rumbaut (2004) most succinctly summarizes the importance of these temporal distinctions when he states, "time in the United States for these immigrant children thus was not solely a measure of length of exposure to American life, but also an indicator of qualitatively different life stages and sociodevelopmental contexts at the time of immigration" (p. 1163).

In terms of nativity and the determination of immigrant generations, immigrant children and their immigrant parents both constitute the first generation. The second generation is conventionally defined as a person who is native-born of at least one immigrant parent. Ramakrishnan (2004) argues that a distinction should be made between those with two immigrant parents and those with only one. He finds that those with one immigrant parent and one native-born parent are better off socioeconomically than those with two immigrant parents (the true second generation). Therefore, he concludes that those with only one immigrant parents might be better referred to as the 2.5 generation. The first and second generations combined are referred to as immigrant or foreign-born stock. The third generation consists of those who are native-born to second-generation parents but in most large datasets, the third generation cannot be distinguished from the fourth or higher generations. Those immigrants who arrived in the new country as children are commonly referred to as the 1.5 generation (Hurh 1990; Rumbaut 1991), though there is little consistency in the literature about what is the cut-off age for this group.

Besides nativity, the three main temporal measurements for immigrant children are age-at-arrival, duration, and period or year of arrival. First, age at arrival is particularly important for immigrant children because it determines when they enter the host country's education system as well as what developmental stage they learn the dominant language and begin to learn the customs and culture of the host society. Myers *et al.* (2009) find though that age at arrival is more important for some outcome indicators (e.g., language proficiency) than for other outcome indicators like homeownership. Second, duration or the length of residence in the host society determines how long an immigrant has had to learn the ropes (Portes and Rumbaut 2006). Conventionally, longer duration in a host society is positively associated with language acquisition, socioeconomic advancement, and acculturation. However, Zhou (1997) points out the long duration does not necessarily equate to better outcomes. For example, as children acculturate at different rates than their immigrant parents, family cohesion and bilingualism might be on the decline.

Lastly, the period or year of arrival provides the historical context in which immigrants start their lives in the new country. The period of arrival provides information about the economic conditions, political environment, or policies and programs in place that directly impact the lives of immigrant families as they begin their lives in the host society. The period of arrival is also quite telling of where individuals are situated in the immigration flows from a particular country of origin. For example, Eckstein and Barberia (2002) show how Cuban immigrants in the United States differ socioeconomically, politically, and culturally by when they arrive. Taken together, these temporal factors help to better situate where immigrants are in the adaptation process.

Contexts

For children who immigrated themselves, the migration experience varies across different countries of origin, as does the context of reception. Some may experience a smoother transition than others due to language proficiency of the receiving country, ease of admission, or the resources that their parents possess. Nonetheless, the experience of moving to a new place where they do not have friends, are not familiar with the neighborhood or the school culture can be formidable for anyone. For second-generation children, they do not have a migration experience of their own, but often they are still impacted by the migration experiences of their parents. For some, it may be that the parents endured extreme hardships as boat people or as border crossers on foot, while other immigrant parents may have directly located into some of the wealthiest neighborhoods with highly regarded school systems. Whatever the case may be, children of immigrants are closely tied to the migration experience of their parents and its consequences.

Beyond the actual context of migration, the children of immigrants face certain contexts of reception that may facilitate faster acculturation or increased socioeconomic progress. In contrast, some children are located in contexts that hinder academic, social, or cultural incorporation. The socioeconomic prospects for the children of immigrants are contingent on several factors. First, the socioeconomic resources of their parents in terms of their educational and occupational attainment as well as their earnings are particularly important. These will have a significant effect on where immigrant families can locate which in turn impacts the schools the children will attend as well as the safety and resources of the neighborhood. Second, the availability of a co-ethnic community in terms of emotional and social support as well as a potential source of social capital for the education of their children (Kasinitz *et al.* 2008). Third, the legal status of immigrant parents and their children can be a key determinant in where they settle, how they access schools and employment, and the degree of freedom with which to function in civic life. The following sections outline some of the variations in contexts that contribute to the outcomes for children of immigrants.

Structural contexts of race/ethnicity, gender, and class

During the turn of the twentieth century, the focus in US scholarship was on the ability of Southern and Eastern European white ethnics to assimilate to a white, Anglo-Saxon mainstream that arrived in previous generations. Since the majority of post-1965 immigrants are nonwhites, the revisions of assimilation theory has had to consider the increasing relevance of race and its bearing on the socioeconomic progress of immigrants and their children (Portes and Zhou 1993; Zhou 1997; Waters 1999; Alba and Nee 2003; Portes and Rumbaut 2006). Along with race, researchers also continually emphasize the importance of ethnic diversity within panethnic categories of Asian or Latino for socioeconomic outcomes (Oropesa and Landale 1997). Race and ethnicity shape the identity formation, aspirations, and academic performance of children of immigrants (Portes and Rumbaut 2006).

Unlike immigrants at the turn of the twentieth century who were predominantly poor, the post-1965 immigrants are much more diverse in terms of the human capital and wealth that they bring with them as well as the ways in which they fit into the class structure of the receiving country. Since current immigrants and their children do not belong to a singular socioeconomic class, the discussions around socioeconomic distance (or gap) from the mainstream or intergenerational mobility are complicated. This is especially true when there is socioeconomic diversity even within a particular immigrant group. However, the initial position of immigrant parents in the class structure of the receiving country may not reflect their educational or occupational attainments from their country of origin. Language barriers, foreign degrees, lack of labor market experience or less cultural capital of the new country may contribute to lower class status than might otherwise be warranted. This "downgraded" class status may or may not be permanent for these immigrants but their socioeconomic attainments will certainly have long-term implications for their children's aspirations, resources, and achievements.

Gender is often overlooked when examining the socioeconomic assimilation of the children of immigrants. In fact, the earlier formulations of assimilation theory ignore it almost entirely. However, the educational and economic transformations in the latter half of the twentieth century have impacted the lives of women and men in significantly different ways. Within this changing context, the socioeconomic prospects for the children of immigrants must take into consideration gendered paths of mobility or assimilation along with race and class (Park *et al.* 2011). In her research on the educational experiences of Dominicans, Anglophone West Indians, and Haitians, Lopez (2003) explains that racialization and gendered processes not only influence the experiences of these youth but they also shape the outlooks of social mobility attainment.

Ultimately, the broader structural contexts within the receiving country can widen, constrict, or alter the socioeconomic mobility paths for the children of immigrants. Therefore, they cannot be ignored but simultaneously, they only represent a part of the context of reception that must be taken into consideration. The local community (including co-ethnic communities), schools, and the family are also important settings in which children of immigrants grow up. Hence, both types of contexts impact the outcomes for the children of immigrants. As Zhou and Bankston state, "the effect of an immigrant culture varies depending not only on the social structures of the ethnic community on which the immigrant culture is based, but also on the social structures of the larger society of which the immigrant culture is a part" (1998: 12).

Neighborhood, local, and co-ethnic community

Some maintain that the local context of reception is the single most important factor in determining the opportunities and barriers to socioeconomic adjustment and advancement. The local context of reception can be operationalized in many ways including government policies toward a particular immigrant group, the labor market, and or intergroup dynamics (Portes and Rumbaut 1996). The local context impacts the children of immigrants in much of the same ways as it does for other children in their neighborhoods. Those in middle-class neighborhoods with abundant economic and social resources as well as safe spaces for school and play are more likely to have better educational and social outcomes. In contrast, those in immigrant families who reside in neighborhoods with a high concentration of poverty, high unemployment, violence, and/or under-funded schools face significant challenges in their daily lives as well as in their socioeconomic outcomes.

Zhou and Bankston (1998) suggest that for those immigrant families who find themselves in socioeconomically marginalized neighborhoods, the co-ethnic community provides a buffer between the negative impacts of the locality and the children of immigrants growing up within it. Even for those who have less human capital or resources, their children can draw from and benefit from the social capital afforded to them by the individuals with higher socioeconomic status within their ethnic community (Kasinitz *et al.* 2008). The ethnic community provides the support as well as exerting a degree of control over their youth that frequently produces positive educational achievements. The strategy of selective acculturation into positive aspects of the mainstream society while maintaining interactions within the ethnic community to buffer against the negative aspects of the immediate local surroundings frequently explains the success of immigrants located in relatively poor neighborhoods.

Schools and the beginnings of socioeconomic attainment

The neighborhoods in which these children of immigrants live also determine the schools they attend. Again, the outcomes for the children of immigrants are highly varied with youth enrolling "in schools that range from well-functioning, with a culture of high expectations and a focus on achievement, to dysfunctional, with an ever-present fear of violence, distrust, low expectations, and institutional anomie" (Suarez-Orozco *et al.* 2008: 40). High aspirations and socioeconomic success are more common among children in middle-class neighborhoods with well-resourced school districts, effective programs for supplemental education, and other programs to encourage educational success. On the other hand, children in working class or poor neighborhoods that are segregated racially, economically, and linguistically face the high likelihood of lower socio-economic success. These segregated places are often inextricably linked to "overcrowded, understaffed schools that have high rates of turnover among teachers and other staff, are poorly resourced and maintain low academic expectations, and are plagued by hostile peer cultures and the ever-present threat of violence" (Suarez-Orozco *et al.* 2008: 40). Consequently, the children of immigrants in these kinds of schools are often vulnerable to lower expectations and academic achievement and ultimately, higher drop-out rates. As discussed in the previous section, the capacity of immigrant families to foster selective acculturation for their children within these neighborhoods is especially important.

Beyond the socioeconomic context of the school, studies of immigrant children in the classroom show that they often feel that they are neglected while the most disruptive students receive the most attention. This is particularly true for the children who have limited English proficiency. For immigrant children specifically, their own English proficiency is an extremely important factor in their academic success. In many new destinations that have little experience with immigrants and in resource-poor neighborhoods, classes or programs for English acquisition may not exist or may be extremely under-funded. The No Child Left Behind policy in the United States, as argued by Suarez-Orozco *et al.* (2008), has exacerbated the disadvantage of these students who are not only pressured to learn English but are also pushed to pass standardized tests they do not understand. This may lead to discouraged students who may eventually see very few options beyond dropping out.

Immigrant families and intergenerational relationships

Immigrant parents, regardless of their own background, come to the United States with the hope of a better life for their children. Often they are willing to take jobs for which they may be overqualified and accept lower wages in exchange for opportunities unparalleled in their country of origin. For many, language acquisition and/or acculturation are much more gradual than the case is for their children. Through school and the media, children learn to speak English relatively quickly. Owing to parent–child role reversal and the dependence of parents on their children for information or interactions outside the home, the parents may lose their parental authority over their children. The need to preserve parental authority may be particularly pervasive in neighborhoods that can have a negative influence on their children. As a protection strategy discussed in previous sections, immigrant parents look to their co-ethnic community to serve as a buffer between their children and the neighborhood or even the ill effects of mainstream culture.

A second issue to consider is the relationship between immigrant parents and their children as it relates to the pace of acculturation. As Portes and Rumbaut (1996) explain, both the parent and children generations simultaneously go through the adaptation process of learning the language and/or "the ropes" in the United States. However, "the rates at which they do so and the extent to which this learning combines with retention of the home culture varies, with decisive consequences for the immigrant family" (1996: 240). There are several possible relationships that can occur across generations. First, the refusal to acculturate by both generations is referred to *consonant* resistance to acculturation. These families are often those whose lives are entirely insulated in ethnic enclaves with limited English proficiency and little contact with those outside the community. Second, the willingness and effort by both generations to acculturate is referred to as *consonant* acculturation. Often times, the immigrant parents come with high socioeconomic status and settle their families in more integrated or predominantly white neighborhoods. The third scenario would be when parents do not acculturate but their children do. This is referred to as *dissonant* acculturation. Lastly, there is what is called *selective acculturation* which is akin to the segmented assimilation notion that some of the most successful children of immigrants are those that selectively and strategically choose only certain aspects of both cultures to maximize the likelihood of success.

Differing views of whether to and how much to acculturate can often lead to conflict and tension between immigrant parents and their children. Additionally, it may increase the distance felt between generations and perhaps jeopardizes the closeness of the family. This in turn can further accelerate the acculturation of the children while parents may retreat further into their co-ethnic community. Ultimately, the children of immigrants and their parents may find relative socioeconomic success within different communities and family ties might be their only connection. It is unclear whether the children of immigrants will continue to maintain strong, cohesive ethnic communities for their children or if they will become a part of the continuously changing mainstream society.

Shifting contours of the twenty-first century

Waves of immigration have consistently increased diversity in receiving countries and immigrants in the past decade continue this tradition in several ways. Racially or ethnically, turn of the twentieth-century immigration in the United States brought significant numbers of southern and eastern Europeans to a northern and western European mainstream while the majority of post-1965 immigrants came from Asia and Latin America. By 2009, the share of new immigrants (those who arrived in past decade) from Europe shrank from what it was in 2000 while it remained steady for Latino immigrants. On the other hand, the share of new immigrants from Asia and other parts of the world like Africa are gradually increasing. The increasing racial and ethnic diversity of immigrants and their children may be received with ambivalence in high immigration receiving nations. The researchers in Alba and Waters' book (2011) consistently found evidence for upward mobility across case studies in the United States and Europe. It remains to be seen whether a new ethnic pluralism or pressures of traditional assimilation will prevail for the children of immigrants.

Beyond the shifting racial and ethnic diversity of new immigrants in the twenty-first century, their socioeconomic profile is also changing. At the turn of the twentieth century, most newly arrived immigrants were thought to be from poor rural areas bringing little education or money to start their lives in the United States. One of the fundamental features of the United States 1965 immigration legislation was the preference and greater admission of skilled immigrants. The immigrant population began to reflect a socioeconomic polarization and disparity similar to those previously observed between whites and blacks (Rumbaut and Komaie 2010). However, the immigrant population is slowly becoming skewed more toward higher socioeconomic status. In the past decade, an increasing number of immigrants are entering the United States with high levels of education and wealth. For example, almost 60 percent of new immigrants from Asia (those arriving after 2000) have at least a bachelor's degree. Furthermore, new immigrants are arriving with lower levels of poverty than in previous decades.

Third, at the end of the twentieth century, an increasing number of immigrants began to settle in areas that have had little to no experience with immigrant populations. These "new destinations" have been more likely to be rural, suburban, or smaller metro areas than the established gateways of the past. Because these new destinations have not previously had many immigrants, many of them do not have the assimilation machines (institutional, non-profit organizations, ethnic enclaves, etc.) in place to help immigrants adapt and integrate to the broader community (Massey 2008). Research on the settlement of immigrants in new destinations has begun to emerge where schools may be ill-equipped to incorporate children of immigrants who are not proficient in English or are from different backgrounds. For immigrant children specifically, the schools may not be equipped to handle limited or non-English speakers. The schools may also not know how to involve immigrant parents because of linguistic, cultural, or social barriers. Besides the expected difficulty of moving to a new place, these immigrant children may also face a social environment that may be particularly difficult to navigate. Their parents may experience similar issues in their workplace and in other contexts as they try to establish a life in a new environment. Given the strain that all members of the family may feel, it can have negative consequences for these children in the longer term. Immigrants introduce racial/ethnic as well as cultural diversity to these communities and it is uncertain whether the children of immigrants growing up in new destinations will experience rapid assimilation or perpetual "otherness."

References and further reading

Alba, R. (2005) "Bright vs. blurred boundaries: Second-generation assimilation and exclusion in France, Germany, and the United States" *Ethnic and Racial Studies* 28(1): 20–49.

Alba, R. and Nee, V. (2003) *Remaking the American Mainstream: Assimilation and the Contemporary Immigration.* Cambridge, MA: Harvard University Press.

Alba, R. and Waters, M. C. (eds) (2011) *The Next Generation: Immigrant Youth in a Comparative Perspective.* New York: New York University Press.

Boyd, M. (2002) "Educational attainments of immigrant offspring: Success or segmented assimilation" *International Migration Review* 36(4): 1037–60.

Crul, M. and Vermeulen, H. (2003) "The second generation in Europe" *International Migration Review* 37(4): 965–86.

Eckstein, S. and Barberia, L. (2002) "Grounding immigrant generations in history: Cuban Americans and their transnational ties." *International Migration Review* 36(3): 799–837.

Gans, H. (1992) "Second-generation decline: Scenarios for the economic and ethnic futures of the post-1965 American Immigrants" *Ethnic and Racial Studies* 15(2): 173–92.

Gordon, M. (1964) *Assimilation in American Life: The Role of Race, Religion, and National Origins.* New York: Oxford University Press.

Hernandez, D. J. (ed.) (1999) *Children of Immigrants: Health, Adjustment, and Public Assistance.* National Research Council and Institute of Medicine Board on Children Youth and Families. Washington, DC: National Academy Press.

Hurh, W. M. (1990) "The "1.5 generation": A paragon of Korean-American pluralism. *Korean Culture* 11(1): 21–31.

Kasinitz, P., Mollenkopf, J. H., and Waters, M. C. (eds) (2004) *Becoming New Yorkers: Ethnographies of the New Second Generation.* New York: Russell Sage Foundation.

Kasinitz, P., Mollenkopf, J. H., Waters, M. C., and Holdaway, J. (2008) *Inheriting the City: The Children of Immigrants Come of Age.* Cambridge, MA: Harvard University Press.

Lopez, N. (2003) *Hopeful Girls, Troubled Boys: Race and Gender Disparity in Urban Education.* New York: Routledge.

Massey, D. S. (ed.) (2008) *New Face in New Places: The Changing Geography of American Immigration.* New York: Russell Sage Foundation.

Mather, M. (2009) "Children in immigrant families chart new path." *Reports on America.* Washington, DC: Population Reference Bureau.

Myers, D., Gao, X., and Emeka, A. (2009) "The gradient of immigrant age-at-arrival effects on socioeconomic outcomes in the US" *International Migration Review* 43(1): 205–29.

Oropesa, R. S. and Landale, N. (1997) "Immigrant legacies: Ethnicity, generation, and children's familial and economic lives" *Social Science Quarterly* 78(2): 399–416.

Park, J. and Myers, D. (2010) "Intergenerational mobility in the post-1965 immigration era: Estimates by an immigrant generation cohort method" *Demography* 47(2): 369–92.

Park, J., Nawyn, S., and Benetsky, M. (2011) "Gender and socioeconomic intergenerational mobility of post-1965 immigrants and second generation" Paper presented at the annual meetings of the American Sociological Association, Las Vegas.

Park, R. E. and Burgess, E. W. (1921) *Introduction to the Science of Sociology.* Chicago, IL: University of Chicago Press.

Park, R. E., Burgess, E. W., and McKenzie, R. D. (1925) *The City: Suggestions for the Study of Human Nature in the Urban Environment.* Chicago, IL: University of Chicago Press.

Perlmann, J. and Waldinger, R. (1997) "Second generation decline? Children of immigrants, past and present—a reconsideration" *International Migration Review* 31(4): 893–922.

Piore, M. J. (1979) *Birds of Passage: Migrant labor and Industrial Societies.* New York: Cambridge University Press.

Portes, A. and Rumbaut, R. G. (1996) *Immigrant America: A Portrait,* 2nd edition. Los Angeles, CA: University of California Press.

——(2001) *Legacies: The Story of the Immigrant Second Generation.* Berkeley, CA: University of California Press and Russell Sage Foundation.

——(2006) *Immigrant America: A Portrait.* Third Edition. Los Angeles, CA: University of California Press.

Portes, A. and Zhou, M. (1993) "The new second generation: Segmented assimilation and its variants among post-1965 immigrant youth." *Annals of the American Academy of Political and Social Science* 530(1): 74–98.

Ramakrishnan, S. K. (2004) "Second-generation immigrants? The '2.5 generation' in the United States" *Social Science Quarterly* 85(2): 380–99.

Rumbaut, R. G. (1991) "The agony of exile: A study of the migration and adaptation of Indochinese refugee adults and children." In F. L. Ahearn and J. L. Athey (eds), *Refugee Children: Theory, Research, and Services.* Baltimore, MD: Johns Hopkins University Press, pp. 53–91.

——(1997) "Paradoxes (and Orthodoxies) of Assimilation" *Sociological Perspectives* 40(3): 483–511.

——(2004) "Ages, life stages, and generational cohorts: Decomposing the immigrant first and second generations in the United States" *International Migration Review* 38(3): 1160–1205.

Rumbaut, R. G. and Komaie, G. (2010) "Immigration and adult transitions" *The Future of Children* 20(1): 43–66.

Rumbaut, R. G. and Portes, A. (eds). (2001) *Ethnicities: Children of Immigrants in America.* Berkeley, CA: University of California and Russell Sage Foundation.

Silberman, R. (2011) "The employment of second generations in France: The republican model and the November 2005 riots." In R. Alba and M. C. Waters (eds), *The Next Generation: Immigrant Youth in a Comparative Perspective.* New York: New York University Press.

Suárez-Orozco, C., Suárez-Orozco, M. M., and Todorova, I. (2008) *Learning a New Land: Immigrant Students in American Society.* Cambridge, MA: The Belknap Press of Harvard University Press.

United Nations (2009) *International Migration.* New York: US Department of Economics and Social Affairs, Population Division.

Warner, W. L. and Srole, L. (1945) *The Social Systems of American Ethnic Groups.* New Haven, CT: Yale University Press.

Waters, M. (1999) *Black Identities: West Indian Immigrant Dreams and American Realities.* New York: Russell Sage Foundation.

Zhou, M. (1997) "Growing up American: The challenge confronting immigrant children and children of immigrants" *Annual Review of Sociology* 23: 63–95.

Zhou, M. and Bankston, C. L. (1998) *Growing Up American: How Vietnamese Children Adapt to Life in the United States.* New York: Russell Sage Foundation.

Zúñiga, V. and Hernández-León, R. (eds) (2005) *New Destinations: Mexican Immigration in the United States.* New York: Russell Sage Foundation.

27

International adoption

Andrea Louie

Transnational adoption has been celebrated as a form of altruism through which children orphaned by war, natural disasters, or other circumstances are given new homes and the opportunity for better lives. However, it is important to remember that adoption also represents the movement of children, often too young to give consent, across national, and often racial boundaries to become a permanent part of their new families. In this sense, transnational adoption has been critiqued by some, as much as it has been celebrated by others, both for the procedural irregularities that sometimes involve the trafficking of children or the adoption of children who are not true orphans, and for the broader inequalities that define the transfer of children from poorer to wealthier nations, and from the global south to the global north.

These critiques do not intend to diminish the altruism of those who wish to adopt, nor the potential positive aspects of adoption itself. Indeed, many proponents of adoption argue that the transnational adoption system works effectively, giving homes to children who need them. But it is also important to understand key issues associated with the politics of international adoption and the rights of children that frame international adoption as a very specific type of migration.

This chapter places the movement of international adoptees within a broader context of shifting historical and geopolitical conditions, and unequal global flows. Drawing in part on my own research with US families who have adopted from China, and more broadly on the growing transnational adoption literature, I provide an overview of the very specific type of migration that international adoption represents. This form of migration is shaped by the circumstances that orphan children or compel birth parents to relinquish their children for adoption, and the policies and politics within both sending and receiving countries that regulate adoption practices and shape the reception of adoptees into these countries.

I discuss the cultural and political economy of transnational adoption, sketching out the shifting historical and geopolitical contexts that open up adoption flows. I also address more critical approaches toward adoption relating to the commodification and trafficking of children and discussions of adoption as the creation of a forced diaspora (Hubinette 2007).

A history of transnational adoption

The circumstances under which international adoptions have occurred have varied throughout history, both in terms of the ways in which children became orphaned and the processes by which international adoptions were facilitated. Marre and Briggs (2009: 1) observe that though international adoption was initially a way to rescue children orphaned by war, it has now become a means for infertile couples and others to create a family. They further observe that what began as an effort to provide temporary foster care to World War I orphans eventually transformed into the adoption of war orphans following World War II and subsequent wars in Asia and Latin America, and more recently into the adoption of "abandoned" Asian and Eastern European children (2009: 29, see also Tobias Hubinette's "Orphan Trains to Babylifts" in Trenka *et al.* 2006, for a comprehensive history of international adoption.) However, they emphasize that "Even this new form of transnational adoption has been marked by the geographies of unequal power, as children move from poorer countries to wealthier ones—and the forces that make a country rich and powerful are above all historical. In this sense, transnational adoption has been shaped by the forces of colonialism, the Cold War, and globalization" (2009: 1–2).

Briggs and Marre emphasize that our current understandings of international adoption as a permanent way to form a family through the adoption of children from another country have not always defined transnational adoption practices. Noting that international adoption involves specific understandings of children's rights, and of the relationship between the United States and other nations, they cite historian Christina Klein's work that argues that the desire of US families to adopt war orphans reflected a broader paternalistic attitude that the United States developed toward other countries after World War II (Briggs and Marre 2009: 5). Combined with the efforts of evangelical Christians such as Harry and Bertha Holt to adopt Korean War orphans including Amerasian children, this also signaled a shift in how adoptees were viewed in relation to broader US society. Following the Korean War in 1953, the Holts, farmers from the state of Oregon on the west coast of the United States, adopted eight Amerasian children, lobbying Congress to pass special legislation to allow them to do so. In 1956, they opened Holt International, an adoption agency with a Christian mission statement, and began bringing Korean War orphans to the United States and placing them with adoptive families. They later expanded their services to include adoptions from 14 countries in total, including Cambodia, China, Ethiopia, Guatemala, Haiti, India, and Uganda (Holt International website).

Briggs and Marre note that for the Holts and others, international adoption was initially seen as involving the saving of underprivileged children by wealthier nations. They observe that "the programs took for granted that children would be converted religiously, nationally, and socially: they would become little Americans, or Swedes, or Norwegians" (Briggs and Marre 2009: 8). This assimilative approach framed how adoptee's identities were shaped by their parents, and the degree to which issues of racism were addressed for these children, most of whom were children of color adopted by white families.

Complex and varied socio-historical circumstances led to adoption flows from Latin America, former socialist nations in Eastern Europe and the Soviet Union, and from Africa. In Latin America, the past neocolonial involvement of the United States has shaped adoption flows from countries such as Guatemala to the United States (Leinaweaver and Seligmann 2009: 4). Seligmann (1990: 4) notes that "A review of available statistics demonstrates starkly the rise and fall of transnational adoption in tandem with the increase and decline of civil war and violence in distinct regions of Latin America (Selman 2004; Briggs 2005)." Adoption from the former Soviet Union and former Soviet Republics such as Kazakhstan and the Ukraine, and post-Socialist Eastern European countries such as Romania, began following the dissolution of the Soviet Union in 1991. Adoptions from the former Soviet Union grew exponentially between 1992 and 2001, from 324 to 4, 279 (Evan P. Donaldson Adoption Institute n.d.). Adoptions from Africa saw an increase in the 1990s, with children from Ethiopia and Madagascar being sent to France. After 2003, the numbers of children adopted from Ethiopia to France, Spain, and the United States continued to rise (Selman 2009: 587–88).

According to Peter Selman, numbers of intercountry adoptions (ICA) have increased steadily over the past fifty years, "to an estimated total worldwide of over 45,000 a year in 2004" (Selman 2009: 575). However, contrary to predications for continued growth, numbers fell by 17 percent over the next few years. Selman notes that, "There are well over 100 countries involved in sending children for ICA and it is impossible to review trends in all of these" (Selman 2009: 581). However, he does observe some overall shifts in analyzing data since 1997. For example, while in 1997, 67 percent of children adopted internationally into Spain were from Latin America, by 2000, only 21 percent were from Latin America, and Eastern Europe now accounted for 47 percent of adoptions to Spain (Selman 2009: 582). In addition, while adoption from Asia (primarily China) constituted 54 percent of intercountry adoptions in 2005, Africa was the only continent to show an overall growth in the number of adoptions in 2007, and will likely be the only one showing future growth (Selman 2009: 583). The overall decline in international adoptions since 2004 can be explained by a decline in the availability of children for adoption from "key states of origin" (Selman 2009: 589).

Adoptees versus other immigrants

In recent years, transnational adoption has been a growing area of research, reflecting both the increasing number of internationally adopted children, and the coming of age of significant numbers of Korean and other transnational and transracial adoptees who are themselves engaging in scholarship, activism, and creative expression related to adoption. Transnational adoption can be explored from a number of perspectives, both academic and non-academic. However, within the context of this volume, it is important to specifically examine how adoptees are positioned both legally and socially in relation to other types of migrants. As noted above, like broader migration patterns, international adoption flows are the product of global inequities that result in movements occurring primarily in one direction—from poorer to richer nations, primarily in North America and Europe. These patterns are not new, nor are they coincidental. In general, the top sending and receiving countries have remained the same over the past few years. Peter Selman's study, focusing on the top 20 receiving countries, finds that intercountry adoptions increased 42 percent between 1998 and 2004. His data show that the countries receiving the highest number of international adoptees in 2004 were the USA, Spain, France, Italy, Canada, the Netherlands, Sweden, Norway, Germany, and Switzerland, in that order. The top sending countries to the US are China, Russia, Guatemala, South Korea, Kazakhstan, the Ukraine, India, Haiti, Ethiopia, and Colombia (Selman 2009: 37). Selman notes, however, "the paradox that the countries sending the most children in recent years have not been the poorest or those with the highest birth rates" (2009: 38). Thus, adoptions are not solely determined by these factors, but rather are mediated by governmental policies and other social, cultural, or historical factors.

In addition, adoption flows, like other migration flows are often gendered. However, these patterns too are complex. Selman notes that while the majority of children adopted from China, India, and Vietnam are girls, more boys were adopted from South Korea, because girls were often adopted domestically. China is well known for and has also been criticized by other nations, by anti-abortion advocates, and others, for its One Child Policy, which has indirectly resulted in high rates of infant abandonment of Chinese girls. At the same time, Kay Johnson (2004) has shown that there are a host of historical, cultural, political, and economic factors that lead to female infant abandonment, including the lack of a social security policy in China, and the continued belief predominant in rural areas that girls become part of their husbands' families and therefore will not be able to care for their aging parents.

But while the Chinese government has been critiqued for what are viewed as its oppressive policies that regulate family size and a woman's fertility, these same circumstances facilitate the availability of children for adoptive parents. Many of these girls have been adopted internationally, to the United States, Canada, Spain, Great Britain, and other North American and European countries. Many parents desire Asian girls because they view them as model minorities who are docile and malleable (Dorow 2005). Unlike other racial minorities, Asian Americans enjoy a racial status that is between black and white, though closer to white (Zhou 2005). The history of the United States has produced a racial system that is framed within a black-white binary (Ancheta 2010), into which other minorities are slotted as "constructive blacks" or "constructive whites." As scholar Robert Lee argues, the model minority myth, which portrayed Asian Americans as successful, trouble free immigrants, arose in the 1950s in the context of the Cold War efforts to spread the image of the United States as a liberal democracy that treats its minorities well. At the same time, these false conceptions were used against other underperforming US minority groups, particularly blacks and Latinos who were characterized as lacking in cultural values, and therefore as undeserving of government aid in the form of welfare and other programs.

For Chinese girls, the circumstances under which they became available for adoption—in the view of many adoptive parents, as healthy infants whose only crime was to have been born as girls—lessen prospective parents' anxieties about their health and the circumstances of their relinquishment. Some narratives surrounding female Chinese adoptees frame their adoption from China as involving a degree of altruism in rescuing girls from these circumstances in which they are not wanted. However, Johnson's (2004) research also shows that issues of infant abandonment are highly complex, indicating that many Chinese parents would not relinquish their infant girls if a sufficient social security network were available for rural families and if government policy allowed for the birth of more than one child without fines or other forms of punishment.

Another complex dimension of international adoption relates to the specific national and international policies that regulate the movement of adoptees. These often differ from those that both spur and govern other forms of migration. In some ways, adoptee migration flows parallel migration patterns more broadly in that they trace similar patterns from poorer to richer nations. However, there are also important distinctions between adoptees and other migrants, just as there exists great variation within migrant populations themselves. Voluntary migrants most often plan in advance for their emigration, which is usually a strategy to secure better employment, further one's education, or reunite with family members. At the same time, they often face strict legal barriers from both their countries of origin and receiving countries that restrict and regulate their transnational movement. For example, US immigration laws favor certain classes of immigrants, including those with specific professional skills or those with family already in the United States. The 1965 Immigration and Nationality Act, or the Hart–Celler Act, created special categories of immigration that gave preference to skilled and professional laborers and also included provisions for family reunification. The immigrant adjustment process also varies, depending on their level of presocialization to US culture. Some immigrants come with English fluency and advanced degrees, and struggle little with finding employment and navigating everyday social life and bureaucracies. Others who lack literacy even in their native languages and who come with few economic or educational resources struggle more.

Adoptees, on the other hand, are a very different kind of migrant. Once placed for adoption, adoptee paperwork travels through separate channels from that of other migrants. For example, though still governed by state regulations on both sending and receiving ends, US citizens who adopt from abroad are allowed to file form I-600 to the US Citizenship and Immigration Services office, titled "Petition to Classify Orphan as an Immediate Relative." Depending on the child's visa and whether or not the adoption has been finalized by both countries, the child may be granted citizenship immediately upon entering US soil per the Child Citizenship Act of 2000.

Adoptees also face major transitions as they become part of families who usually come from different cultural, religious, and often "racial" backgrounds than their caretakers in their countries of birth. Though young children are viewed as being malleable, and many appear to adjust very smoothly, the shift from orphanage or foster care to living with a new family can be overwhelming for some. Though most adoptees grow up in families that are middle to upper class in socioeconomic background and may therefore have access to resources to which not all immigrants may initially have available to them, for many, adoption represents a significant loss, even trauma, from feeling abandoned by birth parents to having been removed from the familiar settings of their birth countries, usually without their consent.

In this sense, then, adoptees are in some ways more similar to refugees than they are to voluntary migrants. Like refugees, few travel of their own free will, but rather are brought to other countries via circumstances beyond their control. As children made parentless due to war, environmental disaster, poverty, ethnic or racial conflict, or other complex social or cultural factors, they are, as Swedish scholar and international adoptee Tobias Hubinette (2007: 177) asserts, a forced and marginalized diaspora. Hubinette argues that under these circumstances, they are required to identify with and perform whiteness and that "this ethnic instability leads to severe psychic violence and physical alienation" (2007: 178–9). His argument serves as a critique of the celebration of hybrid, border-crossing identities that is common in portrayals of transnational migration and cosmopolitanism. Elsewhere, he compares international adoption, which he considers a form of "forced migration" that has resulted in the movement of "almost half a million children" to western countries since 1950, to the Atlantic slave trade, the coolie trade, and the trafficking of women and children (Hubinette in Trenka 2006: 142–3). Though he acknowledges key differences between these practices, he remarks that "both practices are driven by insatiable consumer demand, private market interests, and cynical profit making, and both use a highly advanced system of pricing where the young, the healthy, and the light-skinned are most valued" (2006: 143). His perspective may be viewed as a somewhat extreme viewpoint on adoption as a form of migration. However, there have been numerous other critiques of adoption practices.

Critiques of adoption

While international adoption has often been celebrated as a way to help children without permanent homes and to create new multicultural families, the overall system that drives adoption, which as Hubinette discusses above assigns unequal values to children of different backgrounds, has been critiqued on many levels. Though some may say they prefer international adoption for a variety of reasons that may include an interest in other countries and cultures, the high costs and other challenges associated with adopting a healthy white infant from the US also factor into the decisions of many parents to turn to international adoption to form a family. My research, carried about between 2001 and 2009 in St Louis, Missouri and the San Francisco Bay Area of California focused primarily on how white and Asian American adoptive parents conceived of Chineseness as a racial and cultural form as they attempted to help their children craft identities. Most parents I interviewed for my own research on Chinese adoption also insisted that their primary motivation for adoption was their own desire to have a child, and not to engage in a form of altruism. However, it remains a point of contention among many adoption activists and scholars that international adoptees are often preferred over domestic adoptees of color (Ortiz and Briggs 2005), and that the costs associated with adoption correlate with both race and national origins, causing some to speak of adoption in terms of "baby markets" (Goodwin 2010).

Another pressing critique surrounds the regulation of adoption. As a form of intercountry migration, adoption is regulated very differently from other forms of immigration, and thus raises different sets of issues. How can it be ensured that children's rights are protected—that they are indeed orphans without family to care for them in their home countries? Do children need to be adopted abroad, away from their countries of birth, and to grow up with little knowledge of these origins, or can options be provided for adoption or fostering in their birth countries? The movement of children across national borders to become part of new families carries numerous other potential issues relating to who has the right to make decisions regarding which children are adopted, or whether international adoption should occur at all. Historically, even acts viewed as humanitarian efforts such as the 1975 Operation Babylift from Vietnam have raised controversy for the removal of 2,000 children from their homeland, many of whom had not actually been orphaned. Following the fall of Vietnam to the Communists, the United States frantically scrambled to evacuate Vietnamese war orphans to safety, loading them onto cargo planes, in some cases placing infants in boxes. It was later discovered that many of these children still had living parents and relatives who wished to raise them, though in many cases they had already been placed with new US families (Bergquist 2009). Similar situations have occurred in 2007, when a French non-profit organization tried to airlift Sudanese children from Dafur, despite warnings from the French government that the children had not been verified as orphans and the fact that adoption is prohibited by Muslim law.

It is unfortunate that in some cases adoption has been associated with child trafficking and other illegal means of coercing mothers to relinquish their children who are then sold. Child trafficking schemes attached to adoption have been exposed in many countries, including Guatemala, Cambodia, and Vietnam (Schuster Institute for Investigative Journalism 2011). In some of these cases, adoption programs have been closed down or temporarily halted when these schemes have been uncovered.

In response to these and other concerns, sending and receiving countries have in some cases engaged in international efforts to regulate transnational adoption, based on the premise that these children's futures should be determined by their own governments and fellow citizens, and not by foreigners, no matter how good their intentions may be. Indeed, the Hague Adoption Convention (1993) stipulates that orphaned children should ideally be placed with family members, or adopted domestically as a second choice. International adoption should only be seen as a last resort, and only be done with the permission of the child's birth country. Though not all nations have agreed to comply, the convention's aim is to prevent child trafficking and ensure that children's rights and interests are protected. The United Nations Convention on Rights of the Child of 1989 similarly establishes basic rights for children under 18, which include rights to be protected in the case of adoption. It states that "the child, for the full and harmonious development of his or her personality, should grow up in a family environment, in an atmosphere of happiness, love, and understanding" (1989: Preamble) (as quoted in Seligmann 2009). These regulations, which have not yet been accepted by all countries, aim to ensure that children who are adopted internationally have been orphaned or voluntarily relinquished by their parents, and that there are no intermediaries who are misleading birth families and/or profiting from the sale of their children for adoption.

However, the question of adoption as a human rights issue can be complex. There may be conflicting perspectives on what actions best protect the rights of children. Research by

Leinaweaver shows that Peruvian adoption workers view transnational adoption as a means to "promote" the rights of children, while work by Cardarello in Brazil indicates that adoption is sometimes viewed as a form of child trafficking that impinges on children's rights (Leinaweaver and Seligmann 2009: 3).

What are a nation's responsibilities to care for its own children, and at what point does international adoption become a form of commodifying children for sale abroad? The notion of adoptees as commodities has also been at the center of critiques leveled at South Korea, which has received accusations that it is exporting its own children and turning international adoption into a form of national income. These critiques came to a head during the 1988 Olympics, which were held in Seoul, South Korea, during which the government was critiqued for using its children as an export commodity. South Korean children have been adopted to the United States, Sweden, France, and numerous other locations. Despite its rapid economic development and rising living standards, traditional ideas regarding out of wedlock births and the adoption of children who were not of one's bloodline had not changed significantly (Freundlich and Lieberthal 2005). While international adoption had traditionally been seen as a last resort for underdeveloped, impoverished nations to find homes for children who did not have parents, or whose parents could not care for them, it is clear that there are ethical issues involved in a nation's decision to make its children available for adoption in the first place. Kim Park Nelson writes that, "Transnational adoptions have become so common that they have resulted in measurable income streams to some birth countries, to the annual tune of $15–20 million in South Korea (estimated 2001 GDP of $865 billion), $5 million in Guatemala (estimate 2001 GDP of $48.3 billion) and $2 million in Honduras (estimated 2001 GDP of $17 billion)" (2006: 96).

Another ethical issue stemming from the removal of children from their "birth countries" and cultures has shaped contemporary approaches toward raising adopted children. Largely in response to critiques from first and second wave Korean adoptees who had been raised in colorblind atmospheres without much acknowledgment of their Korean origins or their status as racial minorities, newer generations of adoptive parents have endeavored to expose their children to what they term their "birth cultures." This issue is not a new one within the context of domestic US adoption. While some scholars such as Rita Simon (2000) argued that transracial adoption did not lead to racial identity issues, in 1972, the National Association of Black Social Workers released an official statement in opposition to the adoption of black children by white families, asserting that white families would not be equipped to teach these children about African American culture or how to live as racial minorities in US society. Contrary to the notion that "love is all you need" these social workers emphasized that children were not just part of families, but also communities, and that removing them from these communities was akin to "cultural genocide."

Racial, cultural, and national belonging

The above sections illustrate that international adoption is undergirded by sets of complex motivations that shape the fates of adopted children. Children arrive not as blank slates who can be melded seamlessly into their adoptive families, but with specific histories that are sometimes embodied in the physical features that in the case of transracial adoptees mark their "difference." As discussed in the previous section, contemporary adoption practices have evolved in response to previous concerns about establishing cultural identities for adoptees.

The next section of this chapter will discuss transracial adoption to Europe and the United States, the destination of the majority of international adoptees and the focus of most of the literature on the subject. While studies such as Heather Jacobson's (2008) have shown that even in same-race adoptions, some parents take an interest in the "birth cultures" of their children, this chapter will focus primarily on transracial international adoption—the adoption of children of color by white families in the global north.

According to the Evan P Donaldson Institute, over one-quarter of a million children have been transnationally adopted into the United States between 1971 and 2001. Between the years of 1991 and 2001, transnational adoptions to the United States more than doubled. Adoption numbers are similarly significant for Sweden. Tobias Hubinette (n.d.) notes that, "Statistics Sweden (SCB) has identified 43,882 international adoptees in Sweden born between 1932–2001 and coming from more than 130 countries … The international adoptees represent 1–2 percent of all generations born from the beginning of the 1970s, and still around one thousand children arrive annually to Sweden. In total, the international adoptees constitute 15 percent of all non-white immigrants in the country." While Hubinette's statistics indicate that in the case of Sweden, international adoptees represent a significant portion of the non-white immigrant population of the country, other research has shown that adoptive parents often place immigrants and adoptees into different categories (Howell and Marre 2006, cited in Howell 2009). Adoptees are viewed as differing from immigrants in large part due to the socializing efforts of their parents. Howell (2003: 159) asserts that adoptive parents attempt to make their children essentially Norwegian by dressing them in Norwegian clothing, teaching them traditional folk tales, and fostering other aspects of Norwegian culture. Similarly, Yngvesson (2007: 566) observes that in the 1970s and 1980s, adoptees were seen as externally distinct from other Swedes, but as "completely Swedish" on the inside. She notes that publications by Sweden's Adoption Centre "contrasted" adopted and immigrant children, asserting that immigrants maintained their traditional ways upon moving to Sweden, while adoptees became Swedish because they were raised by Swedish parents. She also notes, however, that as adoptees grew to adulthood and realized that they were being racialized and discriminated against in ways similar to immigrants, these notions were soon debunked. In the case of Spain, Marre and Briggs (2009: 228) notes that international adoptions are not viewed as a form of international migration, as immigrants are viewed as having "integration difficulties" in contrast to the smoother transitions adopted children were imagined to make. And ironically, while adoptive parents were interested in the cultures of their children's birth countries, Marre and Briggs also note that parents downplayed the fact that there were "possible similarities" between the two groups (228).

In the field of China adoption research, critics have noted that while parents may feel more comfortable with families similar to their own, they may be creating very narrow versions of Chinese culture that are disconnected from the actual practices of Chinese and Chinese American families (Anagnost 2000; Eng 2003; Dorow 2006). They assert that the decontextualized, aestheticized versions of "birth culture" that adoptive parents create may merely serve to neatly slot adoptee heritages into the majority white adoptive cultures. Critics, including academics, adoption professionals, and adoptees themselves, point to the dangers in aestheticizing and celebrating children's birth cultures at the expense of attention to issues of race (Anagnost 2000). They argue that cultural practices and artifacts should not be taken out of context, and that local minority communities representing the child's background should not be ignored at the expense of focusing on the country of birth. The issues surrounding the cultural and racial positioning of adoptees reflect broader issues regarding how adoptee experiences can be understood *vis-à-vis* other migrant groups, as they are on the one hand part of families to which their belongingness is emphasized, and on the other they remained linked to their countries of origin by their personal histories and often by their phenotypical features.

Debates over what constitutes "birth cultures" and how they are imagined and implemented within the context of adoptive family lives are significant, in that they reflect tensions between an adoptee's "racial" and cultural roots, and how these origins remain meaningful in the context of the racial and cultural politics of their country of residence. Discourses of colorblindness and assimilation that permeate US multiculturalism may have the dual effect of reducing "difference" to a cultural realm to be celebrated in the context of diversity, and dismissing discussions of race to something that only existed in the past.

Recent works in critical race theory and adoption in the context of both the United States and Europe have discussed the processes by which international transracial adoptees are racialized and exoticized in relation to both domestic black adoptees (Ortiz and Briggs 2005) and other racial minority immigrants, thus shedding light on the racial politics surrounding perceptions of international adoptees. At the same time, in both North American and Europe, culture has become the focus of the adoptee's difference, often as a way to diminish the focus on the adoptee's racial differences, but also as part of broader racial and multicultural projects. There is some disagreement among adoption researchers as to the salience of racism in contemporary contexts, and of the relative power of culture to provide a basis for the flexible creation of new identities in what some consider to be a post-racial society. Norwegian anthropologist Signe Howell (2009: 160) argues that:

> issues of race are more in evidence in the United States than in Europe. Howell and Melhuus (2007), Howell and Marre (2006), and Marre (2007) have argued that race is not regarded as relevant in transnational adoption in Norway and Spain. Prospective adoptive parents in the Scandinavian countries may not specify racial preferences in their applications. Surveys show, however, that adoptive parents are anxious about racism as their children grow up and leave home.

However, for many, the concern is that given the celebratory focus on the cultural distinctiveness of adoptees rather than the potential implications of their minority status, adoptees may not be prepared to go out into the world from their sheltered family lives as people of color living in a majority white society. While anti-immigrant sentiments fueled by fears of labor competition and other forms of xenophobia may shape attitudes toward new immigrants to North America or Europe, particularly non-white ones, adopted children of similar racial backgrounds to those of immigrant populations may be welcomed into communities. However, it is important to consider the interplay between discourses of color blindness that imply that adoptees' racial origins are irrelevant, and the broader politics of race that affect adoptees outside the home. Unlike immigrants who experience similar racial and ethnic environments both in and outside the home, transracial adoptees are often raised in predominantly white homes and environments, but may be lumped together with other people of color outside the safe haven of their families.

The language of kinship

The study of adoptive families represents an opportunity to examine new forms of kinship and family that traverse national borders, whether in practice or in the imagination. Anthropologist Signe Howell refers to "kinning" processes that bring adopted children into Norwegian families. Other works discuss the ways that adoptees (and/or their parents) endeavor to create or uncover bonds of kinship, whether genetic or of commonality, with fellow adoptees. Toby Volkman (2010) writes of the sustained efforts on the part of adoptive parents to locate siblings for their children through the use of DNA technology. This trend points to the perceived power of having biological connections for adopted individuals who may not know anyone who is genetically related to them. Most adoptees of course do have genetic relatives, but their ties to them have often been severed.

The discontinuity that marks the adoptee's transition from their country of birth to their new countries of citizenship distinguishes theirs from the experiences of other migrants, particularly those who maintain strong transnational ties to friends and family in their home country. These ties are usually facilitated by personal connections, and other forms of social, cultural, and economic capital that enable migrants to sustain these ties. However, for the majority of adoptees who lack kinship ties or access to other social networks, transnational ties may be difficult to build and sustain.

Korean adoptees, many of whom from the first two waves are now adults, have criticized the Korean government for misinformation, inconsistencies in paperwork, and general lack of knowledge regarding their adoption histories (Trenka 2009). While many Korean adoptees have successfully carried out searches for birth families, others have been stymied by a lack of transparency in their adoption records, or sometimes purposeful misinformation, as in the case of Deann Borshay Liem, who chronicled her search for her birth family in the film "First Person Plural." The fact that many international adoptees do have birth families back in their countries of origin greatly complicates the notion of adoption as involving a clean break between a child's country of origin and his or her new start as part of another family (Yngvesson 2010).

It is not uncommon for adoptees, either individually or with families and travel groups to engage in roots-searching activities, birth family searches, or forms of activism, thereby forging new transnational relationships and networks (Yngvesson 2005; Kim 2010). Eleana Kim's work documents this process for Korean adoptees who travel to Korea on homeland tours and are faced with messages from the Korean government that complicate their understandings of their Koreanness (Kim 2010). Barbara Yngvesson discusses the experiences of Swedish adoptees "returning" to their roots in Chile. In some ways, their endeavors are not totally dissimilar from those of many second, third, and fourth generation descendants of migrants who no longer retain direct connections to the homeland and need to construct them anew. In both cases, roots-seekers must contend with governmental discourses of belonging and exclusion, which impose assumptions about their racial and cultural identities (Louie 2004; Kim 2007). These travels usually represent temporary transnational movements, and are therefore not strictly a form of migration. However, while non-adopted descendants of migrants may be able to access some genealogical and historical information about their families, this is often more difficult for adoptees. Instead, adoptees who are unable to or do not desire to locate birth families can form other types of connections with fellow adoptees and others that might also be transnational in nature. International adoptees from Korea, for example, have formed a number of organizations, some in Korea itself, to advocate for adoptee issues, including ASK (Adoptee Solidarity Korea), which is trying to hold the Korean government to its promise to end Korean adoption within the next few years, and TRACK (Truth and Reconciliation for the Adoption Community of Korea), which aims to achieve "full knowledge of past and present Korean adoption practices to protect the human rights of adult adoptees, children, and families." Jane Jeong Trenka blog: (http://justicespeaking.wordpress.com/objective-Replacement?/).

Adoptees are also engaged in various forms of cultural production and expression, including filmmaking (Borshay Liem 2000) and creative writing (Kwon Dobbs 2007; Trenka 2009), in which they give voice to their diverse experiences. Though they share many similarities with other migrants, including feelings of displacement, loss, and of being in-between cultures, it is also important to acknowledge the specificity of their journeys.

Transnational adoption will likely continue in one form or another in the years to come. However, as advocates work to reform adoption practices so that they are in the best interest of the children, to increase opportunities for the domestic adoption of children within their countries of birth, or even to improve conditions for birth mothers so that they may not need to relinquish their children in the first place, one wonders what the future of transnational adoption will look like. Will it continue at its present numbers, or at some point, might transnational adoption slow or perhaps disappear altogether?

References and further reading

Anagnost, A. (2000) "Scenes of misrecognition: Maternal citizenship in the age of transnational adoption" *Positions: East Asia Cultures Critique* 8(2): 389–421.

Ancheta, A. (2010) "Neither black nor white." In J. Wu and T. Chen (eds), *Asian American Studies Now: A Critical Reader*. New Brunswick, NJ: Rutgers University Press, pp. 21–34.

Bergquist, K. Sook, J. (2009) "Operation Babylift of baby abduction? Implications of the Hague Convention on the humanitarian evacuation and 'rescue' of children" *International Social Work* 52(5): 621–33.

Borshay, L. D. (2000) *First Person Plural*, [DVD] Berkeley, CA: Mu Films.

Dorow, S. K. (2005) *Transnational Adoption: A Cultural Economy of Race, Gender and Kinship*. New York: NYU Press.

Dorow, S. K. (2006) "Racialized choices: Chinese adoption and the 'white noise' of blackness" *Critical Sociology*. 32(2–3): 357–79.

Eng, D. L. (2003) "Transnational adoption and queer diasporas" *Social Text* 76(21.3): 1–37.

Evan B. Donaldson Adoption Institute (n.d.) *International Adoption Facts*.

Freundlich, M. and Kim Libreta, J. (2000) *The Gathering of the First Generation of Adult Korean Adoptees: Adoptees' Perceptions of International Adoption*. New York: Evan B. Donaldson Adoption Institute.

Goodwin, M. (2010) *Baby Markets: Money and the New Politics of Creating Families*. Cambridge: Cambridge University Press.

Holt International Website. www.holtinternational.org/historical.shtml.

Howell, S. (2007) *The Kinning of Foreigners: Transnational Adoption in a Global Perspective*. Brooklyn, NY: Berghahn Books.

Howell, S. (2009) "Adoption of the unrelated child: Some challenges to the anthropological study of kinship" *Annual Review of Anthropology* 38: 149–66.

Howell, S. L. (2003) "Kinning: the creation of life trajectories in transnational adoptive families" *Journal of the Royal Anthropological Institute* 9(3): 465–84.

Hubinette, T. (n.d) "The international adoptees of Sweden and the theory of multiple burdens." www.tobiashubinette.se/multiple_burdens.pdf.

——(2006) "Orphan trains to Babylifts: Colonial trafficking, empire building, and social engineering." In J. J. Trenka, J. C. Oparah, and S. Y. Shin (eds), *Outsiders Within: Writing on Transracial Adoption*. Cambridge, MA: South End Press, pp. 139–49.

——(2007) *Asian Bodies Out of Control: Examining the Adopted Korean Existence. Asian Diasporas: New Formations, New Conceptions*. R. Parrenas and L. Siu (eds), Stanford, CA: Stanford University Press.

Jacobson, H. (2008) *Culture Keeping: White Mothers, International Adoption, and the Negotiation of Family Difference*. Nashville, TN: Vanderbilt University Press.

Johnson, K. (2004) *Wanting a Daughter, Needing a Son: Abandonment, Adoption, and Orphanage Care in China*. St Paul, MN: Yeong and Yeong.

Kim, E. (2007) "Our adoptee, our alien: Transnational adoptees as specters of foreignness and family in South Korea" *Anthropological Quarterly*, 80(2): 497–531.

——(2010) *Adopted Territory: Transnational Korean Adoptees and the Politics of Belonging*. Durham, NC: Duke University Press.

Kwon Dobbs, J. (2007) *Paper Pavilion*. Buffalo, IN: White Pine Press.

Lee, R. (1999) *Orientals*. Philadelphia, PA: Temple University Press.

Leinaweaver, J. B. and Seligmann, L. J. (2009) "Introduction: Cultural and political economies of adoption in Latin America" *Journal of Latin American and Caribbean Anthropology* 14(1): 1–19.

Louie, A. (2004) *Chineseness Across Borders: Renegotiating Chinese Identities in China and the US*. Durham, NC: Duke University Press.

Marre, D. and Briggs, L. (2009) *International Adoption: Global Inequalities and the Circulation of Children*. New York: NYU Press.

National Association of Black Social Workers (1972) "Position statement on trans-racial adoption." The Adoption History Project. darkwing@oregon.edu/~adoption.

Ortiz, A. T. and Briggs, L. (2003) The culture of poverty, crack babies, and welfare cheat: The making of the "Healthy White Baby Crisis." *Social Text* 76(21.3): 39–57.

Park Nelson, K. (2006) "Shopping for children in the international marketplace." In J. J. Trenka, J. C. Oparah, and S. Y. Shin (eds), *Outsiders Within: Writing on Transracial Adoption*. Cambridge, MA: South End Press.

Schuster Institute for Investigative Journalism. Fraud and Corruption in International Adoptions. www.brandeis.edu/investigate/adoption/index.html.

Seligmann, L. J. (2009) "The cultural and political economies of adoption in Andean Peru and the United States" *Journal of Latin American and Caribbean Anthropology* 14(1): 115–39.

Selman, P. (2009) "The rise and fall of intercountry adoption in the 21st century" *International Social Work* 52(5): 575–94.

Simon, R. and Alstein, H. (1994) *The Case for Transracial Adoption*. New York: University Publishing Association.

Simon, R. J. and Altstein, H. (2000) *Adoption Across Borders: Serving the Children in Transracial and Intercountry Adoptions*. Lanham, MD: Rowman & Littlefield.

Trenka, J. J. (2009) *Fugitive Visions: An Adoptee's Return to Korea*. Minneapolis, MN: Graywolf Press.

Trenka, J., Oparah, J. J., and Shin, S. Y. (2006) *Outsiders Within: Writing on Transracial Adoption*. Cambridge, MA: South End Press,.

——(n.d.) *Chinese Adoptee Links blog*, http://chineseadopteelinks.wordpress.com/about/.

Volkman, T. A. (2005) *Cultures of Transnational Adoption*. Durham, NC: Duke University Press.

Yngvesson, B. (2010) *Belonging in an Adopted World: Race, Identity, and Transnational Kinship*. Chicago, IL: University of Chicago Press.

——(2007) "Refiguring kinship in the space of adoption" *Anthropological Quarterly* 80(2): 561–79.

——(2005) "Going 'home': Adoption, loss of bearings and the mythology of roots." In T. Volkman (ed.), *Cultures of Transnational Adoption*. Durham, NC: Duke University Press.

Zhou, M. (2004) "Are Asian Americans becoming white?" *Contexts* 3(1): 29–37.

Part VII
Migrants and the state

Popular and scholarly discourse about the experience of international migration commonly focuses on migrants' cultural orientation and on the impact of social structure as the key factors in determining outcomes. However, a growing body of research refers to the influence of a third entity—the nation-state—as shaping migrants' entry, adaptation, mobility, and fate. In fact, resources and limitations encountered by migrants—both individually and collectively—are to a considerable degree shaped by the actions of nation-states.

Both sending and receiving states regulate a variety of activities that shape migrants' lives, including primary and secondary education, language training, recruitment, emigration control, naturalization, political incorporation, regulation of work status, health care, and access to various public benefits. This section examines how governments and nation-states act with regard to immigrants.

In their chapter on borders, boundaries rights, and politics, Roger Waldinger and Thomas Soehl, note that since migration involves people "voting with their feet" against the country of origin and for the host society; it is an inherently political act. At the same time, they observe that international migration is also politically destabilizing, as it poses potentially threatening questions to both the country of origin and the host society about their relations to the migrant population. Further, the political status of the migrant population itself is also uncertain. The authors identify several reasons why migration scholars have neglected the issue. Finally, they review and assess the ways though which scholars have tackled the study of immigrant politics in order to highlight central issues in the field.

In his chapter on regulation, recruitment, and control, Matthew Light reviews the ways that nation-states control international migration. He considers the history of migration regulation, explores the range of variation in national immigration policies, and evaluates reasons that contemporary industrialized democracies have for developing their policies. Finally, the chapter examines new directions for research, including normative theories of immigration policy and the creation of immigration policy in developing countries.

In her chapter on unauthorized migrants, sociologist Cecilia Menjivar contends that we should view undocumented immigration in terms of its political and economic construction rather than from a legalistic perspective. She points out that undocumented workers respond to the same circumstances and cultures of migration as legally sanctioned migrants, and decide to migrate in response to recruitment efforts originating in the host society. Accordingly, their being labeled as illegal often reflects an effort by the host society government to manage contradictory demands from anti-immigrant movements, on the one hand, and employers who continue to seek migrant labor, on the other.

Noting that undocumented immigrants are often ineligible for health care and education, unable to contact police, and subject to family-splitting deportation policies, Menjivar argues that they unjustly suffer at the hands of the host society, often in ways that are harmful to it as well. Since the host society bears some culpability for their presence, she asserts that migrants' undocumented status should be treated as an issue of citizenship rather than one of criminality.

In her chapter on migration and health, Guillermina Jasso explores health characteristics across different migration streams and examines whether health improves or deteriorates in the destination country. She does this by drawing on the US New Immigrant Survey to develop a conceptual framework, examine the empirical challenges, and present estimates of health selection and health change. She concludes that health deteriorates due to the hardship of dealing with migration and the visa process but then improves as migration-related stress ends, and increasing familiarity with the host society allows the migrant to navigate the destination country's health environment to mitigate its harms and enhance its benefits.

In his chapter on naturalization, Thomas Janoski summarizes quantitative data and the historical record of naturalization policies from several countries to develop an empirically-based understanding of various nations' willingness to extend citizenship to migrants. This offers a more objective and systematic way of evaluating naturalization than is availed by repeating clichés about the extent to which a country is or is not open to migrants. Addressing methodological issues and the value of cross-national and macro-sociological studies, Janoski concludes that naturalization is not a simple result of immigration, but rather, a complex political process in itself.

In her chapter on education, Ramona Fruja Amthor focuses on the US experience to summarize current research and policy debates about immigrants and education by comparing two periods of migration. In the early twentieth century, immigrants with largely European origins attended schools committed to fostering assimilation via the inculcation of American values, cultural practices and the English language. From the mid-1960s until the present, immigrants from Latin America, Asia, and other non-European settings to the United States have entered schools in a wide range of communities—ranging from impoverished inner-city locations to affluent suburbs—that are more concerned with matters of diversity and cultural preservation. Amthor summarizes important findings about the experience of the sizeable and diverse population of contemporary immigrant student in the United States and addresses current debates surrounding the implications of gender, mental health, discrimination, class differences, ethnic networks and permanence of settlement in determining achievement among contemporary immigrant students.

Given the recent growth in both the numbers of migrants and the impacts of globalization that open a wide array of possibilities for them, nation-states increasingly seek to understand, control, and direct the actions of their citizens abroad. Interrogating this phenomenon, Brendan Mullan and Cristían Doña-Reveco present a historical overview of host societies' relations with emigrants. In it, they discuss the relationship between migrant remittances and sending states' economic development and assess the reciprocal political relationship between emigrants and their state of origin. Finally, the authors explore various relationship between states, emigrants, and concepts of citizenship and offer suggestions for future research.

Newcomers' consumption of public welfare has been a major reason for opposition to immigration in many countries. Accordingly, debates regarding the type, extent, and timing of state-provided social services for immigrants reflect deep ideological divides in many countries. Those against the extension of welfare benefits to immigrants assert that such programs attract immigrants, engender a "culture of dependency" and are an unsustainable strain on the state. In contrast, others recognize the benefits migrants offer to host societies' economies, dwindling populations and welfare systems.

In their chapter on immigrants and the welfare state in Western societies, Xavier Escandell and Alin M. Ceobanu examine the debates on the role of immigration and the future sustainability, coverage, and configuration of existing welfare state programs in order to reveal different states' policies, structures, and attitudes that pertain to including immigrants economically and politically. The article concludes with suggestions as to how states might respond to the challenges and opportunities posed by increased immigration.

28

The political sociology of international migration

Borders, boundaries, rights, and politics

Roger Waldinger and Thomas Soehl

International migration is an inherently political phenomenon. In leaving home, the migrants vote with their feet, *against* the home state and *for* the receiving state, preferring a state with the resources needed to provide public goods and make markets work over one that can't. In so doing, the migrants also do what *neither* state wants: their departures/entries illuminate problems of state capacity on both sides of the chain, highlighting the home state's inability to retain its people while underscoring the receiving state's inability to control its borders to the extent that the populace wants. Once across the border, migrants simultaneously become foreigners *in* the country *where they live* while becoming foreign *to* the country *from which they came*. Consequently, international migration always raises the question of the migrants' attachment to body politics newly encountered as well as left behind.

Unfortunately, there is no carefully specified perspective for understanding how these twin attachments are made, transformed, or cut off. Despite growing interest, politics remains an underdeveloped topic in migration studies, whether the concern has to do with receiving society *immigrant* politics or sending society *emigrant* politics. As we will show in the next section, this lacuna derives from prevailing intellectual biases, whether having to do with those that focus on individual action or those that emphasize social processes. We will then identify central issues entailed in the study of migrant politics—whether home or host country oriented—reviewing and assessing the ways in which scholars have tackled this problem.

Why politics falls out

Assimilation

Assimilation remains the most influential approach to the study of the migrant experience on the receiving society side of the border. Yet politics is nowhere to be found in any of the influential statements of this perspective. Case in point is Alba and Nee's (2003: 235) seminal, *Remaking the Mainstream: Assimilation and Contemporary Immigration*, where politics receives barely any mention. The longest treatment is a paragraph long, emphasizing that the European immigrants of the nineteenth and early twentieth centuries "inserted themselves qua groups into political pro-cesses … in ways that created tangible rewards for ethnic membership … " (156). As for citizenship, a matter of great political controversy *and* substantial scholarship, it gets no reference at all.

How could it be otherwise? The strength of Alba and Nee's account lies in its rational choice approach: immigrants cast off ethnic ways and attachments, connecting with the mainstream and adopting its practices, because orientations toward the host country and its expectations yield the greatest rewards. Hence, the immigrant search to get ahead gradually but inexorably leads to the decline of an ethnic difference.

Since "conflict and disagreement"—*not* the disappearance of difference—are the "defining features of political life" (Pearson and Citrin 2006: 220), a theory of political assimilation cannot simply forecast diffusion into some undifferentiated mainstream: no such thing exists. Politically, the population that Alba and Nee describe as the mainstream is divided, whether by ideology, class, region, religion, or some material interest. Bereft of sociological meaning, the mainstream is instead a claim, an ideological tool that insiders and outsiders use to struggle over who is what. Moreover, assimilation into the mainstream and a corresponding diffusion of identity is *not* what receiving society publics want. Rather, they clamor that the foreigners become nationals, replacing the particularism imported from abroad with the particularism found in their new home. Last, whereas the framework advanced by Alba and Nee understands boundaries to be informal, the relevant political boundaries involve the inherently formal conditions of legal status and citizenship. Those bright political boundaries exercise long-term consequences at both individual and societal levels: initial non-incorporation impedes political participation at any point in the process, whether before or after citizenship acquisition (Hochschild and Mollenkopf 2009). As long as the migrants remain outside the body politic, they have limited ability to influence "who gets what" let alone "who is what," a factor in turn structuring the society in which they now live.

Transnationalism

Transnationalism is the popular intellectual alternative to assimilation and deservedly so, as it demonstrates how international migration inherently generates cross-border connections, which then gradually yield a "transnational social field" linking migrants and stay-at-homes.

In highlighting these cross-border connections and their ubiquity, interest in transnationalism has broadened the scope of inquiry, moving it beyond the traditional preoccupations with immigrant assimilation or integration in which everything of importance transpires *within* the boundaries of destination states. Though enlightening, this new sensitivity yields little more than a richer, broader description, as it lacks a framework to explain how migrants manage these cross-state conditions, under which conditions, with what success, and for how long.

Ironically, the intellectual difficulties resemble the shortcomings afflicting assimilation approaches. Just like assimilation, transnationalism highlights the migrants' agency, with the difference that the story gets pulled back to the point of origin. Rather than starting on the receiving side of the border, the proponents of transnationalism note that the motivations impelling migration—the search for a better life—make migration a survival strategy for kin and significant others left at home. While these cross-state ties are ubiquitous, they are put in place by masses of individuals taking a common, parallel, but *uncoordinated* path in the effort to get ahead. Though the migrants are therefore likely to be highly connected, it is not clear how or why they should identify with any home country political collectivity, whether at local, regional, or national levels.

Just like assimilation, transnationalism also neglects the structures impeding engagement with the body politic left behind, as upon movement to a new state migrants suffer the dual exclusion associated with their status as emigrants—being citizens abroad—and as immigrants—being aliens where they actually live. While home states can and do follow "their" emigrants abroad, they are not "unbound," but rather constrained by the costs and logistics of creating a political infrastructure in a foreign country, not to speak of concerns that visible home country activity might spark anti-immigrant reactions. Unfortunately, the transnational perspective has not acknowledged these obstacles, nor explained how they might be transcended. Just as seriously it lacks an account of the factors that might promote the persistence of homeland attachments, notwithstanding the many changes that so often lead migrants to shift focus to the country of reception as settlement deepens.

Migrants' perspectives: from migration to mobilization

Where might we look for insight into the processes by which international migrants, impelled into cross-border mobility by their own private concerns, follow a path to political engagement? One source is Piore's classic *Birds of Passage* (1979). Here, Piore emphasizes settlement: initially oriented toward return, seeking to help their families by sojourning in a rich country, the migrants live together, with little sense of connection, either to one another or to the new country where they live. They take as many jobs as they can find, seeking to quickly accumulate the savings needed to go home and invest in a farm or a new business. But the strategy that works in the short term becomes increasingly problematic as time wears on: as the migrants spend more time with one another and more money on their own consumption, leaving less to be sent home abroad, their time horizon expands.

A time in the receiving society deepens, orientations shift, as migrants' expectations regarding the terms and conditions of work converge with those of the society around them. Once content to fill the unstable, undesirable jobs at the bottom of the hierarchy, content with lowest quality dwellings, they increasingly want more. Since from here it is a short step to some collective action, whether wildcat or more organized strikes or concerted activity of some other sort, the model developed by Piore tells us how the transition from migrant laborer to political subject might occur. Though highly stylized, this model receives ample support from research conducted across a broad range of contexts, whether focusing on protests among foreign workers in Europe in the 1970s and 1980s or among Latino immigrants in the United States.

While accurately depicting the changing mentality and comportment of the classic migrant laborer, as an account of political behavior, Piore's model falls short on at least two counts. Following the prevailing trend in the literature, it pushes emigrant politics off the agenda: once the migrants' frame of reference shifts from "there" to "here," receiving society issues are all that matters. More importantly it takes for granted that the possibility that the receiving society permits such a shift. After all, the underlying psychological and social mechanisms should be the same among Pakistani migrants to the Persian Gulf or Filipino migrant workers to Singapore, as among Mexicans in Los Angeles or Algerians in Paris. Yet the latter two possess something lacked by the former two, namely a set of formal rights: at the minimum, freedom of expression and assembly and to judicial relief, regardless of legal or citizenship status, often to more expanded social rights, including labor protection by the sending state and its agencies and involvement in organized labor. The question, therefore, has to do with the origins of these rights and the factors embedding them in the political environment that the migrants confront in the society where they settle. To pursue that issue, we need to shift perspective and examine the contours of migrant political behavior from the standpoint of the host societies and states that they encounter. Later, we will return to questions of emigrant politics.

The receiving context: closure and incorporation

Political incorporation and citizenship

We begin with citizenship, a multidimensional concept touching on issues of rights, legal status, participation in the polity, membership, and belonging. Zeroing in on several of these dimensions, we can see how the contradictions and tensions among them create the environment in which migrants are both politicized *and* become political actors themselves.

The bounded polity

Citizenship has two faces: it is internally inclusive, establishing legal equality for members of the state, but also externally exclusive, as only citizens possess unconditional access to the territory and full political rights. Using the term introduced by Rogers Brubaker (1992), citizenship is an object as well an instrument of closure.

This dimension of citizenship is key in maintaining the coherence between the identity of the population *in* the state and that of the people *of* the state. While the view that society = nation = state represents the liberal ideal, an "imagined community" (Anderson 2006) in which the polity takes the form of the rule of likes over likes, international migrations challenge this isomorphism of states, societies, and people. Maintaining that national, imagined community *demands* that the people be bounded, lest there be no members with interests reflected in and represented by *their* state. Because the community of citizens needs the stability and commitment that comes with membership, the internal boundary of citizenship necessarily confronts foreigners wanting political membership in the territory where they actually live; passage across that internal frontier is *never* guaranteed. Believing in the idea of the national community, nationals endeavor to implement it, making sure that membership is only available to some, and signaling to the newcomers that acceptance is contingent on conformity. Hence, rather than an atavism slated to disappear, anti-immigrant sentiment is the dark side of the commitment to a national community.

Territory and rights

While the boundaries of the polity are tightly guarded, the boundaries of its territory are much more permeable, as almost all allow the influx of aliens, whether immigrants (both legal and undocumented), visitors, foreign students or temporary workers. While potential migrants have no claims on the state they hope to enter as long as they are on the "wrong" side of the border they wish to cross, the situation takes on very different form, as soon as that border is successfully traversed. While lacking the full entitlements of citizens, or the less complete protections of legal resident aliens, contemporary migrants *all* "have a right to have rights," the basic fundament of citizenship as famously described by Arendt (1951). Today even the undesirables are no longer cast of out of humanity, as in the mid-twentieth-century world she depicted. It is precisely because they are so enabled, that contemporary migrants have the capacity to strike and protest when their aspirations change in the way that Piore suggests.

From where do those rights come? Some analysts hail the advent of "post-national citizenship," claiming that foreign residents share the same core rights enjoyed by citizens, thanks to the protection of an international human rights discourse/regime and the advent of post-national membership where personhood complements and partly replaces nationality (Soysal 1994). These scholars, however, concede that any "post-national citizenship" extends to legal residents only, leaving unauthorized migrants at the mercy of the host state; they also note that international conventions or discourses yield strongest impacts *within* state boundaries, but not at the *external* boundary, where states exercise greater latitude.

An alternative view contends that migrants' rights derive from the fundamental traits of the polities into which they move. The receiving societies of North America, Europe, and the Antipodes are more than nation states guarding borders and access to membership: they are liberal democracies whose constitutions and legal orders demand an expansive distribution of rights (Joppke 1998). Indeed, the history of the United States—the case in which immigration is most deeply rooted in the country's tradition—underscores the degree to which migrants' rights derive from the nature of the polity itself. US courts recognized aliens' legal personhood and rights to protection in the late nineteenth century by US courts, decisions that subsequently provided the basis for additional rights (Bosniak 2006). Furthermore, the nature of liberal polities is such that migrants will enjoy the support of fully established allies, equipped with the knowledge and resources needed to defend migrant rights they see as embedded in existing statutes and also fight for expanded migrant rights.

Though contemporary migrants to democratic states enjoy a baseline of rights, it is unstable and uncertain, capable of expanding, but also contracting. Toleration was long the *de facto* policy in the rich, receiving state democracies; since the 1990s, greater efforts at border control have increasingly been linked to intensified efforts at internal control, leaving unauthorized migrants with a narrower margin of rights and an increased risk of deportation. Legal residents are better protected; however, even their rights can be rolled back, as indicated by trends in the United States since the mid-1990s.

Moreover, migrants' capacity for political participation falls far short of that enjoyed by citizens. Most importantly, voting rights are more limited; nowhere have non-citizens gained the right to vote in national elections. Consequently, exclusion from citizenship inevitably produces a divide between democracy and demography, a gap particularly large in the United States, where only one-third of the foreign-born population possesses US citizenship and another third lacks legal resident status (Passell and Cohn 2009). In the United States, therefore, the question of "who is what" has had a steadily widening impact on "who gets what." Non-citizens are poorer than citizens, a gap that has substantially widened over the past four decades. Moreover, the poorest of the non-citizens are those most firmly excluded from the polity: two-thirds of the immigrants with less than a high school education are in the United States illegally. But these are also the people whom the citizens entitled to influence policy and most likely to engage with politics are *least* inclined to help. Whereas the median voter has always been more selective—better educated, more affluent—than the median citizen, that discrepancy has remained relatively unchanged; by contrast, the gap between the median voter and the median non-citizen (legal or otherwise) has grown, as the latter has fallen increasingly behind the former. Consequently, redistribution has become increasingly unattractive to the median voter, who would have to share with non-citizens; because the burden of America's growing inequality has disproportionately been born by non-citizens, the motivations to cut up the pie in a more equitable way have correspondingly declined (McCarty et al. 2006).

Crossing the divide: becoming a citizen

Thus, although some scholars have described a "devaluation of citizenship," there is every reason to think that citizenship as status, and not just citizenship as rights, remains crucial. Hence, a crucial issue remains the ways in which persons who have crossed over the *external*, territorial boundary can later move across the *internal* boundary of citizenship. This brings us to the questions of the rules of citizenship acquisition and the modalities by which citizenship is also an object of closure. As mentioned above all nation-states make naturalization—the acquisition of the country's citizenship to those who haven't been assigned at birth contingent on a set of requirements. For example a significant period of *legal* presence in the territory is a minimum requirement in most states. But beyond that substantial differences remain.

These differences are often linked to typologies of citizenship regimes, with the classic distinction contrasting ethnic and civic definitions of citizenship. In the former the barriers for access to the political community for migrants and their children are very high while in the latter the barriers are much lower. The analytical value and utility of this distinction however is open to question—especially when it attempts to sort whole countries into these boxes. But even particular policies that govern the acquisition of citizenship are often hard to categorize. Thus, a host country might insist on fluency in its language as a precondition for naturalization or even for admission to the territory as a long-term resident. But is that a sign of civic conception because it emphasizes the importance of communication in the common public sphere or is it rather an element of an ethnically defined boundary around the citizenry? Moreover, within any particular stylized citizenship variant, policies toward citizenship differ, as shown by Bloemraad (2006), comparing two countries falling into the "civic" citizenship category, the United States and Canada. The United States takes a *laissez-faire* approach toward citizenship acquisition: while legal immigrants face relatively few impediments in accessing citizenship, they have to do it on their own, with little direct or indirect encouragement from the state. In Canada, by contrast, the state actively encourages the newcomers to become Canadians. The consequences can be seen in contrasting rates of naturalization: the foreigners arriving in Canada become citizens at roughly twice the rate of their counterparts who instead head for the United States.

Brubaker (1992: 21) defines the state as a "membership organization, an association of citizens." But just as citizenship can take more than one form, involving status as well as rights, so membership has more than one dimension. While membership can be equated with status, as in the statement above, it is also a claim, to be used in order to obtain citizenship, but also to contest the citizenship claim of others, whether would-be citizens or those who already possess that status. Thus, just as rights are not an exclusive privilege of citizens, citizenship does not guarantee equal rights, as indicated by the many groups of citizens (minorities, women, the working poor) who remain fundamentally disadvantaged despite citizenship's promise of equality. Possessing nationality in the country where they reside, they are nonetheless second-class citizens.

Regardless of formal citizenship regime and foreign-born persons' own citizenship status, the very fact of foreign birth is likely to put belonging in question, rendering the immigrants' claims for membership vulnerable to those with different conceptions of the national community. Precisely because immigration comprises a social dilemma that liberal societies cannot escape, it is a source of continuing controversy, reminding the immigrants that people like them, indeed, often their own kinsmen and compatriots, are not wanted. Moreover, foreign origins, even if distant, can be grounds for doubt. Thus, even in the United States, dominant group members view minorities as susceptible to dual loyalties and hence less patriotic than "unhyphenated" Americans.

Thus, the dual quality of membership allows it to be unpacked into two dimensions, one relating to citizenship status, the other relating to the political culture in which citizenship can be practiced. Here we could draw a distinction between monistic political cultures, such as those of contemporary France or the early twentieth century United States and its insistence that immigrants "swat the hyphen," and the more pluralistic political cultures of the settler societies of North America and the Antipodes at the turn of the twenty-first century. Rather than reproducing yet another dualism, these differences are better thought of as continuous in form, and also the object of struggle, over which different groups, committed to different visions of the national community, engage in conflict. And unlike the politics of citizenship status regimes, where powerful forces are pushing toward some degree of convergence, variations in political culture are so deeply embedded in national histories as to produce continuing cross-state differences.

Navigating the context: political opportunity structures and group identity

The population movements across borders that converge on democratic societies produce a new political phenomenon: persons who begin their lives in the new country formally excluded from the polity. As we have argued above, presence on the territory of a democratic state provides the potential for participation in politics, with politics conceptualized in so wide a fashion as to encompass any form of civic or collective activity, beyond the private, and possibly, religious sphere. But that potential is highly contested, due to immigrants' foreign origin and the controversies inevitably sparked by ongoing immigration. Moreover, the scope for participation varies, depending on the nature of the regimes that allow immigrants to formally enter the polity of the society in which they reside. Even that passage does not ensure full membership: possessing status citizenship, immigrants may be treated as second-class citizens and/or so perceive themselves, conditions that will affect their ability to engage with and belong in the body politic to which they have become newly attached.

Thus another defining characteristic of the migrant experience are the controversies inevitably unleashed by international migration, which may both trigger engagement with politics and at the same time furnish the seeds out of which identity is made. On the one hand, adverse political reactions to the influx of foreigners are an endemic condition of the rich democracies. On the other hand, immigrants and their offspring learn more than the ropes of the countries were they reside: they come to absorb many of its expectations and values, including an aspiration to membership. Precisely, because the cultural assimilation and political re-socialization of the foreigners is so successful, adverse reactions to immigration and efforts to restrict the national community *can* provide a catalyst to an ethnic response, generating a perception of "linked fate," diminishing the impact of class differences among persons sharing a common ethnic origin. Furthermore, as long as immigrants and their descendants remain socioeconomically and geographically distinct, even while talking and behaving much like dominant group members, ethnicity and interest are likely to converge. For these reasons, ethnicity is likely to provide an effective means of political claims-making and mobilization, as a result of which immigrants and their offspring are likely to follow a distinct path as they enter and move through the new body politic.

These traits are generic to the migrant situation in the advanced democracies, though differences in immigration histories, citizenship regimes, and political cultures give rise to significant variation. Equally important is the way in which the *specific* conditions of the political environment link up with the political claims making of migrant actors themselves. This way of framing the question is central to the political opportunity structure (POS) approach. This perspective has long been used by the social movement literature: here it has been used to explain how country specific institutional arrangements shape the tactics and identities of political actors that engage in protest and other forms of collective action. More recently, POS has been employed to study the political mobilization of minorities and immigrants, either to account for variation across differently categorized minorities within a country or across different nation-state contexts (Koopmans *et al.* 2005).

Following the POS approach minority identities are formed and dissolved in the very process of making political claims. For example, the way in which states categorize their population in respect to immigrant background (i.e. foreigners vs. natives in Germany and Switzerland versus racial/ethnic categories in England) shapes the ways in which immigrants make political claims and ultimately also come to define their political and social identity. Thus in Britain, where policy is decidedly framed in multi-ethnic/multi-racial terms, immigrant groups were much more likely to make claims framed in an anti-discrimination and unequal treatment while in France "the absence of a legal and discursive framework of equal opportunity and anti-discrimination … gives migrants few opportunities for demands against racial, ethnic or cultural biases in social institutions" (Koopmans *et al.* 2005: 141).

In principle, the POS approach should provide an opportunity to analyze the interdependence between migrant political actors and their context. In reality most studies focus on the environmental determinants, leaving the process by which the context shapes migrants' claims making underspecified and giving "minimal attention to being devoted to the strategic choices made by immigrant ethnic actors themselves" (Bousetta 2000: 235). For example, while POS approaches generally demonstrate the match between opportunity structure and the kind of claims that immigrants pursue, they don't explain how or why, implying that there is a natural fit between the opportunity structure and the kinds of claims and identities that immigrant groups tend to pursue.

A part of the problem is that POS assumes what needs to be explained: both clearly defined ethnic groups and of self-conscious, fully informed political actors are taken as given. Other approaches suffer from similar shortcomings. For example, in the United States, ethnic politics has long provided the main paradigm for studying the political incorporation of immigrants, focusing on the factors that shape the political participation of minorities, the coalitions they establish, and the extent to which they can realize their policy goals. Yet, as Lee (2008) notes in a recent critical review, a "preordained identity to politics link" is often taken for granted, distorting "our understanding of race and ethnicity, especially when taken as prior to, rather than subject to, empirical study" (p. 461). Similarly, in political psychology the political relevance of ethnic identifications functions as a common tacit assumption, though the specific meanings and salience of those identities is rarely explored.

Of course there are significant differences across populations (and countries): not all arrive with the same resources or undergo the same experiences: some are more homogeneous than others; some arrive under adverse circumstances, some enter under more favorable conditions, encountering a warmer welcome. Still, political opportunity structures do not confront ethnic or immigrant "groups" as such; rather, they are encountered by specific political entrepreneurs from immigrant or ethnic populations, who in turn, seek to mobilize or organize their putative co-ethnics. For these ethnic political entrepreneurs, the level of cohesion or "groupness" or differentiation within a community becomes a central component of the political opportunity structure.

The sending context: emigrant politics and emigration policy

Looked at from the standpoint of the receiving society, international migration imports a foreign element, comprising a presence on the host state's territory, but largely standing outside its polity. But the same picture appears somewhat different, if looked at from the standpoint of *emigrants* and the sending states from which they come.

In this light, the fact that international migrations inherently yield cross-border connections provides the point of departure. The many exchanges linking places of origin and destination effectively knit "here" and "there" together, facilitating and motivating continued involvement with home country politics, while diminishing its costs (Soehl and Waldinger 2010). However, it is movement into a new, separate political environment that enhances migrants' potential to influence home matters. Residence in a rich country gives the migrants resources not possessed before; that the rich country is also democratic yields the rights needed to put those resources to political use; because the receiving state's borders keeps out the tentacles of the sending state migrants also gain political protection against home state interests that might seek to control them (Waldinger 2011).

Though migration can be a source of homeland leverage for those still interested in the place left behind, displacement to the territory of a different state, representing a new people yields impacts that work in the opposite direction. Homeland political involvement tends to entail high costs and low benefits. While not the only reason to participate in politics, pursuit of material benefits—whether individual or collective—is one of the factors that lead people to spend time and effort on political matters. Home states, however, can do relatively little for the migrants in the territory where they actually live (Fitzgerald 2009) reducing motivations to purely symbolic or intrinsic rewards, which are unlikely to be compelling for most. Options for participation are also limited, with obstacles high. Although home country political parties maintain foreign branches and candidates travel abroad to garner expatriate support and material assistance, campaigning on foreign soil costs considerably more than on native grounds, especially if the former is a developing and the latter a developed society. Where they exist, expatriate electoral systems might attract greater migrant attention, but none can reproduce the national voting infrastructure on the territory of another country.

Absent mobilization, the pressures to detach from home country politics intensify. Political life is fundamentally social: participation responds to the level and intensity of political involvement in one's own social circles, which in turn generate political information. However, the circumstances of settlement are likely to lead to spiraling dis-engagement. Even areas of high ethnic density rarely possess the ethnic institutional completeness and political infrastructure that would stimulate engagement with home country matters. The migrants' status as immigrants orients them toward receiving state institutions, and media practices—even if conveyed via a mother tongue—provide at best modest coverage of home country developments. Absent powerful inducements, clear signals, and the examples of significant others, the costs of participation may easily outweigh its benefits. Since, by contrast, immigrants often realize that they will settle in the places where they live and where political participation is also easier, disconnection from home country politics is the typical pattern.

On the other hand, almost all migrations include at least some persons who remain impelled by homeland matters. Even though the rank-and-file may disengage, migration generates resources and provides protection for the minority of homeland activists, furnishing them with significant leverage. Moreover, the hard core is rarely alone, as there is often a large constituency that resonates to the homeland call, at least occasionally. In general, social identities change more slowly than social connections: even if no longer sending remittances or making periodic trips home, many immigrants retain an emotional attachment to their country of origin. Consequently, symbolic, homeland-oriented ethnicity persists, providing a base for homeland activists to mobilize (or manipulate).

Towards a political sociology of migration

Population movements across borders are propelled by a search to get ahead, as access to the territory of a rich country opens up resources unavailable in the poorer countries from which the migrants come. Though the populace may grumble, employers in the rich democracies of the north have repeatedly shown themselves ready to accept foreign workers. Likewise, sending states, which often decry the discrimination and exploitation that the emigrants encounter, nonetheless welcome the remittances earned through hard labor on foreign soil.

While economically driven, international migrations inevitably yield unintended, deeply significant political consequences, disrupting the neat congruence between "nations" and states thought to underpin the contemporary political order. As seen from the perspective of receiving states, migration changes the location of *aliens*, moving them from foreign territories on to native grounds. As seen from the perspective of sending states, migration shifts the location of *nationals*, transferring from the homeland on to foreign soil abroad. Either way, state, society, and nation are no longer one and the same.

As aliens, immigrants start off outside the polity, which is why the standard political science concerns related to formal political participation initially do not apply. Rather, the crux of the matter involves the relationship between the *politics of immigration* and *immigrant politics*. The former entails the rights and entitlements associated with the liminal status of alien residence on the territory of another people as well as the policies affecting the passage across the internal boundary of citizenship and into the polity. The latter, by contrast, concerns the means and mechanisms by which aliens engage in political activity and possibly acquire citizenship, foreigners learn the rules of a new national political situation, and foreign-born, naturalized citizens gain political incorporation and acceptance.

A mirror set of questions asks what happens when both emigrants and sending states try to keep up the connection to the body politic left behind. *Emigrant politics* concerns the efforts of the emigrants to engage with the homeland polity, whether seeking to create new states, overthrow regimes, lobby host governments on behalf of home states, participate in home state elections, change home state electoral and citizenship laws so as to allow for expatriate voting and dual citizenship. Those activities interact with the *politics of emigration*: sending state policies oriented toward the expatriates, seeking either to resolve the problems of *citizens living abroad*, where they suffer from the liabilities of alien status, or reconnecting the *emigrants* back to the place from which they came.

While these are the general parameters governing the politics of migration, patterns on the ground inevitably take a distinct form, affected by political environments in home and host societies, circumstances of migration, the resources that migrants both import and acquire, as well as the historical experience of both entry *and* exit. In the end, neither scholars, nor states, nor migrants can escape the political consequences generated by population movements across state boundaries, which is why the students of migration need to put the political sociology of migration at the top of their research agenda.

References and further reading

Alba, R. D. and Nee, V. (2003) *Remaking the American Mainstream: Assimilation and Contemporary Immigration.* Cambridge, MA: Harvard University Press.

Anderson, B. R. (2006) *Imagined Communities: Reflections on the Origin and Spread of Nationalism.* London: Verso.

Arendt, H. (1951) *The Origins of Totalitarianism.* New York, Harcourt.

Bloemraad, I. (2006) *Becoming a Citizen: Incorporating Immigrants and Refugees in the United States and Canada.* Berkeley, CA: University of California Press.

Bosniak, L. (2006) *The Citizen and the Alien: Dilemmas of Contemporary Membership.* Princeton, NJ: Princeton University Press.

Bousetta, H. (2000) "Institutional theories of immigrant ethnic mobilisation: Relevance and limitations" *Journal of Ethnic and Migration Studies* 26(2): 229–45.

Brubaker, R. (1992) *Citizenship and Nationhood in France and Germany.* Cambridge, MA: Harvard University Press.

——(2004) *Ethnicity Without Groups*. Cambridge, MA: Harvard University Press.

Fitzgerald, D. (2009) *A Nation of Emigrants: How Mexico Manages its Migration*. Berkeley CA: University of California Press.

Hochschild, J. and Mollenkopf, J. (eds) (2009) *Bringing Outsiders In Transatlantic Perspectives on Immigrant Political Incorporation*. Ithaca, NY: Cornell University Press.

Joppke, C. (1998) "Immigration challenges the nation state." In C. Joppke (ed.) *Challenge to the Nation-State: Immigration in Western Europe and the United States*. Oxford: Oxford University Press.

Koopmans, R., Statham, P., Giugni, M., and Passy, F. (2005) *Contested Citizenship: Immigration and Cultural Diversity in Europe*. Minneapolis, MN: University of Minnesota Press.

Lee, T. (2008) "Race, immigration, and the identity-to-politics link" *Annual Review of Political Science* 11: 457–78.

McCarty, N., Poole, K. T., and Rosenthal, H. (2006) *Polarized America: The Dance of Ideology and Unequal Riches*, Cambridge, MA: MIT Press.

Passel, J. S. and Cohn, D'V. (2009) *A Portrait of Unauthorized Immigrants in the United States*. Washington, DC: Pew Hispanic Center. http://pewhispanic.org/files/reports/107.pdf (accessed January 13 2010).

Pearson, K. and Citrin, J. (2006) "The political assimilation of the fourth wave." In T. Lee and K. Ramakishnan (eds), *Transforming Politics, Transforming America*. Charlottesville, VA: University of Virginia Press, pp. 217–42.

Piore, M. J. (1979) *Birds of Passage: Migrant Labor and Industrial Societies*. Cambridge: Cambridge University Press.

Soysal, Y. N. (1994) *Limits of Citizenship: Migrants and Postnational Membership in Europe*. Chicago, IL: University of Chicago.

Waldinger, R. (2011) "Immigrant Transnationalism," *Sociopedia ISA* Newbury Park, CA: Sage.

Waldinger, R. and Soehl, T. (2010) "Making the connection: Latino immigrants and their cross-border ties" *Ethnic and Racial Studies* 33(9): 1489–510.

29

Regulation, recruitment, and control of immigration

Matthew Light

Introduction

Scholars of immigration policy have traditionally investigated why and how national governments regulate the entry into their territory of foreign citizens for the purpose of permanent
resettlement. In recent decades, immigration policy research has broadened its focus to include
more aspects of the regulation of human mobility, and has become more integrated with related
bodies of scholarly literature. In what follows, we first consider the historical background to the
contemporary regulation of migration. We then explore the range and causes of variation in
immigration policies in contemporary industrialized democracies. Finally, we examine some
promising new directions for research, including normative theories of immigration policy, and
immigration policy in developing countries.

The historical context of the control of immigration

Contemporary immigration policy debates implicitly assume institutional arrangements concerning
states, borders, and citizenship that only emerged in roughly their current form toward the late
nineteenth century. To speak of "immigration" assumes that states distinguish strictly between
"citizens" and "foreigners;" that foreigners are subject to special restrictions on their entry to the
territory of another state; and finally that there actually *are* potential immigrants—people who both
can and would like to relocate to another country. Some 70 years ago, Karl Polanyi noted until the
early modern period, most Europeans—in particular the enserfed peasant population—were not
even formally free to emigrate. The nineteenth-century mass emigration of Europeans to countries
such as the United States, Canada, Australia, and Argentina only become possible following the
construction of a market economy based on formally free labor (Polanyi 1957 [1944]).

Indeed, for much of human history, "coerced" long-distance migration has been at least as
important as "voluntary" migration. The historical peak of coerced long-distance migration
began around 1600 and lasted until the abolition of the Atlantic slave trade in 1820 and included
the transportation of African slaves and European indentured servants and convicts to the New
World. A less well-known example of coerced mass-migration was the organized resettlement
of serfs and convicts to Siberia and the other far reaches of the Russian Empire, which was

undertaken to secure the state's claim to these remote and sparsely populated territories (Eltis 2002). Thus, coerced migration can have both economic and geopolitical functions for the governments that organize it.

Torpey (2000) has produced the most comprehensive analysis of the historical development of immigration policy, and its primary enforcement tools, the passport and the visa. As he notes, *foreigner* only became a meaningful concept in western societies during the early modern period, since this construct itself presupposes territorial states that distinguish systematically between their own subjects and those of other states. Moreover, early modern European states were less concerned with restricting the *entry* of foreigners than with restricting the *emigration* of their own subjects, whether the humble (needed for military service and tax revenue) or the skilled (needed to prevent a "brain drain" of valuable human capital). Through devices such as Tudor England's "Poor Laws" and similar mechanisms in other European countries, states sought to regulate the mobility of the poor, compel them to work, and punish those who were willfully unemployed. European states tended to perceive immigration as a boon—new subjects, free of charge!—rather than as an undesirable phenomenon that should be severely restricted. To take one example, the Russian Empire enthusiastically recruited European scientists, officials, skilled workers, and peasants from the seventeenth to nineteenth centuries.

The nineteenth century constituted a brief "golden age" of both emigration and immigration—at least for Europeans, most of whom were now legally free to leave their home countries. In addition, the major destinations (including North America, Australia, Argentina, and some other European colonial offshoots) were experiencing rapid economic growth and labor shortages, and thus were highly receptive to mass immigration (although not to all immigrants, as noted below). European emigration was also facilitated by new modes of transportation, notably the development of regular steamship service (Zolberg 1999a). This combination of free emigrants, receptive destination countries, and improved transport made possible an unprecedented boom in European immigration to the various "new Europes."

However, a much more restrictive regulatory mood set in during the closing decades of the nineteenth century and ultimately brought this brief golden age to an end. Torpey argues that the trend toward restrictive immigration policies was caused by geopolitical shifts, including the increasing tension in the international system that culminated in the outbreak of World War I, as well as the growth of revolutionary movements in the world, leading to the Russian Revolution of 1917. In this more unstable political environment, immigration came to be seen as a threat to existing regimes. Moreover, this drive for "regime preservation" frequently took on explicitly racialized overtones. A study by Zolberg (1999a) points to the role of ethnic and racial anxieties in immigration restrictions in the United States, where Chinese and Japanese immigration to the Pacific coast states aroused highly organized opposition among whites. In the 1880s, this anti-Asian movement successfully lobbied Congress to ban East Asian immigration to the United States, a prohibition which remained in effect until the 1950s. In subsequent decades, immigration from southern and eastern Europe also came under political attack. The United States did contain a pro-immigrant political coalition, which included big business, the Catholic Church, Jewish organizations, and urban political machines. However, these advocates of liberal immigration policies were ultimately vanquished by an anti-immigrant coalition that included organized labor, social and intellectual elites, and populist political forces (Zolberg 1999a: 307). As a result, a series of laws in the 1920s severely limited immigrant admissions, and imposed strict quotas based on the "national origins" of immigrants. As Zolberg notes, the defeat of business interests in the US immigration policy debate during this period demonstrates that immigration policy cannot be explained fully by reference to the economic concerns of the powerful. (We shall return to this theme in the discussion of immigration policy formation below.)

In roughly the same period, restrictive immigration policies also spurred the development of new administrative techniques to control international mobility. In particular, as Torpey notes, the now-ubiquitous passport and visa system of controlling international travel began to emerge only in the late nineteenth century, and became truly universal only with World War I. The establishment of this system marked the final stage in the establishment of modern mobility controls in democratic, capitalist states. After about 1920, most such states' policies provided for relatively free internal migration and emigration; and on the other hand, strict restrictions on immigration. However, not all states adhered to such policies. Thus, in the Soviet Union and most of its post-World War II satellites, emigration was severely limited, internal migration was strictly regulated, and immigration was by and large undesired.

Varieties of immigration policy in the developed world

While the scientific study of immigration policy first emerged in the United States, contemporary scholars now increasingly examine policies in other developed countries, notably in western Europe, as well as in the developing world, in order to explain variations between national policies. Gary Freeman's (1995) distinction between "traditional" and "non-traditional" countries of immigration still constitutes a good starting point. Freeman's "traditional" countries of immigration are primarily "the English-speaking [primarily white] settler societies" of Australia, Canada, New Zealand, and the United States in which "migration was critical to their founding and national development." (Although this article does not specifically reference non-English speaking countries in which European immigration has played a comparable role, such as Argentina and Israel, presumably they also belong in this category.) In contrast, Freeman argues that in European societies mass immigration is a more recent phenomenon. He writes that some northern European countries such as the United Kingdom and Germany began to receive labor immigrants in the post-World War II period, and other countries, primarily in the Mediterranean basin, have begun to experience large-scale immigration only in the last few decades (Freeman 1995: 882).

For Freeman, what ultimately turns on this distinction is a country's basic policy orientation toward immigration. For "traditional" countries of immigration, he argues, immigration "was integral to their founding and development as nations ... and they stand alone today in encouraging mass immigration for permanent settlement" (Freeman 1995: 887). As a result, while anti-immigrant sentiment may occasionally be intense (especially at the local and regional level), immigration retains a certain basic acceptance as a permanent feature of national life, and national policies do not ban or severely restrict immigration. He argues that European states see immigration (at least for permanent settlement) as unnatural, accept it reluctantly, and limit it wherever possible.

However, closer examination of the history of immigration policies both in Europe and the United States partially undermines, or at least makes more complex, Freeman's distinction between "traditional" and "non-traditional" countries of immigration. In the United States, immigration policy has always been highly contested, and basic policy approaches have varied widely between historical periods, from a highly open one (for most of the nineteenth century), to a virtually closed one (in the mid-twentieth century), to a much more open one (since the mid-1960s). A useful reference that summarizes the history of US immigration policy from the nineteenth century to the early 1990s is provided by Ueda (1994).

As noted above, by the 1920s, the US immigration policy discourse had turned decisively against immigration. Policies in place from the 1920s until roughly the 1960s were marked by strict quotas on new immigrants, "national origins" rules, as well a virtual ban on immigration from East Asia. However, post-World War I legislation also saw the creation of certain "non-quota categories" exempt from limitation, which included spouses and other close relatives of

US citizens ("family reunification"), certain professional categories, and, importantly, Western Hemisphere immigration.

After World War II, changing political circumstances gradually brought about the transformation of US immigration policy from a restrictive one based on racialized national origins quotas to a more open one based on family reunification and, to a much lesser extent, recruitment of immigrants with specialized skills. As Ueda notes, it is probably not a coincidence that immigration policy reforms in the post-World War II United States coincided with the abolition of official racial segregation in the 1950s and 1960s (Ueda 1994: 44). In part, both these developments may have resulted from the declining intellectual legitimacy of pseudo-scientific racism, which as we saw informed earlier US immigration policy debates. Geopolitical factors also seem to have played a role in immigration policy changes. The US government, which was then engaged in global political competition with the Soviet Union and its allies, feared that overtly racist policies (such as the total exclusion of East Asians) would alienate newly independent developing countries.

In this political context, the 1965 Hart–Celler Act abolished the system of racialized exclusion and national-origins restrictions, while retaining some features of earlier legislation, such as the distinction between quota and non-quota immigrants. The act also created the modern system of "worldwide" immigration, in which Congress sets quotas for annual admissions of so-called "visa immigrants" from all over the world, without distinction between the Eastern and Western Hemispheres. It also provided for unlimited admission of certain categories, mainly spouses, children, and parents of US citizens. Indeed, Hart–Celler made "family reunification" the cornerstone of US immigration policy by allocating more immigrant visas on the basis of applicants' kinship with US citizens and permanent residents, rather than on the basis of their skills or recruitment by employers. The act thus set the stage for the renewal of large-scale immigration to the United States, although now primarily from the developing world, and not from Europe, as in the past. It also laid the foundations for contemporary policy debates. We now examine two such debates, one concerning the proper response to undocumented labor migration from Latin America, and another concerning the relative importance of skills and family reunification in US immigration policies.

"Undocumented immigrants" could be defined as non-citizens who are present in a country without holding a legal status there. Yet, while concise, such a definition is misleading. First, "the state" itself is a complex of institutional and individual actors, who frequently proceed at cross-purposes, and serve different interests. Second, even nominally prohibited forms of mobility are in fact desired by powerful actors within the state and the private sector. Thus, Zolberg argues that the US government implicitly tolerates the presence of millions of undocumented immigrants in the United States, albeit under conditions that maximize their utility as a labor force while preventing their permanent integration into American society (Zolberg 1999b). In the same vein, Massey *et al.* (2002) argue that in recent decades, restrictive US policies have actually stimulated the growth of the undocumented population and also created more opportunities for the oppression and exploitation of the undocumented.

The exclusion of the Western Hemisphere from quota limitation during the 1920s eventually made Latin America, and specifically Mexico, the leading source of immigrants to the United States (Massey *et al.* 2002: 31). But unlike the European immigrants who predominated before World War I, contemporary Mexican migrants come to the United States from a neighboring country with strong historical links to the US Southwest. Until quite recently, most Mexican migrants arrived in the United States with the intention of working temporarily to save (or send home) money before returning to Mexico. Indeed, from 1942 to 1964, the US Immigration and Naturalization Service (or INS) operated the so-called *Bracero* (roughly, "field hand") program, which provided Mexican guest workers with temporary authorization to work in the United States, primarily for agricultural employers in Texas and other south-western states (Massey *et al.* 2002: 45). Even after the *Bracero* system was formally wound up, large-scale undocumented temporary labor migration from Mexico continued until the mid-1980s. Although formally illegal, no significant attempts were made to combat such migration, again, mainly at the behest of the same agricultural employers who formerly backed the *Bracero* program.

This situation changed abruptly in 1986, with the passage of the Immigration Reform and Control Act (IRCA). IRCA's proponents put it forward as a measure to prevent undocumented immigration. Among other provisions, it authorized an immediate 50 percent increase in funding for INS enforcement, mainly to be used in actual monitoring of the border. Also, for the first time in US history, IRCA imposed criminal liability upon employers who knowingly employed undocumented immigrants (Massey et al. 2002: 49). According to Massey, however, these labor force control measures have failed, because they concentrated on interdiction of migrants rather than supervision of workplaces, and created little credible threat of sanctions against employers. Fearing arrest and deportation, Mexican workers are now forced to accept lower wages and other exploitative labor practices (Massey et al. 2002: 122).

In addition, migrant workers (primarily men) increasingly shun the hazards of frequent border crossings and instead bring their wives and children to live with them in the United States, which in turn has contributed to the rapid growth of the permanent Mexican-American population in the decades since IRCA (Massey et al. 2002: 129). These findings suggest that undocumented labor immigration is difficult to control through the essentially repressive measures provided by IRCA and subsequent legislation, which ignore the economic incentives for Mexico–US labor migration, the social networks and geographic proximity that facilitate it, and the ability of powerful actors (such as US employers of Mexican migrants) to blunt the impact of migration enforcement or turn it to their own advantage.

US immigration policy has been criticized from a very different direction by the economist George Borjas, who has called for major revisions to the criteria for selecting legal immigrants (Borjas 1999). Borjas proposes stricter limits on family reunification as well as the creation of a new category of skills-based immigrant visas. The revised US policy would thus be somewhat similar to the Canadian "point system," in which prospective immigrants are admitted based on "points," which they receive for their educational level and English or French proficiency. The government sets the minimum point score required to qualify for an immigrant visa to Canada. Borjas argues that the United States should emulate Canada's system.

In particular, he claims that the current US system of family reunification (FR) has undesirable social and economic consequences. He claims that FR has led to an influx of less-skilled workers from developing countries, who compete with other less-skilled workers in the US labor market, thus driving down their wages. He also contends that less-skilled immigrants' children partially replicate their lower educational attainment, thus creating more entrenched economic inequality in American society. And Borjas argues that because post-1965 immigration is primarily from Latin America, it is leading to the formation of large Spanish-speaking ethnic enclaves, and thus impeding the integration of immigrants. Borjas states unequivocally that his proposal to limit FR and seek out higher-skilled immigrants is intended to promote the interests of native-born American citizens (primarily less-skilled American workers), rather than those of immigrants (Borjas 1999: 187). This raises deeper philosophical questions about the ethics of immigration policy, to which we return at the end of this chapter.

Likewise, Borjas's proposal that the United States model its immigration policy on Canada's point system raises important theoretical questions regarding the value of comparative research. Borjas overlooks important differences between the two countries that may make some features of Canada's experience difficult to replicate in the United States. As Jeffrey Reitz has noted, since World War II the Canadian government has pursued mass immigration much more enthusiastically than its American counterpart, as a means to stimulate the development of Canada's vast and sparsely populated territory (Reitz 2004). Compared to the United States, there appears to be much higher public acceptance of high levels of immigration, and calls to restrict immigration drastically are more muted than in Canada's southern neighbor (Reitz 2004: 110). One explanation for the greater public acceptance of immigration is that as a result of the point system, Canadian immigrants tend to have higher educational levels and lower poverty levels than American ones, although this may now be changing (Reitz 2004: 120). Also, as compared with the United States, Canadian immigrants are drawn far less from any single country or world region, and the scale of undocumented immigration is much smaller in Canada (Reitz 2004: 103–5). Perhaps as a result, the official policy of "multiculturalism" first enunciated in the 1970s seems to have widespread popular support, although as Reitz notes the actual content of "multiculturalism" as a policy is open to question (Reitz 2004: 123–4).

Yet, contra Borjas, Canada's very different circumstances may make its policies difficult to implement in the United States. In particular, Canada borders only the United States, and is geographically remote from Latin America and other parts of the developing world. In contrast, the United States borders Latin America, and has a long history of drawing temporary labor migration from it. While it would certainly be possible to admit more highly skilled immigrants to the United States as Borjas proposes, significantly limiting Latin American migration as he also proposes may simply not be feasible. As Massey's research suggests, immigration cannot be turned on and off like a faucet at the will of policy-makers. The United States is probably destined to remain a major destination of Latin American labor migration for the foreseeable future. This suggests while US legislators have some control over the conditions under which this migration will take place, including in particular whether it will be legally authorized, it is unlikely that they can fully suppress it.

Just as comparing immigration in the United States and Canada can help inform immigration policy and theoretical debates, a developing scholarly literature on European immigration has also enriched theoretical debates regarding the determinants of immigration policy. Thus, some 20 years ago, Rogers Brubaker explored differing attitudes toward nationhood in nineteenth-century France and Germany and their consequences for each country's policies on naturalization of immigrants and the citizenship of immigrants' children (Brubaker 1992). As Brubaker argues, in France there emerged a form of national identification based on allegiance to French civic ideals, and this led to relatively easy naturalization and to blanket attribution of citizenship to children of immigrants born in France. In Germany, in contrast, a discourse of nationhood focused on ethnic identity led to a rejection of immigration and a policy of attributing citizenship only to the children of Germans.

Like Brubaker, Saskia Sassen has also examined the history of immigration policy in Europe before the twentieth century. Her work suggests that immigration in the Old World is actually far more "constitutive" than authors such as Freeman acknowledge (Sassen 1999). Sassen has charted a pre-1900 European history marked by both widespread permanent international migration and by cross-border cyclical or seasonal migration networks. In particular, she draws attention to aspects of immigration policy in nineteenth-century France that Brubaker's work does not emphasize. In contrast to his focus on the importance of ideas of "nationhood" in shaping national immigration policies, Sassen notes that French recruitment of immigrants (notably from Italy and Poland) and generous citizenship and naturalization policies actually resulted importantly from France's low birthrate and the state's desire to replenish the population (Sassen 1999: 65–8). In short, European states have a long history of using immigration to promote other policy goals.

A similar process of re-evaluation is under way with respect to more recent European history, notably regarding immigration in Germany, the largest western European country. In the post-World War II period, the government of the Federal Republic of Germany (also known as West Germany) famously claimed that Germany was "not a country of immigration." In fact, however, Germany was a major destination for millions of international migrants in the post-war decades. These included ethnic Germans from communist East Germany and other Soviet bloc states, and a large and growing population of *Gastarbeiter* ("guest workers") recruited from Turkey and other Mediterranean countries, who were admitted on a temporary labor basis and were not initially promised the option of permanent resettlement (Martin 2004). Although recruitment of guest workers was halted in 1973, many of the current workers did not want to go home. Accordingly, permanent residence and limited family reunification rights were accorded to them. As will be discussed below, these rights frequently came from court decisions, rather than changes in legislation initiated by the government. In addition, German laws continued to severely limit immigrants' access to naturalization and continued to attribute citizenship to children by descent only.

However, over the last decade, substantial policy evolution has taken place in Germany. After years of center-right dominance, in 2002 a new center-left government adopted major legislation that acknowledges that Germany is indeed a country of immigration, calls for active recruitment of high-skilled immigrants, and provides for facilitated naturalization of long-term foreign residents and a partial right of citizenship for the German-born children of immigrants (Martin 2004: 245–50). Moreover, one could also question whether Germany's approach to labor migration was ever particularly harsh. In contrast to the United States, Germany's guest workers generally had a legal status and were integrated into the German social welfare system. Indeed, they ultimately gained permanent residence and access to FR as a result of German court decisions that cited migrants' rights under the German constitution (Joppke 1998: 284). We have already noted Zolberg's caution to distinguish between a state's official discourse on immigration and the actual effects of its policies. In the case of Germany's labor migrants, the official policy of rejecting immigration was belied by the reality of permanent legal residence. The major change in policy is really the acknowledgment that a large proportion of permanent residents may become German citizens with full political rights.

Thus, both the contemporary German experience of policy evolution toward greater recognition of immigration (Martin 2004; Joppke 2008) and the nineteenth-century French experience of deliberate recruitment of immigrants for demographic replacement (Sassen 1999) suggest that immigration policy may be less rooted in a country's historical and cultural heritage than the distinction between "traditional" and "non-traditional" countries seems to imply. Rather, in many cases, the immediate political motivations of powerful social actors may be decisive in shaping immigration policy. In the next section of this chapter, we examine in more depth how scholars have approached the determinants of immigration policy.

The formation of immigration policies and anti-immigrant movements

A substantial scholarly corpus has grown up examining why contemporary developed states admit immigrants at all, what factors influence their admission criteria, and how opposition to immigration emerges. Within this corpus, we can distinguish economic and political explanations. A leading example of the former is Sassen's hypothesis that economic globalization has created both increased demand for immigration in the developed world and increased supply of it from developing countries (Sassen 2001). On the demand side, Sassen claims that globalization has led to a need for workers in low-wage service positions. On the supply side, the increasing exposure of people in developing countries to a global economy and mass culture, and improved means of transport and communication that facilitate travel, have made them more receptive to emigration.

In contrast to Sassen's emphasis on global economic forces, other writers focus on specific political processes that shape immigration policies, with attention both to conflicts between political and economic elites and the mass public, as well as to the role of specific governmental institutions. Thus, Freeman, in an argument somewhat similar to Borjas's, argues that "those who benefit from immigration in direct and concrete ways are better placed to organize than are those who bear immigration's costs [because] immigration tends to produce concentrated benefits and diffuse costs" (Freeman 1995: 885). Like Borjas, Freeman identifies employers of less-skilled labor, as well as the families of existing immigrants, as major beneficiaries of liberal immigration policies; such groups constitute lobbies on behalf of continued liberal immigration policies. In contrast to this interest-group approach, Hollifield (2004) situates immigration policy within the context of evolving norms and institutions of human rights protection. In the post-World War II period, he argues, liberal institutions and human rights norms have made it harder for democratic states to limit immigration or rid themselves of unwanted immigrants through harsh measures such as mass expulsions. Finally, Joppke (1998) has offered a partial synthesis, in which he distinguishes between the policy formation process in the United States and Europe. For Joppke, US immigration policy is dominated by "client politics" in which ethnic and business lobbies combine to frustrate anti-immigration initiatives. In Europe, while such lobbies are far less effective, in some European countries restrictions on immigration are tempered by judicial enforcement of human rights norms. We can see this dynamic in the case of German guest workers, who acquired permanent residence rights through court decisions in their favor.

Theorists of immigration policy also examine the origin of anti-immigrant movements. Above, we reviewed Zolberg's account of the nineteenth- and twentieth-century United States, and in particular his emphasis on the role of racialized anti-immigration movements in lobbying Congress to enact new restrictions on immigration. In contrast to Zolberg's emphasis on ideological and racialized sources of opposition to immigration, some other scholars have looked more to economic factors to explain the emergence of such movements. Jeanette Money distinguishes between opposition to the arrival of immigrants as newcomers who fit into the economy in particular ways, and hostility to specific immigrant groups that derives from racism, ethnic prejudice, or generalized xenophobia (Money 1999). Based on case studies of contemporary Australia, France, and Britain, Money argues (somewhat like Borjas) that migrant inflows eventually saturate local labor markets in particular high-immigration regions, and also lead to increased fiscal charges as a result of increased consumption of publicly funded services. These economic and fiscal pressures generate regional anti-immigrant sentiment, which sometimes can bring about restrictive changes to national policies. While Money herself favors liberal immigration policies, which she regards as a matter of social justice, she also argues that the economic and fiscal consequences of immigration need to be acknowledged and dealt with, both as a matter of equity and in order to make immigration politically sustainable. Thus, in her view, businesses that employ immigrants should be compelled to accept more of the financial costs associated with services to immigrants (Money 1999: 220).

Conclusion: emerging and future directions for research

The closing section of this chapter examines some promising new directions for immigration policy research. These new research agendas include normative questions of immigration policy, international migration between developing countries, and rapid urbanization in the developing world.

Many of the works we have discussed above have touched on normative questions. Thus, Borjas, Freeman, and Money suggest that the interests of immigrants and at least some segments of receiving societies may not always be fully aligned, and Joppke and Hollifield point to the moral and legal claims of longstanding immigrant residents for permanent residence, FR, and other rights. For that matter, Torpey's discussion of the gradual monopolization of control over immigration by the modern state also implicitly raises the question of whether such control is indeed legitimate. Given all the normative questions that are generated by empirical studies of immigration policy, it is encouraging that political philosophers are now addressing these questions.

In this vein, Benhabib (2004) applies insights from moral philosophy to contemporary immigration debates. Drawing on authors such as Kant and Arendt, Benhabib identifies "the paradox of democratic legitimacy." That is, she argues, the very act of constituting a political community, while it is necessary for creating democratic rights on the part of members of that community, inevitably also creates a category of outsiders with limited rights. Benhabib attempts to reconcile the rights of members of the political community to determine their own future, and as she puts it, "the rights of others"—immigrants. Benhabib proposes what she calls "disaggregated citizenship," meaning that certain obligations, such as providing haven for refugees, are incumbent on all states, and the corresponding rights are in effect universal. Yet, she also accepts the legitimacy of national citizenship, albeit in a form that is at least partially porous and open to outsiders.

Two other trends in international migration research both concern migration within and between countries in the developing world. While "south–south" migration is not new, it is certainly receiving increased attention, in part because the migration networks involving countries in the developing world are growing rapidly. A case in point is the republics of the former Soviet Union (or USSR), where labor migration is booming. In particular, contemporary Russia is a destination for millions of labor migrants from Central Asia and the Caucasus, and this migration network is now among the most numerically significant in the world. Yet, this immigration is taking place under an authoritarian political regime that is also characterized by regional balkanization and highly flawed law enforcement institutions. My own work has examined the nexus of authoritarian rule and official malfeasance in a case study of the policing of labor migrants in Moscow, Russia, who now number in the millions (Light 2010). As I argue, in contemporary Russia, despite the federal government's explicit constitutional authority over migration, implementation of migration policy is importantly controlled at the local level. Local policy directives (often unpublished) to the police and other law enforcement can create a partially symbiotic relationship between restrictive regional migration policies and official corruption.

Another highly significant form of migration taking place today is the acceleration of urbanization in developing countries. For the first time in human history, most human beings now reside in urban rather than in rural areas. This mass migration has taken place in part *within* national boundaries, thus removing it from what would traditionally be considered the bailiwick of immigration policy scholarship—migration across borders. Yet, the regulation of urbanization in the developing world is ripe for analysis by immigration scholars, for as Torpey reminds us, internal migration is no less subject to state authority than cross-border migration, and like immigration, the governance of internal migration has also evolved and been contested over many centuries.

A particularly dramatic contemporary example of the urbanization of the developing world is the huge outpouring of Chinese peasants into their country's major cities, which is estimated to involve 150 to 200 million people (Fan 2008). Because of the residential registration (or *hukou*) system that officially binds all Chinese citizens to their legal places of residence, whether urban or rural, peasants moving to the cities often face official rejection and legal discrimination.

Known as the "floating population," such peasant migrants experience conditions similar to those of undocumented immigrants in developed economies, even including the risk of forced repatriation to their official places of residence, as well as deprivation of social and political rights. In effect, China has created a kind of urban citizenship for a privileged minority of Chinese residents, while the peasant majority and migrant workers are denied many of the benefits of the country's economic boom (Fan 2008: 53). In the long term, the floating population's struggle for rights may lead to political conflict, which could have ramifications far beyond China's borders.

In conclusion, the study of immigration policy in recent years has developed in new directions, building on traditional areas of strength, such as the recruitment of permanent immigrants in traditional countries of settlement, while adding new dimensions, such as a more comparative and systematic approach, as well as attention to new countries of immigration and other forms of immigration. We can now look forward to a discussion of immigration policy that will be increasingly informed by broader theoretical and normative questions in the study of global migration phenomena.

References and further reading

Benhabib, S. (2004) *The Rights of Others: Aliens, Residents, and Citizens*. Cambridge: Cambridge University Press.

Borjas, G. J. (1999) *Heaven's Door: Immigration Policy and the American Economy*. Princeton, NJ: Princeton University Press.

Brubaker, R. (1992) *Citizenship and Nationhood in France and Germany*. Cambridge, MA: Harvard University Press.

Eltis, D. (2002) Introduction: Migration and agency in global history. In D. Eltis (ed.), *Coerced and Free Migration: Global Perspectives*. Stanford, CA: Stanford University Press, pp. 1–32.

Fan, C. C. (2008) *China on the Move: Migration, the State, and the Household*. London: Routledge.

Freeman, G. P. (1995) "Modes of immigration politics in liberal democratic states" *International Migration Review* 29(4): 881–902.

Hollifield, J. F. (2004) "The emerging migration state" *International Migration Review* 38(3): 885–912.

Joppke, C. (1998) "Why liberal states accept unwanted immigration" *World Politics* 50(2): 226–93.

Light, M. (2010) "Policing migration in Soviet and post-Soviet Moscow" *Post-Soviet Affairs* 26(4): 275–313.

Martin, P. L. (2004) "Germany: Managing migration in the twenty-first century." In W. A. Cornelius, T. Tsuda, P. L. Martin, and J. F. Hollifield (eds), *Controlling Immigration: A Global Perspective*. Stanford, CA: Stanford University Press, pp. 221–53.

Massey, D. S., Durand, J. and Malone, N. J. (2002) *Beyond Smoke and Mirrors: Mexican Immigration in an Era of Economic Integration*. New York: Russell Sage Foundation.

Money, J. (1999) *Fences and Neighbors: The Political Geography of Immigration Control*. Ithaca, NY: Cornell University Press.

Polanyi, K. (1957) [1944]) *The Great Transformation: The Political and Economic Origins of Our Times*. Boston, MA: Beacon Press.

Reitz, J. G. (2004) Canada: Immigration and nation-building in the transition to a knowledge economy. In W. A. Cornelius, T. Tsuda, P. L. Martin, and J. F. Hollifield (eds), *Controlling Immigration: A Global Perspective*. Stanford, CA: Stanford University Press, pp. 97–133.

Sassen, S. (1999) *Guests and Aliens*. New York: New Press.

——(2001) *The Global City: New York, London, Tokyo*. Princeton, NJ: Princeton University Press.

Torpey, J. (2000) *The Invention of the Passport: Surveillance, Citizenship, and the State*. Cambridge: Cambridge University Press.

Ueda, R. (1994) *Postwar Immigrant America: A Social History*. Boston, MA: Bedford/St Martin's.

Zolberg, A. R. (1999a) The Great Wall Against China: Responses to the First Immigration Crisis, 1885–1925. In Lucassen, J. and Lucassen, L. (eds) *Migration, Migration History, History: Old Paradigms and New Perspectives*. Bern: Peter Lang, pp. 291–317.

——(1999b) "Matters of state: Theorizing immigration policy." In C. Hirschman, P. Kasinitz, and J. Dewind (eds), *The Handbook of International Migration: The American Experience*. New York: Russell Sage Foundation, pp. 71–93.

30

Undocumented (or unauthorized) immigration

Cecilia Menjívar

The US Department of Homeland Security (DHS hereafter) (Hoefer *et al.* 2010) defines unauthorized residents as:

> all foreign-born non-citizens who are not legal residents. Most unauthorized residents either entered the United States without inspection or were admitted temporarily and stayed past the date they were required to leave. Unauthorized immigrants applying for adjustment to lawful permanent resident status under the Immigration and Nationality Act (INA) Section 245(i) are unauthorized until they have been granted LPR status, even though they may have been authorized to work. Persons who are beneficiaries of Temporary Protected Status (TPS)—an estimated several hundred thousand—are not technically authorized but were excluded from the legally resident immigrant population because data are unavailable in sufficient detail to estimate this population.

Therefore, the unauthorized immigrant population (or commonly denominated "undocu-mented") is composed, roughly in equal parts, of individuals who arrive with temporary visas to the United States through a designated point of entry, such as an airport or a border port of entry, and then stay in the country after their visas expire ("visa over-stayers") as well as of individuals who enter the country without inspection (entry without inspection or EWIs). However, as the DHS's definition above indicates, there are also individuals who might be in the process of regularizing their status (from a temporary visa to a permanent one such as legal permanent residence) and are already in the country, who are also counted under the category of undocumented because technically they do not yet hold a permanent visa (e.g., "green card"). It is useful, therefore, to keep in mind three points regarding the undocumented population in the United States. First, there are several ways for an individual to become undocumented; only approximately half of the undocumented in the country have crossed the Mexico-US border. Second, not all individuals who move in to permanent legal statuses come into the country with those statuses; many are here and then apply through employment, marriage, or family reunification for those permanent visas. And third, issues regarding undocumented immigration are not unique to the United States, as other major immigrant-receiving countries around the world also face questions around unauthorized migratory flows. Importantly for the United States and other cases, whatever the technical category of entry, a fundamental point to highlight is the central position of the receiving state in shaping these categories. The United States case I discuss is one in a broader global trend, as states in major receiving countries today, through their laws, create the different categories of admission (and exclusion), provide avenues for individuals to change from one category of admission to another, and in general, trace the contours of the immigrants' legality. In the United States, as in other countries then, categories of admission fluctuate according to the economic and political environment of the country at a particular historical junction so that often a group that was previously admitted legally can become unauthorized (and vice versa) with the stroke of a pen. It is this relationship between the state and undocumented immigration that I would like to underscore in this chapter.

Highlighting the role of the state in shaping undocumented immigration necessitates a shift of focus from examining undocumented immigration as a group of individuals possessing this characteristic (and how this legal status might affect their lives), to how the category into which they are classified is created, recreated, and transformed. Examining undocumented immigration as simply a legal category can presuppose an individual characteristic independent of the milieu in which it is created, perhaps even individual volition in the matter, and a status devoid of the political meaning that migrant legality has. Instead, a focus on how the broader context produces these legal categories can lead to conceptualizing immigrant legality as a sociopolitical condition (see De Genova 2002), an angle that moves us away from a focus on "undocumented status" as a naturalized category that deemphasizes the role of the state in its creation, to one that allows us to bring in the central place of the receiving state in actively producing this category. In doing so, I follow other scholars (De Genova 2002; Calavita 2005; Ngai 2005; Chavez 2008) to draw attention to the constructedness of immigrant legal categories, as well as the role of the state in making, unmaking, and reproducing these legal classifications. Thus, rather than starting out assuming categories of legality as a given, as definitional aspects of an immigrant's identity, I would like to call attention to the "preeminently political identity" (see De Genova 2002) of immigrants' legality to underscores the power of the state in constituting and reconstituting immigrants through the legal categories it creates.

Shifting the focus to what the state does through its laws, and to the political considerations in the creation of the undocumented category, also allows us to give attention to how the category of undocumented immigration has shifted and continues to change over time. At certain points in history there have been economic and political demands that have required the creation of policies of admission for certain groups of immigrants, and when those demands no longer apply, categories of admission change. As Sassen (1998: 56) observes, migratory flows, "do not just happen; they are produced. And migrations do not involve just any possible combination of countries; they are patterned." And whereas political expediency can dictate the creation of new categories of admission, the other side of the coin is the creation of categories of exclusion. It is important to note that individuals who are admitted legally (whether they come into the country through a visa program or through a particular admission category, or once in the country are given the opportunity to regularize their status) often come from the same socioeconomic, political, and cultural contexts where the unauthorized also originate. Individuals in those contexts are usually exposed to similar incentives for migration, to the same forces that shape their decision to migrate, and thus often will initiate their own migration, whether they have a visa or not. Thus, individual immigrants with and without visas often come from the same regions or a country, and sometimes even from the same families. Thus, within the overall context, some individuals have the resources to secure a visa or a permit to migrate, others will not. These observations blur strict distinctions between the unauthorized (or undocumented) and the legal, documented population.

In the pages that follow I will first situate my argument in historical context by examining how a legal program created to provide laborers in the context of a labor shortage gave rise to a flow of undocumented immigration from the same communities in Mexico where documented (legal) migration flows originated. I also focus on a case in which political demands and international relations shaped the admissions policy of the immigrants, a case of officially sanctioned refugees with unrecognized refugee flows. This case also helps to de-link the common association between labor migration flows with undocumented immigration. These cases help to illustrate the economic and political exigencies behind the creation of the unauthorized immigration flows to the United States that we see today. I then move to contemporary trends to provide a brief overview of the estimates of the undocumented population today, and in the last section I provide some examples, ranging from the immediate sphere of the family to contacts with other institutions in society, of experiences of immigrants who live in undocumented statuses in the United States.

Undocumented immigration in historical context

The cyclical nature of the US economy requires flexibility in the supply of laborers that often is difficult to meet, and unmatched labor requirements are often fulfilled with immigrant labor. At different points in history various immigrant groups have filled this demand, with the US government creating programs to bring in these laborers. For instance, the expansion of cattle ranches and agricultural production in the latter part of the nineteenth century was met through programs created to bring in Asian laborers—Chinese, Japanese, Filipinos—to work in these sectors. But when the demand for these laborers declines, the visa programs under which these laborers migrated are terminated.

There are several important links between these worker programs and their ending for unauthorized migration. Often, these programs last for years, allowing the laborers to establish communities and cement roots and sometimes even bring family members with them. Also, the programs themselves often fail to bring in enough authorized laborers to meet the labor demands; with more workers required at one end and laborers available at the other, a parallel migratory flow composed of unauthorized workers is created. Furthermore, sometimes these programs are large scale and bring a substantial number of workers from certain regions into the sending countries. When the visa programs end, a "culture of migration" has already been created, social networks through which individuals migrate are well established, and thus, the formal ending of these worker programs does not ensure that the actual migration will also be discontinued (Massey *et al.* 2002). The *de jure* termination of these labor migration programs is seldom accompanied by a *de facto* ending of the migration flow because important social forces have already been set in motion for migration to continue.

This was the case of the *Bracero* Program, a program created under a binational agreement between the United States and Mexico to supply Mexican workers between 1941 and 1945 to alleviate the labor shortage in agriculture and to maintain food supply during war mobilization in the context of World War II (WWII). As Massey *et al.* (2002) note, this program was conceived originally as a temporary measure to alleviate the labor shortage, but with the booming post-war economy, California and Texas growers asked Congress to extend this program. Although the program provided needed agricultural laborers, the demand was barely met with the number of visas that Congress allocated, and thus, laborers without visas were attracted to work opportunities and joined those who came (with authorization) under the program to the fields of the US southwest. With the recession following the Korean War, the public grew hostile at the laborers' presence and demanded that the federal government do something about controlling this immigration, even as agricultural growers continued to press Congress for more workers (Massey *et al.* 2002). Thus, in 1954 the Immigration and Naturalization Service launched "Operation Wetback" to deport the laborers, but the program continued in place until it ended by Congress in 1963 (in practice in 1964); approximately 5 million Mexicans migrated in the program's 22-year history.

Although conditions had been created at both ends for laborers to continue migrating for work, undocumented immigration from Mexico would not have grown had it not been for a new change to US immigration law. As Massey *et al.* (2002) argue, unauthorized migration from Mexico to the United States probably would have not grown had it not been for a new US policy of imposing numerical limits on the number of visas allocated to Mexicans (and other Western Hemisphere countries), which had previously been exempted from these limits. Rising unemployment and high inflation in the early 1970s made Mexican migration a salient topic once again. Congress responded with the 1976 Immigration and Nationality Act that imposed the 20,000-per-country visa limit that the United States had in place for other regions of the world, to Western Hemisphere countries, including Mexico. Thus, the number of visas that Mexicans could apply for was dramatically reduced, from a theoretically unlimited supply to 20,000 per year (Massey *et al.* 2002). With social links between potential Mexican migrants and Mexicans already in the United States already well established through decades of migration and associated processes already in motion, but without access to the visas potential migrants had before the passing of the 1976 law, undocumented immigration from Mexico increased dramatically from the late 1970s on. From one year to the next, this new law closed a path for many Mexicans to migrate with visas to the United States, but the law could not cut off the social and economic ties that Mexican migrants had already created through decades of large-scale migration.

Economic pressures for labor demands often play a central part in the creation of migration flows through laws originally created only for temporary periods. However, there are political factors that also have shaped the creation, dissolution, and general treatment of migratory flows from politically conflictive regions of the world. This practice has a long history but was more emphatically applied in the United States in the context of the Cold War. In this ideological battle, individuals exiting politically conflictive regions were seen as voting with their feet and thus serving the political objectives of the receiving state. As such, interstate relations between sending and receiving states became critical determinants of whether migrants originating in politically conflictive regions would be admitted as refugees (or whether they fell outside legal parameters to join the ranks of the unauthorized population). Indeed, as Zolberg *et al.* (1989) observed, defining a particular group of immigrants as refugees is not a decision based solely on persecution or unsafe conditions in the country of origin but, even more importantly, on the fact that a receiving state recognizes them as deserving asylum and assistance. The classic example of the relationship between foreign policy and admissions from politically conflictive regions is the Cuban-Haitian case. Whereas thousands of Cubans were welcomed without close inspection of their motives for departure, during the same years Haitians were systematically excluded, classified as undocumented, and deemed deportable, even though they were fleeing political persecution and a generalized context of state violence. A similar paradoxical case was exemplified in the contrasting case of Chileans on the one hand, and Vietnamese, Laotian, and Cambodians on the other in the mid-1970s, where inter-state relations between the United States and these countries dictated the reception that these émigrés received in the United States.

In certain cases, particularly when migrants originate in conflictive regions that are in relatively close geographic proximity to the United States, a lack of government reception to these migrants creates a real potential for unauthorized flows to emerge. This was the case of the Central Americans (mostly from Guatemala and El Salvador) who migrated to the United States during the political conflicts that raged in their countries in the 1980s. From the outset these conflicts were viewed as essentially a Cold War situation, another possibility for Communism to expand and thus where it needed to be contained, and as a result the United States became deeply involved mostly through financing the military operations of the governments involved in the conflicts. Against this background, and with the history of the close link between refugee and foreign policy, it would have been politically antithetical for the US government to receive formally (with a policy of reception as it had done with other refugee flows) the refugees that the Central American conflicts were generating. Thus, upon their arrival on US shores, the Central Americans were categorized as another undocumented migration flow. As most of these refugees lacked an entry US visa because they could not procure one in their country, they had to cross Mexico on their way north, and in the eyes of the public (and policy makers) individuals fleeing political violence were easily lumped together under the general "undocumented labor migration flow."

In the three decades since large-scale Central American migration has been under way, under pressure from human rights groups, these migrants have been extended limited opportunities to regularize their status or to apply for temporary protection at different points in time. But in general, the policies that have shaped their reception in the United States have left them largely unprotected legally. Indeed, together with Mexicans, Guatemalans, and Salvadorans (and recently, Hondurans too) lead the list of the largest nationality groups of undocumented immigrants in the United States today. Following my argument here, this is not a coincidence. Indeed, a close examination of the history of the legislation that has shaped these migration flows makes it easy to see how the state, responding to economic and political pressures at particular historical junctions, has been pivotal in their creation and maintenance, and thus in creating and recreating the different legal categories into which these immigrants have been categorized.

Current trends and estimates

According to 2009 estimates by the DHS (Hoefer *et al.* 2010) there were 10.8 million undocumented immigrants in the United States in 2009, or roughly 4 percent of the nation's population (or 6.5 percent of the workforce) (Passel and Cohn 2009). Of the nation's 39 million foreign born, 30 percent are estimated to be undocumented. Until the 1990s this population was highly concentrated in a handful of states. However, from the 1990s on, it has increased rapidly and also has become more geographically dispersed, mostly as a result of border policies that have redirected the flow and made crossing, particularly among previous seasonal migrant workers, far more difficult (see Massey *et al.* 2002). Thus, border policies have had the unintended consequence of increasing the number of undocumented in the country because, rather than engaging in a risky journey back and forth, these individuals have stayed put (Massey *et al.* 2002).

Starting in 2006, the growth of this population has stabilized and has even shown a declining trend, particularly in some states like California. For instance, whereas in 1990 California was home to 42 percent of the total undocumented population in the country, by 2008 this share had declined to 22 percent (Passel and Cohn 2009). In the most recent estimates, the DHS estimates that the overall decline of the unauthorized population was 7 percent between 2008 and 2009, from 11.6 million to 10.8 million, a decline attributed to the general economic downturn associated with the recession started in 2008 (Hoefer *et al.* 2010). According to these estimates, California houses one quarter of the entire undocumented population, Texas is home to 16 percent, Florida's share is 7 percent, Illinois and New York each houses 5 percent, and other states, like Arizona and Georgia share just under 5 percent of the total (Hoefer *et al.* 2010). Thus, although close to half of the undocumented population is still concentrated in only three states (California, Texas, and Florida), this population is more dispersed today than two decades earlier, being present in all 50 states. But if we look at undocumented immigrants in the labor force (not the total undocumented population), we see a different picture: in 2008 these states were Nevada, California, Arizona, New Jersey, and Florida (in that order) (Passel and Cohn 2009). Thus, although there are undocumented immigrants living in all states today, this geographical dispersion is highly uneven, as undocumented workers constitute approximately 10 percent of the workforce in California and Arizona, but only 2.5 percent in the Midwest and Plains states (Passel and Cohn 2009).

In terms of their sociodemographic profile, about 62 percent of the total unauthorized population comes from Mexico, with increasing numbers from Asia and Central America (approximately 12 percent come from Guatemala, El Salvador and Honduras combined), and Asia (about 6 percent from India, China, and the Philippines) (Hoefer *et al.* 2010). Passel and Cohn (2009) note that approximately half of undocumented immigrants live with immediate family members (47 percent, in contrast to 21 percent among US born), and that three-quarters of households headed by undocumented immigrants consist of married or cohabiting couples with children. Hoefer *et al.* (2010) estimate that this population is primarily of working age: only 12 percent are under 18 and 4 percent over 55. As well, 73 percent of the children of unauthorized immigrants are US citizens by birth (Passel and Cohn 2009). Thus, the number of "mixed-status families" (families that contain a mix of citizens and non-citizen members) (see Fix and Zimmerman 2001) has increased rapidly, a situation that significantly blurs the distinction between the undocumented population and the US-born and/or the legal permanent resident populations. And as Fix and Zimmerman (2001) note, mixed-status families are themselves complex; they not only include individuals with various legal statuses, but these statuses change with time, as when a person legalizes their status or legal permanent residents naturalize. For instance, whereas there were about 2.7 million US-born children living in mixed-status families in 2003, there were 4 million in 2008 (Passel and Cohn 2009).

Effects of undocumented status

The state, through its laws, shapes migrants' paths of incorporation and their futures in their adopted homeland. Immigrants' legal status shapes who they are, how they relate to others, their participation in local communities, and their continued relationship with their homelands. While in theory a universal set of rights is available to everyone, regardless of status, Bloch (2010) notes that in practice, undocumented immigrants do not benefit from existing rights frameworks because of their legal status. Indeed, an immigrant's legal status can affect anything from the immigrants' access to welfare benefits and health care (Portes and Rumbaut 2006) to their vulnerability and domestic violence among the women (Salcido and Adelman 2004). It also affects their chances in the labor market, job prospects, earnings (Massey *et al.* 2002), and their religious involvement (Menjívar 2006). Indeed, legal statuses today create a class of immigrants with rights and privileges that stands in contrast with legal immigrants.

I will use a series of examples to illustrate in depth how legal status can make a difference in the lives of immigrants. The cases will exemplify how an undocumented status can shape dynamics within the intimate space of the family, including its composition and separation, as well as how it impacts relations between the family and other institutions in society. An undocumented status of family members, particularly of adult family members, can create a disconnection between families and institutions such as schools, health services, and law enforcement agencies, which happens even when there are US-born children.

Sphere of the family

An immediate consequence of being an undocumented immigrant is the possibility of an imminent deportation. Parents can be separated from children and women and men in couples can be separated. It is important to note that these separations can last indefinitely, as immigration law is structured in such a way that individuals wait for years if not decades for their cases to be processed or for an opportunity to enter (or re-enter) the country. The backlogs of visa applications are notoriously huge. In addition, the waiting time for admission through family reunification varies widely for each national group and therefore petitioning for a family member to immigrate legally does not mean that this person can come into the country immediately. For instance, a Mexican who is petitioned by a sibling to immigrate must wait approximately 19 years to receive a visa, whereas potential immigrants in western European countries wait only a couple of years (if at all). Thus, often individuals opt for migrating without a visa (or overstay their temporary visas) if they want to be reunited with their loved ones. Once in the country, these individuals also enter the labor force, working jobs that pay little without benefits. But to them, the advantage is that they live with their families while earning wages that are usually higher than those in the origin country. However, individuals who are out of status (or undocumented), are always at risk of deportation while they conduct their daily lives. And when individuals are deported and separated from their families, no one knows when or if they will see each other again. However, their lives go on and important decisions are made during these uncertain times. Given that there are approximately 4 million US-born children who live in a household where at least one parent is undocumented or in the process of legalizing their status, family separation resulting from deportation has profound effects on the non-undocumented population as well.

In other cases, the parent or parents migrate without a visa, but given the dangers involved in this migration, they leave the children in the care of family members back in the home country. These family separations are also uncertain, and close family members can spend years without seeing each other. During these separations the parents in the United States send remittances and gifts to the children left behind, but these gifts seldom make up for the emotional proximity that comes from living under the same roof. Sometimes the children reproach the parents for leaving them behind, but the parents see no other alternative for providing the best they can for their children (Menjívar and Abrego 2009). In some cases, the parents and children spend such a long time separated that they find little in each other to recognize as a family when they are reunited again. These family separations, however, are closely linked to the structure of immigration law and the categories of admission in place that create situations in which many of these family members must wait for years to reunite.

Another area that is affected by an individual's legal status is domestic violence. For women in situations of domestic violence, legal status can make a difference between life and death. When the male partners are permanent legal residents or US citizens and the women in these cases are not, the "papers" that they lack can be used as a weapon for manipulation. According to Salcido and Adelman (2004), the partners often threaten them with withdrawing the women's legal permanent resident application (a process initiated by the partners if they are citizens or permanent legal residents) if the women report the abuse to the authorities. And although immigrant women in situations of domestic violence can self-petition for permanent legal residence without a family member initiating the process, the requirements for the application include police reports and other documentation that the women lack due to the fear of reporting the abuse. Salcido and Adelman (2004) describe the case of how Chave, a woman who had applied for her permanent legal residence through her husband, fell in and out of legality and regularly risked losing the opportunity to regularize her status because her husband would hide the INS mail that came with paperwork for her. In addition to suffering physical violence with him, he would undermine her legalization process as a way to control her. In Chave's words, "When he hears the mail coming he jumps to get it, and takes everything. That is how he hid that [INS] envelope [requiring a response within 90 days] ... " (Salcido and Adelman 2004: 166).

Links to other institutions

Legal status deeply influences the links that immigrants establish with different institutions in society. Often, individuals who are undocumented or in the process of regularizing their status try to avoid contact with service providers and law enforcement agencies in order to avoid calling attention to themselves. This is particularly the case when laws denying social services to undocumented immigrants are enacted. For instance, Nora, a Guatemalan woman who lived in Phoenix, Arizona (Menjívar and Bejarano 2004), simply smiled when asked if she could count on the US police for protection. She explained that she was aware that the police are more helpful in the United States than the police were in Guatemala, but would not call them in case of need because she was still undocumented and feared deportation if the authorities detected her status. Her fear was so extreme that once she almost lost her life rather than calling the police. While she was working the night shift at a McDonald's, three men robbed the establishment at gunpoint. The robbers shoved all the employees into a huge freezer, but did not lock it. Nora managed to get out, but instead of calling the police, however, she grabbed a broomstick, hit one of the men and knocked him unconscious. She got his gun and threatened the other two men that she would kill their friend if they did not leave. While she was arguing with the men, a manager called the police and the situation was resolved. Only when the police arrived did Nora drop the gun. The managers and the police thanked her, but also asked her not to do this again. She added: "At that moment, while I was holding the men, I kept on thinking, what do I do? If I call the police, I'll get deported. Yes, I was nervous [with the gun], but I was even more nervous to have to talk to the police."

As the case of Nora attests, migrants often go through lengths in order to avoid detection by authorities. This also happens when immigrants risk their own health so as to avoid contact with health care professionals to avoid the risk of deportation. They often prefer to treat themselves at home when they are ill. For instance, Miguel, a Salvadoran immigrant in Phoenix explained that whenever he or anyone of his family gets sick, they first try to use some home remedies—like herbal teas, honey, cinnamon, and cloves for a cold. If the ailment does not go away, they use Tylenol, Advil, or the like. If that does not work, they call on friends to see what they can recommend or to get their friends' left over prescription medications that had proven effective. He said that he did not share medicine just because it is a cheaper option for those, like himself, who do not have health insurance, but because doing so is "safer" as they do not want to meet with any public health professionals.

As I mentioned earlier, often undocumented individuals live in what Fix and Zimmerman (2001) refer to as "mixed-status families," that is, undocumented parents or children live with documented (mostly US citizen) children or siblings, or several members of a family each having a different legal status. Thus, in the same families there are children who have the privilege of citizenship—and thus access to goods and benefits in society—those in the process of regularizing their status, and undocumented ones who lack even the most basic rights, such as access to funding for higher education and to health care, and who can be deported at any moment. Membership in such mixed-status families can have unforeseen consequences for the children, as within the same family legal status can channel siblings to different paths. The immigrants' and the children's relations with different institutions in society will be equally dissimilar. And in some cases the parents' legal status keeps US-born children from obtaining benefits to which they are entitled. In fact, there are many eligible citizen children with non-citizen parents who do not participate in benefit programs because the parents are unaware that their children are eligible or are afraid of the consequences of benefit receipt for their legal status and eventual legal citizenship (Hagan *et al.* 2003). Thus, the legal instability of the adult immigrants also affects the children's potential for success.

Individuals' legal status also shapes in fundamental ways their perceptions of their educational aspirations, and potential trajectories and achievements. Abrego (2008) examined these effects in Los Angeles. One of the students in her study described the stigmatizing experience of knowing that with her undocumented status she could not enter college (legally, she could attend but she would need to pay out-of-state-state tuition). This is how the student explained her thoughts to Abrego:

> I felt *so* bad! Because my friends knew my grades and they would ask me, "What school did you apply to?" And I was like, "No, I didn't." "How come you haven't applied?!" … And one friend, she knew about my situation and she said, "You know what? I feel so bad because your grades are much better than mine and I'm able to go to a university and you're not." I felt like crying. … All they do senior year is talk about college. "I applied here and I applied there" and I didn't even bother applying because I knew the answer—I couldn't pay for it.
>
> (Abrego 2008: 718)

The case of the Umaña family in Phoenix illustrates the central place that an ambivalent legal status has for the educational plans and fortunes of its members, and this is manifested across various legal statuses. Carlos and Isabel Umaña have three children, all born in El Salvador and now in their 20s, Marisa, Israel, and Federico. Theirs is a textbook case of a "mixed-status" family (Fix and Zimmerman 2001). Each of the five members has a different place *vis-à-vis* immigration law; only Carlos is "fully" documented as Isabel emphasized. Carlos applied for legalization through the Nicaraguan Adjustment and Central American Relief Act (NACARA), one of the relief programs available to Guatemalans and Salvadorans and is now a permanent legal resident, but the process took so long that the two boys turned 21 during the long wait for Carlos's green card, which has complicated matters for the boys' own applications. Isabel is "in the process" of regularizing her status; she has completed all the requirements is still waiting for her green card, which, for three years already, "is coming any moment." Twenty-seven year old Marisa submitted a legalization application through the NACARA program, but is still waiting for the application to be adjudicated. Twenty-four year old Ismar's paperwork got lost twice in the immigration offices, which means that he has spent years without any documents, but finally received a social security card but it does not allow him to work. And 23-year-old Francisco, the youngest, married a young woman from Utah and received a social security card that has allowed him to enroll in a program that will train him in law enforcement.

Given the unstable legal statuses of the members of these family members they have found it difficult to find better paying jobs. But what really frustrates Isabel, the mother, is that, except for Francisco, no one in the family has been able to continue with their education. This was a dream the parents had when they brought the children to live with them years ago; indeed, it was the reason why the parents brought them over instead of remitting monthly. Isabel worries that the dream may never materialize. In her words,

> Look, my husband and I went to the university in El Salvador; he has one year of electrical engineering and I have two years of law [school]. We know the value of an education. But look at our situation now. Marisa dropped out of community college because she can't go on without financial aid … she is not eligible. Israel, he graduated from high school here, but because of the papers, he's still cutting grass with his father. And they are all getting older and as you and I know, the longer they stay out of school the harder it will be for them to come back. I want to continue too; I'm not a dumb person. We can discuss philosophy and law, if you'd like. Modesty aside, I was a very good student. I have taken 38 credits at the community college, but when will I finish? When will I transfer and get my degree? We're not even talking about law school anymore … that's gone. But for now, only Francisco is lucky. God willing, he will take advantage and educate himself.

Discussion/conclusion

The points I have outlined here highlight the enduring power of the state in producing and reproducing immigrant legality. I discussed how undocumented immigration is produced and reproduced through immigration policy and have argued that an immigrant's legal status is not simply an individual characteristic affecting certain outcomes or even neatly separate from legal statuses in practice. This emphasis has brought to light the key links between immigrants' legal statuses and state policies and how immigrants' legal statuses fluctuate and are constructed and produced based on economic and political exigencies at different historical junctions. However, immigrants' legal statuses have real consequences and affect a whole range of activities, from the intimate sphere of family dynamics, including domestic violence, to links between individuals and families and various social institutions. My argument therefore underscores the central place of the state in defining who belongs and who is excluded, both in the US case as in others around the world. As De Genova (2002: 422) observes, "Illegality," then, both theoretically and practically, is a social relation that is fundamentally inseparable from citizenship."

Legal categories mark immigrants not only as non-nationals but also as deportable and thus become marks of exclusion. Not all groups have equal access to permanent statuses, an aspect of immigration law that undermines the assumption of equality of status and belonging. How immigrants live their legal status (e.g., how undocumented immigrants navigate contacts with different social institutions and how their legal status affects their relations with their family members) has important repercussions for their incorporation in society and for citizenship (as belonging) in general. This observation allows us to see legal status as an important axis of stratification that can shape immigrants' assimilation in critical ways. Indeed, attention to new forms of inequality stemming from the receiving state's immigrant policies has allowed Douglas Massey (2007) to argue forcefully that legal status now joins race, class, and gender as a central axis of stratification in American society.

References and further reading

Abrego, L. (2008) "Legitimacy, social identity, and the mobilization of law: The effects of assembly bill 540 on undocumented students in California" *Law & Society Inquiry* 33(3): 709–34.
Bloch, A. (2010) "The right to rights? Undocumented migrants from Zimbabwe living in South Africa" *Sociology* 44(2): 233–50.

Calavita, K. (2005) *Immigrants at the Margins: Law, Race, and Exclusion in Southern Europe*. New York: Cambridge University Press.

Chavez, L. R. (2008) *The Latino Threat: Constructing Immigrants, Citizens, and the Nation*. Stanford, CA: Stanford University Press.

De Genova, N. P. (2002) "Migrant 'illegality' and deportability in everyday life" *Annual Review of Anthropology* 31: 419–47.

Fix, M. and Zimmerman, W. (2001) "All under one roof: Mixed-status families in an era of reform" *International Migration Review* 35(2): 397–419.

Hagan, J., Rodriguez, N., Capps, R., and Kabiri, N. (2003) "The effects of recent welfare and immigration reforms on immigrants' access to health care" *International Migration Review* 37(2): 444–63.

Hoefer, M., Rytina, N., and Baker, B. C. (2010) *Estimates of the Unauthorized Immigrant Population Residing in the United States: January 2009*. Office of Immigration Statistics, Policy Directorate, Department of Homeland Security.

Massey, D. S. (2007) *Categorically Unequal: The American Stratification System*. New York: Russell Sage.

Massey, D. S., Durand J., and Malone. N. J. (2002) *Beyond Smoke and Mirrors: Mexican Immigration in an Era of Economic Integration*. New York: Russell Sage Foundation.

Menjívar, C. (2006) "Liminal legality: Salvadoran and Guatemalan immigrants' lives in the United States" *American Journal of Sociology* 111(4): 999–1037.

Menjívar, C. and Abrego, L. (2009) Parents and children across borders: Legal instability and intergenerational relations in Guatemalan and Salvadoran families." In N. Foner (ed.), *Across Generations: Immigrant Families in America*. New York: New York University Press, pp. 160–89.

Menjívar, C. and Bejarano, C. (2004) "Latino immigrants' perceptions of crime and of police authorities: A case study from the Phoenix Metropolitan area" *Ethnic and Racial Studies* 27(1): 120–48.

Ngai, M. M. (2005) *Impossible Subjects: Illegal Aliens and the Making of Modern America*. Princeton, NJ: Princeton University Press.

Passel, J. S. and Cohn, D. (2009) *A Portrait of the Undocumented Immigrants in the United States*. Pew Hispanic Center. http://pewhispanic.org/files/reports/107.pdf (accessed May 1 2010).

Portes, A. and Rumbaut, R. G. (2006) *Immigrant America: A Portrait*, 3rd edn. Berkeley, CA: University of California Press.

Salcido, O. and Adelman, A. (2004) "'He has me tied with the blessed and damned papers': Undocumented-immigrant battered women in Phoenix, Arizona" *Human Organization* 63(2): 162–72.

Sassen, S. (1998) *Globalization and Its Discontents: Essays on the New Mobility of People and Money*. New York: New Press.

Zolberg, A., Suhrke, A. and Aguayo, S. (1989) *Escape from Violence: Conflict and the Refugee Crisis in the Developing World*. New York: Oxford University Press.

31

Migration and health

Guillermina Jasso

Introduction

Two questions dominate research on migration and health—the health selection question, which seeks to learn the direction of selection on health across different migration streams; and the health change question, which seeks to learn whether health improves or deteriorates in the destination country. To address these questions, this chapter explores the theoretical framework for studying selection, examines the empirical challenges, and summarizes recent estimates of health selection and health change.

The two questions represent the health-focused expression of the first two of the four central questions in the study of migration:

1 What are the migrant's characteristics and behavior at entry?
2 How do the migrant's characteristics and behavior change with time in the destination country?
3 What are the characteristics and behavior of the children of immigrants?
4 What are the impacts on the origin and destination countries?

The first question encompasses questions about the forces of selectivity; it is called the *selection question*. The second question pertains to the migrant's trajectory after immigration; it is called the *assimilation question*. The third question covers everything that pertains to the children of immigrants; it is called the *second-generation question*. Finally, the fourth question seeks to assess the myriad effects of immigration on both origin and destination countries and their residents; it is called the *impacts question*.

Of course, the third and fourth central questions are also important in the study of migration and health. For example, there is great interest in understanding parental transmission of health effects as well as the effects of migration on healthcare costs in the destination country. But the first two questions are fundamental.

The selection question embeds several mechanisms, including the prospective migrant's *desire to move* and choice of a destination country and including as well the actions of individuals and governments in both countries to encourage or discourage the move—*in extremis*, forcing or preventing it. The key element in the selection question is the connection between the prospective migrant's characteristics—such as socioeconomic location and health—and the desire to move, also called *migrant energy*. The apt phrase "migrant energy" appears in several literatures. For example, the social scientist Aderanti Adepoju is quoted as saying, "There is hardly any prosperous country that is not based on migrant energy" (Sawyerr 2010), and the historian Richard Gott (2005: 45) discusses "the injection of migrant energy" in Cuba in the late eighteenth and early nineteenth centuries.

Meanwhile, the assimilation question also embeds several mechanisms, including the extent and pace of adaptation to the destination country. There is keen interest in assessing the migrant's characteristics at specific periods of duration in the destination country—for example, at 5, 10, 15, 20 years after migration—relative to the native population in the destination country and also the migrant's counterparts who remain in the origin country. A key question is the extent to which migrant energy remains at work, affecting assimilation.

Thus, the selection and assimilation questions lead to several empirical questions on health, including three to be addressed below: (1) the direction of health selection out of the origin country; (2) the health level of new immigrants in the destination country; and (3) health change among immigrants.

Studying these questions is not easy. This is because many things intervene, including family dynamics, legal restrictions on migration, and the migration process itself.

The classical research prescription was to compare movers and stayers. If there were no government restrictions on exit or entry and no interference from family dynamics, the contrast between movers and stayers in the population of an origin country would be fully informative about self-selection. But given government policies and family dynamics, the actual movers may (1) include tied movers and forced movers, and (2) miss tied stayers and forced stayers. Accordingly, a challenge in the study of selection is to correctly identify those who self-select into a move. One approach, discussed below, is to directly measure the desire to move.

Studying health selection involves additional challenges, due to the effects of the migration process on health. We distinguish between three sources of health effects: visa stress, migration stress, and the health-relevant environment in the destination country. If there are no restrictions on migration, there is no visa stress. For example, people from Puerto Rico who move to the United States experience migration stress but no visa stress. Visa stress may cause health to deteriorate, even if only temporarily. Thus, assessing immigrant health soon after arrival may be too late to obtain a pure and undistorted view of health selection; visa stress may have begun much earlier. For that reason, the research prescription is to assess immigrant health at the time of the migration decision.

Theoretical and empirical analysis of migration and health produce stylized stories. For example, in one such story—known as the healthy immigrant effect—new immigrants are healthier than stayers in the origin country and healthier as well than natives in the destination country but over time their health declines so that they lose the initial health advantage over natives in the destination country (Stephen *et al.* 1994; Antecol and Bedard 2006; Biddle *et al.* 2007). The decline may be associated with several mechanisms, including exposure to negative effects and inability to extract positive effects.

However, given visa stress, the pervasive effects of legal status, and the dramatic diversity among the foreign-born—including, for example, naturalized citizens and illegals, world-class scientists and persons with no formal schooling—a more accurate story may follow two lines. First, among legal immigrants, health declines temporarily due to visa stress, migration stress, and exposure to the new health environment; but with the passage of time, visa stress and

G. Jasso

migration stress end, and the immigrant learns to navigate the new environment, mitigating its health harms and extracting its health benefits. Second, among the unauthorized, visa stress never ends, and the circumstances of daily life, coupled with deficits in the destination country language, may make it difficult to deal effectively with the new country's health environment.

Theoretical framework for studying migration and health

Modeling selection

Is it the healthy or the unhealthy or the in-between who desire to move? To address this question, we start with a general selection model and then apply it to health.

Consider a population with two characteristics. One characteristic is the desire to move; which as above we call migrant energy, denoted E. The other characteristic, denoted X, may be schooling, skill, income, wealth, health, status, or any characteristic which may potentially influence the desire to move or with respect to which the forces of selectivity are to be assessed. The basic selection equation is thus written:

$$E = f(X) \tag{31.1}$$

The graph of the selection function may be monotonic or nonmonotonic. If monotonic, selection may be *positive*, *negative*, or *zero*. That is, migrant energy may increase, or decrease, as X increases, or be independent of it. Its rate of change may also differ.

In the context of health, a major question pertains to the direction of selection with respect to health (Jasso *et al.* 2004, 2005; Palloni and Arias 2004; Akresh and Frank 2008). *A priori* it is useful to distinguish between migration streams. For example, Jasso *et al.* (2004, 2005) argue that in migration streams where economic considerations play a part, and to the extent that skill levels are higher among healthier people, the gains from migrating will be greater for healthier individuals and thus migrants will be positively self-selected on health.

Other migration streams, however, such as older immigrants or immigrants who do not plan to work, may display negative or zero health selection profiles. Refugees, who are urgently fleeing, may display a zero health selection profile—the desire to move may be independent of their healthiness—although as survivors of extreme situations they may possess higher levels of health. However, if the greater the healthiness, the greater the desire to flee, then refugees, too, may display positive health selection.

Immigrants primarily attracted to the American social and political climate may have zero selection on health, as the "freedom gains" from life in the United States would not necessarily vary by health.

Of course, selection need not be monotonic with respect to X, as has been recognized at least since Lee (1966), who discussed two forms of *extremal selection* (J-shaped and U-shaped), in which the desire to move first decreases as X increases, then subsequently increases. Another type of nonmonotonic selection is what Chiquiar and Hanson (2005) call *intermediate selection*, in which the desire to move increases to a maximum and subsequently declines.

The selection profiles are linked both to deeper mechanisms at work in migration processes and to a variety of important consequences of migration. For example, "brain drain" concerns arise in positive selection, and, with diminished urgency, in extremal selection, but not in negative selection.

Modeling migrant health

Five key ideas arise in modeling migrant health:

1   The legal aspects of migration—obtaining an exit visa and/or an entry visa—may be highly stressful, generating *visa stress* (Kasl and Berkman 1983; Vega and Amaro 1994; Jasso 2003; Jasso *et al.* 2004, 2005). Nowadays entry visas are more widespread than exit visas, but not too long ago many countries required exit visas (for example, Nazi Germany in 1933–45 and the Soviet Bloc countries before 1989), and some still do (e.g., Cuba).
2   Living in a foreign country may be highly stressful, generating *migration stress.*
3   Each sociogeographic locale has its own *exposure effects* on health, such as effects associated with the food, altitude, environmental pollutants, climate, etc. These effects are a mix of positive and negative effects.
4   Understanding selection—the relation between the desire to move and migrant characteristics—requires defining the point in time at which the *migration decision* occurs. What matters for assessing selection patterns is the individual's characteristics at that point. If these characteristics can change after the migration decision—for example, if health deteriorates due to visa stress, or if it improves due to exposure effects—then it is critical to measure the migrant's characteristics at the time of the migration decision. Thus, health selection refers to the migrant's health at the time of the migration decision, not after arrival at destination. The time of the migration decision is roughly when the first steps are taken to begin the migration process. As discussed above, in the case of most legal permanent residents to the United States, that point is reasonably construed as the filing of the first application that starts the visa process.
5   The challenge in studying immigrant health is to isolate the selection effect and the visa stress, migration stress, and exposure effects.

US immigrant visa process

All foreign-born in the United States can be classified according to their legal status. Table 31.1 outlines the basic types of legal status. Table 31.1 also shows the employment constraints; these are especially relevant given that in the United States health insurance is obtained through employment.

How many people are in each of the categories in Table 31.1? According to the US Census Bureau (American Community Survey, 2010 1-year estimates), in 2010 there were an estimated 39,955,854 foreign-born persons. Of these, an estimated 17,476,082 (or about 43.7 percent) had become US citizens (group 1 in Table 31.1). Thus, based on the Census Bureau figures, the total in the LPR, nonimmigrant, and unauthorized groups (groups 2, 3, and 4 in Table 31.1) would be about 22,479,772. Meanwhile, the Department of Homeland Security (DHS) estimates that on average, in Fiscal Year 2008, there were 1,830,000 legal temporary residents and that, as of January 1 2010, there were 12,630,000 legal permanent residents (LPR) and 10,790,000 unauthorized residents—for a total of 25,250,000. Ignoring differences in reference period, the Census Bureau estimate and the DHS estimate of the size of the three noncitizen groups combined differ by about 2.8 million. Whether one or more of the estimates is too low or too high—i.e., how to resolve the discrepancy—is a topic for further research.

As shown in Table 31.2, the United States admits about a million persons a year to legal permanent residence; these include both new arrivals and persons who are already in the United States with a temporary visa or in unauthorized status and adjust to LPR. The system of visa

G. Jasso

Table 31.1 Types of foreign-born persons in the United States and their employment restrictions

1. Legal permanent residents (LPR) who have become citizens
   May exercise any occupation except President and Vice-President of the United States
2. Legal permanent residents who have not become citizens
   May exercise any occupation except those reserved for citizens
3. Legal temporary residents (nonimmigrants)
3.1. Authorized to work–no restrictions (except on occupations reserved for citizens)
3.2. Authorized to work–with restrictions (such as hours of work or specific employer)
3.3. Not authorized to work
4. Unauthorized residents
   Not authorized to work

Table 31.2 Recent annual flows of new legal permanent residents to the United States

Fiscal year(s)	All immigrants	Excluding IRCA
A. Average annual flow		
1991–1995	1,046,063	781,848
1996–2000	773,021	771,307
2001–2005	980,478	980,344
2006–2010	1,119,850	1,119,735
B. Annual flow		
2006	1,266,264	1,266,047
2007	1,052,415	1,052,322
2008	1,107,126	1,107,010
2009	1,130,818	1,130,735
2010	1,042,625	1,042,563

Notes

Flows of new legal permanent residents (LPR) represent all persons granted legal permanent residence during the period. In most years, over half of all new LPRs are already living in the United States. Through Fiscal Year 2000 the figures in the "Excluding IRCA" column refer to the total, non-IRCA-legalization number of new LPRs. This number was reported as "total non-legalization" in Table 4 of the INS and DHS Yearbooks through the 2004 Yearbook. The Yearbooks for 2005–10 do not report the non-IRCA-legalization total, but it is possible to obtain it by subtracting the IRCA legalization total from the grand total in Table 7. During the period 1991–2010 IRCA legalizations declined from a high of over a million in 1991 to less than a thousand in every year since 1998, with a low of 8 in 1999 and totals of 188, 217, 93, 116, 83, and 62 in Fiscal Years 2005–2010, respectively (DHS Yearbooks, Table 4 through 2004, Table 7 thereafter).

allocation provides numerically unlimited visas to the spouses, minor children, and parents of adult US citizens. Numerically limited visas are granted to three main categories of immigrants: (1) family immigrants, comprised of the adult children and siblings of US citizens and the spouses and children of LPRs; (2) employment immigrants, comprised of five subcategories; and (3) diversity immigrants (winners of the lottery visas designated for persons from countries underrepresented in recent immigration). Two additional categories of LPR visas have subsets of both numerically limited and numerically unlimited type. These are: (4) humanitarian immigrants (including refugees, asylees, and parolees); and (5) legalization immigrants, that is, illegal immigrants who are becoming legal, including registry-provision immigrants (who qualify in virtue of length of illegal residence) and cancellation-of-removal immigrants, plus immigrants targeted by special legalization legislation (such as the Nicaraguan Adjustment and Central American Relief Act of 1997, or NACARA). The unauthorized may also become legal if they qualify for a visa under one of the other categories above.

The *principal* is the person who qualifies for the visa. The three categories of immediate relatives of US citizens—spouse, parent, minor child—are, with few exceptions, for principals only. All other categories provide LPR visas not only for the principal but also for the spouse and minor children of the principal, except for the category for spouses of LPRs and a few categories designated for "unmarried" principals, in which case "accompanying relative" visas are available only for minor children.

The process of applying for an immigrant visa is arduous and time-consuming. Persons waiting for numerically limited visas may have to wait many years (currently the upper extreme is almost 23 years for applicants from the Philippines in the sibling category). For most immigrants the date of the first application is a convenient date to represent the date of the migration decision. Exceptions include refugees, whose migration decision, as well as admission to the United States with a nonimmigrant refugee document, predates the filing for LPR.

The prospective immigrant must pass a medical examination to ensure that he or she is not inadmissible on medical grounds. The medical grounds for inadmissibility are grouped into four categories: (1) communicable disease of public health significance (e.g., tuberculosis or syphilis); (2) lack of required vaccinations (e.g., for polio and hepatitis B); (3) physical or mental disorders with harmful behavior; and (4) drug abuse or addiction. Thus, US immigration law plays a part in shaping the immigrant's health status at admission to legal permanent residence.

Thus, US immigration law shapes the migrant population—both legal immigrants and illegal migrants. As well, it distorts the link between migrant energy and the X characteristics involved in selection mechanisms, in at least two ways: (1) persons ineligible for LPR may not move, no matter how great their migrant energy, or may move as an illegal; and (2) persons with a long wait for an LPR visa may drop out of the queue, or become illegal.

This brief sketch of the US visa process suggests that migration streams may be visa-specific, as well as country- and gender-specific.

Selected migration process subpopulations

As noted above, a key challenge is to disentangle the effects of visa stress, migration stress, and US exposure. Some subpopulations may prove useful in this regard. These include groups that experience migration stress but not visa stress (such as persons born in Puerto Rico) or born in the United States to foreign parents (such as foreign students) who raise them abroad since childhood and groups that experience visa stress but not migration stress (such as persons brought to the United States as young children by parents who were unauthorized or who had long-term legal temporary employment, such as foreign correspondents and employees of international organizations).

All persons living in the United States—whether natives or immigrants—are subject to the set of US exposure effects. However, natives have had a longer time than immigrants in which to learn how to mitigate negative exposure effects and intensify positive exposure effects—as well as the benefits of more extensive networks. Accordingly, the challenge is to discern how US exposure affects health trajectory. Plausibly, negative effects dominate at first, but as learning about the environment occurs, the positive effects may dominate. Comparison between natives and immigrants at different US durations and with a variety of resources for learning about the US environment (knowledge of English, schooling level, contact with natives) will assist in discerning the trajectory.

Selected migration process sequences

The migration process sequence also can be useful in disentangling the effects of visa stress and migration stress. Among persons who arrive with an immigrant visa, visa stress is experienced in the origin country, concluding when the prospective immigrant, already approved by a consular official overseas, is admitted to the United States by a border official. Then begin both migration stress and US exposure. Persons who do not need an immigrant visa, such as those born in Puerto Rico, become subject to migration stress and US exposure at the same time as new-arrival LPRs.

The situation is different for persons who adjust to LPR in the United States. Depending on the extent of previous US residence, the prospective immigrant may experience all three sources of stress at the same time—visa stress, migration stress, and the early possibly negative effects of US exposure.

It is likely that health deteriorates during the visa process and during the initial time of US residence—due to visa stress and migration stress. Health assessments during those periods may mask the true selection effect. Further, experiencing both visa stress and migration stress at the same time may exacerbate the negative effects—reminiscent of the classical conjecture about the stresses associated with reaching puberty and transitioning to middle school at the same time (Simmons and Blyth 1987).

Immigrant selection as glimpsed in the destination country

There is no necessary relation between health selection and health relative to natives in the destination country. As Soldo *et al.* (2002) put it, "The theory of positive migrant selection yields no predictions about the health of migrants relative to the population at place of destination." The most skilled in one country may resemble the relatively lower-skilled in another. A country with positive selection on health may produce migrants who rank toward the bottom of the health distribution in the destination country.

Modeling health change

As noted, among applicants for legal permanent residence, the migration decision is followed by the process of applying for permanent residence. This process is highly stressful, and health may decline. The magnitude of visa stress and of the associated health decline may differ across migration streams. For example, visa stress may be greater for immigrants requiring an affidavit of support. As well, the start of visa stress may be earlier than the start of the LPR visa process for some immigrants, including refugees and those with previous illegal experience.

LPR is eventually obtained. At that point, visa stress ends, and we may conjecture that healthiness begins an upward trajectory. As with the decline, aspects of the recovery period may also vary by immigrant stream. Except for normal aging, one might imagine that following the recovery period, healthiness returns to its original level, unless visa stress has been so severe or prolonged that the body's physiology is altered (Seeman *et al.* 1997; Smith 1999). Note that the exact trajectory may differ across migration streams. For example, among immigrants with conditional visas, visa stress does not end at admission to LPR; and among refugees, visa stress may end at the time of temporary (nonimmigrant) admission.

As discussed above, migration stress begins at inception of US residence. It, too, may end, and its effects characterized by decline and recovery.

US exposure effects may be positive or negative. If negative, the trajectory may be upward, as the new immigrant learns to mitigate the harms and extract the benefits in the United States.

Selection mechanisms for return migration

As seen above, the second central question in the study of migration focuses on the immigrant career—the extent and pace of incorporation in the destination country—inclusive of the skill trajectory, the wealth trajectory and the health trajectory. Incorporation not only bears the imprint of the initial selection but also it generates a new selection—selection out of the destination country, including return to the origin country (Massey *et al.* 1987; Palloni and Arias 2004; Wong *et al.* 2007).

Thus, with respect to health, a new question arises, concerning the direction of the return selection. Do the healthiest leave the destination country? Or the unhealthiest? Or is there intermediate or extremal selection? A priori it would seem that origin-country conditions are pivotal, in particular, the quality and cost of healthcare. A US immigrant from a country with a universal healthcare system may choose to return if in ill health, while a US immigrant from a country without quality healthcare may choose to return only if in robust health.

Empirical framework

Data requirements for addressing health selection and health change are stringent. Analyzing health selection requires information on the desire to move and on health at the time of the migration decision. Assessing health relative to the native population requires information on health at the start of a well-defined point in the immigrant career, such as admission to legal permanent residence. Analyzing health change requires information on health at two well-defined points. Finally, understanding migrant behavior requires understanding the environment migrants face in the destination country—an environment defined by the migrant's legal status, in particular, whether the migrant has LPR.

Here we summarize results based on the New Immigrant Survey (NIS), a longitudinal study of probability samples from cohorts of immigrants newly admitted to legal permanent residence. The data satisfy the requirements for analyzing health selection and health change. In the years ahead, there will no doubt be additional data sources with the requisite data, for both the United States and other countries around the world.

Selected NIS information for studying migrant health

The analyses summarized here are based on the first round of the 2003 cohort (NIS-2003-1). The data pertain to the main sampled immigrants who are in the Adult Sample (age 18 and older) and who were not overseas and thus received all the questionnaires ($N = 8,253$). They are a subset of the main sampled immigrants ($N = 8,573$), for whom the response rate was 68.6%. For succinct overview of the NIS project, see Jasso (2008); for fuller overview and for data or documentation, see Jasso (2011) and the project website (http://nis.princeton.edu).

NIS Health Information

The NIS-2003-1 provides subjective assessments of overall health (1) at the time of the migration decision ("at the time of that first filing that started the process for the immigrant visa that you now have"), and (2) at the time of the interview. Previous research suggests that subjective assessment of overall health accord well with objective measures (Ware *et al.* 1978; Wallace and Herzog 1995).

As already discussed, the assessment of health at the time of the migration decision is especially important for studying health selection, because, except for certain immigrants such as refugees and illegals, the measure pertains to health at a time before the start of visa stress.

The subjective health assessments provide five response categories: excellent, very good, good, fair, and poor. These are coded 1 to 5, with 1 representing poor and 5 representing excellent.

The analysis of health change relies on an NIS question that asks the respondent whether his or her health at the time of the interview is worse, the same, or better than it was "right before you most recently came to the United States to live." These are coded with −1 for worse, 0 for same, and +1 for better.

NIS information on the desire to move to the United States

Selection, as we saw above, is about the desire to move—migrant energy—and it may vary in strength across migrants, producing the selection profile. NIS data include questions on the desire for LPR and earlier LPR applications which make it possible to approximate migrant energy E. The main question is: "In what year did you first think that someday you might like to have legal permanent residence in the United States?" Response categories include "always", "never", and a specific year.

To measure the number of years that the respondent has wanted LPR, a new variable, called E-years, is defined as follows. If the respondent answered the question above with "Never," E-years is coded zero. If the respondent answered with a specific year, E-years is coded by year of admission to LPR (2003) minus the year of first wanting LPR. If the respondent answered with "Always," E-years is coded with the age at admission to LPR. If the respondent did not answer the question but did answer other questions on the year of earlier applications to LPR as a principal, E-years is coded using the earliest year mentioned (subtracting this year from 2003). This measure of desire for LPR ranges from zero to the age at admission to LPR of the oldest immigrant. It has the advantage that it quantifies the number of years that the respondent wanted LPR, reminiscent of Jacob's 14 years working for permission to marry Rachel. However, it has the disadvantage that it is sensitive to the respondent's age; thus, a control for age must be included when this measure is used.

Another way to circumvent the influence of age on E-years is to define the proportion of life wanting LPR. This new measure, E-proplife, is the ratio of E-years to age at admission to LPR. This measure ranges from zero to one.

Both E-years and E-proplife are sensitive to the wait for numerically limited visas. A solution is to always use controls for visa category and country of origin, which jointly determine the visa wait.

Other NIS information for studying health

NIS data provide extensive information on country of birth and visa class of admission. A total of 168 origin countries are represented in the NIS Adult Sample. Of these, 150 are represented among male respondents and 154 among female respondents.

Visa data provide information for distinguishing migration streams, including whether the immigrant is a principal or an accompanying spouse, whether the immigrant has a numerically unlimited or numerically limited visa, if numerically limited, whether the visa is a family, work, humanitarian, diversity, or legalization visa. We distinguish 19 broad visa categories. A further binary variable indicates whether the visa is a conditional visa. Additionally, a binary variable was constructed to indicate previous illegal experience; persons with illegal experience include not only persons with legalization visas but also persons who achieved LPR with a variety of other visas (notably spouse of US citizen).

Specification of the health selection equation

To assess the direction of health selection, we begin with the general equation (31.1) and specify its empirical counterpart:

$$E^* = \alpha + \sum \beta_c Hlt_c + \sum \upsilon_k Visa_k + \gamma_j COB_j + e \qquad (31.2)$$

where $E^\star$ denotes the particular measure of migrant energy E; Hlt denotes the five-category variable for the health assessment at the time the first application was filed; visa and country of birth are represented by dummy variables (or, put differently, the equation includes visa and country fixed effects); and e denotes the random error. Equations in which the dependent variable is E-years also include as a regressor the respondent's age at admission to LPR. The omitted health category is "poor". In an analysis of variance (ANOVA) framework, this specification would be equivalent to obtaining the means of the five health categories (the main effects), controlling for country, visa, and age. Equation (3.2) is estimated in gender-specific versions.

Because the visa class for spouses of US citizens is large (approximately one-third of all adult LPRs) and because the employment and diversity categories are small (but important), the NIS sample was stratified. All results summarized below are based on analyses which use sampling weights to adjust for the sample stratification.

Inclusion of the visa and country dummies controls for differences in E or its measures across migration streams defined by visa and origin country. The country and visa dummies also capture the effects of waiting for numerically limited visas. Thus, the coefficients of the health dummies indicate the pattern of health selection net of visa and country effects.

The pattern of the health coefficients indicates the type of selection. Given that "poor" is the omitted category, if the coefficients are all positive and increase from "fair" to "excellent", the health selection is monotonic and positive. If the coefficients are all negative and decreasing, the selection is negative. If the coefficients are not positive and increasing or negative and decreasing, then the selection is nonmonotonic. For example, if the coefficients first increase, then decrease, there is intermediate selection (inverse U-shaped). In contrast, if the coefficients decrease from zero and subsequently increase, then the selection is extremal (U-shaped).

Specification of the health change equation

To assess the direction of health change after LPR, we specify the basic equation:

$$HC^* = \beta_0 + \beta_1 Age + \beta_2 E^* + \beta_3 TimeLPR + e \qquad (31.3)$$

where $HC^\star$ denotes a measure of health change, Age refers to age at the time of the interview, $E^\star$ denotes a measure of migrant energy, and TimeLPR denotes the time in years elapsed between admission to LPR and the interview.

The measure of health change used below is the respondent's assessment about whether health at the time of the interview is worse, the same, or better than it was right before coming to the United States to live. Accordingly, we specify an ordered-logit specification.

Controls are included, as follows. Among immigrants whose US residence began at admission to LPR, visa stress ended at admission to LPR unless they had conditional visas. Thus, immigrants whose US residence began at admission to LPR differ from immigrants whose US residence began before admission to LPR in that, while both groups experience migration stress and US exposure effects between inception of US residence and the baseline interview, only the group whose US residence predates LPR experiences visa stress during that interval.

Accordingly, we use the information on whether the immigrant is an adjustee or a new arrival to proxy inception of US residence and define a three-category variable, with one category for new arrivals and two categories for adjustees, those with and those without illegal experience. We include as well a variable to indicate a conditional visa.

Migrant energy should exert positive effects on health. The greater the migrant energy, the stronger the embrace of the destination country and the more rapid the process of extracting its health benefits.

Thus, the measure of time in the United States since LPR captures the combined effects of US exposure and migration stress since admission to LPR, net of age, the conditional visa and adjustee variables, and migrant energy.

Immigrant health selection

The results on immigrant health selection summarized here, based on NIS data on new legal immigrants in 2003, indicate that, on average, health selection is positive—unambiguously positive among women, likely positive among men. However, this positive selection covers a wide diversity of selection profiles among migration streams.

Selection profiles for the top five countries of birth indicate that immigrants from India exhibit extremal (U-shaped) selection, as do men from China, while men from El Salvador exhibit negative selection. Women from Mexico exhibit a pattern of intermediate (inverse U-shaped) selection veering on positive selection, while men from Mexico have a multi-peak pattern that veering toward intermediate selection—thus roughly consistent with Chiquiar and Hanson's (2005) results for skill and wage selection—intermediate among men, positive among women. Most of the country-specific selection profiles are nonmonotonic. Only one is negative (among men from El Salvador). Besides the profile for women from Mexico, only two other profiles—for women from China and El Salvador—exhibit a hint of a possibility of positive selection.

Estimation of health selection profiles by visa category indicates that women who immigrate with parent-of-US-citizen visas exhibit positive selection, but young daughters of US citizens exhibit negative selection. Men who marry US citizens exhibit intermediate selection, while women who marry US citizens could have intermediate or extremal profiles. Diversity principals of both sexes exhibit extremal profiles, as do male legalization principals and women with illegal experience. Men with illegal experience exhibit positive health selection—the only such category other than mothers of US citizens.

Finally, a close look at the 18 migration streams for which sample size enables estimation of selection profiles defined by both visa, country, and gender indicates that only one group has unambiguous positive health selection—female spouses of Indian-born employment principals—and only three groups have unambiguous negative health selection—employment principals of both sexes from the Philippines and diversity principal men from Ethiopia. The remaining 14 migration streams have nonmonotonic health selection profiles, mostly extremal (including male employment principals from India), with two intermediate selection profiles among women. Interestingly, Mexico-born mothers of US citizens display U-shaped selection if they had illegal experience but inverse U-shaped selection if they had no illegal experience.

Immigrant health in the eye of the destination country

Health selection is fundamental and far-reaching. The estimates reviewed above provide a rich portrait of selection. Yet selection is not quite visible in the destination country. Whether an immigrant stream is drawn from the top or the bottom or the middle of an origin country's hierarchy is less important in the destination country than where it fits in the hierarchies of the destination country. That women from Mexico are probably positively selected on health would be masked if health levels in Mexico are far below those in the United States; and that men from

El Salvador are negatively selected would be masked if health levels in El Salvador are far above those in the United States. Thus, high levels of healthiness can co-exist with negative selection, and vice versa; and the link is more complicated when the selection is nonmonotonic.

Estimates based on NIS data indicate that, seen from the vantage point of the United States, men from India and the Philippines seem to be in much better health than those from Mexico and China. Yet their selection profiles are similar (U-shaped for China and India, inverse U-shaped for Mexico and the Philippines). Moreover, the negative selection of men from El Salvador disappears into a health distribution with its highest peak at excellent health. Similarly, the positively selected mothers of US citizens seem only average relative to other immigrants in the United States, and the negatively selected daughters of US citizens are among the healthier immigrants.

Of course, the new LPRs may be taking steps to improve their health. One such step is obtaining health insurance. At the time of the baseline interview, 42.4 percent had health insurance. The visa categories associated with high and low fractions of health coverage are not surprising. Visa classes with fractions covered greater than the overall 42.4 percent are employment principal and spouse (70.5 and 71.7 percent, respectively), spouses of native-born US citizens (60 percent), spouses of foreign-born US citizens (48.4 percent), and refugee-asylee-parolee principals and spouses (51.2 percent and 60.2 percent, respectively). Particularly low coverage rates are found among parents, minor children, siblings, and siblings-in-law of US citizens and among diversity principals and spouses—all in the 24–28 percent range.

As for origin country, countries in the top ten whose immigrants have high fractions covered are India (49.1 percent), Philippines (47.9 percent), and Colombia (43.8 percent). At the other extreme, countries with low fractions covered are Vietnam and Haiti (in the 29–30 percent range) and the Dominican Republic (22.4 percent).

But the immigrant career is just beginning. It will be important to examine healthcare coverage at the second and subsequent rounds of data collection.

From a vantage point in the destination country, selection does its job of producing immigrants, and social scientists probe the process, but what really matters is the new array of immigrants. As befits a country of immigrants, a democratic country of immigrants, the immigrants' selection origins may count for little—unless they influence what happens next, in this case, the health trajectory.

Immigrant health trajectory after LPR

At admission to legal permanent residence, visa stress ends for all immigrants except those with conditional visas—chiefly spouses of US citizens and of LPRs in marriages of less than 2 years' duration and employment-based investor immigrants—whose visas are conditional for two years and who must apply for removal of the conditionality restrictions. The immigrants are in various stages of the migration stress sequence. Among those who have lived for many years in the United States, migration stress has concluded; among those who are coming to the United States for the first time, it is just beginning. Recovery from visa stress may not be instantaneous, depending on the severity of the stress; similarly, recovery from migration stress may vary in duration. Meanwhile, everyone, in company with the native-born, faces the health-relevant aspects of the US environment, the challenge being to mitigate negative effects and accentuate positive effects, something which is learned with time in the United States.

Estimates of the health change equation indicate that selection has a continuing—and positive—effect on health.

Men show a strong effect of time in the United States since receiving legal permanent residence, with their health improving with every passing day; women, on the other hand are on average at best on a plateau, not recovering from visa stress and migration stress and/or not yet extracting benefits from the US environment. The estimates also suggest that experiencing all three sources of health change at the same time takes its toll—adjustees show less health improvement than new arrivals.

These results are based on a survey conducted soon after admission to legal permanent residence. Subsequent rounds of the New Immigrant Survey will make it possible to track health change. Visa stress, already ended for most of the cohort, will end for all with the removal of conditionality restrictions. Migration stress presumably will run its course. The effects of US exposure will continue, and it will be possible to assess whether, and how, immigrants learn to extract greater health benefits and mitigate health harms. As well, it will be possible to assess whether, and how, migrant energy continues to exert its positive effect on health.

Discussion

Classically, there are two main questions about immigrant health—the health selection question, which seeks to learn the direction of selection on health across different migration streams, and the health change question, which seeks to learn whether health improves or deteriorates in the destination country, relative to both nonmigrants in the origin country and natives in the destination country.

This chapter highlighted several important features of migration and health. First, government restrictions on exit and entry coupled with family dynamics make it difficult to infer health selection from movers and stayers. Accordingly, we discussed a new approach—directly measuring the desire to move and estimating the selection function, viz., the desire to move as a function of the migrant's health. Second, there are three distinct sources of health change—visa stress, migration stress, and exposure effects in the destination country. Because one of these, visa stress, can predate arrival in the destination country, measuring health upon arrival is too late to provide an undistorted view of health selection. Third, migration streams—defined by origin country, visa class, and gender—have distinctive health selection profiles. Fourth, disentangling the effects of visa stress, migration stress, and destination-country exposure requires careful attentiveness to both the migration stream features and the dates of the migration decision, admission to legal permanent residence, and subsequent removal of LPR conditionality restrictions.

We summarized estimates of the health selection equation and the health change equation based on data from the New Immigrant Survey. The results are consistent with a model in which health deteriorates due to the hardships of the visa process, hardships which are intensified if the migrant goes through the visa process after moving to the destination country, but then improves, as visa stress and migration stress end, migrant energy exerts a positive effect on health, and the migrant learns how to navigate the destination country's health environment, mitigating its harms and extracting its benefits.

But chronic visa stress—as among the unauthorized—may prevent health improvement, even if migration stress ends and even if the migrant masters the destination country's health environment.

References and further reading

Akresh, I. R. and Frank, R. (2008) "Health selection among new immigrants" *American Journal of Public Health* 98(11): 2058–64.
Antecol, H. and Bedard, K. (2006) "Unhealthy assimilation: Why do immigrants converge to American health status levels?" *Demography* 43(2): 337–60.

Biddle, N., Kennedy, S., and McDonald, J. T. (2007) "Health assimilation patterns among Australian immigrants" *The Economic Record* 83(260): 16–30.

Chiquiar, D. and Hanson, G. H. (2005) "International migration, self-selection, and the distribution of wages: Evidence from Mexico and the United States" *Journal of Political Economy* 113(2): 239–81.

Gott, R. (2005) *Cuba: A New History*. New Haven, CT: Yale University Press.

Jasso, G. (2003) "Migration, human development, and the lifecourse." In J. T. Mortimer and M. Shanahan (eds), *Handbook of the Lifecourse*. New York: Kluwer, pp. 331–64.

——(2008) "New immigrant survey." In W. A. Darity Jr. (ed.), *International Encyclopedia of the Social Sciences*, Second Edition, Volume 5. Detroit, MI: Macmillan Reference USA, pp. 499–500.

——(2011) "Migration and stratification" *Social Science Research* 40(5): 1292–1336.

Jasso, G., Massey, D. S., Rosenzweig, M. R. and Smith, J. P. (2004) "Immigrant health—selectivity and acculturation." In N. B. Anderson, R. A. Bulatao, and B. Cohen (eds), *Critical Perspectives on Racial and Ethnic Differences in Health in Late Life*. Washington, DC: National Academy Press, pp. 227–66.

——(2005) "Immigration, health, and New York City: Early results based on the US new-immigrant cohort of 2003" *Economic Policy Review* 11(2): 127–51.

Kasl, S. V. and Berkman, L. (1983) "Health consequences of the experience of migration" *Annual Review of Public Health* 4: 69–90.

Lee, E. S. (1966) "A theory of migration" *Demography* 3(1): 47–57.

Massey, D. S., Alarcón, R., Durand, J., and González, H. (1987) *Return to Aztlan: The Social Processes of International Migration from Western Mexico*. Berkeley, CA: University of California Press.

Palloni, A. and Arias, E. (2004) "Paradox lost: Explaining the Hispanic adult mortality advantage" *Demography* 41(3): 385–415.

Sawyerr, S. (2010) "Workshop: Reducing tears of migration." *Tell Magazine*. www.tellng.com.

Seeman, T. E., Singer, B. H., Rowe, J. W., Horwitz, R. I., and McEwen, B. S. (1997) "Price of adaptation—Allostatic load and its health consequences" *Archives of Internal Medicine* 157(19): 2259–68.

Simmons, R. G. and Blyth, D. A. (1987) *Moving into Adolescence: The Impact of Pubertal Change and School Context*. New York: Aldine.

Smith, J. P. (1999) "Healthy bodies and thick wallets: The dual relation between health and economic status" *Journal of Economic Perspectives* 13(2): 145–66.

Soldo, B. J., Wong, R., and Palloni, A. (2002) "Migrant health selection: Evidence from Mexico and the US." Paper presented at the annual meeting of the Population Association of America, Atlanta, Georgia, May 2002.

Stephen, E. H., Foote, K., Hendershot, G. E., and Schoenborn, C. A. (1994) *Health of the Foreign-Born Population: United States, 1989–90*. Advance Data from Vital and Health Statistics, No. 241, 14 February 1994. Hyattsville, MD: National Center for Health Statistics.

US Department of Homeland Security, Office of Immigration Statistics (2002–10) *Yearbook of Immigration Statistics*. Washington, DC: Government Printing Office.

US Department of State (n.d.) Various issues. "Visa Bulletin." Posted online.

US Immigration and Naturalization Service (1979–2001) *Statistical Yearbook of the Immigration and Naturalization Service*. Washington, DC: Government Printing Office.

Vega, W. and Amaro, H. (1994) "Latino outlook: Good health, uncertain prognosis" *Annual Review of Public Health* 15: 39–67.

Wallace, R. B., and Herzog, R. (1995) "Overview of the health measures in the health and retirement study" *The Journal of Human Resources* 30: S84–S107.

Ware, J., Davies-Avery, A., and Donald, C. (1978) *General Health Perceptions*. R1987/5. Santa Monica. CA: RAND.

Wong, R., Palloni, A., and Soldo, B. J. (2007) "Wealth in middle and old age in Mexico: The role of international migration" *International Migration Review* 41(1): 127–51.

32

Micro- and macro-explanations of naturalization

Thomas Janoski

The study of naturalization—immigrants becoming a citizens of their new country—has gone through significant change in the past 20 years. The first major change moved from focusing almost exclusively on the USA and other settler countries to a broader array of receiving countries in Europe and Asia. Most early studies were dominated by assimilation and naturalization in the American experience. Since the 1990s, this American focus has given way to the micro-analysis of naturalization processes in advanced industrialized countries, the naturalization of different sending country immigrants in the same receiving country, and the movement from overall assimilation to segmented assimilation. The second major change was toward the more macro-political and cultural facets of immigration laws in individual sending countries, followed by an emerging literature on the comparison of naturalization regimes in different countries. Along with these two changes are some knotty questions about how to theorize and measure naturalization.

The micro- and macro-approaches just mentioned have differing foci and significance. The micro-examination of immigrants' willingness to become citizens and their eventual integration into society has important impacts on immigrants/citizens social mobility, self-esteem, political rights and participation, and, more generally, their overall life-chances. This has an especially strong effect on the first generation of immigrants, but also on the second and third generations who may do better.

The macro-social study of the nationality policies of a receiving country themselves are important gauges of how states and societies accept or reject foreigners and long-term residents. Activist groups in countries with high naturalizations react more strongly against anti-foreigner protests, demonstrations, and murders. Their reactions are different because naturalized immigrants can vote, organize, and protest. For instance, French conservative parties and anti-immigrant leader La Pen attacked the *jus soli* principle and obtained stricter nationality policies. But students and naturalized immigrants worked together through *SOS Racisme* and other groups to prevent the government from enacting more anti-immigrant demands. When the French socialists regained power, they reversed the *jus soli* decision (Hargreaves 1995; Feldblum 1999). In many ways, the political and cultural forces that explain these policies and politics can be altered once their significance and social bases are understood. The key difference is that countries with liberal nationality policies lay the base for the political organization of immigrants so that they can protect themselves and pursue their own livelihood, while countries with difficult nationality policies make it nearly impossible for immigrants to protect themselves in the political arena and they have to rely on the kindnesses of strangers (i.e., citizens) to protect their homes and families. As a result, access to citizenship can make a difference in everyday lives and can actually be a matter of life or death.

This chapter will make three main points: (1) naturalization rates vary quite a bit between receiving countries, and this raises a number of methodological issues about how to measure naturalization, (2) the long tradition of micro-sociological studies of naturalization have sharpened and expanded their focus beyond the USA, and (3) macro-sociological theories are a relatively new area that uncover unexamined forces in cross-national studies.

The extent and measurement of naturalization

In the last four decades, nationality rates in advanced industrialized countries have varied widely. From 1980 to 1984, naturalization rates (the acquisitions of citizenship divided by the foreign population) ran as high as nearly 10,000 per 100,000 foreigners in Canada to less than 500 per 100,000 foreigners in Germany. Canada's more open policies averaged a nationality rate 10 times larger than Germany. From 2000 to 2005, the rates were over 12,000 and 2,000 for the same two countries: still a large difference. The naturalization rates for other countries can be seen in Table 32.1 (for data see US-INS 1972–2003; OECD 1976–2005, 2006–9; US-CIS 2004–6; Waldrauch 2006; Baker 2009; Janoski 2010).

In open countries (top of Table 32.1), immigrants can quickly become citizens, vote, and form interest groups; but in more closed countries, immigrants rarely vote and are often subject to deportation if they lose their jobs or get in legal trouble. In open countries immigrant children born in the receiving country automatically obtain citizenship, while in closed countries such children have to wait for nationality as an adult, which can be a process fraught with difficulties.

The largest issue drawn between open and closed countries concerns whether a country has *jus soli*—birth on home soil confers citizenship to the child of native or foreign parents—or *jus sanguinis*—the blood of the citizen parents provides citizenship (Liang 1994b). *Jus soli* creates a large number of new citizens by citizens being born from non-citizens on home soil. A narrow view of naturalization would only consider those persons who have officially gone through the naturalization process that often includes a waiting or residency period, applications, and various tests (perhaps an oath). The wide rate includes *jus soli* births, which exist only in countries that have *jus soli*, and the other types of "citizenship acquisition" (the OECD term for naturalization). Table 32.1 includes both rates and they only differ for the *jus soli* countries (Australia, Canada, France, Ireland, New Zealand, the UK, and the USA; and more recently for Germany and Belgium in a limited way). In most cases the estimates of *jus soli* births are small, but one exception is Ireland where there is little naturalization. Many ignore *jus soli* births and only analyze the "official" rate, but a full analysis of naturalization or nationality would require the wide rate (Waldrauch 2006; Janoski 2010). Even micro-studies would need to consider this since all of the third-generation and often half the second-generation immigrants are actually *jus soli* births in *jus soli* but not in *jus sanguinis* countries.

Given that one makes a choice about which naturalization rates to study, the explanation of these still massive differences can be approached from the micro- or macro-level.

Micro-theories of naturalization

Micro-theories explain individual decisions and characteristics that lead to naturalization. The first group of theories focused on the social psychology of assimilation. This began in the 1920s in the

Table 32.1 Wide and Narrow Naturalization Rates per 100,000 Aliens from 1970 to 2005 (Countries ranked according to 1970–74 wide naturalization rates.)

Country	1970–74	1975–79	1980–84	1985–89	1990–95	1995–99	2000–05
Canada[a]	10,006	14,659	9,865	8,856	11,268	11,963	12,332
	8,364	13,141	8,371	7,274	9,950	10,799	11,286
UK[a]	7,516	5,760	7,275	5,606	3,618	3,509	5,286
	6,031	4,532	6,348	5,552	3,567	2,795	4,777
Australia[a]	5,354	6,944	7,250	8,286	8,571	6,160	4,542
	3,398	5,355	5,666	7,439	8,222	5,666	3,638
New Zealand[a]	3,650	5,968	5,583	5,407	4,818	4,241	4,257
	1,562	3,387	4,015	3,765	3,100	2,916	2,822
US[a]	3,640	6,350	3,775	4,045	4,468	9,066	7,069
	2,047	2,461	2,207	2,465	2,764	7,273	5,665
Denmark	3,185	3,176	3,133	2,829	2,853	3,441	4,596
Finland	4,251	3,003	5,810	6,596	2,233	2,841	4,173
Austria	3,313	2,922	2,960	2,430	2,047	2,464	4,754
Norway	–	5,248[c]	2,854	2,554	3,767	6,556	4,821
Sweden	2,975	3,956	4,836	4,733	5,976	6,445	7,627
Switzerland	2,975	2,287	1,426	1,261	888	1,398	2,313
France[a]	2,959	2,815	2,818	2,670	2,851	3,492	4,889
	1,304	1,418	1,376	1,589	2,177	2,387	3,772
Netherlands	1,731	1,791	2,544	4,628	4,718	9,682	4,821
Belgium	847	819	848	2,764	2,728	3,430	5,615[b]
	847	819	848	2,764	2,728	3,430	5,253
Germany	268	331	314	489	489	1,344	2,642[b]
	268	331	314	489	489	1,344	2,107
Ireland[a]	–	–	2,277	2,465	1,838	2,085	3,104
			269	599	405	681	681
Italy	–	–	117	608	610	892	657
Japan	999	885	967	700	723	1,017	917

Source: OECD 1976-2005), Janoski 2010.
Notes:
[a]Canada, the UK, Australia, Ireland, France, New Zealand and the United States have *jus soli* adjustments over the whole period.
[b]Germany and Belgium started *jus soli* adjustments in 2000.
[c]Norway's naturalization figure is for 1977 to 1979.

USA with the assimilation approach focused on individuals and their social capital and contact with the new culture involving at least some re-socialization toward their new home. The theory was that the more immigrants become like the receiving society, the more they would naturalize. The logic of assimilation theory in explaining variation in naturalization stresses differences in education, occupation, and family status as important aspects of behavior (Bernard 1936; Gordon 1964; Grebler 1966; Garcia 1981; Evans 1988; Massey *et al.* 1998). Portes and Curtis (1987: 355–6) list the causes of assimilation as:

1 Sending Country: younger age, being married, having children, higher education, high parental SES, coming from an urban community, having more work experience, and living in the country prior to one's most current entry.

2 Receiving Country: higher occupation status, more income, owning a home, obtaining more education since arrival, having good language skills, and having extensive knowledge of the receiver society.
3 Social Context: Living and working in cities and neighborhoods with an ethnic mix, and interacting more with neighbors, friends, and kin;
4 Personal Attitudes: Being satisfied with the receiver society and life, having a fading desire to return home, and having low perceptions of discrimination.

The closer immigrants get to being embedded in socio-economic, family, and identity net-works—work with natives, speak the language, marry a native, interact with natives and upwardly mobile immigrants, and internalize native culture—the more likely they will naturalize (Gordon 1964; Portes and Curtis 1987; Liang 1994a). The assimilationist theory became con-nected to social networks and chain migration processes with kin and friends. But the more immigrants stay immersed in an ethnic enclave speaking their original language, the less they will naturalize. The assimilationist approach has yielded an impressive body of research, especially about how individual ethnic groups may differ in their propensity to naturalize.

The assimilationist approach has been criticized because of its ready assumption that immi-grants will abandon their sending country culture for the receiver country culture. Further, assimilationist theory tried to force one model on a diverse array of immigrants. Coupled with multi-cultural perspectives (especially from Canada) and strong ethnic communities among Hispanics and Asians, new theories began to develop.

In the early 1990s, segmented assimilation theories began to stress that immigrants do not easily give up their sending country culture. The special issue of *International Migration Review* in 1997 provided numerous articles indicating that there is increasing evidence that immigrants who naturalize may maintain a complex identity composed of sending and receiving country culture (Portes 1997; Zhou 1997). This meshed with movements in social psychology empha-sizing multiple identities and an increasingly globalized and transnational world. Since then studies have shifted away from a universal micro-theory of naturalization to studies that emphasize how immigrants from different ethnic groups have different behaviors and values that explain high or low naturalization (Liang 1994a; Yang 1994; Zhou 1997; Kasinitz *et al.* 2002; Bean *et al.* 2003, 2006; Zhou and Lee 2007; Gilbertson and Singer 2009). For instance, findings indicate that 41.8 percent of the immigrants admitted from 1978 to 1987 from 10 Hispanic and Asian countries naturalized, while 61.7 percent of Filipino, 65.4 percent of Vietnamese, and only 18.2 percent of Mexican immigrants naturalized (Woodrow-Lafield *et al.* 2004). These more specific studies of each immigrant group explain the diverse reasons why.

Receiving countries vary in the reception that they provide to immigrants. Portes and Rumbaut describe the government's favorable, neutral, and hostile reception of immigrants, and each society's neutral and prejudiced responses (2001: 49–51; Reitz 2003). Matching the gov-ernment and societal responses results in nine combinations: (1) favorable government, neutral society; (2) favorable government, prejudiced society; (3) both neutral, (4) neutral government, prejudiced society, (5) hostile government, neutral society, (6) hostile government, prejudiced society. In their study of 15 sending countries, governments varied but society was prejudiced in most countries (2, 4, and 6), but the most welcoming responses were to Cuban immigrants with positive and neutral (1) and to Filipino immigrants with both neutral (3). Their approach has three clear implications for naturalization: (a) positive responses result in assimilation with straightforward naturalization, (b) mixed responses result in "segmented assimilation" with a clear preference for dual nationality, and (c) hostile acculturation produces countercultural reactions where immigrants avoid naturalization. While positive receptions are preferable, the long-term effects of hostile acculturation can work in opposite directions. On the one hand, the long-term effects of hostile reception can create an underclass that develops a negative or countercultural identity. This appears to be a problem with Mexican immigrants in large American cities where education and employment are sparse and gangs and violence may be a problem (Portes and Rumbaut 2001). The sons and daughters of Afro-Caribbean (Jamaican, Dominican, Puerto Rican, etc.) immigrants with a distinct identity may be re-socialized with the African-American counterculture (Waters 1999). This may lead to lower levels of naturalization. On the other hand, the tightening of restrictions on immigrant rights (e.g., cutting government benefits in the USA or making naturalization more difficult in Europe), can produce rather large increases in naturalization rates to avoid these disadvantages. In this second case, these restrictions may reduce immigration rates in the long-term, but increase naturalization rates in the short-term to avoid restrictive laws.

As a second major approach to micro-social theories, demographic and economic models have a major impact on naturalization. Getting married, having a family, or buying a house result in increased ties to the receiver country. With the exception of well-off migrants, most immigrants often find housing in lower income neighborhoods where housing prices are lower. The decision to purchase a house rather than rent is a big decision. Further, immigrants eventually become very interested in the schools that their children go to and want to see them improve. Each of these decisions increases the probability that their stay in the receiver country is permanent and that naturalization is an important next step.

Economic factors also lead to naturalization. Employment and especially raises, promotions, and social mobility lead to higher likelihood of naturalization, and conversely, unemployment leads to less likelihood (Molho 1986: 105–7). It should also be recognized that economic growth and employment opportunities in the sending country may have an effect. For instance, when growth took off in Ireland in the late 1990s, some Irish immigrants to the USA went back for those opportunities (Barrett 1999).

From the development of segmented assimilation in the USA, attention has increasingly focused on naturalization and citizenship in Europe, especially concerning some of the countries that make citizenship rather difficult to attain. Increasing numbers of studies have been done on Germany (Diehl and Blohm 2003; Anil 2007; Constant et al. 2007; Becker 2009), France (Wihtol de Wenden 1994; Simon 2003), Canada (Tomata 1999), Australia (Evans 1988; Zappalá and Castles 2000), Belgium (Timmerman et al. 2003), Austria (Vieter 1990), Japan (Kashiwazaki 2000); and Europe more generally (Bauer et al. 2000; Crul and Vermuelen 2003; Tübergen et al. 2004; Beuker 2005; Tübergen 2006; Crul and Heering 2008; Maxwell 2010). Many of these studies are of jus sanguinis countries so that the naturalization process extends further into the second and third generation of immigrants, which differs significantly from the USA. So future results may end up producing new micro-theories.

These different factors can be modeled in Figure 32.1 with the various factors leading to higher naturalizations in items 1, 2, 4, 5, and 7a and b leading to higher probabilities of naturalization (item 8), and various home country ties and subcultures leading to negative or countercultural identities (items 3, 6, and 7c and d) and less naturalization.

Micro-theories have their strong points with social psychology, but more generally they have two disadvantages: (1) they are narrowly focused on the process of naturalization of different ethnic groups in one country, not on differences between receiving countries; and (2) since they are based on individual level data, these studies do not help with state-level variables such as different naturalization laws and eager or resistant bureaucracies. In the end, the assimilationist and segmented assimilationist theories are good at addressing individual decisions to naturalize, but taken alone they cannot explain why naturalization rates differ in a number of countries, which is the topic of the next section.

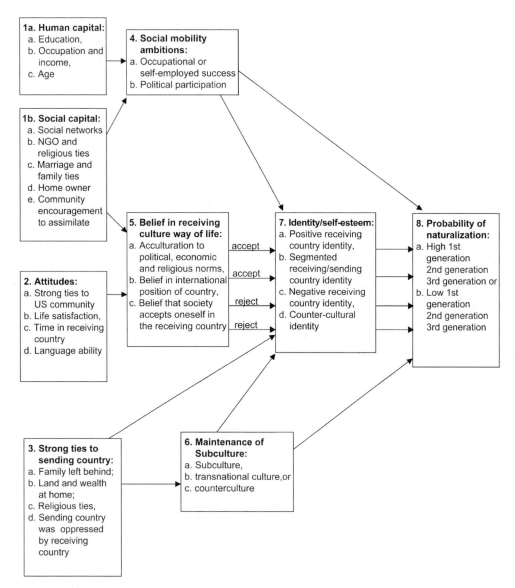

Figure 32.1 Micro-theoretical model explaining naturalization

Macro-explanations of naturalization

Massey *et al.* say that "international migration rarely engaged the interests of theorists working in the historical-structural tradition" (1998: 35). But there has been increasing interest in sociology and political science on naturalization at the macro-level. Much of the macro-social approach compares countries but since this area is so new, many works have examined naturalization laws and policies in particular countries one-by-one. For instance, Bauböck *et al.* (2006: v. 2), Nascimbene (1996) and Aleinikoff and Klusmeyer (2000) have chapters for each of the 15 EU countries, Bauböck *et al.* (2010) addresses the 12 new accession states plus Croatia and Turkey, and

Aleinikoff and Klusmeyer (2000) have individual chapters for Australia, Canada, the USA, Russia, South Africa, the Baltics, Mexico, Israel, and Japan. While these country studies focused on laws and implementation are useful, they do not provide much in the way of causal explanations. But four developing perspectives explicitly target long-term causal mechanisms that explain naturalization rates: (1) the cultural idiom and convergence approaches, (2) the demographic and economic theories, and (3) the political theories of clientelism (capture theory) and left party power, and (4) the various regime theories based on institutions. They are discussed below.

First, the cultural approach provides a direct approach to explaining why some countries are open to naturalizing strangers and their children, while other countries are extremely reluctant. Brubaker's (1989, 1992) work on citizenship and nationhood uses a "cultural idiom" approach—ways of thinking and talking about nationhood. He demonstrates that cultural idioms were either formed in the crucible of the French Revolution or developed indigenously over time in Germany. The French Revolution transformed "belonging" to French society into active participation based on rights and obligations, which fixed itself upon the nation-state. Prior bases for rights in terms of belonging came from the cosmopolitan aristocracy in pre-revolutionary France. Modern citizenship began with an act of closure upon the French nation-state with those who opposed the state being executed and citizens being conscripted to protect the republic. This cultural crucible created the French approach to universality that allows nearly anyone who assimilates and supports French cultural and political norms to become a citizen. Consequently, French naturalization rates have been reported as high for a densely populated European country, and the legal principles of *jus soli* predominate over *jus sanguinis* (Brubaker 1992: 35–49).

Germany did not have an event like the French Revolution, and the development of citizenship was connected to the estate or *Stand*, which was a highly particularistic institution (Brubaker 1992: 50–72). The estate developed into multiple legal systems with community-based notions of belonging in many different regions. The focus was inward with the most extreme example being the closed "home towns," where membership meant you could work and have a livelihood. Although legal development took place within and between numerous German states, laws closed off the poor and the alien Polish and Jewish cultures. The result was a long-lasting and active system of *jus sanguinis* that brought millions of dispersed German ethnics (*Aussiedler*) back from an eastern European diaspora as full-fledged citizens. But the German system erected great barriers against citizenship for Turks and their children because the German law, until recently, totally avoided the legal principle of *jus soli*.

Brubaker's theory is well argued as a macro-social explanation naturalization rates, but there are a few problems. First, his "cultural idioms" resemble genetic codes of citizenship, especially because they locate the unique events that have continuous effects over centuries. The mechanisms of development and the agents acting them out suggest that a constant factor dooms a country to be controlled by its cultural idiom. Second, a theory based on uniqueness provides little guidance in explaining other countries.

Another cultural approach concerns convergence theory. Hollifield (2000) presents a liberal state theory by emphasizing economic forces and chain migration networks that sustain culture through international migration. His political and legal factors are central to a theory that citizenship rights are increasingly enacted for citizens and proposed for immigrants and refugees. He and Joppke (2005) see international institutions as pressuring the state to enact liberal rights. Thus, if economic cycles are controlled, one should see an increase in immigrant rights and open naturalization policies through international pressures. This process has a globalization component as transnational corporations further promote international movements and indirectly promote an international civil society. Similarly, Bauböck (1994) presents a convergence approach using political theory (see also Schmitter Heisler 1992, 1998; Soysal 1994; Freeman 1995, 2006; Jacobson 1996).

Convergence is an interesting but difficult to prove theory. There is often considerable variation in state policy as some states ignore international civil society or at least bend it to their will. And one must be careful in this area not to conflate a general convergence theory with EU integration. While there is a push to make policies consistent, the EU treads lightly in this area. So in many ways, international civil society can be more of a resource for pro-immigration actors than a constraint on each country. Often these convergence theories do not identify the enactors of these policies within each state, not to mention the interest groups who request them. Hollifield refers to political parties in a rather passive way when he says that the "demands for greater immigration control or changes in nationality or citizenship laws will be channeled through political parties and party systems" (2000: 170). As a result, liberal state theory sees political parties as unimportant, which makes change look like it comes from rather general global or cultural needs.

Second, demographic and economic factors have an impact on naturalization. Demographic models see immigration as the result of the declining birth rates (Molho 1986: 105–7). Unlike earlier centuries, all advanced industrialized countries now exhibit declining birth rates, and consequently, receiving countries are in need of replenishing their labor supply. Nonetheless, high immigration itself does not cause high naturalization rates as states may decide on very different citizenship policies. Related to this theory are demographic models where immigration results from the size of countries, crowding, and the distance migrants travel (Molho 1986: 105–7; Massey *et al.* 1998). Population density in the immigrants' country of origin would be a positive factor toward naturalization, but population density in the receiving country has a negative effect. Countries with high population density per square mile often state that their lands are too crowded to allow for increased immigration of foreigners. This theory has a more political component because it claims that the state passes laws to prevent further immigration and more specifically to make naturalization difficult. But these crowding and distance models are clearly not as important as demographic decline explanations. From 1880 to 1950, demographic decline uniquely fit France, and the political component appeared with strong advocates for immigration and naturalization. But other countries arrived at demographic decline after World War II, and by then nearly all advanced industrialized countries experienced declining birth rates.

For economic pull theories, labor shortages in the receiving countries can produce a need for workers that immigration can fill. This aggravates political party polarization. On the other hand, baby booms, women entering the labor force, and immigration create labor market pressures on the native population and may increase competition and eventually unemployment (Janoski 1990). The movement of factories and service jobs from industrialized economies to low wage countries adds to these labor market woes. In the economic push theories, the economic wealth of the receiving country and the poverty of the sending country produce a strong incentive for the sending country's residents to migrate to the wealthier country. For the economic pull theories, labor shortages in the wealthier country produces a need for workers that immigration can fill (Ritchey 1976: 364–75; Petersen 1978: 554–6; Molho 1986; Massey *et al.* 1998). The push-pull framework can also be extended to other factors such as services, public assistance, and racial equity (Ritchey 1976: 375–8).

Third, a variety of political theories focus more clearly on the parties and groups demanding change: Freeman's (2006) theory of clientele politics, and Huber and Stephen's (2001) combination of status group and class conflict. The first theory is Freeman's (1995) theory based on rational choice that uses a two-by-two classification of concentrated or diffuse costs and benefits to emphasize one particular cell—clientelism. This combination of concentrated benefits for employers and immigrant interest groups, and diffuse costs spread throughout the population operates under conditions of low salience with the public having little interest in immigration. Salience is low for the public because immigrants are either spread over the country as a whole or concentrated in a few areas that can be overlooked. The two interest groups then capture the immigration issue and get their bills passed. Freeman (1998, 2006) and Money (1999) have developed this further in a comparative context, but in many ways it is too simple, especially since changing party ideology plays such a small role (Tichenor 2002). Political parties are divided on the issue of immigration as there is a major division among the right between free market employers and traditional nationalists, and the left between universalistic cosmopolitans and protectionist labor. However, the increasing protests about immigration policy from France to the US contradict the low salience aspect of this theory. Consequently, the emphasis has shifted away from clientelism toward interest group politics.

Another approach, which is more institutional than political, is Bloemraad's (2006) work on Canadian and US naturalization processes. She avoids cultural idioms, naturalization law, and the characteristics of immigrants. Instead, she focuses on the reception that immigrants receive *vis-à-vis* naturalization. Canada welcomes and encourages naturalization from the top with significant civil society participation, and the USA has the cooler welcome and relies on nonprofit and local governments operating from the bottom. This institutional approach with two settler countries is convincing. How it would fare with colonizers and noncolonizers is less clear.

Another political approach to explaining naturalization recognizes the overarching constraints of globalization with an independent and important political effect. Political parties in national legislatures have a strong influence on these laws. With the rise of international civil society pressing for a liberal refugee regime, the costs of asylum policies and national security threats bring a restraining influence on immigration and naturalization. After World War II, anti-immigrant parties emerged from the far right, which the more moderate right needs to appease in order to protect their political base. The right's antipathy for immigration and naturalization has increased due to the connection between rising welfare state costs and the provision of benefits for refugees (Gimpel and Edwards 1999).

These political parties and international civil society give rise to major institutional changes. Soysal's (1994) international theory examines a larger human rights regime that gave strong legitimacy to protecting refugees and according rights to people within their own countries, and this regime interacted with the past institutions and policies to produce a third irony. The UN approach led to a number of human rights declarations and accords that were signed after the world recognized the horrors of war and the holocaust. Despite its strong isolationist tendencies, the USA eventually recognized its role as a world leader and joined others in forming the UN. The UN created United Nations Educational, Scientific and Cultural Organization (UNESCO) to push for racial equality and equal treatment, and the UN High Commissioner on Refugees (UNHCR) to persuade states to accept more refugees (Loescher 1993, 2001). This by itself would resonate with cultural convergence theory, but politics becomes more directly involved.

The international refugee regime has politicized immigration and made the issue salient. Left and green parties in red-green coalition governments led the charge for greater immigration and naturalization, while Christian democratic and conservative parties in blue-black coalition governments opposed a more generous and multi-cultural approach. Before the new refugee regime connected to the UN, refugees were simply immigrants who had to make it on their own. After World War II with the development of strong welfare states, the conservatives began to see the rise of welfare state costs and increasing immigration to be closely connected.

In the USA, this led to the Republican revolt against immigration in the last 20 years, followed by restrictive federal legislation (Gimpel and Edwards 1999). Similarly, major restrictions on asylum occurred in Germany in the early 1990s (Green 2004). Thus, the increasing flow of refugees causes right parties to demand restrictions on immigration and naturalization, and left and green parties to increase their pressure for open naturalization in reaction to anti-immigrant forces.

Under conditions of globalization and international civil society, left parties and unions have come to support immigration and especially naturalization. Before World War II, left parties had a strong impulse to protect workers from immigration because the presence of job-seeking immigrants decreases the power of organized labor by increasing the labor supply (Borjas 1995; Briggs 2001). After World War II this approach began to wither and a new approach focused on protecting and even organizing immigrants (Haus 2002; Watts 2003). While the behavior of some labor unions and parties might periodically contradict this statement, each of them increasingly began to change and lead efforts to increase naturalization. Thus, left and green parties have supported more open naturalization policies, liberal and center parties sometimes join in this coalition, and conservative and right-wing parties abhor it.

While left party power has a weakened base in unions and manufacturing, it has picked up support from women's increasing labor force participation and subsequent political power. While women's voting initially showed little difference from men's, an increasing gender gap in most countries has developed around a welfare state that reflects women's and not just men's vulnerabilities to the market, and women's general concern toward "caring" for people in society. Caring values can also be manifested in greater female concern for asylees, who are more often widows and children (Lister 2002; Hobson 2005).

In the fourth approach, long-term institutional differences provide a theory of immigration and racism with an argument that can easily be translated to explain nationality. Pierre Messmer describes colonization in reverse as "the trap set by history" where Europeans have "been accustomed to colonizing the world" and "(n)ow the foreigners are coming here to us" (Freeman 1979: 20). Thus, states that openly grant citizenship do so because they often want to stabilize their empires or what remains of them, and settler countries like Canada and the USA want to control indigenous people and replace them with Europeans. Countries that neither colonize nor settle tend to protect their culture or *volk* from immigration.

Regime approaches describes how countries shape their long-term legal and social approaches to naturalization (Freeman 1979). Four types of regimes are generally addressed: colonizer (imperial or post-colonizers), folk (communitarian or diasporic), the republican (civic registration or libertarian), and settler regimes (multi-cultural or Anglo-Saxon) (Baldwin-Edwards 1991; Faist 1996: 230; Kostakopoulou 2003: 96; Joppke 2005; Castles and Miller 2009: 39). Some regimes are geographical: Scandinavian, Anglo-Saxon, Mediterranean, and Schengen. One problem with some of these regime theories is that their classification schemes put countries into more than one category (e.g., Castles and Miller, Faist, and Baldwin-Edwards), or have empty cells (e.g., Kostakopoulous). The larger issue is that the theories are not empirically tested.

But one regime theory tests four regime types against naturalization data: colonizer, non-colonizer/occupier, settler, and Nordic regime types (Janoski 2010). The colonizers with high colonization have naturalization rates four times as high as the non-colonizers, the settler countries with high rates of indigenous decline have naturalization rates seven times the non-colonizer rates, and the Nordic countries are in between. The theory behind these regimes is as follows. First, states colonize and then the colonizer tries to control the colony by incorporating natives into the bureaucracy and military. The longer the colonization effort lasts, the more the colonizer has problems with social control. The colonizer solves these problems in four stages:

repression, colonial control, military service, and subsequent immigration. In the repression stage, the military of the colonial power uses force to colonize the country, but this creates intolerance and closure toward natives. In the next stage, the colonizing country needs its troops elsewhere and/or gradually realizes that military occupation of the colonized country is very expensive. The colonizer must co-opt many natives into their way of thinking, and many talented and cooperative natives fill administrative, governmental, and police posts. In the third stage, some cooperative natives are sent to the colonizer's schools and universities to improve their work in the colonies. And fourth, colonial natives risk their lives in military service for the colonizer (mercenary units excepted) and create citizenship claims on the state. After these four stages, natives make claims for greater citizenship. And these natives and their families gradually receive citizenship rights in their native lands and in the colonizing country when they immigrate. Countries who only experience the first stage of colonization (e.g., Japan and Germany) maintain parochial and intolerant attitudes toward naturalization (Janoski 2010).

Second, without colonization reaching the social control stage, the state has no incentive to offer naturalization. High emigration and at least some national identity processes create resistance to granting citizenship to foreign immigrants. Middle and lower classes are able to turn emigration into their own economic opportunities and this can also reduce the total demand for legal, political rights, and social rights (Janoski 1990, 1998). Driven to its extreme, the avoidance of immigration can even turn into the persecution and forced emigration of minority religious and ethnic groups.

Third, settler countries develop an inclusive conception of citizenship rights from their interests in territorial expansion combined with a campaign against the rights of indigenous peoples, and in alleviating the subsequent labor shortage with extensive immigration to fill the newly conquered lands. The settler colonies eradicated large segments of their indigenous populations, and in so doing, opened up vast areas of land, which were then perceived as being uninhabited and open to immigrants. After settler countries are established, immigration in the short-term creates status groups competing for jobs and wages (Freeman 1979; Briggs 1992; Hollifield 1992, 2000; Layton-Henry 1992). Eventually, these countries become the most receptive states toward immigrants of diverse races and ethnic groups. The settler model fits Australia, Canada, New Zealand, and the USA.

Fourth, Nordic countries who were non-colonizers are a less institutionalized regime type. They have liberalized their asylum, refugee, and immigration policies toward non-EU countries to create naturalization rates that are higher than non-colonizers and nearly as high as most settler countries. Much of their development has come through cumulative left party power. This is an important example of historical institutions not receiving reinforcement, which leads to the creation of a new regime type from what was formerly a group of non-colonizing countries. Regime theory can be an effective theory, but it is somewhat similar to cultural theory with constants, but these are within groups of countries (i.e., not idiomatic or universalistic as in cultural theories). These five quite diverse theories can be modeled in Figure 32.2.

The various theories discussed (items 1 through 5) lead to higher naturalization rates (item 9), but it is important to look at the actual mechanisms by which this occurs. The most obvious are the actual nationality laws (item 6) but it is important to note that there are informal ways that naturalization rates increase either by state discretion in implementation or through the efforts of NGOs and religious organizations (items 7a and b). Further, the impacts of demographic and economic variables on naturalization come through more community-based influences. The impact of these variables is indicated by country time-series, cross sectional and pooled analyses (9a, b, and c).

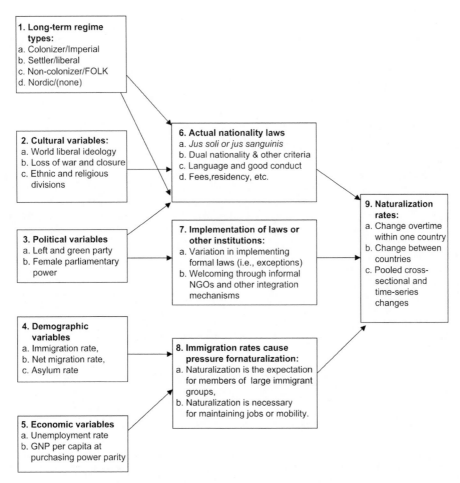

Figure 32.2 Macro-theoretical model predicting naturalization rates

Conclusion

Nationality and naturalization are not a simple result of immigration, but rather a complex political institutional process itself. Naturalization rates themselves can be viewed as a narrow measure of naturalization, or with a much broader concept of *jus soli* births. Given the understanding of these issues, the explanation of micro- and macro-processes has made much progress in the last twenty years. Micro-studies have a long trail of evidence but they are turning toward a much broader array of receiver countries and may change substantively in the future. Macro-approaches have a shorter history, but with their recent success explaining naturalization they face the challenge of integrating individual level analysis to back up their claims.

Changes in naturalization requirements are quite political, religious, and ethnic in their causes. The Cold War led to a 1963 treaty restricting dual citizenship so that opposing countries could not claim the same person as a soldier to fight for them. By the 1990s, a major effort at dual (triple or even more) nationality began and pressures mounted for opening up nationality. Globalization produced some emphasis on transnational citizenship, and the study of transnational, post-national or cosmopolitan citizenship is booming (Baubök 1994; Ong 1998; Bloemraad *et al.*

2008). World and global citizenship are seemingly possible. But since the recent spate of terrorist violence with 9/11 and subsequent wars, integration measures in many countries have produced a renewed tendency toward closure through language tests and proof of social integration (Hansen 2008). It will be interesting to see where these trends will lead naturalization in the next few decades.

References and further reading

Aleinikoff, T. A. and Klusmeyer, D. (eds) (2000) *From Migrants to Citizens: Membership in a Changing World*. Washington, DC: Carnegie Endowment for Peace.

Anil, M. (2007) "Explaining the naturalization practices of Turks in Germany in the wake of the citizenship reform of 1999" *Ethnic and Migration Studies* 33(8): 1363–76.

Baldwin-Edwards, M. (1991) "Immigration after 1992" *Policy and Politics* 19(3): 199–211.

Baker, B. C. (2009) "Trends in naturalization rates: 2008 update" *Homeland Security Fact Sheet*. Washington, DC: Office of Immigration Statistics, US Department of Home Land Security.

Barrett, A. (1999) *Irish Migration: Characteristics, Causes and Consequences*. IZA DP No. 97. Bonn, Germany: Institute for the Study of Labor.

Bauböck, R. (1994) *Transnational Citizenship*. Aldershot: Edward Elgar.

Bauböck, R., Ersbøll, E., Groenendijk, K., and Waldrauch, H. (2006) *Acquisition and Loss of Nationality: Policies and Trends in 15 European States,* Volumes 1 and 2. Amsterdam: Amsterdam University Press.

Bauböck, R., Perchinig, B., and Sievers, W. (eds) (2010) *Citizenship Policies in the New Europe*. Amsterdam: University of Amsterdam Press.

Bauer, T., Lofstrom, M., and Zimmermann, K. (2000) "Immigration policy, assimilation of immigrants, and natives' sentiments toward immigrants: Evidence from 12 OECD countries" *Swedish Economic Policy Review* 7(2): 13–53.

Bean, F., Brown, S., and Rumbaut, R. (2006) "Mexican immigrant political and economic incorporation" *Perspectives on Politics* 4(2): 309–13.

Bean, F. and Stevens, G. (2003) *America's Newcomers and the Dynamics of Diversity*. New York: Russell Sage Foundation.

Becker, B. (2009) "Immigrants' emotional identification with the host society: The example of Turkish parents' naming practices in Germany" *Ethnicities* 9(2): 200–225.

Bernard, W. S. (1936) "Cultural determinants of naturalization" *American Sociological Review* 1(6): 943–53.

Beuker, C. (2005) "Political incorporation among immigrants from ten areas of origin" *International Migration Review* 39(1): 103–40.

Bloemraad, I. (2006) *Becoming a Citizen*. Berkeley, CA: University of California Press.

Bloemraad, I., Korteweg, A., and Yurdakul, G. (2008) "Citizenship and immigration: Multiculturalism, assimilation and challenges to the nation state" *Annual Review of Sociology* 34: 153–79.

Borjas, G. (1995) "Do blacks gain or lose from immigration?" In D. Hamermesh and F. Bean (eds), *Help or Hindrance? The Economic Implications of Immigration for African Americans*. New York: Russell Sage, pp. 51–74.

Briggs, V. (1992) *Mass Immigration and National Interest*. Armonk, NY: Sharpe.

Briggs, V. (2001) *Immigration and American Unionism*. Ithaca, NY: Cornell University Press.

Brubaker, W. R. (1992) *Citizenship and Nationhood in France and Germany*. Cambridge, MA: Harvard University Press.

——(1989) "Citizenship and naturalization: Policies and politics." In W. R. Brubaker (ed.), *Immigration and the Politics of Citizenship in Europe and North America*. Lanham, MD: University Press of America, pp. 99–127.

Castles, S. and Miller, M. (2009) *The Age of Migration*, 5th Edition. London: Palgrave-Macmillan.

Constant, A., Gataulina, L., and Zimmermann, K. F. (2007) "Naturalization proclivities, ethnicity and integration." In *Discussion Paper Series*. Bonn: ISA, pp. 1–26.

Crul, M. and Heering, L. (2008) *The Position of the Turkish and Moroccan Second Generation in Amsterdam and Rotterdam*. Amsterdam: Amsterdam University Press.

Crul, M. and Vermeulen, H. (2003) "The second generation in Europe" *International Migration Review* 37(4): 965–86.

Diehl, C. and Blohm, M. (2003) "Rights or identity? Naturalization processes among 'labor migrants' in Germany" *International Migration Review* 37(1): 133–62.

Evans, M. D. R. (1988) "Choosing to be a citizen: The time-path of citizenship in Australia" *International Migration Review* 22(2): 243–64.

Faist, T. (1996) "Immigration, integration, and the welfare state." In R. Bauböck, A. Heller, and A. Zolberg (eds), *The Challenge of Diversity*. Aldershot: Avebury, pp. 227–58.

——(2000) *The Volume and Dynamics of International Migration and Transnational Social Spaces*. New York: Oxford University Press.

Feldblum, M. (1999) *Reconstructing Citizenship*. Albany, NY: SUNY Press.

Freeman, G. P. (1979) *Immigrant Labor and Racial Conflict in Industrialized Societies*. Princeton, NJ: Princeton University Press.

——(1995) "Modes of immigration politics in liberal democratic states" *International Migration Review* 29(4): 881–902.

——(2006) "National models, policy types and the politics of immigration in liberal democracies" *West European Politics* 29(2): 227–47.

Garcia, J. (1981) "Political integration of Mexican immigrants: Explorations into the naturalization process" *International Migration Review* 15(4): 608–25.

Gilbertson, G. and Singer, A. (2009) "Nationalization under changing conditions of membership: Dominican immigrants in New York City. In N. Foner, R. Rumbaut, and S. Gold (eds), *Immigration Research for a New Century*. New York: Russell Sage, pp. 157–86.

Gimpel, J. and Edwards, J. (1999) *The Congressional Politics of Immigration Reform*. Boston, MA: Allyn Bacon.

Gordon, M. M. (1964) *Assimilation in American Life*. New York: Oxford University Press.

Grebler, L. (1966) "The naturalization of Mexican immigrants in the United States" *International Migration Review* 1(1): 17–32.

Green, S. (2004) *The Politics of Exclusion: Institutions and Immigration Policy in Contemporary Germany*. Manchester: Manchester University Press.

Hansen, R. (2008) "A new citizenship bargain for the age of mobility? Citizenship requirements in Europe and North America." Transatlantic Council on Migration, Migration Policy Institute.

Hargreaves, A. (1995) *Immigration, "Race" and Ethnicity in Contemporary France*. London: Routledge.

Haus, L. A. (2002) *Unions, Immigration and Internationalization: New Challenges and Changing Coalitions in the United States and France*. New York: Palgrave.

Hobson, B. (2005) "Feminist theories of political sociology." In T. Janoski, R. Alford, A. Hicks, and M. Schwartz (eds), *The Handbook of Political Sociology*. New York: Cambridge, pp. 135–52.

Hollifield, J. (1992) *Immigrants, Markets and States: The Political Economy of Post War Europe*. Cambridge, MA: Harvard University Press.

——(2000) "The politics of international migration." In C. Brettell and J. Hollifield. *Migration Theory: Talking Across Disciplines*. London: Routledge, pp. 137–85.

Huber, E. and Stephens, J. (2001) *Development and Crisis of the Welfare State*. Chicago, IL: University of Chicago Press.

Jacobson, D. (1996) *Rights Across Borders*. Baltimore, MD: Johns Hopkins Press.

Janoski, T. (1990) *The Political Economy of Unemployment*. Berkeley, CA: University of California Press.

——(1998) *Citizenship and Civil Society*. Cambridge: Cambridge University Press.

——(2010) *The Ironies of Citizenship: Naturalization and Integration in Advanced Societies*. Cambridge: Cambridge University Press.

Joppke, C. (2005) *Selecting by Origin: Ethnic Migration in the Liberal State*. Cambridge, MA: Harvard University Press.

Kashiwazaki, C. (2000) "Citizenship in Japan: Legal practice and contemporary development." In T. Alexander Aleinikoff and D. Klusmeyer (eds), *From Migrants to Citizens*. Washington, DC: Brookings, pp. 434–74.

Kasinitz, P., Mollenkopf, J., and Waters, M. (2002) "Becoming American/becoming New Yorkers: Ethnographies of the new second generation" *International Migration Review* 34(4): 1020–36.

Kostakopoulou, T. (2003) "Why naturalisation?" *Perspectives on European Politics and Society* 4(1): 85–115.

——(2001) *Citizenship, Identity and Immigration in the European Union*. Manchester: Manchester University Press.

Layton-Henry, Z. (1992) *The Politics of Immigration*. Oxford: Blackwell.

Liang, Z. (1994a) "Social contact, social capital, and the naturalization process: Evidence from six immigrant groups" *Social Science Research* 23(4): 407–37.

——(1994b) "On the measurement of naturalization" *Demography* 31: 525–48.

Lister, R. (2002) "Sexual citizenship." In E. Isin and B. Turner (eds), *Handbook of Citizenship Studies*. Thousand Oaks, CA: Sage, pp. 191–207.

Loescher, G. (1993) *Beyond Charity: International Cooperation and the Global Refugee Crisis*. New York: Oxford University Press.

——(2001) *UNCHR and World Politics*. New York: Oxford.

Massey, D., Arango, J., Hugo, G., Kouaoci, A., Pellegrino, A., and Taylor, J. E. (1998) *Worlds in Motion: Understanding International Migration at the End of the Millennium*. Oxford: Clarendon.

Maxwell, R. (2010) "Evaluating migrant integration: Political attitudes across generations in Europe" *International Migration Review* 44(1): 25–52.

Molho, I. (1986) "Theories of migration: A review" *Scottish Journal of Political Economy* 33(4): 396–419.

Money, J. (1999) *Fences and neighbors: The political geography of immigration control*. Ithaca, NY: Cornell University Press.

Nascimbene, B. (ed.) (1996) *Nationality Laws in the European Union*. London: Butterworths.

Ong, A. (1998) *Flexible Citizenship*. Durham, NC: Duke University Press.

OECD. (1987) *The Future of Immigration* Paris: OECD.

——(1976–2005) *Trends in International Migration*. Paris: OECD.

——(2006–9) *International Migration Outlook*. Paris: OECD.

Petersen, W. (1978) "International migration" *Annual Review of Sociology* 4: 533–75.

Portes, A. (1997) "Immigration theory for a new century: Some problems and opportunities" *International Migration Review* 31(4): 799–825.

——(2000) "Review of worlds in motion" *International Migration Review* 34(131): 976–78.

Portes, A. and Curtis, J. W. (1987) "Changing flags: Naturalization and its determinants among Mexican immigrants" *International Migration Review* 21: 352–71.

Portes, A. and Rumbaut, R. (2001) *Legacies: The Story of the Immigrant Second Generation*. Berkeley, CA: University of California Press.

Reitz, J. (ed.). (2003) *Host Societies and the Reception of Immigrants*. San Diego, CA: Center for Comparative Immigration Studies.

Ritchey, P. (1976) "Explanations of migration." *Annual Review of Sociology* 2: 363–404.

Schmitter Heisler, B. (1992) "The future of immigrant incorporation: Which models? Which concepts?" *International Migration Review* 26(2): 623–45.

——(1998) "Contexts of immigrant incorporation." In H. Kurthen, J. Fijalkowski, and G. Wagner (eds) *Immigration, Citizenship, and the Welfare State in Germany and the United States*. Stamford, CT: JAI Press, pp. 91–106.

Simon, P. (2003) "France and the unknown second generation" *International Migration Review* 37(4): 1091–119.

Soysal, Y. (1994) *The Limits of Citizenship*. Chicago, IL: University of Chicago Press.

Tichenor, D. (2002) *Dividing Lines: The Politics of Immigration Control in America*. Princeton, NJ: Princeton University Press.

Timmerman, C., Vanderwaeren, E., and Crul, M. (2003) "The second generation in Belgium" *International Migration Review* 37(4): 1065–90.

Tomata, F. (1999) "Patterns of acquiring citizenship." In S. Halli and L. Driedger (eds) *Immigrant Canada*. Toronto: University of Toronto Press, pp. 163–82.

Tübergen, F. van (2006) *Immigrant Integration: A Cross-National Study*. New York: LFB.

Tübergen, F. van, Flap, H., and Maas, I. (2004) "The economic incorporation of immigrants in 18 western societies" *American Sociological Review* 69(5): 704–27.

US Department of Homeland Security, Citizenship and Immigration Service (CIS). (2004–6) *Annual Report* Washington, DC Immigration and Naturalization Statistics.

US Department of Justice, Immigration and Naturalization Service (INS) (1972–2003) *Annual Report*. Washington, DC: GPO.

Veiter, T. (1990) "Open problems of the treatment and the rights of ethnic groups in Austria" *Europa Ethnica* 47(2): 74–75.

Waldrauch, H. (2006) "Acquisition of nationality." In R. Bauböck, E. Ersbøll, K. Groenendijk and H. Waldrauch (eds). *Acquisition and Loss of Nationality, Volume 1*. Amsterdam: Amsterdam University Press, pp. 121–82.

Waters, M. (1999) *Black Identities: West Indian Immigrant Dreams and American Realities*. Cambridge, MA: Harvard University Press.

Watts, J. R. (2003) *Immigration Policy and the Challenge of Globalization*. Ithaca, NY: Cornel University Press.

Wihtol de Wenden, C. (1994) "Citizenship and nationality in France." In R. Bauböck (ed.) *From Aliens to Citizens*. Avebury: Aldershot, pp. 85–93.

Woodrow-Lafield, K., Xu, X., Kersen, T., and Poch, B. (2004) "Naturalization of US immigrants" *Population Research and Policy Review* 23(3): 187–218.

Yang, P. (1994) "Explaining immigrant naturalization" *International Migration Review* 28(3): 449–77.

Zappalá, G. and Castles, S. (2000) "Citizenship and immigration in Australia." In T. A. Aleinikoff and D. Klusmeyer (eds), *From Migrants to Citizens: Membership in a Changing World*. Washington, DC: Carnegie Endowment, pp. 32–81.

Zhou, M. (1997) "Segmented assimilation: Issues, controversies and recent research on the new second generation" *International Migration Review* 31(4): 975–1008.

Zhou, M. and Lee, J. (2007) "Becoming ethnic or becoming American: Tracing the mobility trajectories of the new second generation in the United States" *DuBois Review* 4(1): 189–205.

33

Immigration and education

Ramona Fruja Amthor

Historical and intellectual development

Education and progress, both personal and social, have been intricately linked in the human imagination and across historical contexts. The link became even more powerful with the introduction of free, open, and eventually compulsory education—for example, from the early days of the "common schools" in mid-nineteenth-century United States, education has carried tremendous symbolic weight in the national imagination. It connected the gains of an education to personal self-improvement, social mobility and the fulfillment and perpetuation of the new republic's virtues. Such potential eventually engendered previously absent support for publically-funded schools from multiple social strata, as each was able to find a relevant promise in this institution. Among these supportive groups were the newest members of society who, ironically, were among the very reasons native-born populations supported free schools that would aid with their integration. Drawing mainly on US-based immigration, this chapter centers on the inter-sections between immigration and education conceptualized both as a social institution and as lived experience. I position the education of immigrants in historical context as well as in the context of assimilation and integration theories, emphasizing the relationship between education and aspects of inequality and social reproduction. After a brief overview of the historical development in this area of inquiry, I highlight major issues in the field—focusing on immigrant education along several relevant social locations—and subsequent critiques. I conclude with potential areas of future investigation.

Newcomers' history with formal educational institutions in the United States is complex and contested. Historical evidence shows the nuanced relationship immigrants had with schools, being both drawn to their promises of integration and success in the new land, while simultaneously resisting their impositions when these were antagonistic to immigrants' own values and intentions. This historical relationship records a tension between "coercion and beneficence, between immigrant acquiescence and resistance" (Olneck 2004: 383). Oversimplification of this history may lead to erroneous conclusions about the possibilities of immigrant incorporation through education, both historically and now. For example, despite some common social angst regarding immigrants' desire to use schools for separatist intentions—and resist linguistic and cultural integration—historical research highlights immigrants' desire for schools and education that has been, in fact, consistent. Their contemporary aims for education are not in contrast with a "golden age" of seamless integration that has allegedly ceased to exist in our fragmented society. On the contrary, immigrants seem to want from education today what they have historically wanted: integration and mobility in the new society along with a fair recognition of their identities (Olneck 2009). Similarly, interpretations of this history range from the critiques of aggressive Americanization of immigrants through education—portrayed as a compelling force that stripped newcomers of their identities—to the subsequent critiques of thoroughly "bleak" views of American history that overlook education's genuinely progressive facet that benefited immigrants in their transition.

Immigrants' history with educational institutions, therefore, and their experiences in those contexts highlight essential ideological positions about social progress, national agendas and other issues with an important legacy into the present. As immigration sociologist Michael Olneck (2004) has argued, "research on immigrants and education illuminates important societal beliefs and aspirations, responses to social change, prevailing educational policies and practices, and continuous debates about multiculturalism" (p. 381). It is thus an essential scholarly area that addresses perennial issues, albeit a newer one in the longer history of immigration studies.

Of the 71 million children in the United States in 2009, 24 percent had an immigrant parent. The increase in immigrants' number in educational institutions—currently one in five students is an immigrant or the child of an immigrant—enriches these institutions and poses important questions about how they are to respond. This, however, is far from being a new phenomenon. Indeed, questions about how to address immigrant integration and how schools should participate in the process—as major acculturating, if not assimilating institutions—are long-standing and have coincided with major immigration waves or turning points in the United States, its ideological orientations and economic situation. For example, the middle of the nineteenth century (with the spread of the "common schools"), the beginning of the twentieth (known for its Americanization movement), as well as the "intercultural education" movement between the two world wars and the subsequent multicultural education approaches emerging out the 1960s Civil Rights Movement, all exemplify such recurrent attempts at addressing the education and integration of minorities and immigrants. With the post-1965 immigration and its exponential increase in immigrants of previously banned origins, integration in the social fabric continues to capture policy, public, and scholarly debates. Current so-called "dilemmas" over immigrants' integration simply continue a quintessential narrative in American history.

The connection of this national narrative with education became clearer as social science research on immigration and education has emerged more visibly in the last four decades. This new interest was paralleled by the later increase in attention to children and youth in studies of immigration, an interest prompted by the post-1965 immigrants' descendants ("the new second generation") and their adaptation (e.g., Portes and Zhou 1993; Kao and Tienda 1995; Portes and Rumbaut 2001; Suárez-Orozco and Suárez-Orozco 2001). Historical research on immigrants and schools in the United States—although mostly originating in education research and not necessarily immigration research—has focused on the schools' role in the integrative movements from the common school era of the mid-nineteenth century and through the Americanization movement of the early twentieth century. Research on how educational institutions respond to immigrants has continued from the historical contexts to contemporary ones, along with interest in immigrant students' patterns of educational achievement and the newer attention to their various experiences with schools.

The ethos of the Civil Rights Movement, even if initially focused on native-born minorities, prompted a shift in the focus and tone of research with immigrants in general and with immigrant youth and students in particular. More research emerged justified by a sense of concern and care *for* the needs of immigrants and their well-being in the new society. While initially the value of pre-migration social resources was ignored or denigrated, in the 1970s, scholars paid increased attention to the positive effects of migrants' social and cultural practices which facilitated their survival and success post-arrival, including interest in education.

A fascination with immigrant achievement also emerged in the 1970s, as research studies began to look at academic performance by group, beginning with some attention to cohorts in the early 1900s. Even if these historical studies are considered limited due to data access and variable operationalization—which made it difficult to separate the effects of ethnicity per se from other relevant factors (Olneck 2004)—these studies found relatively consistent rank ordering in achievement. The children of Northern Europeans were doing as well as native-born white Americans, Eastern European Jews better or the same as native-born white Americans, while non-Jewish central and southern Europeans were at serious disadvantage. Later studies, as Michael Olneck (2004) explains in his historical overview, would account for both structural and cultural factors, because in considering the issues of achievement, "cultural factors do not operate in a vacuum; nor are they impervious to material and historical circumstances" (p. 394).

The interest in immigrants' educational attainment by group continues today, including attention to the intersection of cultural and structural factors, especially since certain groups remain in disadvantaged positions and their prospects at social mobility are thus limited in the newer knowledge-based economy. Studies have increased to highlight disconcerting trends, for example, for Latino youth whose drop-out rates and lower educational attainment are disproportionally high compared to other groups. Alejandro Portes and Ruben Rumbaut's ambitious Children of Immigrants Longitudinal Study (CILS) of over five thousand immigrant youth of seventy-seven nationalities in San Diego and Dade County, Florida, and the Longitudinal Immigrant Student Adaptation Study (LISA) led by Carola and Marcelo Suarez-Orozco (1997–2002)—as well as other studies, both in the United States and Canada—confirm trends of disproportional achievement across groups. These findings drew attention to important variables for achievement and their uneven distribution across immigrant origins, placing some at higher likelihood of success just as in the historical context:

> [A]s in historical data, observed variations in school performance and attainment among contemporary immigrant groups to some extent reflect the consequences of differences among groups in socioeconomic status, parental education, parental literacy, parental proficiency in English, nativity, and the like. In some cases, observed advantages can be attributed almost entirely to background factors correlated with ethnic group membership"
> (Olneck 2004: 395).

In addition to large-scale patterns of educational attainment as a variable in socio-economic opportunity, newer attention to the lived experiences of immigrant students prompted interest in smaller, focused studies that opened up their experienced worlds both in school and out. Through mixed methods and the possibilities that ethnographic research tools enable, these studies have emphasized the nuances of experience—both positive and challenging—that immigrant youth face (i.e., adaptation and acculturation, language acquisition with the resulting family dynamics; parent-child and peer relationships; school contexts, educational aspirations and achievement as understood by the youth themselves; the importance of gender in differentiated adaptation; the development of identity in light of age maturation coupled with transition to a new society; psychological adjustment and so on). Different patterns of educational adaptation became apparent and important and they were not defined only in terms of performance, but also in terms of school experiences, raising questions about what schools could do better to respond to immigrants' evident and less visible educational needs.

Many of these relatively recent accounts highlight the complexities of loss and gain involved in immigration. This juxtaposition is a more recent interest, given that less than five decades ago, maintaining and valuing a student's ethnic heritage and the identities that were shaped by it were not generally a concern of educators. The rise of the Civil Rights Movement, however, along with the US ethnic revival of the 1970s and the increasingly popular post-colonial narratives of resistance and ethnic heritage have generated an interest in exploring the experience of immigration from more angles than one, including the losses in family relationships, language, and identity. Paying special attention to the experiences of the young through extensive, cross-disciplinary research, immigration emerged even more clearly as one of the most stressful human experiences (e.g., Aronowitz 1984; Igoa 1995; Choi *et al.* 2006). For example, approximately 85 percent experience separation from their families and need to go through the process of reunification and its psychological ramifications. It became increasingly apparent that these complexities are not left outside the classrooms' doors and that schools are often unequipped to address these issues. On the contrary, schools can become complicit in the difficulties experienced by youth in the new country, and the current accumulation of findings, both quantitative and qualitative, provide a clearer understanding of the issues affecting the education of immigrants and their experiences with this process in the United States.

Major claims and developments

Education in the context of immigration has to be understood in conjunction with the evolution of sociological theory about immigrant assimilation and its variants. The early centrality of the assimilationist model (Park 1950; Gordon 1964) carried very important implications for the role of education, given that educational success was meant to offer, at least in part, the means for that upward assimilation and acculturation. Historical analyses of schools do point to ways in which they facilitated this process and were intentionally used to that end. From the basic elements of literacy and language acquisition, cultural elements, and content knowledge necessary for new positions on the economic ladder, education had the potential to enhance each new generation's socio-economic standing and, importantly, enhance the acculturation process.

Once critiques of the assimilationist model emerged as requiring modification (Alba and Nee 1997)—and pointing to substantial economic and residential mobility being directly proportional to the immigrants' human capital—the clear differentiation in prospects raised important questions about the means by which some immigrants acquire more human capital and how schools might be complicit in that process. In addition, the very "progress assumption" was heavily scrutinized, given the inverse relationship between immigrant youth length of stay in the US and their health and educational aspirations. Disadvantaged by skin color in the racialized social structure (Waters 1999), as well as by residence in inner-cities with few mobility ladders, today's non-white, less educated immigrants were shown as vulnerable to downward or segmented assimilation (Portes and Zhou 1993; Portes and Rumbaut 2001) or second-generation decline (Gans 1992). While the highly educated immigrants seem to follow a "utopic" path towards success and fast mobility—some even bypassing the generational pattern of previous immigrant groups—the lower skilled ones and their children experience the "dystopic" consequences of simply trying to survive (Suarez-Orozco 2000). As the optimistic notion of straight-line assimilation has been replaced by evidence of segmented assimilation, closer attention to the educational and in-school experiences of immigrants became essential. Such studies would be able to illuminate in what ways schools' reception of immigrants and response to their needs structure their experiences and ultimately their opportunities in the new society. The assumption that education will evidently offer opportunities across the spectrum of immigrant groups was placed under scrutiny, especially since opportunities that initially appeared abundant, progressively diminished in light of forces rooted in the social context (Portes and Rumbaut 2001).

What became important, therefore, in the newer social analyses, were the ways various social locations and factors intersected with achievement and adaptation in schools, given that these outcomes could vary significantly. A number of studies do show that many immigrant youth fare academically as well as or better than their native peers, carrying positive attitudes towards school work, teachers, and achievement. Others, however, highlight problems in educational adaptation and lack of appropriate preparation as an obstacle to social mobility across generations. Such factors include reception encountered in schools, class and access to support systems, generational status, gender, as well as ethnicity and national origin along with shifts in the development of identity. In what follows, I offer a brief overview of these major factors associated with immigrants' divergent educational experiences and attainment.

While multiple social institutions impact the transition and experience of immigrants in their new society, for children and youth, the most sustained interaction outside of the family is with the school. The kinds of schools children enter have tremendous impact on their educational outcomes which, in turn, impact their future opportunities. Interaction between immigrants and schools depends not only on immigrant characteristics as it may usually be assumed (e.g., parental educational attainment, level of educational engagement, etc.) but also to a great extent on the ways schools are structured, financed, and led. Local dynamics are important, since different schools vary in how they receive immigrants (Hernandez 2004). Nevertheless, systematic studies have shown characteristics of schools which do well with immigrant youth reception and those which are more likely to be detrimental and become "fields of endangerment" (Suarez-Orozco et al. 2008). Many of these schools have a high percentage of students who are poor; the racial and ethnic composition demonstrate segregation; many teachers are not certified to teach in the areas assigned to them; drop-out rates and suspensions are comparatively higher, while daily attendance rate is lower; scores are low on state-administered proficiency tests; and an achievement gap by ethnic and racial group exists among those who attend the school.

For many immigrant students, schools share a good number of these traits, and for the majority of the students studied, schools were highly racially and economically segregated and enrolling low income students (Suarez-Orozco et al. 2008). According to ethnographic observations, schools that responded well to immigrants displayed good leadership with involved principals who were present and visible in the school context, affirmed students' cultures and languages through teachers' positive attitudes and various programs, and resources were made available for academic tutoring and improvement. Schools located in areas with poorer funding and where violent outbursts were common placed newcomers in precarious positions, leaving them in fear of violence and bullying. Inter-ethnic animosity often becomes tangible and intimidating (Centrie 2000) and students experience a "triple segregation" (Suarez-Orozco, et al. 2008)—racial, economic, and linguistic. When schools are not able to generate environments where students, teachers, and staff engage with diversity and multiculturalism in a genuine sense (Ngo 2010), members of different groups tend to misread each other and often operate based on stereotypes (Olneck 2004). Teachers tend to respond to students depending on their level of conformity to popularized perceptions of specific immigrant groups (e.g., Asians as "model minorities"—see Centrie 2000; or Latinos as disengaged and unruly—see Trueba 1988). They tend to express positive feelings towards certain immigrants as better than others, as well as negative juxtapositions with native minorities who are positioned as lacking the positive values of some newcomers.

Struggling schools often correlate with lower income neighborhoods—given that in the United States most school funding comes from the state and relies heavily on property taxes—so social class also becomes a central variable in the educational experiences of immigrant children and youth. This is especially important since among current immigrants in the USA, a fraction are more educated than the overall population, while another is significantly less educated (Bean and Stevens 2003). As a result, the possibilities of immigrant success are much more contingent than expressed in the popular representations of immigrant success. The highly-educated (or affluent) immigrants often possess the human and social capital, as well as the legal resources to join the native-born middle to upper classes with relative ease. They simultaneously maintain fruitful ethnic networks and affiliations with cultural and educational associations that ensure the transmission of cultural capital to their children. These children, in turn, make the most rapid strides among immigrant youth, entering the middle class themselves through access to better and even elite educational opportunities (Louie 2004).

Working class and poor immigrants, on the other hand, tend to lack comparable financial and cultural resources, with a large fraction residing in segregated neighborhoods. The situation of undocumented students becomes even more precarious as the anxiety about their status can couple with being locked out of the educational opportunity structure once they graduate from high school (Seif 2004). The initial point of settlement, correlated with resources at arrival, often sets poorer immigrant students on a more difficult trajectory for social mobility, beginning with the comparatively poor schools and social isolation from more successful groups (Zhou and Bankston 1994). Moreover, the success of immigrant youth is no longer simply a matter of attaining higher levels of education—or better salaries—than the previous generation. Most of the immigrant youth can show success by those variables simply because their parents are struggling at the bottom (Zhou 1997). For example, the children of Mexican immigrants (the current largest single immigrant nationality in the USA) show an improvement in educational attainment by 3 years compared to their parents. This improvement is important but it still leaves them with only approximately 12 years of schooling and thus no significant access to careers that would positively affect their standing. In addition, current demographics show that by the third generation this improvement achieved by the second generation does not continue (Trejo and Grogger 2002).

In the longitudinal studies conducted thus far, underfunded schools in low-income neighborhoods were most likely to produce profiles of immigrant students who were categorized as "low achievers" or "decliners," while "high achievers" were least likely to attend the underfunded, segregated schools. Dominicans, Mexicans, and Latin Americans were most likely to attend such schools, in comparison to the much lower likelihood among Chinese students, a comparison that clearly translates into the later patterns of academic achievement we see across these immigrant groups. It is also consistent with other findings which examine the overlap between race and class in the USA and how immigrants' phenotype defines the type of neighborhood they settle in. Latino immigrants tend to live in impoverished neighborhoods with high Latino populations, as do black immigrants with native-born African-Americans. In contrast, Asian immigrants are relatively less constrained in the racialized structure and tend to encompass a larger proportion of middle class newcomers—they thus tend to be less confined in residential settlement (Louie 2004; Portes and Rumbaut 2006) and this has tremendous implications for school choice as well.

Generational status has also proven to be a very important variable, an interest prompted by the well-being and achievement of "the new second generation." Once longitudinal comparisons were made across generations, competing trends emerged about the achievement of immigrant youth. Worrisome findings showed declining grade point averages among the second generation as well as low college graduation rates among such groups as Latinos (Portes and Rumbaut 2001; Fry 2002). Data from the National Longitudinal Study of Adolescent Health were used to show that first-generation youth of Hispanic, Asian, and African heritage do obtain more education than their parents, but the second generation and third or later generations generally lose ground (Perreira *et al.* 2006). These differences in dropout rates were connected to differences in human, cultural, and social capital. In fact, almost half of the difference in the dropout probability between Hispanic and white students (out of a total difference of 14 percent) was found to stem from the greater prevalence of poverty among Hispanic students. English proficiency was also a key factor in explaining the high Hispanic dropout rate (Lofstrom 2007).

Nevertheless, competing findings complicate the picture, as first-generation immigrant youth also tend to be academically outpaced by their native-born peers. Despite the optimism of the first generation (Kao and Tienda 1995) and their "dual frame of reference" (Ogbu 1991), newcomers struggle more with language acquisition for academic contexts and may also struggle with problems related to legal status and low socio-economic status. Limited English-proficiency youth are less likely to enroll in and complete postsecondary degrees, more likely to be employed in low-earning jobs and end up being paid much less in adulthood (Bleakley and Chin 2004). When it comes to academic English, the 1.5 generation (born elsewhere but immigrating before the age of 12) has an advantage, while the second generation and beyond benefit from initial immersion in the language and recognition through citizenship. By the third generation, however, factors such as racism, poverty, and acculturation to anti-academic peer norms may play a role in diminishing the academic achievement and school engagement of youth of immigrant descent.

The language advantage of the second generation is not simply a factor in facilitating understanding of academic content, but also in providing access to students' social interactions in school and in helping to overcome barriers reported by first-generation students in relationships with native-born peers and teachers. While family and community networks were found to be among the most important factors in immigrants' adaptation and success (Portes and Rumbaut 2001), school-based supportive relationships are also key to immigrant students' academic engagement and subsequent success. Engagement is a crucial factor, measured in the extent to which students are connected to what, how, and with whom they are learning (Suarez-Orozco, *et al.* 2008). All students need this to succeed and all face challenges that might deteriorate academic engagement levels, but for immigrant students such challenges emerge in ways specific to the migration process. Academic engagement comprises cognitive, behavioral, and relational aspects, with the last one proving critical in supporting academic outcomes in schools. Relational engagement enables access to details about curriculum and college admissions as well as bureaucratic processes, the labor market, advice, and advocacy (Stanton-Salazar 2004). For immigrant students, positive relationships with peers, teachers, and other school staff provide protective frameworks such as role modeling and a sense of belonging which, in turn, translate into increased motivation and achievement.

This kind of relational engagement in school-based relationships, however, is not uniformly achieved among immigrant students. One of the major variations emerged along gender differences. A number of studies consistently positioned immigrant girls as outperforming boys across ethnic groups (e.g., Portes and Rumbaut 2001; Rong and Brown 2001), as boys were found with significantly lower grades, lower levels of engagement with classes and homework, as well as lower career and educational goals. Several factors were connected to this gap, including parental support for girls' education in the new country and much stricter social controls than for sons. Girls were also less likely than boys to develop oppositional relationships with schools as a result of perceived racism, hostility or lack of connection with teachers and school staff (Qin-Hilliard and Orozco 2004). This correlates with teachers' own reports of having more negative expectations of boys than girls, raising questions again about the need to diversify the teaching force which continues to be mainly white, middle-class, and female. As boys reported being more disengaged relationally in school than girls, they did not necessarily express specific disinterest in learning. As a result, boys' lower academic performance may not be caused by lack of academic interest, but the interaction of low social support, hostile experiences in school, and negative teacher expectations (Qin-Hilliard and Orozco 2004). This finding was important in suggesting that negative social relations in school could be an important factor in explaining immigrant boys' lower achievement compared to girls.

Because schools are such an integral part of immigrant children and youths' lives, they participate in more than just structuring the students' academic attainment and career trajectories. Schools, in fact, become important sites for the construction of identity, especially as they interact with other social worlds students inhabit simultaneously, such as the family, peer groups and religious communities (Phelan *et al.* 1993). As they negotiate these boundaries, immigrant youth often find that the transition from one context to another is not simple—in fact, one of the better-documented aspects of the immigration experience refers to the tensions that arise as children and youth try to fulfill multiple roles that would be acceptable to both families and peers (Garcia Coll and Magnuson 1997). As they acquire and adapt to new cultural scripts—at a faster rate than their parents, who do not interact with acculturating school environments—children and youth acquire necessary language skills (Wong Filmore 2005; Qin 2006) and opportunities. At the same time, however, as they become interpreters and cultural guides for less acculturated family members (Faulstich Orellana 2003), the newly gained cultural capital can still be at odds with familial norms. Youth thus become caught in the tensions between the two worlds and the subsequent possible alienation from families (Zhou 1997; Qin 2006).

This is a process that schools need to recognize as they respond to students' behaviors and engagement in schools, creating spaces for students to develop positive ethnic identities just as they also adapt to the new context. It is social competence in both cultures that has been found as the more advantageous alternative for these youth's success, aiming to blend the positive elements of both realms, through such means as "accommodation without assimilation" (Gibson 1988) or "selective acculturation" which appears to lead to better academic achievement (Portes *et al.* 2005). However, developing this healthy and productive sense of ethnic identity depends not only on individual inclination toward ethnic identification, but also on the possibilities of recognition found in the context of reception (Phinney *et al.* 2001). Schools, therefore, play an essential role in this process, needing to pay close attention to identity formation and processes of negative social mirroring (Suarez-Orozco *et al.* 2008) which impact youth's sense of self. If "street culture" and related activities often offer youth better spaces for self-expression and confidence-building than schools, the likelihood that youth will turn to those alternative spaces is much higher. Especially in segregated and impoverished areas, some youth ultimately take counterproductive and possibly self-destructive trajectories, confirming fears in this regard repeatedly expressed by immigrant parents (Zhou 2003).

Main critiques

While major developments in understanding immigration and education were closely connected to the development of sociological theory on trajectories of immigrant incorporation, the accumulated research has also demonstrated some shortcomings in light of subsequent findings. The problem of "segmented assimilation" or "second-generation decline" which spurred much attention to the role of education turned out to be also a major source of critique—both because of how some of the mechanisms of decline were positioned in the literature and because that decline itself may not be as frequent or dramatic as initially shown.

First, the problem with representing the mechanisms of decline eventually emerged from research conducted from the segmented assimilation perspective that has shown how immigrant youth often adopt the orientations of native-born, co-ethnic peers. In areas closed out of the opportunity structure and with substandard schools, such attitudes often referred to oppositional identities toward schooling and even violent activity through gang association. These findings were initially used to highlight factors which may, along with other elements, contribute to immigrant achievement decline and how some immigrants maintained their particular national and linguistic markers to distinguish themselves from the native-born underclass and thus maintain a chance at upward mobility. While these arguments further demonstrated social inequalities along race and class in the receiving society, they were also later critiqued for blaming the decline of immigrants' success on the already disadvantaged native minorities.

Second, the focus on generational "decline" itself has also come under scrutiny in the context of a general focus in the research literature on the challenges encountered by immigrants throughout their transition and, specifically, in the educational context as well. Newer studies generated what appeared to be counterintuitive findings regarding the declining adaptation and well-being of immigrants, suggesting more variation in immigrants' prospects and even optimistic possibilities (Kasinitz et al. 2008). The most recent large-scale study based on the coming of age of immigrant children in New York (Kasinitz et al. 2008) found that from educational and occupational achievement to earnings and labor force participation, each immigrant second generation group studied was upwardly mobile both in comparison to its first generation parents and to its native-born reference group. This also echoed some earlier studies which showed that, while children in immigrant families experience a greater risk of living in poverty than those in native-born families, this is mostly due to the poverty rates in the first generation—by the second generation there is only a slightly higher chance (i.e., by 2 percent; Hernandez 2004). In contrast to a decline characteristic to the second generation, a "second generation advantage" was posited as the ability to draw on positive elements of both cultures, English fluency and acquiring jobs comparable to those of native New Yorkers their age. While the means by which this is accomplished, through the savvy use of positive social capital and selective acculturation techniques is not a new concept (Portes and Rumbaut 2001), when applied to the wider range of impact found on the children of immigrants in the study, these findings highlighted a more hopeful interpretation of immigrant integration.

The findings can also be contextualized in international perspective through the International Comparative Study of Ethnocultural Youth (Berry et al. 2006) which also suggests a great deal of variation in acculturation strategies and adaptation. Psychological and sociocultural adaptation was measured for a sample of 5000 adolescents in 13 countries, suggesting that, when compared to national peers, immigrant youth showed slightly fewer psychological problems, behavior problems and better school adjustment, as well as expressing the same level of life satisfaction and self-esteem as native peers. A major thrust of the study was its emphasis on the fact that, even in the absence of big differences between the immigrants and the national samples, there were nevertheless large variations within the immigrant groups themselves. These differences were connected to how the acculturation processes took place for different groups and individuals, reminding of the importance of the context of reception which often welcomes immigrants in different ways. Schools, therefore, as part of this receiving context, could participate in attenuating the discrepancies in educational experiences. This issue of inter-group variation takes the argument back to the centrality of other kinds of inequality in social location and divisions along the lines of race, ethnicity, and class. If some of the more recent findings cast a more optimistic light on the prospects of immigrant youth, there should remain, nevertheless, valid concern regarding the experiences of second generation young adults who are coming of age in contexts quite different from a large metropolis with a dynamic economy and more openness to immigrants, like New York City. At the same time, these studies help reiterate the sentiment that negative outcomes for immigrant youth are not and should not be unavoidable (Berry and Sam 1997).

Continued relevance of the issue

If, as suggested by the more recent critiques, optimistic prospects are to be increased and expanded across all immigrant origin groups, the role of education cannot be overstated. This is a multi-faceted issue, referring not only to the economic implications of educational attainment in the current economic conditions, but also to the dimensions of human dignity and quality of life that are either enabled or hindered by the kind of education immigrant children and youth have access to in the new society. In cases where schools are still underfunded and underprepared to engage fruitfully the diverse human experiences that migration has brought into their classrooms, attention to this issue is far from being resolved. Moreover, continued discrepancies in achievement and social mobility among groups, especially in light of the modern economy remain central. Economically, successful transitions to adulthood depend on a combination of credentialing, educational achievement, the acquisition of marketable skills and abilities, as well as physical and mental health. The coupling of success with mental health is also important, since the educational attainment of certain groups, such as the Chinese, is not necessarily complemented by healthy psychological adaptation (Qin 2006). Their academic attainment tends to belie struggles with inter-generational and inter-cultural tensions, as well as the pressures of doing well despite language barriers and bullying.

Beyond the actual experiences in schools, immigrants' transitions to higher education or the workforce are structured by interactions among ethnicity, gender, social class, policy implementation and the conditions of the labor market. For youth who are undocumented, the availability of free, public education until the age of 18 ceases and major obstacles to obtaining further education and the necessary credentials intervene. Despite desires to earn higher education degrees, many youth in this situation have their life trajectories significantly altered by the lack of higher education funds for undocumented youth. This has long-term implications because their accumulation of human, cultural, and social capital is likely to impact the well-being of their own children. In general, parental low educational attainment is likely to place children at a disadvantage both in immediate economic terms (access to certain resources while growing up, including quality health care; Duncan and Brooks-Gunn 1997) and in the long-run, given the children's own educational attainment. This correlation appears repeatedly in the assessment of discrepancies in attainment among current immigrant youth (Perreira et al. 2006).

Beyond the personal achievement and sense of possibility in the new society, the value of education for immigrants extends into wider-scale economic implications. Current population projections suggest that by 2030, approximately two thirds of the elderly are estimated to be white (from the generation born between 1946 and 1964), compared to only 59 percent of working-age adults and only 52 percent of children and youth (Hernandez 2004). By 2040, due to immigration of mostly Hispanic and Asian background, the number of non-Hispanic white youth is estimated to drop to less than 50 percent. The argument is thus made that the well-being, adjustment, and productivity of immigrant and minority youth today is essential to the projected well-being of the country (Hernandez 2004). Paying attention to the educational attainment of these children and youth and investing in it is, in fact, in the economic interest of the entire nation. Education thus remains an essential issue to consider, not only for the sake of the immigrants themselves, but also for the overall national well-being, as newcomers and native populations live in an intricate mutual dependence.

Future developments

The relative novelty of attention to education in immigrants' lives and the complexity of the issue warrant continued work in this area and multiple directions would prove fruitful, both at the institutional, structural levels and that of lived experience. The several larger-scale studies conducted so far provided invaluable data that has offered a tremendous beginning in our understanding of the factors that impact immigrant youth's educational opportunities and experiences. Conducted in metropolitan areas and with specific groups of immigrants, these studies offered an initial direction for such research and more would be important, not only in similar locations but also expanding the types of contexts and populations considered. Areas that were more recently impacted by immigration and are continuing to adjust their institutions—including the schools—would provide great comparison points, as would inclusion of groups which are comparatively understudied (including those of African and European origin). These additional directions would further nuance our accounts of experience across groups, as well as continue the existing efforts in this regard for pan-ethnic groups and various refugee groups. Additionally, the dynamics of migration in globalization have prompted attention outside the initial destination country. This implies an increased need to examine the processes of return migration and how educational institutions respond to the complex situations of educating nationals who are, in fact, immigrants in their own countries and experience difficulties in transitioning to their "home" country.

Existing research highlights negative characteristics of schools and surrounding areas which prove detrimental to immigrant youth's life trajectories, as well as some that have proven positive. Further work in this area would be illuminating, investigating in further depth the institutional dynamics which make success possible for immigrant youth—in other words, we need to understand further what successful schools do in serving immigrant youth justly and how such environments emerge and sustain themselves. This would be relevant both in terms of the student experience and regarding the external pressures schools face in producing certain results in standardized measurements, pressures which usually further hinder the academic well-being of newcomers (Linn 2000). Also, in curricular terms, the potentials of multicultural education approaches for academic success have been examined to a great extent for national minorities, but only more recently have these been expanded to include specific implications for current immigrant youth. Some findings suggest that even when implemented with good intentions, multicultural education principles for schools with many immigrant students fall short of their great potential (Ngo 2010). How more schools use this resource to serve their immigrant students is an area that deserves further attention, as does inviting all involved parties in revealing and reflecting on their needs and aspirations for the educational process. We need further examination of overlaps and disconnects among the various positions of students, parents, teachers, and community leaders, as well as positive options for the gaps that emerge. Overall, expanding on these areas of inquiry would enhance current understanding of positive responses and results in the education of immigrant youth. Offering more optimistic models is essential in an area that is often overshadowed by the justified difficulties prompted by pursuing an education in the migration process.

References and further reading

Alba, R. and Nee, V. (1997) "Rethinking assimilation theory for a new era of immigration" *International Migration Review* 31(4): 826–74.

Aronowitz, M. (1984) "The social and emotional adjustment of immigrant children: A review of the literature" *International Migration Review* 18(2): 237–57.

Bean, F. and Stevens, G. (2003) *America's Newcomers and the Dynamics of Diversity*. New York: Russell Sage Foundation.

Berry, J., Phinney, J., Sam D., and Vedder. (2006) *Immigrant Youth in Cultural Transition: Acculturation, Identity, and Adaptation Across National Contexts*. New York: Routledge.

Berry, J. and Sam, D. (1997) "Acculturation and adaptation." In J. Berry, M. Segall, and C. Kagitcibasi (eds), *Handbook of Cross-cultural Psychology, Volume 3: Social Behavior and Applications*. Boston, MA: Allyn and Bacon, pp. 291–326.

Bleakley, H. and Chin, A. (2004) "Language skills and earnings: Evidence from childhood immigrants" *Review of Economics and Statistics* 86(2): 481–96.

Centrie, C. (2004). *Identity Formation of Vietnamese Immigrant Youth in an American High School*. El Paso, TX: Lfb Scholarly Pub Llc.

Choi, H., Meininger, J. C., and Roberts, R. E. (2006) "Ethnic differences in adolescents' mental distress, social stress and resources" *Adolescence* 41: 163–283.

Duncan, G. J. and Brooks-Gunn, J. (eds) (1997) *Consequences of Growing up Poor*. New York: Russell Sage Foundation.

Faulstich Orellana, M. (2003) "Responsibilities of children in Latino immigrant homes" *New Directions for Youth Development* 100: 25–39.

Hernandez, D. (2004) "Children and youth in immigrant families: Demographic, social and educational issues." In B. A. Banks and C. McGee Banks (eds), *Handbook of Multicultural Education*. San Francisco, CA: Jossey-Bass, pp. 404–19.

Fry, R. (2002) "Latinos in higher education: Many enroll, too few graduate." *Pew Hispanic Center Report*. Pew Hispanic Center. Sept. 5, 2002.

Gans, H. (1992) "Second generation decline: Scenarios for the economic and ethnic futures of the post-1965 American immigrants" *Ethnic and Racial Studies* 15(2): 173–92.

Garcia Coll, C. and Magnuson, K. (1997) "The psychological experience of immigration: A developmental perspective." In A. Booth, A. C. Crouter, and N. Landale (eds), *Immigration and the Family: Research and Policy on US Immigrants*. Mahwah, NJ: Lawrence Erlbaum Associates, pp. 91–132.

Gibson, M. A. (1988) *Accommodation without Assimilation: Sikh Immigrants in an American High School*. Ithaca, NY: Cornell University Press.

Gordon, M. (1964). *Assimilation in American Life*. New York: Oxford.

Igoa, C. (1995) *Inner World of the Immigrant Child*. New York: St Martin's.

Kao, G. and Tienda, M. (1995) "Optimism and achievement: The educational performance of immigrant youth" *Social Science Quarterly* 76(1): 1–19.

Kasinitz, Mollenkopf, J., Waters, M., and Holdaway, J. (2008) *Inheriting the City: The Second Generation Comes of Age*. New York: Russell Sage Foundation.

Linn, B. (2000) "Testing and accountability" *Educational Researcher* 29(2): 4–17.

Lofstrom, M. (2007) *Why are Hispanic and African-American Dropout Rates so High?* Institute for the Study of Labor (IZA) University of Bonn. http://ftp.iza.org/dp3265.pdf.

Louie, V. (2004) *Compelled to Excel: Immigration, Education and Opportunity among Chinese Americans*. Palo Alto, CA: Stanford University Press.

Ngo, B. (2010) *Unresolved Identities: Discourse, Ambivalence, and Urban Immigrant Students*. Albany, NY: State University of New York Press.

Ogbu, J. (1991) "Immigrant and involuntary minorities in comparative perspective." In M. A. Gibson and J. U. Ogbu (eds), *Minority Status and Schooling: A Comparative Study of Immigrant and Involuntary Minorities*. New York: Garland Press, pp. 3–36.

Olneck, M. (2009) "What have immigrants wanted from American schools? What do they want now? Historical and contemporary perspectives on immigrants, language, and American schooling" *American Journal of Education* 115(3): 379–406.

——(2004) "Immigrants and education in the United States." In B. A. Banks and C. McGee Banks (eds), *Handbook of Multicultural Education*. San Francisco, CA: Jossey-Bass, pp. 381–403.

Park, R. (1950) *Race and Culture*. Glencoe, IL: The Free Press.

Perreira, K. M., Harris, K. M., and Lee, D. (2006) "Making it in America: High school completion by immigrant and native youth" *Demography* 43(3): 511–36.

Qin, D. B. (2008) "Doing well vs. feeling well: Understanding family dynamics and the psychological adjustment of Chinese immigrant adolescents" *Journal of Youth and Adolescence* 37(1): 22–35.

——(2006) "Our child doesn't talk to us anymore: Alienation in immigrant Chinese families" *Anthropology and Education Quarterly* 37(2): 162–79.

Phelan, P., Davidson, L. D., and Yu, H. C. (1993) "Students' multiple worlds: Navigating the borders of family, peer and school cultures." In P. Phelan and L. D. Davidson (eds), *Renegotiating Cultural Diversity in American School.* New York: Teachers College Press, pp. 52–88.

Phinney, J. S., Romero, I., Nava, M., and Huang, D. (2001). "The role of language, parents, and peers in ethnic identity among adolescents in immigrant families" *Journal of Youth and Adolescence* 30(2): 135–53.

Portes, A., Fernández-Kelly, P., and W. Haller (2005) "Segmented assimilation on the ground: The new second generation in early adulthood" *Ethnic and Racial Studies* 28(6): 1000–40.

Portes, A. and Rumbaut, R. (2001) *Legacies: The Story of the Second Generation.* Berkeley, CA: University of California Press.

Portes, A. and Rumbaut, R. (2006) *Immigrant America: A Portrait.* Berkeley, CA: University of California Press.

Portes, A. and Zhou, M. (1993) "The new second generation: Segmented assimilation and its variants" *Annals of the American Academy of Political and Social Sciences* 530(1): 74–96.

Rong, X. L. and Brown, F. (2001) "The effects of immigrants generation and ethnicity on educational attainment among young African American and Caribbean Black in the United States" *Harvard Educational Review* 71(3): 536–68.

Seif, H. (2004) "'Wise Up!' Undocumented Latino youth, Mexican-American legislators, and the struggle for higher education access." *Latino Studies* 2(2): 210–30.

Suarez-Orozco, C. and Suarez-Orozco, M. (2001) *Children of Immigration.* Cambridge, MA: Harvard University Press.

Suarez-Orozco, M. (2000) "Everything you ever wanted to know about assimilation but were afraid to ask" *Daedalus Journal of the American Academy of Arts and Sciences* 129(4): 1–30.

Suárez-Orozco, C. and Baolian Qin-Hilliard, D. (2004) "Immigrant boys' experiences in US schools." In N. Way and J. Chu (eds), *Adolescent Boys: Exploring Diverse Cultures of Boyhood.* New York: New York University Press, pp. 295–316.

Suarez-Orozco, C., Suarez-Orozco, M. and Todorova, I. (2008) *Learning a New Land: Immigrant Students in American Society.* Cambridge, MA: The Belkap Press of Harvard University Press.

Stanton-Salazar, R. D. (2004) "Social capital among working-class minority students." In M. Gibson, A. Gandara, and J. Peterson Koyama (eds), *School Connections: US Mexican Youth, Peers and School Achievement.* New York: Columbia University Press, pp. 18–38.

Suarez-Orozco, C. and Suarez-Orozco, M. (2001). *Children of Immigration.* Cambridge, MA: Harvard University Press.

Trejo, S. and Grogger, J. (2002) *Falling Behind or Moving Up? The Intergenerational Progress of Mexican Americans.* San Francisco, CA: Public Policy Institute of California.

Trueba, H. T. (1988) "Culturally based explanations of minority students' academic achievement" *Anthropology and Education Quarterly* 1(9): 270–87.

Waters, M. C. (1999) *Black Identities: West Indian Immigrant Dreams and American Realities.* Cambridge, MA: Harvard University Press.

Wong Fillmore, L. (2005) "When learning a second language means losing the first." In M. M. Suárez-Orozco, C. Suárez-Orozco, and D. B. Qin (eds), *The New Immigration: An Interdisciplinary Reader.* New York: Routledge, pp. 289–308.

Zhou, M. (1997) "Segmented assimilation: Issues, controversies, and recent research on the new second generation" *International Migration Review* 31(4): 825–58.

——(2003) "Making it in urban America: Challenges and prospects for the children of contemporary immigrants." In L. Roulleau-Berger (ed.), *Youth and Work in the Post-Industrial City of North America and Europe.* Leiden, the Netherlands: Brill Academic Publishers, pp. 265–82.

Zhou, M. and Bankston, C. L. III. (1994) Social capital and the adaptation of the second generation: The case of Vietnamese youth in New Orleans. *International Migration Review* 28(4): 821–45.

34

Emigration and the sending state

Brendan Mullan and Cristián Doña-Reveco

Emigrants are in another state's grip, so governments of countries of emigration must develop creative ways to manage citizens abroad, preserve their national loyalty, and extract their resources.

(Fitzgerald 2009: 4)

… sending countries around the world, from Turkey to Mexico, have recently shifted their view towards their emigrants, from 'traitors' to 'compatriots' abroad.

(Joppke 2011: 1)

Introduction

It is by now a truism that international migration is a process, not an event. As evidenced by the contributions to this handbook, the cultural, demographic, economic, political, and social causes, content, and consequences of international migration as a process are well documented. However, there remain lacunae and among all the processes embedded within international migration, the complexities of the reciprocal relationship between the sending state and its emigrants has recently begun to receive the detailed attention and critical analysis that it deserves (Gamlen 2008; Fitzgerald 2009; Délano 2010, 2011; Kapur 2010; Joppke 2011).

Despite a weakening in new migration flows across the world because of the global economic crisis that began in 2008, more than 215 million people (3 percent of the world population) were living outside their country of origin in 2010 (World Bank 2011). The Mexican–US migration, corridor is the world's largest with 11.6 million migrants in 2010.[1] These migration flows are a relatively recent phenomenon. For most of history, subjects of a polity could not leave their polity or could only do so with great logistical and legal difficulty. These barriers to exit were slowly eradicated with the agricultural, industrial, and urban revolutions and the emergence of states, nation-states, and concomitant new forms of social, political, and economic organization and institutions that gave rise to dramatically changed views on and patterns of international migration.

While international migrants have historically maintained socio-economic and emotional ties to their nations of origin (Shain 2005), the post 1945 era has been one of increasing nation-states' awareness of and concern for their citizens and communities abroad and the various political, economic, and socio-cultural roles and impact these communities may play and exert in their countries of origin (González Gutiérrez 2006; Agunias 2009). As Kapur succinctly summarizes "the impact of emigration on the sending country depend critically on the selection effects: who leaves, how many leave, why they leave, the legal basis on which they leave, where they go, how they fare, and how long they have been gone" (Kapur 2010: 7).

The migration of highly skilled professionals from the "undeveloped south" to the "developed north," massive outflows of undocumented migrants, the closed borders of Eastern Europe during the Cold War, the increasing importance of remittances to local economies, and the role of emigrant exiles and expatriates in the development of perceptions with regard to their country of destination have all served to focus the attentions of the state on its emigrant population. Similarly, dramatically improved transportation and travel systems and infrastructures, along with radical advances in information technology and media enabled emigrants to communicate easily and affordably with their families, communities, and related constituencies in their countries of origin. Governments in sending countries have struggled to understand, control, and direct the impact of their diasporas on their political, social, and economic institutions and infrastructure. This struggle is deeply intertwined with the rapidly changing political, cultural, technological, and socio-economic practices and processes subsumed under the term "globalization."

Globalization's elusiveness as a concept adds to the complexity of understanding the relationship between sending states and their emigrants. Often viewed as a primarily economic phenomenon, globalization represents the increasing interaction, or integration, of national economic systems through the growth in international trade, investment, capital, and labor (migration) flows. This economic interpretation when combined with the rapid increase in cross-border political social, cultural, and technological exchange that has created extensive world-wide transnational human and social networks sets the stage on which we may survey the relationship between the sending state and its emigrants. States' connection to, communication with, and control of their emigrant expatriate populations are conditioned by the new circumstances of globalization.

Following an historical overview, which includes a discussion of the different forms and structures that states have used to maintain or reinforce the relationship with their diasporas and a brief examination of emigration as a human right, we discuss the relationship between sending states' and economic development with a particular focus on the function and impact of migrant remittances, both economic and social, and of alternative mechanisms of capital flows. Further, we analyze the implications, opportunities, and challenges for the sending state of *brain drain*, its corollary *brain gain,* and their change to *brain circulation*, and we assess the reciprocal political relationship between emigrants (exiles and expatriates) and their state of origin. We conclude with some assessment of how states, emigration, and concepts of citizenship are interlinked and we offer some suggestions for future research on the relationship between the state and its emigrants.

Historical overview

The Magna Carta of 1215 specifies that:

> It shall be lawful in the future for anyone to leave our kingdom, and to return, safely and securely, by land or by water, and without violating our trust, but not during war or for some other brief period, nor if the good of the kingdom will be affected.
>
> (Dale 1991: 3060)

This clause is relevant because it introduces the right of individuals to emigrate and because it introduces the idea that sovereign allegiance is not territorially bound. Ever since, from the early formative period of the monarch-led territorial state, through the differentiation and separation of the institutions of government from the monarch as a person, to the post-Westphalian concept of the sovereign nation-state, the "state" has had the role of creating and implementing solutions and regulations for human state-boundary crossing movement in the form of legislative migration policies and administrative implementation of those regulations.

International migration has played a key role in the rise and fall of empires, states, and coalitions of states as the world moved through the major political and economic stages of mercantilism, colonialism, industrialization, post-industrialization, and globalization. Historical classifications typically approximate international migration into several broad stages: European dominated, colonization-driven migration from about 1500 to 1800, imperialism, coercion, and industrialization-driven migration between Europe and the New World from about 1800 to 1915, limited international migration in the inter-war years and up to about 1950, and the post-1950 emergence of migration as a "managed" complex multi-faceted global phenomenon (see Massey *et al.* 1993; Goldin *et al.* 2011).

Because of the limited state involvement in emigration, the endurance of free travel as a liberal ideal until the first third of the twentieth century, and the relative youthfulness of today's nation-states, economic considerations have outweighed political considerations in explaining the dynamics of international migration. The independence of the Americas in the late eighteenth century and early nineteenth century, the industrial revolution, and the process of European colonization which led to the age of mass migration since the first half of the nineteenth century—Polanyi's *Great Transformation*—refocused the right to emigration debate from a natural law-based justification to the rights of citizens in liberal democracies and liberal economic ideologies (Zolberg 2007). The policies of sending countries, particularly those with colonies, varied during the eighteenth and nineteenth centuries, as their laissez-faire economic and political doctrines shifted. For example, in Great Britain and France as the governing ideology moved from Mercantilism to Malthusianism, the debate over emigration moved as well. Conceptual interpretations of emigration, which had been deemed as treason to the Crown with artisans prohibited from migrating shifted with rapid population growth to a more utilitarian perspective of "shoveling out paupers" (Green 2005: 273; Zolberg 2007) signaling a clear change to the encouragement of emigration for reasons of economic and domestic policy. However, even though emigration was seen as positively enlarging empires, those emigrating without the intention to return automatically lost their original nationality. In Great Britain this only changed when the nationality law of 1889 included citizens abroad as members of the nation (Green 2005).

As Italy and Germany reorganized into recognizable nation-states in the nineteenth century, emigration policies and practices were "closely entwined" with the concept of the nation (Gabaccia *et al.* 2007). From a minimal preoccupation, Germany became concerned with emigration as a debilitating force on nation building and encouraged emigration only to German colonies or to areas where emigrants could maintain and sustain German language, traditions, and customs. Italy similarly actively promoted the idea that emigrants were going to *Italianize* the countries of reception making emigration a form of "free" colonization. For Germany and Italy citizenship was defined as belonging to a racialized group of equals following the concept of *Jus sanguinis*. Italian and German emigrants would lose their nationality only if they served an enemy power during time of war or if the individual voluntarily renounced their nationality (Gabaccia *et al.* 2007).

The post-1918 redrawing of the European map led to about 9.5 million refugees between the early post war and the mid-1920s. Interwar conflicts and civil wars between 1918 and 1939 also created huge numbers of refugees. As examples, between 280,000 and 330,000 people of Jewish descent left Germany escaping the Nazi regime and other 150,000 after the *anschluss*. The Spanish Civil war (1936–9), led to the displacement of more than 3 million people within Spain and about half a million refuges after the war ended. All of this has dubbed the twentieth century the "century of refugees" (Bade 2003: 197)

Democratic states have also attempted to control the exit of its citizens in the late twentieth century and after. For example, Israel sought to attract and retain citizens for politically strategic nation-strengthening reasons. Emigration is discouraged in Israel for demographic conditions. Because of Israel's relatively small and slow growing population, especially when compared to that of Palestine, "emigration imperils Jewish Israeli's sense of security on both practical and ideological levels, [and] is treated as a serious threat indeed" (Gold 2007: 289). Although in the early days of the Israeli Republic emigration was considered almost immoral, more recently there have been governmental policies destined to regain connections with Jewish communities abroad and make them part of the Jewish state and nation (Gold 2007).

Sending states now realize that it is neither feasible nor desirable to stop emigration but that maintaining or improving relationships with their diasporic communities abroad can be beneficial regardless of the reason for departure. The post-1945 era saw a significant re-conceptualization and re-interpretation of the relationship between individuals and states *vis-à-vis* the right to leave and return to one's country of origin. Article 13 of United Nations' 1948 Universal Declaration of Human Rights normatively defines the relationship between the nation-state and its emigrants and clearly specifies emigration as a human right.[2]

While western democratic societies' governments and people generally acknowledged and accepted the right to emigrate as a basic human right, this is and was not true for the people and governments of much of the non-western world (East Europe during the Cold War, the Southern Cone of America, large swathes of Africa and Asia). In many non-western societies the rights to leave and return to any country were ignored; the Berlin Wall was the physical representation of the impossibility to leave and exiles were only very rarely, if ever, allowed to return to their countries of origin. The Human Rights declaration and other human rights instruments around the world do allow for exceptions. The United Nations details these exceptions in the 1966[3] International Covenant on Civil and Political Rights, which states that the right of emigration and of free movement within one's own country (the first paragraph of Article 13) "shall not be subject of restriction except on those which are provided by law, are necessary to protect national security, public order (*ordre public*), public health or morals or the rights and freedoms of others" (Chetail 2003: 48). This broader interpretation of the right to leave and return has opened the possibility for states to curtail the right to emigration through claims that such emigration would be a risk to national security, health, or morality. In sum, the 1948 Declaration sets a precedent on the relationship between the individual and the state. Citizens of a nation-state were now not compelled to remain in their country and could, theoretically at least, leave and return at any moment.

Development and migration in sending countries

The relationship between migration and development remains unsettled (Portes 2007; Hanson 2008; de Haas 2008; Castles and Miller 2009). In 2010 worldwide, inward remittance flows, arguably the most studied and cited impact of international migration on development, from the 215 million people or 3 percent of the world population who live outside their countries of origin exceeded US$440 billion in 2010 (World Bank 2011) while, as a traditional comparison, the net official development assistance from the OECD countries accounted for only US$128 billions. Countries receive foreign direct investment, official development assistance, and private debt/portfolio equity in addition to remittance flows. Figure 34.1 shows these resource flows into all developing countries over the period 1995 to 2010.

The World Bank (2011) emphasizes the resilience of remittances to downturn as a result of the 2008 economic crisis[4] when compared to other resource flows to developing countries. This resiliency is attributed to the cumulation of migrant remittances over years which generates a sustainable remittance momentum, the small marginal impact of remittance transmittance on migrants' incomes, increasing duration of migration, and if economic recession does force migrants to return, they will bring their accumulated savings with them. Foreign direct investment and private debt and portfolio equity show no such resilience to economic crises. The magnitude of remittances is impressive: India and China lead, each with over $50 billion received in 2010, followed by Mexico and the Philippines with over $20 billion each; France, Germany, Bangladesh, Belgium, Spain, and Nigeria round out the top 10, each with over $10 billion in remittances received. When remittances received are measured as a percentage of GDP, the top 10 countries are almost all lesser developed countries with Tajikistan receiving 35 percent of its 2009 GDP in remittances, and Tonga, Lesotho, Moldova, Nepal, Lebanon, and Samoa all depending on remittances for over 20 percent of their GDP (World Bank 2011).

Remittances are a direct result of migration being deployed by families in low income countries as household income supplementation strategy. Empirical evidence strongly suggests that these remittances have a direct, albeit not immediate, effect on the development of the areas of origins of migrants. In summarizing remittances' positive and negative micro- and

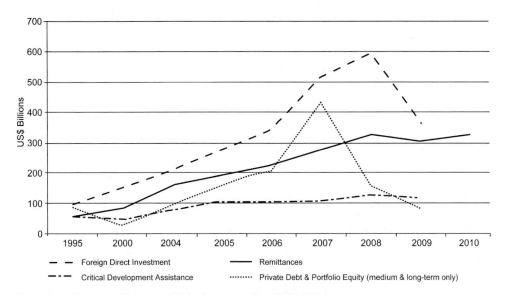

Figure 34.1 Resource flows to developing countries 1995–2010.
Source: World development indicators database and World bank Migration and Remittances Unit 2010

macro-impacts on sending countries, Goldin *et al.* (2011) usefully distinguish between remittances' short-term household poverty reduction, medium-term macroeconomic boost, and long-term human capital base build up effects. The impact of remittances is, however, mostly invisible to the non-migrant population. At the micro level (household or farm level) remittances allow the purchase of consumer goods that otherwise would have not been available. It also can provide improved access for family members to education or health care. In a second, later, stage remittances may allow migrant-sending households or farms to increase their investment in local production often encouraging subsequent state participation and sponsorship. The multiplier effect of remittances on the local economy is felt through taxes on the goods bought with remittances and possible additional employment to meet the extra demand generated through remittance expenditures.

Remittances can have negative impacts on the receiving economies. At the micro level remittances can produce marked inequalities between those households that receive them and those who do not. The resulting remittance-based relative poverty can increase migration propensities among non-remittance receiving households thus contributing to the cumulative causation of migration. At a more macro level, remittances do not replace government strategies to deal with lack of infrastructure, development, and poverty on sending regions.

While direct financial (cash) remittances are the usual mechanism through which emigrants create a micro- and, perhaps eventually, a macro-economic stimulus to sending states, such mechanisms are now deemed to be not enough to access emigrants' capital abroad. Remittances are drawn from emigrants' current income flows and those flows are subject to the conventional vagaries of labor markets especially given the current global economic crisis: unemployment, delayed payment of wages, wage reductions, currency exchange rate fluctuations, and excessive remittance transmission charges. Similarly, not all emigrants remit part of their income to their countries of origin, even if they are successful and established labor force participants abroad. Sending countries now seek to tap their emigrants' accumulated savings through innovative financial instruments and approaches that may target previously untargeted sources of capital investment. Most prominent among these instruments are diaspora bonds, a potentially stable and inexpensive source of external finance for sending countries, which are issued by developing countries and marketed to emigrants in rich countries (Ketkar and Ratha 2011).

India, Israel, and to a lesser extent Lebanon, have the most established and successful record of raising hard currency financing from their emigrants and diasporas with Israel having raised an estimated $25 billion since the 1950s and India $11 billion since the early 1990s (Ketkar and Ratha 2009). For Israel, diaspora bonds underpin its sovereign debt rating while for India, struggling with the aftermath of geopolitical turbulence in the late 1990s, the diaspora bond funded India Millennium Deposits of 2000 emphasized diaspora funding's significance for the country's overall creditworthiness ratings (Ketkar and Ratha 2011). The World Bank is reportedly advising several nations about diaspora bonds with Kenya, Nigeria, and the Philippines all expressing interest and an increasingly "desperate" Greece also pursuing the idea (*Economist* 2011: 69). While significant diaspora bond funding is in its infancy and can be problematic as a means to underwrite physical and human capital infrastructure development in sending countries, as evidenced by a recent failure of an Ethiopian diaspora-bond issue, the concept remains under consideration by both sending countries' governments and, more recently, by private sector companies.

Less tangible but no less important social, cultural, and human capital migrant remittances also have beneficial and deleterious effects on sending communities. Levitt (1998) examines how sending societies' individuals, families, and communities are affected by the flow of "ideas, behaviors, identities, and social capital." Kapur (2010), focusing on the impact of emigration on

India, generalizes social remittances to incorporate "ideas transmission," or the "flow of ideas embedded in human capital, both through returning migrants as well as from Diaspora members living abroad," (Kapur 2010: 159). These flows are facilitated today not just through the physical return of migrants or the continued circular migration of individuals but also through advances in and ease of use of modern communication media technologies which enable emigrants to communicate easily and affordably with their families, communities, and related constituencies in their countries of origin. Such intellectual, social, and human capital remittances can also exacerbate tensions among non-migrant households in the sending area through a heightened awareness of gender inequities, increased work and child care responsibilities, and extended family care and living responsibilities brought on by the absence of husbands and other family members.

Remittances are not a replacement for national and local development policies. States should continue their engagement on infrastructure projects in the remittance receiving areas and not simply relegate development to home town associations or to the migrants themselves. Connecting sending areas with other regions through improved roads and communications facilities the extension of the impact of remittances and saving as well as increases the multiplier effects of remittances. For example, notwithstanding some criticism, the Mexican Government's *Tres por Uno* (three for one) program, where each dollar sent by a community is paired by the local, state, and federal government expenditure, is one of many good examples of policies to increase the impact of remittances in the development of communities of origin (González Gutiérrez 2006; Goldin *et al.* 2011).

Human capital flight and circulation

First highlighted in the analysis of Indian physicians and nurses in Britain in the 1960s, the notion of brain drain rapidly became an example of the perils that emigration brought to developing countries. This "specter" (Goldin *et al.* 2011: 179) lures highly educated human capital from low income countries by richer countries. This process of skilled migration negatively impacts the development opportunities of the sending countries. Examples abound: the flight of doctors from India (Kapur 2010), Cuba (Pedraza 2007), and Africa (Goldin *et al.* 2011), and university graduates in general (Docquier and Marfouk 2006).

The original argument was that this highly skilled human capital was educated in the countries of origin often at the expenses of the local governments which finance their educations in state run public universities, only for them to leave to former imperial powers or core countries where these migrants would be offered better income, security, and professional development. Although this is a real problem for some countries, it is important to also look at the characteristics of local labor markets to contextualize the process in terms of period and time of occurrence.

It is not clear whether those highly skilled emigrants "would have been as productive at home" (Goldin *et al.* 2011: 181). These migrations occur in a context of low investment in the areas where these migrants are most productive and in countries with high unemployment. It is probable then, that without this migration, the number of unemployed highly skilled would increase pressuring wages down and decreasing chances of development as well. The sending country, although it is still produces a loss in a percentage of graduates, remains with a more manageable number of highly skilled professionals.

Unlike the 1960s' original brain drain flows and patterns, contemporary globalization patterns have increased interdependence, exchange, and communications which in turn has led to new forms of highly skilled migration; those of brain gain, brain circulation, and brain exchange. These new forms of highly skilled migration point to a more positive outlook where less developed economies can gain from the transference of knowledge that pre-supposes the migration of their own professionals to the developed countries even if they stay in the country of migration.

The return of highly skilled migrants, although limited in number, can have extraordinary impacts on the development opportunities of the country of origin. As mentioned above, through "social remittances," these migrants bring social and cultural resources, intellectual capital, and ideas that have mostly positive effects in the areas of origin. Brain circulation, the continuous back and forth migration of highly skilled migrants, not only creates a diaspora network, but when well channeled can directly impact the areas of expertise of the migrant without mandating permanent return to the country of origin. With mixed results, United Nations Development Program and United Nation Volunteers have developed since 1976 the Transference of Knowledge through Expatriate Nationals (TOKTEN) program designed to increase the involvement of highly skilled emigrants on development projects. Although this program is currently under way in four sending countries, other nations have developed "diaspora engagement policies" or initiatives. The Philippines, Argentina, and Colombia have created their own interesting policies to canalize projects of their own (González Gutiérrez 2006; Goldin et al. 2011).

The impact of the migration of the highly skilled on the country of origin does not end with the transference of knowledge. These emigrants bridge sending and receiving countries and economies providing networks, financial, and cultural expertise that allows companies to reduce risk and costs in political negotiations in the receiving country. Although emigrant entrepreneurs tend not to aid the economy of the sending country in the short or medium term, if sending country conditions are attractive for investment, overseas business émigrés can be a resource to incite and connect investors from the receiving country with opportunities in the sending country. Even in certain political contexts that might otherwise prove politically endangering for the sending country, investments from expatriates have not stopped. In China, for example, about 70 percent of China's total foreign direct investments between 1985 and 2000 came from overseas Chinese (Goldin et al. 2011). These investments flows were not affected by the Tiananmen Square protests or any other political crisis in the mainland.

Political opposition from abroad: the role of exiles

Historically, governments exiled opponents to quiet political opposition; exiles define themselves in opposition to the current government of the sending nation, having left their country due to real or perceived threats to their personal security and their challenge to claims for political loyalty demanded by sending country regimes. Traditionally, exile was a component of elitist politics and not a mass movement. In the twentieth century this process changed from a three tier structure (expelling state, individual, receiving state) to a four-tier structure with the inclusion of international public and civil society in the form of non-governmental or humanitarian organizations (Sznajder and Roniger 2009). Exile also became a more global movement following the German *anschluss*, exile from the Southern Cone of America between 1960 and 1990, exile from many newly independent post-colonial states, and exile from authoritarian regimes in the middle-east and from former soviet dependencies. The main difference between "conventional" emigrants and political exiles is that the latter not only live in a contiguous struggle against the government of the home country to create the political conditions to allow them to return, but they also refuse to seek or settle into any stable life or life-style pattern while abroad (Shain 2005). In fact, a common theme that appears in interviews and biographies of exiles is that many of them lived for years with their luggage ready to return at the first possibility (Sznajder and Roniger 2009).

Moreover, political exiles not only serve as a lobby group in the receiving country to influence policies against the country of origin, but they have also been used by the latter as instruments to engage and intervene in the political affairs of other countries. As the recent history of Iraq demonstrates, exiles are often severely conflicted as to their political loyalties. Attempts to depose their native government can be perceived as a patriotic mission or as treason regardless of their final objective, imperiling the reconstruction of the polity if they succeed in replacing the government. In sum, as Shain summarizes, "political exiles tend to test the limits of and reshape concepts such as loyalty, obligation, and 'the national interest'" (Shain 2005: xiv).

Living in countries with different political systems can undoubtedly influence emigrants' experiences of politics and activism. The re-emergence and resuscitation of the Latin American left in the 1970s and 1980s was influenced by exiles' experiences, mostly in liberal democracies world-wide, but primarily in the social democratic regimes of northern Europe and in the countries of the Soviet Bloc (Sznajder and Roniger 2009; Goldin et al. 2011). The democratic state-building and business entrepreneurial expertise and networks developed by exiles while abroad have been of utmost relevance in the reconstruction of previously dictatorial and authoritarian states (Shain 2005; Goldin et al. 2011).

The process of exiles' return to the sending state is often fraught with difficulty, uncertainty, and unease. Their return has a direct impact on families that have developed under very different circumstances and there are political and economic tensions surrounding the definitions and constructions of the future nation between those who stayed behind and those who left. Tensions between non-exiles who remained in the sending country, often feeling aggrieved that exiles lived in safe and secure world, studying or becoming economically secure, while they suffered tyrannical government repression, can produce cleavages in definitions of collective national identity (Sznajder and Roniger 2009).

As time passes and former exiles are no longer enemies of the state and other emigrants continuously send remittances or engage with their countries of origin, sending nations have increasingly become interested in the role of emigrants in state construction from outside, implying an understanding by the state that nationality and belonging does not end at the political border. States encourage nationals of shared heritage to increase and maintain their loyalty to their state of origin through the celebration of national days, shared religious festivities, and other cultural activities. The objective of the state is not only to mobilize political support abroad, to secure remittances and to control political activity but also to extend participation in a highly interconnected world (Oestergaard-Nielsen 2003).

In political terms, the extension of participation has been marked by incorporating emigrants in the foreign policy of the country of origin. Bilaterally, states uses emigrants to lobby for improved commercial relations such as free trade agreements or better labor visa agreements. For example, one of the objectives of the creation of the Office of the President for Mexicans Abroad during the government of Vicente Fox in Mexico was to reconnect with Mexicans in the US in order to utilize their capacities to lobby for better treatment of undocumented and irregular migrants in the United States which could pave the road for a comprehensive migration agreement (Brand 2006; González Gutiérrez 2006).

A second form of political engagement and participation promoted by sending countries is to give nationals abroad voting rights. Currently, while about 115 countries allow some form of overseas voting, there still exist some de facto barriers to political and electoral participation (Ellis and Wall 2007). Extending the franchise to emigrants remains a second stage in the involvement of emigrants with their country of origin. In fact, it is mostly only after emigrants have achieved considerable economic power and influence—through remittances, for example—that they will lobby national policy makers for this right. Moreover, when processes of political

417

democratization in the home country reach a point where local political parties are able to evaluate the potential impact of overseas votes on their own constituencies 'decisions are then made to block or support legislations related to extending political rights to nationals abroad' (Lafluer 2011). This is directly connected with the size of the diaspora and the reasons for which these emigrants left the country. Large populations abroad might be seen as "dangerous" in that their participation can put those that remain in the homeland at a disadvantage, particularly considering that most of the decisions will not directly affect those living elsewhere in the world. Finally, as with Mexico, when a large component of the diaspora is in opposition to the current government or when the allies of former dictators are still active participants of political decisions, as in Chile, political parties are less inclined to support this type of legislation, because they fear that it could only help the current government and therefore produce an imbalance in the political system (Oestergaard-Nielsen 2003; Lafluer 2011).

Concluding on citizenship

We have explored, described, and explained many of the relationships and interactions between a nation-state and its emigrants that occur within the context of a socio-political agreement or contract between the state and its members. This contract can be understood in general terms as citizenship. Citizenship however has as a primary condition a territorial basis where the state claims a binding authority enforced through the legitimate use of physical force (Weber 1947). In the case of emigrants, states cannot enforce their authority since emigrants are not within the territory of the state.

An alternative, more inclusive of emigrants but still territorially based, characterization of citizenship as a "status bestowed on those who are full members of a community" (Marshall 1964: 84) considers citizenship as comprised of: civil citizenship encompassing rights related with individual freedoms and associated with judiciary institutions; political citizenship involving the rights to participate in the political life of a nation; and social citizenship ranging from the right to basic economic security to the possibility to participate in the social heritage and life of the society. Today, the locus of citizenship and the ensuing different interpretations of citizenship is a central and critical debate in migration studies (Samers 2010).

Reviewing the literature, Kivisto and Faist (2007) found no less than 20 characterizations of citizenship in the last 20 years continuum-framed from the perspective of belonging to a supranational state (world, global or universal citizenship), to belonging to no state or to more than one state simultaneously (post-national, transnational or multicultural citizenship) or to particular aspects of being a citizen (cyber, environmental or gendered citizenship) to name a few. Much less studied is the perspective of the sending state on citizenship. States have attempted to incorporate emigrants back to their community via the offering of the possibility of maintaining or recuperating their citizenship (and nationality) of origin, thus obtaining a dual or multiple citizenship. Emigrants have responded by using all or some aspects of the citizenship offered by their countries of origin in what Fitzgerald (2009) has named *citizenship à la carte*, (see below); but these areas of research remain nascent.

Although not new, dual citizenship has expanded greatly since the end of the Cold War and is defined by the acquisition by an emigrant of the nationality of the receiving country while maintaining their original national citizenship. Historically dual citizenship has been disapproved by governments due to fear of divided loyalties and concomitant difficulties of state security (Shain 2005; Kivisto and Faist 2007; Samers 2010). The biggest concern was that the state could no longer "claim a monopoly on the membership of its citizenry" (Kivisto and Faist 2007: 103), thus impeding the state from using violent means to maintain its authority.

The increased acceptance of dual citizenship is related to the increase in migration flows, the end of empires and the shifting interest in the countries of origin. Nation-states increasingly realize that the preservation of their emigrants' citizenship is strongly related to their identification as member of a community of origin. This national identification with the *imagined community* (Anderson 1991) allows citizens to be more active in the defense of the homeland while abroad. Also, by maintaining their citizenships of origin, emigrants are more likely travel back to the home country and send remittances not only to families but also to encourage larger scale development projects as described above (Kivisto and Faist 2007; Fitzgerald 2009).

Emigrants have responded to this changing conceptualization of citizenship by capitalizing on some or all of what dual citizenship entails but we need to know much more about emigrants' knowledge, attitude, and practice of dual or multiple citizenships. Fitzgerald (2009) notes that the impact of large emigration flows and the increase in velocity of international transfers have compelled the nation-state to establish a new social contract with its citizens abroad, *citizenship à la carte*, originating in the need to maintain connection with emigrants it has also, at least indirectly, been seemingly enthusiastically adopted by the emigrants. The state will offer an association "based on voluntary membership, a choice of multiple political affiliation, and an emphasis in rights over obligations" (Fitzgerald 2009: 35), which provides emigrants with a mechanism of decision over when and how to send remittances, participate in elections, serve military conscription, and to send their children to be educated in the homeland and so forth

In sum, relations between the state of origin and its emigrants need further research. The changing characteristics of the state, the world's interdependency, social and financial remittances, the participation of emigrants in the development of their homeland, as well as the conditions of citizenship are spaces where emigrants and the state intersect. In a world of compressed time and space, the nation-state still has responsibilities towards its emigrants first among which is to protect its citizens at their place of destination. The right to not migrate involves providing individuals and families with the possibilities to live their lives in their places of origin and to achieve social and economic development without having to move to a different country. This includes the possibility to exercise its personal liberties free from want and fear which are at the center of the notion of human security and human rights.

Notes

1 In 2010, excluding migration from the former Soviet Union, the top migration corridors were Mexico–USA, Bangladesh–India, Turkey–Germany, China–Hong Kong, India–UAE, China–USA, Philippines–USA, Afghanistan–Iran, India–USA, Puerto Rico–USA, and West Bank/Gaza–Syrian Arab Republic (World Bank, 2011).
2 Article 13(2) of the Declaration states: "*Everyone has the right to leave any country, including his own, and to return to his country*" (www.un.org/en/documents/udhr/).
3 This Covenant entered in effect in 1976.
4 The World Bank notes that some high income countries do not report or provide data on remittances (Canada, Qatar, Singapore, and the UAE) even though they are important migrant destination counties.

References and further reading

Agunias, D. R. (2009) *Closing the Distance: How Governments Strengthen Ties with their Diasporas*. Washington, DC: Migration Policy Institute.
Anderson, B. (1991) *Imagined Communities: Reflections on the Origin and Spread of Nationalism*. London: Verso.
Bade, K. J. (2003) *Migration in European History*. Malden, MA: Blackwell.
Brand, L. A., (2006) *Citizens Abroad: Emigration and the State in the Middle East and North Africa*. Cambridge: Cambridge University Press.

Castles, S. and Miller, M. (2009) *The Age of Migration: International Population Movements in the Modern World*. New York: Guilford Press.

Chetail, V. (2003) "Freedom of movement and transnational perspectives: A human rights perspective." In T. A. Aleinikoff and V. Chetail (eds), *Migration and International Legal Norms*. The Hague: T.M.C. Asser, pp. 47–60.

Dale, S. (1991) "The Flying Dutchman dichotomy: The international right to leave v. the sovereign right to exclude" *Dickenson Journal of International Law* 9(2): 359–85.

De Hass, H. (2008) *Migration and Development: A Theoretical Perspective*. Working Paper No. 9, International Migration Institute, University of Oxford.

Délano, A. (2011) *Mexico and its Diaspora in the United States: Policies of Emigration Since 1848*. New York: Cambridge University Press.

——(2010) "Immigrant integration vs. transnational ties? The role of the sending state" *Social Research* 77(1): 237.

Docquier F. and Marfouk A. (2006) "International Migration by Education Attainment, 1990–2000." In C. Ozden and M. Schiff (eds), *International Migration, Remittances, and the Brain Drain*. Washington, DC: The World Bank, pp. 151–200.

Ellis, A. and Wall, A. (2007) *Voting from Abroad: The International IDEA Handbook*. Stockholm: International IDEA.

Fitzgerald, D. (2009) *A Nation of Emigrants: How Mexico Manages its Migration*. Berkeley, CA: University of California Press.

Gabaccia, D. R., Hoerder, D., and Walaszek, A. (2007) "Emigration and nation building during the mass migrations from Europe." In N. L. Green and F. Weil (eds), *Citizenship and Those Who Leave: The Politics of Emigration and Expatriation*. Urbana, IL: University of Illinois Press, pp. 63–90.

Gamlen, A. (2008) *Why Engage Diasporas?* COMPAS working papers, no. 63. Oxford, Centre on Migration, Policy and Society.

Gold, S. J. (2007) "Israeli emigration policy." In N. L. Green and F. Weil (eds), *Citizenship and Those Who Leave: The Politics of Emigration and Expatriation*. Urbana, IL: University of Illinois Press, pp. 283–304.

Goldin, I., Cameron, G., and Balarajan, M. (2011) *Exceptional People: How Migration Shaped Our World and Will Define Our Future*. Princeton, NJ: Princeton University Press.

González Gutiérrez, C. (ed.) (2006) *Relaciones Estado-diáspora: Aproximaciones Desde Cuatro Continentes*. Two Volumes. México, DF: Secretaría de Relaciones Exteriores.

Green, N. L. (2005) "The politics of exit: Reversing the immigration paradigm" *Journal of Modern History* 77(2): 263–89.

Hanson, G. (2008) *International Migration and Development*. Washington, DC: The International Bank for Reconstruction and Development.

Joppke, C. (2011) *The Role of the Sending State and Society in Immigrant Integration*. Analytic and Synthetic Notes CARIM-AS 2011/33. Florence: Robert Schuman Centre for Advanced Studies, European University Institute.

Kapur, D. (2010) *Diaspora, Development, and Democracy: The Domestic Impact of International Migration from India*. Princeton, NJ: Princeton University Press.

Ketkar, S. L. and Ratha, D. (2009) *Innovative Financing for Development*. Washington, DC: World Bank.

——(2011) "Diaspora bonds: tapping the diaspora during difficult times." In S. Plaza and D. Ratha (eds), *Diaspora for Development in Africa*. Washington, DC: World Bank, pp. 127–44.

Kivisto, P. and Faist, T. (2007) *Citizenship: Discourse, Theory, and Transnational Prospects*. Malden, MA: Blackwell Pub.

Lafleur, J. M. (2011) "Why do states enfranchise citizens abroad? Comparative insights from Mexico, Italy and Belgium" *Global Networks* 11(4): 481–501.

Levitt, P. (1998) "Social remittances: Migration driven local-level forms of cultural diffusion" *International Migration Review* 32(4): 926–48.

Massey, D. S., Arango, J., Hugo, G., and Kouaouci, A. (1993) "Theories of international migration: A review and appraisal" *Population and Development Review* 19(3): 431–66.

Marshall, T. H., (1964) *Class, Citizenship, and Social Development; Essays*. Garden City, NY: Doubleday.

Oestergaard-Nielsen E. ed. (2003) *International Migration and Sending Countries: Perceptions, Policies, and Transnational Relations*. Basingstoke: Palgrave Macmillan.

Pedraza, S. (2007) *Political Disaffection in Cuba's Revolution and Exodus*. New York: Cambridge University Press.

Portes, A. (2007) "Migration, development, and segmented assimilation: A conceptual review of the evidence" *The Annals of the American Academy of Political and Social Science* 610(1): 73–97.

Samers, M. (2010) *Migration*. London: Routledge.

Shain, Y. (2005) *The Frontier of Loyalty*. Ann Arbor, MI: The University of Michigan Press.

Sznajder, M. and Roniger, L. (2009) *The Politics of Exile in Latin America*. New York: Cambridge University Press.

The Economist (2011) "Milking migrants" *The Economist* August 20: 69.

Weber, M., (1947) *Max Weber: The Theory of Social and Economic Organization*. New York: Free Press.

Zolberg, A. R. (2007) "The exit revolution." In N. L. Green and F. Weil (eds), *Citizenship and Those Who Leave: The Politics of Emigration and Expatriation*. Urbana, IL: University of Illinois Press, pp. 33–60.

World Bank (2011) *Migration and Remittances Factbook 2011*. Washington, DC: World Bank.

35

Immigration and the welfare state in Western societies

Ethnic heterogeneity, redistribution and the role of institutions

Xavier Escandell and Alin M. Ceobanu

Introduction

During the first decade of this century, there has been increasing popular pressure for more restrictive immigration policies across the globe. While multiple issues have catalyzed the expanding ambivalence towards immigration world-wide, one important dimension of this unease stems from the perception that migrants pose a financial burden on the state. Debates over the type, extent, and timing of state-provided social services for immigrants reflect deep ideological divides in many countries. Those against the extension of welfare benefits to immigrants assert that programs attract immigrants (the "magnet hypothesis"), engender a "culture of dependency," and are an unsustainable strain on the state (Borjas 2002). These studies focus on cost–benefit analyses and assess the impact immigrants have on specific social protection programs. In contrast, others recognize the importance migrants have on the host societies' economy and the future sustainability of the welfare system (Bean and Stevens 2003). Moreover, many Western societies see immigration as a viable solution to the demographic challenge posed by growing elderly populations requiring services and a shrinking younger population whose labor and taxes help subsidize such resources (Castles and Miller 2003). In this chapter, we examine the debates on the role of immigration and the future sustainability, coverage, and configuration of existing welfare state programs on both sides of the Atlantic.

One strand of the social scientific scholarship examining the relationship between welfare state provisions and immigrant integration policies focuses on the repercussions of extending or limiting social benefits and rights to immigrants (Freeman 2009). The results of such scholarship are mixed. One key insight from the literature on social rights extension to migrants is that Western democracies face a "progressive dilemma" between sustaining an inclusive welfare state system (including, for example, health care, and public education) for some types of migrants, while simultaneously keeping popular support for welfare state policies (Brettell and Hollifield 2000). Some scholars observe that societies that extend social welfare benefits to migrants are likely to adopt universal personhood rights and tend to be more lenient regarding the type of membership they extend to migrants allowing dual citizenship, for example, as in the case of Sweden (Soysal 1994). Others show that in a context of increased immigration, there is a tendency to restrict social and political rights to immigrants (Freeman 2009). Still others show that robust welfare systems may result, in some cases, in more restrictive immigration policies over time (Koopmans 2010). What these diverse findings show is that how societies approach access to welfare benefits has repercussions for understanding how immigrants are integrated socially and into labor markets and also shapes public opinions towards immigration, immigrants, and what it means to be a member of the state (Sainsbury 2006).

In examining this relationship between welfare state systems and immigration policies, some have argued that the European social policy model is undergoing a process of "Americanization." In other words, the European public is increasingly expressing anti-immigrant sentiments which are tied to perceptions of how much immigrants use and benefit from social and welfare services (Freeman 2009). Welfare chauvinism may be due, in part, to the abandonment of Keynesian economic redistribution principles and the embrace of a more "American" neoliberal model regarding social policies in which attitudes of individual responsibility prevail (Wilson 1996). In the context of the United States, such individualistic approaches are congruent with popular views that robust welfare services are a drain on the economy. In the context of Europe, there may also, however, be other potential explanations which warrant further study. Contrary to their counterparts in the United States, Europeans may not necessarily want to dismantle the social welfare system and privatize services *per se*, but, rather, may wish to implement restrictive policies in order to protect it for citizens by excluding migrants' access to these services. While these ideological principles are subject to continued discussion, one key issue that can inform future policy developments is whether increased ethnic heterogeneity because of immigration erases the class-based in-group-solidarity necessary to sustain a universal welfare state system based on high taxation levels. Furthermore, in the absence of such solidarity towards immigrants, do Western democracies run the risk of perpetuating a system in which immigrants constitute the "new urban underclass?"

To address these issues, we explore several themes of actuality: the above mentioned liberal paradox western democracies face, the welfare magnet hypothesis and the emergence of welfare chauvinism from an empirical and cross-national comparative perspective. These themes are not exhaustive of the multiple nuances of the relationship between the state and immigration. They are, nonetheless, key in examining future policy developments in western societies. Given the extensive variations of institutional arrangement regarding the organization of social protection systems and immigration policies across countries, an investigation of the relationship between the welfare state and practices associated with entitlement, exclusion, and overall political and social membership is timely (Geddes 2003: 152). We conclude with remarks on how the state might respond to the challenges and opportunities posed by increased immigration to Western societies.

The liberal paradox and immigration regimes

Some scholars argue that forces of globalization and transnationalism have created both opportunities for the expansion of social rights to immigrants as well as the curtailment of such rights (Brettell and Hollifield 2000). They address this contradiction, arguing that as modern states deal with the forces of globalization, they are caught in a "liberal paradox." That is, states face increased pressures for economic openness (i.e., in trade, investments, and labor) while also experiencing demands for border "closure" as favored by powerful political actors and apprehensive publics. As

Hollifield *et al.* (2008: 68) argue, "the central challenge is how to maintain openness and at the same time protect the rights of individuals and citizens as well as denizens [non-citizens]." States are thus pulled between state-centric endogenous demands (e.g. immigration and border control policies) and supranational calls for an untethered market economy and greater attention to personhood and human rights (Soysal 1994). Public policies seeking to reconcile these tensions vary a great deal across countries leading to different integration outcomes in terms of labor market participation and overall social and political incorporation.

In the absence of unified global migration policies (and consequently a lack of coordination between developed and developing countries), it is unavoidable that some political con-stituencies will argue that certain migration flows are tied to levels of accessibility to social protection systems (Hollifield 2007). Efforts to pass Proposition 187 in California limiting immigrants' access to benefits; the 1996 passing of the Personal Responsibility and Work Opportunity Reconciliation Act (commonly known as the welfare reform act), where US citizenship became a criterion for eligibility to welfare; as well as immigration restrictions in some European countries (particularly those with universal welfare states and in particular those with strong pension schemes for the elderly) are examples of one approach to address these concerns (Gran and Clifford 2000). Similarly, since the European Union's expansion towards central and Eastern Europe, individual member states have temporarily imposed restrictions on workers from these new member states (to avoid what Boeri and Brücker (2005) call "welfare shopping").

Rising negative attitudes toward immigrants (and their use of welfare benefits) are paralleled by changing trends regarding actual use of benefits. While earlier studies in the United States showed that immigrants were less likely than natives to use welfare benefits (Tienda and Jensen 1986), recent studies have shown an increase in immigrants' use of certain programs (Van Hook *et al.* 1999). As Jennifer Van Hook (2003) shows, the actual impact of immigrants' usage of welfare *vis-à-vis* natives' is dependent on the type of immigrants (e.g. refugees versus economic migrants), familial poverty levels and whether individuals versus immigrant households are used as the unit of analysis (Van Hook 2003; see also Bean and Van Hook 1998). In Europe too, there is evidence showing that immigrants (especially non-EU immigrants) are increasingly becoming users of unemployment and family benefits (Boeri and Brücker 2005). However, it is important to note that immigrants' access to these benefits is often the result of their payroll taxed contributions to the national systems and that overall immigrant aggregate contributions often outweighs their levels of usage.

Cross-nationally there is great variation in the use of social protection systems, the types of institutional arrangements to ensure accessibility or restriction to benefits, as well as public per-ceptions of how rights to legal (and second generation) immigrants should be granted. For example, easier access to naturalization in Europe is tied to more restrictive attitudes towards extension of social rights to documented immigrants (Ceobanu and Escandell 2011). Just as public opinion pressures shape the future development of the welfare state, the structure and type of welfare state configuration are central to understand the effects that immigration inte-gration policies have on immigrants' labor market participation and their dependency of the welfare state (Koopmans 2011). Figure 35.1 shows this cyclical relationship. Thus, across Western societies, different institutional structures shape the types of social policies created to address migrants' social rights, participation in the labor market, and social and political integration into host societies which ultimately affect public perceptions (Soysal 1994; Sainsbury 2006).

Within the social sciences, scholars have proposed different typologies of welfare state regimes (see Arts and Gelissen 2002). Although not addressing how different regimes deal with immigra-tion per se, Esping-Andersen's (1990) seminal work has provided a useful typology, identifying

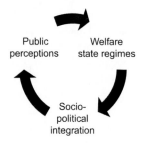

Public
perceptions

Welfare
state regimes

Socio-
political
integration

Figure 35.1 Mechanism between public perceptions, welfare state regimes, and immigrant's
socio-political integration

three types of welfare state regimes: liberal, conservative-corporatist, and social democratic. Based on Esping-Andersen's typology, we argue that two of its central characteristics (the degree of commodification and kind of social stratification and solidarity), can help explain the current and future development of immigration policy in Western societies (Moreno Fuentes and Bruquetas Callejo 2011). There is clear evidence that high decommodification (the degree to which social services are rendered as a social right) and strong universalism of Scandinavian, social-democratic countries influenced the development of an immigrant-inclusive type of welfare state (Arts and Gelisen 2002). In terms of stratification and solidarity, universal models with highly redistributive systems of benefits provide equal access to social rights for immigrants including unrestricted access to welfare state arrangements. However, the relative openness of the system is paralleled by strict immigration control in terms of entry and residency which are tied to access to benefits.

In contrast, when a system displays low decommodification levels (as in the liberal Anglo-Saxon model), higher individualistic tendencies and reliance on immigrants' labor market participation is the mechanism for access to benefits. The liberal model, based on low income redistribution fosters a division in the population between a minority of low-income state dependents and a majority able to afford private insurance plans (Arts and Gelisen 2002: 141). The system fosters stigmatization and prejudice by the majority population. Moreover, characterized by a minimal involvement of the state in providing services, immigrants are expected to be beneficiaries of specific governmental programs defined to remedy their situation of poverty and marginalization. The provisions of services (e.g., social work, community services, and means-tested benefits such as food stamps) are often highly politicized and many believe immigrants should not be entitled to them.

Third, moderate decommodification and reliance on the market participation to service its members is a predominant feature in the conservative-corporatist model associated with Central Western European countries such as Germany. Regardless of nationality, immigrants have access—like the rest of the population—to social protection benefits through their individual payroll taxes to the national system of social protection. Anti-immigrant discourses pursued by ultra-right-wing political elites, however, are increasingly being tied to the expansion of social protection benefits that target minorities. Moreover, some have argued for a fourth model commonly found in Mediterranean countries (e.g., Italy and Spain) which are characterized by universal health and education programs; unemployment benefits, and pension schemes coupled with the expectation that traditional family ties will act as providers of services. As in the previous model, immigrants benefit from their contributions to the national system of social security, and through residence, have access to health and education benefits (Moreno 2006). In the first decade of the new millennium, southern Europe has become a new site for anti-immigrant sentiments toward sub-Saharan, North African, and Latin American immigrants.

Not only does the *type* of welfare state regime influence the integration of migrants into host societies, but so too do different types of membership granted to immigrants. Several studies have explored how type of citizenship influences whether or not migrants have access to social benefits (Bloemraad *et al.* 2008). Soysal's (1994) seminal work on post-national forms of membership additionally draws attention to other political membership models which provide frameworks through which migrants are incorporated in the polity. Like Esping-Andersen and others, Soysal is interested in the variations across institutional structures. She distinguishes between membership models of organizational configuration: *Corporatist, Statist, Liberal,* and *Fragmental.* A central tenant in Soysal's classification is that migrants have different capacities and institutional constraints across countries to formally create advocacy groups that help them attain formal political representation in host societies. The centralized corporatist model is character-ized by the function of corporate groups, such as faith-based organizations and occupational associations, which play key roles in the incorporation process of new immigrants. In the statist model (as seen in France), the state is a centralized administrative unit that organizes incor-poration and is the main provider of social services. In contrast, the liberal model does not have a centralized administration or formal collective groups actively aiding the incorporation of migrants. It is important to note that not all countries neatly fit into these typologies. Hybrids exist, such as the case of Germany, which Soysal characterizes as statist-corporatist. In terms of organizational structure, Germany follows the patterns visible in corporatist models but the state plays a strong role in the political order bringing it more in line with statist models.

While there is some consensus that states confront the forces of globalization by adopting a more inclusive (post-national) form of membership, the literature corroborates that particularly since 9/11, there has been a resurgence of the view that citizenship regimes should play a pivotal role in determining foreigner's models of inclusion and access to welfare benefits (Bloemraad *et al.* 2008). In fact, one feature across the models discussed is that regardless of the institutional arrangement of their social protection systems and immigration policies, the surge of anti-immigrant sentiments are framed in terms of citizenship rights and benefits' access. With these differences in mind, and with the understanding that attitudes toward immigration are mediated by the larger contextual and institutional structures, we turn to one of the central controversies regarding attitudes toward immigration and perceived impact on the welfare state benefits.

The "magnet hypothesis" and welfare chauvinism

The notion that countries with robust welfare state systems are more desirable destinations for immigrants is a topic of significant debate. Using the United States as his empirical setting, George Borjas (2002) argues that countries with welfare-states characterized by high decommodification levels are in theory, more attractive to low-skilled immigrants whose socio-economic position is more vulnerable *vis-à-vis* non-immigrants. Borjas (2002: 1120) argues that "income differences across countries influence a person's decision of whether to move to the United States—regardless of whether these differences arise in the labor market or in the safety net provided by the welfare state." In addition, a more extreme position asserts that in order to alleviate potential abuses of the system, citizenship and naturalization are a necessary requirement for immigrants to receive welfare benefits and be eligible for affirmative action programs (Huntington 2004). Similarly, Koopmans (2011: 8) argues that immigrants' incentives for developing language proficiency and improving human capital are lower in these societies and foster a culture of dependency. From this perspective, countries with robust welfare state systems supposedly become a magnetic "pull factor" which attracts immigrants (Borjas 2002). Over time, concerns also arise that continued immigration flows will endanger the very financial existence of the welfare state system (Borjas 2002). From this perspective, countries with higher social inequality are more appealing to skilled immigrants, whereas countries with generous welfare states are more attractive to unskilled immigrants resulting in what Koopmans (2010) would characterize as a "negative selection" process.

Numerous scholars have questioned this opportunistic explanation for why immigrants naturalize and focus on specific favorable contexts that encourage migrants to seek out citizenship. Van Hook *et al.* (2006) using a social-contextual approach, show that immigrants' pursuit of naturalization depends not only on material benefits but also symbolic benefits (Bloemraad *et al.* 2008). For example, they show that in the United States, aggregate levels of favorable attitudes and public views towards immigration at the state level positively influence the likelihood of naturalization. This study further confirms that the probability of naturalization increased as much for welfare non-recipients as recipients of benefits, demonstrating that benefits levels do not significantly add to the motivations for naturalization beyond what access explains (p. 16). Furthermore, other research has shown that the level of highly skilled immigration is not associated with the benefit available in the receiving societies. Skilled immigrants are less interested in the generosity of the welfare state and are more favorably perceived by the more conservative political establishment (Chiswick 1999).

Focusing on intergroup relations and building on literature exploring social capital and generalized forms of trust, some scholars argue that as host societies become more ethnically heterogeneous, there are lower levels of support for welfare programs and generalized forms of trust/social capital (Putnam 2007). In many European countries, as immigrants have increasingly become users of welfare state benefits (Boeri and Brücker 2005), they also become the object of discrimination echoing the experiences ethnic and racial minorities have faced historically in the United States

The relationship between diversity, solidarity, and redistribution, as it specifically relates to migrants' use of welfare state programs and popular perceptions of this usage (including backlash toward welfare policies in general) has generated a great deal of scholarly debate in recent years (see Freeman 2009 for a review). As the United States and European societies have become more multi-ethnic, increasing lack of solidarity across ethnic and racial lines has blossomed and migrants are often blamed for the unsustainability of current levels of welfare provisions. Crepaz (2008) for example, argues that when minorities become the most predominant users of welfare benefits, they become the object of "nativist resentment," and forms of "welfare chauvinism" emerge. Nativist resentment refers to the pure rejection of minorities based on racial and religious attributes, and is often accompanied by the criminalization of immigrants (Crepaz 2008). Welfare chauvinism, on the other hand, is related to "the fear among groups in the native population (and settled immigrants) that certain new immigrant groups take away jobs, housing, and social services" (Faist 1994: 440). Thus, resentment stems from perceptions that immigrants benefit more than they contribute to the welfare state system (Crepaz and Damron 2009). As these perceptions become more widespread, the legitimacy and support for welfare state arrangements become more difficult to sustain.

In response to public scrutiny and the current global economic recession, some development economists (mainly conducting research in Africa), go so far as to argue that ethnic diversity is associated with poor economic conditions and social failures (La Ferrara 2002). Some sustain that growing ethnic diversity disrupts conceptions of community where ideas of "us," (the recognized and legitimate users of services) are pitted against the interests and contributions of "others" (strangers "undeserving" of such services). In the United States, as perceptions that minorities benefit more from the welfare system increase, the legitimacy of the very system has been put into question by majority populations (Alesina and La Ferrara 2002). Alesina and Glaeser (2004) demonstrated that significant differences in social spending between the United States and European countries could be accounted for by racial diversity. Moreover, migrants in comparison with other groups (e.g., the unemployed, elderly, and families in need of social assistance) have traditionally been perceived to be less "deserving" of state's benefits as they are also viewed as having put themselves in a situation of welfare dependency (van Oorschot 2008). Van Oorschot (2008) shows that Europeans perceive immigrants as less deserving of state assistance because they are in less need than others (e.g., elderly people), have contributed less to the system, and, overall, are perceived as less similar to the native population and less likeable, grateful, and compliant to European standards. Along these lines, Bay and Pedersen (2006) examined the relationship between attitudes toward unconditional income redistribution policies and ethnic heterogeneity in Norway. They found that many initial supporters of an unconditional basic income policy changed positions when told it would include non-citizens living in Norway (p. 432). Similarly, Gilens (1999) found that in the United States when recipients share common racial background with local populations, support towards the welfare state increases. New cross-national comparative studies seems to corroborate that multiethnic societies show higher levels of negative views toward redistributive policies (Freeman 2009).

Scholars examining the relationship between welfare states and socio-economic integration have been critiqued by others who argue that while there is potential conflict between ethnic diversity and solidarity, it remains debatable whether such tensions are universal or inevitable (Crepaz 2008; Johnson *et al.* 2010: 354). To understand the factors that mediate attitudes toward diversity and redistribution, these scholars argue that one needs to take into account the very institutions and policies aimed at regulating access to social rights (Crepaz 2008). For example, the socio-contextual approach assumes that state and country levels of support for immigration settlement might influence the type of responses immigrants have toward the very states hosting them and institutions providing services (Van Hook *et al.* 2006). From this perspective one can ask whether it is actually greater institutional and social support received by immigrants that determines the likelihood of naturalization rather than the opposite: where naturalization is viewed as a means to access social rights. In this light, institutions and welfare state regimes are thus perceived to have the capacity to shape attitudes and outcomes, such as community, solidarity, and national identity, among others (Crepaz and Damron 2009: 439). These scholars contend that the more welfare states decommodify individuals, the less welfare chauvinism there is (Crepaz 2008). Given that institutions and political environments set the stage for specific inter-group relationships to flourish, such environments can also diminish the development on anti-immigrant sentiment. Thus, countries with more advanced and universal social protection systems, avoid stigmatization and social categorization, and are more likely to foster social cohesiveness and help socially integrate immigrants into host societies. Crepaz and Damron (2009: 456) conclude that extensive welfare states are in a better position to absorb immigrants and reduce overall levels of welfare chauvinism *vis-à-vis* countries with more restricted welfare systems.

A recent study, by Koopmans (2010) shows a completely different picture, one in which labor market participation is lower in countries with more robust welfare state systems. In the Netherlands and Sweden, countries which have embraced multicultural integration policies, labor market participation is lower compared to Austria, Germany, and Switzerland which traditionally "chose to retain high barriers to migrants becoming full citizens and made residence rights dependent on performance in the labor market and the absence of a criminal record." Koopmans (2010) shows that in countries with limited welfare state systems, such as the UK, immigrants show better rates of labor participation. Other research, however, has been more tempered at establishing the causal mechanism between immigration and social and labor integration of immigrants. Regardless of the actual level of integration, immigration is becoming a source of political contention and may shape the future development of the welfare state especially as the financial crisis imposes further constraints to the European social policy model. While it is premature to state that Europe is undergoing a process of "Americanization," anti-welfare attitudes may become more predominant as western societies become more multiethnic. The challenge for liberal states is to continue to adopt more inclusive policies aimed at including non-citizens without lowering the provision levels for the majority of the population.

Future theoretical directions

There is a vast literature suggesting that the lack of social and labor integration incentivizes the development of welfare chauvinism among general populations. This is paralleled in the United States by growing activism of numerous political constituencies calling for the dismantlement of government programs and drastic cuts in public spending. In the context of Europe, however, these relationships need further theorizing. Are immigration and immigrants and their impact on the welfare state services a convenient narrative, what Pau Pierson would call an obfuscating strategy, for those with a neoliberal agenda? We argue that the realities of increasing ethnic and racial heterogeneity in contemporary western societies can serve as a political tool to pitch "natives" against "newcomers" in efforts to garner support for the retrenchment of the welfare state (Pierson 1994). Needless to say, as negative public perceptions towards immigration surge, states will continue to find themselves under pressure to legitimate their role in regulating and addressing inequality. In exploring the relationship between ethnic diversity and forms of solidarity and redistribution, the interplay of larger politico-institutional, socio-demographic, and economic factors need to be taken into account.

Politico-institutional and contextual considerations

The existing research discussed above, points in different directions when it comes the role institutions play in the integration of immigrants. While some argue that institutions and their policies can set the tone for better inclusion, others assert that generous welfare systems and multicultural policies create incentives for immigration but not necessarily assimilation. The risk of viewing citizens and non-citizens as two diametrically opposed constituencies to which the welfare regimes have to respond powerfully exemplifies the liberal paradox (Hollifield *et al.* 2008). Hollifield and colleagues (2008) further argue that if individual human and civil rights were to be abandoned, ignored or tampered with, then *liberal* states run the risk of undermining their own legitimacy and anti-immigration policies may come into conflict with their *raison d'être* (p. 97). While moving towards a "post-national" form of membership as proposed by Soysal (1994) does not fit the post 9/11 geopolitical environment, the very transformation of borders and identities as a result of transnationalism bring new challenges to the nation-state (Vertovec 2004). These new identities are transforming the very institution of citizenship and political membership. While western societies are increasingly allowing dual citizenship (Portes and DeWind 2007), even non-citizens and undocumented migrants have a fluid, complex, and contradictory relationship with the nation state. For example, in some countries undocumented migrants have access to medical benefits in public hospitals but at the same time may be on a national deportation list. So the very patient that is put on a waiting list for a kidney transplant may also be on another ministry's list to be deported. The nation-state is likely to be trapped in these contradictions as different types of immigrants are perceived by the general public as competitors for scarce resources.

We believe that further research is needed in examining the effects that multicultural policies (or lack thereof) have across different welfare systems in explaining majority-minority relations. For example, cross-national, comparative, longitudinal studies on public views toward the government's responsibility toward different beneficiaries (such as the sick, elderly, and the unemployed) *vis-à-vis* immigrants can help to tease out the politico-institutional aspects of intergroup relations (Blekesaune 2007).

Boeri and Brücker (2005) argue that "welfare shopping" can be prevented through minimal contributions and compensations (e.g., increase the generosity of unemployment benefits in the high immigration areas) and can have a positive effect on reducing negative attitudes toward immigration. They suggest tapping into Europe's social cohesion funds to finance assistance schemes for individuals from member states that do not have such benefits (e.g., means-tested benefits) but this can only be materialized if the European social policy model based on social transfers is maintained, financially supported and endorsed. Boeri and Brücker (2005: 673) suggest a policy scheme where:

> new members that do not have social assistance of the last-resort type (i.e., means-tested assistance that is paid without conditions on employment history, age or health, for example) could be required to introduce minimum guaranteed income schemes (MGI) at home. This would reduce the incentives to move for the most disadvantage citizens in the new member nations (these often include ethnic minorities with a high propensity to move).

The migration that is driven by access to social benefits in receiving societies thus requires coordination between sending and receiving societies. They further suggest that such coordination is similar to the approach used by the United States toward Puerto Rico or by Western Länder in the case of German unification (Boeri and Brücker 2005). Debates about establishing a similar US "welfare reform act" in the context of Europe is especially relevant as the EU revisits proposals to integrate Turkey into the union and continues to experience demographic pressures from North African countries.

Other pressing theoretical problems that require further research concern the directionality of the causal mechanisms between the actual institutional structures of the welfare state, immigrants' labor market integration, and public attitudes toward redistributive policies. As shown in Figure 35.1, collective values are a motivating force in determining the institutional structures of the welfare state. These, in turn, are key for immigrants' political integration which ultimately affects the general public perceptions toward immigration. The circular nature of these processes call for prudence when trying to establish what factors are causing which effects. To argue that naturalization, for example, is part of a strategic calculation to access welfare benefits may, in fact, be more the result of more inviting contexts in terms of overall attitudes and labor market opportunities. Jennifer Van Hook and colleagues argue that the recommended policies derived from focusing on naturalization as a path toward dependence, is short sighted. Rather, they advocate for the social and economic complexities underlying migrants' decision making processes. Further research is needed to tease out these processes.

Socio-psychological considerations

Research on welfare state and immigration needs to further decipher whether immigration operates as the sole cause or as a mediating contextual factor in changing attitudes toward the welfare state (Freeman 2009). As suggested by Freeman (2009) more empirical and comparative research is needed to assess the interrelationships between public's attitudes toward welfare states and the dynamics of competition and conflict. In expressing competition and conflict, individual level social psychological theories that explore inter- and intra-group dynamics can continue to provide insights about what micro level forces (e.g., national identity or intergroup contact) explain welfare chauvinism (see Ceobanu and Escandell 2010 for a review of the literature on key determinants of anti-immigrant sentiment). In the Canadian case, for example, national identity has considerable significance for attitudes toward the welfare state. Contradicting some of the literature on nationalism and intergroup solidarity, Johnson *et al.* (2010) find that national identity and the welfare state are mutually supportive, in the context of a country with a liberal nationalism (characterized by strong trust towards government as one important dimension of people's ideas of belonging). These findings are not corroborated by cross-national research exploring similar issues. Nationalistic tendencies (national and regional) tend to be associated with anti-immigrant sentiment, and help explain the rejection of multiculturalism, the increase in Islamophobia and overall incorporation of exclusivist postulates in ultra-right-wing and main stream political parties. In efforts to establish future empirical studies to measure the relationships between welfare state attitudes and ideas of redistribution, a focus on national identity requires a deep exploration of each country's history and culture.

Finally, a focus on intergroup relations and the positive and negative aspects of social capital is in order. The literature on social capital can enlighten the mechanism that foster inter-group cooperation (or what sociologist Alejandro Portes would call "bounded solidarity") in increasingly multi-ethnic societies. This would help clarify whether welfare programs aimed at providing resources to immigrant communities are fostering smoother processes of social and labor integration, or whether (as Koopmans suggests), they are creating a new urban underclass of dependent non-citizens that are socially, culturally, and geographically segregated.

References and further reading

Alesina, A. and La Ferrara, E. (2002) "Who trusts others?" *Journal of Public Economics* 85(2): 207–34.

Alesina, A. and Glaeser, E. (2004) *Fighting Poverty in the US and Europe: A World of Difference*. Oxford: Oxford University Press.

Arts, W. A. and Gelissen, J. (2002) "Three worlds of welfare capitalism or more? A state-of-the-art report" *Journal of European Social Policy* 12(2): 137–58.

Bay, A. H. and Pedersen, W. (2006) "The limits of social solidarity" *Acta Sociologica* 49(4): 419–36.

Bean, F. D. and Stevens, G. (2005) *America's Newcomers and the Dynamics of Diversity*. New York: Russell Sage Foundation.

Blekesaune, M. (2007) "Economic conditions and Public attitudes to welfare policies" *European Sociological Review* 23(3): 393–403.

Bloemraad, I., Korteweg, A., and Yurdakul, G. (2008) "Citizenship and immigration: Multiculturalism, assimilation, and challenges to the nation-state" *Annual Review of Sociology* 34: 153–79.

Boeri, T. and Brücker, H. (2005) "Why are Europeans so tough on migrants?" *Economic Policy* 20(44): 629–703.

Bommes, M. and Geddes, A. (eds) (2000) *Immigration and Welfare: Challenging the Borders of the Welfare State* (Routledge/EUI Studies in the Political Economy of Welfare). London and New York: Routledge.

Borjas, G. (2002) "Welfare reform and immigrant participation in welfare programs" *International Migration Review* 36(4): 1093–123.

Brettell, C. B. and Hollifield, J. F. (2000) "Introduction." In C. B. Brettell and J. F. Hollifield (eds) *Migration Theory: Talking Across Disciplines*. New York: Routledge, pp. 1–26.

Castles, S. and Miller M. J. (2003) *The Age of Migration: International Population Movements in the Modern World*. 3rd edition. New York: The Guilford Press.

Ceobanu, A. M. and Escandell, X. (2010) "Comparative analysis of public attitudes towards immigrants and immigration using multinational survey data: A review of theories and research" *Annual Review of Sociology* 36(1): 309–28.

——(2011) "Paths to citizenship? Public views on the extension of rights to legal and second-generation immigrants in Europe" *The British Journal of Sociology* 62(2): 221–40.

Chiswick, B. R. (1999) "Are immigrants favorably self-selected?" *American Economic Review* 89(2): 181–85.

Crepaz, M. M. L. (2008) *Trust Beyond Borders: Immigration, the Welfare State and Identity in Modern Societies*. Ann Arbor, MI: University of Michigan Press.

Crepaz, M. M. L. M. and Damron, R. (2009) "Constructing tolerance: How the welfare state shapes attitudes about immigrants" *Comparative Political Studies* 42(3): 437–63.

Esping-Andersen, G. (1990) *The Three Worlds of Welfare Capitalism*. Cambridge: Polity Press.

Faist, T. (1994) "Immigration, integration and the ethnicization of politics" *European Journal of Political Research* 25(4): 439–59.

Faist, T., Gerdes, J., and Beate, R. (2007) "Dual citizenship as a path-dependent process." In A. Portes and J. DeWind (eds), *Rethinking Migration: New Theoretical and Empirical Perspectives*. New York: Berghahn Books, pp. 90–121.

Freeman, G. P. (2009) "Immigration, diversity, and welfare chauvinism" *The Forum* 7(3): article 7.

Geddes, A. (2003) "Migration and the welfare state in Europe" *Political Quarterly* 74(1): 150–62.

Gilens, M. (1999) *Why Americans Hate Welfare: Race, Media, and the Politics of Antipoverty Policy*. Chicago, IL: University of Chicago Press.

Gran, B. and Clifford, E. (2000) "Rights and ratios: Evaluating the relationship between social rights and immigration" *Journal of Ethnic and Migration Studies* 26(3): 417–47.

Hollifield, J. F. (2007) "The emerging migration state." In A. Portes and J. DeWing (eds), *Rethinking Migration: New Theoretical and Empirical Perspectives*. New York: Berghahn Books, pp. 62–89.

Hollifield, J. F., Hunt, V. F., and Tichenor, D. J. (2008) "The liberal paradox: Immigrants, markets, and rights in the United States" *SMU Law Review* 67.

Huntington, S. P. (2004) *Who are We? America's National Identity and the Challenges it Faces*. New York: Simon and Schuster.

Johnson, R., Banting, K., Kymlicka, and Soroka, S. (2010) "National identity and support for welfare state" *Canadian Journal of Political Science* 42(2): 349–77.

Koopmans, R. (2010) "Trade-offs between equality and difference: Immigrant integration, multiculturalism and the welfare state in cross-national perspective" *Journal of Ethnic and Migration Studies* 36(1): 1–26.

La Ferrara, E. (2002) "Self help groups and income generation in the informal settlements of Nairobi" *Journal of African Economics* 11(1): 61–89.

Moreno Fuentes, F. J. and Bruquetas Callejo, M. (2011) *Immigration and Welfare State in Spain*. Barcelona: Obra Social 'La Caixa".

Moreno, L. (2006) "The model of social protection in Southern Europe: Enduring characteristics?" *Revue Française des Affaires Socials* 1(5): 73–95.

Pierson, P. (1994) *Dismantling the Welfare State? Reagan and Thatcher and the Politics of Retrenchment*. Cambridge: Cambridge University Press.

Portes, A. and DeWind, J. (eds) (2007) 'A cross-Atlantic dialogue: The progress of research and theory in the study of international migration.' In A. Portes and J. DeWind (eds), *Rethinking Migration: New Theoretical and Empirical Perspectives*. New York: Berghahn Books, pp. 1–8.

Putnam, R. (2007) "E. pluribus unum: Diversity and community in the twenty first century—the 2006 Johan Skytte Prize Lecture" *Scandinavian Political Studies* 30(2): 137–74.

Sainsbury, D. (2006) "Immigrants' social rights in comparative perspective: Welfare regimes, forms of immigration and immigration policy regimes" *Journal of European Social Policy* 16(3): 229–44.

Soysal, Y. N. (1994) *The Limits of Citizenship: Migrants and Postnational Membership in Europe*. Chicago, IL: University of Chicago Press.

Tienda, M. and Jensen, L. (1986) "Immigration and public assistance participation: Dispelling the myth of dependency" *Social Science Research* 15(4): 372–400.

Van Hook, J (2005) "Immigrant welfare receipt: Implications for policy." In F. D. Bean and G. Stevens, *America's Newcomers and the Dynamics of Diversity*. New York: Russell Sage Foundation, pp. 66–93.

Van Hook, J. and Bean, F. (1998) "Welfare reform and supplemental security income receipt among immigrants in the United States." In H. Kurthen, J. Fijalkowski, and G. G. Wagner (eds), *Immigration, Citizenship and the Welfare State in Germany and the United States*. Stamford, CT: JAI Press, pp. 139–158.

Van Hook, J., Brown, S. K., and Bean, F. D. (2006) "For love of money? Welfare reform and immigrant naturalization" *Social Forces* 85(2): 643–66.

Van Hook, J., Glick, J. E., and Bean, F. D. (1999) "Immigrant and native public assistance receipt: How the unit of analysis affects research findings" *Demography* 36(1): 111–20.

Van Oorschot, W. (2008) "Solidarity towards immigrants in European welfare states" *International Journal of Social Welfare* 17(1): 3–14.

Vertovec, S. (2004) "Migrant transnationalism and modes of transformation" *International Migration Review* 38(3): 907–1001.

Wilson, W. J. (1996) *When Work Disappears: The World of the New Urban Poor*. New York: Vintage.

Part VIII
Maintaining links across borders

Until relatively recently, most scholars and policy makers assumed that migrants maintained extensive relations with only a single nation state—that of their country of origin (for short-term sojourners) and the host society (for longer-term settlers). In fact, the notion of permanent settlement and straight-line assimilation has been so mythologized in the classic countries of migration that there is a dearth of public awareness about the large fraction of migrants who returned to their countries of origin during the late nineteenth and early twentieth centuries. However, a growing body of research and theorizing has come to recognize that various communities maintain international social, economic, political, familial, religious, and identification links. Consequently, migrants' maintaining links across borders has become a vital area of migration research.

Some individuals and groups are able to work legally and even maintain citizenship in several countries while others must do so while trying to elude authorities. Nevertheless, the ubiquity of globe-spanning networks and accessible forms of communication means that many persons and groups who do not regularly cross borders often exchange affiliations, information, and resources with those in disparate locations while also identifying with far away people and places that they may or may not have actually visited.

To better understand such relationships, scholars have advanced an approach called "transnationalism." Stressing the globalization of political, economic, social, and cultural life, the speed and low cost of modern communication and transportation, the rights revolution that has opened opportunities for incorporation and self-determination among the women and men of formerly excluded ethnic and nationality groups, and the acceptance of expatriates in the polity of many nations, the concept of transnationalism emphasizes the various networks and links (demographic, political, economic, cultural, familial) that exist between two or more locations. From this perspective, migration is not a single, discrete event involving movement from one geographically and socially bounded locality to another. Instead, transnational communities embody and exchange concerns, relationships, resources, needs, and often people immersed in multiple settings.

An alternative model for understanding the interconnection of dispersed people is diaspora. Originally associated with groups encountering forced exile from their homeland—as in the case of Jews, Africans, Armenians, and Indians—in recent years, scholars have applied this concept in a broader if less specific manner to codify a range of interconnections between people, cultures, and nations to represent feelings of longing and displacement but also the potential for reconnection, advancement, and liberation common to migrants and exiles in many settings.

Diaspora and transnationalism are closely related and sometimes overlap—as is the case among Jews who travel back and forth between Israel and North America. However, studies concerning transnationalism often see migrants as pragmatic and emphasize their agency, while those focusing on diaspora describe feelings of loss and dislocation as ubiquitous.

This section features three chapters that explore migrants' maintenance of links across international borders. Gabriel Sheffer's contribution concerns the historical development of diasporas. Drawing on numerous case studies, he explores their transformation as they interact with various communities and nation states and maintain connections with both members and local environments.

Thomas Faist's chapter contends that interest in transnationalism does not follow a coherent theoretical vision, but, rather, involves an eclectic examination of various cross-border phenomena. He identifies major debates associated with the concept, including transnationalism's relationship to globalization, its implications for the viability of the nation state, and the extent to which it is compatible with or likely to supersede identity-related formulations including assimilation and multiculturalism.

Finally, Janet Salaff's chapter describes how the analysis of returned migrants has evolved from an early period when researchers assumed that decision-making concerned maximizing the financial rewards associated with two known environments, to the present era, when rational calculation receives less emphasis and researchers deploy a multiform and nuanced understanding of the process that emphasizes social relationships. These include migrants' involvements in social networks, the impact of peer groups, families, life course issues, gender, and one's status in either setting. The author instructs that rather than being the outcome of careful calculations, migration decisions are often the result of spontaneous or circumstantial concerns. Return migration may be the enduring consequence of a brief "visit" or the availability of a place to stay rather than a considered decision to alter one's life.

36

The historical, cultural, social, and political backgrounds of ethno-national diasporas

Gabriel Sheffer

Working definition

This chapter discusses the substantial importance of the historical backgrounds of ethno-national-religious diasporas, as far as their current existence and their growing roles, actions, and influence on both their homelands and hostlands are concerned. The main related argument is that this aspect of diasporism needs much additional research.

In most theoretical and analytical deliberations and discussions of the nature, composition, behavior, and activities of ethno-national-religious or transnational diasporas there is a strong tendency to argue that the diasporic phenomenon is not old, and to focus on the diasporas' recent and current situation. Thus, there are relatively few attempts to consider the age of the diasporic phenomenon and to categorize various types of diasporas and accordingly to study their historical backgrounds and their impacts on their current states of affairs and positions. Only recently some attention has been given to the very basic fact that the historical background of the diasporic phenomenon in general, and of each diaspora in particular, has an impact on their current situation.

In this vein, the main purpose of this chapter is to generally examine the histories and the cultural, social, and political backgrounds of current "historical" and "modern" established and "incipient" ethno-national diasporas.

Approaches to the study of diasporas

The following is a clarification of the main approaches to the study of the historical emergence, nature, and characterizations of diasporic entities. The essential purpose here is to show that diasporism is an ancient phenomenon, that some "old" diasporas still exist and that the historical factor has significant influence on all diasporas.

The initial study of the characteristics of diasporas began with what might be called the "Diasporic approach." Later the "Transnationalist approach" has emerged. More recently there is growing recognition that these two approaches should be unified or at least coordinated.

This chapter follows the ethno-national-religious approach to the diasporic phenomenon. Thus, following are the main factors of a general diasporas' profile that have historical consequences: the identity of the ethno-national members of diasporas is a non-essentialist pri-mordial one. Such ethno-national-religious diasporas are the outcome of either voluntary migration (e.g., Irish and Turks) or expulsion from their homeland (e.g., the Jews and the Palestinians). These diasporic entities are formed and become established only after migrants voluntarily, but explicitly, decide to permanently settle in one or a number of hostlands. In most cases, the decision to permanently live in a hostland is taken by individuals, families, and small groups after an initial period of residence and adjustment in the hostland. Such decisions need the acceptance and confirmation of the "receiving" hostlands. Unless they become the undisputed majority that controls the country/state to which they emigrated, diasporas remain minority groups. Their core members preserve their ethno-national-religious identity and communal solidarity. Based on a combination of historical primordial psychological/mythical and instrumental factors, the ethnic identity and communal solidarity serve as the twin foun-dations for maintaining diasporas' collective affinities and connections. To maintain and pro-mote such affinities, constant contacts among the diasporas' elites and activist grassroots groups are avowedly preserved. Such ongoing contacts have cultural, social, economic, and political significance for the diasporans, for their hostlands, for their homelands, for other diasporic communities of the same origin, and for other interested and involved actors. These contacts also provide the essential grounds for all activities of diasporic organizations to deal with various aspects of the entities' cultural, social, economic, and political needs in a way that usually complements but at times also contradicts and clashes with the interests of hostlands and their governments. Diasporas adopt and try to implement coherent strategies. In most cases, they apply the communalist strategy. The emergence of diasporic organizations creates the potential for the development of multiple authority and loyalty patterns. To avoid undesirable conflicts with the norms and laws established by the dominant social group and its political organizations in hostlands, most diasporas accept these countries' social and political "rules of the game." At certain periods in their history of integration in hostlands, real or alleged dual, divided, and ambiguous loyalties may create tensions between various social and political groups in the host country and the diaspora. Sometimes such confrontations lead to the intervention of homelands on behalf of their diasporas, or to intervention in the affairs of "their" diasporas. Finally and most importantly, the capability of diasporas to mobilize their members in order to promote or defend their own or their homelands' interests in their hostlands will result in the formation of either conflictual or cooperative triadic, or even four-sided, relationships and exchanges invol-ving homeland, diaspora, hostland, and other interested actors. These relations are now an inherent part of international politics, and influence the behavior of all parties involved.

Some writers in this field classified the diasporas either according to their origin and causes of their emergence and establishment, or according to the cultural, social, political, and economic functions that they perform in their hostlands. Rather, the following distinctions should be made between diasporas, in general, and between the various internal subgroups of diasporas, in particular. The first distinction is between "old/historical," "modern," and "incipient" diasporas. The second distinction is between "state-linked" and "stateless" diasporas. The third distinction applies to the various groups and individuals constituting each diaspora—the "core" and various "peripheries."

The actual historical backgrounds of current diasporas

"Old" diasporas

For many centuries the term "diaspora" was applied almost only to the dispersed ethno-national-religious Greek and especially to the Jewish diasporic entities. During the last decades, however, the term has become exceedingly popular and has been applied to numerous dispersed entities. This is the case not only among scholars in this sphere, but also among many individuals, social groups, politicians, communication persons, and diasporans themselves. By accepting this term and notion, there is a growing realization that the Jewish diaspora is not the only surviving "old historical" diaspora and that it has various similarities to other diasporas of "the same age and younger."

Probably later than the formation of the Jewish diaspora, but still during ancient times, other quite large ethnic diasporas were formed. Indians were among those who formed an old historical diaspora. The Chinese began their emigration out of China and the establishment of a Chinese diaspora also during ancient times. Another well-known old historical diaspora is that of the Armenians. Moreover, various African tribes moved from their countries of origin to other locations and established what also might be called old-historical diasporas. Most of these and other old ethnic diasporas have continued to exist until now.

The first impact of the historical longevity of diasporic existence is connected to their genetic origin. Thus for example, members of these diasporas, especially the Indians, Chinese, and Africans, have maintained their facial and physical marks, which, on the one hand, distinguish them from other ethnic groups in their hostlands, a factor that in certain cases creates tensions and conflicts between the diasporans and the local people, and on the other hand, these features encourage comradeship and cooperation between the diasporans who belong to the same entity.

The later development of modern nationalism (as from the seventeenth or eighteenth centuries) only strengthened the ethno-national-religious connections and ties between members of such historical diasporas and added the modern national element to the ethnic-religious ones that marked the very early beginnings of these entities. In turn, these ethno-national basic factors have strengthened the non-geographical communal affinity, cohesion, and cooperation within these entities and between them and their homelands.

The history and the memories of a diaspora's establishment and survival and especially the ingrained memory of the land of origin, strengthen the non-assimilated core diasporans' connections to their actual or perceived homelands. Members of historical diasporas have maintained legends and true stories about their homelands that are repeated, especially during the various holidays that diasporans celebrate, during religious affairs, and during family and group meetings. Furthermore, these memories are emphasized especially in the educational programs that the diasporas initiate and operate in their hostlands. In certain cases, the result is an urge of diasporans to return to their actual or perceived homeland. These have been the cases, for example, of the Chinese, African, Armenian, Jewish, Indian, and even the Japanese diasporas.

Yet another aspect of the impact of the history of those old diasporas is the painful memories of acute troubles and conflicts that such diasporans have experienced and suffered either in their homelands or hostlands. Such memories influence the way in which these people regard the entire world and their conception of their ethno-national-religious individual and group characteristics.

The historical memories and perspectives that are continuously embraced by diasporans also have substantial impacts on the current culture that these diasporans maintain. This is a result of diasporans' efforts to actually follow historical and cultural patterns. Thus, in addition to their churches, mosques, and synagogues, historical diasporas have established special schools, educational institutes, and organizations for their young and older children. Among other major issues that they are teaching in these special educational institutes is the ethno-national-religious history of the diaspora and its ramifications, the timing and reasons for its members' emigration from the homeland and the basic cultural features of the entire nation.

On both the emotional and the formal and informal levels, the histories of these entities help to strengthen the existence and cohesion of the core groups and the individual members of these entities. Both historical happy memories about good occurrences in the diasporas and stories and memories of disasters strengthen the communal connections and tendencies.

All these historical images and memories have also practical organizational and behavioral meanings. From the organizational point of view, the social and political conflicts between diasporans and hostlands' societies, rulers, and especially governments, and the involved persecutions and deprivations, encourage these entities to establish and maintain their non-geographical cultural and social boundaries and augment cohesion. As far as possible, such diasporans are doing it through well established organized groups and institutions.

Modern diasporas

Some historians who have written about diasporas argue that the "early modern era" of diasporism started at the end of the fifteenth century and lasted until the late eighteenth century. The argument is that this phase in the history of diasporism began with the European discovery of the Americas and later of other continents and countries. It has been argued that following these discoveries there started a growing process of founding the European empires and colonies. In turn, the urge to establish such empires and its actual consequences resulted in the movement of growing numbers of individuals and groups to help in conquering and colonizing more territories and to settle and control them. Such were the cases of the British, Spanish, Portuguese, and French colonies. These migrations enhanced the eventual emergence of modern diasporas rather than of kin-groups in adjacent territories.

The contacts between "colonial" diasporas and their homelands were maintained partly by the existence of relatively strong governments that controlled both those empires and homelands. Among other things, such as military units, equipment, and weapons, homelands' rulers and governments provided means of communications between the homelands and the diasporas. Such networks were, and still are, essential for the continued existence, development, and especially for the relations of diasporans with their homelands. Such processes and linkages between diasporans and their homelands were further enhanced during the early days of the emergence of modern nation-states. The Treaty of Utrecht in 1713 confirmed the existence of ethnicity and ethnic groups that served as the basis for the development of ethno-national states and consequently of "their" ethno-national diasporas.

Relevant for the analysis in this chapter is the combination of three main developments that began to occur as from the mid-eighteenth century. The first development was the European Revolutions of the mid-nineteenth century, known as the "1848 Spring of Nations." This development included a series of political upheavals throughout the European continent, described as a revolutionary wave. While most of the immediate political effects of those revolutions were reversed, the long-term reverberations of the events were far-reaching. These developments marked the beginnings of modern ethno-national homelands for both the local people and for people in the growing diasporas. During that period the numbers of migrants increased quite significantly.

The second development occurred during the nineteenth century, when the Spanish, Portuguese, and Ottoman empires began to crumble and the Holy Roman and Mughal empires collapsed. A main consequence was that "their" diasporas gained greater freedom and autonomy and even sovereignty over the areas where they resided permanently. It meant that settlers began to develop new local identities and reduced their connections with their homelands. It raised the significant question—that is still relevant today—to what extent are these diasporas of their homelands? This applies especially to British, French, Spanish, and Portuguese settlers in North and South America. In any event, following the Napoleonic Wars and the French defeat in Europe, the British Empire became the world's largest and leading power that encouraged British emigration.

The third development was connected to the concurrent processes of industrialization and the emergence of new technologies. Among other things, these developments impacted the ongoing development of new means of transportation and communication, which contributed to the easiness of traveling and communication, and consequently to an increase in waves of migrants to existing imperial or colonial territories as well as to new independent states. Those migrants of different ethno-national backgrounds began to establish and organize diasporas in a more modern fashion.

In most cases, people who previously were citizens of the states that established the empires and colonies soon became the local citizens of the independent or autonomous states that had been formed by the imperial and colonial powers. Thus, as has been noted above, there is still an ongoing debate whether these groups can be regarded as diasporas. These were the cases of the British in what later became the independent United States, Canada, and Australia, and the Spanish and Portuguese in various areas in South America. In Canada the situation became even more complicated, especially as far as the French Canadians thought of themselves and have been regarded by France. In all these cases there have been debates whether the people of French and British origin are French or British diasporas or they are only of French and British origins. However, the emigrants from other homelands to these new states, who were not fully integrated or totally assimilated, actually formed modern organized diasporic entities.

During the late nineteenth and early twentieth centuries there occurred massive ethnic crises that caused new large refugee and migrant movements and therefore an increase of the complexity of their individual, group, and communal realities. On the one hand, this occurred due to the rise of nationalism and racism that caused critical wars, among them the two world wars. On the other hand, and in an interconnected fashion, these large waves of migration were caused by social and economic crises in homelands and by the migrants' hopes to have a better living in hostlands.

Later in the twentieth century there occurred the movement of millions of ethnic refugees and voluntary migrants across Europe, Asia, and northern Africa. Many of these migrants went to the Americas, which became states ready and even encouraging the absorption of such people. Such groups included Jews, Gypsies, and other ethnic minorities from areas under Axis control, as well as various ethnic minorities from areas under Russian and Soviet control following the Russian Revolution, and continuing through the mass forced resettlements under Stalin; Germans; Polish people forced by the Soviet Union to leave their homeland eastwards of the Curzon Line; and Armenians living in the region controlled by the Ottoman Empire The same applies to Chinese, Palestinians, Iraqis, Iranians, Chechens, Albanians, Afghanis, etc.

During the Cold War era large groups of refugees continued to move from areas of inter- and intra-state wars and conflicts, especially from Third World states all over Africa, the Middle East and East Asia. During those periods the migrants had to mostly rely on themselves for their survival and functioning, and only partially on their established or incipient diasporic groups and organizations. In most cases their homelands were engaged with their own difficult problems and therefore there was almost no awareness of whether their diasporas were in trouble, or should be helped and provided with various resources. Thus, most homelands remained indifferent and inactive *vis-à-vis* their diasporas. Simultaneously, most diasporas were not expecting a great deal of intervention in their affairs or on their behalf in those hostlands.

More recently, there has been a noticeable change in this respect. Now most homelands show a growing interest in "their" diasporas. At the same time, members of the historical and modern diasporas also began to show greater interest in their homelands. Therefore, many homeland governments have established special ministries or agencies to develop and keep close relations with their diasporas. For example, this has been the case in France, Italy, Greece, Japan, and Israel. The main reason for this pattern is that homelands have realized that they can culturally, socially, politically, and economically benefit from such close relations, especially when nationalism and ethnicity are not disappearing but rather regaining their power and influence. For their part, diasporas, especially in more democratic and liberal states can and on many occasions want to maintain such relations with their homelands. Also the diasporas' close relations with their homelands benefit those homelands' security and ability to gain cultural and social inspiration, help, and actual resources, especially when these diasporas face persecution or conflict in the hostland.

Incipient diasporas

One of the main results of the above mentioned more recent large waves of voluntary and imposed migrations is the existence and formation of new "incipient diasporas." The main characteristics of these emerging entities distinguishing them from the historical and modern diasporas are the various aspects of their adaptation to their new position in their hostlands, their integration there, and their continuous relations and contacts with their homelands.

During the first years that they live in their new residence locations in hostlands most migrants from the same ethno-national origins are strongly inclined to maintain close relations with their relatives, kin-groups, and former communities in their homelands. Thus, in many cases, the personal history and historical memories of these new diasporans play a major role in their organization and behavior, which is part of their ethno-national identity. When these migrants have not been forcefully expelled from their homelands and when they have relatives there, they are strongly inclined to maintain close relations and connections with the people in their homeland. This is the general inclination since they are not sure whether they will succeed in permanently settling in the hostland and thus may need to return to their homelands. Thus they feel and think that they may need the support of their homeland to ensure their safety and interests during the first years in their hostlands.

In contrast, while these migrants are getting used to the new hostland that does not fully or largely reject them, the first and second generations begin to emotionally and rationally ponder and decide about their degree of integration into the hostland. At that point, one of the main considerations is whether to permanently settle in the hostland or to keep the option of an eventual return to their homeland. Then, when the actual situation and chances for permanently residing in the hostland are adequate, a decision to permanently settle means searching for the best patterns of integration and of these patterns' possible impacts on the maintenance of their ethno-national identity and contacts with the homeland. Reasonable integration and simultaneous wish to remain connected to their homeland, is the main inclination of many first and second generations of these migrants. Eventually, these people become the core members of the emerging diaspora. The migrants who are not anxious to maintain their pure ethno-national identity and contacts with the homeland form the peripheries of those emerging diasporas. Some of them eventually fully integrate in the hostland culture and society and change their identity, and consequently they are lost to their emerging diaspora.

In most cases the next step made by the core members of these incipient diasporas is to organize. More recently, in many cases these steps are made with the support of the homeland that is also interested in keeping the closest possible connections with "their" diaspora. This is partly because of the homelands' own interests and partly because of their concern with those migrants who are still very closely connected to the homeland and may consider a possible return, and who in the meantime support their relatives, kin, and communities at the homeland. Though these days migrants who stay for longer periods in their respective hostlands tend to establish voluntary organizations quite rapidly after their arrival, the main energy and resources invested in this aspect occurs when a quite reasonable number of core members are permanently settled in the hostland, maintain close relations among themselves, and are ready to cooperate and act together. Such a development is an important step on the way to becoming permanent modern diasporas.

The first informal and formal networks and organizations that incipient diasporans shape and establish are mainly in the field of communication. These include newspapers, radio, and television stations, and Internet networks. The main purposes of these organizations and networks are to provide the diasporans and their homelands means for regular communication with each other. Simultaneously, or a little bit later, the organizations that core members establish and operate in hostlands are on the local or state level of the social and political spheres. Their activities are aimed at the hostland's leaders, governments, parties, and social organizations. The main purpose of such politically oriented organizations is lobbying on behalf and in favor of the members of the incipient diaspora.

Another type of organizations that are established by such diasporas are the cultural and educational. In cases when the identity of the incipient diasporans includes strong religious elements, this activity is based on or includes religious organizations that activate churches, mosques, and synagogues, and formal and informal educational organizations, which are mainly aimed to preserve and maintain the historical identity of the members and as far as possible to avoid the "loss" of such members. Realizing the significance of these organizations, some homelands spiritually and financially support them.

As previously noted, one of the first and then regular purposes of all these organizations is to try and draw and then maintain the non-geographic boundaries of these emerging entities. This is an essential task that is aimed at the avoidance of the defection from the community or the "invasion" of unwanted individuals and groups to the emerging community.

From the economic point of view, the relevant networks and organizations that the incipient diasporas are forming have to do with remittances to the people in the homelands. Usually remittances directed to people in the homeland are made by individuals, families, and small groups in the hostland. Since one of the reasons for migration out of the homeland is the economic difficulties experienced by those who eventually migrated and of their families and kin, the money is transferred directly to them. In case the general economic situation in the homeland is difficult, the new organizations that are established by the incipient diaspora try as far as they can to raise and transfer donations to the homeland. Usually the amounts of these donations are small. Only when diasporans are improving their general social, political, and economic situations in the hostlands, do they use their existing organizations and form new organizations that specialize in economic issues to promote and conduct business in and with the homeland.

When individuals and groups are permanently settled in the hostlands and all those cultural, social, political, and economic organizations operate on a regular basis, the processes of turning an incipient diaspora into an established modern diaspora begin to materialize.

The cultural, social, political, and economic backgrounds

Besides the ethno-national identity factor, the most significant interconnected factors influencing the historical development, existence, and actual behavior of diasporas are their ethno-national cultural backgrounds.

The cultural background that diasporans are carrying on is based on their memories and more factual knowledge of their nation's and homeland's history and of the culture that they enjoyed in their hostland. In truly liberal hostlands that are not imposing unbearable pressures on the diasporans to avoid contact with their homeland and its culture, these historical developments are influential.

Among the more significant cultural factors that are related to the people in certain homelands is the religious one. This factor plays a major role among core members of both incipient diasporas and older established diasporas. For example, the importance of the religious factor is very clear among ethno-national Roman Catholic diasporas, such as the Irish, Italian, and Polish; the ethno-national Muslim diasporas, such as the Pakistani, Palestinian, Iraqi, and North Africans; and of course among members of the Jewish diaspora.

Despite the growing image that among the more educated and integrated young diasporans there is a strong tendency to become more secular, not all younger core diasporans are giving up their basic religious belief in their ethno-national-religious identity and their views and activities in this sphere and in the closely related cultural sphere. Though they may not attend all religious events conducted in their communities in hostlands, still those who are not totally integrated into the culture and society of the hostland are not giving up the most fundamental side of their religious belief. More generally, maintaining the most basic religious beliefs and attendance of religious functions daily, end of the week (Fridays, Sabbaths, and Sundays), and holidays, help core diasporans to maintain not only their strict historical religious identity but also their connections to their diasporic entity in their hostlands and to their homeland.

For secular and religious diasporans, the variety of cultural events and activities arranged by diasporic organizations are not less important. Among the most significant activities in this sphere are the above mentioned various educational programs organized and carried out by the entity or by certain groups within it. All such educational institutions dedicate a lot of classes and teachings to the history of the nation and of the diasporas themselves.

It should also be noted that during recent years all these organizations, events, and activities that among other things promote the knowledge of the history of their entities are expanding and becoming more effective in strengthening these diasporas.

The social importance of the roles of family, kin, and social groups in the creation, survival, continued activities, and relations with the homeland cannot be exaggerated. Like the significance of the cultural religious and ethno-national identities, the interlinked history of the social backgrounds both in the homeland and hostland are essential factors that to a great extent determine the continued existence and behavior of diasporas. If not relying on the genetic aspect for diasporans' relations with the homeland and their entities, then the non-essentialist primordial social elements that lie at the heart of diasporas' histories are basic factors in the diasporic phenomenon.

These fundamental social background factors determine, among other things, the possible and actual existence and the degree of porosity of the non-geographical cultural and social boundaries of a diaspora. It is clear that such boundaries are abstract but they create important historical meanings for the diasporans, for the people in their homelands, and for the society in their hostland. On the local, regional, and municipal levels, these boundaries are made noticeable by the diasporans' residence locations. Voluntary or forced diasporans' residence in clearly isolated and identified "ghettoes," or in certain easily recognized districts, mean that such boundaries are not totally abstract but that they are real and meaningful. The actual "spaces" of such locations create recognizable settings that members of other ethnic-religious groups would avoid. In the past such ghettoes were the living spaces of most of the Jewish Diaspora and now such spaces are inhabited by Mexicans, Muslims, and African diasporans.

Such "real" local boundaries make the keeping of the diaspora community easier, on the one hand, and the ability of the various opponents of the diaspora to avoid living there, to follow and to control the diaspora, on the other hand. Generally, such spaces and their boundaries have some practical implications. In cases that such boundaries subsist, one of their meanings is the actual existence of a clearly defined and coherent diaspora community, at least on a specific local level. Inter-connectedly, the maintenance of such boundaries by the diasporans means that the "defection" from the entity, on the one hand, and the "intrusion" into such entities, on the other hand, is either not acceptable or limited.

The size of the diasporic entities on the state, regional, and local levels and their locations in the hostland—in large or small cities, in smaller towns and villages, in the main geographical and political centers, or rather in the geographical peripheries of the hostland—have noticeable effects on various aspects of the social background of individuals and groups of diasporans. These factors have quite clear effects on the social stratification, cohesion, and the historical behavior of these entities.

Thus, residing in smaller communities in the geographical peripheries of a hostland increases the diasporans' continuous need for constant connections between themselves and other members of the same diasporas, especially in the central locations where most or larger groups of the diasporans reside, and the centers of their organizations are located. Living in small communities in isolated areas in a hostland results in the constant search by "older" diasporans for newcomers of the same origin and attempts to enlist these newcomers as active members of the community. The permanent core diasporans in these communities invest efforts and material resources in the drive to attract new migrants and their absorption in the existing local community. The social contacts are established and maintained on the basis of family connections, individual friendships, and groups' ties. These social activities contribute to the nature of the local communities and also might have impacts on the entire entity in a certain country and its relations with the homeland. Once these communities are active the homeland is bound to establish some contacts with them and try to act together to accomplish both the homeland and diasporic goals.

One of the main implications of the ability, or the inability, of the activists and their organizations to enhance social cohesion is the capability, or incapability, to prevent full integration of the members of the diaspora into the hostland society, especially in larger towns and cities. The more effective means to prevent that integration, on the one hand, and to enhance the cohesion of the community, on the other hand, are the above-mentioned parades, seminars, conferences, and meetings.

The current advancing media and means of communication, facilitate the creation of quite complex and extended diasporic social networks. These networks are needed and formed in view of the ideological, political, and economic heterogeneity of the various diasporas.

The political culture of a diasporic entity is also an important basic factor influencing individual diasporans and the entire entity's activities and ability to have an effect on all involved actors. One of the main factors affecting this sphere is the historical non-democratic or democratic inclinations and experiences of the more politically active diasporans and their organizations. When the historical practical political experience and memory is non-democratic and their permanent residence is in democratic hostlands, then during their earlier periods there the diasporans have difficulties in fully understanding the meaning and nature of the democratic regime in general and in such states in particular. One of the consequences is incipient diasporans' relative lack of political activities during their first period of residence in their hostlands.

When incipient diasporans and diasporas turn into permanent and established ones, their involvement in hostland and homeland politics gradually increases. In certain diasporas such increasing involvement happens quickly and in others it develops more slowly. That pace depends on a number of factors: first, after a while in their hostlands growing numbers of such diasporans gain a better understanding of the political system there; second, the actual situation in the hostland—when there are acute real or imagined social or political threats and pressures on the diaspora it is quite natural that the more knowledgeable and active diasporans would do their best to change the situation through political actions; third, positive assistance that the diasporans get from their homelands encourages them to be more politically active; fourth, the actual appearance of political activists in the diaspora, and not less important, or even more important, is the existence of relevant politically oriented diasporic organizations and activists; fifth, the access of the diasporans to the politicians, and even more significantly to the bureaucrats in the hostland; sixth, the right to vote in local and state elections and the rate of voting in such elections. The higher the voting rates the greater are the cooperative relations between the diasporans and the hostlands' politicians and bureaucrats.

The diasporans' strategic policies to tackle their political situation in the hostland and the main strategic alternatives that are open to them are: first, their historical isolation, on the one hand, and participation, on the other hand, in the hostland. Except for vary special entities, such as the Roma, full isolation is unwanted and impossible. However, the strategy of relative isolation has been adopted by various diasporas with the main purpose of keeping, as far as possible, the entity's boundaries, their historical culture including in certain cases the religious affiliation of the members, social and family connections, and connections to the homeland. The second political participatory strategy is that of adopting the well-defined and recognized autonomy of both the individuals and the entire entity through a limited degree of integration into the hostland. Diasporas that adopt this strategy accept the most basic rules of the game in the hostland, but still try to maintain the entity's non-geographical borders fairly closed in order to avoid defection of members. The third strategy is fuller integration in all aspects of the hostland's life, including politics. This includes acceptance of the main cultural characteristics, mixing in the society, joining the state educational system, participating in the various political processes such as elections, running for offices, advertising, using the media, and lobbying. The fourth strategy is connected to the diasporans' wishes and abilities to influence the hostland's politics without undertaking any major responsibility for all actions and statements made by the diasporans. The main actual political issues that traditionally the diasporas decide upon are their general intention, mode, and responsibility for participation in hostlands' political system. In the cases of incipient diasporas, most of these activities are undertaken and performed on an individual level. In most cases of established diasporas the activities are conducted on both the individual and organizational levels. On the local level the contacts and political activities are more frequent and intense. On the state level most activities are conducted by the leaders and heads of the organizations. During recent years more diasporas have established representatives in various international organizations. One of these organizations that is demonstrating interest in diasporas, and in turn these entities have active representatives there, is the UN.

The main tactics that established diasporas use, whose members are full citizens of their hostlands, is participation in elections on the local and state levels. Their voting has an impact on their political contacts and achievements. The voting for both winners and losers in the election buy chances for the diasporans to influence future political developments on the local or state levels. Also, the ability to offer financial and publicity support for candidates and later for those who have been elected pave the way to diasporans' demands for political actions in their favor.

One of the most popular and frequently used means for gaining political influence is lobbying in favor of the diaspora itself and/or the homeland. One of the questions raised in this context is that of the target of the lobbying. Depending on the diaspora's political position and contacts the individual and organizations conduct direct talks with politicians, governmental institutions, and bureaucrats. While on most occasions lobbying is secretly conducted, when the worst comes to the worst, then, simultaneously or separately, in addition to their regular use of the current media, the diasporans make public demands in order to raise questions and get results. Usually these demands are directed to the politicians rather than to the bureaucrats.

Conclusions

This chapter emphasizes the substantial importance of the historical backgrounds of ethno-national-religious diasporas as far as their current existence and their growing roles, actions, and influence on both their homelands and hostlands are concerned.

The first argument is that unlike what has been written in many books and articles, the diasporic phenomenon did not begin in the modern period. There are established diasporas, such as the Jewish, Chinese, Indian, and Armenian, that were formed in ancient time and still exist. Their long historical survival has major influence on their fundamental identity, emotions, and thoughts. The same applies to "modern diasporas." These factors determine the rates of diasporas' connections to individuals, groups, official, and social-political offices and organizations in their homelands.

In various ways historical diasporas have shaped the main aspects of the general phenomenon and the above mentioned profile and patterns of developments of the modern and incipient ethno-national diasporas. However, the existence of these factors does not mean that all such diasporas are exactly similar. The general diasporic phenomenon and each diaspora are heterogeneous, and there is a certain degree of divergence among and inside these entities.

Interconnected to the first main argument is the more specific one, which is that the history of each diaspora has influenced the cultural, social, and political elements determining their ability to survive and be active. After settling permanently in their hostlands diaspora members develop their relations with the hostland and homeland based to an extent on the memories of the historical circumstances that its members experienced.

The third main argument of this chapter is that in view of the few studies and publications about the historical backgrounds of the diasporas and their various impacts on their current cultural-social-political nature and their relations with their homelands, there is a substantial need to enlarge the scope of the studies and publications in this direction. The study of the historical aspect and its impacts will enhance our better understanding of the entire diasporic phenomenon.

References and further reading

Alfonso, C., Kokot, W., and Toloyan, K. (eds) (2004) *Diaspora, Identity and Religion, New Directions in Theory and Research*. New York: Routledge.

Armstrong, J. (1976) "Mobilized and proletarian diasporas" *American Political Science Review* 70(2): 393–408.

Baubock, R. and Faist, T. (eds) (2010) *Transnationalism and Diaspora: Concepts, Theories and Methods*. Amsterdam: Amsterdam University Press.

Ben-Rafael, E. and Sternberg, Y.(eds) (2009) *Transnationalism, Diasporas and the Advent of a New (Dis)Order*. Leiden: Brill.

Braziel, J. and Mannur, A. (eds), (2003) *Theorizing Diasporas. A Reader*. Oxford: Blackwell Publishing Ltd.

Brubaker, R. (2005) "The 'diaspora' diaspora" *Ethnic and Racial Studies* 28(1): 1–9.

Cohen, R. (2008) *Global Diasporas: An Introduction*. New York: Routledge.

Dufoix, S. (2008) *Diasporas*. Berkeley, CA: University of California Press.

Esman, M. (2009) *Diasporas in the Contemporary World*. Cambridge: Polity Press.

Levitt, S. and Khargram, S. (eds) (2007) *The Transnational Studies Reader: Intersections and Innovations*. New York: Routledge.

Miles, W. and Sheffer, G. (1998) "Francophone and zionism: A comparative study of transnationalism and trans-statism" *Diaspora* 7(2): 119–48.

Safran, W. (1999) "Comparing diasporas: A review essay" *Diaspora* 8(3): 255–92.

Shain, Y. (2007) *Kinship and Diasporas in International Affairs*. Ann Arbor, MI: The University of Michigan Press.

Sheffer, G. (1986) "A new field of study: Modern diasporas in international politics." In G. Sheffer (ed.), *Modern Diasporas in International Politics*. London: Croom Helm, pp. 1–15.

——(2006) *Diaspora Politics: At Home Abroad*, Cambridge: Cambridge University Press.

——(2006) "Transnationalism and diasporism" *Diaspora* 15(1): 121–45.

Tololyan, K. (2007) "The contemporary discourse of diaspora studies" *Comparative Studies of South Asia, Africa, and the Middle East* 27(3): 647–55.

Vertovec, S. (1997) "Three meanings of Diaspora" *Diaspora* 6(3): 277–99.

——(2009) *Transnationalism*. New York: Routledge.

37

Transnationalism

Thomas Faist

"Transnationalism" entered the lexicon of migration studies in the early 1990s, over a century after earlier generations of migration researchers had introduced and made extensive use of the concept of assimilation. It did so in rather different circumstances, for whereas assimilation gained currency with relatively little reflection or debate at the moment that migration research was in its early formative period, transnationalism entered a well-developed sociological subfield dealing with migrant incorporation. Several principal advocates assertively promoted the concept, which was rather quickly embraced by many scholars. However, it also confronted by skeptics. The result is that the concept has undergone substantial revision since its earliest formulations, the consequence of an often-spirited dialogue (see Levitt and Jaworsky 2007). Over time, the debate around transnationalism in migration has concerned broader issues in the social sciences, such as nationalism, political power, methodological nationalism, and essentializing ethno-cultural groups.

Those scholars who initially embraced the idea of transnational migration did so because of a conviction that it was necessary to capture the distinctive and characteristic features of the new immigrant streams and groups that have developed in the advanced industrial nations at the core of the capitalist world system. The term has emerged and evolved at a time characterized by high levels of labor migration from economically less developed nations to the most developed, and from similarly high levels of political refugees fleeing conflicts and instability in former communist and Third World nations. The influx of these new labor migrants and refugees has reshaped, not only nation-states with long histories of immigration, the settler states of the United States, Canada, and Australia, but also states that have not been notable as immigrant receiving nations in the earlier phases of industrialization, those of Western Europe and to a lesser extent, Japan. The high levels of immigration, the new locales of settlement, reshaped ethno-cultural mixes, changes in the nature of capitalist economies in a new (post-)industrial epoch, changes in the meaning and significance attached to the idea of citizenship, and the potency of a globalized popular culture have contributed to the conviction that what is novel about the present requires equally novel conceptual tools if we are to make sense of the impact of the new international migration on the receiving, transition, and sending countries. This overview proceeds by examining (1) the initial conceptualizations of the transnational perspective on migration and efforts at systematization; (2) discussions around contentious issues regarding past versus present transnationalism; the extent of transnationalism among migrants;

and transnationalism, states, and politics; and, finally, (3) venues for further research through a transnational optic.

Transnational social formations—also called fields or spaces—consist of combinations of social and symbolic ties and their contents, positions in networks and organizations, and networks of organizations that cut across the borders of at least two nation states. In other words, the term refers to sustained and continuous pluri-local transactions crossing state borders. Most of these formations are located in between the life-world of personal interactions, on the one hand, and the functional systems of differentiated spheres or fields, such as the economy, polity, law, science, and religion. The smallest element of transnational social formations is transactions, that is, bounded communications between social agents such as individual persons. More aggregated levels encompass groups, organizations, and firms. It is an empirical question whether such transnational transactions are global or regional.

Initial conceptualizations

Transnational approaches certainly do not form a coherent theory or set of theories. They can be more adequately described as a perspective, which has found entry into the study of manifold cross-border phenomena. We can delineate several generations of transnational scholarship but focus mostly on those which are relevant for migration research. A first precursor to the use of the concept in migration research, flourishing in the late 1960s and 1970s, asked about the emergence, role, and impact of large-scale, cross-border organizations. This literature, steeped in the field of International Relations, focused its attention on interdependence between states, resulting from the existence and operations of powerful non-state actors, such as multinational companies (Keohane and Nye 1977). Curiously, the interest in this transnational approach quickly disappeared with the onset of debates on globalization from the late 1970s onwards. Perhaps this demise was related to the fact that globalization studies re-centered the interest to how national political economies were reshaped by ever-growing capital flows across borders. Almost two decades later, transnational ideas took root again in a very specific field—international or cross-border migration—and with a decided focus on the agency of a particular type of agent, migrants. It was in social anthropology and later sociology that this lens took hold. This gaze dealt with dense and continuous ties across the borders of nation-states, which concatenate into social formations.

The initial phase ran from the early 1990s until the dawn of the new century. While a number of scholars contributed to this development, cultural anthropologist Nina Glick Schiller and her colleagues Linda Basch and Christina Szanton Blanc have provided the pioneering impetus (Basch *et al.* 1994). Based on this foundation, a number of scholars have contributed to a further elaboration of types of transnational practices, and provided typologies of transnational practices and spaces.

Transnationalism as a new mode of incorporation: Glick Schiller and colleagues

Glick Schiller *et al.* (1994) made two initial points, one historical and the other theoretical. Historically, they contended that there is something qualitatively different about immigrants today compared to their late nineteenth- and early twentieth-century counterparts. Glick Schiller viewed this earlier era's immigrants as having broken off all homeland social relations and cultural ties, thereby locating themselves solely within the socio-cultural, economic, and political orbit of the receiving society. By contrast, she contended, today's immigrants are composed of those whose networks, activities, and patterns of life encompass both their host and home societies. Their lives cut across national boundaries and bring two societies into a single social field.

From this historical comparison, Glick Schiller *et al.* (1994) offered a rationale for a new analytic framework, making a case for the introduction of two new terms: "transnationalism" and "transmigrants." The former refers to "the process by which immigrants build social fields that link together their country of origin and their country of settlement," while the latter refers to the "immigrants who build such social fields" by maintaining a wide range of affective and instrumental social relationships spanning borders (Basch *et al.* 1994: 27). Implicitly, the introduction of these new concepts suggested that existing theoretical frameworks are not up to the task of analyzing the new immigrants. To make their case, the authors presented vignettes. One of them involved a Haitian hometown association located in New York City. While the activities of the association clearly have something to do with immigrant adjustment, it has also initiated various projects in Haiti. This, Glick Schiller and her colleagues contended, distinguishes contemporary mutual aid societies from those in the past, which they argued were solely designed to address the adjustment needs of the immigrants themselves (Basch *et al.* 1994: 145–224). Another example involved white-collar Grenadian immigrants being addressed by Grenada's Minister of Agriculture and Development: Immigrants are at once both Grenadian citizens with an ability to influence friends and relatives who have remained in the homeland and American ethnics capable of undertaking efforts to shape economic and political decisions in the host society. The third example looked to Filipinos and the *Balikbayan* box, a formalized and regulated form of remittance. This illustration suggests is that remittances are not new, but that homeland governments are increasingly likely to embrace their expatriate communities when such an embrace can be economically beneficial.

From these illustrations, the authors made two main conceptual points. First, social science must become "unbound." The argument is that the problem with theories operating as closed systems in which the unit of analysis is ultimately the national state is that they fail to provide room for the wider field of action occupied by contemporary immigrants. Thus, Glick Schiller, *et al.* argued for the necessity of recasting theory from the national to a global systems perspective. They stressed that transnationalism is the product of world capitalism that has produced economic dislocations making immigrants economically vulnerable (Basch *et al.* 1994: 30–4). While sympathetic to the discussions of transnationalism as cultural flows, seen in the work of figures such as Arjun Appadurai and Ulf Hannerz, the main thrust of the authors' argument involved an articulation of a notion of transnational migration that focuses primarily on social relations.

Second, the authors pointed to the multiple and fluid identities of contemporary transmigrants, contending that their manipulation of identities reveals a resistance on the part of transmigrants to "the global political and economic situations that engulf them."

This insight necessitates a need to rethink received ideas regarding class, nationalism, ethnicity, and race. Relying on the Gramscian idea of hegemony, the authors treated each of these aspects of identity as contested and pliable. The real significance of the discussion is that assimilation and cultural pluralism are inadequate to account for the distinctive character of contemporary immigration. From this perspective, whereas assimilation implies the loss of past identity, cultural pluralism advances an essentialist perspective that treats ethnic identities as immutable (Glick Schiller *et al.* 1992: 13–19).

A typology of transnationalism

While Glick Schiller *et al.* (1994) placed transnational social fields in the framework of world systems analysis, this raised the question of how to conceptualize transnational social formations. One answer has been the concept of transnational social space. The idea of transnational spaces entailed considering the migratory system as a boundary-breaking process in which two or more nation states are penetrated by and become a part of a singular new social space. This space involves in part the circulation of ideas, symbols, activities, and material culture. It also involves the border-crossing movements of people who then come to engage in transnational social relations, with implications for immigrant incorporation. Social space does not only refer to physical features, but also to larger opportunity structures, the social life, and the subjective images, values, and meanings that the specific and limited place represents to migrants. Space is thus different from place in that it encompasses or spans various territorial locations. It includes two or more places.

Transnational spaces can be differentiated according to their degree of formalization. The degree of formalization refers both to the internal characteristics of group organization and the extent of common or shared values and symbols. On the one hand there are networks with low levels of formalization, and on the other there are highly formalized institutions. Organizations are characterized by a high degree of formalized relations, for example in terms of hierarchy and control. Communities also show a high degree of formalization, though not in terms of their internal organizational structure but their common values and symbols. There are four ideal types of transnational spaces: areas of contact and diffusion; small groups, particularly kinship systems; issue networks; and communities and organizations (see Table 37.1).

1   *Diffusion in Contact Fields:* This category comprises phenomena such as the exchange of goods, capital, and services between businesses. People engaged in these transactions do not necessarily have sustained or close contact with each other. In some cases, strangers meet at the marketplace or at tourist resorts. Transboundary ties between individuals and organizations may also lead to a diffusion of language, e.g. specialist terms are borrowed from one language and incorporated into another. We also find social and cultural practices diffusing across borders—as in the action repertoires of social movements. Among immigrants, for example, we observe processes that partly point to cultural diffusion from the country of origin to the country of settlement. For example, Kurds in Turkey brought their traditional New Year's celebration (*Newroz*) to Germany, where it became an important symbol of common Kurdish identity. In order to take the wind out of the Kurdish separatists' sails, the Turkish government promptly responded by declaring *Newroz* an official bank holiday in 1996.

2   *Small Groups—Kinship Systems:* Highly formalized transboundary relations within small groups like households and families, or even wider kinship systems, are representative for many migrants. Families may live apart because one or more members work abroad as contract workers (like the former "guestworkers" in Germany), or as posted employees

Table 37.1 Types of transnational social spaces

Degree of formalization	
Low: networks	*High: institutions*
(1) *Diffusion* e.g., fields for the exchange of goods, capital, persons, information, ideas and practices	(2) *Small kinship groups* e.g., households, families
(3) *Issue networks* e.g.,networks of business people, epistemic networks, advocacy networks	(4) *Communities and organizations* e.g., religious groups, political parties, businesses

within multinational companies. Small household and family groups have a strong sense of belonging to a common home. A classic example for such relations are transnational families, who conceive themselves as both an economic unit and a unit of solidarity and who may keep, besides the main house, a kind of shadow household in another country. Transnational families make use of resources inherent in social ties like reciprocity, and also resources existing in symbolic ties, such as solidarity. Economic assets are mostly transferred from abroad to those who continue to run the household "back home."

3 *Issue Networks:* These are sets of ties between persons and organizations in which information and services are exchanged for the purpose of achieving a common goal. Linkage patterns may concatenate into advocacy networks (e.g. human rights), business networks, or science networks. Often, there is a common discourse concerning a specific issue such as human rights or a profession, and such networks and organizations are sometimes even seen as the nucleus of a "global civil society" (see Keane 2003). In contrast to organizations with formal membership, access to these networks is not strictly limited to interested actors. While issue networks look back upon a long tradition in the realm of human rights, and are making steady progress in ecology, they are also emerging among migrants who have moved from the so-called third countries to the European Union (EU). Regarding business networks, persons from emigration states who live abroad constitute an important source of financial transfer and investment, both as immigrant entrepreneurs in their new societies of settlement and with their countries of origin. The governments of sending nations have increasingly initiated programs to attract emigrants' investments. By far the largest set of transnational networks—a set of interlinked local, national, and regional networks—in the world is that of the Overseas Chinese and Indians abroad, promoting trade by providing market information and matching and referral services by utilizing their co-ethnic ties. Such ties alleviate the problems associated with contract enforcement and by providing information about trading opportunities.

4 *Transnational Communities and Organizations:* Communities and organizations constitute highly formalized types of transnational spaces with an inherent potential for a relatively long life-span. Close symbolic ties are characteristic of transnational communities, whereas a more formal internal hierarchy and systematically structured controls over social ties exist within transnational organizations.

Transnational communities comprise dense and continuous sets of social and symbolic ties, characterized by a high degree of intimacy, emotional depth, moral obligation and sometimes even social cohesion. Transnational communities can evolve at different levels of aggregation. The simplest type consists of village communities in interstate migration systems, whose relations are marked by solidarity extended over long periods of time. Members of such communities who are abroad or have returned home often invest in private or public projects for the benefit of the community in question. The quintessential form of transnational communities consists of larger transboundary religious groups and churches. World religions, such as Judaism, Christianity, Islam, Hinduism, and Buddhism existed long before modern states came into existence. Diasporas also belong to the category of transnational communities. In classical renditions, these are groups that experienced the territorial dispersion of their members some time in the past, either due to a traumatic experience, or specialization in long-distance trade. Jews, Palestinians, Armenians, and Greeks can be named as examples here. Generally, members of diasporas have a common memory of their lost homeland, or a vision of an imagined one to be created, while at the same time the immigration country often refuses the respective minority full acknowledgment of their cultural distinctiveness (see Gold 2002).

An early type of transnational organization—interstate non-governmental organizations (INGOS)—developed out of issue networks like the Red Cross, Amnesty International, and Greenpeace. At the other extreme there are organizations which are based in one specific country but whose sphere of influence extends abroad, as with the ethno-nationalist Kurdish Workers' Party PKK. Transnational enterprises constitute a further type of transnational organization. Overall, such transnational communities and organizations must be theoretically linked to transnationalism from above, rather than treating transnationalism from above and from below as discrete parallel phenomena.

What makes transnational communities different from the more familiar form that typified immigrant enclaves in industrializing nations a century ago is that it is located in a space that encompasses two or more nation-states, a situation made possible by time-space compression. Metaphorically, assimilation is associated with the image of "the uprooted" (Handlin 1973 [1951]), and cultural pluralism with "the transplanted" (Bodnar 1985). An appropriate transnational metaphorical alternative may be—borrowing from the novelist Salman Rushdie—the idea of "translated people," that is, migrants are continually engaged in translating languages, cultures, norms, and social and symbolic ties. Transnational migrants forge their sense of identity and their community, not out of a loss or mere replication. Crucially, it is not simply individuals living with one foot in two places that constitute the sole occupants of transnational communities. The latter do not necessarily require individual persons living in two worlds simultaneously or between cultures in a total "global village" of de-territorialized space. What is required, however, is that communities without propinquity link through exchange, reciprocity, and solidarity to achieve a high degree of social cohesion, and a common repertoire of symbolic and collective representations.

Summarizing the various strands of research sketched here, Steven Vertovec (1999: 449–56) points out several recurring themes that shape the ways the term is employed. He identifies six distinct, albeit potentially overlapping or intertwined, uses of the term: (1) as a social morphology focused on a new border spanning social formation; (2) as diasporic consciousness; (3) as a mode of cultural reproduction variously identified as syncretism, creolization, bricolage, cultural translation, and hybridity; (4) as an avenue of capital for transnational corporations (TNCs), and in a smaller but significant way in the form of remittances sent by immigrants to family and friends in their homelands; (5) as a site of political engagement, both in terms of homeland politics and the politics of homeland governments vis-à-vis their émigré communities, and in terms of the expanded role of international non-governmental organizations (INGOs); and (6) and as a reconfiguration of the notion of place from an emphasis on the local to the translocal.

Transnational social spaces and globalization

When comparing transnational and global approaches, transnationalism is an older term, predating globalization by some 10–15 years: around 1970 compared to the early to mid-1980s. Methodologically, most globalization approaches are concerned, in the first instance, with macro-dynamics, whereas accounts of the transnational tend to be more agency-oriented. This is very visible in world systems theory, which is, in essence, a top-down, outside-in approach. In contrast, transnational approaches take an agency-oriented view, usually starting from small groups and networks of mobiles. In its broader meaning, "transnational studies" (Khagram and Levitt 2008) thus tends to be concerned with topics such as migrant networks, traders, and ethnic business constellations, politics of place among migrants and returnees, diasporas, and development, immigrant incorporation—but also social movements and advocacy networks.

Transnational*ism* as a discourse could be regarded as a stepping stone towards globalism and even cosmopolitanism—but also the contrary, reinforcing nationalism. After all, transnationalism refers to the Janus face of cross-border processes and conditions which may foster long-distance nationalism. Nationalist claims are frequently articulated and mobilized within cross-border groups and structures. Nationalism is not always geared toward achieving congruence between national–cultural boundaries and state borders. Nation-building may be confined to sub-state territories without ever crossing the threshold to secession, and it may extend beyond state borders by attempting to bind together populations in a homeland territory and abroad without trying to remove the borders between them or to bring back external kin-populations into the homeland. An example of the former has been, until now, Québec in Canada; an example for the latter has been the Irish diaspora in the USA since the nineteenth century.

Open and contested questions

A number of contentious issues have characterized the debate around transnationalism since the late 1990s: Is transnationalism a mode of immigrant incorporation or is it a mode of activity? If it is a mode of incorporation, is it antithetical to assimilation or multiculturalism? How many transnationals are there? What is the role of national states in forging transnational social ties and spaces?

Migrant Incorporation: Assimilation and Transnationalism—Exclusive or overlapping?

What is the relationship between transnationalism and assimilation? It is noteworthy that the pioneers of this understanding of the transnational challenged the notion that the incorporation of immigrants takes place in the container of the respective nation-state in which immigrants settle for longer periods of time in their life course. In the early Glick Schiller and colleagues (Basch *et al.* 1994) formulation viewed assimilation and transnationalism as contrasting, antithetical modes of incorporation, the former being at the least an alternative to the latter and perhaps—as a form of resistance—a direct challenge to it. Later contributions conceptualized the two as distinct modes of incorporation, which existed side by side, such as assimilation, partial adaption, or integration in transnational groups. More recent arguments point toward assimilation and multi-culturalism as modes of incorporation and transnationalism as distinct activities which may contribute to incorporation in various ways (Kivisto 2005); for example transnationalism, rather than being seen as something that slows assimilation, might actually accelerate the process.

A general consensus has emerged among key proponents of transnationalism that "simulta-neity" is the characteristic relationship between assimilation and transnationalism. The point is that assimilation and transnationalism ought not to be construed as competing alternatives and the reason is clear: whereas assimilation refers to a mode of immigrant incorporation into a receiving society, transnationalism does not. Rather, it is a mode of connection between and across the borders of various states, a mode of connectedness that is achieved to the extent that a dialectical relationship between the movers and stayers in the two worlds is achieved in one or more arenas of social life: familial, religious, economic, political, cultural, and so forth.

How many transnational migrants?

The guiding assumption of the first phase of transnational theorizing was that all, most, or at least a significant percentage of contemporary immigrants were transnational. Alejandro Portes and associates were among the first scholars to offer empirical evidence about the scope of transnationalism, studying three specific immigrant groups in the USA: Colombian, Salvadorans, and Dominicans and three fields, economic, political, and socio-cultural. Their conclusion was that a relatively small minority of immigrants can be defined as transnational. Looking at the economic realm, they focused on self-employed immigrants whose business activities require frequent travel abroad and who depend for the success of their firms on their contacts and associates in another country, primarily their country of origin. They discovered that the percentages of immigrants from each group that were transnational entrepreneurs was very small, ranging between 4 and 6 percent. Similar results were obtained in their examination of the political activities of these three groups. The study examined such practices as memberships in home country political parties, giving money to those parties, taking part in home country electoral activities, membership in civic hometown associations and charity organizations, and giving money to such non-electoral organizations. The percentages of immigrants involved in regular engagements with these practices ranged from 7 percent to 14 percent. While the percentage of migrants engaged in routine and sustained cross-border activities may be small, this does not necessarily lead to the conclusion that transnationalism is a minor side stream (Portes 2003).

National states, politics, and transnationalism

What is new is the role some emigration country governments are playing in attempting to encourage ongoing connections with their expatriate communities. Immigrants in Europe and North America a century ago confronted governments and cultural elites that tended to be overtly hostile; today's counterparts, in contrast, frequently find their emigrants to be useful economically, and sometimes politically and culturally as well. Thus, rather than condemning their decision to exit or enticing them to return, they instead work to create relationships with the immigrants that are beneficial to the homeland.

Moreover, for a viable transnational community to be established and to sustain itself over time, a continual pattern of involvement with both governmental and civic institutions in the homeland and receiving country are essential. This is because transnational immigrants *qua* transnational immigrants are engaged in activities designed to define and enhance their position in the immigration region, while simultaneously seeking to remain embedded in a participatory way in the everyday affairs of the homeland community, be that national or local or both. What is distinctive about this type of community without propinquity is that over time the transnational social space thus carved out makes the dichotomous character of host society concerns versus homeland concerns if not irrelevant, at least less pronounced and at some level part of a transcendent structure of border-crossing social relations. Instruments include dual citizenship, tax incentives for investments by expatriates, additional social security schemes and consular services abroad. Vice versa, there are manifold efforts of diasporas to engage in "homeland" politics. Migrant transnational activities are part of broader transnational politics, expressed in studies of social movements and advocacy networks. This literature mainly does not address competitors to the state, such as multinational companies, or flows across the borders of states, such as transnational migration, but emphasizes issues prevalent in the public spheres and involving mobilization of target groups around various issues, such as the environment, production chains, human rights, gender, religion, or crime (see collection in Khagram and Levitt 2008).

Outlook: beyond methodological nationalism and groupism

Current scholarship has taken off with the criticism of methodological nationalism and groupism. Methodologically, both criticisms are crucial points of departure toward developing a transnational or transboundary methodology. First, studies in a transnational vein are critical of methodological nationalism (Wimmer and Glick Schiller 2003), that is, the often unstated assumption that national society or the national state is the "natural "unit of analysis and of data collection. Yet there is a need to go beyond criticism and explicitly name the reference points for transnational analysis. Second, the concomitant danger of groupism (Brubaker 2004) refers to studies that treat diasporic and transnational communities as units that are stable over time, and of overriding importance for the individual identities and social practices of their members. Migrant formations can be built around various categorical distinctions, such as ethnicity, race, gender, schooling, professional training, political affiliation, and sexual preference. Ethnicity constitutes a particularly vexing issue in transnational studies. On the one hand, a transnational approach should be able to overcome the ethnic bias inherent in much migration scholarship. The fallacy is to label migrants immediately by ethnic or national categories. Often scholars presuppose prematurely that categories such as Turks, Brazilians, and so forth matter a lot for all realms and purposes, since they often do in public discourse. On the other hand, methods should enable researchers to trace actually existing social formations, such as networks of reciprocity built around ethnic markers, which are of great importance, for example, in informal transfer systems of financial remittances. This means to turn the issue of the importance of ethnicity into an empirical question.

Thus, future research should be concerned less with accounting for cross-border ties and flows of fixed categories of persons or groups, but focuses more on changing boundaries. This is so because social spaces denote dynamic processes, not static notions of ties and positions. The main point is a concern with boundaries demarcating social spaces in a wider sense—in particular, on how the boundaries themselves come into existence and change. Boundaries may refer to distinctions along categories such as groups, organizations, and cultural differences. In general, if it makes sense, as the critique of methodological nationalism charges, that national states—and, by implication, ethnic or national groups—are not quasi-natural entities, it is of prime importance to get a distance to fixed notions of social formations and their boundaries. It is then useful to start with less obtrusive concepts such as boundaries and spaces. This way offers a chance to look at changing boundaries—in relation to existing ones (e.g. national states) and to new ones (emergent properties of transnational and global systems), and explore how old spaces are transformed and new spaces emerge. It is not an approach cognizant that borders and, more broadly, boundaries, are ever shifting and changing.

Looking at cross-border transactions is intimately connected to changing boundaries along economic, political, and cultural lines. Boundary changes are essentially a question of power constellations. The creation, maintenance, and enforcement of boundaries are functions of power, be it authoritative (non-)decision-making or symbolic power of generating frames through which persons, groups, and events are slotted. Just take geographical mobility across borders and boundaries. States make rules of admission and membership; they exercise the power of ascription in that they and other agents are involved in definitions of "us" and "them," or desirable and undesirable migrants. The early transnational migration literature portrayed the power aspect as dichotomous. Transnationalism from above referred to the practices of multinational corporations, or international institutions, such as the IMF's structural adjustment programs in the 1990s. By contrast, transnationalism from below was supposedly found in grassroots transnational enterprise, social movements, and migrant networks—and challenged the institutionalized power structures. In early formulations one almost gets the impression that transnational migrants are a cross-border substitute for the lost working class as a historical subject of social transformation. Such a conceptualization of above vs. below is misleading, however. As we know, practices from below may also reproduce authoritarian structures or exclusion along gender, class, religious, ethnic or racial lines (e.g. Goldring and Krishnamurti 2008). In short, the above and below are found in all social formations, however small and grassroots they may (appear to) be. If this is plausible, then we need to turn to a more nuanced discussion of borders and boundaries within social spaces going beyond and intersecting places such as nation-states. It is important to unpack the notion of power and identify the social mechanisms which are at work in the making and unmaking of boundaries in social spaces.

The search for mechanisms indicating change of boundaries leads to a distinction of two crucial fields, namely, first, accounting for the integration of social spaces and, second, accounting for changing boundaries in social spaces. The first realm has received some attention. Transnational ties can concatenate in various forms of transnational social spaces, namely transnational reciprocity in kinship groups, transnational circuits in exchange-based networks, and transnational communities such as diasporas, characterized by high degrees of diffuse solidarity. Thus, mechanisms such as various forms of exchange, reciprocity, and solidarity are operative in ensuring the integration of cross-border social formations. What has received much less attention is the transformation of boundaries in intersecting social spaces. We need to understand how boundaries in such spaces change, are redrawn, reinforced or transformed.

It is therefore helpful to think about how boundaries change and by which mechanisms such transformations occur. Social boundaries interrupt, divide, circumscribe, or segregate distributions of persons and groups within social spaces which cross the borders of national states. Shifting boundaries are indications of the changing of institutions, practices, and cognitions. The dynamics of changing boundaries can be nicely captured in the debate on the newness of migrant transnational social spaces. Some transnational scholars early on claimed the newness of such phenomena. It did not take long until historically minded social scientists showed convincingly that not only have return migration and occasional visits to home regions existed for quite some time (Foner 2005), but also that transnational communities, with dense internal ties both within states of immigration and toward regions of emigration, have likewise existed for a long time. Max Weber, for example, spoke of the *Auslandsgemeinschafte* of German immigrants in South and North America in the late nineteenth century.

Certainly, these cases were not as widespread as they are today, and were not further encouraged by means of instant long-distance communication. Yet these technological changes would not have translated into social change if it had not been for the right toward collective self-determination, and boundary shifts in thinking and acting upon cultural diversity which have produced the new trends. Among these socio-political processes are a higher extent of tolerating cultural pluralism (multiculturalism) and dual citizenship provisions, in conjunction with other changes in the national and international political contexts. All of these have added new dimensions to and altered the scope and thrust of transnational cultural, political, and economic involvements.

It is useful to analyze actual boundaries as the institutionalization of the relations and differentials of power. There are four types of how boundaries are being redrawn (inspired by the typology in Zolberg and Long 1999): First, existing boundaries become porous, as in the case of dual citizenship when more and more national states tolerate overlapping membership in nations. Second, boundaries may shift, as when lines between "us" and "them" do not run along national lines but along religious ones. This has happened in many states in Western Europe over the past three decades. Public debates have come not to portray nationalities but conflicts between Muslims and "us" as relevant trench lines. Third, boundaries can be maintained or even reinforced, as in the extension of border control in the European Union to both the patrolling of exterior borders, the emergence of buffer zones with adjacent countries, and an increase in controls internal to national states. And fourth, new boundaries emerge, as evidenced by the portrayal and public policies toward transnational activities. While transnational practices of highly skilled and prosperous migrants are celebrated by immigration country and increasingly also emigration country governments as a significant contribution to the competitiveness of national economies, transnational ties of other categories of so-called low-skilled migrants are often seen as contributing to segregation and self-exclusion. Or, to give another example, transnational ties may represent a security risk, as in the case of terrorists, on the one hand, but international migrants are also cast as a new type of development agent, on the other hand. The exact mechanisms of boundary genesis and changes need to be researched in order to gauge how new societal formations emerge across borders but also in what ways well-entrenched institutions such as national states and international organizations change and adapt.

References and further reading

Basch, L. Glick Schiller, N., and Szanton Blanc, C. (1994) *Nations Unbound: Transnational Projects, Postcolonial Predicaments, and Deterritorialized Nation-States*. Longhorne, MA: Gordon and Breach.

Bodnar, J. (1985) *The Transplanted. A History of Immigrants in Urban America*. Bloomington, IN: Indiana University Press.

Brubaker, R. (2004) *Ethnicity Without Groups*. Cambridge, MA: Harvard University Press.

Faist, T. (2000) *The Volume and Dynamics of International Migration and Transnational Social Spaces*. Oxford: Oxford University Press.

Foner, N. (2005) *In a New Land: A Comparative View of Immigration*. New York: New York University Press.

Glick Schiller, N., Basch, L. and Blanc-Szanton, C. (1994) *Nations Unbound: Transnational Projects, Postcolonial Predicaments, and Deterritorialized Nation-states*. Amsterdam: Gordon and Breach Publishers.

Gold, S. J. (2002) *The Israeli Diaspora*. Seattle, WA: University of Washington Press.

Goldring, L. and Krishnamurti, S. (eds) (2007) *Organizing the Transnational: Labour, Politics, and Social Change*. Vancouver: University of British Columbia Press.

Handlin, O. (1973) [1951]. *The Uprooted. The Epic Story of the Great Migrations that made the American People*. 2nd edition enlarged. Boston, MA: Little, Brown.

Keane, J. (2003) *Global Civil Society*. Cambridge: Cambridge University Press.

Keohane, R. O. and Nye, J. S. (1977) *Power and Interdependence: World Politics in Transition*. Boston, MA: Little, Brown.

Kivisto, P. (2005) *Incorporating Diversity: Rethinking Assimilation in a Multicultural Age*. Boulder, CO: Paradigm Publishers.

Khagram, S. and Levitt, P. (eds). (2008) *The Transnational Studies Reader: Intersections and Innovations*. London: Routledge.

Levitt, P. and Nadya Jaworsky, B. (2007) "Transnational migration studies: Past developments and future trends" *Annual Review of Sociology* 33: 129–56.

Portes, A. Guarnizo, L. E., and Landolt, P. (1999) "The study of transnationalism: Pitfalls and promise of an emergent research field" *Ethnic and Racial Studies* 22(2): 217–37.

Portes, A. (2003) "Conclusion: Theoretical convergences and empirical evidence in the study of immigrant transnationalism" *International Migration Review* 37(3): 874–92.

Smith, M. P. and Guarnizo, L. E. (1998) *Transnationalism from Below*. New Brunswick, NJ: Transaction Publishers.

Vertovec, S. (1999) "Conceiving and researching transnationalism" *Ethnic and Racial Studies* 22(2): 447–62.

Wimmer, A. and Glick Schiller, N. (2003) "Methodological nationalism, the social sciences, and the study of migration: An essay in historical epistemology" *International Migration Review* 37(3): 576–610.

Zolberg, A. R. and Woon, L. L. (1999) "Why Islam is like Spanish: Cultural incorporation in Europe and the United States" *Politics and Society* 27(1): 5–38.

38

Return migration

Janet W. Salaff

Introduction

Return migration researchers have raised issues that parallel discussions of migration, which contrast rational decision-making with decision-making embedded in social norms and culture. However, migration and return migration differ in crucial ways: return migrants have experienced their home culture either directly or indirectly. Therefore, most analyses of this population must include issues of belonging, identity, and emotions.

This review of issues related to return migration mainly focuses on voluntary, rather than forced, migration (illegal immigrants' and asylum-seekers' repatriation, etc.). It will begin with a discussion of alternative frameworks of decision-making, and then describe the literature on return migration and transnationalism and identities; these include long-term studies and studies that focus on various statuses. Finally, it will conclude with a discussion of the costs migrants encounter in adaptation.

Frameworks

Voluntary exits and returns from a country can be seen as a form of decision-making. March (1994) described the two prevailing models of decision-making. Economics-rooted decisions are based on the logic of consequences, a form of bounded rational decision-making. In contrast, relationship-based decisions are founded in a logic of appropriateness, based on how other individuals in similar situations choose to act. Social relations, emotional factors, and identity issues all affect decision-making, so the social network literature can be helpful when analyzing these issues.

Rational decision-making

According to classic studies, economic factors were the most important motivations for migration. Labor migration was seen as a migratory cycle, that begins when working-age migrants leave their place of origin and seek employment in a more advanced economic area. After a substantial period working abroad, they return home after having achieved their goals. Here, action depends on anticipated future effects, and alternatives are weighed in terms of expected outcomes. These theories assume knowledge of alternatives and their consequences, which is referred to as the logic of consequences, because potential migrants supposedly evaluate their future moves based on economic outcomes. Some researchers have attributed the return of immigrants to their homeland to their failure to achieve prosperity abroad. This line of thought also associates migration and economic determinism, and is popular among neo-economists who consider possible migrants to be evaluating the worth of their labor at home and abroad.

In the field of migration, rational decision-making frameworks are variations of the push–pull model. These take the individual actor as the unit of analysis, and assume that the individual evaluates the alternatives of remaining or returning based on how they will affect their liveli-hood. According to the push–pull model, suffering individuals leave their residence for another country after assessing their plight. Reasons for moving might include poverty or political upheaval. According to this model, migrants cut most ties with their home country in order to emigrate; immigrants are considered to be "uprooted" into the host society without any social anchors. These "rootless" individuals are thus considered to be especially open to assimilation: a straight-line absorption into the new culture. The model implies that the receiving country, especially those in North America, is so superior to the origin country that migrants would never even consider returning. Analysis of migrants' remittances is central to this economic-based schema; researchers attempt to predict whether labor migrants would return when a cer-tain threshold of accumulation or capital is reached. This is one approach to the study of return migration (Meyers 1998).

From this perspective, most return migration is attributed to economic factors: those who return to their country of origin are said to be pursuing economic gains. Countries that have prospered and have tried to encourage emigrants to return include Ireland, China, Hong Kong, Singapore, Korea, Taiwan, and Malaysia.

In a similar vein, many researchers have discussed the economic contributions of those edu-cated abroad who return. The boom in advanced technologies in Beijing and Bangalore has been attributed to these returnees (Zweig et al. 2006). As a result, political leaders encourage students educated abroad to return and improve the social and economic conditions of their home country. In the People's Republic of China, these bearers of modernity who were edu-cated abroad are rewarded upon their return with professional opportunities and cash. Recently, researchers have focused on the labor market as a motivation for those educated abroad to return to their home country and have looked at governmental policies intended to motivate skilled expatriate students to return. The Canadian government, in an attempt to retain edu-cated youth from abroad, has changed its immigration policy; these changes make it easier for international students to work after graduation, with the goal of encouraging foreign students to stay in Canada. However, few researchers have conducted a detailed evaluation of the particular social positioning among international students, in order to demonstrate that they are remaining in Canada for material reasons. It is likely that a host of social relationships also figure in whe-ther they return to their native land or remain in the host country. One would also like to see comparisons of another sort: for example, a study of returnees in comparison with those that do not return.

Overall, this push–pull view of outgoing and return migration has been criticized. On the one hand it is seen as "oversocialized" because it portrays migrants as passive agents whose migration is the result of macro-societal forces. On the other it is viewed as an "under-socialized" economic theory that considers migration to be driven only by individual calcula-tions (Boyd 1989). Taking its place is the current trend of research that reveals the activism of migrants and that embeds them in their social relations.

Social and cultural embeddedness: social networks

Researchers have realized that migration involves more complex issues than a simple calculation of earnings. They revised the earlier narrow emphasis on economic determinants that excluded the socio-cultural issues involved in migration decision-making, and tried to incorporate the multiple factors prompting migration.

Boyd (1989) took a new approach in her seminal article, arguing that migrants' social networks are central to the dynamics of their lives. She theorized that embeddedness in social, political, and cultural contexts influences their conduct in the sphere of migration as in other realms. Others have expanded on her research, demonstrating that individuals do not abandon the relationships that affected them before, during, and after their migration (Levitt 2002).

More research is required about how social relations interact with economic factors to influence return migration. Clearly, both social and economic factors contribute to young people's desire to return to their homeland. For instance, Aranda (2006) found that for Puerto Ricans, favorable economic conditions in their home country (such as employment or business opportunities) encourage return migration from the United States when migration networks link the two locations. These networks passed on information, and provided a welcoming environment for those making quick decisions to return (Aranda 2006).

There has been some progress in the field of social factors. Sociologists and geographers studying social and cultural embeddedness have developed theories about social categories and interactions during the return process. They describe these stimuli to leave and then to return as the "bandwagon effect," which refers to a relationship-based logic of appropriateness, in which decision-makers consider what is an appropriate action in a particular situation by following what other individuals would do under similar conditions.

In particular former colonies (e.g., Hong Kong, the West Indies, and some African countries), migration to study abroad is seen as a form of social status (Waters 2005). The metropolis is seen as a superior place to get educated, and parents work hard to obtain the resources to send their children abroad for education. Return migration is often prompted by the expectations of the parents of these children. As well, youth educated abroad who see many of their classmates returning home are likely to follow.

Transnationalism

The development of the concept of transnationalism was an important juncture in the study of international migration. Researchers in this field focus on how migrants' networks cross international borders. They argue for a reconceptualization of international migrants as transnational migrants, describing migrants as having two worlds, or as in-between travelers who have social networks in their homeland and their host country. The diverse social networks of migrants (e.g., family, friends, and former colleagues) cross borders and form complex relationships between members, which affect migrants' decisions. The study of migration networks involves following the migration paths of individuals and families and exploring the nature of contact between individuals, especially family members, as they leave their homeland, arrive in the host country, and continue to maintain contact with their country of origin.

By exploring a wide range of cross-border activities, scholars can incorporate two important conceptual issues: the internal complexity of migrants' social networks and the external complexity of migrants' transnational social networks (Gielis 2009). External complexity (relationships between migrants living in a host country and their homeland) is particularly relevant here. For many researchers, the external complexity of migrants' social networks is closely related to whether or not they will return to their homeland. Most empirical research on this issue has focused on the second generation; diverse ethnic and migrant groups have been studied to explore how transnationalism affects the return migration process (Levitt 2009; King and Christou 2010).

How does transnationalism lead people back to their homeland? Researchers have proposed several ways that maintaining these ties prompts return migration. First, transnational visits bring young people into contact with peers in their homeland and help them feel that they belong there. Next, for second-generation young people who have never lived in their homeland for long periods, ties to relatives in the homeland reduce the cost of "trying it out." For example, Salaff, and others have reported that young people who want to return to Hong Kong often find it problematic to find housing for temporary stays. Much migration is unplanned and spontaneous, based on a chance opportunity, so individuals without any contacts in the homeland may be deterred by the enormity of this venture (Salaff et al. 2008). In contrast, those with personal links are more likely to take the plunge.

Another aspect is language: when a language is particularly difficult to learn (for example Asian languages with pictorial script), familiarity with the native tongue is important (Danico 2004). Transnationals are often better able to maintain two languages. Return migrants who are familiar with the language have a greater range of job prospects than others.

Selectivity clearly makes a difference; families that do not wish to return to their homeland are unlikely to maintain transnational relations with those back home. As well, Menjívar reported that state regulations may intervene; even when families desire to maintain contact with those back home, passport and visa difficulties may make contact impossible (Menjívar 2000).

Identities

A person's identity is embedded in lived structures in many ways, affecting everyday life and the sociocultural realities in which those lives are lived (DiMaggio 1997). Those that study return migration pay special attention to emigrants' social–psychological identities. They note that migrants have many ideological and mental associations with home, and these have become an important focus of research.

In most cases, researchers find internally formed and externally imposed understandings of ethnic identity, home, and belonging alongside other pragmatic and practical reasons for returning home. This requires locating in a concrete manner the actual contacts that young people have with their homelands. Cassarino (2004) proposed this potentially fruitful approach, theorizing that social networks underlie identities.

Migrant generations

Dreams of homeland surely vary by migrant generation, since their knowledge or skill with a new homeland acquired over a period of time differ dramatically. The term "migration generation" is used to distinguish migrants by the social structures in which they are embedded at their lifecycle stage at immigration. Immigrants who arrive as adults are classified as "first-generation" or their dependent children are classified as "1.5 generation;" and those born in the host country are classified as "second-generation" immigrants. These classifications are associated with Mannheim's concept of political generation (Mannheim 1952).

The first generation tends to imagine the homeland vividly, colored by its experiences in the host nation. Few second-generation young people have lived in their home country, so it is important to identify the activating mechanisms that prompt them to turn a dream into reality. The lifecycle stage at which individuals immigrate is linked to their choice of residence through the social structures in which they are embedded. These structures shape their experiences of, and attachment to, their host country and country of origin. Migration generation theorists predict that structures in the place in which migrants grew up are most binding. This suggests that individuals born in the home of the ancestors are more likely then those born in a host country to feel connected to their homeland and to wish to return. First and 1.5 generation immigrants have lived in multiple locations, so they are likely to feel conflicted over where "home" is. Those who are born and raised in the host country (the second generation) and are full participants in the school system with its attending youth structures, tend to be most determined to remain in the host country.

Studies have also linked migration generation and cultural identity to immigrants' language facility. Language fluency is a portal to insider experiences. To feel at home, an individual must be familiar with cultural idioms and artifacts (Swidler 1986). Their age at family resettlement shapes youths' cultural tool-kit and choice of social contacts. Language fluency, the ability to speak fluently in the mother tongue is associated with social networks (Danico 2004). Youths who left their homeland at an older age tend to be more comfortable in their native tongue and to seek out peers who share their language. Immigrant parents can include them in ethnic events, thereby socializing them into the mother culture. Returning to their homeland, they will be able to converse with others and build local social networks. Embedded in social groups that prioritize their ethnic home, they are more open to return migration. In contrast, those who leave their country at a younger age tend to be more fluent in the host country's language, easing their acceptance by non-ethnic peers. Involvement in local peer networks may induce them to remain in the host country.

As young immigrants mature and develop committed relationships, their partners' social networks are added to their own; this is yet another example of how age is related to the development of social networks. This multiplying of social networks complicates the choice to stay or return.

Methods

The methods used to study return migrants have shifted along with the emphasis on social relations. Writers find biographical methods most useful, to help locate common experiences in people's lives which can help generate hypotheses. As well, the exploration of respondents' of narratives provides rich understanding of their motives and the occasions prompting their return to the homeland (Potter et al. 2010).

Studies over time contribute to the understanding of return migration. They can document who returns under what circumstances, and can also compare those who do not return with those who do; these comparisons can be very illuminating.

Three books have notably focused on migrants over time. Smith (2006) traced the cross-border visits of Mexican immigrants in New York over two generations. He was most interested in how young people participated in ritual activities in Mexico; after traveling there with their parents, he wondered how they maintained their relationships over time. He followed a number of Mexican villagers who had migrated to New York over two generations, and documented how changing levels of interest in ritual activities increased in tandem with transnationalism. He linked increasing cross-border activities to the life cycle, reporting that as teenagers, the migrants did not always show interest in their homeland. But a few years later, married with children, they became more interested in the homeland. This interest did not always lead to return migration, but led to return visits for holidays and ritual occasions. This approach ties embeddedness closely to return migration, by showing how embeddedness forms.

Salaff et al. (2010) studied a number of Hong Kong families for almost two decades. These families included first-generation migrants who became transnationals because they were unable to earn a living in the host country. Several eventually returned to Hong Kong, while others remained in Canada. From our interest in return migration, we note that the children of these transnational migrants followed their parents; some moved to Canada for their education, and planned to return to Hong Kong. This study emphasized nonintentional migration activities; many subjects planned to move, but lacked full information about the land abroad. Their returns were unplanned, based on chance, rather than planned excursions.

In another longitudinal study, Olwig (2007) reported cross-border migration activities of three Caribbean kinship group by means of their life histories. While not completely a study over time, the life history method was a close substitute. She found that kin ties were primary in the location of families and their members over time. Some members aimed to go to north America or England for a professional education, planning to return to the West Indies, but marriage and other issues often intervened. Others, in contrast, did not intend to return to their West Indies' home, but followed family members back. This research project demonstrates that taking time into account highlights the role of relationships in decision-making.

Returnees of different statuses

Researchers that have applied a biographical approach have reported that return migration intersects with liminal events, life-cycle transitions such as graduation, marriage, or retirement, or unexpected events such as the aging and illness of a parent (Ni Laoire 2008). Hence, studies of return migration have also distinguished between migrants of different statuses, including graduating students and job seekers who have studied abroad. Migrants who have held jobs and then retired also face the decision of whether to remain in the adopted country or return to the homeland.

Returning students

Whether or not students that study abroad will return to their home of origin is intensely debated and has important political and economic implications. Researchers using an economic model to study returns argue that return migration is related to economic opportunities; this argument has been made forcefully about the young people that come from rapidly-developing China and India, and other countries. However, few economic studies have explored the social relationships that students maintain in their home country prior to return.

The findings of studies that combine both paradigms, economic and social, are most interesting. Youths who maintain ties with family and friends in the home country as well as in the host country are more likely to return home after graduation. Part of the attraction is social capital from contacts that can help them find work. Researchers have also traced how work in North America can lead young people back to their home country through the relationships formed with similar others in the work place. Saxenian et al. (2002) reported that these work ties can give rise to transnational entrepreneurship; a young person becomes interested in starting an investment in the home country, and applies skills and knowledge obtained in the North American workplace, often inviting a workmate to join the enterprise.

The study of identity issues often focuses on students. By spending years in the host country at a liminal time in their lives, students often take on the values of those around them. If they are immigrants, the socialization institutions will have an even more pronounced effect on them. This is especially true in Canada, where the philosophy of multiculturalism has led to attempts to incorporate newcomers. While immigrant youths make friends and find potential partners, they are influenced by the surrounding norms. A considerable body of research has focused on Hong Kong immigrants to Canada and Australia in the 1990s, because of the unprecedented large population leaving at one historical moment. This research has shown how the values of the host country influence students, and how students maintain these values even after returning to their homeland. Still, proponents of segmented assimilation point out that not all native values are discarded; the young person is likely to maintain their basic values, but with new nuances.

Parents are often unhappy at the changes in the behavior of children who return home. No matter how they may try to re-infuse their child with Chinese cultural values, the intercultural experience of being acculturated into Western culture may result in children lacking the assimilation strategy of intercultural relations. They may be unable to manage their cultural identities in a way that allows them to integrate the two cultural systems in how they think and behaving (Berry 1998).

Female and male students appear to differ with regard to the factors that determine their intentions to stay in the study country or return home (Olwig 2007). Young women are more likely to delay their decision to return until they find the right partner, and the partner's decision to return has considerable weight. In contrast, young male students are more likely to state that they decide where to live and would choose a partner that agrees with this decision. These findings suggest that social and emotional factors are as important as economic factors in the decisions of transplanted residents to return home or to stay in the host country.

Retired workers

Those who have worked for decades abroad and are about to retire must decide where to spend their later years. Articles devoted to this topic illustrate the complexity of retirees' decisions (Haug 2008). Most striking was the importance of the location of meaningful others. Individuals who had raised their families in the host country typically want to stay with their families; their children and grandchildren were often tightly tied to the new land. If the parents had not maintained close ties with their homeland, they were also less likely to wish to return. Some retirees had only visited home a few times before they retired, and were struck by the changes in their homelands and felt they were strangers there. This is another example of how social relations affect the return voyage.

Adaptation

Researchers have noted the social costs and social and cultural adjustments experienced by returnees to the country of origin. Having left their original home, migrants have broken their social networks. Some experience material losses, having given up jobs and sold their homes, and some governments provide programs, counseling services to returned migrants, aimed at helping with the re-integration process (Ralph 2009).

One major difficulty originates in relationships with locals. Returnees may feel that they have experiences that locals do not have, but these experiences are not outwardly apparent; some migrants report feeling different but not being visibly different. At the minimum, they will feel separation and alienation from others who have not left (Ralph 2009). Others may be suspicious about returnees, feeling that they changed during their residence abroad. This was documented in a study of first generation returnees to the Republic of Ireland (Ralph 2009). Second generation return migrants typically face other problems. Other issues are compounded by racism and gender, as seen in the experiences of migrants returning to the West Indies from England. These young people are accused of having "gone British" and face resentment when they return. It is difficult for those who have not left home to imagine life abroad, and they may accuse returnees of giving up their culture. Returnees are often alienated from locals and may feel most comfortable with other returnees (Potter *et al.* 2010).

Chan and Chan's (2010) study about integration in workplaces in Hong Kong revealed that colleagues act as barriers to integration. Workplace competition and envy is common. We can speculate that social networks contribute to these problems; employees who return to work in an environment where coworkers have not been abroad must integrate into tight and complicated networks. Coworkers feel they must prove that they are as good as returnees, and may achieve this goal by making the returnees look bad. Chan reported that workers are more likely to be accepted by coworkers in firms and industries with many sources of employees, when the employees did not all go to school together. His research clarifies the defense mechanisms of the returnees, and how they make sense of the difficulties.

Family issues are also important: returnees may face a range of difficulties related to integrating the entire family. For children born abroad, this return can be especially traumatic. Even for spouses who may have once lived in the ancestral land, return can be problematic, because their lifestyle overseas was usually very different.

We have explored the ways that social relations shape return migration experiences. Returnees are attracted back to their native land, or the land of their forefathers, through a variety of mechanisms. Economic opportunities figure among these, but to focus on these experiences alone is to miss the rich fabric of social relations that also attract returnees. To begin with, researchers of transnational migration have found that those most likely to return have maintained transnational ties with their home country. Next, the timing of returns is usually associated with lifecycle transitions. These may be transitions to the returnee, as for example graduation from school abroad or the loss of a job or a broken relationship. A transition can occur in the homeland to the wider kinship group, as with the passing of a close relative.

Next, the experiences of return also are imbued with social issues. How confident is the return migrant in this voyage? Having kin to receive them eases the costs of a tentative return. Those that can expect a receptive homecoming are much more likely to take the plunge. They can anticipate ahead of time how they will fit into the local society better, and they may be able to count on housing, or at least the kind of advice that they need for day-to-day living until they get used to the "new" place.

The reception of the returnee by the locals, especially those that have never lived abroad, significantly shapes the feelings of success. These experiences are seen in adjustments by the families that the returnees bring with them, and workplace integration. Integration into the wider society through friends, neighbors, and others has also been pointed at as a feature of the returnees experiences. In sum, a strict analysis based on economic calculations can neither predict who will return the nor account for the experiences of return migration.

References and further reading

Aranda, E. M. (2006) *Emotional Bridges to Puerto Rico: Migration, Return Migration, and the Struggles of Incorporation.* Lanham, MD: Rowman and Littlefield.
Berry, J. (1998) "Intercultural relations in plural societies" *Canadian Psychology* 40(1): 12–21.
Boyd, M. (1989) "Family and personal networks in international migration: Recent developments and new agendas" *International Migration Review* 23(3): 638–69.

Cassarino, J.-P. (2004) "Theorising return migration: The conceptual approach to return migrants revisited" *International Journal on Multicultural Societies* 6(2): 253–79.

Chan, K.-B. and Chan, W.-W. V. (2010) "The return of the native: Globalization and the adaptive responses of transmigrants" *World Futures* 66(6): 398–434.

Danico, M. Y. (2004) *The 1.5 Generation: Becoming Korean American in Hawai'i*. Honolulu, HI: The University of Hawai'i Press.

DiMaggio, P. J. (1997) "Culture and cognition" *Annual Review of Sociology* 23: 263–87.

Gielis, R. (2009) "A global sense of migrant places: Towards a place perspective in the study of migrant transnationalism" *Global Networks* 9(2): 271–87.

Haug, S. (2008) "Migration networks and migration decision-making" *Journal of Ethnic and Migration Studies* 34(4): 585–605.

King, R. and Christou, A. (2010) "Cultural geographies of counter-diasporic migration: Perspectives from the study of second-generation 'returnees' to Greece" *Population, Space and Place* 16(2): 103–19.

Levitt, P. (2002) "The ties that change: Relations to the ancestral home over the life cycle." In P. Levitt and M. C. Waters (eds), *The Changing Face of Home: The Transnational Lives of the Second Generation*, New York: Russell Sage Foundation, pp. 123–44.

——(2009) "Roots and routes: Understanding the lives of the second generation transnationally" *Journal of Ethnic and Migration Studies* 35(7): 1225–42.

Mannheim, K. (1952) "The problem of generations." In K. Mannheim (ed.), *Essays on the Sociology of Knowledge*, New York: Routledge and Kegan Paul, pp. 276–322.

March, J. G. (1994) *A Primer on Decision Making: How Decisions Happen*. New York: The Free Press.

Menjívar, C. (2000) *Fragmented Ties: Salvadoran Immigrant Networks in America*. Berkeley, CA: University of California Press.

Meyers, D. (1998) *Migrant Remittances to Latin America: Reviewing the Literature*. Los Angeles, CA: The Tomás Rivera Policy Institute.

Ni Laoire, C. (2008) "Settling back? A biographical and life-course perspective on Ireland's recent return" *Irish Geography* 41(2): 195–210.

Olwig, K. F. (2007) *Caribbean Journeys: An Ethnography of Migration and Home*. Durham, NC: Duke University.

Potter, R. B., Conway, D., and St Bernard, G. (2010) "'Racism in a melting pot.?' Trinidadian mid-life transnational migrants' views on race and colour-class on return to their homes of descent" *Geoforum* 41(5): 805–13.

Ralph, D. (2009) "Home is where the heart is? Understandings of 'home' among Irish-born return migrants from the United States" *Irish Studies Review* 17(2): 183–200.

Salaff, J., Wong, S., and Greve, A. (2010) *Hong Kong Movers and Stayers: Narratives of Family Migration*. Chicago, IL: University of Illinois Press.

Salaff, J., Shik, A., and Greve, A. (2008) "Like sons and daughters of Hong Kong: The return of the young generation" *The China Review* 8(1): 31–57.

Saxenian, A., Motoyama, Y., and Quan, X. (2002) *Local and Global Networks of Immigrant Professionals in Silicon Valley*. San Francisco, CA: Public Policy Institute Of California.

Smith, R. C. (2006) *Mexican New York*. Berkeley, CA: University of California Press.

Swidler, A. (1986) "Culture in action: Symbols and strategies" *American Sociological Review* 51(2): 273–86.

Waters, J. L. (2005) "Transnational family strategies and education in the contemporary Chinese diaspora" *Global Networks* 5(4): 359–77.

Zweig, D., Chung, S. F., and Vanhonacker, W. (2006) "Rewards of technology: Explaining China's reverse migration" *Journal of International Migration and Integration* 7(4): 449–71.

Part IX
Methods for studying
international migration

The study of international migration is a diverse project shaped by many academic disciplines, research methods, and approaches to social research. While this area of investigation has long been a significant focus of certain academic fields, in recent years, disciplines that were not previously concerned with the topic have begun to study it as well. This burgeoning interest in studying international migration notwithstanding, few academic disciplines have created research methods and techniques that are specifically devoted to it. Instead, they have relied upon approaches commonly used within the discipline at large.

Here we offer nine chapters that describe research techniques developed specifically for the study of international migration. It is our hope that this section will provide readers with two ways of improving their migration research. First, these chapters offer an excellent summary of the diverse tools and techniques used to examine a topic that specialists increasingly regard as multi-disciplinary. Second, the chapters will assist readers in mastering research methods specifically designed for the collection and analysis of data on international migration.

A consensus of migration scholars increasingly understand their endeavor to be multi-disciplinary in nature. They contend that to achieve a well-rounded understanding of the topic, one must bring together theories, data, and findings from many academic fields. The chapters in this section facilitate this goal. By learning about these methods, students and scholars will be able to evaluate and integrate the findings of multi-disciplinary research on immigrants.

The section begins with one of the most commonly applied tools used for the study of international migration: census analysis. National censuses provide high-quality, credible data about both the total numbers of international migrants as well as a large amount of social, demographic, and economic information about their characteristics, ways of life, settlement patterns and behaviors. Karen Woodrow-Lafield describes the kinds of questions that are best answered via census data and suggests useful techniques for measuring variables that are not easily accessible—such as religious or sub-ethnic differences. She also explains how census practices have changed over time and reflects on the challenges involved in making inter-national comparisons using data from different countries. Finally, she shows how census analysis can be refined by supplementing it with other data sources.

Mariano Sana and Becky Conway's chapter on surveys and ethnosurveys describes a method uniquely appropriate for the study of international migration—one that collects data from migrant populations in both the country of origin and the destination. This approach combines a random sample survey conducted prior to migration with a snowball-based collection of data among members of the original sample now in the host society. While the resulting data are not fully random or representative, they are based upon both qualitative and quantitative methods. Accordingly, the technique is well suited for capturing the social and bi-national dimensions of international migration.

Patricia Fernandez Kelly summarizes the history of ethnographic research for the study migrants. She then describes her own use of the method to acquire rich, comparative accounts of the experience of several nationalities of immigrant youth as they deal with social networks, identity issues, and employment.

Chien Juh Gu provides valuable information about conducting in-depth interviews with members of migrant communities who have very different cultural orientations than the researcher. Topics include the researcher's role as an insider or outsider to the subject population, the affects of structural position (race/gender/class) on the interview encounter, language use, cultural sensitivity, and research ethics. Gillian Stevens and Hiromi Ishizawa's chapter explores measuring time, a topic of vital importance, given the emphasis on time-related phenomena such as assimilation, returns to human capital, cohort effects, and generational issues in the study of international migration. The article codifies time-related aspects of migration and introduces techniques by which the effects of time can be analyzed.

Steven Gold summarizes how photographs and other visual data, including images made by immigrants, by researchers or acquired from archives, can be used to document immigrants' experiences, facilitate interactions between researchers and respondents, pose and answer research questions, and teach students and colleagues about international migration.

In her chapter on online communities and diaspora studies, Emily Noelle Ignacio discusses the potential benefits and limitations of conducting discursive analysis online, particularly with regard to the study of diasporic communities. While the method offers new levels of access to discussions about membership, belonging, social networks and other topics of interest to students of migration, it is also subject to various distortions. To avoid such liabilities, Ignacio instructs that those who wish to do online research, should be prepared to research the context within which the poster is physically located; the context(s) that the poster is responding to; the context of the site itself; and the context(s) that any respondent may be located in. In addition, the use of other data gathering techniques should be considered and findings critically evaluated to insure their veracity and utility.

Irene Bloemraad, whose research combines surveys, census data and other sources of information collected from the same nationalities in different locations, describes how comparative methods can be used to examine how structures, culture, norms, institutions, and other processes affect collective outcomes. Bloemraad describes different types of comparisons, from comparisons of migrant groups to geographic areas to comparisons across time. She then details different ways for designing comparisons, using similarities and/or differences between comparison groups to yield theoretical or conceptual advances.

Rigoberto Rodriguez's chapter on action research with immigrants describes the use of various methods that engage people and communities in the research process to produce findings and actions that can address shared concerns. Most action research projects rely on four interlocking tenets of participation, critical knowledge attainment, social action and change, and empowerment. The chapter provides an overview of action research scholarship, introduces citizenship theory as a means of enhancing awareness of social inequalities that impact immigrants, and presents a case study of an action research project devoted to improving the health conditions in Boyle Heights, a predominantly Mexican-American and Mexican immigrant community located in Los Angeles, California.

39

Census analysis

Karen A. Woodrow-Lafield

Introduction

The primary purposes for census-taking vary across nations. For the majority, censuses are the source of information on the migrant stock, but certain countries with population registers already have excellent data and censuses are not necessary. For the United States, the census is constitutionally mandated every 10 years for purposes of apportioning political representation among the states according to the distribution of the population. Just as dramatic changes occurred over time in implementing this count as technologies evolved from hand calculations and early tabulating machines to efficient, high capacity computers, the US Census Bureau's mission of providing timely, relevant, and quality data about the people and economy of the United States has evolved to include not only the crucial topics of people, housing, business, and governments, for which the major resource has historically been the decennial census of population and housing, but also information from other sources (surveys, administrative statistics, and other information), such as through the *Statistical Abstract* annual series. The US 2010 Census is the re-engineered census, with the American Community Survey (ACS) designed for collecting detailed social and economic characteristics nationally and subnationally on a continuous basis. With respondent participation on a mandatory basis, the ACS was gradually implemented and fully fielded by 2010. Similarly, Canada initiated the National Household Survey (NHS) in conjunction with the 2011 Census, for which participation is voluntary.

Censuses include persons according to residence rules—*de jure criteria*, or legal residence, or *de facto criteria*, or "usual residence," the place where a person lives and sleeps most of the time or the place they consider their usual residence. Thus, the US census with *de facto* residence rules includes unauthorized residents as counted in their usual place of residence in the United States. Mexico's census is by *de jure* criteria, thus encompassing those migrants sojourning north of the border. China's 2010 census counted residents at their usual place of residence rather than according to *hukuo*, place of household registration, and this marked the first application of this residence criterion and first inclusion of international migrants.

Residence rules for US national surveys, the ACS and the Current Population Survey (CPS) differ from the decennial census, with more inclusiveness of the working population and, implicitly, such special populations as temporary migrants and unauthorized residents. Conducted monthly, the CPS gathers employment and labor force participation data, and the March interview contains supplemental social and economic characteristics. The CPS rule is a version of usual residence that includes everyone in a housing unit who considers the unit as their usual residence or who has no other usual residence plus any temporarily absent individuals for whom the unit is considered usual residence. The ACS concept of residence is "current residence" with everyone interviewed who is in the housing unit on the day of interview who is living or staying there for more than 2 months, regardless of whether or not they maintain a usual residence elsewhere, or who does not have a usual residence elsewhere. If a person who usually lives in the housing unit is away for more than two months at the time of the survey contact, he or she is not a current resident of that unit. This rule recognizes that people can have more than one place where they live or stay over the course of a year, and for those whose residence changes seasonally, such as migrant groups, these conceptual differences may affect where persons are counted in time.

Most countries have had a complete census, typically on a periodic basis, such as every ten years in years ending in "0" or "1," for a long period as in the case of the United States or a shorter period (1990–2010) as in the case of China, or every five years as in Canada. Nationally representative surveys often augment census-taking. China conducts a population sample census in years ending in "5." Census-taking is subject to change for reasons of costs, privacy concerns, and various crises. Censuses may be postponed, as were the 2000 round censuses until 2005 or 2006 for Nicaragua, Colombia, Peru, and El Salvador. The UN provides technical and financial assistance in national censuses in order to enhance the value of data for the international community. Temporal comparability may differ over time for several reasons.

Migration is a key component in demographic change for a specific population and in changing the contour of the world population. In the US case, international migration events are outnumbered by internal migration events, due to job mobility, individual preferences, rural–urban shifts, and economic restructuring, but international migration contributes to population growth. In recent decades, industrial expansion in China has resulted in a large "floating population" of workers living near those industrial centers, but those population shifts were not easily captured with hukou-based census-taking. Considerable population growth occurred in Mexico near maquiladoras located at the US–Mexico border.

Upon the December 14 2010 release of the first results from the US 2010 Census, the US population count (308.7 million) seemed much as anticipated based on comparison with the middle estimate (308.5 million) from demographic analysis (US Census Bureau 2010). A decade ago, the 2000 census count showed the greatest national population increase ever and increased populations for each of the 50 states, was higher than the demographic estimate by 6 million, 2 million more than the 1990 census net undercount of 4 million, and sparked immediate reassessment of net immigration for the 1990s. The number of unauthorized residents in 2000 was estimated to be substantially greater than in 1990 with the increase happening in the late 1990s (Bean *et al.* 2001). Again emphasizing the value of census analysis for understanding migration, regular and irregular, the Mexican Census 2010 count was considerably higher than expected, leading to speculation that migration into the United States over the decade had been less than assumed.

Data, questions, and issues

Censuses of major destination nations, especially the United States, Canada, and Australia, have generally included the major questions for studying migration. The key questions that are recommended and most related to migration are place of birth, citizenship, and place of residence

5 years ago (Massey and Clemens 2008). Additional questions that may be considered useful in analyzing migration are race, Hispanic origin, ancestry, parental birthplace, date of entry or immigration, language spoken, and departures of household family members. Data on international migrants are easily accessible from the United Nations according to official statistics (censuses, national surveys, or population registers) on the foreign-born or the foreign population enumerated in the countries or areas of the world with classification by origin, sex, and age (UN DESA 2008). National data is available for country of origin as either country of birth or country of citizenship. A global bilateral international migration database based on the 2000 round of population censuses for OECD countries and non-OECD destination countries includes demographic characteristics, duration of stay, labor market characteristics, education, and place of birth (Dumont *et al.* 2010).

Place of birth is not typically detailed as to specific area within a foreign country which may sometimes result in incomplete information, although, for natives, place of birth may be detailed as to specific area and permit measuring lifetime migration within the nation of birth. Formal citizenship in the United States is set forth in the Fourteenth Amendment as *jus soli* or citizenship by birthright, *jus sanguines* (right of blood) or citizenship as inherited from parents (born abroad of American parents) or derivative, and citizenship conferred through naturalization, sometimes referred to as administrative assimilation. Individuals are increasingly adopting dual or multiple citizenships and maintaining transnational ties. More nations are permitting dual citizenship and abandoning earlier commitment to the Hague Convention of 1930 which stated that each nation is responsible for determining who may be a citizen or national of their country and declared that dual nationality, or dual citizenship, was undesirable, but, in 1997, a new European Convention on Nationality was adopted which accepts the concept of multiple nationalities, subject to regulation. Colombia, Vietnam, Jamaica, Brazil, Ecuador, Mexico, Philippines, and the Dominican Republic permit dual citizenship, but Cuba, China, and Korea do not. National censuses are generally limited to information on whether an individual holds that nation's citizenship without ascertaining multiple citizenships. Place of prior residence is meant to measure the net in-flow for a recent time period, and many experts regard this response data as factually based and preferable to any response as to the events of immigration, entry, or last arrival.

Until 2011, Canadian censuses had included a question on place of birth since the 1871 Census, and questions on citizenship and year of immigration were initiated with the 1901 Census. The 2001 and 2006 Censuses included place of birth, citizenship, landed immigrant status and year of landing, plus these censuses renewed data collection on birthplace of parents which had been previously included in the 1971 Census. Canada adopted an official policy of diversity and multiculturalism in the 1970s, and Canadian census data are richly detailed on ethnicity and religious affiliation. In tandem with immigration policies based on a point system and targeted limits on immigrants and refugees, Canada has settlement policies for which census analyses are informative. Because "landed immigrant status" and "year of landing" refer to the granting of permanent resident status, these Canadian census data are highly appropriate for analyzing the association of length of official Canadian residence with integration indicators, although experiences before achieving landed immigrant status may be missed. However, non-permanent resident status is ascertained, and about 10 percent of these are US-born citizens (Michalowski and Norris 2005; Statistics Canada 2010). The 2011 Census covered only basic demographic characteristics, and the NHS included detailed questions about citizenship, immigration, and language.

Since the 1850 census, the US census included data collection on the nativity (place of birth) of the population, with other questions and sampling bases varying among censuses (Gibson and

Jung 2006). Over 1980–2000, data about place of birth, US citizenship, residence 5 years ago, language, ancestry, and year of entry into the United States (for anyone born outside the United States) were gathered on the detailed questionnaire administered to the one-in-six sample, and the Integrated Public-Use Microdata Samples are a tremendous asset for researchers. With the 2010 census, this time series ended, and new data from the ACS became available for analyzing broad and detailed patterns. The place of birth, US citizenship, and year of US entry items on the ACS questionnaire are similar to the predecessor decennial census questions, and new questions are being included, such as date of naturalization on the 2008 ACS. Ancestry information depicts origins of past migrants plus their descendants as subjectively defined; ancestry refers to ethnic origin, descent, roots, heritage, or a place of birth of a person or his or her ancestors as they wish to respond. For example, the Arab ancestry population was treated in an analysis of 2000 census data, looking at persons providing Lebanese, Egyptian, Syrian, Palestinian, Jordanian, Moroccan, Iraqi, or other Arab ancestry responses (de la Cruz and Brittingham 2003). English language proficiency, how well spoken, is the basis for understanding linguistic assimilation as well as linguistic isolation.

A remarkable change with China's 2010 census consisting of a short form and a long form is inclusion of place of birth for the first time with a smaller eight-question survey, and foreigners are expected to be enumerated, possibly including unauthorized migrants and internal migrant workers to whom special efforts have been directed. Sending unauthorized migrants to Japan and the United States, China is a destination for unauthorized residents from such countries as Indonesia, Philippines, and Thailand from which legal workers have been allowed, with some estimated as having become undocumented.

Place of prior residence is sometimes specific to area within a country for purposes of assessing internal migration that occurred over a defined period. In the US case, there have been extensive studies of internal migration patterns of the foreign-born and native-born populations across metropolitan areas, states, and regions (Frey and Liaw 1998; Rogers and Raymer 1999; Kritz and Gurak 2004). China's 2000 Population Census was a detailed 10 percent sample survey that included intricate questions related to migration of household members residing outside the household for less than 6 months, of household members residing outside the household for more than 6 months, and of household members temporarily residing in the current location and away from their place of household registration for less than 6 months (Liang and Ma 2004). Each individual was questioned about his or her *hukou* status and place of household registration, place of birth, and date of arrival in the current location. Those who had moved in the last five years were asked about county and province of origin, original residence as rural or urban, reason for migration, and province of prior residence.

Since 1890, the US census classifies individuals who were born in a foreign country, but who had at least one parent who was an American citizen, as native rather than as foreign born. Questions about birthplace of parents allow classification of the native population by parentage: native of native parentage (both parents native), native of foreign parentage (both parents foreign-born) and native of mixed parentage (one parent native and one parent foreign born). The term foreign stock includes the foreign-born population and the native population of foreign or mixed parentage. A question on birthplace of parents was included in the US census from 1870 to 1970, but, starting in the 1980 census, the question on ancestry (based on self-identification) replaced the question on birthplace of parents. Questions on birthplace of parents, along with other nativity and immigration questions, were included on selected CPSs in 1979–91 (Woodrow 1992) and regularly included on the monthly CPS beginning in 1994. One option in intergenerational analysis has been to focus on those children residing with a foreign-born parent. A second option has been utilizing the CPS data for nativity, immigration, and birthplace of parents for intergenerational analyses of specific groups of first generation immigrants and second generation Americans. At the turn of the century, about 22 percent were of foreign birth or ancestry, consisting of 11.8 percent foreign-born and 10.6 percent with foreign-born parents, based on pooling samples in 1998–2002 (Rumbaut 2004).

Asking about a date of migrating to a country would elicit accurate responses only if migration were a single, nonrepeatable event, but migration is often a dynamic process of making repeated trips of variable durations or progressing through stages. In answering a question about date of entry or immigration, the meaning of individuals' responses may be imprecise. To measure net inflow for a recent time period, date of entry is regarded as subject to conceptual limitations stemming from migration circularity and status irregularity because respondents may answer in terms of last arrival, an earlier arrival, coming to stay, or obtaining legal documents (Massey 2010). The commonly used question on date of entry or immigration is also subject to limitations for assessing socioeconomic advancement due to inclusion of temporary migrants or individuals having dual residence for the most recent period and return migration or emigration.

Latin American countries are improving census quality as well as expanding information about international migration, and, in the past two decades, Mexico has particularly expanded national surveys for studying migration. Following inclusion on several household surveys of questions about household members living outside the country, this was a sample topic in the Mexico's Population and Housing Census 2000. Intended to estimate emigration levels and characteristics, the questions were about whether any members of the household had left to live abroad within the prior 5 years with further questions on sex, age at departure, month and year of departure, country of destination, country of present residence, and month and year of return of each such member were recorded. These data proved useful, although subject to omission of whole household emigration (Hill and Wong 2005). Census data on Dominicans living abroad provided better estimates than estimates conventionally used in policy debates (Larson and Sullivan 1987).

Crucial to migration analyses of census data are issues of coverage and accuracy. Not surprisingly, the relevance of migration analyses and census inclusion of key questions may depend on the prominence of migration for the country, especially for destination countries. For countries of mass emigration, census data would be less useful than the data at destination.

Analyzing migration from censuses

Population growth and distribution

International migration

From 1850 to 1930, the US foreign-born population increased from 2.2 million to 14.2 million, reflecting that period's large-scale immigration from Europe. As a percentage of total population, the foreign-born population rose from 9.7 percent in 1850, fluctuated in the 13 percent to 15 percent range from 1860 to 1920, and dropped to 11.6 percent in 1930, partly resulting from return migration after wage increases in European countries. Immigration was low during the 1930s and 1940s and, by 1950 the US foreign-born population had declined to 10.3 million or 6.9 percent of the total population, and with high old-age mortality and only slightly increased immigration in the 1950s and 1960s, the foreign-born population dropped to 9.6 million in 1970 or only 4.7 percent. With post-1965 immigration from Latin America, Asia, and elsewhere, the decennial censuses have shown increases in the foreign-born population from 9.6 million in 1970 to 14.1 million in 1980, to 19.8 million in 1990, and to 31.1 million in 2000, or from 4.7 percent in 1970 to 6.2 percent in 1980, to 7.9 percent in 1990, and to 11.1 percent in 2000. By 2009, the foreign-born share of 12.5 percent surpassed the historical high of 11.6 percent in 1930. This level of representation exceeds the 9.5 percent share of international migrants in the European countries in 2010, although specific countries have higher percentages, such as Germany with 13.1 percent and Switzerland with 23.2 percent.

Beyond the straightforward counting of foreign-born persons present in the census data of a country, population characteristics by period of migration or date of entry are indicative of newly arrived immigrants and migration flows, although these counts differ from actual population flows which may or may not be measured through administrative statistics. Initial migrants may reverse migrate or make another migration or have been lost through mortality. Because date of arrival is subject to response error, asking about place of residence 5 years ago is a preferable measure for recent migration.

As apparent in the preceding paragraph, comparison of population stocks across time may suggest the net flows or net change. Detailed demographic analyses may reveal estimated net immigration, emigration, or net migration. US decennial censuses previously provided benchmarking data as to international migration components of population change, and the ACS is now the basis for three measures of year-to-year change in the foreign population. These are (1) change in the total foreign population from one survey year to the next; (2) the number reporting year of US entry 1 year prior to the current survey year; and (3) the number reporting residing abroad one year prior to the current survey year (Norris and Costanza 2005; Grieco 2008, 2009). The latter is the basis for the net international migration component in US population estimates, and, in conjunction with year-of-entry details, are useful for evaluating 2010 Census coverage (US Bureau of the Census 2010). During the past decade, the Hispanic population seemed to be becoming more widely dispersed and both new and traditional destination areas of Hispanic settlement depend on immigration for population growth due to domestic outmigration (Lichter and Johnson 2009).

Internal migration

With expanded questions, China's 2010 Census documented a vast internal migration, concluding that more than 261 million citizens—nearly one in five—were living in places other than where China's household registration process had indicated that they did. Most of those were probably migrant laborers who have swelled big cities in search of higher-paying jobs so as to send money back to families that remain in rural areas (Wines and LaFraniere 2011).

Based on US Census 2000 data on current place of residence and place of residence five years ago, gross and net mobility/migration data were available for various levels of geography with demographic, family, or household characteristics with county-to-county migration flow data for counties and other entities by selected characteristics. Migration patterns in the 1990s were in the context of high immigration, extensive housing construction and low interest rates, economic growth and low inflation, and high employment and labor demand. Nearly one of every two persons lived elsewhere in 1995 from the 2000 residence. Retirement migration to Florida continued, making that state first on net increase from internal migration. The pattern of black migration to the South that was visible in the 1960–90 censuses was even more clearly demonstrated in the 2000 census as a major return migration to the Southern region that included highly educated individuals, especially to Georgia, Texas, and Maryland, at the expense of New York, California, and Illinois (Frey 2004). In a sharp shift to the trend since 1940, more people left California in the late 1990s than moved to California from elsewhere in the United States, and this loss was offset with movers from abroad to California.

Instead of asking about place of residence 5 years ago as had recent US decennial censuses, the ACS asks for residence 1 year prior to the enumeration date, which varies depending upon when the respondent is interviewed for the survey. This narrower time interval is somewhat preferable given that the concept of the net migrant is flawed in obscuring the nature and quantity of changes within an area composed of smaller areas and diverse populations (Rogers 1995).

Unauthorized migration and immigration status

In evaluating coverage of the US 1980 census, census demographers for the first time estimated a resident unauthorized population of 2.1 million, including one million Mexicans (Warren and Passel 1987). When the 1980 census count exceeded the initial demographic estimate of the total resident population, there was a possibility that millions of undocumented residents were present. Without a question on legal status, unauthorized estimates were developed indirectly. The final undercoverage estimates by age, sex, and race hypothesized total resident populations of legally resident persons (counted and uncounted), "counted" undocumented persons, and alternative figures of "uncounted" undocumented persons. Recombining the information showed a hypothetical minimum undercount for the foreign-born population that was substantially higher than the overall rate and comparable to that of the nonwhite population, primarily because the undercoverage rate for the undocumented population was hypothesized as high. Measuring unknown immigration with the basic population accounting equation relies upon accuracy in census enumeration as foreign-born, gauging foreign-born coverage, and accounting for lawful permanent residents and lawful temporary residents included in the census.

Tracking geographic impacts of US immigration is exacerbated by the absence of local population registers, considerable internal migration, and sizeable undocumented migration from non-bordering and bordering countries. Application of residual methodologies with US census surveys over 1980–2009 illustrated the magnitude of unauthorized migration and likely geographic impacts. The first empirical study of the geographic distribution of undocumented residents (Passel and Woodrow 1984) showed that in 1980 undocumented residents were concentrated in California, New York, Texas, Florida, Illinois, and New Jersey, the same areas as immigrants in general. Subsequent studies showed a more spatially dispersed unauthorized population decades although the greatest concentration still resided in California (US Department of Homeland Security 2011). From early to more recent studies of the US unauthorized population, findings consistently showed the majority was male, Hispanic (Mexican and other Central American), and recently arrived. Numbers of unauthorized residents born in Guatemala, Honduras, El Salvador, and Nicaragua as included in Mexican census data are likely too small to be measurable with residual techniques, these migrant groups in transit to the Mexico–US border are represented in apprehensions at the Mexico–US border as well as in casualties of migrant-focused crimes. Even in the US case, census and survey data on the foreign-born population are subject to response and nonresponse errors to which are added various errors accruing from the estimation technique (Woodrow-Lafield 1995; Massey and Capoferro 2004).

Emigration

Although countries typically measure in-migrants with administrative systems and censuses, scarcely any have measurement systems for emigration, relying on intercensal comparisons and other countries' data for foreign-born populations and lawfully admitted individuals. With an increasing foreign-born population, the accuracy of measuring components of net immigration became more crucial for population estimates, projections, and census evaluation. Intercensal survival techniques using successive censuses appeared to show emigration of 1.1 million foreign-born persons for 1960–70 (with age and sex detail) (Keely and Kraly 1978). With unknown unauthorized migration and unknown emigration of legally admitted persons, after the 1980 census, US demographers focused on an alien address registration system to develop an estimate for legally resident aliens by demographic and temporary or lawful permanent residence categories, with a bonus of legal emigration estimates (Warren and Passel 1987). This evaluation gave an estimate that 1.2 million legally resident immigrants had emigrated in the 1970s and about 0.5 million aliens emigrated for 1965–70. Subsequent studies to estimate the US population by legal and unauthorized residence required assumptions about emigration of lawful permanent residents. Drawing upon these studies, Woodrow (1991a) developed a range for foreign-born emigration in the 1980s of 1.0 to 2.1 million. Emigration estimates for US population programs are currently developed with a similar methodology comparing survey data on foreign-born and native-born populations, yielding estimates ranging between 2.0 and 2.6 million for 2000–2010 (USCB 2010).

In principle, one strategy for measuring emigration would be to conduct multiple country surveys in order to link individuals on current and previous place of residence, but this would scarcely be feasible for studying emigration from major receiving countries for which there are many origin source countries. Even with a specific focus on origin-destination linked country surveys within a migration system, there are few examples. A notable one is the Netherlands Interdisciplinary Demographic Institute-Eurostat project in 1997–8 involving origin countries in Africa and the Middle East and destination as the European Union (Bilsborrow 2007). Households were designated as migrant households on the basis of having a member who had emigrated at any time in the past 10 years which seemed a broad definition. A related strategy would be to conduct surveys in the host or destination country with some mechanism for introducing those individuals who are not present and emigrated, even if their characteristics would be only partially revealed. Such a mechanism exists through network sampling with a consanguineal counting rule that links nonresident relatives with the host population (Woodrow 1991b; Woodrow-Lafield 1996). Only those who emigrated without leaving behind a relative in the host country would be outside this consanguineally linked transnational population. In the 1980s, the method seemed promising for identifying the US emigrant population, given the alternatives of extrapolation of past trends or applying the intercensal technique with unknown unauthorized migration.

As mentioned earlier in the case of Mexico, some sending countries, such as Georgia, Moldova, Poland, and Tunisia, included emigration questions on the 2000 round of censuses, that is, asking about persons absent from the household, with greater success more likely for recent emigrants (past 5 years), emigrants with close ties in the country through family or proximity, and emigrants on registration systems in their origin countries (Chudinovskikh et al. 2008). This approach is not without problems, however, and may not be the best way for identifying migrants for multi-country surveys (Beauchemin and González Ferrer 2011). Particularly for smaller national populations, receiving country statistics on immigrants can be more helpful than this approach.

From the Mexico Census 2010, 1.1 million Mexicans had migrated abroad in 2005–10, and 723,000 remained abroad at the time of the interview and 351,000 had already returned. These implied 145,000 net migrants to the US and 70,000 return migrants for that period. Comparing with about 240,000 net migrants per year between 1995 and 2000 based on the 2000 Census, the number of international migrants decreased by 31.9 percent. There was a peak of about 450,000 net migrants that occurred between 2000 and 2005 (Stevenson 2011).

Addressing gaps, managing controversies, and future policies

Gaps

Among the most serious gaps in studying migration with census data, small origin populations remain elusive without population census data adequate for showing their detailed characteristics. Even censuses in the major destination countries are limited in studying populations and migration dynamics for such origins as Thailand or Panama. Innovative research is possible for smaller populations, such as Hidalgo and Bankston (2011). Their focus was intermarriage for Thai American immigrants over 1980–2000, specifically examining marriage of foreign-born women with non-Thai men. Historically associated with the US military presence in Thailand, Thai American intermarriage has become demilitarized but there may be some legacy effects toward continuing intermarriage of Thai-born women with native men. Sometimes, focusing on the ethnic, ancestral, or language group is sufficient for substantive and analytical purposes.

A useful variable is the percent foreign-born in community as representation of co-ethnics as a measure of social capital or social ties (Liang 1994; Yang 1994). At the country-level, economists include as an influence for international migration the stock of previous migrants from the source country living in the destination—the "friends and relatives" effect. One rationale is that having these friends and relatives may reduce the overall loss of ethnic capital in the source country, and another is that these networks lower migration costs through helping with loans or giving resources (Hatton and Williamson 2002). The "friends and relatives" effect does not seem to persist over time as much as demographic and economic factors (Clark et al. 2002).

Researchers may employ a variety of techniques to study socio-demographic outcomes for origin or special status groups, e.g., refugees or unauthorized high school graduates, living in a city or metropolitan area (Gold et al. 2008). Census sources are severely limited for causal modeling of international migration processes and for generational and assimilation analyses, although, subject to evaluations, parental birthplace may be incorporated into the 2013 ACS (Grieco 2009). Data are often rich on socioeconomic measures but weak as to migrant characteristics and timing of events. For example, census survey-based studies show human capital measures as associated with having naturalized by the census date, but many initial characteristics are unknown such as immigration status, English proficiency, educational attainment, and occupational background. On a measurement basis, demographers attempt to make the most of available census and survey sources in studying dynamic migration change.

Census surveys typically do not include questions about immigration status—legal status—because individuals would be unlikely to provide such private details to the government and individuals might then avoid census-takers. Special survey techniques have been investigated for providing more reliable data than from the residual analyses discussed earlier as to the number, characteristics, and distribution of unauthorized and lawfully resident populations. These techniques involve a series of questions about immigration status that do not require an individual to self-identify as unauthorized (GAO 2006; Massey 2010).

In studying certain groups that are defined on the basis of ethnic and religious markers, especially groups such as Middle Easterners or Jews for whom current US censusing and classification procedures put their likely responses on the race question into the "white" category, researchers do not have direct response data from national census surveys, given prohibitions against asking individuals about religious affiliations. An alternative approach with US census data is to draw upon country of birth, reported ancestries or ethnic origins (or parental place of birth, when available in earlier censuses), for identifying foreign-born and native-born individuals as Jewish (Waldinger and Lichter 1996) or as Middle Easterners, e.g., Arab, Armenian,

Iranian, or Israeli for Los Angeles (Bozorgmehr *et al.* 1996). Language spoken is another crucial characteristic in triangulation for group identification. US census data, however, appear rich in comparison with French census data lacking racial and ethnic characteristics due to an historical prohibition on acquiring such details.

Census controversies and inadequacies

Census controversies persist with attacks for privacy concerns due to follow-up contacts in regard to non-returned census forms and the detailed nature of questions about race and other socio-economic characteristics. In part, these concerns reflect lack of understanding of census data uses for public policy, but increasing mistrust in government is relevant.

In the US case, the presumed and measured presence of millions of unauthorized residents resulted in pre-1980 and pre-1990 litigation to prohibit inclusion of unauthorized residents in the apportionment counts. That issue diminished with reengineering of the 2010 Census that limited the actual census to only ten basic questions without any questions on place of birth and citizenship that would have been necessary for excluding estimated unauthorized residents from the apportionment counts. A new challenge arose when certain advocacy groups sought briefly to rally anti-census sentiment in reaction to US immigration policies.

Reengineering censuses and/or harmonizing censuses

As findings from the 2010 round of censuses emerge, US social scientists and demographers will be analyzing data from the American Community Survey with a backward look to detailed social and economic characteristics data from Census 2000. Whether ACS data are to become regarded as a truly rich resource for studying US foreign-born population, from larger origin groups to smaller origins, and whether studies have useful comparability with those from earlier US Censuses remain open questions. The first 5-year data set of 2005–9 ACS 5-year estimates was released in December 2010, providing detailed information for groups or areas as small as 20,000. In the future, the ACS sample size may be increased from 2.9 million to 3.5 million housing units in order to enhance data quality for small areas.

The national statistical agencies of Canada, Mexico, and the United States formed a North American Migration Working Group (NAMWG) shortly after the 2000 census round for documenting existing sources of migration data and working toward the development of harmonized data on migration flows between the three countries. For binational or joint studies, researchers have had to resolve a number of issues as to data comparability (Pryor and Long 1987; Norris and Costanza 2005). Even as social scientists were beginning to utilize and evaluate ACS data releases in 2010 for communities in the United States, imminent changes to the Canadian and UK censuses may adversely affect the quantity and quality of migration data (Boyd 2010). In 2011, Canada replaced the long-form survey questionnaire for which participation was mandatory and included the several immigration and citizenship questions on the NHS which is voluntary. Some demographers are concerned that the NHS will have serious nonresponse problems with recent immigrants and other groups, jeopardizing analyses of immigrant wellbeing and assimilation. Following its 2011 census, the British National Office of Statistics may not conduct another census and may instead draw upon existing public and private databases as informational sources—an integrated population statistics system.

As apparent from the advent of the US ACS, the Canadian NHS, and the possible British ONS integrated population statistics system, there is a new era of census-taking with both promises of detailed data on a continuous basis and reservations about census level quality in addition to traditional concerns about response and nonresponse. Immigration scholars and migration analysts must be attentive to national agency roles in shaping census-taking.

Public policy

In the US case, the presence of irregular migration as defined by survey-based studies has brought considerable debate over immigration policies and border enforcement. A series of immigration, trade, and welfare reforms are the backdrop for concerns about an accumulation of perceived and real inadequacies and brokenness, along with unanticipated consequences. The control and abatement of unauthorized immigration may be perceived by some as a difficult social policy issue. Research should guide policy formulation, and sounder policy-making would follow from sharpening this link and from more research about migration dynamics, migrant populations, and demographic and economic impacts of immigration. Policies on North American economic integration, migration and labor mobility, and border enforcement may change toward remedying the US situation with Mexico, the primary origin of US unauthorized migrants (Massey *et al.* 2002; Massey 2009).

References and further reading

Bean, F. D., Corona, R., Tuirán, R., Woodrow-Lafield, K. A., and Van Hook, J. (2001) "Circular, invisible, and ambiguous migrants: Components of difference in estimates of the number of unauthorized Mexican migrants in the United States" *Demography* 38(August): 411–22.

Beauchemin, C. and González-Ferrer, A. (2011) "Sampling international migrants with origin-based snowballing method: New evidence on biases and limitations" *Demographic Research* 25(3): 103–34.

Bilsborrow, R. (2007) "Surveys of international migration: Issues and tips. Sixth Coordination Meeting on International Migration and Development" New York: Population Division, United Nations.

Boyd, M. (2010) "Letter from the Chair" *World on the Move* 17(Fall): 1–22.

Bozorgmehr, M., Der-Martirosian, C., and Sabagh, G. (1996) "Middle Easterners: A new kind of immigrant." In R. Waldinger and M. Bozorgmehr (eds), *Ethnic Los Angeles*. New York: Russell Sage Foundation, pp. 345–78.

Chudinovskikh, O., Anich, R., and Bisogno, E. (2008) "Measuring emigration at the census: Lessons learned from four country experiences." Joint UNECE/Eurostat Work Session on Migration Statistics, Geneva, Switzerland, March 3–5.

Clark, X., Hatton, T. J., and Williamson, J. G. (2002) "Where do US immigrants come from? Policy and sending country fundamentals." NBER Working Paper 8998. Cambridge, MA: National Bureau of Economic Research, June.

De la Cruz, G. P. and Brittingham, A. (2003) "The Arab population." US Census 2000, Census 2000 Brief, C2KBR-23. Washington, DC: US Census Bureau. December.

Dumont, J.-C., Spielvogel, G., Widmaier, S. (2010) "International migrants in developed, emerging, and developing countries: An extended profile. OECD Social, Employment, and Migration Working Papers No. 114", www.oecd.org/els/workingpapers.

Frey, W. H. (2004) "The new great migration: Black Americans' return to the South, 1965–2000." Center on Urban and Metropolitan Policy, The Living Cities Census Series. Washington, DC: The Brookings Institution, May.

Frey, W. H. and Liaw, K.-L. (1998) "The impact of recent immigration on population redistribution within the United States." In J. P. Smith and B. Edmonston (eds), *The Immigration Debate*. Washington, DC: National Academy Press.

Gibson, C. and Jung, K. (2006) "Historical census statistics on the foreign-born population of the United States: 1850 to 2000." Population Division Working Paper No. 81. Washington, DC: US Bureau of the Census.

Gold, S. J., Wibert, W. N., Bondartsova, V., Melcher, J., Post, L. A., and Biroscak, B. J. (2008) "Estimation of the Number of Immigrants and Refugees in Lansing (Michigan), 2005–7." A report prepared for the Family and Community Vitality Focus Area of the Innovation in University-Community Research Collaboration Grants. East Lansing, MI: Michigan State University.

Grieco, E. M. (2008) "Estimating net international migration for the United States." Presentation, Joint ECE-EUROSTAT Work Session on Migration Statistics, Geneva, March 3–5.

——(2009) "Update on activities of the US Census Bureau on immigration and the foreign-born." UN/POP/MIG-8CM/2009/13, Eighth Coordination Meeting on International Migration. New York: Population Division, United Nations, November 16–17.

Hatton, T. J. and Williamson, J. G. (2002) "What fundamentals drive world migration?" NBER Working Paper 9159. Cambridge, MA: National Bureau of Economic Research, September.

Hidalgo, D. A. and Bankston III, C. L. (2011) "The demilitarization of Thai American marriage migration, 1980–2000" *Journal of International Migration and Integration* 12(1): 85–99.

Hill, K. and Wong, R. (2005) "Mexico-US migration: Views from both sides of the border" *Population and Development Review* 31(March): 1–18.

Keely, C. B. and Kraly, E. P. (1978) "Recent net alien immigration to the United States: Its impact on population growth and native fertility" *Demography* 15(3): 267–83.

Kritz, M. M. and Gurak, D. T. (2004) "Immigration and a changing America." *The American People: Census 2000.* New York City and Washington, DC: Russell Sage Foundation and Population Reference Bureau.

Larson, E. and Sullivan, T. (1987) "'Conventional numbers' in immigration research: The case of the missing Dominicans" *International Migration Review* 21(Winter): 1474–97.

Liang, Z. (1994) "Social contact, social capital, and the naturalization process: Evidence from six immigrant groups" *Social Science Research* 23(4): 407–37.

Liang, Z. and Ma, Z. (2004) "China's floating population: New evidence from the 2000 Census" *Population and Development Review* 30(September): 467–88.

Lichter, D. T. and Johnson, K. M. (2009) "Immigrant gateways and Hispanic migration to new destinations" *International Migration Review* 43(3): 496–518 (accessed March 12, 2011).

Massey, D. S. (2009) Testimony, 'Securing the borders and America's points of entry, what remains to be done,' The Senate Committee on the Judiciary, Subcommittee on Immigration, Refugees and Border Security, May 20.

Massey, D. S. (2010) "Immigration statistics for the twenty-first century" *The Annals* 63(1): 124–40.

Massey, D. S. and Clemens, M. (2008) "Five actions on migration data to make urgent research possible." Commission on International Migration, Data for Development Research, Center for Global Development, Global Forum on Migration and Development 2008.

Massey, D. S. and Capoferro, C. (2004) "Measuring unauthorized migration" *International Migration Review* 38(Fall): 1075–1102.

Massey, D. S., Durand, J., and Malone, N. J. (2002) *Beyond Smoke and Mirrors: Mexican Immigration in an Era of Economic Integration.* New York: Russell Sage Foundation.

Michalowski, M. and Norris, D. (2005) "Concepts and definitions to identify the stock of international migrants: The Canadian case study." Presentation, Joint ECE/EUROSTAT Seminar on Migration Statistics, Geneva, March 21–23.

Norris, D. and Costanza, J. (2005) "Measuring migration across US borders: A comparison and evaluation of migration data and data sources in Canada and the United States." Paper presented at the 25th International Population Conference of the International Union for the Scientific Study of Population, Tours, France.

Passel, J. S. and Woodrow, K. A. (1984) "Geographic distribution of undocumented immigrants: Estimates of undocumented aliens counted in the 1980 Census by state" *International Migration Review* 18(3): 642–671.

Pryor, E. T. and Long, J. F. (1987) "The Canada-United States Joint Immigration Study: Issues in data comparability," *International Migration Review*, 21(4): 1038–66.

Rogers, A. (1990) "Requiem for the net migrant" *Geographical Analysis* 22(4): 283–300.

Rogers, A. and Raymer, J. (1999) "Estimating the regional migration patterns of the foreign-born population in the United States: 1950–90" *Mathematical Population Studies* 7(3): 181–216.

Rumbaut, R. G. (2004) "Ages, life stages, and generational cohorts: Decomposing the immigrant first and second generation in the United States" *International Migration Review* 38(3): 1160–205.

Statistics Canada (2010) Visual census. 2006 Census. Ottawa. Released December 7, 2010. www12.statcan.gc.ca/census-recensement/2006/dp-pd/fs-fi/index.cfm?Lang=ENG&TOPIC_ID=6&prcode=01 (accessed January 21, 2011).

Stevenson, M. (2011) Mexico census: Fewer migrating, many returning. Associated Press. March 4. www.businessweek.com/ap/financialnews/D9LOFETO3.htm (accessed March 12, 2011).

United Nations, Department of Social and Economic Affairs (2008) *Population Division*. The United Nations Global Migration Database (UNGMD).

US Bureau of the Census (2010) "The development and sensitivity analysis of the 2010 Demographic Analysis estimates" Washington, DC: Population Division. December 6.

US Department of Homeland Security (2011) "Estimates of the unauthorized immigrant population residing in the United States: January 2010." In M. Hoefer, N. Rytina, and B. C. Baker (eds), Population Estimates, Office of Immigration Statistics. February.

US Government Accountability Office. (2006) *Estimating the Undocumented Population: A "Grouped Answers" Approach to Surveying Foreign-born Respondents*. GAO-06-775. September.

Waldinger, R. and Lichter, M. (1996) "Anglos: Beyond ethnicity?" In R. Waldinger and M. Bozorgmehr (eds), *Ethnic Los Angeles*, New York: Russell Sage Foundation, pp. 413–44.

Warren, R. and Passel, J. S. (1987) "A count of the uncountable: Estimates of undocumented aliens counted in the 1980 Census" *Demography* 24(3): 375–93.

Wines, M. and LaFraniere, S. (2011) "New census finds China's population growth has slowed" *New York Times*, April 28.

Woodrow, K. A. (1991a) "Project D5: Preliminary estimates of emigration component." *Preliminary Research and Evaluation Memorandum No. 78.*

——(1991b) "Using census and survey data to measure undocumented immigration and emigration from the United States" *Statistical Journal of the United Nations Economic Commission for Europe* 7(4): 241–51.

——(1992) "A consideration of the effect of immigration reform on the number of undocumented residents in the United States" *Population Research and Policy Review* 11(2): 117–44.

Woodrow-Lafield, K A. (1995) "An analysis of net immigration and census coverage evaluation" *Population Research and Policy Review* 14(2): 173–204.

Woodrow-Lafield, K. A. (1996) "Emigration from the United States: Multiplicity survey evidence" *Population Research and Policy Review* 15(2): 171–99.

Yang, P. Q. (1994) "Explaining immigrant naturalization" *International Migration Review* 28(3): 449–77.

40

Surveys and ethnosurveys

Mariano Sana and Becky Conway

Collecting data through surveys

Throughout the twentieth century surveys became the preferred universal method for the collection of data on individuals and households. The popularity of surveys hinges on two scientific strengths: statistical representativeness—based on proper sampling—and standardization—the principle of using exactly the same tools to collect comparable data from different subjects. The most desirable properties of survey data, such as maximum validity and reliability and minimum or no bias, are thought to be achieved when representativeness and standardization are secured. All of these are thoroughly addressed themes in survey methodology textbooks. A third advantage of collecting data from a sample of the population is of a practical nature. Surveys cost only a fraction of what their alternative, a population census, costs.

The present chapter addresses some specific survey developments as they pertain to the study of international migration—internal migration will not be considered. Our coverage is necessarily modest given space constraints. First, we review a specific type of migration survey, the ethnosurvey, outlining the principles on which it is based. Migration surveys have always been besieged by complex problems related to locality (migrants are by definition mobile and thus difficult to sample) and validity (migration surveys usually cover sensitive topics). In addressing these challenges, the ethnosurvey reconsiders the two fundamental strengths of social surveys outlined above: representativeness and standardization. After reviewing the ethnosurvey, we address other migration surveys that seek to address the same challenges. Afterward, we briefly refer to probabilistic surveys of US migrants in the United States. We close by considering two recent developments in social survey research that are of central interest to migration survey practitioners and might change, or are already changing, some crucial aspects of survey data collection.

Let us list as well what we will not do. As the focus of this chapter is surveys, we do not consider other sources of immigration statistics, including censuses and government administrative records. While we will refer to specific survey migration research projects, we will not attempt to offer a catalog of all of them. Omissions will be inevitable. We will not discuss the advantages and disadvantages of surveys for the study of international migration, the many substantial challenges faced by migration surveys, and issues of questionnaire design. As a comprehensive treatment of these issues, the volume by Bilsborrow and colleagues (1984) remains a primary reference text for migration survey practitioners. The reader interested in a comprehensive coverage of international migration surveys may also consult Fawcett and Arnold (1987), an insightful piece in need of an update. Finally, while we briefly refer to studies conducted elsewhere, the emphasis is on surveys addressing migration to, or immigrants in, the United States.

Migration surveys and the ethnosurvey

The main organization collecting data through social surveys is the government, but non-governmental entities carry out surveys as well. In the United States, there are two large government surveys suitable for the study of migrants. One is the Current Population Survey (CPS), a monthly survey of about 50,000 households, which is the main source of information on the characteristics of the US labor force. The other one is the American Community Survey (ACS), which produces population data for small areas annually—an improvement over the 10-year gap between censuses. Assuming no significant omissions of specific subpopulation groups, both surveys produce statistically representative data. However, both suffer from an important limitation: they do not provide information on the legal status of immigrants. (The US population census is no substitute, as it too lacks data on legal status of the foreign-born.) Of course, whether this limitation is relevant depends on the research questions being pursued, and notwithstanding the omission of legal status, the CPS and the ACS are widely used in the study of migrants in the United States. An example of non-governmental large survey is the New Immigrant Survey (NIS), a nationally representative multi-cohort longitudinal study of new legal immigrants and their children, which samples its subjects from government administrative records on newly admitted lawful permanent residents. The NIS has information on an impressive array of variables, many more than the CPS and the ACS, but while the latter lack information on legal status, the NIS does not have undocumented immigrants in its sample frame to begin with.

In short, the major surveys available for the study of immigrants in the United States provide a wealth of data but are also affected by significant constraints. Again, the importance of these constraints depends on the questions that guide the analysis. When those questions focus on the experience of immigrants in their host country national surveys are likely to be useful, but when the questions pertain to migration as a process that contemplates the experience of migrants before and after migration, they are bound to be less helpful. The same can be said of a number of Mexican government-sponsored surveys that collect data on the context of emigration and the migration experience of those who have returned to Mexico. While US surveys omit returned migrants, Mexican surveys omit those who remain in the United States.

A binational approach to Mexico–US migration

Since international migration is a process that takes place in at least two countries, it is clear that single-country data sources are insufficient to provide a complete picture of the phenomenon. The most prominent data collection effort aimed at covering both sides of the border is the Mexican Migration Project (MMP). The MMP began in 1982 with the goal of gathering a wealth of social and economic information to better understand the complexities of the Mexico–US migration process. The first product of this endeavor was the volume *Return to Aztlan* (Massey *et al.* 1987), which reported findings from the first four MMP surveys in as many survey sites (called "communities" in MMP terminology) in Western Mexico. Since its beginnings, the

MMP has carried out 128 surveys in Mexican communities. Each Mexican survey is followed by interviews of members of that same community who have settled in the United States. The latter are located via chain referrals—or "snowball sampling." Typically, each Mexican survey consists of 200 households from the selected site, with the goal of interviewing 20 migrants from the same community for a matching US sample—a goal that has at times been difficult to meet. As of today, the MMP has compiled data on 138,711 individuals and 21,475 households, of which 922 are located in the United States.

Over time, the MMP has diversified the location and size of the communities it samples so that it has achieved a more or less balanced coverage of the rural–urban continuum and of places both with and without a tradition of migration to the United States. Yet, the MMP communities are neither chosen at random nor are they part of a stratified sample design. Adding that the US samples are drawn from contacts in a snowball fashion, it is clear that the MMP cannot claim statistical representativeness for its data. It may strike some as odd that the largest continuous survey data collection effort on Mexico–US migration does not benefit from one of the two main strengths of survey research, as outlined in our first paragraph above.

In fact, lack of statistical representativeness is the only outcome that can be expected from surveys that shed light on the migration process—and as we review below, this constraint is not unique to the MMP, but present in all bi- or multinational migration surveys. Migration scholars know that, far from resembling a one-time definitive move, international migration is most often a nuanced process that involves multiple locations and transitions. Once international migration is understood as a process, migrant communities—such as those Mexican *barrios*, towns, and *ranchos* where migration to the US is commonplace—must be conceptualized as transnational communities. When only one border is involved, we can think of them as binational communities. Since each of these binational communities has a fixed location in the country of origin but diffuse locations in the country of destination, proper random statistical sampling becomes, from a practical point of view, either impossible or prohibitively expensive. Simply put, there is not, and in all likelihood there will never be, a statistically representative survey of transnational communities.

Statisticians know that data diversity cannot properly substitute for representative data. A large sample size cannot help either. Each MMP survey is only representative of the community where it was fielded—in fact, it is only representative of the survey site, which may be a subset of the community in question, especially when the community is a medium-sized or large city. When pooled together the MMP samples are not representative of Mexico. The MMP provides a set of weights to account for different sampling fractions in each survey site, but that is unrelated to statistical representativeness. Hence, the MMP data are not appropriate to produce national-level estimates. What the ethnosurvey is best for is to study migration as a social process and to do so from a binational perspective. Statistical inference of population characteristics using the MMP is inappropriate, but data diversity and large sample size are very helpful for statistical modeling of social processes, a perfectly legitimate use of the MMP data.

In sum, the MMP statistical approach does not claim national (or binational) representativeness but it does benefit from the rigor of random sampling in selected communities, and it exploits its now massive sample size and data diversity for statistical modeling of international migration as a social process. Careful consideration would likely conclude that this is the most feasible methodological course of action to gather data on international migration once migrant communities are conceptualized as spanning more than one country.

In addition to its binational approach, the other defining characteristic of the MMP challenges the second established strength of survey research that we mentioned at the outset: standardization.

Criticisms of survey standardization

The standardization principle is ingrained in the survey research ethos. As Floyd Fowler puts it: "Standardized measurement that is consistent across all respondents ensures that comparable information is obtained about everyone who is described" (Fowler 2002: 4). This principle governs every aspect of the interview process, including the environment in which the interview is carried out, the interviewer's behavior throughout the interaction and, of course, the formulation of the questions: "Survey questions are supposed to be asked exactly the way they are written, with no variation or wording changes. Even small changes in the way questions are worded have been shown, in some instances, to have significant effects on the way questions are answered" (Fowler 2002: 119).

The standardization principle has been criticized by social scientists on validity grounds. Formulating the same question in exactly the same way to two different respondents does not guarantee that they will interpret the question in exactly the same way. The traditional approach to standardization seeks to eliminate any undue influence of the interviewer over the respondent by denying the interviewer any freedom to depart from the script, even when the respondent asks for clarifications. This "prohibition against interaction" is intended to ensure reliability, but it potentially undermines the validity of survey data (Suchman and Jordan 1990). This and other criticisms eventually led survey methodologists to settle for an approach that maximizes the advantages of structured interviews while allowing for some flexibility in interviewing techniques (Maynard *et al.* 2002).

The ethnosurvey

The ethnosurvey was conceived in the early 1980s, at a time when the standardized approach to interviewing was being questioned. The perennial concern over validity was maximized by the sensitive nature of some of the questions in the MMP survey, including those on illegal border crossings, legal status while in the United States, and financial matters.

Essentially, the ethnosurvey is not a type of survey but a multimethod approach to research on a complex social process, first applied in the study by Massey *et al.* (1987) that gave birth to the MMP. In combining the quantitative approach of social surveys with the qualitative approach of anthropological inquiry, the ethnosurvey seeks to employ the strength of each to minimize the weaknesses of the other (Massey 1987).

In the ethnosurvey, the scientific rigor of random sampling is applied in a small number of study sites, and it is combined with tools of qualitative inquiry such as participant observation, archival research and in-depth interviews with key community informants. It can be inferred that the ethnosurvey research team is necessarily interdisciplinary. Data are collected at the individual, household, community, and state levels to place subsequent analysis in full context. A key feature of the ethnosurvey is the collection of retrospective life histories that account for the fundamental events in the lives of the respondents, including employment, migration, marriage, fertility, and property ownership. The resulting data are suitable for both the careful presentation of case studies and the quantitative rigor of event history analysis. Finally, and as we mentioned earlier, the ethnosurvey acknowledges the binational nature of migrant communities by implementing parallel sampling, i.e., sampling the community of origin in Mexico and migrants from that community who have settled in the United States (Massey 1987).

When it comes to the interview interaction, the ethnosurvey "yields an interview that is informal, non-threatening, and natural, that allows the interviewer some discretion about how and when to ask sensitive questions; yet it produces a standard set of data" (Massey 1987: 1506).

In practice, the interviewer does not have a questionnaire with scripted questions, but a set of forms that she/he needs to fill in. To correctly fill in each box in each of these forms, "it is absolutely essential that interviewers understand clearly what information is being sought in each table of the questionnaire" (Massey et al. 1987: 13). Given this, considerably more time needs to be allotted for interviewer training in an ethnosurvey than in a mainstream social survey.

While the ethnosurvey approach is informed by the strengths of survey and ethnographic research, it is different from both. Fundamental differences with standardized surveys include: (a) the survey instrument is not fully structured and the questions are not worded in advance, (b) instead of being banned from departures from the interview script, or even following any script at all, the interviewers have freedom to conduct the interviews in the way they deem best, (c) instead of focusing on procedure, interviewer training is mostly concerned with securing the fieldworkers' correct understanding of the information that needs to be captured. Yet, for all these departures from standardization, the ethnosurvey is not an in-depth ethnographic interview, fundamentally because (a) the interviewer does not have an interview guide, but an actual set of constructs—future variables in a data set—for which he/she needs to collect specific information, (b) the meaning of the constructs is defined in advance, i.e. there is no meaning-construction work to be shared between interviewer and respondent, (c) the data is to be used in a quantitative manner, which makes precision in the information collected a primary concern and recording/transcribing of interviews generally unnecessary, as there is no analysis to be done of the interview per se and no particular interest in research questions not developed in advance and already embedded in the interview forms, (d) finally, while ethnographies are typically conducted by single individuals, the ethnosurvey is team work.

Other studies based on bi- or multinational approaches

A number of international migration studies have followed the MMP model. The Health and Migration Survey (HMS) study was set up to examine the health consequences of migration from Mexico to the United States. Like the MMP, the HMS also employed a binational approach, with surveys conducted in one Mexican state and two US cities—San Diego and Houston. Unlike the MMP, the HMS produced panel data. In 1996, it collected data from households in six Mexican communities, returned to those same households in 1998 and, at the same time, added households from two new communities. In 1999, the researchers returned to all households, and then in 2002, they conducted yet another round of follow-up interviews while adding new households from a new community.

The HMS drew its US samples from a roster of addresses in an area canvassed by the survey team. This method produces a statistically representative sample of the immigrant neighborhood in the US, but its main strength probably lies in minimizing the risk of missing immigrants who are not closely connected to the networks of those interviewed in Mexico, a clear possibility in the chain-referral snowball approach of the MMP (Beauchemin and Gonzalez-Ferrer 2010). Unlike the MMP, the key survey respondent in the HMS was the "señora," or the primary woman in the household, either the wife of a male head or the household head herself. In addition to data comparable to the MMP's, the HMS questionnaire also gathered information on health—a notoriously absent topic in the MMP questionnaire—including detailed histories about reproductive health and migration of mothers, as well as the health of their young children, with particular attention paid to the role of social support and social networks (Kanaiaupuni et al. 2005).

The MMP co-directors, Douglas Massey and Jorge Durand, followed on their own footsteps with the Latin American Migration Project (LAMP), which carried out the first round of data collection in Puerto Rico in 1998. Since then, the LAMP has fielded surveys in the Dominican

Republic, Paraguay, Nicaragua, Costa Rica, Haiti, Peru, Guatemala, El Salvador, and Colombia—the surveys in Paraguay and Guatemala were made possible by association with other research projects, and all of the surveys benefited from collaboration with local scholars. At the time of writing, the LAMP had data on 7,103 households in these countries. Four of these studies (Puerto Rico, Dominican Republic, Nicaragua, and Costa Rica) included parallel sampling with households interviewed in the United States, Spain (from the Dominican Republic) and Costa Rica (from Nicaragua).

Ethnosurvey-inspired research projects have also been implemented in other regions of the world. The Migrations between Africa and Europe (MAFE) study, which began its data collection in 2008, seeks to explore migration patterns from Senegal to France, Italy, and Spain, from the Democratic Republic of Congo to Belgium and the United Kingdom, and from Ghana to the Netherlands and the United Kingdom. The MAFE study design builds on the MMP ethnosurvey and the Push and Pull Factors in International Migration project, to which we refer below. Like the ethnosurvey, this project involves intensive interviewer training as well as the collection of life histories for event history analysis. Randomization was used for the selection of the survey sites in the country of origin, subject to some constraints—for example, in most African countries the survey was only implemented in the capital city. For the surveys at destination, the MAFE relied on a variety of sampling techniques. For example, for the Senegalese surveys, municipal population registries in Spain provided an ideal sampling frame—including both documented and undocumented migrants. In France and Italy, however, there were no registries available and the researchers had to resort to quota sampling, recruiting respondents through a variety of channels to minimize biases (Beauchemin and Gonzalez-Ferrer 2010).

Another example of a survey research project methodologically linked to the MMP ethnosurvey is the Polish Migration Project (PMP), started in 2005, which explores migration from Poland to Germany. Unlike the MMP, however, in the PMP the interviews were conducted in an almost fully standardized fashion. Also unlike the MMP, data collection does not prioritize the household head, but a household member chosen at random. Finally, a balance between migrants and nonmigrants is achieved by means of a stratified sample design. Similarities with the original ethnosurvey persist in that the study is multimethod, gathers data from a diverse number of sites, and collects retrospective longitudinal life histories for event history analysis (Massey et al. 2008).

Above we mentioned the Push and Pull Factors in International Migration project. It is worth referring to it here given the large body of literature that it originated. This study focused on the migration flows from Morocco and Senegal to Spain, Ghana and Egypt to Italy, and Turkey and Morocco to the Netherlands. The surveys in the African countries were fielded in 1996–8. The selection of countries of origin was not arbitrary. It secured the coverage of both long-established and more recent migration flows, a sizeable migration flow in each case, regional differentiation in socioeconomic development and access to migrants from these countries in Europe (Schoorl et al. 2000: 14). As in the case of the MMP and the MAFE, then, constraints on statistical representativeness were countered with an emphasis on diversity of study sites. Like the MMP, the study sampled respondents in both the country of origin and the country of destination, but there was no link between them. The reader seeking more background on early migration surveys in Europe should consult the Push and Pull Factors study 2000 report (Schoorl et al. 2000: 10–12).

We conclude our review by shifting to a different region of the world. The China International Migration Project (CIMP) is explicitly modeled after the MMP, including the multimethod approach, multiple survey sites and parallel sampling, multilevel data collection and an ethnosurvey questionnaire applied to 200 households in each community (Liang et al. 2008). The surveys were fielded in eight towns of Fujian Province between October 2002 and March

2003. The US interviews—all of them in New York City—of migrants from the selected towns were conducted in the summer of 2003. The CIMP's ethnosurvey questionnaire is very similar to the questionnaires employed by MMP and LAMP, with modifications appropriate to the Chinese case. For example, it includes questions on cadre status and limits detailed inquiry on migration trips to the US sample—due to low levels of return migration, respondents in Fujian were typically not the migrants themselves, but relatives who knew no more than very basic information about the trip. This low prevalence of return migration, in turn, led the researchers to conduct a higher proportion of interviews in the United States than is typical in MMP surveys: 25 to 40 interviews in the United States for every survey in China—the typical MMP target is 20 US interviews.

Surveying immigrants in the United States

The MMP and its ethnosurvey have contributed enormously to a better understanding of the social process of Mexico–US migration, but the bulk of the MMP data was collected in Mexico. In addition, the MMP US samples are not based on random sampling. The study of Mexican immigrants—and immigrants from other nationalities—in the United States via probabilistic sampling has been undertaken by other research projects. As we noted above, a statistically representative survey of transnational communities would be impractical and prohibitively expensive, but at the local level, probabilistic sampling can be implemented.

For over two decades a number of probabilistic surveys have been fielded in Southern California (see Marcelli 2006), and these surveys included both interviews of unauthorized and legal immigrants with two goals: (1) drawing inference concerning both the migration and the immigrant incorporation processes, and (2) producing estimates of the unauthorized immigrant population in the area. The latter goal is achieved by regressing legal status on relevant predictors using the survey data and applying the estimated coefficients to the Public Use Microdata Samples (PUMS) from the census—something that of course should not be attempted if the US samples were produced using chain-referral methods.

Producing estimates of the unauthorized immigrant population in a given area may or may not be a major goal of a survey study, but probabilistic samples of immigrants in specific, urban, US locations have proven operationally demanding but possible. To the HMS surveys mentioned earlier and the Southern California surveys we add the Durham, North Carolina surveys reported by Parrado et al. (2005) and the surveys of Brazilian and Dominican immigrants in Boston conducted between June and September of 2007 (Marcelli et al. 2009a,b). All of these surveys involved the patient construction of otherwise inexistent sample frames in order to maximize the likelihood of interviewing a significant number of immigrants from the target population. These sample frames were produced by field teams that canvassed residential areas selected on the basis of census information and/or reports from local informants, members of community-based organizations. While it worked very effectively in the HMS and the Durham and Boston surveys, canvassing is not the only choice for sample-frame construction. Other choices, such as a census-based random sample in targeted blocks, a snowball sample using community groups to select the seeds, and an intercept-point survey collected at community gathering sites, are reviewed in an experiment conducted by McKenzie and Mistiaen (2009).

Two recent developments

Most recently, two developments stand out. First, community-based participatory research (CBPR) has taken the front seat in the study of immigrants in the US through social surveys, especially when unauthorized immigrants are included in the sample frame. CBPR integrates members of the community being studied into all stages of the research project in a mutually beneficial partnership with the researchers. From the point of view of the community, this partnership secures that the new knowledge produced by the study is relevant and efficiently used to target community needs and improve its members' well-being. Thus, it is not surprising that CBPR has so far been almost exclusively applied to health research—or, in the case of migration studies, research concerned with the health of migrant populations. For researchers working in other fields, it is harder to make a case for a practical benefit for the community in exchange for its involvement. From the point of view of the researchers, the account from Parrado and colleagues serves as an apt example: "In our case, community involvement was of key importance to gain access to a difficult-to-reach population, develop a flexible survey instrument, increase data quality, and ground our findings within the cultural realities of Durham migrants" (Parrado et al. 2005: 211). In short, community involvement legitimizes both the research methods and the research results. This legitimacy is needed to address a fundamental problem raised by Josephson (1970), who reported significant resistance to a survey for a public health research project in a low-income neighborhood of New York City when community members questioned the intentions of the survey and trusted neither the institution responsible for it nor the (detached) researchers in charge. It is clear that CBPR can be particularly useful for survey research projects that need to reach undocumented migrants, a population with a justified instinct to avoid disclosing sensitive information to strangers.

The surveys mentioned above of Mexican immigrants in Durham and Brazilian and Dominican immigrants in the Boston Metropolitan Area are examples of CBPR. The study in North Carolina combined CBPR, targeted random sampling and parallel sampling in sending and receiving areas to sample a difficult-to-reach migrant population and study a sensitive issue: HIV risk. The similarities with the MMP approach are apparent. The novelty is the mix of the ethno-survey with CBPR. There is a precedent worth reviewing in a survey of an "underground," hard-to-reach population of largely uncertain documentation status: Haitian immigrants in Southern Florida (Stepick and Stepick 1990). The researchers spent about five years engaged in anthropological work in the community prior to their survey, an involvement that is to be credited for the high response rates when the survey began. The researchers were able to obtain representative results by drawing random samples from a map of census blocks where the community was concentrated. They also hired Haitians to conduct the interviews—being tri-lingual was a crucial requirement for interviewers in this case—and the interviewers had con-siderable flexibility in the implementation of the survey instrument as a way to increase rapport as well as gain acceptance to do the interviews in the first place. Even though Stepick and Stepick did not explicitly call their study an "ethnosurvey" or a "community-based participatory study," their research was indeed a combination of both.

CBPR hinges on the assumption that members of the community being studied can con-structively participate in the research process, and that this participation will be effective by virtue of their being part of the community. Since they are part of the community, they pre-sumably possess background knowledge that should be useful for the study; they would know how to relate to the research subjects, and so on. Their proximity to the survey setting should be valuable. This thinking is consistent with results from an experiment reported by Sana and Weinreb (2008), who formulated the following question: given survey errors, specifically data inconsistencies, who is best suited to fix them? Using carefully altered MMP data in an experiment involving MMP personnel and data users, they showed evidence that fieldworkers have an advantage over those who have never been to the field, even when the latter were regular users of the MMP data. They concluded that field experience gives fieldworkers an instinctual edge that results from their familiarity with the setting and culture where the data were collected. Thus, solving inconsistencies is not simply a matter of common sense.

The evidence then points to likely data quality gains that arise from closer proximity of the interviewers to the survey setting—which implies closer proximity, or less social distance, between the interviewer and the respondent. While this expectation would strike many as commonsense, it questions a norm established since the early development of survey research. The "stranger-interviewer norm" (Weinreb *et al.* 2011) posits that, in order to collect unbiased and valid data, the interviewer must have no prior social relationship with the respondent. CBPR practice questions this norm: the involvement of community members in the survey process suggests closer proximity between interviewers and respondents than allowed by the norm, even if a direct relationship between the interviewer and the respondent is absent. The same can be said of the popular practice of matching interviewers and respondents along key demographic attributes such as gender, race, or ethnicity. There is an undeniable tension between a long-established norm that dictates that interviewers must be strangers, and the practice of employing interviewers who stand closer and closer to the respondent in terms of gender, race, ethnicity, community membership, or social distance defined in a variety of ways. This tension is exacerbated by the second major recent development in the field of survey research: the ongoing erosion of the stranger-interviewer norm or, at the very least, the open questioning of its soundness.

Social surveys, including the MMP ethnosurvey, have traditionally assumed that more valid data is collected when there is no prior relationship between interviewer and respondent. In no CBPR survey of which we are aware did the researchers allow the interviewers to interview people they directly knew, even though the interviewer was someone from the same community as the respondent—which in the case of the Durham and Boston surveys means someone from the same ethnic group, who speaks the same language, and lives nearby. Working with data from a (non-migration) survey in Kenya in which a significant number of interviews had accidentally violated the stranger–interviewer norm, Weinreb (2006) found that validity seemed to be improved, and social desirability bias reduced, in interviews in which the interviewer was the ultimate insider: namely, when the interviewer and respondent were not just from the same community, but actually knew each other. As he eloquently argues, "the basic proposition that respondents are more honest with strangers than with insiders … draws on assumptions about microsocial relations that at best are inconsistent with and at worst antithetical to a large body of social theory at the micro level" (Weinreb 2006: 1016). In short, everything we claim to know about trust, truth-telling, intimacy, and deception suggests that people are more likely to practice the first three of these with those whom they know well, and more likely to resort to the latter with those whom they do not know.

A systematic, controlled experiment to test the validity of the stranger-interviewer norm is in order, and that is precisely what took place in a town in the Dominican Republic in the summer of 2010. In that setting, the researchers manipulated the recruitment of interviewers and the assignment of interviewers to respondents so as to generate survey data from three types of interviews: outsider interviews (where the interviewer was from out of town), local–stranger interviews (where the interviewer was local but there was no relationship between interviewer and respondent), and insider interviews (where the interviewer and respondent knew each other prior to the interview). A stratified sample design guaranteed that each of these three groups was properly randomized. The effects of type of interview on the data collected will be analyzed by means of statistical inference (for example, concerning social desirability bias) and, for some questions, direct validation. Preliminary results seem to be mixed, depending on the types of questions asked (Weinreb *et al.* 2011) but no details were available at the time of writing. By the time this book is published, the reader should be able to look for publications presenting the full range of results from the Dominican experiment, the first systematic empirical test of the stranger-interviewer norm.

References and further reading

Beauchemin, C. and Gonzalez-Ferrer, A. (2010) "Multi-country surveys on international migration: An assessment of selection bias in destination countries." MAFE Working Paper 3.

Bilsborrow, R. E., Oberai, A. S. and Standing, G. (1984) *Migration Surveys in Low Income Countries: Guidelines for Survey Questionnaire and Design*. London: Croom Helm.

Fawcett, J. T. and Arnold, F. (1987) "The role of surveys in the study of international migration: An appraisal" *International Migration Review* 21(4): 1523–40.

Fowler, F. J. (2002) *Survey Research Methods*. Thousand Oaks, CA: Sage Publications, Applied Social Research Methods Series v. 1. 3rd edition.

Josephson, E. (1970) "Resistance to community surveys" *Social Problems* 18(1): 117–29.

Kanaiaupuni, S. M., Donato, K. M., Thompson-Colon, T., and Stainback, M. (2005) "Counting on kin: Social networks, social support and child health" *Social Forces* 83(3): 1137–64.

Liang, Z. Chunyu, M. D., Zhuang, G., and Ye, W. (2008) "Cumulative causation, market transition, and emigration from China" *American Journal of Sociology* 114(3): 706–37.

Marcelli, E. (2006) "Effects of unauthorized migration." In J. Loucky, J. Armstrong, and L. J. Estrada, *Immigration in America Today: An Encyclopedia*. Westport, CT: Greenwood Press, pp. 82–7.

Marcelli, E., Holmes, L., Estella, D., da Rocha, F., Granberry, P., and Buxton, O. (2009a) *(In)Visible (Im) Migrants: The Health and Socioeconomic Integration of Brazilians in Metropolitan Boston*. San Diego, CA: Center for Behavioral and Community Health Studies, San Diego State University.

Marcelli, E., Holmes, L., Troncoso, M., Granberry, P., and Buxton, O. (2009b) *Permanently Temporary? The Health and Socioeconomic Integration of Dominicans in Metropolitan Boston*. San Diego, CA: Center for Behavioral and Community Health Studies, San Diego State University.

Massey, D. S. (1987) "The ethnosurvey in theory and practice" *International Migration Review* 21(4): 1498–522.

Massey, D. S., Kalter, F., and Pren, K. A. (2008) "Structural economic change and international migration from Mexico and Poland" *Kölner Zeitschrift für Soziologie and Sozialphsychologie* 60: 134–62.

Massey, D. S., Alarcón, R., Durand, J., and González, H. (1987) *Return to Aztlan: The Social Process of International Migration from Western Mexico*. Berkeley, CA: University of California Press.

Maynard, D. W., Houtkoop-Steenstra, H., Schaeffer, N. C., and van der Zouwen, J. (eds) (2002) *Standardization and Tacit Knowledge: Interaction and Practice in the Survey Interview*. New York: John Wiley & Sons.

McKenzie, D. J. and Mistiaen, J. (2009) "Surveying migrant households: A comparison of census-based, snowball, and intercept point surveys" *Journal of the Royal Statistical Society: Series A (Statistics in Society)* 172(2): 339–60.

Parrado E. A., McQuiston, C., and Flippen, C. A. (2005) "Participatory survey research – Integrating community collaboration and quantitative methods for the study of gender and HIV risks among Hispanic migrants" *Sociological Methods & Research* 34(2): 204–39.

Sana, M. and Weinreb, A. A. (2008) "Insiders, outsiders, and the editing of inconsistent survey data" *Sociological Methods & Research* 36(4): 515–41.

Schoorl, J., Heering, L., Esveldt, I., Groenewold, G., van der Erf, R., Bosch, A., de Valk, H., and de Bruijn, B. (2000) "Push and pull factors of international migration: A comparative report." Luxembourg: Office for Official Publications of the European Communities.

Stepick, A. and Stepick, C. D. (1990) "People in the shadows: Survey research among Haitians in Miami" *Human Organization* 49(1): 64–77.

Suchman, L. and Jordan, B. (1990) "Interactional troubles in face-to-face survey interviews" *Journal of the American Statistical Association* 85(409): 232–41.

Weinreb, A. A. (2006) "The limitations of stranger-interviewers in rural Kenya" *American Sociological Review* 71(6): 1014–39.

Weinreb, A. A., Sana, M. and Stecklov, G. (2011) "Outsider, locals, and insiders: Results from a Methodological Experiment on Data Collection." Paper presented at the Annual Meeting of the Population Association of America, Washington DC, March 31–April 2.

41

Making sense of the other

Ethnographic methods and immigration research

Patricia Fernández-Kelly

Introduction

In this chapter I aim to show how ethnographic research can enhance our understanding of immigration adding value to broad generalizations through the discovery of details at the micro-level. How immigrants process information, define themselves *vis-à-vis* mainstream populations, and adapt to conditions of tolerance or hostility constitute relevant questions in the production of knowledge and the design of policy. Because immigration amplifies ordinary experience, it accentuates phenomena of general interest, including changes in family composition, multiple adaptations to external pressures, mobility in the labor market, and evolving ideas about race and ethnicity. Thus, the ethnographic study of immigration yields knowledge that illuminates the experience of multiple groups, not solely immigrants; its relevance is substantive and practical; theoretical as well as instrumental. Research about immigrants may be regarded, in the words of Robert K. Merton, as a "strategic site" for broad sociological analysis (Merton 1987).

The chapter is divided into two parts. The first one, comprising four sections, gives attention to the evolution of ethnography noting that it first emerged as part of a mission to design rigorous approaches to data collection. In the second part, also comprising four sections, I offer an example from my own research to illustrate ways in which ethnographic research may be applied to the understanding of immigration. I also suggest ways in which findings from that exercise may illuminate equivalent phenomena in other social contexts. In the concluding section I briefly revisit the central argument of the paper.

Rethinking ethnography

Ethnography came of age during the first decades of the twentieth century as a means to memorialize cultures at risk of being absorbed or eliminated by Western expansion, colonial intrusion, and the advent of modernity. From the outset, the ethnographic agenda entailed a conviction in sharp divides between the world of ethnographers and the world of informants, whether located in New Guinea (Malinowski 1922), Samoa (Mead 1928 [2001]), Polynesia

(Firth 1925), the Andaman Islands (Radcliffe-Brown 1922 [1967]), Southern Sudan (Evans Pritchard 1940 [1960]), or Ghana (Fortes 1940). By the turn of the twentieth century, however, those assumed boundaries were being questioned. Immigration played a central role in those debates insofar as it thrust peoples from disparate geographic locations into contact with one another in factories, schools, neighborhoods, and even combat zones. As urbanization grew so did an interest in the study of immigrants, many of whom labored in cities and worked in industrial facilities. Thomas and Znaniecky's (1918–20) foundational study of Polish workers in the United States and Poland is a case in point. The Chicago School of Sociology, which introduced innovations in ethnographic research, was virtually coterminous with the study of immigration (Wirth 1928 [1998]) as were studies of migrant workers in southern Africa, all of them involving fieldwork (Richards 1939; van Velsen 1960; Wallerstein 1965; Arrighi 1967).

As more people moved from rural to urban settings within their own countries, or crossed international borders in search of opportunity, differences in background between professional observers and those being observed began to blur. By the mid-twentieth century, the availability of rapid air transportation, and advanced communications technology further enhanced the capacity of researchers to apply ethnographic methods to the study of populations in advanced industrial countries (Gille and Riain 2002; Glick Schiller 2003). In the United States that trend accelerated after the passage of the 1965 Immigration and Nationality Act, which enabled newcomers from points other than Europe—mostly Asia and Latin America—to settle in American towns and cities. Nearly unprecedented hostility against immigrants after the 9/11 attack further pushed the study of immigration to center stage. Even more recently, new immigrant flows in Asia and Europe have invigorated immigration research. The proliferation of ethnographic studies on that subject in various locations (Orellana 2001; Gold 2002; Levitt 2003; Ostergaard-Nielsen 2003; Sayad 2004; Fitzgerald 2006, 2010; Massey 2010) is but the latest effect of a long and sustained focus on the immigrant experience. Such studies hark back to the origins of ethnography and, more broadly, anthropology, a discipline that evolved slowly in Europe since the sixteenth century.

The anthropological quandary

The modern roots of anthropology—and therefore ethnography—are found in the period of Great Discoveries that brought Europeans both accurate and distorted reports about previously unknown races, cultures, and languages. Gutenberg's invention of the printing press in the 1450s allowed for the spread of information originating in many parts of the globe. By the eighteenth century, museums and private cabinets of curiosities were commonplace in centers of higher learning while military and commercial victories continued to sustain a belief in European superiority (Hodgen 1967; Harris 1968 [2001]). Puzzlement about the multiplicity of human phenotypes, colorations, and ways of life was filtered through the optic of colonial domination. Anthropology reflected the biases of European conquerors and colonialists producing evolutionary frameworks at the peak of which stood the Caucasian man and at whose bottom Africans were equated with the primitive origins of humanity (Gould 1981). By and large, nineteenth-century anthropologists, viewed non-European societies as windows onto the pre-industrial past.

The beginning of the twentieth century witnessed the advent of a narrower, more scientifically oriented Anthropology. Led by Franz Boas, scholars broke away from the focus on panhuman questions to advocate research based on detailed and local studies of artifacts, languages, and cultures. The new approach was a reaction against three trends in the preceding period: (1) grand speculative theories with little empirical foundation; (2) evolution as a single theoretical model; and (3) the characterization of so-called primitive societies as early developmental stages long surpassed by Europeans. Boas' emphasis on historical particularities was as much a search for scientific rigor as a denunciation of political doctrines masquerading as science. Ethnography emerged in this context, as a means to abandon speculation and focus on direct observation, a precondition of the modern quest for improved knowledge.

The repudiation of conjectural, evolutionary schemes created new requirements for the collection of data through immersion in the field and face-to-face interaction with individuals and groups outside the anthropologist's immediate milieu. In-depth interviews, an offshoot of that project; were inspired by scientific ambition and a commitment to the rigorous collection of empirical data. The image of "Franz Boas stepping off the boat in an Eskimo village with his suitcase in hand, preparing for a long stay in residence" (Wallace 1972: 469) provided a powerful new paradigm in the Kuhnian sense that dislodged a tradition of library scholarship and of uncritical use of the comparative method (Sanday 1979). While *primitives* and *natives* had been used in the nineteenth and early twentieth centuries as silent illustrations of imperial theory, interviews made *subjects* visible and their voices audible. Paradoxically, especially in the light of more recent criticisms, ethnographic methods, including in-depth interviews, emerged and were refined as tools to advance precision and to contest ideological pronouncements.

The sociological counterpart

Boas's yearning for accuracy and rigor was shared by sociology, a discipline almost devoid of systematic methodologies during the nineteenth century. Early attempts of sociologists to obtain verifiable information were crude with some exceptions. Charles Booth produced a monumental series on London partly focusing on rural-urban migration and broadly relying on the copious but nonsystematic gathering of facts (Booth 1889–91; 1892–97; 1902). In France, Frédéric Le Play made extensive studies of family budgets and contributed to the development of statistical sampling through his *monographic method* of collating data obtained by field research (Le Play 1870). Herbert Spencer, who wrote against a backdrop of increasing industrialization and internal migration in England, assembled vast amounts of observations conducted by other people, and used them to illustrate and support his own ideas (Spencer 1873).

By the early 1900s, however, the *Methodological Note* comprising the greater portion of a volume in Thomas and Znaniecki's *Polish Peasant in Europe and America* (1918–20) marked a turning point in the pursuit of rigor, at the center of which were both immigration as a subject and ethnography as a methodological approach. Unencumbered by anthropology's penchant for the exotic, sociologists were mostly concerned with processes of urbanization and modernity. Early community studies and studies of immigration relied on, and were used to refine the interview method as part of surveys (see, for example, Lynd and Lynd 1929 [1959]). In the 1920s, scholars like Robert E. Park and E. W. Burgess (1921) promoted direct contact with immigrants and workers in the new American metropolis. By the 1940s Robert K. Merton had perfected the focus interview and used it as part of his investigation of patterns of social life (Merton *et al.* 1948).

Sociologists systematized the interview method as part of broader approaches that included participant observation, oral histories, ethnographic description, and ethnological comparisons. They also used the interview to collect aggregate data susceptible of quantitative analysis (Blau and Duncan 1967). While in anthropology, the dividing line between professional observers and those observed was assumed to be culture, in sociology, class—as well as culture—constituted main demarcations. In both cases the interview relied on induction, offering an analogue to controlled observation and experimental manipulation.

The ethnographer's claim to rigor, however, was not to remain unchallenged. As ethnographic studies gained popularity, new questions emerged about their effectiveness in the search of scientific knowledge. A central concern entailed the control of subjective interferences that may distort observation, warp description and render explanation useless. I explore this point next.

Questioning the inquirer

Throughout its trajectory, ethnography—understood as a repertory of approaches and techniques involving direct interaction with members of an observed population (Willis 2000)—has aimed to *make sense of the other* but increasingly blurred lines separating observers from those being observed have fueled new questions about its value to the scientific mission. This is especially true about the interview method.

There are at least two ways to address the advantages and limitations of in-depth interviews. One encompasses a review and explanation of procedures to obtain data. In that case, the task is mostly descriptive and pedagogical. The second, more difficult endeavor, centers on the evolving relationship between professional observers and those being observed as part of a contested process to pinpoint meanings, establish cognitive boundaries, and develop internally plausible narratives about specific phenomena—the reasons behind individual decisions to migrate, for example, the way in which immigrants adapt to labor markets, or the way they self define in terms of race and ethnicity. The goal, in that sense, is not to take the statements of informants at face value—fading memories, the imprecision of language, and the play of emotions diminish the self-evident character of spoken accounts—but to identify experiential patterns as described by individuals sharing common characteristics. An interview may at first appear as little more than a personal account but when compared to other, similar interviews with individuals displaying common features it becomes part of a totality reflecting structural conditions and collective responses.

Michael Burawoy, a major force in innovative research, has developed qualitative methodologies flexible enough to connect social structure and individual agency. Towards that purpose, he proposes the *extended case method* which:

> applies reflexive science to ethnography in order to extract the general from the unique, to move from the "micro" to the "macro", and to connect the present to the past in anticipation of the future, all by building on preexisting theory.
>
> (Burawoy 1991: 5)

In that framework, theoretical formulations must be rubbed against empirical realities and conclusions resulting from that exercise must be used to reconstruct and refine theory.

Unlike quantitative methods, the logic behind ethnographic research, including interviews, continued interaction, and participant observation, is not primarily to generalize findings to large universes but to obtain an in-depth understanding of the factors accounting for social action. That involves: (a) exploring meanings assigned by individuals to their own behavior and that of others; (b) questioning the meanings imposed by the researcher upon the same actions; (c) uncovering the sui generis logic behind events; and (d) articulating coherent explanations about concrete areas of experience. The ethnographer's role is not necessarily to "settle the matter" but to raise questions that can be subsequently pursued through various methodologies. Triangulation, that is, the iteration between theoretical propositions and quantitative and qualitative analyses, is the foundation of science both as a process and as a result (Denzin 1988). Or, to paraphrase Michael H. Agar (1985), quantitative strategies can be used to discern the extent to which a phenomenon occurs in a larger universe; qualitative research is most appropriate to elucidate what the phenomenon means or, in fact, whether it exists at all (see also, Wolcott 2008; Fetterman 2009; Murchison 2010).

Exploring alternatives

In other words, between the radical belief promoted by post-modernist conjecture that all attempts to know lapse into subjectivity, and the equally extreme assumption that true understanding derives solely from objective criteria, another possibility exists: the conceptualization of scientific knowledge as a product of contestation, iteration, and inter-subjective exchanges. In that scheme, the premise is not that subjectivity necessarily interferes with scientific knowledge but that it can be harnessed to attain a fuller understanding of empirical realities. The question then becomes how to manage—rather than evict—subjectivity in the service of rigorous analysis.

The most expeditious way to tackle that question is by combining the strengths of different methodologies. In that design, quantitative and qualitative studies become the centerpiece of a learning process in which cognitive distance and proximity complement one another. The perspective gained from surveys, for example, is supplemented by the depth achieved through ethnographic research. Quantitative methodologies are best suited to describe the characteristics of a population, the frequency and character of behaviors and the correlation between constructed variables. Ethnography can be used to elucidate the sequence that connects those related variables.

Ethnographic research thus demands complete commitment to the task of understanding (Sanday 1979; Wolcot 2008). This, in turn, requires the cultivation of empathy—an ability to see things the way individuals and groups see them who are removed from the observer's immediate environment. Michael Piore puts it this way: "What interviews can reveal is not a set of specific answers to specific questions … [but] *patterns* of responses. Each answer, whether true or false, is a piece of that pattern. Individual responses cannot be interpreted in isolation" (Piore 1978: 81). Even in small samples, motifs emerge that cannot be attributed to personal idiosyncrasy. And, as Fitzgerald (2006) has aptly shown, the identification of common themes through ethnographic research cannot be discounted in attempts at generalization. Even a limited number of patterned responses merits explanation and can inform the design of large surveys.

The ethnographer may therefore resort to an iterative exercise of comparison to ascertain whether emerging findings are eccentric or not. Cross-checking information through archival research or the examination of census data can also aid the process of discovery and verification. Every interview produces information unique to the person being interviewed but also themes that recur as other members of the same group are brought into the conversation. By identifying and recording those salient themes, the researcher will soon come into contact with configurations of significance. In the next section, I illustrate this proposition on the basis of my own research.

Ethnography in the study of immigration

The Children of Immigrants Longitudinal Survey (CILS), spearheaded by sociologists Alejandro Portes and Rubén Rumbaut, is the most ambitious study of second-generation immigrants in the United States. It consists of repeated panels of interviews with immigrant children and, in some cases, their parents over a period spanning more than a decade. A sample, comprising more than 6000 youngsters between the ages of 11 and 14, was originally interviewed in 1993, in schools located in Miami, Florida, and San Diego, California, two important gateways for immigration, especially after the passage of the 1965 Immigration and Nationality Act. By the time the project concluded in 2006 extensive survey data had been collected on the trajectory of children of immigrants from early adolescence through their mid- and late 20s. It was possible, as a result, to pinpoint normative outcomes in the life trajectories of youngsters distinguished by national origin, length of residency in the United States, levels of education, etc. CILS also provided a glimpse into subjects such as perceptions, aspirations, and questions surrounding identity formation.

As part of CILS, I designed and implemented several ethnographic projects conceived as supplements to the larger survey. Here, I describe one of those studies to illustrate the application of ideas outlined in the previous sections.

Murdering the alphabet: children of immigrants and expressive entrepreneurship

In 2002, in collaboration with sociologists Lisa Konczal and William Haller, I set out to explore various dimensions of *segmented assimilation*. That concept was coined nearly a decade earlier (Portes and Zhou 1993) giving rise to controversies regarding established and revised explanations of the dynamics behind immigrant incorporation. Older accounts assumed an eventual melding of immigrants and their children into mainstream America—including economic ascent, higher levels of education, and compliance to normative values. The theory of segmented assimilation showed that progression to be far from obvious. CILS data, in particular, revealed the significance of social networks and human and material resources intervening at the local level to facilitate or impede assimilation. Clear differences emerge when children of immigrants are viewed in terms of national origin, socio-economic and educational status, race, and sex. For example, second-generation Chinese, Indian, and Cuban immigrants face negligible rates of incarceration while the offspring of Jamaicans, Haitians, and Mexicans confront a high probability of imprisonment (Portes and Rumbaut 2001). Operating at the mid-range level, segment assimilation theory occupies a salutary space equidistant between grandiose speculation and narrow detail (Merton 1987). It neither indulges in wishful thinking, as some straight assimilationists do (Gordon 1964; Alba 2003; Waldinger and Feliciano 2004), nor does it devolve into the inconsequential review of individual cases. The basic assumptions of segmented assimilation—that personal and material assets matter to children's ability to abide by or disconnect from normative expectations—are what I took to *the field* in 2002, when I designed an implemented an ethnographic module for the CILS project.

By that year, youngsters who had been first interviewed in their early teens had become adult men and women. They were young enough to remember their high school graduation but sufficiently mature to have started families, obtained professional degrees, managed businesses, or run afoul of the law. My hope was to learn more about the links connecting childhood to adulthood and about how they vary in consonance with the quality and quantity of resources—material as well as human—available to the young. I was especially interested in the manifold ways in which children evaluate information and use it to advance their own interests.

My colleagues and I selected Miami as a research location because it is a main point of destination for immigrants and also a focus of the CILS study. The first challenge was to select a large enough sub-sample from the original data base to provide insight into a range of experiences reflecting those of the larger surveyed population. Bill Haller took the lead in developing a directory of potential respondents containing equivalent numbers of young women and men, high, middle, and low-income families, business people, salaried and waged workers, and individuals with penal records. Taken as a whole our cases represented a microcosm of the broad universe under investigation by the CILS project. Fifty-five individuals were included in the sub-sample.

The original CILS sample was collected in accordance with stochastic methods and thus included a wide array of nationalities. For our ethnographic study we focused primarily on Cubans, West Indians, and Central Americans because they had the best potential for yielding significant information on several aspects of segmented assimilation. In Miami-Dade County, Cubans are the dominant population in terms of numbers and political salience. They also exemplify successful incorporation through business formation and self-employment. West Indians, especially Jamaicans and Haitians, command attention not only because of their fast growth rates but also because of their physical distinctiveness, which poses unique challenges as they seek inclusion in the larger society. Central Americans, Nicaraguans in particular, display adjustments that merit investigation as they become part of an overarching Cuban enclave in Miami. Taken together, the three groups illustrate a wide range of social, economic, racial, and ethnic adaptations.

I had a special interest in young people with arrest records and penal experience largely because they present an opportunity to improve our understanding of patterns of compliance, resistance, and opposition to normative standards. By cross-referencing social security numbers we located a good number of pertinent examples in the web pages of Florida's correctional facilities. Interviews involving individuals with jail and prison records are notoriously difficult to secure. We vigorously pursued such cases through diverse methods including the hand delivery of letters of introduction, the assurance of confidentiality, and the offer of substantial fees for interview time. Eleven such cases were included in our final report.

The next step was to design a lithe and efficient instrument for in-depth interviewing. An interview schedule is not the same as a survey questionnaire. To confuse the two will result in the accumulation of information hardly useful to accomplish the purpose of ethnographic research, that is, an understanding of processes and the connection between various phases of individual experience. With that in mind, we constructed an interview schedule focusing on five rubrics: (a) biographical/demographic profile; (b) household composition and resource flows; (c) social networks; (d) Identities; and (e) perceptions and outlook on success and failure. A limited number of questions were included under each of those headings.

The first rubric—biographic profile—was meant to situate an interlocutor in time and space. To do this is a matter of ethical and instrumental necessity. From an ethical point of view, offering interviewees an opportunity to relate their personal history is an expression of respect and a form of recognition that every life is unique and valuable (Wolcott 2008). On the practical side, biographical profiles yield useful demographic data—place of birth, migration and educational trajectory, marital status, etc.—and tend to facilitate rapport between the interviewer and the person being interviewed. It is revelatory of the human condition that, when given a chance, most of us won't shy away from reflecting upon our own lives. That is largely because humans are meaning-seeking and meaning-making creatures—when adequately implemented, the tools of ethnography offer a channel to realize a fundamental human craving: the articulation of meaningful narratives. No ethnography should be undertaken without an interest in the biographical accounts of informants.

The second rubric—household composition and resource flows—was aimed at obtaining information about the character, quantity, and quality of assets available to children of immigrants and other members of their households. Such information can add depth to our understanding of social class and economic standing, a critical goal given children's divided fates which often relate to economic inequalities. Next were issues concerning social networks which, according to the postulates of segmented assimilation theory, are decisive in promoting or retarding immigrant progress. Finally, we surmised, ideas about individual and collective identities, as well as outlooks on failure and success would provide insight into the relationship between cognitive systems and behavioral outcomes. An additional item in the interview schedule was whether, in the opinion of our informants, we should include other topics not already covered. I do not subscribe to notions of reflexivity that require the full participation of informants in interpretative tasks—it is the ethnographer who must be held responsible for interpretation—but I fully concur with those who maintain that research can always be improved by taking seriously the insights of informants (Haney 1996). When completed, our interview schedule did not exceed two typed pages. Brevity was intended to promote the collection of usable information; prolonged interviews often result in the accumulation of verbiage of little consequence for understanding social phenomena.

Interviews conducted with this instrument lasted between one and two hours. Our research team, consisting of three individuals, completed 55 interviews in 20 days. With one exception, all interviews took place in the homes of those interviewed. This is important because homes as well as places of employment offer a bounty of visual information that allows the researcher to supplement data collected through conversation. As in the natural sciences, a focus on *habitat* greatly facilitates the task of the researcher. In some cases, other members of the family were present and were able to contribute ideas. We accomplished approximately 110 hours of direct exchange with members of the sub-sample. We also engaged in participant observation and assembled copious notes about physical context. When scheduling and transportation are included, our team spent in excess of 250 hours conducting fieldwork.

All interviews were recorded and then coded though the use of an instrument I designed in 1995 to enable a rapid identification of major topical strands and patterns emerging from interview comparison. That coding instrument is divided into three sections. The first one consists of a summary of the interview with an eye on materials, such as direct quotations, suitable for analysis or inclusion in reports, articles, or books. The second section identifies and discusses major *thematic patterns* emerging from the interview. One of them, in this case, was the widespread belief in personal responsibility among children of immigrants regardless of economic condition or level of education. Prosperous entrepreneurs as much as incarcerates believe that they are the masters of their own fates notwithstanding huge differences in access to wealth and human capital. Almost without exception, they assign little significance to material assets when evaluating the outcomes of their lives, a testimony to normative processes of socialization in the United States that focus on individual character and stamina rather than contextual effects. The third section in the coding instrument cross-references and compares interview narratives to identify commonalities and differences in the experience of youngsters. It was informative to learn, for instance, that in a sample of 55 individuals differentiated by class, national provenance, sex, and race, 20 percent were involved in non-traditional occupations that ranged from graffiti art to the operation of an Internet casino, illustrating what I later conceptualized as "expressive entrepreneurship."

In other words, the coding instrument condenses and organizes information in ways that facilitate analysis beyond the hermeneutic capacity of gifted investigators; it focuses on specific questions and thematic patterns that any properly trained professional can master. Its format is consistent with the broader aims of ethnography, which is to uncover patterns in the narratives articulated by interviewees (Burawoy 1991; Wolcott 2008). Our research design was informed by theory and the data collected were used to augment theoretical knowledge about segmented assimilation.

Identity matters

The study described in the previous section yielded a wealth of information. An extended account of findings may be found in Fernández-Kelly and Konczal (2008). Most significant were insights regarding collective self definitions. Second-generation Cubans, for example are deeply affected by the exile experience of their elders. Two decades ago it was possible to imagine a decline of anti-Castro sentiment in Miami as older Cubans passed away and more temperate political feelings prevailed, the result of Americanization among second- and third-generation Cuban Americans. That, however, has not occurred; younger Cubans cling to, and even magnify intense feelings of anger against the Castro regime, partly as a means to honor their parents' suffering and acknowledge the legitimacy of their struggle. That insight alone begs for additional research about the formation of political thought across generations.

Equally interesting was to learn that young men and women of Cuban descent feel wholly Cuban and wholly American. Paraphrasing one of them, the Cuban self is about family, comfort, food, music, and dance but the American self is about political participation, personal independence, and financial success. Among Nicaraguans living in Miami, to be Hispanic is to adhere to the Cuban success story. Nicaraguans have faced paramount difficulties in terms of assimilation—including uncertainty about their legal status after fleeing the Sandinista Revolution. Facing discrimination because of their national provenance and modest class position, many young Nicaraguans feel socially excluded. As a result, they subsume their national origin under the pan-ethnic term, Hispanic, which in Miami is associated to the Cuban success story. West Indians, especially Haitians and Jamaicans face even more extreme choices in terms of identity, with some embracing cultural forms originating among native born Blacks and others emphasizing their immigrant distinctiveness to distinguish themselves from African Americans. Each of these findings illustrates processes of segmented assimilation. They also represent a new starting point for further investigating whether such patterns represent temporal or durable adaptations. Therefore, our study was both a way to flesh out the experience of second-generation immigrants whose general characteristics and typical life paths were known through the CILS longitudinal survey, and an opportunity to raise new questions susceptible of further inquiry.

Expressive entrepreneurship revisited

Our most important discovery concerned a comparatively large number of youngsters in the sub-sample who were deliberately shunning conventional work to embrace forms of creative self-employment. Youngsters in affluent and low-income families saw independent business formation as a means to design an aesthetic and meaningful life, different from the toil and instrumental struggle of their parents. "My father and mother," said a young Cuban man in his mid-twenties, "never had any enjoyment; all they did was work in their store so that my sister and I could have a better future. To me [a better future] means freedom and beauty, and excitement. I don't want a minuscule life." The young man under consideration, a budding photographer, saw art as a vehicle to escape the stifling constraints of the formal labor market. He came from a family of means but others in the sub-sample—working-class Cubans, Dominicans, Nicaraguans, Guatemalans, Haitians, and Jamaicans—had similar aspirations: they saw themselves as lyricists, actors, composers, light designers, rap artists, and musicians. One of them was proud to report that he managed a virtual casino on the Internet, "to achieve maximum freedom."

On the basis of my interviews with such youngsters, I introduced the notion of *expressive entrepreneurship* to designate new trends in employment whereby individuals circumvent the formal labor market as a way to gain independence and fulfill creative ambitions. I related this to intergenerational shifts in aspirations but also to changes in the economy. In an age characterized by the relocation of manufacturing—and even high-end service jobs—to overseas locations, youngsters of all kinds are less able to secure well paying and stable employment.

Rather than becoming cheap labor (in the case of low-income groups) or accepting the strict demands of the globalized rat race (in the case of educated, professionally bound groups) young people are resorting to expressive entrepreneurship. In doing that, they are also attempting to shape alternatives to labor as lived out by previous generations.

The last two sentences in the previous paragraph may be seen as an interpretation founded on ethnographic research but they are also the formulation of a new hypothesis calling for further inquiry. The limited number of cases included in our sample precludes any form of generalization. Nevertheless, even a small number of cases emerging from empirical research, sharing similar characteristics, and pointing towards the same rationale are sufficient to spur additional investigation. It is at this point that triangulation matters (Denzin 1989). Resorting to other methodologies, including archival, historical, and census research, as well as quantitative data collection and analysis can yield evidence to support or modify the formulated hypothesis. It is worth noting in that respect that census figures place "arts, entertainment, and recreation" as one of the fastest growing sectors of the US economy, a fact consistent with the rationale behind expressive entrepreneurship. The arts, entertainment, and recreation industry is expected to grow by 15 percent by 2018. Job growth will reflect, among other factors, increasing incomes and leisure time (US Department of Labor 2010–11). Independent artists, writers, and performers represent one of the most rapidly expanding occupations (US Census, Bureau of Labor Statistics 2011). In addition, recent studies carried out among non-immigrant youngsters suggest that expressive entrepreneurship may be a broader trend encompassing not solely immigrant youths but also the children of native-born Americans (Sullivan 2011). Questions about the conceptual validity of expressive entrepreneurship remain open until it becomes possible to establish the magnitude of the phenomenon and the degree to which it represents a transitory adaptation or a durable tendency.

Conclusion

In this chapter I have recorded some pivotal moments in the evolution of ethnography as part of a foundational tool box in the social sciences. I described ethnographic research as part of an effort to gain a more precise understanding of empirical realities concealed first by purely theoretical speculations and, more recently, by quantitative analyses. Paradoxical in this development has been the recurrent suspicion that qualitative approaches reduce the degree of rigor required by scientific research. In fact qualitative and quantitative research methods are complementary to one another.

In the second part of this chapter, I provided an abridged account of an ethnographic research project concerning a specific subject—the experience of children of immigrants regarding social networks, identity, and employment. On the basis of field work begun in 2002, I showed the correspondence between theory, qualitative methodology, and conceptualization meant to enhance or reconstruct initial theoretical assumptions. That account illustrates a manner of reasoning. It also represents a procedure to collect and interpret information based on a continued interchange between sociological ideas and narratives elicited through a purposive dialogue initiated by depth interviews. Scholarly interpretations and the testimonies of immigrant youngsters were approached with a similar mixture of skepticism and empathy. I discussed expressive entrepreneurship—the tendency of youthful populations to shun formal labor markets to seek meaning and independence in creative forms of self-employment—as a concept that complements and enhances our understanding of segmented assimilation.

Ethnography represents a bountiful methodological approach not as a way to evict subjectivity, but as a course to deeper understanding through structured inter-subjective exchanges.

The capacity for selection and interpretation is part of that procedure. While the findings of ethnographic research cannot be overly generalized, those of quantitative analyses are often generalized without attention to hidden forms of significance and meaning. The risk in the first case is anecdotal babble; in the second it is the blind accumulation of generalities through technically sophisticated methodologies but with a flimsy connection to reality. Were it not for ethnographic research, our understanding of ourselves and *others* would be diminished. How else are we to learn but by asking those whose experience concerns us? Perhaps the sole posing of that question is the best way to justify ethnographic enquiry as part of the pathways traversed in the pursuit of knowledge.

References and further reading

Alba, R. (2003) *Remaking The American Mainstream: Assimilation and Contemporary Immigration*. Cambridge, MA: Harvard University Press.

Agar, M. H. (1985) *Speaking of Ethnography*. Thousand Oaks, CA: Sage Publications.

Arminger, G. and Borhnstedt, G. W. (1987) "Making it count even more: A review and critique of Stanley Lieberson's 'Making it Count: The Improvement of Social Theory and Research." In C. C. Clogg (ed.), *Sociological Methodology*. San Francisco, CA: Jossey-Bass, pp. 366–72.

Arrighi, G. (1967) *The Political Economy of Rhodesia*. New York: Mouton.

Blau, P. M. and Duncan, O. D. (1967) *The American Occupational Structure*. New York: John Wiley.

Booth, C. (1889–91) *Life and Labour of the People in London*. London: Macmillan.

Buford May, R. A. and McCoy, M. P. (2000) "Do you see what I see? Examining a collaborative ethnography" *Qualitative Inquiry* 6(1): 65–87.

Burton, A. (1991) "Dividing up the struggle: The consequences of 'split' welfare work for union activism." In Burawoy *et al.* (eds), *Ethnography Unbound: Power and Resistance in the Modern Metropolis*. Berkeley, CA: University of California Press, pp. 85–99.

Burgess, E. W. (1925) "The growth of the city: An introduction to a research project." In R. Park, E. W. Burgess, and R. D. McKenzie (eds), *The City*. Chicago, IL: University of Chicago Press, pp. 47–62.

Denzin, N. K. (1989) *Interpretive Biography*. Newbury Park, CA: Sage Publications;.

Evans-Pritchard, E. (1940 [1969]) *The Nuer: A Description of the Modes of Livelihood and Political Institutions of a Nilotic People*. Oxford: Clarendon Press.

Fernández-Kelly, P. and Konczal, L. (2008) "Murdering the alphabet: Identity and entrepreneurship among second-generation Cubans, West Indians, and Central Americans" *Ethnic and Racial Studies*, 28(6): 1153–81.

Fetterman, D. M. (2009) *Ethnography: Step-by-Step*. Thousand Oaks, CA: Sage Publications.

Firth, R. (1925) "The Māori carver" *Journal of the Polynesian Society* 34(136): 277–91.

Fitzgerald, D. (2006) "Towards a theoretical ethnography of migration" *Qualitative Sociology* 29(1): 1–24.

——(2010) "Mixing methods and crossing boundaries in the study of international migration" (COMCAD Arbeitspapiere – working papers; 73) Bielefeld: COMCAD – Center on Migration, Citizenship and Development.

Fortes, M. (1940) *African Political Systems* (ed., with E. E. Evans-Pritchard). London: International African Institute.

Gille, Z. and Ó Riain, S.(2002) "Global ethnography" *Annual Review of Sociology* 28: 271–96.

Glick Schiller, N. (2003) "The centrality of ethnography in the study of transnational migration." In N. Foner (ed.), *American Arrivals: Anthropology Engages the New Immigration*. Santa Fe, NM: School of American Research Press, pp. 99–128.

Gold, S. J. (2002) *The Israeli Diaspora*. Seattle, WA: University of Washington Press/Routledge.

Gordon, M. (1964) *Assimilation in American Life*. New York: Oxford University Press.

Gould, S. J. (1981) *The Mismeasure of Man*. New York: Norton.

Haney, L. (1996) "Homeboys, babies, men in suits: The state and the reproduction of male dominance" *American Sociological Review* 61(5): 759–78.

Harris, M. (1968 [2001]) *The Rise of Anthropological Theory; A History of Theories of Culture*, Updated Edition. Lanham, MD: Altamira Press.

Hodgen, M. T. (1964) *Early Anthropology in the Sixteenth and Seventeenth Centuries*, Philadelphia, PA: University of Pennsylvania Press.

Le Play, F. (1870) *L'Organisation du Travail*. Tours : A. Mame et Fils.

Levitt, P. (2003), "You know. Abraham was really the first immigrant: Religion and transnational migration" *International Migration Review* 37(3): 847–74.

Lynd, R. S. and Lynd, H. M. (1929 [1959]) *Middletown: A Study in Modern American Culture*. New York: Harcourt Brace Javanovich.

Malinowski, B. (1922) "Argonauts of the Western Pacific: An account of native enterprise and adventure in the archipelagoes of Melanesian New Guinea" *Studies in Economics and Political Science*, no. 65. London: Routledge and Kegan Paul.

Massey, D. S. (2010) *New Faces in New Places: The Changing Geography of American Immigration*. New York: Russell Sage Foundation.

Mead, M. (1928 [2001]) *Coming of Age in Samoa*. New York: Harper's Perennial Modern Classics.

Merton, R. K. (1987) "Three fragments from a sociologist's notebooks: Establishing the phenomenon, specified ignorance, and strategic research materials" *Annual Review of Sociology* 13: 1–28.

Merton, R. K., West, P. S., and Jahoda, M. (1948) *Patterns of Social Life: Explorations in the Sociology and Social Psychology of Housing*. New York: Bureau of Applied Social Research, Columbia University.

Murchison, J. (2010) *Ethnography Essentials: Designing, Conducting, and Presenting Your Research*. Somerset, NJ: Jossey-Bass.

Orellana, M. F., Thorne, B., Chee, A., and Lam, W. S. E. (2001) "Transnational childhoods: The participation of children in processes of family migration" *Social Problems* 48(4): 572–91.

Østergaard-Nielsen, E. (2003) "The politics of migrants' transnational political practices" *International Migration Review* 37(3): 760–86.

Park, R. E. and Burgess, E. W. (1921) *Introduction to the Science of Sociology*. Chicago, IL: University of Chicago Press.

Piore, M. J. (1978) "Qualitative research techniques in economics." In J. Van Maanen (ed.), *Qualitative Methodology*. Newbury Park CA: Sage Publishers, pp. 71–86.

Portes, A. and Zhou, M. (1993) "The new second generation: Segmented assimilation and its variants" *Annals of the National Academy of Political and Social Science* 530: 74–96.

Portes, A. and Rumbaut, R. (2001) *Legacies: The Story of the Immigrant Second Generation*. Berkeley, CA: University of California Press.

Radcliffe-Brown, A. R. (1922 [1967]) *The Andaman Islanders*. New York: The Free Press.

Richards, I. A. (1939) *Land, Labour and Diet in Northern Rhodesia: An Economic Study of the Bemba Tribe*. London: Oxford University Press.

Sanday, P. R. (1979) "The ethographic paradigm(s)." In J. Van Maanen (ed.), *Qualitative Methodology*. Newbury Park: Sage Publications, p. 19.

Sayad, A. (2004) *The Suffering of the Immigrant*. Cambridge: Polity Press.

Spencer, H. (1873) *Descriptive Sociology*. London: Williams and Norgate.

Sullivan, E. R. (2011) "The youth mystique: Downward mobility and emerging adulthood." A Thesis presented in partial fulfillment of the Requirements for the Degree of Bachelor of Arts. Princeton University, Department of Sociology.

Thomas, W. I. and Znaniecki, F. (1918–20) *The Polish Peasant: Monograph of an Immigrant Group*. Chicago, IL: University of Chicago Press.

Staughton, R. (1929) *Middletown, a Study in American Culture*. New York: Harcourt, Brace and Company.

US Department of Labor, Bureau of Labor Statistics (2011) *Statistical abstract: Labor Force, Employment and Earning Projections*, Table 620.

US Department of Labor, "Bureau of Labor Statistics" (2010–11) *Occupational Outlook Handbook* (www.bls.gov/ooh/).

van Velsen, Jan (1960) "Labour migration as a positive factor in the continuity of Tonga tribal society" *Economic Development and Cultural Change* 8(3): 265–78.

Waldinger, R. and Feliciano, C. (2004) "Will the new second generation experience 'downward assimilation?' Segmented assimilation re-assessed" *Ethnic and Racial Studies* 27(3): 376–402.

Wallace, A. F. C. (1972) "Paradigmatic processes in culture change" *American Anthropologist* 74(3): 467–78.

Wallerstein, I. (1965) "Migration in West Africa: The political perspective." In H. Kuper (ed.), *Urbanization and Migration in West Africa*. Berkeley, CA: University of California Press, pp. 148–59.

Weber, M. (1949) *The Methodology of the Social Sciences*) Glencoe, IL: Free Press.

Willis, P. (2000) *The Ethnographic Imagination*. London: Polity.

Wirth, L. (1928 [1998]) *The Ghetto*. New Brunswick, NJ: Transaction.

Wolcott, H. (2008) *Ethnography: A Way of Seeing*. Lanham, MD: Altamira Press.

42

Interviews

Chien-Juh Gu

Introduction

Qualitative interviewing is often used in migration studies, but there has been little discussion concerning the application of this research method to immigrant subjects. Even before interviews are conducted, a number of questions arise: Why are interviews important for studying immigrants? What interview methods are used in empirical research and what are their principles? What factors need to be considered when interviewing immigrants and why? How does a researcher's role affect interview dynamics? What interview strategies are useful when interviewing women, men, and adolescents? How should undocumented immigrants be approached? How does the interviewer earn the trust of interviewees? How is the interviewees' consent acquired? How should sensitive questions be posed? What language should be used when interviewees are not native speakers? How should interviews conducted in a foreign language be transcribed and reported? How should the interviewer dress for an interview? Is giving gifts unethical? What are the strengths and weaknesses of interview methods? How are interviews used in a multiple method approach and in team research? To address these issues, this chapter provides reviews interview methods and discusses their applications to immigrant subjects.

The chapter begins with an introduction of the two particular interview methods: in-depth interviews and life history interviews. Following this introduction, I discuss various issues that need to be considered during the interview process with immigrants. These issues include the researcher's role as an insider or outsider, structural positions (race/gender/class) in the interview encounter, language use, cultural sensitivity, and ethics. To address these issues, I draw examples from my own research of Taiwanese immigrants and integrate studies by other scholars.[1]

Interview methods

Interviewing is used in both quantitative and qualitative research, and its format can vary greatly. Basically involving asking questions and getting responses, interviewing can be conducted in a one-on-one interaction, as a group discussion, or even over the phone. It may be completed in five minutes, be a one-time exchange that lasts from 30 minutes to a few hours, or be conducted over multiple, lengthy sessions. Interview questions can be structured (such as in surveys), semi-structured, or unstructured; their purposes vary for different disciplines and projects, ranging from opinion polling to academic analysis. The following review focuses on face-to-face qualitative interviewing in social sciences.

Booth was the first to use interviewing in social research, in his 1886 study, which combined survey, unstructured interviews, and ethnographic observations (Converse 1987 cited in Fontana and Frey 2005: 699). Booth's approach influenced later community research, including the studies by DuBois (1899) and Lynd and Lynd (1929). The Chicago School, which was developed in the early twentieth century, relied greatly on informal interviews, personal documents, and observations in ethnographic studies. Although quantitative survey research has been a dominant approach in social sciences since World War II, in-depth interviewing has been broadly employed in qualitative research—particularly in ethnographies—and remains significant. From classic studies, such as *Street Corner Society* (Whyte 1943), *Boys in White* (Becker *et al.* 1961), and *Black Metropolis* (Drake and Cayton 1970), to contemporary works such as *Portraits of White Racism* (Wellman 1993) and *Opting Out* (Stone 2008), qualitative interviewing has been an important data collection method.

Qualitative interviewing seeks to understand the subjects' life experiences in great depth, coherence, and density (Weiss 1994). As Fontana and Frey (2005) state, interviewing is one of the most powerful tools we can employ to understand fellow humans; it is not merely listening to what the subjects have to say, but an active collaboration between the interviewer and the interviewee. During the interview process, both the interviewee and the interviewer engage in the construction of meaning (Mishler 1986). Qualitative interviewing seeks to empower respondents, by giving them a voice and by positioning them in the center of their stories (Mishler 1986; Holstein and Gubrium 2003). This objective is similar to several theoretical approaches and political agendas, such as symbolic interactionism, feminism, and post-colonialism. For instance, symbolic interactionists consider interviewing to be a social interaction in which meaning emerges in the communication process; both parties present themselves and are influenced by each other's presentation of self (De Santis 1980; Berg 2009). Feminists advocate equal status between the researchers and the subjects. They argue that interviewers should disclose their personal information to their interviewees in order to achieve this goal (Oakley 1981; Cotterill 1992). Post-colonialist scholars underline the multiplicity of local culture and indigenous voices (During 1998). Although they each have a different focus, these approaches all highlight the subjectivity and agency of the researched.

In immigration studies, interview-based research has gained increased visibility and significance. Examples include *Urban Villagers* (Gans 1962), *Gendered Transitions* (Hondagneu-Sotelo 1994), *The Transnational Villagers* (Levitt 2001), *Mexican New York* (Smith 2006), and *The Israeli Diaspora* (Gold 2002), just to name a few. Many migration scholars have relied on qualitative interviewing to acquire in-depth knowledge of the immigrants' life experiences. This approach not only gives the immigrants a voice, but the vivid portraits of each community bring immigrant experiences to life.

Before discussing specific issues concerning interviewing immigrants, in-depth interviews and life history interviews are discussed. This section reviews the overall principles of the two methods and then focuses on data collection.

In-depth interviews

In-depth interviewing is a popular method in qualitative research. It is usually conducted as a one-on-one encounter between an interviewer and an interviewee, with the goal being to understand the interviewee's perceptions and experiences. In qualitative interviewing, the researcher and the interviewee are "conversational partners" (Rubin and Rubin 2004). This means that the interview format is a conversation between two parties. However, the two parties are not in equal positions (Kvale 1996; Rubin and Rubin 2004; Berg 2009). Although the interviewee does most of the talking, the interviewer designs and directs the conversation. In other words, the interviewer maintains a certain amount of intentional control over the interview process. The interview should have a smooth conversational flow and allow great flexibility for the interviewee to express himself or herself. Moreover, it should be kept on target, centering on the topics that the interviewer planned to explore in the interview.

Creating a conversational partnership is essential to a successful interview, which relies on establishing and maintaining a good rapport. Various factors can affect the rapport between the interviewer and the interviewee, just as reactivity (that is, how the interviewee responds to the questions) can affect the interview. The factors discussed most often center on the interviewer's appearance and personal characteristics. An interviewer's overt physical characteristics, such as hairstyle, mode of dress, race, and gender, create a first impression for the interviewee. These characteristics can affect the interviewee's consent to participate in an interview (De Santis 1980). The interviewer's individual attributes, such as mood, personality, and experience, will influence both how an interviewer asks questions and how the interviewee perceives the researcher and answers questions. In other words, the interviewer brings his or her own emotions, values, and biases into the interview (Rubin and Rubin 2004). Although qualitative interviewing is by no means value-free or neutral of a researcher's judgment (Bowman et al. 1984), such influences and biases can be reduced by the researchers' remaining self-aware. As Berg (2009: 132) suggests, the interviewer should be a "self-conscious performer," carefully preparing and rehearsing the lines, roles, and actions that will be carried out in the interview in advance.

Qualitative interviews use open-ended questions, often loosely structured around topical themes in a project. They allow flexible and in-depth expressions of emotions, experiences, and opinions. An interviewer should remain open-minded to new directions, interpretations, and sub-themes during the interview process. Unlike surveys in which a standard questionnaire is used, qualitative interview questions are not fixed and can be modified during the interview process. Because of the open-ended format, unexpected answers often emerge. Questions are often followed by further probing, to attain explanations or clarification. Thus, the interviewer needs to be sensitive and catch important clues in order to acquire more extensive information. Intensive and active listening is, therefore, important for accomplishing this task. As Rubin and Rubin (2004) argue, the interviewer must learn to capture cultural meanings in context in qualitative interviewing (that is, to "hear data"). The pattern of questioning can also be modified, depending on what works in the actual interview. Furthermore, interviewees have different speaking styles and respond to questions in varied ways. Some are talkative and self-revelatory, while others need frequent probing to elaborate; some are informative while others have little to say about the topic. The researcher must modify questions and customize questioning approaches to suit each interviewee. In other words, maintaining a flexible question design allows the interviewer to closely follow the interviewee's train of thought.

To hear data in qualitative interviewing requires cultural sensitivity. Cultural sensitivity facilitates the interview as well as the data interpretation and analysis. The interviewer and the interviewee often come from different worlds, which could result in different understandings of the same word. As Johnson (2001) points out, interviewers' commonsense cultural knowledge often influences what they hear, which may not reflect what the interviewees say or mean. Therefore, researchers must be aware of their own cultural assumptions and be careful about the terms used in questioning; they must also learn to understand the subjects' cultural definitions and recognize words that convey rich connotative meanings for the people being studied (Rubin and Rubin 2004). Non-verbal clues, such as facial expressions, body gestures, and grunts, are also important for seeing cultural meanings in context. In other words, interviewers must hear both what subjects say and how they say it in order to discern the layered meanings of the participants' perceptions (Gorden 1987; Johnson 2001). Verbal and non-verbal channels of communication between an interviewer and an interviewee convey messages and meanings for social interpretations.

Qualitative interviewing is often combined with participant observation in field research. Instead of conducting interviews in more formal one-on-one encounters, researchers may talk to their subjects in the field while participating in the subjects' social lives. Sometimes called "ethnographic interviews," this type of qualitative interviewing is usually unstructured and is seldom recorded. Researchers document their conversations and observations in the field by writing journals (field notes), which become the main data for analysis. Ethnographic interviewing is more advantageous than one-time formal interviewing because of the researcher's participation in the field. By being there, the fieldworker acquires a broad understanding of the subjects, their surrounding environment and their social relations. This understanding helps to guide research directions and construct interview questions, thereby refining the researcher's reflexivity in the research process (Briggs 1983; Whyte 1984). In addition, a rapport can be established with the subjects prior to interviews. Although ethnographic interviewing and one-on-one formal interviewing have different formats and procedures, they share major principles of execution. Many scholars conduct both formal and ethnographic interviews; some use interviews as their main data, while others use them as a supplement.

Life history interviews

The life history interview is a qualitative research method for gathering information on the subjective essence of a person's entire life (Atkinson 1998). Through a guided interview, the interviewee tells stories of what has happened in his or her life, including important events, people, feelings, and experiences. In a life history interview, the interviewee is a storyteller, giving a personal narrative of his or her life as a whole. Every interview is, thus, a mini-autobiography. The storyteller chooses what and how to tell the audience their life story through a guided conversation. In contrast to in-depth interviews, which usually center on a particular topic, the life history method focuses on an individual's experiences through different stages of life. Life history interviews require a longer time for data collection but gather more comprehensive information about the subject than other types of interviews.

The life history interview has been used primarily in anthropological work, but has also been used in other disciplines (see McCall and Wittner 1990). Anthropologists use the life story as the unit of study for individual case research; historians, on the other hand, use life story materials to enhance their understanding of local history; and sociologists use life stories to explore relationships and group interactions (Atkinson 1998). The life history method has also been applied to disciplines such as education, health sciences, and women's studies (Cole and Knowles 2001).

The life history method takes a longitudinal approach to conducting interviews. The less structured the interviews, the better the interviewer can get subjects to tell their stories (Atkinson 1998). A life history interview typically begins with questions that attempt to understand the circumstances into which the interviewee was born, such as questions about the subject's birth, family members and special events or childhood traditions. Asking about childhood memories deepens understanding of the interviewee, his or her relations with others, and the surrounding community. Religious beliefs and practices, cultural traditions in the family, relationships with family members, leisure activities, and neighborhood environment are examples of initial questioning areas. Questions then move on to the next stage of life: the school years. Example questions include, but are not limited to: What was it like in elementary school? What was it like in middle school? What are your best and worst memories about school? What were your teachers and peers like? What did you learn about yourself during your school years? How was your college experience? Finally, the interview moves on to adulthood, including work and romantic relationships. During each stage of questioning, efforts should be made to acquire in-depth and extensive understanding of the subject's life experiences. In particular, the interviewer should pay close attention to significant life events, people, and personal feelings involved in the process and in relationships. Throughout the process of collecting and interpreting life stories, maintaining trusting and close relationships with interviewees is important to the acquisition of in-depth insights (Watson 1985).

In contrast to verbatim transcription, which is often used with in-depth interviews, life story interviews should be written in the first person, using the interviewees' own words (Atkinson 1998). Each interview becomes a flowing narrative in the words of the person telling the story. These personal narratives are then examined in order to understand single lives in detail, as well as the individual's role in the community. In other words, the interviewees are the first interpreters of the stories told. Through the story tellers' personal constructions of reality, the researchers discover what they plan to learn from the subjects (Holstein and Gubrium 1995).

McCall and Wittner (1990) argue that life histories deepen existing knowledge because researchers are forced to examine their own assumptions, in relation to the subjects' experiences. By incorporating more actors into scholarly conceptions, the life history method helps researchers to understand the complexities of social life and the process of change. In particular, life stories illuminate a person's evolution of their self-concept over time. They help to understand a person's subjective meaning and interpretations of his or her life story, as well as the contexts in which such meaning and interpretations are produced at different points in a person's life.

Although not yet a prevalent research tool in immigration studies, life history interviews have been adopted by some scholars (e.g., Smith 2006; Gabrielli et al. 2007; Ling 2007). There are two main reasons the life history method is particularly suitable for studying human migration. First, contemporary international migration is rarely a one-time action or event; rather, it is a developmental social process (Massey 1986). The ability of the life history method to trace this process from the social actor's viewpoint makes it a proper approach for immigration research. In fact, as early as a century ago, Thomas and Znaniecki (1927) stressed the importance of life histories (what they called "personal life-records") in their classic work, *The Polish Peasant*. Second, relocating oneself and one's family to a new society is one of the most drastic actions that a person can take in their lifetime (Gold 1997). International migration is a significant life event, bringing fundamental changes to the immigrants' lives. The life history approach is a great tool for exploring issues relevant to this action. How do individuals adapt to these changes? How does a person's self-concept evolve during the migration process? How do immigrants' significant relations change over time? This method also empowers immigrants, as it highlights the subjects' subjective interpretations.

Applications to immigrant interviews

"Good interview research goes beyond formal rules and encompasses more than the technical skills of interviewing to also include personal judgment about which rules and questioning techniques to involve or not invoke" (Kvale and Brinkmann 2009: 87). With general interview principles as the foundation, specific strategies and techniques can vary, depending on the research topic and the researched group. Immigrants are a unique population. They have relocated from another society, often don't speak the host country's language, and have varied migration backgrounds. Many immigrants have experienced dramatic changes in their social and economic lives as a result of immigration; for instance, some were forced to leave their countries due to special circumstances such as wars or disasters. The extent of immigrants' acculturation and adaptation vary, as do their social practices and cultural traditions. Therefore, a variety of factors need to be taken into consideration when adopting interview methods for studying immigrants. This section looks at four issues: the influences of structural positions (such as gender, class, and race) on the interview; language use in conducting and reporting interviews; cultural factors to be considered in the interview process; and ethics.

Structural positions

Many method books have discussed the idea that interviewers' observable features (age, gender, race, hairstyle, clothing, manner of speech, etc.) and personality attributes (moods, interests, experiences, biases, etc.) affect both how subjects respond to an interview and what the researchers hear in that interview (Gubrium and Holstein 2001; Rubin and Rubin 2004; Berg 2009). However, interviewees' perceptions of and responses to the interview are also shaped by their own structural positions and life experiences. As a result, being aware of the influences of both parties' characteristics helps a researcher to adopt effective interview strategies and to prevent biases.

Unlike ethnographic studies, in which researchers spend months or years with their subjects to develop trust, understanding, and relationships, interview data are often collected within a few hours. Making a good impression in the first 10 minutes is essential for completing a successful interview. As Berg (2009: 131) points out, "the interviewee's conception of the interviewer centers around aspects of appearance and demeanor." This conception affects the interviewees' interactions with the interviewer and how they answer the interview questions. For instance, how interviewers dress for the interview is one of the first impressions given to the interviewees. The principle is to dress appropriately—do not dress too formally or fancy when interviewing immigrant laborers; do not appear sloppy when interviewing immigrant entrepreneurs. It is important to present a polite, patient, and friendly overall demeanors when conducting interviews. While clothing and manners seem easy to manage, other factors such as gender, race, and social class are much more complicated.

Race/ethnicity and insider vs. outsider status

The insider-outsider controversy was heated in the 1970s, when white people comprised 98 percent of all social scientists (Moore 1973). Much of the scholarly concern centered on whether and how researchers' race affected studies of racial minorities (see Merton 1972; Moore 1973; Baca Zinn 1979). Even today, when the demographic composition of the profession is much more diverse, the issue of race/ethnicity and insider-outsider retains its importance in empirical and epistemological discussions in social research. In fact, race or ethnicity is not the only element to constitute a researcher's insider or outsider status. Other factors, such as gender, sexuality, immigrant status, nationality, social class, and residential region, can also become a major distinction between researchers and the researched, and sometimes these differentiations are multifaceted rather than dichotomous. It is, therefore, useful to understand the potential impact of insider-outsider positions in interview-based research.

The researcher's role as an insider or outsider affects both subject recruitment and the interview process. There are advantages and disadvantages to each of these two roles. When the researcher belongs to the immigrant group under study, it is easy to collect information, locate informants and communicate with subjects because of their shared cultural background. Moreover, it is likely that the subjects will be willing to share their experiences, because they expect the interviewer will have a good understanding of them or will want to help a fellow immigrant. However, there are also some drawbacks when the interviewer is an insider. When coming from the same culture, the researcher could easily take certain things for granted and miss important clues in the subjects' stories. Some subjects hesitate to be interviewed by a fellow immigrant, because they have concerns about their anonymity and confidentiality. In some cases, insider researchers end up taking on more responsibilities than they can handle, due to their reciprocity ideal and their informants' expectations (Baca Zinn 1979).

In contrast, out-group interviewers benefit from their outsider status in that they tend to make fewer assumptions about the researched group. Because of their cultural gap with the subjects, out-group researchers are more likely to ask questions that insiders do not typically pose, sometimes leading to important discoveries. However, there are also obstacles that out-group researchers must overcome when studying an immigrant group: understanding the group's culture and migration history; finding key informants to help them collect information and locate interviewees; speaking the language; and earning the subjects' trust. Many outsider researchers therefore conduct fieldwork in addition to interviews in order to strengthen their ties with the researched community.

Race/ethnicity is probably the most apparent characteristic for defining insiders and outsiders, as a great number of contemporary immigrants do not belong to the mainstream racial group in the host society, and many are non-white. As Dunbar *et al.* (2001) suggest, interviewing racialized populations requires very special attention and caution because the social context of a racialized experience differs significantly from the mainstream culture. Interviewers must be deeply familiar with the lives of respondents in order to elicit a full version of the interviewee's story. Self-disclosure on the part of the insider interviewer is sometimes helpful in facilitating the in-depth expression of an interviewee's emotions and life experiences. Reflexivity, empathy, and sensitivity are also valuable assets that can help researchers to capture the complexities of ethnic minorities' lives.

Immigrants can be seen as outsiders, regardless of their own racial backgrounds or those of the interviewers. In a study of homeless immigrants in Copenhagen, Järvinen (2003) discovered that her interviewers treated immigrant subjects as "guests" of the country. The native Danish interviewers asked whether the immigrants intended to "go home," and took a defensive position when the interviewees criticized "their country." Such host-guest interaction reveals an insider-outsider distinction unconsciously drawn by native-born interviewers, which is a problem that should be avoided when interviewing immigrants.

Gender, age, and social class

Gender is another major factor that influences interview dynamics and results. Interviewers and interviewees are shaped by culturally ascribed meanings of masculinity and femininity, so their gender will affect both the interaction atmosphere and the extent to which personal experiences are shared. Cross-sex interviewing appears to be more challenging than same-sex interviewing, as feelings of discomfort and limited self-disclosure occur more frequently in cross-sex interactions. For instance, women volunteer more personal information to female interviewers than to male interviewers (Padfield and Procter 1996); women interviewers could sometimes appear too flatteringly attentive to male interviewees (De Santis 1980); and the interview relationship could be goaded toward becoming a sexual one in some encounters, although infrequently (Weiss 1994). Such gendered phenomena may also hold true in immigrant communities, suggesting caution when interviewing the opposite sex.

Taking gender effects into account, scholars have suggested different strategies for interviewing men and women, which are also useful for interviewing immigrants. Schwalbe and Wolkomir (2001) contend that masculine selves lead to little disclosure of emotions and the exaggeration of rationality, autonomy, and control by men. Interviewers should adopt indirect approaches and avoid questions that threaten a male subject's masculine self, such as economic failure and stress. Asking for stories (instead of direct questions about emotionally loaded topics) and shifting the focus to the contexts (rather than actions) are some useful ways to elicit in-depth expressions from men.

Female subjects had been excluded from social science studies until the 1970s (Reinharz and Chase 2001). In immigration research, the long-missing voices of women did not begin to be heard until the 1980s (see Pedraza 1991; Pessar 2003; Curran *et al.* 2006). Socialized into their gender role, women tend to be self-silencing and soft-spoken, especially when men are present. Interviewing women, therefore, needs an approach that differs from that of studying men (Reinharz and Chase 2001). Feminist scholars have advocated a feminist methodology that highlights women's standpoints and subjectivities. They argue that when women interview women, sisterhood bonds and the interviewer's self-disclosures are essential approaches for encouraging and hearing women's voices in interviewing (Oakley 1981; DeVault 2004). Whether they adopt the feminist methodology or not, scholars who study immigrant women share the goal of unfolding the women's subjective experiences (see Gabaccia 1992; Kelson and DeLaet 1999; Hondagneu-Sotelo 2003).

Age and social class are two other factors that shape the power dynamics in interviewing. Eder and Fingerson (2003) argue that children and adolescents are socially disadvantaged and disempowered groups, so interviewing them requires a different approach to interviewing adults. They suggest that creating a natural context, conducting a brief observation before the interview and interviewing in a group setting are all useful methods. In a study of second-generation immigrants, Wolf (1997) conducted four focus groups to solicit the perceptions of Filipino youth concerning their intergenerational conflicts. The group settings allowed these immigrant children to freely express their psychological struggles with two competing cultural traditions, a topic that may not have been as easy to discuss in other contexts. Hearing similar stories from their peers allowed their adolescents to open up and share their own experiences. They felt that they were not alone in their cultural tug with their parents, and could be well understood. This study exemplifies the importance of group settings for interviewing adolescences.

Immigrants of different socio-economic backgrounds may perceive research differently and thus call for different interview strategies. For instance, immigrant laborers may be exhausted simply by everyday survival and be difficult to approach for interviews; they may also be unfamiliar with research processes and interview interactions. Researchers need to be patient and flexible when scheduling interviews with laborers, and explain the purpose and process of research clearly. Questions need to be asked in lay terms that are easy to understand; asking for examples and stories are useful in helping subjects to express their opinions. The purpose of recording and acquiring consent should be explained politely, but the interviewer should not insist if subjects feel uncomfortable with a tape recorder. Some laborers and refugees may be suspicious of interviews. Researchers can seek assistance or an introduction from non-profit organizations familiar to the subjects, or conduct fieldwork in the subjects' communities to establish relationships and networks before interviews take place. In Malpica's (2002) study, in-depth interviews were arranged at the end of the project, after the researcher had earned the trust of day laborers through participant observation. While there might be fewer obstacles when interviewing immigrants who are highly educated and understand the nature of research interviews, establishing networks with co-ethnics remains useful for locating interviewees.

Some immigrant communities proscribe interaction between the sexes, or particular age or status groups. Researchers need to be aware of and sensitive to these cultural taboos. For instance, Muslim women are not allowed to be alone with a man who is not a relative, and older Muslim men may not feel they are being taken seriously when interviewed by a woman (Wenger 2003). In Asian communities, within which occupation-based social hierarchies are evident, student interviewers may not be able to gain access to entrepreneurs or organizational leaders. Such factors need to be taken into consideration when choosing interviewers.

Of course, the extent of the influence resulting from a researcher's social characteristics can neither be measured nor easily verified. It is also impossible to isolate any single factor from the intersecting effects of gender, ethnicity, social class, age, sexual orientation, and immigrant status (among others) on an interview encounter. However, being aware of potential influences helps to keep the researcher attentive while observing and interpreting the interviewees' responses. It also helps prevent reactivity and makes good use of the advantages that such influences can bring to research. In particular, if the researcher hires assistants to conduct the interviews, then the interviewer's structural positions and their potential impact on the interview become a necessary consideration.

Language

Many immigrants are non-native-speakers. Since the main purpose of qualitative interviews is to gather in-depth information about the subjects' perceptions and experiences, using a language with which the subjects feel comfortable helps them to express themselves freely and vividly. Before the interview, the researcher can ask what language the subject would like to use for the interview, or can proceed in whatever language the subject speaks while in conversation. Speaking in the subject's native tongue is beneficial to the research in many ways. For example, the subjects are able to express themselves well and describe their life experiences in great depth. Language is the carrier of cultural meaning and reflects the speaker's ways of thinking. During my interviews, several second generation subjects tried to communicate in Taiwanese, while several first generation interviewees started our conversations in English (both were their second language). In both situations, I went along with the language the interviewees chose to speak, but the subjects switched to their first language after a few minutes. It was obvious that they expressed themselves best in their first language. Without having to switch between two languages, subjects can speak their minds using complex vocabularies and sophisticated expressions. Such vivid illustrations of meaning are exactly what the researcher wishes to capture in qualitative interviews.

Moreover, a connection between the researcher and the researched can be established more easily when they speak the same language. In my research, I often sensed the subjects' excitement and feeling of closeness when I spoke their mother tongue. My position as an outside researcher immediately turned into that of an insider, thereby establishing a special bond. By speaking the same language, the subjects knew that I was "one of them" and that I understood their culture. This feeling of closeness is valuable, because immigrants live in a foreign land and often feel alienated. For instance, several subjects in my study traveled one hour every Sunday to attend a Taiwanese church, so they could hear the language that they dearly missed. Many participants ordered Taiwanese CDs and videos from overseas in order to feel less homesick.

Being able to speak their native language brings their home to them, which means a lot to many subjects. When a researcher makes the effort to learn the interviewees' language, it is certainly appreciated and the friendship between the two parties can be more easily established.

While I believe that language proficiency and linguistic competence are valuable assets in interview research, there are alternatives. When the principle researcher does not speak the immigrants' language, a translator can be used to conduct the interview. Researchers can also hire interviewers who speak the language, or can interview those immigrants who speak fluent language of the host society. The problem with this last solution, however, is that the translation process can result in the loss of connotation, because cultural meanings are embedded in language. Therefore, I encourage researchers to conduct interviews in the subjects' native language whenever possible, in order to document the vibrant expressions subjects will use to illustrate their own thoughts. When interviewers are hired, researchers should be present at some, if not all, of the interviews. It is difficult to oversee the interview process if the researcher is absent. There should also be frequent communication with the interviewers, to discuss any concerns or problems that may arise throughout the research process.

Researchers inevitably face issues of transcription and translation when compiling data and writing reports for interviews conducted in a foreign language. The following approaches are what I have found to be most effective: first, interviews should be transcribed in the language spoken during the interview, even if they must be translated into another language for reports. In my opinion, verbatim transcripts are the best way to document interviews because they allow researchers to review the entire conversation and trace clues in the stories. These clues, which sometimes include inconsistencies or contradictions, help to outline the complexities and nuances of individual life experiences. Moreover, when transcribing interviews, subjects' emotional expressions (e.g., smile, hesitation, confusion, pause, etc.) should be noted, to capture the covert contexts of their stories. Second, data analysis should be conducted before translating the interviews into another language, in order to keep the analyses as close to the original contexts as possible. Third, when publishing interviews, all translations should reflect the original cultural meanings as closely as possible. This may include using idiomatic languages and keeping grammatical errors intact to zealously reflect the subjects' minds and expressions.

In reality, scholars use different strategies that are conditioned by the purpose and resources of a project, the researcher's writing style, and the readers of the research reports. Some researchers transcribe only portions of their interviews; some translate the interviews before data analysis; some re-write the subjects' narratives in perfect native language; and some write interview excerpts in two languages. As there are no absolute rules, scholars must make judgment and allow flexibility in the research process. Sometimes, figuring out what works best for a project takes some trial-and-error.

Cultural sensitivity

No immigration study can succeed without understanding the culture of the immigrant group being researched. Immigrants come from countries where the economic, political, social, and cultural contexts are often quite different from those of the receiving society. These contexts shape and continue to affect individuals' perceptions and behavior in the host society. Culture is an essential, yet complicated matter in immigrants' social practices and emotional lives (Foner 1997; Gu 2010). In particular, adult immigrants who grew up in another society often maintain a strong culture of origin, the result of socialization's profound influence, even among the most acculturated. In a global era where transnational migration is fairly common, immigrants' continuous exposure to their original culture is inevitable, and its impact on their lives cannot be overlooked. Studying immigrants requires a thorough comprehension of their culture and sensitivity to their social norms.

Culture is important in the interview process in several ways. For instance, asking subjects to sign a consent form could be a potential cause of anxiety. For instance, Taiwan's colonization history and China's communist background may cause immigrants from the two countries to be suspicious or to fear signing formal documents such as consent forms. In my research with Taiwanese immigrants, oral consent was used and recorded at the beginning of every interview. This approach helped me to earn the subjects' trust and facilitated the interviews. For illegal immigrants, the risks inherent in signing their names on a formal document could prevent them from participating in research. Earning trust and using oral consent are, therefore, crucial in this instance. Studies of undocumented immigrants have particularly benefited from fieldwork because it helps to build mutual understanding and trust between the researcher and the researched, thereby facilitating subjects' consent to interviews (see Hondagneu-Sotelo 1994; Valenzuela 2003). Moreover, Cornelius (1982) suggested that conducting fieldwork in immigrants' communities of origin could help in locating and interviewing undocumented immigrants in the United States, through the networks and friendships that a researcher establishes with their co-ethnics back home.

Some topics could be sensitive to immigrants, thus requiring cautious wording in inquiry, such as undocumented status, income and finances, mental illness, sexuality, and drug use. Understanding immigrants' perceptions, stigmas, or taboos regarding these topics will help the interviewer to phrase questions in non-intimidating ways. When inquiring about an immigrant's legal status, Cornelius (1982) suggests less threatening questions such as "Are you thinking about getting papers?" "Would you like to get papers?" "Did you have trouble getting into the country?" and "Are you in the process of getting papers?" When asking about income and family finances, I usually use sequent questions that start with the most indirect one, such as "It must be tough managing all the expenses (e.g., house, children's education and medical bills). Is one income enough? Do you receive financial support from relatives back home? How do you manage your family finances?" If the conversation goes smoothly and the interviewee seems open when answering relevant questions, I would then ask "Do you mind if I ask about your household income?" In contrast, if the interviewee appears reserved and hesitant, I would switch to another topic and give it another try at the end of the interview, when the subject has opened up more. As Weiss (1994) suggests, a reliable research relationship should be established before asking sensitive questions.

Another sticky issue that arose during my interviews is the usage of "Taiwanese" and "Chinese." Some subjects identified themselves as "Chinese" and corrected me during the interview when I referred to them as "Taiwanese." In contrast, those who identified themselves as Taiwanese became offended when I referred them as "Chinese." One subject spent a lot of time emphasizing the importance of Taiwanese identity. Although national identity is not a focus of my research, I soon realized the sensitivity associated with these two terms. To avoid generating tension, I used "immigrants from Taiwan" in my description and then followed with whatever term the subject used in conversation. When interviewing immigrants who are sensitive to specific term usages for any reason, the interviewer should recognize the subject's discomfort and rephrase the questions. Interviewers can also ask interviewees to explain how different terms are used and perceived in the immigrant community.

In the above examples, the keys to successful interviews include indirect questions and attentive observation. It is particularly important for topics associated with stigmas, such as mental illness, addiction, and homosexuality. In my interviews with Taiwanese immigrants, I used non-stigmatized terms such as "hardship," "stress," and "psychological struggles" to discuss mental health issues (Gu 2006). These neutral terms did not provoke anxiety or hesitation. On the contrary, the subjects were very willing to talk about their difficulties and emotions. Many appreciated the opportunity to reflect upon their lives, and some found the interviews to be "therapeutical," as one subject commented.

Another approach to discussing sensitive issues is to explain the purpose of the topic before asking the questions (Weiss 1994). When the subjects understand why certain questions are asked and why the information is important, they may be more likely to collaborate with the interviewer in the discussion. Sexuality, homesickness, and illegal employment are a few examples. Another way to initiate the discussion is to start with general observations on the topic or with other people's stories, and then ask the subjects to comment. For instance: "Some people have said that drug use is a serious problem in your community. Is it true?" "How prevalent is the problem?" "Have you seen anyone you know suffering from drug problems? Could you describe the situation?" "What do you think is the major cause of the problem?" Similar topics for which this approach can apply include gambling, economic failure, and generational conflicts. When it comes to sensitive issues, some people feel more comfortable talking about what they see in general or using other people's stories to express their opinions, rather than talking about themselves. Although it is done indirectly, the interviewees' own experiences are often revealed in this way.

Cultural sensitivity helps researchers to avoid tension, establish rapport, and choose appropriate approaches for collecting data. Its importance cannot be stressed enough. In addition, it is equally important to be cautious when writing up findings on sensitive topics. Pseudonyms must be used, especially in direct quotes, to ensure subjects' anonymity and protect their privacy. Since indirect questions and alternative terms are often used to ask sensitive issues, it is likely that interviewees also use indirect expressions in their answers. Researchers must be careful in their interpretations, making sure the subjects' narratives are appropriately analyzed and avoiding over-interpretations.

Ethics

Is it ethical to pay or give gifts to subjects? In principle, scholars believe that subjects benefit from having the opportunities to participate in and contribute to a study (Weiss 1994). Research will eventually benefit the subjects once scholarly understanding of the subjects' lives is enhanced by collecting data from them. In reality, however, it is not uncommon for a study to offer gift cards, small presents, or cash as an incentive or compensation to participants for their time. Weiss (1994) contends that payment can be an important incentive for low-income respondents to participate in research, but might not be necessary for middle-class interviewees. In my opinion, presenting gifts is not merely an ethical matter but also an issue of cultural appropriateness. In some cultures, such as Asian traditions, giving gifts is an important norm in social interactions. Giving presents can serve as a friendly gesture in a culturally appropriate way, setting the tone for good rapport.

I have witnessed the awkwardness that can ensue from not presenting gifts, and the difference gifts can make to the interview process. During the first few interviews I conducted, I did not bring any presents. I sensed some disappointment from my respondents when I arrived at their homes, and realized that giving gifts is an important norm in Taiwanese culture. Later, I began bringing presents to interviews, usually a small fruit basket. As a result, rapport was quickly established. For my second project, I budgeted gifts into my research proposal, and gave subjects a university mug and a small bottle of Michigan maple syrup; these gifts conveyed gratitude in a culturally appropriate way. After each interview, I sent a thank-you card to express my appreciation for their time and assistance.

In sum, I believe that giving payment or gifts is not a right or wrong issue. Rather, its justification involves the careful consideration of various factors, such as the subjects' cultures, the research budget, and the rationales of a study. Usually, the material rewards that researchers offer are not large amounts that could dramatically change the subjects' financial condition. Therefore, gifts may convey more of a cultural than a material meaning. I suggest that researchers make their own judgments in the field and allow some flexibility when their budgets permit. Interviewees differ from research project to research project. Their cultures vary, and the nature of each project differs. Giving small presents to the subjects might seem insignificant but can help to establish a rapport and to facilitate the process of data collection.

Conclusion

Qualitative interviewing serves as a powerful tool for data collection. Its major strengths lie in its focus on subjects' voices, as well as in its ability to show the richness and complexity of life experiences. Through interviewing, researchers acquire an in-depth understanding of interviewees' perceptions and feelings. In particular, life history interviewing allows researchers to capture subjects' life trajectories, selfhood evolvement, and changes in social relations over time. Compared to surveys, interview methods are more time consuming and labor intensive. Interviewers need rigorous training and actual practice to develop skills and accumulate empirical experience. Compared to ethnography, interviews lack the opportunity to observe subjects in dynamic social situations, but provide more subjective interpretations of the researched. They also allow researchers to systematically analyze interviewees' narratives by using coding techniques suggested by grounded theory or by using computer software. Research reports that use interview excerpts are able to situate subjects in the center of their stories, which is a powerful way to show subjective accounts of the researched population.

Qualitative interviewing is often combined with other research methods in data collection (especially with ethnography); using multiple methods has been a contemporary trend in social research. Each research method has its own strengths and weaknesses, so adopting more than one method can take advantage of the varied pros and cons of different methods, thereby obtaining a more comprehensive understanding of the researched population or social phenomenon. Teamwork is another approach used for studying immigrant communities. For instance, *Gatherings in Diaspora* (1998) was written by the New Ethnic and Immigrant Congregations Project fellows, led by Warner and Wittner. Although they came from varied demographic, religious, and disciplinary backgrounds, the team worked together to produce a book that is coherent in theme but that covers diverse immigrant congregations. Another example is Horton's *The Politics of Diversity* (1995). A research team conducted this study of Monterey Park, in California, led by Horton. The team members' multiethnic backgrounds allowed them to collect data from different sources and in different languages. This approach is particularly effective for studying an immigrant community that is composed of varied ethnic groups.

Interview research is a craft (Kvale and Brinkmann 2009). Researchers as interviewers are the main instruments in interview research. Their knowledge, abilities, and sensitivity are crucial to the quality of the knowledge produced. Good craftsmanship requires both practical skills and personal insights, which can be learned through field observations, training, and extensive practice. In this chapter, I have introduced two qualitative research methods, in-depth interviews and life history interviews. I also provided a great number of examples for discussing various issues in interview contexts, including the outsider-insider status, structural positions, language, cultural sensitivity, and ethics. Incorporating my own reflections and other scholars' perspectives, I hope these discussions offer insights for migration researchers. Interviewing is a fascinating research tool. Through interviews, immigrants' marginal positions are reversed and their unvoiced stories are heard. The richness and complexity of data that interview methods acquire far surpass those collected by other research methods.

Note

1 Many of the examples are derived from my two projects with Taiwanese immigrants in the Chicago metropolitan area. For the first project, I conducted 54 in-depth interviews with Taiwanese immigrants and their adult children. Using semi-structured questions, these interviews lasted from one to four hours and were conducted in three languages (Mandarin, Taiwanese, and English). This project was published as *Mental Health among Taiwanese Americans: Gender, Immigration, and Transnational Struggles* (Gu 2006). For the second project, I conducted interviews with 21 Taiwanese immigrant women. Using the life history method, these interviews ranged from three to 12 hours and were conducted in Mandarin or Taiwanese. This project is the foundation of my second book, which is still in progress. The 75 subjects that I have interviewed varied greatly in terms of gender, age, social class, ethnicity of origin, occupation, and marital status.

References and further reading

Atkinson, R. (1998) *The Life Story Interview*. New York: Sage.

Baca Zinn, M. (1979) "Field research in minority communities: Ethical, methodological and political observations by an insider" *Social Problems* 27(2): 209–19.

Becker, H. S., Geer, B., Hughes, E. C., and Strauss, A. L. (1961) *Boys in White: Student Culture in Medical School*. Chicago, IL: University of Chicago Press.

Berg, B. L. (2009) *Qualitative Research Methods for the Social Sciences*, 7th edition. Boston, MA: Allyn and Bacon.

Bowman, B., Bowman, G. W., and Resch, R. C. (1984) "Humanizing the research interview: A posthumous analysis of LeRoy Bowman's approach to the interview process" *Quality and Quantity* 18(2): 159–71.

Briggs, C. L. (1983) "Questions for the ethnographer: A critical examination of the role of the interview in fieldwork" *Semiotica* 46(2/4): 233–61.

Cole, A. L. and Knowles, J. G. (2001) *Lives in Context: The Art of Life History Research*. New York: Rowman and Littlefield.

Converse, J. M. (1987) *Survey Research in the United States: Roots and Emergence 1890–1960*. Berkeley, CA: University of California Press.

Cornelius, W. A. (1982) "Interviewing undocumented immigrants: Methodological reflections based on fieldwork in Mexico and the US" *International Migration Review* 16(2): 378–404.

Cotterill, P. (1992) "Interviewing women: Issues of friendship, vulnerability, and power" *Women's Studies International Forum* 15(5–6): 593–606.

Curran, S. R., Shafer, S., Donato, K. M., and Garip, F. (2006) "Mapping gender and migration in sociological scholarship: Is it segregation or integration?" *International Migration Review* 40(1): 199–223.

De Santis, G. (1980) "Interviewing as social interaction" *Qualitative Sociology* 2(3): 72–98.

DeVault, M. (2004) "Talking and listening from women's standpoint: Feminist strategies for interviewing and analysis." In S. N. Hesse-Biber and M. L. Yaiser (eds), *Feminist Perspectives on Social Research*. Oxford: Oxford University Press, pp. 227–50.

Drake, S. C. and Cayton, H. R. (1970) *Black Metropolis*. New York: Harcourt, Brace.

DuBois, W. E. B. (1899) *The Philadelphia Negro: A Social Study*. Philadelphia, PA: Ginn.

Dunbar, Jr. C., Rodriguez, D., and Parker, L. (2001) "Race, subjectivity, and the interview process." In J. F. Gubrium and J. A. Holstein (eds), *Handbook of Interview Research*. Thousand Oaks: Sage, pp. 279–98.

During, S. (1998) "Postcolonialism and globalisation: A dialectical relation after all?" *Postcolonial Studies* 1(1): 31–47.

Eder, D. and Fingerson, L. (2003) "Interviewing children and adolescents." In J. A. Holstein and J. F. Gubrium (eds), *Inside Interviewing*. Thousand Oaks: Sage, pp. 33–54.

Foner, N. (1997) "The immigrant family: Cultural legacies and cultural changes" *International Migration Review* 31(4): 961–74.

Fontana, A. and Frey, J. H. (2005) "The interview: From neutral stance to political involvement." In N. K. Denzin and Y. S. Lincoln (eds), *Handbook of Qualitative Research*. Thousand Oaks: Sage, pp. 695–727.

Gabaccia, D. (ed.) (1992) *Seeking Common Ground: Multidisciplinary Studies of Immigrant Women in the United States*. Westport, CT: Praeger.

Gabrielli, G., Paterno, A., and Strozza, S. (2007) "The dynamics of immigrants' life history: Application to the insertion of Albanian and Moroccan immigrants into some Italian areas" *Population Review* 46(1): 41–55.

Gans, H. J. (1962) *Urban Villagers: Group and Class in the Life of Italian-Americans*. New York: The Free Press.

Gold, S. J. (1997) "Transnationalism and vocabularies of motive in international migration: The case of Israelis in the United States" *Sociological Perspectives* 40(3): 409–27.

Gold, S. J. (2002) *The Israeli Diaspora*. London: Routledge.

Gorden, R. L. (1987) *Interviewing*. Chicago, IL: Dorsey Press.

Gu, C. (2006) *Mental Health Among Taiwanese Americans: Gender, Immigration, and Transnational Struggles*. New York: LFB Scholarly Publishing.

——(2010) "Culture, emotional transnationalism, and mental distress: Family relations and well-being among Taiwanese immigrant women" *Gender, Place and Culture*, 17(6): 687–704.

Gubrium, J. F. and Holstein, J. A. (2001) "From the individual interview to the interview society." In J. F. Gubrium and J. A. Holstein, (eds) *Handbook of Interview Research*. Thousand Oaks, CA: Sage, pp. 3–32.

Holstein, J. A. and Gubrium, J. F. (1995) *The Active Interviews*. Thousand Oaks, CA: Sage.

——(2003) "Inside interviewing: New lenses, new concerns." In J. A. Holstein and J. F. Gubrium, (eds) *Inside Interviewing*. Thousand Oaks, CA: Sage. pp. 3–32.

Hondagneu-Sotelo, P. (1994) *Gendered Transitions: Mexican Experiences of Immigration*. Berkeley, CA: University of California Press.

Hondagneu-Sotelo, P. (ed.) (2003) *Gender and US Immigration: Contemporary Trends*. Berkeley, CA: University of California Press.

Horton, J. (1995) *The Politics of Diversity: Immigration, Resistance and Change in Monterey Park, California*. Philadelphia, PA: Temple University Press.

Järvinen, M. (2003) "Negotiating strangerhood: Interviews with homeless immigrants in Copenhagen" *Acta Sociologica* 46(3): 215–30.

Johnson, J. M. (2001) "In-depth interviewing." In J. F. Gubrium and J. A. Holstein (eds), *Handbook of Interview Research*. Thousand Oaks, CA: Sage, pp. 103–20.

Kelson, G. A. and DeLaet, D. L. (eds.) (1999) *Gender and Immigration*. New York: New York University Press.

Kvale, S. (1996) *Interviews: An Introduction to Qualitative Research Interviewing*. Thousand Oaks, CA: Sage.

Kvale, S. and Brinkmann, S. (2009) *Interviews: Learning the Craft of Qualitative Research Interviewing*, 2nd edition. Thousand Oaks, CA: Sage.

Levitt, P. (2001) *The Transnational Villagers*. Berkeley, CA: University of California Press.

Ling, H. (2007) *Voices of the Heart: Asian American Women on Immigration, Work, and Family*. Dexter, MO: Truman State University Press.

Lynd, R. S. and Lynd, H. M. (1929) *Middletown: A Study in American Culture*. New York: Harcourt, Brace.

Malpica, D. M. (2002) "Making a living in the streets of Los Angeles: An ethnographic study of day laborers" *Migraciones Internacionales* 1(3): 124–48.

Massey, D. S. (1986) "The settlement process among Mexican migrants to the United States" *American Sociological Review* 51(5): 670–87.

McCall, M. M. and Wittner, J. (1990) "The good news about life history." In H. S. Becker and M. M. McCall (eds), *Symbolic Interaction and Cultural Studies*. Chicago, IL: Chicago University Press, pp. 46–89.

Merton, R. K. (1972) "Insiders and outsiders: A chapter in the sociology of knowledge" *American Journal of Sociology* 78(1): 9–48.

Mishler, E. G. (1986) *Research Interviewing: Context and Narrative*. Cambridge, MA: Harvard University Press.

Moore, J. W. (1973) "Social constraints on sociological knowledge: Academics and research concerning minorities" *Social Problems* 21(1): 64–77.

Oakley, A. (1981) "Interviewing women: A contradiction in terms?" In R. A. Voice (ed.), *Doing Feminist Research*. London: Routledge, pp. 30–61.

Padfield, M. and Procter, I. (1996) "The effect of interviewer's gender on the interviewing process: A comparatice enquiry" *Sociology* 30(2): 355–66.

Pedraza, S. (1991) "Women and migration: The social consequences of gender" *Annual Review of Sociology* 17: 303–25.

Pessar, P. R. (2003) "Engendering migration studies: The case of new immigrants in the United States." In P. Hondagneu-Sotelo (ed.) *Gender and US Immigration*. Berkeley, CA: University of California Press, pp. 20–42.

Pessar, P. R. and Mahler, S. J. (2003) "Transnational migration: Bringing gender in" *International Migration Review* 37(3): 812–46.

Reinharz, S. and Chase, S. E. (2001) "Interviewing women." In J. F. Gubrium and J. A. Holstein (eds), *Handbook of Interview Research*. Thousand Oaks, CA: Sage, pp. 221–38.

Rubin, H. J. and Rubin, I. S. (2004) *Qualitative Interviewing: The Art of Hearing Data*, 2nd edition. London: Sage.

Schwalbe, M. L. and Wolkomir, M. (2001) "Interviewing men." In J. F. Gubrium and J. A. Holstein (eds), *Handbook of Interview Research*. Thousand Oaks, CA: Sage, pp. 203–20.

Smith, R. C. (2006) *Mexican New York: Transnational Lives of New Immigrants*. Berkeley, CA: University of California Press.

Stone, P. (2008) *Opting Out: Why Women Really Quit Careers and Head Home*. Berkeley, CA: University of California Press.

Thomas, W. I. and Znaniecki, F. (1927) *The Polish Peasant in Europe and America*. New York: Alfred A. Knopf, Inc.

Valenzuela, Jr. A. (2003) "Day labor work" *Annual Review of Sociology* 29: 307–33.

Warner, R. S. and Wittner, J. G. (1998) *Gatherings in Diaspora: Religious Communities and the New Immigration*. Philadelphia, PA: Temple University Press.

Watson, L. C. (1985) *Interpreting Life Histories: An Autobiographical Inquiry*. New Brunswick, NJ: Rutgers University Press.

Weiss, R. S. (1994) *Learning from Strangers: The Art and Method of Qualitative Interview Studies*. New York: The Free Press.

Wellman, D. T. (1993) *Portraits of White Racism*. Cambridge: Cambridge University Press.

Wenger, G. C. (2003) "Interviewing older people." In J. A. Holstein and J. F. Gubrium (eds), *Inside Interviewing*. Thousand Oaks, CA: Sage, pp. 111–30.

Whyte, W. F. (1943) *Street Corner Society: The Social Structure of an Italian Slum*. Chicago, IL: University of Chicago Press.

——(1984) *Learning from the Field*. London: Sage.

Wolf, D. L. (1997) "Family secrets: Transnational struggles among children of Filipino immigrants" *Sociological Perspectives* 40(3): 457–82.

43

Considering time in analyses of migration

Gillian Stevens and Hiromi Ishizawa

Time is a multi-dimensional concept. It can be tracked from the point of view of individuals, who become older as the calendar pages flip over and who experience noteworthy events during a certain historical time period and at a certain point in their life cycle. Time can also be tracked through the succession of generations. Unfortunately, defining, operationalizing, and analyzing how these dimensions of time are implicated in how migrants and their descendants fare in a destination society is difficult for numerous reasons. In this chapter, we outline some of the complexities and difficulties involved in trying to investigate the various dimensions of time in migrants' lives and present some strategies for dealing with them.

Dimensions of time for migrants

The most elemental aspect of time for all individuals is experienced as aging throughout the life course from the moment of birth to the moment of death. The process of biological maturation from birth until death, which is generally measured through chronological age, is punctuated by important life events such as completion of education, entry into the labor force, and marriage, which often define the entrance or exit from socially defined life course stages such as childhood, adolescence, or young adulthood. Because most societies are heavily age-graded with strong norms and social structures governing the timing of important life events, chronological age is also a good indicator of life course stage.

When investigating outcomes or processes associated with or marked by some important event, numerous dimensions of time can come into play. These include (but are not limited to) the timing of a particular life event in an individual's life course (or the age at which it occurred), the length of time since (or before) the event and the time of observation, the individual's age at observation, and the calendar year (or time period) the event occurred. If the event under consideration is birth, then this collection of dimensions collapses into three: age (at time of observation), calendar year of observation, and calendar year of birth or birth cohort. This trio of variables are often referred to as age, (time) period, and (birth) cohort. For example, a 30-year-old person observed in the year 2000 would be a member of the 1970 birth cohort.

When the event under consideration occurs after birth, then the researcher is faced with a choice of what dimensions of time to consider. Because the act of international migration is typically a significant disruption in an individual's life course and marks the age at which individuals leave one national context to reside in another, the three dimensions of time that are often theoretically important include age at migration, length of residence in the destination country, and age. Age at migration is strongly related to probability that important life events, such as the completion of education, occur in the migrant's country of origin versus their country of destination. The length of residence in the destination country is also strongly linked to processes of adaptation because it takes a span of time for migrants to learn about and to deal with the myriad facets of life in a new country. Finally, after entering a new country, migrants "age in place" both socially and biologically with the starting point of their experience in the destination country having been set by their age at migration.

Figure 43.1 presents a Lexis diagram that shows the relationships between these three processes occurring with the passage of time—aging, increases in experience in a new destination country and the passage of calendar time. The top four diagonal lines each represents a person living a portion of their life in a destination country. The uppermost lifeline, labeled α, depicts a person entering the country at age 35 in 1985 and then leaving in 2000 at age 50. Line β shows a migrant entering the country at age 20 and staying in the country until after 2010. Line δ and line γ show migrants entering at ages 10 and 20 years respectively in 1990 and staying in the country until after 2010. Line ε shows a native-born person born in 1990 who stays in the country through 2010. The vertical line at 2010 crosses four of the lifelines and thereby demonstrates that those four individuals were in the country in that year.

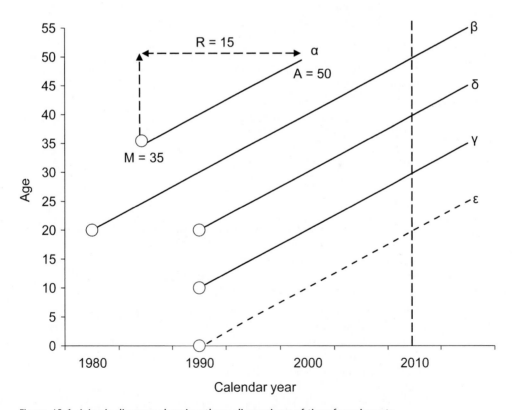

Figure 43.1 A Lexis diagram showing three dimensions of time for migrants

Difficulties

There are at least three difficulties associated with attempts to investigate the impact of these various dimensions of time on migrants' lives in their country of destination. These include problems of measurement, problems of selection, and the statistical confounding among the dimensions of time.

Migration is often considered to be a discrete behavior occurring at one point in calendar time: an individual may move across a border on March 17 2001, for example. But international migration is often a more transitional process in which migrants move back and forth across a border and so it is often difficult to pinpoint when, in either calendar time or at what age, the act of migration occurred. It then becomes more difficult to assess the length of time a migrant has lived in the country of destination. The temporal ambiguity associated with migrating for some individuals also feeds into the more general problem of measurement error—many immigrants give inconsistent responses when asked about the year in which they migrated (Redstone and Massey 2004).

A second problem, especially with the use of cross-sectional or retrospective data, concerns the biases associated with processes of selection. In Figure 43.1, the vertical line crossing the horizontal axis in the year 2010 crosses only three of the lifelines representing migrants and so demonstrates that a cross-sectional survey fielded in 2010 would capture only three of the four migrants who entered during the previous 30 years. This can cause difficulties in interpretation if the migrants who leave the country differ from those who stay. For example, if migrants who are economically unsuccessful in a country of destination are more likely to leave, then those who stay (and who are captured by the survey) consist of the more successful. In the extreme, a survey of migrants could show that migrants who have been in the country the longest are the most successful and this relationship, as seen in the cross-sectional data, could be entirely attributable to the least successful migrants giving up and returning home and not to any process of economic progress among those remaining in the country. The degree of selection in a cross-sectional survey is a function of the strength of the selectivity process and the timing of observation or data gathering.

A third and particularly vexing problem is that the three variables, age, age at migration, and length of residence, are statistically confounded in a manner that is analogous to the "age-period-cohort" problem in demography. If *age* (A), years of *residence* in the destination country (R), and age at *migration* (M), are all measured in the same metric, then

$$A = R + M$$

After some amount of time has passed after migrating, say 15 years, not only has the migrant lived in the country for 15 years and therefore had a decade and a half of experience in the country, he or she is 15 years older and thus has matured in the country, and these two processes, the increasing experience in the destination country and the increasing age, are tethered to a particular point in his or her lifetime, his or her age at migration.

This confounding can be seen in Figure 43.1. The lifeline α shows the confounding for a single migrant who enters the country at age 35 in 1985, lives there for 15 years, and then leaves at age 50 in the year 2000. More generally, if a researcher wished to assess whether migrants who enter the country in early adulthood, say at age 20, did better during the 1990s versus the 1980s, it is impossible to design a clean cross-sectional comparison that holds age at migration constant and differentiates between the impact of differences across time periods (i.e., the 1980s versus the 1990s) and differences in amount of experience. A cross-sectional comparison of migrants β and δ, for example, in 2010, would compare a migrant with 30 years of experience with a migrant with only 20 years of experience. Migrants δ and γ have the same years of experience in the destination country but their ages at migration, 20 and 10 respectively, differ.

The confounding of age, age at migration, and length of residence in the destination country is not problematic if one or two of the three variables are unrelated to the issue under investigation. However, in many situations there are theoretical reasons to believe that all three variables tap important processes that affect the outcome variable. For example, in research on second language proficiency among immigrants, age at onset of second language learning, which is often measured through age at migration, is strongly and negatively related to a migrant's ultimate proficiency in the second language, perhaps because of maturational constraints in second language learning. Research also shows that length of residence in the new country of destination is strongly and positively related to a migrant's proficiency in a second language because learning a new language takes time. Meanwhile, there are reasons to believe that age may also be negatively related to rate of second language learning because of cognitive declines associated with aging. Most research on second language acquisition among immigrants explicitly considers only one, or at most two, of the three variables (Stevens 2006).

Ignoring the statistical confounding

There are numerous approaches to the general problem of statistical confounding between the three (or more) dimensions of time. The most common approach is to ignore it and to consider only one or two of the dimensions of time. However, ignoring the problem can lead to wrong conclusions because the estimates of the independent variables that are considered in the analysis model may be biased. For example, in the regression equation below, Y refers to an outcome variable, α refers to the intercept, the β's to the partial slopes associated with age (A), age at migration (M), and length of residence (R) respectively, and ε to the error term.

$$Y_i = \alpha + \beta_1(A_i) + \beta_2(M_i) + \beta_3(R_i) + \varepsilon_i$$

Because of the statistical confounding among the three independent variables, this equation simplifies to:

$$Y_i = \alpha + (\beta_1 + \beta_2)(M_i) + (\beta_1 + \beta_3)(R_i) + \varepsilon_i$$

As the second regression equation shows, leaving out one of the three independent variables introduces the possibility of bias into the estimated slopes of the two remaining variables.

Tabular analyses do not fare any better. Table 43.1 shows the cross-classification of chronological age and age at migration with the cell values showing the length of years of residence in the destination country according to the migrant's age at migration and his or her age at the time of observation. An individual migrating at 5 would at age 20 have lived 15 years in the country.

If scores on a test of second language proficiency reflect *only* age at migration such that migrants who were able to start learning the language early in life by virtue of their migrating earlier in life outscoring those who migrate later in life, the scores might look like those in Table 43.2. The outcome scores in Table 43.2 show that migrants entering the country at age 5 score, on average, 100%, no matter what their current age or how long they have been in the country while those who enter at age 15 score 90% no matter what their current age or how long they have been in the country, etc.

Table 43.1 The relationships between values of age, age at migration, and years of residence

Age at migration	Chronological age			
	10	20	30	40
5	5	15	25	35
15		5	15	25
25			5	15
35				5

Table 43.2 An array of scores constructed to show pure age-at-migration effects by age at migration and chronological age

Age at migration	Chronological age			
	10	20	30	40
5	100%	**100%**	100%	100%
15		90%	**90%**	90%
25			80%	**80%**
35				70%

If, as is commonly the case in social science research, the sample is delimited by age (such as young adults in their 20s and 30s), then the scores in Table 43.2 can be read as showing several different relationships. For example, because the average score among respondents aged 30 is lower than that of respondents aged 20, age appears to be negatively related to scores on the outcome variable. Alternatively, the bolded scores, which refer to scores for migrants who have been in the country for 15 years are higher than the scores on the diagonal directly below, which refer to migrants who have been in the country for only five years (refer back to Table 43.1). It therefore appears that length of residence is related to the outcome scores. These two interpretations emerge even though the scores were originally constructed to show "pure" age at migration effects. These errors in interpretation are common in literature investigating second language acquisition among migrants. They also potentially occur in studies investigating any outcome among migrants that is theoretically the result of processes tied to each of the three variables.

Solutions to the statistical confounding of age, length of residence and age at migration

Because the statistical confounding between age, length of residence, and age at migration mirrors the confounding between the trio of demographic variables, age, period, and cohort, it is possible to borrow the statistical techniques used by demographers and quantitative social scientists to break the linear dependency. Unfortunately, although there are a variety of approaches, there is no magic bullet.

With cross-sectional data, it is possible to break the statistical confounding by modeling theoretically grounded curvilinear relationships (rather than linear relationships) between one or more of the three variables and the outcome variable (Fienberg and Mason 1985). It is also possible to make assumptions about statistical equalities across selected age or age at migration or length of residence groupings in categorical analyses. Constrained multiple regression analysis (sometimes referred to as multiple classification analysis) assumes, for example, that several age groups, length of residence or age at migration groups have identical effects on the outcome variable (see Mason *et al.* 1973). A recent variant of this approach, the "age–period–cohort–characteristic" model substitutes an aggregate-level characteristics for one of the dimensions (O'Brien 2000) and thereby moves towards a random-effects (rather than fixed effects) modeling strategy (see Yang and Land 2008).

Pitkin and Myers (2011) draw on a demographic approach, standardization, and suggest the calculation of a temporally standardized period-specific index of the outcome variable (such as English proficiency, educational attainment, earnings or homeownership). Their index, which is akin to the well-known *total fertility rate* (a period-specific measure that describes the fertility of a synthetic cohort and assumes constancy in the period-specific array of age-specific fertility rates and a rectangular age distribution), is calculated using data from two censuses (or other repeated cross-sectional surveys). It describes the average age-specific "advancement" of migrants arriving in a particular historical period during a following time span on a particular outcome. It thus takes into account the attributes of age at arrival and age cohorts. A major merit of the index is the ability to compare the extent of migrants' advancement across various outcomes (e.g., occupational advancement versus advances in housing integration) within a given time period. As the authors point out, however, this approach is sensitive to the assumed distribution of ages of arrival. In addition, the indices do not provide estimates of length of residence effects or apply to a specific cohort.

Gathering data at more than one point in time for the same individuals is yet another way to lessen the problems associated with the confounding of age, age at migration, and length of residence. Fixed effects models can be used to identify an effect for each individual thus allowing each respondent to act as his or her own control (Yaffee 2003). In the equation below, which illustrates a simple fixed effects model, Replacement$_i$ refers to the time-invariant effect for individual i, and the β's are the slopes for the three variables age at migration, age, and length of residence.

$$Y_i = [\alpha_i + \beta_1(M_i)] + \beta_2(A_{it}) + \beta_3(R_{it}) + \varepsilon_{it}$$

However, it is necessary to impose constraints on even this simple model. Furthermore, because the variable "age at migration" is time-invariant, the estimates of the true individual-level effects (the α_i) are merged with the effects of age at migration (which is why the terms are shown bracketed together). Thus the model yields age and length-of-residence effects that are not confounded with age-at-migration effects but it does not yield separate age at migration effects.

The solution that is the most theoretically defensible and that is easy to state but difficult to do, is to gather better data. The typical measures of age, age at migration and length of residence are only surrogates for more fundamental concepts and processes that are related to the substantive issue at hand. Length of residence, for example, has been used to measure the extent to which a migrant has been exposed to opportunities to learn a second language. Direct measures of the opportunities to learn the language by measuring the respondents' extent of participation in social contexts (such as schools and workplaces) dominated by the language would break the interdependence between the three variables.

Time and generations

Because of the interest in integration of specific national-origin populations into a host society, social scientists often assess change over time by evoking the concept of generations (Alba 1988).

The concept of "generation" is a complex one but when considering the consequences of migration, it generally includes two elements: genealogical descent and geographic location. Although the exact terminology varies across nation, the first (or foreign-born) generation usually consists of individuals born outside of the country who migrated after birth to the country of destination. The second and succeeding generations are "native-born" and usually enjoy more rights and privileges (such as easier access to citizenship) than the first (foreign-born) generation. Scholars' interest in the progression of generations often rests on the hypothesis that succeeding generations are better integrated (e.g., economically or culturally) into the destination society (and more distant from the origin society) than preceding generations.

Difficulties

One of the difficulties in measuring generational status is produced by the importance of age at migration as a predictor of integration among migrants, i.e., the first generation. Adults who migrated as children are, on average, much more integrated into the destination society than those who migrated later in life. One way to deal with this situation is to carve up the first generation by age at migration calling, for example, those who migrate before age 10 (or 15 or 18) the "1.5" generation thereby acknowledging that early in life migrants are more similar to native-born residents of the country than later in life migrants. This approach can be refined by using "decimal" generations (e.g., 1.25, 1.5 …) to differentiate among child migrants (Oropesa and Landale 1997) and among adults according to their age at migration (Rumbaut 2004).

A second difficulty emerges in measuring the distinctions between the later generations. A simplistic rendering of the succession of generations suggests that foreign-born parents bear and raise (second-generation) native-born children, and these second-generation children bear and raise third-generation children, etc. In reality, the succession of generations quickly twists back on itself. Over a quarter of married foreign-born young adults in the United States have native-born American spouses (Stevens et al. forthcoming). Their children will therefore have one native-born parent and one foreign-born parent. Rumbaut (2004) argues that the nativity of both parents should be used to distinguish the second generation (i.e., respondents with two foreign-born parents) from the 2.5 generation (i.e., those with a foreign-born and a native-born parent).

A third difficulty occurs because of the placement of generations in calendar time and thus the now familiar recurrence of confounding between the three important dimensions of time, which in this case are generation, historical time, and age (Alba 1988). Comparing the attainments or achievements of the second generation with those of the first is often accomplished by using retrospective cross-sectional data gathered at a particular time "t" to compare the accomplishments of the current first-generation (adult) migrants with those of second-generation adults. This comparison conflates changes over historical time with those over generation. For example, if the life line β in Figure 43.1 represents the first foreign-born generation and line ε represents the native-born second generation, and the issue at hand is the proportion completing high school, then the comparison rests on high school completion rates occurring before 1980 for the foreign-born generation and after 2000 for the native-born generation.

A fourth difficulty emerges from the compounding of individual time and generational time in comparisons of the first and second generations. Recent substantive research suggests that dimensions of time appear to be linked across generations within families. Bleakley and Chin (2008) show, for example, that the ages of migration of foreign-born *parents* are related to their (native-born) children's outcomes. Later-born children appear to be advantaged relative to earlier-born children in terms of second language acquisition and perhaps in educational and labor force outcomes as well—a pattern that Smith (2008) refers to as a reverse Cinderella effect. Even if the respondents in the first and second generations are not directly linked at the individual level and the comparison between the first and second generation is at the aggregate level, there is no reason to think that this problem disappears: the comparison may still be affected by the distributions of ages of migration and length of residence within the foreign-born generation.

Conclusions

Untangling the roles of temporal dimensions in research on migrants is difficult. Some of the problems are shared with all other types of social science research, such as the difficulties in operationalizing of concepts. But because migrating is a significant life event that occurs at a particular historical time at a particular age for each migrant, many different dimensions of time are often important. Untangling the effects of age, age at migration, and length of residence in the destination society (or some other set of time dimensions) on the processes of adaptation or reaction to the new society is difficult but not considering how these different dimensions of time impact the processes can lead to wrong conclusions. Trying to consider how processes of adaptation unfold over generations also runs into difficulties, the first and most important of which is how to define and operationalize generational status. The only reason to keep on trying to define, measure, and untangle the various dimensions of time in research on migrants is that time always seems to matter.

References and further reading

Alba, R. D. (1988) "Cohorts and the dynamics of ethnic change." In M. W. Riley, B. J. Huber, and B. B. Hess (eds), *Social Structures and Human Lives*. Newbury Park: Sage Publications, pp. 211–28.

Bleakley, H. and Chin, A. (2008) "What holds back the second generation? The intergenerational transmission of language human capital among immigrants" *Journal of Human Resources* 43(2): 267–98.

Fienberg, S. E. and Mason, W. M. (1985) "Specification and implementation of age, period, and cohort models." In *Cohort Analysis in Social Research: Beyond the Identification Problem* (eds), W. M. Mason and S. E. Fienberg. New York: Springer-Verlag, pp. 45–88.

Mason, K. O., Mason, W. M., Winsborough, H. H., and Poole, W. K. (1973) "Some methodological issues in cohort analysis of archival data" *American Sociological Review* 38(2): 242–58.

O'Brien, R. M. (2000) "Age period cohort characteristic models" *Social Science Research* 29(1): 123–39.

Oropesa, R. S. and Landale, N. (1997) "In search of the new second generation: Alternative strategies for identifying second generation children and understanding their acquisition of English" *Sociological Perspectives* 40(3): 429–55.

Pitkin, J. and Myers, D. (2011) "A summary period measure of immigrant advancement in the US" *Demographic Research* 24(12): 257–92.

Redstone, I. and Massey, D. S. (2004) "Coming to stay: An analysis of the US census question on immigrants' year of arrival" *Demography* 41(4): 721–38.

Rumbaut, R. (2004) "Ages, life stages, and generational cohorts: Decomposing the immigrant first and second generations in the United States" *International Migration Review* 38(3): 1160–205.

Smith, R. C. (2008) "Horatio Alger lives in Brooklyn: Extrafamily support, intrafamily dynamics, and socially neutral operating identities in exceptional mobility among children of Mexican immigrants" *The Annals of the American Academy of Political and Social Science* 620(1): 270–90.

Stevens, G. (2006) "The age-length-onset problem in research on second language acquisition among immigrants" *Language Learning* 56(4): 671–92.

Stevens, G., Ishizawa, H., and Escandell, X. (Forthcoming) "Marrying into the American population: Pathways into cross-nativity marriages" *International Migration Review*.

Yaffee, R. (2003) "A primer for panel data analyses." New York University. Information Technology Services.

Yang, Y. and Land, K. C. (2008) "Age-period-cohort analysis of repeated cross-section surveys: Fixed or random effects" *Sociological Methods and Research* 36(3): 297–326.

44

Using photography in studies of international migration

Steven J. Gold

Introduction

Visual techniques offer much to the study of international migration. Benefits include collecting information about topics of study, generating rapport and easing communication with respondents, comparing groups, refining theoretical analysis, sharing findings, and teaching about results. This chapter offers basic guidelines to assist those studying migration with the use of visual techniques. While much of the discussion focuses on visual sociology, the article also refers to other academic disciplines and approaches to visual representation.

Historical background

According to Howard Becker (1986), a sociologist whose writings have contributed much to the linking of social science and documentary photography, both disciplines trace their origins to the same time and place—France in the 1840s—and both are devoted to exploring society. Becker posits that sociology offers photographers a theoretical footing capable of enriching their projects, while photography's techniques can enhance social scientists' ability to make powerful images.

Visual sociology incorporates two distinct but related activities. The first involves the analysis of existing visual information to learn about the social groups and contexts that produce and use them. The second is the creation of visual documents—photographs, films, videotapes, and the like—as means of recording information about groups and issues.

Social scientists and historians have used photography in their studies of migrant communities and processes for over a century (Stasz 1979). However, both the popularity of photographic methods and the way they have been used vary according to political, technological, and aesthetic trends, and disciplinary norms and practices. Moreover, while scholars of migration have long employed visual data, literature on the use of photography as a research method has only been available for the last three decades.

The discipline of sociology has a lengthy if uneven record of involvement with visual documentation. From 1896 until 1916, the *American Journal of Sociology* (*AJS*) regularly published photographs as part of the Chicago school of urban analysis. Many of these documented immigrants and their communities (Stasz 1979). Most were featured in articles that concerned social reform activities rather than "scientific" studies of society, and many had women authors. However, as sociology became more oriented toward scientific objectivity and quantification, photographs were no longer included in articles and only appeared in the journal to commemorate the death of renowned colleagues.

The exclusion of photographs from *AJS* occurred prior to the time when natural science used photography as a basic technique for data collection, analysis, and presentation. It was also before traditions of serious documentary photography and photojournalism—which both drew upon and contributed to social science and historical knowledge—had been established.

Once these practices became accepted, the potential for migration scholars to both contribute to and benefit from the visual study of society was enhanced. In fact, one of the most significant documentary projects of the first half of the twentieth century—that of The Farm Security Administration, which used documentary photographs taken by Walker Evans, Dorothea Lange, Russell Lee, Arthur Rothstein, and others to convince the American middle class of the viability of the New Deal—was informed by sociology. While the project was supervised by Columbia University economist Roy Stryker, the shooting scripts that directed photographers toward appropriate subject matter were created by Indiana University sociologists Robert and Helen Lynd (1929), the authors of the famous Middletown studies. Many of the FSA images documented issues relevant to migration studies, including displacement, environmental crises, racial segregation, itinerant labor and ethnic communities.

During the 1930s and 1940s, artists and scholars in a number of fields developed methods that would prove useful to the visual exploration of society in general and to migration studies in particular. One of the most ambitious projects was Margaret Mead and Gregory Bateson's *The Balinese Character* (1942), which relied on thousands of still photographs and extensive moving picture footage to document social life on that Indonesian island. Between the wars, European artist/activists were involved in the worker-photographer movement—which encouraged rank and file people to examine their lives and their conflicts with powerful interest groups via documentary photography.

Helping sociologists overcome some of the status-based challenges that resulted in the exclusion of photographs from *AJS* after 1915 was the fact that several leading scholars of the Post War era—including John Berger and Jean Mohr, Howard Becker (1986), Erving Goffman and Pierre Bourdieu—published significant projects that relied upon the analysis of photographs. Moreover, from the 1930s until the 1980s, documentary photography and photojournalism distributed in picture magazines and illustrated newspapers provided the public with almost unlimited opportunities to peruse photographic renderings of social issues and current events.

Since the 1970s, there has been a renewed interest in visual studies of society, with the formation of the International Visual Sociology Association, the establishment of undergraduate and graduate classes on the topic, the publication of numerous books and journal articles and the regular inclusion of paper and didactic sessions devoted to visual studies at professional meetings. Anthropologists, psychologists, historians, jurists, educators, and other scholars as well as journalists, documentarians, social activists and film makers also developed a variety of visual methods to explore the experience of immigrants.

Images and words

Despite popular aphorisms about a picture being worth a thousand words, cameras not lying, and the desire of photographers to make purely visual arguments, scholars using photography to explore or analyze social issues including immigration are encouraged to combine images with text to assist viewers in interpreting what is shown (Becker 1986). As Susan Sontag (1977) reasons, people must rely on knowledge they already possess to interpret what they see in a photograph. Accordingly, text is required to help viewers appreciate what is significant about an image. Authors of visual projects have developed a variety of ways of linking images and text and continue to debate about the extent to which viewers should be either encouraged to draw their own conclusions about what is shown or have its meaning delineated for them. However, few if any circumvent the use of text altogether.

Images and the research process

Visual information is not the sole benefit photography offers to migration researchers. Rather, the use of images can facilitate the process of research more generally. Photography can help to establish rapport with respondents, contextualize and lend specificity to the subject matter in question and jump-start discussions between researchers and interviewees. In addition, the inclusion of images can encourage the viewing audience to join the analytical enterprise, and make presentations more accessible to diverse audiences (Collier and Collier 1986; Harper 1987; Vergara 1997).

In fact, while scholars of migration are often drawn to visual methods in order to access visual documents of migrants' experience, many researchers realize that they learn as much from the social interactions associated with making and analyzing images as they do from contemplating what is depicted in the images themselves.

The use of photographs in migration history

A major concern of migration studies involves the socio-historical context of human movement. In what ways are contemporary migrants and their experience similar to and different from those of an earlier historical period? A goldmine of visual data for the exploration of this topic is available in a growing number of photographic archives. Many such archives are digitized and available on line. Consequently, researchers can access images without leaving their offices or classrooms. Moreover, because many such sources are public, the cost of obtaining and publishing images is often low.

A powerful way of identifying historical processes is provided by re-photographing the same people or location at various intervals and then comparing images of the same setting, group or social process taken during different time periods. Using this approach, Chilean-American visual sociologist Camilo Vergara has photographed inner city neighborhoods over a span of years to capture their changing environments. In one set of images, we witness the transformation of a New York tenement building. Initially fully occupied, it is vacated, boarded up, broken into, demolished, and eventually replaced with low-rise townhomes.

Milton Rogovin (Isay et al. 2003) recorded the changing situation of his neighbors in urban Buffalo, New York, between the 1970s and the early 2000s. The resulting sets of images reveal 30 years in the lives of their subjects. One series documents the progression of a spunky teenager into an adult towering over his own children and ultimately into a hunched elder standing alongside his grandchildren. Having collected these series of images, Rogovin displays them to their subjects and records the person's reflections on the changes that time has wrought on them, their companions and the community that the photographer and subject have shared for decades.

To examine the experience of displacement encountered by refugees from Sudan's civil wars, Judith Aston (2010) developed an interactive web site that juxtaposed anthropologist Wendy

James' ethnographic images of group members engaged in various activities during the 1960s, prior to their flight, with contemporary photographs and videos of the population residing in refugee camps (www.voicesfromthebluenile.org).

Relying upon archival photographs and documents, historian Anna Pegler-Gordon (2009) produced an impressive study of exclusion-era Chinese immigration to the US that shows how photographic technology was used to both create and document racial distinctions among migrants. The study further demonstrates that Chinese immigrants influenced the creation of photographic documentation in such a way as to resist government control and to avoid deportation.

Migrants' images and outlooks

As Pegler-Gordon's (2009) research demonstrates, the content and meaning of photographs is shaped by who took them and for what purpose. Mug shots, surveillance photos, and lurid photo journalism have depicted migrants as exotic, threatening or amoral. At the same time, photographs taken by immigrants themselves offer an alternative view of their identity, one informed by their own perspectives on the host society. Such images allow migrants to identify injustices foisted upon them in the country of origin and record achievements in the point of settlement.

In *Sojourners and Settlers*, a global study of Yemini migration, the authors display "sojourner snapshots," migrants' personal photographs alongside the images taken by academics and documentary photographers (Brumfield 1988). In an effort to make accessible such reflexive images, the *Shades of LA* collection at the Los Angeles Public Library was developed through the collaborative efforts of library staff and immigrant and ethnic communities who came together to scan personal photographs, record associated stories and make them available to scholars, historians, and an interested public (www.lapl.org/catalog/photo_collection_overview.html).

A number of photographers, educators, and activists have involved immigrants in the visual examination of their own communities. Caroline Wang's Photovoice method and similar approaches permit migrants to record and reflect upon their own social conditions and lives (www.comminit.com/en/node/201294/2754). This technique is valuable because it allows migrants to photograph issues that concern them, captures elements of research participants' own subjectivity and has the potential to be empowering. Rather than passively being photographed by scholars or visual artists, community members themselves create and use images a basis for mobilizing action to improve their communities.

The approach—which can be traced back to the worker/photographer movement of the 1920s and 1930s—is increasingly popular and compatible with contemporary communications media and understandings of identity construction, as demonstrated by sociologist Marisol Clark-Ibáñez (2007), who used this method in conjunction with photo-elicitation interviews to document the lives of immigrant children in Los Angeles.

Photography and fieldwork

In the following section, I describe several ways that photography can be used in conjunction with interviewing and participant observation fieldwork to improve research on immigrant communities. These include gaining orientation, developing rapport, and communicating with respondents. I also summarize two case studies wherein images contribute to the discovery and analysis of communal patterns among immigrant populations.

Gaining orientation

When starting a field study, photographs are useful for recording information about people, locations, and events of interest. For example, photographs can document what environments look like, how they provide a context in which groups interact, and who is present at events. The resulting images can be reviewed to assist in recording, coding, and analysis of fieldnotes (Collier and Collier 1986; Suchar 1997).

Academic disciplines tend to value parsimonious and abstract findings that describe social relationships without having to deal with the full range of complexity associated with real people and situations. The most prestigious forms of social research are based on methods like library research, surveys, and analysis of official statistics, which keep investigators distant from the people, processes, and settings that they claim to study (Harper 1987). Even ethnographic data are often collected through gatekeepers and spokespersons in office settings or focus groups distant from the places where the social relations of greatest sociological significance take place. Moreover, in describing what they have discovered, social scientists too often rely on academic abstractions—about which they know a great deal—rather than situational knowledge associated with the setting at hand—about which they know much less (Harper 1987). When researchers describe an occupation as "service work," they gloss over what it is like to actually perform the job; when they refer to social relations as "embedded in networks," they add little to our comprehension of the deep and intricate relationships upon which communities are based. These scholastic tendencies discourage sociologists from acquiring direct knowledge about real people and settings (Gold 2007).

The need to create photographs in research settings can provide a corrective to academic distancing by demanding that researchers get involved with the people and settings that are their objects of study to a degree that exceeds what is generally applied in other methods. For example, Vergara's (1997) photographic explorations of inner-city environments—based on years of immersion within them—offer a more detailed and phenomenologically rich account of urban life than is available in more conventional approaches to the topic.

Scholars using visual methods apply this procedure in their research on migrant communities. To create compelling photographs, one must move out of the air-conditioned offices of restaurants and factories into kitchens, shop floors, and warehouses. To chronicle religious communities, they return to research settings following interviews to observe and photograph holiday celebrations. They also attend communal activities—festivals, classes, weddings, baby showers, political demonstrations, and visit migrants in their homes. In this way, the act of making photographs both requires and encourages researchers to directly encounter individuals and aspects of the social world from which they might have otherwise remained at a distance. Their ability to get near is further reinforced by reliance on wide-angle lenses, which require close proximity to work effectively (Becker 1986). The resulting interactions and images tend to enhance researchers' own insights and their ability to share findings with colleagues.

Developing rapport

Making and sharing photographs can be helpful in generating rapport with respondents. As Collier and Collier (1986) point out in *Visual Anthropology*, many individuals and groups who are unfamiliar with the goals and intentions of social science researchers *can* comprehend the purposes of photographers. In this way, making photographs gives a fieldworker a basis for meeting and interacting with those present in the location of research. The initial interaction leads to return visits when photographs are presented to their participants.

In my own fieldwork, I often begin interviews by showing respondents a series of pictures that I had taken in the course of studying their communities. This allows me to quickly and concretely demonstrate my familiarity with the subject and environment of research in a way that I believe enhances the quality of the interviews that follow. In many cases, such interactions function as photo-elicitation interviews (Harper 2002).

Whenever possible, researchers are encouraged to give copies of images to the people they photograph. Not only does this allow researchers to honor the respondents' willingness to be photographed, it also provides for additional rapport-building interactions and establishes an opportunity for discussing the photos. When individuals are shown pictures of themselves, highly specific comments are sometimes elicited. Such was the case when members of a refugee family poignantly reflected on their experience of downward mobility—from relative affluence in the country of origin to their current austere circumstances in the United States.

E-mailing images

In the last decade, photography, and with it, the visual study of immigrant communities, have been transformed by digital technologies. While the broader implications of this transformation are still being debated, one of digital photography's greatest advantages for migration studies lies in its ability to expand paths of connection with respondents. I realized this as I photographed an Arab American community festival (Gold, 2002). While I had done this kind of photography for years at various events, this was the first time I ever used a digital camera to do so. As I normally do, I introduced myself to participants, spoke with them, asked for permission to take pictures, and then got their address so that I could send a print. In the past, this interaction was not complete for a week or so, during which time I would develop negatives, make prints, and send them (via surface mail) to the person whom I had photographed.

With digital photography, I collected the subjects' e-mail addresses. Not having to develop and print the images, I was able to send them off immediately after the event. This rapid turn-around, coupled with a general access to e-mail among members of the community I researched, allowed me to establish communication with several of the people whom I had photographed.

These connections permitted me to correspond with people I met. Accordingly, I became much more aware of their organizations' activities, and two of the photographs that I took during the festival wound up being published in community publications, which I now read regularly to keep informed of the community's activities. In this way, digital photography and e-mail allowed me to extend rapport with, learn about, and contribute to a community in a manner superior to that which I had used during years of previous experience with film cameras.

Discovery and analysis of social patterns

As suggested by Michael Burowoy's (1991) extended-case method, ethnographic investigations are commonly used to interrogate social life and to reflect on the applicability of theoretical formulations to real world settings. Findings reveal the complex and often unexpected ways that people cope with the situations that they confront. Drawing from this tradition, photographic methods and visual data can be used to contribute to the refinement of general propositions about the behavior of immigrant and ethnic groups as they adapt to new environments

Most fieldwork methodologies encourage researchers to engage in a sequential process of collecting, coding, and analyzing data; memo writing; and revisiting field settings to check their observations, refine findings, and create higher-level generalizations. Visual sociologists appreciate that visual information can be useful in this kind of research, and they have developed a body of literature that describes ways in which photographs can be incorporated (Harper 1987).

As a case in point, Suchar (1997) draws on what he calls Becker's (1986) *interrogatory principle,* whereby images are used to help answer sociological questions suggested by literature review and prior fieldwork. The resulting photos are then analyzed in light of other data to generate supplementary questions. Repeating this cycle allows a researcher to incorporate additional evidence (photographic and otherwise) and produce findings. In the section that follows, I show how the use of visual information allowed me to refine my understanding of collective life among several migrant populations.

Case studies of immigrant collectivism

Communal configurations

Prior to the 1960s, most studies of migrant communities maintained an assimilationist perspective that assumed the sooner immigrants adopted the social practices and forms of association of the host society, the more rapidly they would experience successful adaptation. However, since that time, scholars have noted that retaining social practices from the country of origin as well as co-ethnic interaction patterns can yield social and economic benefits and hence foster successful adaptation to the new setting. Accordingly, a significant body of migration research considers the consequence of retaining or discarding country-of-origin practices, as well as the costs and benefits associated with interacting with host society natives or coethnics.

Studies of immigrant communities associated with *ethnic mobilization* theory suggest that in the modern era, major benefits are garnered by populations who organize on a broad, group-wide, or international scale. Advocates of this perspective posit that local forms of organization and group solidarity are likely to be superseded by group-level patterns. However, many recent immigrant and refugee populations are marked by diversity in terms of background, interests, experiences, identities, and patterns of resettlement. Accordingly, ethnic identification and interaction tends to take place within subgroups that share commonalties rather than at the level of the entire population which is marked by few strong ties. Hence, scholars of migration seek to understand the prevailing forms of group solidarity that exist within various populations. Do small networks predominate? Are broad-based collectives more common? Or is a combination of both forms prevalent? Finally, what group characteristics and contexts are associated with segmented and inclusive solidarity?

My photography-supplemented research informs this debate. I found that Soviet Jews, Vietnamese, and Israeli migrants cooperate at the community-wide level. However, various subgroups of these immigrant populations (based on common background, outlook, relationships, and orientation) have more extensive forms of cooperation than apparent at the level of the ethnic community as a whole. I discerned this as I showed photographs that I had taken in the course of fieldwork to group members. I initially expected respondents to take pride in the upward mobility and organizational accomplishments of their successful countrymen. However, respondents were often unimpressed by the achievements of elite co-nationals. Instead, they expressed feelings of estrangement from those shown in my photos and described the people as self-serving. As suggested by photo-based interviews and other evidence, the strongest ties, at least among these populations, tended to be maintained among those subgroups and networks already sharing high levels of social capital. While group members expressed a desire to develop group-wide alliances, these were difficult to establish and maintain. (See Figure 44.1, which shows that ethnic organizations are made on the basis of particular places of origin.)

Coethnic and outgroup labor in ethnic economies

The above discussion suggests that immigrant collaboration among the groups I studied is most extensive among subgroups characterized by commonalities and close ties. This finding leads to another question: Is there a limit on the benefits provided by closeness among immigrant networks, and if so, under what conditions?

A considerable body of research has focused on the advantages ethnic entrepreneurs receive through forms of connection, integration, and solidarity that occur *within* a single national-origin group. Influential studies have shown how Cuban entrepreneurs work together and hire recently-arrived coethnics to maintain a powerful ethnic economy in Miami, one that offers coethnics better earnings than generally available to Cubans who find jobs in the larger economy. Similar findings are noted in research on Korean, Chinese, and Caribbean migrants in the

Figure 44.1 Association banners in New York City's Chinatown

United States, South Asians in the UK, and Turks in Germany and the Netherlands. Recently, however, a number of scholars have questioned in-group cooperation as they have noted the ways in which ethnic entrepreneurs also take advantage of their connections with other ethnic populations, institutions, and social developments to create jobs, successfully manage businesses, and increase earnings.

Through fieldwork, I found that many migrant groups have a desire to help their countrymen and women by providing jobs and advice. Loyalty alone, however, is a poor basis for running a business. A deeper look reveals that the issue of coethnic employment is a complex one. Among Soviet Jews, Vietnamese, and Israelis, the desire to hire coethnics is often constrained by economic realities involving the costs and accessibility of coethnic workers versus other potential employees who are available in the labor market.

Drawing from Becker's (1986) suggestion to pose sociological questions that can be addressed visually, I sought to find out who is employed in ethnic businesses in order to collect information about the relationship between employers and workers. As I observed and photographed Soviet Jewish, Vietnamese, and Israeli businesses in the United States, I consistently noticed Latinos and members of other groups as employees. This finding contrasted dramatically with prevailing assertions about coethnic cooperation between owners and workers. The consistency of this observation prompted me to look closer, to ask questions about out-group labor, and to collect more photographic and other kinds of information about inter- and intraethnic economic cooperation.

Through this approach, I discovered that entrepreneurs often avoid coethnic workers because they are more likely than out-group members to use their employment experience as an apprenticeship that provides them with the knowledge, connections, and capital needed to start their own businesses. This practice is very common among populations with high rates of self-employment and can be a source of considerable consternation because employers realize that they are training today's coethnic employee to be tomorrow's competitor. Because immigrant business resources and strategies have their origins in shared communal sources, the potential for coethnic competition is considerable.

Rather than employing coethnics, they increasingly relied on Mexican, Chicano, and Central American workers. A Chinese-Vietnamese journalist who had extensive contacts in the Southern California business community explained why many coethnic businesses employed Latinos. "Mexican, no green card, so you pay cheap. I pay you $5 an hour, but I pay Mexican $3 an hour. Mexicans are strong, and if I need to fire him, he just goes." Reliance on Latino workers had become so common that during visits to the Los Angeles garment district, I frequently observed and photographed signs in grammatically flawed Spanish, suggesting that Latino workers were sought by non-coethnic employers (Figure 44.2).

The use of photography helped me notice, document, and explore the use of out–group labor in ethnic businesses. In so doing, I was moved to challenge widely held assertions regarding the role of coethnic cooperation in making these enterprises viable. In recent years, several scholars have published studies validating my findings as they describe the employment of one migrant group by another. My research, influenced by photographic evidence, played a role in contributing to this new approach. In turn, this growing body of work is clarifying our understanding of ethnic economies.

Ethical issues

Participants in research may not wish their picture to be reproduced because it is embarrassing or denies them control over their own identity. Further, some groups maintain cultural or religious

Figure 44.2 Los Angeles garment district

beliefs that restrict or prohibit the making of photographs. Finally, being photographed while engaging in illegal or stigmatized activities can subject a research participant to ridicule, arrest or deportation.

Migration scholars who use images in their work need to be aware of the consequences subjects face when being photographed. This is challenging because researchers and respondents often have very different ideas about the meaning of photography. Universities, funding agencies, disciplinary organizations and other organizations under whose auspices researchers function often require researchers to evaluate the impacts of being included in research as part of

S. J. Gold

their human subjects review process, and mandate that researchers take appropriate steps to insure that subjects are protected. Most often, this is achieved through the use of signed consent forms.

In addition, publishers may demand that researchers produce subjects' permission to display images in books or articles. While artists' and journalists' ability to display images may be justified by concepts like freedom of expression or freedom of the press, social scientists lack such protections. As a consequence, some of the most dramatic and visually compelling images social scientists create may wind up being unpublishable.

It is crucial for researchers using visual materials to protect respondents from the harm that might result from being photographed or otherwise included in research. At the same time, if institutions' review boards address the ethical implications of research solely through the doctrinaire application of bureaucratic and legalistic forms, they may hinder researchers and cast research subjects as passive victims while offering them little in the way of real protection.

An alternative approach to ethical problems emphasizes researchers' commitment to the maintenance of caring and humane relations with the individuals and groups that they are studying (as opposed to mere conformity to legalistic procedures). This should be rooted in a richly contextualized understanding of the ways that those being studied themselves use photography. For example, Eugenia Shanklin (1979) suggests that rather than relying on impersonal, confusing, and legalistic consent forms, researchers making documentary photographs should observe the way that photographs are used by members of the social group under study and conduct their own photography in conformity with these norms.

Collaborative image making

In a manner akin to that suggested by Shanklin, anthropologist Marcus Banks (2001) argues that in certain contexts, members of ethnic groups have considerable control over how images are created, such that photographs made within them reflect not only the perspective of the researcher but also that of the community that is being documented.

Banks describes how he discovered that photographs he took of a religious feast included the outlook of his research subjects, who told him what he should photograph and how he should do so:

> I can see how the "directed" photograph is a collaborative image. It was composed and framed according to my own (largely unconscious) visual aesthetic and is part of my own corpus of documentary images of that feast. But it is also a legitimization and concretization of social facts as my friends saw them.

> (Banks 2001: 46–7)

Like Banks, I realized that a set of images I had taken at several festivals organized by an Arab American organization reflected collaboration. In fact, articles in major Detroit newspapers advertising the events specifically invited non-Arabs to attend, and pointed out that the "Organizers of the Dearborn Arab International Festival … see the event as an opportunity for more non-Arabs to see a side of the Arab-American community they have not experienced." Accordingly, my photography at these events, coupled with efforts to establish good relations with subjects and scholarly work directed toward becoming familiar with Detroit's Arab Americans contributed to the collaborative nature of this project.

The practice of collaborative photography, however, is not foolproof. Laura Lewis cites the case of documentary photos of the inhabitants of a Mexican village that was taken with their permission as nevertheless resulting in what one scholar called "unethical optical violence" being inflicted on them (Rose 2007: 252).

Unfortunately, there is no easy solution for the ethical and bureaucratic problems associated with incorporating images in migration research. However, a combination of due diligence, creativity, and flexibility can allow researchers to enjoy the benefits of visuals without harming subjects or getting into trouble with authorities.

Limitations on the use of photography in migration studies

Despite the many benefits associated with using photographs in studies of immigrant communities, there are liabilities as well. Visuals have the potential to offend research subjects and violate standards of ethical research. Photography can become an end in itself rather than a means of improving research about migration. Further, given the increasing demands for obtaining subjects' permission to reproduce and display images of them, one may be unable to publish images no matter how great their scholarly or aesthetic value.

Conclusions

When integrated with other research techniques, photography has the potential to contribute richness, specificity, and nuance to studies of migration. Visuals offer a sound basis for documenting historical processes and accessing migrants' own outlooks. Showing photographs to respondents can facilitate rapport and yield insightful comments about the nature of the communities in question. The need to take photographs encourages researchers to approach, observe, and think about the social world in a much more focused and empirically based manner than is the case using other methods. E-mailed images can assist researchers in expanding their contacts with members of communities that they are exploring. When created to inform theoretically-defined questions, photographs can yield additional forms of evidence that can be used to refine existing social knowledge. Photographs can allow researchers to document and illustrate the diversity of behavior patterns, thus challenging overly-general characterizations of groups. Photographs taken by members of migrant communities can reflect their outlooks and subjectivity in a manner distinct from that reflected in data collected by social outsiders. Finally, photographs offer a means of sharing analysis and research findings with community members, students, and colleagues.

References and further reading

Aston, J. (2010) "Spatial montage and multimedia ethnography: Using Computers to visualize aspects of migration and social division among a displaced community" *Forum Qualitative Social Research* 11(2): Art 36, www.qualitative-research.net.

Banks, M. (2001) *Visual Methods in Social Research*. Thousand Oaks, CA: Sage.

Bateson, G. and Mead, M. (1942) *Balinese Character: A Photographic Analysis*. New York: New York Academy of Sciences.

Brumfield, J. (1988) "On the photographs." In J. Friedlander (ed.), *Sojourners and Settlers: The Yemeni Immigrant Experience*. Salt Lake, UT: University of Utah Press, pp. 173–85.

Becker, H. S. (1986) *Doing Things Together*. Evanston, IL: Northwestern University Press.

Berger, J. and Mohr, J. (1975) *A Seventh Man*. London: Writers and Readers Publishing Cooperative.

Burawoy, M. (1991) "The extended case method." In: M. Buraway, A. Burton, A. A. Ferguson, and K. J. Fox (eds), *Ethnography Unbound: Power and Resistance in the Modern Metropolis*. Berkeley, CA: University of California Press, pp. 271–87.

Clark-Ibáñez, M. (2007) "Inner-city children in sharper focus: Sociology of childhood and photo-elicitation interviews." In G. Stanczak (ed.), *Visual Research Methods: Image, Society, and Representation*, Thousand Oaks, CA: Sage Publications, pp. 167–96.

Collier, J., Jr. and Collier, M. (1986) *Visual Anthropology* (revised and expanded edition). Albuquerque, NM: University of New Mexico Press.

Gold, S. (2002) The Arab-American community in Detroit, Michigan. *Contexts,* 1(2), 48–55.

——(2007) "Using photography in studies of immigrant communities: Reflecting across projects and populations." In G. C. Stanczak (ed.), *Visual Research Methods: Image, Society and Representation.* Los Angeles, CA: Sage, 2007, pp. 141–66.

Harper, D. (1987) *Working Knowledge: Skill and Community in a Small Shop.* Chicago, IL: University of Chicago Press.

——(2002) "Talking about pictures: A case for photo elicitation" *Visual Studies* 17(1): 13–26.

Isay, D., Miller, D., and Wang, H. (2003) *Milton Rogovin: The Forgotten Ones.* New York: The Quantuck Lane Press.

Lynd, R. S. and Lynd, H. M. (1929) *Middletown: A Study in Contemporary American Culture.* New York: Harcourt, Brace, and Company.

Pegler-Gordon, A. (2009) *In Sight of America: Photography and the Development of US Immigration Policy.* Berkeley, CA: University of California Press.

Rose, G. (2007) *Visual Methodologies* (2nd edn). Thousand Oaks, CA: Sage.

Shanklin, E. (1979) "When a good social role is worth a thousand words." In J. Wager (ed), *Images of Information: Still Photography in the Social Sciences.* Beverly Hills, CA: Sage, pp. 139–45.

Sontag, S. (1977) *On Photography.* New York: Farrar, Strauss & Giroux.

Stasz, C. (1979) "The early history of visual sociology." In Jon Wager (ed.), *Images of Information: Still Photography in the Social Sciences.* Beverly Hills, CA: Sage, pp. 119–36.

Suchar, C. S. (1997) "Grounding visual sociology research in shooting scripts" *Qualitative Sociology* 20(1), 33–55.

Vergara, C. J. (1997) *The New American Ghetto.* New Brunswick, NJ: Rutgers University Press.

45

The challenges of online diaspora research

Emily Noelle Ignacio

Introduction

Because of the spread of global capitalism and innovations in transportation, telecommunications, and technology, as well as changes in citizenship and immigration laws, scholarship on immigration, especially diaspora, has necessarily changed. These changes have made it apparent that scholars cannot adequately capture the experiences of immigrants or understand the effects of structural changes on immigrants if scholars insist upon "home and host country frameworks" (Purkayastha 2009: 95). For example, because members of the diaspora, some belonging to one family (like my own) are scattered all over the world, they have to simultaneously grapple with specific social, political, and economic forces within their host country, their home country, as well as negotiate the interrelationship between various host countries and/or their home country.

Some scholars argue that the evolution of global capitalism and communications technologies have produced a new community of transmigrants "whose daily lives depend on multiple and *constant* interconnections across international borders and whose public identities are configured in relationships to more than one nation-state" (emphasis mine: Glick-Schiller *et al.* 1995: 48). Others choose to examine the identities of diasporic members through the lens of "flexible citizenship" and/or "cosmopolitanism" (Ong 1999; Camroux 2008). These scholars consider ethnic identity a sense of belongingness that "involves not a hypothetical transnationalism but rather a kind of 'long-distance nationals' and/or 'binary nationalisms' that allow the diasporic individual to be both here and there simultaneously" (Camroux 2008: 24). Regardless of the theoretical approach or concepts scholars use to describe this community, it is clear that more research needs to be conducted to better understand and address the effects of globalization on diasporic communities.

In recent years, because of the growing use of the internet to communicate—via email, social forums, videocalling, and videoconferencing—scholars from various disciplines have chosen to study, not only the impact of these mediums on various communities around the world (see, for example, Miller and Slater 2001), but also the use of these mediums in forming and/or maintaining communities (Nakamura 2002; Bernal 2005; Ignacio 2005; Mitra 2006; Helland 2007; Ó Dochartaigh; 2009; Figer and Ynion 2010; Tynes 2011).

For those studying diasporic communities whose members use new technologies to com-municate with one another, online research, including online surveys, might seem an obvious and primary means of collecting empirical data. While I am happy social scientists have embraced online methods to studying communities formed within cyberspace, I also believe that we should continually reflect on whether our research is best served by conducting our studies online, offline, or in both arenas. In this chapter, I first address the seemingly "natural" convergence of two different scholarly communities interested in transnationalism—those who study diasporas and migration and those who conduct research on online communities. Then, I assess the benefits and challenges of conducting online research to study diasporic communities. This essay simultaneously advocates for the continued use of online methods, particularly in the study of diasporic communities, while also offering a cautionary tale on its possible overuse or misuse.

New technological advances and migration studies

Most migration studies, understandably, focus upon the movement of persons from one nation-state to another nation-state. However, there has been long-standing, parallel work on nations as "imagined communities" (Anderson 1983) and borders as "unnatural" (i.e., politically, culturally, and socially constructed boundaries: Rosas 2007; Nevins 2010). The acknowledgment that national borders, identities, and communities are constantly contested and re-constituted has affected research on migration and immigrant communities. We have had to recognize that the concepts that we regularly use to describe various communities are directly impacted by state policies and economic policies (i.e., "citizens," "immigrants," "emigrants," "temporary migrants," etc.) may be limited or inadequate.

Those who study immigrant communities must be open to this destabilization because the legal contours of immigration are not stable and constantly changing in relation to economic and state policies. For example, US immigration policy is currently tied to ideas of "nation" and "national identity," as well as labor needs and ideas of "deserving" political refugees. Yet, it is important for researchers to be open to the possibility that members of diasporic communities will choose to *not* identify with or describe his/her experiences in relation to the statuses created in the host country, and, in some cases, even the "home" country. Some reject legal identities (i.e., migrant, citizen, etc.) and assert pre-nation-state identities (i.e., indigenous identities, see, for example, Murray 2011), while others refuse identities defined by binary oppositions and state boundaries through celebrations of "borderlands consciousness" (Anzaldúa 2007 [1999]; Rosas 2007).

When we move our analyses online, especially when we study communication between diasporic members, the possibilities of witnessing the destabilization and construction of knowledges, identities, and communities can greatly increase (Ignacio 2005; Hepp 2009). Online studies on diasporas, thus far, have revealed the new, unique labels or phrases people use to identify themselves (Hepp 2009) and introduced different ways of understanding the relationships between offline and online communities (Ignacio 2005; Camroux 2008; Hepp 2009), as well as individuals' complicated and often unpredictable relationships to "nations" and states. Given that technological advances are changing the contours of online communities and communication, methodologists are simultaneously exploring the effects of the internet on qualitative methods.

Current uses of online methods

Over the past 15 years, numerous authors have published books and articles on online methods which address the following: (1) the benefits and complications of conducting internet research

(Jones 1999; Miller and Slater 2001; Watson, Peacock, and Jones 2006; Beddows 2008; Hookway 2008; Sampson, Bloor, and Fincham 2008; Lobe and Vehovar 2009; Briassoulis 2010); (2) how to go about conducting internet research (Jones 1999; Beddows 2008; Markham and Baym 2008); and (3) ethical issues with conducting research online (see for example, Battles 2010; Parry 2011).

In this chapter, I hope to contribute to this literature by discussing the benefits and limitations of conducting discursive analysis of online diasporic communities. As stated earlier, while I believe that conducting research via the internet and other communication technologies can greatly advance our understandings of diasporic communities, I also believe that should be aware of certain limitations and challenges they face in exploring new mediums. Because internet communities are "perpendicular communities" (i.e., inextricably linked and responsive to other virtual and non-virtual communities), we must be open to refining our methods as we conduct research and develop new techniques to accommodate new situations (Kendall 1999; Miller and Slater 2001; Ignacio 2005; Beddows 2008). Below, I discuss the promises and challenges of researching diasporic knowledge-productions online.

Discussion of online methods and diaspora studies: benefits

Location

New technologies have made it possible for multiple people located around the world to efficiently communicate with one another. Doing research at online locales opens the possibility of watching articulation in action, especially in forums in which multiple people interact. In the past, these forums involved newsgroups. Now, ideal forums include social networking sites and discussion boards. In these sites, it is possible to witness the effects of these policies and/or histories on the diasporas discussion of culture, nation, history, community, and identity (Ignacio 2005: Bernal 2006; Mitra 2006).

I argue that if one chooses social networking sites (such as Facebook or Twitter) as their location, then one should consider conducting an interpretive, textual or discursive analysis, rather than conduct positivist or, even post-positive, research due to sampling issues. As in research offline, scholars must be careful about sampling bias and, ideally, must try to generate a random sample. Given that, even in 2011, there are still access issues and differences in technological skills, it is likely that diasporic members online—especially those who voluntarily join discussion groups on social networking sites like Facebook—are not "representative" of the whole group. Thus, these sites may not be the best places to conduct online surveys or even troll for information that could be obtained through structured interviews (Beddows 2008; Battles 2010). Textual and/or discursive analyses of postings in these online locales, however, can give us all a glimpse of knowledge formation in these spaces (Denzin 1999; Ignacio 2006).

In these forums, conversation analysis, especially via the method of instances (Psthas 1995; Denzin 1999), allows researchers to examine struggles over identity, meanings, and even the self. Briefly, the method of instances requires the researcher to analyze how people understand and respond to each utterance within the whole context (i.e., the conversation or thread) in which the utterances are spoken (Psthas 1995; Denzin 1999; Ignacio 2005). This method, employed in online forums, enables researchers to witness and analyze the impact of social, political, economic, and cultural issues on identity and community formation, as well as individual voice and choice. In addition, it illuminates the destabilization and re-articulation of inherited concepts and categories established within our fields.

Unique issues: implication of diaspora studies

Limitations: location and contextual concerns

Clearly online research has much to offer scholars of transnational migration and diaspora studies. However, doing internet research is not as simple as it may appear, nor is it the most desirable method depending on the questions one wishes to be answered. Just as there are limitations to each method collected in geographically bounded locales, so, too, are there limitations to data collected online.

First, the direct application of traditional methods (e.g., structured interviews, surveys, and focus groups) online (Beddows 2008; Battles 2010) to online studies fails to account for the importance of the locations of and interactions between scholar and subject. Second, some research calls for multi-faceted approaches and face-to-face ethnographies. For example, Guevarra (2010) and Rodriguez (2010), in order to study the effects of various transnational institutional policies or practices (for example, structural adjustment policies, integrated financial markets, etc.) on individuals' decisions to immigrate, necessarily had to travel to the point of emigration (the Philippines) so they could see policies and practices "in action." The result is a very rich description of the intended and actual practices and policies of cultivating export labor and the effects of these policies on both the images of emigrants/immigrants (in both the home and host countries), as well as the identities and self-assessment of individual emigrants in localized set-tings/communities (Guevarra 2010; Rodriguez 2010). As another example, in order to address the "bind of agency" that affects the choices of migrants, Rhacel Parreñas (2001) interviewed Filipina domestic workers in two, specific, locations—Rome and Los Angeles. In so doing, she was able to explain the differential effects of neoliberal economic policies, not only on national policies involving the importation of labor, but on how those global and intermediate policies affect the daily lives and choices of immigrants.

In all of these studies, it is not only the particular questions the scholars are asking but the importance of location that strengthens their research. Although, technically, each of these scholars could have gotten some of their information via online methods, they had all indicated how face-to-face interactions and the location itself had helped them form (often, at the spur of the moment) questions/statements of where to go next. This is not to say that research on emigration or about immigrants should never be conducted using online methods. As we have seen, many scholars have already conducted informative research online. However, as in all projects which employ the use of textual analysis, online researchers—particularly those who are conducting structured interviews—cannot take note of how the words, the tone, and the overall interaction guided the research. Listening to the tone of one's voice, seeing someone's expressions—not only as they speak, but as they react to others (even if it is just the interviewer) can lead the interviewer toward a more comprehensive understanding of how political econo-mies, state policies, and cultural politics affect persons. Similarly, the interviewer's responses may, also, be affected by this interaction.

Of course, online scholars are also deeply affected by location and the effects of the context that location on the study. Some might assume that interviewer bias may be lessened because bodies are not interacting—because interviewers and interviewees cannot read each other's body language before answering questions or formulating follow up questions. Similarly, some assume that answers to written surveys don't reflect "interviewer bias" or interviewees' desire to answer questions to meet interviewers' expectations. They believe responses to questions asked online are "pure", in that the respondents are (supposedly) not reacting to the interviewer. Those who suggest the purity of online responses fail to account for the researcher/researched relationship that exists online as well as in face-to-face encounters. They also fail to account for the fact that textual responses are often delayed, allowing for less-than-spontaneous answers. (Psthas 1995; Denzin 1999; Ignacio 2006).

The point I am making is that the contexts of offline and online interviews are necessarily different, but contexts always impact research. So, the questions that all scholars should ask are "why should I use online methods? Are they most desirable method to answer my questions?" No matter the method chosen, if it predominantly involves the analysis of text, particularly if it is collected in an open, online community forum, it entails carefully preserving the contexts within which the material was collected (see Chapter 1 of Ignacio 2005). Textual, conversation analysis must be treated carefully because the context is created and circumscribed by various utterances. Furthermore, the timing of the utterances is of utmost importance in this medium.

On immigration and online methods

Weighing benefits and costs

Choosing appropriate online methods

As stated earlier, when studying the experiences of migrants, immigrants, transmigrants, and diasporic communities, it may be tempting to use online methods, because these communities frequently use technological advances to communicate with and support one another. It is true that technological advances, most definitely, have made it easier for both organizations and individuals around the world to transfer funds, transport goods, and communicate. However, no matter what topic we choose to research, methodologists, quantitative and qualitative, always remind us that the most important thing researchers must do is choose the method that will best answer the questions we are asking such that we can best contribute our understandings about that particular area of research.

For example, in the mid-1990s, when thinking through how to conduct research for what later would become my book, *Building Diaspora* (2005), I had to answer three main questions that all researchers have to answer: (1) What is my thesis question? (2) What is/are the best method(s) to use to collect the necessary empirical material for my research? and (3) (if applicable) Where should I conduct this research? For this research, I was interested in observing the process of community and ethnic identity, as well as knowledge-formation among diasporic Filipinos subscribed to an internet newsgroup. I conducted a "nethnography" with a twist, engaging in limited participant observation and then conducting conversational analysis using the "method of instances." I chose to conduct a limited participant observation because I did not want to "taint" the conversations about community and identity by guiding the conversations toward a conversation which the respondents may not have intended to participate. (Thus, I limited my responses in the newsgroup.) I conducted a conversational analysis because I was concerned with the process of knowledge-production. As a result of both the physical locations of the persons involved in the discussion as well as the medium within which they were communicating (i.e., the newsgroup), it was necessary to preserve the context of the conversation and of each utterance so as to best study the complexities of identity formation.

Context

Conversation analysis

Textual, conversation analysis of discussions in an open, online community must be treated carefully because the context is created and circumscribed by strictly by various utterances. If one decides to analyze online conversations for the purpose of analyzing the development of discourses, it is very important to preserve and describe as best as one can the context within which utterances are made. While it is true that, in non-virtual settings, textual and discourse analysts must take into account both intertextuality and culture, online communities have specific contexts that are often created and circumscribed by the participants themselves, so online scholarship entails this additional layer of observations (Voithofer 2006; Watson *et al.* 2006). Online communities are distinguished from non-virtual communities by the fact that communication takes place largely through written words (Watson *et al.* 2006). The timing of the utterances is of utmost importance in this medium. If the data is being collected in real time (i.e., synchronous), the scholar must pay close attention to the timing of utterances, much like musicians are hyperaware of the timing and tone of other musicians, so as to be able to more accurately express the "feel" of the context. If the data are not collected in real time (i.e., asynchronous, such as looking at the threads of conversation in archived groups, social networking sites, etc.), then the researcher should pay close attention, at the very least, to the timestamps of the conversations.

In online communities, context is not only tied to the specific listserve, medium, and/or social networking site (such as Facebook, Twitter, or MySpace), it is also tied to time and, often, a knowledge of a non-virtual context to which the participant is responding. Online communities do not merely reflect non-virtual communities. They are, instead, "perpendicular communities," which are mutually constitutive (Ignacio 2005). Thus, as in all ethnographies, scholars continue to benefit greatly from being as diligent in paying careful attention to the issues in the "outside" world to which the participants respond in order to best analyze the discourse within the online community. Depending on the online community, the researcher has to plan carefully his or her data collection techniques. The timing of the responses, particularly in light of rapidly changing contexts, are often crucial to understanding and analyzing the utterances. Scholars who fail to account for the context of discussions and the timing of utterances will most likely produce incomplete analyses of the "mini-conversations."

As one can imagine, a comprehensive conversational analysis on Twitter becomes immensely difficult if one is following a number of users responding to the same event. Not only does one need to learn the correct hashtags (i.e, a non-hierarchical keyword, term, or phrased assigned to a piece of information) users are writing to communicate with one another. One needs to interpret posts appearing at breakneck speed. As an example of how difficult this chosen method could be (particularly if research is conducted on Twitter) for studying conversations between members of the diaspora, one could point to one event initially "reported" on Twitter, then generated multiple responses:

On April 17 2011, a very young Filipino actor by the name of A. J. Perez died in a horrific car accident. The news of his death was first posted by a fellow Filipino actor named Ogie Diaz (@OgieDiaz) via Twitter. Diasporic Filipinos familiar with either Ogie Diaz or A. J. Perez reacted to the news quickly, furiously retweeting condolences from various celebrities and offering their deepest condolences so frequently that they became "top tweets" of the day. At first glance, this may appear to just be a function of the medium; this is, after all, what Twitter users share—a steady stream of status updates, theirs or others. But, an ethnographer interested in observing the process of community, identity, or even discourse formation on Twitter must account for the specific context of posts and a much larger "non-Twitter" context in order to analyze the phenomenon. An ethnographer would need to account for the following before undertaking an analysis of these tweets.

First, with the click of one button (i.e., the retweet button), Twitter allows users to broadcast someone else's posted message (aka, tweet) to all the people on his or her network. Since many television personalities and other celebrities make their Twitter pages available to all and also allow all Twitter users to sign up for their page as Twitter "followers," it is very easy for one's status update to spread like wildfire on Twitter.

Second, many diasporic Filipinos rely not only on the internet, but also satellite television and ethnic newspapers to either stay in touch with each other or learn about their culture. ABS-CBN, the Philippines' largest media conglomerate, broadcasts widely in the Philippines and worldwide via satellite television. With respect to the above scenario, A. J. Perez was an ABS-CBN "homegrown talent," and Ogie Perez is also under contract with the company. Both (as is the case with all ABS-CBN stars) are heavily promoted by ABS-CBN, appearing not only in the shows within which they star (in this case, *Sabel* and *Mutya*), but also in variety shows (*ASAP*), entertainment news shows (*E-live*), or weekly dramas (*Maalaala Mo Kaya*). Therefore, diasporic Filipinos who are avid Twitter users and who subscribe to "the Filipino channel" (i.e., ABS-CBN), watch their shows online, read about their stars in various local ethnic newspapers, and/or have seen their films would, more likely than not, have seen the news fairly quickly.

To complicate matters, the Filipino diaspora lives and works in over 200 countries. Given that the diaspora operates in different time zones, the tweets and retweets also occurred around the clock.

Furthermore, given the marriage between Twitter, other social networking sites (like Facebook), ABS-CBN and other channels, these tweets appeared on all mediums, at all hours of the day, simultaneously reflecting, creating, and changing both news and context. These are perpendicular worlds.

Researchers interested in approaching this event from a conversation analysis standpoint, then, would have a very challenging task, to say the least. As stated earlier, to do a very thorough conversation analysis, the scholar would have to not only gather the data, but also be very sensitive to the timing of these posts, the influence of outside sources on the contexts, as well as, the ways these posts changed the context. It was overwhelming to have witnessed it in action. Studying the whole phenomenon, using the method of instances, while not impossible, would be a gargantuan task.

Conclusion

Thus, as in all research, scholars must be very clear about the phenomenon that they wish to study, the questions they want to have answered, and the methods and site within which they which to collect their research. If they choose to do online research to study diasporas, they should be aware that, although members of various diasporas use the internet to maintain (or create) ties with loved ones and friends from their homeland or other host countries, we cannot treat the internet merely as a technological tool that helps people communicate. The internet itself is a location within which a context is created by those present in the community in general and at that particular point in time in which people are communicating with one another.

For those wishing to generalize their results towards all diasporic community members, then, conducting research online may not be the best choice given the difficulty of obtaining random samples online. Currently, the data that one can collect on the internet is, as stated, best used for conversation analysis or textual analysis. If scholars are more concerned with knowledge-production, however, then the internet could be a promising site. However, those who wish to do online research, should ideally be prepared to research the (1) context within which the poster is physically located; (2) the context(s) that the poster is responding to; (3) the context of the site itself; and (4) the context(s) that any respondent may be located within. Though this is somewhat doable in asynchronous sites, it can be very difficult to manage in online forums like

Twitter whose context is largely created by the timing of the response. A scholar can, of course, decide to limit the time within which he or she will study the responses on the site, as this is commonly done in both offline and other on-line contexts. However, given that these textual comments are creating the context of the site, the scholar would most likely benefit from continuing to collect data until there is an obvious break in the conversation of a particular topic. In Twitter, for example, this is often delineated by (1) a relatively long break from updating one's status; and (2) an obvious break in the central topic of the status update.

In addition, the researcher should analyze and thoroughly describe for the reader both the text, as well as, the context within which the text was "uttered" and the context created by the text. If the data is being collected in real time (i.e., synchronous research), the scholar must pay close attention to the timing of utterances, much like musicians are hyperaware of the timing and tone of other musicians, so as to be able to more accurately express the "feel" of the context. If the data are not collected in real time (i.e., asynchronous research, such as analyzing threads of conversation in archived groups, social networking sites, etc.), then the researcher should pay close attention, at the very least, to the timestamps of the conversations. In addition, the conversations, often happen very quickly and require much cross-referencing. In other words, online communities have specific contexts that are, often, created and circumscribed by the participants themselves, so online scholarship entails this additional layer of observations.

Most of all, beyond the mechanics of implementing the method, I believe that all scholars who study diasporic communities should examine whether they want to conduct their research solely using online methods, offline methods, or a combination of the two. While it may appear to be convenient or, possibly, even (as in the case of studying communication between diasporic members) the "best" location to conduct one's research, as in all research projects, scholars must examine first if the data that one can collect on the internet will answer his or her research questions.

The internet, for all its widespread use and the ease of gathering an $n > 30$, should not be used as a primary source of quantitative or qualitative data that will be generalized toward the entire diaspora. As stated above and in other methodological texts, hopes for "random sampling" across a whole population is not possible not only because of the continuing digital divide, but also because using the internet is still a voluntary exercise. Thus, any researcher who tries to make the claim that the primary data collected via the internet can be generalized to the community which he or she is studying, unfortunately, necessarily weakens their analysis, and opens up their entire research project to serious scrutiny. Or, scholars who approach the study using methods that are intended to generalize across a population (i.e., through the use of positive or post-positive methods) will, inevitably, have to state in their analysis that their study was not meant to generalize across the entire population, but can offer a glimpse of how knowledge is produced. Thus, I argue, should one decide to study online conversations, one must carefully decide if it is the most appropriate location to help us better understand immigration, transmigration, and/or diaspora.

Acknowledgment

Many thanks to Zachary Beare, Erica Coie, Susan M. Hollister, Stephanie Nawyn, and Alice M. Ritscherle for their patience and for their help in preparing this publication.

Further reading

Anderson, B. (1983) *Imagined Communties: Reflections on the Origin and Spread of Nationalism*. London: Verso Books.

Anzaldua, G. (2007 [1999]) *Borderlands/La Frontera*. San Francisco, CA: Aunt Lute Books.

Battles, H. T. (2010) "Exploring ethical and methodological issues in internet-based research with adolescents" *International Journal of Qualitative Methods* 9(1): 27–39.

Beddows, E. (2008) "The methodological issues associated with internet-based research" *International Journal of Emerging Technologies and Society* 6(2): 124–39.

Bernal, V. (2005) "Eritrea on-line: Diaspora, cyberspace, and the public sphere" *American Ethnologist* 32(4): 660–75.

Bernal, V. (2006). "Diaspora, cyberspace and political imagination: The Eritrean diaspora online" *Global Networks* 6(2): 161–79.

Briassoulis, H. (2010) "Online petitions: New tools of secondary analysis?" *Qualitative Research* 10(6): 715–27.

Camroux, D. (2008) "Nationalizing transnationalism? The Philippine state and the Filipino diaspora" *Les Études du CERI* 152: 2–39.

Denzin, N. K. (1999) "Cybertalk and the method of instances." In S. Jones (ed.), *Doing Internet Research: Critical Issues and Methods for Examining the Net*. Thousand Oaks, CA: Sage Publications, pp. 107–26.

Figer, R. C. and Ynion, W. L. G. (2010) "Religiosity online: Holy connections with the homeland by Filipino migrants in Japan" *Asian Social Science* 6(2): 3–11.

Glick-Schiller, N., Basch, L., and Szanton-Blanc (1995) "From immigrant to transmigrant" *Anthropological Quarterly* 68(1): 48–63.

Guervarra, A. R. (2010) *Marketing Dreams, Manufacturing Heroes: The Transnational Labor Brokering of Filipino Workers*. New Brunswick, NJ: Rutgers University Press.

Helland, C. (2007) "Diaspora on the electronic frontier: Developing virtual connections with sacred homelands" *Journal of Computer-Mediated Communication* 12(3): 956–76.

Hepp, A. (2009) "Localities of diasporic communicative spaces: Material aspects of translocal mediated networking" *Communication Review* 12(4): 327–48.

Hookway, N. (2008) "'Entering the blogosphere': Some strategies for using blogs in social research" *Qualitative Research* 8(1): 91–113.

Ignacio, E. N. (2005) *Building Diaspora: Filipino Community Formation on the Internet*. New Brunswick, NJ: Rutgers University Press.

——(2006) "E-scaping boundaries: Bridging cyberspace and diaspora studies through nethnography." In D. Silver and A. Massanari (eds), *Critical Cyberculture Studies*. New York: NYU Press, pp. 276–95.

Jones, S. (1999) *Doing Internet Research: Critical Issues and Methods for Examining the Net*. Thousand Oaks, CA: Sage Publications.

Kendall, L. (1999) "Recontextualizing cyberspace: Methodological considerations for on-line research." In S. Jones (ed.), *Doing Internet Research: Critical Issues and Methods for Examining the Net*. Thousand Oaks, CA: Sage Publications, pp. 57–74.

Lobe, B. and Vehovar, V. (2009) "Towards a flexible online mixed method design with a feedback loop" *Quality and Quantity* 43(4): 585–97.

Markham, A. N. and Baym, N. K. (2008) *Internet Inquiry: Conversations About Method*. Thousand Oaks, CA: Sage Publications.

Miller. D. and Slater, D. (2001) *The Internet: An Ethnographic Approach*. Oxford: Berg Publishers.

Mitra, A. (2006) "Towards finding a cybernetic safe place: Illustrations from people of Indian origin" *New Media and Society* 8(2): 251–68.

Murray, S. A. (2011) "Immigrant and refugee life narratives of immigration and community organizing in the North Puget Sound region." Paper presented at Stony Brook Ethnography Conference.

Nakamura, L. (2002) *Cybertypes: Race, Ethnicity, and Identity on the Internet*. New York: Routledge Press.

Nevins, J. (2010) *Operation Gatekeeper and Beyond: The War on Illegals and the Remaking of the US-Mexico Boundary*, 2nd edn, London: Routledge Press.

Ó Dochartaigh, N. (2009) "Reframing online: Ulster Loyalists imagine an American audience" *Identities* 16(1): 102–27.

Ong, A. (1999) *Flexible Citizenship: The Cultural Logics of Transnationality*. Raleigh, NC: Duke University Press.

Parreñas, R. (2001) *Servants of Globalization: Women, Migration, Domestic Work*. Palo Alto, CA: Stanford University Press.

Parry, M. (2011) "Harvard researchers accused of breaching students' privacy: Social-network project shows promise and peril of doing social science online" *The Chronicle for Higher Education,* July 10, 2011.

Psthas, G. (1995) *Conversation Analysis*. Thousand Oaks, CA: Sage Publications.

Purkayastha, B. (2009) "Another world of experience? Transnational contexts and the experiences of South Asian Americans" *South Asian Diaspora* 1(1): 85–99.

Rodriguez, R. M. (2010) *Migrants for Export: How the Philippine State Brokers Labor to the World*. Minneapolis, MN: University of Minnesota Press.

Rosas, G. (2007) "The fragile ends of war: Forging the US–Mexico border and borderlands consciousness" *Social Text* 25(2): 81–102.

Sampson, H., Bloor, M. and Fincham, B. (2008) "A price worth paying? Considering the 'cost' of reflexive research methods and the influence of feminist ways of 'doing'" *Sociology* 42(5): 919–33.

Tynes, R. (2007) "Nation-building and the diaspora on Leonenet: A case of Sierra Leone in cyberspace" *New Media and Society* 9(3): 497–518.

Voithofer, R. (2006) "Studying intertextuality, discourse and narratives to conceptualize and contextualize online learning environments" *International Journal of Qualitative Studies in Education (QSE)* 19(2): 201–19.

Watson, M., Peacock, S., and Jones, D. (2006) "The analysis of interaction in online focus groups" *International Journal of Therapy and Rehabilitation* 13(12): 551–57.

46

Comparative methodologies in the study of migration

Irene Bloemraad[1]

All migration research, regardless of methodology, is comparative. An ethnographer, even one studying a specific group of people in a particular setting, constantly compares and contrasts observations. A researcher using data from a thousand survey respondents compares answers using statistical methods. An archival researcher might compare official accounts of a law's passage to the private letters of those involved. The very identification of international migration as a field of study rests on a comparison: scholars assume that there is something unique and noteworthy in the experiences of those who migrate compared to those who do not.

For the purposes of this chapter, "comparative migration research" entails the systematic analysis of a relatively small number of cases. Instead of focusing on individuals as the primary comparison, self-consciously comparative projects are pinned to another unit of analysis: migrant groups, organizations, geographical areas, time periods and so forth. The goal of these studies is to examine how structures, cultures, norms, institutions or other processes affect outcomes through the combination and intersection of causal mechanisms. Comparison is a creative strategy of analytical elaboration using a particular research design.[2]

Comparative studies are thus characterized by their research design and the focus of analysis, *not* by a particular data or methodology. Indeed, comparative migration studies use the full breadth of evidence commonly employed by academic researchers, from in-depth interview data to mass survey responses, and from documentary materials to observations in the field.

In what follows, I first consider why students of migration might want to engage in comparison, and when doing so is more costly than helpful. I then examine what migration researchers compare, from groups to time periods. Finally, I examine how to compare. What are the different logics that drive comparative research? Throughout, the discussion is animated by a deep-seated belief that more studies should employ comparison, but that it must be done with careful thought to what, how, and why we compare.

Why compare?

Comparison is compelling because it reminds us that social phenomena are not fixed or "natural." Through comparison we can de-center what is taken for granted in a particular time or place after we learn that something was not always so, or that it is different elsewhere, or for other people. A well-chosen comparative study can challenge conventional wisdom or show how existing academic theories might be wrong.

Yet the more things you compare—whether people, immigrant groups, organizations, neighborhoods, cities, countries, or time periods—the more background knowledge you need and the more time and resources you must invest to collect and analyze data. This problem applies across methodologies, from the ethnographer who decides to study two research sites instead of one, to the scholar who wants to survey additional people who speak diverse languages. All researchers, but especially students of migration, need to think very hard about *why* comparison makes sense. Introducing additional comparisons into an immigration-related project frequently entails significant costs in time and money, due to the distances involved and the skills needed to deal with distinct populations, and they raise thorny challenges of access and communication.

Comparison is not very useful when the goal is merely to "increase the N," that is, an exercise in expanding the number of cases without considering how those cases advance the project. Those doing in-depth interviewing might feel that interviewing 50 migrants is inherently better than interviewing 40. This might be true if the 10 additional people represent a particular type of experience or a category of individuals that could nuance an evolving argument. But if the goal is merely to increase confidence in the generalizability of results, additional interviews will contribute little if they are not based on probability sampling.[3]

Comparison is most productive when it does analytical weight-lifting. A well-chosen comparison allows a researcher to probe alternative accounts for a particular phenomenon or leverages the researcher's ability to get at certain theoretical ideas or build new concepts. For example, in the project that led to the publication of *Becoming a Citizen* (Bloemraad 2006), I wanted to study how government policies in Canada and the United States influence immigrants' political incorporation. To address concerns that comparing Canada and the United States was like contrasting apples and oranges, due to their different migration streams, I focused on a particular migrant group that had very similar characteristics and migration trajectories on either side of the 49th parallel. Comparing the same group, the Portuguese, in two different countries served as an analytical strategy to undermine alternative accounts of why immigrants' citizenship levels in Canada were so much higher than in the United States. It also allowed me to focus on understanding the mechanisms by which government policy could trickle down to affect individual immigrants' decisions about citizenship and political participation.[4]

In the same project, comparison served a second analytical purpose when I expanded the study to include Vietnamese migrants. Canada and the United States, while alike in many respects, also differ in consequential ways. It was thus difficult to advance the argument that Canadian government support for integration and multiculturalism affected citizenship and political engagement. Critics could reasonably argue that political integration might be driven by a host of other cross-national variations, from welfare state differences to distinct electoral politics. My nascent argument was that Canadian policies had an effect because they funded community-based organizations, provided services and advanced symbolic politics of legitimacy. The logic behind the argument suggested that migrants groups in the United States that received government assistance—such as official refugees like the Vietnamese— would resemble the Canadian pattern more than similarly situated economic and family-reunification migrants, such as the Portuguese. By expanding the comparison to two groups in two countries, I could evaluate whether the mechanisms identified in the first comparison held in a second.[5]

What to compare?

Because academics continuously build on prior research, there is always an inherent comparison between a particular study and the research or thinking that has come before. I term this the *external comparative placement* of a project vis-à-vis the existing literature. Both novice and experienced researchers need to ask the comparative question, "What is the theoretical and substantive edge of my project in relation to others?"

In this way, even a single case study can be "comparative" to the extent that a researcher compares his or her case with existing work. Such comparisons often occur when scholars study an immigrant group that has not been examined before, or when they look at a particular research site—whether a neighborhood or a church—that does not fit the general pattern. Analytically, such a comparison can stretch or modify an existing theory, as Burawoy (1998) recommends in the extended case method, or the case can serve as an anomaly that challenges existing scholarship and helps to generate new theories and ideas. Either as an extension or challenge, the conversation between the new empirical study and the existing literature becomes the comparative mechanism. Such case studies are not, however, formal comparative studies in the sense outlined here.

Migration studies, as Nancy Foner (2005) notes, also invariably contain an implicit or explicit comparison between "here" and "there," emanating from the change in place that occurs with migration. Such here-and-there distinctions can be sharp, but they can also become blurred, empirically and conceptually, as is in studies of transnationalism, which view migration occurring in transnational social fields that span places and sometimes time. Transnational projects, by rejecting sharp geographical or temporal distinctions, usually fall outside the category of formal comparative studies since the point of this work is to erase the hard-set divisions between here and there.[6]

I reserve the term "comparison" for a *specific comparative design internal to the research project*. Such comparisons can take a variety of forms, but they all involve a choice about what, exactly, should be compared. What constitutes a "case"? I first discuss three key comparisons, roughly ordered from most to least common in studies of migration, and then I briefly consider some additional comparative strategies.

Comparing migrant groups

Traditionally, in the United States, comparative migration studies contrast different migrant groups in the same geographical location, be it a city or the country as a whole.[7] Milton Gordon's (1964) classic theorizing on assimilation, for example, draws on a comparison of four groups distinguished by race and religion: blacks, Puerto Ricans, European-origin Catholics, and Jews. More recently, Sofya Aptekar (2009) compares how influential white residents of a New Jersey suburb perceive new high-skilled Chinese and Indian migrants. She argues that local processes of racialization portray the less politically visible Chinese as successful but conformist model minorities, while Asian Indians who challenge local politicians and power holders are viewed as invaders and troublemakers.

The choice of what to compare is not simply choosing a unit of analysis. It is also a theoretical and conceptual choice about what sorts of factors are consequential for a particular outcome of interest. Thus, the decision to compare the educational aspirations of Dominican and Chinese Americans rests on the assumption that national origin (or culture, or homeland economic system, or some other factor for which national origin can act as a proxy) fundamentally matters (Louie 2006). Even if it turns out that national origin does not matter, this "non-finding" is viewed as important because of the general expectation within the academic field, or among the public, that it should matter.

Migration researchers in the United States overwhelmingly assume that national origin matters. Empirically, this assumption often finds support. Thus, Vivian Louie's (2006) comparison of second-generation Dominican and Chinese-origin youth reveals that ethnic, pan-ethnic, and transnational orientations intermingle to give Dominicans a more optimistic view of their social mobility even though most grow up in blighted neighborhoods and their group, on average, has poorer socio-economic outcomes than those of Chinese origin. More broadly, Kasinitz *et al.* (2008) report significant differences between the social, political, and economic trajectories of second-generation and native-born young adults from seven ethno-racial groups in New York City.

The choice to focus on national origin also flows from Americans' longstanding concerns over race and race relations in the United States. Comparing groups defined by national origin, ethnicity, race or religion is "natural" in this context. In France, however, the state—and many researchers—have explicitly rejected race as a social category. Other categories are taken-for-granted, a tendency encouraged by the dearth of ethno-racial statistics. Thus, in an analysis of educational outcomes similar in style to the New York studies, Patrick Simon (2003) contrasts educational trajectories of second generation and native French youth by focusing on social classes, as well as ethno-national groups. Comparative migration researchers should be attentive to the inherent cognitive biases of their discipline or society when deciding what sort of cases to compare.

Geographic comparisons: nations, cities, towns, and other places

Outside the United States, we find a stronger tradition of cross-national migration studies. These studies usually examine how broad differences in countries' laws, policies, economic systems, social institutions and national ideologies affect migration outcomes. An early and influential study in this "national models" tradition is Rogers Brubaker's (1992) comparison of citizenship laws in France and Germany. Legal differences make it easier for immigrants and their children to become French nationals than German citizens, which Brubaker traces back to centuries-long processes of state-building and nation formation. Other researchers ground their cross-national studies in the notion of political or discursive opportunity structures, an idea taken from social movement theorizing. In this vein, Koopmans *et al.* (2005) differentiate five European countries by their relative position on mono- or multicultural group rights and civic or ethnic citizenship. Countries' placement on these two dimensions then drives explanations for immigrants' claims-making and the mobilization of native-born groups sympathetic or hostile to immigrants.

The greater emphasis on cross-national comparison, especially by scholars studying Europe, probably lies in the closer proximity of European countries to each other and greater familiarity with an international literature. Many scholars outside the United States regularly read scholarship produced in the United States, as well as in their own country, leading to comparative questions about the importance of place. Lately, the European Union and related European bodies provide significant funding for cross-national research teams, spurring further geographic comparisons.

In recent years, more and more researchers include the United States as a case comparison. Some early comparisons were done by scholars working outside the United States, such as Jeffrey Reitz's (1998) assessment of immigrants' economic fortunes in the United States, Canada, and Australia and Christian Joppke's (1999) analysis of sovereignty and citizenship ideologies in the United States, Germany, and the United Kingdom. Now more US-based scholars are working on cross-national comparative projects. This group includes early-career researchers such as Margarita Mooney's (2009) comparison of Haitian Catholics' faith in Miami, Montreal, and Paris and senior scholars such Richard Alba's (2005) conceptual and empirical work on cross-national differences in second-generation integration in the United States, France, and Germany. Such studies help evaluate whether theories developed in the United States can be generalized or whether they are instances of American exceptionalism. At the same time, researchers need to be sensitive to the danger of trying to compare places so dissimilar that they reap few or no benefits from the comparative enterprise.[8]

The upshot of most of these cross-national studies is that the societies in which immigrants reside have as much, or even more, influence on process of migration and immigrant incorporation than the characteristics of those who move. This more structural or institutional lens provides a quite different understanding of migration dynamics and outcomes than migrant group comparisons. Because the group approach contrasts immigrants, collectively and individually, such studies tend to highlight the importance of specific immigrant attributes (e.g. immigrants' culture, minority status, etc.), or the interaction of immigrant attributes with the local environment. In the national models or political opportunity structure approach, the characteristics and agency of immigrants is secondary to the overwhelming constraints of macro-level forces (e.g., receiving nations' culture, laws around citizenship, etc.).

Spatial comparisons in migration studies have long privileged the nation-state as the key unit of analysis. This focus has been challenged by transnational scholars and, increasingly, by those who study sub-national places, usually cities, but also regions, provinces/states, and neighborhoods. A dynamic frontier in comparative migration is the comparison of different immigrant-receiving cities and towns.[9]

In Europe, theoretical and empirical interest in cities has been fed by dissatisfaction with national models that view all places in a country as homogeneous instances of the same paradigm. Immigrants' lives are very different in Berlin as compared to a small town in Bavaria, despite their common location in Germany. Nina Glick Schiller and Ayse Çalar (2009) have recently theorized a localities approach to migration that focuses on post-industrial restructuring, while the empirical work of Romain Garbaye (2005) demonstrates that despite a national "French" citizenship model, access to politics for immigrants and the second generation differ significantly depending on local party systems and the organization of municipal government.

In a similar way, immigrants living in relatively progressive San Francisco face different obstacles and opportunities than those in Hazelton, Pennsylvania, the site of a contentious legal battle over local ordinances directed against undocumented migrants. In the United States, interest in local comparisons has been fueled by the twin phenomena of exploding local legislation—pro- and anti-immigrant—in the face of failed federal immigration reforms (Varsanyi 2010), and by immigrants' growing geographic dispersion to new metropolitan areas, suburbs, and destinations in the South and to rural areas that never experienced migration before (Massey 2008; Singer et al. 2008).

Comparison across time

Temporal comparisons are rarer in migration studies. Historians tend to focus on a particular time period, while most social scientists carry out research on current topics. Historians at times speak to contemporary issues to frame a historical study, and social scientists regularly provide a rapid "background" to a particular migrant group or place, but few attempt a sustained comparison of how dynamics "then" replicate or differ from dynamics "now."[10]

This paucity is unfortunate since much of the public debate over immigration—especially in the United States, but also in other countries—poses explicit or implicit questions over whether today's immigrants are "better" than those in the past. Are they integrating more quickly or more slowly? Do they possess more or less human and financial capital than prior waves? Speaking directly to such questions, Nancy Foner (2000) engages in a sustained analysis of the educational outcomes, occupations, ethnic enclaves, race, and gender dynamics of New York's earlier Jewish and Italian migrants as compared to contemporary New Yorkers from a myriad of countries. Similarly, Joel Perlmann (2005) uses statistical analysis to compare the socio-economic trajectories of low-skilled European migrants who arrived at the turn of the twentieth century to recent generations of Mexican migrants. Both accounts offer cautiously optimistic assessments of the fate of contemporary immigrants in the United States.

Other comparisons: groups, organizations, and institutions

Comparisons between migrant groups, places, and time do not exhaust the types of comparisons available to migration scholars. Individual immigrants can be grouped by social class, gender, generation, legal status and other socially relevant labels. Some of these studies are based on extensive field research, such as Cecilia Menjívar's (2000) discussion of how Salvadoran men and women experience and use social networks differently for migration and settlement in San Francisco. Other studies involve "large N" comparisons of demographic or survey data. When done well, such statistical comparisons do not just show that a particular regression coefficient has statistical significance, holding all other variables constant, but they also explain how a particular categorization (male/female; refugee/non-refugee) represents a series of social, economic, cultural or political processes that produce different experiences and outcomes between groups of people.

There are also a host of meso-level organizations and institutions that can be compared, such as civic groups, schools, churches, unions, businesses, and so forth. For example, Angie Chung (2007) compares two community-based groups in Los Angeles that have different organizational structures and alliance strategies in the Korean community. Daniel Faas (2010) investigates the political identities of Turkish minority and ethnic majority students in four different schools, focusing on how educational goals at the European, national, and regional levels influence instruction and identities on the ground.

Faas's study is an example of how migration scholars are increasingly combining comparative strategies. Most common is the study of a few migrant groups in a few carefully chosen countries. These studies follow what Nancy Green (1994) calls a "divergent" comparison model, or what I label a "quasi-experimental" approach (Bloemraad 2006). This strategy is particularly effective in disentangling the relative importance of immigrant characteristics, societal influences and the intersection between the two. Is there a "Chinese" pattern to immigrant settlement, regardless of destination country, or do similarities due to national origin become negligible when we take into account the receiving society? If Chinese settlement in two places is compared to Indian settlement in the same destinations, what stands out: similarities between groups in the same place, or between members of the same group in different places? Or is such a neat distinction impossible?

Other comparative strategies are also possible. Faas's (2010) comparison rests on fieldwork in a university track and a vocational high school in both Germany and Great Britain, allowing him to nuance simple categorizations of "German" or "British" educational institutions. Complex comparisons promise substantial pay-offs if done well, but they are difficult to carry out. The individual researcher quickly becomes overwhelmed by data collection and analysis. Team-based projects alleviate some of these problems, but they come with separate challenges, such as the need for careful planning to collect comparable evidence and for compromise among partners in identifying and explaining key findings.

Unanticipated comparisons and surprising findings

The discussion thus far presumes careful attention to the question of what to compare while a project is in the planning stages, and it assumes that the original comparison remains central to the analysis throughout the project. Yet research often takes unanticipated turns or runs into dead-ends. New data or ideas can force a researcher to modify a project's design. Sometimes the key comparative cases do not turn out to be the ones originally envisioned. In Cinzia Solari's (2006) study of Russian-speaking immigrant homecare workers, she expected that their different understandings of carework—as a matter of professionalism or sainthood—would be gendered. Instead, she found that an institutional comparison better explained migrants' discursive strategies: Jewish migrants, whether men or women, were taught a professional orientation by a long-standing Jewish refugee resettlement agency; Russian Orthodox migrants relied on more haphazard networks that privileged a saintly view of carework.

Null findings are also important, although they are disconcerting for the researcher who put substantial thought into choosing analytically-informed cases. In his study of third and fourth generation Mexican Americans' ethnic identity, Tomás Jiménez (2010) carefully selected two US towns based on their experience with continuous or interrupted Mexican migration. He expected that these different histories would matter, but found that large-scale new migration generated similar experiences and attitudes in both places. While not what he expected, this finding led Jiménez to identify how new migration can "replenish" the ethnicity of those with generations of history in the United States, regardless of place.

How to compare

The choice of what to compare is analytically distinct from decisions about how to compare. *What to compare* involves decisions about the general class of "cases" in the project: are we interested in migrant groups, immigrant-receiving countries, both, or something else altogether? Such decisions are also conceptual and theoretical ones since they privilege one level of analysis over another and they shape the sort of explanations that flow from a project.

How to compare involves decisions about which specific cases one chooses: Kenyan migrants or Peruvians? Amsterdam or San Francisco? Such decisions are also choices about the comparative logics that will drive the analysis and the type of conversation the researcher wants to have with existing theory. Practicalities—including constraints on money, time, the researcher's ability to speak certain languages, and other factors—often means that choices over "what sort" of cases and "which specific" cases intersect. Nonetheless, good comparative designs rest on smart choices about comparative logics.

Most similar comparative designs

Here the researcher chooses specific cases that are very similar in a number of critical respects. The comparison of two or more similar cases allows the researcher to probe whether certain decisive variations produce consequential divergences.[11] When studying particular places, most-similar comparative designs set up a quasi-experimental logic: given that all else is the same, what is the effect of a particular difference on the outcome of interest? This logic drove my comparison of immigrant political incorporation in Canada and the United States (Bloemraad 2006).

The logic behind most-similar comparisons can also apply to other types of cases, such as the study of migrant groups. For example, a researcher could pick two groups with similar migration histories and socio-economic profiles, but which tend to hold different legal statuses. This is the strategy used by Sarah Horton (2004) to explain why Cuban and Mexican migrants are treated differently by staff in a health care clinic in New Mexico. The persuasiveness of such designs rests on readers' willingness to concur with the breadth of similarity between the cases, and that the consequential difference highlighted by the researcher is indeed the critical factor driving dissimilar outcomes.

Most different comparative designs

In these designs, a researcher purposely chooses diametrically opposing cases that vary from each other on a series of characteristics. Such case selection can serve two distinct purposes, based on different comparative logics. One logic builds on Mill's method of similarity. When a number of cases are very different, but produce a similar outcome, this outcome can be explained by identifying the key factor shared across the dissimilar cases. Few migration scholars adopt this strategy, perhaps because of a bias within academia to explaining discrepant, rather than similar, outcomes. Most different designs can nonetheless be fruitful. Although such a strategy was not his initial goal, elements of this logic are embedded in Jiménez's (2010) findings and arguments, and they are found in arguments about how human rights norms and supranational structures generate similar postnational citizenship practices across diverse countries (Soysal 1994).

Other scholars employ most-different cases as manifestations of Weberian ideal types. Within migration studies, Brubaker's (1992) comparison of German and French citizenship is one of the most self-conscious examples of this strategy. While Brubaker offers a detailed, historically grounded examination of nationhood in France and Germany, these two countries become ideal-types for two sorts of immigrant-receiving countries, those with "civic" notions of nationality compared to those with "ethnic" understandings of membership. The logic of ideal-type comparison can also be applied to other comparisons, including migrant groups and meso-level institutions.

Comparison as a conceptual spectrum of cases

Cases can also be chosen because they fit particular categories in a typology. In such research designs, a scholar identifies two or three key characteristics presumed to be important for explaining a particular outcome or phenomenon. Cases are then selected based on those characteristics, and comparisons between cases speak to the importance of the underlying characteristics. In this way, Koopmans and colleagues (2005) distinguish the Netherlands as a civic, multicultural country and France as a civic but monocultural land. Both nations are then distinguished from ethnic, monocultural Germany. Placement within this conceptual grid subsequently explains variations in public claims-making.

This method of case selection can also be extended to choices over which migrant groups to study or other units of analysis. According to a model of segmented assimilation, immigrants' incorporation will vary by how receptive government policy is toward the group, whether members of the group are a racial minority, and the relative strength of the social, human, and financial capital of the group as a whole (Portes and Zhou 1993). An evaluation of this model would thus entail choosing groups that vary along these key dimensions.

The typology approach sits between a variable-oriented and Weberian method of analysis. By identifying characteristics that inform the placement of cases into a typology, the researcher privileges key variables—such as government policy or social capital—over the case as a holistic entity. Thus, for some researchers, the variable itself—its absence or presence, whether it is high, medium or low—becomes the core theoretical thrust of the research; the case serves as an illustration, but is, in a sense, secondary to the argument. For other researchers, however, the overlap of two or three key characteristics cannot be disentangled and isolated from each other. Rather, the particular intersection of the characteristics creates unique configurations that render the cases conceptually distinct from each other.[12] Understood in this more holistic way, the case remains primary, and the analysis fits more closely to the Weberian ideal-type model.

Conclusion

Doing comparative migration research demands careful attention to what sorts of cases will be compared and critical choices over which specific cases will drive the analysis. These choices are not self-evident. Rather, they entail theoretical and conceptual decisions about level of analysis, comparative logics and the particular lens one brings to migration research. This makes comparative research challenging, but it also makes it a highly creative endeavor.

Not all migration research needs to be self-consciously built on a comparative research design. Each additional comparison in a project carries significant costs: data collection and analysis become harder, as does writing about all the moving parts of a project. Even migration projects that are not explicitly comparative contain comparative elements inherent in a scholar's engagement with the existing literature, in the process of data analysis and even in the very identification of migration as a subject of research.

Nevertheless, explicitly comparative research holds out significant advantages. Comparison makes most sense when it contributes directly to theory development, evaluation, or elaboration of an evolving argument. It does not privilege any particular type of data; observational, inter-view, archival, and statistical studies can all be comparative. Importantly, comparative studies can challenge accepted and conventional wisdoms, and lead to innovative new thinking.

Notes

1 My thanks to Nancy Foner, Stephanie Nawyn and Mario Small for helpful comments on an earlier draft of this chapter.
2 There is an extensive literature debating the relative merits of "small-N" (a few cases) and "large-N" (many cases) comparative studies that I do not cover here. I include large-scale statistical studies in this chapter if the primary level of analysis goes beyond individual-level comparisons and is done in the spirit of a configurational approach to theory rather than a "variable-oriented" logic that assumes the independence of explanatory variables. For one important, early formulation of the distinction between case-oriented and variable-oriented comparative research, see Ragin (1987). More recently, Lieberman (2005) has called for a "nested" approach that marries small and large-N analysis in the same project, to leverage the relative strengths of each approach.
3 If a researcher uses a probability sample, increasing the number of cases can improve the precision of estimates generalizable to a larger population and reduce error around coefficients estimates in infer-ential modeling. If, however, cases are not chosen using random selection, as is usually the case with in-depth interviewing, increasing the sample from 40 to 50 has no effect on the statistical general-izability of results. For a related discussion on problematic reasons to "increase your N," see Small (2009).
4 I draw on this personal example, and the other examples outlined below, because I know the studies well. These examples are far from exhaustive of the excellent comparative migration research that exists; other scholars will identify different exemplars of best practices.
5 For a more extensive account on the choices and challenges of putting together this project, see Bloemraad (forthcoming).

6 This is not necessarily so; some transnational studies are comparative in the sense used here. For example, Wendy Roth's (2009) study of panethnic identity formation in sending societies compares two transnational social fields: one between the United States and Puerto Rico, the second between the United States and the Dominican Republic. This comparison allows her to underscore how transnational social fields can vary in consequential ways.

7 For example, Eric Fong and Elic Chan's (2008) statistical review of published immigration research between 1990 and 2004 finds that only 14 percent of studies conducted by US researchers focused on immigrants in general, while 86 percent focused on particular groups. In comparison, 44 percent of publications by Canadian scholars examined immigrants in general, with only 56 percent centered on specific groups.

8 For example, Joppke (1999) concludes, in his comparison of the United States, Germany, and the United Kingdom, that differences in citizenship and immigrant integration are so large it is impossible to draw general lessons beyond the observation that national particularities matter and multiculturalism affects all liberal Western states.

9 In one sense, a focus on cities is not new. Particular US cities, especially Chicago and New York, have generated an enormous volume of influential research over the past century, and beyond the United States, Saskia Sassen (1991) elaborated an early argument for the specificity of global cities, especially their migrant-attracting labor market structures. This research was not, however, focused on comparing cities in order to understand how migration and integration dynamics vary between them; instead, the city became a generalizeable case.

10 On historians reluctance to engage in comparison, and a call for that to change, see Green (1994).

11 Przeworski and Teune (1970) first made this influential distinction between comparing "most similar" and "most different" systems in their work on comparative research. This in turn influenced analytical strategies of causal inference using Mill's method of difference and similarity (Skocpol and Somers 1980).

12 This is the same line of reasoning used by theorists of intersectionality: understanding the experiences of the conceptual category "black women" is not just about putting together "black" experiences and "female" experiences in additive fashion. Rather, black women's experiences are conceptually and qualitatively different from that of black men or white women.

References and further reading

Alba, R. (2005) "Bright vs. blurred boundaries: Second-generation assimilation and exclusion in France, Germany, and the United States" *Ethnic and Racial Studies* 28(1): 20–49.

Aptekar, S. (2009) "Organizational life and political incorporation of two Asian Immigrant groups: A case study" *Ethnic and Racial Studies* 32(9): 1511–33.

Bloemraad, I. (2006) *Becoming a Citizen: Incorporating Immigrants and Refugees in the United States and Canada.* Berkeley, CA: University of California Press.

——(2012) "What the textbooks don't tell you: Moving from a research puzzle to published findings." In C. Vargas-Silva (ed.), *Handbook of Research Methods in Migration*, Cheltenham: Edward Elgar Publishing, pp. 502–20.

Brubaker, W. R. (1992) *Citizenship and Nationhood in France and Germany.* Cambridge, MA: Harvard University Press.

Burawoy, M. (1998) "The extended case method" *Sociological Theory* 16(1): 4–33.

Chung, A. Y. (2007) *Legacies of Struggle: Conflict and Cooperation in Korean American Politics.* Stanford, CA: Stanford University Press.

Faas, D. (2010) *Negotiating Political Identities Multiethnic Schools and Youth in Europe.* Farnham: Ashgate.

Foner, N. (2000) *From Ellis Island to JFK: New York's Two Great Waves of Immigration.* New Haven, CT: Yale University Press.

——(2005) *In a New Land: A Comparative View of Immigration.* New York: New York University Press.

Fong, E. and Chan, E. (2008) "An account of immigration studies in the United States and Canada, 1990–2004" *Sociological Quarterly* 49(3): 483–502.

Garbaye, R. (2005) *Getting Into Local Power: the Politics of Ethnic Minorities in British and French Cities.* Oxford, UK: Blackwell.

Glick Schiller, N. and Çalar, A. (2009) "Towards a comparative theory of locality in migration studies: Migrant incorporation and city scale" *Journal of Ethnic and Migration Studies* 35(2): 177–202.

Gordon, M. M. (1964) *Assimilation in American Life: The Role of Race, Religion and National Origins*. New York: Oxford University Press.

Green, N. (1994) "The comparative method and poststructural structuralism: New perspectives for migration studies" *Journal of American Ethnic History* 13(4): 3–22.

Horton, S. (2004) "Different subjects: The health care system's participation in the different construction of cultural citizenship of cuban refugees and mexican immigrants" *Medical Anthropology Quarterly* 18(4): 472–89.

Jiménez, T. (2010) *Replenished Ethnicity: Mexican Americans, Immigration, and Identity*. Berkeley, CA: University of California Press.

Joppke, C. (1999) *Immigration and the Nation-State: The United States, Germany, and Great Britain*. Oxford: Oxford University Press.

Kasinitz, P., Mollenkopf, J. H., Waters, M. C., and Holdaway, J. (2008) *Inheriting the City: The Children of Immigrants Come of Age*. Cambridge, MA: Harvard University Press.

Koopmans, R., Statham, P., Giugni, M., and Passy, F. (2005) *Contested Citizenship: Immigration and Cultural Diversity in Europe*. Minneapolis, MN: University of Minnesota Press.

Lieberman, E. S. (2005) "Nested analysis as a mixed-method strategy for comparative research" *American Political Science Review* 99(3): 435–52.

Louie, V. (2006) "Second generation pessimism and optimism: How Chinese and Dominicans understand education and mobility through ethnic and transnational orientations" *International Migration Review* 40(3): 537–72.

Massey, D. S. (ed.) (2008) *New Faces in New Places: The Changing Geography of American Immigration*. New York: Russell Sage Foundation.

Menjívar, C. (2000) *Fragmented Ties: Salvadoran Immigrant Networks in America*. Berkeley, CA: University of California Press.

Mooney, M. A. (2009) *Faith Makes Us Live: Surviving and Thriving in the Haitian Diaspora*. Berkeley, CA: University of California Press.

Perlmann, J. (2005) *Italians Then, Mexicans Now: Immigrant Origins and Second-Generation Progress, 1890–2000*. New York: Russell Sage Foundation Press.

Portes, A. and Zhou, M. (1993) "The new second generation: Segmented assimilation and its variants" *Annals of the American Academy of Political and Social Science* 530: 74–96.

Przeworski, A. and Teune, H. (1970) *The Logic of Comparative Social Inquiry*. New York: John Wiley.

Ragin, C. C. (1987) *The Comparative Method: Moving Beyond Qualitative and Quantitative Strategies*. Berkeley, CA: University of California Press.

Reitz, J. G. (1998) *Warmth of the Welcome: The Social Causes of Economic Success for Immigrants in Different Nations and Cities*. Boulder, CO: Westview Press.

Roth, W. D. (2009) "'Latino before the world': The transnational extension of panethnicity" *Ethnic and Racial Studies* 32(6): 927–47.

Sassen, S. (1991) *The Global City: New York, London, Tokyo*. Princeton, NJ: Princeton University Press.

Simon, P. (2003) "France and the unknown second generation: Preliminary results on social mobility" *International Migration Review* 37(4): 1091–1119.

Singer, A., Hardwick, S. W., and Brettell, C. (2008) *Twenty-First Century Gateways: Immigrant Incorporation in Suburban America*. Washington, DC: Brookings Institution Press.

Skocpol, T. and Somers, M. (1980) "The uses of comparative history in macrosocial inquiry" *Comparative Studies in Society and History* 22(2): 174–97.

Small, M. L. (2009) "'How many cases do I need?' On science and the logic of case selection in field based research" *Ethnography* 10(1): 5–38.

Solari, C. (2006) "Professionals and saints: How immigrant careworkers negotiate gendered identities at work" *Gender & Society* 20(3): 301–31.

Soysal, Y. N. (1994) *Limits of Citizenship: Migrants and Postnational Membership in Europe*. Chicago, IL: University of Chicago Press.

Varsanyi, M. (ed.) (2010) *Taking Local Control: Immigration Policy Activism in US Cities and States*. Palo Alto, CA: Stanford University Press.

47

Action research with immigrants

Working with vulnerable immigrant communities

Rigoberto Rodriguez

Introduction

Public, private, non-profit, and public organizations are increasingly using Action Research (AR) to engage individuals and communities to address problems that affect their well-being (Dick 2006, 2009). The proliferating use of AR raises questions about whether there is alignment between the interests of organizations sponsoring AR projects and the communities involved in these projects. Over a decade ago, Hagey (1997, p. 2) called attention to the abuses of AR, especially by principal investigators serving as agents for powers interested in managing the community, infantilizing community leaders and belittling their problem-solving skills, and turning local leaders and young people into research assistants while wresting away their control over the research project. In addition to manipulation, organizations can use AR projects to reinforce political ideologies that marginalize immigrant communities. My research with Mexican immigrants involved in AR projects sponsored by state-organized, private–public partnerships revealed that immigrants were being trained to support, rather than to challenge, broader neo-liberal and neo-conservative political projects that marginalize them (Rodriguez 2007).

A critical examination of AR with immigrants is in order because of the vulnerability of immigrants in a profoundly and persistently antagonistic political environment. As much as immigrants are now a permanent feature of today's highly industrialized societies, so is the nativist and vitriolic discourse that continuously legitimizes the use punitive public policies against working class, vulnerable immigrant populations (Castles and Miller 1998; Castles and Davidson 2000). This anti-immigrant discourse pejoratively casts immigrants as "illegal aliens," that is, as undeserving noncitizens without the right to demand better social conditions (Rosaldo 1997; Chavez 2001, 2008).

This article calls for a normative stance on the use of AR methods when working with vulnerable immigrant communities to ensure that social justice guides the design and implementation of AR projects. AR practitioners should use AR methods that help immigrants build greater legitimacy as social actors in an anti-immigrant context and help them to demand better conditions by challenging practices, politics, and people that weaken their political, civil, and social rights. AR methods that do not advance the legitimacy and interests of immigrants as social actors should not be used, or at the very least should be supplemented by AR strategies that bolster the position of immigrants in society.

There are three issues with the AR scholarship and among AR practitioners, however, that make it challenging to adopt a more normative stance in the use of AR methods with immigrants. First, AR scholars have justifiably resisted making strong demarcations between different AR methods, but taking this position creates a situation where any AR method might be viewed as "good enough" when working with immigrants. Second, the AR literature focused on immigrants generally fails to link the everyday problems faced by immigrants to the broader anti-immigrant ideologies and public policies that actively marginalize them. Finally, at the level of practice, organizations sponsoring AR with immigrant communities are often unaware of the differences between and among AR methods, and can place constraints on the use of AR methods that strengthen immigrant communities.

The first part of this article provides a brief overview of the AR scholarship, showing that the field has avoided drawing hard distinctions between different AR approaches. I propose distinguishing AR methods based on what they conceive as the root cause of the problems that immigrants experience: individual behavior; system fragmentation; or social inequality. The second section shows how the AR immigrant-focused literature tends to define immigrants' needs with little reference to the broader anti-immigrant cultural politics and public policies that create many of everyday problems faced by immigrants. Using a theory of citizenship that shows the connection between anti-immigrant cultural politics and public policies and how these turn Mexican immigrants into a vulnerable group in the United States, I argue that Participatory Action Research (PAR) methods should be used with vulnerable immigrant groups, unless otherwise justified.

In the third section, I present a case study to illustrate how organizations sponsoring AR projects with immigrants can often drive the choice over the AR method, placing many constraints on AR practitioners and immigrant communities in terms of using the PAR approach. This case study also shows how PAR methods were infused into a planning process in order to bolster the legitimacy and power of immigrants as social actors, or "citizens," in a way that the original AR method could not do. The conclusion presents three general lines of inquiry pertaining to the use of PAR with vulnerable immigrant communities.

Action research: definition, tenets, methods, and approaches

AR is an umbrella term referring to various methods that engage people and communities in the research process leading to actions that address problems affecting them. AR today is used across many academic disciplines and in a rich variety of organizational and community settings. However, until recently, AR has been a marginal approach in the broader social sciences, in part due to constraints to institutionalizing AR into academia, such as the Institutional Review Board processes (Greenwood and Levin 1998; Stoecker 2008).

Most AR projects rely on four interlocking tenets of active participation, critical knowledge attainment, social action and change, and empowerment (Greenwood and Levin 1998; Stringer 2007; McIntyre 2008; Velde *et al.* 2009). First, AR requires the active participation of people impacted by an issue. AR democratizes the research process by substantially including local stakeholders as co-researchers who collaboratively choose and define a problem relevant to their lives and jointly design the research activities. The selected problem needs to be relevant to participants' lives to engage and sustain individual and/or collective action leading to useful solutions that benefit the people involved (Greenwood and Levin 1998; Stringer 2007; Velde *et al.* 2009).

Second, AR should lead to greater and more critical knowledge attainment with regards to the chosen problem(s). AR assumes that ordinary people possess complex forms of social knowledge to navigate everyday life. AR practitioners use various qualitative and quantitative methods to help people examine and demystify the connections between practices, programs, and policies to determine what is causing the specific conditions impacting their lives.

Third, AR is geared toward social action and change. AR cannot only be about academic critique; it is about turning people's complex social knowledge into practical strategies and actions to spur transformation of programs, systems, and policies. To this end, the intended outcome of the social change effort is "increased well-being—economic, political, psychological, spiritual—of human persons and communities" (Greenwood and Levin 1998; Reason and Bradbury 2006).

Finally, AR promotes the empowerment of people involved in the process. AR cannot resolve all problems; indeed many AR projects never achieve their intended goals (Greenwood and Levin 1998; Stringer 2007). However, an AR project should build the capacity of individuals and communities to enact social change whether or not they are able to eliminate a problem (Velde *et al.* 2009). At the end of an AR project, a community should have a greater understanding of a problem, a commitment to change it, and a stronger network of allies to impact that problem in the future (Hagey 1997; Stringer 2007; McIntyre 2008).

AR projects, moreover, tend to unfold along a similar set of steps across different contexts. For Stringer (2007) the action research process consists of three steps: look, think, and act. "Look" involves gathering relevant data to build a snapshot of the current situation. "Think" focuses on exploring, analyzing, interpreting, explaining, and theorizing about the current situation (Why are things as they are?). "Act" includes planning and implementing action, along with ongoing evaluation activities. This road map is similar to Suárez-Balcázar's (2009) four-step process of (a) reflection, values, and service needs; (b) identification of community health service needs; (c) brainstorm and identify solutions; and (d) engage in action planning and taking action.

These research and action steps do not necessarily transpire in a linear, sequential fashion. Rather, AR projects are more like a "recursive process that involves a spiral of adaptable steps" (McIntyre 2008: 2). Given the wide variety of contexts within which AR projects occur, McIntyre (2008, pp. 2–3) believes that:

> there is no fixed formula for designing, practicing, and implementing [AR] projects … Rather, there is malleability in how [AR] processes are framed and carried out. In part, that is owing to the fact that [AR] practitioners … , some of whom are community insiders and others who come from outside the community, draw from a variety of theoretical and ideological perspectives that inform their practice.

The view that there is no fixed method or formula for AR projects seems to pervade the broader scholarship, which generally avoids drawing rigid methodological distinctions between and among the broader AR field. McIntyre (2008: 206), for instance, maintains that "similarities [in AR methods] provide a foundation for communication and trust; differences offer possibilities for mutual learning and development." Avoiding rigid demarcations among AR methods is probably driven by a desire to keep the AR field focused on social change, rather than become entangled in theoretical and methodological concerns that are typically the grist of traditional social science disciplines. However, the lack of clear distinctions between approaches and methods raises a problem for AR practitioners working with immigrants: How do practitioners choose an AR method when working with vulnerable immigrants?

I differentiate between three kinds AR methods based on what they assume to be the root cause of the problem(s) that people experience. One set of AR methods assumes that the root cause of a problem is the individual's behavior. This can be seen in health programs that link individual lifestyle choices to health outcomes. For example, a community health program focused on diabetes management can consist of a dynamic and participatory educational work-shop that helps individuals with low literacy skills to learn more about effective nutritional and physical activities (Minkler and Wallerstein 2008). Changing the individual's knowledge, atti-tude, skills, and beliefs through dynamic, action research methods can lead to behaviors that produce better health outcomes for individuals. This individual-level explanation of problems anchors many health and human services programs that use participatory methods to improve health outcomes.

Another set of AR methods assumes that the primary cause behind everyday problems is the fragmentation of social systems. These AR methods are largely inspired by systems theory for organizational and community development (Greenwood and Levin 1998; Weisbord and Janoff 2010). Systems theorists postulate that the lack of effective coordination, communication, and collaboration among various sectors is often the cause of community problems. Accordingly, the solution to these problems rests in organizing a multi-stakeholder process that brings together individuals from different parts of a system to solve an issue collectively. Stakeholders include people with the authority to make institutional decisions, people with technical expertise per-taining to a specific problem, and individuals who will be impacted by the decisions to be made (Weisbord and Janoff 2010). This multi-stakeholder process is bolstered by robust facilitation to ensure effective communication and to build trust, so that people who typically do not interact with each other are able to understand each other's perspective and build more comprehensive and effective solutions.

A third set of AR methods assumes that social inequality is at the root of the problems that communities face in their everyday lives. Social problems are a manifestation of the over-concentration of political, economic, and cultural resources in the hands of political, economic, and technical elites. The inequitable distribution of resources generates debilitating and oppres-sive conditions for some groups. PAR typically begins by identifying a group that is oppressed by systems of exploitation, racism, sexism, and other social structures, and helps the marginalized group(s) experience empowerment by calling attention to racism, discrimination, and other social structures responsible for the conditions and problems they face. Hagey (1997: 2) believes that an essential step in a PAR project is conducting a power analysis using specific concepts that acknowledge institutional responsibility in creating conditions that must be rectified, such as "restitution" or "procedural justice," which acknowledge:

> how relationships are lived, how interactions exclude or refrain from including, how par-ticular elite individuals holding office practice dominance and perpetuate systemic dis-advantage, how racism hurts and humiliates and is denied, how its perpetrators are unwilling to examine their own practices and how resistance to change is manifested … or when institutions have righteous sounding policies that they do not put into daily practice.

Which of these three AR approaches should AR practitioners choose when working with immigrants? There is certainly a place for each of the three AR approaches in working with immigrant communities. Sometimes, the root cause of a problem does lie in the behaviors of individuals or in the lack of effective systems coordination. However, for AR scholars who believe that social inequality is the primary cause of the multiple problems faced by immigrant communities, PAR should be considered the "best practice" unless otherwise justified.

PAR with vulnerable immigrants: social groups and citizenship

What has kept AR scholars and practitioners from calling for the use of PAR as the norm when working with immigrants? In my estimation, the AR literature with immigrants tends to describe the problems impacting immigrants without reference to social inequality as the root cause of their problems. This tendency is illustrated in the following four articles that are fairly representative of the broader literature on AR with immigrants.

The first article is from Balcázar et al. (2009), who developed the Concerns Report Method (CRM) as a systematic participatory process for setting agendas for community change from the perspective of those who share a common predicament. Community members take an active role in developing the community concerns survey through focus groups and interviews with leaders and service providers. They produce a prioritized list of strengths and needs to facilitate agenda setting that can inform policies, services, and programs and to provide evidence for planning new services. Their article, however, does not discuss the relationship between social inequality and the problems identified by immigrants, nor does it discuss the immigrant community's lack of political power to advocate for new services. How will immigrants pressure local authorities for new services without political clout?

Similarly, Ataov et al. (2010: 3) discuss an AR project that sought to integrate immigrants into work life in more meaningful ways in Norway. The AR practitioners used democratic dialogue with different stakeholders at the work site to enhance the environment for greater and dignified integration of immigrants. Their AR project produced encouraging results, demonstrating that intentional dialogue can help create a better work life for immigrants. The article, however, does not discuss the root causes of immigrant worker exploitation in everyday work life. It does not name the labor market dynamics that impact immigrants, such as depressed wages, poor working conditions, discriminatory hiring practices, and so on (Waldinger and Lichter 2003). The article suggests that robust communication, not necessarily structural reform, is sufficient to improve work life conditions for immigrants.

Along the same lines, in an ethnographic AR project with transnational migrants, Sánchez (2009) finds that transnationalism can help immigrants maintain a connection between two or more places without having to sever ties to their countries of origin. Maintaining linguistic and cultural practices gives immigrants a wealth of knowledge that can support AR projects to navigate across borders. This article, however, does not show how these transnational networks and practices are impacted by oppressive social structures that immigrants face in both the country of origin and of destination. As Fox and Rivera-Salgado (2004) show with indigenous migrants from Oaxaca, Mexico, some immigrant communities face racially oppressive and economically exploitative contexts across *Oaxacalifornia,* a social space that runs from Oaxaca and Baja California, Mexico, and California, United States.

These immigrant-focused AR articles, in other words, define immigrants more as a "population" than a "social group." Young (1990) defines a "population" as an abstract concept that can be constructed on the basis of a variable, such as being foreign born. Populations can be constructed without reference to power relationships or social structures that shape the experiences and identity of social groups. By contrast, a social group refers to a community with a shared identity that emerges historically in relationship to other social groups and within specific social structures. A social structure consists of dominant discourses, public policies, and institutional practices that variously empower or disempower social groups.

A notable exception in the AR immigrant literature is Cahill's (2010) article focused on Mexican immigrant youth in Utah. Cahill (2010: 152) describes a PAR project where young immigrant Latinos/as interpreted their personal experiences of marginalization in relation to a broader anti-immigrant discourse. The article shows how Latino/a immigrant youth critically examined and rejected an ideology that defined them as S.W.I.N.E. (Stupid. Wetbacks. Infecting. Nearly. Everyone!!!)—which referred to the "swine flu" epidemic that received a lot of media attention in 2009. The problem with Cahill's article is that she draws only on cultural theory to explain the PAR process. While Anzaldúa's (1987) border culture theory helps understand the anti-immigrant cultural politics and how these impact people from a particular social group, it does not help explain how these cultural politics also provide legitimacy to public policies that create and reinforce an oppressive social structure.

It is important to connect cultural politics and public policies together in order to understand the unequal social structure that turns immigrants into a vulnerable social group. Connecting cultural politics and public policies can be done through a theory of citizenship. Nakano-Glen (2002), in particular, views citizenship as a cultural, political, and legal institution that is actively deployed to establish and regulate a social group's standing in a nation based on the ideologies of race, class, and gender. For Schneider and Ingram (1997), moreover, the social construction of a social group as "undesirable" citizens (through cultural politics) legitimizes the use of punitive public policies directed at them.

This theory of citizenship helps explain why immigrants develop different social group identities through their experience of the social structures in the country of destination. Some immigrant groups might be viewed in positive terms, as desirable citizens, and experience a relatively welcoming social structure. This was largely the case with Cuban exiles in the early 1960s that came into the United States at the height of the Cold War (Garcia 1996; Gonzalez 2011). Other immigrant groups, however, experienced a harsher social structure upon arrival. This was the case with Cuban refugees from the Mariel boat lift of the 1990s, who were from a lower economic group, predominantly non-white, and were labeled as "criminals" (Garcia 1996; Gonzalez 2011). This group did not receive the government benefits of prior Cuban migrants.

That contemporary citizenship politics produce social structures that make immigrant groups vulnerable is clearly evidenced by the recent experiences of Mexican immigrants in the United States. Mexican immigrants are the largest foreign-born population in the United States (Ruggles *et al.* 2010) and have been at the epicenter of contemporary anti-immigrant cultural politics and public policies in the United States. Chavez (2001 2008) has documented the formation of a specifically anti-Mexican immigrant discourse over the last 30 years depicting Mexican immigrants as criminals, invaders, disease bearers, and welfare users. These images are encapsulated in the dehumanizing term, "illegal alien." The image of non-citizen, criminals is also laced with a discourse of the "underclass," which invokes images of gang members, drug traffickers, and welfare dependents bearing multiple "social pathologies" emanating from a "culture of poverty" (Hayes-Bautista 2004).

Even though many studies show that Mexican immigrants have relatively low rates of welfare dependency and high levels of workforce participation (Hayes-Bautista 2004), the anti-Mexican immigrant popular ideologies have persisted and legitimized three general kinds of punitive policies at the federal, state, and local level that marginalize Mexican immigrants. Some of these public policies restrict access to government benefits and public institutions. The Personal Responsibility and Work Opportunity Reconciliation Act (1996) and Illegal Immigration Reform and Immigrant Responsibility Act (1996) are two pieces of federal legislation that, among other draconian measures, further restricted immigrants' access to public benefits. These federal policies attempted to enact at the federal level what California's Proposition 187 (1994) was unable to do. Proposition 187 was a ballot initiative passed by Californian voters to prohibit "illegal" immigrants from using health care, public education, and other social services in California. It was ruled unconstitutional.

Other public policies have intensified the enforcement of federal immigration laws. This includes a litany of border militarization programs across different states bordering Mexico, including: San Diego, California (1994)—"Operation Gatekeeper"; El Paso, Texas (1993)—"Operation Blockade/Hold the Line"; Southern Arizona (1994)—"Safeguard"; and South Texas (1997)—Rio Grande. Enforcement strategies also include the delegation of federal authority to local law enforcement via 287(g) (Nevins 2002) and the Secure Communities Program that uses greater federal–local collaboration to identify "high priority" criminal undocumented immigrants. Enforcement also includes E-Verify, a program requiring businesses to file the Social Security Numbers of employees or risk losing their business licenses. (Social Security Numbers are needed in order to work lawfully in the United States.)

A third set of policies include a host of state laws and local ordinances that place additional restrictions on the everyday life of undocumented immigrants. In my work across Southern California working with Mexican immigrant communities, it is not uncommon to hear the following experiences of undocumented immigrants. Undocumented immigrants find it very difficult to obtain a job because they lack proper authorization to work. Finding a job itself is challenging, whether as a day laborer or domestic worker. If they are hired, they are vulnerable to labor exploitation in terms of low wages, poor working conditions, unstable work, and a lack of health insurance. If they work in the informal economy as street vendors, they are often harassed by city and county officials due to a lack of business permits. In California, moreover, undocumented immigrants are prohibited from obtaining a driver's license. So, if they need to drive a car to get to work, they are exposed to predatory lending when purchasing a car or car insurance. If stopped by local law enforcement for minor traffic infractions, their cars are impounded or immobilized. Depending on the city where they are stopped, the local police officers can request their immigration papers.

In short, the anti-immigrant cultural politics and the federal, state, and local policies they have ushered in together form a social structure that on a daily basis places immigrants in a vulnerable situation. However, perhaps the most deleterious impact of this social structure is that it actively erodes the legitimacy of the immigrant group's right to make claims for better conditions. Defined as "illegal aliens," Mexican immigrants are perceived as lacking the basic civil right to demand better conditions because they should not be in the United States "in the first place." As Rosaldo (1997) argues, these discourses and policies curtail social rights, i.e., the very right to have access to educational, health, housing, employment, and other resources that can enable them to be active citizens in a democratic society.

The everyday problems that immigrants face cannot be divorced from broader social structures. The pervasiveness of anti-immigrant discourses and policies that render immigrants vulnerable supports the normative claim that AR methods with immigrants need to connect the everyday problems to social inequality. Consequently, AR approaches need to help immigrants address the causes that make them vulnerable in the first place and to restore the legitimacy of immigrants as civic actors with the right to demand better conditions. In the following section, I offer a case study that illustrates how the choice of an AR method can make a difference in restoring the right of vulnerable immigrants to engage and demand better conditions. The case study also demonstrates the importance of paying greater attention to on-the-ground dynamics between and among organizations sponsoring AR projects. Sometimes, organizations that sponsor AR projects in immigrant communities are not aware of the difference that AR methods make in working with vulnerable immigrant communities.

Improving health in Boyle Heights, California

This case study describes an AR project to improve the health conditions in Boyle Heights, a predominantly Mexican-American and Mexican immigrant community located in east Los

Angeles, California. Home to approximately 90,000 residents, Boyle Heights is nestled at the intersection of the 5, 10, 60, and 101 Freeways, perhaps the busiest freeway intersection in the United States. The freeway exhaust, coupled with street traffic and emissions from the local industrial buildings, generates very high levels of air pollution, causing inordinately high levels of asthma. The community also suffers from insufficient or inadequate safety, park space, grocery stores with healthy and affordable food options, effective public transportation systems, high-performing schools, health clinics, well-paying jobs with health insurance, accessible quality housing, and other important resources that promote a good quality of life for families.

Over the past 20 years or so, community organizing agencies have emerged to improve these conditions. These organizations include East Los Angeles Community Corporation (www.elacc.org), Inner City Struggle (www.innercitystruggle.org), *Proyecto Pastoral* (www.proyectopastoral.org), and *Unión de Vecinos* (www.uniondevecinos.org). These organizations use community organizing strategies to change public policies and transform systems they consider are the root causes of the neighborhood conditions. These organizations have variously invested in developing a base of grassroots leaders and social and political networks in the neighborhood in order to mobilize them around specific campaigns to improve housing, education, environmental, or other conditions.

In 2009, the largest health foundation in California, The California Endowment (TCE), selected Boyle Heights as the location of a long-term project to improve the health of the community. TCE selected Boyle Heights and 13 other sites throughout California as part of a broader shift toward place-based approaches to healthy communities. This place-based strategy is based on the theory of the social determinants of health and environment, which argues that social, political, and economic processes, either individually or together, interact with the built environment (e.g., land use, transportation systems, and physical structures) to influence a population's health and well-being (Schultz and Northridge 2004). TCE modified this model by including safety and education (Davis *et al.* 2009).

Like the community organizing agencies, TCE understood that policies and systems are often the source of health problems. Using a public health approach, TCE wanted to address the root causes of problems "upstream" (i.e., policies and systems) instead of simply ameliorating the symptoms of the problems "downstream" (i.e., individual behaviors). Recognizing that changing policies and systems is a long-term endeavor, TCE committed to funding local and regional change efforts for a 10-year period, at approximately $2–$3 million per year in Boyle Heights, pending the availability of funds. It also committed to leveraging funds from other sources. To receive funding, the Boyle Heights community needed to produce a strategic plan to transform public policies and systems to improve the community's health. TCE required that community residents be actively engaged in the planning process and throughout the initiative.

On paper, the alignment between TCE and community organizing agencies in Boyle Heights seemed like a dream come true, especially because most foundations tend to fund services to change individual behaviors, rather than to encourage community organizing efforts to try to change systems and policies.

However, TCE established additional parameters to the AR process that threatened to dilute the leadership role of residents and community organizations. Based on experiences with prior projects and additional data analysis, TCE selected 10 health outcomes through a top-down process. Communities were invited to partner with TCE, but communities had to agree to target these 10 outcomes: (1) all children have health coverage; (2) families have improved access to a "health home" that supports healthy behaviors; (3) health and family-focused human services shift resources toward prevention; (4) residents live in communities with health-promoting land use, transportation, and community; (5) children and families are safe from

571

violence in their homes and neighborhoods; (6) communities support healthy youth development; (7) neighborhood and school environments support improved health and healthy behaviors; (8) community health improvements are linked to economic development; (9) health
gaps for boys and young men of color are narrowed; and (10) California has a shared vision of
community health (Anzaldúa 1987). Although TCE's outcomes might be very relevant to the
lives of Boyle Heights residents, TCE's top-down process contradicted the bottom-up approach
of PAR projects, which typically begin with a bottom-up process to build understanding,
ownership, and commitment to change.

In addition, the term "outcome" stems from the professional fields of evaluation research and
health and human services and refers to the overall result of an intervention (Patton 2002).
Importantly, the term "outcome" is a critical element of a larger "logic modeling" method that
includes other constructs, such as "target changes," "strategies," "resources and capacities," and a
theory of "adaptive leadership." The logic modeling process served as the blueprint for the AR
process: local participants were supposed to begin with the end in mind (i.e., the outcome) and
then identify the strategies that would produce target changes, followed by resources and
capacities to support the strategies (Minkler and Wallerstein 2008).

The term "outcome" and the "logic modeling" process was a relatively new and technical
term for the community organizing agencies and the resident leaders they work with. How
could neighborhood residents know what strategies or target changes to select when they
played no role in determining the outcomes in the first place?

In addition to the more or less unfamiliar logic modeling process, TCE also required the
involvement of multiple stakeholder groups throughout the planning process. Communities
were asked to reach out to groups in the fields of health, mental health, education, housing,
transportation, and so on. In this multi-stakeholder process, a person who worked in a health
and human service agency could have as much of a say as a resident impacted by the issues. The
assumption was that professional stakeholders had the same interests as the residents. Yet, the
technical logic modeling process itself arguably privileged professionals with the technical
know-how within these fields. This is important to underscore because, from a PAR perspective, these professionals were part of institutions whose systems and policies disadvantage the
communities in the first place.

Residents and community organizing agencies were supposed to work actively to achieve
outcomes they had no role in shaping; they were supposed to attempt to change policies and
systems using an unfamiliar "logic modeling" framework; and they were supposed to work
within a multi-stakeholder process that advantaged professionals over residents and community
organizing agencies. TCE also retained the power to accept, reject, and fund some strategies
over others at the end of the process. Admittedly, community residents and organizations could
choose not to participate, but doing so would mean losing $2–3 million per year for 10 years of
TCE investments, plus the additional funds it promised to leverage.

I want to emphasize that in my estimation TCE did not actually intend to create these
conditions of inequality for residents and community organizing agencies. TCE seemed truly
committed to resident empowerment. However, as one of the facilitators of the planning process in Boyle Heights, I saw the contradiction between the organization's altruistic purpose and
the AR method it set in motion at the ground level in this specific community. TCE used an
AR method that presupposed that systems fragmentation was the root cause of the health
conditions, rather than a method based on social inequality as a root cause. This is evidenced by
the fact that TCE did not require communities to use a power analysis to understand the differential power relations within and among the collaborative partners, or to view social
inequality as the root cause. (To its credit, after the planning process ended, TCE has adopted

and promoted "structural racialization" as theory to understand how institutions shape the conditions that low-income residents face.)

The political and practical challenge faced at the ground level was not so much how to change the AR method, because this was already set. The challenge was how to infuse PAR principles into an AR project bereft of a theory of social inequality. How could we make sure that community residents, predominantly Spanish-speaking Mexican immigrants, strengthened their position within this AR project? How could we structure power relations within the collaborative to ensure that residents were leading the AR project?

Community residents, community organizing agencies, and social services professionals held a number of intense deliberations around this issue. The result of these debates was a theory of change, a governance structure, management and coordination committees, and learning structures that altogether helped community residents play a significant leadership role throughout the planning process, than it would have been possible otherwise.

A "theory of change" crystallizes the core assumptions guiding an initiative or intervention (Minkler and Wallerstein 2008). The Boyle Heights group agreed that in order to implement the Boyle Heights community plan to achieve the TCE outcomes, neighborhood residents needed to lead the process, with the support of community organizations, service organizations and public agencies. This theory of change was a fundamental moment in introducing PAR principles, for it placed Boyle Heights residents—mostly Spanish-speaking Mexican immigrants—as the leading force or decision-makers of the AR initiative.

The group used this theory of change to craft a governance structure that differentially enfranchised stakeholders based on residency in Boyle Heights. The governance structure consisted of a "General Body" with the ultimate authority over the content of the community plan. General Body members were either "decision-makers" or "supportive partners." A "decision-maker" was either a person or an organization with the power to veto any given proposal. To be a decision-maker, a person needed to be a Boyle Heights resident and attend a certain amount and percent of General Body meetings during the planning process. A community organization could also be a decision-maker if it was located in Boyle Heights and dedicated at least 51 percent of its budget to the Boyle Heights community.

"Supportive partners," on the other hand, referred to every other person or organization serving the neighborhood but not meeting the above criteria. These supportive partners could be businesses, nonprofits or public institutions, such as City and County agencies, schools, and other representatives. Supportive partners could participate at all levels of the planning process, providing ideas, making recommendations, and debating points, but in the end could not veto a proposal. This governance structure essentially enfranchised residents and community organizations as citizens, with decision-making powers. Residents were not just co-researchers in the process; they were place-based citizens.

In addition, the Boyle Heights group established management and coordination committees to support broad-based community engagement. The Steering Committee was responsible for ensuring that the planning process adhered to the theory of change and the original work plan. If the planning process deviated from the original work plan, the Steering Committee needed to present the changes to General Body for authorization. The Community Engagement and Youth Engagement Committees identified, engaged, and supported adult and youth resident participation by providing an array of supports, such as child watch, translation, food, transportation, mentoring, coaching, trainings, among other resources.

Finally, to make sure that community residents had a deep understanding of the 10 outcomes to meaningfully complete the logic modeling process, multiple sessions were held to reinterpret the "outcomes" in the everyday language of community residents. The 10 outcomes were re-articulated and clustered into three content areas: (a) health and access to health systems; (b) community development; (c) youth, schools, and neighborhoods. A work group was formed for each area. Protocols and participation principles were crafted to make sure that youth and adult voices were honored during the work group sessions. Protocols included having a youth, adult, and organizational staff as co-facilitators of the work groups. Stipends were offered to the youth and adult resident co-facilitators, and along with individualized support, such as transportation, coaching, and mentoring so that youth and adult resident co-facilitators strengthened their role as the planning progressed. Participation principles included asking youth and adult residents to speak first, before organizational staff could speak.

The AR project lasted close to 18 months and involved over 1,300 community residents participating in various deliberative meetings. At least 300 neighborhood residents were active decision-makers in the General Body meetings. The planning process culminated with a unanimous consensus in support of the Boyle Heights community plan.

Conclusion: future lines of inquiry

This case study illustrated the significance of using PAR as a normative approach to AR with vulnerable immigrants. Infusing PAR principles into this local AR project amplified the role of neighborhood residents from "co-researchers" to "decision-makers" in this multi-stakeholder process. PAR principles also led the collaborative to establish a robust planning infrastructure consisting of management, coordination, and learning structures to foster substantial input. Ultimately, the AR project positioned Mexican immigrants as "citizens" in this place-based planning process.

This case study also highlights the need to pursue at least three lines of inquiry with regards to AR with immigrants. Although my argument is that PAR should be used as the norm when working with vulnerable immigrants, I believe that future research can focus on various AR methods to better assess their relative strengths and limitations in working vulnerable immigrants. Under what conditions can PAR principles be infused into other AR methods when working with immigrants? Are there conditions under which PAR does not offer the best option?

A second line of inquiry concerns the strengths and limitations of place-based initiatives and their ability to "empower" Mexican immigrants. Place-based initiatives seem to be increasing in number in Los Angeles, across California, and nationally. What are the specific AR methods ad principles that can help immigrant residents of these neighborhoods play a decision-making role, not merely co-researcher, in these place-based initiatives? When should sponsoring organizations step in or out of the AR process to support the empowerment of immigrants? How can we use place-based citizenship as springboard to amplify the citizenship of immigrants in broader society?

The third line of inquiry has to do with the multi-stakeholder institutional terrain upon which these AR projects are often conducted. These multi-stakeholder planning processes are sites of potentially new discursive formations, strategy development, and emergent practices that can generate new ways to solve problems and perhaps point to new cultural politics and public policies. What criteria or process can be used to ensure that the institutional interests of various stakeholders are transparent and contribute to advancing the interests of vulnerable immigrants?

References and further reading

Anzaldúa, G. (1987) *Borderlands La Frontera: The New Mestiza*, San Francisco, CA, Aunt Lute Book Company.
Balcazar, F. E., Garcia-Iriarte, E., and Suarez-Balcazar, Y. (2009) "Participatory action research with Colombian immigrants" *Hispanic Journal of Behavioral Sciences* 31(1): 112–27.

Castles, S. and Davidson, A. (2000) *Citizenship and Migration: Globalization and the Politics of Belonging*. New York: Routledge.

Castles, S. and Miller, M. J. (1998) *The Age of Migration: International Populations Movements in the Modern World*. New York: The Guilford Press.

Chavez, L. R. (2001) *Covering Immigration: Popular Images and the Politics of the Nation*. Berkeley and Los Angeles, CA, University of California, Press.

——(2008) *The Latino Threat: Constructing Immigrants, Citizens, and the Nation*. Stanford, CA: Stanford University Press.

Davis, L. M., Kilburn, M. R., and Schultz, D. J. (2009) *Reparable Harm: Assessing and Addressing Disparities Faced by Boys and Men of Color in California*. Santa Monica, CA: RAND.

Dick, B. (2006) "Action research literature 2004–6: Themes and trends" *Action Research* 4(4): 439–58.

——(2009) "Action research literature 2006–8: Themes and trends" *Action Research* 7(4): 423–41.

Fox, J. and Rivera-Salgado, G. (eds) (2004) *Indigenous Mexican Migrants in the United States*. University of California, San Diego, CA: Center for US-Mexican Studies and the Center for Comparative Immigration Studies.

Garcia, M. C. (1996) *Havana USA: Cuban Exiles and Cuban Americans in South Florida, 1959–1994*. Los Angeles, CA: University of California Press.

Glenn, E. N. (2002) *Unequal Freedom: How Race and Gender Shaped American Citizenship and Labor*. Cambridge, MA: Harvard University Press.

Gonzalez, J. (2011) *Harvest of Empire: A History of Latinos in America*. London: Penguin Books.

Greenwood, D. J. and Levin, M. (1998) *Introduction to Action Research: Social Research for Social Change*. Thousand Oaks, CA: Sage Publications, Inc.

Hagey, R. S. (1997) "The use and abuse of participatory action research" *Chronic Diseases in Canada* 18(1): 1–4.

Hayes-Bautista, D. E. (2004) *La Nueva California: Latinos in the Golden State*. Berkeley, CA: University of California Press.

McIntyre, A. (2008) *Participatory Action Research*. Thousand Oaks, CA: Sage Publications, Inc.

Minkler, M. and Wallerstein, N. (eds) (2008) *Community-based Participatory Research for Health: From Process to Outcomes*. San Francisco, CA: Jossey-Bass.

Nevins, J. (2002) *Operation Gatekeeper: The Rise of the "Illegal Alien" and the Making of the US-Mexico Boundary*. New York: Routledge.

Patton, M. Q. (2002) *Qualitative Research and Evaluation Methods*. Thousand Oaks, CA: Sage Publications, Inc.

Reason, P. and Bradbury, H. (eds) (2006) *Handbook of Action Research*. London: Sage Publications.

Rodriguez, R. (2007) *Enterprising Citizenship: Mexican Immigrant Empowerment and Public-private Partnerships in Santa Ana, California*. Ph.D Dissertation, University of Southern California.

Rosaldo, R. (1997) "Cultural citizenship, inequality, and multiculturalism". In W. V. Flores and R. Benmayor (eds), *Latino Cultural Citizenship*. Boston, MA: Beacon Press, pp. 27–38.

Ruggles, S., Alexander, J. T., Genadek, K., Goeken, R., Schroeder, M. B., and Sobek, M. (2010, 2011). *Statistical Portrait of the Foreign-Born Population in the United States*, 2009. February 17, Pew Hispanic Center.

Sánchez, P. (2009) "Chicana feminist strategies in a participatory action research project with transnational Latina youth" *New Directions for Youth Development* 2009(123): 83–97.

Schneider, A. L. and Ingram, H. (1997) *Policy Design For Democracy*. Lawrence, KA: University Press of Kansas.

Schultz, A. and Northridge, M. E. (2004) "Social determinants of health: Implications for environmental health promotion" *Health Education and Behavior* 31(4): 455–71.

Stoecker, R. (2008) "Challenging institutional barriers to community-based research" *Action Reseach* 6(1): 49–67.

Stringer, T. E. (2007) *Action Research*. Los Angeles, CA: Sage Publications.

Velde, J. V. D., Williamson, D. L., and Ogilvie, L. D. (2009) "Participatory action research: Practical strategies for actively engaging and maintaining participation in immigrant and refugee communities" *Qualitative Health Research* 19(9): 1293–1302.

Waldinger, R. and Lichter, M. I. (2003) *How The Other Half Works: Immigration and the Social Organization of Labor*. Berkeley, CA: University of California Press.

Weisbord, M. and Janoff, S. (2010) *Future Search: Getting the Whole System in the Room for Vision, Commitment, and Action*. San Francisco, CA: Berrett-Koehler Publishers.

Index

Abbink, J. 91
Abrego, L. 363
absent mobilization 342
Abu-Lughod, J.L. 80
academic discourse on climate change 35
academic expectations of migrants' children 315
academic language acquisition 274
academic research, photography in 534
acculturation: complex processes of 40; education
  and immigration 397; group and individual
  phenomenon 39–40; structural assimilation and
  309; theories of 308–10; theories of,
  psychological acculturation and 38–39; see also
  psychological acculturation
Acosta, K.L. 291, 292
action research (AR) with immigrants 564–75;
  anti-immigrant cultural politics 570; California
  Endowment (TCE) 571–72, 573; citizenship
  politics 569; citizenship theory 569; citizenship
  theory, Participatory Action Research (PAR)
  and 565, 569; Concerns Report Method
  (CRM) 568; contexts of 566; critical
  knowledge attainment 566; cultural politics,
  public policies and 569–70; definition of AR
  565; demarcations between AR methods 565,
  566; empowerment of people 566;
  ethnographic AR project with transnational
  migrants 568; everyday problems,
  anti-immigrant ideologies and 565; further
  reading 574–75; future lines of inquiry 574;
  improving health in Boyle Heights, California
  570–74; individual behavior, focus on 567;
  methodological differences and constraints on
  uses of 565; Mexican immigrant youth in Utah
  568–69; normative stance in use of 564–65;
  Participatory Action Research (PAR) 565, 567,

568, 569, 572, 573, 574; procedural justice 567;
process of 566; public policies, intensification of
federal immigration laws and 569–70;
restitutive justice 567; restrictions on everyday
life of undocumented immigrants 570; social
action and change 566; social groups, PAR
with 568–74; social inequality, focus on 567;
social system fragmentation, focus on 567;
tenets, interlocking of AR 565; vulnerability of
immigrants 564; vulnerable immigrants, PAR
with 568–74; welfare dependency 569;
workforce participation 569
Adamo, S.B. 30
adaptation: measurements of 312; migration as 30;
of new second generation 397; return
migration and 466–67; well-being of
immigrants, decline in 404
Adepoju, A. 89, 90
Adler, N.J. 157
adoption, international 319–30; adoptee
paperwork 322–23; adoptees *versus* other
immigrants 321–23; adoption, critiques of
323–25; adoption flows, gendered 321–22;
adoption flows, socio-historical circumstances
and 320–21; "birth cultures" 325, 326–27;
child trafficking and 324; China, adoption from
323–24, 326; commodification 325; consumer
demand 323; cultural belonging 325–27; Evan
P Donaldson Institute 326; families, adoptee
integration with 323; further reading 329–30;
Hague Adoption Convention (1993) 324;
human rights issue 324–25; hybrid,
border-crossing identities 323; Immigration and
Nationality Act (US, 1965) 322; intercountry
adoptions (ICA) 321; kinship, language of
327–29; national and international regulatory

Ebaugh, H.R. and Chafetz, J.S. 264
Echazarra, A. 212
Ecklund, E.H. 264
ecological analysis, climate change and 29
The Economic Basis of Ethnic Solidarity (Bonacich, E. and Modell, J.) 150
economic perspectives 12–27; cumulative causation theory 19; dual labor market theory 17–18; further reading 25–27; heterogeneity among individuals 14–15; initiating causes, theories of 12–13, 13–15, 15–17, 17–18; institutional theory 20; instrumental variables 21; insurance hypothesis 16; investment hypothesis 16; labor migration theories 12; Lewis model 14; macroeconomic level, migration at 14; macroeconomic variables, correlation between 21–22; migrant remittances 20–24; migrant selection 15; negative selection 15; neoclassical theories 13–15; neoclassical theories, statistical testing of 14; network theory 18–19; new economics of labor migration (NELM) 15–17, 18, 19, 21; positive selection 15; remittances and consumption, correlation between 21–24; reversed causality 20–21; rural–urban migration in developing countries 16–17; segmented labor market (SLM) theory 17–18; self-perpetuating causes, theories of 12, 13, 18–19, 20
economics: economic advantage as motivational factor 157; economic crises 191–92; economic mobility, language acquisition and 271; education and economic expansion in US, era of 308; ethnic economies, coethnic and outgroup labor in 537–38; global economic disparities 100–101; global economy and highly-skilled migration 153; hour-glass economy, restructuring toward 308; human trafficking, factors contributing to 124–25; international migration, considerations and dynamics of 411; labor demands, undocumented migration and 358; nativism, causes of 193–95, 199; political support and economic need for highly-skilled migration 155; pull theories 387; return migration, factors in 461
Eder, D. and Fingerson, L. 513
education and immigration 396–408; acculturation 397; adaptation and well-being of immigrants, decline in 404; adaptation of new second generation 397; assimilationist model, critiques of 399–400; children of immigrants, prospects for 315; Children of Immigrants Longitudinal Study (CILS) 398; Civil Rights Movement 397; Civil Rights Movement, ethos of 397–98; claims and developments 399–403; compulsory education, development of 396; critiques 403–5; cultural capital, familial norms

and 403; decline, representation of mechanisms of 404; education, symbolic weight (and value) of 396, 405–6; education aspirations, legal status and 363; education level and language acquisition 274; educational attainment (and adaptation), patterns of 398–99; formal educational institutions, newcomers' history with 396–97; further reading 407–8; future developments 406; generational decline, focus on 404; generational status 401–2; historical perspective 396–99; identity, construction of 403; immigrant achievement, fascination with 398; intellectual development 396–99; inter-group variation, problem of 404–5; International Comparative Study of Ethnocultural Youth 404; language advantage of second generation 402; Longitudinal Immigrant Student Adaptation Study (LISA) 398; lower income neighborhoods, struggling schools and 401; multiculturalism, debates about 397; relational engagement in school-based relationships 402–3; relevance of issue 405–6; schools, interaction between immigrants and 400; schools, sites for the construction of identity 403; segregation of schools 400–401; social progress, ideological positions about 397
education and migration: educational organizations in ethno-national diasporas 443, 444
Egypt as conduit for refugees and immigrants 91–92
Ehrenreich, B. and Hochschild, A.R. 285
Ehrlich, P. 28
Ehrlich, P.R. and Ehrlich, A.H. 29
Ehrlich, P.R. and Holdren, J.P. 29
Eich-Krohm, Astrid xiii, 130, 153–65
Eitzen, S. 145, 146, 148
Ellis, A. and Wall, A. 417
Eltis, D. 346
e-mailing images 535
embeddedness 60, 100, 129, 130, 232, 234, 253, 265, 409, 415, 456, 488, 560; cultural embeddedness 462, 463–65; naturalization and 383; political sociology of international migration 336–37, 338, 340
emigrant politics 334; emigration policy and 341–42
emigration: in census analysis 477–78; measurement of 478; rights to 412
empathy, cultivation of 498
employment and employment opportunities 14, 44, 57, 68, 82, 108, 112, 113, 116, 124, 126, 138, 154–55, 191, 204, 231, 255–56; Americas, migration history in 68; highly-skilled migration, trends in 155, 156, 157, 160; need for, resettlement policies and 113;

imperial trade in Asia 80–81
incipient diasporas 442–43
inclusion over exclusion 140–41
income and finance, topics of 516
incorporation: of migrants through norms of sexuality, intimacy, and affect 220–21; transnationalism and 450–51
in-depth interviews 500–501, 507–9
indigenous nationalism, migrants and 225–36; ancestral rootedness, native-ness and 228; anti-racism, politics of 228–29; Asian Settler Colonialism in Hawaii (Amerasia) 228, 229; autochthony 226–30; belonging, essentialization of 227; border politics 230; capitalist social relations, imposition of 231; coerced immobility 231; colonialism, understandings of 225, 234–35; colonization of indigenous people 229; common rights 234; cultural differences 232; decolonialism 225–26, 234; expropriation 227, 234; further reading 235–36; global system of power 230, 233; indigeneity, representation of 227–28, 233; national state system, logics of 230; nationalism, native nations and 231–32; nationalist narratives, challenge to 233–35; nativism 227; neo-liberalism 232; neo-racism and conflation of migration and colonialism 231–33; Othering, neo-liberalism and 232–33; postcolonialism 226; "Settlers of color and 'immigrant' hegemony: 'Locals' in Hawaii" (Trask, H.K. in Amerasia) 230; spatial and temporal dependence 227; statist politics 228–29; territorialization of life, significance of 231; territorialized understanding of colonization and imperialism 225–26; traditional differences 232
indirect questions in interviews 516–17
individual panethnicity 243–44
Indo-European speakers 77
Indra, D. 114
industrialization 81, 132, 182, 204, 207, 215, 411, 449, 496; ethno-national diasporas 441; industrial development in Americas 68
inequalities and human trafficking 124–25; see also social inequalities
information technology (IT), introduction of 153
initiating causes, theories of 12–13, 13–15, 15–17, 17–18
insider-outsider status in interviews 511–12
institution building 243, 255–56
institutional completeness 251–52
institutional theory 9, 12, 13, 20, 24
insurance hypothesis 16, 17, 21, 22, 23
Integrated Public-Use Microdata Samples (US) 474
integration: adoptee integration with families 323; European Union (EU) common agenda for 198; families, adoptee integration with 323;

immigrant integration, focus on 185; language acquisition and problems of 271; long-term social integration 115; politics of immigration and 60–62; process of, ethnicity and 156; social cohesion and 445; state provisions and migrant integration policies, relationship between 422–23; trading routes, integration of 78–79; welfare states, socio-economic integration and 428; see also resettlement policies and integration of refugees
intellectual development 396–99
interactivity: ethnicity, community perspective on 250, 255–56, 257–58; online diaspora research 546–47
Interdisciplinary Demographic Institute-Eurostat project (1997–98) 478
internal diversities, panethnicity and 241–43
internal migration: within Africa (since 1960s) 87–93; census analysis 476–77; European migration history 53, 56–58; forced migrants 101
international adoption see adoption, international
international civil society: globalization and 389; naturalization and 388
International Comparative Study of Ethnocultural Youth 404
international corporations' encouragement of highly skilled migration 153
international flows of human trafficking 120–21, 123–24
international human rights law 108, 140, 198, 352
International Justice Mission (IJM) 119
international migration: causes and consequences of 2; census analysis 475–76; forms of 1–2; psychological acculturation and 40; research on, trends in 252–54; sending state and 411
International Migration Review (IMR) 180, 181
International Organization for Migration (IOM) 1
International Visual Sociology Association 531
internet: growth in use of 543; immigration scholarship, internet and changes in 543–44
interstate non-governmental organizations (INGOS) 454
inter-subjective exchanges 498, 503
interviews 506–21; age and social class 513–14; attentive listening 516–17; cultural sensitivity 515–17; drug use, topic of 516; ethics 517–18; ethnicity, insider-outsider status and 511–12; further reading 519–21; gender 512–13; gifts 517–18; homesickness, topic of 517; illegal employment, topic of 517; immigrant interviews, applications to 510–11; in-depth interviews 507–9; income and finance, topics of 516; indirect questions 516–17; insider-outsider status 511–12; interview interaction 487–88; interview research 518–19; language 514–15; life history interviews 509–10; linguistic

changing conditions and dangers of 262;
journey of, religion and 261–63; liberal paradox
and immigration regimes 423–26; Manchurian
migrations 84; mass migration, periods of
economic downturns. and 193; migration laws,
bias against Asians in 75; migration rates
(1501–1900) 54; migration systems theory
101–3; motivations of highly skilled 156–57;
patterns of, unprecedented nature of 1, 2;
policies of developed world, varieties of
347–51; politicization of 388–89; race and,
mutuality of 169; reactions to 2; scholarship on,
internet and changes in 543–44; selected
migration process sequences 371–72; status in
census analysis 477; surveys of, complex
problems of 484; surveys of, ethnosurveys and
485; technological advances and migration
studies 544; traditional and non-traditional
countries of 347; transatlantic system of 81, 82;
undertaking of, religion and 260–63
Migrations between Africa and Europe
(MAFE) 489
Miles, Robert 232
Milkman, R. and Wong, K. 137
Milkman, Ruth 135, 136
Miller, A. 218
Miller, D. and Slater, D. 543, 545
Mills, C.W. 11, 560, 562n11
Min, P.G. and Kim, C. 296, 297, 299, 301,
302, 303
Min, Pyong Gap xvi, 5, 145–52, 190, 194
mining 68
Mink, Gwendolyn 134
Minkler, M. and Wallerstein, N. 567, 572, 573
Mishler, E.G. 507
Mitra, A. 543, 545
"mixed-status families" 362–63
mobility transition 53–54
Moch, Leslie 52
modeling health change 372
modeling migrant health 369
modern diasporas 440–42
Modood, T. 174, 176, 190
Mohapatra, S. et al. 1
Mohr, J. 531
Molho, I. 384, 387
Money, J. 352, 353, 388
monographic method 496
monotheistic sects from Western Asia 79–80
Moodley, K. 146
Mooney, M.A. 557
Moore, J.W. 244, 511
Mora, A. and Davila, M.T. 275, 278
Morakvasic, Mirjana 180, 181
Morales, Ofelia Woo 181
Morano Foadi, S. 162
Morawska, E. 2

Moreno Fuentes, F.J. and Bruquetas Callejo, M.
425
Morgan, Charlie V. xvi, 269, 295–306
Morley, D. 233
Morokvasic, M. 207
most-different comparative designs 560
most-similar comparative designs 559–60
Muehlebach, A. 246
Mullan, B. and Doña-Reveco, C. 332
Mullan, Brendan xvi, 409–21
multiculturalism: criticisms against 176; debates
about 397; need for rethinking on 175–76
multinational corporations (MNCs) 155
multiracial people 177
Murchison, J. 498
Murdock, H. 92
Muslim extremism, fear of 198; see also
Islamophobia
Musterd, S. 206, 207, 208
Myers, D. et al. 312
Myers, N. 29
Nagel, J. 240
Naipaul, V.S. 102
Nakamura, L. 543
Nakano-Glen, E. 569
Naples, Nancy 183
Nascimbene, B. 385
nation states: in Africa, manufacture of 87–88;
development of 60; national data, availability of
473; politics and transnationalism 456;
regulatory policies on adoption of, national and
international 322; system of, logics of 230
National Association of Black Social Workers 325
national belonging 325–27
National Council of La Raza 240
National Day Laborer Organizing Network
(NDLON) 142
National Household Survey (NHS, Canada) 471,
480–81
National Origin's Act (US,1924) 190
National Urban Indian Development
Corporation 240
nationalism: development in modern times 439;
nationalist narratives, challenge to 233–35;
native nations and 231–32; resurgence of 88
nationalist sexual norms 220
nationality rates in advanced industrialized
countries 381
Native Americans (First Nation peoples) 240,
245–46
nativism: consequences of 197–99; cultural causes
of 196–97, 199; indigenous nationalism,
migrants and 227; intransigent nativism 198,
199–200; old and new 190–93; political causes
of 195–96, 199; social causes of 196–97, 199;
see also host hostility, nativism and
nativity data 473–74

migrant-sending and-receiving societies 245; political attachment 334; political theories of naturalization 387–88; politicization of immigration 388–89; situation in hostland 446–47; system in hostland, participation in 446; tactics of established diasporas 446–47; undocumented category, considerations in creation of 356; welfare states, politico-institutional and contextual considerations 429–30; *see also* political sociology of international migration

pollution, climate change and 29

Polo, Marco 80

population building (1776–1940) 66–70

population-environment nexus 28–29

population growth: and distribution 475–78; immigration and 307; population stocks, comparison across time 476; and redistribution 82

Porter, J.N. 148

Portes, A. 2, 383, 412, 431, 456

Portes, A. and Curtis, J.W. 382, 383

Portes, A. and DeWind, J. 429

Portes, A. and Macleod, D. 244

Portes, A. and Rumbaut, R. 5, 156, 191, 196, 197, 264, 269, 271, 280, 289, 311, 312, 313, 314, 315, 360, 383, 384, 397, 398, 399, 400, 401, 402, 404, 498, 499

Portes, A. and Sensenbrenner, J. 252

Portes, A. and Zhou, M. 170, 256, 309, 310, 313, 397, 399, 499, 560

Portes, A. *et al.* 403, 455

positive selection 15

post-industrial societies 191

post-national citizenship 337–38

post-traumatic stress disorder (PTSD) 104

postcolonialism 226

Poston, D. and Frisbie Parker, W. 29

Potocky-Tripodi, M. 113

Potter, R.B. *et al.* 464, 467

poverty 17, 19, 24, 69, 91, 101, 127, 251, 262, 270, 310, 314, 317, 323, 350, 414; education and 387, 402, 404; welfare state and 424, 425

Powell, Enoch 192

Prashad, V. 233

Presley, Elvis 59

Price, M. and Benton-Short, L. 205

prior residence data 474

procedural justice 567

prostitutes, Western demand for 90–91

protection: key concern for UNHCR 108; outside of resettlement, expansion of 115–16

Pryor, E.T. and Long, J.F. 480

Przeworski, A. and Teune, H. 562n11

Psthas, G. 545, 547

psychological acculturation 38–51; acculturation, acculturation theory and 38–39; acculturation,

complex processes of 40; acculturation, group and individual phenomenon 39–40; cognition 42; context, cultural differences and 45, 48–49; context, individual differences and 44–45; context, local impact and 45; cultural differences and 45, 48–49; developmental status 41–42; domain 43–44; further reading 49–51; future directions in 48; gender 42; generation 43; international migration and 40; lifespan perspective 41; means 44; motives 44; personality 42; policy implications of 47–48; processes in 46; rewards in 47; risks in 46–47; time considerations 44; within-group variability 40–41

Public Use Microdata Samples (PUMS) 490

"pull factors": climate change 30, 32; forced migrants 100

Purkayastha, B. 156, 184, 543

Push and Pull Factors in International Migration project 489

"push factors": climate change 30, 31, 32, 33, 35, 36

Putnam, R.D. 253, 427

Qian, Z. and Lichter, D.T. 296, 297, 298, 300, 301, 302

Qin, D.B. 47, 403, 405

Qin-Hilliard, D. and Orozco, C. 403

qualitative interviewing 506, 518

quasi-experimental studies 558, 559

queer identities 183

queer social networks 291

queer studies 183

questions for census analysis 472–75

quota laws in US 197

quota limitations 348

race: ethnicity, immigrant intermarriage and 301–2; family, migration and 286–87; insider-outsider status and 511–12; integration process for highly-skilled and 156; international adoption and issues of 327; racial belonging 325–27; racial categorization, panethnicity and 241; racial endogamy 301; racial lumping 239–40; salience of "race" and ethnicity, questioning the presumptions on 172–73

race and migration, changing configuration of 169–79; agency, need for rethinking on 171, 177; automatic coupling of migrant with non-white-raced person 173; British Chinese people 171–72; Chicago School studies of migration and race relations 172; citizenship, need for rethinking on 175–76; communal ties and class solidarities 171; cultural assimilation 175–76; cultural variables 170; diasporas 170; Eastern European migrants, arrival in Western destinations 173–74; ethnic businesses 169; further reading 178–79; globalization, dynamics of 170; identity and belonging 170; identity